T5-DGZ-156

WEST ACADEMIC PUBLISHING'S LAW SCHOOL ADVISORY BOARD

CASES AND MATERIALS ON

ARBITRATION LAW AND PRACTICE

Eighth Edition

■ ■ ■

Thomas E. Carbonneau
Orlando Distinguished Professor of Law
Penn State University

Henry Allen Blair
Robins Kaplan Distinguished Professor of Law
Senior Fellow, Dispute Resolution Institute
Mitchell Hamline School of Law

AMERICAN CASEBOOK SERIES®

444 Cedar Street, Suite 700
St. Paul, MN 55101
1-877-888-1330

Printed in the United States of America

ISBN: 978-1-64242-087-6

To my daughter:
Sara Lucille Carbonneau,
Distinguished graduate of Sarah Lawrence College, licensed in Acupuncture and Chinese Medicine, and gifted thinker and writer.

To ***Amanda Eiko Lindseth***
My sun, my moon, and all my stars.

INTRODUCTION

Arbitration occupies a dominant place in the U.S. legal system. Its significance and stature are now unquestioned. Its existence and impact upon the legal process cannot be ignored. It has become the primary means for adjudicating civil disputes. Arbitration greatly exceeds its traditional range of application. Its use is no longer relegated to commercial relationships and contract disputes between merchants. Its jurisdictional reach extends to the purchase of securities and other consumer transactions. It is the remedy by which employment disputes are resolved. It also addresses controversies that involve federal statutory rights, the regulation of commerce, and fundamental civil liberty guarantees. Few, if any, disputes are deemed inarbitrable. Only criminal liability escapes its reach.

The most controversial question in the current law of arbitration centers upon the validity and enforceability of arbitration agreements. There appears to be resistance among some courts to the enforcement of adhesive arbitration agreements, especially in the context of consumer and employment disputes. This development centers upon class action waivers and is most in evidence among the state and federal courts in California. There, arbitration agreements are more frequently voided on the basis of unconscionability or for a lack of mutuality. The courts in California, it seems, have concluded that legal procedural regularity must be fully maintained in unilateral contracts for arbitration. The U.S. Supreme Court's recent decisions in *Rent-A-Center v. Jackson,* 561 U.S. 63, 130 S. Ct. 2772 (2010), *AT&T Mobility v. Concepcion*, 563 U.S. 321, 131 S. Ct. 1740 (2011), and *Am. Express Co. v. Italian Colors Rest.*, 570 U.S. 228, 133 S. Ct. 2304 (2013), countered that development and its effects. Courts in a few other jurisdictions have periodically invoked the costs of arbitration and their distribution among the contracting parties to nullify arbitration agreements. No matter the basis, opposition to arbitration agreements is confined to a minority of courts (especially state courts). Their reluctance to enforce arbitration agreements is uncharacteristic. In the vast majority of cases, courts give full effect to arbitration agreements.

Arbitral awards are also generally favored by courts and enforced. Vacatur or nullification is a rare result. According to SCOTUS, the Federal Arbitration Act (FAA) codifies a policy that sustains the recourse to arbitration. Further, it limits the judicial supervision of arbitral awards to procedural matters that are vital to the legitimacy of any type of adjudication. Moreover, courts have interpreted the narrow grounds for review restrictively. Recent practice, however, has eroded somewhat the policy of nearly automatic enforcement of awards by developing an action to clarify awards and broadening the evident partiality ground for vacatur with a mandate for arbitrator disclosure. Because of the new emphasis upon disclosures, alleging partiality in either neutral or party-appointed arbitrators has become the most effective means for challenging awards.

The action to clarify awards—despite its practical value—is likely to have a pernicious effect because it may eventually become a vehicle for achieving the ends of adversarial representation. Under the decisional law, it is a common law doctrine that allows courts to remand an award to the arbitral tribunal to have opaque determinations explained or clarified. Spurred by contentious trial practices, losing parties have already asked courts and tribunals to "clarify" arbitral determinations that go against their interests. The procedure thereby introduces merits review into the arbitral process by the back door. Challenging the neutrality of arbitrators on the basis of disclosures and their determinations for a would-be lack of clarity are ominous developments for arbitral autonomy. They underscore the tension in arbitration law between the protection of rights and the functionality of the adjudicatory process. They highlight the difficulty of providing simultaneously for due process in and access to adjudication. The U.S. Supreme Court has nonetheless been unwavering and unequivocal over the last fifty or so years in its support for arbitration. *See, e.g., BG Group v. Argentina,* 134 S. Ct. 1198 (2014). A number of other cases—*Stolt-Nielsen v. AnimalFeeds Int'l Corp.*, 559 U.S. 662, 130 S. Ct. 1758 (2010), *Hall Street Associates v. Mattel,* 552 U.S. 576, 128 S. Ct. 1396 (2008), *Volt Info. Sciences v. Stanford Univ.*, 489 U.S. 468, 109 S. Ct. 1248 (1989), and *Commonwealth Coatings Corp. v. Continental Casualty Co.*, 393 U.S. 145, 89 S. Ct. 337 (1968)—represent the primary deviation from the Court's general practice on arbitration.

Through more than forty-five arbitration cases, the Court has articulated a judicial doctrine that admits of few, if any, exceptions or conditions to the right to arbitrate. All matters but criminal liability fall within the purview of arbitration. Moreover, the arbitrator is the sovereign decider of the merits, the procedure, and even jurisdictional challenges. At this stage in the decisional law on arbitration, it is clear that the Court is using the FAA as a stepping stone to elaborating a judicial law on arbitration. The Court has added significantly to the content of the statute. For example, FAA § 2—unquestionably the key provision of the Act both historically and doctrinally—establishes that the surrender of judicial remedies by contract does not violate public policy; it thereby validates arbitration agreements as a proper exercise of contract freedom. Nonetheless, in the Court's rulings, arbitration agreements are not simply contracts. In the words of Justice Black, when he reacted critically to the majority's endorsement of the separability doctrine in his dissent in *Prima Paint Corp. v. Flood & Conklin Mfg. Co*, 388 U.S. 395 (1967), they are "super" contracts, "[e]levate[d] above all other contractual provisions."

Glossing the FAA, the Court has made arbitration agreements nothing less than the means for correcting the provision of dysfunctional adjudicatory services in American society.

The Court has altered the governing legislation in other respects. The federal preemption doctrine, extended to arbitration by the Court over a number of cases, has been instrumental to the creation and maintenance of the "strong federal policy on arbitration." It guaranteed that a set of uniformly favorable principles to arbitration would apply in all federal and state jurisdictions. In establishing the doctrine, the Court literally rewrote the express content of the FAA, extending the statute's application to state courts and legislatures. Federal preemption also allowed the Court to 'promulgate' an implied federal right to arbitrate. The case law nevertheless acknowledged that several FAA provisions were directed exclusively to federal district courts and the governing legislation did not expressly create federal question jurisdiction. These would-be anomalies, however, did not impede the Court's policy on extending the scope of arbitration. Federalization of the law is well-established; since *Dobson*, 513 U.S. 265 (1995), and *Doctor's Associates, Inc.*, 517 U.S. 681 (1996), it is essentially unquestioned. An expansive view of interstate commerce governs and states cannot enact laws restricting—directly or indirectly—arbitration agreements.

The Court has also exhibited singular determination in upholding the federal policy on arbitration. It admits of no exceptions to settled views and demands compliance with them regardless of logic, legal tradition, or veracity. In this regard, the Court is more perspicacious than it is single-minded or arbitrary. It is generally acknowledged that exceptions, additions, or modifications to legal rules, once recognized, mutate over time and progressively swallow up or transform the original rule. The U.S. law of arbitration would not be as cohesive, viable, or effective were it riddled with the twists and turns of qualification. In fact, the campaign for federalization was waged to create a disciplined, uniform, and unambiguous regulation of arbitration. After all, the goal that is contemplated is nothing less than building a workable system of civil adjudication in U.S. society.

While there are misgivings, debates, and controversies, arbitration—despite imperfections—is in a golden era. The Court sustains every aspect of the operation of the arbitral process in both the domestic and transborder sphere. Doctrine is adapted to achieve the objectives of policy; everything is sacrificed to bring about an accessible form of civil adjudicatory justice. The judicial support not only is consistent, but it is devoid of ambivalence as well. As a consequence, arbitration has expanded its scope of application to new dispute areas and beyond the boundaries of contract itself. With the extension of the contract of arbitration to nonsignatory parties and the deference paid to adhesive agreements, arbitral clauses implied at law may soon become a new feature of the U.S. court doctrine on arbitration. The critique, and possibly impairment, of arbitration can only proceed from the legislative branch. It is to it that forces antagonistic to arbitration have directed their efforts to contain arbitration and arbitrability. Thus far, the efforts of the opponents have been futile.

These course materials convey a comprehensive picture of the arbitral process. In particular, they seek to provide legal professionals with the knowledge and understanding necessary to participate effectively in counseling on arbitration, the drafting of arbitration agreements, conducting arbitral proceedings, and managing court actions relating to arbitration. The principles, rules, and procedural structures that are described are basic to the law of arbitration and apply to all systems of arbitration.

The chapters describe the various stages of an arbitration, define the issues that are vital to its operation, assess the legal doctrines and concepts that regulate it, and point to critical doctrinal and practical developments. In some respects, the availability of recourse to arbitration has changed the face of traditional law-making and lawyering. Arbitration dislodges the application and activity of the traditional judicial process. Although arbitration is effective and valuable, it is hardly without problems and drawbacks. Lawyers and clients need to assess the remedy and make a judgment about its transactional viability. The materials point to problems that are likely to arise in the practice of arbitration law and propose a framework for elaborating solutions.

The volume begins with a presentation of essential terms and definitions. It then introduces the basic statutory law in the area (the FAA and the RUAA). Thereafter, it addresses the major themes in the decisional law on arbitration: federalization, contractual freedom, and arbitrability. It investigates particular applications of the arbitral remedy (traditional and nontraditional), *e.g.*, labor and employment, securities, and consumer arbitration. The issues that relate to the enforcement of arbitral awards are thoroughly outlined and discussed. Finally, the most recent and difficult problems of practice are identified and treated comprehensively.

The presentation emphasizes the importance of practical problems and underscores the fragility of existing rules and the need for professionals in the field to be analytically rigorous as well as creative in their approach to problems. The text that follows seeks to educate through a comprehensive presentation of relevant and timely information, the rigorous analytical evaluation of that data, and the identification of the practical implications of the "findings of fact" and "conclusions of law."

COPYRIGHT ACKNOWLEDGMENTS

The author gratefully acknowledges the copyright permissions granted by the following organizations:

1. The Virginia Law Review Association and Fred B. Rothman & Co. to reprint excerpts from Cohen & Dayton, *The New Federal Arbitration Law*, 12 VA. L. REV. 265, 281 (1926);
2. Juris Publishing, Inc. to reprint a variety of excerpts from my arbitration treatise, entitled "The Law and Practice of Arbitration" (4th edition 2012) and to use "Paul Friedland, Arbitration Clauses for International Contracts" (2d edition 2007) as a general reference.

SUMMARY OF CONTENTS

TABLE OF CONTENTS

Chapter 7. The Enforcement of Domestic Arbitral Awards **585**

TABLE OF CASES

The principal cases are in bold type.

CASES AND MATERIALS ON

ARBITRATION LAW AND PRACTICE

Eighth Edition

CHAPTER 1

EXPLAINING ARBITRATION

■ ■ ■

1. A DEFINITION

There are many impressions of arbitration. Commentators often describe arbitral adjudication as a dim reflection of its judicial counterpart. Lawyers, judges, and legal scholars have traditionally assessed arbitration as a remedy of limited scope and value. Arbitration, they state, does not even approximate the history, practices, and operation of judicial litigation. In contrast to arbitration, legal civilization offers process, stability, and intricate predicates of decision. The legal system is long-standing and well-established. Society believes that trials, courts, and legal rules guarantee the rights of citizenship and maintain the integrity of our republican form of government. However valuable traditionalism may be, society and its institutions are in a state of perpetual transformation. Circumstances change, new needs arise, and past approaches become obsolete. Even the basic features of social organization can be surpassed by time, global developments, and unexpected events.

Today's societies, for example, cannot escape the impact of population growth or the advances of technology. The greater the number of people, the dearer resources become. Scarcity and uneven distribution heighten the pressures of competition. Skirmishes, battles, and war are likelier. Computers may or may not offer a viable solution to these problems. Despite its acceleration and voluminous production, artificial intelligence is artificial because it is not anchored in the human personality. Electronic devices could either facilitate human activity or render it inconsequential. Human trust in computer advances, therefore, should be begrudging. Trepidation is the voice that should be heard and obeyed. The distinction between good and evil, the past and the present has never been more ambiguous. When should established practices be abandoned and the allure of the present embraced? A faltering educational system may not generate the minds necessary to the task. The growth of government and the advent of debt-financing add to the peril. Government policies mask the risks of the future. They are meant to lull citizens into unquestioning acquiescence and eventually indifference. Talent and energy and the recognition and pursuit of opportunity, not the erection of a complex and insidious bureaucracy, constitute the pathway to legitimate and effective social permutations.

In many respects, arbitration is a mechanism that creates helpful choices for people. It empowers citizens to make their own decisions about the resolution of conflict. It thereby solidifies individual identity through the exercise of personal power. It represents a choice about the management of dispute resolution and commercial risk. Arbitration arises from a contract. It is a private and simplified trial procedure for the adjudication of civil (especially contract) disputes. It yields binding determinations through less expensive and more efficient proceedings in which decision-makers are expert and equal treatment of the parties defines fairness. Arbitration is neither negotiation nor mediation. By agreeing to arbitrate, the parties authorize arbitrators to adjudicate their disputes, *i.e.*, to render a final and binding disposition of the matters submitted. The awards (outcomes) can be enforced through the standard legal means that, in this case, strongly favor enforceability. Once the parties appoint the arbitral tribunal, they, as a rule, relinquish control of the proceedings, the dispute, and its resolution to the arbitrators.

Ordinarily, an arbitration agreement is consensual. Despite their unilateral character, adhesive contracts for arbitration are lawful and enforceable. Chapter 6 will discuss concerns about this conclusion in more detail, but the Court's most recent arbitration decision (*Epic Systems v. Lewis*) confirms the legal validity of adhesive arbitral agreements. Parties can also submit existing or prospective disputes to arbitration. The parties have the freedom—the legal right—to engage in arbitration and customize its implementation and operation. By entering into an arbitration agreement, the parties voluntarily abandon their right to judicial relief and, in effect, create a private system of adjudication that is more suited to their pocketbook and priorities.

Prior to the U.S. Supreme Court's contemporary advocacy for arbitration, the arbitral process was relegated to the deeper recesses of commerce—specialized trades and other minor commercial sectors. The Court gradually but steadily expanded the range of the mechanism to include a greater number of transactions, *i.e.* non-union employment disputes and consumer purchases. Moreover, without arbitration, global commerce would have continued to be stymied by the law's conflicts methodology. Arbitral practice delegates the resolution of venue, jurisdictional, and governing law conflicts to the designated arbitrators. It thereby eliminates the reference to national courts that ordinarily jealously protect their jurisdictional prerogatives and determine matters exclusively through the parties' adversarial confrontation. The arbitral process also benefits from a virtually irrebuttable presumption of enforcement for both agreements and awards.

Arbitration responds especially well to the needs of commercial dispute resolution. First, arbitration is generally private and confidential. Arbitral proceedings are not open to the public and awards generally do not contain reasons and, as a rule, have been infrequently published. The recourse to arbitration, therefore, allows commercial parties to maintain their commercial reputation despite disagreement. Second, arbitral adjudication is more flexible and can be less adversarial and protracted than its judicial analogue. Inelaborate proceedings result in an economy of time and money. The commercial experience of the arbitral tribunal lessens the significance of legal precedent, eliminates the need for complex rules of evidence, and limits the expanse of discovery, the use of experts, and other procedures designed to gather information for trial. The arbitral tribunal must provide the parties with a fair and reasonable opportunity to admit evidence and to be heard. The tribunal should decide the matters submitted in a timely fashion. Procedural informality, trusting the arbitrators' professional capabilities, and allowing commercial pragmatism to trump fastidious legal technicalities are the hallmarks of arbitral adjudication.

Third, arbitrating parties have the right to select the arbitrators. The designated arbitrators ordinarily have experience in the relevant business area. Their commercial expertise allows them to reach determinations that are in keeping with notions of fair mercantile conduct. By choosing to arbitrate, therefore, business parties avoid inexpert decision-makers prone to reach inept results. Parties select an uneven number of arbitrators to avoid deadlocks. One arbitrator is usually agreed upon for smaller matters and three-member panels preside over larger cases. A third-party service-provider or a court can designate the sole arbitrator. For establishing the larger panels, each party selects an arbitrator and the two party-appointed arbitrators name a third arbitrator, known as the neutral, who chairs the panel. While the party-appointed arbitrators are expected to act impartially, they are named generally because they have supported positions akin to the designating party's arguments on the issues. In larger cases, the neutral arbitrator generally casts the deciding vote. Each party expects 'its' arbitrator to favor its version of the case or, at a minimum, represent its side of the dispute to the deliberating tribunal. This practice sometimes leads to 'an arbitration-within-an-arbitration', in which each party-appointed arbitrator attempts to persuade the neutral arbitrator of the rectitude of its party's case. This type of arbitrator conduct, however, can lessen the neutrality of the panel and might support claims of partiality. The appointment of a truly neutral arbitrator, therefore, is fundamental to the fairness of the proceeding and the integrity of the determination.

In global commercial litigation, as alluded to earlier, arbitration eliminates the conflicts associated with the assertion of national court jurisdiction, the choice of applicable law, and the enforcement of non-domestic judgments. Arbitration tempers the juridical disparities between different legal traditions and systems. It functions as a *de facto* trans-border legal system, providing an adjudicatory process free of national bias and parochial perceptions and laws, capable of dispensing commercially-sound adjudicatory results. The generally less adversarial tenor of arbitral proceedings also contributes to arbitration's 'business appeal'. In arbitration, commercial parties can effectively protect their interests without engaging in or suffering adversarial histrionics. In a number of ways, arbitration is a type of 'in-house' or informal adjudicatory process through which the usages, interests, values, and concerns of commerce become controlling.

NOTES AND QUESTIONS

1. Arbitration is **private** adjudication with its own rules and procedures. Above all, lawyers and their clients should understand that an agreement to arbitrate is **binding**. When parties sign or acquiesce to an arbitration agreement, they must proceed to arbitration and are bound by the arbitrator's rulings (unless they settle). Settlement may not be feasible or suitable in the arbitral adjudicatory setting. **Appeal** is exceedingly limited in arbitration—nearly nonexistent. For all intents and purposes, the award is final as rendered.

2. A critical question in the law of arbitration is whether the **'privatization'** of civil adjudication through arbitration is in the best interests of society. The rise of arbitration is directly related to issues that surround the management of judicial resources and the protection of legal rights. The weight of the criminal docket has reduced the standing of civil litigation and made it an ancillary concern of the legal system. The costs, delays, and protracted character of court proceedings make civil justice a lesser obligation than the determination of criminal liability. Arbitration is more **accessible** to civil litigants because it is a 'one-off' proceeding the costs of which are paid by the parties. **Economy** is realized through expedition, which substantially reduces lawyer fees. There is no waiting on the docket. Nonetheless, popular arbitrators can have a number of pending cases—a factor that should be considered in selecting arbitrators. In arbitration, the parties can generally afford a merits determination. Arbitral adjudication, therefore, is expeditious, efficient, economical, effective, and enforceable.

3. The choice of arbitration implies an **exchange**: adjudicatory accessibility, efficiency, and functionality *for* judicial rights protection, maintaining the integrity of legal rules through courts, and rulings pursuant to a judicially-crafted substantive law. An arbitral proceeding must assure the neutrality and impartiality of the adjudicators. Thereafter, expertise, alacrity, and finality are the process' primary advantages.

4. Another significant consideration—one that is as critical as **adjudicatory neutrality**—is the fulfillment of society's promise of constitutional justice. A judicial process overwhelmed by the demands of adversarial jousting and the length of criminal trials cannot effectively protect individual legal rights in the civil setting. Judges act as passive referees and the lawyers fight about their fabricated, albeit plausible, narratives. In effect,

trials and legal representation are, at least arguably, alien to veracity. Moreover, a trial system that 'coerces' the parties to settle is hardly a bastion for the **protection of legal rights**. The theory of judicial litigation guarantees absolute fairness, but its operation frequently forgets the litigants' fundamental interests and true concerns—an attribute that itself epitomizes unfairness. The conflict between the operation and objectives of the legal process depreciates judicial litigation. Court trials often never reach finality. The political order contemplated by the social contract is not attained.

5. Arbitration addresses **private law** disputes arising through contract. It does not implicate the political State or its public law obligations. For example, it cannot apply to matters of criminal liability. Nonetheless, the Court has extended arbitration to disputes involving regulatory statutes—thereby allowing arbitration to help fulfill public mandates and public policy objectives. In 1960, SCOTUS expanded arbitration's remedial reach to the maintenance of industrial peace. Decades later, arbitration was applied to disputes in the non-unionized workplace and consumer dissatisfaction with products and services. Today, arbitration can resolve even matters implicating civil rights. As mentioned previously, the Court saw arbitration as a solution to the inaccessibility of civil justice. In addition, to buttress arbitration, the Court created an "emphatic" or "strong" or "liberal" "federal policy favoring arbitration." Further, it **federalized** the U.S. law of arbitration. Both developments enhanced the 'autonomy' of the arbitral process. The history of Western arbitration—specifically, in the U.S., France, and England—establishes that courts are crucial to arbitration's acceptance by and integration into society.

6. You should assess the Court's policy and rulings on arbitration, as well as its support for the process. In effect, the extraordinary result is that the highest court in the United States willingly delegates jurisdiction over civil litigation to a private process regulated by contract and individual parties. Do you believe that the privazation of civil dispute resolution is necessary and justified? Does it support or undermine constitutional integrity? Is civil litigation through courts untenable in modern America? What are the gains and losses associated with the implementation of non-judicial justice?

2. HOW DOES ARBITRATION WORK?

Arbitration is a trial framework—a procedural model for conducting private proceedings. Although it has proven itself to be highly effective, it is not a panacea. In some instances, arbitration can provide a better procedural framework, but it is nothing more or less than an **adjudicatory alternative**—one of several processes for achieving the final and binding resolution of disputes. Like everything else, arbitration has advantages and disadvantages. In each case, the choice of remedial relief—whether to pursue traditional litigation, arbitration, or structured negotiations—must be made on the basis of an understanding of the processes, the circumstances of the dispute, and the ability of the mechanisms to be effective. The choice of an arbitrator is critically important. The capabilities of the arbitrator are the primary factor in establishing the quality and effectiveness of an arbitration.

As noted earlier, parties generally engage in arbitration to achieve quicker results and economy. To expedite the process, arbitrating parties forgo elements of the judicial trial: discovery, appeal, and judicial due process. The bargain for accelerated adjudication, therefore, can disappoint expectations of procedural and substantive fairness. There is little legal recourse against arbitrators or their rulings. Arbitrators are not publicly regulated or certified. They are chosen by the parties and their legal advisors. **Arbitrator malpractice** does not exist. Like judges, arbitrators benefit from **adjudicatory immunity**. Unless the parties customize their recourse to arbitration, the process seems to demand absolute trust in the arbitrator. The arbitrator's desire for reappointment is perhaps the most significant limitation on the exercise of arbitrator discretion.

The arbitration agreement may be the best means for guarding against abuse in arbitration. Parties can require arbitrators to conduct adversarial proceedings—complete with pre-trial discovery, the use of party-appointed expert witnesses, and the exercise of cross-examination—and to follow legal precedent. Arbitrators cannot disregard these provisions without imperiling the enforceability of the award. The parties could also require judicial appeal of all arbitrator rulings or create an appeals process within the arbitration format itself. At this stage, the parties would have come full circle from their point of departure by providing for a **'judicialized'** arbitral proceeding. This prospect lessens considerably the 'alternative' value of arbitral adjudication—its viability as a substitute for the judicial trial. Judicialized arbitration still provides expertise and greater access, but it loses its flexibility and ability to adapt to changes of circumstance.

Providing for an unconventional arbitral mechanism creates a 'front-end load' and enhances the risk of difficulties and the creation of obstacles. Negotiations are longer, more involved, and difficult; legal representation is more significant and expensive; and the transaction itself is more readily frustrated. Such agreements are more likely to become **pathological** than the standard abbreviated reference to arbitration (*i.e.*, any dispute arising under this contract shall be submitted to arbitration—either *ad hoc* or institutional arbitration). The true advantage to judicialized arbitration is that the parties get what they want—at least, wanted at one time. Most parties, however, entrust the determination of such matters to the arbitrators. The future is always uncertain and difficult to predict.

Especially in international arbitration, arbitrators can command substantial compensation (as much as $1,000 to $1,500 per hour for adjudicatory work). The greater the arbitrator's experience and reputation, the higher the fee. Arbitrators add value to the process by their judgment and professional experience. Because of their trial experience, retired judges are frequently appointed as arbitrators. In some respects, arbitration has not strayed far from its inside-the-business origins. The days of the archetypal international arbitrator and global lawyer (Bertold Goldman, F.A. Mann, Pierre Lalive, Jean Robert, Hans Smit, Philippe Fouchard, and Henry de Vries), however, are gone; global commerce is an 'every-day' event; English is its principal means of expression. There are many more people in the field and a great deal more business is done through arbitration. Writings, conferences, journals, and trainings abound. Women attorneys, however, continue to have an insufficient presence in ICA (International Commercial Arbitration). Nonetheless, the exceptions to the rule have made remarkable contributions to the field.

Despite its development and greater breadth, arbitration remains anchored in the singularity of the contract, the demands of the business area, and the needs of the parties. Arbitration's 'magic' is its ability to subdue and discipline the pitfalls of the law and its traditional and possibly dated methodology. Arbitral autonomy is the price for adjudicatory functionality. Arbitration works and it is effective. The risk of the process resides in the inability of correction. If the judgment of the arbitrator fails, there are few remedies to nullify the award. A maverick arbitrator can cause significant, even irreparable harm. Finally, while judicial litigation is founded upon universal distrust, arbitral adjudication is centered upon **trust** in the arbitrators and the necessity of sensible adjudication.

The Stages of an Arbitral Proceeding

Assuming the arbitral agreement is an enforceable contract, the arbitration usually takes place in accordance with the rules of an administering arbitral institution, like the American Arbitration Association (AAA) or JAMS (an acronym that formerly referred to the Judicial Arbitration and Mediation Services and which is now simply the corporate name of an arbitral service-provider). Though commonly used, institutions are not a requirement of the arbitral process. Parties could opt to conduct their arbitrations on an *ad hoc* basis, drafting in detail their own rules to govern the process. When they are used, institutional rules merely constitute a prefabricated set of instructions about how the process should function. Parties adopt these instructions as part of their contract in order to save time and money, freeing them from having to devise their own protocols.

The institutional rules define the stages of the arbitral process: (1) formation of the arbitral tribunal; (2) drafting a submission to establish the tribunal's jurisdiction; (3) selecting the rules of procedure; (4) undertaking the proceedings; (5) concluding the proceedings; (6) the tribunal's deliberations; and (7) the rendering of an award, including a possible award "on agreed terms." The latter represents the result of the parties' negotiations; it is deemed an award to foster the enforceability of the settlement. Otherwise, the settlement would be a contract, the enforcement of which would depend upon standard litigation proceedings.

The Beginning

Following receipt of a **demand** for arbitration, the administering arbitral institution notifies the other party of the demand and requests that it submit an answer. The parties then appoint arbitrators. The supervising institution can supply the parties with lists of arbitrators. Ordinarily, legal counsel makes recommendations about suitable candidates based on experience and general intelligence (the word of mouth in the area). Once the arbitral tribunal is constituted, the parties enter into a submission agreement. The submission establishes the specific elements of the parties' disagreement. Under some arbitral laws and procedures, the parties need not enter into a submission; they can meet with the arbitrators to establish the matters to be arbitrated (a pre-hearing conference). Also, if the parties are unable to agree on the substance of their disagreement prior to the proceeding, the arbitral tribunal can proceed to the arbitration and later establish which questions were submitted to it by the parties for decision. In effect, the arbitrators establish their right to rule just before rendering the award. Such a procedure is controversial because it allows the arbitrators to function both as adjudicators and litigants. This dual role exceeds the ordinary limits of arbitrator power. Jurisdiction to rule is not a decisional, procedural, or interpretative matter. Rather, it relates to the arbitrators' investiture to rule and defines the parties' purpose in agreeing to arbitrate. No matter how experienced and distinguished they might be, the arbitrators are not 'super' parties in the proceeding. They work for the parties and are not themselves participants in the litigation. The advantage to this innovative procedure to establish jurisdiction, however, is the avoidance of substantial delay in holding the arbitration and reducing the possibility that the arbitration might never take place.

Designated parties must agree to serve as an arbitrator. Arbitrators are obligated to disclose any conflicts of interest that might impair their ability to rule in an impartial manner. Conflicts can emerge prior to, during, and after the arbitration. Challenges based on allegations of partiality must be brought in a timely manner and not only to create delay. Allegations of partiality should not be a means of appeal against an unfavorable award or a way to postpone the day of reckoning. Such conduct should be discouraged by the imposition of sanctions either by the arbitrators or the vacatur court. The arbitrators can refuse to serve on the panel or can disqualify themselves. The parties can attempt to disqualify an arbitrator. Transforming the threshold phase of an arbitral proceeding into an adversarial exchange on arbitrator neutrality can undermine the arbitration. The arbitral tribunal, in consultation with the parties and the administering party, chooses a venue for the proceeding. Thereafter, the parties pay the required deposits for arbitrator and administrative fees. The tribunal sets a time for the initial hearing and establishes the objectives of the proceeding.

The Hearings

Parties generally expect arbitration to be a reasonably fair and flexible proceeding. The arbitrators usually have sufficient procedural authority to thwart strident adversarial debates and trial tactics that unnecessarily prolong the proceedings. The parties want to be heard and to make their case. They then want the arbitral tribunal to decide. Arbitral proceedings usually do not include a right to pre-trial discovery. Ordinarily, parties are required to exchange document and witness lists before the proceedings begin—a voluntary and cooperative form of discovery. The arbitral tribunal has the authority to admit and evaluate the evidence. While the arbitrating parties have the right to be heard, neither side can abuse its rights by manufacturing specious arguments, issues, and evidence—thereby delaying the proceeding for litigious advantage.

Evidence and Witnesses

During an arbitral proceeding, the parties make their case through testimony, documents, and advocacy. In many legal systems, the parties' agreement to arbitrate implies a **duty to arbitrate in good faith**. Failing to respond to tribunal requests in a timely fashion, attempting to obfuscate by presenting too many lay or expert witnesses, pursuing the other side's witnesses too stridently, or refusing to comply with the tribunal's requests for specific information—all potentially constitute a breach of the good faith obligation. The arbitral tribunal determines whether non-complying party conduct amounts to a breach of duty; the tribunal can award damages or take the breach into account in reaching its determination. The arbitral tribunal should require that the parties abide by the spirit and letter of their arbitration contract.

The right to **notification** and full **disclosure** are strictly enforced in arbitral proceedings. Direct, *ex parte* communications between the arbitrators and the parties are not permitted. All communications must be directed to a case manager who then supplies both the arbitral tribunal and the other side with the information. This approach avoids any appearance of partiality and maintains the **integrity** and **fairness** of the **process**. During the proceeding, the tribunal can rule on jurisdictional questions and other matters, such as the attachment of assets through interim measures. Interim rulings are akin to a final award. Their enforcement can require court action.

When the parties have completed their presentation of evidence and witnesses and summarized their respective positions, the arbitral tribunal closes the proceedings and adjourns to deliberate. At this stage, new information can only be admitted with the tribunal's permission. Admission of new information also requires that the opposing party have an opportunity to respond. The tribunal's **deliberations** are confidential. The decision can be reached by simple majority vote (usually 2 to 1). With the exception of international practice, arbitral tribunals generally render awards without issuing an opinion or providing reasons, *i.e.*, an explanation of the result.

The Award

The award usually adopts a standard format: A statement of the facts, a listing of the issues, the parties' respective positions, and a disposition of the matters submitted. The exclusion of an opinion to explain the result is intended to discourage judicial challenges against the award—specifically, the surreptitious judicial review of the merits of the arbitral ruling. The administering institution sends the award to the parties usually within thirty days after the hearings and deliberations are completed. The rendering of a final award triggers the payment of outstanding institutional and arbitrator fees from the money deposited by the parties. The administering arbitral institution may withhold the award until all **fees and costs** have been paid. Withholding payment for costs may become a strategy by the losing party to reduce the amount of the award. The winning party's additional cost to secure the award could become the subject of a second arbitral proceeding.

The costs of the arbitration generally are shared equally by the parties. In terms of the payment of attorney's fees, the American Rule generally applies. Each party pays its attorney's fees, unless the agreement contains a 'loser-pays-all' provision. The implementation of such a provision may require the arbitral tribunal to reconvene and to rule upon whether there is a 'losing' party. The tribunal would then apportion costs. Alternatively, the arbitral tribunal may exercise its discretion as to the distribution of costs. The parties can comply voluntarily with the terms of the award or seek to have the award enforced or challenged. The award can be converted to a judicial judgment in an enforcement action. The grounds for **challenging** arbitral awards are limited and narrow. Courts rarely **nullify** arbitral awards. In fact, the challenging party might risk Rule 11 sanctions if its opposition to the award is found to be designed primarily to postpone satisfying the award.

Possible Problems

Arbitrations do not always run smoothly. Parties opposed to participating in an arbitration can create a host of problems to thwart the process. They can challenge the arbitral tribunal's jurisdiction by alleging that the arbitration agreement is nonexistent, an invalid contract, or fails to cover the dispute in question. Also, a party can simply refuse to appear at the proceedings, decline to nominate an arbitrator, or ignore the directives of the administering institution. The tribunal can decide that experts will testify together to avoid any misunderstanding of their positions. In addition, a party can object to the procedures followed in the arbitral proceeding or to the powers of the arbitral tribunal—for example, whether the arbitral tribunal can award punitive damages, whether experts can appear and how they are to be qualified, or whether the arbitrators can order attachments during the proceedings to secure the payment of an eventual award. Further contention can be generated regarding matters of administrative detail—such as whether the place of arbitration is equally convenient for both parties.

NOTES AND QUESTIONS

1. Structuring the arbitral trial may become a significant activity in the legal representation of clients. Lawyers will eventually develop protocols that reconcile different organizations for the arbitral trial. The composition of the arbitral tribunal and the qualifications and experience of arbitrators can also become significant concerns for legal counsel. As a result, counseling may involve the process of selecting arbitrators. The likely collegiality of the tribunal needs to be considered as well. Finally, arbitrators need to assess whether they should accept their appointment. Their expertise may not apply to the particular dispute or the extent of their workload may preclude accepting a new case.

2. As noted earlier, providing for an eccentric arbitration can make it difficult to hire arbitrators or a service-provider. U.S. attorneys who are new to the arbitral process and procedure always express concern about the availability of discovery. They then want to be able to control the appearance and number of witnesses, as well as preserve their prerogative to engage in cross-examination. This attitude could readily clash with the expectations associated with arbitration and its standard practices. It could reflect a lawyer inability to adapt to different adjudicatory platforms. The Court has been, and continues to be, a strong supporter of arbitration in virtually all circumstances. In its view, either party intent or juridical policy make arbitration necessary—perhaps indispensable—to the operation of the American legal system.

3. THE DESTINY OF ARBITRATION

As noted previously, the ascendancy of arbitration has had a substantial impact on law practice. Negotiating and writing arbitration agreements, representing clients in arbitral proceedings, and advocating in award enforcement actions are becoming an integral part of contemporary law firm work. Arbitration's consequences for law practice will vary by state and region. Commercial activity generally fosters the emergence of arbitration. The legal process' sense of arbitral adjudication can also be a factor in the acceptance of, and recourse to, arbitration. In hospitable venues, practicing lawyers must be able to draft arbitration agreements that are responsive to the client's interests and needs. These contracts must intermediate between the necessity of maintaining the principle of legality, the integrity and functionality of adjudication, and client concern for frugality, functionality, fairness, and finality. Nonetheless, 'winning' remains a major motivation both for transactions and adjudication.

Arbitration's enhanced presence in law practice and transactional settings has also generated a sometimes intemperate debate among commentators about fairness in contract and the comparable worth of public and private adjudication. Arbitration's new day has had a ricochet effect upon the remedial mechanism itself. Its chief characteristics can be adjusted in light of the circumstances of application. What was both possible and desirable in self-contained and self-regulating commercial sectors can be impractical and even untoward in dealings between unequal parties with different levels of comprehension and experience.

While arbitral adjudication marries well the interests and needs of **mercantile** groups, it responds much less effectively to the disputes that arise between competing **social** and **political groups**. Technical expertise and flexible trial procedures are not key to the provision of justice in civil liberties and social policy settings. In fact, the systemic features of arbitration may have a detrimental effect in politicized circumstances. Critics of the process have emphasized that arbitration is coerced by dominant parties and the flexibility of arbitral procedure and the exercise of discretion by the arbitrators can minimize the availability of public law rights. Privacy in commercial arbitration preserves competitive advantage and trade secrets, whereas—in consumer and employment matters—it is seen as camouflage for the stronger party's **overreaching**. Further, adapted determinations fashioned by arbitrators can conflict with regulatory policies.

Arbitration makes self-governance possible. In a purely transactional setting, parties can agree to arbitrate either in the form of *ad hoc* or institutional arbitration. In the former, the parties undertake the management and administration of the arbitration, while—in the latter—they delegate those tasks to an arbitral **service-provider**. Institutional arbitration is more expensive, but it provides the benefit of professional experience and the application of well-established arbitral standards. Parties can also require that arbitrators rule according to law or decide the case pursuant to commercially-adapted standards. Further, they can authorize the arbitrators to rule in equity. Awards rendered through established arbitral institutions are likely to present fewer problems of enforcement. Freedom of contract even allows the contracting parties to vary the institutional rules—essentially to craft a customized arbitral procedure. Such modifications could, however, convert an institutional arbitration into an *ad hoc* proceeding, without the associated reduction in costs. The federal courts practice a nearly absolute 'hands-off' **supervisory policy** toward arbitral awards, allowing arbitrations to close themselves off from external scrutiny and to function with nearly complete independence. The legitimacy of the process depends upon the arbitrators and, to a lesser extent, upon the skills and adaptability of legal counsel.

The federal decisional law seeks to maintain the systemic **autonomy** of arbitration, recognizing independence as an indispensable part of arbitration's remedial viability. In effect, the courts have removed any real force to the already narrow statutory grounds for policing arbitral awards. The aggressive judicial protection of arbitration is meant to eliminate dilatory tactics. As a consequence, a consumer who fails to read or understand the standard language of a purchase contract from a manufacturer or who is forced to arbitrate in order to buy goods or services may be left without any recourse against arbitration. Arbitration can only coexist with a **docile judiciary**. Courts may have been difficult to access, but now the legal doctrine on arbitration makes them even more distant. Arbitration is the portal to the consumer economy and the processing of employment disputes. Acquiescence to arbitration grants access to goods, services, and employment. To some degree, arbitral tribunals have become the courts of civil litigation.

The 'reconstruction' of **civil justice** through arbitration may be a beneficial occurrence. Despite some adversarialization, the arbitral procedure has remained adaptable and resilient. The arbitral, legal, and judicial processes may be responding as effectively as possible to new contingencies and providing—in times of economic and political restructuring—a means of maintaining a fundamental **rule of law** in American society. Overburdened courts—saddled with criminal proceedings—are unable to provide sufficient justice services to civil litigants. Arbitration supplies timely access, legal representation, fair hearings, and a final and binding decision. Arbitration may satisfy the domestic need for adjudicatory services in the same way that it fashioned a legal system for **global commerce**. If the movement toward alternative, privatized justice has done nothing else, it has placed enormous responsibility on the legal profession and given it the opportunity to participate in a wholesale but quiet redefinition of law and adjudicatory legitimacy.

4. BASIC DOCTRINES, CONCEPTS, AND FEATURES

(i) Freedom of Contract

The legal principle that governs (at least, theoretically) the law, practice, and regulation of U.S. arbitration is contract freedom. In *Volt Info. Sciences, Inc. v. Board of Trustees of Leland Stanford Junior Univ.*, 489 U.S. 468 (1989), the U.S. Supreme Court established that:

> . . . The FAA does not require parties to arbitrate when they have not agreed to do so . . . nor does it prevent parties who do agree to arbitrate from excluding certain claims from the scope of their arbitration agreement. . . . It simply requires courts to enforce privately negotiated agreements to arbitrate, like other contracts, in accordance with their terms. . . . Arbitration under the Act is a matter of consent, not coercion, and parties are generally free to structure their arbitration agreements as they see fit. . . .

Freedom of contract allows **parties** to write their own rules of arbitration—in effect, to have the agreement to arbitrate establish the law of arbitration for their transaction. The parties, therefore, are the sovereigns of the process. They are the **law-givers**—customizing the process to their adjudicatory needs, discarding unhelpful rules and ineffective procedures, and establishing a process that reflects their sense of fairness, finality, and functionality.

Obviously, freedom of contract privileges the position of the economically stronger and more sophisticated party. Some states, in particular California, afford protection to the weaker party against the dominance of the stronger party. Freedom of contract, therefore, can be rendered ineffectual in circumstances in which power relationships are uneven. In *Mastrobuono v. Shearson Lehman Hutton, Inc.*, 514 U.S. 52 (1995), the Court integrated the objectives of the federal policy favoring arbitration into the freedom of contract principle. Parties were free to establish the modalities of their arbitration as long as their contracts supported the recourse to arbitration. In other words, **freedom of contract** worked only if it resulted in the submission of disputes to arbitration. Finally, the Court in *Hall Street Associates v. Mattel*, 552 U.S. 576 (2008), concluded that party freedom of contract in arbitration ended with the rendition of the award by the arbitrators. Therefore, the parties could not regulate award enforcement by contract agreement. Contract choice no longer governed at this point. The vacatur of awards belonged exclusively to the courts. Enacted law applied by judges was the sole source of authority in the final stage of the arbitral process. The Court appears to have concluded that the law needed to maintain a foothold in the arbitral process perhaps for the sake of the integrity of law and court litigation. It may also have been a means of protecting the limited judicial supervision of awards.

(ii) Arbitration Agreements

A contract for arbitration can take one of two forms: the submission or the arbitral clause. The **submission** is an arbitration agreement in which the parties agree that an existing dispute shall be submitted to arbitration. The **arbitral clause** is a contract under which the parties agree to submit future disputes to arbitration. A contract for arbitration, in either form, must be written and satisfy the requirements of contract validity. Courts have liberally interpreted the writing requirement—a practice that coincides with the federal policy favoring arbitration.

The arbitral clause is the primary arbitration agreement. Ordinarily, the arbitral clause appears as a provision within a larger contract; it, however, can be a legally separate agreement. When it is materially separate from the principal agreement, the arbitral clause must establish to which contractual relationship it applies. In any event, in terms of legal theory, the arbitral clause is always distinct from the main contract. Under the separability doctrine, the arbitral clause is legally **autonomous**. The nullity of the main contract, therefore, cannot invalidate the agreement to arbitrate, unless the moving party establishes—to the satisfaction of the arbitrators or a court—that the nullity specifically affects the arbitration provision.

Once a dispute arises in a transaction governed by an arbitral clause, the parties usually enter into a submission agreement. That agreement defines the specific elements of the dispute, confers jurisdiction upon the arbitral tribunal, and initiates the arbitral proceedings. It should be underscored that a valid arbitration agreement that has not been mutually rescinded by the parties divests the courts of jurisdiction to entertain any matter covered by the agreement, even when a resulting award is incapable of coercive legal enforcement or the arbitral proceeding is being delayed.

(iii) Arbitrability

'Arbitrability', an uncommon word according to 'spell checks', means 'amenable or submissible to arbitration'. It functions in relation to the parties' agreement (**contract arbitrability**) and enacted statutes (**subject-matter arbitrability**). It answers the question of whether a dispute can be resolved through arbitration, and thus is akin to the assertion of jurisdiction. Arbitrability is a means of expressing and balancing the requirements of public policy and contract freedom. Parties must have entered into an arbitration agreement, the scope of which covers the matter at issue. A valid arbitration agreement obligates the parties to arbitrate unless the parties agree to rescind their obligation. While contract is the gateway to arbitration, statutory law can invalidate the contract for arbitration when public law rights are involved. When the U.S.

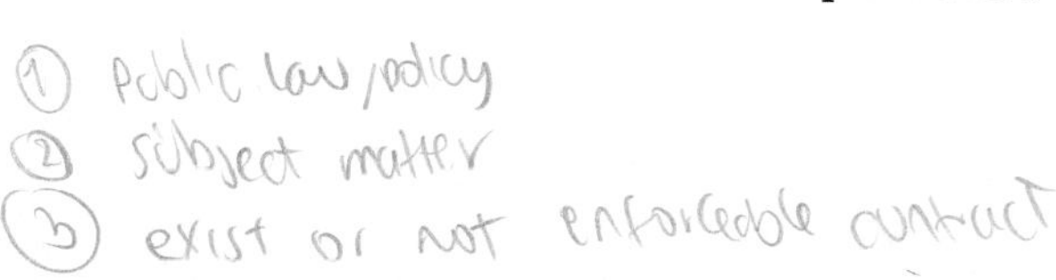

Congress enacts legislation, it can give the courts exclusive jurisdiction to resolve disputes that arise under the statute. The law thereby eliminates the parties' right to agree to arbitration because the Congress believes the rights have significant public importance. They must, therefore, be litigated only in public judicial proceedings. Public policy thereby curtails contract rights. The extent of the curtailment depends upon the statutory language and the courts' interpretation of that language.

In effect, arbitrability represents the dividing line between public and private jurisdiction—the point at which freedom of contract ends and legislative commands begin. Private commercial conduct intersects with the public interest in several areas (for example, anti-trust, securities, bankruptcy, and discrimination law). In the recent past, most arbitration laws and court decisions provided that commercial disputes that interface with the public interest could not be submitted to arbitration. Since *Mitsubishi Motors Corp. v. Soler Chrysler-Plymouth*, 473 U.S. 614 (1985), the federal judiciary has rejected that view of subject-matter inarbitrability. The federal courts now hold that statutory claims, regardless of whether they arise in domestic or international contracts, can be submitted to arbitration. Moreover, the Court has made clear that a very strong presumption of arbitrability applies to statutory rights.

The decisive element is no longer the language of the statute. In fact, the U.S. Supreme Court has never found a statutory provision specific or clear enough to preclude arbitration, and few statutes seem to prevent recourse to arbitration. Rather, party intent governs the question of arbitrability. When the parties agree, without qualification, to the submission of disputes to arbitration, the submission includes all disputes that may arise—even those based on statutory law. This decisional position makes the reference to arbitration stronger, unambiguous, and more comprehensive. The objective of the legal regulation of arbitration no longer is to segregate judicial and arbitral jurisdiction, but rather to promote the independent operation and autonomy of the arbitral process. Arbitrators, not courts, control the arbitration and its operation. The autonomy attributed to arbitration makes the process effective and functional—capable of dispensing civil justice.

Disputes can also be deemed inarbitrable on the basis of contract. Here, the application of the arbitrability doctrine does not involve public policy; the subject matter of the dispute is not an obstacle to arbitrability. Parties invoking this defense might allege that the dispute in question is not covered by the arbitration agreement. Therefore, they cannot be compelled to arbitration simply because they have not agreed to arbitrate. The parties, for example, may have restricted the scope of their arbitral agreement to disputes relating to matters of delivery of specific items. All other disagreements or conflicts arising between them, they could provide further, must be submitted initially to mediation and then (if necessary) to judicial litigation. Disputes relating to the conformity of goods to specifications would not fall within the scope of the agreed-upon reference to arbitration. They would be inarbitrable as a matter of contract law. The parties, however, could submit such a disagreement to arbitration by modifying their contract or entering into a submission agreement when the dispute arises. Inarbitrability as a result of contract can also come about in circumstances in which the agreement to arbitrate cannot be established or is a flawed as a contract. The limitation on arbitration here does not arise from the scope of the arbitration agreement, but rather from whether it exists or is an enforceable contract.

NOTES AND QUESTIONS

1. Does the arbitrability of statutory rights represent a trespass by arbitration into the public domain—an intrusion into the realm of public and judicial jurisdiction? Are contract and statutory disputes indistinguishable? Should the submission of statutory claims to arbitration be accompanied by a requirement that arbitrator determinations on statutory matters be written and reasoned according to law? Would the 'qualified' subject-matter arbitrability of statutory disputes be a better approach? How extensively should arbitrators consider judicial interpretations of the relevant statute when they are confronted with statutory and contractual questions to decide?

2. Which public policies apply to arbitration? Is arbitration itself a public policy? Is it the supreme public policy? Why should it trump or engulf the political regulation of commerce and the implementation of civil liberty guarantees? Is the suggested conflict more theoretical than real? How would you identify and define the public domain?

3. Why should a 'garden variety' reference to arbitration presume the arbitrability of statutory claims? Given the impact on public policy, should the presumption be reversed? Why not have freedom of contract prevail and allow parties to determine—for their transaction—the arbitrability of statutory disputes?

(iv) Separability and *Kompetenz-Kompetenz*

Both concepts are intended to protect the jurisdictional authority of arbitral tribunals and the autonomy of the arbitral process. Prior to their incorporation in the law of arbitration, a party bent on delay would oppose the arbitration by alleging that the principal contract was void—usually for reasons of public policy. The latter allegation was an amorphous basis of opposition—difficult to establish or deny. Because the agreement to arbitrate was generally included in the main contract, it suffered the fate of the other contract provisions. In a word, the parties were not bound to arbitrate because the agreement to arbitrate was *arguably* invalid. The mere allegation that the main contract was invalid, therefore, gave the courts jurisdiction to decide whether a valid contract of arbitration existed. Judicial intervention delayed the arbitration and impeded the implementation of the agreed-upon recourse to arbitration. As a result, dilatory tactics flourished prior to the statutory adoption of *kompetenz-kompetenz*.

The **separability doctrine** provides that the agreement to arbitrate is separate from, and independent of, the main contract. Succinctly stated, the arbitration agreement is a self-standing contract. Allegations of contractual invalidity directed to the main contract do not necessarily affect or apply to the arbitral clause. The challenging party, therefore, must establish that the alleged flaw also reaches the arbitral clause. Otherwise, the reference to arbitration remains unchallenged and intact. The critical issue is whether a court or the arbitral tribunal should decide the impact of the allegation upon the arbitral clause. Recent decisions have expanded the arbitrator's jurisdiction to resolve such issues, thereby further insulating the arbitral process from judicial interference.

At this juncture, the separability doctrine works in tandem with *kompetenz-kompetenz*. The ***kompetenz-kompetenz*** **doctrine** (in English, jurisdiction to rule on jurisdictional challenges) provides that the arbitral tribunal has the authority to decide objections to its authority to rule—specifically, whether an arbitration agreement (the basis of the arbitrators' authority to adjudicate) exists or is a valid and enforceable contract and what it provides in terms of arbitrability and the arbitral process (the scope of the arbitrators' adjudicatory authority). The tribunal can also decide claims that the dispute in question is not covered by the arbitral clause. The tribunal's rulings on jurisdictional matters are subject to judicial scrutiny either at the time of pronouncement (when and if they are rendered in the form of an interim award) or at the enforcement stage of the process (when the rulings are integrated into the final award). Ordinarily, jurisdictional issues are considered at the end of the process when reversal is less likely.

NOTES AND QUESTIONS

1. When separability and *kompetenz-kompetenz* are part of the local law of arbitration, the legal system is favorably disposed to arbitration. The two doctrines not only weaken and defeat delaying strategies, but also empower arbitrators to exercise judge-like powers in defining their own jurisdiction. Lax or delayed judicial supervision, in effect, gives the arbitrators' decision on their jurisdictional authority a substantial presumption of enforceability.

2. How likely is it that arbitrators will find flaws in their jurisdictional investiture when the discovery of such flaws would result in their loss of lucrative adjudicatory work? Courts have no financial stake in jurisdictional determinations. Are courts then not in a better position to reach a determination on jurisdiction? Why does the governing legal standard provide to the contrary?

3. An unusual feature of the U.S. law on arbitration is that it does not expressly recognize or incorporate the *kompetenz-kompetenz* doctrine. The FAA was enacted in 1925 when the Western judicial doctrine on arbitration was embryonic. Moreover, *kompetenz-kompetenz* came into existence in Europe in the 1960s. As a result, FAA § 3 provides that jurisdictional issues pertaining to arbitration (whether a valid agreement exists and whether a dispute is covered by the agreement) are to be decided by a federal district court in the context of determining whether a judicial proceeding should be stayed pending arbitration. Under *First Options of Chicago, Inc. v. Kaplan*, 514 U.S. 938 (1995), however, contracting parties can agree to delegate the determination of jurisdictional questions to the arbitrators. *Kompetenz-kompetenz*, therefore, is available through contract provision. What does the FAA's failure to provide for *kompetenz-kompetenz* say about the statute's underlying objective? Does the parties' ability to provide for it by contract undermine the statutory regime?

(v) The Arbitrators' Remedial Powers

The basic rule of U.S. arbitration law is that arbitrators (as a matter of law) possess the remedial authority necessary to adjudicate the submitted dispute. Arbitral tribunals can award pre- and post-judgment interest. They can issue orders for provisional relief. U.S. arbitration law also provides that arbitrators have the authority to award punitive damages and attorney's fees. The authorization to rule generally presumes the ability to award the necessary relief. If the parties want to restrict the authority of arbitrators, they must so state specifically in the arbitration agreement.

The arbitrators also have the authority to issue orders for the production of evidence by an arbitrating party. When the party refuses to comply, the arbitral tribunal can seek to have its injunction enforced by a court or—under some frameworks for arbitration—can simply take the party's refusal to comply into account in the final award. Ordinarily, the arbitrators' power to order the production of evidence and to enjoin conduct applies only to the parties to the arbitration. Like its counterpart in England, U.S. arbitration law, however, is an exception to the rule. Under FAA § 7, arbitrators can compel non-arbitrating parties to produce evidence or to appear at the proceeding or both. Some federal courts have placed restrictions on the arbitrators' power to subpoena third-parties.

Arbitrators generally rule pursuant to law. Freedom of contract, however, allows parties to agree to another decisional predicate. They can require the arbitrators to rule according to equity, as amiable compositors, or in light of their expertise. Amiable composition empowers arbitrators to disregard a legal result that they believe is unjust after they have established how the law would resolve the dispute. They can then substitute their determination for the legal ruling. Amiable composition relies upon the knowledge, ability, and experience of the arbitrators. It also reflects an occasional adjudicatory reality: Decision-makers come to a conclusion that they believe to be right and interpret the law and the contract accordingly. The concept of amiable composition affords the arbitrators considerable, perhaps untoward discretion. Finally, arbitrators can be authorized to decide matters according to their technical expertise and knowledge. This standard applies to arbitrations in which the application of law is of lesser importance and the matters at issue involve scientific, engineering, or other specialized fields. It is especially well-known and practiced in Latin America.

NOTES AND QUESTIONS

1. Begin thinking about the content of a would-be model arbitration clause. In addition to the agreement to arbitrate disputes, what other stipulations might be necessary? What limits would you incorporate into an arbitration agreement to limit the arbitrator's decisional discretion?

2. Should FAA § 7 allow arbitrators to subpoena non-arbitrating parties? If so, why should an ordinary citizen be subject to the authority of a private arbitrator?

3. How should arbitrators rule? Why?

(vi) Enforcement of Awards

The enforcement of awards is critical to the viability of the arbitration. If arbitrator determinations were not enforceable at law, there would be little, if any, incentive to engage in arbitration. The process would be replete with dilatory tactics and become merely a stepping stone to court litigation. In effect, the expense of engaging in arbitration would render the process useless as an adjudicatory substitute. The coercive enforcement of awards is necessary only when the debtor party does not voluntarily satisfy the award. Courts will either confirm or vacate an award. In some circumstances, the court might remand an award to the arbitrators for clarification or reconsideration. By and large, the judicial policy favoring arbitration dominates enforcement cases. The vast majority of actions for vacatur fail.

Do and should courts merely 'rubber stamp' what arbitrators decide, especially on the application of law? Should the law provide for the automatic enforcement of awards? In ICSID (International Centre for the Settlement of Investment Disputes or World Bank) arbitration, for example, awards are automatically enforced in Signatory States. This practice makes it impossible for courts to disturb the results reached by international arbitrators in litigation between Host States and investors. An internal ICSID committee reviews awards and determines whether they contain a legally justified result to the controversy. Not surprisingly, the diplomats and political representatives often disagree about the 'right' outcome under international law. The lack of consensus often leads to several different committee proceedings and results. This situation adds to the already protracted character of the proceedings.

Would the ICSID rule and procedure be useful in a purely domestic setting? If not, should the parties be able to choose it anyway? *See Hall Street Associates v. Mattel*, 552 U.S. 576 (2008). Why should State policy be allowed to overwhelm contract freedom in these circumstances?

The statutory grounds for the judicial supervision of arbitral awards are limited and exclude by implication judicial merits review. The parties have bargained for a single adjudication. Appellate relief is limited to flagrant procedural abuses that essentially constitute a denial of justice. Under FAA § 10, the parties are entitled to proceedings that are free of corruption, in which they are heard by disinterested arbitrators who decide only the matters submitted pursuant to the stipulations of the agreement. Moreover, the parties must be given notice of the proceedings and treated equally and fairly in terms of making their case through documents, testimonial evidence, witnesses, and advocacy.

Arbitrators can only rule upon the disputes that are legally submitted to them. A ruling on a matter that is 'not submitted' constitutes an excess of authority and can bring about the vacatur of the award (if the excessive ruling is an inseparable part of the award) or a partial enforcement of the award (if the excessive ruling can be severed from the other rulings). According to *Stolt-Nielsen v. AnimalFeeds*, 559 U.S. 662 (2010), arbitrators who fail to provide a legal foundation for their determinations exceed (or rather, fail to fulfill) their professional authority to rule. Their interpretation is merely an a-legal opinion. The Court's statement involved the arbitrators' construction of the parties' arbitration clause, concluding that it permitted class arbitration. Because the arbitrators decided the matter *ex cathedra* and made no reference to any legal basis to justify their conclusions, the Court quashed the arbitrators' decision on the basis of excess of authority. It was an unusual and questionable usage and interpretation of the vacatur ground. The latter point was made in a subsequent case, *Oxford Health Services v. Sutter*, 569 U.S. 564 (2013), which restored the dominance of the deferential judicial policy toward arbitration.

Under the 'equal treatment of the parties' doctrine, the arbitral tribunal must allow each party the same opportunity to make its case. An 'abbreviated' form of due process establishes a functional balance between the rule of law, the guarantee of legal rights, and the means for their implementation. The hearing must be both fair and effective. Awards are also subject to judicial scrutiny under non-statutory (or common law) grounds. These grounds, added by the decisional law to the statutory provision, permit judicial review of the merits of awards. The latter is impliedly excluded by the statute, thereby creating a conflict between the statute and judicial practice. The decisional law thereby allows awards to be assessed by a court for manifest disregard of the law, irrational rulings, or a violation of statutory public policy.

You should think about how to define the various statutory and non-statutory grounds for vacatur. When might arbitrators exceed their powers or manifestly disregard the law? How much do they need to disclose to avoid a challenge of the award for 'evident partiality'? Must actual bias be established to constitute the latter? Why are public policy violations restricted to matters of statutory public policy? When does an arbitral ruling become irrational?

The courts hold that an error of law is insufficient to vacate an arbitral award. Criminal acts by an arbitrator committed during and relating to the arbitration, however. are actionable (*e.g.,* accepting bribes, committing fraud, or intimidating a party). Excess of authority is sometimes interpreted broadly, making it a 'catch-all' provision that is dangerously malleable. Procedural misconduct by arbitrators is virtually impossible to establish given the judicial position that arbitrators have basically unlimited power to conduct the arbitral proceeding. Agreeing to arbitration means that the parties wanted to have arbitrators rule on their dispute and conduct the proceedings. The position is based on the 'benefit of the bargain' theory, a position that has great appeal among courts which favor arbitration.

5. CLASS ACTION WAIVERS

The Court's recent ruling in *Epic Systems v. Lewis*, 584 U.S. ___, 138 S.Ct. 1612 (2018), joined to the prior holding in *AT&T Mobility v. Concepcion*, 563 U.S. 333 (2011), establishes that class action waivers contained in adhesive contracts imposed by the stronger party on the weaker one are lawful and enforceable contracts. In both opinions, the Court invoked the "emphatic federal policy favoring arbitration" which commands, allegedly by congressional directive, the presumptive enforcement of arbitration agreements. The Court also referred to the freedom of contract principle to justify the validity of the contract: The parties had 'voluntarily' entered into the contract and continued to be bound by their decision. Both *Concepcion* and *Epic Systems* illustrate the strength of the judicial support for arbitration and arbitrability. According to Justice Gorsuch in *Epic Systems*:

> Should employees and employers be allowed to agree that any disputes between them will be resolved through one-on-one arbitration? Or should employees always be permitted to bring their claims in class or collective actions, no matter what they agreed with their employers?

As a matter of policy these questions are surely debatable. But as a matter of law the answer is clear. In the Federal Arbitration Act, Congress has instructed federal courts to enforce arbitration agreements according to their terms—including terms providing for individualized proceedings. Nor can we agree with the employees' suggestion that the National Labor Relations Act (NLRA) offers a conflicting command. It is this Court's duty to interpret Congress's statutes as a harmonious whole rather than at war with one another. And abiding that duty here leads to an unmistakable conclusion. The NLRA secures to employees rights to organize unions and bargain collectively, but it says nothing about how judges and arbitrators must try legal disputes that leave the workplace and enter the courtroom or arbitral forum. This Court has never read a right to class actions into the NLRA—and for three quarters of a century neither did the National Labor Relations Board. Far from conflicting, the Arbitration Act and the NLRA have long enjoyed separate spheres of influence and neither permits this Court to declare the parties' agreements unlawful.

[. . .]

Although the Arbitration Act and the NLRA have long coexisted—they date from 1925 and 1935, respectively—the suggestion they might conflict is something quite new. Until a couple of years ago, courts more or less agreed that arbitration agreements like those before us must be enforced according to their terms. . . .

[. . .]

We begin with the Arbitration Act and the question of its saving clause.

Congress adopted the Arbitration Act in 1925 in response to a perception that courts were unduly hostile to arbitration. No doubt there was much to that perception. Before 1925, English and American common law courts routinely refused to enforce agreements to arbitrate disputes. . . . But in Congress's judgment arbitration had more to offer than courts recognized—not least the promise of quicker, more informal, and often cheaper resolutions for everyone involved. . . . So Congress directed courts to abandon their hostility and instead treat arbitration agreements as "valid, irrevocable, and enforceable." 9 U. S. C. § 2. The Act, this Court has said, establishes "a liberal federal policy favoring arbitration agreements." . . . [citation to *Moses H. Cone* and *Prime Paint*] . . . (discussing "the plain meaning of the statute" and "the unmistakably clear congressional purpose that the arbitration procedure, when selected by the parties to a contract, be speedy and not subject to delay and obstruction in the courts").

Not only did Congress require courts to respect and enforce agreements to arbitrate; it also specifically directed them to respect and enforce the parties' chosen arbitration procedures. . . . Indeed, we have often observed that the Arbitration Act requires courts "rigorously" to "enforce arbitration agreements according to their terms, including terms that specify *with whom* the parties choose to arbitrate their disputes and *the rules* under which that arbitration will be conducted." . . .

[. . .]

This is where the employees' argument stumbles. They don't suggest that their arbitration agreements were extracted, say, by an act of fraud or duress or in some other unconscionable way that would render *any* contract unenforceable. Instead, they object to their agreements precisely because they require individualized arbitration proceedings instead of class or collective ones. And by attacking (only) the individualized nature of the arbitration proceedings, the employees' argument seeks to interfere with one of arbitration's fundamental attributes.

We know this much because of *Concepcion*. There this Court faced a state law defense that prohibited as unconscionable class action waivers in consumer contracts. The Court readily acknowledged that the defense formally applied in both the litigation and the arbitration context. . . . But, the Court held, the defense failed to qualify for protection under the saving clause because it interfered with a fundamental attribute of arbitration all the same. It did so by effectively permitting any party in arbitration to demand class wide proceedings despite the traditionally individualized and informal nature of arbitration. This "fundamental" change to the traditional arbitration process, the Court said, would "sacrific[e] the principal advantage of arbitration—its informality—and mak[e] the process slower, more costly, and more likely to generate procedural morass than final judgment." . . . Not least, *Concepcion* noted, arbitrators would have to decide whether the named class representatives are sufficiently representative and typical of the class; what kind of notice, opportunity to be heard, and right to opt out absent class members should enjoy; and how discovery should be altered in light of the class wide nature of the proceedings. . . . All of which would take much time and effort, and introduce new risks and costs for both sides. . . . In the Court's judgment, the virtues Congress originally saw in arbitration, its speed and simplicity

> and inexpensiveness, would be shorn away and arbitration would wind up looking like the litigation it was meant to displace.
>
> Of course, *Concepcion* has its limits. The Court recognized that parties remain free to alter arbitration procedures to suit their tastes, and in recent years some parties have sometimes chosen to arbitrate on a classwide basis. . . . But *Concepcion*'s essential insight remains: courts may not allow a contract defense to reshape traditional individualized arbitration by mandating classwide arbitration procedures without the parties' consent. . . . Just as judicial antagonism toward arbitration before the Arbitration Act's enactment "manifested itself in a great variety of devices and formulas declaring arbitration against public policy," *Concepcion* teaches that we must be alert to new devices and formulas that would achieve much the same result today. . . . And a rule seeking to declare individualized arbitration proceedings off limits is, the Court held, just such a device.
>
> [. . .]
>
> What all these textual and contextual clues indicate, our precedents confirm. In many cases over many years, this Court has heard and rejected efforts to conjure conflicts between the Arbitration Act and other federal statutes. In fact, this Court has rejected *every* such effort to date (save one temporary exception since overruled) [the reference is probably to *Gardner-Denver* and the Civil Rights Act of 1964], with statutes ranging from the Sherman and Clayton Acts to the Age Discrimination in Employment Act, the Credit Repair Organizations Act, the Securities Act of 1933, the Securities Exchange Act of 1934, and the Racketeer Influenced and Corrupt Organizations Act. . . .
>
> [. . .]
>
> The policy may be debatable but the law is clear: Congress has instructed that arbitration agreements like those before us must be enforced as written. While Congress is of course always free to amend this judgment, we see nothing suggesting it did so in the NLRA—much less that it manifested a clear intention to displace the Arbitration Act. . . .

The language of the opinion is unambiguous and its doctrine unmistakable: *Concepcion* is affirmed and the Court is merely following the congressional command in the statute to sustain the contractual reference to arbitration. In its wisdom, **Congress** has chosen to **rehabilitate arbitration** and ordered courts in the United States to enforce arbitration agreements as written by the parties. The majority in *Epic Systems* does not refer to the requirements of contract formation or to the lack of bilateral agreement between the parties. The weakness of one and the strength of the other are not a concern. Possible social policy consequences can be debated, but—as the Court itself emphasizes—**the law is clear**. The Court's institutional and systemic 'duty' is manifest. Its responsibility is to give full effect to categorical legislative commands and the parties' intentions. The law is clear only because of the Court's categorical prior decisional rulings on arbitration. There is, therefore, circularity and a self-fulfilling logic to the Court's ruling in *Epic Systems v. Lewis*.

If you have the proverbial 'inquiring' mind, you might find the Court's genuflection before the altar of legislative power not as credible analytically as the Court would like lawyers and commentators to believe. It is more convincing to view the FAA as the Court's transformation of special interest legislation into a means of providing functional civil justice in the American legal system. *Epic Systems* affirms the judicial reconstruction of the FAA. By upholding adhesive arbitral clauses with class waivers, the Court adds to the autonomy and independence of arbitral adjudication.

The Court's decisions on class waivers have given the U.S. law of arbitration a modest, but visible political character. Lobby groups on the left argue that the ability of manufacturers and employers to rescind unilaterally the right of consumers and employees to engage in class litigation gives the stronger party an unfair advantage and compromises the weaker party's legal rights. This position assumes that class litigation benefits all members of the class, not just the named plaintiffs and their lawyers and that it cures the markets of their flaws. Pro-business lobbyists contend that the ability to eliminate class action lessens the costs of doing business and protects commercial parties from vexatious and extortive litigation. This position minimizes the importance of legal rights and assumes that a fair arbitral process can be constructed between unequal parties. The Court avoided assessing these positions and confined itself to noting (through Justice Scalia in *Concepcion*) that consumers managed to redress their grievances before class litigation was ever instituted. Also, in the Court's view, class litigation was difficult, if not impossible, to integrate into arbitral frameworks because the class action approach to litigation conflicted with arbitration's essential adjudicatory attributes.

The Court ignored the rights deprivation argument. Seemingly, the Court did not want to politicize arbitration. Consumer and employment arbitration represent a very small part of the arbitration business. Its monetary significance is modest. Exposing arbitration to attacks on this basis is very likely to cause more harm than good. The importance of allowing class waivers resides in freeing business from a 'disguised' tax imposed by the legal system through class litigation. The latter is a barrier to commercial profitability; it yields a modest social good and 'confiscates' corporate wealth.

6. THE FEDERAL POLICY ON ARBITRATION

SCOTUS has freely interpreted the FAA for a number of decades through Courts with different leanings and compositions. According to Justice O'Connor, the Court has created an American arbitration law "of its own making." Many of the Court opinions refer to a policy that the Court has made the centerpiece of its decisional law on arbitration. The Court frequently invokes a "strong" or "emphatic" or "liberal" "federal policy favoring arbitration." The Court uses the policy to frame and decide arbitration cases. The policy creates a virtually irrebuttable presumption that arbitration agreements and awards are enforceable. Moreover, the judicial supervision of arbitration hardly budges the needle. Once the parties designate arbitration as their remedy, they are entitled to the benefit [or conscription] of their bargain. In terms of arbitration, the courts give effect to the parties' intent. The Court claims that the federal policy arises from the FAA. It is more accurate to say that the federal policy on arbitration arises from SCOTUS' continuously 'reformist' construction of the statute. The Court has federalized arbitration, thereby providing for the uniform regulation of arbitral agreements and awards. The Court feigns an allegiance to the principle of contract freedom to camouflage its reconfigurations of the FAA.

There is resistance to the SCOTUS doctrine on arbitration, especially from the Ninth Circuit. It has been the principal critic of the Court's doctrine and rulings on arbitration. For the opponents, the chief drawback of the judicial doctrine on arbitration is that it mistakenly establishes that arbitral adjudication and judicial litigation are equivalent processes. The judicial trial is designed to protect legal rights through impartial and neutral procedures and proceedings. Arbitration hearings use their flexibility and ability to adapt to unanticipated and unusual circumstances as well as expertise, expedition, and economy to validate their adjudicatory integrity. Therefore, arbitral hearings and the judicial trial, in many respects, stand in contradistinction to each other. They advance different values and protect different interests. Arbitration seeks to provide commercial justice. It is not the purveyor of legal civilization. Arbitrators do not apply the law in a judicial sense. Arbitration molds adjudication to the specific needs of the parties. Because it is so responsive and adaptable, it occupies an inferior position in the ranking of adjudicatory mechanisms. The prevailing view is that judicial adjudication functions above and beyond the parties' station and comprehension. It is the law—forbidding, detached, and mysterious. It operates elsewhere than the unremarkable and routine. Judicial adjudication privileges authority, rigor, and discipline. It does not adapt to the circumstances of disputes. Parties and their disputes adapt to it.

The unequivocal endorsement of arbitration is the means by which the Court fulfilled its managerial obligations to the legal system. Arbitral proceedings remedied the inadequacies of judicial litigation by providing expertise, expedition, economy, effectiveness, and enforceability. Most importantly, arbitration provided accessibility. The lack of appeal on the merits and limited discovery helped to establish many of arbitration's essential qualities. Practicing a sensible form of procedural fairness was also a contributing factor. Arbitration resulted in a genuine form of *res judicata*. The "strong federal policy favoring arbitration" made possible a functional type of civil justice necessary to the constitutional integrity of the American legal system. This version of civil justice was affordable and workable. It did not require the creation of new courts. The protection of legal rights could be achieved without imposing a ruinous burden on societal resources. Finally, the "emphatic federal policy" allowed the Court to favor arbitrability in the vast majority of, if not all, cases.

7. ARBITRATOR THRESHOLD POWERS

Allocations of decision-making authority can be tricky in arbitration. Distinguishing the powers that arbitrators have from the power of courts, at the outset of the arbitral process, requires awareness of a couple of key U.S. Supreme Court decisions.

In *Howsam v. Dean Witter Reynolds, Inc.*, 537 U.S. 79 (2002), the U.S. Supreme Court held that a dispute—over whether a National Association Securities Dealers (NASD) six-year eligibility requirement for submission precluded arbitration—was a "question of arbitrability" that should be decided by an arbitrator, not the courts. Upon receiving investment advice from Dean Witter, Karen Howsam bought an interest in four limited partnerships. Subsequently, believing that Dean Witter had misrepresented the value of the partnerships, Howsam filed a demand for arbitration pursuant to the Client Service Agreement. The agreement contained an arbitration clause providing for the arbitration of all controversies arising out of a customer's company accounts. The clause allowed the client to select the arbitration forum.

Upon learning of Howsam's attempt to invoke arbitration, Dean Witter filed suit in federal district court asking that the dispute be declared ineligible for arbitration because it was more than six years old. NASD Code Section 10304 states that no dispute "shall be eligible for submission . . . where six (6) years have elapsed from the occurrence or event giving rise to the . . . dispute." The district court ruled that an arbitrator, not the court should interpret the NASD rule. Dean Witter appealed and the Tenth Circuit reversed. According to the appellate court, application of the NASD rule raised questions about the dispute's "arbitrability." Such questions should be resolved by a court, not an arbitrator. The U.S. Supreme Court granted Howsam's petition for *certiorari* because the lower federal courts "reached different conclusions about whether a court or an arbitrator primarily should interpret and apply this particular NASD rule."

In the Court's view, the question of whether parties have submitted a dispute to arbitration, *i.e.*, the "question of arbitrability," is "an issue for judicial determination unless the parties clearly and unmistakably provide otherwise." The phrase "question of arbitrability," however, only applies in limited circumstances:

> . . .where contracting parties would likely have expected a court to decide the gateway matter, where they are not likely to have thought that they had agreed that an arbitrator would do so, and, consequently, where reference of the gateway dispute to the court avoids the risk of forcing parties to arbitrate a matter that they may well not have agreed to arbitrate.

Therefore, " 'procedural questions which grow out of the dispute and bear on its final disposition are presumptively not for the judge, but for an arbitrator to decide.' " Arbitrators should decide "allegation[s] of waiver, delay, or a like defense to arbitrability" because these issues do not raise the question of whether parties agreed to submit a dispute to arbitration. Finally, the Court referred to the language of the Revised Uniform Arbitration Act of 2000 (RUAA) providing that an "arbitrator shall decide whether a condition precedent to arbitrability has been fulfilled." According to the commentary in the RUAA, "in the absence of an agreement to the contrary, issues of procedural arbitrability, *i.e.*, whether prerequisites such as time limits . . . have been met, are for the arbitrator to decide."

Finding that the time-limit rule "closely resembles the gateway questions that this court has found not to be questions of arbitrability," the Court ruled that the application of the NASD time-limit rule was a matter presumptively for the arbitrator, not the judge. Moreover, NASD arbitrators were "comparatively more expert about the meaning of their own rule" and consequently better able to apply it. Accordingly, aligning the ". . . decisionmaker with . . . comparative expertise" better secures a "fair and expeditious resolution of the underlying controversy—a goal of arbitration systems and judicial systems alike."

HOWSAM V. DEAN WITTER REYNOLDS, INC.

537 U.S. 79, 123 S.Ct. 588, 154 L.Ed.2d 491 (2002).

BREYER, JUSTICE.

This case focuses upon an arbitration rule of the National Association of Securities Dealers (NASD). The rule states that no dispute "shall be eligible for submission to arbitration . . . where six (6) years have elapsed from the occurrence or event giving rise to the . . . dispute." NASD Code of Arbitration Procedure § 10304 (1984) (NASD Code or Code). We must decide whether a court or an NASD arbitrator should apply the rule to the underlying controversy. We conclude that the matter is for the arbitrator.

I

The underlying controversy arises out of investment advice that Dean Witter Reynolds, Inc. (Dean Witter), provided its client, Karen Howsam, when, sometime between 1986 and 1994, it recommended that she buy and hold interests in four limited partnerships. Howsam says that Dean Witter misrepresented the virtues of the partnerships. The resulting controversy falls within their standard Client Service Agreement's arbitration clause, which provides:

> "[A]ll controversies . . . concerning or arising from . . . any account . . . , any transaction . . . , or . . . the construction, performance or breach of . . . any . . . agreement between us . . . shall be determined by arbitration before any self-regulatory organization or exchange of which Dean Witter is a member."

The agreement also provides that Howsam can select the arbitration forum. And Howsam chose arbitration before the NASD.

To obtain NASD arbitration, Howsam signed the NASD's Uniform Submission Agreement. That agreement specified that the "present matter in controversy" was submitted for arbitration "in accordance with" the NASD's "Code of Arbitration Procedure." And that Code contains the provision at issue here, a provision stating that no dispute "shall be eligible for submission . . . where six (6) years have elapsed from the occurrence or event giving rise to the . . . dispute." NASD Code § 10304.

After the Uniform Submission Agreement was executed, Dean Witter filed this lawsuit in Federal District Court. It asked the court to declare that the dispute was "ineligible for arbitration" because it was more than six years old. And it sought an injunction that would prohibit Howsam from proceeding in arbitration. The District Court dismissed the action on the ground that the NASD arbitrator, not the court, should interpret and apply the NASD rule. The Court of Appeals for the Tenth Circuit, however, reversed. . . . In its view, application of the NASD rule presented a question of the underlying dispute's "arbitrability"; and the presumption is that a court, not an arbitrator, will ordinarily decide an "arbitrability" question. *See, e.g., First Options of Chicago, Inc. v. Kaplan,* 514 U.S. 938, 115 S.Ct. 1920, 131 L.Ed.2d 985 (1995).

The Courts of Appeals have reached different conclusions about whether a court or an arbitrator primarily should interpret and apply this particular NASD rule. . . . We granted Howsam's petition for *certiorari* to resolve this disagreement. And we now hold that the matter is for the arbitrator.

II

This Court has determined that "arbitration is a matter of contract and a party cannot be required to submit to arbitration any dispute which he has not agreed so to submit." . . . Although the Court has also long recognized and enforced a "liberal federal policy favoring arbitration agreements," . . . it has made clear that there is an exception to this policy: The question whether the parties have submitted a particular dispute to arbitration, *i.e.*, the "*question of arbitrability*," is "an issue for judicial determination [u]nless the parties clearly and unmistakably provide otherwise." . . . We must decide here whether application of the NASD time limit provision falls into the scope of this last-mentioned interpretive rule.

Linguistically speaking, one might call any potentially dispositive gateway question a "question of arbitrability," for its answer will determine whether the underlying controversy will proceed to arbitration on the merits. The Court's case law, however, makes clear that, for purposes of applying the interpretive rule, the phrase "question of arbitrability" has a far more limited scope. . . . The Court has found the phrase applicable in the kind of narrow circumstance where contracting parties would likely have expected a court to have decided the gateway matter, where they are not likely to have thought that they had agreed that an arbitrator would do so, and, consequently, where reference of the gateway dispute to the court avoids the risk of forcing parties to arbitrate a matter that they may well not have agreed to arbitrate.

Thus, a gateway dispute about whether the parties are bound by a given arbitration clause raises a "question of arbitrability" for a court to decide. . . . Similarly, a disagreement about whether an arbitration clause in a concededly binding contract applies to a particular type of controversy is for the court. . . .

At the same time the Court has found the phrase "question of arbitrability" *not* applicable in other kinds of general circumstance where parties would likely expect that an arbitrator would decide the gateway matter. Thus " 'procedural' questions which grow out of the dispute and bear on its final disposition" are presumptively *not* for the judge, but for an arbitrator, to decide. . . . So, too, the presumption is that the arbitrator should decide "allegation[s] of waiver, delay, or a like defense to arbitrability." . . . Indeed, the Revised Uniform Arbitration Act of 2000 (RUAA), seeking to "incorporate the holdings of the vast majority of state courts and the law that has developed under the [Federal Arbitration Act]," states that an "arbitrator shall decide whether a condition precedent to arbitrability has been fulfilled." RUAA § 6(c), and comment 2, 7 U.L.A. 12–13 (Supp.2002). And the comments add that "in the absence of an agreement to the contrary, issues of substantive arbitrability . . . are for a court to decide and issues of procedural arbitrability, *i.e.*, whether prerequisites such as *time limits*, notice, laches, estoppel, and other conditions precedent to an obligation to arbitrate have been met, are for the arbitrators to decide." *Id.*, § 6, comment 2, 7 U.L.A., at 13 (emphasis added).

Following this precedent, we find that the applicability of the NASD time limit rule is a matter presumptively for the arbitrator, not for the judge. The time limit rule closely resembles the gateway questions that this Court has found not to be "questions of arbitrability." . . . Such a dispute seems an "aspec[t] of the [controversy] which called the grievance procedures into play." . . .

Moreover, the NASD arbitrators, comparatively more expert about the meaning of their own rule, are comparatively better able to interpret and to apply it. In the absence of any statement to the contrary in the arbitration agreement, it is reasonable to infer that the parties intended the agreement to reflect that understanding. . . . And for the law to assume an expectation that aligns (1) decision maker with (2) comparative expertise will help better to secure a fair and expeditious resolution of the underlying controversy—a goal of arbitration systems and judicial systems alike.

We consequently conclude that the NASD's time limit rule falls within the class of gateway procedural disputes that do not present what our cases have called "questions of arbitrability." And the strong pro-court presumption as to the parties' likely intent does not apply.

III

Dean Witter argues that, in any event, *i.e.,* even without an anti-arbitration presumption, we should interpret the contracts between the parties here as calling for judicial determination of the time limit matter. Howsam's execution of a Uniform Submission Agreement with the NASD in 1997 effectively incorporated the NASD Code into the parties' agreement. Dean Witter notes the Code's time limit rule uses the word "eligible." That word, in Dean Witter's view, indicates the parties' intent for the time limit rule to be resolved by the court prior to arbitration.

We do not see how that is so. For the reasons stated in Part II, *supra,* parties to an arbitration contract would normally expect a forum-based decision maker to decide forum-specific procedural gateway matters. And any temptation here to place special anti-arbitration weight on the appearance of the word "eligible" in the NASD Code rule is counterbalanced by a different NASD rule; that rule states that "arbitrators shall be empowered to interpret and determine the applicability of all provisions under this Code." NASD Code § 10324.

Consequently, without the help of a special arbitration-disfavoring presumption, we cannot conclude that the parties intended to have a court, rather than an arbitrator, interpret and apply the NASD time limit rule. And as we held in Part II, *supra,* that presumption does not apply.

IV

For these reasons, the judgment of the Tenth Circuit is *Reversed.*

NOTES AND QUESTIONS

1. How would you define a "gateway question" in light of the Court's opinion? How does the Court explain the notion of "arbitrability"?

2. Who decides what circumstances or issues constitute a "gateway question" and a question of arbitrability? Why? Does the result favor or disfavor arbitration? In what way(s)?

3. What is a "procedural question"? What impact does it have on the jurisdictional question?

4. Does freedom of contract play any role in the Court's ruling? What about the federal policy favoring arbitration?

Green Tree Fin. Corp. v. Bazzle, 539 U.S. 444 (2003), involved consolidated cases about loan contracts between Green Tree, homeowners, and purchasers of mobile homes. The arbitral clause in the loan agreements provided for the arbitration of all disputes "by one arbitrator selected by us with consent of you." Individual cases eventually were certified as a class and compelled to arbitration. The arbitral clause made no mention of classwide arbitration. On appeal, the South Carolina Supreme Court held that, under state contract law, the silence of the agreement on classwide arbitration permitted the claims to be submitted to class action arbitration. On appeal to the Court, the consideration of whether the agreement allowed for classwide arbitration created a number of divisions within the Court—four Justices formed a plurality; one Justice authored a concurring-dissenting opinion; and four Justices dissented. The split did not appear to reflect ideological differences among the Justices. Rather, it indicated analytical disagreement about an important issue of arbitration law.

Justice Breyer wrote the plurality opinion. In addressing the issue, the Court returned to an opaque concept of arbitrability that it originally propounded in *First Options of Chicago, Inc. v. Kaplan*, 514 U.S. 938 (1995). In *Kaplan*, the Court stated that courts decide the basic issues of arbitrability (whether there is a valid contract of arbitration that covers the question of litigation), unless the parties authorize the arbitrators to rule on these matters. *Howsam v. Dean Witter Reynolds, Inc.* confirmed this division of labor between the courts and arbitrators—unless the parties provided otherwise, the courts decided the threshold arbitrability matters, while the arbitrators ruled upon issues that pertained to the implementation of the arbitration (*e.g.*, the application of a time-limit bar to the submitted claim). *Bazzle* adds that the interpretation of the content of the arbitration agreement also falls within the sovereign decisional authority of the arbitrator. Simply stated, "Under the terms of the parties' contracts, the question—whether the agreement forbids class arbitration—is for the arbitrator to decide."

The impact of the plurality opinion upon the law of arbitration was generally favorable. The determination was not antagonistic to arbitration because it extended the scope of the arbitrator's discretion, limited the role of the courts in regard to the arbitral process, and enhanced the systemic autonomy of arbitration. This appraisal was supported by the fact that the four dissenting Justices, as well as the concurring Justice, did not express animosity toward arbitration in their disagreement with the plurality.

The analytical factor that separated the court into two camps centered upon the distinction between substantive and procedural arbitrability. Chief Justice William Rehnquist wrote the principal dissenting opinion. Advancing the view that *Kaplan* and *Howsam* were distinguishable, the dissent asserted that the courts must decide to what the parties have agreed. Determining what the agreement provided was not simply a matter of implementing the agreed-upon recourse to arbitration. According to the Chief Justice, the question in *Bazzle* fell within the orbit of *Kaplan,* not *Howsam*:

> I think that the parties' agreement as to how the arbitrator should be selected is much more akin to the agreement as to what shall be arbitrated, a question for the courts under *First Options*, than it is to 'allegations of waiver, delay, or like defenses to arbitrability,' which are questions for the arbitrator under *Howsam*.

According to the dissent, the parties had not agreed to classwide arbitration and the South Carolina Supreme Court "imposed a regime that was contrary to the express agreement of the parties. . . ." The state court's failure to implement the parties' actual intent in the contract justified the reversal of its decision.

The case also raised of a state law question. Justice Thomas dissented on the basis that the Federal Arbitration Act should not govern "a state court's interpretation of a private arbitration agreement." Chief Justice Rehnquist acknowledged that state contract law regulated contracts of arbitration, but emphasized that state laws that contravened federal law were subject to preemption. Finally, Justice Stevens—who concurred and ideally would have upheld the South Carolina Supreme Court rather than remand the case—concluded that: "There is nothing in the Federal Arbitration Act that precludes . . . [the] determinations by the Supreme Court of South Carolina." According to Justice Stevens, that court held "as a matter of state law that class-action arbitrations [were] permissible if not prohibited by the applicable arbitration agreement, and that the agreement between [the] parties [was] silent on the issue."

When the Court granted *certiorari* in *Bazzle*, the expectation among commentators was that it would decide the vexed question of **classwide arbitration** and begin the formal elaboration of a basic standard of fairness in consumer arbitration—including the possible unconscionability or limited validity of arbitration agreements in this setting. It is clear—at least ostensibly—that those matters did not occur to, let alone preoccupy, the Court. By ruling on a boundary-line issue—in effect, characterizing the class action question as an interpretation of a valid agreement to arbitrate and delegating the question to the arbitrator as a matter of **procedural arbitrability** (for the plurality) or by having a court interpret the content of the arbitration agreement to determine whether it excluded classwide arbitration (for the three-member dissent)—the Court stated that the fairness and legitimacy questions in consumer arbitration were a matter to be determined by the arbitrating parties' contract and the arbitrators' interpretation of the parties' contractual intent. This conclusion reinforces the view, also stated in *Kaplan*, that the practice of arbitration should not be allowed to generate too much judicial litigation. Justice Breyer's view, expressed here and elsewhere, was that bringing arbitration issues before courts foiled arbitration's *raison d'être*. The Court thereby substantially buttressed the independence and autonomy of arbitration.

GREEN TREE FIN. CORP. V. BAZZLE

539 U.S. 444, 123 S.Ct. 2402, 156 L.Ed.2d 414 (2003).

BREYER, JUSTICE.

This case concerns contracts between a commercial lender and its customers, each of which contains a clause providing for arbitration of all contract-related disputes. The Supreme Court of South Carolina held (1) that the arbitration clauses are silent as to whether arbitration might take the form of class arbitration, and (2) that, in that circumstance, South Carolina law interprets the contracts as permitting class arbitration. . . . We granted *certiorari* to determine whether this holding is consistent with the Federal Arbitration Act. . . .

We are faced at the outset with a problem concerning the contracts' silence. Are the contracts in fact silent, or do they forbid class arbitration as petitioner Green Tree Financial Corp. contends? Given the South Carolina Supreme Court's holding, it is important to resolve that question. But we cannot do so, not simply because it is a matter of state law, but also because it is a matter for the arbitrator to decide. Because the record suggests that the parties have not yet received an arbitrator's decision on that question of contract interpretation, we vacate the judgment of the South Carolina Supreme Court and remand the case so that this question may be resolved in arbitration.

I.

In 1995, respondents Lynn and Burt Bazzle secured a home improvement loan from petitioner Green Tree. The Bazzles and Green Tree entered into a contract, governed by South Carolina law, which included the following arbitration clause:

> "ARBITRATION—All disputes, claims, or controversies arising from or relating to this contract or the relationships which result from this contract . . . *shall be resolved by binding arbitration by one arbitrator selected by us with consent of you.* This arbitration contract is made pursuant to a transaction in interstate commerce, and shall be governed by the Federal Arbitration

> Act. . . . THE PARTIES VOLUNTARILY AND KNOWINGLY WAIVE ANY RIGHT THEY HAVE TO A JURY TRIAL, EITHER PURSUANT TO ARBITRATION UNDER THIS CLAUSE OR PURSUANT TO A COURT ACTION BY U.S. [SIC] [us] (AS PROVIDED HEREIN). . . . The parties agree and understand that the arbitrator shall have all powers provided by the law and the contract. These powers shall include all legal and equitable remedies, including, but not limited to, money damages, declaratory relief, and injunctive relief." . . . (emphasis added, capitalization in original).

Respondents Daniel Lackey and George and Florine Buggs entered into loan contracts and security agreements for the purchase of mobile homes with Green Tree. These agreements contained arbitration clauses that were . . . identical to the Bazzles' arbitration clause. . . .

At the time of the loan transactions, Green Tree apparently failed to provide these customers with a legally required form that would have told them that they had a right to name their own lawyers and insurance agents and would have provided space for them to write in those names. . . . The two sets of customers before us now as respondents each filed separate actions in South Carolina state courts, complaining that this failure violated South Carolina law and seeking damages.

In April 1997, the Bazzles asked the court to certify their claims as a class action. Green Tree sought to stay the court proceedings and compel arbitration. On January 5, 1998, the court both (1) certified a class action and (2) entered an order compelling arbitration. Green Tree then selected an arbitrator with the Bazzles' consent. And the arbitrator, administering the proceeding as a class arbitration, eventually awarded the class $10,935,000 in statutory damages, along with attorney's fees. The trial court confirmed the award, and Green Tree appealed to the South Carolina Court of Appeals claiming, among other things, that class arbitration was legally impermissible.

[. . .]

The South Carolina Supreme Court withdrew both cases from the Court of Appeals, assumed jurisdiction, and consolidated the proceedings. . . . That court then held that the contracts were silent in respect to class arbitration, that they consequently authorized class arbitration, and that arbitration had properly taken that form. We granted *certiorari* to consider whether that holding is consistent with the Federal Arbitration Act.

II

The South Carolina Supreme Court's determination that the contracts are silent in respect to class arbitration raises a preliminary question. Green Tree argued there, as it argues here, that the contracts are not silent—that they forbid class arbitration. And we must deal with that argument at the outset, for if it is right, then the South Carolina court's holding is flawed on its own terms; that court neither said nor implied that it would have authorized class arbitration had the parties' arbitration agreement forbidden it.

Whether Green Tree is right about the contracts themselves presents a disputed issue of contract interpretation. THE CHIEF JUSTICE believes that Green Tree is right; indeed, that Green Tree is so clearly right that we should ignore the fact that state law, not federal law, normally governs such matters and reverse the South Carolina Supreme Court outright. THE CHIEF JUSTICE points out that the contracts say that disputes "shall be resolved . . . by one arbitrator selected by us [Green Tree] with consent of you [Green Tree's customer]." And it finds that class arbitration is clearly inconsistent with this requirement. After all, class arbitration involves an arbitration, not simply between Green Tree and a *named customer,* but also between Green Tree and *other* (represented) customers, all taking place before the arbitrator chosen to arbitrate the initial, *named customer's* dispute.

We do not believe, however, that the contracts' language is as clear as THE CHIEF JUSTICE believes. The class arbitrator *was* "selected by" Green Tree "with consent of" Green Tree's customers, the named plaintiffs. And insofar as the other class members agreed to proceed in class arbitration, they consented as well.

Of course, Green Tree did *not* independently select *this* arbitrator to arbitrate its disputes with the *other* class members. But whether the contracts contain this additional requirement is a question that the literal terms of the contracts do not decide. The contracts simply say (I) "selected by us [Green Tree]." And that is literally what occurred. The contracts do not say (II) "selected by us [Green Tree] to arbitrate this dispute and no other (even identical) dispute with another customer." The question whether (I) in fact implicitly means (II) is the question at issue: Do the contracts forbid class arbitration? Given the broad authority the contracts elsewhere bestow upon the arbitrator, the answer to this question is not completely obvious.

At the same time, we cannot automatically accept the South Carolina Supreme Court's resolution of this contract-interpretation question. Under the terms of the parties' contracts, the question—whether the agreement forbids class arbitration—is for the arbitrator to decide. The parties agreed to submit to the arbitrator *"[a]ll* disputes, claims, or controversies arising from or relating to this contract or the relationships which result from this contract." And the dispute about what the arbitration contract in each case means (*i.e.,* whether it forbids the use of class arbitration procedures) is a dispute "relating to this contract" and the resulting "relationships." Hence the parties seem to have agreed that an arbitrator, not a judge, would answer the relevant question. . . . And if there is doubt about that matter—about the " 'scope of arbitrable issues' "—we should resolve that doubt " 'in favor of arbitration.' " . . .

In certain limited circumstances, courts assume that the parties intended courts, not arbitrators, to decide a particular arbitration-related matter (in the absence of "clea[r] and unmistakabl[e]" evidence to the contrary). . . . These limited instances typically involve matters of a kind that "contracting parties would likely have expected a court" to decide. . . . They include certain gateway matters, such as whether the parties have a valid arbitration agreement at all or whether a concededly binding arbitration clause applies to a certain type of controversy. . . .

The question here—whether the contracts forbid class arbitration—does not fall into this narrow exception. It concerns neither the validity of the arbitration clause nor its applicability to the underlying dispute between the parties. Unlike *First Options,* the question is not whether the parties wanted a judge or an arbitrator to decide *whether they agreed to arbitrate a matter*. . . . Rather the relevant question here is what *kind of arbitration proceeding* the parties agreed to. That question does not concern a state statute or judicial procedures. . . . It concerns contract interpretation and arbitration procedures. Arbitrators are well situated to answer that question. Given these considerations, along with the arbitration contracts' sweeping language concerning the scope of the questions committed to arbitration, this matter of contract interpretation should be for the arbitrator, not the courts, to decide. . . .

[. . .]

NOTES AND QUESTIONS

1. What is (if any) the "gateway question" in Bazzle?

2. Why does the South Carolina Supreme Court take such a different position on the question of litigation?

3. Under current law, what is the function of the courts in regard to arbitration? When can courts intervene in the arbitral process?

4. Do you agree with the Court that the arbitrating parties bargained for wide arbitrator interpretation?

5. Is this a salutary result for arbitration? Why and why not?

8. FEDERAL JURISDICTION IN THE 'PENUMBRA'

Though the FAA constitutes effectively a substantive body of arbitral law for the United States, it does not create an independent basis for subject matter jurisdiction. In other words, the mere fact that the FAA applies to a given arbitration contract does not mean that federal courts have jurisdiction. In order to have jurisdiction, as the following case discusses, a court must "look through" the arbitration agreement and determine if there is a jusidictional foundation for federal law in the underlying dispute.

VADEN V. DISCOVER BANK

556 U.S. 49, 129 S.Ct. 1262, 173 L.Ed.2d 206 (2009).

JUSTICE GINSBURG delivered the opinion of the Court.

Section 4 of the Federal Arbitration Act, 9 U.S.C. § 4, authorizes a United States district court to entertain a petition to compel arbitration if the court would have jurisdiction, "save for [the arbitration] agreement," over "a suit arising out of the controversy between the parties." We consider in this opinion two questions concerning a district court's subject-matter jurisdiction over a § 4 petition: Should a district court, if asked to compel arbitration pursuant to § 4, "look through" the petition and grant the requested relief if the court would have federal-question jurisdiction over the underlying controversy? And if the answer to that question is yes, may a district court exercise jurisdiction over a § 4 petition when the petitioner's complaint rests on state law but an actual or potential counterclaim rests on federal law?

The litigation giving rise to these questions began when Discover Bank's servicing affiliate filed a complaint in Maryland state court. Presenting a claim arising solely under state law, Discover sought to recover past-due charges from one of its credit cardholders, Betty Vaden. Vaden answered and counterclaimed, alleging that Discover's finance charges, interest, and late fees violated state law. Invoking an arbitration clause in its cardholder agreement with Vaden, Discover then filed a § 4 petition in the United States District Court for the District of Maryland to compel arbitration of Vaden's counterclaims. The District Court had subject-matter jurisdiction over its petition, Discover maintained, because Vaden's state-law counterclaims were completely preempted by federal banking law. The District Court agreed and ordered arbitration. Reasoning that a federal court has jurisdiction over a § 4 petition if the parties' underlying dispute presents a federal question, the Fourth Circuit eventually affirmed.

We agree with the Fourth Circuit in part. A federal court may "look through" a § 4 petition and order arbitration if, "save for [the arbitration] agreement," the court would have jurisdiction over "the [substantive] controversy between the parties." We hold, however, that the Court of Appeals misidentified the dimensions of "the controversy between the parties." Focusing on only a slice of the parties' entire controversy, the court seized on Vaden's counterclaims, held them completely preempted, and on that basis affirmed the District Court's order compelling arbitration. Lost from sight was the triggering plea—Discover's claim for the balance due on Vaden's account. Given that entirely state-based plea and the established rule that federal-court jurisdiction cannot be invoked on the basis of a defense or counterclaim, the whole "controversy between the parties" does not qualify for federal-court adjudication. Accordingly, we reverse the Court of Appeals' judgment.

I

This case originated as a garden-variety, state-law-based contract action: Discover sued its cardholder, Vaden, in a Maryland state court to recover arrearages amounting to $10,610.74, plus interest and counsel fees.[1] Vaden's answer asserted usury as an affirmative defense. Vaden also filed several counterclaims, styled as class actions. Like Discover's complaint, Vaden's pleadings invoked only state law: Vaden asserted that Discover's demands for finance charges, interest, and late fees violated Maryland's credit laws. . . . Neither party invoked—by notice to the other or petition to the state court—the clause in the credit card agreement providing for arbitration of "any claim or dispute between [Discover and Vaden]."[2] . . .

Faced with Vaden's counterclaims, Discover sought federal-court aid. It petitioned the United States District Court for the District of Maryland for an order, pursuant to § 4 of the Federal Arbitration Act (FAA or Act), . . . compelling arbitration of Vaden's counterclaims.[3] Although those counterclaims were framed under state law, Discover urged that they were governed entirely by federal law, specifically, § 27(a) of the Federal Deposit Insurance Act (FDIA), 12 U.S.C. § 1831d(a). Section 27(a) prescribes the interest rates state-chartered, federally insured banks like Discover can charge, "notwithstanding any State constitution or statute which is hereby preempted." This provision, Discover maintained, was completely preemptive, *i.e.*, it superseded otherwise applicable Maryland law, and placed Vaden's counterclaims under the exclusive governance of the FDIA. On that basis, Discover asserted, the District Court had authority to

---

1 Discover apparently had no access to a federal forum for its suit against Vaden on the basis of diversity-of-citizenship jurisdiction. Under that head of federal-court jurisdiction, the amount in controversy must "excee[d] . . . $75,000." 28 U.S.C. § 1332(a).

2 Vaden's preference for court adjudication is unsurprising. The arbitration clause, framed by Discover, prohibited presentation of "any claims as a representative or member of a class." . . .

3 Section 4 reads, in relevant part:

> "A party aggrieved by the alleged failure, neglect, or refusal of another to arbitrate under a written agreement for arbitration may petition any United States district court which, save for such agreement, would have jurisdiction under title 28, in a civil action or in admiralty of the subject matter of a suit arising out of the controversy between the parties, for an order directing that such arbitration proceed in the manner provided for in such agreement." 9 U.S.C. § 4.

entertain the § 4 petition pursuant to 28 U.S.C. § 1331, which gives federal courts jurisdiction over cases "arising under" federal law.

The District Court granted Discover's petition, ordered arbitration, and stayed Vaden's prosecution of her counterclaims in state court pending the outcome of arbitration. . . . On Vaden's initial appeal, the Fourth Circuit inquired whether the District Court had federal-question jurisdiction over Discover's § 4 petition. To make that determination, the Court of Appeals instructed, the District Court should "look through" the § 4 petition to the substantive controversy between the parties. . . . The appellate court then remanded the case for an express determination whether that controversy presented "a properly invoked federal question." . . .

On remand, Vaden "concede[d] that the FDIA completely preempts any state claims against a federally insured bank." . . . Accepting this concession, the District Court expressly held that it had federal-question jurisdiction over Discover's § 4 petition and again ordered arbitration. . . . In this second round, the Fourth Circuit affirmed, dividing 2 to 1. . . .

Recognizing that "a party may not create jurisdiction by concession," . . . the Fourth Circuit majority conducted its own analysis of FDIA § 27(a), ultimately concluding that the provision completely preempted state law and therefore governed Vaden's counterclaims. [Footnote omitted.] . . .

We granted *certiorari* in view of the conflict among lower federal courts on whether district courts, petitioned to order arbitration pursuant to § 4 of the FAA, may "look through" the petition and examine the parties' underlying dispute to determine whether federal-question jurisdiction exists over the § 4 petition. . . . [Footnote omitted.] . . .

As this case shows, if the underlying dispute is the proper focus of a § 4 petition, a further question may arise. The dispute brought to state court by Discover concerned Vaden's failure to pay over $10,000 in past-due credit card charges. In support of that complaint, Discover invoked no federal law. When Vaden answered and counterclaimed, however, Discover asserted that federal law, specifically § 27(a) of the FDIA, displaced the state laws on which Vaden relied. What counts as the underlying dispute in a case so postured? May Discover invoke § 4, not on the basis of its own complaint, which had no federal element, but on the basis of counterclaims asserted by Vaden? To answer these questions, we first review relevant provisions of the FAA . . . and controlling tenets of federal jurisdiction.

II

In 1925, Congress enacted the FAA "[t]o overcome judicial resistance to arbitration," . . . and to declare " 'a national policy favoring arbitration' of claims that parties contract to settle in that manner." . . . To that end, § 2 provides that arbitration agreements in contracts "involving commerce" are "valid, irrevocable, and enforceable." . . . [Footnote omitted.] Section 4—the section at issue here—provides for United States district court enforcement of arbitration agreements. Petitions to compel arbitration, § 4 states, may be brought before "any United States district court which, save for such agreement, would have jurisdiction under title 28 . . . of the subject matter of a suit arising out of the controversy between the parties." . . . [Footnote omitted.]

The "body of federal substantive law" generated by elaboration of FAA § 2 is equally binding on state and federal courts. . . . "As for jurisdiction over controversies touching arbitration," however, the Act is "something of an anomaly" in the realm of federal legislation: It "bestow[s] no federal jurisdiction but rather requir[es] [for access to a federal forum] an independent jurisdictional basis" over the parties' dispute. . . . [Footnote omitted.] Given the substantive supremacy of the FAA, but the Act's nonjurisdictional cast, state courts have a prominent role to play as enforcers of agreements to arbitrate. . . .

The independent jurisdictional basis Discover relies upon in this case is 28 U.S.C. § 1331, which vests in federal district courts jurisdiction over "all civil actions arising under the Constitution, laws, or treaties of the United States." Under the longstanding well-pleaded complaint rule, however, a suit "arises under" federal law "only when the plaintiff's statement of his own cause of action shows that it is based upon [federal law]." . . . Federal jurisdiction cannot be predicated on an actual or anticipated defense: "It is not enough that the plaintiff alleges some anticipated defense to his cause of action and asserts that the defense is invalidated by some provision of [federal law]." . . .

Nor can federal jurisdiction rest upon an actual or anticipated counterclaim. We so ruled, emphatically, in *Holmes Group,* 535 U.S. 826. Without dissent, the Court held in *Holmes Group* that a federal counterclaim, even when compulsory, does not establish "arising under" jurisdiction. [Footnote omitted.] Adhering assiduously to the well-pleaded complaint rule, the Court observed, *inter alia*, that it would undermine the clarity and simplicity of that rule if federal courts were obliged to consider the contents not only of the complaint but also of responsive pleadings in determining whether a case "arises under" federal law. . . . [Footnote omitted.]

A *complaint* purporting to rest on state law, we have recognized, can be recharacterized as one "arising under" federal law if the law governing the complaint is exclusively federal. . . . Under this so-called "complete preemption doctrine," a plaintiff's "state cause of action [may be recast] as a federal claim for relief, making [its] removal [by the defendant] proper on the basis of federal question jurisdiction." . . . [Footnote omitted.] A state-law-based *counterclaim*, however, even if similarly susceptible to recharacterization, would remain nonremovable. Under our precedent construing § 1331, as just explained, counterclaims, even if they rely exclusively on federal substantive law, do not qualify a case for federal-court cognizance.

III

Attending to the language of the FAA and the above-described jurisdictional tenets, we approve the "look through" approach to this extent: A federal court may "look through" a § 4 petition to determine whether it is predicated on an action that "arises under" federal law; in keeping with the well-pleaded complaint rule as amplified in *Holmes Group*, however, a federal court may not entertain a § 4 petition based on the contents, actual or hypothetical, of a counterclaim.

A

The text of § 4 drives our conclusion that a federal court should determine its jurisdiction by "looking through" a § 4 petition to the parties' underlying substantive controversy. We reiterate § 4's relevant instruction: When one party seeks arbitration pursuant to a written agreement and the other resists, the proponent of arbitration may petition for an order compelling arbitration in

> "any United States district court which, save for [the arbitration] agreement, would have jurisdiction under title 28, in a civil action or in admiralty of the subject matter of a suit arising out of the controversy between the parties." 9 U.S.C. § 4.

The phrase "save for [the arbitration] agreement" indicates that the district court should assume the absence of the arbitration agreement and determine whether it "would have jurisdiction under title 28" without it. . . . Jurisdiction over what? The text of § 4 refers us to "the controversy between the parties." That phrase, the Fourth Circuit said, and we agree, is most straightforwardly read to mean the "substantive conflict between the parties." . . . [Footnote omitted.]

The majority of Courts of Appeals to address the question, we acknowledge, have rejected the "look through" approach entirely. . . . The relevant "controversy between the parties," Vaden insists, is simply and only the parties' discrete dispute over the arbitrability of their claims. She relies, quite reasonably, on the fact that a § 4 petition to compel arbitration seeks no adjudication on the merits of the underlying controversy. Indeed, its very purpose is to have an arbitrator, rather than a court, resolve the merits. A § 4 petition, Vaden observes, is essentially a plea for specific performance of an agreement to arbitrate, and it thus presents principally contractual questions: Did the parties validly agree to arbitrate? What issues does their agreement encompass? Has one party dishonored the agreement?

Vaden's argument, though reasonable, is difficult to square with the statutory language. Section 4 directs courts to determine whether they would have jurisdiction "save for [the arbitration] agreement." How, then, can a dispute over the existence or applicability of an arbitration agreement be the controversy that counts?

The "save for" clause, courts espousing the view embraced by Vaden respond, means only that the "antiquated and arcane" ouster notion no longer holds sway. . . . The "save for" clause, as comprehended by proponents of the "ouster" explanation, was designed to ensure that courts would no longer consider themselves ousted of jurisdiction and would therefore specifically enforce arbitration agreements. . . .

We are not persuaded that the "ouster" explanation of § 4's "save for" clause carries the day. To the extent that the ancient "ouster" doctrine continued to impede specific enforcement of arbitration agreements, § 2 of the FAA, the Act's "centerpiece provision," . . . directly attended to the problem. Covered agreements to arbitrate, § 2 declares, are "valid, irrevocable, and enforceable, save upon such grounds as exist at law or in equity for the revocation of any contract." Having commanded that an arbitration agreement is enforceable just as any other contract, Congress had no cause to repeat the point. . . . [Footnote omitted.]

In addition to its textual implausibility, the approach Vaden advocates has curious practical consequences. It would permit a federal court to entertain a § 4 petition only when a federal-question suit is already before the court, when the parties satisfy the requirements for diversity-of-citizenship jurisdiction, or when the dispute over arbitrability involves a maritime contract. . . . [Footnote omitted.] Vaden's approach would not accommodate a § 4 petitioner who *could* file a federal-question suit in (or remove such a suit to) federal court, but who has not done so. In contrast, when the parties' underlying dispute arises under federal law, the "look through" approach permits a § 4 petitioner to ask a federal court to compel arbitration without first taking the formal step of initiating or removing a federal-question suit—that is, without seeking federal adjudication of the very questions it wants to arbitrate rather than litigate. . . .

B

Having determined that a district court should "look through" a § 4 petition, we now consider whether the court "would have [federal-question] jurisdiction" over "a suit arising out of the controversy" between Discover and Vaden. . . . As explained above, § 4 of the FAA does not enlarge federal-court jurisdiction; rather, it confines federal courts to the jurisdiction they would have "save for [the arbitration] agreement." . . . Mindful of that limitation, we read § 4 to convey that a party seeking to compel arbitration may gain a federal court's assistance only if, "save for" the agreement, the entire, actual "controversy between the parties," as they have framed it, could be litigated in federal court. We conclude that the parties' actual controversy, here precipitated by Discover's state-court suit for the balance due on Vaden's account, is not amenable to federal-court adjudication. Consequently, the § 4 petition Discover filed in the United States District Court for the District of Maryland must be dismissed.

[. . .]

In holding that Discover properly invoked federal-court jurisdiction, the Fourth Circuit looked beyond Discover's complaint and ho[n]ed in on Vaden's state-law-based defense and counterclaims. Those responsive pleadings, Discover alleged, and the Fourth Circuit determined, were completely preempted by the FDIA. . . . The Fourth Circuit, however, misapprehended our decision in *Holmes Group*. Under the well-pleaded complaint rule, a completely preempted counterclaim remains a counterclaim and thus does not provide a key capable of opening a federal court's door. . . .

[. . .]

The dissent would have us treat a § 4 petitioner's statement of the issues to be arbitrated as the relevant controversy even when that statement does not convey the full flavor of the parties' entire dispute. Artful dodges by a § 4 petitioner should not divert us from recognizing the actual dimensions of that controversy. The text of § 4 instructs federal courts to determine whether they would have jurisdiction over "a suit arising out of *the* controversy between the parties"; it does not give § 4 petitioners license to recharacterize an existing controversy, or manufacture a new controversy, in an effort to obtain a federal court's aid in compelling arbitration. [Footnote omitted.]

Viewed contextually and straightforwardly, it is hardly "fortuit[ous]" that the controversy in this case took the shape it did. . . . Seeking to collect a debt, Discover filed an entirely state-law-grounded complaint in state court, and Vaden chose to file responsive counterclaims. Perhaps events could have unfolded differently, but § 4 does not invite federal courts to dream up counterfactuals when actual litigation has defined the parties' controversy. [Footnote omitted.]

As the dissent would have it, parties could commandeer a federal court to slice off responsive pleadings for arbitration while leaving the remainder of the parties' controversy pending in state court. That seems a bizarre way to proceed. In this case, Vaden's counterclaims would be sent to arbitration while the complaint to which they are addressed—Discover's state-law-grounded debt-collection action—would remain pending in a Maryland court. When the controversy between the parties is not one over which a federal court would have jurisdiction, it makes scant sense to allow one of the parties to enlist a federal court to disturb the state-court proceedings by carving out issues for separate resolution. [Footnote omitted.]

Furthermore, the presence of a threshold question whether a counterclaim alleged to be based on state law is totally preempted by federal law may complicate the dissent's § 4 inquiry. This case is illustrative. The dissent relates that Vaden eventually conceded that FDIA § 27(a), not Maryland law, governs the charges and fees Discover may impose. . . . But because the issue is jurisdictional, Vaden's concession is not determinative. . . . The dissent simply glides by the preemption issue, devoting no attention to it, although this Court has not yet resolved the matter.

In sum, § 4 of the FAA instructs district courts asked to compel arbitration to inquire whether the court would have jurisdiction, "save for [the arbitration] agreement," over "a suit arising out of the controversy between the parties." We read that prescription in light of the well-pleaded complaint rule and the corollary rule that federal jurisdiction cannot be invoked on the basis of a defense or counterclaim. Parties may not circumvent those rules by asking a federal court to order arbitration of the portion of a controversy that implicates federal law when the court would not have federal-question jurisdiction over the controversy as a whole. It does not suffice to show that a federal question lurks somewhere inside the parties' controversy, or that a defense or counterclaim would arise under federal law. Because the controversy between Discover and Vaden, properly perceived, is not one qualifying for federal-court adjudication, § 4 of the FAA does not empower a federal court to order arbitration of that controversy, in whole or in part. [Footnote omitted.]

Discover, we note, is not left without recourse. Under the FAA, state courts as well as federal courts are obliged to honor and enforce agreements to arbitrate. . . . Discover may therefore petition a Maryland court for aid in enforcing the arbitration clause of its contracts with Maryland cardholders.

True, Maryland's high court has held that §§ 3 and 4 of the FAA prescribe federal-court procedures and, therefore, do not bind the state courts.[20] But Discover scarcely lacks an available state remedy. Section 2 of the FAA, which does bind the state courts, renders agreements to arbitrate "valid, irrevocable, and *enforceable*." This provision "carries with it duties [to credit and enforce arbitration agreements] indistinguishable from those imposed on federal courts by FAA §§ 3 and 4." . . . Notably, Maryland, like many other States, provides a statutory remedy nearly identical to § 4. See Md. Cts. & Jud. Proc. Code Ann. § 3–207 (Lexis 2006) ("If a party to an arbitration agreement . . . refuses to arbitrate, the other party may file a petition with a court to order arbitration. . . . If the court determines that the agreement exists, it shall order arbitration. Otherwise it shall deny the petition."). See also Walther v. Sovereign Bank, 386 Md.

[20] This Court has not decided whether §§ 3 and 4 apply to proceedings in state courts . . . and we do not do so here.

412, 424, 872 A.2d 735, 742 (2005) ("The Maryland Arbitration Act has been called the 'State analogue . . . to the Federal Arbitration Act.' The same policy favoring enforcement of arbitration agreements is present in both our own and the federal acts." (internal quotation marks and citation omitted)). Even before it filed its debt-recovery action in a Maryland state court, Discover could have sought from that court an order compelling arbitration of any agreement-related dispute between itself and cardholder Vaden. At no time was federal-court intervention needed to place the controversy between the parties before an arbitrator.

* * *

For the reasons stated, the District Court lacked jurisdiction to entertain Discover's § 4 petition to compel arbitration. The judgment of the Court of Appeals affirming the District Court's order is therefore reversed, and the case is remanded for further proceedings consistent with this opinion.

It is so ordered.

CHIEF JUSTICE ROBERTS, with whom JUSTICE STEVENS, JUSTICE BREYER, and JUSTICE ALITO join, concurring in part and dissenting in part.

I agree with the Court that a federal court asked to compel arbitration pursuant to § 4 of the Federal Arbitration Act should "look through" the dispute over arbitrability in determining whether it has jurisdiction to grant the requested relief. But look through to what? The statute provides a clear and sensible answer: The court may consider the § 4 petition if the court "would have" jurisdiction over "the subject matter of a suit arising out of the controversy between the parties." . . .

The § 4 petition in this case explains that the controversy Discover seeks to arbitrate is whether "Discover Bank charged illegal finance charges, interest and late fees." . . . Discover contends in its petition that the resolution of this dispute is controlled by federal law—specifically § 27(a) of the Federal Deposit Insurance Act (FDIA), 12 U.S.C. § 1831d(a) (setting forth the interest rates a state-chartered, federally insured bank may charge "notwithstanding any State constitution or statute which is hereby preempted"). Vaden agrees that the legality of Discover's charges and fees is governed by the FDIA. [Asterisk omitted.] A federal court therefore "would have jurisdiction . . . of the subject matter of a suit arising out of the controversy" Discover seeks to arbitrate. That suit could be an action by Vaden asserting that the charges violate the FDIA, or one by Discover seeking a declaratory judgment that they do not.

The majority is diverted off this straightforward path by the fortuity that a complaint happens to have been filed in this case. Instead of looking to the controversy the § 4 petitioner seeks to arbitrate, the majority focuses on the controversy underlying that complaint, and asks whether "the *whole* controversy," as reflected in "the parties' state-court filings," arises under federal law. . . . [Emphasis added by dissent.] Because that litigation was commenced as a state-law debt-collection claim, the majority concludes there is no § 4 jurisdiction.

This approach is contrary to the language of § 4, and sharply restricts the ability of federal courts to enforce agreements to arbitrate. The "controversy" to which § 4 refers is the dispute alleged to be subject to arbitration. The § 4 petitioner must set forth the nature of that dispute—the one he seeks to arbitrate—in the § 4 petition seeking an order to compel arbitration. Section 4 requires that the petitioner be "aggrieved" by the other party's "failure, neglect, or refusal . . . to arbitrate under a written agreement for arbitration"; that language guides the district court to the specific controversy the other party is unwilling to arbitrate.

[. . .]

There is no reason to suppose "controversy" meant the controversy subject to arbitration everywhere else in the FAA, but something quite different in § 4. The issue is whether there is jurisdiction to compel arbitration to resolve a controversy; why would the pertinent controversy for assessing jurisdiction be anything other than the same one asserted to be subject to arbitration?

The majority looks instead to the controversy the state-court litigation seeks to resolve. This produces the odd result of defining "controversy" more broadly than the § 4 petition itself. Discover's petition does not seek to arbitrate its state-law debt-collection claims, but rather Vaden's allegation that the fees Discover has been charging her (and other members of her proposed class) violate the FDIA. . . . The majority does not appear to question that there would be federal jurisdiction over a suit arising out of the subject matter of that dispute. The majority finds no jurisdiction here, however, because "a federal court could not entertain Discover's state-law debt-collection claim." . . . There is no jurisdiction to compel arbitration of a plainly federal controversy—the FDIA dispute—because there is no jurisdiction to compel arbitration of the debt-collection dispute. But why Discover should have to demonstrate federal jurisdiction over a state-court claim it does not seek to arbitrate is a mystery. . . .

The majority's approach will allow federal jurisdiction to compel arbitration of *entirely* state-law claims. Under that approach the "controversy" is not the one the § 4 petitioner seeks to arbitrate, but a broader one encompassing the "whole controversy" between the parties. . . . If that broader dispute involves both federal and state-law claims, and the "originating" dispute is federal, . . . a party could seek arbitration of just the state-law claims. The "controversy" under the majority's view would qualify as federal, giving rise to § 4 jurisdiction to compel arbitration of a purely state-law claim.

Take this case as an example. If Vaden had filed her FDIA claim first, and Discover had responded with a state-law debt-collection counterclaim, that suit is one that "could be litigated in federal court." . . . As a result, the majority's approach would seem to permit Vaden to file a § 4 petition to compel arbitration of the entirely state-law-based debt-collection dispute, because that dispute would be part and parcel of the "full flavor[ed]," "originating" FDIA controversy. . . . Defining the controversy as the dispute the § 4 petitioner seeks to arbitrate eliminates this problem by ensuring that the *actual dispute* subject to arbitration is federal.

The majority's conclusion that this controversy "is not one qualifying for federal-court adjudication," . . . stems from its mistaken focus on the existing litigation. Rather than ask whether a court "would have" jurisdiction over the "subject matter" of "a" suit arising out of the "controversy," the majority asks only whether the court *does* have jurisdiction over the subject matter of a *particular* complaint. But § 4 does not speak of actual jurisdiction over pending suits; it speaks subjectively of prospective jurisdiction over "the subject matter of a suit arising out of the controversy between the parties." . . . The fact that Vaden has chosen to package the FDIA controversy in counterclaims in pending state-court litigation in no way means that a district court "would [not] have" jurisdiction over the "subject matter" of "a suit" arising out of the FDIA controversy. A big part of arbitration is avoiding the procedural niceties of formal litigation; it would be odd to have the authority of a court to compel arbitration hinge on just such niceties in a pending case.

By focusing on the sequence in which state-court litigation has unfolded, the majority crafts a rule that produces inconsistent results. Because Discover's debt-collection claim was filed before Vaden's counterclaims, the majority treats the debt-collection dispute as the "originating controversy." . . . But nothing would have prevented the same disagreements between the parties from producing a different sequence of events. Vaden could have filed a complaint raising her FDIA claims before Discover sought to collect on any amounts Vaden owes. Because the "originating controversy" in that complaint would be whether Discover has charged fees illegal under federal law, in that situation Discover presumably *could* bring a § 4 petition to compel arbitration of the FDIA dispute. The majority's rule thus makes § 4 jurisdiction over the same controversy entirely dependent upon the happenstance of how state-court litigation has unfolded. Nothing in § 4 suggests such a result.

The majority glosses over another problem inherent in its approach: In many if not most cases under § 4, no complaint will have been filed. . . . What to "look through" to then? The majority instructs courts to look to the "full-bodied controversy." . . . But as this case illustrates, that would lead to a different result had the state-court complaint not been filed. Discover does not seek to arbitrate whether an outstanding debt exists; indeed,

Discover's § 4 petition does not even allege any dispute on that point. . . . A district court would therefore not understand the § 4 "controversy" to include the debt-collection claim in the absence of the state-court suit. Under the majority's rule, the FDIA dispute would be treated as a "controversy" qualifying under § 4 before the state suit and counterclaims had been filed, but not after.

The far more concrete and administrable approach would be to apply the same rule in all instances: Look to the controversy the § 4 petitioner seeks to arbitrate—as set forth in the § 4 petition—and assess whether a federal court would have jurisdiction over the subject matter of a suit arising out of that controversy. The controversy the moving party seeks to arbitrate and the other party will not would be the same controversy used to assess jurisdiction to compel arbitration.

The majority objects that this would allow a court to "hypothesiz[e] discrete controversies of its own design," . . . in an apparent effort to find federal jurisdiction where there is none. Not so. A district court entertaining a § 4 petition is required to determine what "a suit" arising out of the allegedly arbitrable controversy would look like. There is no helping that, given the statute's subjunctive language. But that does not mean the inquiry is the free-form one the majority posits.

To the contrary, a district court must look to the specific controversy—the concrete dispute that one party has "fail[ed], neglect[ed], or refus[ed]" to arbitrate—and determine whether *that* controversy would give rise to a suit under federal law. District courts do that sort of thing often enough; the exercise is closely analogous to the jurisdictional analysis in a typical declaratory judgment action. . . . Looking to the specific controversy outlined in Discover's § 4 petition (whether its fees violate the FDIA), it hardly requires "dream[ing]" to conceive of a lawsuit in which Vaden would claim the FDIA has been violated and Discover would claim it has not. . . .

Nor would respondents' approach allow a § 4 petitioner to simply "recharacterize" or "manufacture" a controversy to create federal jurisdiction. . . . All of the established rules of federal jurisdiction are fully applicable in scrutinizing whether a federal court would have jurisdiction over a suit arising out of the parties' underlying controversy.

[. . .]

Accordingly, petitioners may no more smuggle state-law claims into federal court through § 4 than they can through declaratory judgment actions, or any other federal cause of action. To the extent § 4 brings some issues into federal court in a particular case that may not be brought in through other procedural mechanisms, it does so by "enlarg[ing] the range of remedies available in the federal courts[,] . . . not extend[ing] their jurisdiction." . . .

[. . .]

The correct approach is to accord § 4 the scope mandated by its language and look to "a suit," arising out of the "subject matter" of the "controversy" the § 4 petitioner seeks to arbitrate, and determine whether a federal court would have jurisdiction over such a suit.

The majority concludes by noting that state courts are obliged to honor and enforce agreements to arbitrate. . . . The question here, however, is one of remedy. It is a common feature of our federal system that States often provide remedies similar to those under federal law for the same wrongs. We do not, however, narrowly construe the federal remedies—say federal antitrust or civil rights remedies—because state law provides remedies in those areas as well. . . .

* * *

Discover and Vaden have agreed to arbitrate any dispute arising out of Vaden's account with Discover. Vaden's allegations against Discover have given rise to such a dispute. Discover seeks to arbitrate that controversy, but Vaden refuses to do so. Resolution of the controversy is governed by federal law, specifically the FDIA. There is no dispute about that. In the absence of the arbitration agreement, a federal court "would have jurisdiction . . . of the subject matter of a suit arising out of the controversy between the parties," 9 U.S.C. § 4, whether the suit were brought by Vaden or Discover. The District Court therefore may exercise jurisdiction over this petition under § 4 of the Federal Arbitration Act.

NOTES AND QUESTIONS

1. Which dispute divides the parties and which party wants to submit the matter to arbitration? Is the dispute about debt collection or charging questionable and excessive fees? Can you distinguish these disputes? If so, how? Are they conjoined? If so, what result? Is the majority or dissent more persuasive? Why?

2. Is Discover Bank's filing in state court a "scarlet letter" for jurisdictional purposes? To what strategy does the state court filing testify? Explain your answer and your understanding of the question.

3. Evaluate the majority's claim that the plaintiff's motivation to seek a judicial forum for litigation is "unsurprising." What impact does this factor have, if any, upon the majority's determination?

4. Is the majority opinion a brief for states rights? If so, in what specific respects? Does the majority tout the federal policy favoring arbitration? Where, in the opinion, is such a position evident?

5. What definition of federal jurisdiction does the majority espouse under the FAA? How is the dissent's concept of this matter different?

6. What is the 'look through' doctrine for purposes of FAA § 4? How do the majority and dissent's positions differ on this matter? Is 'look through' a favorable-to-arbitration concept? In what way(s)? When might it conflict with the federal policy on arbitration?

7. How does FAA § 2 provide a resolution or lessening of the tension between the majority and dissenting opinions?

8. How might the Court fill the federal question gap in the FAA? Is recognizing a would-be anomaly sufficient or should a firmer and clearer stance be adopted? What might the latter provide?

9. RIPENESS

In the 'ripeness' cases, the Court concludes that an action for vacatur is premature and that an enforcement proceeding can only take place after the award has been rendered. 'Anticipatory vacatur' is not available and, if it were, it might well frustrate the "emphatic federal policy favoring arbitration."

Assess the effect of the Court's opinion on arbitration doctrine. The Court appears intent upon protecting arbitration from aggressive court scrutiny or almost any court scrutiny. Explain the Court's position on arbitration and the allowable bases upon which to challenge the enforcement of arbitral awards.

VIMAR SEGUROS Y REASEGUROS, S.A. V. M/V SKY REEFER

515 U.S. 528, 115 S.Ct. 2322, 132 L.Ed.2d 462 (1995).

JUSTICE KENNEDY delivered the opinion of the Court.

This case requires us to interpret the Carriage of Goods by Sea Act (COGSA) . . . as it relates to a contract containing a clause requiring arbitration in a foreign country. The question is whether a foreign arbitration clause in a bill of lading is invalid under COGSA because it lessens liability in the sense that COGSA prohibits. Our holding that COGSA does not forbid selection of the foreign forum makes it unnecessary to resolve the further question whether the Federal Arbitration Act . . . would override COGSA were it interpreted otherwise. In our view, the relevant provisions of COGSA and the FAA are in accord, not in conflict.

I.

The contract at issue in this case is a standard form bill of lading to evidence the purchase of a shipload of Moroccan oranges and lemons. The purchaser was Bacchus Associates (Bacchus), a New York partnership that distributes fruit at wholesale throughout the Northeastern United States. Bacchus dealt with Galaxie Negoce, S.A. (Galaxie), a Moroccan fruit supplier. Bacchus contracted with Galaxie to purchase the shipload of fruit and chartered a ship to transport it from Morocco to Massachusetts. The ship was the M/V Sky Reefer, a refrigerated cargo ship owned by M.H. Maritima, S.A., a Panamanian company, and time-chartered to Nichiro Gyogyo Kaisha, Ltd., a Japanese company. Stevedores hired by Galaxie loaded and stowed the cargo. As is customary in these types of transactions, when it received the cargo from Galaxie, Nichiro as carrier issued a form bill of lading to Galaxie as shipper and consignee. Once the ship set sail from Morocco, Galaxie tendered the bill of lading to Bacchus according to the terms of a letter of credit posted in Galaxie's favor.

Among the rights and responsibilities set out in the bill of lading were arbitration and choice-of-law clauses. Clause 3, entitled "Governing Law and Arbitration," provided:

> "(1) The contract evidenced by or contained in this Bill of Lading shall be governed by the Japanese law.
>
> "(2) Any dispute arising from this Bill of Lading shall be referred to arbitration in Tokyo by the Tokyo Maritime Arbitration Commission (TOMAC) of The Japan Shipping Exchange, Inc., in accordance with the rules of TOMAC and any amendment thereto, and the award given by the arbitrators shall be final and binding on both parties." . . .

When the vessel's hatches were opened for discharge in Massachusetts, Bacchus discovered that thousands of boxes of oranges had shifted in the cargo holds, resulting in over $1 million damage. Bacchus received $733,442.90 compensation from petitioner Vimar Seguros y Reaseguros (Vimar Seguros), Bacchus' marine cargo insurer that became subrogated pro tanto to Bacchus' rights. Petitioner and Bacchus then brought suit against Maritima in personam and M/V Sky Reefer in rem in the District Court for the District of Massachusetts under the bill of lading. These defendants, respondents here, moved to stay the action and compel arbitration in Tokyo under clause 3 of the bill of lading and § 3 of the FAA, which requires courts to stay proceedings and enforce arbitration agreements covered by the Act. Petitioner and Bacchus opposed the motion, arguing the arbitration clause was unenforceable under the FAA both because it was a contract of adhesion and because it violated COGSA § 3(8). The premise of the latter argument was that the inconvenience and costs of proceeding in Japan would "lesse[n] . . . liability" as those terms are used in COGSA.

[. . .]

II.

The parties devote much of their argument to the question whether COGSA or the FAA has priority. . . . There is no conflict unless COGSA by its own terms nullifies a foreign arbitration clause, and we choose to address that issue rather than assume nullification *arguendo*. . . . We consider the two arguments made by petitioner. The first is that a foreign arbitration clause lessens COGSA liability by increasing the transaction costs of obtaining relief. The second is that there is a risk foreign arbitrators will not apply COGSA.

A

The leading case for invalidation of a foreign forum selection clause is . . . *Indussa Corp. v. S.S. Ranborg*, 377 F.2d 200 (1967) (en banc). The court there found that COGSA invalidated a clause designating a foreign judicial forum because it "puts 'a high hurdle' in the way of enforcing liability, and thus is an effective means for carriers to secure settlements lower than if cargo [owners] could sue in a convenient forum". . . . The court observed "there could be no assurance that [the foreign court] would apply [COGSA] in the same way as would an American tribunal subject to the uniform control of the Supreme Court." . . . Following *Indussa*, the Courts of Appeals without exception have invalidated foreign forum selection clauses under § 3(8). . . . As foreign arbitration clauses are but a subset of foreign forum selection clauses in general, . . . the *Indussa* holding has been extended to foreign arbitration clauses as well. . . . The logic of that extension would be quite defensible, but we cannot endorse the reasoning or the conclusion of the *Indussa* rule itself.

The determinative provision in COGSA, examined with care, does not support the arguments advanced first in *Indussa* and now by the petitioner. Section 3(8) of COGSA provides as follows:

> "Any clause, covenant, or agreement in a contract of carriage relieving the carrier or the ship from liability for loss or damage to or in connection with the goods, arising from negligence, fault, or failure in the duties or obligations provided in this section, or lessening such liability otherwise than as provided in this chapter, shall be null and void and of no effect." . . .

The liability that may not be lessened is "liability for loss or damage . . . arising from negligence, fault, or failure in the duties or obligations provided in this section." The statute thus addresses the lessening of the specific liability imposed by the Act, without addressing the separate question of the means and costs of enforcing that liability. The difference is that between explicit statutory guarantees and the procedure for enforcing them, between applicable liability principles and the forum in which they are to be vindicated.

The liability imposed on carriers under COGSA 3 is defined by explicit standards of conduct, and it is designed to correct specific abuses by carriers. In the 19th century[,] it was a prevalent practice for common carriers to insert clauses in bills of lading exempting themselves from liability for damage or loss, limiting the period in which plaintiffs had to present their notice of claim or bring suit, and capping any damages awards per package. . . . Thus, § 3 . . . requires that the carrier "exercise due diligence to . . . [m]ake the ship seaworthy" and "[p]roperly man, equip, and supply the ship" before and at the beginning of the voyage, § 3(1), "properly and carefully load, handle, stow, carry, keep, care for, and discharge the goods carried," § 3(2), and issue a bill of lading with specified contents, § 3(3). . . . Section 3(6) allows the cargo owner to provide notice of loss or damage within three days and to bring suit within one year. These are the substantive obligations and particular procedures that § 3(8) prohibits a carrier from altering to its advantage in a bill of lading. Nothing in this section, however, suggests that the statute prevents the parties from agreeing to enforce these obligations in a particular forum. By its terms, it establishes certain duties and obligations, separate and apart from the mechanisms for their enforcement.

Petitioner's contrary reading of § 3(8) is undermined by the Court's construction of a similar statutory provision in *Carnival Cruise Lines, Inc. v. Shute*. . . . There a number of Washington residents argued that a Florida forum selection clause contained in a cruise ticket should not be enforced because the expense and inconvenience of litigation in Florida would "caus[e] plaintiffs unreasonable hardship in asserting their rights" . . . in violation of the Limitation of Vessel Owner's Liability Act. . . . We observed that the clause "does not purport to limit petitioner's liability for negligence" . . . and enforced the agreement over the dissent's argument, based in part on the *Indussa* line of cases, that the cost and inconvenience of traveling thousands of miles "lessens or weakens [plaintiffs'] ability to recover." . . .

If the question whether a provision lessens liability were answered by reference to the costs and inconvenience to the cargo owner, there would be no principled basis for distinguishing national from foreign arbitration clauses. Even if it were reasonable to read § 3(8) to make a distinction based on travel time, airfare, and hotel bills, these factors are not susceptible of a simple and enforceable distinction between domestic and foreign forums. Requiring a Seattle cargo owner to arbitrate in New York likely imposes more costs and burdens than a foreign arbitration clause requiring it to arbitrate in Vancouver. It would be unwieldy and unsupported by the terms or policy of the statute to require courts to proceed case by case to tally the costs and burdens to particular plaintiffs in light of their means, the size of their claims, and the relative burden on the carrier.

Our reading of "lessening such liability" to exclude increases in the transaction costs of litigation also finds support in the goals of the Brussels Convention for the Unification of Certain Rules Relating to Bills of Lading . . . on which COGSA is modeled. Sixty-six countries, including the United States and Japan, are now parties to the Convention . . . and it appears that none has interpreted its enactment of § 3(8) of the Hague Rules to prohibit foreign forum selection clauses. . . . In light of the fact that COGSA is the culmination of a multilateral effort "to establish uniform ocean bills of lading to govern the rights and liabilities of carriers and shippers *inter se* in international trade," . . . we decline to interpret our version of the Hague Rules in a manner contrary to every other nation to have addressed this issue. . . .

It would also be out of keeping with the objects of the Convention for the courts of this country to interpret COGSA to disparage the authority or competence of international forums for dispute resolution. Petitioner's skepticism over the ability of foreign arbitrators to apply COGSA or the Hague Rules, and its reliance on this aspect of *Indussa* . . . must give way to contemporary principles of international comity and commercial practice. As the Court observed in *The Bremen v. Zapata Off-Shore Co.* . . . the historical judicial resistance to foreign forum selection clauses "has little place in an era when . . . businesses once essentially local now operate in world markets." . . . "The expansion of American business and industry will hardly be encouraged," we explained, "if, notwithstanding solemn contracts, we insist on a parochial concept that all disputes must be resolved under our laws and in our courts." . . . *See Mitsubishi Motors Corp. v. Soler Chrysler-Plymouth, Inc.* . . . (if international arbitral institutions "are to take a central place in the international legal order, national courts will need to 'shake off the old judicial hostility to arbitration,' and also their customary and understandable unwillingness to cede jurisdiction of a claim arising under domestic law to a foreign or transnational tribunal") . . . ; *Scherk v. Alberto-Culver Co.* . . . ("A parochial refusal by the courts of one country to enforce an international arbitration agreement" would frustrate "the orderliness and predictability essential to any international business transaction"). . . .

That the forum here is arbitration only heightens the irony of petitioner's argument, for the FAA is also based in part on an international convention. . . . If the United States is to be able to gain the benefits of international accords and have a role as a trusted partner in multilateral endeavors, its courts should be most cautious before interpreting its domestic legislation in such manner as to violate international agreements. That concern counsels against construing COGSA to nullify foreign arbitration clauses because of inconvenience to the plaintiff or insular distrust of the ability of foreign arbitrators to apply the law.

B

Petitioner's second argument against enforcement of the Japanese arbitration clause is that there is no guarantee foreign arbitrators will apply COGSA. This objection raises a concern of substance. The central guarantee of § 3(8) is that the terms of a bill of landing [sic] may not relieve the carrier of the obligations or diminish the legal duties specified by the Act. The relevant question, therefore, is whether the substantive law to be applied will reduce the carrier's obligations to the cargo owner below what COGSA guarantees. . . .

Petitioner argues that the arbitrators will follow the Japanese Hague Rules, which, petitioner contends, lessen respondents' liability in at least one significant respect. The Japanese version of the Hague Rules, it is said, provides the carrier with a defense based on the acts or omissions of the stevedores hired by the shipper, Galaxie . . . [while COGSA] . . . makes nondelegable the carrier's obligation to "properly and carefully . . . stow . . . the goods carried[.]" . . .

Whatever the merits of petitioner's comparative reading of COGSA and its Japanese counterpart, its claim is premature. At this interlocutory stage it is not established what law the arbitrators will apply to petitioner's claims or that petitioner will receive diminished protection as a result. The arbitrators may conclude that COGSA applies of its own force or that Japanese law does not apply so that, under another clause of the bill of lading, COGSA controls. Respondents seek only to enforce the arbitration agreement. The district court has retained jurisdiction over the case and "will have the opportunity at the award-enforcement stage to ensure that the legitimate interest in the enforcement of the . . . laws has been addressed." *Mitsubishi Motors*. . . . Were there no subsequent opportunity for review and were we persuaded that "the choice-of-forum and choice-of-law clauses operated in tandem as a prospective waiver of a party's right to pursue statutory remedies . . . , we would have little hesitation in condemning the agreement as against public policy." *Mitsubishi Motors*. . . . [M]ere speculation that the foreign arbitrators might apply Japanese law which, depending on the proper construction of COGSA, might reduce respondents' legal obligations, does not in and of itself lessen liability under COGSA § 3(8).

Because we hold that foreign arbitration clauses in bills of lading are not invalid under COGSA in all circumstances, both the FAA and COGSA may be given full effect. The judgment of the Court of Appeals is affirmed, and the case is remanded for further proceedings consistent with this opinion.

It is so ordered.

JUSTICE BREYER took no part in the consideration or decision of this case.

JUSTICE O'CONNOR, concurring in the judgment.

I agree with what I understand to be the two basic points made in the Court's opinion. First, I agree that the language of . . . COGSA . . . and our decision in *Carnival Cruise Lines* . . . preclude a holding that the increased cost of litigating in a distant forum, without more, can lessen liability within the meaning of COGSA § 3(8). . . . Second, I agree that, because the District Court has retained jurisdiction over this case while the arbitration proceeds, any claim of lessening of liability that might arise out of the arbitrators' interpretation of the bill of lading's choice of law clause, or out of their application of COGSA, is premature. . . . Those two points suffice to affirm the decision below.

Because the Court's opinion appears to do more, however, I concur only in the judgment. Foreign arbitration clauses of the kind presented here do not divest domestic courts of jurisdiction, unlike true foreign forum selection clauses such as that considered in *Indussa*. . . . That difference is an important one—it is, after all, what leads the Court to dismiss much of petitioner's argument as premature—and we need not decide today whether *Indussa*, insofar as it relied on considerations other than the increased cost of litigating in a distant forum, retains any vitality in the context of true foreign forum selection clauses. . . . As the Court notes, "[f]ollowing *Indussa*, the Courts of Appeals without exception have invalidated foreign forum selection clauses under § 3(8)[.]" . . . I would prefer to disturb that unbroken line of authority only to the extent necessary to decide this case.

JUSTICE STEVENS, dissenting.

The Carriage of Goods by Sea Act (COGSA), enacted in 1936 as a supplement to the 1893 Harter Act, regulates the terms of bills of lading issued by ocean carriers transporting cargo to or from ports of the United States. . . .

Petitioners in this case challenge the enforceability of a foreign arbitration clause, coupled with a choice-of-foreign-law clause, in a bill of lading. . . . The bill, issued by the Japanese carrier, provides (1) that the transaction " 'shall be governed by Japanese law,' " and (2) that any dispute arising from the bill shall be arbitrated in Tokyo. . . . Under the construction of COGSA that has been uniformly followed by the Court[s] of Appeals and endorsed by scholarly commentary for decades, both of those clauses are unenforceable against the shipper because they "relieve" or "lessen" the liability of the carrier. Nevertheless, relying almost entirely on a recent case involving a domestic forum selection clause that was not even covered by COGSA, *Carnival Cruise Lines* . . . , the Court today unwisely discards settled law and adopts a novel construction of § 3(8).

I.

In the 19th century[,] it was common practice for ship owners to issue bills of lading that included stipulations exempting themselves from liability for losses occasioned by the negligence of their employees. Because a bill of lading was (and is) a contract of adhesion, which a shipper must accept or else find another means to transport his goods, shippers were in no position to bargain around these no-liability clauses. Although the English courts enforced the stipulations, . . . this Court concluded, even prior to the 1893 enactment of the Harter Act, that they were "contrary to public policy, and consequently void." . . .

Section 1 of the Harter Act makes it unlawful for the master or owner of any vessel transporting cargo between ports of the United States and foreign ports to insert in any bill of lading any clause whereby the carrier "shall be relieved from liability for loss or damage arising from negligence." In *Knott v. Botany Mills*, 179 U.S. 69, 21 S.Ct. 30, 45 L.Ed. 90 (1900), we were presented with the question whether that prohibition applied to a bill of lading containing a choice-of-law clause designating British law as controlling. . . .

The Court's holding that the choice-of-law clause was invalid rested entirely on the Harter Act's prohibition against relieving the carrier from liability. . . . Since *Knott*, courts have consistently understood the Harter Act to create a flat ban on foreign choice-of-law clauses in bills of lading. . . . Courts have also consistently found such clauses invalid under COGSA, which embodies an even broader prohibition against clauses "relieving" or "lessening" a carrier's liability. . . .

[. . .]

. . . In *Indussa*, the bill of lading contained a provision requiring disputes to be resolved in Norway under Norwegian law. Judge Friendly first remarked on the harsh consequence of "requiring an American consignee claiming damages in the modest sum of $2600 to journey some 4200 miles to a court having a different legal system and employing another language." . . . The decision, however, rested not only on the impact of the provision on a relatively small claim, but also on a fair reading of the broad language in COGSA. Judge Friendly explained:

> "[Section] 3(8) of COGSA says that 'any clause, covenant, or agreement in a contract of carriage * * * lessening [the carrier's liability for negligence, fault, or dereliction of statutory duties] otherwise than as provided in this Act, shall be null and void and of no effect.' From a practical standpoint, to require an American plaintiff to assert his claim only in a distant court lessens the liability of the carrier quite substantially, particularly when the claim is small. Such a clause puts 'a high hurdle' in the way of enforcing liability . . . and thus is an effective means for carriers to secure settlements lower than if cargo could sue in a convenient forum. A clause making a claim triable only in a foreign court would almost certainly lessen liability if the law which the court would apply was neither the Carriage of Goods by Sea Act nor the Hague Rules. Even when the foreign court would apply one or the other of these regimes, requiring trial abroad might lessen the

carrier's liability since there could be no assurance that it would apply them in the same way as would an American tribunal subject to the uniform control of the Supreme Court, and § 3(8) can well be read as covering a potential and not simply a demonstrable lessening of liability." . . .

As the Court notes, . . . the Courts of Appeals without exception have followed *Indussa*. In the 1975 edition of their treatise, Gilmore and Black also endorsed its holding, adding this comment:

> "Cogsa allows a freedom of contracting out of its terms, but only in the direction of increasing the ship owner's liabilities, and never in the direction of diminishing them. This apparent one sidedness is a commonsense recognition of the inequality in bargaining power which both Harter and Cogsa were designed to redress, and of the fact that one of the great objectives of both Acts is to prevent the impairment of the value and negotiability of the ocean bill of lading. Obviously, the latter result can never ensue from the increase of the carrier's duties." . . .

Thus, our interpretation of maritime law prior to the enactment of the Harter Act, our reading of that statute in *Knott*, and the federal courts' consistent interpretation of COGSA, buttressed by scholarly recognition of the commercial interest in uniformity, demonstrate that the clauses in the Japanese carrier's bill of lading purporting to require arbitration in Tokyo pursuant to Japanese law both would have been held invalid under COGSA prior to today.

The foreign arbitration clause imposes potentially prohibitive costs on the shipper, who must travel—and bring his lawyers, witnesses and exhibits—to a distant country in order to seek redress. The shipper will therefore be inclined either to settle the claim at a discount or to forgo bringing the claim at all. The foreign-law clause leaves the shipper who does pursue his claim open to the application of unfamiliar and potentially disadvantageous legal standards, until he can obtain review (perhaps years later) in a domestic forum under the high standard applicable to vacation of arbitration awards. . . . Yet this Court today holds that carriers may insert foreign-arbitration clauses into bills of lading, and it leaves in doubt the validity of choice-of-law clauses.

Although the policy undergirding the doctrine of *stare decisis* has its greatest value in preserving rules governing commercial transactions, particularly when their meaning is well understood and has been accepted for long periods of time, the Court nevertheless has concluded that a change must be made. Its law-changing decision is supported by three arguments: (1) the statutory reference to "lessening such liability" has been misconstrued; (2) the prior understanding of the meaning of the statute has been "undermined" by the *Carnival Cruise* case; and (3) the new rule is supported by our obligation to honor the 1924 "Hague Rules." None of these arguments is persuasive.

II.

The Court assumes that the words "lessening such liability" must be narrowly construed to refer only to the substantive rules that define the carrier's legal obligations. . . . Under this view, contractual provisions that lessen the amount of the consignee's net recovery, or that lessen the likelihood that it will make any recovery at all, are beyond the scope of the statute.

In my opinion, this view is flatly inconsistent with the purpose of COGSA § 3(8). That section responds to the inequality of bargaining power inherent in bills of lading and to carriers' historic tendency to exploit that inequality whenever possible to immunize themselves from liability for their own fault. A bill of lading is a form document prepared by the carrier, who presents it to the shipper on a take-it-or-leave-it basis. . . . Characteristically, there is no arm's-length negotiation over the bill's terms; the shipper must agree to the carrier's standard-form language, or else refrain from using the carrier's services. Accordingly, if courts were to enforce bills of lading as written, a carrier could slip in a clause relieving itself of all liability for fault, or limiting that liability to a fraction of the shipper's damages, and the shipper would have no recourse. COGSA represents Congress' most recent attempt to respond to this problem. By its terms, it invalidates any clause in a bill of lading "relieving" or "lessening" the "liability" of the carrier for negligence, fault, or dereliction of duty.

When one reads the statutory language in light of the policies behind COGSA's enactment, it is perfectly clear that a foreign forum selection or arbitration clause "relieves" or "lessens" the carrier's liability. The transaction costs associated with an arbitration in Japan will obviously exceed the potential recovery in a great many cargo disputes. As a practical matter, therefore, in such a case no matter how clear the carrier's formal legal liability may be, it would make no sense for the consignee or its subrogee to enforce that liability. It seems to me that a contractual provision that entirely protects the shipper from being held liable for anything should be construed either to have "lessened" its liability or to have "relieved" it of liability.

Even if the value of the shipper's claim is large enough to justify litigation in Asia, contractual provisions that impose unnecessary and unreasonable costs on the consignee will inevitably lessen its net recovery. If, as under the Court's reasoning, such provisions do not affect the carrier's legal liability, it would appear to be permissible to require the consignee to pay the costs of the arbitration, or perhaps the travel expenses and fees of the expert witnesses, interpreters, and lawyers employed by both parties.

Judge Friendly and the many other wise judges who shared his opinion were surely correct in concluding that Congress could not have intended such a perverse reading of the statutory text.

More is at stake here than the allocation of rights and duties between shippers and carriers. A bill of lading, besides being a contract of carriage, is a negotiable instrument that controls possession of the goods being shipped. Accordingly, the bill of lading can be sold, traded, or used to obtain credit as though the bill were the cargo itself. Disuniformity in the interpretation of bills of lading will impair their negotiability. . . . Thus, if the security interests in some bills of lading are enforceable only through the courts of Japan, while others may be enforceable only in Liechtenstein, the negotiability of bills of lading will suffer from the uncertainty. COGSA recognizes that this negotiability depends in part upon the financial community's capacity to rely on the enforceability, in an accessible forum, of the bills' terms. Today's decision destroys that capacity.

The Court's reliance on its decision in *Carnival Cruise Lines, Inc.* . . . is misplaced. That case held that a domestic forum selection clause in a passenger ticket was enforceable. As no carriage of goods was at issue, COGSA did not apply to the parties' dispute. Accordingly, the enforceability of the ticket's terms did not implicate the commercial interests in uniformity and negotiability that are served by the statutory regulation of bills of lading. Moreover, the *Carnival Cruise* holding is limited to the enforceability of domestic forum selection clauses. The Court in that case pointedly refused to respond to the concern expressed in my dissent that a wooden application of its reasoning might extend its holding to the selection of a forum outside of the United States. . . . The wooden reasoning that the Court adopts today does make that extension, but it is surely not compelled by the holding in *Carnival Cruise*.

Finally, I am simply baffled by the Court's implicit suggestion that our interpretation of the Harter Act (which preceded the Hague Rules), and the federal courts' consistent interpretation of COGSA since *Indussa* was decided in 1967, has somehow been unfaithful to our international commitments. . . . The concerns about invalidating freely negotiated forum selection clauses that this Court expressed in *The Bremen v. Zapata Off-Shore Co.* . . . have no bearing on the validity of the provisions in bills of lading that are commonly recognized as contracts of adhesion. Our international obligations do not require us to enforce a contractual term that was not freely negotiated by the parties. Much less do they require us to ignore the clear meaning of COGSA—itself the product of international negotiations—which forbids enforcement of clauses lessening the carrier's liability. . . .

The majority points to several foreign statutes, passed by other signatories to the Hague Rules, that make foreign forum selection clauses unenforceable in the courts of those countries. . . . The majority assumes (without citing any evidence) that these statutes were passed in order to depart from the Hague Rules, and that COGSA, our Nation's enactment of the Hague Rules, should therefore be read to mean something different from these statutes. I think the opposite conclusion is at least as plausible: these foreign nations believed nonenforcement of foreign forum selection clauses was consistent with their international obligations, and they passed these statutes to make that explicit. If anything, then, these statutes demonstrate that several foreign countries agree that the United States courts' consistent interpretation of COGSA does not contravene our mutual treaty obligations. . . .

III.

Lurking in the background of the Court's decision today is another possible reason for holding, despite the clear meaning of COGSA and decades of precedent, that a foreign arbitration clause does not lessen liability. It may be that the Court does violence to COGSA in order to avoid a perceived conflict with another federal statute, the Federal Arbitration Act (FAA). . . . The FAA requires that courts enforce arbitration clauses in contracts—including those requiring arbitration in foreign countries—the same way they would enforce any other contractual clause. . . . According to the Court of Appeals, reading COGSA to invalidate foreign arbitration clauses would conflict directly with the terms and policy of the FAA.

Unfortunately, in adopting a contrary reading to avoid this conflict, the Court has today deprived COGSA § 3(8) of much of its force. Its narrow reading of "lessening [of] liability" excludes more than arbitration; it apparently covers only formal, legal liability. . . . Although I agree with the Court that it is important to read potentially conflicting statutes so as to give effect to both wherever possible, I think the majority has ignored a much less damaging way to harmonize COGSA with the FAA.

Section 2 of the FAA . . . intends to place arbitration clauses upon the same footing as all other contractual clauses. Thus, like any clause, an arbitration clause is enforceable, "save upon such grounds" as would suffice to invalidate any other, non-arbitration clause. The FAA thereby fulfills its policy of jettisoning the prior regime of hostility to arbitration. Like any other contractual clause, then, an arbitration clause may be invalid without violating the FAA if, for example, it is procured through fraud or forgery; there is mutual mistake or impossibility; the provision is unconscionable; or, as in this case, the terms of the clause are illegal under a separate federal statute which does not evidence a hostility to arbitration. Neither the terms nor the policies of the FAA would be thwarted if the Court were to hold today that a foreign arbitration clause in a bill of lading "lessens liability" under COGSA. COGSA does not single out arbitration clauses for disfavored treatment; it invalidates any clause that lessens the carrier's liability. Illegality under COGSA is therefore an independent ground "for the revocation of any contract," under FAA § 2. There is no conflict between the two federal statutes.

The correctness of this construction becomes even more apparent when one considers the policies of the two statutes. COGSA seeks to ameliorate the inequality in bargaining power that comes from a particular form of adhesion contract. The FAA seeks to ensure enforcement of freely-negotiated agreements to arbitrate.... [F]oreign arbitration clauses in bills of lading are not freely-negotiated. COGSA's policy is thus directly served by making these clauses illegal; and the FAA's policy is not disserved thereby. In contrast, allowing such adhesionary clauses to stand serves the goals of neither statute.

IV.

The Court's decision in this case is an excellent example of overzealous formalism. By eschewing a commonsense reading of "lessening [of] liability," the Court has drained those words of much of their potency. The result compounds, rather than contains, the Court's unfortunate mistake in the *Carnival Cruise* case.

I respectfully dissent.

NOTES AND QUESTIONS

1. *Vimar* implements the judicial doctrine on arbitration. It relates to international commercial arbitration in that it involves a maritime transaction, the application of maritime statutory law to the trans-border transport of goods, and treaty law. It is also characteristic of the litigation on domestic arbitration in that it involves an alleged conflict between the legislation on arbitration and a regulatory statute. Given the merger of the domestic and international arbitral judicial policy, however, the specific character of the litigation may no longer be significant: What applies internationally also governs domestic arbitral matters. *See Granite Rock Co. v. Int'l Broth. of Teamsters*, 561 U.S. 287 (2010).

2. The majority believes that COGSA and the FAA are not in conflict because submitting a COGSA dispute to arbitration is permissible under Section 3(8) of COGSA. The dissent believes that the contractual reference to arbitration in the bill of lading violates the letter and spirit of Section 3(8) and is, therefore, invalid. The majority takes exception with "the reasoning" and "the conclusion" of the Second Circuit Court of Appeals' decision in *Indussa* by drawing a distinction between the substantive obligations under the legislation and the procedure for the enforcement of these obligations. How characteristic is this distinction of the Court's general decisional methodology on arbitration? Where else has the Court employed this approach? Justice Stevens is highly critical of the majority opinion on this point, but he did not

use the same logic in *Mastrobuono* on the issue of punitive damages and the applicable state law?

3. The precedential significance and relevance of *Carnival Cruise* is another point of disagreement between the majority and dissenting opinions. Which side of the Court has it right? From the perspective of logic and analysis? From the vantage point of policy? Which appraisal is likely to generate a better arbitration law? If Justice Stevens' evaluation is at all convincing, will the logical gaps and tendentious determinations in the majority opinion discredit the U.S. law on arbitration? If the limitations of the majority are so evident, why do so few Justices join the dissent in this and other cases?

4. How do you assess the majority's derisory comments on the transaction costs of litigation abroad? Is the dissent correct in arguing that the increased costs of litigation are a means of discounting or eliminating liability, a consequence prohibited by the legislation? Do the customarily unilateral character of the contract and the foregoing factor amount to undermining the legislative regulation? Is the majority invoking the defense of the sophisticated merchant and simply acquiescing to the self-regulating practices of international merchants? If it is, should it?

5. How do the practice of other nations, the Court's other rulings on international commercial arbitration, and the New York Convention fit into the majority's determination? How "wooden," "mechanical," or "formalistic" is the majority reasoning on this score? How distinguishable is the question in *Vimar* from the issues in *Scherk* and *Mitsubishi*? Justice Stevens observed in *Mitsubishi* that the dispute in *Scherk* was more of an action for breach of a contractual warranty than a statutory claim case. How might that reasoning be applied to *Vimar*? Is Justice Stevens right when he asserts: "Nothing in . . . [the New York Convention] even remotely suggests an intent to enforce arbitration clauses that constitute a 'lessening' of liability under COGSA or the Hague Rules?" 515 U.S. at 554 n.14.

6. How does the **"second look" doctrine** factor into the majority analysis and determination? How does Justice Stevens respond to this doctrinal confection? Can the international adjudicatory mechanism ever be trusted? Is that consideration relevant in the non-conflictualist and non-extraterritorial post-modern era?

7. Gilmore and Black's treatise on admiralty law plays a prominent role in the dissenting opinion. The treatise is the definitive source for the analysis of maritime law rules. The dissent finds substantial support in the treatise. The majority relies very little upon commentators and secondary sources. What does that factor say about the majority opinion? Is the majority correct in concluding that its determination gives full effect to both COGSA and the FAA? Or, is the U.S. version of maritime regulation applicable whenever it is chosen by the parties? Does it matter that the designation is by a unilateral provision? Is the international character of the contract relevant? Does the majority opinion create new law that, in every respect, privileges the rule of the FAA?

PACIFICARE HEALTH SYSTEMS, INC. V. BOOK

538 U.S. 401, 123 S.Ct. 1531, 155 L.Ed.2d 578 (2003).

JUSTICE SCALIA delivered the opinion of the Court.

In this case, we are asked to decide whether respondents can be compelled to arbitrate claims arising under the Racketeer Influenced and Corrupt Organizations Act (RICO) . . . , notwithstanding the fact that the parties' arbitration agreements may be construed to limit the arbitrator's authority to award damages under that statute.

I

Respondents are members of a group of physicians who filed suit against managed-health-care organizations including petitioners PacifiCare Health Systems, Inc., and PacifiCare Operations, Inc. (collectively, PacifiCare), and UnitedHealthcare, Inc., and UnitedHealth Group Inc. (collectively, United). These physicians alleged that the defendants unlawfully failed to reimburse them for health-care services that they had provided to patients covered by defendants' health plans. They brought causes of action under RICO, the Employee Retirement Income Security Act of 1974 (ERISA), and federal and state prompt-pay statutes, as well as claims for breach of contract, unjust enrichment, and in quantum merit. . . .

Of particular concern here, PacifiCare and United moved the District Court to compel arbitration, arguing that provisions in their contracts with respondents required arbitration of these disputes, including those arising under RICO. . . . Respondents opposed the motion on the ground that, because the arbitration provisions prohibit an award of punitive damages, . . . respondents could not obtain "meaningful relief" in arbitration for their claims under the RICO statute, which authorizes treble damages. . . . *See Paladino v. Avnet Computer Technologies, Inc.*, 134 F.3d 1054, 1062 (C.A.11 1998) (holding that where a remedial limitation in an arbitration agreement prevents a plaintiff from obtaining "meaningful relief" for a statutory claim, the agreement to arbitrate is unenforceable with respect to that claim).

The District Court denied petitioners' request to compel arbitration of the RICO claims. . . . The court concluded that given the remedial limitations in the relevant contracts, it was, indeed, "faced with a potential Paladino situation . . . , where the plaintiff may not be able to obtain meaningful relief for allegations of statutory violations in an arbitration forum." . . . Accordingly, it found the arbitration agreements unenforceable with respect to respondents' RICO claims. . . . The Eleventh Circuit affirmed "for the reasons set forth in [the District Court's] comprehensive opinion," . . . and we granted *certiorari*. . . .

II

Petitioners argue that whether the remedial limitations render their arbitration agreements unenforceable is not a question of "arbitrability," and hence should have been decided by an arbitrator, rather than a court, in the first instance. They also claim that even if this question is one of arbitrability, and is therefore properly within the purview of the courts at this time, the remedial limitations at issue do not require invalidation of their arbitration agreements. Either way, petitioners contend, the lower courts should have compelled arbitration. We conclude that it would be premature for us to address these questions at this time.

[. . .]

. . . Two of the four arbitration agreements at issue provide that "punitive damages shall not be awarded [in arbitration]," . . . one provides that "[t]he arbitrators . . . shall have no authority to award any punitive or exemplary damages," . . . and one provides that "[t]he arbitrators . . . shall have no authority to award extra contractual damages of any kind, including punitive or exemplary damages." . . . Respondents insist, and the District Court agreed, . . . that these provisions preclude an arbitrator from awarding treble damages under RICO. We think that neither our precedents nor the ambiguous terms of the contracts make this clear.

Our cases have placed different statutory treble-damages provisions on different points along the spectrum between purely compensatory and strictly punitive awards. . . . [W]e have characterized the treble-damages provision of the False Claims Act . . . as "essentially punitive in nature." . . . [O]n the other hand, we explained that the treble-damages provision . . . of the Clayton Act . . . "is in essence a remedial provision." . . . [W]e noted that "the antitrust private action [which allows for treble damages] was created primarily as a remedy for the victims of antitrust violations." And . . . we stated that "it is important to realize that treble damages have a compensatory side, serving remedial purposes in addition to punitive objectives." Indeed, we have repeatedly acknowledged that the treble-damages provision contained in RICO itself is remedial in nature. . . . [W]e stated that "[b]oth RICO and the Clayton Act are designed to remedy economic injury by providing for the recovery of treble damages, costs, and attorney's fees." And . . . we took note of the "remedial function" of RICO's treble-damages provision.

In light of our case law's treatment of statutory treble damages, and given the uncertainty surrounding the parties' intent with respect to the contractual term "punitive," the application of the disputed language to respondents' RICO claims is, to say the least, in doubt. And *Vimar* instructs that we should not, on the basis of "mere speculation" that an arbitrator might interpret these ambiguous agreements in a manner that casts their enforceability into doubt, take upon ourselves the authority to decide the antecedent question of how the ambiguity is to be resolved. 515 U.S., at 541, 115 S.Ct. 2322. In short, since we do not know how the arbitrator will construe the remedial limitations, the questions whether they render the parties' agreements unenforceable and whether it is for courts or arbitrators to decide enforceability in the first instance are unusually abstract. As in *Vimar*, the proper course is to compel arbitration.

The judgment of the Court of Appeals is reversed, and the case is remanded for further proceedings consistent with this opinion.

It is so ordered.

JUSTICE THOMAS took no part in the consideration or decision of this case.

NOTES AND QUESTIONS

1. Does the opinion in *Pacificare* fit into the *Howsam-Bazzle* doctrine? If so, how?

2. Other than the reference to *Avnet*, it is curious that an agreed-upon arbitral limitation should lead to the unenforceability of the arbitration agreement. Should such a result be confined to circumstances of bargaining inequality between the parties or when the parties are substantially uneven in terms of sophistication? Why should a restrictive reference to arbitration disturb a general agreement to arbitrate?

3. How do you assess the Court's position that the litigation is premature?

4. In your view, is the issue in *Pacificare* an arbitrability question or a gateway matter? If it involves interpreting the contract, is it always a gateway matter?

10. INTERNATIONAL COMMERCIAL ARBITRATION (ICA)

The rise of arbitration in domestic U.S. law is related to the dysfunction of the domestic judicial process. In fact, one of the primary objectives of the federal policy on arbitration is to minimize public expenditures on adjudicatory services and achieve efficiency in, and accessibility to, those services. The prominence of arbitration in international commercial transactions can also be explained in terms of the deficiencies of the process of judicial adjudication. In transnational commercial relations, arbitration is a means by which international merchants avoid the ineffectiveness of national **legal systems** and by which trade policymakers cope with the unbending rule of **national sovereignty**. Whenever a commercial transaction goes beyond national territorial boundaries, it inevitably encounters either a **conflicts-of-law** problem or the barrier of sovereignty, if not both.

Trans-border transactional settings are varied but can be grouped into paradigmatic categories. The most commonplace transaction consists of the standard sales agreement between parties of different nationality who reside in different countries. Another category encompasses mixed commercial and political circumstances in which a private investor enters into, for instance, a construction project with an agency of a foreign government. Finally, the political conduct or policies of a host State can affect the embedded economic interests of foreign nationals. In all of these circumstances, the resolution of claims can be subject to a wide range of sometimes insurmountable problems that defeat the rule of law. Moreover, both parties fear foreign judicial bias, leading each of them to file an action in what they believe to be a hospitable venue. Such approaches represent a waste of time, money, and other resources because the eventual judgments end in a stalemate. At the very least, a trans-border commercial transaction can raise a number of problems: disagreements about choice-of-forum, venue, jurisdiction, choice-of-law, proof and interpretation of foreign law, and the enforcement of judgments.

The following cases illustrate how a trans-border rule of law can be fashioned through arbitration. *Bremen v. Zapata* is not, strictly speaking, an arbitration case. It deals with the validity of forum-selection clauses in international contracts. Arbitration can be considered a type of forum-selection clause that provides not only a venue, but also a framework of litigation. From that perspective, it is a 'super' forum-selection clause. The Court's reasoning regarding party autonomy and the needs of international commerce in *The Bremen* reverberates through *Scherk* and *Mitsubishi.*

THE BREMEN V. ZAPATA OFF-SHORE CO.

407 U.S. 1, 92 S.Ct. 1907, 32 L.Ed.2d 513 (1972).

MR. CHIEF JUSTICE BURGER delivered the opinion of the Court.

We granted certiorari to review a judgment of the United States Court of Appeals for the Fifth Circuit declining to enforce a forum-selection clause governing disputes arising under an international towage contract between petitioners and respondent. The circuits have differed in their approach to such clauses. For the reasons stated hereafter, we vacate the judgment of the Court of Appeals.

In November 1967, respondent Zapata, a Houston-based American corporation, contracted with petitioner Unterweser, a German corporation, to tow Zapata's ocean-going, self-elevating drilling rig *Chaparral* from Louisiana to a point off Ravenna, Italy, in the Adriatic Sea, where Zapata had agreed to drill certain wells.

Zapata had solicited bids for the towage, and several companies including Unterweser had responded. Unterweser was the low bidder and Zapata requested it to submit a contract, which it did. The contract submitted by Unterweser contained the following provision, which is at issue in this case:

> "Any dispute arising must be treated before the London Court of Justice."

In addition the contract contained two clauses purporting to exculpate Unterweser from liability for damages to the towed barge.

After reviewing the contract and making several changes, but without any alteration in the forum-selection or exculpatory clauses, a Zapata vice president executed the contract and forwarded it to Unterweser in Germany, where Unterweser accepted the changes, and the contract became effective.

On January 5, 1968, Unterweser's deep sea tug *Bremen* departed Venice, Louisiana, with the *Chaparral* in tow bound for Italy. On January 9, while the flotilla was in international waters in the middle of the Gulf of Mexico, a severe storm arose. The sharp roll of the *Chaparral* in Gulf waters caused its elevator legs, which had been raised for the voyage, to break off and fall into the sea, seriously damaging the *Chaparral*. In this emergency situation Zapata instructed the *Bremen* to tow its damaged rig to Tampa, Florida, the nearest port of refuge.

On January 12, Zapata, ignoring its contract promise to litigate "any dispute arising" in the English courts, commenced a suit in admiralty in the United States District Court at Tampa, seeking $3,500,000 in damages against Unterweser *in personam* and the *Bremen in rem*, alleging negligent towage and breach of contract. Unterweser responded by invoking the forum clause of the towage contract, and moved to dismiss for lack of jurisdiction or on *forum non conveniens* grounds, or in the alternative to stay the action pending submission of the dispute to the "London Court of Justice." Shortly thereafter, in February, before the District Court had ruled on its motion to stay or dismiss the United States action, Unterweser commenced an action against Zapata seeking damages for breach of the towage contract in the High Court of Justice in London, as the contract provided. Zapata appeared in that court to contest jurisdiction, but its challenge was rejected, the English courts holding that the contractual forum provision conferred jurisdiction.

In the meantime, Unterweser was faced with a dilemma in the pending action in the United States court at Tampa. The six-month period for filing action to limit its liability to Zapata and other potential claimants was about to expire, but the United States District Court in Tampa had not yet ruled on Unterweser's motion to dismiss or stay Zapata's action. On July 2, 1968, confronted with difficult alternatives, Unterweser filed an action to limit its liability in the District Court in Tampa. That court entered the customary injunction against proceedings outside the limitation court, and Zapata refiled its initial claim in the limitation action.

It was only at this juncture, on July 29, after the six-month period for filing the limitation action had run, that the District Court denied Unterweser's January motion to dismiss or stay Zapata's initial action. In denying the motion, that court relied on the prior decision of the Court of Appeals in *Carbon Black Export, Inc. v. The Monrosa*. . . . In that case the Court of Appeals had held a forum-selection clause unenforceable, reiterating the traditional view of many American courts that "agreements in advance of controversy whose object is to oust the jurisdiction of the courts are contrary to public policy and will not be enforced." . . . Apparently concluding that it was bound by the *Carbon Black* case, the District Court gave the forum-selection clause little, if any, weight. Instead, the court treated the motion to dismiss under normal *forum non conveniens* doctrine applicable in the absence of such a clause. . . . Under that doctrine "unless the balance is strongly in favor of the defendant, the plaintiff's choice of forum should rarely be disturbed." . . . The District Court concluded: "The balance of conveniences here is not strongly in favor of [Unterweser] and [Zapata's] choice of forum should not be disturbed."

[. . .]

On appeal, a divided panel of the Court of Appeals affirmed, and on rehearing *en banc* the panel opinion was adopted, with six of the 14 *en banc* judges dissenting. As had the District Court, the majority rested on the *Carbon Black* decision, concluding that "at the very least" that case stood for the proposition that a forum-selection clause "will not be enforced unless the selected state would provide a more convenient forum than the state in which suit is brought." From that premise the Court of Appeals proceeded to conclude that, apart from the forum-selection clause, the District Court did not abuse its discretion in refusing to decline jurisdiction on the basis of forum non conveniens. It noted that (1) the flotilla never "escaped the Fifth Circuit's *mare nostrum*, and the casualty occurred in close proximity to the district court"; (2) a considerable number of potential witnesses, including Zapata crewmen, resided in the Gulf Coast area; (3) preparation for the voyage and inspection and repair work had been performed in the Gulf area; (4) the testimony of the *Bremen* crew was available by way of deposition; (5) England had no interest in or contact with the controversy other than the forum-selection clause. The Court of Appeals majority further noted that Zapata was a United States citizen and "[t]he discretion of the district court to remand the case to a foreign forum was consequently limited," especially since it appeared likely that the English courts would enforce the exculpatory clauses. In the Court of Appeals' view, enforcement of such clauses would be contrary to public policy in American courts under *Bisso v. Inland Waterways Corp*. . . . Therefore, "[t]he district court was entitled to consider that remanding Zapata to a foreign forum, with no practical contact with the controversy, could raise a bar to recovery by a United States citizen which its own convenient courts would not countenance."

We hold, with the six dissenting members of the Court of Appeals, that far too little weight and effect were given to the forum clause in resolving this controversy. For at least two decades we have witnessed an expansion of overseas commercial activities by business enterprises based in the United States. The barrier of distance that once tended to confine a business concern to a modest territory no longer does so. Here we see an American company with special expertise contracting with a foreign company to tow a complex machine thousands of miles across seas and oceans. The expansion of American business and industry will hardly be encouraged if, notwithstanding solemn contracts, we insist on a parochial concept that all disputes must be resolved under our laws and in our courts. Absent a contract forum, the considerations relied on by the Court of Appeals would be persuasive reasons for holding an American forum convenient in the traditional sense, but in an era of expanding world trade and commerce, the absolute aspects of the doctrine of the *Carbon Black* case have little place and would be a heavy hand indeed on the future development of international commercial dealings by Americans. We cannot have trade and commerce in world markets and international waters exclusively on our terms, governed by our laws, and resolved in our courts.

Forum-selection clauses have historically not been favored by American courts. Many courts, federal and state, have declined to enforce such clauses on the ground that they were "contrary to public policy," or that their effect was to "oust the jurisdiction" of the court. Although this view apparently still has considerable acceptance, other courts are tending to adopt a more hospitable attitude toward forum-selection clauses. This view, advanced in the well-reasoned dissenting opinion in the instant case, is that such clauses are prima facie valid and should be enforced unless enforcement is shown by the resisting party to be "unreasonable" under the circumstances. We believe this is the correct doctrine to be followed by federal district courts sitting in admiralty. . . . Not surprisingly, foreign businessmen prefer, as do we, to have disputes resolved in their own courts, but if that choice is not available, then in a neutral forum with expertise in the subject matter. Plainly, the courts of England meet the standards of neutrality and long experience in admiralty litigation. The choice of that forum was made in an arm's-length negotiation by experienced and sophisticated businessmen, and absent some compelling and countervailing reason it should be honored by the parties and enforced by the courts.

The argument that such clauses are improper because they tend to "oust" a court of jurisdiction is hardly more than a vestigial legal fiction. It appears to rest at core on historical judicial resistance to any attempt to reduce the power and business of a particular court and has little place in an era when all courts are overloaded and when businesses once essentially local now operate in world markets. It reflects something of a provincial attitude regarding the fairness of other tribunals. . . . The threshold question is whether that court should have exercised its jurisdiction to do more than give effect to the legitimate expectations of the parties, manifested in their freely negotiated agreement, by specifically enforcing the forum clause.

There are compelling reasons why a freely negotiated private international agreement, unaffected by fraud, undue influence, or overweening bargaining power, such as that involved here, should be given full effect. In this case, for example, we are concerned with a far from routine transaction between companies of two different nations contemplating the tow of an extremely costly piece of equipment from Louisiana across the Gulf of Mexico and the Atlantic Ocean, through the Mediterranean Sea to its final destination in the Adriatic Sea. In the course of its voyage, it was to traverse the waters of many jurisdictions. The *Chaparral* could have been damaged at any point along the route, and there were countless possible ports of refuge. That the accident occurred in the Gulf of Mexico and the barge was towed to Tampa in an emergency were mere fortuities. It cannot be doubted for a moment that the parties sought to provide for a neutral forum for the resolution of any disputes arising during the tow. Manifestly much uncertainty and possibly great inconvenience to both parties could arise if a suit could be maintained in any jurisdiction in which an accident might occur or if jurisdiction were left to any place where the *Bremen* or Unterweser might happen to be found. The elimination of all such uncertainties by agreeing in advance on a forum acceptable to both parties is an indispensable element in international trade, commerce, and contracting. There is strong evidence that the forum clause was a vital part of the agreement, and it would be unrealistic to think that the parties did not conduct their negotiations, including fixing the monetary terms, with the consequences of the forum clause figuring prominently in their calculations. . . .

Thus, in the light of present-day commercial realities and expanding international trade we conclude that the forum clause should control absent a strong showing that it should be set aside. Although their opinions are not altogether explicit, it seems reasonably clear that the District Court and the Court of Appeals placed the burden on Unterweser to show that London would be a more convenient forum than Tampa, although the contract expressly resolved that issue. The correct approach would have been to enforce the forum clause specifically unless Zapata could clearly show that enforcement would be unreasonable and unjust, or that the clause was invalid for such reasons as fraud or overreaching. Accordingly, the case must be remanded for reconsideration.

We note, however, that there is nothing in the record presently before us that would support a refusal to enforce the forum clause. The Court of Appeals suggested that enforcement would be contrary to the public policy of the forum under *Bisso* . . . because of the prospect that the English courts would enforce the clauses of the towage contract purporting to exculpate Unterweser from liability for damages to the *Chaparral.* A contractual choice-of-forum clause should be held unenforceable if enforcement would contravene a strong public policy of the forum in which suit is brought, whether declared by statute or by judicial decision. . . . It is clear, however, that whatever the proper scope of the policy expressed in *Bisso*, it does not reach this case. *Bisso* rested on considerations with respect to the towage business strictly in American waters, and those considerations are not controlling in an international commercial agreement. . . .

[. . .]

This case . . . involves a freely negotiated international commercial transaction between a German and an American corporation for towage of a vessel from the Gulf of Mexico to the Adriatic Sea. As noted, selection of a London forum was clearly a reasonable effort to bring vital certainty to this international transaction and to provide a neutral forum experienced and capable in the resolution of admiralty litigation. Whatever "inconvenience" Zapata would suffer by being forced to litigate in the contractual forum as it agreed to do was clearly foreseeable at the time of contracting. In such circumstances it should be incumbent on the party seeking to escape his contract to show that trial in the contractual forum will be so gravely difficult and inconvenient that he will for all practical purposes be deprived of his day in court. Absent that, there is no basis for concluding that it would be unfair, unjust, or unreasonable to hold that party to his bargain.

[. . .]

The judgment of the Court of Appeals is vacated and the case is remanded for further proceedings consistent with this opinion.

Vacated and remanded.

[. . .]

MR. JUSTICE DOUGLAS, dissenting.

[. . .]

Respondent is a citizen of this country. Moreover, if it were remitted to the English court, its substantive rights would be adversely affected. Exculpatory provisions in the towage [contract] provide (1) that petitioners, the masters and the crews "are not responsible for defaults and/or errors in the navigation of the tow" and (2) that "(d)amages suffered by the towed object are in any case for account of its Owners."

Under our decision in *Dixilyn Drilling Corp.*, . . . "a contract which exempts the tower from liability for its own negligence" is not enforceable, though there is evidence in the present record that it is enforceable in England. That policy was first announced in *Bisso*. . . . Although the casualty occurred on the high seas, the *Bisso* doctrine is nonetheless applicable. . . .

Moreover, the casualty occurred close to the District Court, a number of potential witnesses, including respondent's crewmen, reside in that area, and the inspection and repair work were done there. The testimony of the tower's crewmen, residing in Germany, is already available by way of depositions taken in the proceedings.

All in all, the District Court judge exercised his discretion wisely in enjoining petitioners from pursuing the litigation in England.

[. . .]

NOTES AND QUESTIONS

1. Relief for Zapata is less likely, or perhaps unavailable, in England. The exculpatory clauses probably would be enforced by English courts, resulting in a dismissal of the action against Unterweser. *See* 407 U.S. at 8 n.8. Moreover, even if Unterweser were held liable, the limitation fund in England, as noted in the opinion, is modest. Should these factors, in addition to the public policy against exculpatory clauses in maritime transactions articulated in *Bisso*, be enough to place the litigation within the jurisdiction of U.S. courts and law? Moreover, the incident occurred near a U.S. jurisdiction, involved directly the business assets of a U.S. national, and generally implicated U.S. economic and dispute resolution interests. Why should English courts and law have exclusive jurisdiction over a matter that has no connection or proximity to England or English interests?

2. The Court finds both the policy in *Bisso* and the *Carbon Black* doctrine on forum-selection clauses inapplicable to a trans-border commercial agreement. The Court, in effect, reverses the rule of *Carbon Black*, holding that **forum-selection clauses** are presumptively enforceable in international contracts. The adverse party can rebut the presumption by establishing that enforcement would result in debilitating inconvenience or a denial of justice. In his dissent, Justice Douglas takes a more insidious view of the interplay between the forum-selection clause and the *Bisso* policy against exculpatory clauses:

> It is said that because these parties specifically agreed to litigate their disputes before the London Court of Justice, the District Court, absent "unreasonable" circumstances, should have honored that choice by declining to exercise its jurisdiction. The forum-selection clause, however, is part and parcel of the exculpatory provisions in the towing agreement which, as mentioned in the text, is not enforceable in American courts. For only by avoiding litigation in the

> United States could petitioners hope to evade the *Bisso* doctrine. Judges in this country have traditionally been hostile to attempts to circumvent the public policy against exculpatory agreements. For example, clauses specifying that the law of a foreign place (which favors such releases) should control have regularly been ignored. Thus, in *The Kensington*, . . . the Court held void an exemption from liability despite the fact that the contract provided that it should be construed under Belgian law[,] which was more tolerant. . . .
>
> The instant stratagem of specifying a foreign forum is essentially the same as invoking a foreign law of construction except that the present circumvention also requires the American party to travel across an ocean to seek relief. Unless we are prepared to overrule *Bisso* we should not countenance devices designed solely for the purpose of evading its prohibition. It is argued, however, that one of the rationales of the *Bisso* doctrine, "to protect those in need of goods or services from being overreached by others who have power to drive hard bargains," . . . does not apply here because these parties may have been of equal bargaining stature. Yet we have often adopted prophylactic rules rather than attempt to sort the core cases from the marginal ones. In any event, the other objective of the *Bisso* doctrine, to "discourage negligence by making wrongdoers pay damages," . . . applies here and in every case regardless of the relative bargaining strengths of the parties.

407 U.S. at 24 n.*.

Compare and contrast the majority and dissenting opinions.

3. You should carefully examine the content of the applicable forum-selection clause. Are there problems with its content? For example: (1) to which subject areas does the phrase "any dispute arising" refer; (2) "arising" how and where; (3) what does "treated" mean—adjudication, bureaucratic processing, acknowledgment, or settlement; and (4) what is "the London Court of Justice"? It appears that the sophisticated commercial parties agreed to have "any dispute arising" "treated" before a court in London that does not in fact exist. Do these problems reveal that the parties failed to consider, or to agree upon, an appropriate situs for dispute resolution, and that these failures mean that choice-of-law considerations should dictate which court has jurisdiction? Why should the Court remedy the parties' contractual ineptitudes in these circumstances? Is the contractual failing a proper basis for applying the standard doctrines in *Bisso* and *Carbon Black*?

SCHERK V. ALBERTO-CULVER CO.

417 U.S. 506, 94 S.Ct. 2449, 41 L.Ed.2d 270, *reh'g denied*, 419 U.S. 885, 95 S.Ct. 157, 42 L.Ed.2d 129 (1974).

[. . .]

I.

The United States Arbitration Act, . . . reversing centuries of judicial hostility to arbitration agreements, was designed to allow parties to avoid "the costliness and delays of litigation," and to place arbitration agreements "upon the same footing as other contracts. . . . " . . . Accordingly the Act provides that an arbitration agreement such as is here involved "shall be valid, irrevocable, and enforceable, save upon such grounds as exist at law or in equity for the revocation of any contract." . . . The Act also provides in § 3 for a stay of proceedings in a case where a court is satisfied that the issue before it is arbitrable under the agreement, and § 4 of the Act directs a federal court to order parties to proceed to arbitration if there has been a "failure, neglect, or refusal" of any party to honor an agreement to arbitrate.

In *Wilko v. Swan*, . . . this Court acknowledged that the Act reflects a legislative recognition of the "desirability of arbitration as an alternative to the complications of litigation," . . . but nonetheless declined to apply the Act's provisions. . . .

The Court found that "[t]wo policies, not easily reconcilable, are involved in this case." . . . On the one hand, the Arbitration Act stressed "the need for avoiding the delay and expense of litigation," . . . and directed that such agreements be "valid, irrevocable, and enforceable" in federal courts. On the other hand, the Securities Act of 1933 was "[d]esigned to protect investors" . . . by creating "a special right to recover for misrepresentation. . . . " . . . In particular, the Court noted that § 14 of the Securities Act . . . provides:

> Any condition, stipulation, or provision binding any person acquiring any security to waive compliance with any provision of this subchapter or of the rules and regulations of the Commission shall be void.

The Court ruled that an agreement to arbitrate "is a 'stipulation,' and [that] the right to select the judicial forum is the kind of 'provision' that cannot be waived under § 14 of the Securities Act." . . . Thus, Wilko's advance agreement to arbitrate any disputes subsequently arising out of his contract to purchase the securities was unenforceable under the terms of § 14 of the Securities Act of 1933.

Alberto-Culver, relying on this precedent, contends that the District Court and Court of Appeals were correct in holding that its agreement to arbitrate disputes arising under the contract with Scherk is similarly unenforceable in view of its contentions that Scherk's conduct constituted violations of the Securities Exchange Act of 1934 and rules promulgated thereunder. For the reasons that follow, we reject this contention and hold that the provisions of the Arbitration Act cannot be ignored in this case.

[. . .]

Finally, and most significantly, the subject matter of the contract concerned the sale of business enterprises organized under the laws of and primarily situated in European countries, whose activities were largely, if not entirely, directed to European markets.

Such a contract involves considerations and policies significantly different from those found controlling in *Wilko*. In *Wilko*, quite apart from the arbitration provision, there was no question but that the laws of the United States generally, and the federal securities laws in particular, would govern disputes arising out of the stock-purchase agreement. The parties, the negotiations, and the subject matter of the contract were all situated in this country, and no credible claim could have been entertained that any international conflict-of-laws problems would arise. In this case, by contrast, in the absence of the arbitration provision considerable uncertainty existed at the time of the agreement, and still exists, concerning the law applicable to the resolution of disputes arising out of the contract.

Such uncertainty will almost inevitably exist with respect to any contract touching two or more countries, each with its own substantive laws and conflict-of-laws rules. A contractual provision specifying in advance the forum in which disputes shall be litigated and the law to be applied is, therefore, an almost indispensable precondition to achievement of the orderliness and predictability essential to any international business transaction. Furthermore, such a provision obviates the danger that a dispute under the agreement might be submitted to a forum hostile to the interests of one of the parties or unfamiliar with the problem area involved.

A parochial refusal by the courts of one country to enforce an international arbitration agreement would not only frustrate these purposes, but would invite unseemly and mutually destructive jockeying by the parties to secure tactical litigation advantages. In the present case, for example, it is not inconceivable that if Scherk had anticipated that Alberto-Culver would be able in this country to enjoin resort to arbitration he might have sought an order in France or some other country enjoining Alberto-Culver from proceeding with its litigation in the United States. Whatever recognition the courts of this country might ultimately have granted to the order of the foreign court, the dicey atmosphere of such a legal no-man's-land would surely damage the fabric of international commerce and trade, and imperil the willingness and ability of businessmen to enter into international commercial agreements.

The exception to the clear provisions of the Arbitration Act carved out by *Wilko* is simply inapposite to a case such as the one before us. In *Wilko* the Court reasoned that "[w]hen the security buyer, prior to any violation of the Securities Act, waives his right to sue in courts, he gives up more than would a participant in other business transactions. The security buyer has a wider choice of courts and venue. He thus surrenders one of the advantages the Act gives him. . . ." . . . In the context of an international contract, however, these advantages become chimerical since, as indicated above, an opposing party may by speedy resort to a foreign court block or hinder access to the American court of the purchaser's choice.

Two Terms ago in *The Bremen v. Zapata Off-Shore Co.*, . . . we rejected the doctrine that a forum-selection clause of a contract, although voluntarily adopted by the parties, will not be respected in a suit brought in the United States "unless the selected state would provide a more convenient forum than the state in which suit is brought." . . . Rather, we concluded that a "forum clause should control absent a strong showing that it should be set aside." . . .

An agreement to arbitrate before a specified tribunal is, in effect, a specialized kind of forum-selection clause that posits not only the situs of suit but also the procedure to be used in resolving the dispute. The invalidation of such an agreement in the case before us would not only allow the respondent to repudiate its solemn promise but would, as well, reflect a "parochial concept that all disputes must be resolved under our laws and in our courts. . . . We cannot have trade and commerce in world markets and international waters exclusively on our terms, governed by our laws, and resolved in our courts." . . .

[. . .]

Accordingly, the judgment of the Court of Appeals is reversed and the case is remanded to that court with directions to remand to the District Court for further proceedings consistent with this opinion.

It is so ordered.

MR. JUSTICE DOUGLAS, with whom MR. JUSTICE BRENNAN, MR. JUSTICE WHITE, and MR. JUSTICE MARSHALL concur, dissenting.

[. . .]

This invocation of the "international contract" talisman might be applied to a situation where, for example, an interest in a foreign company or mutual fund was sold to an utterly unsophisticated American citizen, with material fraudulent misrepresentations made in this country. The arbitration clause could appear in the fine print of a form contract, and still be sufficient to preclude recourse to our courts, forcing the defrauded citizen to arbitration in Paris to vindicate his rights.

It has been recognized that the 1934 Act, including the protections of Rule 10b–5, applies when foreign defendants have defrauded American investors, particularly when, as alleged here, they have profited by virtue of proscribed conduct within our boundaries. This is true even when the defendant is organized under the laws of a foreign country, is conducting much of its activity outside the United States, and is therefore governed largely by foreign law. The language of § 29 of the 1934 Act does not immunize such international transactions, and the United Nations Convention provides that a forum court in which a suit is brought need not enforce an agreement to arbitrate which is "void" and "inoperative" as contrary to its public policy. When a foreign corporation undertakes fraudulent action which subjects it to the jurisdiction of our federal securities laws, nothing justifies the conclusion that only a diluted version of those laws protects American investors.

[. . .]

When a defendant, as alleged here, has, through proscribed acts within our territory, brought itself within the ken of federal securities regulation, a fact not disputed here, those laws including the controlling principles of *Wilko,* apply whether the defendant is foreign or American, and whether or not there are transnational elements in the dealings. Those laws are rendered a chimera when foreign corporations or funds unlike domestic defendants, can nullify them by virtue of arbitration clauses, which send defrauded American investors to the uncertainty of arbitration on foreign soil, or, if those investors cannot afford to arbitrate their claims in a far-off forum, to no remedy at all.

Moreover, the international aura which the Court gives this case is ominous. We now have many multinational corporations in vast operations around the world, Europe, Latin America, the Middle East, and Asia. The investments of many American investors turn on dealings by these companies. Up to this day, it has been assumed by reason of *Wilko* that they were all protected by our various federal securities Acts. If these guarantees are to be removed, it should take a legislative enactment. I would enforce our laws as they stand, unless Congress makes an exception.

The virtue of certainty in international agreements may be important, but Congress has dictated that when there are sufficient contacts for our securities laws to apply, the policies expressed in those laws take precedence. Section 29 of the 1934 Act, which renders arbitration clauses void and inoperative, recognizes no exception for fraudulent dealings which incidentally have some international factors. The Convention makes provision for such national public policy in Art. II(3). Federal jurisdiction under the 1934 Act will attach only to some international transactions, but when it does, the protections afforded investors such as Alberto-Culver can only be full-fledged.

NOTES AND QUESTIONS

1. The *Scherk* opinion integrates the *Zapata* doctrine into the resolution of international commercial arbitration cases. The majority's determination that the *Wilko* ruling is either irrelevant or inapplicable to international business transactions attests to the Court's intent to restrict the **extraterritorial reach** of U.S. domestic law and devise special rules for trans-border litigation. The majority opinion also provides a forceful illustration of the conflict that is emerging between the judicial policy on arbitration and the domain of law, in particular, sectors of regulatory activity that have public importance. For example, although it is never stated in these terms, the question in *Scherk* centers upon **subject-matter inarbitrability**: Whether securities claims, specifically those arising under the 1934 Securities Exchange Act, can be submitted to arbitration as a matter of law. The resolution of that question also involves another vital, and equally understated, aspect of arbitration law, namely, the role of contract rights in defining arbitration's scope of application and their impact upon the legal regulation of arbitration. The decision ignores both considerations and places nearly exclusive emphasis upon the judicial policy on trans-border litigation and the perceived needs of international commerce.

There is, therefore, some level of incongruity between the statement of policy and the analytical questions and doctrinal considerations that are raised in *Scherk*. In fact, it is possible to agree with the Court's internationalist policy (the rejection of extraterritoriality and the recognition of the need for the global regulation of commerce) and disagree with the conclusions it reaches on the questions of law that are presented. The policy appears to be unnecessarily intolerant of legal restrictions on arbitration. While the New York Convention obligates contracting States to enforce international arbitral awards on a nondiscriminatory basis and with only a modicum of judicial supervision, it allows them to refuse to enforce arbitral agreements and awards that pertain to an inarbitrable subject matter under their law or which violate their national public policy. The balance between arbitral autonomy and national legal interests achieved in the Convention simply does not factor into the Court's reasoning or elaboration of policy. The Court's view seems to be that any legal curtailment of arbitration *per force* invites greater restrictions, leading inevitably to the collapse of world trade and financial markets. The hyperbole is manifest, but for what effect is the policy exaggerated?

The Court may be concerned about the influence of its ruling upon lower federal courts or the effect of the U.S. decisional law upon courts in other jurisdictions. The discipline of an unequivocal policy and clear doctrine avoids the undermining reference to exceptions or the *ad hoc* invocation of *sui generis* rules. It is also possible that the Court's policy on arbitration reflects systemic concerns: The congressional ratification of the New York Convention establishes law which the Court is obligated to enforce and to safeguard against the historical menace of judicial hostility to arbitration. None of these rationales is particularly convincing or explains how the right to arbitration acquires a constitutional status nearly equivalent to the right of freedom of speech. Despite its many allusions to a congressional mandate, the Court's policy exceeds any legislative endorsement of arbitration and constitutes an example of how the Court fashions law on its own. There are, for example, no congressional statutes that consecrate the importance to the United States of international business transactions or trans-border commerce.

The consistency and unequivocal character of the Court's policy on international arbitration, as well as its eventual merger with the policy on domestic arbitration, can perhaps be best explained by the Court's need to **manage judicial dockets** and administer the federal court system. Because trans-border litigation imposes an additional and more complex burden upon the federal courts, it is critical to make arbitration agreements and awards effective to avoid placing inordinate demands upon national judicial resources. The same 'managerial' rationale explains the compromise of rights that occurred in the federalization of domestic U.S. arbitration law and the extension of domestic arbitration to statutory conflicts.

2. The applicable arbitral clause in *Scherk* provided:

> The parties agree that if any controversy or claim shall arise out of this agreement or the breach thereof and either party shall request that the matter shall be settled by arbitration, the matter shall be settled exclusively by arbitration in accordance with the rules then obtaining of the International Chamber of Commerce, Paris, France, by a single arbitrator, if the parties shall agree upon one, or by one arbitrator appointed by each party and a third arbitrator appointed by the other arbitrators. In case of any failure of a party to make an appointment referred to above within four weeks after notice of the controversy, such appointment shall be made by said chamber. All arbitration proceedings shall be held in Paris, France, and each party agrees to comply in all respects with any award made in any such proceeding and to the entry of a judgment in any jurisdiction upon any award rendered in such proceeding. The laws of the State of Illinois, U.S.A. shall apply to and govern this agreement, its interpretation and performance.

417 U.S. at 508 n.1.

Discuss the positive and negative attributes of the clause.

3. The arbitrability of statutory rights is never expressly mentioned in *Scherk*, although that issue will preoccupy the Court in *Mitsubishi* ten years later. In *Scherk*, the issue never escalates beyond the applicability of domestic precedents and statutes in the context of international business transactions. *Scherk* also establishes that trans-border contracts should be enforced as written in order to remedy the uncertainties of global commerce. By filing a domestic lawsuit, Alberto Culver breached the agreement into which it voluntarily entered. Contract enforcement in *Scherk* divests national courts of jurisdiction and places the authority to rule in the ICC and its arbitrators.

The discussion also centers upon the ***Wilko* bar** to arbitration in securities matters. The Court quickly determines that *Wilko* is inoperative in litigation dealing with international arbitration. It initially makes a number of technical distinctions to support its determination: *Wilko* addressed a conflict between the FAA and the 1933 Securities Act, while *Scherk* pits the codification of the New York Convention in Title 9 against the 1934 Securities Exchange Act. Moreover, despite the enormous similarities between the statutes, "[t]here is no statutory counterpart of 12(2) in the Securities Exchange Act of 1934, and neither 10(b) of that Act nor Rule 10(b)–(5) speaks of a private remedy to redress violations of the kind alleged here." While 10(b)(5) creates "an implied private cause of action," it "does not establish the 'special right' that the Court in *Wilko* found significant." Moreover, the Court identifies a lack of concordance between the jurisdictional "provisions" of the Acts. *See* 417 U.S. at 513–14. Accordingly, these distinctions create "a colorable argument" for sustaining the view that the *Wilko* bar to predispute arbitration agreements in securities contracts does not apply to the international contract in *Scherk*.

MITSUBISHI MOTORS CORP. V. SOLER CHRYSLER-PLYMOUTH, INC.

473 U.S. 614, 105 S.Ct. 3346, 87 L.Ed.2d 444 (1985).

[. . .]

II.

[. . .]

. . . [W]e find no warrant in the Arbitration Act for implying in every contract within its ken a presumption against arbitration of statutory claims. The Act's centerpiece provision makes a written agreement to arbitrate "in any maritime transaction or a contract evidencing a transaction involving commerce . . . valid, irrevocable, and enforceable, save upon such grounds as exist at law or in equity for the revocation of any contract." . . . The "liberal federal policy favoring arbitration agreements," *Moses H. Cone Memorial Hospital,* . . . manifested by this provision and the Act as a whole, is at bottom a policy guaranteeing the enforcement of private contractual arrangements: the Act simply "creates a body of federal substantive law establishing and regulating the duty to honor an agreement to arbitrate." . . .

Accordingly, the first task of a court asked to compel arbitration of a dispute is to determine whether the parties agreed to arbitrate that dispute. . . . Thus, as with any other contract, the parties' intentions control, but those intentions are generously construed as to issues of arbitrability.

There is no reason to depart from these guidelines where a party bound by an arbitration agreement raises claims founded on statutory rights. . . .

[W]e are well past the time when judicial suspicion of the desirability of arbitration and of the competence of arbitral tribunals inhibited the development of arbitration as an alternative means of dispute resolution. . . . Of course, courts should remain attuned to well-supported claims that the agreement to arbitrate resulted from the sort of fraud or overwhelming economic power that would provide grounds "for the revocation of any contract." . . . But, absent such compelling considerations, the Act itself provides no basis for disfavoring agreements to arbitrate statutory claims by skewing the otherwise hospitable inquiry into arbitrability.

That is not to say that all controversies implicating statutory rights are suitable for arbitration. There is no reason to distort the process of contract interpretation, however, in order to ferret out the inappropriate. . . . For that reason, Soler's concern for statutorily protected classes provides no reason to color the lens through which the arbitration clause is read. By agreeing to arbitrate a statutory claim, a party does not forgo the substantive rights afforded by the statute; it only submits to their resolution in an arbitral, rather than a judicial, forum. It trades the procedures and opportunity for review of the courtroom for the simplicity, informality, and expedition of arbitration. We must assume that if Congress intended the substantive protection afforded by a given statute to include protection against waiver of the right to a judicial forum, that intention will be deducible from text or legislative history. . . . Having made the bargain to arbitrate, the party should be held to it unless Congress itself has evinced an intention to preclude a waiver of judicial remedies for the statutory rights at issue. Nothing, in the meantime, prevents a party from excluding statutory claims from the scope of an agreement to arbitrate. . . .

[. . .]

The Bremen and *Scherk* establish a strong presumption in favor of enforcement of freely negotiated contractual choice-of-forum provisions. Here, as in *Scherk*, that presumption is reinforced by the emphatic federal policy in favor of arbitral dispute resolution. And at least since this Nation's accession in 1970 to the Convention, . . . that federal policy applies with special force in the field of international commerce. Thus, we must weigh the concerns of *American Safety* against a strong belief in the efficacy of arbitral procedures for the resolution of international commercial disputes and an equal commitment to the enforcement of freely negotiated choice-of-forum clauses.

[. . .]

We are left, then, with the core of the *American Safety* doctrine—the fundamental importance to American democratic capitalism of the regime of the antitrust laws. . . . Without doubt, the private cause of action plays a central role in enforcing this regime. . . . As the Court of Appeals pointed out:

> "A claim under the antitrust laws is not merely a private matter. The Sherman Act is designed to promote the national interest in a competitive economy; thus, the plaintiff asserting his rights under the Act has been likened to a private attorney-general who protects the public's interest." . . .

The treble-damages provision wielded by the private litigant is a chief tool in the antitrust enforcement scheme, posing a crucial deterrent to potential violators. . . .

The importance of the private damages remedy, however, does not compel the conclusion that it may not be sought outside an American court. Notwithstanding its important incidental policing function, the treble-damages cause of action conferred on private parties by § 4 of the Clayton . . . Act and pursued by Soler here by way of its third counterclaim, seeks primarily to enable an injured competitor to gain compensation for that injury.

[. . .]

There is no reason to assume at the outset of the dispute that international arbitration will not provide an adequate mechanism. To be sure, the international arbitral tribunal owes no prior allegiance to the legal norms of particular states; hence, it has no direct obligation to vindicate their statutory dictates. The tribunal, however, is bound to effectuate the intentions of the parties. Where the parties have agreed that the arbitral body is to decide a defined set of claims which includes, as in these cases, those arising from the application of American antitrust law, the tribunal therefore should be bound to decide that dispute in accord with the national law giving rise to the claim. . . . And so long as the prospective litigant effectively may vindicate its statutory cause of action in the arbitral forum, the statute will continue to serve both its remedial and deterrent function.

Having permitted the arbitration to go forward, the national courts of the United States will have the opportunity at the award-enforcement stage to ensure that the legitimate interest in the enforcement of the antitrust laws has been addressed. The Convention reserves to each signatory country the right to refuse enforcement of an award where the "recognition or enforcement of the award would be contrary to the public policy of that country." . . . While the efficacy of the arbitral process requires that substantive review at the award-enforcement stage remain minimal, it would not require intrusive inquiry to ascertain that the tribunal took cognizance of the antitrust claims and actually decided them.

As international trade has expanded in recent decades, so too has the use of international arbitration to resolve disputes arising in the course of that trade. The controversies that international arbitral institutions are called upon to resolve have increased in diversity as well as in complexity. Yet the potential of these tribunals for efficient disposition of legal disagreements arising from commercial relations has not yet been tested. If they are to take a central place in the international legal order, national courts will need to "shake off the old judicial hostility to arbitration" . . . and also their customary and understandable unwillingness to cede jurisdiction of a claim arising under domestic law to a foreign or transnational tribunal. To this extent, at least, it will be necessary for national courts to subordinate domestic notions of arbitrability to the international policy favoring commercial arbitration.

Accordingly, we "require this representative of the American business community to honor its bargain" . . . by holding this agreement to arbitrate "enforce[able] . . . in accord with the explicit provisions of the Arbitration Act." . . .

The judgment of the Court of Appeals is affirmed in part and reversed in part, and the cases are remanded for further proceedings consistent with this opinion.

It is so ordered.

JUSTICE POWELL took no part in the decision of these cases.

JUSTICE STEVENS, with whom JUSTICE BRENNAN joins, and with whom JUSTICE MARSHALL joins except as to Part II, dissenting.

[. . .]

. . . This Court's holding rests almost exclusively on the federal policy favoring arbitration of commercial disputes and vague notions of international comity arising from the fact that the automobiles involved here were manufactured in Japan. Because I am convinced that the Court of Appeals' construction of the arbitration clause is erroneous, and because I strongly disagree with this Court's interpretation of the relevant federal statutes, I respectfully dissent. In my opinion, (1) a fair construction of the language in the arbitration clause in the parties' contract does not encompass a claim that auto manufacturers entered into a conspiracy in violation of the antitrust laws; (2) an arbitration clause should not normally be construed to cover a statutory remedy that it does not expressly identify; (3) Congress did not intend § 2 of the Federal Arbitration Act to apply to antitrust claims; and (4) Congress did not intend the Convention on the Recognition and Enforcement of Foreign Arbitral Awards to apply to disputes that are not covered by the Federal Arbitration Act.

[. . .]

V.

The Court's repeated incantation of the high ideals of "international arbitration" creates the impression that this case involves the fate of an institution designed to implement a formula for world peace. But just as it is improper to subordinate the public interest in enforcement of antitrust policy to the private interest in resolving commercial disputes, so is it equally unwise to allow a vision of world unity to distort the importance of the selection of the proper forum for resolving this dispute. Like any other mechanism for resolving controversies, international arbitration will only succeed if it is realistically limited to tasks it is capable of performing well, the prompt and inexpensive resolution of essentially contractual disputes between commercial partners. As for matters involving the political passions and the fundamental interests of nations, even the multilateral convention adopted under the auspices of the United Nations recognizes that private international arbitration is incapable of achieving satisfactory results.

In my opinion, the elected representatives of the American people would not have us dispatch an American citizen to a foreign land in search of an uncertain remedy for the violation of a public right that is protected by the Sherman Act. This is especially so when there has been no genuine bargaining over the terms of the submission, and the arbitration remedy provided has not even the most elementary guarantees of fair process. Consideration of a fully developed record by a jury, instructed in the law by a federal judge, and subject to appellate review, is a surer guide to the competitive character of a commercial practice than the practically unreviewable judgment of a private arbitrator.

Unlike the Congress that enacted the Sherman Act in 1890, the Court today does not seem to appreciate the value of economic freedom. I respectfully dissent.

NOTES AND QUESTIONS

1. The *Mitsubishi* opinion introduces a more substantive consideration into the Court's decisional law on international commercial arbitration. From the outset of the opinion, Justice Blackmun recognizes subject-matter arbitrability as the principal question of the case. In keeping with *Scherk*, a domestic law precedent is on point and is determined to be inapplicable in the context of international commercial arbitration. Also, the decision, as in *Scherk*, includes a forceful dissent authored by a member of the Court with long-standing expertise in the area deemed arbitrable by the majority. Unlike *Scherk*, the dissent in *Mitsubishi* does not harness the allegiance of a substantial minority of the Court. Finally, the Court in *Mitsubishi* begins to **commingle** its **rulings** on domestic and international arbitration. The

majority makes significant reference to the federalism trilogy in supporting its conclusions on the question of arbitrability. Although the ruling is still couched in terms of the needs of trans-border commerce, a **unitary policy** on arbitration begins to emerge. As has already been noted, the Court will simply forget the international specialty of the rule of statutory arbitrability once it decides *McMahon* and *Rodriguez*. *See Shearson/Am. Express, Inc. v. McMahon*, 482 U.S. 220 (1987); *Rodriguez v. Shearson/Am. Express, Inc.*, 490 U.S. 477 (1989). There had been an expectation that *Mitsubishi* would provide the Court with the opportunity to refine its policy on international commerce and arbitration. Needless to say, the opinion disappoints that expectation.

2. The arbitral tribunal in *Mitsubishi* consisted of three Japanese lawyers: A former law school dean, a former judge, and a practicing lawyer who had some U.S. legal training and written on Japanese antitrust law. Does an arbitral proceeding in Japan at all resemble a trial proceeding in the United States? Do you believe that the regulatory culture and the antitrust laws in Japan bear any equivalency to their U.S. counterparts? What about private attorneys-general, treble damages, and the discovery features of the applicable U.S. statute? Is the Court right to focus upon the non-national and private character of arbitration? Do those additional considerations argue for the inarbitrability of statutory claims? Is the Court being flippant in its assessment of the situation? Is it at all possible that "the statute will continue to serve both its remedial and deterrent function"? Can there be any doubt that the reference of the antitrust claims to arbitration results in a loss of important legal rights? Would the Court's reasoning be more plausible in a domestic context in which arbitrators might have the requisite adjudicatory experience and legal and cultural knowledge? Does the reasoning in *Mitsubishi per force* entail a substantial diminution of the status of the antitrust legislation and of law itself? While the implied rejection of extraterritoriality is admirable, is it feasible—politically or legally—when it entails a unilateral divestiture of legal authority in circumstances in which there is no international regime of antitrust regulation to fill the void?

3. There are two technical arguments that appear at the end of Part III of the majority opinion. First, the Court states in a footnote:

> [I]n the event the choice-of-forum and choice-of-law clauses operated in tandem as a prospective waiver of a party's right to pursue statutory remedies for antitrust violations, we would have little hesitation in condemning the agreement as against public policy.

Second, in the text of the opinion, the Court observes:

> [T]he national courts of the United States will have the opportunity at the award-enforcement stage to ensure that the legitimate interest in the enforcement of the antitrust laws has been addressed.

Both remarks are intended to allay fears that all legal authority in matters of antitrust has been abdicated to **international arbitrators**. How do you assess the meaning and significance of what the Court is saying in these two passages? Do they constitute effective judicial supervision? Are they intended to do so? As to the first passage, how does it square with the contractualist theory of arbitration? As to the second passage, known as the **'second look' doctrine**, does it coincide with the obligations contained in Articles III and V of the New York Convention? How do you evaluate the general impact of *Mitsubishi* upon the Convention? The majority states: "The utility of the Convention in promoting the process of international commercial arbitration depends upon the willingness of national courts to let go of matters they normally would think of as their own." How should that remark be interpreted and evaluated?

4. As noted earlier, Justice Stevens' dissent reflects his extensive acquaintance with and knowledge of the antitrust laws. Toward the end of his dissent, he compares *Mitsubishi* and *Scherk*, stating that *Scherk* involved basically a non-statutory fraud claim that was "virtually identical to the breach of warranty claim. . . ." Stevens dissented in *Scherk* as a Seventh Circuit judge. His dissent coincided with the result later reached by the Court. As to *Mitsubishi*, Justice Stevens states that it "implicates our fundamental antitrust policies. . . ." Do you agree with his comparative evaluation of the statutory significance of the two cases? Is there simply a difference in expertise that results in a different appraisal? Does Justice Stevens inadequately evaluate the international dimension of the two cases? Does his analysis reflect insularity and sectarianism? Does it deliberately ignore or fail to perceive the advent of global commerce?

How persuasive is Justice Stevens in arguing that the arbitral clause does not apply to the dispute between Soler and Mitsubishi on the basis of contractual interpretation? Is he right that the contract itself limits the scope of the arbitral clause to technical and business disputes in which commercial expertise and adjudicatory informality are especially useful and relevant? Which parties in fact have agreed to arbitration? Which contract contains the arbitral clause? Is there a free-floating agreement to arbitrate? Why do you think the majority avoids these considerations? Which methodology makes for good or legitimate law?

Think about the **corporate configuration** in the case. Solar is a Puerto Rican company seeking to do business in Central America in part to respond to a change in the market demand for its products. Solar is part of or obligated by a Swiss Joint Venture Company created by Chrysler and Mitsubishi. Soler is directly bound by its supply contract with Mitsubishi. Mitsubishi wrote the arbitral clause, the application of which is limited to a few sections of the contract. The content of the arbitral clause evidently protects Mitsubishi's interest and restricts Soler's adjudicatory rights. Does Mitsubishi engage in international lawlessness? Should the 'form' contract have been more balanced? Which law governs the contract, the parties, and the arbitration? Should the contract have contained an 'escape clause' or recognized *force majeure* as a legitimate defense? Where does the blame for non-performance reside? Is the would-be breach the result of fortuitous circumstances? Soler alleges that it is protected by U.S. regulatory law. Is that view correct? If not, can it be defended?

11. FINAL OBSERVATIONS: ARBITRATION'S ORIGINS, PURPOSE, SCOPE, AND FUTURE

In both domestic and international matters, arbitration is being used to repair the adjudicatory deficiencies of judicial litigation. Processing disputes through courts often exceeds the financial capabilities of prospective users of judicial services. Ironically, protracted proceedings prevent parties from having their 'day in court'. Elaborate rules and procedures allow courts to regulate lawyer representational conduct; they have little to do with the parties or their disagreement. In effect, the litigants are third-string players in the trial. Witness and documents lists, discovery requests, on-site inspections, cross-examination, motions, opening and closing statements, conflicts in scheduling, expert witnesses, and randomly-chosen jurors make it likely that the party with the greater resources will prevail. Only wealthy or significantly maimed **litigants** can afford the requisite legal representation. Once the 'tournament' concludes, democratic populism requires that the least capable participants in the process (the jurors) assess the facts, read the court's instructions on the law, and decide on an outcome. When financial disparity or mythical beliefs do not decide the contest, parties can negotiate in the shadows of the litigation and attempt to settle. In fact, abandoning the fantasy of absolute victory and reaching a compromise may be the most rational way to manage the risks of judicial litigation and avoid calamities. Negotiated settlements are often the conclusion—such results have the virtue of being linked to the parties' sense of justice. In contrast to arbitral proceedings, judicial trials rarely go to completion. To some degree, outcomes based on substantive law have become relics. Law firm conference rooms are the modern courthouses. Bargaining strategies subordinate and ultimately replace legal standards.

In trans-border litigation, an **enforceable legal result** is even less likely. There, party conflict can implicate sovereign authority and different legal traditions. Enforcement of the result is precarious. Great instability prevails. Litigation abroad against foreign nationals is riddled with **uncertainty**: where to file a lawsuit, selecting a governing law, distinguishing between common-law and civil-law systems, predicting how the law will be interpreted and applied, establishing appellate remedies and their availability, and—lastly—but not least, gauging the likelihood of enforcing a judgment elsewhere than the place of rendition. When a multinational contract relationship breaks down, the parties seek the familiar; they want to find refuge in their national courts. The petitioned court rules on the propriety of venue, whether it has jurisdiction to rule, and on the law applicable. Determinations reached in different courts are likely to conflict. The consequences are evident: judgments are enforceable only in the jurisdiction in which they were rendered and the financial investment in national court proceedings generally is lost. The **maneuvering** results in an **impasse**. The standard conclusion is that global commercial deals are high-risk ventures that cannot be stabilized because there is no global legal process. The **conflicts methodology** creates a legal quagmire.

In both the international and domestic setting, arbitral adjudication lays bare the shortcomings of the law and court trials. It also provides an effective alternative to loss. In effect, civil litigation becomes possible through the exercise of party choice. Moreover, arbitration ends or supersedes the clamoring for new courts. A party-financed remedy exists and is entirely workable. Each arbitration is a **stand-alone event**. The arbitrators do not have a docket of cases; they do not rule for precedential reasons; the parties can choose to arbitrate and structure the arbitral proceedings through the arbitral clause. Courts do not interfere in the arbitral process and enforce awards with a modicum of scrutiny. SCOTUS federalized the legal regulation of arbitration and created an "emphatic federal policy favoring arbitration." The Court has demonstrated nearly absolute antipathy for imposing legal limits on the enforceability of arbitration agreements and awards.

With the aid of high courts, trans-border NGOs, and an army of national courts compliant on enforcement, the UN and UNCITRAL elaborated a juridical framework by which to create a ***de facto* global system** for the conduct of commerce and worldwide litigation. Development began several years after WW II. It led to the New York Convention, the Model Law on International Commercial Arbitration, the UNCITRAL Arbitration Rules, the Notes on Organizing Arbitral Proceedings, and other documents that permit recent adherents to establish, *ipso facto,* a legal doctrine favorable to arbitration. The support for international commercial arbitration originated in Europe (France especially); thereafter, it became dominant in the United States. The contemporary practice of ICA relies heavily on its North American-Western European (AmEur) origins. The French legal system was the first national process to recognize arbitration as indispensable to international commerce. SCOTUS began moving in that direction in the early 1970s. The Court is now arbitration's strongest and most visible supporter. Currently (09/2018), 159 State parties have ratified the New York Arbitration Convention.

The rise and effectiveness of arbitration could only be achieved with **judicial approbation**. Judicial resistance would have hindered the rise of, and the recourse to, arbitration. The judiciary's willingness to cede power to 'makeshift' adjudication and 'merchant' justice was vital to the establishment of contemporary arbitration. Courts, in fact, collaborated in 'arbitralizing' civil litigation. Contemporary arbitration is not sideshow for specialized trades. It is vital to achieving civil justice in American society and functional civil litigation in international business transactions. Arbitration's rise necessarily implies a decline in the recourse to the rituals of law. With the resort to arbitration in civil justice, well-established legal practices lost some of their standing. In fact, the concept of the civil trial may have been forever altered. Functionality exacts a price. Judicial guidance on the meaning of due process may now be of lesser importance. Merchants and arbitrators generally lack the ability to stand in the juridical shoes of judges. Moreover, legal values may be less workable in today's fast-paced, electronic society. Questions must be answered immediately and those answers need to be instantly available. Human beings have redefined themselves through technology. What was once prized and deemed essential is irrelevant. "Planes, trains, and automobiles" have had a profound effect on **social organization**. Crafting words and structuring syntax to achieve elegant writing is becoming unnecessary, even counterproductive and undesirable. If people's educational skills and outlook are changed, society's perception of courts and litigation will follow suit. Some Western societies now appear ready to jettison a significant part of traditional legal civilization to conserve and redirect social resources.

A critical question in the field today is whether arbitration can break free of its regional mold and become a truly global process. Arbitration and arbitrators could impair the **regulatory authority of States**. Arbitral clauses could vest privately-appointed arbitrators with the power to establish global legal standards. The arbitrators' commonality of background and experience could create a single, uniform set of controlling rules. The entire governance of society itself could be privatized. Currently, the lack of homogeneity prevails. There is profound diversity in the international community. Language, cultural practices, religious beliefs, and political practice and history differ radically and to such an extent that reconciliation or even co-existence may not be realistic. The **acceptance** of AmEur (North American-Western European) arbitration could be impossible in other parts of the world. Latin American jurisdictions, for example, are highly critical of capitalism and distrust the would-be Empire to the North. Leaders in Latin America have long talked about embracing trans-border arbitration, but nothing tangible has emerged. Only Brazil and Chile seem to have effectively incorporated arbitration into their legal systems. The future holds little promise either for capitalism or arbitration on the Latin American continent.

The Middle East has variegated approaches to ICA. Although an Emirate-wide law on arbitration has yet to be enacted in the UAE, Dubai has a Western-friendly approach to global arbitration. **Dubai** entered into an arrangement with the London Court of International Arbitration (LCIA) to establish a significant operational presence in the emirate. The objective was to import Western arbitration instead of modifying local practices and adjusting them to the Western system. Dubai's approach bears some similarity to **Hong Kong's** regulation of ICA; there, relying on its colonial past, it established an arbitration center that serves the entirety of Asia and functions as a commercial gateway for the West to China. In 2012, the Saudis enacted a new arbitration law to participate more effectively in global commerce. It was anticipated that Saudi judges would resist arbitration's intrusion into their adjudicatory responsibilities. The initial cases, however, indicate that **Saudi judge**s are emulating the Western judicial disposition toward arbitration.

The diversity of cultures and political systems in Asia may be the greatest challenge to the acceptance of AmEur arbitration. For example, **Japan** disfavors the recourse to arbitration for cultural reasons. Although there are many recipients of law degrees in Japan, the Japanese bar admits very few members. Adversarialism is not a way of life in Japan. Public confrontations between parties in court are shameful and socially ostracizing. Arbitration has an even **lesser standing**. While Japanese judges are certified and empowered by the government, arbitrators are authorized to rule merely by private contract. Given a choice, Japanese parties would always choose to mediate business conflicts. Japanese commercial parties, however, are realistic. When so obligated, Japanese companies arbitrate with their Western commercial partners in foreign jurisdictions. Japanese companies are involved in numerous international arbitrations each year; moreover, Japanese companies fully and effectively participate in global commerce. Japan has a long-standing arbitration center for the resolution of maritime disputes. The Japanese cultural exception, therefore, has little currency in the **realities** of cross-border business transactions.

Chinese reluctance toward Western arbitration is based upon the regime's practice of maintaining **complete control** over all aspects of national life. Political organization and the distrust of non-Chinese practices create a possibly impenetrable barrier between East and West. The respective political values and methods of governance are alien to each other. Any balanced accommodation is based upon an either-or choice between strict order without freedom or substantial individual liberty and limited regulation. In the West, the market regulates commercial conduct. Western countries, for example, impose no public law limits on arbitral service-providers or arbitrators. Restrictions could compromise the venue's reputation as hospitable to arbitration. It is up to the contracting parties to choose to arbitrate and to decide how to arbitrate. The **arbitrator's allegiance** is to the parties and the resolution of their dispute. The Chinese government, however, lets nothing operate freely. Because there is no individual freedom, there is no freedom of contract. The Hong Kong Arbitration Center will cease to be a viable arbitral institution if it could be influenced by the Chinese government. **Impartiality** is a fundamental value—it is a necessity—of private or public Western adjudicatory processes. As the early CIETAC experience demonstrates, Western business will not participate in an adjudicatory system in which the Chinese government (directly or indirectly) or local practices can dictate the outcome of individual arbitrations. In the Chinese sphere of influence, Western arbitration practices may not be legitimate, chosen, or effective. Such an outcome would restrict ICA to its geographical origins and the political values that prevail in those countries. Delegation of systemic authority to individuals and private activity is exceedingly unlikely in dictatorships and nations that are ideologically unfriendly to commerce and democracy. Democracy may be indispensable to effective, functional arbitration. **Statism** and **cultural myopia** are inadequate platforms upon which to conduct Western business. The exercise of unlimited control by political entities creates an environment that is antagonistic to individual entrepreneurialism. The State represents too great a risk to induce economic risk-taking in the territory in which it reigns.

The Chinese influence will be felt throughout the Far East region. For historical reasons, Japan may or may not be part of the Far Eastern group. Japan and possibly Singapore may be the only foothole for Western parties. It is likely that Chinese influence will work to evict Western arbitral practices from the Far East, **footholes** notwithstanding. The Chinese Communist Party will not delegate adjudicatory authority to foreign individuals or practices. While CIETAC has adjusted to Western arbitral practices, Chinese law has not. Political power remains lodged in the Party and the government. Despite an ability to accommodate, the Chinese government will never cede judicial power to non-governmental entities. The Hong Kong 'solution' (present but compliant) may be the best possible result. As long as all parties to the arbitration are Western, the Hong Kong venue is likely to remain friendly. When Chinese businesses are involved and Chinese economic interests implicated, the arbitration may be converted into a diplomatic event—a dismal result for non-Chinese private commercial parties. The **revolution in civil litigation** undertaken and supervised by national supreme courts in Western legal systems is not an implant that is likely to flourish in the Far East.

What is your assessment of these observations?

CHAPTER 2

FEDERAL AND STATE ARBITRATIONS

■ ■ ■

1. THE FEDERAL ARBITRATION ACT

In the nineteenth century, U.S. courts and law were hostile to arbitration. Such antipathy was characteristic of most legal systems at the time. Judges were unwilling to surrender the power of conducting trials and to be replaced by individuals with little or no legal training. In their view, arbitration was makeshift and approximative justice. Courts were, therefore, reluctant to compel parties to arbitrate. In the words of Mr. Justice Story,

> . . . [w]hen . . . [courts] are asked to . . . compel the parties to appoint arbitrators whose award shall be final, they necessarily pause to consider whether such tribunals possess adequate means of giving redress, and whether they have a right to compel a reluctant party to submit to such a tribunal, and to close against him the doors of the common courts of justice, provided by the government to protect rights and to redress wrongs.

Tobey v. County of Bristol, 23 F. Cas. 1313, 1320–21 (C.C. D. Mass. 1845) (No. 14,065).

In order to be legally binding, the agreement to arbitrate needed to be confirmed by continuous voluntary participation in the arbitral proceeding. Unlike English courts, which reviewed the merits of awards through the case-stated procedure, courts in the United States would enforce awards once they were rendered. Their opposition to arbitration was expressed by attacks on the agreement to arbitrate—in particular the arbitral clause. Under U.S. law, the arbitral clause was subject to unilateral rescission at any time prior to the rendition of an award. The submission agreement could also be avoided prior to the rendering of an award, but, because it was entered into after a dispute arose, it represented a firmer waiver of judicial relief. In an earlier part of his opinion, Mr. Justice Story stated that arbitration agreements were not "against public policy" and that courts "have and can have no just objection to these domestic forums, and will enforce . . . their awards when fairly and lawfully made, without hesitation or question."

The United States Arbitration Act, more commonly known as the Federal Arbitration Act or the FAA, was special interest legislation designed to stabilize commercial transactions in New York City. It was intended to validate the dispute resolution practices of the commercial trades. The FAA, however, was to become landmark legislation that ended the era of judicial hostility to arbitration and made arbitration a vital mechanism of dispute resolution. Its refashioning by SCOTUS over decades created a far different statute that surpassed the objectives that led to its enactment. In many respects, the FAA is a precocious example of modern arbitration legislation; it anticipates the central provisions of more contemporary statutes by some forty to fifty years. It legitimizes arbitration agreements and establishes a strong presumption of enforceability. It also restricts the role of courts in arbitration and provides limited grounds for the judicial supervision of awards. The FAA's eventual objective was to rehabilitate arbitration as an adjudicatory process and give it the systemic autonomy it needed to function effectively. In its current form, the FAA retains most of its original language. Supplementary provisions were added in 1970, 1988, and 1990.

The United States Arbitration Act

§ 1. "Maritime Transactions" and "Commerce" Defined: Exceptions to Operation of Title

"Maritime transactions," as herein defined, means charter parties, bills of lading of water carriers, agreements relating to wharfage, supplies furnished vessels or repairs of vessels, collisions, or any other matters in foreign commerce which, if the subject of controversy, would be embraced within admiralty jurisdiction; "commerce," as herein defined, means commerce among the several States or with foreign nations, or in any Territory of the United States or in the District of Columbia, or between any such Territory and another, or between any such Territory and any State or foreign nation, or between the District of Columbia and any State or Territory or foreign nation, but nothing herein contained shall apply to contracts of employment of seamen, railroad employees, or any other class of workers engaged in foreign or interstate commerce.

§ 2. Validity, Irrevocability, and Enforcement of Agreements to Arbitrate

A written provision in any maritime transaction or a contract evidencing a transaction involving commerce to settle by arbitration a controversy thereafter arising out of such contract or transaction, or the refusal to perform the whole or any part thereof, or an agreement in writing to submit to arbitration an existing controversy arising out of such a contract, transaction, or refusal, shall be valid, irrevocable, and enforceable, save upon such grounds as exist at law or in equity for the revocation of any contract.

§ 3. Stay of Proceedings Where Issue Therein Referable to Arbitration

If any suit or proceedings be brought in any of the courts of the United States upon any issue referable to arbitration under an agreement in writing for such arbitration, the court in which suit is pending, upon being satisfied that the issue involved in such suit or proceeding is referable to arbitration under such an agreement, shall on application of one of the parties stay the trial of the action until such arbitration has been had in accordance with the terms of the agreement, providing the applicant for the stay is not in default proceeding with such arbitration.

§ 4. Failure to Arbitrate under Agreement; Petition to United States Court Having Jurisdiction for Order to Compel Arbitration; Notice and Service Thereof; Hearing and Determination

A party aggrieved by the alleged failure, neglect, or refusal of another to arbitrate under a written agreement for arbitration may petition any United States district court which, save for such agreement, would have jurisdiction under Title 28, in a civil action or in admiralty of the subject matter of a suit arising out of the controversy between the parties, for an order directing that such arbitration proceed in the manner provided for in such agreement. Five days' notice in writing of such application shall be served upon the party in default. Service thereof shall be made in the manner provided by the Federal Rules of Civil Procedure. The court shall hear the parties, and upon being satisfied that the making of the agreement for arbitration or the failure to comply therewith is not in issue, the court shall make an order directing the parties to proceed to arbitration in accordance with the terms of the agreement. The hearing and proceedings, under such agreement, shall be within the district in which the petition for an order directing such arbitration is filed. If the making of the arbitration agreement or the failure, neglect, or refusal to perform the same be in issue, the court shall proceed summarily to the trial thereof. If no jury trial be demanded by the party alleged to be in default, or if the matter in dispute is within admiralty jurisdiction, the court shall hear and determine such issue. Where such an issue is raised, the party alleged to be in default may, except in cases of admiralty, on or before the return day of the notice of application, demand a jury trial of such issue, and upon such demand the court shall make an order referring the issue or issues to a jury in the manner provided by the Federal Rules of Civil Procedure, or may specially call a jury for that purpose. If the jury find[s] that no agreement in writing for arbitration was made or that there is no default in proceeding thereunder, the proceeding shall be dismissed. If the jury find[s] that an agreement for arbitration was made in writing and that there is a default in proceeding thereunder, the court shall make an order summarily directing the parties to proceed with the arbitration in accordance with the terms thereof.

§ 5. Appointment of Arbitrators or Umpire

If in the agreement provision be made for a method of naming or appointing an arbitrator or arbitrators or an umpire, such method shall be followed; but if no method be provided therein, or if a method be provided and any party thereto shall fail to avail himself of such method, or if for any other reason there shall be a lapse in the naming of an arbitrator or arbitrators or umpire, or in filling a vacancy, then upon the application of either party to the controversy the court shall designate and appoint an arbitrator or arbitrators or umpire, as the case may require, who shall act under the said agreement with the same force and effect as if he or they had been specifically named therein; and unless otherwise provided in the agreement the arbitration shall be by a single arbitrator.

§ 6. Application Heard as Motion

Any application to the court hereunder shall be made and heard in the manner provided by law for the making and hearing of motions, except as otherwise herein expressly provided.

§ 7. Witnesses Before Arbitrators; Fees; Compelling Attendance

The arbitrators selected either as prescribed in this title or otherwise, or a majority of them, may summon in writing any person to attend before them or any of them as a witness and in a proper case to bring with him or them any book, record, document, or paper which may be deemed material as evidence in the case. The fees for such attendance shall be the same as the fees of witnesses before masters of the United States courts. Said summons shall issue in the name of the arbitrator or arbitrators or a majority of them and shall be signed by the arbitrators, or a majority of them, and shall be directed to the said person and shall be served in the same manner as subpoenas to appear and testify before the court; if any person or persons so summoned to testify shall refuse or neglect to obey said summons, upon petition the United States court in and for the district in which such arbitrators, or a majority of them, are sitting may compel the attendance of such person or persons before said arbitrator or arbitrators, or punish said person or persons for contempt in the same manner provided by law, for securing the attendance of witnesses or their punishment for neglect or refusal to attend in the courts of the United States.

§ 8. Proceedings Begun by Libel in Admiralty and Seizure of Vessel or Property

If the basis of jurisdiction be a cause of action otherwise justifiable in admiralty, then, notwithstanding anything herein to the contrary the party claiming to be aggrieved may begin his proceeding hereunder by libel and seizure of the vessel or other property of the other party according to the usual course of admiralty proceedings, and the court shall then have jurisdiction to direct the parties to proceed with the arbitration and shall retain jurisdiction to enter its decree upon the award.

§ 9. Award of Arbitrators; Confirmation; Jurisdiction; Procedure

If the parties in their agreement have agreed that a judgment of the court shall be entered upon the award made pursuant to the arbitration, and shall specify the court, then at any time within one year after the award is made any party to the arbitration may apply to the court so specified for an order confirming the award, and thereupon the court must grant such an order unless the award is vacated, modified, or corrected as prescribed in sections 10 and 11 of this title. If no court is specified in the agreement of the parties, then such application may be made to the United States court in and for the district within which such award was made. Notice of the application shall be served upon the adverse party, and thereupon the court shall have jurisdiction of such party as though he had appeared generally in the proceeding. If the adverse party is a resident of the district within which the award was made, such service shall be made upon the adverse party or his attorney as prescribed by law for service of notice of motion in an action in the same court. If the adverse party shall be a nonresident, then the notice of the application shall be served by the marshal of any district within which the adverse party may be found in like manner as other process of the court.

§ 10. Same; Vacation [sic] [Vacatur]; Grounds; Rehearing

(a) In any of the following cases the United States court in and for the district wherein the award was made may make an order vacating the award upon the application of any party to the arbitration—

1. Where the award was procured by corruption, fraud, or undue means.

2. Where there was evident partiality or corruption in the arbitrators, or either of them.

3. Where the arbitrators were guilty of misconduct in refusing to postpone the hearing, upon sufficient cause shown, or in refusing to hear evidence pertinent and material to the controversy; or of any other misbehavior by which the rights of any party have been prejudiced.

4. Where the arbitrators exceeded their powers, or so imperfectly executed them that a mutual, final, and definite award upon the subject matter submitted was not made.

5. Where an award is vacated and the time within which the agreement required the award to be made has not expired the court may, in its discretion, direct a rehearing by the arbitrators.

(b) The United States district court for the district wherein an award was made that was issued pursuant to section 580 of title 5 may make an order vacating the award upon the application of a person, other than a party to the arbitration, who is adversely affected or aggrieved by the award, if the use of arbitration or the award is clearly inconsistent with the factors set forth in section 572 of title 5.

§ 11. Same; Modification or Correction; Grounds; Order

In either of the following cases the United States court in and for the district wherein the award was made may make an order modifying or correcting the award upon the application of any party to the arbitration:

(a) Where there was an evident material miscalculation of figures or an evident material mistake in the description of any person, thing, or property referred to in the award.

(b) Where the arbitrators have awarded upon a matter not submitted to them, unless it is a matter not affecting the merits of the decision upon the matter submitted.

(c) Where the award is imperfect in matter of form not affecting the merits of the controversy.

The order may modify and correct the award, so as to effect the intent thereof and promote justice between the parties.

§ 12. Notice of Motions to Vacate or Modify; Service; Stay of Proceedings

Notice of a motion to vacate, modify, or correct an award must be served upon the adverse party or his attorney within three months after the award is filed or delivered. If the adverse party is a resident of the district within which the award was made, such service shall be made upon the adverse party or his attorney as prescribed by law for service of notice of motion in an action in the same court. If the adverse party shall be a nonresident, then the notice of the application shall be served by the marshal of any district within which the adverse party may be found in like manner as other process of the court. For the purposes of the motion any judge who might make an order to stay the proceedings in an action brought in the same court may make an order, to be served with the notice of motion, staying the proceedings of the adverse party to enforce the award.

§ 13. Papers Filed with Order on Motions; Judgment; Docketing; Force and Effect; Enforcement

The party moving for an order confirming, modifying, or correcting an award shall, at the time such order is filed with the clerk for the entry of judgment thereon, also file the following papers with the clerk:

(a) The agreement; the selection or appointment, if any, of an additional arbitrator or umpire; and each written extension of the time, if any, within which to make the award.

(b) The award.

(c) Each notice, affidavit, or other paper used upon an application to confirm, modify, or correct the award, and a copy of each order of the court upon such an application.

The judgment shall be docketed as if it was rendered in an action.

The judgment so ordered shall have the same force and effect, in all respects, as, and be subject to all the provisions of law relating to, a judgment in an action; and it may be enforced as if it had been rendered in an action in the court in which it is entered.

§ 14. Contracts Not Affected

This title shall not apply to contracts made prior to January 1, 1926.

§ 15. Inapplicability of the Act of State doctrine

Enforcement of arbitral agreements, confirmation of arbitral awards, and execution upon judgments based on orders confirming such awards shall not be refused on the basis of the Act of State doctrine.

§ 16. Appeals

(a) An appeal may be taken from—

(1) an order—

(a) refusing a stay of any action under section 3 of this title,

(b) denying a petition under section 4 of this title to order arbitration to proceed,

(c) denying an application under section 206 of this title to compel arbitration,

(d) confirming or denying confirmation of an award or partial award, or

(e) modifying, correcting, or vacating an award;

(2) an interlocutory order granting, continuing, or modifying an injunction against an arbitration that is subject to this title; or

(3) a final decision with respect to an arbitration that is subject to this title.

(b) Except as otherwise provided in section 1292(b) of title 28, an appeal may not be taken from an interlocutory order—

(1) granting a stay of any action under section 3 of this title;

(2) directing arbitration to proceed under section 4 of this title;

(3) compelling arbitration to proceed under section 206 of this title;

(4) refusing to enjoin an arbitration that is subject to this title.

An Interpretation of the FAA

In *AMF v. Brunswick Corp.,* national competitors, manufacturing electronic equipment for bowling alleys, entered into a litigation settlement which provided that any future disputes regarding advertising would be submitted to a neutral third-party for an advisory opinion. The U.S. District Court for the Eastern District of New York enforced the agreement under the Federal Arbitration Act (FAA). The court reasoned that, because the FAA did not define the term "arbitration," any submission to a third-party constituted an agreement to arbitrate. The court stated that no "magic words such as 'arbitrate' . . . [were] needed to obtain [the] benefits of the Act [the FAA]." Moreover, the term "arbitration" "eludes easy definition" and could be synonymous with mediation and conciliation.

Accordingly, the FAA "provided for [the] enforcement of agreements to 'settle' disputes. . . ."

On the basis of this unusual construction of the FAA, the court compelled AMF and Brunswick to have recourse to their agreed-upon ADR procedure (the non-binding advisory opinion). Despite its title, content, and legislative history, the FAA—in the court's view—was not just an arbitration statute, but legislation broadly applicable to all forms of alternative dispute resolution (ADR).

AMF INC. V. BRUNSWICK CORP.

621 F.Supp. 456 (E.D. N.Y. 1985).

(footnote omitted)

[. . .]

WEINSTEIN, CHIEF JUDGE.

[. . .]

I. Facts

AMF and Brunswick compete nationally in the manufacture of electronic and automatic machinery used for bowling [alleys]. In earlier litigation before this court, AMF alleged that Brunswick had advertised certain automatic scoring devices in a false and deceptive manner. Brunswick responded with counterclaims regarding advertisements for AMF's pinspotter, bowling pins and automatic scorer. In 1983 the parties ended the litigation with a settlement agreement filed with the court. Any future dispute involving an advertised claim of "data based comparative superiority" of any bowling product would be submitted to an advisory third party, the National Advertising Division ("NAD") of the Council of Better Business Bureaus, to determine whether there was experimental support for the claim.

[. . .]

In March and April 1985, Brunswick advertised its product, Armor Plate 3000, in a trade periodical called Bowler's Journal. . . . [T]he advertisement . . . detail[s] the advantages of Armor Plate; and . . . strongly suggests that research supports the claim of durability as compared to wood lanes.

[. . .]

AMF, disputing the content of the advertisement, sought from Brunswick the underlying research data. . . . Brunswick replied that having undertaken the expense of research it would not make the results available to AMF. Thereupon AMF informed Brunswick that it was invoking . . . the settlement agreement and requested that Brunswick provide substantiation to an independent third party. Brunswick responded that its advertisement did not fall within the terms of the agreement. AMF now brings this action to compel Brunswick to submit its data to the NAD for nonbinding arbitration.

[. . .]

III. Law

A. Arbitration

1. The Act

AMF characterizes the settlement agreement as one subject to the Federal Arbitration Act. . . . The Act provides for enforcement of agreements to "settle" disputes arising after the agreement was entered into. In relevant part it reads:

> A written provision in . . . a contract evidencing a transaction involving commerce to settle by arbitration a controversy thereafter arising out of such contract or transaction, or the refusal to perform the whole or any part thereof . . . shall be valid, irrevocable, and enforceable, save upon such grounds as exist at law or in equity for the revocation of any contract.

. . . The issue posed is whether "a controversy" [c]ould be "settled" by the process set forth in the agreement.

Brunswick argues that the parties did not contemplate the kind of arbitration envisaged by the Act because the opinion of the third party is not binding on AMF and Brunswick and the agreement cannot settle the controversy. Arbitration, Brunswick argues, must present an alternative to litigation; that is, it must provide "a final settlement of the controversy between the parties."

Arbitration is a term that eludes easy definition. One commentator has pointed out that "difficulty with terminology seems to have persisted throughout the entire development of arbitration." . . . He suggests that arbitration has become "synonymous with 'mediation' and 'conciliation.' " . . .

The Federal Arbitration Act, adopted in 1925, made agreements to arbitrate enforceable without defining what they were. Contemporary cases provide a broad description of arbitration: "[a] form of procedure whereby differences may be settled.". . . At no time have the courts insisted on a rigid or formalistic approach to a definition of arbitration.

Case law following the passage of the Act reflects unequivocal support of agreements to have third parties decide disputes—the essence of arbitration. No magic words such as "arbitrate" or "binding arbitration" or "final dispute resolution" are needed to obtain the benefits of the Act. . . .

[. . .]

An adversary proceeding, submission of evidence, witnesses and cross-examination are not essential elements of arbitration. . . . The Second Circuit has set a standard of "fundamental fairness" in arbitration; rules of evidence and procedure do not apply with the same strictness as they do in federal courts. . . .

Arbitration is a creature of contract, a device of the parties rather than the judicial process. If the parties have agreed to submit a dispute for a decision by a third party, they have agreed to arbitration. The arbitrator's decision need not be binding in the same sense that a judicial decision needs to be to satisfy the constitutional requirement of a justiciable case or controversy. . . .

2. *Application of the Act to the Facts*

Under the circumstances of this case, the agreement should be characterized as one to arbitrate. Obviously there is a controversy between the parties—is there data supporting Brunswick's claim of superiority. Submission of this dispute will at least "settle" that issue, even though the parties may want to continue related disputes in another forum.

It is highly likely that if Brunswick's claims are found by NAD to be supported that will be the end of AMF's challenge to the advertisement. Should the claims not be found to be supported, it is probable that Brunswick will change its advertising copy. Viewed in the light of reasonable commercial expectations the dispute will be settled by this arbitration. That it may not end all controversy between the parties for all times is no reason not to enforce the agreement.

The mechanism agreed to by the parties does provide an effective alternative to litigation, even though it would not employ an adversary process. That the arbitrator will examine documents *in camera* and *ex parte* does not prevent recognition of the procedure as arbitration since the parties have agreed to this special practice in this unique type of dispute. Courts are fully familiar with the practice since prosecutorial and business secrets often require protection by *ex parte* and *in camera* proceedings during the course of a litigation.

In a confidential-submission scheme, such as the one agreed to here, adversarial hearings cannot take place. But this fact does not militate against application of the Act. Rather it supports arbitration since the special arbitrator may be more capable of deciding the issue than is a court which relies so heavily on the adversary process. Moreover, the particular arbitrator chosen by these parties is more capable than the courts of finding the faint line that separates data supported claims from puffery in the sometimes mendacious atmosphere of advertising copy.

[. . .]

The alternative dispute resolution (ADR) procedure agreed upon in the settlement is designed to reduce the acrimony associated with protracted litigation and to improve the chances of resolving future advertising disputes. This form of ADR is designed to keep disputes of this kind out of court.

The value of this settlement agreement lies largely in the particular experience and skill of the NAD as a resolver of disputes. In the fourteen years since its formation, the NAD has developed its own process of reviewing complaints of deceptiveness, coupling relative informality and confidentiality with safeguards to ensure procedural fairness. . . . To these advantages of the special ADR system designed by the parties is added the unique ability of the NAD to decide what is fair in advertising. A judge might make this inquiry, but ultimately it would have to defer to the very expertise that NAD offers without resort to the courts.

General public policy favors support of alternatives to litigation when these alternatives serve the interests of the parties and of judicial administration. Here AMF and Brunswick agreed in June 1983 that a special ADR mechanism would serve them better than litigation. Such decisions are encouraged by no less an observer than the Chief Justice of the United States. In his words, ADR devices are often superior to litigation "in terms of cost, time, and human wear and tear." . . .

. . . [T]he specific policy of this court is to enforce ADR agreements. In most instances they reduce the need for court trials and save clients' time and money.

A remedy at law would be inadequate since it could only approximate the skilled, speedy and inexpensive efforts available by way of specific performance. A lawsuit would deny AMF the practical specialized experience that the parties agreed to have available for an examination of data-based comparative advertising. A court decision and an NAD decision would have different effects on the parties' reputations within the bowling products industry. In short, a remedy at law falls short of providing many of the advantages of specific performance.

[. . .]

IV. Conclusion

[. . .]

AMF's petition to compel the submission of data pursuant to Paragraph 9 of the settlement agreement of June 30, 1983 is enforceable under the Federal Arbitration Act and pursuant to this court's equity jurisdiction.

[. . .]

So Ordered.

NOTES AND QUESTIONS

1. The decision in *AMF v. Brunswick Corp.* illustrates the dangers of 'adjusting' statutory texts on an *ad hoc* basis to reach an expedient result. The sole purpose of this process is to arrive at a 'desirable' or 'functional' conclusion. The ruling court decides on the legitimacy of the methodology and its impact on the law in the particlar case. In *AMF Brunswick*, the judicial discussion is an evidently flawed construction of the applicable statute. The FAA does not contain any of the definitional indeterminacy that the court attributes to it. It appears that the court believes that it must falsify the law for the sake of its docket.

Is a "super" FAA realistic? Is the court being analytically rigorous or does it engage in a version of what Judge Andrews describes as "practical politics" in *Palsgraf*? What consequences are likely from the application of this methodology?

2. Is the *AMF v. Brunswick Corp.* court correct or plainly wrong? Does it distort well-established concepts of arbitration law to enforce the parties' contract provision and relegate them and their dispute to another forum?

3. How would you describe arbitration? Do you agree with the court that the concept of arbitration is difficult to define?

4. In *Wolsey, Ltd. v. Foodmaker, Inc.*, 144 F.3d 1205 (9th Cir. 1998), the U.S. Court of Appeals for the Ninth Circuit provided a different, albeit related, response to the question of what dispute management processes fall within the ambit of the FAA. The Ninth Circuit held that a provision for nonbinding American Arbitration Association (AAA) arbitration was enforceable under FAA § 2.

In 1991, Wolsey contracted with Foodmaker to obtain the right to develop "Jack in the Box" restaurants in Hong Kong and Macau. The contract contained a dispute resolution provision, establishing a three-step process by which to resolve all disputes: (1) a senior executive officer meeting; (2) non-binding AAA arbitration; and (3) litigation in federal court. In March 1994, Wolsey alleged fraudulent inducement and initiated the dispute resolution process. After meeting with the senior executives of Foodmaker, he filed a demand for AAA arbitration. The arbitral tribunal ruled in favor of Wolsey, but Foodmaker did not comply with the non-binding award. Wolsey filed suit in federal court, alleging new claims based upon statutory law. These claims had not been advanced in the AAA arbitration. Foodmaker, therefore, moved to compel arbitration. The district court denied the motion; Foodmaker appealed to the Ninth Circuit.

The Ninth Circuit determined that, despite the Development Agreement's reference to "non-binding" arbitration, an order to compel arbitration could be issued. The court relied on case law "reflect[ing] unequivocal support of agreements to have third parties decide disputes—the essence of arbitration. No magic words such as 'arbitrate' or 'binding arbitration' or 'final dispute resolution' [were] needed to obtain the benefits of the [FAA]. . . . If the parties [had] agreed to submit for a decision by a third party, they have agreed to arbitration." Referring to the "presumption in favor of arbitrability created by the FAA," the Ninth Circuit underscored that, in *Moses H. Cone Memorial Hosp. v. Mercury Constr. Corp.*, 460 U.S. 1 (1983), the U.S. Supreme Court held that "arbitration need not be binding in order to fall within the scope of the Federal Arbitration Act."

Do you agree with the court's ruling? How does it compare to *AMF-Brunswick*?

5. In *CB Richard Ellis, Inc. v. American Environ. Waste Management*, 1998 WL 903495 (E.D.N.Y. 1998) (unrep. in F. Supp.2d), the Federal Court for the Eastern District held that the FAA governs a contractual provision for the submission of disputes to mediation. American Environmental had agreed to remove waste from commercial properties managed by CB. The contract contained a general clause for the mediation of disputes. When disputes arose, one party filed a judicial action, while the other party alleged that the disagreements should first be submitted to mediation.

The court addressed the question of whether the parties were—pursuant to their contract—obligated to mediate their differences before filing a court action. The court stated that the FAA controlled the determination because, in part, "[b]oth sides agree[d] that the [FAA] . . . govern[ed]" such questions. Why party provision or acquiescence should be so vital to the FAA's scope of application was never explained. Moreover, the court referred to the circuit precedent, namely, *AMF v. Brunswick Corp.* According to the court, the reference in FAA § 2 to the "settlement" of disputes by arbitration allowed the provision (hence the legislation) to cover not only arbitration agreements, but also clauses for the mediation of disputes and other forms of ADR. You should assess the court's reasoning.

What is its likely impact upon the drafting of arbitration agreements and counseling on arbitration? Will courts change the way they think about arbitration?

6. Other courts have been less inclined to interpret the statutory language creatively and expand the FAA's scope of application. In *Heritage Building Systems, Inc.*, 185 S.W.3d 539 (Tex. Ct. App. 2006), the court suggested that the FAA was not an all-purpose ADR statute; it held that, when parties have agreed to arbitrate disputes, it is improper to compel mediation under the FAA at the request of only one of the parties. Presumably, a mutual agreement to proceed to mediation would have been enforceable—not on the basis of the FAA, but rather as a matter of contract. The Seventh Circuit reached a similar conclusion in *Omni Tech Corp. v. MPC Solutions Sales LLC*, 432 F.3d 797 (7th Cir. 2005). There, the court held that a written agreement to submit disputes to an accounting firm for a binding determination did not

constitute an arbitration agreement. Like other types of ADR references, the agreed-upon procedure was enforceable under contract law. The arbitration statute simply was not applicable. Similarly, the Tenth Circuit, in *Salt Lake Tribune Publishing Co., L.L.C. v. Management Planning, Inc.*, 390 F.3d 684 (10th Cir. 2004), held that an appraisal procedure, not intended by the parties to be final and binding in all circumstances, did not sufficiently resemble "classic arbitration" to be arbitration.

The First Circuit ruled in a related vein. In *HIM Portland, LLC v. DeVito Builders, Inc.*, 317 F.3d 41 (1st Cir. 2003), the court determined that "[w]here contracting parties condition an arbitration agreement upon the satisfaction of some condition precedent, the failure to satisfy the specified condition will preclude the parties from compelling arbitration and staying [judicial] proceedings under the FAA."

Commentary

Under Section One, the FAA applies to maritime and commercial matters that are part of interstate commerce or which involve foreign commerce. The U.S. Supreme Court in *Citizens Bank v. Alafabco*, 539 U.S. 52 (2003), took an expansive view of interstate commerce. There, the Court held that commercial lending had a broad impact on the U.S. economy. Moreover, by enacting the FAA, Congress invoked its widest powers under the Commerce Clause. As a result, the FAA applied to transactions "in commerce" and "in the flow" of interstate commerce. It also appears from the language of Section One that the FAA does not apply to the resolution of disputes that arise from employment contracts or relationships. Presumably, the special rights of recourse that might have been available to workers in specialty areas of foreign or interstate commerce could be undermined by the use of arbitration. *Gilmer v. Interstate/Johnson Lane Corp.*, 500 U.S. 20 (1991), directly challenged the exclusion of employment contracts from the purview of the federal legislation on arbitration. There, the Court upheld an arbitral clause that was said to govern disputes arising out of a stock broker's employment contract, notwithstanding the language of Section One.

In 2001, the U.S. Supreme Court issued its landmark ruling in *Circuit City Stores, Inc. v. Adams*, 532 U.S. 105 (2001), holding that the employment contract exclusion in FAA § 1 only applied to the employment contracts of interstate transportation workers. Employers, therefore, could require all other employees to submit employment-related disputes to arbitration. Accordingly, the strong federal policy in favor of arbitration generally applied to the enforcement of arbitration agreements in employment relationships.

According to the Court, the FAA was enacted to eliminate the "hostility of American courts to the enforcement of arbitration agreements" and thereby to compel "judicial enforcement of a wide range of written arbitration agreements." Section 2 of the FAA, the Court further stated, provided for the enforceability of any "written provision in any maritime transaction or a contract evidencing a transaction involving commerce to settle by arbitration a controversy thereafter arising out of such contract or transaction." The Court had interpreted Section 2 as "implementing Congress' intent to exercise its commerce power to the full." Section 1, therefore, only exempted "contracts of employment of seamen, railroad employees, or any other class of workers engaged in foreign or interstate commerce" from the FAA's scope of application.

The Court then observed that it "need not assess the legislative history of the exclusion provision." That legislative history became "problematic" when "sources . . . removed from the full Congress" were consulted. Furthermore, the Court saw no contradiction in its position that Congress would exempt from the scope of the statute only workers over whom it had jurisdiction in 1925, namely, seamen and railroad workers, and yet intend the Act to apply to workers over whom—pursuant to its limited Commerce Clause power—it had no control. "It is reasonable to assume that Congress excluded 'seamen' and 'railroad employees' from the FAA for the simple reason that it did not wish to unsettle . . . dispute resolution schemes covering certain workers."

Justices Stevens, Ginsburg, Breyer, and Souter dissented. In their dissenting opinions, the Justices explained that the FAA was originally intended to allow the arbitration of commercial and maritime disputes, and that there was no legislative intent to have the FAA govern in employment matters. The FAA was a "response to the refusal of courts to enforce commercial arbitration agreements, which were commonly used in the maritime context." The original bill, in fact, was drafted by the Committee on Commerce, Trade, and Commercial Law of the American Bar Association (ABA). A sponsor of the bill stated that the FAA intended "to give an opportunity to enforce an agreement [to arbitrate] in commercial contracts and admiralty contracts." The bill was originally opposed by representatives of organized labor, primarily the International Seamen's Union of America, "because of their concern that . . . [it] might authorize federal judicial enforcement of arbitration clauses in employment contracts."

The FAA's legislative history makes clear that it was not intended to be a source of new substantive legal rights. In the words of one of its proponents, the FAA provides for the enforcement of ordinary contractual rights in areas of specialized commercial activity:

> This bill simply provides for one thing, and that is to give an opportunity to enforce an agreement in commercial contracts and admiralty contracts an agreement to arbitrate, when voluntarily placed in the document by the parties to it. It does not involve any new principle of law except to provide a simple method by which

> the parties may be brought before the court in order to give enforcement to that which they have already agreed to. . . . It does nothing more than that. It creates no new legislation, grants no new rights, except a remedy to enforce an agreement [to arbitrate] in commercial contracts and in admiralty contracts.

65 *Cong. Rec.* 1931 (1924) (statement of Rep. Graham). Congress considered the FAA as a means by which commercial parties could gain access to a private adjudicatory remedy through the exercise of their contract rights. It allowed the federal courts to give effect to those agreements. It was deemed a procedural enactment that created a statutory mechanism for enforcing arbitral agreements and awards:

> The principal support for the Act came from trade associations dealing in groceries and other perishables and from commercial and mercantile groups in the major trading centers. . . . Practically all who testified in support of the bill . . . explained that the bill was designed to cover contracts between people in different states who shipped, bought, or sold commodities. . . .

Prima Paint Corp. v. Flood & Conklin Mfg. Co., 388 U.S. 395, 409 n.2 (1967) (Black, J., dissenting).

This historical background demonstrates the enormous distance that separates the FAA's original meaning and purpose at the time of enactment from its current version in the decisional law. The courts have extended the reach of the FAA far beyond the adjudication of specialized commercial claims and have given the right to arbitrate not only a substantive character, but a constitutional stature as well. Moreover, the courts viewed the federalism questions that arose in connection with the FAA as an opportunity to transform the legislation into a substantive law enactment. What began as a procedure for special interests became a cornerstone remedy of civil litigation?

§ 2. Validity, Irrevocability, and Enforcement of Agreements to Arbitrate

A written provision in any maritime transaction or a contract evidencing a transaction involving commerce to settle by arbitration a controversy thereafter arising out of such contract or transaction, or the refusal to perform the whole or any part thereof, or an agreement in writing to submit to arbitration an existing controversy arising out of such a contract, transaction, or refusal, shall be valid, irrevocable, and enforceable, save upon such grounds as exist at law or in equity for the revocation of any contract.

Commentary

Section Two is—historically and doctrinally—the centerpiece provision of the FAA. It establishes the legal validity of arbitration agreements. Section Two recognizes both the arbitral clause and the submission agreement as lawful forms of contract. Neither agreement violates public policy. Arbitral agreements are "valid, irrevocable, and enforceable"—a statement that clearly repudiates the past judicial practice of upholding arbitration agreements only once the arbitral tribunal had rendered an award. Merchants can decide for themselves whether to forgo the courts. An agreement to arbitrate can only be challenged on standard contract formation grounds, *i.e.*, the failure of consideration, adhesion, or unconscionability.

Challenging arbitration agreements for contract deficiencies, however, has not been very successful. The policy support for arbitration permits a great deal of latitude in the definition of contract validity. Unilateral and adhesive contracts for arbitration are often enforced.

In *Harris v. Green Tree Financial Corp.*, 183 F.3d 173 (3d Cir. 1999), the U.S. Court of Appeals for the Third Circuit upheld a broad arbitration clause that granted only one of the contracting parties—the stronger one—the right to litigate certain claims. The court stated that "the mere fact Green Tree retains the option to litigate some issues in court, while the Harrises must arbitrate all claims does not make the arbitration agreement unenforceable. We have held repeatedly that inequality in bargaining power, alone, is not a valid basis upon which to invalidate an arbitration agreement." The court determined that the agreement was not unconscionable.

The California Supreme Court has taken a particularly active role in policing the validity of arbitration agreements. It endorsed a far more expansive concept of unconscionability than the Third Circuit, emphasizing the need for a fully bilateral obligation to arbitrate. That position has influenced a number of other courts.

In *Armendariz v. Foundation Health Psychcare Services, Inc.*, 24 Cal.4th 83, 99 Cal.Rptr.2d 745, 6 P.3d 669 (Ca. 2000), the California high court established minimum requirements for enforcing arbitration agreements. These requirements sought to ease the disparity of position between the parties and to lessen the possible compromise of the weaker party's rights. Under California law, an arbitration agreement imposed by the stronger party was unconscionable if it did not guarantee that the arbitral process protected discovery rights, provided a written decision that made court review possible, impartial arbitrators, complete recovery, and limited costs. In particular, the obligation to arbitrate disputes must be mutual—equally applicable to both parties.

The incorporation of arbitration agreements into general workplace documents has generated litigation. Courts, for example, have wrestled with the question of whether a provision for arbitration in an employee handbook constitutes a valid agreement to arbitrate. Some courts merely require that an agreement to arbitrate be physically discernable; others demand that employers provide some means to effectuate acknowledgement and/or rejection; and yet others seek an explicit and affirmative consent by the employee to the waiver of judicial process. 'Handbook' agreements generally are upheld unless they abusively compromise the legal rights of the employee. Moreover, state contract law cannot discriminate against arbitration contracts.

The 'in writing' requirement is generally construed flexibly by courts. Arbitration agreements need not be signed in order to be effective. E-mail transmissions can establish valid agreements to arbitrate as long as they recite the required language. Illiteracy does not constitute a defense to enforceability as long as there was an opportunity to read the agreement. The federal policy in favor of arbitration attenuates the rigor of contract formation requirements. A broad arbitral agreement subjects all disputes arising under the agreement to arbitration. Any doubts are resolved in favor of arbitration. A "presumption of arbitrability . . . can be overcome only if it may be said with positive assurance that the arbitral clause is not susceptible to the interpretation that it covers the asserted dispute." *Orange Cty. Choppers, Inc. v. Goen Tech. Corp.*, 374 F.Supp.2d 372 (S.D.N.Y. 2005). A broad clause covers disputes that the parties did not anticipate at the time of contracting or that were created by operation of law rather than by the agreement. *See Masco Corp. v. Zurich Am. Ins. Co.*, 382 F.3d 624 (6th Cir. 2004) (when a broad arbitral clause exists, only express provisions excluding a particular dispute or the most commanding evidence will remove a dispute from the forum of arbitration).

A line of cases has developed in the decisional law under FAA § 2 addressing the question of whether an arbitration agreement between private parties could displace the authority and jurisdiction of government agencies to investigate and pursue remedies on behalf of aggrieved claimants. For example, in *Equal Employment Opportunity Commission v. Kidder, Peabody & Co., Inc.*, 156 F.3d 298 (2d Cir. 1998), the U.S. Court of Appeals for the Second Circuit affirmed a district court ruling that an arbitration agreement between an employer and employee precluded the Equal Employment Opportunity Commission (EEOC) from seeking purely monetary relief for the employee under the Age Discrimination in Employment Act (ADEA) in federal court. In its ruling, the court stated that "to allow the EEOC to recover monetary damages would frustrate the purpose of the [Federal Arbitration Act] (FAA) because an employee, having signed the agreement to arbitrate, could avoid arbitration by having the EEOC file in the federal forum seeking back pay on his or her behalf."

In contrast, the U.S. Court of Appeals for the Sixth Circuit held, in a split decision in *Equal Employment Opportunity Commission v. Frank's Nursery & Crafts, Inc.*, 177 F.3d 448 (6th Cir. 1999), that the EEOC was not required to arbitrate a Title VII statutory action—even though the employee signed an arbitration agreement. Given the broad grant of powers by the U.S. Congress to the EEOC, the Sixth Circuit concluded that the provisions of the FAA, preclusion principles, and waiver rules could not be used to treat an EEOC right of action as identical to an employee's own private right of action.

In *EEOC v. Waffle House, Inc.*, 534 U.S. 279 (2002), the U.S. Supreme Court held that an agreement between an employer and an employee to arbitrate workplace disputes did not bar the EEOC from obtaining either injunctive or victim-specific relief. The EEOC had brought suit in state court seeking injunctive relief and back pay, reinstatement, and damages on behalf of an employee who had been discharged after having a seizure at work. The Court held in a 6–3 ruling that the EEOC was not barred from seeking either injunctive or victim-specific relief for the employee. The Court stated that the EEOC had the same authority under the ADA that it had under the Civil Rights Act, namely, the authority to bring injunctive actions to force employers to halt unlawful employment practices. The Court also stated that the FAA "does not mention enforcement by public agencies" and "does not purport to place any restriction on a nonparty's choice of judicial forum." The ADA "clearly makes the EEOC the master of its own case and confers on the agency the authority to evaluate the strength of the public interest at stake." According to the Court, it is both the EEOC's "province" to select a forum and to decide how public resources should be used to obtain victim-specific relief.

The Court affirmed the independent power of the EEOC to investigate and bring its own enforcement actions under Title VII and the ADA. It determined that, because of its independent power, the EEOC was not bound by an arbitration agreement signed by an employee, nor was it limited in its discretion as to what remedies it would seek on behalf of an employee. Just because an employee agreed to arbitrate disputes did not mean that the EEOC, acting upon that employee's allegations of discrimination, was bound by the agreement.

As the Court itself noted, the opinion and its doctrine are likely to have little impact: "the EEOC only files suit in a small fraction of the charges that employees file. . . ." In the "year 2000, the EEOC received 79,896 charges of employment discrimination . . . [and] only filed 291 lawsuits and intervened in 111 others." The Court further recognized that "the EEOC files less than two percent of all antidiscrimination claims [brought] in federal court." Thus, "permitting the EEOC access to victim-specific relief in cases where the employee has agreed to binding arbitration, but has not yet brought a claim in arbitration, will have a *negligible* effect on the federal policy favoring arbitration." And, it remains "an open question whether a settlement or arbitration judgment would affect the validity of the EEOC's claim or the character of relief the EEOC may seek."

In dissent, Justice Thomas argued that, if an employee agreed to arbitration, the EEOC was bound by that agreement because the EEOC could do "on behalf of an employee that which an employee has agreed not to do for himself," namely, to seek monetary relief before a court. Justice Thomas further contended that, while "the EEOC has the statutory right to *bring* suit, it has no statutory entitlement to *obtain* a particular remedy." Thus, "whether a particular remedy is 'appropriate' in any given case is a question for a court and not for the EEOC." Because the employee had waived his right to obtain relief in a judicial forum by signing an arbitration agreement, the EEOC should be precluded from seeking victim-specific relief in a judicial forum.

Participation in a legal proceeding involving the issues subject to arbitrate could constitute a waiver of the right to arbitrate. The issue arose initially in cases involving international commercial arbitration. The question was whether a party seeking interim relief from a court in aid of arbitration breached the arbitration agreement by invoking the jurisdiction of a court. Arbitration agreements in international contracts now contain a provision stating that seeking interim relief from the courts does not violate the obligations under the agreement to arbitrate. Moreover, Article 9 of the UNCITRAL Model Law on International Commercial Arbitration confirms the rule by providing: "It is not incompatible with an arbitration agreement for a party to request, before or during arbitration proceedings, from a court an interim measure of protection and for a court to grant such measure."

In domestic practice, when should a contracting party's conduct be deemed so antagonistic to the agreement to arbitrate that a party should be deprived of its right to compel arbitration or enforce the award? Judicial determinations appear to turn on how extensive the recourse to courts and judicial procedures was and whether the party's conduct prejudiced or burdened significantly the other party. In fact, prejudice to the opposing party is the 'touchstone' of the waiver of the right to arbitrate. Factors to be considered include: the timeliness of the motion to arbitrate, the degree to which the party seeking arbitration has contested the merits in court, extent of motion practice, assent to court orders, and the depth of discovery. *See Hoxworth v. Blinder, Robinson & Co.*, 980 F.2d 912 (3d Cir. 1992).

The California Court of Appeal for the Second District held in *Davis v. Continental Airlines, Inc.*, 59 Cal.App.4th 205, 69 Cal.Rptr.2d 79 (1997), that the defendants waived their right to arbitration by unreasonably delaying their motion to compel arbitration until after engaging in extensive discovery with the plaintiff. The court held that the defendants waived their right to compel arbitration. It cited *Christensen v. Dewor Developments,* 33 Cal.3d 778, 191 Cal.Rptr. 8, 661 P.2d 1088 (1983), stating that "although the burden of proof is heavy on the party seeking to establish waiver, which should not lightly be inferred in light of public policy favoring arbitration, a determination by a trial court that the right to compel arbitration has been waived ordinarily involves a question of fact, which is binding on the appellate court if supported by substantial evidence." The court held that the trial court's finding of a waiver was supported by substantial evidence. The court indicated that a waiver may be found when a party seeking arbitration "has (1) previously taken steps inconsistent with an intent to invoke arbitration, (2) unreasonably delayed in seeking arbitration, or (3) acted in bad faith or with willful misconduct." The court further stated that "mere participation in litigation is not enough" to constitute a waiver and that the party seeking to establish a waiver "must show that some prejudice has resulted from the other party's delay in seeking arbitration."

A Texas court of appeals held in *Vireo P.L.L.C. v. Cates,* 953 S.W.2d 489 (Tex. Ct. App. 1997), that a "plaintiff who sues on an arbitrable claim unconditionally, without having initiated arbitration of the claim or demanding specific performance of the arbitration agreement, creates in the defendant a right of election—the defendant may insist or not upon arbitration, as he chooses." The court further stated that, if the defendant does not insist upon arbitration, the contracting parties have "mutually repudiated the arbitration covenant as a matter of law and waived any right thereunder."

In *Green v. U.S. Cash Advance Illinois*, 724 F.3d 787 (7th Cir. 2013), the Seventh Circuit reversed a district court determination that an arbitration agreement was unenforceable because the designated arbitral administrator was unavailable to administer the arbitration. According to the lower court, the designated administrator was an "integral" or material element in the contract and the inability to perform that part of the bargain voided the entire agreement for arbitration. The plaintiff had borrowed money from the payday lender-defendant. She claimed that U.S. Cash Advance misstated that the annual percentage rate of the loan. The misstatement allegedly constituted a violation of the Truth-in-Lending Act. The loan agreement contained an arbitration agreement, providing, *inter alia*, that all disputes would be "resolved by binding arbitration by one arbitrator by and under the Code of Procedure of the National Arbitration Forum."

In July 2009, as part of a settlement with the Minnesota Attorney General, the NAF announced that it would no longer accept consumer arbitration cases. The lender requested that the trial court appoint a substitute 'arbitrator' under FAA § 5, but the court refused because it determined that the arbitral administrator's specific identity was a material part of the bargain for arbitration. The court's reasoning seemed to assume that the selection of a particular set of arbitral institutional rules also meant that the institution would be the arbitral administrator of the arbitral proceeding or that the institution would serve as the arbitrator through one of its agents. The Seventh Circuit, however, made clear that the parties had agreed to arbitrate their disputes and that the contract provided for the application of the NAF's Code—not the selection of the NAF as the arbitral administrator or "arbitrator."

The first provision of the Code, Rule 1.A, provides that only the NAF or its duly designated agent can administer the Code. The appellate court concluded that Rule 1.A was "unenforceable" because of the NAF's "decision to cease conducting [consumer] arbitrations." Therefore, "an agreement to conduct arbitration under the Forum's Code, with the Forum itself on the sidelines, is valid. . . . All that remains is the selection of an arbitrator, and a district court can use [FAA] § 5 to make the appointment." To allow the unavailability of an arbitral service-provider to void the entire arbitration agreement would infringe upon the parties' agreement to arbitrate their disputes on the basis of an inconsequential factor that could easily be rectified. The clause in the loan agreement did not expressly designate the NAF as the sole possible "arbitrator." According to the Seventh Circuit, its reasoning was confirmed by parallel circumstances in *CompuCredit Corp. v. Greenwood*, 132 S.Ct. 665 (2012). In *CompuCredit Corp.*, the NAF was also designated as the arbitral administrator, but SCOTUS had no problem enforcing the agreement to arbitrate even though the designated institution was unavailable. Incorporating the lower court's "integral part" of the bargain analysis into the arbitral decisional law would necessitate trial proceedings to determine party intent and standard practices in arbitration. "The process would be lengthy, expensive, and inconclusive to boot."

The majority opinion was followed by a powerful dissent:

> Despite the surface simplicity of its logic, the majority has actually made an extraordinary effort to rescue the payday lender defendant from its own folly, or perhaps its own fraud. Because the district court correctly denied the motion to compel arbitration, I respectfully dissent.
>
> [. . .]
>
> The majority's reasoning departs from the contractual foundation of arbitration. It puts courts in the business of crafting new arbitration agreements for parties who failed to come to terms regarding the most basic elements of an enforceable arbitration agreement. Section 5 of the Federal Arbitration Act need not and should not be read to authorize such a wholesale re-write of the parties' contract. It certainly should not be read to rescue an arbitration clause on behalf of the clause's author when the author knew or should have known that its designated arbitrator was unavailable. We should instead follow the reasoning and holding of the Second Circuit in *In re Salomon Inc.*

Shareholders' Derivative Litigation, 68 F.3d 554 (2d Cir. 1995), and leave the parties to the court system when their arbitration agreement fails as utterly as this one does.

[. . .]

§ 3. Stay of Proceedings Where Issue Therein Referable to Arbitration

If any suit or proceedings be brought in any of the courts of the United States upon any issue referable to arbitration under an agreement in writing for such arbitration, the court in which suit is pending, upon being satisfied that the issue involved in such suit or proceeding is referable to arbitration under such an agreement, shall on application of one of the parties stay the trial of the action until such arbitration has been had in accordance with the terms of the agreement, providing the applicant for the stay is not in default proceeding with such arbitration.

Commentary

Section Three of the FAA describes the legal effects of an arbitration agreement that is "valid, irrevocable, and enforceable" under Section Two. A valid agreement to arbitrate divests the courts of jurisdiction to entertain the dispute. A federal court cannot assume jurisdiction over a dispute that is properly the subject of an arbitration agreement. When the court is notified of the existence of an arbitration agreement, it can engage in only two types of inquiry: (1) whether the agreement to arbitrate is a valid contract (a Section Two scrutiny); and (2) whether the dispute in question is covered by ("referable to") arbitration (a Section Three scrutiny that amounts to a determination of the question of contractual inarbitrability). Once this scrutiny has been exercised, the court is obligated by statute to stay the court proceeding "until such arbitration has been had in accordance with the terms of the agreement. . . ."

Recent case law has endorsed an unequivocal approach to granting stays under FAA § 3; that practice is fully in compliance with the "strong federal policy favoring arbitration." The principal, and to some degree preemptory, element of a petition for a stay is the existence of a valid agreement to arbitrate disputes. According to one federal district court, there is "little reason to require that an arbitration be commenced by a defendant against itself before a stay [of a court proceeding] can be ordered." Provided there is an enforceable contract of arbitration, a judicial action can be stayed even though no arbitral proceeding has been initiated. As "long as a written agreement to arbitrate exists[,] there is no specific requirement that arbitration actually be pending before a stay of litigation can be granted." The opinion represents a liberal interpretation of FAA § 3's requirement that "the party applying for the stay is not in default in proceeding with such arbitration." *See Sims v. Montell Chrysler, Inc.*, 317 F.Supp.2d 838 (N.D. Ill. 2004).

Even a non-signatory party can secure a stay under FAA § 3. In *Waste Mgmt., Inc. v. Residuos Indus. Multiquim, S.A. de C.V.*, 372 F.3d 339 (5th Cir. 2004), the Fifth Circuit held that FAA § 3 allows nonsignatories to seek a mandatory stay of litigation in favor of a pending arbitration to which they are not a party, provided the litigation includes an issue referable to arbitration under the agreement. The basic test for granting such a stay is "whether proceeding with the litigation [would] destroy the signatories' right to a meaningful arbitration." There are three factors to consider: (1) the arbitrated and litigated disputes must involve the same operative facts; (2) the claims asserted in the arbitration and litigation must be "inherently inseparable"; and (3) the litigation must have a "critical impact" on the arbitration.

It should be noted that, under the arbitration laws of most national jurisdictions, challenges to the contractual validity of the arbitration agreement and to its scope of application would be referred to the arbitral tribunal. As stated earlier, this procedure reflects the application of the separability and *kompetenz-kompetenz* doctrines. The U.S. statutory law on arbitration does not recognize *kompetenz-kompetenz*. Jurisdictional challenges, therefore, require a court proceeding under the language of Sections Two and Three. Judicial recourse on these grounds invites the use of dilatory tactics and can cause a year or two delay in the commencement of the arbitral proceeding. This omission in the FAA underscores the early date of its enactment and suggests a need to revise and update the legislation.

Despite such gaps, however, the FAA remains a highly functional regulatory framework. In fact, the federal decisional law has recently remedied the *kompetenz-kompetenz* omission. In its ruling in *First Options of Chicago, Inc. v. Kaplan*, 514 U.S. 938 (1995), the U.S. Supreme Court affirmed the power of the courts to rule on jurisdictional challenges under Sections Two and Three of the FAA, but also held that the parties could agree to submit such jurisdictional disputes to the arbitral tribunal. Such contractual grants of authority to arbitrators are likely to become a standard feature of both boilerplate and negotiated arbitration agreements.

Two features of Section Three need to be underscored. The reference at the outset of the provision to actions "brought in any of the courts of the United States" confirms that the FAA is directed to the federal courts. There is no hint of a Congressional intent to impose the FAA rules on state courts or to displace state arbitration law with the federal statute. Also, the last clause of the section provides that a party moving to stay a judicial trial because a valid arbitration agreement encompasses the dispute submitted to the court must "not [be] in default in proceeding with such arbitration." To conserve its right to arbitrate disputes, a party must invoke arbitration in a timely manner. If neither party invokes the agreed-upon arbitral mechanism, the parties' conduct rescinds the agreement to arbitrate—at least for the dispute in question. In effect, the parties are estopped from using the arbitration agreement to block judicial jurisdiction.

Finally, neither Sections Two nor Three provide a defense to the enforcement of arbitration agreements and awards on the basis of the subject matter of the dispute. In fact, the FAA contains no mention whatsoever of the subject-matter inarbitrability defense—not even in Section Ten, which regulates the enforcement of awards. The absence of the defense strongly suggests that the FAA is procedural in character. There was no need to refer to subject matter considerations in any of the FAA provisions because other, more substantive statutes would supply the appropriate limits on the right to arbitrate. Moreover, the FAA is intended to apply to interstate maritime and commercial transactions. There was, therefore, no need to delimit the reach of legislation that already circumscribed itself. It applied only to characteristic commercial disputes.

The Act also does not incorporate public policy into the regulation of arbitral agreements and awards. The courts created an equivalent common law ground in their decisional law, but the legislation itself contains no mention of public policy. As with subject-matter inarbitrability, it may have been the expectation of Congress that other, more substantive statutes would define the role of public policy in arbitration on a subject-matter-by-subject-matter basis, thereby maintaining the FAA's procedural focus. However explained, the lack of reference in the FAA to subject-matter inarbitrability and public policy remains puzzling if for no other reason than they are standard concepts in most laws of arbitration. Their exclusion may have invited the decisional law to embark upon the curtailment of both defenses. At present, neither defense has a vital presence in the U.S. law of arbitration. Arbitration is now lawfully applied to all types of disputes, ranging from the standard commercial and maritime conflicts to disputes about statutory rights and consumer claims, with little mention of the impact of this wide jurisdiction upon the domain of public law.

In *Arthur Andersen LLP*, the Court addressed the issue of whether non-signatory parties are entitled to relief under FAA §§ 3 and 16.

ARTHUR ANDERSEN LLP V. CARLISLE

556 U.S. 624, 129 S.Ct. 1896, 173 L.Ed.2d 832 (2009).

JUSTICE SCALIA delivered the opinion of the Court.

Section 3 of the Federal Arbitration Act (FAA) entitles litigants in federal court to a stay of any action that is "referable to arbitration under an agreement in writing." . . . Section 16(a)(1)(A), in turn, allows an appeal from "an order . . . refusing a stay of any action under section 3." We address in this case whether appellate courts have jurisdiction under § 16(a) to review denials of stays requested by litigants who were not parties to the relevant arbitration agreement, and whether § 3 can ever mandate a stay in such circumstances.

[. . .]

II

Ordinarily, courts of appeals have jurisdiction only over "final decisions" of district courts. 28 U.S.C. § 1291. The FAA, however, makes an exception to that finality requirement, providing that "an appeal may be taken from . . . an order . . . refusing a stay of any action under section 3 of this title." 9 U.S.C. § 16(a)(1)(A). By that provision's clear and unambiguous terms, any litigant who asks for a stay under § 3 is entitled to an immediate appeal from denial of that motion regardless of whether the litigant is in fact eligible for a stay. Because each petitioner in this case explicitly asked for a stay pursuant to § 3, . . . the Sixth Circuit had jurisdiction to review the District Court's denial.

The courts that have declined jurisdiction over § 3 appeals of the sort at issues here have done so by conflating the jurisdictional question with the merits of the appeal. They reason that because stay motions premised on equitable estoppel seek to expand (rather than simply vindicate) agreements, they are not cognizable under §§ 3 and 4, and therefore the relevant motions are not actually "under" those provisions. . . . The dissent makes this step explicit, by reading the appellate jurisdictional provision of § 16 as "calling for a look-through" to the substantive provisions of § 3 . . . jurisdiction over the appeal, however, "must be determined by focusing upon the category of order appealed from, rather than upon the strength of the grounds for reversing the order." *Behrens v. Pelletier*, 516 U.S. 299, 311, 116 S. Ct. 834, 133 L. Ed. 2d 773 (1996).[3] The jurisdictional statute here unambiguously makes the underlying merits irrelevant, for even utter frivolousness of the underlying request for a § 3 stay cannot turn a denial into something other than "an order . . . refusing a stay of any action under section 3." . . .

---

[3] Federal courts lack subject matter jurisdiction when an asserted federal claim is "so insubstantial, implausible, foreclosed by prior decisions of this Court, or otherwise completely devoid of merit as not to involve a federal controversy." *Steel Co. v. Citizens for Better Environment*, 523 U.S. 83, 89, 118 S. Ct. 1003, 140 L. Ed. 2d 210 (1998) (quoting *Oneida Indian Nation of N.Y. v. County of Oneida*, 414 U.S. 661, 666, 94 S. Ct. 772, 39 L. Ed. 2d 73 (1974)). Respondents have not relied upon this line of cases as an alternative rationale for rejection of jurisdiction, and there are good reasons for treating subject-matter jurisdiction differently, in that respect, from the appellate jurisdiction here conferred. A frivolous federal claim, if sufficient to confer jurisdiction, would give the court power to hear related state-law claims, see 28 U.S.C. § 1367; no such collateral consequences are at issue here. And while an insubstantial federal claim can be said not to "aris[e] under the Constitution, laws, or treaties of the United States," § 1331, insubstantiality of the merits can hardly convert a judge's "order . . . refusing a stay" into an "order . . . refusing" something else. But we need not resolve this question today.

Respondents argue that this reading of § 16(a) will produce a long parade of horribles, enmeshing courts in fact-intensive jurisdictional inquiries and permitting frivolous interlocutory appeals. Even if these objections could surmount the plain language of the statute, we would not be persuaded. Determination of whether § 3 was invoked in a denied stay request is immeasurably more simple and less fact bound than the threshold determination respondents would replace it with: whether the litigant was a party to the contract (an especially difficult question when the written agreement is not signed). It is more appropriate to grapple with that merits question after the court has accepted jurisdiction over the case. Second, there are ways of minimizing the impact of abusive appeals. Appellate courts can streamline the deposition of meritless claims and even authorize the district court's retention of jurisdiction when an appeal is certified as frivolous. . . . And, of course, those inclined to file dilatory appeals must be given pause by courts' authority to "award just damages and single or double costs to the appellee" whenever an appeal is "frivolous." . . .

III

Even if the Court of Appeals were correct that it had no jurisdiction over meritless appeals, its ground for finding this appeal meritless was in error. We take the trouble to address that alternative ground, since if the Court of Appeals is correct on the merits point we will have awarded petitioners a remarkably hollow victory. We consider, therefore, the Sixth Circuit's underlying determination that those who are not parties to a written arbitration agreement are categorically ineligible for relief.

Section 2—the FAA's substantive mandate—makes written arbitration agreements "valid, irrevocable, and enforceable, save upon such grounds as exist at law or in equity for the revocation of a contract." That provision creates substantive federal law regarding the enforceability of arbitration agreements, requiring courts "to place such agreements upon the same footing as other contracts." . . . Section 3, in turn, allows litigants already in federal court to invoke agreements made enforceable by § 2. That provision requires the court, "on application of one of the parties,"[4] to stay the action if it involves an "issue referable to arbitration under an agreement in writing." . . .

Neither provision purports to alter background principles of state contract law regarding the scope of agreements (including the question of who is bound by them). Indeed § 2 explicitly retains an external body of law

[4] Respondents do not contest that the term "parties" in § 3 refers to parties to the litigation rather than parties to the contract. The adjacent provision, which explicitly refers to the "subject matter of a suit arising out of the controversy between the parties," 9 U.S.C. § 4, unambiguously refers to adversaries in the action, and "identical words and phrases within the same statute should normally be given the same meaning." . . . Even without benefit of that canon, we would not be disposed to believe that the statute allows a party to the contract who is not a party to the litigation to apply for a stay of the proceeding.

governing revocation (such grounds "as exist at law or in equity").[5] And we think § 3 adds no substantive restriction to § 2's enforceability mandate. "[S]tate law," therefore, is applicable to determine which contracts are binding under § 2 and enforceable under § 3 "*if* that law arose to govern issues concerning the validity, revocability, and enforceability of contracts generally." . . . Because "traditional principles" of state law allow a contract to be enforced by or against nonparties to the contract through "assumption, piercing the corporate veil, alter ego, incorporation by reference, third-party, beneficiary theories, waiver and estoppel," . . . the Sixth Circuit's holding that nonparties to a contract are categorically barred from § 3 relief was error.

Respondents argue that, as a matter of federal law, claims to arbitration by nonparties are not "referable to arbitration *under* an agreement in writing," 9 U.S.C. § 3 (emphasis added), because they "seek to bind a signatory to an arbitral obligation *beyond* that signatory's strictly contractual obligation to arbitrate." . . . Perhaps that would be true if § 3 mandated stays only for disputes between parties to a written arbitration agreement. But that is not what the statute says. It says that stays are required if the claims are "referable to arbitration under an agreement in writing." If a written arbitration provision is made enforceable against (or for the benefit of) a third party under state contract law, the statute's terms are fulfilled.[6]

Respondents' final fallback consists of reliance upon *dicta* in our opinions, such as the statement that "arbitration . . . is a way to resolve those disputes but only those disputes that the parties have agreed to submit to arbitration," . . . and the statement that "[i]t goes without saying that a contract cannot bind a non-party." . . . The former statement pertained to *issues* parties agreed to arbitrate, and the latter referred to an entity (the Equal Employment Opportunity Commission) which obviously had no third-party obligations under the contract in question. Neither these nor any of our other cases have presented for decision the question whether arbitration agreements that are otherwise enforceable by (or against) third parties trigger protection under the FAA.

Respondents may be correct in saying that courts' application of equitable estoppel to impose an arbitration agreement upon strangers to the contract has been "somewhat loose." . . . But we need not decide here

---

[5] We have said many times that federal law requires that "questions of arbitrability . . . be addressed with a healthy regard for the federal policy favoring arbitration." . . . Whatever the meaning of this vague prescription, it cannot possibly require the disregard of state law *permitting* arbitration by or against nonparties to the written arbitration agreement.

[6] We thus reject the dissent's contention that contract law's long-standing endorsement of third-party enforcement is "a weak premise for inferring an intent to allow third parties to obtain a § 3 stay." . . . It seems to us not weak at all, in light of the terms of the statute. There is no doubt that, where state law permits it, a third-party claim is "referable to arbitration under an agreement in writing." It is not our role to conform an unambiguous statute to what we think "Congress probably intended." . . .

whether the relevant state contract law recognizes equitable estoppel as a ground for enforcing contracts against third parties, what standard it would apply, and whether petitioners would be entitled to relief under it. These questions have not been briefed before us and can be addressed on remand. It suffices to say that no federal law bars the State from allowing petitioners to enforce the arbitration agreement against respondents and that § 3 would require a stay in this case if it did.

* * *

We hold that the Sixth Circuit had jurisdiction to review the denial of petitioners' request for a § 3 stay and that a litigant who was not a party to the relevant arbitration agreement may invoke § 3 if the relevant state contract law allows him to enforce the agreement. The judgment of the Court of Appeals for the Sixth Circuit is reversed, and the case is remanded for further proceedings consistent with this opinion.

It is so ordered.

DISSENT

JUSTICE SOUTER, with whom THE CHIEF JUSTICE and JUSTICE STEVENS join, dissenting.

Section 16 of the Federal Arbitration Act (FAA) authorizes an interlocutory appeal from the denial of a motion under § 3 to stay a district court action pending arbitration. The question is whether it opens the door to such an appeal at the behest of one who has not signed a written arbitration agreement. Based on the longstanding congressional policy limiting interlocutory appeals, I think the better reading of the statutory provisions disallows such an appeal, and therefore respectfully dissent.

Section 16(a) of the FAA provides that "[a]n appeal may be taken from . . . an order . . . refusing a stay of any action under section 3 of this title." . . . The Court says that any litigant who asks for and is denied a § 3 stay is entitled to an immediate appeal. . . . The majority's assumption is that "under section 3" is merely a labeling requirement, without substantive import, but this fails to read § 16 in light of the "firm congressional policy against interlocutory or 'piecemeal' appeals." . . .

The right of appeal is "a creature of statute," . . . and Congress has granted the Federal Courts of Appeals jurisdiction to review "final decisions," 28 U.S.C. § 1291. "This insistence on finality and prohibition of piecemeal review discourage undue litigiousness and leaden-footed administration of justice." . . . Congress has, however, "recognized the need of exceptions for interlocutory orders in certain types of proceedings where the damage of error unreviewed before the judgment is definitive and complete . . . has been deemed greater than the disruption caused by intermediate appeal." . . . Section 16 functions as one such exception, but departures from "the dominant rule in federal appellate practice," . . . are extraordinary interruptions to the normal process of litigation and ought to be limited carefully.

An obvious way to limit the scope of such an extraordinary interruption would be to read the § 16 requirement that the stay have been denied "under section 3" as calling for a look-through to the provisions of § 3, and to read § 3 itself as offering a stay only to signatories of an arbitration agreement. It is perfectly true that in general a third-party beneficiary can enforce a contract, but this is a weak premise for inferring an intent to allow third parties to obtain a § 3 stay and take a § 16 appeal. While it is hornbook contract law that third parties may enforce contracts for their benefit as a matter of course, interlocutory appeals are a matter of limited grace. Because it would therefore seem strange to assume that Congress meant to grant the right to appeal a § 3 stay denial to anyone as peripheral to the core agreement as a nonsignatory, it follows that Congress probably intended to limit those able to seek a § 3 stay.

Asking whether a § 3 movant is a signatory provides a bright-line rule with predictable results to aid courts in determining jurisdiction over § 16 interlocutory appeals. And that rule has the further virtue of mitigating the risk of intentional delay by savvy parties who seek to frustrate litigation by gaming the system. Why not move for a § 3 stay? If granted, arbitration will be mandated, and if denied, a lengthy appeal may wear down the opponent. The majority contends . . . "that there are ways of minimizing the impact of abusive appeals." Yes, but the sanctions suggested apply to the frivolous, not to the far-fetched; and as the majority's opinion concludes, such an attenuated claim of equitable estoppel as petitioners raise here falls short of the sanctionable.

Because petitioners were not parties to the written arbitration agreement, I would hold they could not move to stay the District Court proceedings under § 3, with the consequence that the Court of Appeals would have no jurisdiction under § 16 to entertain their appeal. I would accordingly affirm the judgment of the Sixth Circuit.

NOTES AND QUESTIONS

1. Would you characterize *Arthur Andersen LLP* as an opinion that is favorable to arbitration? Explain.

2. What rights do nonsignatory parties have under the FAA?

3. What doctrinal relationship exists between FAA § 3 and FAA § 16?

4. Does the majority opinion only support the federal policy on arbitration or does it also give effect to the interests of justice? Are these concerns synonymous?

5. Does the dissent confound or enlighten the matter?

6. What is the dissent's primary opposition to the majority opinion?

§ 4. Failure to Arbitrate under Agreement; Petition to United States Court Having Jurisdiction for Order to Compel Arbitration; Notice and Service Thereof; Hearing and Determination

A party aggrieved by the alleged failure, neglect, or refusal of another to arbitrate under a written agreement for arbitration may petition any United States district court which, save for such agreement, would have jurisdiction under Title 28, in a civil action or in admiralty of the subject matter of a suit arising out of the controversy between the parties, for an order directing that such arbitration proceed in the manner provided for in such agreement. Five days' notice in writing of such application shall be served upon the party in default. Service thereof shall be made in the manner provided by the Federal Rules of Civil Procedure. The court shall hear the parties, and upon being satisfied that the making of the agreement for arbitration or the failure to comply therewith is not in issue, the court shall make an order directing the parties to proceed to arbitration in accordance with the terms of the agreement. The hearing and proceedings, under such agreement, shall be within the district in which the petition for an order directing such arbitration is filed. If the making of the arbitration agreement or the failure, neglect, or refusal to perform the same be in issue, the court shall proceed summarily to the trial thereof. If no jury trial be demanded by the party alleged to be in default, or if the matter in dispute is within admiralty jurisdiction, the court shall hear and determine such issue. Where such an issue is raised, the party alleged to be in default may, except in cases of admiralty, on or before the return day of the notice of application, demand a jury trial of such issue, and upon such demand the court shall make an order referring the issue or issues to a jury in the manner provided by the Federal Rules of Civil Procedure, or may specially call a jury for that purpose. If the jury find[s] that no agreement in writing for arbitration was made or that there is no default in proceeding thereunder, the proceeding shall be dismissed. If the jury find[s] that an agreement for arbitration was made in writing and that there is a default in proceeding thereunder, the court shall make an order summarily directing the parties to proceed with the arbitration in accordance with the terms thereof.

Commentary

Section Four authorizes the federal courts to compel party compliance with the agreement to arbitrate. It also implies that the federal courts have a duty to assist the arbitral process when the exercise of coercive legal authority is necessary to the operation of the process. Along with Section Two, this provision expressly reverses the former judicial hostility to arbitration. It commands courts to take an active role in sustaining the contractual recourse to arbitration. One of the parties to the arbitration agreement must invoke the court's jurisdiction and authority by establishing the existence of a written agreement to arbitrate and demonstrating the other party's failure to abide by the contract. Furthermore, the court with proper jurisdiction is the court that would have had jurisdiction over the matter had the parties not agreed to arbitration.

The remainder of the provision is quite complex. Despite the intricacy of the language, the applicable regime appears to be that, before the requested court can issue an order compelling a party to arbitrate, it must ascertain that an arbitration agreement, in fact, does exist. Once the existence of the agreement is established, the requested court must determine whether the recalcitrant party's refusal to comply is unwarranted in the circumstances. The party allegedly in breach of the agreement has the right to request a jury trial on both issues (except in California).

The statement of the applicable procedure appears excessive for an arbitration statute. It reveals a preoccupation with achieving legal procedural regularity in the disposition of issues arising in arbitration law. This feature of the statute is also in evidence in other provisions of the FAA, confirming its status as a set of directives to the federal courts, but also raising questions about the suitability of the statutory approach to the regulation of arbitration. Guaranteeing compliance with constitutional standards of legality in an action to compel arbitration is perhaps unnecessary and counterproductive. Providing for the possible jury determination of the relevant issues invites the type of delay that can frustrate the recourse to arbitration. A court determination of the issues would advance the interests of arbitration without compromising the basic rights of the parties—especially in specialized commercial sectors. The FAA's regulatory focus, in some respects, gives arbitration a secondary status. The chief objective is not to establish a set of rules for the operation of the arbitral process, but rather to integrate arbitration into the substantive and procedural design of the legal system.

According to the Third Circuit in *Guidotti v. Legal Helpers Debt Resolution, L.L.C.*, 716 F.3d 764 (3d Cir. 2013), a motion to compel arbitration may be subject either to FRCP Rule 12(b)(6), which relates to a motion to dismiss for the failure to state a claim, or FRCP Rule 56 applying to motions for summary judgment. The motion to dismiss does not require discovery and can be decided on the basis of the pleadings. The court examines the complaint and supporting documents in a light that favors the plaintiff's case. In effect, the court seeks to determine whether the plaintiff is entitled to relief under any plausible reading of the initial submissions. A motion for summary judgment involves a ruling on the merits of the controversy and, therefore, requires discovery and time for discovery beyond the perusal of the initial pleadings. Limited discovery allows the court to assess whether "a genuine dispute of material fact" exists. The issue in *Guidotti* involved the question of whether the parties—an indebted consumer and a debt settlement service—had entered into an arbitration agreement. In the Third Circuit's view, because the arbitration agreement was included in a document incorporated by reference into the principal contract but without the use of headers, the matter raised meaningful issues of contract formation that warranted at least "limited" discovery. Once the details of contract formation had been established, the court could decide the issue on a summary judgment basis.

The opinion is not standard fare. It does not read as a resounding statement of support for arbitration and arbitrability. In fact, it seems to cast serious doubt upon the likelihood of referring the dispute to arbitration. The court's reasoning is uncharacteristic of the federal court opinions that address arbitration. It refers to "the competing purposes of the FAA" and concludes that a ' "restricted inquiry into factual issues" '

> will be necessary to properly evaluate whether there was a meeting of the minds on the agreement to arbitrate . . . and the non-movant 'must be given the opportunity to conduct limited discovery on the narrow issue concerning the validity of the arbitration agreement. . . . [Footnote omitted.] In such circumstances, Rule 56 furnishes the correct standard for ensuring that arbitration is awarded only if there is 'an express, unequivocal agreement to that effect.'

The case for "[p]re-arbitration discovery," made elsewhere to determine whether the costs of arbitration were prohibitive or whether the contract for arbitration was unconscionable, reads like a return to the days of judicial hostility to arbitration. Insisting upon solid proof of the existence of an arbitration agreement that was reasonably visible to the consumer at the very least creates delayed recourse to arbitration. It pits the equities of the case against the "emphatic federal policy favoring 'unobstructed' recourse to arbitration" and proclaims that the equities should prevail. It is almost as if the court distrusts the ability of arbitral adjudication to respond effectively to the consumer's predicament. Regardless of the court's attempts to justify its approach, its choice and the consequences of that choice are evident. Because the hapless consumer has been exploited by unethical and deceitful merchants, she is entitled to something other than a legal process that sustains the ends of arbitrability.

The court seems to be fully aware of the implications of its ruling but nonetheless feels impelled to render it:

> In so holding, we recognized that our ruling 'may run contrary to the general policy of encouraging the arbitration of disputes,' . . . and we contemplated the possibility of parties trying to dodge their obligations. For example, '[a] party may, in an effort to avoid arbitration, contend that it did not intend to enter into the

agreement which contained an arbitration clause.' . . . Such '[a] naked assertion . . . by a party to a contract that it did not intend to be bound by the terms [of an arbitration clause],' we reasoned, would be 'insufficient to place in issue the 'making of the arbitration agreement' for purposes of the FAA.' . . . But we did not want to cut off legitimate disputes over an alleged agreement to arbitrate when there has been '[a]n unequivocal denial that the agreement had been made, accompanied by supporting affidavits . . . [;] in most cases [that] should be sufficient to require a jury determination on whether there had in fact been a 'meeting of the minds.' . . .

[. . .]

If Guidotti is correct that any document linked in the email that also linked to the SPAA would, like the SPAA, have a DocuSign header, then the fact that neither party has furnished a version of the Account Agreement bearing a DocuSign header is significant. We accordingly hold that Guidotti came forth with enough evidence in response to the Appellants' arbitration motion to trigger . . . the summary judgment standard found in Rule 56 of the Federal Rules of Civil Procedure.

[. . .]

Unlike the District Court, we are persuaded that a genuine issue of material fact remains regarding the agreement to arbitrate. We do not agree, in other words, that, based on her unsworn claim that the Account Agreement did not accompany the package of documents originally emailed to her in September 2009, and based further on the cases relied on by the District Court, Guidotti was entitled to summary judgment on the question of whether the parties had agreed to arbitrate.

Although it is true that neither side has come forth with a version of the Account Agreement that contains the DocuSign header, there has been no showing that all documents provided in the link included in the September 2009 email must necessarily contain the header. Said differently, we have no way of knowing whether some of the documents provided in the email link could have borne the DocuSign header (the ARA and the SPAA, for example) while others did not (perhaps the Account Agreement). The headers certainly cast doubt on the proposition that the Account Agreement was included in the original email, but they do not establish that fact outright. Presumably, limited discovery regarding the email would have cleared up the issue—either the emailed link contained the Account Agreement or it did not—but given that no discovery has taken place, any summary conclusion is unwarranted.

[. . .]

Thus, the District Court should not have denied the Appellants' motion to compel arbitration without first allowing limited discovery and then entertaining their motion under a summary judgment standard. If, after presentation of the evidence uncovered during discovery, a genuine dispute of material fact remained, the Court then should have submitted to a jury (if either party demanded one) the factual question of whether Guidotti was aware of the arbitration clause in the Account Agreement at the time she signed and submitted the SPAA. [Footnote omitted.]

In *Kilgore v. KeyBank, Nat'l Assoc.*, 718 F.3d 1052 (9th Cir. 2013), the Ninth Circuit reversed a lower court denial of a motion to compel arbitration and remanded the matter to the rendering district court with instructions to order arbitration. The litigation consisted of a putative class action brought against the bank that originated and serviced the loans of the former students of a flight training school that had closed its doors. The class was seeking an injunction to prevent the bank from collecting on the loans or reporting defaults to credit agencies. Each student borrowed more than $50,000 to cover tuition and other fees. KeyBank was an "Ohio-based lending giant" and Silver State Helicopter School was the implicated flight school. The promissory note between the bank and student borrowers contained an arbitration clause and a class action waiver, prohibiting both class litigation and the consolidation of cases. The borrower had sixty days after signing the note to reject the arbitration clause.

On the basis of a wide-ranging discussion of both California and federal arbitration precedent, the Ninth Circuit concluded that the FAA obligated courts to command arbitration whenever a dispute was subject to an arbitration agreement. The judicial task was simply to determine whether an agreement to arbitrate existed and applied to the dispute in question. The court acknowledged the existence of the so-called savings clause in FAA § 2; it engendered a judicial discussion of the plaintiff's claim that the arbitration clause was an unconscionable and unenforceable contract. The court concluded that "nothing . . . in the arbitration clause . . . suggests substantive unconscionability." Moreover, the formation and content of the arbitration contract did not sustain allegations of procedural unconscionability. The sixty days to reject arbitration and the clear visibility of the arbitral clause in the contract (independent section, conspicuous headers, and boldface print) made the agreement fair and enforceable. As to the plaintiff's claim for injunctive relief, the court concluded that the plaintiffs' request for injunctive relief did not "fall within the 'narrow exception to the rule that the FAA requires state courts to honor arbitration agreements.' " Neither the requested ban on reporting defaults nor the prohibition against disbursing loans amounted to a "public injunctive remedy," which—under the "central premise of *Broughton-Cruz*"—courts are better suited to assess and award.

A vigorous dissent emphasized the rapacious and collusive practices in which the lender and school engaged. The helicopter school "did not do a good job training . . . pilots, placing them in jobs, or managing its own finances. But it did make a convincing sales pitch." The school "accepted almost all applicants who could get their loans approved." Even though the school lacked enough personnel and equipment to teach and train the admitted students, KeyBank "promptly forked over to [the school the proceeds of the loan] before students took a single class." Both the school and lender knew that there was little market demand for pilots with the school's degree. The school and bank were complicit in perpetrating a fraud on the students:

> Once a student signed a promissory note, KeyBank immediately transferred the full amount of the loans to [the school]. KeyBank then turned a profit by selling the students' loans on the securities market to investors. Defendant Great Lakes Educational Loan Services, Inc., continues to service those loans by collecting payments from students, and notifying credit reporting agencies when students fail to pay.

Finally:

> To make matters worse, the majority opinion strips Kilgore, Fuller, and their classmates of the ability to find recourse in state or federal court. The majority holds that we must compel arbitration in the students' case, a holding at odds with the district court's decision. According to the majority, the arbitration clause was not unconscionable. I disagree.
>
> A contract provision is unenforceable under California law if it is both procedurally and substantively unconscionable. . . . California applies a sliding scale to determine if a contract is unenforceable due to unconscionability. . . . The more substantively unconscionable the contract, the less procedurally unconscionable it must be to be found unconscionable, and vice versa. . . . Here, the arbitration clause is highly procedurally *and* substantively unconscionable.

§ 5. Appointment of Arbitrators or Umpire

If in the agreement provision be made for a method of naming or appointing an arbitrator or arbitrators or an umpire, such method shall be followed; but if no method be provided therein, or if a method be provided and any party thereto shall fail to avail himself of such method, or if for any other reason there shall be a lapse in the naming of an arbitrator or arbitrators or umpire, or in filling a vacancy, then upon the application of either party to the controversy the court shall designate and appoint an arbitrator or arbitrators or umpire, as the case may require, who shall act under the said agreement with the same force and effect as if he or they had been specifically named therein; and unless otherwise provided in the agreement the arbitration shall be by a single arbitrator.

Commentary

Section Five adds to the duty of courts to assist and cooperate with arbitral proceedings. At the request of one of the parties, a court can nominate an arbitrator when the parties cannot agree upon the designation or one party refuses to comply with its contractual obligation to name an arbitrator. The provision recognizes the principle of freedom of contract: The parties, through their agreement, control the procedure for nominating arbitrators. It is only in circumstances in which freedom of contract fails, *i.e.*, when the agreement is silent and no agreement can be reached subsequently or when there is a refusal to comply with the agreed-upon procedure, that the court can intervene (at the request of a party) and remedy the stalemate. While the agreement to arbitrate eliminates judicial authority to rule on the dispute, coercive judicial power surrounds the operation of the arbitral process. When the contractual rule of law fails, the courts can guarantee the enforcement of contractual obligations. Court-designated arbitrators have the same status and authority as party-appointed arbitrators.

Section Five makes no mention of the possible role administering arbitral institutions might play in naming an arbitrator on behalf of a party or initiating a court proceeding to designate an arbitrator. The development of arbitral practice has made such procedures commonplace. Once again, the omission indicates that, even though the FAA is a viable arbitration statute, some of its content needs to be aligned with the contemporary development of arbitral practice. Finally, Section Five adopts a rebuttable preference for a sole arbitrator. From a practical perspective, such a preference facilitates judicial supervision and the efficiency of arbitration. Designating one or two members of a three-member panel along with a neutral arbitrator would require more extensive court intervention and further consideration of the arbitration agreement.

§ 6. Application Heard as Motion

Any application to the court hereunder shall be made and heard in the manner provided by law for the making and hearing of motions, except as otherwise herein expressly provided.

Commentary

Section Six establishes equivalency between court proceedings relating to arbitration and any other action filed before the federal courts. Motions pertaining to arbitral proceedings shall not be subject to any extraordinary administrative requirements. The statute, however, reserves the right to amend ordinary court procedures, presumably to advance the interests of the arbitral process.

§ 7. Witnesses Before Arbitrators; Fees; Compelling Attendance

The arbitrators selected either as prescribed in this title or otherwise, or a majority of them, may summon in writing any person to attend before them or any of them as a witness and in a proper case to bring with him or them any book, record, document, or paper which may be deemed material as evidence in the case. The fees for such attendance shall be the same as the fees of witnesses before masters of the United States courts. Said summons shall issue in the name of the arbitrator or arbitrators or a majority of them and shall be signed by the arbitrators, or a majority of them, and shall be directed to the said person and shall be served in the same manner as subpoenas to appear and testify before the court; if any person or persons so summoned to testify shall refuse or neglect to obey said summons, upon petition the United States court in and for the district in which such arbitrators, or a majority of them, are sitting may compel the attendance of such person or persons before said arbitrator or arbitrators, or punish said person or persons for contempt in the same manner provided by law, for securing the attendance of witnesses or their punishment for neglect or refusal to attend in the courts of the United States.

Commentary

Section Seven gives arbitrators unique evidence-gathering powers. The adjudicatory authority of the arbitrators extends to nonarbitrating parties who can be ordered to appear and testify or to comply with requests for documents or other evidentiary elements. The language of Section Seven is unequivocal: "[t]he arbitrators ... may summon ... *any* person. . . ." (Emphasis added). Therefore, when the FAA governs the arbitral proceeding, arbitrators have the same subpoena powers as a court of law. If the third party refuses to comply with the order, the arbitral tribunal can petition the appropriate federal court to compel the party to comply, under penalty of the court's power to impose sanctions for contempt. In issuing its order, the arbitral tribunal must satisfy ordinary notification requirements and a majority of the arbitrators must sign the order.

Granting arbitrators subpoena power over third-parties generally is unique. The drafters of the FAA intended to give the arbitrators the tools necessary to engage in effective record-building. Arbitrators could not decide without access to, and an understanding of, the facts. Despite its practical utility in the gathering of evidence, the ability of arbitrators to enjoin third-parties violates the contractual foundation of arbitration. The affected third-parties never agreed to participate in the arbitration and, because the arbitration is a private and consensual proceeding, there is no legal basis upon which to subject them to the arbitrators' adjudicatory authority, except for the language of Section Seven. The provision implies that arbitration implicates the public interest—a position that is manifestly inconsistent with the contractual definition of arbitral adjudication in Section Two. Such extensive powers may have made sense within the confines of specialized commercial communities, but—once the reach of the arbitral process is given more general application—providing for the exercise of arbitral powers beyond the arbitrating parties, even for the exclusive purpose of evidence-gathering, should be reconsidered.

The federal courts are divided on the question. The Third Circuit, in *Hay Group, Inc. v. E.B.S. Acquisition Corp.*, 360 F.3d 404 (3d Cir. 2004), held that FAA § 7 conferred limited subpoena powers on arbitrators and did not give them the authority to compel nonparties to comply with prehearing discovery requests. In *Stolt-Nielsen S.A. v. Celanese AG*, 430 F.3d 567 (2d Cir. 2005), the Second Circuit held that FAA § 7 should be broadly construed to allow arbitrators to subpoena any evidence that is material to the case. Arbitrators could compel nonparties to testify and produce documents at both preliminary and final hearings.

§ 8. Proceedings Begun by Libel in Admiralty and Seizure of Vessel or Property

If the basis of jurisdiction be a cause of action otherwise justifiable in admiralty, then, notwithstanding anything herein to the contrary the party claiming to be aggrieved may begin his proceeding hereunder by libel and seizure of the vessel or other property of the other party according to the usual course of admiralty proceedings, and the court shall then have jurisdiction to direct the parties to proceed with the arbitration and shall retain jurisdiction to enter its decree upon the award.

Commentary

Section Eight deals with maritime litigation and the seizure of assets for the satisfaction of claims. It essentially transposes the jurisdictional rules from the judicial to the arbitral setting. The presence of the "res" is necessary to the assertion of arbitral jurisdiction and the accompanying judicial supervision of the process.

§ 9. Award of Arbitrators; Confirmation; Jurisdiction; Procedure

If the parties in their agreement have agreed that a judgment of the court shall be entered upon the award made pursuant to the arbitration, and shall specify the court, then at any time within one year after the award is made any party to the arbitration may apply to the court so specified for an order confirming the award, and thereupon the court must grant such an order unless the award is vacated, modified, or corrected as prescribed in sections 10 and 11 of this title. If no court is specified in the agreement of the parties, then such application may be made to the United States court in and for the district within which such award was made. Notice of the application shall be served upon the adverse party, and thereupon the court shall have jurisdiction of such party as though he had appeared generally in the proceeding. If the adverse party is a resident of the district within which the award was made, such service shall be made upon the adverse party or his attorney as prescribed by law for service of notice of motion in an action in the same court. If the adverse party shall be a nonresident, then the notice of the application shall be served by the marshal of any district within which the adverse party may be found in like manner as other process of the court.

Commentary

Section Nine establishes that a party, within one year of the rendering of the award, may apply to a court for an order confirming the award. The provision recites the standard requirements for court jurisdiction and for effectuating the enforcement procedure. The provision takes the principle of contractual freedom into account: The parties may choose the court that will issue the order confirming the award prospectively in their agreement. Judicial confirmation of the award begins the process of coercive enforcement of the award against the noncomplying party.

In *Photopaint Tech., LLC v. Smartlens Corp.*, 335 F.3d 152 (2d Cir. 2003) the Second Circuit held that the FAA establishes a one-year statute of limitations for the judicial confirmation of arbitral awards. Even though FAA § 9 was written in the conditional tense, it should be interpreted as being imperative. The Fourth and Eighth Circuits, however, read the provision as permissible, allowing confirmations beyond the one-year time period. The conflict in interpretation has created a split in the federal circuits on this matter. A rigorous rule on the proscription of confirmation actions could have a negative impact upon arbitration by making it less effective and more expensive. It could also be argued that a one-year prescriptive rule enhances the finality and efficacy of the arbitral process.

§ 10. Same; Vacation [sic] [Vacatur]; Grounds; Rehearing

(a) In any of the following cases the United States court in and for the district wherein the award was made may make an order vacating the award upon the application of any party to the arbitration—

1. Where the award was procured by corruption, fraud, or undue means.

2. Where there was evident partiality or corruption in the arbitrators, or either of them.

3. Where the arbitrators were guilty of misconduct in refusing to postpone the hearing, upon sufficient cause shown, or in refusing to hear evidence pertinent and material to the controversy; or of any other misbehavior by which the rights of any party have been prejudiced.

4. Where the arbitrators exceeded their powers, or so imperfectly executed them that a mutual, final, and definite award upon the subject matter submitted was not made.

5. Where an award is vacated and the time within which the agreement required the award to be made has not expired the court may, in its discretion, direct a rehearing by the arbitrators.

(b) The United States district court for the district wherein an award was made that was issued pursuant to section 580 of title 5 may make an order vacating the award upon the application of a person, other than a party to the arbitration, who is adversely affected or aggrieved by the award, if the use of arbitration or the award is clearly inconsistent with the factors set forth in section 572 of title 5.

Commentary

Section Ten articulates the grounds upon which a federal district court with appropriate jurisdiction can refuse to confirm and enforce an arbitral award. The action, known as "vacatur" of the award, nullifies the award through coercive legal means. The basis for denying legal effect to an arbitral award is quite limited. In the main, it centers upon significant procedural deficiencies. The paucity of grounds and their narrowness reflect the FAA's liberal regulatory policy. The spirit of that policy has been reinforced by the decisional law. Any one of the four grounds in Section Ten could have become a significant obstacle to the enforcement of awards. The courts could have broadly construed the words "undue means," "evident partiality," "misconduct," or "imperfect execution of powers" and conducted a relatively rigorous scrutiny of awards. Federal courts have engaged in a modest and lenient review of awards that sometimes borders on the perfunctory. A nearly irrebuttable presumption exists in the federal case law that arbitral awards, once rendered, are legally enforceable.

As to the statutory grounds themselves: they are only four in number; they avoid any reference to a substantive basis for review (thereby, impliedly eliminating the possibility of a merits review of awards); they expressly relegate judicial scrutiny to violations of basic procedural fairness; and they indicate, by their number and content, a statutory policy favoring the enforcement of awards. Parties can obtain judicial relief from an award only when the arbitral trial was manifestly unfair and arbitrator abuse characterized the proceeding. Arbitral proceedings must conform to the minimum guarantees of due process: the right to receive notice, to be heard, and to have the arguments presented considered by the tribunal.

Grounds (a) and (b): The presence of wholesale illegitimacy, such as bribery, threats of violence, or other forms of intimidation, will invalidate an award. In all likelihood, the determination in the award reflects the corruption of the process through "undue means," rather than a disinterested evaluation of the evidence and the arguments. In *Superadio Ltd. Partnership v. Winstar Radio Productions, LLC*, 446 Mass. 330, 844 N.E.2d 246 (2006), the Massachusetts Supreme Judicial Court held that "undue means" under the Massachusetts arbitration law meant "underhanded, conniving, or unlawful" behavior that is similar to corruption or fraud.

Grounds (c) and (d): The arbitrators must also avoid slightly more technical violations of their adjudicatory mandate. Their conduct of the proceedings cannot "prejudice" the right of either party to a fair hearing. They cannot rule on matters not submitted and must provide the parties with a ruling that resolves the dispute. The decisional law liberally construes these statutory requirements. Arbitrators are not required to conduct proceedings in a judicial manner, but rather must satisfy rudimentary procedural standards. The vast majority of awards are enforceable because most arbitrators are capable of conducting proceedings that satisfy minimal requirements of professional adjudication. Both *Stolt-Nielsen v. AnimalFeeds International Corp.*, 559 U.S. 662 (2010), and *Rent-A-Center v. Jackson*, 561 U.S. 63 (2010), however, have enhanced considerably the prospect of judicial supervision of awards and their merits. *Stolt-Nielsen* requires arbitrators to provide a 'legal basis' for their rulings; *Rent-A-Center* enhances the supervisory powers of the courts at the threshold of the process by creating a second *kompetenz-kompetenz* doctrine to decide jurisdictional issues pertaining to the validity and interpretation of the arbitration agreement.

Ground (e): In those rare instances in which an award is vacated, the court can order the arbitrators to rehear the matter and render another award, provided the arbitration agreement has not lapsed and the court believes a rehearing serves the best interest of the parties and justice. Resubmission of the matter to the original arbitrators obviates the need to begin the adjudicatory process anew. The resubmission procedure, however, also signifies that corrective judicial supervision not only is exceptional and limited to significant procedural flaws, but its impact may be relegated to a reconsideration of the matter by the arbitrators. The courts' function then is to preserve whenever and however possible the parties' reference to arbitration. The content of Section Ten, therefore, guarantees the systemic autonomy of the arbitral process by strictly limiting judicial supervision and by having the courts safeguard the results of the process.

Section Ten impliedly eliminates the judicial review of the merits of awards because it contains no grounds for conducting the supervision of awards on that basis and its list of grounds for review is presumably exhaustive. Moreover, the provision contains no reference to the subject-matter inarbitrability defense or the public policy exception to the enforcement of arbitral awards. Apparently, U.S. domestic arbitral awards cannot be challenged on a substantive law basis. The absence of these grounds makes the domestic U.S. law of arbitration rather unique. As noted earlier, it is likely that the limitation in Section One of the statute's scope of application to maritime and commercial matters implies a subject-matter inarbitrability defense and that Congress intended to delineate the subject matter and public policy limits on arbitration in other statutes that addressed directly the subject matter deemed inapposite for arbitral adjudication.

The decisional law has added several common law grounds for effectuating the judicial supervision of arbitral awards. They include: "manifest disregard of the law"; violations of public policy; and capricious, arbitrary, or irrational arbitral determinations. Most of these grounds overlap with each other and are interpreted by the courts in a restrictive manner. They arose primarily in the special setting of labor and, to a lesser extent, maritime arbitration and gradually were interpreted to have a more general application. Their existence in the decisional law contradicts the statutory language and purpose of Section Ten and the judicial policy favoring arbitration. They continue to function in part because of inertia and the general judicial confusion that surrounds their implementation. Suffice it to say that it is difficult to challenge an award on any of these common law bases, even on the ground of public policy violations.

§ 11. Same; Modification or Correction; Grounds; Order

In either of the following cases the United States court in and for the district wherein the award was made may make an order modifying or correcting the award upon the application of any party to the arbitration:

(a) Where there was an evident material miscalculation of figures or an evident material mistake in the description of any person, thing, or property referred to in the award.

(b) Where the arbitrators have awarded upon a matter not submitted to them, unless it is a matter not affecting the merits of the decision upon the matter submitted.

(c) Where the award is imperfect in matter of form not affecting the merits of the controversy.

The order may modify and correct the award, so as to effect the intent thereof and promote justice between the parties.

Commentary

Section Eleven makes possible the enforcement of awards that contain formalistic errors. It substantiates the view that the FAA intends to foster the reference to arbitration, establish a supportive bond between the judicial and arbitral processes, and eliminate the dilatory undermining of the arbitral process. Under Section Eleven, U.S. federal courts, upon the request of one of the parties, have the power to modify or correct awards for inadvertent technical errors that might preclude enforcement. The rationale for the provision is a general "interests of justice" justification. The errors in question must be "evident" and unrelated to the merits of the determination. The provision has not become a source of litigious obfuscation.

Ground (b) of Section Eleven recognizes implicitly a severance procedure that is commonplace in arbitration laws. In circumstances in which arbitrators exceed their authority and rule on matters not submitted to arbitration, the court may enforce that part of the award that is valid by severing it from those portions that represent an illicit exercise of adjudicatory authority. The award then is partially enforced. As noted in ground (b), severance of the award is possible only when the various parts of the award are not interrelated or interdependent.

In 2000, the U.S. Supreme Court held that the FAA's venue provisions, §§ 9–11, were permissive in character. They allowed motions to confirm, vacate, or modify an arbitration award to be brought either in the district where the award had been rendered or in any district proper under the general venue statute. *See Cortez Byrd Chips, Inc. v. Bill Harbert Constr. Co.*, 529 U.S. 193 (2000).

The general venue statute provides for venue in a diversity action in "a judicial district in which a substantial part of the events or omissions giving rise to the claim occurred, or a substantial part of property that is the subject of the action is situated." 28 U.S.C. § 1391(a)(2). The Court explained that "the three venue sections of the FAA [were] best analyzed together, owing to their contemporaneous enactment and the similarity to their pertinent language."

The Court warned that "[e]nlightenment [would] not come merely from parsing the language [of the statute]." Instead, the Court looked to the statute's legislative history:

> When the FAA was enacted in 1925, it appeared against the backdrop of a considerably more restrictive general venue statute than the one current today. At the time, the practical effect of 28 U.S.C. § 112(a) was that a civil suit could usually be brought only in the district in which the defendant resided. The statute's restrictive application was all the more pronounced due to the courts' general inhospitality to forum selection clauses. Hence,

> even if an arbitration agreement expressly permitted [an] action to be brought in the district in which arbitration had been conducted, the agreement would probably prove to be in vain. The enactment of the special venue provisions in the FAA thus had an obviously liberalizing effect, undiminished by any suggestion, textual or otherwise, that congress meant simultaneously to foreclose a suit where the defendant resided. Such a consequence would have been as inexplicable in 1925 as it would be passing strange 75 years later.

The Court stated that interpreting the FAA venue provisions to require motions to confirm, vacate, or modify the award only in the district where the arbitration took place "would be more clearly at odds with both the FAA's 'statutory policy of rapid and unobstructed enforcement of arbitration agreements,' or with the desired flexibility of parties in choosing a site for arbitration." The Court pointed out that "[a]lthough the location of the arbitration may well be the residence of one of the parties, or have some other connection to a contract at issue, in many cases the site will have no relation whatsoever to the parties or the dispute." The Court further explained that "parties may be willing to arbitrate in any inconvenient forum, say, for the convenience of the arbitrators, or to get a panel with special knowledge or experience, or as part of some compromise, but they might well be less willing to pick such a location if any future court proceedings had to be held there." The Court was concerned that the flexibility to make those types of practical choices would be "inhibited by a venue rule mandating the same inconvenient venue if someone later sought to vacate or modify the award."

The Court also noted that a restrictive interpretation of the venue provisions would put them in "needless tension" with FAA § 3 which "provides that any court in which an action 'referable to arbitration under an agreement in writing' is pending 'shall on application of one of the parties stay the trial of the action until such arbitration has been had in accordance with the terms of the agreement.' " The Court explained that the existing precedent gives "a court with the power to stay the action under § 3 . . . the further power to confirm any ensuing arbitration award." Under a restrictive interpretation of the venue provisions, if an arbitration were held outside the district of that litigation, a subsequent proceeding to confirm, modify, or vacate the award could not be brought in the district of the original litigation, a result that the Court found unacceptable.

Finally, the Court held that a restrictive "interpretation would create anomalous results in the aftermath of arbitrations held abroad." FAA §§ 204, 207, and 302 "together provide for liberal choice of venue for actions to confirm awards subject to the 1958 Convention on the Recognition and Enforcement of Foreign Arbitral Awards and the 1975 Inter-American Convention on International Commercial Arbitration. But reading §§ 9–11 to restrict venue to the site of the arbitration would preclude any action under the FAA in courts of the United States to confirm, modify, or vacate awards rendered in foreign arbitrations not covered by either convention." The Court noted that "[a]lthough such actions would not necessarily be barred for lack of jurisdiction, they would be defeated by restrictions on venue, and anomalies like that are to be avoided when they can be." The Court admitted that "[t]here have been, and perhaps there still are, occasional gaps in the venue laws, [but] Congress does not in general intend to create venue gaps, which take away with one hand what Congress had given by way of jurisdictional grant with the other. Thus, in construing venue statutes it is reasonable to prefer the construction that avoids leaving such gaps."

The Court concluded by explaining that "[a]ttention to practical consequences . . . points away from the restrictive reading of §§ 9–11 and confirms the view that the liberalizing effect of the provisions in the day of their enactment was meant to endure through treating them as permitting, not limiting, venue choice today." Therefore, the Court held that the permissive view of FAA venue provisions prevailed.

Finally, it should be noted that U.S. courts have recognized a common law right to seek the clarification of awards from rendering tribunals. The action is intended to respond to circumstances in which the court of confirmation simply does not understand what the tribunal determined. Rather than vacate an incomprehensible award for "indefiniteness," the court remands the award to the arbitrators for clarification. There is no authorization for the procedure in the statute and FAA § 11 seems, in fact, to prohibit it. It contradicts the *functus officio* doctrine and it can permit courts to conduct a merits review of awards and to force arbitrators to adopt a judicial disposition of the dispute. In the context of adversarial representation, it is likely to cause delays and increased costs. Although it is intended to be pragmatic, the action to clarify may well undermine the autonomy of arbitration. *See Hardy v. Walsh Manning Securities, L.L.C.*, 341 F.3d 126 (2d Cir. 2003); *Office and Professional Employees Int'l Union, Local 471 v. Brownsville Gen. Hosp.*, 186 F.3d 326 (3d Cir. 1999).

§ 12. Notice of Motions to Vacate or Modify; Service; Stay of Proceedings

Notice of a motion to vacate, modify, or correct an award must be served upon the adverse party or his attorney within three months after the award is filed or delivered. If the adverse party is a resident of the district within which the award was made, such service shall be made upon the adverse party or his attorney as prescribed by law for service of notice of motion in an action in the same court. If the adverse party shall be a nonresident then the notice of the application shall be served by the marshal of any district within which the adverse party may be found in like manner as other process of the court. For the purposes of the motion any judge who might make an order to stay the proceedings in an action brought in the same court may make an order, to be served with the notice of motion, staying the proceedings of the adverse party to enforce the award.

§ 13. Papers Filed with Order on Motions; Judgment; Docketing; Force and Effect; Enforcement

The party moving for an order confirming, modifying, or correcting an award shall, at the time such order is filed with the clerk for the entry of judgment thereon, also file the following papers with the clerk:

(a) The agreement; the selection or appointment, if any, of an additional arbitrator or umpire; and each written extension of the time, if any, within which to make the award.

(b) The award.

(c) Each notice, affidavit, or other paper used upon an application to confirm, modify, or correct the award, and a copy of each order of the court upon such an application.

The judgment shall be docketed as if it was rendered in an action.

The judgment so ordered shall have the same force and effect, in all respects, as, and be subject to all the provisions of law relating to, a judgment in an action; and it may be enforced as if it had been rendered in an action in the court in which it is entered.

§ 14. Contracts Not Affected

This title shall not apply to contracts made prior to January 1, 1926.

Commentary

Sections Twelve, Thirteen, and Fourteen state that the FAA applies to contracts made after January 1, 1926, and they deal with the technical requirements for filing various motions. They are generally self-explanatory.

§ 15. Inapplicability of the Act of State doctrine

Enforcement of arbitral agreements, confirmation of arbitral awards, and execution upon judgments based on orders confirming such awards shall not be refused on the basis of the Act of State doctrine.

Commentary

Section Fifteen is mistakenly situated in the domestic section of the U.S. law of arbitration. It regulates the impact of the Act of State doctrine upon the enforcement of arbitral agreements and awards. Act of State applies primarily, if not exclusively, in the transborder context, more than likely when a U.S. national or entity alleges that it is aggrieved by the conduct of a foreign State that has taken place within the state's territorial borders. Act of State functions as an objection to U.S. judicial jurisdiction in much the same manner as sovereign immunity. Under the latter, it is alleged that the foreign State cannot be sued before national courts because of its status as a foreign State: It is immune from suit because it is sovereign. Under the former, the foreign State cannot be held accountable for its conduct before a U.S. court because its actions took place within its own territory and were undertaken to further the public interest of the foreign nation. The matter is nonjusticiable because it implicates U.S. foreign policy interests and thereby the constitutional separation of powers doctrine under which the Executive Branch has exclusive authority over the diplomatic interests of the United States.

Unlike Sovereign Immunity, Act of State is unique to U.S. law; it arose and is embedded in U.S. constitutional considerations. It has received the steadfast support of the U.S. Supreme Court. It arises in cases that involve state conduct roughly equivalent to the exercise of eminent domain powers in the domestic setting. The state has allegedly confiscated foreign investor property for a public purpose (giving rise under international law to a duty to provide some form of compensation).

Although it could have an impact upon the domestic enforcement of transborder agreements and awards, the doctrine clearly has little, if anything, to do with the enforcement of domestic arbitration agreements and awards. Assuming the provision functions in the international context, it establishes a very useful rule, reflecting the received wisdom of transborder arbitration practice. In effect, neither Sovereign Immunity nor the Act of State doctrine should be used to frustrate the recourse to arbitration or the enforcement of awards. Once a State agrees to arbitrate, it is deemed to have waived its sovereign right not to be sued. It has agreed to adjudicate its disputes before the arbitral tribunal, and U.S. courts will enforce that implied contractual waiver of immunity under the Foreign Sovereign Immunities Act. Moreover, the State's action, allegedly done for a public purpose within its territory, will not allow it to escape its contractual obligation to arbitrate or to be bound by an arbitral award. As long as the dispute is covered by the agreement to arbitrate, its public law character will not hinder the conduct of the arbitration or frustrate the viability of the award. Nationalizing foreign investor property will not terminate the obligation to arbitrate disputes.

It should be noted that the provisions of Section Fifteen also apply to judicial judgments confirming arbitral awards. When a party refuses to comply with the award rendered by the arbitral tribunal, the other party will seek judicial confirmation of the award and its compulsory enforcement. The request to confirm the award will be opposed by an action for vacatur. If the award is confirmed, the court issues a judgment for the execution of the award. In effect, the award is transformed into a judicial judgment and, at this stage, is no longer an arbitral award. Section Fifteen makes clear that the Act of State doctrine, although it could preclude the enforcement of an ordinary judicial judgment, cannot be used to challenge a judicial judgment that provides for the enforcement of an arbitral award.

§ 16. Appeals

(a) An appeal may be taken from—

(1) an order—

(a) refusing a stay of any action under section 3 of this title,

(b) denying a petition under section 4 of this title to order arbitration to proceed,

(c) denying an application under section 206 of this title to compel arbitration,

(d) confirming or denying confirmation of an award or partial award, or

(e) modifying, correcting, or vacating an award;

(2) an interlocutory order granting, continuing, or modifying an injunction against an arbitration that is subject to this title; or

(3) a final decision with respect to an arbitration that is subject to this title.

(b) Except as otherwise provided in section 1292(b) of title 28, an appeal may not be taken from an interlocutory order—

(1) granting a stay of any action under section 3 of this title;

(2) directing arbitration to proceed under section 4 of this title;

(3) compelling arbitration to proceed under section 206 of this title;

(4) refusing to enjoin an arbitration that is subject to this title.

Commentary

Section Sixteen was enacted in 1988. Together, Sections Fifteen and Sixteen constitute the most recent amendments to the domestic provisions of the FAA—an effort by Congress to modernize somewhat the 1925 legislation by adding provisions that reflect contemporary developments in arbitration law. Despite the relative complexity of its language, Section Sixteen makes a simple and straightforward point: It confirms and gives legislative stature to the decisional law creation of an "emphatic federal policy favoring arbitration." In essence, under the provision, the right of interlocutory appeal exists against any court order that is antagonistic to the pursuit of arbitration, *e.g.*, an order refusing to stay a judicial proceeding in favor of arbitration or refusing to compel arbitration. There is, however, no right of appeal against an interlocutory order that supports the recourse to arbitration. The order of a federal court, for example, that confirms the parties' right and obligation to proceed with arbitration is final.

On the one hand, the dichotomy of regimes clearly favors the interests of arbitration and aligns itself with the FAA policy to legitimate and support arbitration. The gravamen of Section Sixteen also furthers the establishment of a bond of cooperation between the judicial and arbitral processes. One commentator describes the significance of Section Sixteen in these terms:

> It is a pro-arbitration statute designed to prevent the appellate aspect of the litigation process from impeding the expeditious disposition of an arbitration. Its inherent acknowledgment is that arbitration is a form of dispute resolution designed to save the parties time, money, and effort by substituting for the litigation process the advantages of speed, simplicity, and economy associated with arbitration. Its theme is that judicial involvement in the process should be kept to the barest minimum to avoid undermining those goals.

D. Siegel, *Practice Commentary*, TITLE 9 ARBITRATION U.S. CODE ANN. 1996 CUM. ANN. POCKET PT. 306 (1996).

On the other hand, the blatant use of a double standard and the heavy-handed restriction of rights against arbitration, characteristic features of the contemporary U.S. decisional law on arbitration, undermine the regulatory integrity of the legislation. It is one thing to safeguard arbitration against outright juridical bias and to proclaim the right of contractual recourse to arbitration within specialized and self-regulating communities and demand federal judicial compliance with that policy. It is, however, quite another matter to exempt arbitration from ordinary legal rules, especially when it reaches more widely into the community. Arbitration's need for systemic autonomy and independence from judicial intervention does not require a complete elimination of legal restrictions. The law may have had to favor arbitration to protect it from the prejudice of the courts, but, once arbitration attained lawful standing, the protective treatment itself became abusive. It distorts the necessary balance between the functional autonomy of the arbitral process and the safeguarding of legal rights.

The substance of Section Sixteen appears to confirm that the sin of would-be judicial antipathy toward arbitration can never be fully expiated. The atonement must be constantly reaffirmed, and the price of redemption escalates whenever any thought of rights protection is entertained. Not only is the sin of judicial hostility to be avoided, but any semblance or reminder of it, no matter how pale or remote, also must be cast aside, lest the legal system return inexorably to its sinful ways. The literalism of this theology forces the legal system to divest itself of any sense of regulatory equilibrium, to engage in overly zealous rule-making, and to abandon its primary mission of rights protection.

In early December 2000, the U.S. Supreme Court handed down its opinion in *Green Tree Financial Corp.—Alabama v. Randolph*, 531 U.S. 79 (2000). In its opinion, the Court—through the late Chief Justice Rehnquist—addressed a number of issues of contemporary arbitration law, including a matter involving the exercise of judicial review with respect to arbitral awards. In that regard, the Court held that, when a district court compels the parties to arbitrate their differences and dismisses all claims brought before it by the litigation, that determination constitutes a "final decision" under FAA § 16(a)(3) and it is subject to appeal under the FAA statutory provision.

The Court summarized the procedural history of the litigation in the following terms:

> The Court of Appeals for the Eleventh Circuit . . . held that it had jurisdiction to review the District Court's order because that order was a final decision. . . . The Court of Appeals looked to § 16 of the Federal Arbitration Act (FAA), 9 U.S.C. § 16, which governs appeal from a District Court's arbitration order, and specifically § 16(a)(3), which allows appeal from "a final decision with respect to an arbitration that is subject to this title." The Court determined that a final, appealable order within the meaning of the FAA is one that disposes of all the issues framed by the litigation, leaving nothing to be done but execute the order. The Court of Appeals found the District Court's order within that definition.
>
> [. . .]
>
> We granted *certiorari* . . . , and we now affirm the Court of Appeals with respect to the [jurisdictional question]. . . .

Part II of the Court's opinion was a unanimous disposition. In some respects, however, it could be seen as the most controversial segment of the Court's opinion. In reaching its determination, the Court does not appear to reinforce the federal policy in favor of arbitration; it disregards the lower court distinction between "embedded" and "independent" proceedings in defining 'finality'; and it advances a generally strained interpretation of that term.

First, the Court took exception with the petitioners' construction of FAA § 16 as "generally permit[ting] immediate appeal of orders hostile to arbitration, whether the orders are final or interlocutory, but bars appeal of interlocutory orders favorable to arbitration." Prior to *Green Tree*, as noted earlier, it was generally acknowledged that FAA § 16 was a pro-arbitration provision that created a double standard expressly favoring arbitration. The petitioners were entirely correct in their assessment of the provision: it was meant to delay the reconsideration of judicial holdings in favor of arbitration and to subject unfavorable dispositions to immediate review. For reasons which go unstated and are difficult to determine, the Court refused to recognize that feature of FAA § 16 and chose to give the provision a more ordinary and even-handed application:

> Section 16(a)(3), however, preserves immediate appeal of any "final decision with respect to an arbitration," regardless of whether the decision is favorable or hostile to arbitration. And as petitioners and respondent agree, the term "final decision" has a well-developed and longstanding meaning. It is a decision that "ends the litigation on the merits and leaves nothing more for the court to do but execute the judgment" . . . Because the FAA does not define "a final decision with respect to an arbitration" or otherwise suggest that the ordinary meaning of "final decision" should not apply, we accord the term its well-established meaning. . . .

Second, the Court also disregarded the longstanding distinction between "embedded" and "independent" proceedings in determining whether court action in regard to arbitration is "final":

> We disagree [with petitioners' position]. It does not appear that, at the time of § 16(a)(3)'s enactment, the rules of finality were firmly established in cases like this one, where the District Court both ordered arbitration and dismissed the remaining claims. We also note that at that time, Courts of Appeals did not have a uniform approach to finality with respect to orders directing arbitration in "embedded" proceedings. The term "final decision," by contrast, enjoys a consistent and longstanding interpretation. Certainly the plain language of the statutory text does not suggest that Congress intended to incorporate the rather complex independent/embedded distinction, and its consequences for finality, into § 16(a)(3). We therefore conclude that where, as here, the District Court has ordered the parties to proceed to arbitration, and dismissed all the claims before it, that decision is "final" within the meaning of § 16(a)(3), and therefore appealable.

Third, the Court concluded that "final decision" under FAA § 16 means the termination of litigation with regard to the issues brought before the court. That an action to vacate, confirm, or modify the award may be brought once the compelled arbitration is completed did not alter the

Court's view that the lower court action with respect to the arbitration was final:

> The District Court's order directed that the dispute be resolved by arbitration and dismissed respondent's claims with prejudice, leaving the court nothing to do but execute the judgment. That order plainly disposed of the entire case on the merits and left no part of it pending before the court. The FAA does permit parties to arbitration agreements to bring a separate proceeding in a district court to enter judgment on an arbitration award once it is made (or to vacate or modify it), but the existence of that remedy does not vitiate the finality of the District Court's resolution of the claims in the instant proceeding. . . . The District Court's order was therefore "a final decision with respect to an arbitration" within the meaning of § 16(a)(3), and an appeal may be taken. . . .

FAA § 16(a)(3) governs the appeals process against court orders relating to arbitration. The statutory provision upholds the federal policy in favor of arbitration by prohibiting interlocutory relief against court orders that stay litigation pending arbitration. While a dismissal of the judicial proceeding constitutes a final order, a stay merely "administratively close[s]" the case and amounts to a postponement. *See South Louisiana Cement, Inc. v. Van Aalst Bulk Handling, B.V.*, 383 F.3d 297 (5th Cir. 2004). *See also Jeffers v. D'Alessandro*, 169 N.C.App. 455, 612 S.E.2d 447 (2005) (slip copy) (order to compel arbitration is not a "final judgment" and cannot be certified for appeal). Thereafter, the court either will assist the arbitrators in the conduct of the arbitral proceedings when it is requested or entertain a petition to confirm or vacate the resulting award. Upon confirming the award for purposes of enforcement, the court, in effect, has dismissed the court action. An order to that effect would be subject to appeal under FAA § 16. The appeal, however, may be foreclosed by *res judicata* because of the confirmation of the award.

The *Rooker-Feldman* doctrine is relevant to FAA § 16. It is intended to prevent "a party losing in state court from seeking what in substance would be appellate review of the state judgment [in the lower federal courts] based on the losing party's claim that the state judgment itself violate[d] the loser's federal rights." It originated in *Rooker v. Fidelity Trust Co.*, 263 U.S. 413 (1923) and *District of Columbia Court of Appeals v. Feldman*, 460 U.S. 462 (1983). It is meant to discourage forum-shopping and the relitigation of cases based on a strained federal rights argument. It works *in tandem* with FAA § 16 in that it generally precludes reconsideration of an order to compel arbitration. The preclusion of appeal under *Rooker-Feldman* obviously is not temporary or merely delayed. Moreover, it applies to the jurisdictional divide between state and federal courts, rather than to the exercise of appellate jurisdiction among federal courts on arbitration matters. *Rooker-Feldman* is a bar when a party challenges the application of law in a state court litigation, but not when the challenge is directed to the constitutionality of the state law that was applied in the proceeding before the state court.

Pieper v. American Arbitration Association, 336 F.3d 458 (6th Cir. 2003), *cert. denied*, 540 U.S. 1182 (2004), demonstrates the standard application of the doctrine. After being compelled to arbitrate by an Ohio state court, Pieper filed suit before a federal district court alleging that "the dispute was not properly subject to arbitration and seeking injunctive relief that would bar [the] AAA from beginning the arbitration hearings." The federal court concluded that it lacked subject matter jurisdiction to engage in the appellate review of state court proceedings. On appeal, the ruling was upheld because "under the *Rooker-Feldman* doctrine[,]" the lower federal court "was without jurisdiction to grant relief" because *Rooker-Feldman* "generally prohibits federal courts from reviewing state-court judgments."

Despite the clarity of its application in the foregoing case, *Rooker-Feldman* raises a number of unresolved issues that indicate it may not work in concert with FAA § 16 in all circumstances. When a state court denies a motion to compel arbitration, federal law would command interlocutory recourse to an appellate court. Does *Rooker-Feldman* foreclose recourse to the lower federal courts in this instance? Does that mean that recourse to federal appellate courts also is precluded? These circumstances also raise the possible arguments that either the state court applied a state law contrary to the FAA—which, therefore, should be preempted—or the state court misconstrued the applicable law such that it denied the affected party its federal right to arbitrate under FAA § 2. The latter argument assumes that FAA § 2 does in fact create such a right and some sort of accompanying federal question jurisdiction. The case law acknowledges the "anomalies," but has not proposed any resolution of the issue.

These unprovided-for complications at least raise the question of whether *Rooker-Feldman* is intended only to have a pro-arbitration effect, allowing state court determinations favorable to arbitration to escape lower federal court scrutiny. The doctrine was articulated in a federalism-jurisdictional context and not in circumstances of support for or compliance to the federal policy on arbitration. It is difficult to imagine how state court proceedings that prevent the recourse to arbitration under state law would not result in an action before federal courts. The issue, however, has yet to receive a full airing in the decisional law.

NOTES AND QUESTIONS

1. In what sense does the FAA typify the common law approach to the enactment of statutory law? Does the statute convey a complete picture of the

arbitral process? Is the portrait of arbitration that emerges from the legislation sufficient for purposes of advising a client on the decision of whether to arbitrate? What other knowledge might be necessary or useful to accomplish this task? The commentary characterizes the FAA as a document that principally intermediates between the arbitral process and the fundamental aspects of the U.S. legal process and gives primary attention to legal considerations rather than the regulation of arbitration. Is that a fair and realistic assessment of the statute?

2. At the time of its enactment and for some years beyond, the FAA was seen as a procedural enactment. As the analysis of the FAA demonstrates (in Section One), even proponents of the legislation argued that it created "no new rights" but for the enforcement mechanism in Section Ten. Do you agree? How would you argue that the FAA establishes a federal right to arbitrate? If such a right exists, does it have constitutional standing? Does arbitration raise federal-question jurisdiction? Is the contractual right to arbitrate equivalent to First Amendment rights or federal statutory rights attributed to securities investors? How might such a right be vindicated, if at all, in diversity litigation before the federal courts or before state courts when state law governs a case sounding in interstate commerce?

3. You should pay particular attention to Section One and the FAA's scope of application. Try to discover what makes the FAA a federal law enactment. Also, isolate those features of Section One that restrict the reach of the FAA to specialized commercial communities. Do you agree that the FAA originated as special interest legislation, meant to allow arbitration to function in remote sectors of society? Does a fair reading of the text of the FAA or of the character of arbitral adjudication support a wider reach to the remedy? What might justify an "unfair" reading? In articulating your responses, consider the following view of the function of arbitration from Cohen & Dayton, *The New Federal Arbitration Law*, 12 VA. L. REV. 265 (1926):

> Not all questions arising out of contracts ought to be arbitrated. It is a remedy peculiarly suited to the disposition of the ordinary disputes between merchants as to questions of fact—quantity, quality, time of delivery, compliance with terms of payment, excuses for non-performance, and the like. It has a place also in the determination of the simpler questions of law—the questions of law which arise out of these daily relations between merchants as to the passage of title, the existence of warranties, or the questions of law which are complementary to the questions of fact which we have just mentioned.

Id. at 281, *cited in Prima Paint Corp. v. Flood & Conklin Mfg. Co.*, 388 U.S. 395, 409 n.13 (1967) (Black, J. dissenting).

4. The two critical provisions of the FAA are Sections Two and Ten which deal with the arbitral agreement and award. Why are these provisions indispensable to the regulatory framework? You should assess critically the

grounds for the vacatur of awards and arrive at an assessment of their viability as grounds for exercising judicial scrutiny. Also, what other provisions of the FAA appear significant to you and for what reasons?

2. UNIFORM ARBITRATION ACT (2000)

In August 2000, the National Conference of Commissioners on Uniform State Laws (NCCUSL) "approved and recommended for enactment in all the states" the Uniform Arbitration Act (2000). The vote was nearly unanimous (Alabama abstained and the Michigan and Rhode Island state delegations were absent).

The Uniform Arbitration Act was first drafted in 1955. It had not been revised since 1956. The Uniform Arbitration Act of 1956 was adopted in forty-nine jurisdictions. These jurisdictions included the District of Columbia, Puerto Rico, and the U.S. Virgin Islands. Only four states did not enact some version of the uniform law: Alabama, Georgia, Mississippi, and West Virginia. Some states were counted among the adopting jurisdictions because their enacted law on arbitration was modeled upon the FAA and "substantially similar" to the uniform law.

A number of the adopting states enacted special arbitration provisions in addition to the uniform law. These provisions related to and promoted international commercial arbitration. The laws generally were modeled upon or inspired by the UNCITRAL Model Law on International Commercial Arbitration. Such laws are in force in the following state jurisdictions: California, Colorado, Connecticut, Florida, Georgia, Hawaii, Illinois, Maryland, North Carolina, Ohio, Oregon, and Texas.

The work of modernizing the uniform legislation began in 1996 with the creation of a NCCUSL drafting committee. The need for revisions was spurred by the rapid character of developments in the field of arbitration. Despite the high quality of the 1955 uniform law, the increased scope of application for arbitration and the greater sophistication of arbitral doctrine demanded a more elaborate uniform legislative framework.

According to a "Summary" provided by the NCCUSL (available at: http://www.uniformlaws.org/actsummary.aspx?title=Arbitration%20Act%20(2000) (last visited Dec. 3, 2018)), the two principal achievements of the 1955 Uniform Arbitration Act were: (1) the reversal of the common law rule that disfavored pre-dispute agreements to arbitrate; and (2) the articulation of the basic phases and procedures of an arbitral trial. The new law, the 2000 RUAA, allegedly adds to the advances made by its predecessor. It seeks to avoid any federal preemption issues by endorsing rules that are compliant with the federal law on arbitration. It characterizes itself as a default act, many of the provisions of which can be waived or modified by contract. It adds to the regulation of the previous law by addressing: provisional relief, consolidation of different arbitrations, the need for arbitrator disclosures, the civil immunity of arbitrators, the procedural discretion and authority of the arbitrator—specifically as it relates to record-building, and the award of exemplary relief (punitive damages and attorney's fees). The "Summary" does not address the compositional disparity between the two statutes. The RUAA is a less accessible, more opaque, and chaotic statutory framework.

As approved, the Uniform Arbitration Act (2000) incorporates principles and concepts that were developed in the contemporary case law on arbitration—*e.g.*, on arbitrator disclosure and impartiality and the awarding of punitive damages and attorney's fees. In the final analysis, however, the RUAA (2000) is not ready-made for immediate and unqualified adoption in any state jurisdiction. The 1955 version of the uniform law had been such a document. Because it constituted a fully comprehensive statement of regulatory principles on arbitration, the 1956 Act represented a substantial improvement over the narrow procedural focus of the FAA. The successor law, however, is simply not in the same qualitative league in terms of content, organization, and drafting methodology. The new law suffers from severe deficiencies in language. Simply and pointedly stated, the statute is poorly written. To most arbitration attorneys, the RUAA is a problematic statutory statement. Not only are many of its provisions inelegantly rendered, but the inadequacies of language also give rise to ambiguities and confusion about the rule that is being propounded.

The drafting committee appears to have addressed a number of controversial developments in the law either by siding with one position on the question or by taking no position whatsoever—leaving it to judges or legislatures to decide on a suitable rule. The inconsistency of the approach is likely to invite controversy and to undermine the credibility of the suggested provisions. The Revised Uniform Arbitration Act (2000) represents a failed attempt to legislate when a significant, perhaps landmark, law on arbitration could easily have been elaborated. Thus far, the UAA (2000) has been adopted in seventeen states (Alaska, Arkansas, Arizona, Colorado, Florida, Hawaii, Michigan, Minnesota, Nevada, New Jersey, New Mexico, North Carolina, North Dakota, Oklahoma, Oregon, Utah, and Washington). It also was adopted in the District of Columbia. It has been endorsed by the American Bar Association, the American Arbitration Association, the National Academy of Arbitrators, and the National Arbitration Forum.

Selected Provisions

[. . .]

SECTION 4. EFFECT OF AGREEMENT TO ARBITRATE; NONWAIVABLE PROVISIONS.

(a) Except as otherwise provided in subsections (b) and (c), a party to an agreement to arbitrate or to an arbitration proceeding may waive or, the parties may vary the effect of, the requirements of this [Act] to the extent permitted by law.

(b) Before a controversy arises that is subject to an agreement to arbitrate, a party to the agreement may not:

(1) waive or agree to vary the effect of the requirements of Sections 5(a), 6(a), 8, 17(a), 17(b), 26, or 28;

(2) unreasonably restrict the right under Section 9 to notice of the initiation of an arbitration proceeding;

(3) unreasonably restrict the right under Section 12 to disclosure of any facts by a neutral arbitrator; or

(4) waive the right under Section 16 of a party to an agreement to arbitrate to be represented by a lawyer at any proceeding or hearing under this [Act], but an employer and a labor organization may waive the right to representation by a lawyer in a labor arbitration.

(c) A party to an agreement to arbitrate or arbitration proceeding may not waive, or the parties may not vary the effect of, the requirements of this section or Sections 3(a), (c), 7, 14, 18, 20(c) or (d), 22, 23, 24, 25(a) or (b), 29, 30, 31, or 32.

NOTES AND QUESTIONS

1. What principle of U.S. arbitration law is illustrated by the content of Section 4(a)? What qualifications are introduced in regard to the basic principle? When can parties establish their own rules of arbitration?

2. State and explain the content of Section 4(b)(1). What provisions of the law are imperative or mandatory? What do you think of the drafting techniques used here and elsewhere in the statute?

3. Compare Section 4(b)(1) and 4(b)(4) in terms of drafting technique. Which provision is clearer and more accessible? Also, explain the significance of the distinction in Section 4(b)(4).

4. Compare and explain the distinctions that are made in Section 4(b) and (c). What are these provisions meant to say? Could it be stated in plain English?

SECTION 6. VALIDITY OF AGREEMENT TO ARBITRATE.

(a) An agreement contained in a record to submit to arbitration any existing or subsequent controversy arising between the parties to the agreement is valid, enforceable, and irrevocable except upon a ground that exists at law or in equity for the revocation of a contract.

(b) The court shall decide whether an agreement to arbitrate exists or a controversy is subject to an agreement to arbitrate.

(c) An arbitrator shall decide whether a condition precedent to arbitrability has been fulfilled and whether a contract containing a valid agreement to arbitrate is enforceable.

(d) If a party to a judicial proceeding challenges the existence of, or claims that a controversy is not subject to, an agreement to arbitrate, the arbitration proceeding may continue pending final resolution of the issue by the court, unless the court otherwise orders.

NOTES AND QUESTIONS

1. Assess Section 6(a). What is an "agreement contained in a record"? Is this an obtuse way of defining the "in-writing" requirement for arbitration agreements? Does it promote understanding to state that the term "means information that is inscribed on a tangible medium or that is stored in an electronic or other medium and is retrievable in perceivable form"? Is this comprehensible English or caricaturial definition? How would you define the "in-writing" requirement?

2. Does Section 6(b) reject or ignore *First Options of Chicago, Inc. v. Kaplan*, 514 U.S. 938 (1995), and its recognition of *kompetenz-kompetenz* by party provision?

3. Under Section 6, courts—it appears—have exclusive authority to decide questions of contract inarbitrability, namely, "whether an agreement to arbitrate exists or [whether] a controversy is subject to an agreement to arbitrate." Arbitrators, it seems, are only empowered to decide matters that follow in the wake of the resolution of the central issue of arbitrability, *i.e.*, "whether a condition precedent to arbitrability has been fulfilled and whether a contract containing a valid agreement to arbitrate is enforceable." In a word, courts decide jurisdiction and arbitrators interpret the contract.

Section 6(b) and (c) fail to acknowledge that the parties can agree to authorize the arbitrators to rule on matters of contract inarbitrability. By omitting any reference to this possibility, the drafters misrepresented the current law. *First Options of Chicago, Inc. v. Kaplan*, 514 U.S. 938 (1995), established that contracting parties can empower arbitrators to decide questions of contract inarbitrability. To the extent that Section 6(c) suggests otherwise (as it appears to do), it is inaccurate.

The *Reporter's Notes* provide an explanation for the statutory language. As to the impact of *Kaplan* upon the judicial and arbitral authority to decide, the Reporter provides the following commentary:

> 2. Section 6(b) and (c) reflect the decision of the Drafting Committee to include language in the RUAA [the Revised Uniform Arbitration Act] that incorporates the holdings of the vast majority of state courts and the law that has developed under the FAA that, in the absence of an agreement to the contrary, issues of substantive arbitrability, *i.e.*, whether a dispute is encompassed by an agreement to arbitrate, are for a court to decide and issues of procedural arbitrability, *i.e.*, whether prerequisites such as time limits, notice, laches, estoppel, and other conditions precedent to an obligation to arbitrate have been met, are for the arbitrators to decide. . . .
>
> In particular it should be noted that Section 6(b) which provides for courts to decide substantive arbitrability is subject to waiver under Section 4(a). This approach is not only the law in most States, as noted above, but also follows Supreme Court precedent under the FAA that if there is no agreement to the contrary, questions of substantive arbitrability are for the courts to decide. *First Options of Chicago, Inc. v. Kaplan*, 514 U.S. 938 (1995). Some arbitration organizations, such as the American Arbitration Association in its rules on commercial arbitration disputes, provide that arbitrators, rather than courts, make the initial determination as to substantive arbitrability. . . .

Do these statements absolve the deficiencies of the codification? Why did the drafters resort to such an arcane and opaque method of stating rules? Why make the text of a proposed law on such an important topic so difficult of access?

4. Section 6(c) is also cast in cumbersome and impenetrable language. The *Reporter's Notes* explain that it establishes the decisional domain of the arbitrator. Once arbitrators are properly invested with the authority to rule, they decide all matters relating to the contract and its interpretation. They also make decisions regarding the proceedings. Can you provide an explanation of the distinction being made by the Reporter between "procedural" and "substantive" arbitrability? How is the distinction reflected in the text of the statute?

5. As to Section 6(d), the Reporter rightly provides that: "Section 6(d) follows the practice of the American Arbitration Association and most other arbitration organizations that if arbitrators are appointed and either party challenges the substantive arbitrability of a dispute in a court proceeding, the arbitrators in their discretion may continue the arbitration hearings unless a court issues an order to stay the arbitration or makes a final determination that the matter is not arbitrable."

A clearer and more useful statement of the law on matters of inarbitrability might have read as follow:

> Challenges to the validity and enforceability of the arbitration agreement can be brought on the ground that the subject matter of the dispute is inarbitrable as a matter of law or because the agreement to arbitrate allegedly is deficient as a contract or, if a valid contract, does not cover the dispute in question.
>
> (i) The legislature ordinarily decides whether nonjudicial recourse (like arbitration) can be had to resolve disputes that arise under a statute or other enactment. Statutory language that prohibits nonjudicial recourse should be clear and express, making the legislature's intent unmistakable. In particular, it should establish whether the nonwaiver of judicial remedies applies to the rights or remedies or both that are created or made available under the statute. Whenever possible, ambiguities in the statute should be construed to favor the recourse of arbitration.
>
> (ii) Contract problems with regard to the reference to arbitration can arise as to the existence or scope of the arbitration agreement. If no agreement exists or if the agreement is contractually flawed to the point of unenforceability, the reference to arbitration is excluded. If the dispute is beyond the governing arbitral clause's scope of application, arbitration becomes available only through a submission.
>
> (iii) Unless the parties' agreement provides otherwise, courts decide matters of contract inarbitrability. If the parties provide to the contrary in their agreement, these issues can be resolved by the arbitrators.

How do you assess the promulgated statutory text and the suggested provision?

SECTION 8. PROVISIONAL REMEDIES.

(a) Before an arbitrator is appointed and is authorized and able to act, the court, upon [motion] of a party to an arbitration proceeding and for good cause shown, may enter an order for provisional remedies to protect the effectiveness of the arbitration proceeding to the same extent and under the same conditions as if the controversy were the subject of a civil action.

(b) After an arbitrator is appointed and is authorized and able to act:

> (1) the arbitrator may issue such orders for provisional remedies, including interim awards, as the arbitrator finds necessary to protect the effectiveness of the arbitration proceeding and to promote the fair and expeditious resolution of the controversy, to

the same extent and under the same conditions as if the controversy were the subject of a civil action, and

(2) a party to an arbitration proceeding may move the court for a provisional remedy only if the matter is urgent and the arbitrator is not able to act timely or the arbitrator cannot provide an adequate remedy.

(c) A party does not waive a right of arbitration by making a [motion] under subsection (a) or (b).

NOTES AND QUESTIONS

1. Section 8 responds to a problem that arose in the contemporary practice of arbitration and for which most institutional rules now provide a solution. Once a demand for arbitration is filed, an answer follows and the parties must begin the process of naming arbitrators. In the interval, prior to the constitution of the arbitral tribunal, problems may arise regarding securing evidence and enforcement assets. Institutional rules generally provide for the appointment of an interim or emergency arbitrator. The Uniform Law addresses these problems through motions to the courts. Which method is preferable? What practical problems can be associated with each approach?

2. Explain the function of interim or provisional relief in arbitration.

3. What is the purpose and meaning of Section 8(c)?

SECTION 10. CONSOLIDATION OF SEPARATE ARBITRATION PROCEEDINGS

(a) Except as otherwise provided in subsection (c), upon [motion] of a party to an agreement to arbitrate or to an arbitration proceeding, the court may order consolidation of separate arbitration proceedings as to all or some of the claims if:

(1) there are separate agreements to arbitrate or separate arbitration proceedings between the same persons or one of them is a party to a separate agreement to arbitrate or a separate arbitration proceeding with a third person;

(2) the claims subject to the agreements to arbitrate arise in substantial part from the same transaction or series of related transactions;

(3) the existence of a common issue of law or fact creates the possibility of conflicting decisions in the separate arbitration proceedings; and

(4) prejudice resulting from a failure to consolidate is not outweighed by the risk of undue delay or prejudice to the rights of or hardship to parties opposing consolidation.

(b) The court may order consolidation of separate arbitration proceedings as to some claims and allow other claims to be resolved in separate arbitration proceedings.

(c) The court may not order consolidation of the claims of a party to an agreement to arbitrate if the agreement prohibits consolidation.

NOTES AND QUESTIONS

1. Section 10 seeks to codify new principles of arbitration law. It provides rules on the "[c]onsolidation [o]f [s]eparate [a]rbitration [p]roceedings." Like the previous sections, the provision addresses an important aspect of the contemporary U.S. arbitration practice. The critical issue pertaining to consolidation in arbitration is whether party consent is necessary to allow courts to join separate, but related arbitrations. The interplay between *Nereus* and *Boeing* made that much of the law evident. *See Compania Espanola de Petroleos, S.A. v. Nereus Shipping, S.A.*, 527 F.2d 966 (2d Cir. 1975), *cert. denied*, 426 U.S. 936 (1976); *Government of the United Kingdom of Great Britain v. Boeing, Co.*, 998 F.2d 68 (2d Cir. 1993). It is difficult to understand why the provision is not anchored in the clear majority view that mutual party consent is a requisite to consolidation. Instead, mutual party provision on the matter is positioned as an exception to the general proposition that courts can consolidate arbitrations upon the request of *one* of the arbitrating parties. A string of conditions accompanies the statement of the courts' authority to consolidate.

2. What do you make of Section 10(a)(1)? How do you interpret the distinction between "separate agreements to arbitrate" and "separate arbitration proceedings"? Is it meaningful? Is it necessary? Who are the "third" people? What conditions are the drafters attempting to create? Are they trying to establish that the judicial consolidation of separate arbitrations is possible only if the affected parties are parties to an existing arbitration agreement or proceeding? Why did they not just say that?

3. Consolidation raises doctrinal and administrative problems. Why does Section 10 not even recognize these aspects of the process? How would you revise the provision to incorporate these aspects?

4. Section 10(a)(2) and (3) state clearly the settled law on consolidation. There must be a common nexus of facts and issues between the arbitrations and the submission of these related claims to different tribunals would create the possibility of conflicting determinations. Paragraph (4), however, appears to state that the use of judicial consolidation depends upon whether the court concludes that consolidation is less harmful than nonconsolidation in terms of delay and the protection of the rights of the party opposing consolidation. The rule attributes very broad discretion to the courts in ordering consolidation. Does giving such power to the courts contribute to the autonomy of the arbitral process? Is judicial intermeddling likely in light of the wide reach of the rule? Why are courts supreme in matters of arbitral consolidation and not elsewhere

in the arbitral process? Is the rule a fair reflection of the position of the decisional law?

5. Section 10(b) allows for the partial consolidation of claims. Partial consolidation has not been a significant aspect of the case law on or the practice of arbitration—and perhaps for good reason. Although the proposed rule establishes an additional option in matters of consolidation, it is difficult to assess or appreciate its practical utility. In fact, it is likely to generate a number of problems: It increases the use of judicial discretion when existing court options already are too numerous; it further complicates an already complex and controversial procedure; and it is likely to create jurisdictional debates and onerous problems of administration. The wisdom that underlies this provision is, to say the least, questionable.

The *Reporter's Notes* provide the following justification for the consolidation provisions that appear in the UAA (2000):

> As in the judicial forum, consolidation effectuates efficiency in conflict resolution and avoidance of conflicting results. By agreeing to include an arbitration clause, parties have indicated that they wish their disputes to be resolve in such a manner. In many cases, moreover, a court may be the only practical forum within which to effect consolidation. . . . Furthermore, it is likely that in many cases one or more parties, often non-drafting parties, will not have considered the impact of the arbitration clause on multiparty disputes. By establishing a default provision which permits consolidation (subject to various limitations) in the absence of a specific contractual provision, Section 10 encourages drafters to address the issue expressly and enhances the possibility that all parties will be on notice regarding the issue.

6. There is no doubt that consolidation is a highly practical device that can remedy the deficiencies of duplicative litigation. That benefit, however, does not respond to the critical concern and necessary doctrinal limit that contracting parties *agree* to when they agree to arbitrate their disputes. Arbitration agreements do not ordinarily come with jurisdictional presumptions of expansive application that allows them to be stretched beyond their stated scope of application. Courts may be the best vehicles for achieving the benefits of consolidation, but arbitration should and must remain, according to a now classical expression, a "matter of consent . . . not coercion." *See Volt Info. Sciences, Inc. v. Board of Trustees of Leland Stanford Junior Univ.*, 489 U.S. 468 (1989). Further, the Reporter's commentary seems to be saying that, by establishing an overly aggressive statutory rule on consolidation, parties will have a stronger incentive to address the matter of consolidation themselves in their agreement to avoid the rule's application. This rationalization for the rule and its content is unlikely to persuade anyone.

Finally, the UAA (2000) should adopt a position on consolidation that "embodies the fundamental principle of judicial respect for the preservation and enforcement of the terms of agreements to arbitrate." ". . . [T]he legitimate expectations of contracting parties [should] limit the ability of courts to consolidate proceedings."

SECTION 12. DISCLOSURE BY ARBITRATOR.

(a) Before accepting appointment, an individual who is requested to serve as an arbitrator, after making a reasonable inquiry, shall disclose to all parties to the agreement to arbitrate and arbitration proceeding and to any other arbitrators any known facts that a reasonable person would consider likely to affect the impartiality of the arbitrator in the arbitration proceeding, including:

> (1) a financial or personal interest in the outcome of the arbitration proceeding; and
>
> (2) an existing or past relationship with any of the parties to the agreement to arbitrate or the arbitration proceeding, their counsel or representatives, a witness, or another arbitrator.

(b) An arbitrator has a continuing obligation to disclose to all parties to the agreement to arbitrate and arbitration proceeding and to any other arbitrators any facts that the arbitrator learns after accepting appointment which a reasonable person would consider likely to affect the impartiality of the arbitrator.

(c) If an arbitrator discloses a fact required by subsection (a) or (b) to be disclosed and a party timely objects to the appointment or continued service of the arbitrator based upon the fact disclosed, the objection may be a ground under Section 23(a)(2) for vacating an award made by the arbitrator.

(d) If the arbitrator did not disclose a fact as required by subsection (a) or (b), upon timely objection by a party, the court under Section 23(a)(2) may vacate an award.

(e) An arbitrator appointed as a neutral arbitrator who does not disclose a known, direct, and material interest in the outcome of the arbitration proceeding or a known, existing, and substantial relationship with a party is presumed to act with evident partiality under Section 23(a)(2).

(f) If the parties to an arbitration proceeding agree to the procedures of an arbitration organization or any other procedures for challenges to arbitrators before an award is made, substantial compliance with those procedures is a condition precedent to a [motion] to vacate an award on that ground under Section 23(a)(2).

NOTES AND QUESTIONS

1. Section 12 establishes rules on a matter that has become of critical practical significance in the U.S. law of arbitration—"[d]isclosure[s] [b]y [a]rbitrator[s]." By and large, the provision is more limpid than the rules stated

in the foregoing Sections. Moreover, the proposed rules are relatively standard and uncontroversial. At the outset, in Section 12(a), the drafters establish a basic duty of disclosure (which is central to arbitrator impartiality and the enforceability of awards). Prospective arbitrators have a duty to disclose to the arbitrating parties, the administering arbitral institutions, and to the other arbitrators personal, professional, financial, or other information that might compromise their ability to decide disputes in an impartial fashion.

2. The duty has several elements: It applies before the arbitrator accepts the appointment as an arbitrator, requires the prospective arbitrator to engage in "a reasonable inquiry," and involves a disclosure to the arbitrating parties and other arbitrators. The disclosures consist of "any known facts" that a "reasonable person" might think could affect an individual's ability to assess the submitted matters impartially. Under the rule, prospective arbitrators then must disclose two basic types of information: An interest ("financial or personal") in the outcome of the matter, and relationships ("existing or past") with any individual involved in the arbitration ("parties to the agreement to arbitrate or the arbitration proceeding, their counsel or representative, witnesses, or other arbitrators"). According to Section 12(b), the obligation to disclose facts material to impartiality continues after the initial appointment (presumably, throughout the proceeding). The same elements are used to define the scope of the duty.

3. How would you advise prospective arbitrators about what constitutes "a reasonable inquiry"? What is meant by a "known fact[ ]"? Is there a proximate cause dilemma to determining what facts or circumstances might affect impartiality? What does the "reasonable person" standard mean in this context? Is it likely that a rule of disclosure will result inevitably in overdisclosure? Should the rule be the same for neutral and party-designated arbitrators?

4. The rule of disclosure does not seem to arise from a situation of actual abuse, but rather it appears to be intended to be a preventive measure. It can create administrative burdens and delay the recourse to arbitration. It also may generate challenges to awards if disclosure standards are overly rigorous or ill-defined.

If the goal was to strengthen the integrity of arbitration, there were more practical and effective methods to guarantee the professionalism and disinterest of the arbitrators. Institutional rules, for example, could require that party arbitrators be chosen from a pool of neutrals established by the institutions. Institutional administrators could set arbitrator compensation and conduct their own examination of arbitrators on their lists. Also, all tribunals could consist of a sole arbitrator appointed by the institutional administrator or a court. If the real issue is that parties cannot be trusted to appoint objective arbitrators, the function of appointment should be shifted to another actor within the process.

It should be noted that the tradition of partisan arbitrators has not undermined or compromised other forms of arbitration. Labor arbitrators generally are perceived as favoring the union member-worker over management; this circumstance explains the high frequency of awards that apply reinstatement remedies. In addition, maritime arbitrators are appointed on the basis of whether they favor the interests of the ship owner, the party leasing the vessel, the owner of the cargo that was transported, or the insurers who are implicated in the property loss. These forms of arbitration continue to be dominant despite the usage of partisan arbitrators.

If you were asked to advise a would-be czar of adjudication, how would you assess the development of the regime of arbitrator disclosure? Is it necessary or in the best interest of arbitration?

5. Despite its positive attributes, Section 12 could be improved in a number of respects. In places, it suffers from the drawbacks that plague the entire statute. Word choice generally is poor; the syntax is sometimes awkward to the point of confusion; and the statement of the rule can itself become an obstacle to communicating the meaning of the intended regulation. Section 12 could be rewritten to read:

> Arbitrator Impartiality—The Duty of Disclosure and the Disqualification of Arbitrators
>
> The Arbitrator's Duty to be Impartial and to Disclose Information Pertaining to Impartiality. All arbitrators must be impartial. Prospective arbitrators must disclose to the arbitrating parties and to the other arbitrators information that affects or might affect their ability to rule in an impartial fashion.
>
> Prior to accepting their appointment, arbitrators must take stock of their business, financial, and personal interests and review their past and existing social and business associations and relationships. They must then disclose facts that might be likely to affect their ability to be impartial or which might create an appearance of partiality if the circumstances were not disclosed. The information should be communicated to the administering institution which will convey it to the parties and the arbitral tribunal. In fulfilling this obligation, prospective arbitrators must exercise due diligence and the professional care that is incumbent upon individuals who exercise arbitral functions and participate in the arbitral process. Finally, arbitrators are held to the duty to investigate and to disclose throughout the arbitral proceeding.
>
> Based upon the investigation and disclosure, arbitrators can withdraw or reject the offer of appointment or can disqualify or recuse themselves. Moreover, a nominating party can refuse to finalize an appointment or can revoke its appointment of an arbitrator at the outset of the proceeding. An objection to the continued service of an arbitrator at a later stage of the proceeding shall be submitted to the arbitral tribunal. The tribunal shall decide whether the objection has

been made in good faith and whether removal of the challenged arbitrator is warranted.

In the event that an arbitrator is disqualified and removed by the tribunal, that arbitrator is entitled to reasonable compensation for services rendered, provided such services were of reasonable professional quality. The arbitral tribunal shall determine the amount of any compensation that is owed and shall direct the parties to provide funds for such compensation. Moreover, the tribunal shall—in consultation with the administering agency—provide for the appointment of a replacement arbitrator. Replacement arbitrators shall be appointed in the same basic manner as the original arbitrators and shall have the same authority as the original arbitrators. The parties, however, can agree to proceed with a truncated tribunal.

Neutral arbitrators are held to a very high standard of impartiality. As a consequence, they must satisfy the duty of investigation and disclosure with utmost care. Even minor failures in this regard can result in the neutral arbitrator's removal. Removal of a neutral arbitrator must be done through the joint action of the remaining members of the arbitral tribunal and the administering institution. It may also involve a court action.

In the event that the tribunal concludes that the challenge to an arbitrator was motivated by bad faith and/or by an intent to delay or sabotage the arbitration, it may impose sanctions upon the party who acted in bad faith.

When an arbitrator fails to disclose information that is reasonably available and that information has a clear bearing upon the question of arbitrator impartiality, the tribunal can presume that the arbitrator is partial and, as a result, can disqualify the arbitrator.

Evident partiality discovered and established after the award is rendered can result in the vacatur or nonenforcement of the award.

If the parties so provide, these provisions can be supplemented or replaced by institutional or other rules pertaining to arbitrator disqualification.

Compare the suggested provision with its promulgated counterpart in the statute. What are the principal differences? Do the suggested emendations constitute an improvement? Do they make matters worse? Why? When should the failure to disclose or inadequate disclosure lead to the vacatur of the award? Are there less draconian remedies, like remand or the reformation of the submission? Should all disclosure issues be settled at the head of the process?

6. The *Reporter's Notes* add the following explanations for the statutory language and content of Section 12:

[. . .]

The problem of arbitrator partiality is a difficult one because consensual arbitration involves a tension between abstract concepts of impartial justice and the notion that parties are entitled to a decision-maker of their own choosing, including an expert with the biases and prejudices inherent in particular worldly experience. Arbitrating parties frequently choose arbitrators on the basis of prior professional or business associations, or pertinent commercial expertise. . . . The competing goals of party choice, desired expertise and impartiality must be balanced by giving parties "access to all information which might reasonably affect the arbitrator's partiality." . . . Other factors favoring early resolution of the partiality issues by informed parties are legal and practical limitations on post-award judicial policing of such matters.

[. . .]

A greater number of other courts, mindful of the tradeoff between impartiality and expertise inherent in arbitration, have placed a higher burden on those seeking to vacate awards on grounds of arbitrator interests or relationships. . . .

2. In view of the critical importance of arbitrator disclosure to party choice and perceptions of fairness and the need for more consistent standards to ensure expectations in this vital area, the Drafting Committee determined that the RUAA should set forth affirmative requirements to assure that parties should have access to all information that might reasonably affect the potential arbitrator's neutrality. . . .

The Drafting Committee decided to delete the requirement of disclosing "any" financial or personal interest in the outcome or "any" existing or past relationship and substituted the terms "a" financial or personal interest in the outcome or "an" existing or past relationship. The intent was not to include de minimis interests or relationships. For example, if an arbitrator owned a mutual fund which as part of a large portfolio of investments held some shares of stock in a corporation involved as a party in an arbitration, it might not be reasonable to expect the arbitrator to know of such investment and in any event the investment might be of such an insubstantial nature so as not to reasonably affect the impartiality of the arbitrator.

3. The fundamental standard of Section 12(a) is an objective one: disclosure is required of facts which a reasonable person would consider likely to affect the arbitrator's impartiality in the arbitration proceeding. . . . The Drafting Committee adopted the "reasonable person" test with the intent of making clear that the subjective views of the arbitrator or the parties are not controlling. However, parties may agree to higher or lower standards for disclosure under Section

> 4(b)(3) so long as they do not "unreasonably restrict" the right to disclosure and also may establish mechanisms for disqualification. . . .
>
> Section 12(a) requires an arbitrator to make a "reasonable inquiry" prior to accepting an appointment as to any potential conflict of interests. The extent of this inquiry may depend upon the circumstances of the situation and the custom in a particular industry. For instance, an attorney in a law firm may be required to check with other attorneys in the firm to determine if acceptance of an appointment as an arbitrator would result in a conflict of interest on the part of that attorney because of representation by an attorney in the same law firm of one of the parties in another matter.
>
> Once an arbitrator has made a "reasonable inquiry" as required by Section 12(a), the arbitrator will be required to disclose only "known facts" that might affect impartiality. The term "knowledge" (which is intended to include "known") is defined in Section 1(5) to mean "actual knowledge."
>
> [. . .]
>
> 5. Special problems are presented by tripartite panels involving "party-arbitrators"—that is, in situations such as where each of the arbitrating parties selects an arbitrator and a third, neutral arbitrator is jointly selected by the party-arbitrators. . . . In some such cases, it may be agreed that the party-arbitrators are not regarded as "neutral" arbitrators, but are deemed to be predisposed toward the party which appointed them. . . . However, in other situations even the party arbitrators may have a duty of neutrality on some or all issues. The integrity of the process demands that party-arbitrators, like other arbitrators, disclose pertinent interests and relationships to all parties as well as other members of the arbitration panel. It is particularly important for the neutral arbitrator to know the interest of the party arbitrator, for example, if the party arbitrator is being paid on a contingent-fee basis. Thus, Section 12(a) and (b) apply to party arbitrators but under a "reasonable person" standard for someone in the position of a party and not a neutral arbitrator.
>
> [. . .]

Do these remarks lessen the possible apprehensions about the rule of disclosure? Do they convince you that disclosures are necessary and beneficial to arbitration? After reading these remarks, can you better advise prospective arbitrators?

SECTION 14. IMMUNITY OF ARBITRATOR; COMPETENCY TO TESTIFY; ATTORNEY'S FEES AND COSTS.

(a) An arbitrator or an arbitration organization acting in that capacity is immune from civil liability to the same extent as a judge of a court of this State acting in a judicial capacity.

(b) The immunity afforded by this section supplements any immunity under other law.

(c) The failure of an arbitrator to make a disclosure required by Section 12 does not cause any loss of immunity under this section.

(d) In a judicial, administrative, or similar proceeding, an arbitrator or representative of an arbitration organization is not competent to testify, and may not be required to produce records as to any statement, conduct, decision, or ruling occurring during the arbitration proceeding, to the same extent as a judge of a court of this State acting in a judicial capacity. This subsection does not apply:

(1) to the extent necessary to determine the claim of an arbitrator, arbitration organization, or representative of the arbitration organization against a party to the arbitration proceeding; or

(2) to a hearing on a [motion] to vacate an award under Section 23(a)(1) or (2) if the [movant] establishes prima facie that a ground for vacating the award exists.

(e) If a person commences a civil action against an arbitrator, arbitration organization, or representative of an arbitration organization arising from the services of the arbitrator, organization, or representative or if a person seeks to compel an arbitrator or a representative of an arbitration organization to testify or produce records in violation of subsection (d), and the court decides that the arbitrator, arbitration organization, or representative of an arbitration organization is immune from civil liability or that the arbitrator or representative of the organization is not competent to testify, the court shall award to the arbitrator, organization, or representative reasonable attorney's fees and other reasonable expenses of litigation.

NOTES AND QUESTIONS

1. Section 14 has fewer problems than other statutory sections, but its overall quality remains mixed. Both its content and presentation could be substantially improved. As a preliminary matter, it seems peculiar to group the topics of arbitrator immunity, arbitral confidentiality, and attorney's fees together. They are not generally associated with one another. Moreover, each topic appears to receive abbreviated consideration. Because of their importance

in arbitral practice, these topics should command a larger presence in the framework of the uniform law.

2. As to specific features, Section 14(a) establishes that arbitral immunity is equivalent to the immunity enjoyed by state judges when they act in their judicial capacity. Why is this a sound rule? What does it say about arbitration and the arbitral process from a regulatory perspective? Is there a downside to the statement? Do all states provide judges with full or nearly full immunity? What consequences might flow upon arbitration law if they do not? Could limited or perfunctory immunity generate "back door" federalism issues? How?

The immunity extends to "[a]n arbitrator or an arbitration organization." Expanding the reach of the immunity to cover arbitral institutions at least raises an issue of policy. The proposed rule reflects the current practice of the institutions themselves. Whether a self-proclaimed exemption from professional malpractice laws should be integrated into the uniform law remains a matter of debate. The wholesale incorporation of a nearly absolute institutional privilege appears to be unwise on its face—although there are powerful arguments for its inclusion. The drafters, therefore, could have created a separate and more limited form of immunity for arbitral institutions that would have nonetheless provided protection from disappointed parties who were intent upon subverting the process. What type of limited immunity might have been adopted? Is limited immunity workable? Can the administration of arbitrations survive without immunity?

3. A few linguistic details in Section 14(a), (b), and (c) call for additional comment. The phrase "arbitration organization" is used instead of the more usual "arbitral institution." No explanation is provided for the change in word usage, although Section 1 of the Act defines the new phrase. That definition, however, is not very helpful. It is too generalized to provide any real clarification. An illustration of what constitutes an "[a]rbitration organization" might have made the new term more understandable. Moreover, the phrase "[a]n arbitrator or an arbitration organization acting in such capacity" is not only awkward, but it is also ungrammatical. "Capacity" cannot be equated with the prior objects—"arbitrator" and "arbitration organization." It would have been correct and stylistically acceptable to state: "arbitrators or arbitral institutions acting in their [arbitral] capacity." Rigorous use of language is hardly inapposite in a statutory context.

4. Section 14(d)(1) and (2) appear to establish a rule of confidentiality for arbitral proceedings. They create a privilege that shields both arbitrators and agents of the administering arbitral institution from orders that they testify or produce documents regarding the arbitration. The privilege applies to orders emanating from either judicial or administrative or even other types of tribunals. It is the same privilege enjoyed by state court judges in the exercise of their official capacities. The privilege does not apply when the tribunal is adjudicating a claim between an arbitrator, the supervising arbitral institution, or an agent of the institution *and* one of the arbitrating parties or

in circumstances in which the award is being challenged and a serious basis for vacatur exists.

Although the first exception above is stated in language that is broad and imprecise, it appears reasonable to conclude that it relates to circumstances in which an arbitrating party allegedly owes money to an arbitrator or to the administering arbitral institution. The collection of a debt requires proof of its existence and of the party's failure to pay. The privilege of confidentiality yields to evidentiary needs here in part because the delinquent party should not be protected from accountability. The exception, however, does not gauge its impact upon the autonomy of the arbitral process. To some extent, it also invites dilatory tactics by allowing a party to undermine the confidentiality of the process by withholding payment of its share of the costs and fees. In addition, it is not clear from current practice that the nonpayment of arbitral fees and costs constitute a problem sufficient to justify an exception to the rule of confidentiality. The institutional practice of requiring deposits at the beginning and replenishing them throughout the arbitration appears to have been effective (up-to-now) in dealing with such issues.

5. Eliminating confidentiality for purposes of vacatur is part of standard practice. In fact, once a challenge to an award has been lodged and goes to decision, there is little that is not eventually known about the arbitration, the arbitral proceedings, and the arbitral award. Requiring the challenging party to establish a *prima facie* basis for vacatur effectively reduces the prospect that the arbitration will be rehearsed in public for purposes of enforcement. What constitutes a *prima facie* ground and how it should be established are unresolved questions. The underlying objective, however, is clear—to require the party seeking vacatur to have a serious reason for challenging the award. Otherwise, the rule of confidentiality remains intact and fully functional. When confidentiality is operative, it becomes nearly impossible to constitute a record of the arbitration. As a consequence, the vacatur action—in all probability—will fail.

6. Arbitral confidentiality, expressed as "competency to testify," touches upon a number of vital issues of arbitration law. Section 14 of the uniform law takes an enlightened position on these matters. In contrast to the recommendation made in Section 14(d)(2), it has been standard practice to allow parties to challenge the confirmation of the award upon any of the stated statutory grounds. In effect, the exercise of that right meant that whatever transpired in the arbitration and led to the award would be divulged in order to allow the court to evaluate the challenger's petition. The party's right to lodge an action to vacate an award, in effect, gave the court the authority to review *de novo* the arbitral award and process. The exercise of such review authority obviously breached arbitral autonomy and contradicted the judicial policy in favor of arbitration. Through the device of confidentiality, the drafters of the uniform law created an ingenious means by which to circumvent the standard vacatur practice and to enhance the autonomy and functionality of arbitration.

Moreover, through Section 14(d), arbitration gains the type of confidentiality protection that generally had been available only for mediation (given the perceived need for unreserved party participation in that process). A guarantee of confidentiality, extended to include arbitral institutional actors, adds to the attractiveness of arbitration as a dispute resolution process. Under current practice, courts have assumed a highly interventionist posture in such matters. Arbitral actors and proceedings are fully vulnerable to external demands for information. The privilege that has been created proposes to remedy this feature of judicial practice.

7. Section 14(3) reinforces the underlying policy (announced in various places in Section 14) of limiting judicial recourse in regard to arbitration. It provides for the award of penalties against parties who unsuccessfully challenge the immunity or testimonial privilege of an arbitrator, an arbitral institution, or the institution's agents. The cause of action must involve and advance an issue already determined by the statute, namely, that the arbitrator is immune from adjudicatory malpractice liability and incompetent to testify. When the claim can be resolved simply by reference to the statute, the court must award the other party attorney's fees and other costs. It is curious that the drafters did not use the adjective "frivolous" or the phrase "the failure to state a cause of action" to describe the circumstances that were contemplated by the statutory provision. Instead, they chose to use a cumbersome restating technique that renders the provision awkward to read and difficult to understand. The restating technique, however, makes the provision very precise. The precision that the drafters attempted to integrate into the uniform law, however, sometimes seems more characteristic of and more appropriate for a contract document or an instructional manual than a statute.

8. Finally, the reference to attorney's fees in the title of the section is misleading (at least, initially). The topic of the attribution of attorney's fees is a relatively unsettled question in U.S. arbitration law. It should not appear in the title of a section unless that section contains controlling rules on the matter. The topic of attorney's fees is addressed in Section 21(b), the title of which, ironically, does not reveal that it addresses that issue.

9. The *Reporter's Notes* add the following explanations for the statutory language and content in Section 14:

[. . .]

> Arbitral immunity has its origins in common law judicial immunity and in most jurisdictions tracks it directly. The key to this identity is the "functional comparability" of the role of arbitrators and judges. . . .
>
> In addition to the grant of immunity from a civil action, arbitrators are also generally accorded immunity from process when subpoenaed or summoned to testify in a judicial proceeding in a case arising from

their service as arbitrator. . . . This full immunity from any civil proceedings is what is intended by the language in Section 14(a).

2. Section 14(a) also provides to an entity acting as an arbitration organization the same immunity as is provided to an individual acting as an arbitrator. Extension of judicial immunity to those arbitration organizations is appropriate to the extent that they are acting "in certain roles and with certain responsibilities" that are functionally comparable to those of a judge. . . . This immunity to neutral arbitration organizations is because the duties that they perform in administering the arbitration process are the functional equivalent of the comparable role and responsibility of judges in administering the adjudication process in a court of law. There is substantial precedent for this conclusion. . . .

Also the provision draws no distinction between neutral arbitrators and advocate arbitrators. Both types of arbitrators are covered by this provision.

10. A possible rewriting of Section 14 might read as follows:

Section 14. Arbitrator Immunity.

Arbitrators are immune from any form of civil liability in the performance of their adjudicatory functions as arbitrators. Arbitrator immunity is like the civil immunity enjoyed by state court judges when the latter act in their official capacity, except that arbitrator immunity is generally unqualified.

Arbitrators do not cease to be immune because they failed to disclose information under Section 12, they have been disqualified or removed, or the award they rendered was not enforceable.

A person who disregards the civil immunity of an arbitrator and files a civil action for damages, alleging that the arbitrator failed to properly exercise his/her functions as an arbitrator, is subject to paying the arbitrator's attorney's fees and costs for the litigation, if the court rules that the arbitrator is immune from suit under the applicable statute.

Arbitral institutions who administer arbitrations enjoy a more limited qualified immunity. These institutions are immune from civil liability in the performance of their functions, provided the breach of their professional duty does not reach a level of gross negligence, wanton disregard, or recklessness.

Section [14–1]. Confidentiality of the Proceedings.

Parties engage in arbitration with a view to resolving their disputes privately. In order to maintain the confidentiality of arbitration, arbitrators and agents of arbitral institutions cannot be compelled to testify about or produce documents concerning the arbitration by a court of law or an administrative or other tribunal. Moreover, information that such parties may voluntarily communicate is not admissible in such proceedings.

Post-award disclosures of otherwise confidential information regarding the arbitration can result in the assessment of civil liability against an arbitrator or an arbitral institution. Arbitral immunity is not applicable in these circumstances. Such disclosures also constitute a breach of the ethical standards that apply to arbitrators and arbitral institutions. Other participants in the arbitration are encouraged to maintain the confidentiality of the proceedings. Wherever possible, contracts or arbitral rulings should provide for the assessment of penalties for the violation of arbitral confidentiality by these other parties.

The rule of arbitral confidentiality does not apply to actions for the payment of fees and other costs brought by an arbitrator or an arbitral institution against a party to the arbitral proceedings. In an action for the vacatur of an award, a record of the arbitral proceedings can only be constituted if the party opposing the award establishes *prima facie* a serious basis for possible vacatur. Otherwise, the rule of confidentiality applies to any information pertaining to the arbitration.

Attempts to undermine the rule of confidentiality by bringing actions that violate its requirements shall result in the award of attorney's fees and court costs.

Section [14–2]. Arbitrating Party Immunity.

Parties who participate in an arbitration are entitled to the same immunity from civil liability that litigating parties enjoy in a court proceeding that takes place under state law. This immunity, whether absolute or qualified, does not exempt them from the obligation to arbitrate in good faith or the sanctions that could be imposed by the arbitrators for the breach of that duty. At all times during the arbitration, unless the parties' agreement provides otherwise, the parties are subject to the authority of the arbitral tribunal. Moreover, the parties remain responsible for the payment of arbitral fees and costs.

Section [14–3]. Extraordinary Sanctions.

Whenever party conduct undermines arbitrator immunity or arbitral confidentiality and the party's conduct is particularly egregious and threatens the functionality of the arbitral process, a court can award punitive damages in addition to attorney's fees and costs to discourage such behavior.

Section [14–2] and [14–3] add new elements to the content of Section 14 that were not included by the drafting committee. The provision of immunity to arbitrators and arbitral institutions logically raises the question of whether an immunity privilege should be extended to the arbitrating parties. Immunity would apply to arbitrating party conduct during the arbitral proceedings, in particular as to the advocacy undertaken by the parties. The proposed rule acknowledges that a duty to arbitrate in good faith exists and applies to the parties and to the proceedings. The protection of the right to advocate would not necessarily conflict with that duty. Also, allowing for party advocacy (as established, defined, and regulated by state law) would not exempt the arbitrating parties from the authority of the arbitral tribunal or financial liability for arbitral fees and costs.

Proposed Section [14–3] is basically self-explanatory. It provides additional support for the rules of immunity and confidentiality by increasing possible sanctions for violations. Despite the controversial character of punitive damages in domestic law, their availability could reinforce the functional operation of the arbitral process. If flagrant violations of express rules are not discouraged, they are likely to become standard practice. The resolution of such matters could be left to the discretion of a reconstituted arbitral tribunal, but the procedural difficulty and delay of so doing argues strongly for court disposition of these issues. Judicial action undertaken to sustain the arbitral process as established by the parties should not be seen as interference.

SECTION 15. ARBITRATION PROCESS.

(a) An arbitrator may conduct an arbitration in such manner as the arbitrator considers appropriate for a fair and expeditious disposition of the proceeding. The authority conferred upon the arbitrator includes the power to hold conferences with the parties to the arbitration proceeding before the hearing and, among other matters, determine the admissibility, relevance, materiality and weight of any evidence.

(b) An arbitrator may decide a request for summary disposition of a claim or particular issue:

(1) if all interested parties agree; or

(2) upon request of one party to the arbitration proceeding if that party gives notice to all other parties to the proceeding, and the other parties have a reasonable opportunity to respond.

(c) If an arbitrator orders a hearing, the arbitrator shall set a time and place and give notice of the hearing not less than five days before the hearing begins. Unless a party to the arbitration proceeding makes an objection to lack or insufficiency of notice not later than the beginning of the hearing, the party's appearance at the hearing waives the objection. Upon request of a party to the arbitration proceeding and for good cause shown, or upon the arbitrator's own initiative, the arbitrator may adjourn the hearing from time to time as necessary but may not postpone the hearing to a time later than that fixed by the agreement to arbitrate for making the award unless the parties to the arbitration proceeding consent to a later date. The arbitrator may hear and decide the controversy upon the evidence produced although a party who was duly notified of the arbitration proceeding did not appear. The court, on request, may direct the arbitrator to conduct the hearing promptly and render a timely decision.

(d) At a hearing under subsection (c), a party to the arbitration proceeding has a right to be heard, to present evidence material to the controversy, and to cross-examine witnesses appearing at the hearing.

(e) If an arbitrator ceases or is unable to act during the arbitration proceeding, a replacement arbitrator must be appointed in accordance with Section 11 to continue the proceeding and to resolve the controversy.

NOTES AND QUESTIONS

1. Section 15 deals with the "[a]rbitration [p]rocess." This heading is not altogether accurate because the provision, overall, addresses the arbitrator's authority to conduct the arbitral proceeding. The phrase "arbitration process" connotes something larger than the proceedings themselves. A more accurate title, therefore, could have been used.

2. The content of Section 15 is characteristic of the compositional approach used throughout the new uniform law: In essence, the content of the section articulates rules in arcane legalese, and thereby generates propositions that are awkward to the point of being incomprehensible. The most striking feature of Section 15 is its conceptual disarray; there is no discernible organizational order to the elaboration or positioning of the various rules. The content of these rules also lacks cohesion and balance—minor matters are linked to broader policy concerns for no discernible reason or objective. Propositions refer indiscriminately to fundamental procedural concerns and the incidents that flow from the micro-management of the arbitral process. This approach and its consequences are simply not commensurate with the goal of drafting a model statute—one that will seriously affect law practice and the protection of rights for some time to come. Do you agree with this assessment? Is it a fair [and balanced] evaluation? Do you think the new uniform is helpful to the practice of law in the area of arbitration? Is the RUAA a statute or a "how to" manual? Which framework is more workable in practice: The RUAA or the FAA?

3. The *Reporter's Notes* provide a number of clarifications to the content of Section 15. Compared to the actual statutory text, these notes represent a much clearer expression of the objective that underlies the statutory language and of the law it is meant to articulate:

> 1. Section 15 is a default provision and under Section 4(a) is subject to the agreement of the parties. Section 15(a) is intended to give an arbitrator wide latitude in conducting an arbitration subject to the parties' agreement and to determine what evidence should be considered. It should be noted that the rules of evidence are inapplicable in an arbitration proceeding except that an arbitrator's

refusal to consider evidence material to the controversy which substantially prejudices the rights of a party are grounds for vacatur under Section 23(a)(3). . . .

2. As the use of arbitration increases, there are more cases that involve complex issues. In such cases arbitrators are often involved in numerous pre-hearing matters involving conferences, motions, subpoenas, and other preliminary issues. Although the present UAA makes no specific provision for arbitrators to hold pre-hearing conferences or to rule on preliminary matters, arbitrators likely have the inherent authority to do such. Numerous cases have concluded that in arbitration proceedings, procedural matters are within the province of the arbitrators. . . .

Additionally, many arbitration organizations whose rules may govern particular arbitration proceedings provide for pre-hearing conferences and the ruling on preliminary matters by arbitrators. . . .

Section 15(a) is intended to allow arbitrators broad powers to manage the arbitration process both before and during the hearing. This section makes the authority of arbitrators to hold prehearing conferences explicit and is meant to provide arbitrators with the authority in appropriate cases to require parties to clarify issues, stipulate matters, identify witnesses, provide summaries of testimony, to allow discovery, and to resolve preliminary matters. However, it is also the intent of Section 15(a) not to encourage either extensive discovery or a form of motion practice. While such methods as discovery or prehearing conferences may be appropriate in some cases, these should only be used where they 'aid in the fair and expeditious disposition of the arbitration proceeding.' The arbitrator should keep in mind the goals of an expeditious, less costly, and efficient procedure. . . .

[. . .]

Section 15(b) is intended to allow arbitrators to decide a request for summary disposition but only after a party requesting summary disposition gives appropriate notice and opposing parties have a reasonable opportunity to respond. . . .

4. Despite the Committee's intent and the Reporter's clarifications, problems remain. The proposed language tracks, to some degree, the major subject-matter themes of Section 15, but it also departs from the content of the section in a number of significant respects. First, in Section 15(a), the drafters underscore the arbitrator's power to order pre-hearing conferences. In fact, under Section 15(a), the arbitrator's procedural powers are three-fold: (1) to conduct "fair and expeditious" hearings; (2) to hold pre-hearing conferences with the parties; and (3) to rule on evidentiary matters (those matters pertaining to the "admissibility, relevance, materiality, and weight" of the evidence). The order and organization of the provision again is chaotic and

makes it difficult to isolate and understand its basic focus. Section 15(c) is an excellent illustration of how to micro-manage the arbitration process through a variety of unrelated statements that, it seems, are simply grouped together by happenstance. The final statement in Section 15(c) appears to "come out of the blue" and to invite court interference with the arbitral process. The lack of context and cohesion in the provision, in effect, makes it difficult to assess the import of the various statements.

5. Section 15(c), (d), and (e) are generally acceptable rules of arbitral regulation; it is, however, difficult to place them logically under the rubric "Arbitration Process." They appear to relate to different facets of the proceedings or procedure. For example, the appointment of a replacement arbitrator in Section 15(e) could be integrated with a section on arbitrator appointment or could stand on its own. There also are interpretative problems that accompany the looseness of the organization. In Section 15(d), reference is made to the essential components of the arbitral trial triggered by the arbitrator under Section 15(c). It is difficult to understand why this section was not presented as a centerpiece provision on arbitral due process. Instead, it is buried inside an already disorganized section and conveys the impression that it is the standard that applies exclusively to would-be evidentiary hearings. Finally, Section 15(e) provides for adjudication by majority rule in arbitrations governed by the statute. The rule propounded reflects standard practice, but—once again—it does not directly implicate the management of the arbitral proceedings. Rather, it establishes the predicate for legitimate decision-making in arbitration.

6. A rewritten Section 15 might read as follows:

Section 15. Arbitrator Authority to Conduct the Proceedings.

> The arbitral tribunal must conduct the arbitral proceedings in a fair and expeditious manner. In particular, the tribunal must provide the parties with an opportunity to be heard and to respond to the allegations made by the other side.
>
> As to matters of procedure, unless the parties' agreement or the applicable institutional rule provide otherwise, the tribunal has the authority to establish the time and place of the hearings. In exercising this authority, the tribunal must give reasonable notice to the parties. Adjournments of the proceedings are at the tribunal's discretion, but must be granted when requested by a party and good cause is shown. Moreover, the tribunal may order pre-hearing conferences to decide evidentiary matters. The tribunal can also engage in the summary disposition of issues if all of the parties so request or if one party makes such a request with reasonable notice to the other parties.
>
> In granting adjournments, the tribunal must remain mindful of any time-limits that have been established in regard to the arbitration. All arbitrators must be present at the proceedings. The tribunal,

however, may rule on the basis on the evidence presented even when parties—who have been duly-notified—fail to appear and to present their case. Objections to the arbitrators' determination of procedural matters must be made in a timely fashion. Entering an appearance or participating in the proceedings without indicating an opposition to the determination can constitute a waiver of the right to make an objection.

[. . .]

SECTION 17. WITNESSES; SUBPOENAS; DEPOSITIONS; DISCOVERY.

(a) An arbitrator may issue a subpoena for the attendance of a witness and for the production of records and other evidence at any hearing and may administer oaths. A subpoena must be served in the manner for service of subpoenas in a civil action and, upon [motion] to the court by a party to the arbitration proceeding or the arbitrator, enforced in the manner for enforcement of subpoenas in a civil action.

(b) In order to make the proceedings fair, expeditious, and cost effective, upon request of a party to or a witness in an arbitration proceeding, an arbitrator may permit a deposition of any witness to be taken for use as evidence at the hearing, including a witness who cannot be subpoenaed for or is unable to attend a hearing. The arbitrator shall determine the conditions under which the deposition is taken.

(c) An arbitrator may permit such discovery as the arbitrator decides is appropriate in the circumstances, taking into account the needs of the parties to the arbitration proceeding and other affected persons and the desirability of making the proceeding fair, expeditious, and cost effective.

(d) If an arbitrator permits discovery under subsection (c), the arbitrator may order a party to the arbitration proceeding to comply with the arbitrator's discovery-related orders, issue subpoenas for the attendance of a witness and for the production of records and other evidence at a discovery proceeding, and take action against a noncomplying party to the extent a court could if the controversy were the subject of a civil action in this State.

(e) An arbitrator may issue a protective order to prevent the disclosure of privileged information, confidential information, trade secrets, and other information protected from disclosure to the extent a court could if the controversy were the subject of a civil action in this State.

(f) All laws compelling a person under subpoena to testify and all fees for attending a judicial proceeding, a deposition, or a discovery proceeding as a witness apply to an arbitration proceeding as if the controversy were the subject of a civil action in this State.

(g) The court may enforce a subpoena or discovery-related order for the attendance of a witness within this State and for the production of records and other evidence issued by an arbitrator in connection with an arbitration proceeding in another State upon conditions determined by the court so as to make the arbitration proceeding fair, expeditious, and cost effective. A subpoena or discovery-related order issued by an arbitrator in another State must be served in the manner provided by law for service of subpoenas in a civil action in this State and, upon [motion] to the court by a party to the arbitration proceeding or the arbitrator, enforced in the manner provided by law for enforcement of subpoenas in a civil action in this State.

NOTES AND QUESTIONS

1. The *Reporter's Notes* provide the following clarifications on Section 16:

> 1. The Drafting Committee considered but rejected a proposal to add "or any other person" after "an attorney." A concern was expressed about incompetent and unscrupulous individuals, especially in securities arbitration, who hold themselves out as advocates.
>
> 2. This section is not intended to preclude, where authorized by law, representation in an arbitration proceeding by individuals who are not licensed to practice law either generally or in the jurisdiction in which the arbitration is held.

2. The content of Section 17 corresponds to its title. The drafting improvement, however, does not progress much further. The "rag-tag" order and the lack of composition that prevail elsewhere in the uniform law quickly take over the content of this section. Given their subject-matter interrelationship, Section 17 could easily have been merged with Section 15. The sections, in effect, both deal with the arbitrator's power to conduct arbitral proceedings. Indeed, the rationale for having two separate sections of the uniform law address the same subject-matter is far from clear.

3. Section 17(a), (d), (f), and (g) address, in relevant part, the arbitrator's power to issue subpoenas for purposes of evidence-gathering in the form either of documents or the testimony of witnesses. It is not clear, except by implication, that the arbitrator's authority to issue subpoenas applies to both arbitrating and nonarbitrating parties. The FAA articulates a clearer position on that matter. The phrase: "An arbitrator may issue a subpoena for the attendance of a witness. . . ." implies that the arbitrator's subpoena powers extend to non-arbitrating third-parties. It, however, would make for a more comprehensible and workable rule to state directly that:

> Arbitrators possess the authority to issue subpoenas for the purpose of evidence-gathering. They can issue subpoenas to the arbitrating parties or third-parties. The subpoena power is meant to provide a means by which arbitrators can secure both documentary and testimonial evidence that would otherwise be inaccessible but which

the arbitrators deem necessary to the proceeding and, possibly, to the determination of the dispute. In the event that the subpoenaed party refuses to comply, the arbitrator can file a motion to compel enforcement before a court of competent jurisdiction.

4. Section 17(a) further provides that an arbitrator can use the subpoena power to gather evidence "at any hearing." It is unclear why the drafters used such an open-ended phrase, but surely they must have intended to allow for coercive evidence-gathering by arbitrators in any arbitral proceeding in which an arbitrator sits as a member of an arbitral tribunal. Further, the administration of oaths is included in the arbitrator's procedural powers. Does this mean that the law of perjury now applies in an arbitral setting? Institutional rules do not address this matter. Is the contemplated oath-taking then mere window dressings or, at best, a type of individual psychological compulsion? Does the provision simply allow arbitrators to do what they want or is this a matter now for the arbitration agreement? In the final analysis, would you agree that a law so unclear and riddled with ambiguities should not serve as the model statute in an area that is as dynamic and vital as arbitration?

5. The remainder of the provision deals with the deposition of witnesses, conduct of discovery, and issuance of protective orders related to privileged information. The statute seems to give arbitrators a great deal of authority in the conduct of such matters. It appears that arbitrators decide what is procedurally "appropriate" with a view to making the arbitral "proceeding fair, expeditious, and cost effective." The latter phrase is used three times in the provision and may have some general regulatory and doctrinal significance, although there is no express indication to that effect in the statute. Section 17(g) addresses the jurisdictional problems that might arise in an interstate arbitral context and seems to provide for the type of judicial assistance that would proceed from the application of full faith and credit principles. The exact meaning and objective of the provision are again difficult to discern without the assistance of the *Reporter's Notes*.

6. The *Reporter's Notes* provide for the following clarifications of the various matters addressed:

> 1. Presently, UAA Section 7 provides an arbitrator only with subpoena authority for the attendance of witnesses and production of documents at the hearing (RUAA Section 17[a]) or to depose a witness who is unable to attend a hearing (RUAA Section 17[b]). Section 17(b) allows an arbitrator to permit a hearing deposition only where it will insure that the proceeding is "fair, expeditious, and cost effective." This standard is also required in Section 17(c) concerning prehearing discovery and in Section 17(g) regarding the enforcement of subpoenas or discovery orders by out-of-state arbitrators. Note that Section 17(a) and (b) are not waivable under Section 4(b) because they go to the inherent power of an arbitrator to provide a fair hearing by

insuring that witnesses and records will be available at an arbitration proceeding.

[. . .]

3. The approach to discovery in Section 17(c) is modeled after the Center for Public Resources (CPR) Rules for Non-Administered Arbitration of Business Disputes, R. 10 and United Nations Commission on International Trade Law (UNCITRAL) Arbitration Rules, Arts. 24(2), 26. The language follows the majority approach under the case law of the UAA and FAA that, unless the contract specifies to the contrary, the discretion rests with the arbitrators whether to allow discovery. The purpose of the discovery procedure in Section 17(c) is to aid the arbitration process and ensure an expeditious, efficient and informed arbitration, while adequately protecting the rights of the parties. Because Section 17(c) is waivable under Section 4, the provision is intended to encourage parties to negotiate their own discovery procedures. Section 17(d) establishes the authority of the arbitrator to oversee the prehearing process and enforce discovery-related orders in the same manner as would occur in a civil action, thereby minimizing the involvement of (and resort of the parties to) the courts during the arbitral discovery process.

At the same time, it should be clear that in many arbitrations discovery is unnecessary and that the discovery contemplated by Section 17(c) and (d) is not coextensive with that which occurs in the course of civil litigation under federal or state rules of civil procedure. Thus, the parties could decide to eliminate or limit discovery in their arbitration agreement.

[. . .]

5. The simplified, straightforward approach to discovery reflected in Section 17(c)–(e) is premised on the affirmative duty of the parties to cooperate in the prompt and efficient completion of discovery. The standard for decision in particular cases is left to the arbitrator. The intent of Section 17, similar to Section 8(b) which allows arbitrators to issue provisional remedies, is to grant arbitrators the power and flexibility to ensure that the discovery process is fair and expeditious.

6. In Section 17 most of the references involve "parties to the arbitration proceeding." However, sometimes arbitrations involve outside, third parties who may be required to give testimony or produce documents. Section 17(c) has been changed so that the arbitrator should take the interests of such "affected persons" into account in determining whether and to what extent discovery is appropriate and Section 17(b) has been broadened so that a "witness" who is not a party can request the arbitrator to allow that person's testimony to be presented at the hearing by deposition if that person is unable to attend the hearing.

7. The Drafting Committee has made clear in Section 17(d) that if an arbitrator allows discovery, the arbitrator has the authority to issue subpoenas for a discovery proceeding such as a deposition. . . .

[. . .]

The Drafting Committee decided that the present approach of courts to safeguard the rights of third parties while insuring that there is sufficient disclosure of information for a full and fair hearing is adequate. Further development in this area should be left to case law because (1) it would be very difficult to draft a provision to include all the competing interests when an arbitrator issues a subpoena or discovery order against a nonparty [*e.g.*, courts seem to give lesser weight to nonparty's claims that an issue lacks relevancy as opposed to nonparty's claims that a matter is protected by privilege]; (2) state and federal administrative laws allowing subpoenas or discovery orders do not make special provisions for nonparties; and (3) the courts have protected well the interests of nonparties in arbitration cases.

10. Section 17(g) is intended to allow a court in State A (the State adopting the RUAA) to give effect to a subpoena or any discovery-related order issued by an arbitrator in an arbitration proceeding in State B without the need for the party who has received the subpoena first to go to a court in State B to receive an enforceable order. This procedure would eliminate duplicative court proceedings in both State A and State B before a witness or record or other evidence can be produced for the arbitration proceeding in State B. . . .

[. . .]

SECTION 20. CHANGE OF AWARD BY ARBITRATOR.

(a) On [motion] to an arbitrator by a party to an arbitration proceeding, the arbitrator may modify or correct an award:

(1) upon a ground stated in Section 24(a)(1) or (3);

(2) because the arbitrator has not made a final and definite award upon a claim submitted by the parties to the arbitration proceeding; or

(3) to clarify the award.

(b) A [motion] under subsection (a) must be made and notice given to all parties within 20 days after the movant receives notice of the award.

(c) A party to the arbitration proceeding must give notice of any objection to the [motion] within 10 days after receipt of the notice.

(d) If a [motion] to the court is pending under Sections 22, 23, or 24, the court may submit the claim to the arbitrator to consider whether to modify or correct the award:

(1) upon a ground stated in Sections 24(a)(1) or (3);

(2) because the arbitrator has not made a final and definite award upon a claim submitted by the parties to the arbitration proceeding; or

(3) to clarify the award.

(e) An award modified or corrected pursuant to this section is subject to Sections 19(a), 22, 23, and 24.

NOTES AND QUESTIONS

1. Section 20 permits the clarification of an award upon remand to the rendering tribunal. Who determines when clarification is in order: The court in an action to confirm or vacate, a party to the action, a third-party (like the administering arbitral institution)? What is the basis for seeking a clarification? When does a lack of clarity exist? When is it sufficient for a remand? What result if the rendering tribunal cannot be reconstituted or refuses to act because it believes the award is clear or for some other reason?

2. What happens if the rendering tribunal renders another award that is, in the court's or party's view, just as unclear?

3. Can a lack of clarity be distinguished from dissatisfaction with the result? How?

4. Is clarification different from correction, vacatur, or appeal? Explain.

SECTION 21. REMEDIES; FEES AND EXPENSES OF ARBITRATION PROCEEDING.

(a) An arbitrator may award punitive damages or other exemplary relief if such an award is authorized by law in a civil action involving the same claim and the evidence produced at the hearing justifies the award under the legal standards otherwise applicable to the claim.

(b) An arbitrator may award reasonable attorney's fees and other reasonable expenses of arbitration if such an award is authorized by law in a civil action involving the same claim or by the agreement of the parties to the arbitration proceeding.

(c) As to all remedies other than those authorized by subsections (a) and (b), an arbitrator may order such remedies as the arbitrator considers just and appropriate under the circumstances of the arbitration proceeding. The fact that such a remedy could not or would not be granted by the court is not a ground for refusing to confirm an award under Section 22 or for vacating an award under Section 23.

(d) An arbitrator's expenses and fees, together with other expenses, must be paid as provided in the award.

(e) If an arbitrator awards punitive damages or other exemplary relief under subsection (a), the arbitrator shall specify in the award the basis in fact justifying and the basis in law authorizing the award and state separately the amount of the punitive damages or other exemplary relief.

NOTES AND QUESTIONS

1. Section 21 is innovative by comparison to other statutory frameworks. It accurately reflects the contemporary status of remedial relief in U.S. arbitration law. It authorizes arbitrators to award both punitive damages and attorney's fees. They may also order relief that they believe is "just and appropriate under the circumstances." The statutory text provides for sensible limitations on the arbitrators' discretion to award damages. How does this compare to the power granted under the FAA?

2. The source of limitations, however, is unclear. Does the law or party agreement establish the qualifications in Section 21(a), (b), and (c)? What sanction can be imposed if the arbitrator misapplies the law on damages? How or can the arbitrator misapplication of law be distinguished from excess of authority or manifest disregard?

3. Does Section 21(e) imply that there is a procedure for the judicial review of the merits of arbitrator determinations on punitive damages?

4. What result if the law chosen by the parties or the law of the place or seat of the arbitration allows punitive damages but the law of the place of enforcement prohibits them or allows them on a more restrictive basis? Which law governs in these circumstances? Why? Is full faith and credit or federal preemption relevant?

SECTION 22. CONFIRMATION OF AWARD.

After a party to an arbitration proceeding receives notice of an award, the party may make a [motion] to the court for an order confirming the award at which time the court shall issue a confirming order unless the award is modified or corrected pursuant to Section 20 or 24 or is vacated pursuant to Section 23.

SECTION 23. VACATING AWARD.

(a) Upon [motion] to the court by a party to an arbitration proceeding, the court shall vacate an award made in the arbitration proceeding if:

(1) the award was procured by corruption, fraud, or other undue means;

(2) there was:

(A) evident partiality by an arbitrator appointed as a neutral arbitrator;

(B) corruption by an arbitrator; or

(C) misconduct by an arbitrator prejudicing the rights of a party to the arbitration proceeding;

(3) an arbitrator refused to postpone the hearing upon showing of sufficient cause for postponement, refused to consider evidence material to the controversy, or otherwise conducted the hearing contrary to Section 15, so as to prejudice substantially the rights of a party to the arbitration proceeding;

(4) an arbitrator exceeded the arbitrator's powers;

(5) there was no agreement to arbitrate, unless the person participated in the arbitration proceeding without raising the objection under Section 15(c) not later than the beginning of the arbitration hearing; or

(6) the arbitration was conducted without proper notice of the initiation of an arbitration as required in Section 9 so as to prejudice substantially the rights of a party to the arbitration proceeding.

(b) A [motion] under this section must be filed within 90 days after the [movant] receives notice of the award pursuant to Section 19 or within 90 days after the [movant] receives notice of a modified or corrected award pursuant to Section 20, unless the [movant] alleges that the award was procured by corruption, fraud, or other undue means, in which case the [motion] must be made within 90 days after the ground is known or by the exercise of reasonable care would have been known by the [movant].

(c) If the court vacates an award on a ground other than that set forth in subsection (a)(5), it may order a rehearing. If the award is vacated on a ground stated in subsection (a)(1) or (2), the rehearing must be before a new arbitrator. If the award is vacated on a ground stated in subsection (a)(3), (4), or (6), the rehearing may be before the arbitrator who made the award or the arbitrator's successor. The arbitrator must render the decision in the rehearing within the same time as that provided in Section 19(b) for an award.

(d) If the court denies a [motion] to vacate an award, it shall confirm the award unless a [motion] to modify or correct the award is pending.

SECTION 24. MODIFICATION OR CORRECTION OF AWARD.

(a) Upon [motion] made within 90 days after the [movant] receives notice of the award pursuant to Section 19 or within 90 days after the [movant] receives notice of a modified or corrected award pursuant to Section 20, the court shall modify or correct the award if:

(1) there was an evident mathematical miscalculation or an evident mistake in the description of a person, thing, or property referred to in the award;

(2) the arbitrator has made an award on a claim not submitted to the arbitrator and the award may be corrected without affecting the merits of the decision upon the claims submitted; or

(3) the award is imperfect in a matter of form not affecting the merits of the decision on the claims submitted.

(b) If a [motion] made under subsection (a) is granted, the court shall modify or correct and confirm the award as modified or corrected. Otherwise, unless a motion to vacate is pending, the court shall confirm the award.

(c) A [motion] to modify or correct an award pursuant to this section may be joined with a [motion] to vacate the award.

NOTES AND QUESTIONS

1. Sections 23 and 24 are basically comparable to the corresponding grounds in the FAA.

2. Can you improve them in some fashion?

3. Are they clear and free of ambiguity?

4. Are they economically drafted and presented?

Conclusions

It is difficult to envisage the Uniform Arbitration Act (2000) as a successful statutory framework. One distinguished arbitration expert has described it in part as passing the "doing no harm" test. *See* James H. Carter, *Uniform Law Commissioners Adopt Revised UAA*, 5–3 ADR CURRENTS 1, 11 (2000). *See also* AMERICAN ARBITRATION ASSOCIATION, DISPUTE RESOLUTION TIMES 1 (July–September 2000). Even a modestly positive assessment, however, seems questionable. Missing a chance to excel and dominate can be costly. In these circumstances, history may not repeat itself. In some respects, the new uniform law adopts the character and tonality of a procedural manual, rather than a statute. It contains too much "legalese" in word and structure and its pursuit of would-be precision often renders the propounded rules distorted and conceptually inaccessible. The lack of compositional clarity and misguided doctrinal content are present in too many provisions. The proposed statute leaves far too much work to its reader to do, and it communicates effectively to far too few of them. It is a 'constitution' not born of intelligence and elegant language, but of the cavils of petty committee politics.

In the final analysis, how do you evaluate UAA (2000) as a statutory text? Does it contribute to the golden age of arbitration law? Does it codify universal propositions for the legal regulation of arbitration? Are the

Reporter's Notes a better statement of prospective legal rules on arbitration?

CHAPTER 3

FEDERALIZATION

■ ■ ■

1. INITIAL STEPS

The FAA was enacted during the era of *Swift v. Tyson*, 41 U.S. (16 Pet.) 1 (1842). *Swift* provided that federal courts hearing state law cases on a diversity basis were bound by state court opinions only when the cases before them involved state constitutions or statutes. When such laws were not involved, the federal courts were free to devise their own rules of decision independently of state court rulings. *Erie R.R. Co. v. Tompkins*, 304 U.S. 64 (1938), overruled *Swift v. Tyson*, providing that "there is no general federal common law," and that "Congress has no power to declare substantive rules of common law applicable in a state, whether they be local in their nature or general, whether they be commercial law or a part of the law of torts." 304 U.S. at 78. In effect, *Erie* reversed the prior doctrine by requiring federal courts, in cases of diversity jurisdiction, to apply state substantive law except when the controversy was governed by the U.S. Constitution or an Act of Congress. Federal courts, of course, were still required to follow federal procedural law in all cases.

Viewing the enactment of the FAA from the perspective of *Erie*, the question became whether the federal law on arbitration—providing for the enforceability of arbitration agreements—was merely a set of procedural regulations or a unique piece of legislation that created substantive rights and was therefore binding upon the federal courts in all cases. More specifically, in a diversity of citizenship case involving purely state interests, could the provisions of the FAA dislodge the application of a less favorable or perhaps antagonistic (but otherwise controlling) state statute or decisional law?

Under *Erie*, the displacement of applicable state law on arbitration could be seen as an impermissible preemptive application of general federal common law. Although clearly protective of federalism principles, such an interpretation could have fragmented any national consensus on arbitration and undermined the FAA's clear mandate to make arbitration an autonomous and viable alternative adjudicatory process. In this setting, another view of the federalism issue, progressively elaborated in the court construction of the FAA in diversity cases, could be advanced. Because *Erie* mandates the application of state law in all diversity cases except those in which the U.S. Constitution or federal legislation is controlling, the courts could deem that the FAA was applicable as a federal enactment, holding—in effect—that the FAA represents more than the enactment of merely procedural regulations and that it actually creates substantive rights. According to a commentator, "[t]o be consistent with *Erie*, a court creating federal common law need only ground its authority to do so on some federal enactment other than the diversity grant." Field, *The Scope of Federal Common Law*, 99 Harv. L. Rev. 881, 888 (1986). In this regard, the decision in *Prima Paint Corp. v. Flood & Conklin Mfg. Co.*, 388 U.S. 395 (1967), has landmark significance. The Court upheld the Second Circuit's view that: "[A]rbitration clauses as a matter of federal law are 'separable' from the contracts in which they are embedded, and . . . where no claim is made that fraud was directed to the arbitration clause itself, a broad arbitration clause will be held to encompass arbitration of the claim that the contract itself was induced by fraud." 388 U.S. at 402, 404.

Prima Paint also is noteworthy for the U.S. Supreme Court's definition of the FAA's systemic stature and underlying legislative purpose. In *Prima Paint*, the Court underscored the primary intent and ultimate objective of the federal legislation on arbitration, and it expressed its judicial resolve to give full effect to both these aspects of the Act in relevant litigation. The Court further stated that the question in *Prima Paint* "was not whether Congress may fashion federal substantive rules to govern questions arising in simple diversity cases, . . . [but] whether Congress may prescribe how federal courts are to conduct themselves with respect to subject matter over which Congress plainly has power to legislate." 388 U.S. at 405. In other words, *Prima Paint* did not involve the issue of federalism and states' rights, but whether Congress could provide substantive directives to the federal courts in areas in which Congress had specific legislative powers. The Court, in effect, answered the federalism question by implication while appearing to disregard it: Congress could create federal law where it had legislative authority to act. Therefore, in diversity cases in which questions arose regarding the validity of the recourse to arbitration, the federal courts were under an obligation to apply the relevant federal legislation in the area. The only limitation upon the application of federal law in this area appeared to be that the contracts in question containing arbitration clauses must affect interstate commerce.

In *Prima Paint*, the Court articulated what was to become a fundamental tenet of its evolving decisional law on arbitration: That the FAA's purpose to provide for the enforceability of arbitration agreements was manifest, and that objective—buttressed by the reference to contractual freedom—must be given effect in the federal decisional law whenever possible. In the Court's own language, "[i]n so concluding, we not only honor the plain meaning of the statute but also the unmistakably clear congressional purpose that the arbitration procedure, when selected by the parties to a contract, be speedy and not subject to delay and obstruction in the courts." 388 U.S. at 404. Challenges to the validity of arbitration agreements on the basis of state law, therefore, were seen primarily as a dilatory tactic—an attempt to defeat the effect of the arbitration agreement and to frustrate the clear purpose of the federal legislation.

The federal courts grappled earlier with the federalism question in two cases. In *Bernhardt*, the U.S. Supreme Court took an "*Erie*-sensitive" position, holding that the FAA was a federal procedural enactment that could not dislodge the application of state law in federal diversity cases. Allowing claims to be submitted to arbitration through the federal courts in diversity cases might lead to adjudicatory outcomes not otherwise available under state law. The undermining of state law would violate the directive in *Erie*.

In *Robert Lawrence*, the U.S. Second Circuit Court of Appeals advanced a different view of the FAA's status, declaring that it represented the enactment of federal substantive law on arbitration agreements under the constitutional powers of the U.S. Congress. The federal law was applicable in both state and federal courts and also controlled in diversity cases. Judge Medina, in *Robert Lawrence*, anticipates prophetically more than forty years of subsequent litigation on arbitration.

BERNHARDT V. POLYGRAPHIC CO. OF AMERICA

350 U.S. 198, 76 S.Ct. 273, 100 L.Ed. 199 (1956).

(footnotes omitted)

MR. JUSTICE DOUGLAS delivered the opinion of the Court.

[. . .]

[T]he larger question presented here . . . is [ ] whether arbitration touched on substantive rights, which *Erie R.R. Co. v. Tompkins* held were governed by local law, or was a mere form of procedure within the power of the federal courts or Congress to prescribe. Our view is that § 3, so read, would invade the local law field. We therefore read § 3 narrowly to avoid that issue. We conclude that the stay provided in § 3 reaches only those contracts covered by §§ 1 and 2.

The question remains whether, apart from the Federal Act, a provision of a contract providing for arbitration is enforceable in a diversity case.

[. . .]

. . . We deal here with a right to recover that owes its existence to one of the States, not to the United States. The federal court enforces the state-created right by rules of procedure which it has acquired from the Federal Government and which therefore are not identical with those of the state courts. Yet, in spite of that difference in procedure, the federal court enforcing a state-created right in a diversity case is in substance "only another court of the State." The federal court therefore may not "substantially affect the enforcement of the right as given by the State." If the federal court allows arbitration where the state court would disallow it, the outcome of litigation might depend on the courthouse where suit is brought. For the remedy by arbitration, whatever its merits or shortcomings, substantially affects the cause of action created by the State. The nature of the tribunal where suits are tried is an important part of the parcel of rights behind a cause of action. The change from a court of law to an arbitration panel may make a radical difference in ultimate result. Arbitration carries no right to trial by jury that is guaranteed both by the Seventh Amendment and by Ch. 1, Art. 12th, of the Vermont Constitution. Arbitrators do not have the benefit of judicial instruction on the law; they need not give their reasons for their results; the record of their proceedings is not as complete as it is in a court trial; and judicial review of an award is more limited than judicial review of a trial—all as discussed in *Wilko v. Swan*. We said in the *York* case that "The nub of the policy that underlies *Erie R.R. Co. v. Tompkins* is that for the same transaction the accident of a suit by a non-resident litigant in a federal court instead of in a State court a block away should not lead to a substantially different result." . . . There would in our judgment be a resultant discrimination if the parties suing on a Vermont cause of action in the federal court were remitted to arbitration, while those suing in the Vermont court could not be.

[. . .]

The judgment of the Court of Appeals is reversed and the cause is remanded to the District Court for proceedings in conformity with this opinion.

[. . .]

ROBERT LAWRENCE CO. V. DEVONSHIRE FABRICS, INC.

271 F.2d 402, 402–05, 407, 409–10 (2d Cir. 1959).

[. . .]

I

[. . .]

The case involves questions left open by the Supreme Court in *Bernhardt v. Polygraphic Co. of America*. . . . The basic inquiry must be whether the validity and interpretation of the arbitration clause of the contract in this case is governed by Federal Law, *i.e.*, the federal Arbitration Act, or by local Law. . . . [T]he exclusion of diversity cases [from the FAA] would emasculate the federal Arbitration Act . . . [and] we find a reasonably clear legislative intent to create a new body of substantive law relative to arbitration agreements affecting commerce or maritime transactions. Thus we think we are here dealing not with state-created rights but with rights arising out of the exercise by the Congress of its constitutional power to regulate commerce and hence there is involved no difficult question of constitutional law under *Erie.*

[. . .]

[W]e think the text of the Act and the legislative history demonstrate that the Congress based the Arbitration Act in part on its undisputed substantive powers over commerce and maritime matters. To be sure much of the Act is purely procedural in character and is intended to be applicable only in the federal courts. But Section 2['s] declaring that arbitration agreements affecting commerce or maritime affairs are "valid, irrevocable, and enforceable" goes beyond this point and must mean that arbitration agreements of this character, previously held by state law to be invalid, revocable or unenforceable, are now made "valid, irrevocable, and enforceable." This is a declaration of national law equally applicable in state or federal courts. This conclusion flows directly from the realization by the Congress that nothing of significance would have been accomplished without tapping these substantive sources of power. It is these that put teeth into the statute and make it accomplish the salutary and beneficial ends the Congress had in mind.

[. . .]

We, therefore, hold that the Arbitration Act in making agreements to arbitrate "valid, irrevocable, and enforceable" created national substantive law clearly constitutional under the maritime and commerce powers of the Congress and that the rights thus created are to be adjudicated by the federal courts whenever such courts have subject matter jurisdiction, including diversity cases, just as the federal courts adjudicate controversies affecting other substantive rights when subject matter jurisdiction over the litigation exists. We hold that the body of law thus created is substantive not procedural in character and that it encompasses questions of interpretation and construction as well as questions of validity, revocability and enforceability of arbitration agreements affecting interstate commerce or maritime affairs, since these two types of legal questions are inextricably intertwined.

In the case before us there can be little doubt that the transaction in question relates to an interstate shipment of goods and involves "commerce" within the meaning of Sections 1 and 2. We, therefore, find federal law as derived from the Arbitration Act to be controlling.

II

[. . .]

We now turn to the decision of this case and the formulation of the principles of federal substantive law necessary for this purpose.

The District Court held that there could be no finding of an "agreement to arbitrate" until it was judicially resolved whether or not there was fraud in the inception of the contract as alleged by Lawrence. But surely this is an oversimplification of the problem. For example, it would seem to be necessary to answer the following questions before we can decide to affirm or reverse the order appealed from: (1) is there anything in the Arbitration Act or elsewhere to prevent the parties from making a binding agreement to arbitrate any disputes thereafter arising between them, including a dispute that there had been fraud in the inception of the contract; (2) is the exception of Section 2, "save upon such grounds as exist at law or in equity for the revocation of any contract[,]" applicable if such an agreement to arbitrate has been made and the only fraud charged is fraud in inducing the purchase of the goods, rather than fraud in connection with the making of the agreement to arbitrate; (3) did the parties in the case before us make a binding agreement to arbitrate; and (4) is the arbitration clause broad enough to cover the charge of fraud?

That the Arbitration Act envisages a distinction between the entire contract between the parties on the one hand and the arbitration clause of the contract on the other is plain on the face of the statute. Section 2 does not purport to affect the contract as a whole. On the contrary, it makes "valid, irrevocable, and enforceable" only a "written provision in any maritime transaction or a contract evidencing a transaction involving commerce to settle by arbitration a controversy thereafter arising out of such contract or transaction"; and Section 3 provides for the granting of a stay in any suit or proceeding in the federal courts "upon an issue referable to arbitration under an agreement in writing for such arbitration."

[. . .]

Finally, any doubts as to the construction of the Act ought to be resolved in line with its liberal policy of promoting arbitration both to accord with the original intention of the parties and to help ease the current congestion of court calendars. Such policy has been consistently reiterated by the federal courts and we think it deserves to be heartily endorsed . . .

It would seem to be beyond dispute that the parties are entitled to agree, should they desire to do so, that one of the questions for the arbitrators to decide in case the controversy thereafter arises, is whether or not one of the parties was induced by fraud to make the principal contract for the delivery of the merchandise. Surely there is no public policy that would stand as a bar to an agreement of such obvious utility, as is demonstrated by the facts of this case. The issue of fraud seems inextricably enmeshed in the other factual issues of the case. Indeed, the difference between fraud in the inducement and mere failure of performance by delivery of defective merchandise depends upon little more than legal verbiage and the formulation of legal conclusions. Once it is settled that arbitration agreements are "valid, irrevocable, and enforceable" we know of no principle of law that stands as an obstacle to a determination by the parties to the effect that arbitration should not be denied or postponed upon the mere cry of fraud in the inducement, as this would permit the frustration of the very purposes sought to be achieved by the agreement to arbitrate, *i.e.* a speedy and relatively inexpensive trial before commercial specialists.

[. . .]

PRIMA PAINT CORP. V. FLOOD & CONKLIN MFG. CO.

388 U.S. 395, 87 S.Ct. 1801, 18 L.Ed.2d 1270 (1967).

[. . .]

. . .The Court of Appeals for the Second Circuit dismissed Prima Paint's appeal. . . . It held that the contract in question evidenced a transaction involving interstate commerce; that under the controlling *Robert Lawrence Co.* decision a claim of fraud in the inducement of the contract generally—as opposed to the arbitration clause itself—is for the arbitrators and not for the courts; and that this rule—one of "national substantive law"—governs even in the face of a contrary state rule. We agree, albeit for somewhat different reasons, and we affirm the decision below.

[. . .]

Having determined that the contract in question is within the coverage of the Arbitration Act, we turn to the central issue in this case: whether a claim of fraud in the inducement of the entire contract is to be resolved by the federal court, or whether the matter is to be referred to the arbitrators. . . .

With respect to cases brought in federal court involving maritime contracts or those evidencing transactions in "commerce," we think that Congress has provided an explicit answer. That answer is to be found in § 4 of the Act, which provides a remedy to a party seeking to compel compliance with an arbitration agreement. Under § 4, with respect to a matter within the jurisdiction of the federal courts save for the existence of an arbitration clause, the federal court is instructed to order arbitration to proceed once it is satisfied that "the making of the agreement for arbitration or the failure to comply [with the arbitration agreement] is not in issue." Accordingly, if the claim is fraud in the inducement of the arbitration clause itself—an issue which goes to the "making" of the agreement to arbitrate—the federal court may proceed to adjudicate it. But the statutory language does not permit the federal court to consider claims of fraud in the inducement of the contract generally. Section 4 does not expressly relate to situations like the present in which a stay is sought of a federal action in order that arbitration may proceed. But it is inconceivable that Congress intended the rule to differ depending upon which party to the arbitration agreement first invokes the assistance of a federal court. We hold, therefore, that in passing upon a § 3 application for a stay while the parties arbitrate, a federal court may consider only issues relating to the making and performance of the agreement to arbitrate. In so concluding, we not only honor the plain meaning of the statute but also the unmistakably clear congressional purpose that the arbitration procedure, when selected by the parties to a contract, be speedy and not subject to delay and obstruction in the courts.

There remains the question whether such a rule is constitutionally permissible. The point is made that, whatever the nature of the contract involved here, this case is in federal court solely by reason of diversity of citizenship, and that since the decision in *Erie R.R. Co. v. Tompkins*, federal courts are bound in diversity cases to follow state rules of decision in matters which are "substantive" rather than "procedural," or where the matter is "outcome determinative." . . . The question in this case, however, is not whether Congress may fashion federal substantive rules to govern questions arising in simple diversity cases. Rather, the question is whether Congress may prescribe how federal courts are to conduct themselves with respect to subject matter over which Congress plainly has power to legislate. The answer to that can only be in the affirmative. And it is clear beyond dispute that the federal arbitration statute is based upon and confined to the incontestable federal foundations of "control over interstate commerce and over admiralty." . . .

[. . .]

MR. JUSTICE BLACK, with whom MR. JUSTICE DOUGLAS and MR. JUSTICE STEWART join, dissenting.

The Court here holds that the United States Arbitration Act, as a matter of federal substantive law, compels a party to a contract containing a written arbitration provision to carry out his "arbitration agreement" even though a court might, after a fair trial, hold the entire contract—including the arbitration agreement—void because of fraud in the inducement. The Court holds, what is to me fantastic, that the legal issue of a contract's voidness because of fraud is to be decided by persons designated to arbitrate factual controversies arising out of a valid contract between the parties. And the arbitrators who the Court holds are to adjudicate the legal validity of the contract need not even be lawyers, and in all probability will be nonlawyers, wholly unqualified to decide legal issues, and even if qualified to apply the law, not bound to do so. I am by no means sure that thus forcing a person to forgo his opportunity to try his legal issues in the courts where, unlike the situation in arbitration, he may have a jury trial and right to appeal, is not a denial of due process of law. I am satisfied, however, that Congress did not impose any such procedures in the Arbitration Act. And I am fully satisfied that a reasonable and fair reading of that Act's language and history shows that both Congress and the framers of the Act were at great pains to emphasize that nonlawyers designated to adjust and arbitrate factual controversies arising out of valid contracts would not trespass upon the courts' prerogative to decide the legal question of whether any legal contract exists upon which to base an arbitration.

[. . .]

IV.

. . . The plain purpose of the Act as written by Congress was this and no more: Congress wanted federal courts to enforce contracts to arbitrate and plainly said so in the Act. But Congress also plainly said that whether a contract containing an arbitration clause can be rescinded on the ground of fraud is to be decided by the courts and not by the arbitrators. Prima here challenged in the courts the validity of its alleged contract with F & C as a whole, not in fragments. If there has never been any valid contract, then there is not now and never has been anything to arbitrate. If Prima's allegations are true, the sum total of what the Court does here is to force Prima to arbitrate a contract which is void and unenforceable before arbitrators who are given the power to make final legal determinations of their own jurisdiction, not even subject to effective review by the highest court in the land. That is not what Congress said Prima must do. It seems to be what the Court thinks would promote the policy of arbitration. I am completely unable to agree to this new version of the Arbitration Act, a version which its own creator in *Robert Lawrence* practically admitted was judicial legislation. Congress might possibly have enacted such a version into law had it been able to foresee subsequent legal events, but I do not think this Court should do so.

I would reverse this case.

NOTES AND QUESTIONS

1. The central issue in *Prima Paint* involves the consideration of several allied issues which contributes to the complexity of the determination and to the vigorous debate between the majority and dissenting opinions. The primary question in *Prima Paint* is whether a party's allegation of contractual fraud—specifically, fraud in the inducement of the agreement—might void both the main contract and the arbitral clause. If the claim has any credibility, *i.e.*, states a *prima facie* case, jurisdiction over the parties' dispute should be redirected to the courts, because the arbitral tribunal has no legal basis upon which to exercise its adjudicatory authority. The foundation of its authority, the arbitral clause, is suspect and, therefore, inoperative (at least, temporarily). If the court ruling on the matter finds the claim of fraud in the

inducement to be unfounded, presumably the reference to arbitration would be reinvigorated and the arbitral tribunal would assert jurisdiction over the resolution of the other contract disputes.

Prima Paint, therefore, raises a threshold jurisdictional issue. Does the claim of contractual invalidity vest jurisdiction with the courts or the arbitral tribunal to rule upon the impact of that claim upon the agreement to arbitrate? A party seeking to frustrate the agreement to arbitrate or complicate the determination of the matter could simply allege that the contract is void for any number of reasons. Under the contract theory of arbitral adjudicatory authority, the judicial process would always intervene to decide this initial question, thereby creating an opportunity at least to delay the arbitration and to undermine the autonomy of the arbitral mechanism.

The majority's answer to this dilemma, between the legal doctrine propounding the necessity of a valid contractual reference to arbitration and the policy favoring arbitral independence, is the separability doctrine. As in many other legal systems, the policy to foster arbitration overrides the law—here, by proclaiming that the arbitral clause is a separate contract that stands on its own. Allegations of contractual deficiency must be directed specifically at the clause itself; the deficiency of the main agreement does not necessarily impinge upon the arbitration agreement. The separability doctrine heightens the adverse party's burden of proof, makes dilatory objections less likely, and avoids the reference to the courts by maintaining the arbitral tribunal's jurisdiction.

Is there any textual support in the FAA for the separability doctrine? Does state contract law provide a better doctrinal foundation for separability? Is the separability doctrine sufficient to address the jurisdictional problem that has been raised? Who decides on its application to the facts of the case?

2. *Prima Paint* not only announces the federal policy surge toward arbitration, but indicates as well the pattern of the Court's decision-making in the area. In almost every subsequent Court decision on arbitration (*Kaplan* is an exception), the majority opinion is accompanied by a dissent. The majority opinion advocates an unequivocal determination in favor of arbitration and depreciates significantly applicable rules of law that might hinder its underlying policy objective. Logic and accuracy do not restrict the majority reasoning. The dissent, usually undertaken by a well-respected and scholarly member of the Court (Black in *Prima Paint*, Douglas in *Scherk*, Stevens in *Mitsubishi* and *Vimar*, Thomas in *Terminix* and *Mastrobuono*, for example), emphasizes the legal dimension of the issue raised, consults comprehensively the legislative history, and accurately portrays the law in the area.

Criticism of the respective approaches notwithstanding, there is an unmistakable legislative quality to the content of the majority opinions that makes short shrift of legal analysis, while the dissents generally constitute persuasive lawyers' briefs on behalf of the role and integrity of law. Throughout its evolution, the U.S. decisional law on arbitration appears to have functioned on the basis of a dialectic opposition between policy and law, beginning with

Prima Paint and continuing through *Scherk*, *McMahon*, *Terminix*, *Mastrobuono*, and *Vimar*.

3. Justice Black's dissenting opinion warrants its own analysis. It, too, announces the future, but on the opposing side. Do you agree with Justice Black that arbitrators are "wholly unqualified to decide legal issues" and their mission is "to adjust and arbitrate factual controversies"? Do these remarks smack of judicial hostility to arbitration? Might the majority be right to take its unequivocal policy position to ward off any rise in the judicial antipathy toward arbitration? What view of arbitration and its form of adjudication is commanded by the statute? Does Justice Black's assertion conflict with the statutory definition of arbitration?

It is clear that Justice Black disagrees with the majority on all the significant issues raised in the *Prima Paint* litigation. In his view, the separability doctrine has a dubious origin, places arbitration agreements in a privileged position that exempts them from the legal requirements of contract validity, and should not be allowed to permit arbitral fact-finders to rule on legal questions. Moreover, principles of general federal common law that are vaguely attached to federal statutory enactments like the separability doctrine should not displace the application of state law in a diversity context especially when the transaction in question eludes the federal statute's scope of application. The majority opinion constitutes an untoward "mutilation" of the statute.

Given this disagreement, assess the following excerpts from Justice Black's dissent:

i) "The Court thus holds that the Arbitration Act, designed to provide merely a procedural remedy which would not interfere with state substantive law, authorizes federal courts to fashion a federal rule to make arbitration clauses 'separable' and valid."

ii) "The only advantage of submitting the issue of fraud to arbitration is for the arbitrators."

iii) "Fraud, of course, is one of the most common grounds for revoking a contract. If the contract was procured by fraud, . . . there is absolutely no contract, nothing to be arbitrated."

iv) "The language of . . . [the FAA] . . . could not, I think, raise doubts about . . . [its] meaning except to someone anxious to find doubts."

4. Finally, Justice Black's dissent raises concerns about the statutory basis for the federal separability doctrine. Although the Court relies on Section Four of the FAA as the statutory anchor for the doctrine, there is, as Justice Black opines, little in the content of the provision to justify that interpretation. Moreover, simply applying the separability doctrine, no matter what the statutory or federalism objections might be, does not directly or indirectly create jurisdiction in the arbitral tribunal to rule on the validity of the arbitral clause. The legal system needs to further recognize and grant arbitrators the

power to rule on jurisdictional challenges that proceed from allegations that there is either no arbitration agreement or a defective one. Neither the FAA nor the case law gives effect to the *kompetenz-kompetenz* doctrine which is the necessary corollary of separability. In fact, Section Three of the FAA appears to give courts the exclusive power to determine whether a valid arbitration exists, and—as a consequence—whether there is a legal basis for the arbitral tribunal's exercise of adjudicatory authority.

Does the federal separability doctrine imply that arbitrators have jurisdiction to rule on jurisdiction? How does that square with the language of Section Three? Is there a gap in the law? Does it matter? You should consider the holding in *First Options v. Kaplan*, *infra*, in evaluating these questions.

5. The vitality of the separability doctrine was recently reaffirmed by the U.S. Supreme Court in *Buckeye Check Cashing, Inc. v. Cardegna*, 546 U.S. 440 (2006). There, it made clear that the separability doctrine was an essential part of U.S. arbitration law and dictated practice in both state and federal courts: "We reaffirm today that, regardless of whether the challenge is brought in federal or state court, a challenge to the validity of the contract as a whole, and not specifically to the arbitration clause, must go to the arbitrator." The Court made evident the settled law on the question:

> . . . [A]s a matter of substantive federal arbitration law, an arbitration provision is severable from the remainder of the contract. . . . [U]nless the challenge is to the arbitration clause itself, the issue of the contract's validity is considered by the arbitrator in the first instance. . . . [T]his arbitration law applies in state as well as federal courts.

The Court concluded that Florida public policy and contract law, and even its concept of criminal culpability, did not overwhelm separability or federal preemption: "We simply reject[ ] the proposition that the enforceability of the arbitration agreement turn[s] on the state legislature's judgment concerning the forum for enforcement of the state-law cause of action." Additionally, the Court declared that separability arose from FAA § 2, as well as §§ 3 and 4, thereby making it fully enforceable in state courts.

At the outset of its opinion, the Court made a distinction between different types of challenges that could be lodged against arbitration agreements. It recognized two types of challenges: (1) *Southland*-like challenges and (2) challenges to the "contract as a whole." In a footnote, the Court identified a third type of challenge, *i.e.*, whether a contract (presumably, of arbitration) was entered into by the parties. These brief statements constitute a rudimentary outline of the jurisdictional doctrine of *kompetenz-kompetenz* and principles of arbitration law that are recognized as basic law in other, like-minded jurisdictions, like France and England.

It appears that the Court was establishing a distinction between subject matter and contractual inarbitrability and elaborating the basis for a challenge on either ground. *Southland* challenges involve the application of statutes that provide for the exclusive resolution of dispute through courts. When the parties agreed to arbitrate such disputes, courts must decide whether the arbitration agreement is effective in light of the statutory subject matter barrier to arbitration. The consideration of that question inexorably leads to another which is even more decisive: Whether the "blocking" statute's jurisdictional exclusivity (if it is state legislation) is preempted by federal law under FAA § 2.

The Court's two additional statements in this matter relate to inarbitrability based on contract, rather than subject matter. They represent the traditional basis upon which to bring jurisdictional challenges to the arbitral tribunal in most legal systems. Arbitrator authority to rule can be challenged on the basis that the parties never entered into an arbitration agreement. The Court recognized this ground in the footnote. A challenge can also be brought on the basis that a contract to arbitrate exists, but is deficient in formation and unenforceable. Finally, a party could argue that the agreement to arbitrate is good as a contract, but it does not apply or extend to the controversy at hand. In some legal systems, the tribunal's right to rule can be opposed because, although the arbitral clause is fully enforceable and applicable, it has not been correctly applied according to its terms in the litigation in question. In other words, the instituted arbitration deviates from the agreed-upon provisions in the contract that relate, presumably, to material matters.

It would be useful to have a complete and systemic statement from the Court on these issues, rather than haphazard and elliptical statements periodically given in various cases. The lack of clarity and structure creates uncertainties and ambiguities in practice and litigation. The situation is the consequence of court-made law that adds a great deal of content to the controlling statute. A revision of the FAA should address such critical issues and provide a full framework of rules to govern them. For a recent application of *Buckeye, see Rubin v. Sona Int'l Corp.*, 457 F.Supp.2d 191 (S.D.N.Y. 2006) (Westlaw reg. req.) (court rejects the distinction between void and voidable contracts and holds that the arbitrator decides the enforceability of an arbitration agreement, "unless the challenge is to the arbitration clause itself").

2. THE FEDERALISM TRILOGY

The full implications of the ruling in *Prima Paint* on federalism and the status of the FAA were elaborated by the courts over time. In this context, the U.S. Supreme Court decided three cases in the mid-1980s that clarified the policy underlying its arbitration doctrine and confirmed the consequences of that doctrine on federalism. The Court's rulings in *Moses H. Cone Memorial Hospital v. Mercury Constr. Corp.*, 460 U.S. 1 (1983), *Southland Corp. v. Keating*, 465 U.S. 1 (1984), and *Dean Witter Reynolds v. Byrd*, 470 U.S. 213 (1985), made clear that the Court viewed the FAA as having a fundamental Congressional objective. The Court would uphold that objective regardless of state law.

Moses H. Cone involved a contract dispute between a North Carolina hospital and an Alabama building contractor. The contract for the construction of additions to the hospital's main building provided that disputes would be resolved by the architect within a specified period of time. If the dispute went unresolved, it would be submitted to binding arbitration. When a dispute arose over costs and could not be resolved, the hospital filed an action before a North Carolina court seeking, in part, a declaratory judgment that there was no right to arbitrate "under the contract due to waiver, latches, estoppel, and failure to make a timely demand for arbitration." 460 U.S. at 7. The building contractor then filed an action before the federal district court to compel arbitration under Section Four of the FAA. The district court stayed the action pending resolution of the hospital's suit in state court. On appeal, the Fourth Circuit reversed the stay and issued instructions to compel arbitration. The U.S. Supreme Court upheld the appellate opinion.

MOSES H. CONE MEMORIAL HOSP. V. MERCURY CONSTRUCTION CORP.

460 U.S. 1, 103 S.Ct. 927, 74 L.Ed.2d 765 (1983).

JUSTICE BRENNAN delivered the opinion of the Court.

[. . .]

IV

Applying the *Colorado River* factors to this case, it is clear that there was no showing of the requisite exceptional circumstances to justify the District Court's stay.

The Hospital concedes that the first two factors mentioned in *Colorado River* are not present here. There was no assumption by either court of jurisdiction over any res or property, nor is there any contention that the federal forum was any less convenient to the parties than the state forum. The remaining factors, avoidance of piecemeal litigation, and the order in which jurisdiction was obtained by the concurrent forums, far from supporting the stay, actually counsel against it.

A

There is no force here to the consideration that was paramount in *Colorado River* itself, the danger of piecemeal litigation.

The Hospital points out that it has two substantive disputes here, one with Mercury, concerning Mercury's claim for delay and impact costs, and the other with the Architect, concerning the Hospital's claim for indemnity for any liability it may have to Mercury. The latter dispute cannot be sent to arbitration without the Architect's consent, since there is no arbitration agreement between the Hospital and the Architect. It is true, therefore, that if Mercury obtains an arbitration order for its dispute, the Hospital will be forced to resolve these related disputes in different forums. That misfortune, however, is not the result of any choice between the federal and state courts; it occurs because the relevant federal law requires piecemeal resolution when necessary to give effect to an arbitration agreement. Under the Arbitration Act, an arbitration agreement must be enforced notwithstanding the presence of other persons who are parties to the underlying dispute but not to the arbitration agreement. If the dispute between Mercury and the Hospital is arbitrable under the Act, then the Hospital's two disputes will be resolved separately, one in arbitration, and the other (if at all) in state-court litigation. Conversely, if the dispute between Mercury and the Hospital is not arbitrable, then both disputes will be resolved in state court. But neither of those two outcomes depends at all on which court decides the question of arbitrability. Hence, a decision to allow that issue to be decided in federal rather than state court does not cause piecemeal resolution of the parties' underlying disputes. Although the Hospital will have to litigate the arbitrability issue in federal rather than state court, that dispute is easily severable from the merits of the underlying disputes.

[. . .]

This refusal to proceed was plainly erroneous in view of Congress's clear intent, in the Arbitration Act, to move the parties to an arbitrable dispute out of court and into arbitration as quickly and easily as possible. The Act provides two parallel devices for enforcing an arbitration agreement: a stay of litigation in any case raising a dispute referable to arbitration, 9 U.S.C. § 3, and an affirmative order to engage in arbitration, § 4. Both of these sections call for an expeditious and summary hearing, with only restricted inquiry into factual issues. Assuming that the state court would have granted prompt relief to Mercury under the Act, there still would have been an inevitable delay as a result of the District Court's stay. The stay thus frustrated the statutory policy of rapid and unobstructed enforcement of arbitration agreements.

C

[. . .]

The basic issue presented in Mercury's federal suit was the arbitrability of the dispute between Mercury and the Hospital. Federal law in the terms of the Arbitration Act governs that issue in either state or federal court. Section 2 is the primary substantive provision of the Act, declaring that a written agreement to arbitrate "in any maritime transaction or a contract evidencing a transaction involving commerce . . . shall be valid, irrevocable, and enforceable, save upon such grounds as exist at law or in equity for the revocation of any contract."

Section 2 is a congressional declaration of a liberal federal policy favoring arbitration agreements, notwithstanding any state substantive or procedural policies to the contrary. The effect of the section is to create a body of federal substantive law of arbitrability, applicable to any arbitration agreement within the coverage of the Act. In *Prima Paint Corp. v. Flood & Conklin Mfg. Corp.*, [w]e held that the language and policies of the Act required the conclusion that the [contractual] fraud issue was arbitrable. Although our holding in *Prima Paint* extended only to the specific issue presented, the courts of appeals have since consistently concluded that questions of arbitrability must be addressed with a healthy regard for the federal policy favoring arbitration. We agree. The Arbitration Act establishes that, as a matter of federal law, any doubts concerning the scope of arbitrable issues should be resolved in favor of arbitration, whether the problem at hand is the construction of the contract language itself or an allegation of waiver, delay, or a like defense to arbitrability.

[W]e emphasize that our task in cases such as this is not to find some substantial reason for the exercise of federal jurisdiction by the district court; rather, the task is to ascertain whether there exist "exceptional" circumstances, the "clearest of justifications," that can suffice under *Colorado River* to justify the surrender of that jurisdiction. Although in some rare circumstances the presence of state-law issues may weigh in favor of that surrender, . . . the presence of federal-law issues must always be a major consideration weighing against surrender.

D

[. . .]

. . .But in a case such as this, where the party opposing arbitration is the one from whom payment or performance is sought, a stay of litigation alone is not enough. It leaves the recalcitrant party free to sit and do nothing, neither to litigate nor to arbitrate. If the state court stayed litigation pending arbitration but declined to compel the Hospital to arbitrate, Mercury would have no sure way to proceed with its claims except to return to federal court to obtain a § 4 order, a pointless and wasteful burden on the supposedly summary and speedy procedures prescribed by the Arbitration Act.

[. . .]

Affirmed.

JUSTICE REHNQUIST, with whom THE CHIEF JUSTICE and JUSTICE O'CONNOR join, dissenting.

In its zeal to provide arbitration for a party it thinks deserving, the Court has made an exception to established rules of procedure. The Court's attempt to cast the District Court's decision as a final judgment fails to do justice to the meaning of the word "final," to the Act of Congress that limits the jurisdiction of the courts of appeals, or to the district judges who administer the laws in the first instance.

[. . .]

NOTES AND QUESTIONS

1. According to the majority opinion, what is the essential purpose of the FAA? What sections of the FAA support the Court's interpretation of the gravamen of the legislation? Is the FAA still special interest legislation or has arbitration acquired a more prominent remedial function in the legal system?

2. Why should the state court be denied jurisdiction in the circumstances of *Moses H. Cone*? Even if a federal court lawfully asserted jurisdiction, wouldn't state law control the contract and the merits of the litigation? What if the parties have provided for state court jurisdiction and/or the application of state law in their contract? Would or should that factor change the outcome?

3. How do you interpret the Court's reference to "a body of federal substantive law of arbitrability" in defining the content of Section Two? What meaning does the Court appear to attach to the concept of "arbitrability"?

4. On the one hand, the majority states that the FAA creates "a body of federal substantive law of arbitrability, applicable to any arbitration agreement within the coverage of the Act." On the other hand, it also claims that "state courts, as much as federal courts, are obliged to grant stays of litigation under § 3 of the Arbitration Act." Are these two statements consistent? Does this mean the state courts must apply the FAA and disregard the provisions of state law on arbitration? What impact does this have on federalism concerns?

5. At footnote 32, 460 U.S. at 26, in the opinion (not reproduced *supra*), the court makes the following observation:

> The Arbitration Act is something of an anomaly in the field of federal-court jurisdiction. It creates a body of federal substantive law establishing and regulating the duty to honor an agreement to arbitrate, yet it does not create any independent federal-question jurisdiction.

The observation is significant on a number of grounds: First, the Court no longer debates whether the FAA is a procedural or substantive enactment. Despite the clear legislative history to the contrary, the Court recognizes that the FAA is the vehicle for the creation of new federal rights. The basic right appears to be the right to engage in, or provide for, arbitration with a corollary duty upon the courts to enforce the contractual promise to arbitrate. Ascertaining when this right becomes enforceable by federal and state courts seems to be the essential question in *Moses H. Cone* and subsequent cases. Is it a right of constitutional magnitude? Must there be a separate basis for the application of federal law?

Second, relatedly and as significantly, the Court characterizes the FAA as an "anomaly" for jurisdictional purposes. The Act, the Court continues, does not create "federal-question jurisdiction" for purposes of litigation involving arbitration. The observation gains importance in relation to the later decisional law. Indeed, the most recent cases pose the question, albeit critically in dissent, of whether the Court's construction of the FAA has not, in effect, resulted in the creation of federal-question jurisdiction for purposes of arbitration. Such a result challenges fundamental principles of federalism, the legislative history of the statute, and the express language of Section One.

Further in the same footnote, given the would-be anomalous lack of federal-question jurisdiction, the Court declares that "there must be diversity of citizenship or some other independent basis for federal jurisdiction" before a federal court can issue an order to compel arbitration under Section Four of the Act in a diversity case governed by state law. The answer begs the question: Under *Erie*, diversity of citizenship is a sufficient basis for asserting federal court jurisdiction, but not for applying federal law. Diversity alone should not compel or authorize a federal court to apply the FAA, unless the statute and the right to arbitrate have constitutional dimensions.

At another point in footnote 32, 460 U.S. at 26, the *Moses Cone* Court states:

> [A]lthough enforcement of the Act is left in large part to the state courts, it nevertheless represents federal policy to be vindicated by the federal courts where otherwise appropriate.

This statement contravenes fundamental federalism principles. What happened to the position in *Prima Paint* that the FAA stood as a Congressional directive to the federal courts on matters of arbitration? Can the view that state courts are primarily responsible for the practical enforcement of the FAA ever be reconciled with the language of Section One? The position that the FAA is binding upon state courts has now crept into the Court's decisional law and will be underscored and consecrated in later opinions.

In footnote 34, 460 U.S. at 26, the Court articulates a basis for integrating state courts into the arbitration regime established by the FAA. First, because of the operation of common law principles, most state courts, in the Court's view, have agreed voluntarily to be bound by the stay provision in Section Three of the Act. State court practice eliminates any need to clarify the allegedly ambiguous jurisdictional reference in Section Three to actions brought "in any of the courts of the United States." Whether the state court precedent is either so voluminous or so clear on the question is certainly debatable, but the Court's discovery of ambiguity in the language of Section Three is strained at best and contradicts its reading of the provision in *Prima Paint* (not to mention the legislative history of the statute).

Second, and this reasoning gets to the nub of the federalism question and more readily explains the motivation of the holding, the Court observes that a disparity in the enforcement of arbitration agreements among the federal and state courts would undermine the Congressional intent underlying the FAA. This practical rationale is persuasive in some respects, but it is hardly a solution to the federalism issue and state rights problems that are generated by the Court's holding. In advancing this justification, the Court refers to "Congress's intent to mandate enforcement of all covered arbitration agreements." 460 U.S. at 27. If "covered . . . agreements" include all those clauses that are the subject of litigation before the federal and state courts, then the FAA applies to any and all agreements to arbitrate. And, the law of arbitration has been federalized.

Southland Corp. v. Keating, decided a year later, provides some clarification as to the direction and motivation of the Court's decisional law on arbitration. The consequences upon federalism concerns are just as substantial. The discussion relating to the assertion of federal authority is more significant. 465 U.S. 1 (1984). *Keating* centered upon the constitutionality of a section of the California Franchise Investment Law (CAL. CORP. CODE § 31512 (West 1977)) which had been interpreted to require exclusive judicial adjudication of claims brought under the statute. Keating's claim, brought on behalf of Seven-Eleven franchisees against Southland Corporation (the Seven-Eleven franchiser) alleged, among other things, that Southland had breached its fiduciary duty and violated the disclosure requirements of the California Franchise Investment Law. After the trial court held the nonwaiver provisions of the Franchise Investment Law valid, the California court of appeals determined that, if the Franchise Investment Law rendered arbitration agreements unenforceable, it conflicted with the provisions of the FAA and was, therefore, invalid under the Supremacy Clause of the U.S. Constitution. 109 Cal.App.3d 784, 167 Cal.Rptr. 481, 493–94 (1980). The California Supreme Court interpreted the investment law provision to require exclusive judicial adjudication of claims brought under the statute; it held that claims asserted under the investment law were inarbitrable; and it further concluded that the California statute did not contravene the federal legislation on arbitration. 31 Cal.3d 584, 604, 183 Cal.Rptr. 360, 645 P.2d 1192 (1982).

The U.S. Supreme Court concluded that the federal legislation created a duty not only upon the federal courts, but also upon the state courts to apply the federal policy on arbitration embodied in the FAA. "In enacting section 2 of the Federal Act, Congress declared a national policy favoring arbitration and withdrew the power of the states to require a judicial forum for the resolution of claims which the contracting parties agreed to resolve by arbitration." 465 U.S. 1, 10 (1984). Agreeing with the appellate court, the Court further held that, "in creating a substantive rule applicable in state as well as federal courts, Congress intended to foreclose state legislative attempts to undercut the enforceability of arbitration agreements. We hold that § 31512 of the California Franchise Investment Law violates the supremacy clause." *Id.* at 16.

SOUTHLAND CORP. V. KEATING

465 U.S. 1, 104 S.Ct. 852, 79 L.Ed.2d 1 (1984).

CHIEF JUSTICE BURGER delivered the opinion of the Court.

[. . .]

III

. . . [T]he California Franchise Investment Law provides:

> Any condition, stipulation or provision purporting to bind any person acquiring any franchise to waive compliance with any provision of this law or any rule or order hereunder is void. . . .

The California Supreme Court interpreted this statute to require judicial consideration of claims brought under the State statute and accordingly refused to enforce the parties' contract to arbitrate such claims. So interpreted the California Franchise Investment Law directly conflicts with § 2 of the Federal Arbitration Act and violates the Supremacy Clause.

In enacting § 2 of the Federal Act, Congress declared a national policy favoring arbitration and withdrew the power of the states to require a judicial forum for the resolution of claims which the contracting parties agreed to resolve by arbitration. . . . Congress has thus mandated the enforcement of arbitration agreements.

We discern only two limitations on the enforceability of arbitration provisions governed by the Federal Arbitration Act: they must be part of a written maritime contract or a contract "evidencing a transaction involving commerce" and such clauses may be revoked upon "grounds as exist at law or in equity for the revocation of any contract." We see nothing in the Act indicating that the broad principle of enforceability is subject to any additional limitations under State law. . . .

The Federal Arbitration Act rests on the authority of Congress to enact substantive rules under the Commerce Clause. In *Prima Paint Corp. v. Flood & Conklin Manufacturing Co.*, the Court examined the legislative history of the Act and concluded that the statute "is based upon . . . the incontestable federal foundations of 'control over interstate commerce and over admiralty.'" The contract in *Prima Paint*, as here, contained an arbitration clause. One party in that case alleged that the other had committed fraud in the inducement of the contract, although not of the arbitration clause in particular, and sought to have the claim of fraud adjudicated in federal court. The Court held that, notwithstanding a contrary state rule, consideration of a claim of fraud in the inducement of a contract "is for the arbitrators and not for the courts[ ]" . . . . The Court relied for this holding on Congress' broad power to fashion substantive rules under the Commerce Clause.

. . . The statements of the Court in *Prima Paint* that the Arbitration Act was an exercise of the Commerce Clause power clearly implied that the substantive rules of the Act were to apply in state as well as federal courts. As Justice Black observed in his dissent, when Congress exercises its authority to enact substantive federal law under the Commerce Clause, it normally creates rules that are enforceable in state as well as federal courts.

In *Moses H. Cone Memorial Hospital v. Mercury Construction Corp.*, we reaffirmed our view that the Arbitration Act "creates a body of federal substantive law" and expressly stated what was implicit in *Prima Paint*, *i.e.*, the substantive law the Act created was applicable in state and federal courts. . . .

Although the legislative history is not without ambiguities, there are strong indications that Congress had in mind something more than making arbitration agreements enforceable only in the federal courts. . . .

[. . .]

. . .We are unwilling to attribute to Congress the intent, in drawing on the comprehensive powers of the Commerce Clause, to create a right to enforce an arbitration contract and yet make the right dependent for its enforcement on the particular forum in which it is asserted. And since the overwhelming proportion of all civil litigation in this country is in the state courts, we cannot believe Congress intended to limit the Arbitration Act to disputes subject only to federal court jurisdiction. Such an interpretation would frustrate Congressional intent to place "[a]n arbitration agreement . . . upon the same footing as other contracts, where it belongs."

In creating a substantive rule applicable in state as well as federal courts, Congress intended to foreclose state legislative attempts to undercut the enforceability of arbitration agreements. We hold that § 31512 of the California Franchise Investment Law violates the Supremacy Clause.

[. . .]

JUSTICE STEVENS, concurring in part and dissenting in part.

The Court holds that an arbitration clause that is enforceable in an action in a federal court is equally enforceable if the action is brought in a state court. I agree with that conclusion. Although Justice O'Connor's review of the legislative history of the Federal Arbitration Act demonstrates that the 1925 Congress that enacted the statute viewed the statute as essentially procedural in nature, I am persuaded that the intervening developments in the law compel the conclusion that the Court has reached. I am nevertheless troubled by one aspect of the case that seems to trouble none of my colleagues.

For me it is not "clear beyond question that if this suit had been brought as a diversity action in a Federal District Court, the arbitration clause would have been enforceable." The general rule prescribed by § 2 of the Federal Arbitration Act is that arbitration clauses in contracts involving interstate transactions are enforceable as a matter of federal law. That general rule, however, is subject to an exception based on "such grounds as exist at law or in equity for the revocation of any contract." I believe that exception leaves room for the implementation of certain substantive state policies that would be undermined by enforcing certain categories of arbitration clauses.

[. . .]

A state policy excluding wage claims from arbitration . . . or a state policy of providing special protection for franchisees, such as that expressed in California's Franchise Investment Law, can be recognized without impairing the basic purposes of the federal statute. Like the majority of the California Supreme Court, I am not persuaded that Congress intended the pre-emptive effect of this statute to be "so unyielding as to require enforcement of an agreement to arbitrate a dispute over the application of a regulatory statute which a state legislature, in conformity with analogous federal policy, has decided should be left to judicial enforcement." . . .

[. . .]

JUSTICE O'CONNOR, with whom JUSTICE REHNQUIST joins, dissenting.

[. . .]

Today, the Court takes the facial silence of § 2 as a license to declare that state as well as federal courts must apply § 2. In addition, though this is not spelled out in the opinion, the Court holds that in enforcing this newly-discovered federal right state courts must follow procedures specified in § 3. The Court's decision is impelled by an understandable desire to encourage the use of arbitration, but it utterly fails to recognize the clear congressional intent underlying the FAA. Congress intended to require federal, not state, courts to respect arbitration agreements.

[. . .]

One rarely finds a legislative history as unambiguous as the FAA's. That history establishes conclusively that the 1925 Congress viewed the FAA as a procedural statute, applicable only in federal courts, derived, Congress believed, largely from the federal power to control the jurisdiction of the federal courts.

[. . .]

Since *Bernhardt*, a right to arbitration has been characterized as "substantive," and that holding is not challenged here. But Congress in 1925 did not characterize the FAA as this Court did in 1956. Congress believed that the FAA established nothing more than a rule of procedure, a rule therefore applicable only in the federal courts.

[. . .]

B

The structure of the FAA itself runs directly contrary to the reading the Court today gives to § 2. §§ 3 and 4 are the implementing provisions of the Act, and they expressly apply only to federal courts. § 4 refers to the "United States district court[s]," and provides that it can be invoked only in a court that has jurisdiction under Title 28 of the United States Code. As originally enacted, § 3 referred, in the same terms as § 4, to "courts [or court] of the United States." There has since been a minor amendment in § 4's phrasing, but no substantive change in either section's limitation to federal courts.

[. . .]

IV

The Court . . . rejects the idea of requiring the FAA to be applied only in federal courts partly out of concern with the problem of forum shopping. The concern is unfounded. Because the FAA makes the federal courts equally accessible to both parties to a dispute, no forum shopping would be possible even if we gave the FAA a construction faithful to the congressional intent. In controversies involving incomplete diversity of citizenship there is simply no access to federal court and therefore no possibility of forum shopping. In controversies with complete diversity of citizenship the FAA grants federal court access equally to both parties; no party can gain any advantage by forum shopping. Even when the party resisting arbitration initiates an action in state court, the opposing party can invoke FAA § 4 and promptly secure a federal court order to compel arbitration. . . .

[. . .]

V

Today's decision adds yet another chapter to the FAA's already colorful history. In 1842 this Court's ruling in *Swift v. Tyson* set up a major obstacle to the enforcement of state arbitration laws in federal diversity courts. In 1925 Congress sought to rectify the problem by enacting the FAA; the intent was to create uniform law binding only in the federal courts. In *Erie* (1938), and then in *Bernhardt* (1956), this Court significantly curtailed federal power. In 1967 our decision in *Prima Paint* upheld the application of the FAA in a federal court proceeding as a valid exercise of Congress's

Commerce Clause and Admiralty powers. Today the Court discovers a federal right in FAA § 2 that the state courts must enforce. Apparently confident that state courts are not competent to devise their own procedures for protecting the newly discovered federal right, the Court summarily prescribes a specific procedure, found nowhere in § 2 or its common law origins, that the state courts are to follow.

Today's decision is unfaithful to congressional intent, unnecessary, and, in light of the FAA's antecedents and the intervening contraction of federal power, inexplicable. Although arbitration is a worthy alternative to litigation, today's exercise in judicial revisionism goes too far. I respectfully dissent.

NOTES AND QUESTIONS

1. Prior to 1925, the federal courts were obligated under the rule of *Swift v. Tyson* to apply general federal common law in diversity cases. At that time, there were few state statutes on arbitration and no federal legislation on the topic. Only states with significant commercial activity, like New York, had enacted legislation on arbitration. Accordingly, in the absence of federal laws, federal courts sitting in diversity cases refused to enforce agreements to arbitrate. The FAA was intended to remedy that problem in the context of *Swift v. Tyson.* By creating a statutory mechanism for the enforcement of arbitration agreements and awards, the FAA allowed the federal courts to uphold the party reference to arbitration. The same result would apply regardless of whether the litigation took place in New York state court or before a federal district court. The FAA was intended to allow the community of merchants to resolve their disputes through the customary mechanism of arbitration despite *Swift v. Tyson*, the absence of federal law, or the lack of state legislation.

Erie changed considerably the setting in which the FAA was to function. The goal of finding a basis for federal court action now was obsolete. The objective became a competition for primacy between the federal and state law in diversity cases. Should the FAA yield to state laws on arbitration that might not espouse the same regulatory disposition? *Erie* clearly dictated the primacy of state law. Once the context of application for the FAA shifted from remedying a gap in the *Swift* doctrine to an *Erie* problem of the competing jurisdiction of substantive law, the institutional standing of the FAA was transformed. The FAA was no longer a procedural enactment, but rather the vehicle of substantive federal rights. It represented Congress' power over the federal courts and the Congressional exercise of Commerce Clause power over interstate commerce. It was not special interest legislation, but rather a statement of federal policy on arbitration.

These circumstances explain the considerable distance traveled between the enactment of the FAA and the rulings in *Prima Paint* and *Keating.* The FAA's legislative history describes the enactment of an entirely different statute from the one depicted in modern case law. Once the FAA was integrated into the *Erie* debate, it became a different statutory regime, legislation the application of which far exceeded the express language of its provisions or its original intent. With *Keating*, the FAA not only was binding upon the federal courts in diversity cases (that much already was clear in *Prima Paint*) and binding upon state courts in cases touching upon interstate commerce (*Moses H. Cone*), but it also literally vacated the power of states to enact statutes that contradicted, directly or indirectly, the federal policy on arbitration. In effect, the U.S. law on arbitration had been federalized. The Court constrained the legislative authority of states to enacting laws that guaranteed the "unobstructed enforcement" of arbitration agreements.

Does the foregoing discussion coincide with the majority or the dissent's sense of the FAA's origins and purpose? Does it coincide with your evaluation of the FAA? Has the decisional law wrongfully used its judicial powers of decision? Or was the "adaptation" of the FAA necessary and inevitable, and, therefore, justified?

2. According to Justice O'Connor's dissent, "*Bernhardt* held that the duty to arbitrate a contract dispute is . . . 'substantive' . . . and therefore a matter normally governed by state law in federal diversity cases." The word substantive means that the issue is "outcome-determinative." What does this view of *Bernhardt* add to the federalism debate on arbitration? Isn't arbitration a mere form of trial, a choice of remedy?

3. When Justice Stevens advocates for the continued operation of state authority in the arbitration area, is he also making the case for the inarbitrability defense? What plan does Justice Stevens articulate for the peaceful coexistence of arbitration and state legislative authority? To what does Justice Stevens refer when he speaks of the exercise of good judgment in evaluating the scope of the FAA? Do you agree that the case law has focused on "sterile generalizations," rather than considered analysis?

4. The majority opinion is quite straightforward: A provision in a state statute that mandates the resolution of statutory disputes exclusively through the courts is unconstitutional because it contravenes the provisions of the FAA. The FAA is controlling because it reflects the exercise of Congressional authority over interstate commerce and, under the Supremacy Clause, that power overrides state authority.

The Court makes a variety of noteworthy contentions in the footnotes of the opinion. In footnote 10, the Court states: "In holding that the Arbitration Act preempts a state law that withdraws the power to enforce arbitration agreements, we do not hold that §§ 3 and 4 of the Arbitration Act apply to proceedings in state courts. The Federal Rules do not apply in such state court proceedings." On what basis does the Court discriminate between the applicability of the various provisions of the federal statute? Can Sections Two and Three be separated on a substantive basis? What substantive or procedural role remains for the states in the area of arbitration in light of this decision?

In footnote 11: "If we accepted this analysis [Justice Stevens' argument for the peaceful coexistence of arbitration and state legislative authority], states could wholly eviscerate congressional intent to place arbitration agreements 'upon the same footing as other contracts' . . . simply by passing statutes such as the Franchise Investment Law. We have rejected this analysis because it is in conflict with the Arbitration Act and would permit states to override the declared policy requiring enforcement of arbitration agreements." Is the Court's distrust of states warranted? Why is compromise untenable? Is there an element of exaggeration to the Court's position?

Dean Witter Reynolds v. Byrd is the final segment of the federalism trilogy. *Byrd* involved a dispute between a customer and the Dean Witter Reynolds securities brokerage firm. Byrd filed a complaint against Dean Witter Reynolds in a U.S. district court, claiming jurisdiction based on the existence of a federal question as well as diversity of citizenship, alleging violations of the U.S. Securities Act of 1934 and of various state law provisions relating to securities regulation. The broker-dealer contract, however, contained an arbitration agreement. Based upon that agreement, Dean Witter filed a motion to sever the pendant state claims and compel arbitration, staying arbitration pending the resolution of the federal court action. Both at the federal trial and appellate levels, the motion to sever the pendant state claims and compel arbitration was denied because of the "intertwining" doctrine, barring the arbitration of state law claims that are factually inseparable from claims under the federal securities act. According to the appellate court reasoning, the intertwining doctrine maintained the federal courts' "exclusive jurisdiction over the federal securities claim" by preventing the earlier arbitral determination of the state claim to bind the federal proceeding through collateral estoppel. Also, "by declining to compel arbitration, the courts avoid bifurcated proceedings and perhaps redundant efforts to litigate the same factual question twice."

The U.S. Supreme Court reversed the decision, holding that the pendant state claims should be compelled to arbitration. In a unanimous opinion, the Court stated that "the Act leaves no place for the discretion by a district court, but instead mandates that district courts *shall* direct the parties to proceed to arbitration on issues as to which an arbitration agreement has been signed." The Court emphasized the underlying controlling Congressional intent of the federal legislation on arbitration, namely, "that the purpose behind the act's passage was to ensure judicial enforcement of privately made agreements to arbitrate and [we] therefore reject the suggestion that the overriding goal of the FAA was to provoke the expeditious resolution of claims."

DEAN WITTER REYNOLDS, INC. V. BYRD

470 U.S. 213, 105 S.Ct. 1238, 84 L.Ed.2d 158 (1985).

JUSTICE MARSHALL delivered the opinion of the Court.

[. . .]

III

The Arbitration Act provides that written agreements to arbitrate controversies arising out of an existing contract "shall be valid, irrevocable, and enforceable, save upon such grounds as exist at law or in equity for the revocation of any contract." 9 U.S.C. § 2. By its terms, the Act leaves no place for the exercise of discretion by a district court, but instead mandates that district courts shall direct the parties to proceed to arbitration on issues as to which an arbitration agreement has been signed. §§ 3, 4. Thus, insofar as the language of the Act guides our disposition of this case, we would conclude that agreements to arbitrate must be enforced, absent a ground for revocation of the contractual agreement.

It is suggested, however, that the Act does not expressly address whether the same mandate, to enforce arbitration agreements, holds true where, as here, such a course would result in bifurcated proceedings if the arbitration agreement is enforced. Because the Act's drafters did not explicitly consider the prospect of bifurcated proceedings, we are told, the clear language of the Act might be misleading. Thus, courts that have adopted the view of the Ninth Circuit in this case have argued that the Act's goal of speedy and efficient decisionmaking is thwarted by bifurcated proceedings, and that, given the absence of clear direction on this point, the intent of Congress in passing the Act controls and compels a refusal to compel arbitration. They point out, in addition, that in the past the Court on occasion has identified a contrary federal interest sufficiently compelling to outweigh the mandate of the Arbitration Act . . . and they conclude that the interest in speedy resolution of claims should do so in this case. . . .

[. . .]

The legislative history of the Act establishes that the purpose behind its passage was to ensure judicial enforcement of privately made agreements to arbitrate. We therefore reject the suggestion that the overriding goal of the Arbitration Act was to promote the expeditious resolution of claims. The Act, after all, does not mandate the arbitration of all claims, but merely the enforcement, upon the motion of one of the parties, of privately negotiated arbitration agreements. The House Report accompanying the Act makes clear that its purpose was to place an arbitration agreement "upon the same footing as other contracts, where it belongs" and to overrule the judiciary's long-standing refusal to enforce agreements to arbitrate. This is not to say that Congress was blind to the potential benefit of the legislation for expedited resolution of disputes. . . . Nonetheless, the passage of the Act was motivated, first and foremost, by a congressional desire to enforce agreements into which parties had entered, and we must not overlook this principal objective when construing the statute, or allow the fortuitous impact of the Act on efficient dispute resolution to overshadow the underlying motivation. Indeed, this conclusion is compelled by the Court's recent holding in *Moses H. Cone Memorial Hospital v. Mercury Construction Corp.* in which we affirmed an order requiring enforcement of an arbitration agreement, even though the arbitration would result in bifurcated proceedings. . . .

We therefore are not persuaded by the argument that the conflict between two goals of the Arbitration Act, enforcement of private agreements and encouragement of efficient and speedy dispute resolution, must be resolved in favor of the latter in order to realize the intent of the drafters. The preeminent concern of Congress in passing the Act was to enforce private agreements which parties had entered, and that concern requires that we rigorously enforce agreements to arbitrate, even if the result is "piecemeal" litigation, at least absent a countervailing policy manifested in another federal statute. . . . By compelling arbitration of state-law claims, a district court successfully protects the contractual rights of the parties and their rights under the Arbitration Act.

[. . .]

NOTES AND QUESTIONS

What remains of Justice Black's view in *Prima Paint* and of Justice Stevens' position in *Keating* that there could be a logical, rational, and substantively sound reconciliation of arbitration policy with the traditional values and function of the legal system? The federalism trilogy, *Moses H. Cone, Keating*, and *Byrd*, leaves little doubt about its ultimate contribution: It effectively federalizes the domestic U.S. law of arbitration. The Court discovers in the FAA a "strong federal policy supporting arbitration" and a Congressional command to the courts to enforce it. It employs a triple constitutional reference to expand the reach of the FAA and to achieve a uniform national legal position on arbitration: A broad view of interstate commerce under the Commerce Clause, the dominance of federal law under the Supremacy Clause, and the constitutional power of the Congress to direct the conduct of the federal courts. As a result, the FAA is binding upon federal courts in diversity cases and upon state courts ruling on matters that have some linkage to interstate commerce. The FAA also overrides the legislative authority of states to regulate arbitration given the supremacy of federal law. In effect, all statutes and litigation in the United States that implicate arbitration must conform to the provisions and underlying policy of the FAA.

From *Prima Paint* to the federalism trilogy, the Court supports the autonomy of the arbitral process at the price of substantially undermining, if not eradicating, state authority in the area. The Court's decisional law emphasizes the FAA's mandate and the need to eliminate judicial hostility to arbitration. There is a judicial duty to recognize and give effect to arbitration agreements. The Court's pronouncements also add content to the FAA and heighten its systemic standing. The Court is determined to achieve a cohesive and coherent national law and policy on arbitration. The two cases that follow first cast doubt on the process of federalization (*Volt*) and then unequivocally confirm the federalization of the American law of arbitration (*Terminix*).

3. FEDERALIZED ARBITRATION REAFFIRMED

Terminix v. Dobson, decided in 1995, aligns itself perfectly with the federalism trilogy, thereby reaffirming the judicial policy on federalization. In *Terminix*, an Alabama homeowner entered into a termite protection agreement with a local Terminix franchiser. The agreement contained a dispute resolution provision, which stated that "any controversy or claim" arising under the contract "shall be settled exclusively by arbitration." When the owner sold the home to another Alabama resident, the parties discovered that the house was swarming with termites, leading the new owner to file suit in state court against the seller and Terminix. The termite protection contract had been transferred to the new owner at the time of the sale. Terminix and its franchiser, however, objected to the assertion of jurisdiction by the state court on the basis of the arbitral clause in the contract and Section 2 of the FAA. On appeal, the Alabama Supreme Court upheld the trial court's refusal to stay the court action pending arbitration, stating that the federal law on arbitration was inapplicable to the transaction because the transaction's connection to interstate commerce was too slight. The U.S. Supreme Court disagreed and reversed the determination.

Throughout the majority opinion, Justice Breyer restates the basic propositions associated with the "hospitable" federal court "inquiry" into matters of arbitration. The primary purpose for the enactment of the FAA in 1925 was to purge the judiciary of its antiarbitration bias. The FAA's protection of arbitration from judicial prejudice applies wherever federal law can reach; in particular, the federal courts must apply the provisions of the FAA even when they exercise diversity jurisdiction over state litigation; state courts also must apply the FAA whenever a basis for applying federal law can be found, even in cases the merits of which are otherwise governed by state law. In effect, the Court stands firm on the federalization policy articulated in the federalism trilogy, in particular, *Southland Corp. v. Keating* ("we find it inappropriate to reconsider what is by now well-established law"). The Court holds fast to the notion that "the Federal Arbitration Act pre-empts state law" and that "state courts [let alone federal courts] cannot apply state statutes that invalidate arbitration agreements." The Court declares unequivocally: "[T]he Act does displace state law to the contrary."

ALLIED-BRUCE TERMINIX COS., INC. V. DOBSON

513 U.S. 265, 115 S.Ct. 834, 130 L.Ed.2d 753 (1995).

(footnotes omitted)

JUSTICE BREYER delivered the opinion of the Court.

This case concerns the reach of § 2 of the Federal Arbitration Act. That section makes enforceable a written arbitration provision in "a contract *evidencing* a transaction *involving* commerce." Should we read this phrase broadly, extending the Act's reach to the limits of Congress' Commerce Clause power? Or, do the two underscored words, "involving" and "evidencing," significantly restrict the Act's application? We conclude that the broader reading of the Act is the correct one; and we reverse a State Supreme Court judgment to the contrary.

[. . .]

II

Before we can reach the main issues in this case, we must set forth three items of legal background.

First, the basic purpose of the Federal Arbitration Act is to overcome courts' refusals to enforce agreements to arbitrate. . . . The origins of those refusals apparently lie in " 'ancient times,' " when the English courts fought " 'for extension of jurisdiction, all of them being opposed to anything that would altogether deprive every one of them of jurisdiction.' " . . . American courts initially followed English practice. . . . When Congress passed the Arbitration Act in 1925, it was "motivated, first and foremost, by a . . . desire" to change this antiarbitration rule. . . . It intended courts to "enforce [arbitration] agreements into which parties had entered," . . . and to "place such agreements 'upon the same footing as other contracts' ". . . .

Second, some initially assumed that the Federal Arbitration Act represented an exercise of Congress' Article III power to "ordain and establish" federal courts. . . . In 1967 [in *Prima Paint*], however, this Court held that the Act "is based upon and confined to the incontestable federal foundations of 'control over interstate commerce and over admiralty.' " The Court considered the following complicated argument: (1) The Act's provisions (about contract remedies) are important and often outcome-determinative, and thus amount to "substantive" not "procedural" provisions of law; (2) *Erie R.R. Co. v. Tompkins* . . . made clear that federal courts must apply state substantive law in diversity cases . . . ; therefore (3) federal courts must not apply the Federal Arbitration Act in diversity cases. This Court responded by agreeing that the Act set forth substantive law, but concluding that, nonetheless, the Act applied in diversity cases because Congress had so intended. The Court wrote: "Congress may prescribe how federal courts are to conduct themselves with respect to subject matter over which Congress plainly has power to legislate." . . .

Third, the holding in *Prima Paint* led to a further question. Did Congress intend the Act also to apply in state courts? Did the Federal Arbitration Act pre-empt conflicting state antiarbitration law, or could state courts apply their anti-arbitration rules in cases before them, thereby reaching results different from those reached in otherwise similar federal diversity cases? In *Southland Corp. v. Keating*, this Court decided that Congress would not have wanted state and federal courts to reach different outcomes about the validity of arbitration in similar cases. The Court concluded that the Federal Arbitration Act pre-empts state law; and it held that state courts cannot apply state statutes that invalidate arbitration agreements. . . .

We have set forth this background because respondents, supported by 20 state attorneys general, now ask us to overrule *Southland* and thereby to permit Alabama to apply its anti-arbitration statute in this case. . . . Nothing significant has changed in the 10 years subsequent to *Southland*; no later cases have eroded *Southland*'s authority; and, no unforeseen practical problems have arisen. Moreover, in the interim, private parties have likely written contracts relying upon *Southland* as authority. Further, Congress, both before and after *Southland*, has enacted legislation extending, not retracting, the scope of arbitration. *See, e.g.*, 9 U.S.C. § 15 (eliminating the Act of State doctrine as a bar to arbitration); 9 U.S.C. §§ 201–208 (international arbitration). For these reasons, we find it inappropriate to reconsider what is by now well-established law.

. . . We must decide in this case whether that Act used language about interstate commerce that nonetheless limits the Act's application, thereby carving out an important statutory niche in which a State remains free to apply its antiarbitration law or policy. We conclude that it does not.

III

The Federal Arbitration Act, § 2, provides that a

> "written provision in any maritime transaction or *a contract evidencing a transaction involving commerce* to settle by arbitration a controversy thereafter arising out of such contract or transaction . . . shall be valid, irrevocable, and enforceable, save upon such grounds as exist at law or in equity for the revocation of any contract." 9 U.S.C. § 2 (emphasis added).

The initial interpretive question focuses upon the words "involving commerce."

[. . .]

After examining the statute's language, background, and structure, we conclude that the word "involving" is broad and is indeed the functional equivalent of "affecting."

[. . .]

Finally, a broad interpretation of this language is consistent with the Act's basic purpose, to put arbitration provisions on "the same footing" as a contract's other terms. . . . Conversely, a narrower interpretation is not consistent with the Act's purpose, for (unless unreasonably narrowed to the flow of commerce) such an interpretation would create a new, unfamiliar, test lying somewhere in a no-man's land between "in commerce" and "affecting commerce," thereby unnecessarily complicating the law and breeding litigation from a statute that seeks to avoid it.

[. . .]

IV

Section 2 applies where there is "a contract *evidencing a transaction* involving commerce." The second interpretive question focuses on the underscored words. Does "evidencing a transaction" mean only that the transaction (that the contract "evidences") must turn out, *in fact*, to have involved interstate commerce? Or, does it mean more?

[. . .]

We find the interpretive choice difficult, but for several reasons we conclude that the first interpretation ("commerce in fact") is more faithful to the statute than the second ("contemplation of the parties"). First, the "contemplation of the parties" interpretation, when viewed in terms of the statute's basic purpose, seems anomalous. That interpretation invites litigation about what was, or was not, "contemplated." Why would Congress intend a test that risks the very kind of costs and delay through litigation (about the circumstances of contract formation) that Congress wrote the Act to help the parties avoid? . . .

Moreover, that interpretation too often would turn the validity of an arbitration clause on what, from the perspective of the statute's basic purpose, seems happenstance, namely whether the parties happened to think to insert a reference to interstate commerce in the document or happened to mention it in an initial conversation. After all, parties to a sales contract with an arbitration clause might naturally think about the goods sold, or about arbitration, but why should they naturally think about an interstate commerce connection?

Further, that interpretation fits awkwardly with the rest of § 2. That section, for example, permits parties to agree to submit to arbitration "an existing controversy arising out of" a contract made earlier. Why would

Congress want to risk non-enforceability of this later arbitration agreement (even if fully connected with interstate commerce) simply because the parties did not properly "contemplate" (or write about) the interstate aspects of the earlier contract? The first interpretation, requiring only that the "transaction" in fact involve interstate commerce, avoids this anomaly, as it avoids the other anomalous effects growing out of the "contemplation of the parties" test.

Second, the statute's language permits the "commerce in fact" interpretation. That interpretation, we concede, leaves little work for the word "evidencing" (in the phrase "a contract evidencing a transaction") to perform, for every contract evidences some transaction. But, perhaps Congress did not want that word to perform much work. The Act's history, to the extent informative, indicates that the Act's supporters saw the Act as part of an effort to make arbitration agreements universally enforceable. They wanted to "get a Federal law" that would "cover" areas where the Constitution authorized Congress to legislate, namely "interstate and foreign commerce and admiralty." . . . Members of Congress, looking at that phrase, might have thought the words "any contract" standing alone went beyond Congress's constitutional authority. And, if so, they might have simply connected those words with the later words "transaction involving commerce," thereby creating the phrase that became law. Nothing in the Act's history suggests any other, more limiting, task for the language.

[. . .]

Finally, we note that an *amicus curiae* argues for an "objective" ("reasonable person" oriented) version of the "contemplation of the parties" test on the ground that such an interpretation would better protect consumers asked to sign form contracts by businesses. We agree that Congress, when enacting this law, had the needs of consumers, as well as others, in mind. . . . Indeed, arbitration's advantages often would seem helpful to individuals, say, complaining about a product, who need a less expensive alternative to litigation. . . .

We are uncertain, however, just how the "objective" version of the "contemplation" test would help consumers. Sometimes, of course, it would permit, say, a consumer with potentially large damage claims, to disavow a contract's arbitration provision and proceed in court. But, if so, it would equally permit, say, local business entities to disavow a contract's arbitration provisions, thereby leaving the typical consumer who has only a small damage claim (who seeks, say, the value of only a defective refrigerator or television set) without any remedy but a court remedy, the costs and delays of which could eat up the value of an eventual small recovery.

In any event, § 2 gives States a method for protecting consumers against unfair pressure to agree to a contract with an unwanted arbitration provision. States may regulate contracts, including arbitration clauses, under general contract law principles and they may invalidate an arbitration clause "upon such grounds as exist at law or in equity for the revocation of any contract." . . . What States may not do is decide that a contract is fair enough to enforce all its basic terms (price, service, credit), but not fair enough to enforce its arbitration clause. The Act makes any such state policy unlawful, for that kind of policy would place arbitration clauses on an unequal "footing," directly contrary to the Act's language and Congress's intent. . . .

For these reasons, we accept the "commerce in fact" interpretation, reading the Act's language as insisting that the "transaction" in fact "involve" interstate commerce, even if the parties did not contemplate an interstate commerce connection.

V

The parties do not contest that the transaction in this case, in fact, involved interstate commerce. In addition to the multistate nature of Terminix and Allied-Bruce, the termite-treating and house-repairing material used by Allied-Bruce in its (allegedly inadequate) efforts to carry out the terms of the Plan, came from outside Alabama.

Consequently, the judgment of the Supreme Court of Alabama is reversed and the case is remanded for further proceedings consistent with this opinion.

It is so ordered.

JUSTICE O'CONNOR, concurring.

I agree with the Court's construction of § 2 of the Federal Arbitration Act. As applied in federal courts, the Court's interpretation comports fully with my understanding of congressional intent. A more restrictive definition of "evidencing" and "involving" would doubtless foster prearbitration litigation that would frustrate the very purpose of the statute. As applied in state courts, however, the effect of a broad formulation of § 2 is more troublesome. The reading of § 2 adopted today will displace many state statutes carefully calibrated to protect consumers, *see, e.g.*, Mont. Code Ann. § 27–5–114(2)(b) (1993) (refusing to enforce arbitration clauses in consumer contracts where the consideration is $5,000 or less), and state procedural requirements aimed at ensuring knowing and voluntary consent, *see, e.g.*, U.S.C. Code Ann. § 15–48–10(a) (Supp.1993) (requiring that notice of arbitration provision be prominently placed on first page of contract). I have long adhered to the view . . . that Congress designed the Federal Arbitration Act to apply only in federal courts. But if we are to apply the Act in state courts, it makes little sense to read § 2 differently in that context. In the end, my agreement with the

Court's construction of § 2 rests largely on the wisdom of maintaining a uniform standard.

I continue to believe that Congress never intended the Federal Arbitration Act to apply in state courts, and that this Court has strayed far afield in giving the Act so broad a compass. . . . [O]ver the past decade, the Court has abandoned all pretense of ascertaining congressional intent with respect to the Federal Arbitration Act, building instead, case by case, an edifice of its own creation. I have no doubt that Congress could enact, in the first instance, a federal arbitration statute that displaces most state arbitration laws. But I also have no doubt that, in 1925, Congress enacted no such statute.

Were we writing on a clean slate, I would adhere to that view and affirm the Alabama court's decision. But, as the Court points out, more than 10 years have passed since *Southland*, several subsequent cases have built upon its reasoning, and parties have undoubtedly made contracts in reliance on the Court's interpretation of the Act in the interim. After reflection, I am persuaded by considerations of *stare decisis* . . . to acquiesce in today's judgment. Though wrong, *Southland* has not proved unworkable, and, as always, "Congress remains free to alter what we have done." . . .

Today's decision caps this Court's effort to expand the Federal Arbitration Act. Although each decision has built logically upon the decisions preceding it, the initial building block in *Southland* laid a faulty foundation. I acquiesce in today's judgment because there is no "special justification" to overrule *Southland*. . . . It remains now for Congress to correct this interpretation if it wishes to preserve state autonomy in state courts.

JUSTICE SCALIA, dissenting.

[. . .]

. . . For the reasons set forth in Justice Thomas' opinion, which I join, I agree with the respondents (and belatedly with Justice O'Connor) that *Southland* clearly misconstrued the Federal Arbitration Act.

I do not believe that proper application of *stare decisis* prevents correction of the mistake. Adhering to *Southland* entails a permanent, unauthorized eviction of state-court power to adjudicate a potentially large class of disputes. Abandoning it does not impair reliance interests to a degree that justifies this evil. . . .

I shall not in the future dissent from judgments that rest on *Southland*. I will, however, stand ready to join four other Justices in overruling it. . . .

For these reasons, I respectfully dissent from the judgment of the Court.

JUSTICE THOMAS, with whom JUSTICE SCALIA joins, dissenting.

I disagree with the majority at the threshold of this case, and so I do not reach the question that it decides. In my view, the Federal Arbitration Act (FAA) does not apply in state courts. I respectfully dissent.

I

In *Southland Corp. v. Keating*, this Court concluded that § 2 of the FAA "appl[ies] in state as well as federal courts," . . . and "withdr[aws] the power of the states to require a judicial forum for the resolution of claims which the contracting parties agreed to resolve by arbitration". . . . In my view, both aspects of *Southland* are wrong.

A

Section 2 of the FAA declares that an arbitration clause contained in "a contract evidencing a transaction involving commerce" shall be "valid, irrevocable, and enforceable, save upon such grounds as exist at law or in equity for the revocation of any contract." . . . On its face, and considered out of context, § 2 draws no apparent distinction between federal courts and state courts. But not until 1959, nearly 35 years after Congress enacted the FAA, did any court suggest that § 2 applied in state courts. . . . No state court agreed until the 1960's. . . . This Court waited until 1984 to conclude, over a strong dissent by Justice O'Connor, that § 2 extends to the States. . . .

The explanation for this delay is simple: the statute that Congress enacted actually applies only in federal courts. At the time of the FAA's passage in 1925, laws governing the enforceability of arbitration agreements were generally thought to deal purely with matters of procedure rather than substance, because they were directed solely to the mechanisms for resolving the underlying disputes. . . . It would have been extraordinary for Congress to attempt to prescribe procedural rules for state courts. . . . And because the FAA was enacted against this general background, no one read it as such an attempt. . . .

Indeed, to judge from the reported cases, it appears that no state court was even asked to enforce the statute for many years after the passage of the FAA. Federal courts, for their part, refused to apply state arbitration statutes in cases to which the FAA was inapplicable. . . . Their refusal was not the outgrowth of this Court's decision in *Swift v. Tyson*. . . . Rather, federal courts did not apply the state arbitration statutes because the statutes were not considered substantive laws. . . . In short, state arbitration statutes prescribed rules for the state courts, and the FAA prescribed rules for the federal courts.

It is easy to understand why lawyers in 1925 classified arbitration statutes as procedural. An arbitration agreement is a species of forum-selection clause: without laying down any rules of decision, it identifies the adjudicator of disputes. A strong argument can be made that such forum-selection clauses concern procedure rather than substance. . . . And if a contractual provision deals purely with matters of judicial procedure, one might well conclude that questions about whether and how it will be enforced also relate to procedure.

The context of § 2 confirms this understanding of the FAA's original meaning. Most sections of the statute plainly have no application in state courts, but rather prescribe rules either for federal courts or for arbitration proceedings themselves. . . .

Despite the FAA's general focus on the federal courts, of course, § 2 itself contains no such explicit limitation. But the text of the statute nonetheless makes clear that § 2 was not meant as a statement of substantive law binding on the States. After all, if § 2 really was understood to "creat[e] federal substantive law requiring the parties to honor arbitration agreements," *Southland,* then the breach of an arbitration agreement covered by § 2 would give rise to a federal question within the subject-matter jurisdiction of the federal district courts. Yet the ensuing provisions of the Act, without expressly taking away this jurisdiction, clearly rest on the assumption that federal courts have jurisdiction to enforce arbitration agreements only when they would have had jurisdiction over the underlying dispute. In other words, the FAA treats arbitration simply as one means of resolving disputes that lie within the jurisdiction of the federal courts; it makes clear that the breach of a covered arbitration agreement does not itself provide any independent basis for such jurisdiction. Even the *Southland* majority was forced to acknowledge this point, conceding that § 2 "does not create any independent federal-question jurisdiction under 28 U.S.C. § 1331 or otherwise." . . . But the reason that § 2 does not give rise to federal-question jurisdiction is that it was enacted as a purely procedural provision. For the same reason, it applies only in the federal courts.

The distinction between "substance" and "procedure" acquired new meaning after *Erie*. . . . Thus, in 1956 [in *Bernhardt,*] we held that for *Erie* purposes, the question whether a court should stay litigation brought in breach of an arbitration agreement is one of "substantive" law. . . . But this later development could not change the original meaning of the statute that Congress enacted in 1925. Although *Bernhardt* classified portions of the FAA as "substantive" rather than "procedural," it does not mean that they were so understood in 1925 or that Congress extended the FAA's reach beyond the federal courts.

When Justice O'Connor pointed out the FAA's original meaning in her *Southland* dissent, . . . the majority offered only one real response. If § 2 had been considered a purely procedural provision, the majority reasoned, Congress would have extended it to all contracts rather than simply to maritime transactions and "contract[s] evidencing a transaction involving [interstate or foreign] commerce." Yet Congress might well have thought that even if it could have called upon federal courts to enforce arbitration agreements in every single case that came before them, there was no federal interest in doing so unless interstate commerce or maritime transactions were involved. This conclusion is far more plausible than *Southland's* idea that Congress both viewed § 2 as a statement of substantive law and believed that it created no federal-question jurisdiction.

Even if the interstate commerce requirement raises uncertainty about the original meaning of the statute, we should resolve the uncertainty in light of core principles of federalism. . . . To the extent that federal statutes are ambiguous, we do not read them to displace state law. Rather, we must be "absolutely certain" that Congress intended such displacement before we give preemptive effect to a federal statute. . . . In 1925, the enactment of a "substantive" arbitration statute along the lines envisioned by *Southland* would have displaced an enormous body of state law: outside of a few States, predispute arbitration agreements either were wholly unenforceable or at least were not subject to specific performance. Far from being "absolutely certain" that Congress swept aside these state rules, I am quite sure that it did not.

B

Suppose, however, that the first aspect of *Southland* was correct: § 2 requires States to enforce the covered arbitration agreements and preempts all contrary state law. There still would be no textual basis for *Southland's* suggestion that § 2 requires the States to enforce those agreements through the remedy of specific performance, that is, by forcing the parties to submit to arbitration. A contract surely can be "valid, irrevocable and enforceable" even though it can be enforced only through actions for damages. Thus, on the eve of the FAA's enactment, this Court described executory arbitration agreements as being "valid" and as creating "a perfect obligation" under federal law even though federal courts refused to order their specific performance. . . .

To be sure, §§ 3 and 4 of the FAA require that federal courts specifically enforce arbitration agreements. These provisions deal, respectively, with the potential plaintiffs and the potential defendants in the underlying dispute: § 3 holds the plaintiffs to their promise not to take their claims straight to court, while § 4 holds the defendants to their promise to submit to arbitration rather than making the other party sue them. Had this case arisen in one of the "courts of the United States," it is § 3 that would have been relevant. Upon proper motion, the court would have been obliged to grant a stay pending arbitration, unless the contract between the parties did not "evidenc[e] a transaction involving [interstate] commerce." . . . Because this case arose in the courts of Alabama, however, petitioners are forced to contend that § 2 imposes precisely the same obligation on all courts (both federal and state) that § 3 imposes solely on federal courts. Though *Southland* supports this argument, it simply cannot be correct, or § 3 would be superfluous.

[. . .]

II

[. . .]

. . . I see no reason to think that the costs of overruling *Southland* are unacceptably high. Certainly no reliance interests are involved in cases like the present one, where the applicability of the FAA was not within the contemplation of the parties at the time of contracting. In many other cases, moreover, the parties will simply comply with their arbitration agreement, either on the theory that they should live up to their promises or on the theory that arbitration is the cheapest and best way of resolving their dispute. In a fair number of the remaining cases, the party seeking to enforce an arbitration agreement will be able to get into federal court, where the FAA will apply. And even if access to federal court is impossible (because § 2 creates no independent basis for federal-question jurisdiction), many cases will arise in States whose own law largely parallels the FAA. Only Alabama, Mississippi, and Nebraska still hold all executory arbitration agreements to be unenforceable, though some other States refuse to enforce particular classes of such agreements. . . .

[. . .]

. . . In short, we have never actually held, as opposed to stating or implying in dicta, that the FAA requires a state court to stay lawsuits brought in violation of an arbitration agreement covered by § 2.

Because I believe that the FAA imposes no such obligation on state courts, and indeed that the statute is wholly inapplicable in those courts, I would affirm the Alabama Supreme Court's judgment.

NOTES AND QUESTIONS

1. The majority opinion recites and confirms the content of the law as it existed prior to *Volt*. It is significant that the Court perceived no conflict between *Volt* and *Terminix*; it, in fact, cites the language in *Volt* to sustain some of its reasoning in *Terminix*.

The majority also adds new elements to its analytical justification of its arbitration doctrine. First, it advances the view that the judicial policy on arbitration should be sufficiently straightforward to avoid creating complex and self-defeating judicial litigation on arbitration, "thereby unnecessarily complicating the law and breeding litigation from a statute that seeks to avoid it." 513 U.S. at 275. "Why would Congress intend a test that risks the very kind of cost and delay through litigation . . . that Congress wrote the Act to help the parties avoid." *Id.* at 278. Second, the majority undercuts the significance of the FAA's legislative history by questioning its utility and accuracy as a means of gauging the underlying intent of the statute, *e.g.*, "The Act's history, to the extent informative. . . ." *Id.* at 279. Third, the Court describes at some length the advantages of arbitration for achieving consumer protection, dismissing the need to protect consumers from unilateral agreements to arbitrate. *Id.* at 280–81.

What do these elements add to the debate about the federalization of the U.S. law of arbitration? How do they work to sustain the Court's view that the FAA dislodges the application of contrary state statutes and is binding upon state courts? Which of these rationalizations is the weakest? The most persuasive? Is the Court right at one level and wrong at another level?

As a final matter, what does the Court's disregard of legislative history indicate to you? If you were drafting the history of a bill for Congress, is there any way to make it more persuasive to the courts who might read it?

2. Do you agree with Justice O'Connor that the federal law of arbitration is "an edifice of . . . [the Court's] own creation" and that the Court in its arbitration decisions "has strayed far afield"? Do you believe that the majority agrees with Justice O'Connor's evaluation? What type of law-making does the Court engage in if what Justice O'Connor says is true? Is this a proper foundation for the law of arbitration? How do you assess and explain Justice O'Connor's "acquiescence" to the majority view? What role does *stare decisis* play here? Does she really concur or is her opinion a dissenting evaluation with no hope of ever being adopted by the Court? How does Justice O'Connor's "acquiescence" compare to the "evil" perceived by Justice Scalia?

3. Justice Thomas makes a number of highly persuasive points regarding the FAA's legislative history and the text of its provisions. Why do you think the majority is not persuaded? What really separates the majority from Justice Thomas' analytic reasoning and assessment of the statute and case law?

Evaluate Justice Thomas' criticism of the majority's position that Section Two of the FAA is a substantive provision binding upon state courts, while Sections Three and Four are merely procedural and govern only federal proceedings. What do Justice Thomas' criticisms indicate about the flaws in the majority's reasoning and general approach? On a related matter, is Justice Thomas correct to believe that, if Section Two were a substantive provision, it would create federal-question jurisdiction? Is this an indirect but logically inescapable effect of the case law? Explain.

Finally, assess Justice Thomas' statements regarding the cost of overruling *Keating*. Are these reasons more realistic than those advanced by the majority? In particular, you should note that there is nearly universal state law conformity with the provisions of the FAA. Does this make the federalism debate unnecessary or is the uniformity of law its consequence?

Doctor's Associates, Inc. v. Casarotto is a more recent U.S. Supreme Court ruling on the question of the supremacy of the FAA over state laws on arbitration. The 8 to 1 decision adds nothing new to the Court's doctrine on arbitration, but rather confirms the strength of the federalization development. Justice Thomas files a brief dissent based upon his position in *Terminix*. With *Casarotto*, the Court's stance on this question of arbitration law becomes completely unambiguous.

DOCTOR'S ASSOCIATES, INC. V. CASAROTTO

517 U.S. 681, 116 S.Ct. 1652, 134 L.Ed.2d 902 (1996).

JUSTICE GINSBURG delivered the opinion of the Court.

This case concerns a standard form franchise agreement for the operation of a Subway sandwich shop in Montana. When a dispute arose between parties to the agreement, franchisee Paul Casarotto sued franchisor Doctor's Associates, Inc. (DAI) and DAI's Montana development agent, Nick Lombardi, in a Montana state court. DAI and Lombardi sought to stop the litigation pending arbitration pursuant to the arbitration clause set out on page nine of the franchise agreement.

The Federal Arbitration Act declares written provisions for arbitration "valid, irrevocable, and enforceable, save upon such grounds as exist at law or in equity for the revocation of any contract." Montana law, however, declares an arbitration clause unenforceable unless "[n]otice that [the] contract is subject to arbitration" is "typed in underlined capital letters on the first page of the contract." Mont. Code Ann. § 27–5–114(4) (1995). The question here presented is whether Montana's law is compatible with the federal Act. We hold that Montana's first-page notice requirement, which governs not "any contract," but specifically and solely contracts "subject to arbitration," conflicts with the FAA and is therefore displaced by the federal measure.

I

Petitioner DAI is the national franchisor of Subway sandwich shops. In April 1988, DAI entered [into] a franchise agreement with respondent Paul Casarotto, which permitted Casarotto to open a Subway shop in Great Falls, Montana. The franchise agreement stated, on page nine and in ordinary type: "Any controversy or claim arising out of or relating to this contract or the breach thereof shall be settled by Arbitration. . . ." . . .

In October 1992, Casarotto sued DAI and its agent, Nick Lombardi, in Montana state court, alleging state-law contract and tort claims relating to the franchise agreement. DAI demanded arbitration of those claims, and successfully moved in the Montana trial court to stay the lawsuit pending arbitration.

The Montana Supreme Court reversed. The Montana Supreme Court held that Mont. Code Ann. § 27–5–114(4) rendered the agreement's arbitration clause unenforceable. The Montana statute provides:

> "Notice that a contract is subject to arbitration . . . shall be typed in underlined capital letters on the first page of the contract; and unless such notice is displayed thereon, the contract may not be subject to arbitration."

Notice of the arbitration clause in the franchise agreement did not appear on the first page of the contract. Nor was anything relating to the clause typed in underlined capital letters. Because the State's statutory notice requirement had not been met, the Montana Supreme Court declared the parties' dispute "not subject to arbitration."

[. . .]

The Montana Supreme Court read our decision in *Volt Information Sciences, Inc.* as limiting the preemptive force of § 2 and correspondingly qualifying *Southland* and *Perry*. As the Montana Supreme Court comprehended *Volt*, the proper inquiry here should focus not on the bare words of § 2, but on this question: Would the application of Montana's notice requirement "undermine the goals and policies of the FAA"? Section 27–5–114(4), in the Montana court's judgment, did not undermine the goals and policies of the FAA, for the notice requirement did not preclude arbitration agreements altogether; it simply prescribed "that before arbitration agreements are enforceable, they be entered [into] knowingly."

[. . .]

I

Section 2 of the FAA provides that written arbitration agreements "shall be valid, irrevocable, and enforceable, save upon such grounds as exist at law or in equity for the revocation of any contract." Repeating our observation in *Perry*, the text of § 2 declares that state law may be applied "if that law arose to govern issues concerning the validity, revocability, and enforceability of contracts generally." Thus, generally applicable contract defenses, such as fraud, duress or unconscionability, may be applied to invalidate arbitration agreements without contravening § 2.

Courts may not, however, invalidate arbitration agreements under state laws applicable only to arbitration provisions. By enacting § 2, we have several times said, Congress precluded States from singling out arbitration provisions for suspect status, requiring instead that such provisions be placed "upon the same footing as other contracts." Montana's § 27–5–114(4) directly conflicts with § 2 of the FAA because the State's law conditions the enforceability of arbitration agreements on compliance with a special notice requirement not applicable to contracts generally. The FAA thus displaces the Montana statute with respect to arbitration agreements covered by the Act.

The Montana Supreme Court misread our *Volt* decision and therefore reached a conclusion in this case at odds with our rulings. *Volt* involved an arbitration agreement that incorporated state procedural rules, one of which, on the facts of that case, called for arbitration to be stayed pending the resolution of a related judicial proceeding. The state rule examined in *Volt* determined only the efficient order of proceedings; it did not affect the enforceability of the arbitration agreement itself. . . .

Applying § 27–5–114(4) here, in contrast, would not enforce the arbitration clause in the contract between DAI and Casarotto; instead, Montana's first-page notice requirement would invalidate the clause. The "goals and policies" of the FAA, this Court's precedent indicates, are antithetical to threshold limitations placed specifically and solely on arbitration provisions. The State's prescription is thus inconsonant with, and is therefore preempted by, the federal law.

* * *

For the reasons stated, the judgment of the Supreme Court of Montana is reversed, and the case is remanded for further proceedings not inconsistent with this opinion.

It is so ordered.

JUSTICE THOMAS, dissenting.

For the reasons given in my dissent last term in *Allied-Bruce Terminix Cos. v. Dobson* I remain of the view that § 2 of the Federal Arbitration Act does not apply to proceedings in state courts. Accordingly, I respectfully dissent.

NOTES AND QUESTIONS

1. *Casarotto* makes the direction of the judicial policy on arbitration abundantly clear on questions of federalism. State law provisions cannot contravene the letter or spirit of the FAA as interpreted by the U.S. Supreme Court.

2. Justice Ginsburg states that arbitration agreements can be regulated by laws applying to all contracts; in effect, state laws cannot single out arbitration agreements for discriminating treatment.

3. Because arbitration agreements are contracts of adjudication, are they ordinary contracts? What room does this pronouncement leave to the states in terms of regulation?

4. If state law prohibits the enforcement of contracts that are against public policy, would a state law providing that public policy include protection

against predispute waivers of judicial remedies in consumer transactions be invalid?

5. Finally, assess the Court's integration of the *Volt* decision as support for its result in *Casarotto.*

KINDRED NURSING CENTERS, LTD. P'SHIP V. CLARK

___ U.S. ___, 137 S. Ct. 1421, 1424, 197 L.Ed. 2d 806 (2017).

JUSTICE KAGAN delivered the opinion of the Court.

The Federal Arbitration Act (FAA or Act) requires courts to place arbitration agreements "on equal footing with all other contracts." *DIRECTV, Inc.* v. *Imburgia*, 577 U. S. ___, ___ (2015) (slip op., at 6) (*quoting Buckeye Check Cashing, Inc.* v. *Cardegna*, 546 U. S. 440, 443 (2006)); *see* 9 U. S. C. § 2. In the decision below, the Kentucky Supreme Court declined to give effect to two arbitration agreements executed by individuals holding "powers of attorney"—that is, authorizations to act on behalf of others. According to the court, a general grant of power (even if seemingly comprehensive) does not permit a legal representative to enter into an arbitration agreement for some-one else; to form such a contract, the representative must possess specific authority to "waive his principal's fundamental constitutional rights to access the courts [and] to trial by jury." *Extendicare Homes, Inc.* v. *Whisman*, 478 S. W. 3d 306, 327 (2015). Because that rule singles out arbitration agreements for disfavored treatment, we hold that it violates the FAA.

I

Petitioner Kindred Nursing Centers L. P. operates nursing homes and rehabilitation centers. Respondents Beverly Wellner and Janis Clark are the wife and daughter, respectively, of Joe Wellner and Olive Clark, two now- deceased residents of a Kindred nursing home called the Winchester Centre.

At all times relevant to this case, Beverly and Janis each held a power of attorney, designating her as an "attorney-in-fact" (the one for Joe, the other for Olive) and affording her broad authority to manage her family member's affairs. In the Wellner power of attorney, Joe gave Beverly the authority, "in my name, place and stead," to (among other things) "institute legal proceedings" and make "contracts of every nature in relation to both real and personal property." . . . In the Clark power of attorney, Olive provided Janis with "full power . . . to transact, handle, and dispose of all matters affecting me and/or my estate in any possible way," including the power to "draw, make, and sign in my name any and all . . . contracts, deeds, or agreements." . . .

Joe and Olive moved into the Winchester Centre in 2008, with Beverly and Janis using their powers of attorney to complete all necessary paperwork. As part of that process, Beverly and Janis each signed an arbitration agreement with Kindred on behalf of her relative. The two contracts, worded identically, provided that "[a]ny and all claims or controversies arising out of or in any way relating to . . . the Resident's stay at the Facility" would be resolved through "binding arbitration" rather than a lawsuit. . . .

When Joe and Olive died the next year, their estates (represented again by Beverly and Janis) brought separate suits against Kindred in Kentucky state court. The com- plaints alleged that Kindred had delivered substandard care to Joe and Olive, causing their deaths. Kindred moved to dismiss the cases, arguing that the arbitration agreements Beverly and Janis had signed prohibited bringing their disputes to court. But the trial court denied Kindred's motions, and the Kentucky Court of Appeals agreed that the estates' suits could go forward. . . .

The Kentucky Supreme Court, after consolidating the cases, affirmed those decisions by a divided vote. . . . The court began with the language of the two powers of attorney. The Wellner document, the court stated, did not permit Beverly to enter into an arbitration agreement on Joe's behalf. In the court's view, neither the provision authorizing her to bring legal proceedings nor the one enabling her to make property-related contracts reached quite that distance. . . . By contrast, the court thought, the Clark power of attorney extended that far and beyond. Under that document, after all, Janis had the capacity to "dispose of all matters" affecting Olive. . . . "Given this extremely broad, universal delegation of authority," the court acknowledged, "it would be impossible to say that entering into [an] arbitration agreement was not covered." . . .

And yet, the court went on, both arbitration agreements—Janis's no less than Beverly's—were invalid. That was because a power of attorney could not entitle a representative to enter into an arbitration agreement without *specifically* saying so. The Kentucky Constitution, the court explained, protects the rights of access to the courts and trial by jury; indeed, the jury guarantee is the sole right the Constitution declares "sacred" and "inviolate." . . . Accordingly, the court held, an agent could deprive her principal of an "adjudication by judge or jury" only if the power of attorney "expressly so pro- vide[d]." . . . And that clear-statement rule—so said the court—complied with the FAA's demands. True enough that the Act precludes "singl[ing] out arbitration agreements." . . . But that was no problem, the court asserted, because its rule would apply not just to those agreements, but also to some other contracts implicating "fundamental constitutional rights." . . . In the future, for example, the court would bar the holder of a "non-specific" power of attorney from entering into a contract "bind[ing] the principal to personal servitude." . . .

Justice Abramson dissented, in an opinion joined by two of her colleagues. In their view, the Kentucky Supreme Court's new clear-statement rule was "clearly not . . . applicable to 'any contract' but [instead] single[d] out arbitration agreements for disfavored treatment." . . . Accordingly, the dissent concluded, the rule "r[a]n afoul of the FAA." . . .

We granted certiorari. . . .

II A

The FAA makes arbitration agreements "valid, irrevocable, and enforceable, save upon such grounds as exist at law or in equity for the revocation of any contract." 9 U. S. C. § 2. That statutory provision establishes an equal-treatment principle: A court may invalidate an arbitration agreement based on "generally applicable contract defenses" like fraud or unconscionability, but not on legal rules that "apply only to arbitration or that derive their meaning from the fact that an agreement to arbitrate is at issue." *AT&T Mobility LLC* v. *Concepcion*, 563 U. S. 333, 339 (2011). The FAA thus preempts any state rule dis- criminating on its face against arbitration—for example, a "law prohibit[ing] outright the arbitration of a particular type of claim." *Id.*, at 341. And not only that: The Act also displaces any rule that covertly accomplishes the same objective by disfavoring contracts that (oh so coincidentally) have the defining features of arbitration agreements. In *Concepcion*, for example, we described a hypothetical state law declaring unenforceable any contract that "disallow[ed] an ultimate disposition [of a dispute] by a jury." *Id.*, at 342. Such a law might avoid referring to arbitration by name; but still, we explained, it would "rely on the uniqueness of an agreement to arbitrate as [its] basis"—and thereby violate the FAA. *Id.*, at 341 (*quoting Perry* v. *Thomas*, 482 U. S. 483, 493, n. 9 (1987)).

The Kentucky Supreme Court's clear-statement rule, in just that way, fails to put arbitration agreements on an equal plane with other contracts. By the court's own account, that rule (like the one *Concepcion* posited) serves to safeguard a person's "right to access the courts and to trial by jury." . . . In ringing terms, the court affirmed the jury right's unsurpassed standing in the State Constitution: The framers, the court explained, recognized "that right and that right alone as a divine God-given right" when they made it "the *only* thing" that must be " 'held sacred' " and " 'inviolate.' " . . . So it was that the court required an explicit statement before an attorney-in-fact, even if possessing broad delegated powers, could relinquish that right on another's behalf. . . . ("We say only that an agent's authority to waive his principal's constitutional right to access the courts and to trial by jury must be clearly ex- pressed by the principal"). And so it was that the court did exactly what *Concepcion* barred: adopt a legal rule hinging on the primary characteristic of an arbitration agreement—namely, a waiver of the right to go to court and receive a jury trial. . . . Such a rule is too tailor-made to arbitration agreements—subjecting them, by virtue of their defining trait, to un- common barriers—to survive the FAA's edict against singling out those contracts for disfavored treatment.[1]

And the state court's sometime-attempt to cast the rule in broader terms cannot salvage its decision. The clear- statement requirement, the court suggested, could also apply when an agent endeavored to waive other "fundamental constitutional rights" held by a principal. . . . But what other rights, really? No Kentucky court, so far as we know, has ever before demanded that a power of attorney explicitly confer authority to enter into contracts implicating constitutional guarantees. Nor did the opinion below indicate that such a grant would be needed for the many routine contracts—executed day in and day out by legal representatives—meeting that description. For example, the Kentucky Constitution protects the "inherent and inalienable" rights to "acquir[e] and protect[ ] property" and to "freely communicat[e] thoughts and opinions." Ky. Const. § 1. But the state court nowhere cautioned that an attorney-in-fact would now need a specific authorization to, say, sell her principal's furniture or commit her principal to a non- disclosure agreement. (And were we in the business of giving legal advice, we would tell the agent not to worry.) Rather, the court hypothesized a slim set of both patently objectionable and utterly fanciful contracts that would be subject to its rule: No longer could a representative lacking explicit authorization waive her "principal's right to worship freely" or "consent to an arranged marriage" or "bind [her] principal to personal servitude." . . . Placing arbitration agreements within that class reveals the kind of "hostility to arbitration" that led Congress to enact the FAA. *Concepcion*, 563 U. S., at 339. And doing so only makes clear the arbitration-specific character of the rule, much as if it were made applicable to arbitration agreements and black swans.[2]

B

The respondents, Janis and Beverly, primarily advance a different argument—based on the distinction between contract formation and contract enforcement—to support the decision below. Kentucky's clear-statement rule, they begin, affects only contract formation, because it bars agents without explicit authority from entering into arbitration agreements. And in their view, the FAA has "no application" to "contract formation issues." . . . The Act, to be sure, requires a State to enforce all

[1] Making matters worse, the Kentucky Supreme Court's clear-statement rule appears not to apply to other kinds of agreements relinquishing the right to go to court or obtain a jury trial. Nothing in the decision below (or elsewhere in Kentucky law) suggests that explicit authorization is needed before an attorney-in-fact can sign a settlement agreement or consent to a bench trial on her principal's behalf. . . . Mark that as yet another indication that the court's demand for specificity in powers of attorney arises from the suspect status of arbitration rather than the sacred status of jury trials.

[2] We do not suggest that a state court is precluded from announcing a new, generally applicable rule of law in an arbitration case. We simply reiterate here what we have said many times before—that the rule must in fact apply generally, rather than single out arbitration.

arbitration agreements (save on generally applicable grounds) once they have come into being. But, the respondents claim, States have free rein to decide—irrespective of the FAA's equal-footing principle—whether such contracts are validly created in the first instance. . . .

Both the FAA's text and our case law interpreting it say otherwise. The Act's key provision, once again, states that an arbitration agreement must ordinarily be treated as "valid, irrevocable, and enforceable." 9 U. S. C. § 2 . . . . By its terms, then, the Act cares not only about the "enforce[ment]" of arbitration agreements, but also about their initial "valid[ity]"—that is, about what it takes to enter into them. Or said otherwise: A rule selectively finding arbitration contracts invalid because improperly formed fares no better under the Act than a rule selectively refusing to enforce those agreements once properly made. Precedent confirms that point. In *Concepcion*, we noted the impermissibility of applying a contract defense like duress "in a fashion that disfavors arbitration." 563 U. S., at 341. But the doctrine of duress, as we have elsewhere explained, involves "unfair dealing at the contract formation stage." . . . Our discussion of duress would have made no sense if the FAA, as the respondents contend, had nothing to say about contract formation.

And still more: Adopting the respondents' view would make it trivially easy for States to undermine the Act—indeed, to wholly defeat it. As the respondents have acknowledged, their reasoning would allow States to pronounce *any* attorney-in-fact incapable of signing an arbitration agreement—even if a power of attorney specifically authorized her to do so. . . . And why stop there? If the respondents were right, States could just as easily declare *everyone* incompetent to sign arbitration agreements. (That rule too would address only formation.) The FAA would then mean nothing at all—its provisions rendered helpless to prevent even the most blatant discrimination against arbitration.

III

As we did just last Term, we once again "reach a conclusion that . . . falls well within the confines of (and goes no further than) present well-established law." . . . The Kentucky Supreme Court specially impeded the ability of attorneys-in-fact to enter into arbitration agreements. The court thus flouted the FAA's command to place those agreements on an equal footing with all other contracts.

Our decision requires reversing the Kentucky Supreme Court's judgment in favor of the Clark estate. As noted earlier, the state court held that the Clark power of attorney was sufficiently broad to cover executing an arbitration agreement. . . . The court invalidated the agreement with Kindred only because the power of attorney did not specifically authorize Janis to enter into it on Olive's behalf. In other words, the decision below was based exclusively on the clear-statement rule that we have held violates the FAA. So the court must now enforce the Clark-Kindred arbitration agreement.

By contrast, our decision might not require such a result in the Wellner case. The Kentucky Supreme Court began its opinion by stating that the Wellner power of attorney was insufficiently broad to give Beverly the authority to execute an arbitration agreement for Joe. . . . If that interpretation of the document is wholly independent of the court's clear-statement rule, then nothing we have said disturbs it. But if that rule at all influenced the construction of the Wellner power of attorney, then the court must evaluate the document's meaning anew. The court's opinion leaves us uncertain as to whether such an impermissible taint occurred. We therefore vacate the judgment below and return the case to the state court for further consideration. See *Marmet Health Care Center, Inc.* v. *Brown*, 565 U. S. 530, 534 (2012) (*per curiam*) (vacating and remanding another arbitration decision because we could not tell "to what degree [an] alternative holding was influenced by" the state court's erroneous, arbitration-specific rule). On remand, the court should determine whether it adheres, in the absence of its clear- statement rule, to its prior reading of the Wellner power of attorney.

For these reasons, we reverse in part and vacate in part the judgment of the Kentucky Supreme Court, and we remand the case for further proceedings not inconsistent with this opinion.

It is so ordered.

NOTES AND QUESTIONS

1. Notably, the Court had previously, in an exceptionally rare *per curiam* opinion, overturned a West Virginia rule that an arbitration clause in a nursing home admission agreement, adopted prior to an occurrence of negligence resulting in a personal injury or wrongful death, would not be enforced to compel arbitration of a dispute concerning the negligence. *Marmet Health Care Center, Inc. v. Brown*, 565 U.S. 530 (2012). The Kentucky rule at issue in *Kindred* accomplished much the same outcome as the West Virginia rule at issue in *Marmet*, but it did so without overtly discriminating against arbitration. Why then does a nearly unanimous Court—only Justice Thomas dissents in *Kindred*—nevertheless overtun the Kentucky rule? What, in a sentence or two, is the real problem?

2. Though Justice Thomas continues to disagree, *Kindred* makes clear that a strong majority of the Court accepts that the FAA constitutes a body of substantive federal law, equally applicable in state and federal courts. Like *Southland Corp. v. Keating*, *Kindred* reached the U.S. Supreme Court on appeal from a state high court.

3. Unlike the statutory rules at issue in *Southland* or *Doctor's Associates*, the state rule implicated in *Kindred* was a common law rule. Should

that have made more of a difference than it seems to have made in the anlaysis? In thinking about this question, recall that FAA § 2 preserves "generally applicable" contract law defenses. Contract law, in the main, is created by state common law. In other words, each state's highest court generally has authority to create and revise general contract law.

4. In Chapter 7, you'll read *AT&T Mobility LLC v. Concepcion*, 563 U.S. 333, 339 (2011), a decision repeatedly cited by the Court in *Kindred*. What is the principle or rule that the Court in *Kindred* extracts from *Concepcion*?

Interestingly, Justice Kagan authors the majority opinion in *Kindred*. She is joined by every other Justice except Justice Thomas. Nevertheless, Justice Kagan, along with the other more liberal members of the Court, dissented from *Concepcion*. Whatever else that might mean, it indicates that, as of 2017, several core pinciples from *Concepcion* seem to have earned the full support of a majority of the Court.

PRESTON V. FERRER

552 U.S. 346, 128 S.Ct. 978, 169 L.Ed.2d 917 (2008).

JUSTICE GINSBURG delivered the opinion of the Court.

As this Court recognized in *Southland Corp.* v. *Keating*, 465 U.S. 1 (1984), the Federal Arbitration Act (FAA or Act) . . . establishes a national policy favoring arbitration when the parties contract for that mode of dispute resolution. The Act, which rests on Congress' authority under the Commerce Clause, supplies not simply a procedural framework applicable in federal courts; it also calls for the application, in state as well as federal courts, of federal substantive law regarding arbitration. . . . More recently, in *Buckeye Check Cashing, Inc.* v. *Cardegna*, 546 U.S. 440 (2006), the Court clarified that, when parties agree to arbitrate all disputes arising under their contract, questions concerning the validity of the entire contract are to be resolved by the arbitrator in the first instance, not by a federal or state court.

The instant petition presents the following question: Does the FAA override not only state statutes that refer certain state-law controversies initially to a judicial forum, but also state statutes that refer certain disputes initially to an administrative agency? We hold today that, when parties agree to arbitrate all questions arising under a contract, state laws  lodging primary jurisdiction in another forum, whether judicial or administrative, are superseded by the FAA.

I

This case concerns a contract between respondent Alex E. Ferrer, a former Florida trial court judge who currently appears as "Judge Alex" on a Fox television network program, and petitioner Arnold M. Preston, a California attorney who renders services to persons in the entertainment industry. Seeking fees allegedly due under the contract, Preston invoked the parties' agreement to arbitrate "any dispute . . . relating to the terms of [the contract] or the breach, validity, or legality thereof . . . in accordance with the rules [of the American Arbitration Association]." . . .

Preston's demand for arbitration, made in June 2005, was countered a month later by Ferrer's petition to the California Labor Commissioner charging that the contract was invalid and unenforceable under the California Talent Agencies Act (TAA). . . . Ferrer asserted that Preston acted as a talent agent without the license required by the TAA, and that Preston's unlicensed status rendered the entire contract void. [Footnote omitted.]

The Labor Commissioner's hearing officer, in November 2005, determined that Ferrer had stated a "colorable basis for exercise of the Labor Commissioner's jurisdiction." . . . The officer denied Ferrer's motion to stay the arbitration, however, on the ground that the Labor Commissioner lacked authority to order such relief. Ferrer then filed suit in the Los Angeles Superior Court, seeking a declaration that the controversy between the parties "arising from the [c]ontract, including in particular the issue of the validity of the [c]ontract, is not subject to arbitration." . . . As interim relief, Ferrer sought an injunction restraining Preston from proceeding before the arbitrator. Preston responded by moving to compel arbitration.

In December 2005, the Superior Court denied Preston's motion to compel arbitration and enjoined Preston from proceeding before the arbitrator "unless and until the Labor Commissioner determines that . . . she is without jurisdiction over the disputes between Preston and Ferrer." . . . During the pendency of Preston's appeal from the Superior Court's decision, this Court reaffirmed, in *Buckeye*, that challenges to the validity of a contract providing for arbitration ordinarily "should . . . be considered by an arbitrator, not a court." . . .

In a 2-to-1 decision issued in November 2006, the California Court of Appeal affirmed the Superior Court's judgment. The appeals court held that the relevant provision of the TAA . . . vests "exclusive original jurisdiction" over the dispute in the Labor Commissioner. . . . *Buckeye* is "inapposite," the court said, because that case "did not involve an administrative agency with exclusive jurisdiction over a disputed issue." . . . The dissenting judge, in contrast, viewed *Buckeye* as controlling; she reasoned that the FAA called for immediate recognition and enforcement of the parties' agreement to arbitrate and afforded no basis for distinguishing prior resort to a state administrative agency from prior resort to a state court. . . .

The California Supreme Court denied Preston's petition for review.... We granted *certiorari* to determine whether the FAA overrides a state law vesting initial adjudicatory authority in an administrative agency....

II

An easily stated question underlies this controversy. Ferrer claims that Preston was a talent agent who operated without a license in violation of the TAA. Accordingly, he urges, the contract between the parties, purportedly for "personal management," is void and Preston is entitled to no compensation for any services he rendered. Preston, on the other hand, maintains that he acted as a personal manager, not as a talent agent, hence his contract with Ferrer is not governed by the TAA and is both lawful and fully binding on the parties.

Because the contract between Ferrer and Preston provides that "any dispute . . . relating to the . . . validity, or legality" of the agreement "shall be submitted to arbitration." . . . Preston urges that Ferrer must litigate "his TAA defense in the arbitral forum." . . . Ferrer insists, however, that the "personal manager" or "talent agent" inquiry falls, under California law, within the exclusive original jurisdiction of the Labor Commissioner, and that the FAA does not displace the Commissioner's primary jurisdiction....

The dispositive issue, then, contrary to Ferrer's suggestion, is not whether the FAA preempts the TAA wholesale.... The FAA plainly has no such destructive aim or effect. Instead, the question is simply who decides whether Preston acted as personal manager or as talent agent.

III

[. . .]

Section 2 "declare[s] a national policy favoring arbitration" of claims that parties contract to settle in that manner.... That national policy, we held in *Southland*, "appli[es] in state as well as federal courts" and "foreclose[s] state legislative attempts to undercut the enforceability of arbitration agreements." . . . The FAA's displacement of conflicting state law is "now well-established . . . and has been repeatedly reaffirmed." [Footnote omitted.]

A recurring question under § 2 is who should decide whether "grounds . . . exist at law or in equity" to invalidate an arbitration agreement. In *Prima Paint Corp.* v. *Flood & Conklin Mfg. Co.*, 388 U.S. 395, 403–404 (1967), we held that attacks on the validity of an entire contract, as distinct from attacks aimed at the arbitration clause, are within the arbitrator's ken.

The litigation in *Prima Paint* originated in federal court, but the same rule, we held in *Buckeye,* applies in state court.... The plaintiffs in

Buckeye alleged that the contracts they signed, which contained arbitration clauses, were illegal under state law and void *ab initio*. . . . Relying on *Southland*, we held that the plaintiffs' challenge was within the province of the arbitrator to decide. . . .

Buckeye largely, if not entirely, resolves the dispute before us. The contract between Preston and Ferrer clearly "evidenc[ed] a transaction involving commerce," . . . and Ferrer has never disputed that the written arbitration provision in the contract falls within the purview of § 2. Moreover, Ferrer sought invalidation of the contract as a whole. In the proceedings below, he made no discrete challenge to the validity of the arbitration clause. . . . [Footnote omitted.] Ferrer thus urged the Labor Commissioner and California courts to override the contract's arbitration clause on a ground that *Buckeye* requires the arbitrator to decide in the first instance.

IV

Ferrer attempts to distinguish *Buckeye* by arguing that the TAA merely requires exhaustion of administrative remedies before the parties proceed to arbitration. We reject that argument.

A

The TAA regulates talent agents and talent agency agreements. "Talent agency" is defined, with exceptions not relevant here, as "a person or corporation who engages in the occupation of procuring, offering, promising, or attempting to procure employment or engagements for an artist or artists." . . . The definition "does not cover other services for which artists often contract, such as personal and career management (i.e., advice, direction, coordination, and oversight with respect to an artist's career or personal or financial affairs)." . . . The TAA requires talent agents to procure a license from the Labor Commissioner. . . . "In furtherance of the [TAA's] protective aims, an unlicensed person's contract with an artist to provide the services of a talent agency is illegal and void." . . . [Footnote omitted.]

Section 1700.44(a) of the TAA states:

> In cases of controversy arising under this chapter, the parties involved shall refer the matters in dispute to the Labor Commissioner, who shall hear and determine the same, subject to an appeal within 10 days after determination, to the superior court where the same shall be heard *de novo*.

Absent a notice of appeal filed within ten days, the Labor Commissioner's determination becomes final and binding on the parties. . . . [Footnote omitted.]

The TAA permits arbitration in lieu of proceeding before the Labor Commissioner if an arbitration provision "in a contract between a talent agency and [an artist]" both "provides for reasonable notice to the Labor Commissioner of the time and place of all arbitration hearings" and gives the Commissioner "the right to attend all arbitration hearings." . . . This prescription demonstrates that there is no inherent conflict between the TAA and arbitration as a dispute resolution mechanism. . . .

Procedural prescriptions of the TAA thus conflict with the FAA's dispute resolution regime in two basic respects: First, the TAA, in § 1700.44(a), grants the Labor Commissioner exclusive jurisdiction to decide an issue that the parties agreed to arbitrate, . . . second, the TAA, in § 1700.45, imposes prerequisites to enforcement of an arbitration agreement that are not applicable to contracts generally. . . .

B

Ferrer contends that the TAA is nevertheless compatible with the FAA because § 1700.44(a) merely postpones arbitration until after the Labor Commissioner has exercised her primary jurisdiction. . . . The party that loses before the Labor Commissioner may file for *de novo* review in Superior Court. See § 1700.44(a). At that point, Ferrer asserts, either party could move to compel arbitration under Cal. Civ. Proc. Code Ann. § 1281.2 (West 2007), and thereby obtain an arbitrator's determination prior to judicial review. . . .

That is not the position Ferrer took in the California courts. In his complaint, he urged the Superior Court to declare that "the [c]ontract, including in particular the issue of the validity of the [c]ontract, *is not subject to arbitration*," and he sought an injunction stopping arbitration "unless and until, *if ever*, the Labor Commissioner determines that he/she has no jurisdiction over the parties' dispute." . . . [[E]mphasis added.] Ferrer also told the Superior Court: "[I]f . . . the Commissioner rules that the [c]ontract is void, Preston may appeal that ruling and have a hearing de novo *before this Court*." . . . [[E]mphasis added.]

Nor does Ferrer's current argument—that § 1700.44(a) merely postpones arbitration—withstand examination. Section 1700.44(a) provides for *de novo* review in Superior Court, not elsewhere. [Footnote omitted.] Arbitration, if it ever occurred following the Labor Commissioner's decision, would likely be long delayed, in contravention of Congress' intent "to move the parties to an arbitrable dispute out of court and into arbitration as quickly and easily as possible." . . . If Ferrer prevailed in the California courts, moreover, he would no doubt argue that judicial findings of fact and conclusions of law, made after a full and fair *de novo* hearing in court, are binding on the parties and preclude the arbitrator from making any contrary rulings.

A prime objective of an agreement to arbitrate is to achieve "streamlined proceedings and expeditious results." . . . That objective would be frustrated even if Preston could compel arbitration in lieu of *de novo* Superior Court review. Requiring initial reference of the parties' dispute to the Labor Commissioner would, at the least, hinder speedy resolution of the controversy.

Ferrer asks us to overlook the apparent conflict between the arbitration clause and § 1700.44(a) because proceedings before the Labor Commissioner are administrative rather than judicial. . . . Allowing parties to proceed directly to arbitration, Ferrer contends, would undermine the Labor Commissioner's ability to stay informed of potentially illegal activity . . . and would deprive artists protected by the TAA of the Labor Commissioner's expertise. . . .

In *Gilmer* v. *Interstate/Johnson Lane Corp.*, 500 U.S. 20 (1991), we considered and rejected a similar argument, namely, that arbitration of age discrimination claims would undermine the role of the Equal Employment Opportunity Commission (EEOC) in enforcing federal law. The "mere involvement of an administrative agency in the enforcement of a statute," we held, does not limit private parties' obligation to comply with their arbitration agreements. . . .

Ferrer points to our holding in *EEOC* v. *Waffle House, Inc.*, 534 U.S. 279, 293–294 (2002), that an arbitration agreement signed by an employee who becomes a discrimination complainant does not bar the EEOC from filing an enforcement suit in its own name. He further emphasizes our observation in *Gilmer* that individuals who agreed to arbitrate their discrimination claims would "still be free to file a charge with the EEOC." . . . Consistent with these decisions, Ferrer argues, the arbitration clause in his contract with Preston leaves undisturbed the Labor Commissioner's independent authority to enforce the TAA. . . . And so it may. [Footnote omitted.] But in proceedings under § 1700.44(a), the Labor Commissioner functions not as an advocate advancing a cause before a tribunal authorized to find the facts and apply the law; instead, the Commissioner serves as impartial arbiter. That role is just what the FAA-governed agreement between Ferrer and Preston reserves for the arbitrator. In contrast, in *Waffle House* and in the *Gilmer* aside Ferrer quotes, the Court addressed the role of an agency, not as adjudicator but as prosecutor, pursuing an enforcement action in its own name or reviewing a discrimination charge to determine whether to initiate judicial proceedings.

Finally, it bears repeating that Preston's petition presents precisely and only a question concerning the forum in which the parties' dispute will be heard. . . . "By agreeing to arbitrate a statutory claim, a party does not forgo the substantive rights afforded by the statute; it only submits to their resolution in an arbitral . . . forum." . . . So here, Ferrer relinquishes no substantive rights the TAA or other California law may accord him. But under the contract he signed, he cannot escape resolution of those rights in an arbitral forum.

In sum, we disapprove the distinction between judicial and administrative proceedings drawn by Ferrer and adopted by the appeals court. When parties agree to arbitrate all questions arising under a contract, the FAA supersedes state laws lodging primary jurisdiction in another forum, whether judicial or administrative.

V

Ferrer's final attempt to distinguish *Buckeye* relies on *Volt Information Sciences, Inc.* v. *Board of Trustees of Leland Stanford Junior Univ.*, 489 U.S. 468 (1989). *Volt* involved a California statute dealing with cases in which "[a] party to [an] arbitration agreement is also a party to a pending court action . . . [involving] a third party [not bound by the arbitration agreement], arising out of the same transaction or series of related transactions." Cal. Civ. Proc. Code Ann. § 1281.2(c) (West 2007). To avoid the "possibility of conflicting rulings on a common issue of law or fact," the statute gives the Superior Court authority, *inter alia*, to stay the court proceeding "pending the outcome of the arbitration" or to stay the arbitration "pending the outcome of the court action." . . .

Volt Information Sciences and Stanford University were parties to a construction contract containing an arbitration clause. When a dispute arose and Volt demanded arbitration, Stanford sued Volt and two other companies involved in the construction project. Those other companies were not parties to the arbitration agreement; Stanford sought indemnification from them in the event that Volt prevailed against Stanford. At Stanford's request, the Superior Court stayed the arbitration. The California Court of Appeal affirmed the stay order. Volt and Stanford incorporated § 1281.2(c) into their agreement, the appeals court held. They did so by stipulating that the contract—otherwise silent on the priority of suits drawing in parties not subject to arbitration—would be governed by California law. . . . Relying on the Court of Appeal's interpretation of the contract, we held that the FAA did not bar a stay of arbitration pending the resolution of Stanford's Superior Court suit against Volt and the two companies not bound by the arbitration agreement.

Preston and Ferrer's contract also contains a choice-of-law clause, which states that the "agreement shall be governed by the laws of the state of California." . . . A separate saving clause provides: "If there is any conflict between this agreement and any present or future law," the law prevails over the contract "to the extent necessary to bring [the contract] within the requirements of said law." . . . Those contractual terms, according to

Ferrer, call for the application of California procedural law, including § 1700.44(a)'s grant of exclusive jurisdiction to the Labor Commissioner.

Ferrer's reliance on *Volt* is misplaced for two discrete reasons. First, arbitration was stayed in *Volt* to accommodate litigation involving third parties who were strangers to the arbitration agreement. Nothing in the arbitration agreement addressed the order of proceedings when pending litigation with third parties presented the prospect of inconsistent rulings. We thought it proper, in those circumstances, to recognize state law as the gap filler.

Here, in contrast, the arbitration clause speaks to the matter in controversy; it states that "any dispute . . . relating to . . . the breach, validity, or legality" of the contract should be arbitrated in accordance with the American Arbitration Association (AAA) rules. . . . Both parties are bound by the arbitration agreement; the question of Preston's status as a talent agent relates to the validity or legality of the contract; there is no risk that related litigation will yield conflicting rulings on common issues; and there is no other procedural void for the choice-of-law clause to fill.

Second, we are guided by our more recent decision in *Mastrobuono* v. *Shearson Lehman Hutton, Inc.*, 514 U.S. 52 (1995). Although the contract in *Volt* provided for "arbitration in accordance with the Construction Industry Arbitration Rules of the American Arbitration Association," . . . Volt never argued that incorporation of those rules trumped the choice-of-law clause contained in the contract. . . . Therefore, neither our decision in *Volt* nor the decision of the California appeals court in that case addressed the import of the contract's incorporation by reference of privately promulgated arbitration rules.

In *Mastrobuono*, we reached that open question while interpreting a contract with both a New York choice-of-law clause and a clause providing for arbitration in accordance with the rules of the National Association of Securities Dealers (NASD). . . . [Footnote omitted.] The "best way to harmonize" the two clauses, we held, was to read the choice-of-law clause "to encompass substantive principles that New York courts would apply, but not to include [New York's] special rules limiting the authority of arbitrators.". . .

Preston and Ferrer's contract, as noted, provides for arbitration in accordance with the AAA rules. . . . One of those rules states that "[t]he arbitrator shall have the power to determine the existence or validity of a contract of which an arbitration clause forms a part." . . . The incorporation of the AAA rules, and in particular Rule 7(b), weighs against inferring from the choice-of-law clause an understanding shared by Ferrer and Preston that their disputes would be heard, in the first instance, by the Labor Commissioner. Following the guide *Mastrobuono* provides, the "best way to harmonize" the parties' adoption of the AAA rules and their selection of

California law is to read the latter to encompass prescriptions governing the substantive rights and obligations of the parties, but not the State's "special rules limiting the authority of arbitrators." . . .

* * *

For the reasons stated, the judgment of the California Court of Appeal is reversed, and the case is remanded for further proceedings not inconsistent with this opinion.

It is so ordered.

JUSTICE THOMAS, dissenting.

As I have stated on many previous occasions, I believe that the Federal Arbitration Act (FAA) . . . does not apply to proceedings in state courts. . . . Thus, in state-court proceedings, the FAA cannot displace a state law that delays arbitration until administrative proceedings are completed. Accordingly, I would affirm the judgment of the Court of Appeals.

NOTES AND QUESTIONS

1. Judge Alex or Ferrer is seeking to avoid paying his manager or talent agent based upon a technical provision of a California statute. It is not (it seems) that the representative did not render services, but rather than he lacked a license to render such services in a particular lawful capacity. Surely, Ferrer would be subject to a plea for restitutionary relief were his litigation strategy to work, unless his real claim was that the services were never rendered, unnecessary, defective, or otherwise worthless.

2. The clash of state law with the FAA's basic aim and underlying policy is at the core of the litigation in *Preston v. Ferrer*. Why would arbitration be objectionable for either party? Why does Ferrer, in particular, object to the submission of the dispute to arbitration? What remedy does California state law command in these circumstances? What public interest consideration is being served (at least, arguably) by the state legislative framework? How is that objective intolerable to the federal interest?

3. Could tolerance and mutuality be practiced in these circumstances? Why not allow the Labor Commissioner to decide on her jurisdiction first or have her decide the merits subject to arbitral or judicial appeal?

CHAPTER 4

CONTRACT FREEDOM

■ ■ ■

1. INTRODUCTION: THE DECISIONAL LAW

The U.S. Supreme Court has taken a strong interest in promoting the recourse to arbitration and protecting the autonomous and operation of the arbitral process. To borrow a phrase from Justice O'Conner, the Court has built an edifice of arbitration law of its own making. *See Allied-Bruce Terminix Cos. v. Dobson*, 513 U.S. 265 (1995) (O'Connor, Justice, concurring) ("[O]ver the past decade, the Court has abandoned all pretense of ascertaining congressional intent with respect to the Federal Arbitration Act, building instead, case by case, an edifice of its own creation. . . ."). This decisional law has modified substantially the language and objectives of the FAA.

The Court has federalized the law of arbitration by requiring that federal courts sitting in diversity and state courts apply the FAA whenever disputes impinge (no matter how slightly) upon interstate commerce. Notwithstanding exclusionary language, the courts have ruled that the FAA governs employment contracts and authorizes arbitration in various consumer areas (HMOs, banking and brokerage services, and the purchase of goods, like computers). This is a significantly greater range of application than the language of FAA § 1 contemplates.

Furthermore, the Court has repeatedly emphasized the significance of contract freedom in the U.S. law of arbitration, reiterating in various cases that "[a]rbitration under the Act is a matter of consent, not coercion. . . ." *Volt Info. Sciences, Inc. v. Board of Trustees of Leland Stanford Junior Univ.*, 489 U.S. 468, 479 (1989). As a result, an arbitration agreement has the force of law for the parties' transaction. The parties can even reverse the effect of federalization by providing for the application of a state law to their arbitration, even though the transaction involves interstate commerce and the state law contains provisions that conflict with the FAA. The parties can also modify the terms of the FAA itself through a written stipulation. For instance, the Court in *First Options of Chicago, Inc. v. Kaplan*, 514 U.S. 938 (1995), ruled that the parties could confer *kompetenz-kompetenz* authority upon the arbitrators if they agreed to remove contract inarbitrability questions from the jurisdiction of the courts and authorized the arbitrators to rule on these matters. The arbitration agreement, therefore, can be the source of governing law in U.S. arbitral practice.

Section Two is the most significant provision of the FAA. It legitimizes arbitral adjudication and provides that agreements to arbitrate represent a lawful exercise of the parties' freedom of contract. Section Two also provides that arbitration agreements are subject to ordinary contract defenses. In its pursuit of an "emphatic" federal policy "favoring arbitration," the Court has virtually eliminated the barrier of adhesion for the formation of arbitration agreements. Arbitral clauses that are imposed unilaterally as a pre-condition to employment by the economically dominant party without any possibility of negotiation are valid and enforceable. According to the Court's interpretation of Section Two, it seems that the bargain for arbitration is—as a matter of law—always beneficial for the parties to the transaction regardless of whether they knew of or saw the provision for arbitration or voluntarily agree to it.

Finally, in U.S. arbitration law, there is virtually no subject-matter inarbitrability defense. The Court interprets the federal policy supporting arbitration as mandating a "hospitable" approach to questions of arbitrability. Accordingly, all disputes arising under a contract—whether statutory or contractual in character—can be submitted to arbitration. The FAA does not contain an express or even implied restriction on the type of dispute that can be lawfully submitted to arbitration. *See Shearson/Am. Express, Inc. v. McMahon,* 482 U.S. 220 (1987); *Rodriguez de Quijas v. Shearson/Am. Express, Inc.*, 490 U.S. 477 (1989). As the Court correctly observes, individual statutes establish whether Congress intended disputes arising under them to be resolved exclusively by courts. Moreover, the Court never finds any statement of congressional policy clear enough to prevent parties from submitting disputes to arbitration. The parties' disagreement about a statutory matter, the Court states, has no consequences beyond the boundaries of their particular transaction. The law is applied to purely individual conduct and has no systemic effect. Most, if not all, claims arising under regulatory laws that apply to commercial conduct (securities regulation, antitrust, and RICO), those pertaining to federal statutes that create individual rights (*e.g.*, ADA, ADEA, ERISA, and Family Medical Leave Act), and those that implicate civil rights (Title VII of the Civil Rights Act of 1964 as amended by the Civil Rights Act of 1991) can, therefore, be submitted to arbitration—despite their direct link to public policy.

2. CONTRACT FREEDOM

Volt Information Sciences v. Board of Trustees of Leland Stanford Junior University, 489 U.S. 468 (1989), introduced and emphasized the role of contract freedom in the Court's doctrine on arbitration. The Court applied the freedom of contract principle in two subsequent cases. The first, *Mastrobuono v. Shearson Lehman Hutton, Inc.*, 514 U.S. 52 (1995), generated a strong, albeit solitary, dissent. To some degree, the decision in

Mastrobuono contradicts the reasoning and the ruling in *Volt*, yet endorses its view of the significance of contract freedom in the law of arbitration. In the second case, *First Options of Chicago, Inc. v. Kaplan*, 514 U.S. 938 (1995), a unanimous opinion, the Court defines with greater specificity the role of freedom of contract in arbitration and explores in more detail the consequences of its position upon the legal regulation of arbitration.

Volt Information Sciences

Volt Information Sciences involved a contractual agreement between Stanford University and Volt Information Sciences, Inc., one of several contractors working on a large construction project on the Stanford campus. Its contract, to install a system of electrical conduits, contained standard provisions on dispute resolution and choice-of-law, respectively providing for arbitration and the application of local law. A dispute arose between Volt and Stanford regarding compensation for extra work allegedly performed by the contractor. Volt demanded arbitration and Stanford initiated a legal action in which it sued Volt for breach of contract and fraud and also sought indemnification from two other contractors not bound by an arbitration agreement. The California courts denied Volt's motion to compel arbitration and ordered a stay of the arbitral proceeding. According to state procedural law, California courts have discretion to stay arbitral proceedings pending the resolution of related litigation against third parties not bound by the arbitration agreement. The purpose of the provision is to avoid conflicting rulings on the same matter by different tribunals:

> Section 1281.2 (c) [of the CAL. CIV. PROC. CODE ANN. (West 1982)] provides, in pertinent part, that when a court determines that "[a] party to the arbitration agreement is also a party to a pending court action or special proceeding with a third party, arising out of the same transaction or series of related transactions and there is a possibility of conflicting rulings on a common issue of law or fact [,] . . . the court (1) may refuse to enforce the arbitration agreement and may order intervention or joinder of all parties in a single action or special proceeding; (2) may order intervention or joinder as to all or only certain issues; (3) may order arbitration among the parties who have agreed to arbitration and stay the pending court action or special proceeding pending the outcome of the arbitration proceeding; or (4) may stay arbitration pending the outcome of the court action or special proceeding." 489 U.S. at 471, n.3.

The question before the U.S. Supreme Court was two-fold: Had the parties in *Volt* intended to have California law govern not only the contract, but also any ensuing arbitration and, if so, was the applicable law valid under the Supremacy Clause of the Federal Constitution given that the application of state law resulted in a stay of the arbitration proceeding? In turn, these issues engendered a more wide-ranging, albeit circuitous, question: Could party intent be used to defeat the agreed-upon recourse to arbitration? In other words, although the parties agreed to resolve their contractual disputes through arbitration, they would have expressly provided for the application of a state law that could, upon the exercise of judicial discretion, undermine that intent.

California state courts held that the choice-of-law clause (mandating the application of local law) also governed the arbitration agreement. Because California law applied and its procedural law allowed courts to stay arbitral proceedings in circumstances of "intertwining" arbitral and legal proceedings, Volt's request to compel arbitration could lawfully be denied. This determination permitted state law to frustrate the rationale of and predominate over the FAA. In practical terms, it simply provided Stanford, the noncomplying party, with a loophole by which to avoid arbitration.

In prior rulings, primarily in the federalism trilogy, the Court held unequivocally that state legislation could not block the recourse to arbitration. The aim of promoting adjudicatory efficiency in these cases was not a sufficiently significant concern to override the FAA's policy mandate. The content of prior rulings would have predicted an espousal by the majority of the basic approach and content of the dissenting opinion. In arguing for a reversal, the dissenting justices emphasized the state law's detrimental impact upon and inconsistency with the provisions of the FAA and its objectives. State law, after all, was being used to thwart agreed-upon recourse to arbitration.

With an impressive 6 to 2 majority, the Court nonetheless held in *Volt* that the parties' contractual intent was clear (or, at least, the state court's interpretation of it could not be challenged) and that the intent to have state law govern could effectively defeat the agreement to arbitrate. The Court's previous preoccupation with elaborating legal rules uniformly favorable to arbitration was nowhere to be found. Now, the Court was of the view that the FAA meant to have arbitration agreements enforced as written. According to the Court, parties who expressly agree to arbitrate disputes also can agree, by implication from a choice-of-law provision, to undo that agreement whenever a court decides to exercise its discretion to stay arbitral proceedings under state procedural law. Because the dissent represented the views of the Court's two most liberal members, ideological differences appear to be at the heart of the determination. Rather than a statement on arbitration law, *Volt* seems to reflect the majority's adherence to the concept of sanctity of contract which, in turn, acts as a vehicle for expressing a particular concept of the role of government and of the place of the individual in society.

VOLT INFORMATION SCIENCES, INC. V. BOARD OF TRUSTEES OF LELAND STANFORD JUNIOR UNIVERSITY

489 U.S. 468, 109 S.Ct. 1248, 103 L.Ed.2d 488 (1989).

(footnotes omitted)

[. . .]

CHIEF JUSTICE REHNQUIST delivered the opinion of the Court.

Unlike its federal counterpart, the California Arbitration Act, Cal. Civ. Proc. Code Ann. § 1280 *et seq.* (West 1982), contains a provision allowing a court to stay arbitration pending resolution of related litigation. We hold that application of the California statute is not pre-empted by the Federal Arbitration Act in a case where the parties have agreed that their arbitration agreement will be governed by the law of California.

[. . .]

Appellant devotes the bulk of its argument to convincing us that the Court of Appeal erred in interpreting the choice-of-law clause to mean that the parties had incorporated the California rules of arbitration into their arbitration agreement. . . . Appellant acknowledges, as it must, that the interpretation of private contracts is ordinarily a question of state law, which this Court does not sit to review. But appellant nonetheless maintains that we should set aside the Court of Appeal's interpretation of this particular contractual provision for two principal reasons.

Appellant first suggests that the Court of Appeal's construction of the choice-of-law clause was in effect a finding that appellant had "waived" its "federally guaranteed right to compel arbitration of the parties' dispute," a waiver whose validity must be judged by reference to federal rather than state law. This argument fundamentally misconceives the nature of the rights created by the FAA. . . .

. . . § 4 of the FAA does not confer a right to compel arbitration of any dispute at any time; it confers only the right to obtain an order directing that "arbitration proceed in the manner provided for in [the parties'] agreement." Here the Court of Appeal found that, by incorporating the California rules of arbitration into their agreement, the parties had agreed that arbitration would not proceed in situations which fell within the scope of Calif. Code Civ. Proc. Ann. § 1281.2(c) (West 1982). This was not a finding that appellant had "waived" an FAA-guaranteed right to compel arbitration of this dispute, but a finding that it had no such right in the first place, because the parties' agreement did not require arbitration to proceed in this situation. Accordingly, appellant's contention that the contract interpretation issue presented here involves the "waiver" of a federal right is without merit.

Second, appellant argues that we should set aside the Court of Appeal's construction of the choice-of-law clause because it violates the settled federal rule that questions of arbitrability in contracts subject to the FAA must be resolved with a healthy regard for the federal policy favoring arbitration. . . . These [cited] cases of course establish that, in applying general state-law principles of contract interpretation to the interpretation of an arbitration agreement within the scope of the Act . . . due regard must be given to the federal policy favoring arbitration, and ambiguities as to the scope of the arbitration clause itself resolved in favor of arbitration.

But we do not think the Court of Appeal offended the *Moses H. Cone* principle by interpreting the choice-of-law provision to mean that the parties intended the California rules of arbitration, including the § 1281.2(c) stay provision, to apply to their arbitration agreement. There is no federal policy favoring arbitration under a certain set of procedural rules; the federal policy is simply to ensure the enforceability, according to their terms, of private agreements to arbitrate. Interpreting a choice-of-law clause to make applicable state rules governing the conduct of arbitration, rules which are manifestly designed to encourage resort to the arbitral process, simply does not offend the rule of liberal construction set forth in *Moses H. Cone*, nor does it offend any other policy embodied in the FAA.

The question remains whether, assuming the choice-of-law clause meant what the Court of Appeal found it to mean, application of Cal. Civ. Proc. Code Ann. § 1281.2(c) is nonetheless pre-empted by the FAA to the extent it is used to stay arbitration under this contract involving interstate commerce. It is undisputed that this contract falls within the coverage of the FAA, since it involves interstate commerce, and that the FAA contains no provision authorizing a stay of arbitration in this situation. Appellee contends, however, that §§ 3 and 4 of the FAA, which are the specific sections claimed to conflict with the California statute at issue here, are not applicable in this state-court proceeding and thus cannot pre-empt application of the California statute. While the argument is not without some merit, we need not resolve it to decide this case, for we conclude that even if §§ 3 and 4 of the FAA are fully applicable in state-court proceedings, they do not prevent application of Cal. Civ. Proc. Code Ann. § 1281.2(c) to stay arbitration where, as here, the parties have agreed to arbitrate in accordance with California law.

The FAA contains no express pre-emptive provision, nor does it reflect a congressional intent to occupy the entire field of arbitration. . . . But even when Congress has not completely displaced state regulation in an area, state law may nonetheless be pre-empted to the extent that it actually conflicts with federal law, that is, to the extent that it "stands as an obstacle to the accomplishment and execution of the full purposes and objectives of Congress." . . . The question before us, therefore, is whether application of Cal. Civ. Proc. Code Ann. § 1281.2(c) to stay arbitration under this contract in interstate commerce, in accordance with the terms of the arbitration agreement itself, would undermine the goals and policies of the FAA. We conclude that it would not.

The FAA was designed "to overrule the judiciary's long-standing refusal to enforce agreements to arbitrate" . . . and to place such agreements " 'upon the same footing as other contracts' " . . . While Congress was no doubt aware that the Act would encourage the expeditious resolution of disputes, its passage "was motivated, first and foremost, by a congressional desire to enforce agreements into which parties had entered." . . . Accordingly, we have recognized that the FAA does not require parties to arbitrate when they have not agreed to do so . . . nor does it prevent parties who do agree to arbitrate from excluding certain claims from the scope of their arbitration agreement. It simply requires courts to enforce privately negotiated agreements to arbitrate, like other contracts, in accordance with their terms. . . .

In recognition of Congress' principal purpose of ensuring that private arbitration agreements are enforced according to their terms, we have held that the FAA pre-empts state laws which "require a judicial forum for the resolution of claims which the contracting parties agreed to resolve by arbitration." . . . But it does not follow that the FAA prevents the enforcement of agreements to arbitrate under different rules than those set forth in the Act itself. Indeed, such a result would be quite inimical to the FAA's primary purpose of ensuring that private agreements to arbitrate are enforced according to their terms. Arbitration under the Act is a matter of consent, not coercion, and parties are generally free to structure their arbitration agreements as they see fit. . . . Where, as here, the parties have agreed to abide by state rules of arbitration, enforcing those rules according to the terms of the agreement is fully consistent with the goals of the FAA, even if the result is that arbitration is stayed where the Act would otherwise permit it to go forward. By permitting the courts to "rigorously enforce" such agreements according to their terms, . . . we give effect to the contractual rights and expectations of the parties, without doing violence to the policies behind the FAA.

The judgment of the Court of Appeals is *Affirmed.*

JUSTICE O'CONNOR took no part in the consideration or decision of this case.

JUSTICE BRENNAN, with whom JUSTICE MARSHALL joins, dissenting.

The litigants in this case were parties to a construction contract which contained a clause obligating them to arbitrate disputes and making that obligation specifically enforceable. The contract also incorporated provisions of a standard form contract prepared by the American Institute of Architects and endorsed by the Associated General Contractors of

America; among these general provisions was § 7.1.1: "The Contract shall be governed by the law of the place where the Project is located." When a dispute arose between the parties, Volt invoked the arbitration clause, while Stanford attempted to avoid it (apparently because the dispute also involved two other contractors with whom Stanford had no arbitration agreements).

The Federal Arbitration Act requires courts to enforce arbitration agreements in contracts involving interstate commerce. . . . The California courts nonetheless rejected Volt's petition to compel arbitration in reliance on a provision of state law that, in the circumstances presented, permitted a court to stay arbitration pending the conclusion of related litigation. Volt, not surprisingly, suggested that the Supremacy Clause compelled a different result. The California Court of Appeal found, however, that the parties had agreed that their contract would be governed solely by the law of the State of California, to the exclusion of federal law. In reaching this conclusion the court relied on no extrinsic evidence of the parties' intent, but solely on the language of the form contract that the " 'law of the place where the project is located' " would govern.

This Court now declines to review that holding, which denies effect to an important federal statute, apparently because it finds no question of federal law involved. I can accept neither the state court's unusual interpretation of the parties' contract, nor this Court's unwillingness to review it. I would reverse the judgment of the California Court of Appeal.

I

Contrary to the Court's view, the state court's construction of the choice-of-law clause is reviewable for two independent reasons.

A

[. . .]

[T]he right of the parties to have their arbitration agreement enforced pursuant to the FAA could readily be circumvented by a state-court construction of their contract as having intended to exclude the applicability of federal law. It is therefore essential that, while according due deference to the decision of the state court, we independently determine whether we "clearly would have judged the issue differently if [we] were the state's highest court".

B

Arbitration is, of course, "a matter of contract and a party cannot be required to submit to arbitration any dispute which he has not agreed so to submit.". . . . I agree with the Court that "the FAA does not require parties to arbitrate when they have not agreed to do so.". . . . Since the FAA merely requires enforcement of what the parties have agreed to, moreover, they are free if they wish to write an agreement to arbitrate outside the coverage of the FAA. Such an agreement would permit a state rule, otherwise pre-empted by the FAA, to govern their arbitration. The substantive question in this case is whether or not they have done so. And that question, we have made clear in the past, is a matter of federal law.

[. . .]

The Court recognizes the relevance of the *Moses H. Cone* principle but finds it unoffended by the Court of Appeal's decision, which, the Court suggests, merely determines what set of procedural rules will apply. I agree fully with the Court that "the federal policy is simply to ensure the enforceability, according to their terms, of private agreements to arbitrate," . . . but I disagree emphatically with its conclusion that that policy is not frustrated here. Applying the California procedural rule, which stays arbitration while litigation of the same issue goes forward, means simply that the parties' dispute will be litigated rather than arbitrated. Thus, interpreting the parties' agreement to say that the California procedural rules apply rather than the FAA, where the parties arguably had no such intent, implicates the *Moses H. Cone* principle no less than would an interpretation of the parties' contract that erroneously denied the existence of an agreement to arbitrate.

While appearing to recognize that the state court's interpretation of the contract does raise a question of federal law, the Court nonetheless refuses to determine whether the state court misconstrued that agreement. There is no warrant for failing to do so. The FAA requires that a court determining a question of arbitrability not stop with the application of state-law rules for construing the parties' intentions, but that it also take account of the command of federal law that "those intentions [be] generously construed as to issues of arbitrability." . . . Thus, the decision below is based on both state and federal law, which are thoroughly intertwined. In such circumstances the state-court judgment cannot be said to rest on an "adequate and independent state ground" so as to bar review by this Court.

II

Construed with deference to the opinion of the California Court of Appeal, yet "with a healthy regard for the federal policy favoring arbitration," it is clear that the choice-of-law clause cannot bear the interpretation the California court assigned to it.

[. . .]

III

Most commercial contracts written in this country contain choice-of-law clauses, similar to the one in the Stanford-Volt contract, specifying which State's law is to govern the interpretation of the contract. . . . Were every state court to construe such clauses as an expression of the parties' intent to exclude the application of federal law, as has the California Court of Appeal in this case, the result would be to render the Federal Arbitration Act a virtual nullity as to presently existing contracts. I cannot believe that the parties to contracts intend such consequences to flow from their insertion of a standard choice-of-law clause. Even less can I agree that we are powerless to review decisions of state courts that effectively nullify a vital piece of federal legislation. I respectfully dissent.

NOTES AND QUESTIONS

1. The majority argues that the parties are bound by their contractual provisions as stipulated and that rigorous contract enforcement reinforces rather than undermines the consensual foundation of arbitration. The dissent addresses the case from the perspective of the federalism trilogy: State law in *Volt* undermines the right to arbitrate in a transaction involving interstate commerce, contravenes the provisions of the FAA, and is therefore unconstitutional under the Supremacy Clause.

In some measure, the disagreement between the various members of the Court exemplifies the clash between liberal and conservative ideologies. The majority stands upon the principle of *pacta sunt servanda* (party agreements must be observed) and refuses to relieve Volt of the burden of its errors in contractual strategy, while the dissent is willing to manipulate the sanctity of contract to achieve an outcome that achieves its brand of social justice and furthers the federal policy on arbitration. In this sense, the question of the FAA's legal status has little presence in the division that *Volt* creates in the Court. It is ancillary to the unstated but driving controversy about the function and meaning of legal rules, the judicial role in interpreting and applying law, and the ultimate mandate of judicial adjudication. Arguably, *Volt*, given the ideological substratum of the opinion and its position of dissonance in the decisional law, is not a ruling on arbitration at all, but rather a political colloquy within the Court on the larger questions that attend the operation of law.

2. A number of issues appear to have escaped the Court's attention. These issues arguably have some significance to the analysis and outcome, and they could have been used to reinforce the conclusions of either the majority or dissent. For example, the sophisticated business status of the parties could have sustained the majority's argument for the discipline of contract. By the same token, the boilerplate character of the choice-of-law clause would have added to the credibility of the dissent's position that the parties' intent was to arbitrate disputes and that the reference to a disabling state law was pure happenstance and of no, or of amendable, legal effect. In your view, are there other important elements or issues that fail to figure with deserved prominence in the Court's opinion? Why do you find these considerations vital? Why do you think the Court ignores them? Are some elements emphasized by the Court negligible?

3. The arbitral clause in *Volt* provided:

> "All claims, disputes and other matters in question between the parties to this contract, arising out of or relating to this contract or the breach thereof, shall be decided by arbitration in accordance with the Construction Industry Arbitration Rules of the American Arbitration Association then prevailing unless the parties mutually agreed [sic] otherwise. This agreement to arbitrate . . . shall be specifically enforceable under the prevailing arbitration law."

489 U.S. at 470, n.1.

What did the parties intend through the language of this provision? Did they agree to submit their transactional disputes to arbitration? Did they want California law to force them into judicial adjudication? What is the significance of the reference to the AAA rules? What is meant by the phrase "the prevailing arbitration law"? Does it refer to the California arbitration law, provided it either comports with the parties' intent to arbitrate their disputes or is in accord with the general disposition of the FAA on arbitration, or simply to the FAA standing alone? Is this provision an example of inadequate drafting skills even for a standard clause? Should the lawyer who wrote the provision be liable in malpractice when the client's intent to arbitrate is frustrated?

4. The binding character of party choice in contract and its impact upon the FAA's policy on arbitration are the doctrinal centerpiece of the *Volt* opinion. The exercise of party choice, especially in contracts that include a reference to arbitration, can become a rather complex matter. The parties clearly have a legal right to choose the law that governs their contractual relationship. When they decide to arbitrate disputes, the parties also can choose a law to govern the procedural aspects of their arbitration. The law governing the contract and the law governing the arbitration can be the same law or a different law.

In *Volt*, the contractor adopted the standard practice of choosing the customer's law to govern the contract. No express choice-of-law was made as to the law governing the arbitration. The silence of the contract on this question was broken only by a reference to the AAA institutional rules of arbitration. Such rules do not constitute a law of arbitration. Party choice on the question, therefore, either was nonexistent or could be implied from and equated with the choice-of-law provision as to the contract. The Court chooses to use the methodology of implication to select California arbitration law as the law governing the arbitration. The silence of the clause as to the arbitral choice-of-law, however, could also mean that the parties simply omitted to choose a law governing the arbitration. It could also be addressed by holding that a sophisticated business party should reasonably be expected to write a complete contract. The gap in the arbitration agreement could be filled in a number of ways. Any one of the following laws could be selected as the governing law of arbitration. The arbitration law at the place of arbitration because it is the law of the territorial venue. The arbitration law at the likely place of the enforcement of the award because the award will affect local assets. The arbitration law at the place where lawsuits are filed in connection with the arbitration because the ruling court is most familiar with its own law. The arbitration law of the place that has the greatest connection with the designated institutional rules of arbitration to facilitate familiarity, enforcement, and sound decision-making. A uniform statutory law or common law of arbitration in order to promote the harmony of laws and to avoid giving choice-of-law an outcome determinative effect. Or, the FAA when federal courts can be implicated in the matter through diversity or federal-question jurisdiction because the statute is favorable to arbitration.

This list of possible options may not be exhaustive. It illustrates the dangers of not exercising party choice in a transactional setting and the difficulty of providing a remedy when gaps are left in the contract. How would you resolve the choice-of-law problem in *Volt*? Who should make the determination as to which law of arbitration applies when the agreement is silent? What factors should influence the choice? What assumptions might be useful in filling the gap? Should the choice-of-law as to contract always be an influential factor or should silence on this specific question always be resolved in favor of the application of federal law?

5. The *Volt* decision made commercial lawyers, large commercial law firms, and the arbitration bar in general shudder. Can you identify and explain the reasons for their reaction? Why should the opinion induce apprehension? What rationale might lurk in the fine points of the opinion? Is there any basis for considering *Volt* a decisional anomaly?

6. The reasoning and result in *Volt* could be tested by applying radical solutions to the issues in the case that reflect the contemporary judicial policy of always finding a means to sustain the reference to arbitration. For example, why couldn't Stanford's disputes with the two other contractors simply be joined or consolidated with the projected arbitration between Volt and Stanford? Why couldn't the California courts exercise their statutory discretion in that fashion? What are the likely legal and doctrinal objections? Shouldn't such objections succumb to the policy imperative underlying the FAA?

7. The majority opinion perceives no conflict between the provision in the California arbitration statute and the FAA. In fact, the majority believes that the statutory provision for the consolidation or stay of arbitral proceedings is in the best interest of justice. How does the majority reconcile this view with its holding in *Keating*? Is it plausible? In this regard, you should assess the Court's reasoning in footnote five of the opinion:

> [W]e think the California arbitration rules which the parties have incorporated into their contract generally foster the federal policy favoring arbitration.... [T]he FAA itself contains no provision designed to deal with the special practical problems that arise in multiparty contractual disputes when some or all of the contracts at issue include agreements to arbitrate. California has taken the lead in fashioning a legislative response to this problem, by giving courts authority to consolidate or stay arbitration proceedings in these

> situations in order to minimize the potential for contradictory judgments.

489 U.S. at 476 n.5.

Does this language simply ignore the problem and the fact that the California provision frustrates party recourse to arbitration?

8. In footnote six of the opinion, the Court states that the effect of *Keating*, and presumably of the other cases on arbitration, was to obligate state courts to apply Sections One and Two of the FAA, characterizing them as "substantive" provisions of the legislation. The Court, however, declares that the obligation never included Sections Three and Four, which refer expressly to the federal courts. Is the distinction persuasive? What are its practical implications? Does such a ruling provide for a cohesive doctrine on arbitration?

9. The relatively new doctrinal notion that causes a shift in the *Volt* Court's reasoning on arbitration is the view of contractualism: Under the FAA, arbitration agreements are enforceable according to their specific contract language. The emphasis of the decisional law moves from protecting the contractual right to arbitrate (the reversal of judicial hostility to arbitration) to the enforcement of stipulated obligations in the contract of arbitration (party autonomy). "[W]e have recognized that the FAA does not require parties to arbitrate when they have not agreed to do so." Even the dissent, in its footnote four, agrees with the new doctrinal emphasis:

> [T]he FAA does not pre-empt state arbitration rules, even as applied to contracts involving interstate commerce, when the parties have agreed to arbitrate by those rules to the exclusion of federal arbitration law. I would not reach that question, however, because I conclude that the parties have made no such agreement.

Does the integration of the "contractualist" addendum in the Court's developing arbitration doctrine make sense in terms of the practical reality of commercial contracting or of the judicial enforcement of contracts? Would parties agree to arbitrate disputes and also agree that state law could surprise them into a nonagreement to arbitrate? Does the "contractualist" view respond to the conflict between federal and state law in *Volt*? Is it simply a means of conveniently sidestepping that issue? Why does contractualism appear to have the Court's unanimous support?

10. With *Volt*, conflicts and contradictions begin to surface in the Court's reasoning and rulings on arbitration both in terms of the federalism issue and in regard to the coherence of doctrine. The emphatic character of the Court's initial pronouncements on arbitration and federalism left little room for flexibility and the subtleties of exceptions. After *Volt*, how would you summarize the basic tenets of the Court's arbitration doctrine, especially as it relates to federalism and the standing of the FAA? Can you articulate a set of propositions that might predict the content of future rulings?

Mastrobuono

Mastrobuono falls squarely in the Court's federalization policy. Despite *Mastrobuono*'s factual and decisional similarity to *Volt,* the Court rules against the application of state law. In doing so, the Court places a qualification upon the freedom of contract principle articulated in *Volt*. In effect, after *Mastrobuono,* party choice of state law will be fully respected only when the choice-of-law fosters the recourse to arbitration or when the parties have expressly recognized that the state law contains a restriction on the right to arbitrate and expressly agree that the restriction is applicable to their arbitration.

The plaintiffs in *Mastrobuono* opened a securities account with Shearson Lehman Hutton and signed a standard client's agreement. Paragraph thirteen contained an arbitral clause under which the parties agreed to resolve disputes through NASD arbitration. It also provided for the application of New York law to the agreement. After closing the account, the plaintiffs filed suit alleging that Shearson personnel mishandled their funds. The brokerage company, however, prevailed on its motion to stay the court proceeding and to compel arbitration.

Thereafter, an arbitral tribunal awarded the plaintiffs $160,000 in compensatory damages and $400,000 in punitive damages. Shearson appealed, arguing that New York law governed the arbitration and that the rule in *Garrity v. Lyle Stuart, Inc.*, 40 N.Y.2d 354, 386 N.Y.S.2d 831, 353 N.E.2d 793 (1976), a landmark state case, prohibited the arbitrators from awarding punitive damages. The U.S. Supreme Court granted *certiorari* to consider whether "a contractual choice-of-law provision may preclude an arbitral award of punitive damages that otherwise would be proper." The Court answered in the negative, reversing the federal district court and the Seventh Circuit Court of Appeals. The latter courts had held that the arbitral tribunal had no authority to award punitive damages under New York law.

For the majority, Justice Stevens stated that the reference to arbitration was a matter of contract choice. The purpose of the judicial implementation of the FAA was to enforce arbitration agreements as written. The Court borrowed language from *Volt* to justify its interpretation of the federal legislation:

> But it does not follow that the FAA prevents the enforcement of agreements to arbitrate under different rules than those set forth in the Act itself. Indeed, such a result would be quite inimical to the FAA's primary purpose of ensuring that private agreements to arbitrate are enforced according to their terms. *Arbitration under the act is a matter of consent, not coercion,* and parties are generally free to structure their arbitration agreements as they see fit. Just as they may limit by contract the issues which they

> will arbitrate . . . so too may they specify by contract the rules under which that arbitration will be conducted. 514 U.S. at 57 (emphasis added) (quoting *Volt*, 489 U.S. at 479).

The majority in *Mastrobuono* then asserted that *Volt* legitimated its determination.

MASTROBUONO V. SHEARSON LEHMAN HUTTON, INC.

514 U.S. 52, 115 S.Ct. 1212, 131 L.Ed.2d 76 (1995).

JUSTICE STEVENS delivered the opinion of the Court.

New York law allows courts, but not arbitrators, to award punitive damages. In a dispute arising out of a standard-form contract that expressly provides that it "shall be governed by the laws of the State of New York," a panel of arbitrators awarded punitive damages. The District Court and Court of Appeals disallowed that award. The question presented is whether the arbitrators' award is consistent with the central purpose of the Federal Arbitration Act to ensure "that private agreements to arbitrate are enforced according to their terms." *Volt Information Sciences, Inc.* . . .

[. . .]

II

Earlier this Term, we upheld the enforceability of a predispute arbitration agreement governed by Alabama law, even though an Alabama statute provides that arbitration agreements are unenforceable. . . . After determining that the FAA applied to the parties' arbitration agreement, we readily concluded that the federal statute pre-empted Alabama's statutory prohibition. . . .

Petitioners seek a similar disposition of the case before us today. Here, the Seventh Circuit interpreted the contract to incorporate New York law, including the *Garrity* rule that arbitrators may not award punitive damages. Petitioners ask us to hold that the FAA pre-empts New York's prohibition against arbitral awards of punitive damages because this state law is a vestige of the " 'ancient' " judicial hostility to arbitration. . . . Petitioners rely on *Southland Corp. v. Keating* . . . and *Perry v. Thomas* . . . , in which we held that the FAA pre-empted two California statutes that purported to require judicial resolution of certain disputes. In *Southland*, we explained that the FAA not only "declared a national policy favoring arbitration," but actually "withdrew the power of the states to require a judicial forum for the resolution of claims which the contracting parties agreed to resolve by arbitration." . . .

Respondents answer that the choice-of-law provision in their contract evidences the parties' express agreement that punitive damages should not be awarded in the arbitration of any dispute arising under their contract.

Thus, they claim, this case is distinguishable from *Southland* and *Perry*, in which the parties presumably desired unlimited arbitration but state law stood in their way. Regardless of whether the FAA pre-empts the *Garrity* decision in contracts not expressly incorporating New York law, respondents argue that the parties may themselves agree to be bound by *Garrity*, just as they may agree to forgo arbitration altogether. In other words, if the contract says "no punitive damages," that is the end of the matter, for courts are bound to interpret contracts in accordance with the expressed intentions of the parties—even if the effect of those intentions is to limit arbitration.

We have previously held that the FAA's pro-arbitration policy does not operate without regard to the wishes of the contracting parties. In *Volt Information Sciences, Inc.*, . . . the California Court of Appeal had construed a contractual provision to mean that the parties intended the California rules of arbitration, rather than the FAA's rules, to govern the resolution of their dispute. . . . Noting that the California rules were "manifestly designed to encourage resort to the arbitral process," . . . and that they "generally foster[ed] the federal policy favoring arbitration," . . . we concluded that such an interpretation was entirely consistent with the federal policy "to ensure the enforceability, according to their terms, of private agreements to arbitrate." . . . After referring to the holdings in *Southland* and *Perry*, which struck down state laws limiting agreed-upon arbitrability, we added:

> "But it does not follow that the FAA prevents the enforcement of agreements to arbitrate under different rules than those set forth in the Act itself. Indeed, such a result would be quite inimical to the FAA's primary purpose of ensuring that private agreements to arbitrate are enforced according to their terms. Arbitration under the Act is a matter of consent, not coercion, and parties are generally free to structure their arbitration agreements as they see fit. Just as they may limit by contract the issues which they will arbitrate . . . so too may they specify by contract the rules under which that arbitration will be conducted." *Volt*, 489 U.S. at 479.

Relying on our reasoning in *Volt*, respondents thus argue that the parties to a contract may lawfully agree to limit the issues to be arbitrated by waiving any claim for punitive damages. On the other hand, we think our decisions in *Allied-Bruce*, *Southland*, and *Perry* make clear that if contracting parties agree to include claims for punitive damages within the issues to be arbitrated, the FAA ensures that their agreement will be enforced according to its terms even if a rule of state law would otherwise exclude such claims from arbitration. Thus, the case before us comes down to what the contract has to say about the arbitrability of petitioners' claim for punitive damages.

III

Shearson's standard-form "Client Agreement," which petitioners executed, contains 18 paragraphs. The two relevant provisions of the agreement are found in Paragraph 13. The first sentence of that paragraph provides, in part, that the entire agreement "shall be governed by the laws of the State of New York." . . . The second sentence provides that "any controversy" arising out of the transactions between the parties "shall be settled by arbitration" in accordance with the rules of the National Association of Securities Dealers (NASD), or the Boards of Directors of the New York Stock Exchange and/or the American Stock Exchange. . . . The agreement contains no express reference to claims for punitive damages.

The choice-of-law provision, when viewed in isolation, may reasonably be read as merely a substitute for the conflict-of-laws analysis that otherwise would determine what law to apply to disputes arising out of the contractual relationship. Thus, if a similar contract, without a choice-of-law provision, had been signed in New York and was to be performed in New York, presumably "the laws of the State of New York" would apply, even though the contract did not expressly so state. In such event, there would be nothing in the contract that could possibly constitute evidence of an intent to exclude punitive damages claims. Accordingly, punitive damages would be allowed because, in the absence of contractual intent to the contrary, the FAA would pre-empt the *Garrity* rule. . . .

Even if the reference to "the laws of the State of New York" is more than a substitute for ordinary conflict-of-laws analysis and, as respondents urge, includes the caveat, "detached from otherwise-applicable federal law," the provision might not preclude the award of punitive damages because New York allows its courts, though not its arbitrators, to enter such awards. . . . In other words, the provision might include only New York's substantive rights and obligations, and not the State's allocation of power between alternative tribunals. Respondents' argument is persuasive only if "New York law" means "New York decisional law, including that State's allocation of power between courts and arbitrators, notwithstanding otherwise-applicable federal law." But, as we have demonstrated, the provision need not be read so broadly. It is not, in itself, an unequivocal exclusion of punitive damages claims.

The arbitration provision (the second sentence of Paragraph 13) does not improve respondents' argument. On the contrary, when read separately this clause strongly implies that an arbitral award of punitive damages is appropriate. It explicitly authorizes arbitration in accordance with NASD rules; the panel of arbitrators in fact proceeded under that set of rules. The NASD's Code of Arbitration Procedure indicates that arbitrators may award "damages and other relief." NASD Code of Arbitration Procedure 3741(e) (1993). While not a clear authorization of punitive damages, this provision appears broad enough at least to contemplate such a remedy. Moreover, as the Seventh Circuit noted, a manual provided to NASD arbitrators contains this provision:

> "B. Punitive Damages
>
> "The issue of punitive damages may arise with great frequency in arbitrations. Parties to arbitration are informed that arbitrators can consider punitive damages as a remedy." . . .

Thus, the text of the arbitration clause itself surely does not support—indeed, it contradicts—the conclusion that the parties agreed to foreclose claims for punitive damages.

Although neither the choice-of-law clause nor the arbitration clause, separately considered, expresses an intent to preclude an award of punitive damages, respondents argue that a fair reading of the entire Paragraph 13 leads to that conclusion. On this theory, even if "New York law" is ambiguous, and even if "arbitration in accordance with NASD rules" indicates that punitive damages are permissible, the juxtaposition of the two clauses suggests that the contract incorporates "New York law relating to arbitration." We disagree. At most, the choice-of-law clause introduces an ambiguity into an arbitration agreement that would otherwise allow punitive damages awards. As we pointed out in *Volt*, when a court interprets such provisions in an agreement covered by the FAA, "due regard must be given to the federal policy favoring arbitration, and ambiguities as to the scope of the arbitration clause itself resolved in favor of arbitration." . . .

Moreover, respondents cannot overcome the common-law rule of contract interpretation that a court should construe ambiguous language against the interest of the party that drafted it. . . .

[. . .]

We hold that the Court of Appeals misinterpreted the parties' agreement. The arbitral award should have been enforced as within the scope of the contract. The judgment of the Court of Appeals is, therefore, reversed.

It is so ordered.

JUSTICE THOMAS, dissenting.

In *Volt Information Sciences, Inc.*, . . . we held that the Federal Arbitration Act . . . simply requires courts to enforce private contracts to arbitrate as they would normal contracts—according to their terms. This holding led us to enforce a choice-of-law provision that incorporated a state procedural rule concerning arbitration proceedings. Because the choice-of-law provision here cannot reasonably be distinguished from the one in *Volt*, I dissent.

I

A

[. . .]

[In *Volt*], [w]e concluded that even if the FAA preempted the state statute as applied to other parties, the choice-of-law clause in the contract at issue demonstrated that the parties had agreed to be governed by the statute. Rejecting Volt's position that the FAA imposes a pro-arbitration policy that precluded enforcement of the statute permitting the California courts to stay the arbitration proceedings, we concluded that the Act "simply requires courts to enforce privately negotiated agreements to arbitrate, like other contracts, in accordance with their terms." . . . As a result, we interpreted the choice-of-law clause "to make applicable state rules governing the conduct of arbitration" . . . even if a specific rule itself hampers or delays arbitration. We rejected the argument that the choice-of-law clause was to be construed as incorporating only substantive law, and dismissed the claim that the FAA preempted those contract provisions that might hinder arbitration.

We so held in *Volt* because we concluded that the FAA does not force arbitration on parties who enter into contracts involving interstate commerce. Instead, the FAA requires only that "arbitration proceed in the manner provided for in [the parties'] agreement." . . . Although we will construe ambiguities concerning the scope of arbitrability in favor of arbitration, . . . we remain mindful that "as with any other contract, the parties' intentions control." . . . Thus, if the parties intend that state procedure shall govern, federal courts must enforce that understanding. "There is no federal policy favoring arbitration under a certain set of procedural rules; the federal policy is simply to ensure the enforceability, according to their terms, of private agreements to arbitrate." *Volt*. . . .

B

In this case, as in *Volt*, the parties agreed to mandatory arbitration of all disputes. As in *Volt*, the contract at issue here includes a choice-of-law clause. Indeed, the language of the two clauses is functionally equivalent: whereas the choice-of-law clause in *Volt* provided that "[t]he Contract shall be governed by the law of [the State of California]," the one before us today states, in Paragraph 13 of the Client's Agreement, that "[t]his agreement . . . shall be governed by the laws of the State of New York." New York law forbids arbitrators from awarding punitive damages . . . and permits only courts to award such damages. As in *Volt*, petitioners here argue that the New York rule is "anti-arbitration," and hence is pre-empted by the FAA. In concluding that the choice-of-law clause is ambiguous, the majority essentially accepts petitioners' argument. *Volt* itself found precisely the same argument irrelevant, however, and the majority identifies no reason to think that the state law governing the interpretation of the parties' choice-of-law clause supports a different result.

The majority claims that the incorporation of New York law "need not be read so broadly" as to include both substantive and procedural law, and that the choice of New York law "is not, in itself, an unequivocal exclusion of punitive damages claims." . . . But we rejected these same arguments in *Volt*, and the *Garrity* rule is just the sort of "state rule[ ] governing the conduct of arbitration" that Volt requires federal courts to enforce. . . . "Just as [the parties] may limit by contract the issues which they will arbitrate, so too may they specify by contract the rules under which that arbitration will be conducted." . . . To be sure, the majority might be correct that *Garrity* is a rule concerning the State's allocation of power between "alternative tribunals," . . . although *Garrity* appears to describe itself as substantive New York law. Nonetheless, *Volt* makes no distinction between rules that serve only to distribute authority between courts and arbitrators (which the majority finds unenforceable) and other types of rules (which the majority finds enforceable). Indeed, the California rule in *Volt* could be considered to be one that allocates authority between arbitrators and courts, for it permits California courts to stay arbitration pending resolution of related litigation. . . .

II

The majority relies upon two assertions to defend its departure from *Volt*. First, it contends that "[a]t most, the choice-of-law clause introduces an ambiguity into an arbitration agreement." . . . We are told that the agreement "would otherwise allow punitive damages awards," because of Paragraph 13's statement that arbitration would be conducted "in accordance with the rules then in effect, of the National Association of Securities Dealers, Inc." It is unclear which NASD "rules" the parties mean, although I am willing to agree with the majority that the phrase refers to the NASD Code of Arbitration Procedure. But the provision of the NASD Code offered by the majority simply does not speak to the availability of punitive damages. It only states:

> "The award shall contain the names of the parties, the name of counsel, if any, a summary of the issues, including the type(s) of any security or product, in controversy, the damages and other relief requested, the damages and other relief awarded, a statement of any other issues resolved, the names of the arbitrators, the dates the claim was filed and the award rendered, the number and dates of hearing sessions, the location of the hearings, and the signatures of the arbitrators concurring in the award." NASD Code of Arbitration Procedure § 41(e) (1985).

It is clear that § 41(e) does not define or limit the powers of the arbitrators; it merely describes the form in which the arbitrators must announce their decision. The other provisions of § 41 confirm this point. . . . The majority cannot find a provision of the NASD Code that specifically addresses punitive damages, or that speaks more generally to the types of damages arbitrators may or may not allow. Such a rule simply does not exist. The Code certainly does not require that arbitrators be empowered to award punitive damages; it leaves to the parties to define the arbitrators' remedial powers.

The majority also purports to find a clear expression of the parties' agreement on the availability of punitive damages in "a manual provided to NASD arbitrators." . . . But Paragraph 13 of the Client Agreement nowhere mentions this manual; it mentions only "the rules then in effect of the [NASD]." The manual does not fit either part of this description: it is neither "of the [NASD]," nor a set of "rules."

First, the manual apparently is not an official NASD document. The manual was not promulgated or adopted by the NASD. Instead, it apparently was compiled by members of the Securities Industry Conference on Arbitration (SICA) as a supplement to the Uniform Code of Arbitration, which the parties clearly did not adopt in Paragraph 13. Petitioners present no evidence that the NASD has a policy of giving this specific manual to its arbitrators. Nor do petitioners assert that this manual was even used in the arbitration that gave rise to this case. More importantly, there is no indication in the text of the Client's Agreement that the parties intended this manual to be used by the arbitrators.

Second, the manual does not provide any "rules" in the sense contemplated by Paragraph 13; instead, it provides general information and advice to the arbitrator, such as "Hints for the Chair." . . . The manual is nothing more than a sort of "how to" guide for the arbitrator. One bit of advice, for example, states: "Care should be exercised, particularly when questioning a witness, so that the arbitrator does not indicate disbelief. Grimaces, frowns, or hand signals should all be avoided. A 'poker' face is the goal." . . .

Even if the parties had intended to adopt the manual, it cannot be read to resolve the issue of punitive damages. When read in context, the portion of the SICA manual upon which the majority relies seems only to explain what punitive damages are, not to establish whether arbitrators have the authority to award them. . . .

[. . .]

My examination of the Client Agreement, the choice-of-law provision, the NASD Code of Procedure, and the SICA manual demonstrates that the parties made their intent clear, but not in the way divined by the majority. New York law specifically precludes arbitrators from awarding punitive damages, and it should be clear that there is no "conflict," as the majority puts it, between the New York law and the NASD rules. The choice-of-law provision speaks directly to the issue, while the NASD Code is silent. Giving effect to every provision of the contract requires us to honor the parties' intent, as indicated in the text of the agreement, to preclude the award of punitive damages by arbitrators.

III

Thankfully, the import of the majority's decision is limited and narrow. This case amounts to nothing more than a federal court applying Illinois and New York contract law to an agreement between parties in Illinois. Much like a federal court applying a state rule of decision to a case when sitting in diversity, the majority's interpretation of the contract represents only the understanding of a single federal court regarding the requirements imposed by state law. As such, the majority's opinion has applicability only to this specific contract and to no other. But because the majority reaches an erroneous result on even this narrow question, I respectfully dissent.

NOTES AND QUESTIONS

1. The majority and dissenting opinions have dramatically different interpretations of the applicable precedent. For the majority, *Volt* sustains the result reached in *Mastrobuono*, while the dissent believes that the cases as decided cannot be reconciled. Which view do you find more persuasive and why? How would you describe the holding in *Volt* and its relationship to *Mastrobuono*?

2. What is the doctrinal status and content of the Court's contract freedom view of arbitration after the ruling in *Mastrobuono*?

3. The majority stated that an independent "conflict-of-laws analysis" might point to the application of New York law, but would preclude the application of the New York bar on the award of punitive damages by arbitrators because the parties had not expressly decided to exclude such damages in their agreement, thereby making the state law provision subject to pre-exemption by the federalization policy. Moreover, even if the parties intended New York law to govern their contractual obligations, including their reference to arbitration, the choice of New York law would "include only New York's substantive rights and obligations, and not the state's allocation of power between alternative tribunals." Further, "[w]e think the best way to harmonize the choice-of-law provision with the arbitration provision is to read 'the laws of the State of New York' to encompass substantive principles that New York courts would apply, but not to include special rules limiting the authority of arbitrators. Thus, the choice-of-law provision covers the rights and duties of the parties, while the arbitration clause covers arbitration. . . ." The distinction is clear and imaginatively drawn. How persuasive is it?

4. Further, the Court argued that the reference in the agreement to NASD arbitration rules provided some justification for allowing the arbitrators to award punitive damages. Suffice it to state that the NASD Code of

Arbitration Procedure, although it refers to the question of punitive damages in arbitration, does not establish a clear institutional rule on that score. As the Court itself admits, "[w]hile not a clear authorization of punitive damages, this provision appears broad enough at least to contemplate such a remedy." Finally, equity demands that the cost and burden of the contract ambiguity be shouldered by the party opposing the award of punitive damages when that party drafted the contract and created the ambiguity between the choice-of-law and arbitration provisions. "The reason for this rule is to protect the party who did not choose the language from an unintended or unfair result." And, "the choice-of-law clause introduces an ambiguity into an arbitration agreement that would otherwise allow punitive damages awards."

5. Justice Thomas' dissenting analysis is trenchant and comprehensive. How do you evaluate his response to the majority position that the choice of New York law did not include the allocation of power to alternative tribunals? Which side of the Court has the more accurate appraisal of the NASD Code of Arbitration Procedure and the SICA manual? Is there deliberate distortion on the part of the majority? Can its position be squared with the facts?

6. Finally, you should consider the general question of whether arbitrators can be authorized, by law or by contract, to award punitive damages. How would you support the *Garrity* rule and how would you argue against it? As a matter of public policy, should parties be able to contract about the right?

Kaplan

In *Kaplan*, the Court holds that courts rather than arbitral tribunals have jurisdiction to resolve questions of arbitrability (presumably, contract inarbitrability: Whether a contract of arbitration exists and covers a specific dispute or set of disputes), unless the agreement to arbitrate provides that the arbitral tribunal has the authority to decide the matter. To buttress its determination, the Court espouses expressly a contract freedom view of arbitration and of arbitration law in general, under which the contract of arbitration can basically function as a completely self-contained system of arbitration law. This view of arbitration reduces matters of arbitration and the public interest in adjudication to a question of contractual consent between the parties in individual cases.

The Kaplans were private investors and the owners of an investment company (MKI). They, individually, and MKI, as a separate business entity, incurred substantial losses during the October 1987 stock market crash and thereafter in other stock transactions. First Options, a brokerage firm that clears stock trades on the Philadelphia Stock Exchange, was their creditor. First Options, MKI, and the Kaplans entered into four "work out" agreements to repay the debts, only one of which (between First Options and MKI) contained an arbitration agreement. When efforts to collect the debts failed, First Options filed a demand for arbitration against MKI and the Kaplans. The Kaplans refused to submit to arbitration and challenged the agreement to arbitrate. The arbitral tribunal nonetheless asserted jurisdiction and rendered an award against both MKI and the Kaplans. The question submitted to the Court was whether the arbitral tribunal had jurisdiction to adjudicate the disputes between First Options and the Kaplans.

The Court was unanimous in its resolution of the question. The Court's reasoning can be divided into three basic and inter-related parts. First, the Court—seemingly modifying, deserting, or forgetting its position that arbitration is a "mere form of trial"—acknowledges the "practical importance" of the arbitrability question to the party opposing arbitration, recognizing that arbitration involves the abandonment of the right to the judicial resolution of disputes. Second, it declares that the courts (rather than arbitral tribunals) have primary authority to resolve the arbitrability question, grounding its holding in and portraying its determination as a standard of review question. Finally, in a substantially, if not completely, contradictory corollary, the Court proclaims the contract of arbitration as the true source of final authority on the arbitrability question.

At the outset of the opinion, the Court describes the arbitrability question as a narrow concern, but concedes that it "has a certain practical significance." In particular, who decides whether there is a legal basis for compelling the parties to arbitrate can make "a critical difference" to the party resisting arbitration. By agreeing to arbitrate, a party abandons the right to obtain a judicial resolution of contractual disputes, even though some limited judicial supervision of arbitral awards is available. The Court now appears to believe that the waiver of rights gives the arbitrability question importance because it signifies that the parties, in effect, have chosen a form of justice other than judicial justice.

As a consequence, the Court concludes that the "emphatic federal policy" favoring arbitration does not govern the arbitrability question. In fact, on the threshold matter of arbitrability, the appropriate standard of review consists of a fully independent form of judicial review that replaces the normally "hospitable" federal court "inquiry" into issues of arbitration law. While all other arbitration questions are governed by the favorable federal policy, the Court believes that substantial unfairness would result if an unwilling, and—more importantly—an unobligated, party were forced to arbitrate. The Court creates a presumption that the arbitrability question is to be decided by the courts. To rebut the presumption, the party seeking to submit the arbitrability question to arbitration must submit persuasive evidence of the parties' agreement to have recourse to arbitration on the question of arbitrability. "Courts should not assume that the parties agreed to arbitrate arbitrability unless there is 'clear and unmistakable' evidence that they did so."

The two basic substantive segments of the *Kaplan* holding cannot coexist. On the one hand, the Court views arbitrability as a critical rights determination and mandates judicial disposition of the issue; on the other hand, it rules that the question, no matter how significant, can be reassigned to arbitral disposition through the vehicle of a private contract. At this point, none of the Court's complex reasoning on the standard of review question matters because arbitration clauses (especially adhesive ones) will now routinely include a reference of arbitrability questions to the arbitral tribunal. In the consumer and commercial context, courts will simply be excluded from the jurisdictional phase of arbitration by party agreement. The power of a contract clearly trumps the judicial authority to supervise or decide any aspect of arbitration law.

FIRST OPTIONS OF CHICAGO, INC. V. KAPLAN

514 U.S. 938, 115 S.Ct. 1920, 131 L.Ed.2d 985 (1995).

(footnotes omitted)

JUSTICE BREYER delivered the opinion of the Court.

In this case we consider two questions about how courts should review certain matters under the [F]ederal Arbitration Act . . . : (1) how a district court should review an arbitrator's decision that the parties agreed to arbitrate a dispute, and (2) how a court of appeals should review a district court's decision confirming, or refusing to vacate, an arbitration award.

I

[. . .]

We granted *certiorari* to consider two questions regarding the standards that the Court of Appeals used to review the determination that the Kaplans' dispute with First Options was arbitrable. . . . First, the Court of Appeals said that courts "should independently decide whether an arbitration panel has jurisdiction over the merits of any particular dispute." . . . First Options asked us to decide whether this is so (*i.e.*, whether courts, in "reviewing the arbitrators' decision on arbitrability," should "apply a *de novo* standard of review or the more deferential standard applied to arbitrators' decisions on the merits") when the objecting party "submitted the issue to the arbitrators for decision." . . . Second, the Court of Appeals stated that it would review a district court's denial of a motion to vacate a commercial arbitration award (and the correlative grant of a motion to confirm it) "*de novo*." . . . First Options argues that the Court of Appeals instead should have applied an "abuse of discretion" standard. . . .

II

The first question—the standard of review applied to an arbitrator's decision about arbitrability—is a narrow one. To understand just how narrow, consider three types of disagreement present in this case. First, the Kaplans and First Options disagree about whether the Kaplans are personally liable for MKI's debt to First Options. That disagreement makes up the *merits* of the dispute. Second, they disagree about whether they agreed to arbitrate the merits. That disagreement is about the *arbitrability* of the dispute. Third, they disagree about *who should have the primary power to decide the second matter*. Does that power belong primarily to the arbitrators (because the court reviews their arbitrability decision deferentially) or to the court (because the court makes up its mind about arbitrability independently)? We consider here only this third question.

Although the question is a narrow one, it has a certain practical importance. That is because a party who has not agreed to arbitrate will normally have a right to a court's decision about the merits of its dispute (say, as here, its obligation under a contract). But, where the party has agreed to arbitrate, he or she, in effect, has relinquished much of that right's practical value. The party still can ask a court to review the arbitrator's decision, but the court will set that decision aside only in very unusual circumstances. . . . Hence, who—court or arbitrator—has the primary authority to decide whether a party has agreed to arbitrate can make a critical difference to a party resisting arbitration.

We believe the answer to the "who" question (*i.e.*, the standard-of-review question) is fairly simple. Just as the arbitrability of the merits of a dispute depends upon whether the parties agreed to arbitrate that dispute . . . so the question "who has the primary power to decide arbitrability" turns upon what the parties agreed about *that* matter. Did the parties agree to submit the arbitrability question itself to arbitration? If so, then the court's standard for reviewing the arbitrator's decision about that matter should not differ from the standard courts apply when they review any other matter that parties have agreed to arbitrate. . . . That is to say, the court should give considerable leeway to the arbitrator, setting aside his or her decision only in certain narrow circumstances. . . . If, on the other hand, the parties did not agree to submit the arbitrability question itself to arbitration, then the court should decide that question just as it would decide any other question that the parties did not submit to arbitration, namely independently. These two answers flow inexorably from the fact that arbitration is simply a matter of contract between the parties; it is a way to resolve those disputes—but only those disputes—that the parties have agreed to submit to arbitration. . . .

We agree with First Options, therefore, that a court must defer to an arbitrator's arbitrability decision when the parties submitted that matter to arbitration. Nevertheless, that conclusion does not help First Options win this case. That is because a fair and complete answer to the standard-of-review question requires a word about how a court should decide whether the parties have agreed to submit the arbitrability issue to arbitration. And, that word makes clear that the Kaplans did not agree to arbitrate arbitrability here.

When deciding whether the parties agreed to arbitrate a certain matter (including arbitrability), courts generally (though with a qualification we discuss below) should apply ordinary state-law principles that govern the formation of contracts. . . . The relevant state law here, for example, would require the court to see whether the parties objectively revealed an intent to submit the arbitrability issue to arbitration. . . .

This Court, however, has (as we just said) added an important qualification, applicable when courts decide whether a party has agreed that arbitrators should decide arbitrability: Courts should not assume that the parties agreed to arbitrate arbitrability unless there is "clea[r] and unmistakabl[e]" evidence that they did so. In this manner the law treats silence or ambiguity about the question "*who* (primarily) should decide arbitrability" differently from the way it treats silence or ambiguity about the question "*whether* a particular merits-related dispute is arbitrable because it is within the scope of a valid arbitration agreement"—for in respect to this latter question the law reverses the presumption. . . .

But, this difference in treatment is understandable. The latter question arises when the parties have a contract that provides for arbitration of some issues. In such circumstances, the parties likely gave at least some thought to the scope of arbitration. And, given the law's permissive policies in respect to arbitration . . . one can understand why the law would insist upon clarity before concluding that the parties did not want to arbitrate a related matter. . . . On the other hand, the former question—the "who (primarily) should decide arbitrability" question—is rather arcane. A party often might not focus upon that question or upon the significance of having arbitrators decide the scope of their own powers. . . . And, given the principle that a party can be forced to arbitrate only those issues it specifically has agreed to submit to arbitration, one can understand why courts might hesitate to interpret silence or ambiguity on the "who should decide arbitrability" point as giving the arbitrators that power, for doing so might too often force unwilling parties to arbitrate a matter they reasonably would have thought a judge, not an arbitrator, would decide. . . .

On the record before us, First Options cannot show that the Kaplans clearly agreed to have the arbitrators decide (*i.e.*, to arbitrate) the question of arbitrability. . . .

[. . .]

We conclude that, because the Kaplans did not clearly agree to submit the question of arbitrability to arbitration, the Court of Appeals was correct in finding that the arbitrability of the Kaplan/First Options dispute was subject to independent review by the courts.

III

We turn next to the standard a court of appeals should apply when reviewing a district court decision that refuses to vacate . . . or confirms . . . an arbitration award. . . .

[. . .]

We believe . . . that the majority of Circuits is right in saying that courts of appeals should apply ordinary, not special, standards when reviewing district court decisions upholding arbitration awards. For one thing, it is undesirable to make the law more complicated by proliferating review standards without good reasons. More importantly, the reviewing attitude that a court of appeals takes toward a district court decision should depend upon "the respective institutional advantages of trial and appellate courts," not upon what standard of review will more likely produce a particular substantive result. . . . The law, for example, tells all courts (trial and appellate) to give administrative agencies a degree of legal leeway when they review certain interpretations of the law that those agencies have made. . . . But, no one, to our knowledge, has suggested that this policy of giving leeway to agencies means that a court of appeals should give extra leeway to a district court decision that upholds an agency. Similarly, courts grant arbitrators considerable leeway when reviewing most arbitration decisions; but that fact does not mean that appellate courts should give extra leeway to district courts that uphold arbitrators. First Options argues that the Arbitration Act is special because the Act, in one section, allows courts of appeals to conduct interlocutory review of certain antiarbitration district court rulings (*e.g.*, orders enjoining arbitrations), but not those upholding arbitration (*e.g.*, orders refusing to enjoin arbitrations). . . . But that portion of the Act governs the timing of review; it is therefore too weak a support for the distinct claim that the court of appeals should use a different standard when reviewing certain district court decisions. The Act says nothing about standards of review.

We conclude that the Court of Appeals used the proper standards for reviewing the District Court's arbitrability determinations.

[. . .]

The judgment of the Court of Appeals is affirmed.

It is so ordered.

NOTES AND QUESTIONS

1. Do you agree with the Court that arbitration "is simply a matter of contract between the parties"? Is this an overstatement? What regulatory role remains for the law under this view?

Assess the implications of the following statement upon the law of arbitration. The statement is from the Court's discussion of appropriate standards of judicial review: "[I]t is undesirable to make the law more complicated by proliferating review standards without good reasons." Is the machinery of law and of rights protection simply too cumbersome to implement? How does the ADR philosophy fit into the statement?

The question of arbitrability is central to the legal regulation of arbitration. It involves, in some instances, determining whether a valid arbitration agreement exists and, if so, whether it covers the dispute in question. As the Court itself observes, the agreement's validity and scope of application establish the boundary between judicial and arbitral jurisdiction, between public and private adjudication, and represent the parties' willingness to waive their legal right to judicial relief. Given the importance of the choice, it would seem that the law should determine when it has been made.

In *Kaplan*, the Court had the opportunity to integrate the *kompetenz-kompetenz* doctrine into the U.S. law of arbitration. It does so indirectly by holding that arbitrators can rule upon the validity and scope of arbitration agreements, if the arbitration agreement authorizes them to rule on these matters. For all intents and purposes, the *Kaplan* holding amounts to an adoption of the *kompetenz-kompetenz* doctrine on an *ad hoc*, contract basis. It is, however, curious that the Court neither refers to the *kompetenz-kompetenz* doctrine nor acknowledges the relevance of Section Three of the FAA, which provides for court determination of contract inarbitrability questions.

Is the suggestion accurate? Does *Kaplan* effectively overrule or render ineffective part of the holding in *Prima Paint*? What does the judge's observation say about the evolution and content of the Court's doctrine on arbitration? Is there some misunderstanding here that proceeds from the lack of a cohesive doctrinal architecture?

2. For a curious twist on the First Options of Chicago, Inc. doctrine, see *Awuah v. Coverall North Am. Inc.*, 554 F.3d 7 (1st Cir. 2009). There, the court entertained the argument that "the arbitral forum [was] illusory" in the circumstances of a franchise agreement between Coverall and its Franchisees. The latter were mostly recent immigrants who had agreed to provide janitorial cleaning services. They were ill-educated, had poor linguistic skills, and very limited resources. They sued for a litany of contract claims and Coverall sought to compel arbitration pursuant to the franchise agreement. The question ostensibly before the court of appeals was who (a court of or an arbitrator) would decide whether the arbitration agreement was unconscionable.

The contract provided for arbitration under the AAA Rules. AAA Rule 7(a) "codifies" Kaplan and generally the *kompetenz-kompetenz* doctrine by providing that arbitrators have the "power to rule on [their] own jurisdiction, including any objections with respect to the existence, scope or validity of the arbitration agreement."

The arbitration agreement also contained a severance provision, and severe limits on the arbitrator's power to modify the contract. It further provided that the parties would share the costs of arbitration and that the losing party would pay the winning party's attorney's fees. Moreover, class action arbitrations were barred.

The appellate court ruled that the arbitrator should decide whether the arbitral clause was sufficiently fair to be enforceable, *i.e.*, the arbitrator should rule on the unconscionability question. In other words, when the franchisees alleged that the agreement was unconscionable, the arbitrator was authorized by AAA Rule 7(a) to rule on the enforceability of the challenged agreement. The court, however, distinguished that question from the franchisees' claim that the arbitral forum was "illusory" on the basis of the exorbitant front-end and general costs of arbitration. The latter, the court asserted, created a question of whether the franchisees could have "access to the arbitrator." Relying on *Green Tree Fin. Corp.—Alabama v. Randolph*, 531 U.S. 79 (2000), the court emphasized that the costs of the private remedy might foreclose plaintiff access to arbitration. Whether this was the case, *i.e.*, whether the provision for arbitration was illusory, was a critical threshold consideration—separable from, and anterior to, unconscionability and the validity and enforceability of the arbitral clause, and was to be decided by the lower court.

Do you agree with the court's reasoning? Does it undermine or impair party prerogatives under First Options of Chicago, Inc. and the jurisdictional and decisional sovereignty of the arbitrator under *Howsam v. Dean Witter Reynolds, Inc.*, 537 U.S. 79 (2002) and *Green Tree Fin. Corp. v. Bazzle*, 539 U.S. 444 (2003)? The court quotes its prior ruling in *Kristian v. Comcast Corp.*, 446 F.3d 25, 37 (1st Cir. 2006), and contends that: "If arbitration prevents plaintiffs from vindicating their rights, it is no longer a 'valid alternative to traditional litigation.'" What does that statement mean and what does it do to AAA Rule 7(a)? Isn't the ruling a circumvention of the principle that arbitrators have the right to rule initially on their jurisdiction? It seems to bypass the arbitrator's authority and to restore judicial power over arbitration.

RENT-A-CENTER, WEST, INC. V. JACKSON

561 U.S. 63, 130 S.Ct. 2772, 177 L.Ed. 2d 403 (2010).

JUSTICE SCALIA delivered the opinion of the Court.

We consider whether, under the Federal Arbitration Act (FAA or Act), . . . a district court may decide a claim that an arbitration agreement is unconscionable, where the agreement explicitly assigns that decision to the arbitrator.

I

On February 1, 2007, the respondent here, Antonio Jackson, filed an employment-discrimination suit under Rev. Stat. § 1977, 42 U.S.C. § 1981, against his former employer in the United States District Court for the District of Nevada. The defendant and petitioner here, Rent-A-Center, West, Inc., filed a motion under the FAA to dismiss or stay the proceedings, 9 U.S.C. § 3, and to compel arbitration, § 4. Rent-A-Center argued that the Mutual Agreement to Arbitrate Claims (Agreement), which Jackson signed on February 24, 2003 as a condition of his employment there, precluded Jackson from pursuing his claims in court. The Agreement provided for arbitration of all "past, present or future" disputes arising out of Jackson's employment with Rent-A-Center, including "claims for discrimination" and "claims for violation of any federal . . . law." . . . It also provided that "[t]he Arbitrator, and not any federal, state, or local court or agency, shall have exclusive authority to resolve any dispute relating to the interpretation, applicability, enforceability or formation of this Agreement including, but not limited to any claim that all or any part of this Agreement is void or voidable." . . .

Jackson opposed the motion on the ground that "the arbitration agreement in question is clearly unenforceable in that it is unconscionable" under Nevada law . . . Rent-A-Center responded that Jackson's unconscionability claim was not properly before the court because Jackson had expressly agreed that the arbitrator would have exclusive authority to resolve any dispute about the enforceability of the Agreement. It also disputed the merits of Jackson's unconscionability claims.

The District Court granted Rent-A-Center's motion to dismiss the proceedings and to compel arbitration. The court found that the Agreement " ' "clearly and unmistakenly *[sic]*" ' " gives the arbitrator exclusive authority to decide whether the Agreement is enforceable, . . . (quoting *Howsam v. Dean Witter Reynolds, Inc.,* 537 U.S. 79, 83 (2002)), and, because Jackson challenged the validity of the Agreement *as a whole,* the issue was for the arbitrator, . . . (citing *Buckeye Check Cashing, Inc. v. Cardegna,* 546 U.S. 440, 444–445 (2006)). The court noted that even if it were to examine the merits of Jackson's unconscionability claims, it would have rejected the claim that the agreement to split arbitration fees was substantively unconscionable under Nevada law. It did not address Jackson's procedural or other substantive unconscionability arguments.

Without oral argument, a divided panel of the Court of Appeals for the Ninth Circuit reversed in part, affirmed in part, and remanded. . . . The court reversed on the question of who (the court or arbitrator) had the authority to decide whether the Agreement is enforceable. It noted that "Jackson does not dispute that the language of the Agreement clearly assigns the arbitrability determination to the arbitrator," but held that where "a party challenges an arbitration agreement as unconscionable, and thus asserts that he could not meaningfully assent to the agreement, the threshold question of unconscionability is for the court." . . . The Ninth Circuit affirmed the strict Court's alternative conclusion that the fee-sharing provision was not substantively unconscionable and remanded for consideration of Jackson's other unconscionability arguments. . . . Judge Hall dissented on the ground that "the question of the arbitration agreement's validity should have gone to the arbitrator, as the parties 'clearly and unmistakably provide[d]' in their agreement." . . .

We granted certiorari, 558 U.S. ___ (2010).

II

A

The FAA reflects the fundamental principle that arbitration is a matter of contract. Section 2, the "primary substantive provision of the Act," . . . provides:

> "A written provision in . . . a contract evidencing a transaction involving commerce to settle by arbitration a controversy thereafter arising out of such contract . . . shall be valid, irrevocable, and enforceable, save upon such grounds as exist at law or in equity for the revocation of any contract." . . .

The FAA thereby places arbitration agreements on an equal footing with other contracts . . . and requires courts to enforce them according to their terms. . . . Like other contracts, however, they may be invalidated by "generally applicable contract defenses, such as fraud, duress, or unconscionability." . . .

The Act also establishes procedures by which federal courts implement § 2's substantive rule. Under § 3, a party may apply to a federal court for a stay of the trial of an action "upon any issue referable to arbitration under an agreement in writing for such arbitration." Under § 4, a party "aggrieved" by the failure of another party "to arbitrate under a written agreement for arbitration" may petition a federal court "for an order directing that such arbitration proceed in the manner provided for in such agreement." The court "shall" order arbitration "upon being satisfied that the making of the agreement for arbitration or the failure to comply therewith is not in issue." . . .

The Agreement here contains multiple "written provision[s]" to "settle by arbitration a controversy," § 2. Two are relevant to our discussion. First, the section titled "Claims Covered By The Agreement" provides for arbitration of all "past, present or future" disputes arising out of Jackson's employment with Rent-A-Center. . . . Second, the section titled "Arbitration Procedures" provides that "[t]he Arbitrator . . . shall have exclusive authority to resolve any dispute relating to the . . . enforceability

. . . of this Agreement including, but not limited to any claim that all or any part of this Agreement is void or voidable." . . . The current "controversy" between the parties is whether the Agreement is unconscionable. It is the second provision, which delegates resolution of that controversy to the arbitrator, that Rent-A-Center seeks to enforce. Adopting the terminology used by the parties, we will refer to it as the delegation provision.

The delegation provision is an agreement to arbitrate threshold issues concerning the arbitration agreement. We have recognized that parties can agree to arbitrate "gateway" questions of "arbitrability," such as whether the parties have agreed to arbitrate or whether their agreement covers a particular controversy. See, *e.g., Howsam,* 537 U.S., at 83–85; *Green Tree Financial Corp. v. Bazzle,* 539 U.S. 444, 452 (2003) (plurality opinion). This line of cases merely reflects the principle that arbitration is a matter of contract.[1] See *First Options of Chicago, Inc. v. Kaplan,* 514 U.S. 938, 943 (1995). An agreement to arbitrate a gateway issue is simply an additional, antecedent agreement the party seeking arbitration asks the federal court to enforce, and the FAA operates on this additional arbitration agreement just as it does on any other. The additional agreement is valid under § 2 "save upon such grounds as exist at law or in equity for the revocation of any contract," and federal courts can enforce the agreement by staying federal litigation under § 3 and compelling arbitration under § 4. The question before us, then, is whether the delegation provision is valid under § 2.

---

[1] There is one caveat. *First Options of Chicago, Inc. v. Kaplan,* 514 U.S. 938, 944 (1995), held that "[c]ourts should not assume that the parties agreed to arbitrate arbitrability unless there is 'clea[r] and unmistakabl[e]' evidence that they did so." The parties agree the heightened standard applies here. . . . The District Court concluded the "Agreement to Arbitrate clearly and unmistakenly *[sic]* provides the arbitrator with the exclusive authority to decide whether the Agreement to Arbitrate is enforceable." . . . The Ninth Circuit noted that Jackson did not dispute that the text of the Agreement was clear and unmistakable on this point. . . . He also does not dispute it here. What he argues now, however, is that it is not "clear and unmistakable" that his *agreement* to that text was valid, because of the unconscionability claims he raises. . . . The dissent makes the same argument. . . .

This mistakes the subject of the *First Options* "clear and unmistakable" requirement. It pertains to the parties' *manifestation of intent,* not the agreement's *validity.* As explained in *Howsam v. Dean Witter Reynolds, Inc.,* 537 U.S. 79, 83 (2002), it is an "interpretive rule," based on an assumption about the parties' expectations. In "circumstance[s] where contracting parties would likely have expected a court to have decided the gateway matter," *ibid.,* we assume that is what they agreed to. Thus, "[u]nless the parties clearly and unmistakably provide otherwise, the question of whether the parties agreed to arbitrate is to be decided by the court, not the arbitrator." *AT&T Technologies, Inc. v. Communications Workers,* 475 U.S. 643, 649 (1986).

The *validity* of a written agreement to arbitrate (whether it is legally binding, as opposed to whether it was in fact agreed to—including, of course, whether it was void for unconscionability) is governed by § 2's provision that it shall be valid "save upon such grounds as exist at law or equity for the revocation of any contract." Those grounds do not include, of course, any requirement that its lack of unconscionability must be "clear and unmistakable." And they are not grounds that *First Options* added for agreements to arbitrate gateway issues; § 2 applies to all written agreements to arbitrate.

B

There are two types of validity challenges under § 2: "One type challenges specifically the validity of the agreement to arbitrate," and "[t]he other challenges the contract as a whole, either on a ground that directly affects the entire agreement (*e.g.*, the agreement was fraudulently induced), or on the ground that the illegality of one of the contract's provisions renders the whole contract invalid." . . . In a line of cases neither party has asked us to overrule, we held that only the first type of challenge is relevant to a court's determination whether the arbitration agreement at issue is enforceable. (Footnote omitted). . . . That is because § 2 states that a "written provision" "to settle by arbitration a controversy" is "valid, irrevocable, and enforceable" *without mention* of the validity of the contract in which it is contained. Thus, a party's challenge to another provision of the contract, or to the contract as a whole, does not prevent a court from enforcing a specific agreement to arbitrate. "[A]s a matter of substantive federal arbitration law, an arbitration provision is severable from the remainder of the contract." . . . (the severability rule is based on § 2).

But that agreements to arbitrate are severable does not mean that they are unassailable. If a party challenges the validity under § 2 of the precise agreement to arbitrate at issue, the federal court must consider the challenge before ordering compliance with that agreement under § 4. In *Prima Paint,* for example, if the claim had been "fraud in the inducement of the arbitration clause itself," then the court would have considered it. . . . "To immunize an arbitration agreement from judicial challenge on the ground of fraud in the inducement would be to elevate it over other forms of contract," . . . . In some cases the claimed basis of invalidity for the contract as a whole will be much easier to establish than the same basis as applied only to the severable agreement to arbitrate. Thus, in an employment contract many elements of alleged unconscionability applicable to the entire contract (outrageously low wages, for example) would not affect the agreement to arbitrate alone. But even where that is not the case—as in *Prima Paint* itself, where the alleged fraud that induced the whole contract equally induced the agreement to arbitrate which was part of that contract—we nonetheless require the basis of challenge to be directed specifically to the agreement to arbitrate before the court will intervene.

Here, the "written provision . . . to settle by arbitration a controversy," . . . that Rent-A-Center asks us to enforce is the delegation provision—the provision that gave the arbitrator "exclusive authority to resolve any dispute relating to the . . . enforceability . . . of this Agreement,". . . . The "remainder of the contract," . . . is the rest of the agreement to arbitrate claims arising out of Jackson's employment with Rent-A-Center. To be sure this case differs from *Prima Paint, Buckeye,* and *Preston,* in that the arbitration provisions sought to be enforced in those cases were contained in contracts unrelated to arbitration—contracts for consulting services, . . . check-cashing services, . . . and "personal management" or "talent agent" services. . . . In this case, the underlying contract is itself an arbitration agreement. But that makes no difference.[3] Application of the severability rule does not depend on the substance of the remainder of the contract. Section 2 operates on the specific "written provision" to "settle by arbitration a controversy" that the party seeks to enforce. Accordingly, unless Jackson challenged the delegation provision specifically, we must treat it as valid under § 2, and must enforce it under §§ 3 and 4, leaving any challenge to the validity of the Agreement as a whole for the arbitrator.

C

The District Court correctly concluded that Jackson challenged only the validity of the contract as a whole. Nowhere in his opposition to Rent-A-Center's motion to compel arbitration did he even mention the delegation provision. . . . Rent-A-Center noted this fact in its reply: "[Jackson's response] fails to rebut or otherwise address in any way [Rent-A-Center's] argument that the Arbitrator must decide [Jackson's] challenge to the enforceability of the Agreement. *Thus, [Rent-A-Center's] argument is uncontested.*" . . .

The arguments Jackson made in his response to Rent-A-Center's motion to compel arbitration support this conclusion. Jackson stated that "the *entire agreement* seems drawn to provide [Rent-A-Center] with undue advantages should an employment-related dispute arise." . . . (emphasis added). At one point, he argued that the limitations on discovery "further suppor[t][his] contention that the *arbitration agreement as a whole* is substantively unconscionable." . . . (emphasis added). And before this Court, Jackson describes his challenge in the District Court as follows: He "opposed the motion to compel on the ground that the *entire arbitration agreement,* including the delegation clause, was unconscionable." . . . (emphasis added). That is an accurate description of his filings.

As required to make out a claim of unconscionability under Nevada law, . . . he contended that the Agreement was both procedurally and substantively unconscionable. It was procedurally unconscionable, he argued, because it "was imposed as a condition of employment and was non-negotiable." . . . But we need not consider that claim because none of

[3] The dissent calls this a "breezy assertion," . . . but it seems to us self-evident. When the dissent comes to discussing the point, . . . it gives no logical reason why an agreement to arbitrate one controversy (an employment-discrimination claim) is not severable from an agreement to arbitrate a different controversy (enforceability). There is none. Since the dissent accepts that the invalidity of one provision *within an arbitration agreement* does not necessarily invalidate its other provisions, . . . it cannot believe in some sort of magic bond between arbitration provisions that prevents them from being severed from each other. According to the dissent, it is fine to sever an invalid provision within an arbitration agreement when severability is a matter of state law, but severability is not allowed when it comes to applying *Prima Paint Corp. v. Flood & Conklin Mfg. Co.,* 388 U.S. 395 (1967).

Jackson's substantive unconscionability challenges was specific to the delegation provision. First, he argued that the Agreement's coverage was one sided in that it required arbitration of claims an employee was likely to bring—contract, tort, discrimination, and statutory claims—but did not require arbitration of claims Rent-A-Center was likely to bring—intellectual property, unfair competition, and trade secrets claims. . . . This one-sided-coverage argument clearly did not go to the validity of the delegation provision.

Jackson's other two substantive unconscionability arguments assailed arbitration procedures called for by the contract—the fee-splitting arrangement and the limitations on discovery—procedures that were to be used during arbitration under *both* the agreement to arbitrate employment-related disputes *and* the delegation provision. It may be that had Jackson challenged the delegation provision by arguing that these common procedures *as applied* to the delegation provision rendered *that provision* unconscionable, the challenge should have been considered by the court. To make such a claim based on the discovery procedures, Jackson would have had to argue that the limitation upon the number of depositions causes the arbitration of his claim that the Agreement is unenforceable to be unconscionable. That would be, of course, a much more difficult argument to sustain than the argument that the same limitation renders arbitration of his factbound employment-discrimination claim unconscionable. Likewise, the unfairness of the fee-splitting arrangement may be more difficult to establish for the arbitration of enforceability than for arbitration of more complex and fact-related aspects of the alleged employment discrimination. Jackson, however, did not make any arguments specific to the delegation provision; he argued that the fee-sharing and discovery procedures rendered the *entire* Agreement invalid.

Jackson's appeal to the Ninth Circuit confirms that he did not contest the validity of the delegation provision in particular. His brief noted the existence of the delegation provision, . . . but his unconscionability arguments made no mention of it. . . . He also repeated the arguments he had made before the District Court . . . that the "entire agreement" favors Rent-A-Center and that the limitations on discovery further his "contention that the arbitration agreement as a whole is substantively unconscionable". . . . Finally, he repeated the argument made in his District Court filings, that under state law the unconscionable clauses could not be severed from the arbitration agreement. . . .[4] The point of this

[4] Jackson's argument fails. The severability rule is a "matter of substantive federal arbitration law," and we have repeatedly "rejected the view that the question of 'severability' was one of state law, so that if state law held the arbitration provision not to be severable a challenge to the contract as a whole would be decided by the court." . . . For the same reason, the Agreement's statement that its provisions are severable, . . . does not affect our analysis.

argument, of course, is that the Agreement *as a whole* is unconscionable under state law.

Jackson repeated that argument before this Court. At oral argument, counsel stated: "There are certain elements of the arbitration agreement that are unconscionable and, under Nevada law, which would render the *entire arbitration agreement* unconscionable." . . . (emphasis added). And again, he stated, "we've got both certain provisions that are unconscionable, that under Nevada law render the *entire agreement* unconscionable . . . , and that's what the Court is to rely on." . . . (emphasis added).

In his brief to this Court, Jackson made the contention, not mentioned below, that the delegation provision itself is substantively unconscionable because the *quid pro quo* he was supposed to receive for it—that "in exchange for initially allowing an arbitrator to decide certain gateway questions," he would receive "plenary post-arbitration judicial review"—was eliminated by the Court's subsequent holding in *Hall Street Associates, L.L.C. v. Mattel, Inc.,* 552 U.S. 576 (2008), that the nonplenary grounds for judicial review in § 10 of the FAA are exclusive. . . . He brought this challenge to the delegation provision too late, and we will not consider it. (Footnote omitted.). . .

We reverse the judgment of the Court of Appeals for the Ninth Circuit.

It is so ordered.

JUSTICE STEVENS, with whom JUSTICE GINSBURG, JUSTICE BREYER, and JUSTICE SOTOMAYOR join, dissenting.

Neither petitioner nor respondent has urged us to adopt the rule the Court does today: Even when a litigant has specifically challenged the validity of an agreement to arbitrate he must submit that challenge *to the arbitrator* unless he has lodged an objection to the particular line in the agreement that purports to assign such challenges to the arbitrator-the so-called "delegation clause."

The Court asserts that its holding flows logically from *Prima Paint Corp. v. Flood & Conklin Mfg. Co.,* 388 U.S. 395 (1967), in which the Court held that consideration of a contract revocation defense is generally a matter for the arbitrator, unless the defense is specifically directed at the arbitration clause. . . . We have treated this holding as a severability rule: When a party challenges a contract, "but not specifically its arbitration provisions, those provisions are enforceable apart from the remainder of the contract." . . . The Court's decision today goes beyond *Prima Paint.* Its breezy assertion that the subject matter of the contract at issue-in this case, an arbitration agreement and nothing more-"makes no difference," . . . is simply wrong. This written arbitration agreement is but one part of a broader employment agreement between the parties, just as the arbitration clause in *Prima Paint* was but one part of a broader contract for services between those parties. Thus, that the subject matter of the agreement is exclusively arbitration makes *all* the difference in the *Prima Paint* analysis.

I

Under the . . . FAA, . . . parties generally have substantial leeway to define the terms and scope of their agreement to settle disputes in an arbitral forum. "[A]rbitration is," after all, "simply a matter of contract between the parties; it is a way to resolve those disputes—but only those disputes-that the parties have agreed to submit to arbitration.". . . . The FAA, therefore, envisions a limited role for courts asked to stay litigation and refer disputes to arbitration.

Certain issues—the kind that "contracting parties would likely have expected a court to have decided"—remain within the province of judicial review. . . . These issues are "gateway matter[s]" because they are necessary antecedents to enforcement of an arbitration agreement; they raise questions the parties "are not likely to have thought that they had agreed that an arbitrator would" decide. . . . Quintessential gateway matters include "whether the parties have a valid arbitration agreement at all," . . . "whether the parties are bound by a given arbitration clause," . . . ; and "whether an arbitration clause in a concededly binding contract applies to a particular type of controversy,". . . . It would be bizarre to send these types of gateway matters to the arbitrator as a matter of course, because they raise a " 'question of arbitrability.' " . . . (Footnote omitted.).

"[Q]uestion[s] of arbitrability" thus include questions regarding the existence of a legally binding and valid arbitration agreement, as well as questions regarding the scope of a concededly binding arbitration agreement. In this case we are concerned with the first of these categories: whether the parties have a valid arbitration agreement. This is an issue the FAA assigns to the courts. (Footnote omitted.) Section 2 of the FAA dictates that covered arbitration agreements "shall be valid, irrevocable, and enforceable, save upon such grounds as exist at law or in equity for the revocation of any contract." . . . "[S]uch grounds," which relate to contract validity and formation, include the claim at issue in this case, unconscionability. . . .

Two different lines of cases bear on the issue of *who* decides a question of arbitrability respecting validity, such as whether an arbitration agreement is unconscionable. Although this issue, as a gateway matter, is typically for the court, we have explained that such an issue can be delegated to the arbitrator in some circumstances. When the parties have purportedly done so, courts must examine two distinct rules to decide whether the delegation is valid.

The first line of cases looks to the parties' intent. In *AT & T Technologies*, we stated that "question[s] of arbitrability" may be delegated to the arbitrator, so long as the delegation is clear and unmistakable. . . . We reaffirmed this rule, and added some nuance, in *First Options*. Against the background presumption that questions of arbitrability go to the court, we stated that federal courts should "generally" apply "ordinary state-law principles that govern the formation of contracts" to assess "whether the parties agreed to arbitrate a certain matter (including arbitrability)." . . . But, we added, a more rigorous standard applies when the inquiry is whether the parties have "agreed to arbitrate arbitrability": "Courts should not assume that the parties agreed to arbitrate arbitrability unless there is clear and unmistakable evidence that they did so."[3] . . . JUSTICE BREYER's unanimous opinion for the Court described this standard as a type of "revers[e]" "presumption"[4]—one in favor of a judicial, rather than an arbitral, forum. . . . Clear and unmistakable "evidence" of agreement to arbitrate arbitrability might include, as was urged in *First Options*, a course of conduct demonstrating assent (footnote omitted) . . . as is urged in this case, an express agreement to do so. In any event, whether such evidence exists is a matter for the court to determine.

The second line of cases bearing on who decides the validity of an arbitration agreement, as the Court explains, involves the *Prima Paint* rule. . . . That rule recognizes two types of validity challenges. One type challenges the validity of the arbitration agreement itself, on a ground arising from an infirmity in that agreement. The other challenges the validity of the arbitration agreement tangentially—via a claim that the entire contract (of which the arbitration agreement is but a part) is invalid for some reason. . . . Under *Prima Paint*, a challenge of the first type goes to the court; a challenge of the second type goes to the arbitrator. . . . The *Prima Paint* rule is akin to a pleading standard, whereby a party seeking to challenge the validity of an arbitration agreement must expressly say so in order to get his dispute into court.

In sum, questions related to the validity of an arbitration agreement are usually matters for a court to resolve before it refers a dispute to arbitration. But questions of arbitrability may go to the arbitrator in two instances: (1) when the parties have demonstrated, clearly and unmistakably, that it is their intent to do so; or (2) when the validity of an arbitration agreement depends exclusively on the validity of the substantive contract of which it is a part.

---

[3] We have not expressly decided whether the *First Options* delegation principle would apply to questions of arbitrability that implicate § 2 concerns, *i.e.*, grounds for contract revocation. I do not need to weigh in on this issue in order to resolve the present case.

[4] It is a "revers[e]" presumption because it is counter to the presumption we usually apply in favor of arbitration when the question concerns whether a particular dispute falls within the scope of a concededly binding arbitration agreement. . . .

II

We might have resolved this case by simply applying the *First Options* rule: Does the arbitration agreement at issue "clearly and unmistakably" evince petitioner's and respondent's intent to submit questions of arbitrability to the arbitrator? (Footnote omitted.) The answer to that question is no. Respondent's claim that the arbitration agreement is unconscionable undermines any suggestion that he "clearly" and "unmistakably" assented to submit questions of arbitrability to the arbitrator. See Restatement (Second) of Contracts § 208, Comment *d* (1979) ("[G]ross inequality of bargaining power, together with terms unreasonably favorable to the stronger party, may confirm indications that the transaction involved elements of deception or compulsion, or may show that the weaker party had no meaningful choice, no real alternative, or did not in fact assent or appear to assent to the unfair terms"). . . . (Footnote omitted.) The fact that the agreement's "delegation" provision suggests assent is beside the point, because the gravamen of respondent's claim is that he never consented to the terms in his agreement.

In other words, when a party raises a good-faith validity challenge to the arbitration agreement itself, that issue must be resolved before a court can say that he clearly and unmistakably intended to *arbitrate* that very validity question. This case well illustrates the point: If respondent's unconscionability claim is correct—*i.e.,* if the terms of the agreement are so one-sided and the process of its making so unfair—it would contravene the existence of clear and unmistakable assent to arbitrate the very question petitioner now seeks to arbitrate. Accordingly, it is necessary for the court to resolve the merits of respondent's unconscionability claim in order to decide whether the parties have a valid arbitration agreement under § 2. Otherwise, that section's preservation of revocation issues for the Court would be meaningless.

[. . .]

III

Rather than apply *First Options,* the Court takes us down a different path, one neither briefed by the parties nor relied upon by the Court of Appeals. In applying *Prima Paint,* the Court has unwisely extended a "fantastic" and likely erroneous decision. . . . (Footnote omitted.)

As explained at the outset . . . , this case lies at a seeming crossroads in our arbitration jurisprudence. It implicates cases such as *First Options,* which address whether the parties intended to delegate questions of arbitrability, and also those cases, such as *Prima Paint,* which address the severability of a presumptively valid arbitration agreement from a potentially invalid contract. The question of "Who decides?"—arbitrator or court—animates both lines of cases, but they are driven by different concerns. In cases like *First Options,* we are concerned with the parties' intentions. In cases like *Prima Paint,* we are concerned with *how* the parties challenge the validity of the agreement.

Under the *Prima Paint* inquiry, recall, we consider whether the parties are actually challenging the validity of the arbitration agreement, or whether they are challenging, more generally, the contract within which an arbitration clause is nested. In the latter circumstance, we assume there is no infirmity *per se* with the arbitration agreement, *i.e.,* there are no grounds for revocation of the arbitration agreement itself under § 2 of the FAA. Accordingly, we commit the parties' general contract dispute to the arbitrator, as agreed.

The claim in *Prima Paint* was that one party would not have agreed to contract with the other for services had it known the second party was insolvent (a fact known but not disclosed at the time of contracting). . . . There was, therefore, allegedly fraud in the inducement of the contract—a contract which also delegated disputes to an arbitrator. Despite the fact that the claim raised would have, if successful, rendered the embedded arbitration clause void, the Court held that the merits of the dispute were for the arbitrator, so long as the claim of "fraud in the inducement" did not go to validity of "*the arbitration clause* itself." . . . (emphasis added). Because, in *Prima Paint,* "no claim ha[d] been advanced by Prima Paint that [respondent] fraudulently induced it to enter into the agreement to arbitrate," and because the arbitration agreement was broad enough to cover the dispute, the arbitration agreement was enforceable with respect to the controversy at hand. . . .

The *Prima Paint* rule has been denominated as one related to severability. Our opinion in *Buckeye,* set out these guidelines:

> "First, as a matter of substantive federal arbitration law, an arbitration provision is severable from the remainder of the contract. Second, unless the challenge is to the arbitration clause itself, the issue of the contract's validity is considered by the arbitrator in the first instance." . . .

Whether the general contract defense renders the entire agreement void or voidable is irrelevant. . . . All that matters is whether the party seeking to present the issue to a court has brought a "discrete challenge," . . . , "to the validity of the . . . arbitration clause." . . .

Prima Paint and its progeny allow a court to pluck from a potentially invalid *contract* a potentially valid *arbitration agreement.* Today the Court adds a new layer of severability—something akin to Russian nesting dolls-into the mix: Courts may now pluck from a potentially invalid *arbitration agreement* even narrower provisions that refer particular arbitrability disputes to an arbitrator. . . . I do not think an agreement to arbitrate can ever manifest a clear and unmistakable intent to arbitrate its own validity.

But even assuming otherwise, I certainly would not hold that the *Prima Paint* rule extends this far.

In my view, a general revocation challenge to a standalone arbitration agreement is, invariably, a challenge to the " 'making' " of the arbitration agreement itself . . . and therefore, under *Prima Paint,* must be decided by the court. A claim of procedural unconscionability aims to undermine the formation of the arbitration agreement, much like a claim of unconscionability aims to undermine the clear-and-unmistakable-intent requirement necessary for a valid delegation of a "discrete" challenge to the validity of the arbitration agreement itself. . . . Moreover, because we are dealing in this case with a challenge to an independently executed arbitration agreement—rather than a clause contained in a contract related to another subject matter—any challenge to the contract itself is also, necessarily, a challenge to the arbitration agreement. (Footnote omitted.) They are one and the same.

The Court, however, reads the delegation clause as a distinct mini-arbitration agreement divisible from the contract in which it resides—which just so happens also to be an arbitration agreement. . . . Although the Court simply declares that it "makes no difference" that the underlying subject matter of the agreement is itself an arbitration agreement, . . . that proposition does not follow from—rather it is at odds with—*Prima Paint*'s severability rule.

Had the parties in this case executed only one contract, on two sheets of paper—one sheet with employment terms, and a second with arbitration terms—the contract would look much like the one in *Buckeye.* There would be some substantive terms, followed by some arbitration terms, including what we now call a delegation clause—*i.e.,* a sentence or two assigning to the arbitrator any disputes related to the validity of the arbitration provision. . . . If respondent then came into court claiming that the contract was illegal as a whole for some reason unrelated to the arbitration provision, the *Prima Paint* rule would apply, and such a general challenge to the subject matter of the contract would go to the arbitrator. Such a challenge would not call into question the making of the arbitration agreement or its invalidity *per se.*

Before today, however, if respondent instead raised a challenge specific to "the validity of the agreement to arbitrate"—for example, that the agreement to arbitrate was void under state law—the challenge would have gone to the court. That is what *Buckeye* says. . . . But the Court now declares that *Prima Paint*'s pleading rule requires more: A party must lodge a challenge with even greater specificity than what would have satisfied the *Prima Paint* Court. A claim that an *entire* arbitration agreement is invalid will not go to the court unless the party challenges the *particular sentences* that delegate such claims to the arbitrator, on some contract ground that is particular and unique to those sentences. . . .

It would seem the Court reads *Prima Paint* to require, as a matter of course, infinite layers of severability: We must always pluck from an arbitration agreement the specific delegation mechanism that would—but for present judicial review—commend the matter to arbitration, even if this delegation clause is but one sentence within one paragraph within a standalone agreement. And, most importantly, the party must identify this one sentence and lodge a specific challenge to its validity. Otherwise, he will be bound to pursue his validity claim in arbitration.

Even if limited to separately executed arbitration agreements, however, such an infinite severability rule is divorced from the underlying rationale of *Prima Paint*. The notion that a party may be bound by an arbitration clause in a contract that is nevertheless invalid may be difficult for any lawyer—or any person—to accept, but this is the law of *Prima Paint*. It reflects a judgment that the " 'national policy favoring arbitration' " . . . outweighs the interest in preserving a judicial forum for questions of arbitrability—*but only when questions of arbitrability are bound up in an underlying dispute*. . . . When the two are so bound up, there is actually no gateway matter at all: The question "Who decides" is the entire ball game. Were a court to decide the fraudulent inducement question in *Prima Paint,* in order to decide the antecedent question of the validity of the included arbitration agreement, then it would also, necessarily, decide the merits of the underlying dispute. Same, too, for the question of illegality in *Buckeye;* on its way to deciding the arbitration agreement's validity, the court would have to decide whether the contract was illegal, and in so doing, it would decide the merits of the entire dispute.

In this case, however, resolution of the unconscionability question will have no bearing on the merits of the underlying employment dispute. It will only, as a preliminary matter, resolve who should decide the merits of that dispute. Resolution of the unconscionability question will, however, decide whether the arbitration agreement *itself* is "valid" under "such grounds as exist at law or in equity for the revocation of any contract." . . . As *Prima Paint* recognizes, the FAA commits those gateway matters, specific to the arbitration agreement, to the court. . . . Indeed, it is clear that the present controversy over whether the arbitration agreement is unconscionable is *itself severable* from the merits of the underlying dispute, which involves a claim of employment discrimination. This is true for all gateway matters, and for this reason *Prima Paint* has no application in this case.

IV

While I may have to accept the "fantastic" holding in *Prima Paint*, . . . I most certainly do not accept the Court's even more fantastic reasoning today. I would affirm the judgment of the Court of Appeals, and therefore respectfully dissent.

NOTES AND QUESTIONS

1. RAC is the Court's first application of the holding in *First Options of Chicago, Inc. v. Kaplan*, 514 U.S. 938 (1995). The company uses the arbitral clause to regulate any prospective arbitration. It also establishes the threshold authority of the arbitrator. The company, in effect, incorporates a *Kaplan* jurisdictional delegation clause into the arbitral clause and establishes *kompetenz-kompetenz* by contract. The jurisdictional delegation is related to, but distinct from, the adhesive character of the bargain.

2. The plaintiff-consumer claims that the arbitral clause is unconscionable and unenforceable—a matter that it believes should be resolved by a court. The Ninth Circuit agrees. The majority of the U.S. Supreme Court disagrees (5 to 4). Its ruling is intended to privilege the power and authority of the arbitrator at the outset of the process and to give effect to party provision, even when it is unilateral in character.

3. By alleging that the arbitral clause was unconscionable, the plaintiff-consumer did not directly attack the delegation provision giving the arbitrator the authority to decide whether the arbitral clause was a valid contract. Commentators have asserted that the majority opinion establishes a second separability doctrine that applies to the provisions of the arbitral clause.

BG GROUP, PLC V. REPUBLIC OF ARGENTINA

572 U.S. 25, 134 S.Ct. 1198, 188 L.Ed.2d 220 (2014).

JUSTICE BREYER delivered the opinion of the Court.

Article 8 of an investment treaty between the United Kingdom and Argentina contains a dispute-resolution provision, applicable to disputes between one of those nations and an investor from the other. . . . The provision authorizes either party to submit a dispute "to the decision of the competent tribunal of the Contracting Party in whose territory the investment was made," *i.e.*, a local court. Art. 8(1). And it provides for arbitration

> "(i) where, after a period of eighteen months has elapsed from the moment when the dispute was submitted to the competent tribunal . . . , the said tribunal has not given its final decision; [or]
>
> "(ii) where the final decision of the aforementioned tribunal has been made but the Parties are still in dispute." Art. 8(2)(a).

The Treaty also entitles the parties to agree to proceed directly to arbitration. Art. 8(2)(b).

This case concerns the Treaty's arbitration clause, and specifically the local court litigation requirement set forth in Article 8(2)(a). The question before us is whether a court of the United States, in reviewing an arbitration award made under the Treaty, should interpret and apply the local litigation requirement *de novo*, or with the deference that courts ordinarily owe arbitration decisions. That is to say, who—court or arbitrator—bears primary responsibility for interpreting and applying the local litigation requirement to an underlying controversy? In our view, the matter is for the arbitrators, and courts must review their determinations with deference.

I

A

In the early 1990[s], the petitioner, BG Group PLC, a British firm, belonged to a consortium that bought a majority interest in an Argentine entity called MetroGAS. MetroGAS was a gas distribution company created by Argentine law in 1992, as a result of the government's privatization of its state-owned gas utility. Argentina distributed the utility's assets to new, private companies, one of which was MetroGAS. It awarded MetroGAS a 35-year exclusive license to distribute natural gas in Buenos Aires, and it submitted a controlling interest in the company to international public tender. BG Group's consortium was the successful bidder.

At about the same time, Argentina enacted statutes providing that its regulators would calculate gas "tariffs" in U. S. dollars, and that those tariffs would be set at levels sufficient to assure gas distribution firms, such as MetroGAS, a reasonable return.

In 2001 and 2002, Argentina, faced with an economic crisis, enacted new laws. Those laws changed the basis for calculating gas tariffs from dollars to pesos, at a rate of one peso per dollar. The exchange rate at the time was roughly three pesos to the dollar. The result was that MetroGAS' profits were quickly transformed into losses. BG Group believed that these changes (and several others) violated the Treaty; Argentina believed the contrary.

B

In 2003, BG Group, invoking Article 8 of the Treaty, sought arbitration. The parties appointed arbitrators; they agreed to site the arbitration in Washington, D. C.; and between 2004 and 2006, the arbitrators decided motions, received evidence, and conducted hearings. BG Group essentially claimed that Argentina's new laws and regulatory practices violated provisions in the Treaty forbidding the "expropriation" of investments and requiring that each nation give "fair and equitable treatment" to investors from the other. Argentina denied these claims, while also arguing that the arbitration tribunal lacked "jurisdiction" to hear the dispute.... According to Argentina, the arbitrators lacked jurisdiction because: (1) BG Group was not a Treaty-protected "investor"; (2) BG Group's interest in MetroGAS was not a Treaty-protected "investment"; and (3) BG Group initiated arbitration without first litigating its claims in Argentina's courts, despite Article 8's requirement. . . . In Argentina's view, "failure by BG to bring its grievance to Argentine courts for 18 months renders its claims in this arbitration inadmissible." . . .

In late December 2007, the arbitration panel reached a final decision. It began by determining that it had "jurisdiction" to consider the merits of the dispute. In support of that determination, the tribunal concluded that BG Group was an "investor," that its interest in MetroGAS amounted to a Treaty-protected "investment," and that Argentina's own conduct had waived, or excused, BG Group's failure to comply with Article 8's local litigation requirement. . . . The panel pointed out that[,] in 2002, the President of Argentina had issued a decree staying for 180 days the execution of its courts' final judgments (and injunctions) in suits claiming harm as a result of the new economic measures. . . . In addition, Argentina had established a "renegotiation process" for public service contracts, such as its contract with MetroGAS, to alleviate the negative impact of the new economic measures. . . . But Argentina had simultaneously barred from participation in that "process" firms that were litigating against Argentina in court or in arbitration. . . . These measures, while not making litigation in Argentina's courts literally impossible, nonetheless "hindered" recourse "to the domestic judiciary" to the point where the Treaty implicitly excused compliance with the local litigation requirement. . . . Requiring a private party in such circumstances to seek relief in Argentina's courts for 18 months, the panel concluded, would lead to "absurd and unreasonable result[s]." . . .

On the merits, the arbitration panel agreed with Argentina that it had not "expropriate[d]" BG Group's investment, but also found that Argentina had denied BG Group "fair and equitable treatment." . . . It awarded BG Group $185 million in damages. . . .

C

In March 2008, both sides filed petitions for review in the District Court for the District of Columbia. BG Group sought to confirm the award under the New York Convention and the Federal Arbitration Act. . . . Argentina sought to vacate the award in part on the ground that the arbitrators lacked jurisdiction. . . .

The District Court denied Argentina's claims and confirmed the award. . . . But the Court of Appeals for the District of Columbia Circuit reversed. . . . In the appeals court's view, the interpretation and application of Article 8's local litigation requirement was a matter for courts to decide *de novo, i.e.,* without deference to the views of the arbitrators. The Court of

Appeals then went on to hold that the circumstances did not excuse BG Group's failure to comply with the requirement. Rather, BG Group must "commence a lawsuit in Argentina's courts and wait eighteen months before filing for arbitration." . . . Because BG Group had not done so, the arbitrators lacked authority to decide the dispute. And the appeals court ordered the award vacated. . . .

BG Group filed a petition for *certiorari.* Given the importance of the matter for international commercial arbitration, we granted the petition. . . .

II

As we have said, the question before us is who—court or arbitrator—bears primary responsibility for interpreting and applying Article 8's local court litigation provision. Put in terms of standards of judicial review, should a United States court review the arbitrators' interpretation and application of the provision *de novo*, or with the deference that courts ordinarily show arbitral decisions on matters the parties have committed to arbitration? . . .

In answering the question, we shall initially treat the document before us as if it were an ordinary contract between private parties. Were that so, we conclude, the matter would be for the arbitrators. We then ask whether the fact that the document in question is a treaty makes acritical difference. We conclude that it does not.

III

Where ordinary contracts are at issue, it is up to the parties to determine whether a particular matter is primarily for arbitrators or for courts to decide. . . . If the contract is silent on the matter of who primarily is to decide "threshold" questions about arbitration, courts determine the parties' intent with the help of presumptions.

On the one hand, courts presume that the parties intend courts, not arbitrators, to decide what we have called disputes about "arbitrability." These include questions such as "whether the parties are bound by a given arbitration clause," or "whether an arbitration clause in a concededly binding contract applies to a particular type of controversy." . . .

On the other hand, courts presume that the parties intend arbitrators, not courts, to decide disputes about the meaning and application of particular procedural preconditions for the use of arbitration. . . . These procedural matters include claims of "waiver, delay, or a like defense to arbitrability." . . . And they include the satisfaction of " 'prerequisites such as time limits, notice, laches, estoppel, and other conditions precedent to an obligation to arbitrate.' " . . .

The provision before us is of the latter, procedural, variety. The text and structure of the provision make clear that it operates as a procedural condition precedent to arbitration. It says that a dispute "shall be submitted to international arbitration" if "one of the Parties so requests," as long as "a period of eighteen months has elapsed" since the dispute was "submitted" to a local tribunal and the tribunal "has not given its final decision." Art. 8(2). It determines when the contractual duty to arbitrate arises, not whether there is a contractual duty to arbitrate at all. . . . Neither does this language or other language in Article 8 give substantive weight to the local court's determinations on the matters at issue between the parties. To the contrary, Article 8 provides that only the "arbitration decision shall be final and binding on both Parties." Art. 8(4). The litigation provision is consequently a purely procedural requirement—a claims-processing rule that governs when the arbitration may begin, but not whether it may occur or what its substantive outcome will be on the issues in dispute.

Moreover, the local litigation requirement is highly analogous to procedural provisions that both this Court and others have found are for arbitrators, not courts, primarily to interpret and to apply. . . .

Finally, as we later discuss in more detail, . . . we can find nothing in Article 8 or elsewhere in the Treaty that might overcome the ordinary assumption. It nowhere demonstrates a contrary intent as to the delegation of decisional authority between judges and arbitrators. Thus, were the document an ordinary contract, it would call for arbitrators primarily to interpret and to apply the local litigation provision.

IV

A

We now relax our ordinary contract assumption and ask whether the fact that the document before us is a treaty makes a critical difference to our analysis. The Solicitor General argues that it should. He says that the local litigation provision may be "a condition on the State's consent to enter into an arbitration agreement." . . . He adds that courts should "review *de novo* the arbitral tribunal's resolution of objections based on an investor's non-compliance" with such a condition. . . . And he recommends that we remand this case to the Court of Appeals to determine whether the court-exhaustion provision is such a condition. . . .

1

We do not accept the Solicitor General's view as applied to the treaty before us. As a general matter, a treaty is a contract, though between nations. Its interpretation normally is, like a contract's interpretation, a matter of determining the parties' intent. . . .

The Solicitor General does not deny that the presumption discussed in Part III, *supra* (namely, the presumption that parties intend procedural preconditions to arbitration to be resolved primarily by arbitrators), applies both to ordinary contracts and to similar provisions in treaties when those provisions are not also "conditions of consent." . . . And, while we respect the Government's views about the proper interpretation of treaties, . . . we have been unable to find any other authority or precedent suggesting that the use of the "consent" label in a treaty should make a critical difference in discerning the parties' intent about whether courts or arbitrators should interpret and apply the relevant provision.

We are willing to assume with the Solicitor General that the appearance of this label in a treaty can show that the parties, or one of them, thought the designated matter quite important. But that is unlikely to be conclusive. For parties often submit important matters to arbitration. And the word "consent" could be attached to a highly procedural precondition to arbitration, such as a waiting period of several months, which the parties are unlikely to have intended that courts apply without saying so. . . . While we leave the matter open for future argument, we do not see why the presence of the term "consent" in a treaty warrants abandoning, or increasing the complexity of, our ordinary intent-determining framework. . . .

2

In any event, the treaty before us does not state that the local litigation requirement is a "condition of consent" to arbitration. Thus, we need not, and do not, go beyond holding that, in the absence of explicit language in a treaty demonstrating that the parties intended a different delegation of authority, our ordinary interpretive framework applies. We leave for another day the question of interpreting treaties that refer to "conditions of consent" explicitly. . . .

B

A treaty may contain evidence that shows the parties had an intent contrary to our ordinary presumptions about who should decide threshold issues related to arbitration. But the treaty before us does not show any such contrary intention. We concede that the local litigation requirement appears in (1) of Article 8, while the Article does not mention arbitration until the subsequent paragraph, (2). Moreover, a requirement that a party exhaust its remedies in a country's domestic courts before seeking to arbitrate may seem particularly important to a country offering protections to foreign investors. And the placing of an important matter prior to any mention of arbitration at least arguably suggests an intent by Argentina, the United Kingdom, or both, to have courts rather than arbitrators apply the litigation requirement.

These considerations, however, are outweighed by others. As discussed . . . , the text and structure of the litigation requirement set forth in Article 8 make clear that it is a procedural condition precedent to arbitration—a sequential step that a party must follow before giving notice of arbitration. The Treaty nowhere says that the provision is to operate as a substantive condition on the formation of the arbitration contract, or that it is a matter of such elevated importance that it is to be decided by courts. International arbitrators are likely more familiar than are judges with the expectations of foreign investors and recipient nations regarding the operation of the provision. . . . And the Treaty itself authorizes the use of international arbitration associations, the rules of which provide that arbitrators shall have the authority to interpret provisions of this kind. . . .

The upshot is that our ordinary presumption applies and it is not overcome. The interpretation and application of the local litigation provision is primarily for the arbitrators. Reviewing courts cannot review their decision *de novo*. Rather, they must do so with considerable deference.

C

The dissent interprets Article 8's local litigation provision differently. In its view, the provision sets forth not a condition precedent to arbitration in an already-binding arbitration contract (normally a matter for arbitrators to interpret), but a substantive condition on Argentina's consent to arbitration and thus on the contract's formation in the first place (normally something for courts to interpret). It reads the whole of Article 8 as a "unilateral standing offer" to arbitrate that Argentina and the United Kingdom each extends to investors of the other country. . . . And it says that the local litigation requirement is one of the essential " 'terms in which the offer was made.' " . . . .

While it is possible to read the provision in this way, doing so is not consistent with our case law interpreting similar provisions appearing in ordinary arbitration contracts. . . . Consequently, interpreting the provision in such a manner would require us to treat treaties as warranting a different kind of analysis. And the dissent does so without supplying any different set of general principles that might guide that analysis. That is a matter of some concern in a world where foreign investment and related arbitration treaties increasingly matter.

Even were we to ignore our ordinary contract principles, however, we would not take the dissent's view. As we have explained, the local litigation provision on its face concerns arbitration's timing, not the Treaty's effective date; or whom its arbitration clause binds; or whether that arbitration clause covers a certain kind of dispute. . . . The dissent points out that Article 8(2)(a) "does not simply require the parties to wait for 18 months before proceeding to arbitration," but instructs them to do something—to "submit their claims for adjudication." . . . That is correct. But the something they must do has no direct impact on the resolution of their dispute, for as we previously pointed out, Article 8 provides that only the decision of the arbitrators (who need not give weight to the local court's decision) will be "final and binding." Art. 8(4). The provision, at base, is a claims-processing rule. And the dissent's efforts to imbue it with greater significance fall short.

The treatises to which the dissent refers also fail to support its position. . . . Those authorities primarily describe how an offer to arbitrate in an investment treaty can be accepted, such as through an investor's filing of a notice of arbitration. . . . They do not endorse the dissent's reading of the local litigation provision or of provisions like it.

To the contrary, the bulk of international authority supports our view that the provision functions as a purely procedural precondition to arbitrate. . . .

In sum, we agree with the dissent that a sovereign's consent to arbitration is important. We also agree that sovereigns can condition their consent to arbitrate by writing various terms into their bilateral investment treaties. . . . But that is not the issue. The question is whether the parties intended to give courts or arbitrators primary authority to interpret and apply a threshold provision in an arbitration contract—when the contract is silent as to the delegation of authority. We have already explained why we believe that where, as here, the provision resembles a claims-processing requirement and is not a requirement that affects the arbitration contract's validity or scope, we presume that the parties (even if they are sovereigns) intended to give that authority to the arbitrators. . . .

V

Argentina correctly argues that it is nonetheless entitled to court review of the arbitrators' decision to excuse BG Group's noncompliance with the litigation requirement, and to take jurisdiction over the dispute. It asks us to provide that review, and it argues that even if the proper standard is "a [h]ighly [d]eferential" one, it should still prevail. . . . Having the relevant materials before us, we shall provide that review. But we cannot agree with Argentina that the arbitrators " 'exceeded their powers' " in concluding they had jurisdiction. . . .

The arbitration panel made three relevant determinations:

(1) "As a matter of treaty interpretation," the local litigation provision "cannot be construed as an absolute impediment to arbitration," . . . ;

(2) Argentina enacted laws that "hindered" "recourse to the domestic judiciary" by those "whose rights were allegedly affected by the emergency measures," . . . ; that sought "to prevent any judicial interference with the emergency legislation," . . . ; and

that "excluded from the renegotiation process" for public service contracts "any licensee seeking judicial redress," . . . ;

(3) under these circumstances, it would be "absurd and unreasonable" to read Article 8 as requiring an investor to bring its grievance to a domestic court before arbitrating. . . .

The first determination lies well within the arbitrators' interpretive authority. Construing the local litigation provision as an "absolute" requirement would mean Argentina could avoid arbitration by, say, passing a law that closed down its court system indefinitely or that prohibited investors from using its courts. Such an interpretation runs contrary to a basic objective of the investment treaty. Nor does Argentina argue for an absolute interpretation.

As to the second determination, Argentina does not argue that the facts set forth by the arbitrators are incorrect. Thus, we accept them as valid.

The third determination is more controversial. Argentina argues that neither the 180-day suspension of courts' issuances of final judgments nor its refusal to allow litigants (and those in arbitration) to use its contract renegotiation process, taken separately or together, warrants suspending or waiving the local litigation requirement. We would not necessarily characterize these actions as rendering a domestic court-exhaustion requirement "absurd and unreasonable," but at the same time we cannot say that the arbitrators' conclusions are barred by the Treaty. The arbitrators did not " 'stra[y] from interpretation and application of the agreement' " or otherwise " 'effectively "dispens[e]" ' " their " 'own brand of . . . justice.' " . . .

Consequently, we conclude that the arbitrators' jurisdictional determinations are lawful. The judgment of the Court of Appeals to the contrary is reversed.

It is so ordered.

JUSTICE SOTOMAYOR, concurring in part

I agree with the Court that the local litigation requirement at issue in this case is a procedural precondition to arbitration (which the arbitrators are to interpret), not a condition on Argentina's consent to arbitrate (which a court would review *de novo*) . . . Importantly, in reaching this conclusion, the Court acknowledges that "the treaty before us does not state that the local litigation requirement is a 'condition of consent' to arbitration." . . . The Court thus wisely "leave[s] for another day the question of interpreting treaties that refer to 'conditions of consent' explicitly." . . . I join the Court's opinion on the understanding that it does not, in fact, decide this issue.

I write separately because, in the absence of this express reservation, the opinion might be construed otherwise. The Court appears to suggest in *dictum* that a decision by treaty parties to describe a condition as one on their consent to arbitrate "is unlikely to be conclusive" in deciding whether the parties intended for the condition to be resolved by a court. . . . Because this suggestion is unnecessary to decide the case and is in tension with the Court's explicit reservation of the issue, I join the opinion of the Court with the exception of Part IV-A-1.

The Court's *dictum* on this point is not only unnecessary; it may also be incorrect. It is far from clear that a treaty's express use of the term "consent" to describe a precondition to arbitration should not be conclusive in the analysis. We have held, for instance, that "a gateway dispute about whether the parties are bound by a given arbitration clause raises a 'question of arbitrability' for a court to decide." [*Howsam*] . . . . And a party plainly cannot be bound by an arbitration clause to which it does not consent. . . . [*Granite Rock*; *Volt*]. . . .

Consent is especially salient in the context of a bilateral investment treaty, where the treaty is not an already agreed-upon arbitration provision between known parties, but rather a nation state's standing offer to arbitrate with an amorphous class of private investors. In this setting, a nation-state might reasonably wish to condition its consent to arbitrate with a previously unspecified investor counterparty on the investor's compliance with a requirement that might be deemed "purely procedural" in the ordinary commercial context. . . . Moreover, as The Chief Justice notes, "[i]t is no trifling matter" for a sovereign nation to "subject itself to international arbitration" proceedings, so we should "not presume that any country . . . takes that step lightly." . . .

Consider, for example, the United States-Korea Free Trade Agreement, which as the Court recognizes, . . . includes a provision explicitly entitled "Conditions and Limitations on Consent of Each Party." Art. 11.18, Feb. 10, 2011. That provision declares that "[n]o claim may be submitted to arbitration" unless a claimant first waives its "right to initiate or continue before any administrative tribunal or court . . . any proceeding with respect to any measure alleged to constitute a breach" under another provision of the treaty. . . . If this waiver condition were to appear without the "consent" label in a binding arbitration agreement between two commercial parties, one might characterize it as the kind of procedural " 'condition precedent to arbitrability' " that we presume parties intend for arbitrators to decide. . . . But where the waiver requirement is expressly denominated a "condition on consent" in an international investment treaty, the label could well be critical in determining whether the states party to the treaty intended the condition to be reviewed by a court. After all, a dispute as to consent is "the starkest form of the question whether the parties have agreed to arbitrate." . . . And we ordinarily presume that parties intend for courts to decide such questions because otherwise arbitrators might "force unwilling parties to arbitrate a matter they reasonably would have thought a judge . . . would decide." [*Kaplan*]. . . .

Accordingly, if the local litigation requirement at issue here were labeled a condition on the treaty parties' "consent" to arbitrate, that would in my view change the analysis as to whether the parties intended the requirement to be interpreted by a court or an arbitrator. As it is, however, all parties agree that the local litigation requirement is not so denominated. . . . Nor is there compelling reason to suppose the parties silently intended to make it a condition on their consent to arbitrate, given that a local court's decision is of no legal significance under the treaty, . . . and given that the entire purpose of bilateral investment agreements is to "reliev[e] investors of any concern that the courts of host countries will be unable or unwilling to provide justice in a dispute between a foreigner and their own government,". . . . Moreover, Argentina's conduct confirms that the local litigation requirement is not a condition on consent, for rather than objecting to arbitration on the ground that there was no binding arbitration agreement to begin with, Argentina actively participated in the constitution of the arbitral panel and in the proceedings that followed. . . .[1]

In light of these many indicators that Argentina and the United Kingdom did not intend the local litigation requirement to be a condition on their consent to arbitrate, and on the understanding that the Court does not pass on the weight courts should attach to a treaty's use of the term "consent," I concur in the Court's opinion.

CHIEF JUSTICE ROBERTS, with whom JUSTICE KENNEDY joins, dissenting.

The Court begins by deciding a different case, "initially treat[ing] the document before us as if it were an ordinary contract between private parties." . . . The "document before us," of course, is nothing of the sort. It is instead a treaty between two sovereign nations: the United Kingdom and Argentina. No investor is a party to the agreement. Having elided this

---

1 The dissent discounts the significance of Argentina's conduct on the ground that Argentina "object[ed] to the [arbitral] tribunal's jurisdiction to hear the dispute." . . . But there is a difference between arguing that a party has failed to comply with a procedural condition in a binding arbitration agreement and arguing that noncompliance with the condition negates the existence of consent to arbitrate in the first place. Argentina points to no evidence that its objection was of the consent variety. This omission is notable because Argentina knew how to phrase its arguments before the arbitrators in terms of consent; it argued separately that it had not consented to arbitration with BG Group on the ground that BG was not a party to the license underlying the dispute. . . . [*Kaplan*] is not to the contrary, as that case held that "arguing the arbitrability issue to an arbitrator" did not constitute "clea[r] and unmistakabl[e]" evidence sufficient to override an indisputably applicable presumption that a court was to decide whether the parties had agreed to arbitration. . . . The question here, by contrast, is whether that presumption attaches to begin with—that is, whether the local litigation requirement was a condition on Argentina's consent to arbitrate (which would trigger the presumption) or a procedural condition in an already binding arbitration agreement (which would not). That Argentina apparently took the latter position in arbitration is surely relevant evidence that the condition was, in fact, not one on its consent.

rather important fact for much of its analysis, the majority finally "relax[es] [its] ordinary contract assumption and ask[s] whether the fact that the document before us is a treaty makes a critical difference to [its] analysis." . . . It should come as no surprise that, after starting down the wrong road, the majority ends up at the wrong place.

I would start with the document that is before us and take it on its own terms. That document is a bilateral investment treaty between the United Kingdom and Argentina, in which Argentina agreed to take steps to encourage U. K. investors to invest within its borders (and the United Kingdom agreed to do the same with respect to Argentine investors). . . . The Treaty does indeed contain a completed agreement for arbitration—between the signatory countries. Art. 9. The Treaty also includes, in Article 8, certain provisions for resolving any disputes that might arise between a signatory country and an investor, who is not a party to the agreement.

One such provision—completely ignored by the Court in its analysis—specifies that disputes may be resolved by arbitration when the host country and an investor "have so agreed." Art. 8(2)(b), . . . No one doubts that, as is the normal rule, whether there was such an agreement is for a court, not an arbitrator, to decide. [*Kaplan*]. . . .

When there is no express agreement between the host country and an investor, they must form an agreement in another way, before an obligation to arbitrate arises. The Treaty by itself cannot constitute an agreement to arbitrate with an investor. How could it? No investor is a party to that Treaty. Something else must happen to create an agreement where there was none before. Article 8(2)(a) makes clear what that something is: An investor must submit his dispute to the courts of the host country. After 18 months, or an unsatisfactory decision, the investor may then request arbitration.

Submitting the dispute to the courts is thus a condition to the formation of an agreement, not simply a matter of performing an existing agreement. Article 8(2)(a) constitutes in effect a unilateral offer to arbitrate, which an investor may accept by complying with its terms. To be sure, the local litigation requirement might not be absolute. In particular, an investor might argue that it was an implicit aspect of the unilateral offer that he be afforded a reasonable opportunity to submit his dispute to the local courts. Even then, however, the question would remain whether the investor has managed to form an arbitration agreement with the host country pursuant to Article 8(2)(a). That question under Article 8(2)(a) is—like the same question under Article 8(2)(b)—for a court, not an arbitrator, to decide. I respectfully dissent from the Court's contrary conclusion.

I

The majority acknowledges—but fails to heed—"the first principle that underscores all of our arbitration decisions: Arbitration is strictly 'a matter of consent.'" . . . We have accordingly held that arbitration "is a way to resolve those disputes—but only those disputes—that the parties have agreed to submit to arbitration." . . . The same "first principle" underlies arbitration pursuant to bilateral investment treaties. . . . So only if Argentina agreed with BG Group to have an arbitrator resolve their dispute did the arbitrator in this case have any authority over the parties.

The majority opinion nowhere explains when and how Argentina agreed with BG Group to submit to arbitration. Instead, the majority seems to assume that, in agreeing with the United Kingdom to adopt Article 8 along with the rest of the Treaty, Argentina thereby formed an agreement with all potential U. K. investors (including BG Group) to submit all investment-related disputes to arbitration. That misunderstands Article 8 and trivializes the significance to a sovereign nation of subjecting itself to arbitration anywhere in the world, solely at the option of private parties.

A

The majority focuses throughout its opinion on what it calls the Treaty's "arbitration clause," . . . but that provision does not stand alone. Rather, it is only part—and a subordinate part at that—of a broader dispute resolution provision. Article 8 is thus entitled "Settlement of Disputes Between an Investor and the Host State," and it opens without as much as mentioning arbitration. . . . Instead it initially directs any disputing investor and signatory country (what the Treaty calls a "Contracting Party") to court. When "an investor of one Contracting Party and the other Contracting Party" have an investment-related dispute that has "not been amicably settled," the Treaty commands that the dispute "shall be submitted, at the request of one of the Parties to the dispute, to the decision of the competent tribunal of the Contracting Party in whose territory the investment was made." Art. 8(1), . . . (emphasis added). This provision could not be clearer: Before taking any other steps, an aggrieved investor must submit its dispute with a Contracting Party to that Contracting Party's own courts.

There are two routes to arbitration in Article 8(2)(a), and each passes through a Contracting Party's domestic courts. That is, the Treaty's arbitration provisions in Article 8(2)(a) presuppose that the parties have complied with the local litigation provision in Article 8(1). Specifically, a party may request arbitration only (1) "after a period of eighteen months has elapsed from the moment when the dispute was submitted to the competent tribunal of the Contracting Party in whose territory the investment was made" and "the said tribunal has not given its final decision," Art. 8(2)(a)(i), . . . or (2) "where the final decision of the aforementioned tribunal has been made but the Parties are still in dispute," Art. 8(2)(a)(ii), ... Either way, the obligation to arbitrate does not arise until the Contracting Party's courts have had a first crack at the dispute.

Article 8 provides a third route to arbitration in paragraph 8(2)(b)—namely, "where the Contracting Party and the investor of the other Contracting Party have so agreed." . . . In contrast to the two routes in Article 8(2)(a), this one does not refer to the local litigation provision. That omission is significant. It makes clear that an investor can bypass local litigation only by obtaining the Contracting Party's explicit agreement to proceed directly to arbitration. Short of that, an investor has no choice but to litigate in the Contracting Party's courts for at least some period.

The structure of Article 8 confirms that the routes to arbitration in paragraph (2)(a) are just as much about eliciting a Contracting Party's consent to arbitrate as the route in paragraph 8(2)(b). Under Article 8(2)(b), the requisite consent is demonstrated by a specific agreement. Under Article 8(2)(a), the requisite consent is demonstrated by compliance with the requirement to resort to a country's local courts. Whereas Article 8(2)(a) is part of a completed agreement between Argentina and the United Kingdom, it constitutes only a unilateral standing *offer* by Argentina with respect to U. K. investors—an offer to submit to arbitration where certain conditions are met. That is how scholars understand arbitration provisions in bilateral investment treaties in general. . . . And it is how BG Group itself describes this investment treaty in particular. . . .

An offer must be accepted for a legally binding contract to be formed. And it is an "undeniable principle of the law of contracts, that an offer . . . by one person to another, imposes no obligation upon the former, until it is accepted by the latter, *according to the terms in which the offer was made*. Any qualification of, or departure from, those terms, invalidates the offer." . . . This principle applies to international arbitration agreements just as it does to domestic commercial contracts. . . .

By incorporating the local litigation provision in Article 8(1), paragraph 8(2)(a) establishes that provision as a term of Argentina's unilateral offer to arbitrate. To accept Argentina's offer, an investor must therefore first litigate its dispute in Argentina's courts—either to a "final decision" or for 18 months, whichever comes first. Unless the investor does so (or, perhaps, establishes a valid excuse for failing to do so, as discussed below, . . . it has not accepted the terms of Argentina's offer to arbitrate, and thus has not formed an arbitration agreement with Argentina.[1]

Although the majority suggests that the local litigation requirement would not be a "condition of consent" even if the Treaty explicitly called it one, the Court's holding is limited to treaties that contain no such clear

[1] To be clear, the only question is whether BG Group formed an *arbitration* agreement with Argentina. To say that BG Group never formed such an agreement is not to call into question the validity of its various commercial agreements with Argentina.

statement. . . . But there is no reason to think that such a clear statement should be required, for we generally do not require "talismanic words" in treaties. . . . Indeed, another arbitral tribunal concluded that the local litigation requirement was a condition on Argentina's consent to arbitrate despite the absence of the sort of clear statement apparently contemplated by the majority. . . . Still other tribunals have reached the same conclusion with regard to similar litigation requirements in other Argentine bilateral investment treaties. . . .

In the face of this authority, the majority quotes a treatise for the proposition that " '[a] substantial body of arbitral authority from investor-state disputes concludes that compliance with procedural mechanisms in an arbitration agreement (or bilateral investment treaty) is not ordinarily a jurisdictional prerequisite.' " . . . But that simply restates the question. The whole issue is whether the local litigation requirement is a mere "procedural mechanism" or instead a condition on Argentina's consent to arbitrate.

BG Group concedes that other terms of Article 8(1) constitute conditions on Argentina's consent to arbitrate, even though they are not expressly labeled as such. . . . The Court does not explain why the *only other term*—the litigation requirement—should be viewed differently.

Nor does the majority's reading accord with ordinary contract law, which treats language such as the word "after" in Article 8(2)(a)(i) as creating conditions, even though such language may not constitute a "clear statement." . . . The majority seems to regard the local litigation requirement as a condition precedent to performance of the contract, rather than a condition precedent to formation of the contract. . . . But that cannot be. Prior to the fulfillment of the local litigation requirement, there was no contract between Argentina *and BG Group* to be performed. The Treaty is not such an agreement, since BG Group is of course not a party to the Treaty. Neither the majority nor BG Group contends that the agreement is under Article 8(2)(b), the provision that applies "where the Contracting Party and the investor of the other Contracting Party have so agreed." An arbitration agreement must be *formed*, and Article 8(2)(a) spells out how an investor may do that: by submitting the dispute to local courts for 18 months or until a decision is rendered.

Moreover, the Treaty's local litigation requirement certainly does not resemble "time limits, notice, laches, estoppel," or the other kinds of provisions that are typically treated as conditions on the performance of an arbitration agreement, rather than prerequisites to formation. . . . Unlike a time limit for submitting a claim to arbitration, . . . the litigation requirement does not simply regulate the timing of arbitration. As the majority recognizes, . . . the provision does not simply require the parties to wait for 18 months before proceeding to arbitration, but instead requires them to submit their claims for adjudication during that period. And unlike a mandatory pre-arbitration grievance procedure, ... the litigation requirement sends the parties to court—and not just any court, but a court of the host country.

The law of international arbitration and domestic contract law lead to the same conclusion: Because paragraph (2)(a) of Article 8 constitutes only a unilateral standing offer by the Contracting Parties to each other's investors to submit to arbitration under certain conditions, an investor cannot form an arbitration agreement with a Contracting Party under the Treaty until the investor accepts the actual terms of the Contracting Party's offer. Absent a valid excuse, that means litigating its dispute in the Contracting Party's courts to a "final decision" or, barring that, for at least 18 months.

B

The nature of the obligations a sovereign incurs in agreeing to arbitrate with a private party confirms that the local litigation requirement is a condition on a signatory country's consent to arbitrate, and not merely a condition on performance of a pre-existing arbitration agreement. There are good reasons for any sovereign to condition its consent to arbitrate disputes on investors' first litigating their claims in the country's own courts for a specified period. It is no trifling matter for a sovereign nation to subject itself to suit by private parties; we do not presume that any country—including our own—takes that step lightly. . . . But even where a sovereign nation has subjected itself to suit in its own courts, it is quite another thing for it to subject itself to international arbitration. Indeed, "[g]ranting a private party the right to bring an action against a sovereign state in an international tribunal regarding an investment dispute is a revolutionary innovation" whose "uniqueness and power should not be overlooked." . . . That is so because of both the procedure and substance of investor-state arbitration.

[. . .]

Substantively, by acquiescing to arbitration, a state permits private adjudicators to review its public policies and effectively annul the authoritative acts of its legislature, executive, and judiciary. . . . Consider the dispute that gave rise to this case: Before the arbitral tribunal, BG Group challenged multiple sovereign acts of the Argentine Government taken after the Argentine economy collapsed in 2001—in particular, Emergency Law 25,561, which converted dollar denominated tariffs into peso-denominated tariffs at a rate of one Argentine peso to one U. S. dollar; Resolution 308/02 and Decree 1090/02, which established a renegotiation process for public service contracts; and Decree 214/02, which stayed for 180 days injunctions and the execution of final judgments in lawsuits challenging the effects of the Emergency Law. Indeed, in awarding damages to BG Group, the tribunal held that the first three of these enactments violated Article 2 of the Treaty. . . .

Perhaps they did, but that is not the issue. Under Article 8, a Contracting Party grants to private adjudicators not necessarily of its own choosing, who can meet literally anywhere in the world, a power it typically reserves to its own courts, if it grants it at all: the power to sit in judgment on its sovereign acts. Given these stakes, one would expect the United Kingdom and Argentina to have taken particular care in specifying the limited circumstances in which foreign investors can trigger the Treaty's arbitration process. And that is precisely what they did in Article 8(2)(a), requiring investors to afford a country's own courts an initial opportunity to review the country's enactments and assess the country's compliance with its international obligations. Contrast this with Article 9, which provides for arbitration between the signatory countries of disputes under the Treaty without any preconditions. Argentina and the United Kingdom considered arbitration with particular foreign investors to be different in kind and to require special limitations on its use.

The majority regards the local litigation requirement as toothless simply because the Treaty does not require an arbitrator to "give substantive weight to the local court's determinations on the matters at issue between the parties," . . . but instead provides that "[t]he arbitration decision shall be final and binding on both Parties,". . . . While it is true that an arbitrator need not defer to an Argentine court's judgment in an investor dispute, that does not deprive the litigation requirement of practical import. Most significant, the Treaty provides that an "arbitral tribunal shall decide the dispute in accordance with . . . the laws of the Contracting Party involved in the dispute." Art. 8(4). . . . I doubt that a tribunal would give no weight to an Argentine court's authoritative construction of Argentine law, rendered in the same dispute, just because it might not be formally bound to adopt that interpretation.

The local litigation requirement can also help to narrow the range of issues that remain in controversy by the time a dispute reaches arbitration. It might even induce the parties to settle along the way. And of course the investor might prevail, which could likewise obviate the need for arbitration. . . .

None of this should be interpreted as defending Argentina's history when it comes to international investment. That history may prompt doubt that requiring an investor to resort to that country's courts in the first instance will be of any use. But that is not the question. Argentina and the United Kingdom reached agreement on the term at issue. The question can therefore be rephrased as whether it makes sense for either Contracting Party to insist on resort to its courts before being compelled to arbitrate anywhere in the world before arbitrators not of its choosing. The foregoing reasons may seem more compelling when viewed apart from the particular episode before us.

II

Given that the Treaty's local litigation requirement is a condition on consent to arbitrate, it follows that whether an investor has complied with that requirement is a question a court must decide *de novo*, rather than an issue for the arbitrator to decide subject only to the most deferential judicial review. See, *e.g.*, *Adams v. Suozzi*, 433 F. 3d 220, 226–228 (CA2 2005) (holding that compliance with a condition on formation of an arbitration agreement is for a court, rather than an arbitrator, to determine). The logic is simple: Because an arbitrator's authority depends on the consent of the parties, the arbitrator should not as a rule be able to decide for himself whether the parties have in fact consented. Where the consent of the parties is in question, "reference of the gateway dispute to the court avoids the risk of forcing parties to arbitrate a matter that they may well not have agreed to arbitrate." . . .

This principle is at the core of our arbitration precedents. See *Granite Rock Co.*, 561 U.S., at 299. . . . (questions concerning "the formation of the parties' arbitration agreement" are for a court to decide *de novo*). The same principle is also embedded in the law of international commercial arbitration. 2 Born 2792 ("[W]here one party denies ever having made an arbitration agreement or challenges the validity of any such agreement, . . . the possibility of de novo judicial review of any jurisdictional award in an annulment action is logically necessary"). See also Restatement (Third) of U.S. Law of International Commercial Arbitration § 4–12(d)(1) (Tent. Draft No. 2, Apr. 16, 2012) ("a court determines de novo . . . the existence of the arbitration agreement").

Indeed, the question in this case—whether BG Group accepted the terms of Argentina's offer to arbitrate—presents an issue of contract formation, which is the starkest form of the question whether the parties have agreed to arbitrate. In *Howsam v. Dean Witter Reynolds, Inc.*, we gave two examples of questions going to consent, which are for courts to decide: "whether the parties are bound by a given arbitration clause" and "whether an arbitration clause in a concededly binding contract applies to a particular type of controversy." . . . In both examples, there is at least a putative arbitration agreement between the parties to the dispute. The only question is whether the agreement is truly binding or whether it covers the specific dispute. Here, by contrast, the question is whether the arbitration clause in the Treaty between the United Kingdom and Argentina gives rise to an arbitration agreement between Argentina *and BG Group* at all. . . .

The majority never even starts down this path. Instead, it preempts the whole inquiry by concluding that the local litigation requirement is the kind of "procedural precondition" that parties typically expect an arbitrator to enforce. . . . But as explained, the local litigation requirement does not resemble the requirements we have previously deemed presumptively procedural. . . . It does not merely regulate the timing of arbitration. Nor does it send the parties to non-judicial forms of dispute resolution.

More importantly, all of the cases cited by the majority as examples of procedural provisions involve commercial contracts between two private parties. . . . None of them—not a single one—involves an agreement between sovereigns or an agreement to which the person seeking to compel arbitration is not even a party. The Treaty, of course, is both of those things.

The majority suggests that I am applying "a different kind of analysis" from that governing private commercial contracts, just because what is at issue is a treaty. . . . That is not so: The key point, which the majority never addresses, is that there is no completed agreement whatsoever between Argentina and BG Group. An agreement must be formed, and whether that has happened is—as it is in the private commercial contract context—an issue for a court to decide. . . .

The distinction between questions concerning consent to arbitrate and mere procedural requirements under an existing arbitration agreement can at times seem elusive. Even the most mundane procedural requirement can be recast as a condition on consent as a matter of technical logic. But it should be clear by now that the Treaty's local litigation requirement is not a mere formality—not in Buenos Aires, not in London. And while it is true that "parties often submit important matters to arbitration," . . . our precedents presume that parties do not submit to arbitration the most important matter of all: whether they are subject to an agreement to arbitrate in the first place.

Nor has the majority pointed to evidence that would rebut this presumption by showing that Argentina " 'clearly and unmistakably' " intended to have an arbitrator enforce the litigation requirement. . . . As the majority notes, . . . the Treaty incorporates certain arbitration rules that, in turn, authorize arbitrators to determine their own jurisdiction over a dispute. See Art. 8(3). But those rules do not operate until a dispute is properly before an arbitral tribunal, and of course the whole question in this case is whether the dispute between BG Group and Argentina was before the arbitrators, given BG Group's failure to comply with the 18-month local litigation requirement. As a leading treatise has explained, "[i]f the parties have not validly agreed to any arbitration agreement at all, then they also have necessarily not agreed to institutional arbitration rules." 1 Born 870. "In these circumstances, provisions in institutional rules cannot confer any [such] authority upon an arbitral tribunal." . . .

I also see no reason to think that arbitrators enjoy comparative expertise in construing the local litigation requirement. . . . It would be one thing if that provision involved the application of the arbitrators' own rules . . . , or if it were "intertwined" with the merits of the underlying dispute . . . . Neither is true of the litigation requirement. A court can assess compliance with the requirement at least as well as an arbitrator can. Given the structure of Article 8 and the important interests that the litigation requirement protects, it seems clear that the United Kingdom and Argentina thought the same.[2]

III

Although the Court of Appeals got there by a slightly different route, it correctly concluded that a court must decide questions concerning the interpretation and application of the local litigation requirement *de novo*. . . . At the same time, however, the court seems to have simply taken it for granted that, because BG Group did not submit its dispute to the local courts, the arbitral award in BG Group's favor was invalid. Indeed, the court addressed the issue in a perfunctory paragraph at the end of its opinion and saw " 'only one possible outcome' ": "that BG Group was required to commence a lawsuit in Argentina's courts and wait eighteen months before filing for arbitration." . . .

That conclusion is not obvious. A leading treatise has indicated that "[i]t is a necessary implication from [a unilateral] offer that the offer or, in addition, makes a subsidiary offer by which he or she promises to accept a tender of performance." 1 Lord § 5:14, at 1005. On this understanding, an offeree's failure to comply with an essential condition of the unilateral offer "will not bar an action, if failure to comply with the condition is due to the offeror's own fault." . . .

It would be open to BG Group to argue before the Court of Appeals that this principle was incorporated into Article 8(2)(a) as an implicit aspect of Argentina's unilateral offer to arbitrate. Such an argument would find some support in the background principle of customary international law that a foreign individual injured by a host country must ordinarily exhaust local remedies—unless doing so would be "futile." . . . In any event, the issue would be analyzed as one of contract formation, and therefore

[2] JUSTICE SOTOMAYOR contends that "Argentina's conduct confirms that the local litigation requirement is not a condition on consent, for rather than objecting to arbitration on the ground that there was no binding arbitration agreement to begin with, Argentina actively participated in the constitution of the arbitral panel and in the proceedings that followed." . . . But as the arbitral tribunal itself recognized, Argentina *did* object to the tribunal's jurisdiction to hear the dispute. . . . And we have held that "merely arguing the arbitrability issue to an arbitrator"—say, by "filing with the arbitrators a written memorandum objecting to the arbitrators' jurisdiction"—"does not indicate a clear willingness to arbitrate that issue, *i.e.*, a willingness to be effectively bound by the arbitrator's decision on that point." [*Kaplan*]. . . . The concurrence contends that Argentina "apparently" argued its jurisdictional objection in terms of procedure rather than consent, . . . but the one piece of evidence cited—a negative inference from the arbitrator's characterization of Argentina's argument on a subsidiary issue—hardly suffices to distinguish *First Options*.

would be for the court to decide. I would accordingly vacate the decision of the Court of Appeals and remand the case for such an inquiry.

I respectfully dissent.

NOTES AND QUESTIONS

1. The threshold requirement of local litigation is commonplace in Latin American Investment Treaties. What defenses, if any, exist to the requirement of local litigation? What are the origins of the requirement? Does the Calvo Clause provide one explanation for the presence of the provision? Is there also the cynical view that Argentina wanted to render foreign investors 'remedy-less' whenever it undermined their interests? Should the British Foreign Ministry have done a better job of negotiating the BIT? Shouldn't private contract then be capable of voiding the Treaty or parts of it? What did Argentina do to make the local litigation requirement more or less accessible? What consequence did the arbitrators and the courts (including the U.S. Supreme Court) attribute to the Host State's conduct?

2. The other two sides of the Court seem to suggest that the parties never entered into an arbitration agreement. Do you agree? Doesn't the Treaty contain an arbitral clause or—at least—a reference to arbitration? Is the latter enough? How do you reconcile the dichotomous positions?

3. Does Argentina's participation in the arbitration without objection absolve the BG Group of the local litigation requirement? How do the arbitrators interpret the local litigation requirement? Is it more accurate to describe the requirement as "a claims-processing rule"? How does the D.C. Court of Appeals assess the arbitrators' determination? Whose authority controls on these matters? Why does the U.S. Supreme Court grant *certiorari* in this case?

4. Do the factors of sovereignty and treaty-making powers have any bearing on the resolution of the case? Should they or is the matter purely a function of private contract? Assess the Solicitor General's position? Why should it matter or be ignored? What is the impact of the majority determination upon prior cases, like *Bazzle* and *Stolt-Nielsen*? Does the fact, alleged by the majority, that parties generally or often submit important matters to arbitration justify the ratification of the arbitrators' determination?

3. FUNCTUS OFFICIO: A LIMIT ON CONTRACT FREEDOM

KYOCERA CORP. V. PRUDENTIAL-BACHE TRADE SERVICES, INC.

341 F.3d 987 (9th Cir. 2003).

REINHARDT, CIRCUIT JUDGE.

I. BACKGROUND

In 1984, Kyocera Corporation ("Kyocera"), Prudential-Bache Trade Corporation ("Prudential"), and the newly formed LaPine Technology Corporation ("LaPine") began a venture to produce and market computer disk drives. LaPine licensed its proprietary drive design to Kyocera, which manufactured the drives. Prudential's role was generally to stabilize the cash flow of the enterprise: in addition to financing LaPine's inventory and accounts receivable, Prudential purchased, through a subsidiary, the LaPine drives from Kyocera and resold the drives on credit to LaPine, which in turn marketed the drives to its customers.

By the summer of 1986, LaPine—which had never earned a profit—had fallen into serious managerial and financial difficulties. On August 13 and 21, 1986, Kyocera gave written notice that it considered LaPine and Prudential in default due to the failure to pay for delivered drives. Shortly thereafter, Kyocera, Prudential and LaPine began discussions regarding LaPine's reorganization and a restructuring of the relationship among the three companies.

The parties differ on the terms of the final agreement that resulted from the ensuing exchanges. In October and November of 1986, both a general "Definitive Agreement" and a subsidiary, more detailed "Amended Trading Agreement" were prepared. The primary dispute arises out of one term of the "Amended Trading Agreement": LaPine and Prudential claim that all parties agreed that Prudential would no longer purchase drives from Kyocera and resell them to LaPine, and that LaPine would instead purchase drives directly from Kyocera; Kyocera maintains that it never approved any such limitation of Prudential's role. When Kyocera refused to execute the "Amended Trading Agreement" as presented by LaPine and Prudential, LaPine notified Kyocera that it considered Kyocera in breach of contract. On May 7, 1987, LaPine instituted proceedings in federal district court, seeking damages and an injunction compelling Kyocera to continue supplying drives under the alleged terms of the contract.

On September 2, 1987, the district court granted Kyocera's motion to compel arbitration, and a panel of three arbitrators was convened. Arbitration proceeded in two phases. The arbitration panel first determined in "Phase I" that, under California law, Kyocera had entered into a contract by accepting LaPine and Prudential's version of the "Amended Trading Agreement," which required Kyocera to sell drives directly to LaPine. Again applying California law, the arbitrators then determined in "Phase II" that Kyocera breached this contract and that the breach was the proximate cause of damage to LaPine. On August 25, 1994, the arbitrators issued their final decision, unanimously awarding LaPine and Prudential $243,133,881 in damages and prejudgment interest against Kyocera.

Kyocera filed a motion in district court to "Vacate, Modify and Correct the Arbitral Award." The motion relied on the arbitration clause of the parties' "Definitive Agreement," which stated that:

> The arbitrators shall issue a written award which shall state the bases of the award and include detailed findings of fact and conclusions of law. The United States District Court for the Northern District of California may enter judgment upon any award, either by confirming the award or by vacating, modifying or correcting the award. The Court shall vacate, modify or correct any award: (i) based upon any of the grounds referred to in the Federal Arbitration Act, (ii) where the arbitrators' findings of fact are not supported by substantial evidence, or (iii) where the arbitrators' conclusions of law are erroneous.

Accordingly, Kyocera asserted that (i) there existed grounds for vacatur pursuant to the Federal Arbitration Act ("FAA") . . . (ii) the arbitration panel's factual findings were unsupported by substantial evidence, and (iii) the panel made various errors of law. LaPine and Prudential, in turn, moved to confirm the panel's award.

The district court denied Kyocera's motion and granted the motion of LaPine and Prudential. . . . The Court concluded that the Federal Arbitration Act granted federal courts the jurisdiction to review arbitration decisions only on certain enumerated grounds, and that private parties could not by contract enlarge this statutory standard of review. . . .

A. LaPine I

Kyocera timely appealed. It argued, almost exclusively, that the district court erred in applying only the Federal Arbitration Act standard, and not the broader contractual provisions for review. . . .

A divided panel of this court reversed the district court's determination that it was bound to apply only the statutory grounds for review, holding that federal court review of an arbitration agreement is not necessarily limited to the standards set forth in the Federal Arbitration Act. . . . Rather, the majority recognized that Supreme Court precedent required that private agreements to arbitrate be implemented on their own terms and according to their own procedural rules, and then extended that principle to provisions regarding the grounds on which federal courts may review arbitration proceedings. . . . The majority held that when parties resort to the use of an arbitral tribunal[,] . . . they may leave in place the limited court review provided by the FAA, or they may agree to remove that insulation and subject the result to a more searching court review of the arbitral tribunal's decision, for example a review for substantial evidence and errors of law. . . .

The majority then declined to review the district court's decision rejecting Kyocera's arguments under the statutory standard. Therefore, although we affirmed the district court's determination that Kyocera presented no basis for modifying the arbitral award on statutory grounds, . . . we remanded to allow the district court to apply the parties' contractually expanded standard of review of unsupported factual findings or errors of law. . . . No party requested en banc rehearing of our decision.

Judge Kozinski provided the deciding vote in LaPine I, although he noted in his tie-breaking concurrence that the question presented was "closer than most." . . . He recognized that although the Supreme Court cases "say that parties may set the time, place and manner of arbitration[,] none says that private parties may tell the federal courts how to conduct their business." . . . He further acknowledged that "[n]owhere has Congress authorized courts to review arbitral awards under the standard the parties here adopted." . . . Nevertheless, despite the fact that the private parties' agreed-upon standard of review was neither authorized by Congress nor compelled by the Supreme Court, Judge Kozinski concluded that the "supported by substantial evidence or erroneous legal conclusion" standard was sufficiently similar to the standard used in reviewing administrative and bankruptcy decisions, and the standard used in reviewing state court decisions on habeas corpus, to permit the district court to apply the contractual agreement's standard of review without difficulty. His decision would have been different, he stated, "if the agreement provided that the district judge would review the award by flipping a coin or studying the entrails of a dead fowl." . . .

JUDGE MAYER dissented. He stated simply and clearly that:

> [w]hether to arbitrate, what to arbitrate, how to arbitrate, and when to arbitrate are matters that parties may specify contractually. . . . However, Kyocera cites no authority explicitly empowering litigants to dictate how an Article III court must review an arbitration decision. Absent this, they may not. Should parties desire more scrutiny than the Federal Arbitration Act authorizes courts to apply, "they can contract for an appellate arbitration panel to review the arbitrator's award[;] they cannot contract for judicial review of that award."

B. LaPine II

Given that LaPine I affirmed the district court's application of the statutory grounds for review, the court on remand reviewed the arbitration decision according to the non-statutory standards specified in . . . the "Definitive Agreement," addressing each arbitration phase separately. On April 4, 2000, the district court confirmed the arbitration panel's "Phase I" decision on contract formation. . . . The court held that the arbitrators' "conclusions are not only legally sound but they are amply supported by the undisputed facts." . . .

On October 2, 2000, the district court similarly confirmed most of the arbitrators' "Phase II" decision on contract breach and damages. However, the court "vacated" Finding of Fact number 135—which recited that LaPine achieved an operating profit in 1987 when in fact the accounting record showed an operating loss for that year—and "remanded" the case to the arbitral panel "for its consideration as to the effect, if any, of the vacation of Finding of Fact 135 on its damage award."

Although one panel member was deceased, the remaining two members of the arbitral panel issued a letter stating that the vacatur of Finding of Fact 135 had no effect on the damages award, because the panel's valuation methodology did not rely on actual profit figures for that year. On March 6, 2001, the district court confirmed the arbitrators' "Phase II" award, and on March 9, the court entered judgment in favor of Prudential and LaPine. Again, Kyocera timely appealed.

A three-judge panel of this court unanimously affirmed the district court's confirmation of the arbitral panel's award. . . . Kyocera timely filed a request for rehearing en banc, and on December 17, 2002, we granted that request. . . . We now affirm the district court's confirmation of the arbitral panel's award. In so doing, we correct the law of the circuit regarding the proper standard for review of arbitral decisions under the Federal Arbitration Act.

II. DISCUSSION

[. . .]

In this case, we need not speculate as to whether the arbitration panel properly applied complex California contract law to a complex factual dispute, because we conclude that Congress has explicitly prescribed a much narrower role for federal courts reviewing arbitral decisions. The Federal Arbitration Act . . . enumerates limited grounds on which a federal court may vacate, modify, or correct an arbitral award. Neither erroneous legal conclusions nor unsubstantiated factual findings justify federal court review of an arbitral award under the statute, which is unambiguous in this regard. Because the Constitution reserves to Congress the power to determine the standards by which federal courts render decisions, and because Congress has specified the exclusive standard by which federal courts may review an arbitrator's decision, we hold that private parties may not contractually impose their own standard on the courts. We therefore review the arbitral panel's determination only on grounds authorized by the statute, and affirm the confirmation of the arbitration award.

[. . .]

B. The Grounds for Review

We now determine whether our decision in LaPine I, allowing private parties to impose on the federal courts a broader standard of review than the grounds authorized by statute, constitutes . . . an error. . . .

. . . [T]he Federal Arbitration Act allows a federal court to correct a technical error, to strike all or a portion of an award pertaining to an issue not at all subject to arbitration, and to vacate an award that evidences affirmative misconduct in the arbitral process or the final result or that is completely irrational or exhibits a manifest disregard for the law. These grounds afford an extremely limited review authority, a limitation that is designed to preserve due process but not to permit unnecessary public intrusion into private arbitration procedures.

Congress had good reason to preclude more expansive federal court review. Arbitration is a dispute resolution process designed, at least in theory, to respond to the wishes of the parties more flexibly and expeditiously than the federal courts' uniform rules of procedure allow. . . . Broad judicial review of arbitration decisions could well jeopardize the very benefits of arbitration, rendering informal arbitration merely a prelude to a more cumbersome and time-consuming judicial review process. Congress's decision to permit sophisticated parties to trade the greater certainty of correct legal decisions by federal courts for the speed and flexibility of arbitration determinations is a reasonable legislative judgment that we have no authority to reject.

Despite Congress's reasonable decision to adopt a narrow standard for judicial review of arbitration decisions, and despite the fact that Congress nowhere intimated that the federal courts were authorized to apply any other standard, the LaPine I panel concluded that private parties may contract for a more expansive (or less deferential) standard of review. The Third and Fifth Circuits agree with this conclusion. . . . These circuits generally emphasize that the purpose of the Federal Arbitration Act is to enforce the terms of private arbitration agreements, including terms specifying the scope of review of arbitration decisions. . . . In *Volt*, the Supreme Court determined that "[j]ust as [private parties] may limit by contract the issues which they will arbitrate, so too may they specify by contract the rules under which that arbitration will be conducted." . . . The circuits mentioned above would expand *Volt* so as to provide that, just as the Federal Arbitration Act's default rules for how arbitration is to be conducted may be superceded by private contract, . . . so too may the Act's statutory standards governing federal court review . . . be superseded by private contract.

Three circuits [the Tenth, Seventh, and Eighth Circuits] appear to reject the proposition that private parties may dictate how federal courts shall conduct their proceedings. . . .

These three circuits distinguished *Volt*'s holding that private parties' contractual agreements can alter the form and substance of the arbitration proceeding itself—a holding not contested here—from the question whether such agreements may alter statutorily prescribed federal court review of the proceeding. . . .

We agree with the Seventh, Eighth, and Tenth Circuits that private parties have no power to determine the rules by which federal courts proceed, especially when Congress has explicitly prescribed those standards. Pursuant to *Volt*, parties have complete freedom to contractually modify the arbitration process by designing whatever procedures and systems they think will best meet their needs—including review by one or more appellate arbitration panels. Once a case reaches the federal courts, however, the private arbitration process is complete, and because Congress has specified standards for confirming an arbitration award, federal courts must act pursuant to those standards and no others. Private parties' freedom to fashion their own arbitration process has no bearing whatsoever on their inability to amend the statutorily prescribed standards governing federal court review. Even when Congress is silent on the matter, private parties lack the power to dictate how the federal courts conduct the business of resolving disputes. . . . A fortiori, private parties lack the power to dictate a broad standard of review when Congress has specifically prescribed a narrower standard.

We therefore overrule LaPine I, affirm the district court's 1995 conclusion, and hold that a federal court may only review an arbitral decision on the grounds set forth in the Federal Arbitration Act. Private parties have no power to alter or expand those grounds, and any contractual provision purporting to do so is, accordingly, legally unenforceable.

[. . .]

III. CONCLUSION

Private parties have no authority to dictate the manner in which the federal courts conduct judicial proceedings. That power is reserved to Congress—and when Congress is silent on the issue, the courts govern themselves. Here, because Congress has determined that federal courts are to review arbitration awards only for certain errors, the parties are powerless to select a different standard of review—whether that standard entails review by seeking facts unsupported by substantial evidence and errors of law or by "flipping a coin or studying the entrails of a dead fowl." . . . Private parties may design an arbitration process as they wish, but once an award is final for the purposes of the arbitration process, Congress has determined how the federal courts are to treat that award. We hold that the contractual provisions in this case providing for federal court review on grounds other than those set forth in the Federal Arbitration Act are invalid and severable. We further hold that Kyocera has shown no cause for relief under the standard provided in the Federal Arbitration Act. . . .

[. . .]

NOTES AND QUESTIONS

1. In *Hughes Training, Inc. v. Cook*, 254 F.3d 588 (5th Cir. 2001), *cert. denied*, 534 U.S. 1172 (2002), the U.S. Supreme Court let stand a Fifth Circuit ruling that, when parties contract for a certain standard of review to govern the arbitration process, that standard governs the district court's review of the arbitration award. Moreover, that standard of review did not conflict with the FAA when the arbitration procedures, including the standard of review, were unambiguously incorporated into an employment agreement that stated, "the arbitration process 'shall be conducted in accordance with the [Employment Problem Resolution Procedures.]' " The Fifth Circuit held that "[i]t was not unfair for the arbitration agreement to include a standard of review that allowed the district court to assess the arbitrator's legal and factual conclusions." It noted, "Although the supplemental standard of review incorporated into the arbitration agreement benefited [the employer] in this instance, it was equally available to [the employee] had the award been unfavorable to her."

2. In *Puerto Rico Telephone Co., Inc. v. U.S. Phone Mfg. Corp.*, 427 F.3d 21 (1st Cir. 2005), the First Circuit adopted a middle-of-the-road position on the question of the validity and enforceability of opt-in agreements. The contract involved in the litigation provided for AAA arbitration in Puerto Rico and further stated that Puerto Rican law governed the contract. The tribunal rendered an award for damages in the amount of $2.5 million. The defendant opposed the award and argued that, by selecting Puerto Rico as the arbitral venue and Puerto Rican law as the law of the contract, the parties had implicitly contracted for the application of the local arbitration statute that contained a higher standard of review against arbitral awards.

In its holding, the court made two essential points: First, ordinary (or "garden variety") factual or legal errors do not warrant judicial supervision or justify the judicial second-guessing of arbitrator rulings; second, and more germane to the issue of opt-in agreements, the mere inclusion of a generic choice-of-law in the contract was not a sufficient basis for requiring the application of the chosen state law as to the scope of review of arbitral awards.

In effect, the judicial supervision standard in FAA § 10 could only be displaced by clear contract language providing for the application of a different standard.

In so holding, the court assessed the rulings of other federal circuits on the issue. Generally, the Ninth and Tenth Circuits prohibit the practice, followed closely by the Seventh and Eighth Circuits. These courts see such clauses as an intrusion upon federal jurisdictional authority and as having an undermining impact upon arbitration. The Third, Sixth, and now First Circuit give effect to private agreements to arbitrate and enforce opt-in provisions as long as they do not conflict with the strong federal policy on arbitration and contain specific and precise language providing for the displacement of the FAA standard.

3. In *Hoeft v. MVL Group, Inc.*, 343 F.3d 57 (2d Cir. 2003), the Second Circuit held that private parties cannot dictate the basis for the exercise of a federal court's authority to review an arbitral award. The court determined that review for manifest disregard of the law, although not an express part of FAA § 10, cannot be limited by the parties' agreement. The Second Circuit thereby joined the Seventh, Eighth, Ninth, and Tenth Circuits' position that "private parties have no power to determine the rules by which federal courts proceed" in the supervision of arbitral awards.

In *Hoeft*, a dispute arose over payment; the parties were unable to resolve it. The stock purchase agreement included special provisions to determine the amount of a deferred portion of the payment that MVL would make to the Hoefts in the following year. The amended stock purchase agreement included an arbitration clause that stated that, in the event that the parties disagreed on the amount of the payment and could not reach a resolution despite their reasonable best efforts, "such dispute shall be resolved by Stephen Sherrill, whose decision in such matters shall be binding and conclusive upon each of the parties hereto and shall not be subject to any type of review or appeal whatever."

Stephen Sherrill arbitrated the dispute and rendered an award in favor of the Hoefts for $1,402,565. When the Hoefts filed a motion to confirm the award, the award debtor responded with a motion to vacate the award on the grounds that Sherrill exceeded his powers and manifestly disregarded the law. The district court granted the motion to vacate the award stating that, although the arbitrator had not exceeded his powers, he had manifestly disregarded the law in calculating the amount owed.

On appeal, the Second Circuit concluded that parties "may not divest the courts of their statutory and common-law authority to review" arbitral awards under FAA § 10(a) or on the basis of the decisional law grounds. The Hoefts argued that contracting parties could exclude judicial review for manifest disregard of the law because it was not a part of the express statutory language. The court, however, reasoned that the decisional standard was just as vital to the supervision of arbitral awards as the statutory grounds. Moreover, although freedom of contract may be instrumental to arbitration, it did not encompass judicial review: "Unlike arbitration, however, judicial review is not a creature of contract, and the authority of the federal court to review an arbitration award . . . does not derive from a private agreement." *See Insurance Corp. of Ireland v. Compagnie des Bauxites de Guinee*, 456 U.S. 694, 701 (1982). Federal courts are "not [the] rubber stamps" of contract stipulations; they cannot be deprived by private agreement of their authority to review arbitral awards. Referring to *Bowen v. Amoco Pipeline Co.*, 254 F.3d 925, 936 n.8 (10th Cir. 2001), the court concluded that: "[I]n the absence of clear authority to the contrary, parties may not interfere with the judicial process by dictating how the federal courts operate."

4. The U.S. Court of Appeals for the Eighth Circuit also embraced a view of public judicial authority that made it impervious to contractual modifications. Such modifications could be effective only if the parties' intent and language were unmistakable. In *Schoch v. InfoUSA, Inc.*, 341 F.3d 785 (8th Cir. 2003), *cert. denied*, 540 U.S. 1180 (2004), InfoUSA bought Schoch's business and entered into a three-year employment agreement with Schoch. InfoUSA also granted Schoch the option to purchase 360,000 shares of InfoUSA stock. The options vested over a four-year period and could "be exercised for up to three months after termination of employment or consulting relationship." Schoch attempted to exercise his option to purchase shares. InfoUSA refused, claiming that Schoch's three-month period to exercise his option had already expired.

Both parties agreed to arbitrate the dispute. The arbitrator decided that Schoch's option had not expired and awarded him $1,632,000 in damages. The district court granted Schoch's motion to confirm the award. The Eighth Circuit affirmed on appeal.

InfoUSA opposed the arbitral award, asserting—*inter alia*—that a heightened standard of review applied. The Eighth Circuit, however, determined that the parties had not expressed "in crystal-clear language" their intent to have a heightened form of judicial scrutiny apply. Reiterating its reasoning in *UHC Management Co. v. Computer Sciences Corp.*, the Eighth Circuit stated: "It is not clear . . . that parties have any say in how a federal court will review an arbitration award when Congress has ordained a specific, self-limiting procedure for how such a review is to occur [under the FAA]. . . . Congress did not authorize *de novo* review of such an award on its merits; it commanded that when the exceptions do not apply, a federal court has no choice but to confirm." *UHC Management*, 148 F.3d 992, 997 (8th Cir. 1998). The court further stated that "if parties could contract for heightened judicial review, '[their] intent to do so must be clearly and unmistakably expressed.' "

HALL STREET ASSOCIATES, L.L.C. v. MATTEL, INC.

552 U.S. 576, 128 S.Ct. 1396, 170 L.Ed.2d 254 (2008).

JUSTICE SOUTER delivered the opinion of the Court.*

The Federal Arbitration Act (FAA or Act), 9 U.S.C. § 1 *et seq.*, provides for expedited judicial review to confirm, vacate, or modify arbitration awards. §§ 9–11 (2000 ed. and Supp. V). The question here is whether statutory grounds for prompt vacatur and modification may be supplemented by contract. We hold that the statutory grounds are exclusive.

I

This case began as a lease dispute between landlord, petitioner Hall Street Associates, L. L. C., and tenant, respondent Mattel, Inc. The property was used for many years as a manufacturing site, and the leases provided that the tenant would indemnify the landlord for any costs resulting from the failure of the tenant or its predecessor lessees to follow environmental laws while using the premises. . . .

Tests of the property's well water in 1998 showed high levels of trichloroethylene (TCE), the apparent residue of manufacturing discharges by Mattel's predecessors between 1951 and 1980. After the Oregon Department of Environmental Quality (DEQ) discovered even more pollutants, Mattel stopped drawing from the well and, along with one of its predecessors, signed a consent order with the DEQ providing for cleanup of the site.

After Mattel gave notice of intent to terminate the lease in 2001, Hall Street filed this suit, contesting Mattel's right to vacate on the date it gave, and claiming that the lease obliged Mattel to indemnify Hall Street for costs of cleaning up the TCE, among other things. Following a bench trial before the United States District Court for the District of Oregon, Mattel won on the termination issue, and after an unsuccessful try at mediating the indemnification claim, the parties proposed to submit to arbitration. The District Court was amenable, and the parties drew up an arbitration agreement, which the court approved and entered as an order. One paragraph of the agreement provided that

> "[t]he United States District Court for the District of Oregon may enter judgment upon any award, either by confirming the award or by vacating, modifying or correcting the award. The Court shall vacate, modify or correct any award: (i) where the arbitrator's findings of facts are not supported by substantial evidence, or (ii) where the arbitrator's conclusions of law are erroneous." . . .

* Justice Souter delivered the opinion of the Court. Justice Scalia joins all but footnote 7 of this opinion.

Arbitration took place, and the arbitrator decided for Mattel. In particular, he held that no indemnification was due, because the lease obligation to follow all applicable federal, state, and local environmental laws did not require compliance with the testing requirements of the Oregon Drinking Water Quality Act (Oregon Act); that Act the arbitrator characterized as dealing with human health as distinct from environmental contamination.

Hall Street then filed . . . [a motion to vacate or correct the award] . . . on the ground that failing to treat the Oregon Act as an applicable environmental law under the terms of the lease was legal error. The District Court agreed, vacated the award, and remanded for further consideration by the arbitrator. The court expressly invoked the standard of review chosen by the parties in the arbitration agreement, which included review for legal error, and cited *LaPine Technology Corp. v. Kyocera Corp.*, 130 F.3d 884, 889 (CA9 1997), for the proposition that the FAA leaves the parties "free . . . to draft a contract that sets rules for arbitration and dictates an alternative standard of review." . . .

On remand, the arbitrator followed the District Court's ruling that the Oregon Act was an applicable environmental law and amended the decision to favor Hall Street. This time, each party sought modification, and again the District Court applied the parties' stipulated standard of review for legal error, correcting the arbitrator's calculation of interest but otherwise upholding the award. Each party then appealed to the Court of Appeals for the Ninth Circuit, where Mattel switched horses and contended that the Ninth Circuit's recent en banc action overruling *LaPine Kyocera Corp. v. Prudential-Bache Trade Servs., Inc.*, 341 F.3d 987, 1000 (2003), left the arbitration agreement's provision for judicial review of legal error unenforceable. Hall Street countered that *Kyocera* (the later one) was distinguishable, and that the agreement's judicial review provision was not severable from the submission to arbitration.

The Ninth Circuit reversed in favor of Mattel in holding that, "[u]nder *Kyocera* the terms of the arbitration agreement controlling the mode of judicial review are unenforceable and severable." . . . [footnote omitted]. . . .

. . . [W]e granted *certiorari* to decide whether the grounds for vacatur and modification provided by §§ 10 and 11 of the FAA are exclusive. . . . We agree with the Ninth Circuit that they are, but vacate and remand for consideration of independent issues.

II

Congress enacted the FAA to replace judicial indisposition to arbitration with a "national policy favoring [it] and plac[ing] arbitration agreements on equal footing with all other contracts." *Buckeye Check Cashing, Inc. v. Cardegna*, 546 U.S. 440, 443, 126 S. Ct. 1204, 163 L. Ed. 2d 1038 (2006). As for jurisdiction over controversies touching arbitration, the Act does nothing, being "something of an anomaly in the field of federal-court jurisdiction" in bestowing no federal jurisdiction but rather requiring an independent jurisdictional basis. *Moses H. Cone Memorial Hospital v. Mercury Constr. Corp.*, 460 U.S. 1, 25, n. 32, 103 S. Ct. 927, 74 L. Ed. 2d 765 (1983); see, *e.g.*, 9 U.S.C. § 4 (providing for action by a federal district court "which, save for such [arbitration] agreement, would have jurisdiction under title 28").[2] But in cases falling within a court's jurisdiction, the Act makes contracts to arbitrate "valid, irrevocable, and enforceable," so long as their subject involves "commerce." § 2. And this is so whether an agreement has a broad reach or goes just to one dispute, and whether enforcement be sought in state court or federal. . . .

The Act also supplies mechanisms for enforcing arbitration awards: a judicial decree confirming an award, an order vacating it, or an order modifying or correcting it. §§ 9–11. An application for any of these orders will get streamlined treatment as a motion, obviating the separate contract action that would usually be necessary to enforce or tinker with an arbitral award in court. [Footnote omitted.] § 6. Under the terms of § 9, a court "must" confirm an arbitration award "unless" it is vacated, modified, or corrected "as prescribed" in §§ 10 and 11. Section 10 lists grounds for vacating an award, while § 11 names those for modifying or correcting one. [Footnote omitted.]

The Courts of Appeals have split over the exclusiveness of these statutory grounds when parties take the FAA shortcut to confirm, vacate, or modify an award, with some saying the recitations are exclusive, and others regarding them as mere threshold provisions open to expansion by agreement.[5] . . . We now hold that §§ 10 and 11 respectively provide the FAA's exclusive grounds for expedited vacatur and modification.

III

Hall Street makes two main efforts to show that the grounds set out for vacating or modifying an award are not exclusive, taking the position, first, that expandable judicial review authority has been accepted as the

---

[2] Because the FAA is not jurisdictional, there is no merit in the argument that enforcing the arbitration agreement's judicial review provision would create federal jurisdiction by private contract. The issue is entirely about the scope of judicial review permissible under the FAA.

[5] The Ninth and Tenth Circuits have held that parties may not contract for expanded judicial review. See *Kyocera Corp. v. Prudential-Bache Trade Servs., Inc.*, 341 F.3d 987, 1000 (9th Cir.2003); *Bowen v. Amoco Pipeline Co.*, 254 F.3d 925, 936 (CA10 2001). The First, Third, Fifth, and Sixth Circuits, meanwhile, have held that parties may so contract. See *Puerto Rico Tel. Co. v. U.S. Phone Mfg. Corp.*, 427 F.3d 21, 31 (1st Cir. 2005); *Jacada (Europe), Ltd. v. International Marketing Strategies, Inc.*, 401 F.3d 701, 710 (CA6 2005); *Roadway Package System, Inc. v. Kayser*, 257 F.3d 287, 288 (CA3 2001); *Gateway Technologies, Inc. v. MCI Telecommunications Corp.*, 64 F.3d 993, 997 (CA5 1995). The Fourth Circuit has taken the latter side of the split in an unpublished opinion, see *Syncor Int'l Corp. v. McLeland*, 120 F.3d 262 (1997), while the Eighth Circuit has expressed agreement with the former side in *dicta*, see *UHC Management Co. v. Computer Sciences Corp.*, 148 F.3d 992, 997–998 (1998).

law since *Wilko v. Swan*, 346 U.S. 427, 74 S. Ct. 182, 98 L. Ed. 168 (1953). This, however, was not what *Wilko* decided. . . .

The *Wilko* Court was explaining that arbitration would undercut the Securities Act's buyer protections when it remarked . . . that "[p]ower to vacate an [arbitration] award is limited," . . . and went on to say that "the interpretations of the law by the arbitrators in contrast to manifest disregard [of the law] are not subject, in the federal courts, to judicial review for error in interpretation." . . . Hall Street reads this statement as recognizing "manifest disregard of the law" as a further ground for vacatur on top of those listed in § 10, and some Circuits have read it the same way. . . . Hall Street sees this supposed addition to § 10 as the camel's nose: if judges can add grounds to vacate (or modify), so can contracting parties.

But this is too much for *Wilko* to bear. Quite apart from its leap from a supposed judicial expansion by interpretation to a private expansion by contract, Hall Street overlooks the fact that the statement it relies on expressly rejects just what Hall Street asks for here, general review for an arbitrator's legal errors. Then there is the vagueness of *Wilko*'s phrasing. Maybe the term "manifest disregard" was meant to name a new ground for review, but maybe it merely referred to the § 10 grounds collectively, rather than adding to them. . . . Or, as some courts have thought, "manifest disregard" may have been shorthand for § 10(a)(3) or § 10(a)(4), the subsections authorizing vacatur when the arbitrators were "guilty of misconduct" or "exceeded their powers." . . . We, when speaking as a Court, have merely taken the *Wilko* language as we found it, without embellishment, . . . and now that its meaning is implicated, we see no reason to accord it the significance that Hall Street urges.

Second, Hall Street says that the agreement to review for legal error ought to prevail simply because arbitration is a creature of contract, and the FAA is "motivated, first and foremost, by a congressional desire to enforce agreements into which parties ha[ve] entered." . . . But, again, we think the argument comes up short. Hall Street is certainly right that the FAA lets parties tailor some, even many features of arbitration by contract, including the way arbitrators are chosen, what their qualifications should be, which issues are arbitrable, along with procedure and choice of substantive law. But to rest this case on the general policy of treating arbitration agreements as enforceable as such would be to beg the question, which is whether the FAA has textual features at odds with enforcing a contract to expand judicial review following the arbitration.

To that particular question we think the answer is yes, that the text compels a reading of the §§ 10 and 11 categories as exclusive. To begin with, even if we assumed §§ 10 and 11 could be supplemented to some extent, it would stretch basic interpretive principles to expand the stated grounds to the point of evidentiary and legal review generally. Sections 10 and 11, after all, address egregious departures from the parties' agreed-upon arbitration: "corruption," "fraud," "evident partiality," "misconduct," "misbehavior," "exceed[ing] . . . powers," "evident material miscalculation," "evident material mistake," "award[s] upon a matter not submitted;" the only ground with any softer focus is "imperfect[ions]," and a court may correct those only if they go to "[a] matter of form not affecting the merits." Given this emphasis on extreme arbitral conduct, the old rule of *ejusdem generis* has an implicit lesson to teach here. Under that rule, when a statute sets out a series of specific items ending with a general term, that general term is confined to covering subjects comparable to the specifics it follows. Since a general term included in the text is normally so limited, then surely a statute with no textual hook for expansion cannot authorize contracting parties to supplement review for specific instances of outrageous conduct with review for just any legal error. "Fraud" and a mistake of law are not cut from the same cloth.

That aside, expanding the detailed categories would rub too much against the grain of the § 9 language, where provision for judicial confirmation carries no hint of flexibility. On application for an order confirming the arbitration award, the court "must grant" the order "unless the award is vacated, modified, or corrected as prescribed in sections 10 and 11 of this title." There is nothing malleable about "must grant," which unequivocally tells courts to grant confirmation in all cases, except when one of the "prescribed" exceptions applies. This does not sound remotely like a provision meant to tell a court what to do just in case the parties say nothing else. [Footnote omitted.]

In fact, anyone who thinks Congress might have understood § 9 as a default provision should turn back to § 5 for an example of what Congress thought a default provision would look like:

> "[i]f in the agreement provision be made for a method of naming or appointing an arbitrator . . . such method shall be followed; but if no method be provided therein, or if a method be provided and any party thereto shall fail to avail himself of such method, . . . then upon the application of either party to the controversy the court shall designate and appoint an arbitrator. . . ."

"[I]f no method be provided" is a far cry from "must grant . . . unless" in § 9.

Instead of fighting the text, it makes more sense to see the three provisions, §§ 9–11, as substantiating a national policy favoring arbitration with just the limited review needed to maintain arbitration's essential virtue of resolving disputes straightaway. Any other reading opens the door to the full-bore legal and evidentiary appeals that can "rende[r] informal arbitration merely a prelude to a more cumbersome and time-consuming judicial review process," . . . and bring arbitration theory to grief in post-arbitration process.

Nor is *Dean Witter,* . . . to the contrary, as Hall Street claims it to be. *Dean Witter* held that state-law claims subject to an agreement to arbitrate could not be remitted to a district court considering a related, nonarbitrable federal claim; the state-law claims were to go to arbitration immediately. . . . Despite the opinion's language "reject[ing] the suggestion that the overriding goal of the [FAA] was to promote the expeditious resolution of claims," . . . the holding mandated immediate enforcement of an arbitration agreement; the Court was merely trying to explain that the inefficiency and difficulty of conducting simultaneous arbitration and federal-court litigation was not a good enough reason to defer the arbitration . . . .

When all these arguments based on prior legal authority are done with, Hall Street and Mattel remain at odds over what happens next. Hall Street and its *amici* say parties will flee from arbitration if expanded review is not open to them. . . . One of Mattel's *amici* foresees flight from the courts if it is. . . . We do not know who, if anyone, is right, and so cannot say whether the exclusivity reading of the statute is more of a threat to the popularity of arbitrators or to that of courts. But whatever the consequences of our holding, the statutory text gives us no business to expand the statutory grounds. [Footnote omitted.]

IV

In holding that §§ 10 and 11 provide exclusive regimes for the review provided by the statute, we do not purport to say that they exclude more searching review based on authority outside the statute as well. The FAA is not the only way into court for parties wanting review of arbitration awards: they may contemplate enforcement under state statutory or common law, for example, where judicial review of different scope is arguable. But here we speak only to the scope of the expeditious judicial review under §§ 9, 10, and 11, deciding nothing about other possible avenues for judicial enforcement of arbitration awards.

[. . .]

Although we agree with the Ninth Circuit that the FAA confines its expedited judicial review to the grounds listed in 9 U.S.C. §§ 10 and 11, we vacate the judgment and remand the case for proceedings consistent with this opinion.

It is so ordered.

JUSTICE STEVENS, with whom JUSTICE KENNEDY joins, dissenting.

May parties to an ongoing lawsuit agree to submit their dispute to arbitration subject to the caveat that the trial judge should refuse to enforce an award that rests on an erroneous conclusion of law? Prior to Congress' enactment of the Federal Arbitration Act (FAA or Act) in 1925, the answer to that question would surely have been "Yes." [Footnote omitted.] Today, however, the Court holds that the FAA does not merely authorize the vacation [sic] [vacatur] or enforcement of awards on specified grounds, but also forbids enforcement of perfectly reasonable judicial review provisions in arbitration agreements fairly negotiated by the parties and approved by the district court. Because this result conflicts with the primary purpose of the FAA and ignores the historical context in which the Act was passed, I respectfully dissent.

Prior to the passage of the FAA, American courts were generally hostile to arbitration. They refused, with rare exceptions, to order specific enforcement of executory agreements to arbitrate. [Footnote omitted.] Section 2 of the FAA responded to this hostility by making written arbitration agreements "valid, irrevocable, and enforceable." . . . This section, which is the centerpiece of the FAA, reflects Congress' main goal in passing the legislation: "to abrogate the general common-law rule against specific enforcement of arbitration agreements," . . . and to "ensur[e] that private arbitration agreements are enforced according to their terms." . . . Given this settled understanding of the core purpose of the FAA, the interests favoring enforceability of parties' arbitration agreements are stronger today than before the FAA was enacted. As such, there is more—and certainly not less—reason to give effect to parties' fairly negotiated decisions to provide for judicial review of arbitration awards for errors of law.

Petitioner filed this rather complex action in an Oregon state court. Based on the diverse citizenship of the parties, respondent removed the case to federal court. More than three years later, and after some issues had been resolved, the parties sought and obtained the District Court's approval of their agreement to arbitrate the remaining issues subject to *de novo* judicial review. They neither requested, nor suggested that the FAA authorized, any "expedited" disposition of their case. Because the arbitrator made a rather glaring error of law, the judge refused to affirm his award until after that error was corrected. The Ninth Circuit reversed.

This Court now agrees with the Ninth Circuit's (most recent) interpretation of the FAA as setting forth the exclusive grounds for modification or vacation [sic] [vacatur] of an arbitration award under the statute. As I read the Court's opinion, it identifies two possible reasons for reaching this result: (1) a supposed *quid pro quo* bargain between Congress and litigants that conditions expedited federal enforcement of arbitration awards on acceptance of a statutory limit on the scope of judicial review of such awards; and (2) an assumption that Congress intended to include the words "and no other" in the grounds specified in §§ 10 and 11 for the vacatur and modification of awards. Neither reason is persuasive.

While § 9 of the FAA imposes a 1-year limit on the time in which any party to an arbitration may apply for confirmation of an award, the statute does not require that the application be given expedited treatment. Of course, the premise of the entire statute is an assumption that the arbitration process may be more expeditious and less costly than ordinary litigation, but that is a reason for interpreting the statute liberally to favor the parties' use of arbitration. An unnecessary refusal to enforce a perfectly reasonable category of arbitration agreements defeats the primary purpose of the statute.

That purpose also provides a sufficient response to the Court's reliance on statutory text. It is true that a wooden application of "the old rule of *ejusdem generis*" . . . might support an inference that the categories listed in §§ 10 and 11 are exclusive, but the literal text does not compel that reading—a reading that is flatly inconsistent with the overriding interest in effectuating the clearly expressed intent of the contracting parties. A listing of grounds that must always be available to contracting parties simply does not speak to the question whether they may agree to additional grounds for judicial review.

Moreover, in light of the historical context and the broader purpose of the FAA, §§ 10 and 11 are best understood as a shield meant to protect parties from hostile courts, not a sword with which to cut down parties' "valid, irrevocable and enforceable" agreements to arbitrate their disputes subject to judicial review for errors of law. [Footnote omitted.] § 2.

Even if I thought the narrow issue presented in this case were as debatable as the conflict among the courts of appeals suggests, I would rely on a presumption of overriding importance to resolve the debate and rule in favor of petitioner's position that the FAA permits the statutory grounds for vacatur and modification of an award to be supplemented by contract. A decision "*not to regulate*" the terms of an agreement that does not even arguably offend any public policy whatsoever, "is adequately justified by a presumption in favor of freedom." . . .

Accordingly, while I agree that the judgment of the Court of Appeals must be set aside, and that there may be additional avenues available for judicial enforcement of parties' fairly negotiated review provisions. . . . I respectfully dissent from the Court's interpretation of the FAA, and would direct the Court of Appeals to affirm the judgment of the District Court enforcing the arbitrator's final award.

JUSTICE BREYER, dissenting.

The question presented in this case is whether "the Federal Arbitration Act . . . *precludes* a federal court from enforcing" an arbitration agreement that gives the court the power to set aside an arbitration award that embodies an arbitrator's mistake about the law. . . . Like the majority [in *dicta*] and Justice Stevens, and primarily for the reasons they set forth,

I believe that the Act does not *preclude* enforcement of such an agreement. . . .

At the same time, I see no need to send the case back for further judicial decisionmaking. The agreement here was entered into with the consent of the parties and the approval of the District Court. Aside from the Federal Arbitration Act itself, . . . respondent below pointed to no statute, rule, or other relevant public policy that the agreement might violate. The Court has now rejected its argument that the agreement violates the Act, and I would simply remand the case with instructions that the Court of Appeals affirm the District Court's judgment enforcing the arbitrator's final award.

NOTES AND QUESTIONS

1. Does the fact that the parties entered into the arbitration agreement during a legal proceeding make any difference to your analysis of its enforceability? If the parties were truly interested in achieving finality and ending their dispute, should they have instructed the court to choose an arbitrator and conferred on the designated arbitrator absolute power to render an award? Does the parties' qualified recourse to arbitration indicate a mixed commitment to the remedy and a possible solution? Should parties be free to choose a tepid recourse to arbitration?

2. The Court rules that FAA §§ 10 & 11 are the "exclusive" basis for the confirmation and vacatur of arbitral awards under the FAA. You should restate that conclusion, incorporating its necessary implications and consequences for the law of arbitration. Why does the majority never expressly assert that opt-in provisions for enhanced judicial review are invalid and unenforceable contracts? Does the omission portend a narrow holding? What factor narrows the holding? What aim does the majority attempt to achieve?

3. Evaluate Hall Street's use of *Wilko* to make its case. Would *Volt Info. Sciences, Inc.* have been a better reference? Was a 'weak-kneed' approach the best that could be achieved in the circumstances?

4. Assess the Court's appraisal of manifest disregard of the law, especially its view that, "Maybe the term 'manifest disregard' was meant to name a new ground for review, but maybe it merely referred to the § 10 grounds collectively, rather than adding to them . . . or . . . [it] may have been shorthand for § 10(a)(3) or § 10(a)(4), the sections authorizing vacatur when the arbitrators were 'guilty of misconduct' or 'exceeded their powers.' " Is the statement speculation or does it redefine manifest disregard? Does the Court overstate the decisional law of the lower courts on the subject?

5. The initial paragraph in Section IV is perhaps the majority's most enigmatic proclamation. Commentators have been baffled in part because federal preemption should invalidate any state arbitration law that expressly and evidently contradicts any basic FAA rule or principle. Arguing that *Hall Street* constituted exclusively an interpretation of the text of the FAA, the

Texas Supreme Court and its California counterpart have ruled *Hall Street* inapplicable to their states' arbitration statutes, allowing these laws to recognize 'opt-in' agreements as valid and enforceable. Is that assessment justifiable? Does it undermine the national character of the legal regulation of arbitration? *See NAFTA Traders, Inc. v. Quinn*, 339 S.W. 3d 84 (Tex. 2011); *Cable Connection, Inc. v. DIRECTV, Inc.*, 44 Cal. 4th 1334, 190 P. 3d 586 (Cal.2008).

6. In its wake, *Hall Street* has generated substantial judicial debate about the continued viability of manifest disregard of the law as a basis for challenging the enforceability of arbitral awards. The Court itself contributed to the discussion by reversing and remanding the Ninth Circuit decision in *Improv West Associates v. Comedy Club,* 555 U.S. 801, 129 S.Ct. 45 (2008). It asked the Ninth Circuit to reconsider its partial vacatur of an award for manifest disregard of the law in light of the ruling in *Hall Street.* The Ninth Circuit upheld its prior determination, holding that manifest disregard remained a viable basis for the nullification of awards. *See* 553 F.3d 1277 (9th Cir. 2009) [the Ninth Circuit held that manifest disregard is merely a judicial gloss on FAA § 10(a)(4)].

Some courts have determined that *Hall Street* sounded the death knell of manifest disregard. *Citigroup Global Markets Inc. v. Bacon*, 562 F.3d 349 (5th Cir. 2009) [in light of *Hall Street,* "manifest disregard of the law as an independent, nonstatutory ground for setting aside an award must be abandoned and rejected."]; *Hereford v. D.R. Horton, Inc.*, 13 So.3d 375 (Ala. 2009); Robert Lewis Rosen Associates v. Webb, 566 F.Supp.2d 228 (S.D.N.Y. 2008). Yet other courts have concluded that manifest disregard remains part of the law of vacatur. *Kashner Davidson Securities Corp. v. Mscisz*, 531 F.3d 68 (1st Cir. 2008); *Ramos-Santiago v. UPS*, 524 F.3d 120 (1st Cir. 2008); *Chase Bank USA, NA v. Hale*, 859 N.Y.S.2d 342 (2008); MasTec North America, Inc. v. MSE Power Systems, 581 F.Supp.2d 321 (N.D.N.Y. 2008); *Coffee Beanery, Ltd. v. WW, L.L.C.*, 300 Fed.App'x 415 (6th Cir. 2008) (unpub.) (the court rules that *Hall Street* only applies to contract expansions of the FAA grounds for vacatur!).

What is your view of the standing of manifest disregard after the ruling in *Hall Street*? Does it and should it continue to have a role in policing arbiral awards? Was its presence in the regulatory scheme always a misnomer or eccentricity? Formulate your opinion in light of the following commentary:

However the ground originated, manifest disregard invites the courts to pass on the merits of arbitrator determinations. Although manifest disregard is invoked with some frequency in enforcement proceedings, it rarely results in the vacatur of awards. In those few cases in which it does, it ordinarily represents circumstances in which the court disagrees with the arbitrators' interpretation or application of law. No matter how episodic, such results conflict with the statutory policy and the decisional law, both of which prohibit the judicial re-evaluation of abitrator rulings on the merits. Despite its generally perfunctory and sometimes controversial character, manifest disregard could play a role in legitimizing arbitrations involving statutory claims, especailly those that address discrimination and civil liberties issues. The publication of redacted awards along with court supervision of arbitrator decisions on statutory claims would allow the law to grow and develop and give the arbitral adjudication of such claims greater transparency. In the final analysis, the contemporary function of manifest disregard is unsettled and subject periodically to variegated interpretations. Its present status demands future adjustments.

CHAPTER 5

STATUTORY ARBITRABILITY

■ ■ ■

Like contractual inarbitrability, the question of subject-matter inarbitrability is of central importance to the law of arbitration. It defines the lawful adjudicatory role of arbitration. Should arbitration function primarily, if not exclusively, as a mechanism for resolving private contractual disputes (relating to performance, delivery, or payment)? Should its jurisdictional reach be expanded to include claims that arise in the context of contractual relationships and involve legal rights created by statute? Extending arbitration to the resolution of regulatory law claims blurs the jurisdictional boundary between judicial and arbitral adjudication, between the role of the law and the function of contract. In effect, arbitration gains, to some degree, a public law-making authority. It affects the rel statutory framework and the underlying public interest by confining some part of its interpretation and implementation to a private adjudicatory process.

For example, a commercial transaction that results in a failure of timely payment or delivery can also implicate laws that are meant to curb economic monopolies. When the transaction contains an arbitral clause, should the law permit the arbitrators to rule both on the breach of contract claim and a counterclaim sounding in antitrust? Would a statutory command for exclusive judicial jurisdiction over the regulatory claim demand a severance of the arbitral and judicial litigation? A stay of arbitration pending the court action? If the claims are so inter-related that severance of the claims is not possible, should judicial or arbitral jurisdiction be favored?

The answers to these questions in the U.S. law of arbitration have been influenced by considerations of arbitral autonomy, the federal policy supporting arbitration, and the Court's decisional law in matters of international commercial arbitration. On the one hand, it can be argued, as a matter of basic doctrine, that some subject-matter limits must be imposed upon and are necessary to the process of arbitral adjudication. The marketplace may be a private arena, but it is also a stage upon which communitarian interests appear and have a role. Bankruptcies involve both the interests of creditors and the public's interest in the orderly dissolution of liability-ridden enterprises. The sale of securities is a private transaction done in the context of a financial market, the integrity of which is of critical importance to society at large. Commercial competition may enhance the profitability of private enterprises, but it also affects the position of consumers and the general operation of the American economic system. The public dimension of the issues raised by commercial conduct can sometimes warrant exclusive judicial jurisdiction.

On the other hand, the possibility of staying or bifurcating arbitral proceedings because of regulatory law claims can invite dilatory tactics and lessen substantially the adjudicatory effectiveness of arbitration. Parties can always manufacture a claim that enables them to shift the litigation to a court (at least, temporarily), thereby causing delay and greater expense (and perhaps frustrating the recourse to arbitration). In the absence of a clear and easily applicable rule for "intertwined" claims, a body of complex and difficult rules needs to be developed, placing greater stress upon the process. As Justice Breyer makes clear in *First Options v. Kaplan*, none of these consequences is desirable in the context of arbitration. Such rulings would eliminate the simplicity and clarity of the reference to arbitration, and they could transform the law of arbitration into a litigious, unworkable, and self-defeating body of principles. This approach would ultimately contravene the letter and spirit of the FAA, especially Section Two, and result in a deterioration of the system of alternative recourse. If the basic precepts of federalism cannot limit the federal policy on arbitration, it is unlikely that any other legal value or principle could thwart it.

Also, the Court's holdings in international arbitration cases have had a direct and profound impact upon the elaboration of a domestic rule of decision on subject-matter inarbitrability. In two significant cases, *Scherk v. Alberto-Culver Co.*, 417 U.S. 506 (1974), and *Mitsubishi Motors Corp. v. Soler Chrysler-Plymouth, Inc.*, 473 U.S. 614 (1985), the Court ruled that international arbitrators could rule upon statutory claims that arose in the performance of an international contract. At the time they were rendered, *Scherk* and *Mitsubishi* were expressly limited to matters involving transborder commercial arbitration. Their reasoning, however, began to creep into domestic arbitration cases. The Court eventually simply forgot about the international specificity of the holdings and integrated them into the domestic decisional law. As a result, precedent prohibiting the domestic recourse to arbitration for the adjudication of certain statutory claims was reversed, engendering a new interpretation of the domestic provisions of the FAA: Nothing in the Act prohibited the submission of statutory disputes to arbitration. Finally, as a result of its holdings in *Scherk* and *Mitsubishi*, the Court came to believe—or at least to state—that arbitration was a "mere form of trial," the use of which had no impact upon the disputed substantive rights. Therefore, the holdings in the international cases became the doctrinal foundation for the Court's elaboration of a domestic law rule that statutory claims could be submitted to arbitration.

The cases and case summaries that follow describe the effect of the U.S. Supreme Court's arbitration doctrine upon the subject-matter inarbitrability defense among the lower federal courts. To some extent, this section anticipates other developments in the course materials dealing with the arbitrability of statutory rights. In particular, the list of judicial determinations on the arbitrability of various statutory rights introduces a vital aspect of the law of securities arbitration as well as labor and employment arbitration. The present classification is more comprehensive of the rights addressed and provides a view of the debate to which the arbitrability of statutory rights question can give rise. The debate dimension of the area is not as evident either in the cases dealing with securities or employment arbitration. Finally, you should be aware throughout your assessment of these judicial rulings that they are the progeny of the international decisional law and its impact upon *McMahon* and *Rodriguez* as well as the ruling in *Gilmer*. That perspective will allow you to properly assess the inter-related doctrine that unites all these various areas of arbitration.

1. SECURITIES

The evolution of the law toward a narrow subject-matter inarbitrability defense is perhaps best illustrated by the emergence of securities arbitration in the investor-consumer sector. The evolution of the law is progressive. There is a large temporal and doctrinal distance between *Wilko v. Swan*, 346 U.S. 427 (1953), and its related cases: *Shearson/American Express, Inc. v. McMahon*, 482 U.S. 220 (1987), and *Rodriguez de Quijas v. Shearson/American Express, Inc.*, 490 U.S. 477 (1989). The opening proposition, stated in *Wilko*, is that the 1933 Securities Act provides for exclusive judicial resolution of claims arising under the securities legislation as a limited exception to the FAA's policy on arbitration. The final proposition, articulated most clearly in *Rodriguez*, reverses the *Wilko* holding because it represents unlawful judicial hostility to arbitration. After *Rodriguez*, claims arising under either the 1933 Securities Act or the 1934 Securities Exchange Act can be submitted to arbitration in U.S. domestic law.

Wilko v. Swan

In *Wilko*, an investor lodged an action against a securities brokerage firm, claiming that the firm had violated Section 12(2) of the 1933 Act. The brokerage contract contained a dispute resolution clause providing for the submission of disputes to arbitration. Notwithstanding its view that the FAA embodied a strong congressional policy supporting arbitration, the Court deemed the arbitration agreement in *Wilko* to be unenforceable. The

Court reasoned that the provision for arbitration countermanded the express policy of the 1933 Act prohibiting investors from waiving certain statutorily established rights, namely, the right to bring suit in any federal or state court, to select a forum from a wide choice of venue, to take advantage of the nationwide service of process provision, and to dispense with the amount in controversy requirement. Moreover, Section 12(2) of the Act expressly gave investors a cause of action to redress claims of misrepresentation against a seller of securities, requiring the defendant to prove its lack of scienter.

Therefore, despite a valid arbitration agreement, securities claims arising under the 1933 Act could not be submitted to arbitration. The Act's nonwaiver of rights provisions, in effect, manifested a congressional intent to create an exception to the FAA's validation of arbitration agreements. These circumstances were exceptional. The policy imperative underlying the 1933 Act took precedent over its counterpart in the FAA. Ordinarily, however, the FAA would have prevailed.

WILKO V. SWAN

346 U.S. 427, 74 S.Ct. 182, 98 L.Ed. 168 (1953).

(footnotes omitted)

MR. JUSTICE REED delivered the opinion of the Court.

[. . .]

The question is whether an agreement to arbitrate a future controversy is a "condition, stipulation, or provision binding any person acquiring any security to waive compliance with any provision" of the Securities Act which § 14 declares "void." We granted *certiorari* to review this important and novel federal question affecting both the Securities Act and the United States Arbitration Act. . . .

As the margin agreement in the light of the complaint evidenced a transaction in interstate commerce, no issue arises as to the applicability of the provisions of the United States Arbitration Act to this suit, based upon the Securities Act. . . .

In response to a Presidential message urging that there be added to the ancient rule of caveat emptor the further doctrine of "let the seller also beware," Congress passed the Securities Act of 1933. Designed to protect investors, the Act requires issuers, underwriters, and dealers to make full and fair disclosure of the character of securities sold in interstate and foreign commerce and to prevent fraud in their sale. To effectuate this policy, § 12(2) created a special right to recover for misrepresentation which differs substantially from the common-law action in that the seller is made to assume the burden of proving lack of scienter. The Act's special right is enforceable in any court of competent jurisdiction—federal or state—and removal from a state court is prohibited. If suit be brought in a federal court, the purchaser has a wide choice of venue, the privilege of nationwide service of process and the jurisdictional $3,000 requirement of diversity cases is inapplicable.

The United States Arbitration Act establishes by statute the desirability of arbitration as an alternative to the complications of litigation. The reports of both Houses on that Act stress the need for avoiding the delay and expense of litigation, and practice under its terms raises hope for its usefulness both in controversies based on statutes or on standards otherwise created. This hospitable attitude of legislatures and courts toward arbitration, however, does not solve our question as to the validity of petitioner's stipulation by the margin agreements to submit to arbitration controversies that might arise from the transactions.

Petitioner argues that § 14 . . . shows that the purpose of Congress was to assure that sellers could not maneuver buyers into a position that might weaken their ability to recover under the Securities Act. He contends that arbitration lacks the certainty of a suit at law under the Act to enforce his rights. He reasons that the arbitration paragraph of the margin agreement is a stipulation that waives "compliance with" the provision of the Securities Act conferring jurisdiction of suits and special powers.

Respondent asserts that arbitration is merely a form of trial to be used in lieu of a trial at law, and therefore no conflict exists between the Securities Act and the United States Arbitration Act either in their language or in the congressional purposes in their enactment. Each may function within its own scope, the former to protect investors and the latter to simplify recovery for actionable violations of law by issuers or dealers in securities.

Respondent is in agreement with the Court of Appeals that the margin agreement arbitration paragraph . . . does not relieve the seller from either liability or burden of proof . . . imposed by the Securities Act. We agree that in so far as the award in arbitration may be affected by legal requirements, statutes or common law, rather than by considerations of fairness, the provisions of the Securities Act control. This is true even though this proposed agreement has no requirement that the arbitrators follow the law. This agreement of the parties as to the effect of the Securities Act includes also acceptance of the invalidity of the paragraph of the margin agreement that relieves the respondent sellers of liability for all "representation or advice by you or your employees or agents regarding the purchase or sale by me of any property. * * *"

The words of § 14 . . . void any "stipulation" waiving compliance with any "provision" of the Securities Act. This arrangement to arbitrate is a "stipulation," and we think the right to select the judicial forum is the kind of "provision" that cannot be waived under § 14 of the Securities Act. While a buyer and seller of securities, under some circumstances, may deal at arm's length on equal terms, it is clear that the Securities Act was drafted with an eye to the disadvantages under which buyers labor. Issuers of and dealers in securities have better opportunities to investigate and appraise the prospective earnings and business plans affecting securities than buyers. It is therefore reasonable for Congress to put buyers of securities covered by that Act on a different basis from other purchasers.

When the security buyer, prior to any violation of the Securities Act, waives his right to sue in courts, he gives up more than would a participant in other business transactions. The security buyer has a wider choice of courts and venue. He thus surrenders one of the advantages the Act gives him and surrenders it at a time when he is less able to judge the weight of the handicap the Securities Act places upon his adversary.

Even though the provisions of the Securities Act, advantageous to the buyer, apply, their effectiveness in application is lessened in arbitration as compared to judicial proceedings. Determination of the quality of a commodity or the amount of money due under a contract is not the type of issue here involved. This case requires subjective findings on the purpose and knowledge of an alleged violator of the Act. They must be not only determined but applied by the arbitrators without judicial instruction on the law. As their award may be made without explanation of their reasons and without a complete record of their proceedings, the arbitrators' conception of the legal meaning of such statutory requirements as "burden of proof," "reasonable care" or "material fact" . . . cannot be examined. Power to vacate an award is limited. While it may be true, as the Court of Appeals thought, that a failure of the arbitrators to decide in accordance with the provisions of the Securities Act would "constitute grounds for vacating the award pursuant to section 10 of the Federal Arbitration Act," that failure would need to be made clearly to appear. In unrestricted submissions, such as the present margin agreements envisage, the interpretations of the law by the arbitrators in contrast to manifest disregard are not subject, in the federal courts, to judicial review for error in interpretation. The United States Arbitration Act contains no provision for judicial determination of legal issues such as is found in the English law. As the protective provisions of the Securities Act require the exercise of judicial discretion to fairly assure their effectiveness, it seems to us that Congress must have intended § 14 . . . to apply to waiver of judicial trial and review.

[. . .]

Two policies, not easily reconcilable, are involved in this case. Congress has afforded participants in transactions subject to its legislative power an opportunity generally to secure prompt, economical and adequate solution of controversies through arbitration if the parties are willing to accept less certainty of legally correct adjustment. On the other hand, it has enacted the Securities Act to protect the rights of investors and has forbidden a waiver of any of those rights. Recognizing the advantages that prior agreements for arbitration may provide for the solution of commercial controversies, we decide that the intention of Congress concerning the sale of securities is better carried out by holding invalid such an agreement for arbitration of issues arising under the Act.

Reversed.

MR. JUSTICE JACKSON, concurring.

I agree with the Court's opinion insofar as it construes the Securities Act to prohibit waiver of a judicial remedy in favor of arbitration by agreement made before any controversy arose. I think thereafter the parties could agree upon arbitration. However, I find it unnecessary in this case, where there has not been and could not be any arbitration, to decide that the Arbitration Act precludes any judicial remedy for the arbitrators' error of interpretation of a relevant statute.

MR. JUSTICE FRANKFURTER, whom MR. JUSTICE MINTON joins, dissenting.

If arbitration inherently precluded full protection of the rights § 12(2) of the Securities Act affords to a purchaser of securities, or if there were no effective means of ensuring judicial review of the legal basis of the arbitration, then, of course, an agreement to settle the controversy by arbitration would be barred by § 14, the anti-waiver provision, of that Act.

There is nothing in the record before us, nor in the facts of which we can take judicial notice, to indicate that the arbitral system as practiced in the City of New York, and as enforceable under the supervisory authority of the District Court for the Southern District of New York, would not afford the plaintiff the rights to which he is entitled.

The impelling considerations that led to the enactment of the Federal Arbitration Act are the advantages of providing a speedier, more economical and more effective enforcement of rights by way of arbitration than can be had by the tortuous course of litigation, especially in the City of New York. These advantages should not be assumed to be denied in controversies like that before us arising under the Securities Act, in the absence of any showing that settlement by arbitration would jeopardize the rights of the plaintiff.

Arbitrators may not disregard the law. Specifically they are, as Chief Judge Swan pointed out, "bound to decide in accordance with the provisions of section 12(2)." On this we are all agreed. It is suggested, however, that there is no effective way of assuring obedience by the arbitrators to the governing law. But since their failure to observe this law "would constitute grounds for vacating the award pursuant to section 10 of the Federal

Arbitration Act," . . . appropriate means for judicial scrutiny must be implied, in the form of some record or opinion, however informal, whereby such compliance will appear, or want of it will upset the award.

We have not before us a case in which the record shows that the plaintiff in opening an account had no choice but to accept the arbitration stipulation, thereby making the stipulation an unconscionable and unenforceable provision in a business transaction. The Securities and Exchange Commission, as *amicus curiae*, does not contend that the stipulation which the Court of Appeals respected, under the appropriate safeguards defined by it, was a coercive practice by financial houses against customers incapable of self-protection. It is one thing to make out a case of overreaching as between parties bargaining not at arm's length. It is quite a different thing to find in the anti-waiver provision of the Securities Act a general limitation on the Federal Arbitration Act.

On the state of the record before us, I would affirm the decision of the Court of Appeals.

NOTES AND QUESTIONS

1. What concept of arbitration does Justice Reed advance on behalf of the majority? If his vision of arbitral adjudication does not necessarily evidence hostility or antipathy, could it be characterized as limited and somewhat deprecatory? Is it fair to say that the majority in *Wilko* underestimates, or at least narrowly reads, the language and the policy of the FAA?

Is Justice Reed correct in asserting that a buyer of securities gives up more legal rights in agreeing to arbitration than consumers of other goods and services? Where or what is the "public law dimension" of this case?

You should analyze the rights protection argument that divides the majority and dissenting opinions. How does the availability of review and the quality of review factor into the rights protection analysis?

2. Do you agree that arbitration represents a vehicle for achieving economy in litigation? Do both sides of the Court share that view? Is it warranted by the text or legislative history of the FAA?

3. Does *Wilko* involve commercial arbitration or consumer arbitration? Or consumer arbitration in a commercial context? Is there any real difference between these forms of arbitration and, if there is, why doesn't the Court make the distinction? What does the language of Section One of the FAA contribute to this discussion?

4. Analyze carefully Justice Jackson's concurring opinion. What is he suggesting as a possible intermediary solution to the conflict between statutory policies? How does his position compare to Justice Black's view in *Prima Paint* and Justice Stevens' position in *Keating* as an attempt at reconciling divergent policies? What makes the "all-or-nothing" approach more attractive to the majority of the Court in all these cases?

5. Do you find Justice Frankfurter's reasons for his confidence in securities arbitration reassuring? Do you believe that his characterization accurately reflects the actual operation of the arbitral remedy? Isn't he describing arbitration between brokers—inside-the-industry arbitration? Is that significant in terms of the result he reaches?

After *Wilko*, lower federal courts consistently held that claims arising under either the 1933 or 1934 Act were inarbitrable because of the public policy interest in securities investor protection. This assessment was grounded in the language of the Acts (the nonwaiver provisions), rather than the provisions of the FAA. The content of the FAA simply was not germane (*i.e.*, its lack of reference to subject-matter inarbitrability or the public policy defense) because its policy imperative was secondary to another Congressional objective as a matter of law.

Shearson/American Express, Inc. v. McMahon

As to the issue of the arbitrability of Exchange Act claims (a question which divided the Court 5–4), the majority opinion in *McMahon* begins with the view that a claim based upon statutorily established rights does not disrupt the ordinarily "hospitable" inquiry into the question of arbitrability. To defeat the implied presumption favoring the arbitrability of claims, the regulatory vehicle must contain, either in its language or legislative history, a congressional command mandating exclusive recourse to the courts for the vindication of claims. Moreover, the burden is upon the party opposing arbitration to establish the existence of such congressional intent.

The Court then advances a technical interpretation of the relevant provisions of the Exchange Act, arguing that the nonwaiver language of the Act applies exclusively to the substantive obligations under the legislation. Because the recourse to arbitration merely represents the selection of a different forum and remedial process, such an agreement—the Court would have us believe—has no impact upon the substantive statutory rights in question. The nonwaiver language, therefore, does not apply to the nonsubstantive provisions of the Act. The Court gives little significance either to the underlying purpose of the Exchange Act (to protect individual investors from overreaching by securities industry professionals) or to the possibility that arbitrators will construe the applicable law differently from judges, especially in light of the fact that the arbitral procedure in these circumstances is established and directed by the securities industry. In effect, the Court chooses to ignore the adhesive character of the contract and the arbitration agreement, neglecting the evident need for consumer protection generated by the facts.

SHEARSON/AMERICAN EXPRESS, INC. V. MCMAHON

482 U.S. 220, 107 S.Ct. 2332, 96 L.Ed.2d 185 (1987).

JUSTICE O'CONNOR delivered the opinion of the Court.

This case presents two questions regarding the enforceability of predispute arbitration agreements between brokerage firms and their customers. The first is whether a claim brought under § 10(b) of the Securities Exchange Act of 1934 (Exchange Act) must be sent to arbitration in accordance with the terms of an arbitration agreement. The second is whether a claim brought under the Racketeer Influenced and Corrupt Organizations Act (RICO) must be arbitrated in accordance with the terms of such an agreement.

I

Between 1980 and 1982, respondents Eugene and Julia McMahon, individually and as trustees for various pension and profit-sharing plans, were customers of petitioner Shearson/American Express Inc. (Shearson), a brokerage firm registered with the Securities and Exchange Commission (SEC or Commission). Two customer agreements signed by Julia McMahon provided for arbitration of any controversy relating to the accounts the McMahons maintained with Shearson. The arbitration provision provided in relevant part as follows:

> "Unless unenforceable due to federal or state law, any controversy arising out of or relating to my accounts, to transactions with you for me or to this agreement or the breach thereof, shall be settled by arbitration in accordance with the rules, then in effect, of the National Association of Securities Dealers, Inc. or the Boards of Directors of the New York Stock Exchange, Inc. and/or the American Stock Exchange, Inc. as I may elect. . . ."

In October 1984, the McMahons filed an amended complaint against Shearson and petitioner Mary Ann McNulty, the registered representative who handled their accounts, in the United States District Court for the Southern District of New York. The complaint alleged that McNulty, with Shearson's knowledge, had violated § 10(b) of the Exchange Act and Rule 10b–5 by engaging in fraudulent, excessive trading on respondents' accounts and by making false statements and omitting material facts from the advice given to respondents. The complaint also alleged a RICO claim and state law claims for fraud and breach of fiduciary duties.

Relying on the customer agreements, petitioners moved to compel arbitration of the McMahons' claims pursuant to § 3 of the Federal Arbitration Act. The District Court granted the motion in part. . . . The court first rejected the McMahons' contention that the arbitration agreements were unenforceable as contracts of adhesion. It then found that the McMahons' § 10(b) claims were arbitrable under the terms of the agreement, concluding that such a result followed from this Court's decision in *Dean Witter Reynolds, Inc. v. Byrd* and the "strong national policy favoring the enforcement of arbitration agreements." The District Court also held that the McMahons' state law claims were arbitrable. . . . It concluded, however, that the McMahons' RICO claim was not arbitrable "because of the important federal policies inherent in the enforcement of RICO by the federal courts." . . .

The Court of Appeals affirmed the District Court on the state law and RICO claims, but it reversed on the Exchange Act claims. . . . With respect to the RICO claim, the Court of Appeals concluded that "public policy" considerations made it "inappropriat[e]" to apply the provisions of the Arbitration Act to RICO suits. The court reasoned that RICO claims are "not merely a private matter." Because a RICO plaintiff may be likened to a "private attorney general" protecting the public interest, the Court of Appeals concluded that such claims should be adjudicated only in a judicial forum. It distinguished this Court's reasoning in *Mitsubishi Motors Corp. v. Soler* . . . concerning the arbitrability of antitrust claims, on the ground that it involved international business transactions and did not affect the law "as applied to agreements to arbitrate arising from domestic transactions." . . .

With respect to respondents' Exchange Act claims, the Court of Appeals noted that under *Wilko v. Swan*, claims arising under § 12(2) of the Securities Act of 1933 are not subject to compulsory arbitration. The Court of Appeals observed that it previously had extended the *Wilko* rule to claims arising under § 10(b) of the Exchange Act and Rule 10b–5. The court acknowledged that *Scherk v. Alberto-Culver Co.* . . . and *Dean Witter Reynolds, Inc. v. Byrd* . . . had "cast some doubt on the applicability of *Wilko* to claims under § 10(b)." The Court of Appeals nevertheless concluded that it was bound by the "clear judicial precedent in this Circuit," and held that *Wilko* must be applied to Exchange Act claims. . . .

We granted *certiorari*, to resolve the conflict among the Courts of Appeals regarding the arbitrability of § 10(b) and RICO claims.

II

The Federal Arbitration Act . . . provides the starting point for answering the questions raised in this case. The Act was intended to "revers[e] centuries of judicial hostility to arbitration agreements" . . . by "plac[ing] arbitration agreements 'upon the same footing as other contracts.' " . . . The Arbitration Act accomplishes this purpose by providing that arbitration agreements "shall be valid, irrevocable, and enforceable, save upon such grounds as exist at law or in equity for the revocation of any contract." The Act also provides that a court must stay its proceedings if it is satisfied that an issue before it is arbitrable under the agreement, § 3; and it authorizes a federal district court to issue an order compelling arbitration if there has been a "failure, neglect, or refusal" to comply with the arbitration agreement, § 4.

The Arbitration Act thus establishes a "federal policy favoring arbitration," *Moses H. Cone Memorial Hospital v. Mercury Construction Corp.*, requiring that "we rigorously enforce agreements to arbitrate." *Dean Witter Reynolds, Inc. v. Byrd.* . . . This duty to enforce arbitration agreements is not diminished when a party bound by an agreement raises a claim founded on statutory rights. As we observed in *Mitsubishi Motors Corp. v. Soler Chrysler-Plymouth, Inc.*, "we are well past the time when judicial suspicion of the desirability of arbitration and of the competence of arbitral tribunals" should inhibit enforcement of the Act " 'in controversies based on statutes.' " . . . Absent a well-founded claim that an arbitration agreement resulted from the sort of fraud or excessive economic power that "would provide grounds 'for the revocation of any contract,' " . . . the Arbitration Act "provides no basis for disfavoring agreements to arbitrate statutory claims by skewing the otherwise hospitable inquiry into arbitrability." . . .

The Arbitration Act, standing alone, therefore mandates enforcement of agreements to arbitrate statutory claims. Like any statutory directive, the Arbitration Act's mandate may be overridden by a contrary congressional command. The burden is on the party opposing arbitration, however, to show that Congress intended to preclude a waiver of judicial remedies for the statutory rights at issue. If Congress did intend to limit or prohibit waiver of a judicial forum for a particular claim, such an intent "will be deducible from [the statute's] text or legislative history".

To defeat application of the Arbitration Act in this case, therefore, the McMahons must demonstrate that Congress intended to make an exception to the Arbitration Act for claims arising under RICO and the Exchange Act, an intention discernible from the text, history, or purposes of the statute. We examine the McMahons' arguments regarding the Exchange Act and RICO in turn.

III

When Congress enacted the Exchange Act in 1934, it did not specifically address the question of the arbitrability of § 10(b) claims. The McMahons contend, however, that congressional intent to require a judicial forum for the resolution of § 10(b) claims can be deduced from § 29(a) of the Exchange Act, which declares void "[a]ny condition, stipulation, or provision binding any person to waive compliance with any provision of [the Act]."

First, we reject the McMahons' argument that § 29(a) forbids waiver of § 27 of the Exchange Act. Section 27 provides in relevant part:

> The district courts of the United States . . . shall have exclusive jurisdiction of violations of this title or the rules and regulations thereunder, and of all suits in equity and actions at law brought to enforce any liability or duty created by this title or the rules and regulations thereunder.

The McMahons contend that an agreement to waive this jurisdictional provision is unenforceable because § 29(a) voids the waiver of "any provision" of the Exchange Act. The language of § 29(a), however, does not reach so far. What the antiwaiver provision of § 29(a) forbids is enforcement of agreements to waive "compliance" with the provisions of the statute. But § 27 itself does not impose any duty with which persons trading in securities must "comply." By its terms, § 29(a) only prohibits waiver of the substantive obligations imposed by the Exchange Act. Because § 27 does not impose any statutory duties, its waiver does not constitute a waiver of "compliance with any provision" of the Exchange Act under § 29(a).

We do not read *Wilko v. Swan* . . . as compelling a different result. In *Wilko*, the Court held that a predispute agreement could not be enforced to compel arbitration of a claim arising under § 12(2) of the Securities Act. The basis for the ruling was § 14 of the Securities Act, which, like § 29(a) of the Exchange Act, declares void any stipulation "to waive compliance with any provision" of the statute. At the beginning of its analysis, the *Wilko* Court stated that the Securities Act's jurisdictional provision was "the kind of 'provision' that cannot be waived under § 14 of the Securities Act." . . . This statement, however, can only be understood in the context of the Court's ensuing discussion explaining why arbitration was inadequate as a means of enforcing "the provisions of the Securities Act, advantageous to the buyer." . . . The conclusion in *Wilko* was expressly based on the Court's belief that a judicial forum was needed to protect the substantive rights created by the Securities Act. . . . *Wilko* must be understood, therefore, as holding that the plaintiff's waiver of the "right to select the judicial forum" . . . was unenforceable only because arbitration was judged inadequate to enforce the statutory rights created by § 12(2).

Indeed, any different reading of *Wilko* would be inconsistent with this Court's decision in *Scherk v. Alberto-Culver Co.* . . . The Court reasoned that arbitration reduced the uncertainty of international contracts and obviated the danger that a dispute might be submitted to a hostile or unfamiliar forum. At the same time, the Court noted that the advantages of judicial resolution were diminished by the possibility that the opposing party would make "speedy resort to a foreign court." . . . The decision in *Scherk* thus turned on the Court's judgment that under the circumstances of that case, arbitration was an adequate substitute for adjudication as a means of enforcing the parties' statutory rights. *Scherk* supports our understanding that *Wilko* must be read as barring waiver of a judicial forum only where arbitration is inadequate to protect the substantive rights at issue. At the same time, it confirms that where arbitration does provide an adequate means of enforcing the provisions of the Exchange Act, § 29(a) does not void a predispute waiver of § 27—*Scherk* upheld enforcement of just such a waiver.

The second argument offered by the McMahons is that the arbitration agreement effects an impermissible waiver of the substantive protections of the Exchange Act. Ordinarily, "[b]y agreeing to arbitrate a statutory claim, a party does not forgo the substantive rights afforded by the statute; it only submits to their resolution in an arbitral, rather than a judicial, forum." *Mitsubishi Motors Corp. v. Soler*. . . . The McMahons argue, however, that § 29(a) compels a different conclusion. Initially, they contend that predispute agreements are void under § 29(a) because they tend to result from broker overreaching. They reason, as do some commentators, that *Wilko* is premised on the belief "that arbitration clauses in securities sales agreements generally are not freely negotiated." . . . According to this view, *Wilko* barred enforcement of predispute agreements because of this frequent inequality of bargaining power, reasoning that Congress intended for § 14 generally to ensure that sellers did not "maneuver buyers into a position that might weaken their ability to recover under the Securities Act." . . .

We decline to give *Wilko* a reading so far at odds with the plain language of § 14, or to adopt such an unlikely interpretation of § 29(a). The concern that § 29(a) is directed against is evident from the statute's plain language: it is a concern with whether an agreement "waive[s] compliance with [a] provision" of the Exchange Act. The voluntariness of the agreement is irrelevant to this inquiry: if a stipulation waives compliance with a statutory duty, it is void under § 29(a), whether voluntary or not. Thus, a customer cannot negotiate a reduction in commissions in exchange for a waiver of compliance with the requirements of the Exchange Act, even if the customer knowingly and voluntarily agreed to the bargain. Section 29(a) is concerned, not with whether brokers "maneuver[ed customers] into" an agreement, but with whether the agreement "weaken[s] their ability to recover under the [Exchange] Act." . . . The former is grounds for revoking the contract under ordinary principles of contract law; the latter is grounds for voiding the agreement under § 29(a).

The other reason advanced by the McMahons for finding a waiver of their § 10(b) rights is that arbitration does "weaken their ability to recover under the [Exchange] Act." . . . That is the heart of the Court's decision in *Wilko*, and respondents urge that we should follow its reasoning. *Wilko* listed several grounds why, in the Court's view, the "effectiveness [of the Act's provisions] in application is lessened in arbitration." . . .

. . . [T]he reasons given in *Wilko* reflect a general suspicion of the desirability of arbitration and the competence of arbitral tribunals . . . most apply with no greater force to the arbitration of securities disputes than to the arbitration of legal disputes generally. It is difficult to reconcile *Wilko*'s mistrust of the arbitral process with this Court's subsequent decisions involving the Arbitration Act. . . .

Indeed, most of the reasons given in *Wilko* have been rejected subsequently by the Court as a basis for holding claims to be nonarbitrable. In *Mitsubishi*, for example, we recognized that arbitral tribunals are readily capable of handling the factual and legal complexities of antitrust claims, notwithstanding the absence of judicial instruction and supervision. Likewise, we have concluded that the streamlined procedures of arbitration do not entail any consequential restriction on substantive rights. . . . Finally, we have indicated that there is no reason to assume at the outset that arbitrators will not follow the law; although judicial scrutiny of arbitration awards necessarily is limited, such review is sufficient to ensure that arbitrators comply with the requirements of the statute. . . .

The suitability of arbitration as a means of enforcing Exchange Act rights is evident from our decision in *Scherk*. Although the holding in that case was limited to international agreements, the competence of arbitral tribunals to resolve § 10(b) claims is the same in both settings. Courts likewise have routinely enforced agreements to arbitrate § 10(b) claims where both parties are members of a securities exchange or the National Association of Securities Dealers (NASD), suggesting that arbitral tribunals are fully capable of handling such matters. And courts uniformly have concluded that *Wilko* does not apply to the submission to arbitration of existing disputes . . . even though the inherent suitability of arbitration as a means of resolving § 10(b) claims remains unchanged. . . .

Thus, the mistrust of arbitration that formed the basis for the *Wilko* opinion in 1953 is difficult to square with the assessment of arbitration that has prevailed since that time. This is especially so in light of the intervening changes in the regulatory structure of the securities laws. Even if *Wilko*'s assumptions regarding arbitration were valid at the time *Wilko* was decided, most certainly they do not hold true today for arbitration procedures subject to the SEC's oversight authority.

[. . .]

In the exercise of its regulatory authority, the SEC has specifically approved the arbitration procedures of the New York Stock Exchange, the American Stock Exchange, and the NASD, the organizations mentioned in the arbitration agreement at issue in this case. We conclude that where, as in this case, the prescribed procedures are subject to the Commission's § 19 authority, an arbitration agreement does not effect a waiver of the protections of the Act. While stare decisis concerns may counsel against upsetting *Wilko*'s contrary conclusion under the Securities Act, we refuse to extend *Wilko*'s reasoning to the Exchange Act in light of these intervening regulatory developments. The McMahons' agreement to submit to arbitration therefore is not tantamount to an impermissible waiver of the McMahons' rights under § 10(b), and the agreement is not void on that basis under § 29(a).

[. . .]

We conclude, therefore, that Congress did not intend for § 29(a) to bar enforcement of all predispute arbitration agreements. In this case, where the SEC has sufficient statutory authority to ensure that arbitration is adequate to vindicate Exchange Act rights, enforcement does not effect a waiver of "compliance with any provision" of the Exchange Act under § 29(a). Accordingly, we hold the McMahons' agreements to arbitrate Exchange Act claims "enforce[able] . . . in accord with the explicit provisions of the Arbitration Act." . . .

IV

Unlike the Exchange Act, there is nothing in the text of the RICO statute that even arguably evinces congressional intent to exclude civil RICO claims from the dictates of the Arbitration Act. This silence in the text is matched by silence in the statute's legislative history. The private treble-damages provision was added to the House version of the bill after the bill had been passed by the Senate, and it received only abbreviated discussion in either House. . . . There is no hint in these legislative debates that Congress intended for RICO treble-damages claims to be excluded from the ambit of the Arbitration Act. . . .

Because RICO's text and legislative history fail to reveal any intent to override the provisions of the Arbitration Act, the McMahons must argue that there is an irreconcilable conflict between arbitration and RICO's underlying purposes. Our decision in *Mitsubishi Motors Corp. v. Soler* . . . already has addressed many of the grounds given by the McMahons to support this claim. In *Mitsubishi*, we held that nothing in the nature of the federal antitrust laws prohibits parties from agreeing to arbitrate antitrust claims arising out of international commercial transactions. Although the holding in *Mitsubishi* was limited to the international context, . . . much of its reasoning is equally applicable here. Thus, for example, the McMahons have argued that RICO claims are too complex to be subject to arbitration. We determined in *Mitsubishi*, however, that "potential complexity should not suffice to ward off arbitration." . . . Antitrust matters are every bit as complex as RICO claims, but we found that the "adaptability and access to expertise" characteristic of arbitration rebutted the view "that an arbitral tribunal could not properly handle an antitrust matter." . . .

Likewise, the McMahons contend that the "overlap" between RICO's civil and criminal provisions renders § 1964(c) claims nonarbitrable. . . . Yet § 1964(c) is no different in this respect from the federal antitrust laws. *Mitsubishi* recognized that treble-damages suits for claims arising under § 1 of the Sherman Act may be subject to arbitration, even though such conduct may also give rise to claims of criminal liability. . . . We similarly find that the criminal provisions of RICO do not preclude arbitration of bona fide civil actions brought under § 1964(c).

The McMahons' final argument is that the public interest in the enforcement of RICO precludes its submission to arbitration. *Mitsubishi* again is relevant to the question. In that case we thoroughly examined the legislative intent behind § 4 of the Clayton Act in assaying whether the importance of the private treble-damages remedy in enforcing the antitrust laws precluded arbitration of § 4 claims. We found that "[n]otwithstanding its important incidental policing function, the treble-damages cause of action . . . seeks primarily to enable an injured competitor to gain compensation for that injury." . . . Emphasizing the priority of the compensatory function of § 4 over its deterrent function, *Mitsubishi* concluded that "so long as the prospective litigant effectively may vindicate its statutory cause of action in the arbitral forum, the statute will continue to serve both its remedial and deterrent function." . . .

[. . .]

Not only does *Mitsubishi* support the arbitrability of RICO claims, but there is even more reason to suppose that arbitration will adequately serve the purposes of RICO than that it will adequately protect private enforcement of the antitrust laws. The special incentives necessary to encourage civil enforcement actions against organized crime do not support nonarbitrability of run-of-the-mill civil RICO claims brought against legitimate enterprises. The private attorney general role for the typical RICO plaintiff is simply less plausible than it is for the typical antitrust plaintiff, and does not support a finding that there is an irreconcilable conflict between arbitration and enforcement of the RICO statute.

In sum, we find no basis for concluding that Congress intended to prevent enforcement of agreements to arbitrate RICO claims. The McMahons may effectively vindicate their RICO claim in an arbitral forum, and therefore there is no inherent conflict between arbitration and the purposes underlying § 1964(c). Moreover, nothing in RICO's text or legislative history otherwise demonstrates congressional intent to make an exception to the Arbitration Act for RICO claims. Accordingly, the McMahons, "having made the bargain to arbitrate," will be held to their bargain. Their RICO claim is arbitrable under the terms of the Arbitration Act.

V

Accordingly, the judgment of the Court of Appeals for the Second Circuit is reversed, and the case is remanded for further proceedings consistent with this opinion.

It is so ordered.

JUSTICE BLACKMUN, with whom JUSTICE BRENNAN and JUSTICE MARSHALL join, concurring in part and dissenting in part.

I concur in the Court's decision to enforce the arbitration agreement with respect to respondents' RICO claims and thus join Parts I, II, and IV of the Court's opinion. I disagree, however, with the Court's conclusion that respondents' § 10(b) claims also are subject to arbitration.

Both the Securities Act of 1933 and the Securities Exchange Act of 1934 were enacted to protect investors from predatory behavior of securities industry personnel. In *Wilko v. Swan*, . . . the Court recognized this basic purpose when it declined to enforce a predispute agreement to compel arbitration of claims under the Securities Act. Following that decision, lower courts extended *Wilko*'s reasoning to claims brought under § 10(b) of the Exchange Act, and Congress approved of this extension. In today's decision, however, the Court effectively overrules *Wilko* by accepting the Securities and Exchange Commission's newly adopted position that arbitration procedures in the securities industry and the Commission's oversight of the self-regulatory organizations (SROs) have improved greatly since *Wilko* was decided. The Court thus approves the abandonment of the judiciary's role in the resolution of claims under the Exchange Act and leaves such claims to the arbitral forum of the securities industry at a time when the industry's abuses towards investors are more apparent than ever.

I

At the outset, it is useful to review the manner by which the issue decided today has been kept alive inappropriately by this Court. As the majority explains, *Wilko* was limited to the holding "that a predispute agreement could not be enforced to compel arbitration of a claim arising under § 12(2) of the Securities Act." . . . Relying, however, on the reasoning of *Wilko* and the similarity between the pertinent provisions of the Securities Act and those of the Exchange Act, lower courts extended the *Wilko* holding to claims under the Exchange Act and refused to enforce predispute agreements to arbitrate them as well.

In *Scherk v. Alberto-Culver Co.*, . . . the Court addressed the question whether a particular predispute agreement to arbitrate § 10(b) claims should be enforced. Because that litigation involved international business concerns and because the case was decided on such grounds, the Court did not reach the issue of the extension of *Wilko* to § 10(b) claims. The Court, nonetheless, included in its opinion dicta noting that "a colorable argument could be made that even the semantic reasoning of the *Wilko* opinion does not control the case before us." . . . There is no need to discuss in any detail that "colorable argument," which rests on alleged distinctions between pertinent provisions of the Securities Act and those of the Exchange Act, because the Court does not rely upon it today. In fact, the "argument" is important not so much for its substance as it is for its litigation role. It simply constituted a way of keeping the issue of the arbitrability of § 10(b) claims alive for those opposed to the result in *Wilko.*

[. . .]

II

There are essentially two problems with the Court's conclusion that predispute agreements to arbitrate § 10(b) claims may be enforced. First, the Court gives *Wilko* an overly narrow reading so that it can fit into the syllogism offered by the Commission and accepted by the Court, namely, (1) *Wilko* was really a case concerning whether arbitration was adequate for the enforcement of the substantive provisions of the securities laws; (2) all of the *Wilko* Court's doubts as to arbitration's adequacy are outdated; (3) thus *Wilko* is no longer good law. . . . Second, the Court accepts uncritically petitioners' and the Commission's argument that the problems with arbitration, highlighted by the *Wilko* Court, either no longer exist or are not now viewed as problems by the Court. This acceptance primarily is based upon the Court's belief in the Commission's representations that its oversight of the SROs ensures the adequacy of arbitration.

A

I agree with the Court's observation that, in order to establish an exception to the Arbitration Act . . . for a class of statutory claims, there must be "an intention discernible from the text, history, or purposes of the statute." . . . Where the Court first goes wrong, however, is in its failure to acknowledge that the Exchange Act, like the Securities Act, constitutes such an exception. This failure is made possible only by the unduly narrow reading of *Wilko* that ignores the Court's determination there that the Securities Act was an exception to the Arbitration Act. The Court's reading is particularly startling because it is in direct contradiction to the interpretation of *Wilko* given by the Court in *Mitsubishi Motors Corp. v. Soler,* . . . a decision on which the Court relies for its strong statement of a federal policy in favor of arbitration. In *Mitsubishi,* we viewed *Wilko* as holding that the text and legislative history of the Securities Act not general problems with arbitration established that the Securities Act constituted an exception to the Arbitration Act. In a surprising display of logic, the Court uses *Mitsubishi* as support for the virtues of arbitration and thus as a means for undermining *Wilko*'s holding, but fails to take into account the most pertinent language in *Mitsubishi.*

. . . The Court's misreading of *Wilko* is possible because, while extolling the policies of the Arbitration Act, it is insensitive to, and disregards the policies of, the Securities Act. This Act was passed in 1933, eight years after the Arbitration Act of 1925 . . . and in response to the market crash of 1929. The Act was designed to remedy abuses in the securities industry, particularly fraud and misrepresentation by securities-industry personnel, that had contributed to that disastrous event. . . . It had as its main goal investor protection, which took the form of an effort to place investors on an equal footing with those in the securities industry by promoting full disclosure of information on investments. . . .

The Court in *Wilko* recognized the policy of investor protection in the Securities Act. It was this recognition that animated its discussion. In reasoning that a predispute agreement to arbitrate § 12(2) claims would constitute a "waiver" of a provision of the Act, *i.e.*, the right to the judicial forum embodied in § 22(a), the Court specifically referred to the policy of investor protection underlying the Act. . . .

In the Court's view, the express language, legislative history, and purposes of the Securities Act all made predispute agreements to arbitrate § 12(2) claims unenforceable despite the presence of the Arbitration Act. . . .

Accordingly, the Court seriously errs when it states that the result in *Wilko* turned only on the perceived inadequacy of arbitration for the enforcement of § 12(2) claims. . . .

The Court's decision in *Scherk* is consistent with this reading of *Wilko*, despite the Court's suggestion to the contrary. . . . Indeed, in reading *Scherk* as a case turning on the adequacy of arbitration, the Court completely ignores the central thrust of that decision. . . . The *Scherk* Court relied on a crucial difference between the international business situation presented to it and that before the Court in *Wilko*, where the laws of the United States, particularly the securities laws, clearly governed the dispute. *Scherk*, in contrast, presented a multinational conflict-of-laws puzzle. In such a situation, the Court observed, a contract provision setting forth a particular forum and the law to apply for possible disputes was "an almost indispensable precondition to achievement of the orderliness and predictability essential to any international business transaction." . . . Accordingly, the *Scherk* decision turned on the special nature of agreements to arbitrate in the international commercial context.

In light of a proper reading of *Wilko*, the pertinent question then becomes whether the language, legislative history, and purposes of the Exchange Act call for an exception to the Arbitration Act for § 10(b) claims. The Exchange Act waiver provision is virtually identical to that of the Securities Act. More importantly, the same concern with investor protection that motivated the Securities Act is evident in the Exchange Act, although the latter, in contrast to the former, is aimed at trading in the secondary securities market. . . . We have recognized that both Acts were designed with this common purpose in mind. Indeed, the application of both Acts to the same conduct . . . suggests that they have the same basic goal. And we have approved a cumulative construction of remedies under the securities Acts to promote the maximum possible protection of investors. . . .

In sum, the same reasons that led the Court to find an exception to the Arbitration Act for § 12(2) claims exist for § 10(b) claims as well. It is clear that *Wilko*, when properly read, governs the instant case and mandates that a predispute arbitration agreement should not be enforced as to § 10(b) claims.

B

Even if I were to accept the Court's narrow reading of *Wilko*, as a case dealing only with the inadequacies of arbitration in 1953, I do not think that this case should be resolved differently today so long as the policy of investor protection is given proper consideration in the analysis. Despite improvements in the process of arbitration and changes in the judicial attitude towards it, several aspects of arbitration that were seen by the *Wilko* court to be inimical to the policy of investor protection still remain. Moreover, I have serious reservations about the Commission's contention that its oversight of the SROs' arbitration procedures will ensure that the process is adequate to protect an investor's rights under the securities Acts.

[. . .]

Even those who favor the arbitration of securities claims do not contend, however, that arbitration has changed so significantly as to eliminate the essential characteristics noted by the *Wilko* Court. Indeed, proponents of arbitration would not see these characteristics as "problems," because, in their view, the characteristics permit the unique "streamlined" nature of the arbitral process. As at the time of *Wilko*, preparation of a record of arbitration proceedings is not invariably required today. Moreover, arbitrators are not bound by precedent and are actually discouraged by their associations from giving reasons for a decision. Judicial review is still substantially limited to the four grounds listed in § 10 of the Arbitration Act and to the concept of "manifest disregard" of the law. . . .

The Court's "mistrust" of arbitration may have given way recently to an acceptance of this process, not only because of the improvements in arbitration, but also because of the Court's present assumption that the distinctive features of arbitration, its more quick and economical resolution of claims, do not render it inherently inadequate for the resolution of statutory claims. Such reasoning, however, should prevail only in the absence of the congressional policy that places the statutory claimant in a special position with respect to possible violators of his statutory rights. As even the most ardent supporter of arbitration would recognize, the arbitral process at best places the investor on an equal footing with the securities-industry personnel against whom the claims are brought.

Furthermore, there remains the danger that, at worst, compelling an investor to arbitrate securities claims puts him in a forum controlled by the securities industry. This result directly contradicts the goal of both securities Acts to free the investor from the control of the market professional. The Uniform Code provides some safeguards but despite them, and indeed because of the background of the arbitrators, the investor has the impression, frequently justified, that his claims are being judged by a forum composed of individuals sympathetic to the securities industry and not drawn from the public. It is generally recognized that the codes do not define who falls into the category "not from the securities industry." . . . Accordingly, it is often possible for the "public" arbitrators to be attorneys or consultants whose clients have been exchange members or SROs. The uniform opposition of investors to compelled arbitration and the overwhelming support of the securities industry for the process suggest that there must be some truth to the investors' belief that the securities industry has an advantage in a forum under its own control. . . .

More surprising than the Court's acceptance of the present adequacy of arbitration for the resolution of securities claims is its confidence in the Commission's oversight of the arbitration procedures of the SROs to ensure this adequacy. Such confidence amounts to a wholesale acceptance of the Commission's present position that this oversight undermines the force of *Wilko* and that arbitration therefore should be compelled because the Commission has supervisory authority over the SROs' arbitration procedures. The Court, however, fails to acknowledge that, until it filed an amicus brief in this case, the Commission consistently took the position that § 10(b) claims, like those under § 12(2), should not be sent to arbitration, that predispute arbitration agreements, where the investor was not advised of his right to a judicial forum, were misleading, and that the very regulatory oversight upon which the Commission now relies could not alone make securities-industry arbitration adequate. It is most questionable, then, whether the Commission's recently adopted position is entitled to the deference that the Court accords it.

The Court is swayed by the power given to the Commission by the 1975 amendments to the Exchange Act in order to permit the Commission to oversee the rules and procedures of the SROs, including those dealing with arbitration. . . . Subsequent to the passage of these amendments, however, the Commission has taken the consistent position that predispute arbitration agreements, which did not disclose to an investor that he has a right to a judicial forum, were misleading and possibly actionable under the securities laws. The Commission remained dissatisfied with the continued use of these arbitration agreements and eventually it proposed a rule to prohibit them, explaining that such a prohibition was not inconsistent with its support of arbitration for resolving securities disputes, particularly existing ones.... While emphasizing the Court's *Wilko* decision as a basis for its proposed rule, the Commission noted that its proposal also was in line with its own understanding of the problems with such agreements and with the "[c]ongressional determination that public investors should also have available the special protection of the federal courts for resolution of disputes arising under the federal securities laws." . . . Although the rule met with some opposition, it was adopted and *remains in force today.*

Moreover, the Commission's own description of its enforcement capabilities contradicts its position that its general overview of SRO rules and procedures can make arbitration adequate for resolving securities claims. The Commission does not pretend that its oversight consists of anything other than a general review of SRO rules and the ability to require that an SRO adopt or delete a particular rule. It does not contend that its "sweeping authority" . . . includes a review of specific arbitration proceedings. It thus neither polices nor monitors the results of these arbitrations for possible misapplications of securities laws or for indications of how investors fare in these proceedings. . . .

Finally, the Court's complacent acceptance of the Commission's oversight is alarming when almost every day brings another example of illegality on Wall Street. Many of the abuses recently brought to light, it is true, do not deal with the question of the adequacy of SRO arbitration. They, however, do suggest that the industry's self-regulation, of which the SRO arbitration is a part, is not functioning acceptably.

[. . .]

. . . Indeed, in light of today's decision compelling the enforcement of predispute arbitration agreements, it is likely that investors will be inclined, more than ever, to bring complaints to federal courts that arbitrators were partial or acted in "manifest disregard" of the securities laws. . . . It is thus ironic that the Court's decision, no doubt animated by its desire to rid the federal courts of these suits, actually may increase litigation about arbitration.

I therefore respectfully dissent in part.

JUSTICE STEVENS, concurring in part and dissenting in part.

Gaps in the law must, of course, be filled by judicial construction. But after a statute has been construed, either by this Court or by a consistent course of decision by other federal judges and agencies, it acquires a meaning that should be as clear as if the judicial gloss had been drafted by the Congress itself. . . .

During the 32 years immediately following this Court's decision in *Wilko v. Swan*, . . . each of the eight Circuits that addressed the issue concluded that the holding of *Wilko* was fully applicable to claims arising under the Securities Exchange Act of 1934. . . . This long-standing interpretation creates a strong presumption, in my view, that any mistake that the courts may have made in interpreting the statute is best remedied by the Legislative, not the Judicial, Branch. The history set forth in Part I of JUSTICE BLACKMUN's opinion adds special force to that presumption in this case.

For this reason, I respectfully dissent from the portion of the Court's judgment that holds *Wilko* inapplicable to the 1934 Act. Like JUSTICE BLACKMUN, however, I join Parts I, II, and IV of the Court's opinion.

NOTES AND QUESTIONS

1. The majority opinion limits the precedential value of *Wilko*, confining its holding to the 1933 Act, and effectively discredits its reasoning. According to the majority, rather than representing a statement of the importance of the policy of protecting investors from broker overreaching, *Wilko* symbolizes a general distrust of arbitration that conflicts with the Court's more recent pronouncements on arbitration. The *Wilko* decision, therefore, only bars arbitration when it is inadequate to protect the substantive statutory rights at issue. *Scherk* is seen as providing that, when arbitration is deemed (presumably by the courts) sufficient to protect the rights at issue, there is no bar to a waiver of a judicial forum. This reconstruction of precedents extends the doctrine, first articulated in *Scherk* and more forcefully stated in *Mitsubishi*, that the existence of statutory rights does not preclude the recourse to arbitration unless there is a legislative command that clearly mandates exclusive judicial disposition of alleged violations. *McMahon*, in effect, ignores the special circumstances, express doctrinal content, and segregation of domestic and international considerations in the prior decisional law.

2. *McMahon* similarly recasts the holding in *Mitsubishi*. A fair reading of *Mitsubishi* suggests that it establishes that antitrust claims are arbitrable in the context of international contracts. As in *Scherk*, the critical element is the fact that the dispute and the agreement to arbitrate are embedded in an international commercial transaction. If U.S. parties could frustrate the recourse to arbitration by alleging violations of domestic antitrust law, the stability of international commerce achieved with predictable dispute resolution through arbitration would be undermined. According to *McMahon*, however, *Mitsubishi* now stands for the proposition that the submission of statutory rights to arbitration does not represent an abandonment or elimination of those rights. Arbitral tribunals, like courts, are able to interpret and apply the governing statutory law. Resorting to the arbitral rather than judicial adjudication of statutory claims merely represents a choice of dispute resolution forum.

3. As to the issue of the arbitrability of RICO claims, the Court in *McMahon* is unanimous in its view that such claims can be submitted to arbitration. While the RICO legislation could readily be seen as involving matters of public policy, there is no express language in the statute or in its legislative history to indicate a congressional intent to preclude party selection of alternative, nonjudicial remedies. Accordingly, under the revamped understanding of *Mitsubishi*, the Court finds itself bound to conclude that RICO claims can be adjudicated through arbitration. The RICO statute does provide for civil claims, and arbitrators are able to assume jurisdiction over such disputes. Apparently, arbitral (like judicial) jurisdiction extends to the award of treble damages.

4. The majority and dissenting opinions render—once again—dichotomous evaluations of the issues and the governing law. The majority relies primarily upon a policy objective (sustaining the recourse to arbitration) and uses precedent and logic to uphold that objective. Although the result that is eventually reached is clear and unambiguous, its foundations are suspect and fragile. In a word, the distortive reasoning generates conceptual confusion because facts are misrepresented and the traditional means of justification are objectively unreliable. The dissent supplies an accurate and cogent account of the statutory language, its legislative history, and the prior case law. In the dissenting opinion, the rule of reason and rational evaluation inform and establish the proposed rule of law. Policy may influence the analysis, but it does not imprison the reasoning in circuitry and foregone conclusions. The approach is lawyerly and judicious, rather than legislative and rhetorical.

5. There is no mention in any segment of *McMahon* either of consumer arbitration or subject-matter inarbitrability. Although arbitration has been commonplace in the securities industry, it applied previously to disputes between the exchanges, brokerage houses, and brokers. The form of securities arbitration at issue in *McMahon* is different in that it involves the integration of customers into the arbitral system. The facts indicate that the McMahons are quite sophisticated financial parties; nonetheless, they are also the clients of the securities industry. Shouldn't this factor have received greater presence in the Court's evaluation of the suitability of arbitration to resolve the securities disputes in question? Aren't the two types of arbitration implied by the circumstances of the case enormously different forms or usages of arbitration, subject to differing regulatory regimes and policy imperatives?

Also, the unilateral character of the arbitral clause should be underscored. In most transactions for the purchase of securities, the broker presents the buyer with a standard customer agreement that contains a boilerplate provision for the arbitration of disputes. Every customer contract contains such an arbitral provision; in fact, buyers cannot purchase securities from any broker without agreeing to arbitrate disputes. This industry-wide practice makes arbitration the exclusive remedy for consumer complaints against brokers and for claims based upon the violation of securities law.

Again, these aspects of the transaction are not highlighted in the majority opinion. Do they have a direct bearing upon the legitimacy of arbitration in the context of securities disputes involving consumers? Aren't such agreements invalid under Section Two of the FAA? Why does the majority invoke the supervisory activities of the SEC in this context? Doesn't the dissent effectively refute the effectiveness of SEC supervision in terms of the operation of the arbitral mechanism? How might the submission agreement contribute to a more legitimate form of securities arbitration involving investors?

It is rather astounding that the topic of subject-matter inarbitrability is never mentioned in the *McMahon* opinion. What the Court terms the "hospitable inquiry into arbitrability" is integrated into and arises from the view that the law of arbitration is a statement of congressional will and policy that is binding upon the courts. The notion that subject-matter inarbitrability is an established and functional part of arbitration law never explicitly enters into the Court's consideration of the question of the arbitrability of securities disputes. The doctrinal view that arbitration gains its adjudicatory legitimacy from the legal system and that the legal system has the authority to place limits upon the arbitral process is, if not ignored, certainly neglected. The thrust of the Court's decisional law is to find interpretative devices by which to eradicate any possible restriction on arbitral adjudication, from aggrandizing the FAA's statutory purpose to eliminating state authority to regulate arbitration, and to having arbitration apply indiscriminately to contractual and statutory disputes.

The Court's singularity of purpose in terms of arbitration admits of no exception or qualification. The doctrine on arbitration is clearly established, but it is not adaptable to new realities or circumstances. The approach yields predictability and fulfills the Court's purpose: Making civil litigation available and workable. Arbitration risks becoming subservient to legal policy and a unidimensional remedy. Two factors are certain: 1. The Court's interest in arbitration is neither doctrinal nor intellectual, but rather profoundly practical; and 2. Contemporary arbitration is experiencing a substantial development and a golden age.

6. It should be noted that the Court was unanimous in its decision to allow for the arbitration of RICO claims. The RICO statute contains no mention of any dispute resolution restriction or prescription. According to the Court's reasoning, there is no statement, therefore, of a countervailing Congressional policy and the FAA can take effect unimpeded. Do you agree with this reasoning? Does the RICO statute not serve the public interest—in fact, a vital public interest? Are RICO claims meant to be settled in a private adjudicatory setting—away from the scrutiny of the public? What happens to the content of the statute if civil RICO claims can be submitted to arbitration? Does the unanimity in the decision express the Court's distaste for RICO and the litigation it generates? Does it indicate loyalty to the FAA's would-be objective or express a desire to manage federal court dockets by purging them of unwanted and undesirable litigation?

7. Assess the following statement from Justice Blackmun's dissent: "It is thus ironic that the Court's decision, no doubt animated by its desire to rid the federal courts of these [investor] suits, actually may increase litigation about arbitration." 482 U.S. at 268. How might such a situation come about?

8. The Court's holding and reasoning in *McMahon* generated a number of significant reactions. Within the arbitration community, applying securities arbitration to employment and consumer disputes appeared untoward. It created a need to adapt the traditional process to the needs of the new litigation. In the wake of *McMahon*, the American Arbitration Association (AAA) quickly developed a set of institutional rules tailored to securities arbitration. Previously, such cases had been governed by the rules for commercial arbitration. The alacrity of the AAA reaction indicated that the *McMahon* opinion was a source of new business for arbitral institutions and that arbitration in securities matters presented problems not normally associated with conventional arbitrations. With an increased volume of cases, new rules were needed to lessen the industry bias in prior procedures, account for the parties' disparity of position, and address the likelihood that most claims would raise questions of regulatory law.

When compared to their commercial counterpart, the AAA rules for securities arbitration differ in only a few, albeit fundamental, respects. First, in regard to the number of arbitrators on the tribunal, the commercial rules provide that generally only one arbitrator shall be appointed unless the parties provide otherwise or the AAA deems a plurality of arbitrators necessary. The securities arbitration rules require a panel of three arbitrators whenever a claim exceeds the relatively modest sum of $20,000. Second, the appointment of arbitrators is slightly more complicated under the rules for securities arbitration. The parties are given two lists of arbitrators—one listing arbitrators affiliated with the securities industry and the other nonaffiliated arbitrators. When the tribunal consists of three arbitrators, at least two must be nonaffiliated. If the arbitration is to be done by a sole arbitrator, that arbitrator must be nonaffiliated. Finally, in regard to the award, the rules for securities arbitration require arbitrators to "include a statement regarding the disposition of any statutory claims," whereas the rules for commercial arbitration mandate only that the award be in writing and signed by a majority of the arbitrators.

9. While the rules for securities arbitration are molded to the special character of these disputes, they may not alleviate the basic danger of having recourse to arbitration in a consumer and regulatory context. The practice of having three-member tribunals and a majority of nonaffiliated arbitrators may not sufficiently protect consumer interests. It may only provide a formalistic safeguard. Industry practice may still set applicable standards and the public interest may never be defined, elaborated upon, or referred to in this private adjudicatory process. Unlike judges, arbitrators may not have the sense of independence necessary to adopt minority, economically questionable, or otherwise "deviant" positions. Finally, mandating that securities arbitrators expressly acknowledge investor claims of statutory violations only provides

superficial recognition of the disputes' public law character. The rules do not mandate a reasoned assessment of the claim, and appeal to a court is no more readily available in these arbitral circumstances than in others.

Although these alterations do not attenuate the juridical dilemma created by the Court's decision, they mitigate the harshness of the *McMahon* result. In *McMahon*, the Court was willing to have investor claims resolved through industry-controlled (SRO) arbitration procedures. By attempting to deal with disparities in position and the public law aspect of the cases, the new AAA rules at least are pointed in the direction of fairness and seek to protect the institution of arbitration from charges of glaring unsuitability and abuse. It bears reiterating, however, that these rules do not resolve the core problems raised by the arbitrability of securities claims: The adhesive character of the arbitral compact, the economic and positional inequality of the parties, and the depreciation of the public interest in preventing individual investor fraud and broker overreaching in a sophisticated, volatile market.

10. Moreover, in its opinion, the *McMahon* Court looked to SEC supervision as a means of justifying its confidence in industry-controlled securities arbitration procedures. If unfairness and injustice surfaced, the Court seemed to reason, the Commission would be there to provide the necessary correction. "Black Monday" (October 19, 1987) demonstrated the fallacy of the Court's reasoning and made the underlying problems with securities arbitration transparent. Following the stock market collapse, an avalanche of investor claims were submitted to the industry-controlled (SRO) arbitral framework. Apparently, the SEC was unable to exercise its anticipated supervisory capabilities. The volume of pending cases and a growing public dissatisfaction with arbitral procedures led the Commission to consider asking for congressional legislation prohibiting mandatory predispute arbitration agreements in investor-broker contracts. It eventually resolved, however, merely to request a study of the problem. As indicated in the dissenting opinion, the depth of regulatory oversight from the Commission envisaged by the *McMahon* Court simply does not exist.

SEC inaction and public outcries of injustice with mandatory arbitration in securities cases may lead to legislative attacks upon the arbitral process. The *McMahon* opinion, in fact, gave rise to a determination in some legislative quarters to oppose the Court's reordering of fundamental juridical priorities. Massachusetts, for example, enacted legislation prohibiting the use of mandatory arbitration clauses in investor-broker contracts. Under the legislation, which took effect in January 1989, brokers were required to inform prospective clients of their legal right to judicial redress of their grievances. Moreover, brokers had to do business with investors who refused to agree to arbitrate. While the legislation was directed at consumer protection, it cast arbitration in an unfavorable light. Because the Massachusetts law arguably conflicted with the federal law on arbitration and the content of the Court's arbitral doctrine, it was attacked on constitutional grounds. The Massachusetts law was struck down at the federal district court level on the ground that it conflicted with the Supreme Court's "forceful endorsement of the arbitration process." This decision was upheld by the Court on appeal.

Rodriguez v. Shearson/American Express, Inc.

Rodriguez de Quijas v. Shearson/American Express, Inc., 490 U.S. 477 (1989), completes the Court's undermining of the subject-matter inarbitrability defense in regard to statutory rights. The Court decides in this case that claims arising under the 1933 Securities Act are arbitrable, overruling and reversing *Wilko* because it embodied a would-be "outmoded presumption of disfavoring arbitration proceedings." Like *McMahon*, the facts of *Rodriguez* involved allegations of consumer fraud in an investor-broker contract for the purchase of securities. The plaintiffs, who had signed a standard contract containing an arbitration clause, claimed violations of both the 1933 Securities Act and the 1934 Securities Exchange Act. In *McMahon*, the Court ruled that 1934 Act claims could be submitted to arbitration; in *Rodriguez*, the issue of litigation was whether the 1933 Act claims should also be deemed arbitrable.

In a 5 to 4 decision, the *Rodriguez* Court used the principles articulated in *Mitsubishi* and *McMahon* to completely discredit the *Wilko* doctrine. The Court, through Justice Kennedy, made much of the fact that arbitration was "merely a form of trial" that did not affect the substantive rights in contest. Arbitral proceedings were an effective means of trial. Moreover, statutory rights did not occupy a privileged position; they, like contractual obligations, could be adjudicated through arbitration. Having recourse to arbitration resulted only in a waiver of the Act's procedural guarantees, not of the substantive statutory rights. The Act's nonwaiver provision applied only to the legislation's substantive provisions.

The majority opinion emphasized that *Wilko* was at odds with the Court's contemporary pronouncements on arbitration: "To the extent that *Wilko* rested on suspicion of arbitration as a method of weakening the protections afforded in the substantive law to would-be complainants, it has fallen far out of step with our current strong endorsement of the federal statutes favoring this method of resolving disputes." *Wilko* was imbued with " 'the old judicial hostility to arbitration' " and did not address the arbitrability question " 'with a healthy regard for the federal policy favoring arbitration' " mandated by the federalism trilogy. The ruling in *McMahon* dictated that *Wilko* could no longer stand as applicable law because the language of the 1933 and 1934 Acts pertaining to judicial remedies was identical: "Indeed, in *McMahon* the Court declined to read § 29(a) of the Securities Exchange Act of 1934, the language of which is in every respect the same as that in § 14 of the 1933 Act, . . . to prohibit enforcement of predispute agreements to arbitrate." Furthermore, an inconsistent interpretation of the provisions of the two acts would impair the functional harmony of the regulatory scheme for the sale of securities: "[T]he inconsistency between *Wilko* and *McMahon* undermines the essential rationale for a harmonious construction of the statutes, which is to discourage litigants from manipulating their allegations merely to cast their claims under one of the securities laws rather than another."

RODRIGUEZ DE QUIJAS V. SHEARSON/ AMERICAN EXPRESS, INC.

490 U.S. 477, 109 S.Ct. 1917, 104 L.Ed.2d 526 (1989).

JUSTICE KENNEDY delivered the opinion of the Court.

The question here is whether a predispute agreement to arbitrate claims under the Securities Act of 1933 is unenforceable, requiring resolution of the claims only in a judicial forum.

I

Petitioners are individuals who invested about $400,000 in securities. They signed a standard customer agreement with the broker, which included a clause stating that the parties agreed to settle any controversies "relating to [the] accounts" through binding arbitration that complies with specified procedures. The agreement to arbitrate these controversies is unqualified, unless it is found to be unenforceable under federal or state law. The investments turned sour, and petitioners eventually sued respondent and its broker-agent in charge of the accounts, alleging that their money was lost in unauthorized and fraudulent transactions.

The District Court ordered all the claims to be submitted to arbitration except for those raised under § 12(2) of the Securities Act. It held that the latter claims must proceed in the court action under our clear holding on the point in *Wilko v. Swan*. . . . The Court of Appeals reversed, concluding that the arbitration agreement is enforceable because this Court's subsequent decisions have reduced *Wilko* to "obsolescence." . . .

II

The *Wilko* case, decided in 1953, required the Court to determine whether an agreement to arbitrate future controversies constitutes a binding stipulation "to waive compliance with any provision" of the Securities Act, which is nullified by § 14 of the Act. The Court considered the language, purposes, and legislative history of the Securities Act and concluded that the agreement to arbitrate was void under § 14. But the decision was a difficult one in view of the competing legislative policy embodied in the Arbitration Act, which the Court described as "not easily reconcilable," and which strongly favors the enforcement of agreements to arbitrate as a means of securing "prompt, economical and adequate solution of controversies." . . .

It has been recognized that *Wilko* was not obviously correct, for "the language prohibiting waiver of 'compliance with any provision of this title' could easily have been read to relate to substantive provisions of the Act without including the remedy provisions." . . . The Court did not read the language this way in *Wilko*, however, and gave two reasons. First, the Court rejected the argument that "arbitration is merely a form of trial to be used in lieu of a trial at law." . . . The Court found instead that § 14 does not permit waiver of "the right to select the judicial forum" in favor of arbitration . . . because "arbitration lacks the certainty of a suit at law under the Act to enforce [the buyer's] rights". . . . Second, the Court concluded that the Securities Act was intended to protect buyers of securities, who often do not deal at arm's length and on equal terms with sellers, by offering them "a wider choice of courts and venue" than is enjoyed by participants in other business transactions, making "the right to select the judicial forum" a particularly valuable feature of the Securities Act. . . .

We do not think these reasons justify an interpretation of § 14 that prohibits agreements to arbitrate future disputes relating to the purchase of securities. The Court's characterization of the arbitration process in *Wilko* is pervaded by . . . "the old judicial hostility to arbitration." . . . That view has been steadily eroded over the years. . . . The erosion intensified in our most recent decisions upholding agreements to arbitrate federal claims raised under the Securities Exchange Act of 1934 . . . under the Racketeer Influenced and Corrupt Organizations (RICO) statutes . . . and under the antitrust laws. To the extent that *Wilko* rested on suspicion of arbitration as a method of weakening the protections afforded in the substantive law to would-be complainants, it has fallen far out of step with our current strong endorsement of the federal statutes favoring this method of resolving disputes.

Once the outmoded presumption of disfavoring arbitration proceedings is set to one side, it becomes clear that the right to select the judicial forum and the wider choice of courts are not such essential features of the Securities Act that § 14 is properly construed to bar any waiver of these provisions. Nor are they so critical that they cannot be waived under the rationale that the Securities Act was intended to place buyers of securities on an equal footing with sellers. *Wilko* identified two different kinds of provisions in the Securities Act that would advance this objective. Some are substantive, such as the provision placing on the seller the burden of proving lack of scienter when a buyer alleges fraud. . . . Others are procedural. The specific procedural improvements highlighted in *Wilko* are the statute's broad venue provisions in the federal courts; the existence of nationwide service of process in the federal courts; the extinction of the amount-in-controversy requirement that had applied to fraud suits when they were brought in federal courts under diversity jurisdiction rather than as a federal cause of action; and the grant of concurrent jurisdiction in the state and federal courts without possibility of removal. . . .

There is no sound basis for construing the prohibition in § 14 on waiving "compliance with any provision" of the Securities Act to apply to these procedural provisions. Although the first three measures do facilitate suits by buyers of securities, the grant of concurrent jurisdiction constitutes explicit authorization for complainants to waive those protections by filing suit in state court without possibility of removal to federal court. These measures, moreover, are present in other federal statutes which have not been interpreted to prohibit enforcement of predispute agreements to arbitrate. . . .

Indeed, in *McMahon* the Court declined to read § 29(a) of the Securities Exchange Act of 1934, the language of which is in every respect the same as that in § 14 of the 1933 Act to prohibit enforcement of predispute agreements to arbitrate. The only conceivable distinction in this regard between the Securities Act and the Securities Exchange Act is that the former statute allows concurrent federal-state jurisdiction over causes of action and the latter statute provides for exclusive federal jurisdiction. But even if this distinction were thought to make any difference at all, it would suggest that arbitration agreements, which are "in effect, a specialized kind of forum-selection clause," . . . should not be prohibited under the Securities Act, since they, like the provision for concurrent jurisdiction, serve to advance the objective of allowing buyers of securities a broader right to select the forum for resolving disputes, whether it be judicial or otherwise. And in *McMahon* we explained at length why we rejected the *Wilko* Court's aversion to arbitration as a forum for resolving disputes over securities transactions, especially in light of the relatively recent expansion of the Securities and Exchange Commission's authority to oversee and to regulate those arbitration procedures. . . .

Finally, in *McMahon* we stressed the strong language of the Arbitration Act, which declares as a matter of federal law that arbitration agreements "shall be valid, irrevocable, and enforceable, save upon such grounds as exist at law or in equity for the revocation of any contract." Under that statute, the party opposing arbitration carries the burden of showing that Congress intended in a separate statute to preclude a waiver of judicial remedies, or that such a waiver of judicial remedies inherently conflicts with the underlying purposes of that other statute. . . . But as Justice Frankfurter said in dissent in *Wilko*, so it is true in this case: "There is nothing in the record before us, nor in the facts of which we can take judicial notice, to indicate that the arbitral system . . . would not afford the plaintiff the rights to which he is entitled." . . . Petitioners have not carried their burden of showing that arbitration agreements are not enforceable under the Securities Act.

The language quoted above from § 2 of the Arbitration Act also allows the courts to give relief where the party opposing arbitration presents "well-supported claims that the agreement to arbitrate resulted from the sort of fraud or overwhelming economic power that would provide grounds 'for the revocation of any contract.' " . . . This avenue of relief is in harmony with the Securities Act's concern to protect buyers of securities by removing "the disadvantages under which buyers labor" in their dealings with sellers. Although petitioners suggest that the agreement to arbitrate here was adhesive in nature, the record contains no factual showing sufficient to support that suggestion.

III

. . . We now conclude that *Wilko* was incorrectly decided and is inconsistent with the prevailing uniform construction of other federal statutes governing arbitration agreements in the setting of business transactions. Although we are normally and properly reluctant to overturn our decisions construing statutes, we have done so to achieve a uniform interpretation of similar statutory language . . . and to correct a seriously erroneous interpretation of statutory language that would undermine congressional policy as expressed in other legislation. . . .

It also would be undesirable for the decisions in *Wilko* and *McMahon* to continue to exist side by side. Their inconsistency is at odds with the principle that the 1933 and 1934 Acts should be construed harmoniously because they "constitute interrelated components of the federal regulatory scheme governing transactions in securities." . . . In this case, for example, petitioners' claims under the 1934 Act were subjected to arbitration, while their claim under the 1933 Act was not permitted to go to arbitration, but was required to proceed in court. That result makes little sense for similar claims, based on similar facts, which are supposed to arise within a single federal regulatory scheme. In addition, the inconsistency between *Wilko* and *McMahon* undermines the essential rationale for a harmonious construction of the two statutes, which is to discourage litigants from manipulating their allegations merely to cast their claims under one of the securities laws rather than another. For all of these reasons, therefore, we overrule the decision in *Wilko*.

[. . .]

The judgment of the Court of Appeals is

Affirmed.

JUSTICE STEVENS, with whom JUSTICE BRENNAN, JUSTICE MARSHALL, and JUSTICE BLACKMUN join, dissenting.

The Court of Appeals refused to follow *Wilko v. Swan*, . . . a controlling precedent of this Court. As the majority correctly acknowledges, . . . the Court of Appeals therefore engaged in an indefensible brand of judicial activism. We, of course, are not subject to the same restraint when asked to upset one of our own precedents. But when our earlier opinion gives a statutory provision concrete meaning, which Congress elects not to amend during the ensuing 3 1/2 decades, our duty to respect Congress' work product is strikingly similar to the duty of other federal courts to respect our work product.

In the final analysis, a Justice's vote in a case like this depends more on his or her views about the respective lawmaking responsibilities of Congress and this Court than on conflicting policy interests. Judges who have confidence in their own ability to fashion public policy are less hesitant to change the law than those of us who are inclined to give wide latitude to the views of the voters' representatives on nonconstitutional matters. . . . As I pointed out years ago, *Alberto-Culver Co. v. Scherk*, there are valid policy and textual arguments on both sides regarding the interrelation of federal securities and arbitration Acts. . . . None of these arguments, however, carries sufficient weight to tip the balance between judicial and legislative authority and overturn an interpretation of an Act of Congress that has been settled for many years.

I respectfully dissent.

NOTES AND QUESTIONS

1. As with the *McMahon* and other arbitration opinions, the Court's reasoning in *Rodriguez* is calculated to achieve policy objectives. For example, the argument that arbitration is "merely a form of trial" with no impact upon substantive rights is far from convincing. In the U.S. legal system, procedure is a central facet of justice. In both theory and practice, arbitration is a reduced form of adjudication to which parties consent because they want to avoid the length and delays of the legal process. Judicial and arbitral proceedings are two different forms of justice, responding to different adjudicatory goals. Party consent, knowingly and freely given, is at the core of arbitral adjudication.

Statutory rights are not equivalent to commercial contract claims that measure contract performance and the contracting parties' pecuniary interests. Securities regulation is intended to eradicate fraud and overreaching in the sale of stocks. It seeks to stabilize the American financial marketplace. Statutory rights, such as those contained in the securities legislation, antitrust statutes, and RICO, implicate the public interest. They deal with the general welfare of society by affording individuals special protections and prohibiting conduct deemed reprehensible in the trade. These statutes define basic precepts of community order and thereby establish public policy. As a consequence, they are implemented by social institutions invested with public authority and exercising public legal authority.

The Court anchors its reasoning in the need to expunge judicial hostility to arbitration. The central issue of the American law of arbitration, however, is no longer one of legitimating arbitration, but rather establishing the basic boundaries, function, and identity of the process. As contractual freedom must not impinge upon the public order to remain workable in the legal order, so must arbitration acquire some essential contours and basic limitations. By invoking the danger of judicial hostility, the Court is battling a chimerical risk, an historical ghost that has ceased to influence the reality of the process. In any event, a fair reading of *Wilko* should not lead to a construction of the opinion as a decision hostile to arbitration.

2. The dissent in *Rodriguez* grounds its criticism in a separation of powers argument and the need to have the Court respect legislative authority in establishing law. According to Justice Stevens, when the Court's "earlier opinion gives a statutory provision concrete meaning, which Congress elects not to amend during the ensuing 3 1/2 decades, our duty to respect Congress' work product is strikingly similar to the duty of other federal courts to respect our work product."

The dissent's reference to judicial respect for congressional prerogatives is perspicacious because it now appears that the only means of restoring balance and integrity to the American law of arbitration is through the exercise of legislative authority. *Rodriguez* confirms the Court's determination to eliminate any meaningful role for the subject-matter inarbitrability defense in the American law of arbitration. Arguably, the elimination creates an imbalance between private prerogatives and public duties and attributes to arbitration an adjudicatory task that it is ill-prepared and unsuited to perform. "Dumping" unwanted judicial caseloads into arbitral jurisdiction can only harm the arbitral process in the long run, especially when it requires arbitrators to rule upon socially significant issues that are regulated by statute. In the end, society may not only be riddled with an inefficient judicial process, but it may also have lost a workable alternative mechanism for specialty claims.

In keeping with the analysis of *McMahon*, do you think that the decision in *Rodriguez* should result in Congressional action to amend the provisions of the FAA to exclude *bona fide* claims based on statutory rights from the purview of arbitration and to prevent arbitrators from exercising public jurisdictional authority by prohibiting them, for example, from awarding punitive or treble damages? In addition, should some thought be given to adding a public policy exception to the statutory grounds for vacating awards? Such a provision could stand as a symbol of the dividing line between judicial and arbitral jurisdiction. It also would allow courts an additional basis by which to police the validity and enforceability of arbitration agreements. Would the latter allow the courts too much supervisory authority?

2. CIVIL RIGHTS

ALEXANDER V. GARDNER-DENVER CO.

415 U.S. 36, 94 S.Ct. 1011, 39 L.Ed.2d 147 (1974).

MR. JUSTICE POWELL delivered the opinion of the Court.

This case concerns the proper relationship between federal courts and the grievance-arbitration machinery of collective-bargaining agreements in the resolution and enforcement of an individual's rights to equal employment opportunities under Title VII of the Civil Rights Act of 1964. . . . Specifically, we must decide under what circumstances, if any, an employee's statutory right to a trial de novo under Title VII may be foreclosed by prior submission of his claim to final arbitration under the nondiscrimination clause of a collective-bargaining agreement.

I

In May 1966, petitioner Harrell Alexander, Sr., a black, was hired by respondent Gardner-Denver Co. (the company) to perform maintenance work at the company's plant in Denver, Colorado. In June 1968, petitioner was awarded a trainee position as a drill operator. He remained at that job until his discharge from employment on September 29, 1969. The company informed petitioner that he was being discharged for producing too many defective or unusable parts that had to be scrapped.

On October 1, 1969, petitioner filed a grievance under the collective-bargaining agreement in force between the company and petitioner's union. . . . No explicit claim of racial discrimination was made.

Under Art. 4 of the collective-bargaining agreement, the company retained 'the right to hire, suspend or discharge (employees) for proper cause.' Article 5, § 2, provided, however, that 'there shall be no discrimination against any employee on account of race, color, religion, sex, national origin, or ancestry,' and Art. 23, § 6(a), stated that '(n)o employee will be discharged, suspended or given a written warning notice except for just cause.' The agreement also contained a broad arbitration clause covering 'differences aris(ing) between the Company and the Union as to the meaning and application of the provisions of this Agreement' and 'any trouble aris(ing) in the plant.' Disputes were to be submitted to a multistep grievance procedure, the first four steps of which involved negotiations between the company and the union. If the dispute remained unresolved, it was to be remitted to compulsory arbitration. The company and the union were to select and pay the arbitrator, and his decision was to be 'final and binding upon the Company, the Union, and any employee or employees involved.' The agreement further provided that '(t)he arbitrator shall not amend, take away, add to, or change any of the provisions of this Agreement, and the arbitrator's decision must be based solely upon an interpretation of the provisions of this Agreement.' The parties also agreed that there 'shall be no suspension of work' over disputes covered by the grievance arbitration clause.

The union processed petitioner's grievance through the above machinery. In the final pre-arbitration step, petitioner raised, apparently for the first time, the claim that his discharge resulted from racial discrimination. The company rejected all of petitioner's claims, and the grievance proceeded to arbitration. Prior to the arbitration hearing, however, petitioner filed a charge of racial discrimination with the Colorado Civil Rights Commission, which referred the complaint to the Equal Employment Opportunity Commission on November 5, 1969.

At the arbitration hearing on November 20, 1969, petitioner testified that his discharge was the result of racial discrimination and informed the arbitrator that he had filed a charge with the Colorado Commission because he 'could not rely on the union.' The union introduced a letter in which petitioner stated that he was 'knowledgeable that in the same plant others have scrapped an equal amount and sometimes in excess, but by all logical reasoning I . . . have been the target of preferential discriminatory treatment.' The union representative also testified that the company's usual practice was to transfer unsatisfactory trainee drill operators back to their former positions.

On December 30, 1969, the arbitrator ruled that petitioner had been 'discharged for just cause.' He made no reference to petitioner's claim of racial discrimination. The arbitrator stated that the union had failed to produce evidence of a practice of transferring rather than discharging trainee drill operators who accumulated excessive scrap, but he suggested that the company and the union confer on whether such an arrangement was feasible in the present case.

On July 25, 1970, the Equal Employment Opportunity Commission determined that there was not reasonable cause to believe that a violation of Title VII of the Civil Rights Act of 1964 . . . had occurred. The Commission later notified petitioner of his right to institute a civil action in federal court within 30 days. Petitioner then filed the present action in the United States District Court for the District of Colorado, alleging that his discharge resulted from a racially discriminatory employment practice in violation of § 703(a)(1) of the Act. . . .

The District Court granted respondent's motion for summary judgment and dismissed the action. . . . The court found that the claim of racial discrimination had been submitted to the arbitrator and resolved adversely to petitioner. It then held that petitioner, having voluntarily elected to pursue his grievance to final arbitration under the nondiscrimination clause of the collective-bargaining agreement, was bound by the arbitral decision and thereby precluded from suing his employer under Title VII. The Court of Appeals for the Tenth Circuit affirmed *per curiam* on the basis of the District Court's opinion. . . .

. . . We reverse.

II

Congress enacted Title VII of the Civil Rights Act of 1964 . . . to assure equality of employment opportunities by eliminating those practices and devices that discriminate on the basis of race, color, religion, sex, or national origin. . . . Cooperation and voluntary compliance were selected as the preferred means for achieving this goal. To this end, Congress created the Equal Employment Opportunity Commission and established a procedure whereby existing state and local equal employment opportunity agencies, as well as the Commission, would have an opportunity to settle disputes through conference, conciliation, and persuasion before the aggrieved party was permitted to file a lawsuit. In the Equal Employment Opportunity Act of 1972, . . . Congress amended Title VII to provide the Commission with further authority to investigate individual charges of discrimination, to promote voluntary compliance with the requirements of Title VII, and to institute civil actions against employers or unions named in a discrimination charge.

Even in its amended form, however, Title VII does not provide the Commission with direct powers of enforcement. The Commission cannot adjudicate claims or impose administrative sanctions. Rather, final responsibility for enforcement of Title VII is vested with federal courts. The Act authorizes courts to issue injunctive relief and to order such affirmative action as may be appropriate to remedy the effects of unlawful employment practices. . . . Courts retain these broad remedial powers despite a Commission finding of no reasonable cause to believe that the Act has been violated. . . . Taken together, these provisions make plain that federal courts have been assigned plenary powers to secure compliance with Title VII.

In addition to reposing ultimate authority in federal courts, Congress gave private individuals a significant role in the enforcement process of Title VII. Individual grievants usually initiate the Commission's investigatory and conciliatory procedures. And although the 1972 amendment to Title VII empowers the Commission to bring its own actions, the private right of action remains an essential means of obtaining judicial enforcement of Title VII. . . . In such cases, the private litigant not only redresses his own injury but also vindicates the important congressional policy against discriminatory employment practices. . . .

Pursuant to this statutory scheme, petitioner initiated the present action for judicial consideration of his rights under Title VII. The District Court and the Court of Appeals held, however, that petitioner was bound by the prior arbitral decision and had no right to sue under Title VII. Both courts evidently thought that this result was dictated by notions of election of remedies and waiver and by the federal policy favoring arbitration of labor disputes. . . . We disagree.

III

Title VII does not speak expressly to the relationship between federal courts and the grievance-arbitration machinery of collective-bargaining agreements. It does, however, vest federal courts with plenary powers to enforce the statutory requirements; and it specifies with precision the jurisdictional prerequisites that an individual must satisfy before he is entitled to institute a lawsuit. . . . There is no suggestion in the statutory scheme that a prior arbitral decision either forecloses an individual's right to sue or divests federal courts of jurisdiction.

In addition, legislative enactments in this area have long evinced a general intent to accord parallel or overlapping remedies against discrimination. . . . [T]he legislative history of Title VII manifests a congressional intent to allow an individual to pursue independently his rights under both Title VII and other applicable state and federal statutes. The clear inference is that Title VII was designed to supplement, rather than supplant, existing laws and institutions relating to employment discrimination. In sum, Title VII's purpose and procedures strongly suggest that an individual does not forfeit his private cause of action if he first pursues his grievance to final arbitration under the nondiscrimination clause of a collective-bargaining agreement.

In reaching the opposite conclusion, the District Court relied in part on the doctrine of election of remedies. That doctrine, which refers to situations where an individual pursues remedies that are legally or factually inconsistent, has no application in the present context. In submitting his grievance to arbitration, an employee seeks to vindicate his contractual right under a collective-bargaining agreement. By contrast, in filing a lawsuit under Title VII, an employee asserts independent statutory rights accorded by Congress. The distinctly separate nature of these contractual and statutory rights is not vitiated merely because both were violated as a result of the same factual occurrence. And certainly no inconsistency results from permitting both rights to be enforced in their respectively appropriate forums. The resulting scheme is somewhat analogous to the procedure under the National Labor Relations Act, as amended, where disputed transactions may implicate both contractual and statutory rights. Where the statutory right underlying a particular claim may not be abridged by contractual agreement, the Court has recognized that consideration of the claim by the arbitrator as a contractual dispute under the collective-bargaining agreement does not preclude subsequent consideration of the claim by the National Labor Relations Board as an unfair labor practice charge or as a petition for clarification of the union's representation certificate under the Act. . . . There, as here, the relationship between the forums is complementary since consideration of the claim by both forums may promote the policies underlying each. Thus, the rationale behind the election-of-remedies doctrine cannot support the decision below.

We are also unable to accept the proposition that petitioner waived his cause of action under Title VII. To begin, we think it clear that there can be no prospective waiver of an employee's rights under Title VII. It is true, of course, that a union may waive certain statutory rights related to collective activity, such as the right to strike. . . . These rights are conferred on employees collectively to foster the processes of bargaining and properly may be exercised or relinquished by the union as collective-bargaining agent to obtain economic benefits for union members. Title VII, on the other hand, stands on plainly different ground; it concerns not majoritarian processes, but an individual's right to equal employment opportunities. Title VII's strictures are absolute and represent a congressional command that each employee be free from discriminatory practices. Of necessity, the rights conferred can form no part of the collective-bargaining process since waiver of these rights would defeat the paramount congressional purpose behind Title VII. In these circumstances, an employee's rights under Title VII are not susceptible of prospective waiver. . . .

The actual submission of petitioner's grievance to arbitration in the present case does not alter the situation. Although presumably an employee may waive his cause of action under Title VII as part of a voluntary settlement, mere resort to the arbitral forum to enforce contractual rights constitutes no such waiver. Since an employee's rights under Title VII may not be waived prospectively, existing contractual rights and remedies against discrimination must result from other concessions already made by the union as part of the economic bargain struck with the employer. It is settled law that no additional concession may be exacted from any employee as the price for enforcing those rights. . . .

Moreover, a contractual right to submit a claim to arbitration is not displaced simply because Congress also has provided a statutory right against discrimination. Both rights have legally independent origins and are equally available to the aggrieved employee. This point becomes apparent through consideration of the role of the arbitrator in the system of industrial self-government. As the proctor of the bargain, the arbitrator's task is to effectuate the intent of the parties. His source of authority is the collective-bargaining agreement, and he must interpret and apply that agreement in accordance with the 'industrial common law of the shop' and the various needs and desires of the parties. The arbitrator, however, has no general authority to invoke public laws that conflict with the bargain between the parties[.]

[. . .]

IV

The District Court and the Court of Appeals reasoned that to permit an employee to have his claim considered in both the arbitral and judicial forums would be unfair since this would mean that the employer, but not the employee, was bound by the arbitral award. In the District Court's words, it could not 'accept a philosophy which gives the employee two strings to his bow when the employer has only one.' . . . This argument mistakes the effect of Title VII. Under the *Steelworkers* trilogy, an arbitral decision is final and binding on the employer and employee, and judicial review is limited as to both. But in instituting an action under Title VII, the employee is not seeking review of the arbitrator's decision. Rather, he is asserting a statutory right independent of the arbitration process. An employer does not have 'two strings to his bow' with respect to an arbitral decision for the simple reason that Title VII does not provide employers with a cause of action against employees. An employer cannot be the victim of discriminatory employment practices. . . .

The District Court and the Court of Appeals also thought that to permit a later resort to the judicial forum would undermine substantially the employer's incentive to arbitrate and would 'sound the death knell for arbitration clauses in labor contracts.' . . . Again, we disagree. The primary incentive for an employer to enter into an arbitration agreement is the union's reciprocal promise not to strike. . . . It is not unreasonable to assume that most employers will regard the benefits derived from a no-strike pledge as outweighing whatever costs may result from according employees an arbitral remedy against discrimination in addition to their judicial remedy under Title VII. Indeed, the severe consequences of a strike may make an arbitration clause almost essential from both the employees' and the employer's perspective. Moreover, the grievance-arbitration machinery of the collective-bargaining agreement remains a relatively inexpensive and expeditious means for resolving a wide range of disputes, including claims of discriminatory employment practices. Where the collective-bargaining agreement contains a nondiscrimination clause similar to Title VII, and where arbitral procedures are fair and regular, arbitration may well produce a settlement satisfactory to both employer and employee. An employer thus has an incentive to make available the conciliatory and therapeutic processes of arbitration which may satisfy an employee's perceived need to resort to the judicial forum, thus saving the employer the expense and aggravation associated with a lawsuit. For similar reasons, the employee also has a strong incentive to arbitrate grievances, and arbitration may often eliminate those misunderstandings or discriminatory practices that might otherwise precipitate resort to the judicial forum.

V

Respondent contends that even if a preclusion rule is not adopted, federal courts should defer to arbitral decisions on discrimination claims where: (i) the claim was before the arbitrator; (ii) the collective-bargaining agreement prohibited the form of discrimination charged in the suit under Title VII; and (iii) the arbitrator has authority to rule on the claim and to fashion a remedy. Under respondent's proposed rule, a court would grant summary judgment and dismiss the employee's action if the above conditions were met. The rule's obvious consequence in the present case would be to deprive the petitioner of his statutory right to attempt to establish his claim in a federal court.

At the outset, it is apparent that a deferral rule would be subject to many of the objections applicable to a preclusion rule. The purpose and procedures of Title VII indicate that Congress intended federal courts to exercise final responsibility for enforcement of Title VII; deferral to arbitral decisions would be inconsistent with that goal. Furthermore, we have long recognized that 'the choice of forums inevitably affects the scope of the substantive right to be vindicated.' . . . Respondent's deferral rule is necessarily premised on the assumption that arbitral processes are commensurate with judicial processes and that Congress impliedly intended federal courts to defer to arbitral decisions on Title VII issues. We deem this supposition unlikely.

Arbitral procedures, while well suited to the resolution of contractual disputes, make arbitration a comparatively inappropriate forum for the final resolution of rights created by Title VII. This conclusion rests first on the special role of the arbitrator, whose task is to effectuate the intent of the parties rather than the requirements of enacted legislation. Where the collective-bargaining agreement conflicts with Title VII, the arbitrator must follow the agreement. To be sure, the tension between contractual and statutory objectives may be mitigated where a collective-bargaining agreement contains provisions facially similar to those of Title VII. But other facts may still render arbitral processes comparatively inferior to judicial processes in the protection of Title VII rights. Among these is the fact that the specialized competence of arbitrators pertains primarily to the law of the shop, not the law of the land. . . . Parties usually choose an arbitrator because they trust his knowledge and judgment concerning the demands and norms of industrial relations. On the other hand, the resolution of statutory or constitutional issues is a primary responsibility of courts, and judicial construction has proved especially necessary with respect to Title VII, whose broad language frequently can be given meaning only by reference to public law concepts.

Moreover, the factfinding process in arbitration usually is not equivalent to judicial factfinding. The record of the arbitration proceedings is not as complete; the usual rules of evidence do not apply; and rights and procedures common to civil trials, such as discovery, compulsory process, cross examination, and testimony under oath, are often severely limited or unavailable. . . . And as this Court has recognized, '[a]rbitrators have no obligation to the court to give their reasons for an award.' . . . Indeed, it is the informality of arbitral procedure that enables it to function as an efficient, inexpensive, and expeditious means for dispute resolution. This same characteristic, however, makes arbitration a less appropriate forum for final resolution of Title VII issues than the federal courts.

It is evident that respondent's proposed rule would not allay these concerns. Nor are we convinced that the solution lies in applying a more demanding deferral standard. . . . As respondent points out, a standard that adequately insured effectuation of Title VII rights in the arbitral forum would tend to make arbitration a procedurally complex, expensive, and time-consuming process. And judicial enforcement of such a standard would almost require courts to make *de novo* determinations of the employees' claims. It is uncertain whether any minimal savings in judicial time and expense would justify the risk to vindication of Title VII rights.

A deferral rule also might adversely affect the arbitration system as well as the enforcement scheme of Title VII. Fearing that the arbitral forum cannot adequately protect their rights under Title VII, some employees may elect to bypass arbitration and institute a lawsuit. The possibility of voluntary compliance or settlement of Title VII claims would thus be reduced, and the result could well be more litigation, not less.

We think, therefore, that the federal policy favoring arbitration of labor disputes and the federal policy against discriminatory employment practices can best be accommodated by permitting an employee to pursue fully both his remedy under the grievance-arbitration clause of a collective-bargaining agreement and his cause of action under Title VII. The federal court should consider the employee's claim *de novo*. The arbitral decision may be admitted as evidence and accorded such weight as the court deems appropriate.

The judgment of the Court of Appeals is reversed.

Reversed.

NOTES AND QUESTIONS

1. In comparison to more contemporary judicial decisions on arbitration, *Gardner-Denver* is a museum piece—both as to its reasoning and result. The Court gives primary importance to the objectives underlying the federal statute, attributes a unique character to the activity of the judicial branch of government, and actually states that arbitration is not necessarily suitable for the adjudication of all claims.

2. Under *Gardner-Denver,* the employee can either participate in collective-bargaining arbitration and then file a lawsuit or take the Title VII claim directly to court and forgo completely the grievance-arbitration machinery under the CBA. Which method would be better for an employee? Employer? Why?

3. How do you evaluate the Court's distinction regarding the source of rights? The arbitrator has jurisdiction to rule on contract but not statutory claims. What makes these rights so different in terms of importance? Are congressional objectives more central than workplace objectives?

4. Could a labor arbitrator rule on a Title VII claim if the employee (once the dispute arose) agreed to arbitrate the matter and to forgo all reference to judicial remedies? What result is mandated here by *Gardner-Denver*?

5. Does the opinion unnecessarily undermine arbitral autonomy? Why not have special labor arbitrators hear Title VII claims instead of having separate recourse to the courts?

6. Does *Gardner-Denver* share *Wilko*'s antagonism toward arbitration?

7. How should the reasoning in *Gardner-Denver* apply to a non-union setting involving an employment contract?

GILMER V. INTERSTATE/JOHNSON LANE CORP.

500 U.S. 20, 111 S.Ct. 1647, 114 L.Ed.2d 26 (1991).

JUSTICE WHITE delivered the opinion of the Court.

The question presented in this case is whether a claim under the Age Discrimination in Employment Act of 1967 (ADEA) . . . can be subjected to compulsory arbitration pursuant to an arbitration agreement in a securities registration application. The Court of Appeals held that it could . . . and we affirm.

I

Respondent Interstate/Johnson Lane Corporation (Interstate) hired petitioner Robert Gilmer as a Manager of Financial Services in May 1981. As required by his employment, Gilmer registered as a securities representative with several stock exchanges, including the New York Stock Exchange (NYSE). . . . His registration application, entitled "Uniform Application for Securities Industry Registration or Transfer," provided, among other things, that Gilmer "agree[d] to arbitrate any dispute, claim or controversy" arising between him and Interstate "that is required to be arbitrated under the rules, constitutions or by-laws of the organizations with which I register." . . . Of relevance to this case, NYSE Rule 347 provides for arbitration of "[a]ny controversy between a registered representative and any member or member organization arising out of the employment or termination of employment of such registered representative." . . .

Interstate terminated Gilmer's employment in 1987, at which time Gilmer was 62 years of age. After first filing an age discrimination charge with the Equal Employment Opportunity Commission (EEOC), Gilmer subsequently brought suit in the United States District Court for the Western District of North Carolina, alleging that Interstate had discharged him because of his age, in violation of the ADEA. In response to Gilmer's complaint, Interstate filed in the District Court a motion to compel arbitration of the ADEA claim. In its motion, Interstate relied upon the arbitration agreement in Gilmer's registration application, as well as the

Federal Arbitration Act. . . . The District Court denied Interstate's motion, based on this Court's decision in *Alexander v. Gardner-Denver Co.* . . . and because it concluded that "Congress intended to protect ADEA claimants from the waiver of a judicial forum." . . . The United States Court of Appeals for the Fourth Circuit reversed, finding "nothing in the text, legislative history, or underlying purposes of the ADEA indicating a congressional intent to preclude enforcement of arbitration agreements." . . . We granted *certiorari* . . . to resolve a conflict among the Courts of Appeals regarding the arbitrability of ADEA claims.

II

[. . .]

It is by now clear that statutory claims may be the subject of an arbitration agreement, enforceable pursuant to the FAA. . . .

Although all statutory claims may not be appropriate for arbitration, "[h]aving made the bargain to arbitrate, the party should be held to it unless Congress itself has evinced an intention to preclude a waiver of judicial remedies for the statutory rights at issue." . . . In this regard, we note that the burden is on Gilmer to show that Congress intended to preclude a waiver of a judicial forum for ADEA claims. . . . If such an intention exists, it will be discoverable in the text of the ADEA, its legislative history, or an "inherent conflict" between arbitration and the ADEA's underlying purposes. . . . Throughout such an inquiry, it should be kept in mind that "questions of arbitrability must be addressed with a healthy regard for the federal policy favoring arbitration." . . .

III

Gilmer concedes that nothing in the text of the ADEA or its legislative history explicitly precludes arbitration. He argues, however, that compulsory arbitration of ADEA claims pursuant to arbitration agreements would be inconsistent with the statutory framework and purposes of the ADEA. Like the Court of Appeals, we disagree.

A

Congress enacted the ADEA in 1967 "to promote employment of older persons based on their ability rather than age; to prohibit arbitrary age discrimination in employment; [and] to help employers and workers find ways of meeting problems arising from the impact of age on employment." . . . To achieve those goals, the ADEA, among other things, makes it unlawful for an employer "to fail or refuse to hire or to discharge any individual or otherwise discriminate against any individual with respect to his compensation, terms, conditions, or privileges of employment, because of such individual's age." . . . This proscription is enforced both by private suits and by the EEOC. In order for an aggrieved individual to bring suit under the ADEA, he or she must first file a charge with the EEOC and then wait at least 60 days. . . . An individual's right to sue is extinguished, however, if the EEOC institutes an action against the employer. . . . Before the EEOC can bring such an action, though, it must "attempt to eliminate the discriminatory practice or practices alleged, and to effect voluntary compliance with the requirements of this chapter through informal methods of conciliation, conference, and persuasion." . . .

As Gilmer contends, the ADEA is designed not only to address individual grievances, but also to further important social policies. . . . We do not perceive any inherent inconsistency between those policies, however, and enforcing agreements to arbitrate age discrimination claims. It is true that arbitration focuses on specific disputes between the parties involved. The same can be said, however, of judicial resolution of claims. Both of these dispute resolution mechanisms nevertheless also can further broader social purposes. The Sherman Act, the Securities Exchange Act of 1934, RICO, and the Securities Act of 1933 all are designed to advance important public policies, but, as noted above, claims under those statutes are appropriate for arbitration. "[S]o long as the prospective litigant effectively may vindicate [his or her] statutory cause of action in the arbitral forum, the statute will continue to serve both its remedial and deterrent function." . . .

We also are unpersuaded by the argument that arbitration will undermine the role of the EEOC in enforcing the ADEA. An individual ADEA claimant subject to an arbitration agreement will still be free to file a charge with the EEOC, even though the claimant is not able to institute a private judicial action. Indeed, Gilmer filed a charge with the EEOC in this case. In any event, the EEOC's role in combating age discrimination is not dependent on the filing of a charge; the agency may receive information concerning alleged violations of the ADEA "from any source," and it has independent authority to investigate age discrimination. . . . Moreover, nothing in the ADEA indicates that Congress intended that the EEOC be involved in all employment disputes. Such disputes can be settled, for example, without any EEOC involvement. . . . Finally, the mere involvement of an administrative agency in the enforcement of a statute is not sufficient to preclude arbitration. For example, the Securities Exchange Commission is heavily involved in the enforcement of the Securities Exchange Act of 1934 and the Securities Act of 1933, but we have held that claims under both of those statutes may be subject to compulsory arbitration. . . .

Gilmer also argues that compulsory arbitration is improper because it deprives claimants of the judicial forum provided for by the ADEA. Congress, however, did not explicitly preclude arbitration or other nonjudicial resolution of claims, even in its recent amendments to the ADEA. . . . Moreover, Gilmer's argument ignores the ADEA's flexible approach to resolution of claims. The EEOC, for example, is directed to pursue "informal methods of conciliation, conference, and persuasion," . . . which suggests that out-of-court dispute resolution, such as arbitration, is consistent with the statutory scheme established by Congress. In addition, arbitration is consistent with Congress' grant of concurrent jurisdiction over ADEA claims to state and federal courts. . . .

B

In arguing that arbitration is inconsistent with the ADEA, Gilmer also raises a host of challenges to the adequacy of arbitration procedures. Initially, we note that in our recent arbitration cases we have already rejected most of these arguments as insufficient to preclude arbitration of statutory claims. . . .

Gilmer first speculates that arbitration panels will be biased. . . . [W]e note that the NYSE arbitration rules, which are applicable to the dispute in this case, provide protections against biased panels. The rules require, for example, that the parties be informed of the employment histories of the arbitrators, and that they be allowed to make further inquiries into the arbitrators' backgrounds. . . . In addition, each party is allowed one peremptory challenge and unlimited challenges for cause. . . . Moreover, the arbitrators are required to disclose "any circumstances which might preclude [them] from rendering an objective and impartial determination." . . . The FAA also protects against bias, by providing that courts may overturn arbitration decisions "[w]here there was evident partiality or corruption in the arbitrators." . . . There has been no showing in this case that those provisions are inadequate to guard against potential bias.

Gilmer also complains that the discovery allowed in arbitration is more limited than in the federal courts, which he contends will make it difficult to prove discrimination. It is unlikely, however, that age discrimination claims require more extensive discovery than other claims that we have found to be arbitrable, such as RICO and antitrust claims. Moreover, there has been no showing in this case that the NYSE discovery provisions, which allow for document production, information requests, depositions, and subpoenas, . . . will prove insufficient to allow ADEA claimants such as Gilmer a fair opportunity to present their claims. Although those procedures might not be as extensive as in the federal courts, by agreeing to arbitrate, a party "trades the procedures and opportunity for review of the courtroom for the simplicity, informality, and expedition of arbitration." . . . Indeed, an important counterweight to the reduced discovery in NYSE arbitration is that arbitrators are not bound by the rules of evidence. . . .

A further alleged deficiency of arbitration is that arbitrators often will not issue written opinions, resulting, Gilmer contends, in a lack of public knowledge of employers' discriminatory policies, an inability to obtain effective appellate review, and a stifling of the development of the law. The

NYSE rules, however, do require that all arbitration awards be in writing, and that the awards contain the names of the parties, a summary of the issues in controversy, and a description of the award issued. . . . In addition, the award decisions are made available to the public. . . . Furthermore, judicial decisions addressing ADEA claims will continue to be issued because it is unlikely that all or even most ADEA claimants will be subject to arbitration agreements. Finally, Gilmer's concerns apply equally to settlements of ADEA claims, which, as noted above, are clearly allowed.

It is also argued that arbitration procedures cannot adequately further the purposes of the ADEA because they do not provide for broad equitable relief and class actions. As the court below noted, however, arbitrators do have the power to fashion equitable relief. . . . Indeed, the NYSE rules applicable here do not restrict the types of relief an arbitrator may award, but merely refer to "damages and/or other relief." . . . The NYSE rules also provide for collective proceedings. . . . But "even if the arbitration could not go forward as a class action or class relief could not be granted by the arbitrator, the fact that the [ADEA] provides for the possibility of bringing a collective action does not mean that individual attempts at conciliation were intended to be barred." . . . Finally, it should be remembered that arbitration agreements will not preclude the EEOC from bringing actions seeking class-wide and equitable relief.

C

An additional reason advanced by Gilmer for refusing to enforce arbitration agreements relating to ADEA claims is his contention that there often will be unequal bargaining power between employers and employees. Mere inequality in bargaining power, however, is not a sufficient reason to hold that arbitration agreements are never enforceable in the employment context. Relationships between securities dealers and investors, for example, may involve unequal bargaining power, but we nevertheless held in *Rodriguez de Quijas* and *McMahon* that agreements to arbitrate in that context are enforceable. . . . There is no indication in this case, however, that Gilmer, an experienced businessman, was coerced or defrauded into agreeing to the arbitration clause in his registration application. As with the claimed procedural inadequacies discussed above, this claim of unequal bargaining power is best left for resolution in specific cases.

IV

In addition to the arguments discussed above, Gilmer vigorously asserts that our decision in *Alexander v. Gardner-Denver Co.* . . . and its progeny . . . preclude arbitration of employment discrimination claims. Gilmer's reliance on these cases, however, is misplaced.

In *Gardner-Denver*, the issue was whether a discharged employee whose grievance had been arbitrated pursuant to an arbitration clause in a collective-bargaining agreement was precluded from subsequently bringing a Title VII action based upon the conduct that was the subject of the grievance. In holding that the employee was not foreclosed from bringing the Title VII claim, we stressed that an employee's contractual rights under a collective-bargaining agreement are distinct from the employee's statutory Title VII rights:

> "In submitting his grievance to arbitration, an employee seeks to vindicate his contractual right under a collective-bargaining agreement. By contrast, in filing a lawsuit under Title VII, an employee asserts independent statutory rights accorded by Congress. The distinctly separate nature of these contractual and statutory rights is not vitiated merely because both were violated as a result of the same factual occurrence. . . ."

We also noted that a labor arbitrator has authority only to resolve questions of contractual rights. . . . The arbitrator's "task is to effectuate the intent of the parties" and he or she does not have the "general authority to invoke public laws that conflict with the bargain between the parties." . . . By contrast, "in instituting an action under Title VII, the employee is not seeking review of the arbitrator's decision. Rather, he is asserting a statutory right independent of the arbitration process." . . . We further expressed concern that in collective-bargaining arbitration "the interests of the individual employee may be subordinated to the collective interests of all employees in the bargaining unit." . . .

[. . .]

There are several important distinctions between the *Gardner-Denver* line of cases and the case before us. First, those cases did not involve the issue of the enforceability of an agreement to arbitrate statutory claims. Rather, they involved the quite different issue whether arbitration of contract-based claims precluded subsequent judicial resolution of statutory claims. Since the employees there had not agreed to arbitrate their statutory claims, and the labor arbitrators were not authorized to resolve such claims, the arbitration in those cases understandably was held not to preclude subsequent statutory actions. Second, because the arbitration in those cases occurred in the context of a collective-bargaining agreement, the claimants there were represented by their unions in the arbitration proceedings. An important concern therefore was the tension between collective representation and individual statutory rights, a concern not applicable to the present case. Finally, those cases were not decided under the FAA, which, as discussed above, reflects a "liberal federal policy favoring arbitration agreements." . . . Therefore, those cases provide no basis for refusing to enforce Gilmer's agreement to arbitrate his ADEA claim.

V

We conclude that Gilmer has not met his burden of showing that Congress, in enacting the ADEA, intended to preclude arbitration of claims under that Act. Accordingly, the judgment of the Court of Appeals is *Affirmed.*

JUSTICE STEVENS, with whom JUSTICE MARSHALL joins, dissenting.

Section 1 of the Federal Arbitration Act (FAA) states:

> "[N]othing herein contained shall apply to contracts of employment of seamen, railroad employees, or any other class of workers engaged in foreign or interstate commerce." . . .

The Court today, in holding that the FAA compels enforcement of arbitration clauses even when claims of age discrimination are at issue, skirts the antecedent question whether the coverage of the Act even extends to arbitration clauses contained in employment contracts, regardless of the subject matter of the claim at issue. In my opinion, arbitration clauses contained in employment agreements are specifically exempt from coverage of the FAA. . . .

I

[. . .]

Notwithstanding the apparent waiver of the issue below, I believe that the Court should reach the issue of the coverage of the FAA to employment disputes because resolution of the question is so clearly antecedent to disposition of this case. On a number of occasions, this Court has considered issues waived by the parties below and in the petition for certiorari because the issues were so integral to decision of the case that they could be considered "fairly subsumed" by the actual questions presented. . . .

[. . .]

II

The Court, declining to reach the issue for the reason that petitioner never raised it below, nevertheless concludes that "it would be inappropriate to address the scope of the § 1 exclusion because the arbitration clause being enforced here is not contained in a contract of employment. . . . Rather, the arbitration clause at issue is in Gilmer's securities registration application, which is a contract with the securities exchanges, not with Interstate." . . . In my opinion the Court too narrowly construes the scope of the exclusion contained in § 1 of the FAA.

There is little dispute that the primary concern animating the FAA was the perceived need by the business community to overturn the common-law rule that denied specific enforcement of agreements to arbitrate in contracts between business entities. . . . At the Senate Judiciary Subcommittee hearings on the proposed bill, the chairman of the ABA committee responsible for drafting the bill assured the Senators that the bill "is not intended [to] be an act referring to labor disputes, at all. It is purely an act to give the merchants the right or the privilege of sitting down and agreeing with each other as to what their damages are, if they want to do it. Now that is all there is in this." . . .

Given that the FAA specifically was intended to exclude arbitration agreements between employees and employers, I see no reason to limit this exclusion from coverage to arbitration clauses contained in agreements entitled "Contract of Employment." In this case, the parties conceded at oral argument that Gilmer had no "contract of employment" as such with respondent. Gilmer was, however, required as a condition of his employment to become a registered representative of several stock exchanges, including the New York Stock Exchange (NYSE). Just because his agreement to arbitrate any "dispute, claim or controversy" with his employer that arose out of the employment relationship was contained in his application for registration before the NYSE rather than in a specific contract of employment with his employer, I do not think that Gilmer can be compelled pursuant to the FAA to arbitrate his employment-related dispute. Rather, in my opinion the exclusion in § 1 should be interpreted to cover any agreements by the employee to arbitrate disputes with the employer arising out of the employment relationship, particularly where such agreements to arbitrate are conditions of employment.

My reading of the scope of the exclusion contained in § 1 is supported by early judicial interpretations of the FAA. As of 1956, three Courts of Appeals had held that the FAA's exclusion of "contracts of employment" referred not only to individual contracts of employment, but also to collective-bargaining agreements. . . . Indeed, the application of the FAA's exclusionary clause to arbitration provisions in collective-bargaining agreements was one of the issues raised in the petition for certiorari and briefed at great length in *Lincoln Mills* and its companion cases. . . . Although the Court decided the enforceability of the arbitration provisions in the collective-bargaining agreements by reference to § 301 of the Labor Management Relations Act, . . . it did not reject the Courts of Appeals' holdings that the arbitration provisions would not otherwise be enforceable pursuant to the FAA since they were specifically excluded under § 1. . . .

III

Not only would I find that the FAA does not apply to employment-related disputes between employers and employees in general, but also I would hold that compulsory arbitration conflicts with the congressional purpose animating the ADEA, in particular. As this Court previously has noted, authorizing the courts to issue broad injunctive relief is the cornerstone to eliminating discrimination in society. . . . The ADEA, like Title VII of the Civil Rights Act of 1964, authorizes courts to award broad, class-based injunctive relief to achieve the purposes of the Act. . . . Because commercial arbitration is typically limited to a specific dispute between the particular parties and because the available remedies in arbitral forums generally do not provide for class-wide injunctive relief, . . . I would conclude that an essential purpose of the ADEA is frustrated by compulsory arbitration of employment discrimination claims. Moreover, as Chief Justice Burger explained:

> "Plainly, it would not comport with the congressional objectives behind a statute seeking to enforce civil rights protected by Title VII to allow the very forces that had practiced discrimination to contract away the right to enforce civil rights in the courts. For federal courts to defer to arbitral decisions reached by the same combination of forces that had long perpetuated invidious discrimination would have made the foxes guardians of the chickens." . . .

In my opinion the same concerns expressed by Chief Justice Burger with regard to compulsory arbitration of Title VII claims may be said of claims arising under the ADEA. The Court's holding today clearly eviscerates the important role played by an independent judiciary in eradicating employment discrimination.

IV

When the FAA was passed in 1925, I doubt that any legislator who voted for it expected it to apply to statutory claims, to form contracts between parties of unequal bargaining power, or to the arbitration of disputes arising out of the employment relationship. In recent years, however, the Court "has effectively rewritten the statute," and abandoned its earlier view that statutory claims were not appropriate subjects for arbitration. . . . Although I remain persuaded that it erred in doing so, the Court has also put to one side any concern about the inequality of bargaining power between an entire industry, on the one hand, and an individual customer or employee, on the other. . . . Until today, however, the Court has not read § 2 of the FAA as broadly encompassing disputes arising out of the employment relationship. I believe this additional extension of the FAA is erroneous. Accordingly, I respectfully dissent.

NOTES AND QUESTIONS

1. In his dissent, Justice Stevens emphasizes that the contract in question is an employment contract and does not itself contain an arbitral

clause. Does the obligation to arbitrate exist by ricochet as well as by adhesive provision? Which parties agreed to arbitration? Is the agreement to arbitrate a valid contract? What does Section One of the FAA say about arbitral provisions in employment contracts?

2. Would the existence of a submission agreement alter the reasoning or result in *Gilmer*? What concerns of legality and policy would the use of a submission address in the *Gilmer* facts? Would it address the most fundamental concern? What is the most fundamental concern in *Gilmer*?

3. The majority addresses in some detail Gilmer's objections to the use of arbitration to adjudicate age discrimination claims. Evaluate the Court's statements and what they imply about the Court's attitude toward questions raised in arbitration litigation. Do you find any of the Court's statements reassuring in terms of the adjudication of political rights in arbitration?

4. At the end of the majority opinion, Justice White characterizes the agreement to arbitrate as a set of "trade-offs" accepted by the employee and minimizes the "mere inequality of bargaining position" between the parties to the agreement. Are these statements an accurate reflection of the reality of the employment situation? Don't they make the contract and the circumstances of the transaction the exclusive vehicle of legal regulation? What is left of the role of law and basic fairness? Aren't these characterizations truly astounding and a radical departure from prior judicial practice?

5. Focus upon the dissent's reference to the FAA's legislative history in terms of its application to labor matters and to the history of the arbitration of labor grievances at the end of Section II of the opinion. Doesn't the reference to these factors effectively refute the majority's absolute position on arbitration? Why doesn't the majority take this history into account? Does historical fact become irrelevant to the judicial decision-making in this area? In what other cases has the Court used legislative history in its rationale? Is it usually done in dissent, as in *Gilmer*? Is it fair to say that the Court has strayed quite far from its position in *Alexander v. Gardner-Denver Co.*? Do employees still have a "second bite at the apple"?

14 PENN PLAZA LLC V. PYETT

556 U.S. 247, 129 S.Ct. 1456, 173 L.Ed.2d 398 (2009).

JUSTICE THOMAS delivered the opinion of the Court.

The question presented by this case is whether a provision in a collective-bargaining agreement that clearly and unmistakably requires union members to arbitrate claims arising under the Age Discrimination in Employment Act of 1967 (ADEA) . . . is enforceable. The United States Court of Appeals for the Second Circuit held that this Court's decision in *Alexander* v. *Gardner-Denver Co.*, 415 U.S. 36, 94 S. Ct. 1011, 39 L. Ed. 2d 147 (1974), forbids enforcement of such arbitration provisions. We disagree and reverse the judgment of the Court of Appeals.

I

Respondents are members of the Service Employees International Union, Local 32BJ (Union). Under the National Labor Relations Act (NLRA), 49 Stat. 449, as amended, the Union is the exclusive bargaining representative of employees within the building-services industry in New York City, which includes building cleaners, porters, and doorpersons. . . . In this role, the Union has exclusive authority to bargain on behalf of its members over their "rates of pay, wages, hours of employment, or other conditions of employment." . . . Since the 1930's, the Union has engaged in industry-wide collective bargaining with the Realty Advisory Board on Labor Relations, Inc. (RAB), a multiemployer bargaining association for the New York City real-estate industry. The agreement between the Union and the RAB is embodied in their Collective Bargaining Agreement for Contractors and Building Owners (CBA). The CBA requires union members to submit all claims of employment discrimination to binding arbitration under the CBA's grievance and dispute resolution procedures.

[. . .]

Petitioner 14 Penn Plaza LLC is a member of the RAB. It owns and operates the New York City office building where, prior to August 2003, respondents worked as night lobby watchmen and in other similar capacities. Respondents were directly employed by petitioner Temco Service Industries, Inc. (Temco), a maintenance service and cleaning contractor. In August 2003, with the Union's consent, 14 Penn Plaza engaged Spartan Security, a unionized security services contractor and affiliate of Temco, to provide licensed security guards to staff the lobby and entrances of its building. Because this rendered respondents' lobby services unnecessary, Temco reassigned them to jobs as night porters and light duty cleaners in other locations in the building. Respondents contend that these reassignments led to a loss in income, caused them emotional distress, and were otherwise less desirable than their former positions.

At respondents' request, the Union filed grievances challenging the reassignments. The grievances alleged that petitioners: (1) violated the CBA's ban on workplace discrimination by reassigning respondents on account of their age; (2) violated seniority rules by failing to promote one of the respondents to a handyman position; and (3) failed to equitably rotate overtime. After failing to obtain relief on any of these claims through the grievance process, the Union requested arbitration under the CBA.

After the initial arbitration hearing, the Union withdrew the first set of respondents' grievances—the age-discrimination claims—from arbitration. Because it had consented to the contract for new security personnel at 14 Penn Plaza, the Union believed that it could not legitimately object to respondents' reassignments as discriminatory. But the Union continued to arbitrate the seniority and overtime claims, and, after several hearings, the claims were denied.

In May 2004, while the arbitration was ongoing but after the Union withdrew the age-discrimination claims, respondents filed a complaint with the Equal Employment Opportunity Commission (EEOC) alleging that petitioners had violated their rights under the ADEA. Approximately one month later, the EEOC issued a Dismissal and Notice of Rights, which explained that the agency's " 'review of the evidence . . . fail[ed] to indicate that a violation ha[d] occurred,' " and notified each respondent of his right to sue. . . .

Respondents thereafter filed suit against petitioners in the United States District Court for the Southern District of New York, alleging that their reassignment violated the ADEA and state and local laws prohibiting age discrimination. [Footnote omitted.] Petitioners filed a motion to compel arbitration of respondents' claims pursuant to § 3 and § 4 of the Federal Arbitration Act (FAA), 9 U.S.C. §§ 3, 4. [Footnote omitted.] The District Court denied the motion because under Second Circuit precedent, "even a clear and unmistakable union-negotiated waiver of a right to litigate certain federal and state statutory claims in a judicial forum is unenforceable." . . . Respondents immediately appealed the ruling under § 16 of the FAA, which authorizes an interlocutory appeal of "an order . . . refusing a stay of any action under section 3 of this title" or "denying a petition under section 4 of this title to order arbitration to proceed." . . .

The Court of Appeals affirmed. . . . According to the Court of Appeals, it could not compel arbitration of the dispute because *Gardner-Denver*, which "remains good law," held "that a collective bargaining agreement could not waive covered workers' rights to a judicial forum for causes of action created by Congress." . . . The Court of Appeals observed that the *Gardner-Denver* decision was in tension with this Court's more recent decision in *Gilmer* v. *Interstate/Johnson Lane Corp.*, 500 U.S. 20 (1991), which "held that an individual employee who had agreed individually to waive his right to a federal forum *could* be compelled to arbitrate a federal age discrimination claim." [Emphasis in the original opinion.] . . . The Court of Appeals also noted that this Court previously declined to resolve this tension in *Wright* v. *Universal Maritime Service Corp.*, 525 U.S. 70 (1998), where the waiver at issue was not "clear and unmistakable." . . .

The Court of Appeals attempted to reconcile *Gardner-Denver* and *Gilmer* by holding that arbitration provisions in a collective-bargaining agreement, "which purport to waive employees' rights to a federal forum with respect to statutory claims, are unenforceable." . . . As a result, an individual employee would be free to choose compulsory arbitration under *Gilmer*, but a labor union could not collectively bargain for arbitration on behalf of its members. We granted *certiorari,* 552 U.S. 1178, 128 S. Ct. 1223

(2008), to address the issue left unresolved in *Wright*, which continues to divide the Courts of Appeals, [footnote omitted] and now reverse.

II

A

[. . .]

In this instance, the Union and the RAB, negotiating on behalf of 14 Penn Plaza, collectively bargained in good faith and agreed that employment-related discrimination claims, including claims brought under the ADEA, would be resolved in arbitration. This freely negotiated term between the Union and the RAB easily qualifies as a "conditio[n] of employment" that is subject to mandatory bargaining under § 159(a). . . . The decision to fashion a CBA to require arbitration of employment-discrimination claims is no different from the many other decisions made by parties in designing grievance machinery.[5]

Respondents, however, contend that the arbitration clause here is outside the permissible scope of the collective-bargaining process because it affects the "employees' individual, non-economic statutory rights." . . . We disagree. Parties generally favor arbitration precisely because of the economics of dispute resolution. . . . As in any contractual negotiation, a union may agree to the inclusion of an arbitration provision in a collective-bargaining agreement in return for other concessions from the employer. Courts generally may not interfere in this bargained-for exchange. "Judicial nullification of contractual concessions . . . is contrary to what the Court has recognized as one of the fundamental policies of the National Labor Relations Act—freedom of contract." . . .

As a result, the CBA's arbitration provision must be honored unless the ADEA itself removes this particular class of grievances from the NLRA's broad sweep. . . . It does not. This Court has squarely held that the ADEA does not preclude arbitration of claims brought under the statute. . . .

In *Gilmer*, the Court explained that "[a]lthough all statutory claims may not be appropriate for arbitration, 'having made the bargain to arbitrate, the party should be held to it unless Congress itself has evinced

[5] JUSTICE SOUTER claims that this understanding is "impossible to square with our conclusion in [*Alexander* v.] *Gardner-Denver* . . . that 'Title VII . . . stands on plainly different ground' from 'statutory rights related to collective activity': 'it concerns not majoritarian processes, but an individual's right to equal employment opportunities.' " . . . (dissenting opinion) (quoting *Gardner-Denver)* . . . As explained below, however, JUSTICE SOUTER repeats the key analytical mistake made in *Gardner-Denver's dicta* by equating the decision to arbitrate Title VII and ADEA claims to a decision to forgo these substantive guarantees against workplace discrimination. . . . The right to a judicial forum is not the nonwaivable "substantive" right protected by the ADEA. . . . Thus, although Title VII and ADEA rights may well stand on "different ground" than statutory rights that protect "majoritarian processes," . . . the voluntary decision to collectively bargain for arbitration does not deny those statutory antidiscrimination rights the full protection they are due.

an intention to preclude a waiver of judicial remedies for the statutory rights at issue.' " . . . And "if Congress intended the substantive protection afforded by the ADEA to include protection against waiver of the right to a judicial forum, that intention will be deducible from text or legislative history." . . . The Court determined that "nothing in the text of the ADEA or its legislative history explicitly precludes arbitration." . . . The Court also concluded that arbitrating ADEA disputes would not undermine the statute's "remedial and deterrent function." . . . In the end, the employee's "generalized attacks" on "the adequacy of arbitration procedures" were "insufficient to preclude arbitration of statutory claims," . . . because there was no evidence that "Congress, in enacting the ADEA, intended to preclude arbitration of claims under that Act." . . .

The *Gilmer* Court's interpretation of the ADEA fully applies in the collective-bargaining context. Nothing in the law suggests a distinction between the status of arbitration agreements signed by an individual employee and those agreed to by a union representative. This Court has required only that an agreement to arbitrate statutory antidiscrimination claims be "explicitly stated" in the collective-bargaining agreement. *Wright*, 525 U.S., at 80. . . . The CBA under review here meets that obligation. Respondents incorrectly counter that an individual employee must personally "waive" a "[substantive] right" to proceed in court for a waiver to be "knowing and voluntary" under the ADEA. . . . As explained below, however, the agreement to arbitrate ADEA claims is not the waiver of a "substantive right" as that term is employed in the ADEA. . . . Indeed, if the "right" referred to in § 626(f)(1) included the prospective waiver of the right to bring an ADEA claim in court, even a waiver signed by an individual employee would be invalid as the statute also prevents individuals from "waiv[ing] rights or claims that may arise after the date the waiver is executed." § 626(f)(1)(C).[6]

Examination of the two federal statutes at issue in this case, therefore, yields a straightforward answer to the question presented: The NLRA provided the Union and the RAB with statutory authority to collectively bargain for arbitration of workplace discrimination claims, and Congress did not terminate that authority with respect to federal age-discrimination

[6] Respondents' contention that § 118 of the Civil Rights Act of 1991 . . . precludes the enforcement of this arbitration agreement also is misplaced. . . . Section 118 expresses Congress' support for alternative dispute resolution: "Where appropriate and to the extent authorized by law, the use of alternative means of dispute resolution, including . . . arbitration, is encouraged to resolve disputes arising under" the ADEA. . . . Respondents argue that the legislative history actually signals Congress' intent to preclude arbitration waivers in the collective-bargaining context. In particular, respondents point to a House Report that, in spite of the statute's plain language, interprets § 118 to support their position. . . . But the legislative history mischaracterizes the holding of *Gardner-Denver*, which does not prohibit collective bargaining for arbitration of ADEA claims. . . . Moreover, reading the legislative history in the manner suggested by respondents would create a direct conflict with the statutory text, which encourages the use of arbitration for dispute resolution without imposing any constraints on collective bargaining. In such a contest, the text must prevail. . . .

claims in the ADEA. Accordingly, there is no legal basis for the Court to strike down the arbitration clause in this CBA, which was freely negotiated by the Union and the RAB, and which clearly and unmistakably requires respondents to arbitrate the age-discrimination claims at issue in this appeal. Congress has chosen to allow arbitration of ADEA claims. The Judiciary must respect that choice.

B

The CBA's arbitration provision is also fully enforceable under the *Gardner-Denver* line of cases. Respondents interpret *Gardner-Denver* and its progeny to hold that "a union cannot waive an employee's right to a judicial forum under the federal antidiscrimination statutes" because "allowing the union to waive this right would substitute the union's interests for the employee's antidiscrimination rights." . . . The "combination of union control over the process and inherent conflict of interest with respect to discrimination claims," they argue, "provided the foundation for the Court's holding [in *Gardner-Denver*] that arbitration under a collective-bargaining agreement could not preclude an individual employee's right to bring a lawsuit in court to vindicate a statutory discrimination claim." . . . We disagree.

1

The holding of *Gardner-Denver* is not as broad as respondents suggest. The employee in that case was covered by a collective-bargaining agreement that prohibited "discrimination against any employee on account of race, color, religion, sex, national origin, or ancestry" and that guaranteed that "[n]o employee will be discharged . . . except for just cause." . . . The agreement also included a "multistep grievance procedure" that culminated in compulsory arbitration for any "differences aris[ing] between the Company and the Union as to the meaning and application of the provisions of this Agreement" and "any trouble aris[ing] in the plant." . . .

The employee was discharged. . . . He filed a grievance with his union claiming that he was " 'unjustly discharged.' " . . . Then at the final prearbitration step of the grievance process, the employee added a claim that he was discharged because of his race. . . .

The arbitrator ultimately ruled that the employee had been " 'discharged for just cause,' " but "made no reference to [the] claim of racial discrimination." . . . After obtaining a right-to-sue letter from the EEOC, the employee filed a claim in Federal District Court, alleging racial discrimination in violation of Title VII of the Civil Rights Act of 1964. The District Court issued a decision, affirmed by the Court of Appeals, which granted summary judgment to the employer because [of the submission to arbitration]. . . .

This Court reversed the judgment on the narrow ground that the arbitration was not preclusive because the collective-bargaining agreement did not cover statutory claims. . . . Because the collective-bargaining agreement gave the arbitrator "authority to resolve only questions of contractual rights," his decision could not prevent the employee from bringing the Title VII claim in federal court "regardless of whether certain contractual rights are similar to, or duplicative of, the substantive rights secured by Title VII." . . .

[. . .]

The Court's decisions following *Gardner-Denver* have not broadened its holding to make it applicable to the facts of this case. In *Barrentine* v. *Arkansas-Best Freight System, Inc.*, 450 U.S. 728 (1981), the Court considered "whether an employee may bring an action in federal district court, alleging a violation of the minimum wage provisions of the Fair Labor Standards Act, . . . after having unsuccessfully submitted a wage claim based on the same underlying facts to a joint grievance committee pursuant to the provisions of his union's collective-bargaining agreement." . . . The Court held that the unsuccessful arbitration did not preclude the federal lawsuit. Like the collective-bargaining agreement in *Gardner-Denver*, the arbitration provision under review in *Barrentine* did not expressly reference the statutory claim at issue. . . .

McDonald v. *West Branch,* 466 U.S. 284 (1984), was decided along similar lines. The question presented in that case was "whether a federal court may accord preclusive effect to an unappealed arbitration award in a case brought under [42 U.S.C. § 1983]." . . . The Court declined to fashion such a rule, again explaining that "because an arbitrator's authority derives solely from the contract, . . . an arbitrator may not have authority to enforce § 1983" when that provision is left unaddressed by the arbitration agreement. . . . Accordingly, as in both *Gardner-Denver* and *Barrentine*, the Court's decision in *McDonald* hinged on the scope of the collective-bargaining agreement and the arbitrator's parallel mandate.

The facts underlying *Gardner-Denver*, *Barrentine*, and *McDonald* reveal the narrow scope of the legal rule arising from that trilogy of decisions. Summarizing those opinions in *Gilmer*, this Court made clear that the *Gardner-Denver* line of cases "did not involve the issue of the enforceability of an agreement to arbitrate statutory claims." . . . Those decisions instead "involved the quite different issue whether arbitration of contract-based claims precluded subsequent judicial resolution of statutory claims. Since the employees there had not agreed to arbitrate their statutory claims, and the labor arbitrators were not authorized to resolve such claims, the arbitration in those cases understandably was held not to preclude subsequent statutory actions." . . .[7] *Gardner-Denver* and its progeny thus do not control the outcome where, as is the case here, the collective-bargaining agreement's arbitration provision expressly covers both statutory and contractual discrimination claims.[8]

2

We recognize that apart from their narrow holdings, the *Gardner-Denver* line of cases included broad *dicta* that was highly critical of the use of arbitration for the vindication of statutory antidiscrimination rights. That skepticism, however, rested on a misconceived view of arbitration that this Court has since abandoned.

First, the Court in *Gardner-Denver* erroneously assumed that an agreement to submit statutory discrimination claims to arbitration was tantamount to a waiver of those rights. . . . For this reason, the Court stated, "the rights conferred [by Title VII] can form no part of the collective-bargaining process since waiver of these rights would defeat the paramount congressional purpose behind Title VII." . . .

The Court was correct in concluding that federal antidiscrimination rights may not be prospectively waived, . . . but it confused an agreement to arbitrate those statutory claims with a prospective waiver of the substantive right. The decision to resolve ADEA claims by way of arbitration instead of litigation does not waive the statutory right to be free from workplace age discrimination; it waives only the right to seek relief from a court in the first instance. . . . This "Court has been quite specific in holding that arbitration agreements can be enforced under the FAA without contravening the policies of congressional enactments giving employees specific protection against discrimination prohibited by federal law." . . . The suggestion in *Gardner-Denver* that the decision to arbitrate statutory discrimination claims was tantamount to a substantive waiver of

[7] JUSTICE SOUTER'S reliance on *Wright* v. *Universal Maritime Service Corp.*, 525 U.S. 70 (1998), to support its view of *Gardner-Denver* is misplaced. . . . *Wright* identified the "tension" between the two lines of cases represented by *Gardner-Denver* and *Gilmer*, but found "it unnecessary to resolve the question of the validity of a union-negotiated waiver, since it [was] apparent . . . on the facts and arguments presented . . . that no such waiver [had] occurred." . . . And although his dissent describes *Wright's* characterization of *Gardner-Denver* as "raising a 'seemingly absolute prohibition of union waiver of employees' federal forum rights,' " . . . it wrenches the statement out of context: "Although [the right to a judicial forum] is not a substantive right, see *Gilmer*, . . . and *whether or not Gardner-Denver's* seemingly absolute prohibition of union waiver of employees' federal forum rights *survives Gilmer, Gardner-Denver* at least stands for the proposition that the right to a federal judicial forum is of sufficient importance to be protected against less-than-explicit union waiver in a CBA," . . . [emphasis added by the majority opinion]. *Wright* therefore neither endorsed *Gardner-Denver's* broad language nor suggested a particular result in this case.

[8] Because today's decision does not contradict the holding of *Gardner-Denver*, we need not resolve the *stare decisis* concerns raised by the dissenting opinions. . . . But given the development of this Court's arbitration jurisprudence in the intervening years, . . . *Gardner-Denver* would appear to be a strong candidate for overruling if the dissents' broad view of its holding . . . were correct. . . .

those rights, therefore, reveals a distorted understanding of the compromise made when an employee agrees to compulsory arbitration.

In this respect, *Gardner-Denver* is a direct descendant of the Court's decision in *Wilko* v. *Swan*, 346 U.S. 427 (1953), which held that an agreement to arbitrate claims under the Securities Act of 1933 was unenforceable. . . . The Court subsequently overruled *Wilko* and, in so doing, characterized the decision as "pervaded by . . . 'the old judicial hostility to arbitration.' " . . . The Court added: "To the extent that *Wilko* rested on suspicion of arbitration as a method of weakening the protections afforded in the substantive law to would-be complainants, it has fallen far out of step with our current strong endorsement of the federal statutes favoring this method of resolving disputes." . . . The timeworn "mistrust of the arbitral process" harbored by the Court in *Gardner-Denver* thus weighs against reliance on anything more than its core holding. . . . Indeed, in light of the "radical change, over two decades, in the Court's receptivity to arbitration," . . . reliance on any judicial decision similarly littered with *Wilko's* overt hostility to the enforcement of arbitration agreements would be ill advised.[9]

Second, *Gardner-Denver* mistakenly suggested that certain features of arbitration made it a forum "well suited to the resolution of contractual disputes," but "a comparatively inappropriate forum for the final resolution of rights created by Title VII." . . . According to the Court, the "factfinding process in arbitration" is "not equivalent to judicial factfinding" and the "informality of arbitral procedure . . . makes arbitration a less appropriate forum for final resolution of Title VII issues than the federal courts." . . . The Court also questioned the competence of arbitrators to decide federal statutory claims. . . .

These misconceptions have been corrected. For example, the Court has "recognized that arbitral tribunals are readily capable of handling the factual and legal complexities of antitrust claims, notwithstanding the absence of judicial instruction and supervision" and that "there is no reason

---

[9] JUSTICE STEVENS suggests that the Court is displacing its "earlier determination of the relevant provisions' meaning" based on a "preference for arbitration." . . . But his criticism lacks any basis. We are not revisiting a settled issue or disregarding an earlier determination; the Court is simply deciding the question identified in *Wright* as unresolved. . . . And, contrary to JUSTICE STEVENS' accusation, it is the Court's fidelity to the ADEA's text—not an alleged preference for arbitration—that dictates the answer to the question presented. As *Gilmer* explained, nothing in the text of Title VII or the ADEA precludes contractual arbitration, . . . and JUSTICE STEVENS has never suggested otherwise. Rather, he has always contended that permitting the "compulsory arbitration" of employment discrimination claims conflicts with his perception of "the congressional purpose animating the ADEA." . . . The *Gilmer* Court did not adopt JUSTICE STEVENS' personal view of the purposes underlying the ADEA, for good reason: That view is not embodied within the statute's text. Accordingly, it is not the statutory text that JUSTICE STEVENS has sought to vindicate—it is instead his own "preference" for mandatory judicial review, which he disguises as a search for congressional purpose. This Court is not empowered to incorporate such a preference into the text of a federal statute. . . . It is for this reason, and not because of a "policy favoring arbitration," . . . that the Court overturned *Wilko* v. *Swan*. . . . And it is why we disavow the antiarbitration *dicta* of *Gardner-Denver* and its progeny today.

to assume at the outset that arbitrators will not follow the law." . . . An arbitrator's capacity to resolve complex questions of fact and law extends with equal force to discrimination claims brought under the ADEA. Moreover, the recognition that arbitration procedures are more streamlined than federal litigation is not a basis for finding the forum somehow inadequate; the relative informality of arbitration is one of the chief reasons that parties select arbitration. Parties "trad[e] the procedures and opportunity for review of the courtroom for the simplicity, informality, and expedition of arbitration." . . . In any event, "[i]t is unlikely . . . that age discrimination claims require more extensive discovery than other claims that we have found to be arbitrable, such as RICO and antitrust claims." . . . At bottom, objections centered on the nature of arbitration do not offer a credible basis for discrediting the choice of that forum to resolve statutory antidiscrimination claims.[10]

Third, the Court in *Gardner-Denver* raised in a footnote a "further concern" regarding "the union's exclusive control over the manner and extent to which an individual grievance is presented." . . . The Court suggested that in arbitration, as in the collective-bargaining process, a union may subordinate the interests of an individual employee to the collective interests of all employees in the bargaining unit. . . .

We cannot rely on this judicial policy concern as a source of authority for introducing a qualification into the ADEA that is not found in its text. Absent a constitutional barrier, "it is not for us to substitute our view of . . . policy for the legislation which has been passed by Congress." . . . Congress is fully equipped "to identify any category of claims as to which agreements to arbitrate will be held unenforceable." . . . Until Congress amends the ADEA to meet the conflict-of-interest concern identified in the *Gardner-Denver dicta*, and seized on by respondents here, there is "no reason to color the lens through which the arbitration clause is read" simply because of an alleged conflict of interest between a union and its members. . . . This is a "battl[e] that should be fought among the political branches and the industry. Those parties should not seek to amend the statute by appeal to the Judicial Branch." . . .

The conflict-of-interest argument also proves too much. Labor unions certainly balance the economic interests of some employees against the needs of the larger work force as they negotiate collective-bargain agreements and implement them on a daily basis. But this attribute of organized labor does not justify singling out an arbitration provision for disfavored treatment. This "principle of majority rule" to which

[10] Moreover, an arbitrator's decision as to whether a unionized employee has been discriminated against on the basis of age in violation of the ADEA remains subject to judicial review under the FAA. 9 U.S.C. § 10(a). "[A]lthough judicial scrutiny of arbitration awards necessarily is limited, such review is sufficient to ensure that arbitrators comply with the requirements of the statute." . . .

respondents object is in fact the central premise of the NLRA. . . . It was Congress' verdict that the benefits of organized labor outweigh the sacrifice of individual liberty that this system necessarily demands. Respondents' argument that they were deprived of the right to pursue their ADEA claims in federal court by a labor union with a conflict of interest is therefore unsustainable; it amounts to a collateral attack on the NLRA.

In any event, Congress has accounted for this conflict of interest in several ways. As indicated above, the NLRA has been interpreted to impose a "duty of fair representation" on labor unions, which a union breaches "when its conduct toward a member of the bargaining unit is arbitrary, discriminatory, or in bad faith." . . . This duty extends to "challenges leveled not only at a union's contract administration and enforcement efforts but at its negotiation activities as well." . . . Thus, a union is subject to liability under the NLRA if it illegally discriminates against older workers in either the formation or governance of the collective-bargaining agreement, such as by deciding not to pursue a grievance on behalf of one of its members for discriminatory reasons. . . . Respondents in fact brought a fair representation suit against the Union based on its withdrawal of support for their age-discrimination claims. . . . Given this avenue that Congress has made available to redress a union's violation of its duty to its members, it is particularly inappropriate to ask this Court to impose an artificial limitation on the collective-bargaining process.

In addition, a union is subject to liability under the ADEA if the union itself discriminates against its members on the basis of age. . . . Union members may also file age-discrimination claims with the EEOC and the National Labor Relations Board, which may then seek judicial intervention under this Court's precedent. . . . In sum, Congress has provided remedies for the situation where a labor union is less than vigorous in defense of its members' claims of discrimination under the ADEA.

III

Finally, respondents offer a series of arguments contending that the particular CBA at issue here does not clearly and unmistakably require them to arbitrate their ADEA claims. . . . But respondents did not raise these contract-based arguments in the District Court or the Court of Appeals. To the contrary, respondents acknowledged on appeal that the CBA provision requiring arbitration of their federal antidiscrimination statutory claims "is sufficiently explicit" in precluding their federal lawsuit. . . . In light of respondents' litigating position, both lower courts assumed that the CBA's arbitration clause clearly applied to respondents and proceeded to decide the question left unresolved in *Wright*. We granted review of the question presented on that understanding.

[. . .]

Respondents also argue that the CBA operates as a substantive waiver of their ADEA rights because it not only precludes a federal lawsuit, but also allows the Union to block arbitration of these claims. . . . Petitioners contest this characterization of the CBA . . . and offer record evidence suggesting that the Union has allowed respondents to continue with the arbitration even though the Union has declined to participate. . . . But not only does this question require resolution of contested factual allegations, it was not fully briefed to this or any court and is not fairly encompassed within the question presented. . . . Thus, although a substantive waiver of federally protected civil rights will not be upheld, . . . we are not positioned to resolve in the first instance whether the CBA allows the Union to prevent respondents from "effectively vindicating" their "federal statutory rights in the arbitral forum." . . . Resolution of this question at this juncture would be particularly inappropriate in light of our hesitation to invalidate arbitration agreements on the basis of speculation. . . .

IV

We hold that a collective-bargaining agreement that clearly and unmistakably requires union members to arbitrate ADEA claims is enforceable as a matter of federal law. The judgment of the Court of Appeals is reversed, and the case is remanded for further proceedings consistent with this opinion.

It is so ordered.

JUSTICE STEVENS, dissenting.

JUSTICE SOUTER'S dissenting opinion, which I join in full, explains why our decision in *Alexander* v. *Gardner-Denver Co.*, 415 U.S. 36 (1974), answers the question presented in this case. My concern regarding the Court's subversion of precedent to the policy favoring arbitration prompts these additional remarks.

Notwithstanding the absence of change in any relevant statutory provision, the Court has recently retreated from, and in some cases reversed, prior decisions based on its changed view of the merits of arbitration. Previously, the Court approached with caution questions involving a union's waiver of an employee's right to raise statutory claims in a federal judicial forum. After searching the text and purposes of Title VII of the Civil Rights Act of 1964, the Court in *Gardner-Denver* held that a clause of a collective-bargaining agreement (CBA) requiring arbitration of discrimination claims could not waive an employee's right to a judicial forum for statutory claims. . . . The Court's decision rested on several features of the statute, including the individual nature of the rights it confers, the broad remedial powers it grants federal courts, and its expressed preference for overlapping remedies. . . . The Court also noted the problem of entrusting a union with certain arbitration decisions given the potential conflict between the collective interest and the interests of an individual employee seeking to assert his rights. . . .

The statutes construed by the Court in the foregoing cases and in *Wilko* v. *Swan*, 346 U.S. 427 (1953), have not since been amended in any relevant respect. But the Court has in a number of cases replaced our predecessors' statutory analysis with judicial reasoning espousing a policy favoring arbitration and thereby reached divergent results. I dissented in those cases to express concern that my colleagues were making policy choices not made by Congress. . . .

Today the majority's preference for arbitration again leads it to disregard our precedent. Although it purports to ascertain the relationship between the Age Discrimination in Employment Act of 1967 (ADEA), the National Labor Relations Act, and the Federal Arbitration Act, the Court ignores our earlier determination of the relevant provisions' meaning. The Court concludes that "[i]t was Congress' verdict that the benefits of organized labor outweigh the sacrifice of individual liberty" that the system of organized labor "necessarily demands," even when the sacrifice demanded is a judicial forum for asserting an individual statutory right. . . . But in *Gardner-Denver* we determined that "Congress' verdict" was otherwise when we held that Title VII does not permit a CBA to waive an employee's right to a federal judicial forum. Because the purposes and relevant provisions of Title VII and the ADEA are not meaningfully distinguishable, it is only by reexamining the statutory questions resolved in *Gardner-Denver* through the lens of the policy favoring arbitration that the majority now reaches a different result. [Asterisk omitted.]

[. . .]

As was true in *Rodriguez de Quijas*, there are competing arguments in this case regarding the interaction of the relevant statutory provisions. But the Court in *Gardner-Denver* considered these arguments, including "the federal policy favoring arbitration of labor disputes," . . . and held that Congress did not intend to permit the result petitioners seek. In the absence of an intervening amendment to the relevant statutory language, we are bound by that decision. It is for Congress, rather than this Court, to reassess the policy arguments favoring arbitration and revise the relevant provisions to reflect its views.

JUSTICE SOUTER, with whom JUSTICE STEVENS, JUSTICE GINSBURG, and JUSTICE BREYER join, dissenting.

The issue here is whether employees subject to a collective-bargaining agreement (CBA) providing for conclusive arbitration of all grievances, including claimed breaches of the Age Discrimination in Employment Act of 1967 (ADEA), . . . lose their statutory right to bring an ADEA claim in court, § 626(c). Under the 35-year-old holding in *Alexander* v. *Gardner-*

Denver Co. . . . , they do not, and I would adhere to *stare decisis* and so hold today.

I

Like Title VII of the Civil Rights Act of 1964, . . . the ADEA is aimed at " 'the elimination of discrimination in the workplace,' " . . . and, again like Title VII, the ADEA "contains a vital element. . . : It grants an injured employee a right of action to obtain the authorized relief". . . . "Any person aggrieved" under the Act "may bring a civil action in any court of competent jurisdiction for legal or equitable relief," 29 U.S.C. § 626(c), thereby "not only redress[ing] his own injury but also vindicat[ing] the important congressional policy against discriminatory employment practices,". . . .

Gardner-Denver considered the effect of a CBA's arbitration clause on an employee's right to sue under Title VII. One of the employer's arguments was that the CBA entered into by the union had waived individual employees' statutory cause of action subject to a judicial remedy for discrimination in violation of Title VII. Although Title VII, like the ADEA, "does not speak expressly to the relationship between federal courts and the grievance-arbitration machinery of collective-bargaining agreements," . . . we unanimously held that "the rights conferred" by Title VII (with no exception for the right to a judicial forum) cannot be waived as "part of the collective bargaining process." . . . We stressed the contrast between two categories of rights in labor and employment law. There were "statutory rights related to collective activity," which "are conferred on employees collectively to foster the processes of bargaining[, which] properly may be exercised or relinquished by the union as collective-bargaining agent to obtain economic benefits for union members." . . . But "Title VII . . . stands on plainly different [categorical] ground; it concerns not majoritarian processes, but an individual's right to equal employment opportunities." . . . Thus, as the Court previously realized, *Gardner-Denver* imposed a "seemingly absolute prohibition of union waiver of employees' federal forum rights." . . .[1]

We supported the judgment with several other lines of complementary reasoning. First, we explained that antidiscrimination statutes "have long evinced a general intent to accord parallel or overlapping remedies against discrimination," and Title VII's statutory scheme carried "no suggestion . . . that a prior arbitral decision either forecloses an individual's right to sue or divests federal courts of jurisdiction." . . . We accordingly concluded that "an individual does not forfeit his private cause of action if he first pursues his grievance to final arbitration under the nondiscrimination clause of a collective-bargaining agreement." . . .

---

1 *Gardner-Denver* also contained some language seemingly prohibiting even individual prospective waiver of federal forum rights . . . an issue revisited in *Gilmer* v. *Interstate/Johnson Lane Corp.* . . . and not disputed here.

Second, we rejected the District Court's view that simply participating in the arbitration amounted to electing the arbitration remedy and waiving the plaintiff's right to sue. We said that the arbitration agreement at issue covered only a contractual right under the CBA to be free from discrimination, not the "independent statutory rights accorded by Congress" in Title VII. . . . Third, we rebuffed the employer's argument that federal courts should defer to arbitral rulings. We declined to make the "assumption that arbitral processes are commensurate with judicial processes," . . . and described arbitration as "a less appropriate forum for final resolution of Title VII issues than the federal courts." . . .

Finally, we took note that "[i]n arbitration, as in the collective bargaining process, the interests of the individual employee may be subordinated to the collective interests of all employees in the bargaining unit," . . . a result we deemed unacceptable when it came to Title VII claims. In sum, *Gardner-Denver* held that an individual's statutory right of freedom from discrimination and access to court for enforcement were beyond a union's power to waive.

Our analysis of Title VII in *Gardner-Denver* is just as pertinent to the ADEA in this case. The "interpretation of Title VII . . . applies with equal force in the context of age discrimination, for the substantive provisions of the ADEA 'were derived *in haec verba* from Title VII,'" and indeed neither petitioners nor the Court points to any relevant distinction between the two statutes. . . . Given the unquestionable applicability of the *Gardner-Denver* rule to this ADEA issue, the argument that its precedent be followed in this case of statutory interpretation is equally unquestionable. . . . And "[c]onsiderations of *stare decisis* have special force" over an issue of statutory interpretation, which is unlike constitutional interpretation owing to the capacity of Congress to alter any reading we adopt simply by amending the statute. . . . Once we have construed a statute, stability is the rule, and "we will not depart from [it] without some compelling justification." . . . There is no argument for abandoning precedent here, and *Gardner-Denver* controls.

II

The majority evades the precedent of *Gardner-Denver* as long as it can simply by ignoring it. The Court never mentions the case before concluding that the ADEA and the National Labor Relations Act, . . . "yiel[d] a straightforward answer to the question presented," . . . that is, that unions can bargain away individual rights to a federal forum for antidiscrimination claims. If this were a case of first impression, it would at least be possible to consider that conclusion, but the issue is settled and the time is too late by 35 years to make the bald assertion that "[n]othing in the law suggests a distinction between the status of arbitration agreements signed by an individual employee and those agreed to by a union representative." . . . In fact, we recently and unanimously said that the principle that "federal forum rights cannot be waived in union-negotiated CBAs even if they can be waived in individually executed contracts . . . assuredly finds support in" our case law, *Wright*, . . . and every Court of Appeals save one has read our decisions as holding to this position . . . ("an individual may prospectively waive his own statutory right to a judicial forum, but his union may not prospectively waive that right for him. All of the circuits to have considered the meaning of *Gardner-Denver* after *Gilmer,* other than the Fourth, are in accord with this view").

Equally at odds with existing law is the majority's statement that "[t]he decision to fashion a CBA to require arbitration of employment-discrimination claims is no different from the many other decisions made by parties in designing grievance machinery." . . . That is simply impossible to square with our conclusion in *Gardner-Denver* that "Title VII . . . stands on plainly different ground" from "statutory rights related to collective activity": "it concerns not majoritarian processes, but an individual's right to equal employment opportunities." . . . ("[N]otwithstanding the strong policies encouraging arbitration, 'different considerations apply where the employee's claim is based on rights arising out of a statute designed to provide minimum substantive guarantees to individual workers' "). . . .

When the majority does speak to *Gardner-Denver*, it misreads the case in claiming that it turned solely "on the narrow ground that the arbitration was not preclusive because the collective-bargaining agreement did not cover statutory claims." . . . That, however, was merely one of several reasons given in support of the decision, . . . and we raised it to explain why the District Court made a mistake in thinking that the employee lost his Title VII rights by electing to pursue the contractual arbitration remedy. . . . One need only read *Gardner-Denver* itself to know that it was not at all so narrowly reasoned, and we have noted already how later cases have made this abundantly clear. . . .

. . . Indeed, if the Court can read *Gardner-Denver* as resting on nothing more than a contractual failure to reach as far as statutory claims, it must think the Court has been wreaking havoc on the truth for years, since (as noted) we have unanimously described the case as raising a "seemingly absolute prohibition of union waiver of employees' federal forum rights." *Wright* . . . .[2] Human ingenuity is not equal to the task of reconciling statements like this with the majority's representation that *Gardner-*

[2] The majority seems inexplicably to think that the statutory right to a federal forum is not a right, or that *Gardner-Denver* failed to recognize it because it is not "substantive." . . . But *Gardner-Denver* forbade union waiver of employees' federal forum rights in large part because of the importance of such rights and a fear that unions would too easily give them up to benefit the many at the expense of the few, a far less salient concern when only economic interests are at stake. . . .

Denver held only that "the arbitration was not preclusive because the collective-bargaining agreement did not cover statutory claims." . . .[3]

Nor, finally, does the majority have any better chance of being rid of another of *Gardner-Denver's* statements supporting its rule of decision, set out and repeated in previous quotations: "in arbitration, as in the collective-bargaining process, a union may subordinate the interests of an individual employee to the collective interests of all employees in the bargaining unit," . . . an unacceptable result when it comes to "an individual's right to equal employment opportunities." . . . The majority tries to diminish this reasoning, and the previously stated holding it supported, by making the remarkable rejoinder that "[w]e cannot rely on this judicial policy concern as a source of authority for introducing a qualification into the ADEA that is not found in its text." . . .[4] It is enough to recall that respondents are not seeking to "introduc[e] a qualification into" the law; they are justifiably relying on statutory-interpretation precedent decades old, never overruled, and serially reaffirmed over the years. . . . With that precedent on the books, it makes no sense for the majority to claim that "judicial policy concern[s]" about unions sacrificing individual antidiscrimination rights should be left to Congress.

For that matter, Congress has unsurprisingly understood *Gardner-Denver* the way we have repeatedly explained it and has operated on the assumption that a CBA cannot waive employees' rights to a judicial forum to enforce antidiscrimination statutes. . . . And Congress apparently does not share the Court's demotion of *Gardner-Denver's* holding to a suspect judicial policy concern: "Congress has had [over] 30 years in which it could have corrected our decision . . . if it disagreed with it, and has chosen not to do so. We should accord weight to this continued acceptance of our earlier holding." . . .

---

[3] There is no comfort for the Court in making the one point on which we are in accord, that *Gardner-Denver* relied in part on what the majority describes as "broad *dicta* that was highly critical of the use of arbitration for the vindication of statutory antidiscrimination rights." . . . I agree that *Gardner-Denver's* " 'mistrust of the arbitral process' . . . has been undermined by our recent arbitration decisions," . . . but if the statements are "*dicta*," their obsolescence is as irrelevant to *Gardner-Denver's* continued vitality as their currency was to the case's holding when it came down; in *Gardner-Denver* itself we acknowledged "the federal policy favoring arbitration," . . . but nonetheless held that a union could not waive its members' statutory right to a federal forum in a CBA.

[4] The majority says it would be "particularly inappropriate" to consider *Gardner-Denver's* conflict-of-interest rationale because "Congress has made available" another "avenue" to protect workers against union discrimination, namely, a duty of fair representation claim. . . . This answer misunderstands the law, for unions may decline for a variety of reasons to pursue potentially meritorious discrimination claims without succumbing to a member's suit for failure of fair representation. . . . More importantly, we have rejected precisely this argument in the past, making this yet another occasion where the majority ignores precedent. . . . And we were wise to reject it. When the Court construes statutes to allow a union to eliminate a statutory right to sue in favor of arbitration in which the union cannot represent the employee because it agreed to the employer's challenged action, it is not very consoling to add that the employee can sue the union for being unfair.

III

On one level, the majority opinion may have little effect, for it explicitly reserves the question whether a CBA's waiver of a judicial forum is enforceable when the union controls access to and presentation of employees' claims in arbitration, . . . which "is usually the case,". . . . But as a treatment of precedent in statutory interpretation, the majority's opinion cannot be reconciled with the *Gardner-Denver* Court's own view of its holding, repeated over the years and generally understood, and I respectfully dissent.

NOTES AND QUESTIONS

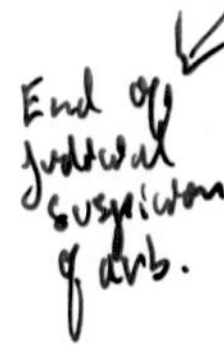

1. The significance of *14 Penn Plaza* can hardly be understated. It represents the reversal, in effect, of a major precedent in both arbitration law and civil rights, at the point at which the two converge. In some respects, it speaks to the end of an era and the beginning of another. Can you speculate as to the transition that is being arguably effectuated? How does the majority discredit the ruling in *Gardner-Denver*? Which policy is triumphant?

2. What did *Gardner-Denver* provide before it underwent a "make-over"? Justice Souter's dissenting opinion is particularly eloquent on this score. It is perhaps Justice Souter's most persuasive and analytically sophisticated writing on arbitration (or, more accurately, civil rights). As between the majority and Justice Souter's dissent, which opinion better achieves the best interest of the United States?

3. What does Justice Stevens' dissent add to the debate?

4. Do you agree with the majority's characterization of *Gardner-Denver*? Why and why not?

5. What law-making function does *Gilmer* now play in the arbitrability debate?

6. Do you believe that Justice Thomas and the other members of the majority (all conservatives) trust the labor unions? How would he (or they) answer that question? What about the union conflict-of-interest argument?

7. Is arbitration, once chosen, final, binding, and jurisdictionally exclusive in all contexts and circumstances after *14 Penn Plaza*?

8. Does *14 Penn Plaza* add fuel to the fire of the critics of arbitration and prepare a confrontation on the floor of the Congress that may foil the Court's "work product" on arbitration that has been in-the-making for more than fifty years? How might the Court have taken that factor into account? Should or could it have?

9. Explain what Justice Souter means when he says at the end of his opinion, that "the majority [opinion] . . . may have little effect."

10. How does each side of the Court use the notions of *stare decisis* and judicial restraint?

11. What do you make of the fact that Justice Powell authored the opinion in *Gardner-Denver* and Justice Thomas spoke for the majority in *14 Penn Plaza*?

3. BANKRUPTCY

IN RE STATEWIDE REALTY CO.

159 B.R. 719 (Bankr. D.N.J. 1993).

[. . .]

The Federal Arbitration Act establishes a strong federal policy which favors arbitration, and which requires that agreements to arbitrate are rigorously enforced even where a party bound by such an agreement asserts a claim based on statutory rights. . . .

The controlling precedent in this circuit for a determination of whether the Bankruptcy Code provisions are in conflict with the arbitration clause is *Hays & Co. v. Merrill Lynch, Pierce, Fenner & Smith, Inc.*, 885 F.2d 1149 (3d Cir.1989). . . .

The court in *Hays* held that a trustee is bound by the terms of an arbitration clause to the same extent as the debtor would be, but that the trustee's Code § 544(b) claims are not subject to arbitration because they are not derivative of the debtor, and the trustee accordingly is not bound by the terms of the arbitration clause in the agreement. . . . Moreover, relying on *McMahon*, the *Hays* court held that the district court erred in its determination that it could exercise discretion to decline to enforce the arbitration clause. It found that the trustee did not meet its burden of demonstrating that the Bankruptcy Code provisions, policy or legislative history demonstrated any conflict with enforcement of an arbitration clause in a non-core proceeding brought by the trustee to enforce a claim of the estate in district court. . . . Furthermore, surveying the Supreme Court arbitration cases . . . , the Third Circuit concluded that it could "no longer subscribe to a hierarchy of congressional concerns that places bankruptcy law in a position of superiority over that [Arbitration] Act." . . . The Third Circuit reasoned in *Hays* that it was no longer good law to conclude that the policies of the Bankruptcy Code outweigh the policies of the Arbitration Act.

The reasoning of the *Hays* court has been followed in recent decisions in other jurisdictions. . . .

[. . .]

Guided by the foregoing analysis, the court finds that in the matter *sub judice*, the Debtor likewise fails to demonstrate that enforcement of the arbitration clause in the Management Agreement is contrary to the provisions or purpose of the Bankruptcy Code. The Debtor points to no

Code provision, policy or portion of legislative history that demonstrates that arbitration should not be compelled.

[. . .]

The fact that the matter before the court is a core proceeding does not mean that arbitration is inappropriate. . . . The description of a matter as a core proceeding simply means that the bankruptcy court has the jurisdiction to make a full adjudication. However, merely because the court has the authority to render a decision does not mean it should do so. The discussion in *Hays* regarding core and non-core proceedings is not read by this court as suggesting that core proceedings may not be subject to arbitration. Rather, it appears that the *Hays* court sought to distinguish between actions derived from the debtor, and therefore subject to the arbitration agreement, and bankruptcy actions in essence created by the Bankruptcy Code for the benefit ultimately of creditors of the estate, and therefore not encompassed by the arbitration agreement.

[. . .]

In the present matter, in terms of efficiency, arbitration is perhaps better suited to resolve the disputes of all the parties. The former partners are presently in arbitration with Hilton International. The addition of the Debtor to the proceeding will enable all claims to be resolved in one forum. In any event, the factors of cost and expediency do not weigh mightily against arbitration. The fact that arbitration may not be as efficient or as expeditious has been held not to justify refusal to enforce arbitration clauses in itself, even in bankruptcy. . . .

As a general rule, the policy behind Chapter 11 Reorganization recognizes the expedient and economic resolution of business affairs. However, inquiry regarding conflict between the statutes should not be [so] broad as to swallow the policies of the Arbitration Act, especially when confirmation is not delayed by arbitration. . . . Following the reasoning of *Hays* in this case, the court cannot perceive any greater impact on the Bankruptcy Code in compelling arbitration than denying it. . . .

[. . .]

NOTES AND QUESTIONS

1. In the court's view, is there no public policy interest in the Bankruptcy Code or does the public policy interest in arbitration simply outweigh the public policy interest in bankruptcy?

2. What is the public's stake in bankruptcy and in arbitration? What do the relevant statutes provide? If you were a judge balancing those interests, what line would you draw?

3. How do you assess the distinction between core and non-core proceedings? Should it make arbitration less or more likely?

4. Finally, assess the last paragraph of the opinion. Is the court saying that arbitrability is acceptable because privatization does not matter in that setting? If the recourse to arbitration is of no consequence, why not leave such matters in the jurisdiction of a public entity? Should arbitration always fully trump judicial recourse? Why can't the two processes be combined and work hand-in-hand? In your view, what is in the public interest after these two cases?

Several federal circuits have expanded the reach of arbitration in bankruptcy matters. They have lessened the significance of the previously central distinction between "core and non-core" matters and emphasized that the recourse to arbitration would be prohibited only if it jeopardized the objectives of the Bankruptcy Code. According to the U.S. Second Circuit, for example, bankruptcy courts do not have the discretion to override an arbitration agreement unless they find that the bankruptcy proceedings are based on provisions of the Bankruptcy Code that "inherently conflict" with the Arbitration Act or that the arbitration of the claim would "necessarily jeopardize" the objectives of the Bankruptcy Code. In *MBNA Am. Bank, N.A. v. Hill*, 436 F.3d 104 (2d Cir. 2006), the lower court had held that the consumer's claim that MBNA violated the automatic stay provision of the Bankruptcy Code was a "core" bankruptcy proceeding and the bankruptcy court was the most appropriate forum for resolving the dispute. The appellate court disagreed, holding that the bankruptcy court must enforce the arbitration agreement between debtor and creditor and ordering the class action to arbitration.

The Third Circuit has ruled in a similar vein. In *In re Mintze*, 434 F.3d 222 (3d Cir. 2006), it held that a bankruptcy court does not have the authority to deny enforcement to an otherwise valid arbitration agreement. In so holding, the court referred to *Hays and Co. v. Merrill Lynch, Pierce, Fenner & Smith, Inc.*, 885 F.2d 1149 (3d Cir. 1989). It stated that the "core/non-core" distinction had been vital to determining whether a bankruptcy court has jurisdiction to adjudicate fully the proceeding, but the court could refuse to enforce the arbitration agreement only if there was an inherent conflict between the objectives of the Arbitration Act and the Bankruptcy Code. The inherent conflict requirement applies to both core and non-core matters.

MINTZE V. AMERICAN GENERAL FIN. SERV., INC.

434 F.3d 222 (3d Cir. 2006).

ROTH, CIRCUIT JUDGE.

[. . .]

III.

AGF argues that the Bankruptcy Court lacked the discretion to deny enforcement of the arbitration clause in the mortgage agreement. The District Court held, and Mintze contends, that the Bankruptcy Court had such discretion and that it was within its bounds of discretion when it ruled against AGF. . . .

A.

Bankruptcy proceedings are divided into two categories: core and non-core. . . . The distinction between the two categories is relevant because the type of proceeding may determine the ultimate authority of the bankruptcy court. In a core proceeding, a bankruptcy court has "comprehensive power to hear, decide and enter final orders and judgments." . . . In addition, the bankruptcy court can make findings of fact and conclusions of law. In contrast, the bankruptcy court's authority is significantly limited in non-core proceedings. In a non-core proceeding, the bankruptcy court is allowed only to make proposed findings of fact and proposed conclusions of law, which it submits to the district court. . . .

The core/non-core distinction does not, however, affect whether a bankruptcy court has the discretion to deny enforcement of an arbitration agreement. . . . It merely determines whether the bankruptcy court has the jurisdiction to make a full adjudication. Because this distinction does not affect whether the Bankruptcy Court had the discretion to deny arbitration, we will accept the parties' stipulation that the proceeding was a "core" proceeding for the purposes of deciding whether the Bankruptcy Court had discretion.

B.

[. . .]

The FAA has established a strong policy in favor of arbitration. . . . It requires rigorous enforcement of arbitration agreements. . . . By itself, the FAA mandates enforcement of applicable arbitration agreements even for federal statutory claims. . . .

The FAA's mandate can, however, be overridden. If a party opposing arbitration can demonstrate that "Congress intended to preclude a waiver of judicial remedies for the statutory rights at issue," the FAA will not compel courts to enforce an otherwise applicable arbitration agreement. . . . To overcome enforcement of arbitration, a party must establish congressional intent to create an exception to the FAA's mandate with respect to the party's statutory claims. . . .

Shortly after the Supreme Court decided *McMahon,* we applied its standard to a bankruptcy case that is similar to the present case. *See Hays,* 885 F.2d 1149. In *Hays,* we held that where a party seeks to enforce a debtor-derivative pre-petition contract claim, a court does not have the discretion to deny enforcement of an otherwise applicable arbitration clause. . . . *Hays* involved a trustee to the debtor's estate, bringing causes of action against a brokerage firm that managed two corporate accounts for the debtor. The complaints alleged federal and state securities violations, as well as some statutory claims created by the Bankruptcy Code. The *Hays* Court was presented with the question whether the Bankruptcy Code conflicts with the FAA "in such a way as to bestow upon a district court discretion to decline to enforce an arbitration agreement" with respect to the trustee's claims. Applying the *McMahon* standard, we said that

> the district court lacked the authority and discretion to deny enforcement of the arbitration clause *unless* [the trustee] had met its burden of showing that the text, legislative history, or purpose of the Bankruptcy Code conflicts with the enforcement of an arbitration clause in a case of this kind, that is, *a non-core proceeding brought by a trustee to enforce a claim of the estate in a district court.*

Hays, 885 F.2d at 1156–57 (emphasis added). We held that whether the *McMahon* standard is met determines whether the court has the discretion to deny enforcement of an otherwise applicable arbitration clause. . . . The starting point is *McMahon.* The Bankruptcy Court and District Court, however, applied the *McMahon* standard after determining that the Bankruptcy Court had the discretion to deny arbitration. Those courts applied *McMahon* to determine whether the Bankruptcy Court *should* have exercised its discretion, rather than to determine whether it had the discretion to exercise. This approach is not what is required by *McMahon* and *Hays.*

Mintze contends, and the District Court held, that our *Hays* decision primarily applies to non-core proceedings. . . .

We disagree with this interpretation—that the application of *Hays* is limited to non-core proceedings. First, *Hays* applied the Supreme Court's *McMahon* standard, which applies to all statutory claims subject to applicable arbitration clauses, not just to those claims arising in non-core bankruptcy proceedings. Second, the *Hays* decision did not seek to distinguish between core and non-core proceedings; rather, it sought to distinguish between causes of action derived from the debtor and bankruptcy actions that the Bankruptcy Code created for the benefit of the creditors of the estate. . . . Third, the two cases that the District Court cited from other circuits to support its holding that the Bankruptcy Court did not abuse its discretion, actually support the contention that *Hays* applies to *core* proceedings. The District Court cited *United States Lines* and *National Gypsum.* Both of these cases expressly state that a finding that a proceeding is a core proceeding does not automatically give a bankruptcy court the discretion to deny arbitration. Rather, those cases indicate that the *McMahon* standard must still be satisfied before a bankruptcy court has such discretion. . . .

We find that the standard we articulated in *Hays* applies equally to core and non-core proceedings. . . . Where an otherwise applicable arbitration clause exists, a bankruptcy court lacks the authority and discretion to deny its enforcement, *unless* the party opposing arbitration can establish congressional intent, under the *McMahon* standard, to preclude waiver of judicial remedies for the statutory rights at issue.

IV.

We conclude that the Bankruptcy Court lacked the authority and the discretion to deny enforcement of the arbitration provision in the contract between Mintze and AGF. The FAA mandates enforcement of arbitration when applicable unless Congressional intent to the contrary is established. Mintze has failed to demonstrate through statutory text, legislative history, or the underlying purposes of the Bankruptcy Code that Congress intended to preclude waiver of judicial remedies for her claims. . . .

NOTES AND QUESTIONS

1. How is the opinion a pronouncement on jurisdiction?

2. Does the FAA and the federal policy on arbitration have any authority in the court's reasoning?

3. Why does the court abandon the distinction between "core" and "non-core" matters?

4. Describe the objectives of the Bankruptcy Code. What public policy interests are considerations in the Code's objectives?

4. ANTITRUST DISPUTES

MITSUBISHI MOTORS CORP. V. SOLER CHRYSLER-PLYMOUTH, INC.

473 U.S. 614, 105 S.Ct. 3346, 87 L.Ed.2d 444 (1985).

JUSTICE BLACKMUN delivered the opinion of the Court.

The principal question presented by these cases is the arbitrability, pursuant to the Federal Arbitration Act . . . and the Convention on the Recognition and Enforcement of Foreign Arbitral Awards, . . . of claims arising under the Sherman Act . . . and encompassed within a valid arbitration clause in an agreement embodying an international commercial transaction.

I.

Petitioner-cross-respondent Mitsubishi Motors Corporation . . . is a Japanese corporation . . . and has its principal place of business in Tokyo, Japan. Mitsubishi is the product of a joint venture between, on the one hand, Chrysler International, S.A. (CISA), a Swiss corporation registered in Geneva and wholly owned by Chrysler Corporation, and, on the other, Mitsubishi Heavy Industries, Inc., a Japanese corporation. The aim of the joint venture was the distribution through Chrysler dealers outside the continental United States of vehicles manufactured by Mitsubishi and bearing Chrysler and Mitsubishi trademarks. Respondent-cross-petitioner Soler Chrysler-Plymouth, Inc. . . . is a Puerto Rico corporation with its principal place of business in Pueblo Viejo, Guaynabo, Puerto Rico.

On October 31, 1979, Soler entered into a Distributor Agreement with CISA which provided for the sale by Soler of Mitsubishi-manufactured vehicles within a designated area, including metropolitan San Juan. . . . On the same date, CISA, Soler, and Mitsubishi entered into a Sales Procedure Agreement . . . which, referring to the Distributor Agreement, provided for the direct sale of Mitsubishi products to Soler and governed the terms and conditions of such sales. . . . Paragraph VI of the Sales Agreement, labeled "Arbitration of Certain Matters," provides:

> "All disputes, controversies or differences which may arise between [Mitsubishi] and [Soler] out of or in relation to Articles I–B through V of this Agreement or for the breach thereof, shall be finally settled by arbitration in Japan in accordance with the rules and regulations of the Japan Commercial Arbitration Association." . . .

Initially, Soler did a brisk business in Mitsubishi-manufactured vehicles. . . . In early 1981, however, the new-car market slackened. Soler ran into serious difficulties in meeting the expected sales volume, and by the spring of 1981 it felt itself compelled to request that Mitsubishi delay or cancel shipment of several orders. . . . About the same time, Soler attempted to arrange for the transshipment of a quantity of its vehicles for sale in the continental United States and Latin America. Mitsubishi and CISA, however, refused permission for any such diversion, citing a variety of reasons, and no vehicles were transshipped. Attempts to work out these difficulties failed. Mitsubishi eventually withheld shipment of 966 vehicles, apparently representing orders placed for May, June, and July 1981 production, responsibility for which Soler disclaimed in February 1982. . . .

The following month . . . Mitsubishi sought an order, pursuant to 9 U.S.C. 4 and 201, to compel arbitration in accord with . . . the Sales Agreement. . . . Shortly after filing the complaint, Mitsubishi filed a request for arbitration before the Japan Commercial Arbitration Association. . . .

Soler denied the allegations and counterclaimed against both Mitsubishi and CISA. . . . In the counterclaim premised on the Sherman Act, Soler alleged that Mitsubishi and CISA had conspired to divide markets in restraint of trade. To effectuate the plan, according to Soler, Mitsubishi had refused to permit Soler to resell to buyers in North, Central, or South America vehicles it had obligated itself to purchase from Mitsubishi; had refused to ship ordered vehicles or the parts, such as heaters and defoggers, that would be necessary to permit Soler to make its vehicles suitable for resale outside Puerto Rico; and had coercively attempted to replace Soler and its other Puerto Rico distributors with a wholly owned subsidiary which would serve as the exclusive Mitsubishi distributor in Puerto Rico. . . .

After a hearing, the District Court ordered Mitsubishi and Soler to arbitrate each of the issues raised in the complaint and in all the counterclaims save two and a portion of a third. With regard to the federal antitrust issues, it recognized that the Courts of Appeals, following *American Safety Equipment Corp. v. J.P. Maguire & Co.*, 391 F.2d 821 (2d Cir. 1968), uniformly had held that the rights conferred by the antitrust laws were " 'of a character inappropriate for enforcement by arbitration.' " . . . The District Court held, however, that the international character of the Mitsubishi-Soler undertaking required enforcement of the agreement to arbitrate even as to the antitrust claims. It relied on *Scherk v. Alberto-Culver Co.* . . .

The United States Court of Appeals for the First Circuit affirmed in part and reversed in part. 723 F.2d 155 (1983). . . .

Finally, after endorsing the doctrine of *American Safety*, precluding arbitration of antitrust claims, the Court of Appeals concluded that neither this Court's decision in *Scherk* nor the Convention required abandonment of that doctrine in the face of an international transaction. . . . Accordingly, it reversed the judgment of the District Court insofar as it had ordered submission of "Soler's antitrust claims" to arbitration. . . .

We granted certiorari primarily to consider whether an American court should enforce an agreement to resolve antitrust claims by arbitration when that agreement arises from an international transaction. . . .

II.

[. . .]

. . . [W]e find no warrant in the Arbitration Act for implying in every contract within its ken a presumption against arbitration of statutory claims. The Act's centerpiece provision makes a written agreement to arbitrate "in any maritime transaction or a contract evidencing a transaction involving commerce . . . valid, irrevocable, and enforceable, save upon such grounds as exist at law or in equity for the revocation of any contract." . . . The "liberal federal policy favoring arbitration agreements," *Moses H. Cone Memorial Hospital,* . . . manifested by this provision and the Act as a whole, is at bottom a policy guaranteeing the enforcement of private contractual arrangements: the Act simply "creates a body of federal substantive law establishing and regulating the duty to honor an agreement to arbitrate." . . .

Accordingly, the first task of a court asked to compel arbitration of a dispute is to determine whether the parties agreed to arbitrate that dispute. . . . Thus, as with any other contract, the parties' intentions control, but those intentions are generously construed as to issues of arbitrability.

There is no reason to depart from these guidelines where a party bound by an arbitration agreement raises claims founded on statutory rights. . . . [W]e are well past the time when judicial suspicion of the desirability of arbitration and of the competence of arbitral tribunals inhibited the development of arbitration as an alternative means of dispute resolution. . . . Of course, courts should remain attuned to well-supported claims that the agreement to arbitrate resulted from the sort of fraud or overwhelming economic power that would provide grounds "for the revocation of any contract." . . . But, absent such compelling considerations, the Act itself provides no basis for disfavoring agreements to arbitrate statutory claims by skewing the otherwise hospitable inquiry into arbitrability.

That is not to say that all controversies implicating statutory rights are suitable for arbitration. There is no reason to distort the process of contract interpretation, however, in order to ferret out the inappropriate. . . . For that reason, Soler's concern for statutorily protected classes provides no reason to color the lens through which the arbitration clause is read. By agreeing to arbitrate a statutory claim, a party does not forgo the substantive rights afforded by the statute; it only submits to their resolution in an arbitral, rather than a judicial, forum. It trades the procedures and opportunity for review of the courtroom for the simplicity, informality, and expedition of arbitration. We must assume that if Congress intended the substantive protection afforded by a given statute to include protection against waiver of the right to a judicial forum, that intention will be deducible from text or legislative history. . . . Having made the bargain to arbitrate, the party should be held to it unless Congress itself has evinced an intention to preclude a waiver of judicial remedies for the statutory rights at issue. Nothing, in the meantime, prevents a party from excluding statutory claims from the scope of an agreement to arbitrate. . . .

* * *

Later, the U.S. District Court, District of Minnesota, held that a domestic antitrust claim is arbitrable. In *Hunt v. Up North Plastics, Inc.*, 980 F.Supp. 1046 (D. Minn. 1997), plaintiff filed suit on his own behalf and on behalf of a putative class of plaintiffs who purchased silage products from the defendants. He alleged that Up North, Ag-Bag, and Poly America, Inc. conspired to fix prices and allocate customers of silage products in violation of federal antitrust laws. Based on the arbitration clause in the sale invoices, Up North and Poly America moved to dismiss the class action.

The court granted Up North's and Poly America's motion. In doing so, it rejected Hunt's argument that domestic antitrust actions were inarbitrable. Although the Eighth Circuit had not yet expressly overruled *Helfenbein v. International Indus., Inc.*, 438 F.2d 1068 (8th Cir. 1971) (declaring that domestic antitrust violations are not subject to arbitration), the court explained that a number of recent decisions nevertheless undermined that holding.

The court asserted that the U.S. Supreme Court's decisions in *Mitsubishi Motors Corp. v. Soler Chrysler-Plymouth, Inc.*, 473 U.S. 614 (1985), which held that a foreign antitrust dispute is arbitrable, and *Shearson/American Express, Inc. v. McMahon,* 482 U.S. 220 (1987), which held that federal securities claims are arbitrable, "call into question the rationale of earlier cases exempting antitrust and other statutory claims from arbitration." It further stated that a number of other circuits—including the Ninth and Eleventh Circuit—have found domestic antitrust disputes arbitrable. And, lastly, it emphasized that the decision in *Swenson's Ice Cream Co. v. Corsair Corp.*, 942 F.2d 1307 (8th Cir. 1991), expressly states that, since the U.S. Supreme Court handed down its rulings in *Mitsubishi* and *Shearson/American Express,* the rule in *Helfenbein* "may no longer be a correct statement of the law." Consequently, the court held that the antitrust claim was arbitrable.

The prior law—stated in the opinion in *American Safety (infra)*—demonstrated a higher regard for the public interest, and placed a higher social value and legal significance upon antitrust regulation. Because the antitrust laws represented an expression of U.S. capitalism and economic organization, disputes arising under these statutes had to be resolved in a public forum by agents appointed to safeguard the public interest. The privatization of such matters was simply untenable in light of their impact upon the public interest. Is the public interest now different? Is antitrust no longer important? Why should privatization trump public law regulation? Are we dealing with "new paradigms"? If so, what are they?

AMERICAN SAFETY EQUIPMENT CORP. V. J.P. MAGUIRE & CO.

391 F.2d 821 (2d Cir. 1968).

(footnotes omitted)

FEINBERG, CIRCUIT JUDGE:

These two appeals by American Safety Equipment Corp. (ASE) are from orders of the United States District Court for the Southern District of New York . . . which stayed, pending arbitration, two declaratory judgment actions by ASE. . . . The merits of these actions are not now directly in question, but the propriety of directing arbitration is. We conclude that the court should have decided itself at least some of the issues it referred to the arbitrators. Accordingly, we remand for further proceedings.

[. . .]

The basic question we must resolve is whether the district court erred in staying ASE's actions and ordering arbitration of ASE's antitrust allegations. . . .

[. . .]

. . . The basic issue was aptly phrased by this court fifteen years ago in *Wilko v. Swan*, 201 F.2d 439, 444 (2d Cir. 1953):

> We think that the remedy a statute provides for violation of the statutory right it creates may be sought not only in any "court of competent jurisdiction" but also in any other competent tribunal, such as arbitration, unless the right itself is of a character inappropriate for enforcement by arbitration * * *.

The question before us is whether the statutory right ASE seeks to enforce is "of a character inappropriate for enforcement by arbitration." . . .

[. . .]

A claim under the antitrust laws is not merely a private matter. The Sherman Act is designed to promote the national interest in a competitive economy; thus, the plaintiff asserting his rights under the Act has been likened to a private attorney-general who protects the public's interest. . . . Antitrust violations can affect hundreds of thousands—perhaps millions—of people and inflict staggering economic damage. . . . We do not believe that Congress intended such claims to be resolved elsewhere than in the courts. . . . [I]n fashioning a rule to govern the arbitrability of antitrust claims, we must consider the rule's potential effect. For the same reason, it is also proper to ask whether contracts of adhesion between alleged monopolists and their customers should determine the forum for trying antitrust violations. Here again, we think that Congress would hardly have intended that. . . .

. . . [T]he claim here is that the agreement itself was an instrument of illegality; in addition, the issues in antitrust cases are prone to be complicated, and the evidence extensive and diverse, far better suited to judicial than to arbitration procedures. Moreover, it is the business community generally that is regulated by the antitrust laws. Since commercial arbitrators are frequently men drawn for their business expertise, it hardly seems proper for them to determine these issues of great public interest. As Judge Clark said concerning the analogous situation in *Wilko v. Swan*, 201 F.2d at 445 (dissenting opinion):

> Adjudication by such arbitrators may, indeed, provide a business solution of the problem if that is the real desire; but it is surely not a way of assuring the customer that objective and sympathetic consideration of his claim which is envisaged by the Securities Act.

Appellee Hickok seems to argue that all these considerations are irrelevant because ASE does not seek damages, apparently conceding that a treble damage claim would not be arbitrable. We do not regard this distinction as significant if it is meant to persuade us that arbitrators rather than courts should declare whether contract provisions violate the Sherman Act. On the other hand, if Hickok is merely emphasizing that ASE's antitrust claims are actually being asserted as a defense to an action for royalties, we agree that questions of separability are present here, and we refer to them below. However, the problem of which forum should determine those questions remains; we believe it is governed by the same considerations discussed above.

We express no general distrust of arbitrators or arbitration; our decisions reflect exactly the contrary point of view. . . . Moreover, we do not deal here with an agreement to arbitrate made after a controversy has already arisen. . . . We conclude only that the pervasive public interest in enforcement of the antitrust laws, and the nature of the claims that arise in such cases, combine to make the outcome here clear. In some situations Congress has allowed parties to obtain the advantages of arbitration if they "are willing to accept less certainty of legally correct adjustment," . . . but we do not think that this is one of them. In short, we conclude that the antitrust claims raised here are inappropriate for arbitration.

[. . .]

NOTES AND QUESTIONS

1. Is the submission of antitrust disputes to international arbitrators the same as the submission of such claims to domestic arbitrators? What differences exist between the two sets of circumstances?

2. Of what relevance is the U.S. Supreme Court's view that arbitration is a mere form of trial that has no effect upon substantive rights in the context of the foregoing antitrust decisions?

3. What meaning do you attribute to the phrase: "A claim under the antitrust laws is not merely a private matter."? How would the court in *Hunt v. Up North Plastics* define "a private matter" or the public interest?

4. How persuasive do you find the opinion in *American Safety?*

5. Assume that an employer provides in the employee's employment contract that a reason for summary dismissal of any employee is "the employer's reasonable belief that the employee endorsed, supported,

contributed to, encouraged, or had an abortion." The contract also contains an arbitration clause, making "any and all disputes" between the employee and the employer subject to arbitration. Further, assume that an employee is dismissed because of the abortion clause. Are disputes pertaining to the termination arbitrable? Could a U.S. attorney intervene with a lawsuit on behalf of the employee?

5. TRUTH-IN-LENDING ACT CLAIMS

In *Randolph v. Green Tree Financial Corp.—Alabama*, 178 F.3d 1149 (11th Cir. 1999), *aff'd in part, rev'd in part*, 531 U.S. 79 (2000), the U.S. Court of Appeals for the Eleventh Circuit held that Truth-in-Lending Act (TILA) claims were inarbitrable when the arbitral remedy could not ensure the vindication of statutory rights.

The facts of the case involved the purchase of a mobile home, a financing agreement, and an arbitration clause contained in the latter contract. The plaintiff alleged that Green Tree's financial documents violated the TILA and that the TILA precluded the arbitration of disputes arising under its statutory framework. When Randolph filed her action before the district court, she also sought to certify a class of individuals who had entered into similar agreements with Green Tree. In response, Green Tree moved to compel arbitration and to stay or dismiss the court action. The district court denied the request for certification. It also ruled that the other issues raised in the complaint were subject to arbitration. It issued an order to compel arbitration and dismissed Randolph's claims with prejudice.

The appellate court considered whether the TILA precluded the enforcement of the arbitral clause in the agreement. It held that, because the arbitral clause failed to provide the minimum guarantees required to ensure that the plaintiff could vindicate her statutory rights under TILA, it was unenforceable. The court nonetheless acknowledged the strong federal policy favoring arbitration. It stated that inherent weaknesses in the procedural apparatus of the arbitration, in and of themselves, should not render an arbitral clause unenforceable. Some procedural flaws, however, present such barriers to the would-be litigants' exercise of their statutory rights that they render the agreement to arbitrate unenforceable. In such circumstances, the reference to arbitration defeats the remedial purpose of the statute. In *Paladino*, for example, the court held that forcing the plaintiff to bear the brunt of substantial arbitration costs combined with steep filing fees constituted a legitimate basis upon which to hold that arbitration did not comport with statutory intent.

Moreover, the arbitration clause in the instant case did not address the question of the distribution of filing fees and arbitration costs. The clause did not incorporate a standard set of rules (like those of the

American Arbitration Association) that provide guidance on these matters. In the court's view, it was, therefore, possible that the parties would have to negotiate these issues before they could even proceed with arbitration. The court was disturbed by the fact that there was no guarantee that a successful plaintiff who received a modest award would not be saddled with the exorbitant arbitral costs:

> The arbitration clause in this case raises serious concerns with respect to filing fees, arbitrators' costs and other arbitration expenses that may curtail or bar a plaintiff's access to the arbitral forum, and thus falls within our holding in *Paladino*. This clause says nothing about the payment of filing fees or the apportionment of the costs of arbitration. It neither assigns an initial responsibility for filing fees or arbitrators' costs, nor provides for a waiver in cases of financial hardship. It does not say whether consumers, if they prevail, will nonetheless be saddled with fees and costs in excess of any award. It does not say whether the rules of the American Arbitration Association, which provide at least some guidelines concerning filing fees and arbitration costs, apply to the proceeding, whether some other set of rules applies, or whether the parties must negotiate their own set of rules.
>
> [. . .]
>
> Accordingly, we conclude that the arbitration clause in this case is unenforceable, because it fails to provide the minimum guarantees required to ensure that Randolph's ability to vindicate her statutory rights will not be undone by steep filing fees, steep arbitrators' fees, or other high costs of arbitration. . . .

The court did not reach the issue of whether TILA precludes all arbitration agreements.

NOTES AND QUESTIONS

1. Does the opinion in *Randolph* announce a new standard for the determination of arbitrability questions? What might that new standard be?

2. The U.S. Court of Appeals for the Third Circuit held that claims arising under the Truth-In-Lending Act ("TILA") and the Electronic Fund Transfer Act ("EFTA") were arbitrable even though class action relief may not be available in arbitration. In the court's assessment, the affected statutes were not enacted to guarantee access to class action procedures. *See Johnson v. West Suburban Bank*, 225 F.3d 366 (3d Cir. 2000), *cert. denied*, 531 U.S. 1145 (2001).

* * *

On an issue of first impression, the Third Circuit examined the statutory language, the legislative history, and the statutory purpose of both the TILA and the EFTA. It found that, while TILA contemplates class actions, it does not create a right to bring such suits. Rather, the statute creates civil liability for lenders who fail to give the required disclosures. The lender is subject both to actual and statutory damages. The court reasoned that "the right to proceed to a class action, insofar as the TILA is concerned, is a procedural one that arises from the Federal Rules of Civil Procedure." The TILA does not create a right to class action litigation. The court also found that "Congress did not address the role of arbitration in the legislative history" of the statute.

"Because nothing in the legislative history or the statutory text of the TILA clearly expresses congressional intent to preclude the ability of parties to engage in arbitration, Johnson must demonstrate that arbitration irreconcilably conflicts with the purposes of the TILA." Johnson unpersuasively argued, according to the court, that "class actions are central to TILA's purposes, because the statute's civil damages provisions are not remedial, but rather, given the frequent absence of actual damages, are designed to deter unfair credit practices." The court also found that plaintiffs who sign valid arbitration agreements and "lack the procedural right to proceed as part of a class . . . retain the full range of rights created by the TILA." Additionally, the court held that "when the right made available by a statute is capable of vindication in the arbitral forum, the public policy goals of that statute do not justify refusing to arbitrate." "While arbitrating claims that might have been pursued as part of class actions potentially reduces the number of plaintiffs seeking to enforce the TILA against creditors, arbitration does not eliminate plaintiff incentives to assert rights under the Act."

In assessing legislative intent in the various implicated statutes, the court stated that it was obligated to "give equal consideration to Congress' policy goals in enacting the FAA." "The statute was intended to overcome judicial hostility to agreements to arbitrate." Arbitration has some well-established advantages: "[I]t is usually cheaper and faster than litigation; it can have simpler procedural and evidentiary rules; it normally minimizes hostility and is less disruptive of ongoing and future business dealings among the parties; and it is often more flexible in regard to scheduling." Therefore, the congressional intent to promote arbitration carried with it equal, if not more, weight than the policy concerns argued by Johnson for the protection of class actions under the TILA.

COMPUCREDIT CORP. V. GREENWOOD

565 U.S. 95, 132 S.Ct. 665, 181 L.Ed. 2d 586 (2012).

JUSTICE SCALIA delivered the opinion of the Court.

We consider whether the Credit Repair Organizations Act (CROA), 15 U.S.C. § 1679 *et seq.*, precludes enforcement of an arbitration agreement in a lawsuit alleging violations of that Act.

I

Respondents are individuals who applied for and received an Aspire Visa credit card marketed by petitioner CompuCredit Corporation and issued by Columbus Bank and Trust, now a division of petitioner Synovus Bank. In their applications they agreed to be bound by a provision which read: "Any claim, dispute or controversy (whether in contract, tort, or otherwise) at any time arising from or relating to your Account, any transferred balances or this Agreement (collectively, 'Claims'), upon the election of you or us, will be resolved by binding arbitration. . . ." . . .

In 2008, respondents filed a class-action complaint against CompuCredit and Columbus in the United States District Court for the Northern District of California, alleging, as relevant here, violations of the CROA. The claims largely involved the defendants' allegedly misleading representation that the credit card could be used to rebuild poor credit and their assessment of multiple fees upon opening of the accounts, which greatly reduced the advertised credit limit.

The District Court denied the defendants' motion to compel arbitration of the claims, concluding that "Congress intended claims under the CROA to be non-arbitrable." . . . A panel of the United States Court of Appeals for the Ninth Circuit affirmed, Judge Tashima dissenting. . . . We granted certiorari, 563 U.S. ___, 131 S.Ct. 2874, 179 L.Ed.2d 1187 (2011).

II

The background law governing the issue before us is the Federal Arbitration Act (FAA), 9 U.S.C. § 1 . . . enacted in 1925 as a response to judicial hostility to arbitration. . . . As relevant here, the FAA provides:

> "A written provision in any maritime transaction or a contract evidencing a transaction involving commerce to settle by arbitration a controversy thereafter arising out of such contract or transaction . . . shall be valid, irrevocable, and enforceable, save upon such grounds as exist at law or in equity for the revocation of any contract." 9 U.S.C. § 2.

This provision establishes "a liberal federal policy favoring arbitration agreements." . . . It requires courts to enforce agreements to arbitrate according to their terms. . . . That is the case even when the claims at issue are federal statutory claims, unless the FAA's mandate has been "overridden by a contrary congressional command." . . . Respondents contend that the CROA contains such a command.

That statute regulates the practices of credit repair organizations, defined as certain entities that offer services for the purpose of "(i) improving any consumer's credit record, credit history, or credit rating; or (ii) providing advice or assistance to any consumer with regard to any activity or service described in clause (i)." [Footnote omitted.] 15 U.S.C. § 1679a(3). In its principal substantive provisions, the CROA prohibits certain practices, § 1679b, establishes certain requirements for contracts with consumers, § 1679d, and gives consumers a right to cancel, § 1679e. Enforcement is achieved through the Act's provision of a private cause of action for violation, § 1679g, as well as through federal and state administrative enforcement, § 1679h.

III

Like the District Court and the Ninth Circuit, respondents focus on the CROA's disclosure and nonwaiver provisions. The former . . . sets forth a statement that the credit repair organization must provide to the consumer before any contract is executed. § 1679c(a). One sentence of that required statement reads, " 'You have a right to sue a credit repair organization that violates the Credit Repair Organization Act.' " The Act's nonwaiver provision states, "Any waiver by any consumer of any protection provided by or any right of the consumer under this subchapter—(1) shall be treated as void; and (2) may not be enforced by any Federal or State court or any other person." § 1679f(a).

The Ninth Circuit adopted the following line of reasoning, urged upon us by respondents here: The disclosure provision gives consumers the "right to sue," which "clearly involves the right to bring an action in a court of law." . . . Because the nonwaiver provision prohibits the waiver of "any right of the consumer under this subchapter," the arbitration agreement—which waived the right to bring an action in a court of law—cannot be enforced. . . .

The flaw in this argument is its premise: that the disclosure provision provides consumers with a right to bring an action in a court of law. It does not. Rather, it imposes an obligation on credit repair organizations to supply consumers with a specific statement set forth (in quotation marks) in the statute. The only consumer right it *creates* is the right to receive the statement, which is meant to describe the consumer protections that the law *elsewhere* provides. The statement informs consumers, for instance, that they can dispute the accuracy of information in their credit file and that " '[t]he credit bureau must then reinvestigate and modify or remove inaccurate or incomplete information.' " . . . That description is derived from § 1681i(a), which sets out in great detail the procedures to be followed by a credit bureau in the event of challenges to the accuracy of its information. Similarly, the required statement informs consumers that they may " 'cancel your contract with any credit repair organization for any reason within 3 business days from the date you signed it' "—the right created and set forth in more detail in § 1679e. And the "right to sue" language describes the consumer's right to enforce the credit repair organization's "liab[ility]" for "fail[ure] to comply with any provision of this subchapter" provided for in § 1679g(a). [Footnote omitted.] Thus, contrary to the dissent's assertion, our interpretation does not "[r]educ[e] the required disclosure to insignificance". . . . The disclosure provision informs consumers of their right to enforce liability for *any* failure to conform to the statute—information they might otherwise not possess. It is the dissent's interpretation that effectively reduces a portion of the CROA to a nullity. Interpreting the "right to sue" language in § 1679c(a) to "create" a right to sue in court not only renders it strikingly out of place in a section that is otherwise devoted to giving the consumer notice of rights created elsewhere; it also renders the creation of the "right to sue" elsewhere superfluous.

Respondents suggest that the CROA's civil-liability provision, § 1679g . . . . , demonstrates that the Act provides consumers with a "right" to bring an action in court. They cite the provision's repeated use of the terms "action," "class action," and "court"—terms that they say call to mind a judicial proceeding. These references cannot do the heavy lifting that respondents assign them. It is utterly commonplace for statutes that create civil causes of action to describe the details of those causes of action, including the relief available, in the context of a court suit. If the mere formulation of the cause of action in this standard fashion were sufficient to establish the "contrary congressional command" overriding the FAA, . . . valid arbitration agreements covering federal causes of action would be rare indeed. But that is not the law. In *Gilmer*[,] we enforced an arbitration agreement with respect to a cause of action created by the Age Discrimination in Employment Act of 1967 (ADEA) which read, in part: "Any person aggrieved may bring a civil action in any court of competent jurisdiction for such legal or equitable relief as will effectuate the purposes of this chapter." 29 U.S.C. § 626(c)(1). In *McMahon*[,] we enforced an arbitration agreement with respect to a cause of action created by a provision of the Racketeer Influenced and Corrupt Organizations Act (RICO) which read, in part: "Any person injured in his business or property by reason of a violation of section 1962 of this chapter may sue therefor in any appropriate United States district court and shall recover threefold the damages he sustains and the cost of the suit. . . ." 18 U.S.C. § 1964(c). And[,] in *Mitsubishi Motors*[,] we enforced an arbitration agreement with respect to a cause of action created by a provision of the Clayton Act which read, in part: "[A]ny person who shall be injured in his business or property by reason of anything forbidden in the antitrust laws may sue therefor in any district court of the United States . . . and shall recover threefold the damages by him sustained, and the cost of suit, including a reasonable attorney's fee." 15 U.S.C. § 15(a). Thus, we have repeatedly recognized that contractually required arbitration of claims satisfies the statutory prescription of civil liability in court. . . . To be sure, none of the statutes described above contained a nonwaiver provision, as the statute before us does. But if a cause-of-action provision mentioning judicial enforcement does not create a right to initial judicial enforcement, the waiver of initial judicial enforcement is not the waiver of a "right of the consumer," § 1679f(a). It takes a considerable stretch to regard the nonwaiver provision as a "congressional command" that the FAA shall not apply. [Footnote omitted.]

Moreover, if one believes that § 1679g's contemplation of court suit (combined with § 1679f(a)) establishes a nonwaivable right to initial judicial enforcement, one must also believe that it establishes a nonwaivable right to initial judicial enforcement in *any* competent judicial tribunal, since it contains no limitation. We think it clear, however, that this mere "contemplation" of suit in any competent court does not *guarantee* suit in all competent courts, disabling the parties from adopting a reasonable forum-selection clause. And just as the contemplated availability of all judicial forums may be reduced to a single forum by contractual specification, so also can the contemplated availability of judicial action be limited to judicial action compelling or reviewing initial arbitral adjudication. The parties remain free to specify such matters, so long as the *guarantee* of § 1679g—*the guarantee of the legal power to impose liability*—is preserved.

Respondents and the dissent maintain that if the CROA does not create a right to a judicial forum, then the disclosure provision effectively requires that credit repair organizations mislead consumers. We think not. The disclosure provision is meant to describe the law to consumers in a manner that is concise and comprehensible to the layman—which necessarily means that it will be imprecise. The required statement says, for example, that the CROA " 'prohibits deceptive practices by credit repair organizations,' " 15 U.S.C. § 1679c(a). This is in some respects an overstatement, and in some respects an understatement, of the "Prohibited practices" set forth in § 1679b. It would include, for example, deception apart from "the offer or sale of the services of the credit repair organization," § 1679b(a)(4). Yet we would not hold, in order to prevent the required statement from being "misleading," that a consumer has a right to be protected from deceptive practices beyond those actually covered by § 1679b. So also with respect to the statement's description of a "right to sue." This is a colloquial method of communicating to consumers that they have the legal right, enforceable in court, to recover damages from credit repair organizations that violate the CROA. We think most consumers would understand it this way, without regard to whether the suit in court has to be preceded by an arbitration proceeding. Leaving that possibility out may be imprecise, but it is not misleading—and certainly not so misleading as to demand, in order to avoid that result, reading the statute to contain a guaranteed right it does not in fact contain.

IV

At the time of the CROA's enactment in 1996, arbitration clauses in contracts of the type at issue here were no rarity. Quite the contrary, the early 1990's saw the increased use of arbitration clauses in consumer contracts generally, and in financial services contracts in particular. . . .

Had Congress meant to prohibit these very common provisions in the CROA, it would have done so in a manner less obtuse than what respondents suggest. When it has restricted the use of arbitration in other contexts, it has done so with a clarity that far exceeds the claimed indications in the CROA. [Footnote omitted.] . . . That Congress would have sought to achieve the same result in the CROA through combination of the nonwaiver provision with the "right to sue" phrase in the disclosure provision, and the references to "action" and "court" in the description of damages recoverable, is unlikely.

* * *

Because the CROA is silent on whether claims under the Act can proceed in an arbitrable forum, the FAA requires the arbitration agreement to be enforced according to its terms. The judgment of the Ninth Circuit is reversed, and the case is remanded for further proceedings consistent with this opinion.

It is so ordered.

[. . .]

JUSTICE SOTOMAYOR with whom JUSTICE KAGAN joins, concurring in the judgment.

Claims alleging the violation of a statute, such as the Credit Repair Organizations Act (Act), . . . are generally subject to valid arbitration agreements unless Congress evinces a contrary intent in the text, history, or purpose of the statute. . . . I agree with the Court that Congress has not shown that intent here. But for the reasons stated by the dissent, I find this to be a much closer case than the majority opinion suggests.

The Act creates a cause of action in its liability provision, see § 1679g(a), denominates the cause of action a "right to sue" in the mandatory disclosure statement, § 1679c(a), and then provides that "right[s]" may not be waived, § 1679f(a). Those for whom Congress wrote the Act—lay readers "of limited economic means and . . . inexperienced in credit matters," § 1679(a)(2)—reasonably may interpret the phrase "right to sue" as promising a right to sue *in court*. And it is plausible to think that

Congress, aware of the impact of its words, intended such a construction of the liability provision.

But while this interpretation of the Act is plausible, it is in my view no more compelling than the contrary construction that petitioners urge. As the majority opinion notes, the disclosure provision does not itself confer a cause of action, and the liability provision that does is materially indistinguishable from other statutes that we have held not to preclude arbitration. In my mind[,] this leaves the parties' arguments in equipoise, and our precedents require that petitioners prevail in this circumstance. This is because respondents, as the opponents of arbitration, bear the burden of showing that Congress disallowed arbitration of their claims, and because we resolve doubts in favor of arbitration. . . . Of course, if we have misread Congress' intent, then Congress can correct our error by amending the statute.

I add one more point. The majority opinion contrasts the liability provision of the Act with other, more recently enacted statutes that expressly disallow arbitration. I do not understand the majority opinion to hold that Congress must speak so explicitly in order to convey its intent to preclude arbitration of statutory claims. We have never said as much, and on numerous occasions have held that proof of Congress' intent may also be discovered in the history or purpose of the statute in question. . . . I agree with the dissent that the statutes the majority opinion cites shed little light on the thoughts of the Congress that passed the Act. But the Act's text is not dispositive, and respondents identify nothing in the legislative history or purpose of the Act that would tip the balance of the scale in favor of their interpretation.

JUSTICE GINSBURG, dissenting.

Congress enacted the Credit Repair Organizations Act (CROA) to protect consumers "who have experienced credit problems"—"particularly those of limited economic means"—against the unfair and deceptive practices of credit repair organizations. 15 U.S.C. § 1679(a). Central to the legislation, Congress sought to arm consumers with information needed to make intelligent decisions about purchasing a repair organization's services. To that end, Congress directed that, "before [execution of] any contract . . . between [a] consumer and [a] credit repair organization," the organization must make certain disclosures. One of the required disclosures reads:

> "You have a right to sue a credit repair organization that violates the [CROA]. This law prohibits deceptive practices by [such] organizations." § 1679c(a).

The Act's civil-liability provision describes suits consumers may bring in court: individual and class actions for damages (actual and punitive) and attorneys' fees. A further provision renders void any purported waiver of any protection or right the Act grants to consumers.

The Court today holds that credit repair organizations can escape suit by providing in their take-it-or-leave-it contracts that arbitration will serve as the parties' sole dispute-resolution mechanism. The "right to sue," the Court explains, merely connotes the vindication of legal rights, whether in court or before an arbitrator. That reading may be comprehensible to one trained to "think like a lawyer." But Congress enacted the CROA with vulnerable consumers in mind—consumers likely to read the words "right to sue" to mean the right to litigate in court, not the obligation to submit disputes to binding arbitration.

In accord with the Ninth Circuit, I would hold that Congress, in an Act meant to curb deceptive practices, did not authorize credit repair organizations to make a false or misleading disclosure—telling consumers of a right they do not, in fact, possess. If the Act affords consumers a nonwaivable right to sue in court, as I believe it does, a credit repair organization cannot retract that right by making arbitration the consumer's sole recourse.

[. . .]

II

Three sections of the CROA, considered together, indicate Congress' intention to preclude mandatory, creditor-imposed, arbitration of CROA claims. See 15 U.S.C. §§ 1679c(a), 1679g, and 1679f. Before entering into any consumer contract, credit repair organizations must give potential customers a written statement of rights they possess under that Act and related consumer-protection laws. § 1679c(a). Congress dictated every word of the required notification. Credit repair organizations must tell consumers, in plain terms, how they may enforce their rights: "You have a right to sue a credit repair organization that violates the Credit Repair Organization Act." . . .

The "right to sue" refers to the claim for relief Congress afforded consumers in § 1679g. "Any person" who violates another's rights under the CROA "shall be liable" for actual damages and attorneys' fees, and may be liable for punitive damages as well. § 1679g(a)(1)–(3). The Act sets out the factors "the court shall consider" in determining the amount of punitive damages "the court may allow" aggrieved consumers to recover, either individually or as a class. § 1679g(a)(2) and (b). The liability created here, in § 1679g, is precisely what the consumer, in light of § 1679c, may sue to enforce.

The Act renders void and unenforceable "[a]ny waiver by any consumer of any protection provided by or *any right* of the consumer under this subchapter." § 1679f (emphasis added). [Footnote omitted.] The rights listed in § 1679c(a) rendered nonwaivable by § 1679f are the "right to sue" and the "right to cancel [a] contract . . . for any reason within 3 business days from the date [the consumer] signed it."[4]

The question on which this case turns is what Congress meant when it created a nonwaivable "right to sue." Recall that Congress' target audience in the CROA is not composed of lawyers and judges accustomed to nuanced reading of statutory texts, but laypersons who receive a disclosure statement in the mail. Recall, as well, Congress' findings that these individuals are often "of limited economic means and . . . inexperienced in credit matters." § 1679(a)(2). Attributing little importance to this context, the Court construes the right to sue as "the legal right, enforceable in court, to recover damages . . . without regard to whether the suit in court has to be preceded by an arbitration proceeding." *Ante,* at 672. I read Congress' words without that sophisticated gloss: The right to sue, I would hold, means the right to litigate in court.

[. . .]

NOTES AND QUESTIONS

1. Do you find the inclusion in the Act of the right to a statement peculiar from a regulatory standpoint or does the peculiarity of the requirement arise from its construction by the majority? Discuss.

2. Does the CROA contain uncharacteristic and poorly thought-out statutory language?

3. When the majority criticizes the dissent's construction of the Act, it states that the dissent's interpretation demands that the statutory language engage in heavy-lifting. What does this mean? Is it an accurate criticism? Doesn't the majority itself belabor the terms of the legislation to sustain hair-splitting distinctions?

4. In your view, does the CROA create a consumer right to sue credit repair organizations in court? Explain.

5. Is the statutory language referring to the 'right to sue' unclear or obtuse? Is it impossible to decipher what Congressional intent underlies the phrase? Is the majority or dissent entitled, therefore, to rewrite the legislation? Does arbitration's current reputation and stature complicated the determination?

---

[4] Two provisions, although described by § 1679c(a) as consumer "right[s]," are not rendered nonwaivable by § 1679f because they are not "right[s] . . . under this subchapter." Rather, the "right to dispute inaccurate information in your credit report" and the "right to obtain a copy of your credit report" referred to in § 1679c(a) are rights conferred elsewhere in the U.S. Code. See § 1681i(a), § 1681j. Section 1679f also makes nonwaivable the " *protection[s]* provided . . . under this subchapter" (emphasis added); these protections include the prohibition of certain business practices, see § 1679b, and the provision, in writing, of certain contractual terms and conditions, see § 1679d.

6. Does the majority's analysis imply a reference to FAA § 2? Explain.

7. According to the majority, when might the arbitration of federal statutory claims become a rarity? Does that possibility explain the Court's true motive for its conclusion?

8. Assess the Court's observation that a non-waiver provision does not constitute a "congressional command" to exclude the FAA.

9. Evaluate the Court's reference to *Gilmer*, *McMahon*, and *Mitsubishi*.

10. Does the majority forget to consider the factor of adhesion in reaching its assessment?

11. Is the statutory reference to a right to sue no more than a reference to the liability of credit repair organizations without any identification or consideration of the process or entity that might establish it?

12. Is the issue of the case as close as Justice Sotomayor suggests in her concurring opinion? Assess her reasoning and the basis for her decision. Is her appraisal of the dimensions of the case dispositive?

13. The dissent emphasizes transactional circumstances, the intended beneficiaries of the legislation, and the self-evident purpose of the enactment. Are these considerations a better means of constructing an accurate appraisal of the Act?

14. Which side of the Court advances the emphatic federal policy favoring arbitration? Where does justice reside—in the arbitrability of statutory claims or consumer protection?

6. MCCARRAN-FERGUSON ACT

The McCarran-Ferguson Act (15 U.S.C. § 1012) establishes the generally preemptive effect of state law in the regulation of the business of insurance and the interpretation of insurance contracts. The statute provides (15 U.S.C. § 1012[b]): "No Act of Congress shall be construed to invalidate, impair, or supersede any law enacted by any state for the purpose of regulating the business of insurance . . . unless such Act specifically relates to the business of insurance." Insurance contracts can involve interstate commerce and contain arbitration agreements, thereby triggering the application of the FAA. When an insurance company becomes insolvent and the relevant contract provides for the arbitration of liquidation matters, does the FAA apply to the enforcement of the arbitration agreement or do state law provisions on liquidation requiring exclusive judicial recourse in such circumstances control?

There is no U.S. Supreme Court precedent directly on point. In *U.S. Dept. of Treasury v. Fabe*, 508 U.S. 491 (1993), the Court reversed a Sixth Circuit opinion on the status of an Ohio liquidation statute, but failed to clarify the relationship between the FAA and the McCarran-Ferguson Act. The circuits are split on the question. The Second and Ninth Circuits have held that the McCarran-Ferguson Act does not preclude the application of the FAA, while the Fifth, Sixth, and Tenth Circuits have held that the Act "reverse preempts" the FAA.

7. LEGAL MALPRACTICE CLAIMS AND FEE DISPUTES

On February 20, 2002, the ABA Committee on Ethics and Professional Responsibility issued Formal Opinion 02–425. In that document, the committee addressed the ethical propriety of retainer agreements between attorneys and clients that contain arbitral clauses which require fee disputes and malpractice claims be submitted to arbitration. While the committee concluded that such contract provisions did not violate ethical standards, it conditioned their ethical acceptability upon a number of factors. First, the client's acceptance of the agreement to arbitrate such disputes must be based upon informed consent. Second, the effect of the arbitration agreement cannot be to limit or exclude the lawyer's liability exposure to the client:

> It is ethically permissible to include in a retainer agreement with a client a provision that requires the binding arbitration of fee disputes and malpractice claims provided that (1) the client has been fully apprised of the advantages and disadvantages of arbitration and has been given sufficient information to permit her to make an informed decision about whether to agree to the inclusion of the arbitration provision in the retainer agreement, and (2) the arbitration provision does not insulate the lawyer from liability or limit the liability to which she would otherwise be exposed under common and/or statutory law.

In explaining its position, the committee emphasized the distinction between fee disputes and professional malpractice claims. Many, if not most, bar associations have implemented arbitral procedures for addressing fee disputes. Rule 1.5 of the Model Rules of Professional Responsibility (MRPR) authorize "fee arbitration programs"; in fact, there are ABA Model Rules for Fee Arbitration. The MRPR, however, does not address instances in which the arbitral procedure applies to malpractice claims.

In particular, MRPR Rules 1.8(h) forbids lawyers from limiting their malpractice liability through contract unless such agreements are recognized at law as lawful and the subscribing client is represented independently. Moreover, a lawyer owes a client fiduciary duties that include "a duty to explain matters" under MRPR Rule 1.4(b). In terms of arbitration agreements in a professional services contract, the duty would oblige the attorney to explain effectively what arbitration is and its benefits and drawbacks. The explanation must be sufficient to allow the client to achieve "informed consent." Finally, the incorporation of an arbitral clause in a retainer agreement also implicates MRPR Rule 1.7(b) that addresses conflict of interest situations. According to the committee, Comment [6] to Rule 1.7 was particularly relevant; it provides: "If the probity of a lawyer's own conduct in a transaction is in serious question, it may be difficult or impossible for the lawyer to give a client detached advice."

Despite all of these misgivings, the committee concluded that agreements to arbitrate malpractice claims were ethically supportable. It aligned its reasoning to the judicial reasoning that ordinarily applies to matters of arbitration. That reasoning usually sustains the recourse to arbitration and is intended to eliminate any obstacles that might stand in the way of the reference to arbitration. For example, the committee stated that: "The mere fact that a client is required to submit disputes to arbitration rather than litigation does not violate Rule 1.8(h) [prohibiting the lawyer from limiting liability], even though the procedures implicated by various mandatory arbitration provisions can markedly differ from typical litigation procedures." It is difficult to understand when the evident differences between arbitral and judicial adjudication would be sufficient to trigger restraint in this area. Apparently, the unavailability of punitive damages in arbitration (as opposed to court proceedings) would be enough to mandate that the client be "independently represented in making the agreement."

The committee does not appear to appreciate the substantial conflict of interest that the unilateral incorporation of an arbitral clause in a retainer agreement represents. It cannot be rationally or plausibly argued that the attorney is not representing his/her own interest primarily and depriving the client of important procedural rights and protections against his/her lack of competence. Arbitration, in this and other settings, can serve no other purpose than limiting the lawyer's liability. There cannot be any fiduciary dimension to conduct that is manifestly self-serving and antagonistic to one side. It is nearly unthinkable that attorneys should attempt to deprive their clients of access to the courts and judicial proceedings.

HENRY V. GONZALEZ

18 S.W.3d 684 (Tex. Ct. App. 2000).

[. . .]

The record contains evidence, and the parties do not dispute, that an arbitration agreement existed between the parties, as it was contained within the attorney/client contract signed by Gonzalez. We have determined that Henry and Hearn's termination of the contract did not affect the validity of the internal arbitration agreement. Therefore, Henry and Hearn satisfied their burden of proof to establish their right to the remedy of arbitration. To overcome the application of the arbitration clause to him, Gonzalez was then required to establish some ground for revocation of the arbitration agreement. . . .

Gonzalez argues two grounds for revocation of the arbitration agreement: (1) the application of the arbitration clause to this case violates public policy, and; (2) fraudulent inducement. Gonzalez's public-policy contentions are unfounded because well established caselaw favors mandatory arbitration and holds that arbitration does not deny parties their right to a jury trial, as a matter of law. . . .

To the extent Gonzalez argues that he was fraudulently induced to sign the contract containing the arbitration clause due to his decreased mental capacity and the fact that the arbitration clause was not conspicuous, his argument fails. An allegation that the contract itself was fraudulently induced is a matter to be decided by the arbitrator. . . . Fraudulent inducement to sign the contract, thus, cannot support the trial court's order denying Henry and Hearn's motion to compel arbitration, as a matter of law.

To the extent Gonzalez argues he was fraudulently induced to agree to arbitration, his argument also fails. Although this question usually requires a fact determination by the trial court, Gonzalez had the burden to prove this issue, and under the "no evidence" standard of review, this court may determine whether the record contains any evidence to support the trial court's judgment. We hold that it does not. . . .

[. . .]

The matters in controversy fall within the scope of the arbitration agreement because the factual allegations forming the bases of the Gonzalezes' legal malpractice and breach of fiduciary duty causes of action necessarily arose from Henry and Hearn's representation of the Gonzalezes under the attorney/client contract. The Gonzalezes' DTPA cause of action falls within the scope of the arbitration agreement because the actions forming the basis of this cause of action related to "the providing of services" by Henry and Hearn to the Gonzalezes, necessarily related to that relationship, and were so factually interwoven with the contract that such action could not stand alone. . . .

We sustain Henry and Hearn's first, second, and third points of error. We need not reach the fourth point of error. Because the evidence shows that a valid arbitration agreement existed, no other ground exists to hold the arbitration agreement revocable, and the claims raised fell within the scope of this agreement, the trial court had no discretion but to compel arbitration. . . .

Dissenting opinion by: PHIL HARDBERGER, CHIEF JUSTICE.

[. . .]

The legal and ethical implications of arbitration provisions in contracts between attorneys and their clients have been the subject of a number of articles. . . . The essence of these articles is that whatever public policy may be served by enforcing arbitration agreements is more than offset by the public policy of not allowing attorneys to take advantage of their clients. Trust is the essential ingredient in an attorney-client relationship. The great majority of clients are not even close to being in an equal bargaining position with their attorneys. They go to an attorney so the attorney can tell them what to do, not vice-versa.

In a serious personal injury case, such as this, clients are typically deeply in grief and overwhelmed by the circumstances that have come upon them. Pain and disability have entered their lives, and the breadwinner is no longer able to bring home wages for the family. As bills pour in, with no offsetting income, a true state of desperation exists. Are we then to allow attorneys, who represent such clients, to take away their rights to a jury should legal malpractice occur? I agree with the commentators in the cited articles and with the laws established in other jurisdictions that conclude that such a practice is against public policy. Certainly it should be against public policy in the absence of some additional protections for the client, which do not exist in the case.

The traditional advantages of arbitration may not be so advantageous in the context of a legal malpractice claim. For example, the savings of cost and time would likely be more of a disadvantage to the attorney alleged to have committed malpractice than to the client because the client's new attorney will typically be handling the claim on a contingency basis. . . . In addition, the ability to pursue the claim in court may provide the client with a bargaining advantage in negotiating with an attorney who seeks to avoid litigation and its potential negative publicity. . . .

More importantly, the fundamental fiduciary nature of the attorney-client relationship dictates against an attorney's ability to impose an arbitration condition on a client. Clients are often in vulnerable positions, requiring them to bestow a large amount of trust in their attorneys. "The client's vulnerability vis-à-vis the attorney is often exacerbated by the client's current legal situation. . . . He is neither expecting, nor emotionally prepared, to 'do battle' with his chosen attorney to protect his own rights." . . . Applying general contractual principles to an arbitration provision in the attorney-client context ignores the practical reality that in most instances the attorney and his or her client are not engaged in an arm's length transaction during their initial negotiations. . . .

Attorneys generally have a greater advantage over their clients in an arbitration setting. Attorneys are trained to conduct arbitration to the best advantage of their clients, in this case themselves. . . . Since one of the "selling points" of arbitration is the ability to proceed without an attorney, the client with the malpractice claim may not seek additional counsel, leaving the trained attorney with a distinct advantage. . . .

In a profession that is called upon to police itself, how can we justify allowing attorneys to take advantage of those who call upon their services? We cannot. Although the traditional contractual defenses, like unconscionability, may be available to clients who are taken advantage of, such a situation should never be allowed to arise. Clients who are in a weaker bargaining position may not be able to meet the burden of proving unconscionability. . . . This does not mean that the attorney would not have taken advantage of his or her client. It simply means that the legal definition of unconscionability, created by attorneys, is an uncertain road for an already burdened client.

Recognizing these public policy concerns, other states have prohibited or limited the inclusion of arbitration provisions in attorneys' engagement letters. For example, Pennsylvania has adopted a rule that permits an arbitration provision in an engagement letter only if: (1) the advantages and disadvantages are fully disclosed by the attorney; (2) the client is advised of his right to consult independent counsel and is given the opportunity to do so; and (3) the client's consent is in writing. . . . Both the District of Columbia and Michigan have taken a more restrictive approach and prohibit arbitration clauses in engagement letters unless the client has the advice of independent counsel. . . . Finally, Ohio has taken the most restrictive approach and simply prohibits pre-dispute arbitration agreements between attorneys and their clients. . . . Ohio reasons that requiring a client to hire a lawyer in order to hire a lawyer sends the wrong message. . . .

Public policy mandates that some restrictions must be placed on an attorney's ability to include an arbitration provision in an engagement letter. Because no such restrictions were imposed in this case, I would conclude that the arbitration clause violates public policy and affirm the trial court's ruling. I respectfully dissent.

NOTES AND QUESTIONS

1. Despite the divisive nature of the debate on the question of the arbitrability of legal malpractice claims, courts are likely to reach the conclusion that such disputes are arbitrable. Such a conclusion would be in keeping with the forceful general trend in the area and would coincide with the determinations of various bar groups on the ethical propriety of arbitration agreements in retainer agreements.

2. It could be argued that the particular character of these claims warrants an adapted form of arbitration, the characteristics of which respond to the issues and interests that underlie these matters. While it appears contradictory to allow attorneys to deny their clients the traditional remedies

typically available, there seems to be little basis for disallowing the arbitration of legal malpractice claims (given the strength of the policy in favor of arbitration) or for making special accommodations for these controversies inside the arbitration process. Notwithstanding the self-evident double standard, the breach of trust, and the contractual unfairness, this battle on subject-matter inarbitrability appears to be as likely of defeat as all the others.

3. Attorneys (and clients), therefore, must consider the content of a generally suitable agreement. In attempting to draft an arbitration clause or contract, parties should understand the rules that generally apply to the crafting of arbitral agreements. The standard arbitration agreement is simple and economical as well as straightforward. It, however, only manages to get the parties to arbitration and to an arbitral institution. It is easy to enforce but offers no protection except to authorize the arbitrators and the arbitral institution to act at their discretion. An overly complex agreement obviously is much more difficult to negotiate and runs the risk of complicating enforcement or making enforcement impossible. It could become a pathological contract that creates stalemate, results in the useless expenditure of resources, and could lead to undesirable solutions. A balanced approach—one that intermediates between being binding and fair—may be the best approach.

4. In arriving at such an agreement, the parties should consider the following factors and aspects (stated roughly in order of importance):

(i) Scope or range of the agreement to arbitrate—what disputes do the parties agree to submit to arbitration—tort, contract, statutory, regulatory, jurisdictional;

(ii) Appointment of arbitrators—who qualifies to be an arbitrator and how should arbitrators be selected; are there specific qualifications; what is the desired number;

(iii) Remedies and damages—what remedies are available in the arbitration—compensatory, punitive, and injunctive relief (a failure to exclude probably means that the relief is available); what about attorney's fees;

(iv) Basis for arbitral rulings—do the arbitrators rule according to law, equity, amiable composition, technical expertise, or some combination of these factors;

(v) Type of arbitral trial—formal, informal, legal, flexible; what about cross-examination, expert witnesses, discovery, or time constraints;

(vi) Content of the award—should reasons be supplied; within the award or apart from it;

(vii) Allocation of arbitral costs and fees—determined by whom and on what basis;

(viii) Standard of review—prior to *Hall Street Associates*, some federal circuits allowed parties to provide for a merits review by courts of arbitral rulings on the law; now, such provisions are unenforceable;

(ix) Selection of institutional rules;

(x) Selection of a law governing the general contract, the arbitration agreement, and the arbitration;

(xi) Obligation to arbitrate in good faith;

(xii) Potential liability of the arbitrator in the event of the vacatur of the award; waiver of fees if the award is set aside.

The agreement should be carefully crafted and worded.

CHAPTER 6

FAIRNESS IN ADHESIVE ARBITRATION

■ ■ ■

1. INTRODUCTION: DISPARATE PARTIES AND ADHESIVE CONTRACTING

Arbitration derives its power from choice and commitment. Arbitration constitutes the choice to opt-out of public courts and, instead, commit to have disputes adjudicated by private decision makers chosen by the parties. As you have seen in previous chapters, the arbitral process allows parties in conflict to focus a dispute resolution process on their actual needs rather than on abstracted and impersonal ideals of justice or, more cynically, on the procedural jockeying that serves only to line lawyers' pockets.

In some circumstances, though, arbitration starts to look less like a choice and more like an unavoidable requirement of buying consumer goods or services, being employed, or getting medical care. Arbitration, in these situations, is imposed on weaker parties and may be part of a scheme that results in the curtailment or outright deletion of their legal rights.

In the United States, a vast majority of consumer contracts with cellular phone companies, internet providers, internet search engines, retailers, travel companies, cable companies, and even utilities providers contain arbitration provisions. Virtually every consumer product purchased includes with it an obligation to arbitrate any disputes with the retailer or manufacturer. At least half of all non-unionized employment agreements contain mandatory arbitration provisions. Finally, more and more patients are obligated to arbitrate any disputes that they have with their health insurance and care providers. As two journalists have put it, "[f]rom birth to death, the use of arbitration has crept into nearly every corner of Americans' lives, encompassing moments like having a baby, going to school, getting a job, buying a car, building a house and placing a parent in a nursing home." Jessica Silver-Greenberg & Michael Corkery, *A 'Privatization of the Justice System': In Arbitration, a Bias Toward Business*, N.Y. TIMES, Nov. 2, 2015, at B4.

All of these contexts share common features. They involve a contract between a commercial party and an individual—what we will refer to as disparate parties. The commercial party drafts an arbitral clause and sticks it in boilerplate that the individual likely does not read or understand. The standardized nature of boilerplate gives the individual little or no opportunity to negotiate. Instead, the individual's options are to accept the boilerplate terms proposed by the commercial party or walk away from the deal.

The use of arbitration in mass-market transactions is relatively new. For many years, even after the passage of the FAA in 1925, arbitration served primarily as a forum for resolution of commercial disputes. In part, this narrow focus was a consequence of the limited range of disputes that were amenable to resolution in arbitration. Cases like *Wilko v. Swan*, which you saw in Chapter 5, indicated that many statutory rights were not arbitrable. Given that the relationships between commercial parties and individuals are often intermediated by a web of statutory protections, arbitration between disparate parties was simply not feasible or efficient.

The Court, however, systematically dismantled *Wilko* and its legacy, expanding the substantive scope of arbitration throughout the 1980s and 90s. *See, e.g., Rodriguez de Quijas v. Shearson/American Express Inc.,* 490 U.S. 477 (1989) (overruling Wilko). Today, virtually all civil issues, including statutory rights, can be resolved in arbitration.

This jurisprudential shift presented an opportunity for commercial parties to keep consumers', workers', and patients' claims out of court and away from juries. Accordingly, corporate counsel began to include arbitration clauses in an expanding range of adhesive contracts. The result was that arbitration embraced more disputants and different types of relationships between them. Arbitration no longer applied just to relatively evenly-matched commercial parties. It began to apply to *unequally* situated individuals versus business entities.

Critics use the terms "mandatory arbitration" or "forced arbitration" to describe these sorts of mass-market arbitration agreements. This terminology may be evocative, but it is also misleading, at least in the sense that all arbitration agreements constitute a binding commitment. The phrasing underscores how politicized, and frequently devoid of doctrinal precision, evaluations of adhesive arbitration have become. Nevertheless, concerns over adhesive arbitration deserve serious attention. It is no exaggeration to say that arbitration today faces a legitimacy crisis at least partially due to its expanding use between commercial parties and individuals.

Mass-market arbitration agreements are routinely delivered to us through boilerplate we never read. These agreements bar access to public courts and replace it with what many critics regard as an inferior, stingier form of arbitral justice. Additionally, these agreements frequently strip away the right to aggregate claims in class actions or other similar mechanisms.

A growing number of scholars, politicians, consumer rights advocates, journalists, and even many judges have taken exception to the fairness of mass-market arbitration agreements. These objections fall into four broad categories:

- Objections based on the formation of the arbitral contract;
- Objections to the fairness of the arbitral process itself;
- Objections to class action waivers; and
- Objections based on the outcomes or remedies of the arbitral process.

This Chapter evaluates each of these objections. It concludes by examining particular issues implicated by disparate party arbitrations in the employment context.

2. OBJECTIONS TO FORMATION

The covert way in which boilerplate terms and conditions are delivered raises questions about formation of the arbitration contract. Traditionally, assent has been the doctrinal and theoretical hallmark of contract law. Most normative justifications for contract rest on the notion that autonomous individuals should be free to form, revise, and pursue their own plans and conceptions of what it means to live a fulfilling, meaningful life. A quintessentially important component of this freedom involves a person being able to exchange an entitlement or property right she has in order to get something else that she values more. Parties are free to make bad exchanges, so long as they are really choosing to make them. Contract law does not protect parties from lousy deals, but it generally prevents coerced or forced ones.

Boilerplate contracting bears scant resemblance to this traditional understanding of mutual assent. Boilerplate terms are delivered on a take-it-or-leave-it basis with little or no opportunity for negotiation. Sometimes the delivery occurs online, through so-called browsewrap, which requires that a recipient clink on a link, often itself difficult to find, in order to access the terms and conditions. Of course, clinking on the link hardly ensures that the recipient will actually see, read, or understand any particular term, including the arbitration clause buried somewhere in the fine print of the page. Sometimes the delivery occurs online through clickwrap, which presents the terms to the recipient and then requires her to click "I agree." Again, however, the mere fact that terms are presented does not mean that the recipient is aware of the existence or meaning of any particular contractual provision. Of course, sometimes the delivery occurs offline through physical paper, which may be included with the provision of goods or services, in fine-print. Whatever the method of transmission, overwhelming empirical evidence, not to mention our own lived experience, demonstrates that no one reads standardized terms and conditions.

To get around the problems created by the unilateral character of adhesive contracting, U.S. courts have refocused contract formation on constructive notice, finding that if a reasonable person in the position of the recipient of boilerplate would have or should have seen the terms, the recipient will be bound by those terms. Assent has become purely hypothetical, no longer tethered to even the remotest requirement of actual acceptance or understanding. Everyone knows that no one reads the terms. So, no one seriously contends that individuals are accepting or understanding the boilerplate presented to them. The question has merely become whether the recipient should have somehow been aware that terms were present. Constructive awareness coupled with inaction amounts to assent. This refocusing may constitute a gerrymandering of the terms "agreement" and "assent." *See, e.g.,* MARGARET JANE RADIN, BOILERPLATE: THE FINE PRINT, VANISHING RIGHTS, AND THE RULE OF LAW 30 (2013).

On the other hand, a number of courts and commentators defend boilerplate contracting on the basis that it results in lower costs (or higher wages) for individuals. Boilerplate can be viewed as simply another product or service attribute. Most individuals do not understand every attribute of the goods or services they purchase. Instead, most people contract for the general gist of whatever it is that they are buying, concentrating on a few salient terms of the deal that really matter to them.

For instance, a majority of buyers of smartphones probably do not understand or think about the subtle differences in microprocessors that the manufacturer might use. Instead, they are interested in things like the price, size of the screen, the camera, and perhaps the memory available. They leave the rest of the details to the manufacturer to sort out. The same could be true of legal terms like arbitration provisions.

Perhaps the critical feature of a mass-market transaction is the price at which that transaction takes place. If the inclusion of an arbitration provision in boilerplate reduces the cost of the transaction (or increases wages), it may be that most people, most of the time, would accept the deal as welfare enhancing. *See, e.g.,* Christopher R. Drahozal, *"Unfair" Arbitration Clauses*, 2001 U. ILL. L. REV. 695, 741 (noting that even "one-sided arbitration clauses" may be beneficial to individuals "if the resulting cost savings are passed on to consumers through reductions in the price of goods and services, to employees through higher wages"). Boilerplate could be economizing on transaction costs, reaching an outcome that a majority of individuals prefer. As Judge Frank Easterbrook has said, "[p]eople are free to opt for bargain-basement adjudication" because "[i]n competition, prices adjust and both sides gain. 'Nothing but the best' may be the motto of a particular consumer but is not something the legal system foists on all consumers." *Carbajal v H & R Block Tax Services, Inc*, 372 F3d 903, 906 (7th Cir 2004) (Easterbrook).

With these competing views of boilerplate in mind, consider the following materials.

MEYER V. UBER TECHNOLOGIES, INC.

868 F.3d 66 (2nd Cir. 2017).

(footnotes omitted)

CHIN, CIRCUIT JUDGE.

In 2014, plaintiff-counter-defendant-appellee Spencer Meyer downloaded onto his smartphone a software application offered by defendant-counter-claimant-appellant Uber Technologies, Inc. ("Uber"), a technology company that operates, among other things, a ride-hailing service. Meyer then registered for an Uber account with his smartphone. After using the application approximately ten times, Meyer brought this action on behalf of himself and other similarly situated Uber accountholders against Uber's co-founder and former Chief Executive Officer, defendant-appellant Travis Kalanick, alleging that the Uber application allows third-party drivers to illegally fix prices. The district court joined Uber as a defendant and denied motions by Kalanick and Uber to compel arbitration. In doing so, the district court concluded that Meyer did not have reasonably conspicuous notice of and did not unambiguously manifest assent to Uber's Terms of Service when he registered. The district court held that Meyer therefore was not bound by the mandatory arbitration provision contained in the Terms of Service.

For the reasons set forth below, we vacate and remand for further proceedings consistent with this opinion.

BACKGROUND

A. *The Facts*

The facts are undisputed and are summarized as follows: Uber offers a software application for smartphones (the "Uber App") that allows riders to request rides from third-party drivers. On October 18, 2014, Meyer registered for an Uber account with the Uber App on a Samsung Galaxy S5 phone running an Android operating system. After registering, Meyer took ten rides with Uber drivers in New York, Connecticut, Washington, D.C., and Paris.

In support of its motion to compel arbitration, Uber submitted a declaration from Senior Software Engineer Vincent Mi, in which Mi represented that Uber maintained records of when and how its users registered for the service and that, from his review of those records, Mi was able to identify the dates and methods by which Meyer registered for a user account. Attached to the declaration were screenshots of the two screens that a user registering in October 2014 with an Android-operated smartphone would have seen during the registration process.

The first screen, at which the user arrives after downloading the application and clicking a button marked "Register," is labeled "Register" and includes fields for the user to enter his or her name, email address, phone number, and a password (the "Registration Screen"). The Registration Screen also offers the user the option to register via a Google+ or Facebook account. According to Uber's records, Meyer did not sign up using either Google+ or Facebook and would have had to enter manually his personal information.

After completing the information on the Registration Screen and clicking "Next," the user advances to a second screen labeled "Payment" (the "Payment Screen"), on which the user can enter credit card details or elect to make payments using PayPal or Google Wallet, third-party payment services. According to Uber's records, Meyer entered his credit card information to pay for rides. To complete the process, the prospective user must click the button marked "REGISTER" in the middle of the Payment Screen.

Below the input fields and buttons on the Payment Screen is black text advising users that "[b]y creating an Uber account, you agree to the TERMS OF SERVICE & PRIVACY POLICY." . . . The capitalized phrase, which is bright blue and underlined, was a hyperlink that, when clicked, took the user to a third screen containing a button that, in turn, when clicked, would then display the current version of both Uber's Terms of Service and Privacy Policy. Meyer recalls entering his contact information and credit card details before registering, but does not recall seeing or following the hyperlink to the Terms and Conditions. He declares that he did not read the Terms and Conditions, including the arbitration provision.

When Meyer registered for an account, the Terms of Service contained the following mandatory arbitration clause:

> **Dispute Resolution**
>
> You and Company agree that any dispute, claim or controversy arising out of or relating to this Agreement or the breach, termination, enforcement, interpretation or validity thereof or the use of the Service or Application (collectively, "Disputes") will be settled by binding arbitration, except that each party retains the right to bring an individual action in small claims court and the right to seek injunctive or other equitable relief in a court of competent jurisdiction to prevent the actual or threatened infringement, misappropriation or violation of a party's copyrights, trademarks, trade secrets, patents or other intellectual property rights. You acknowledge and agree that you

> and Company are each waiving the right to a trial by jury or to participate as a plaintiff or class User in any purported class action or representative proceeding. Further, unless both you and Company otherwise agree in writing, the arbitrator may not consolidate more than one person's claims, and may not otherwise preside over any form of any class or representative proceeding. If this specific paragraph is held unenforceable, then the entirety of this "Dispute Resolution" section will be deemed void. Except as provided in the preceding sentence, this "Dispute Resolution" section will survive any termination of this Agreement.

. . . . The Terms of Service further provided that the American Arbitration Association ("AAA") would hear any dispute, and that the AAA Commercial Arbitration Rules would govern any arbitration proceeding.

[. . .]

[The district court denied defendants' motions to compel arbitration, concluding that Meyer did not have reasonably conspicuous notice of the Terms of Service and did not unambiguously manifest assent to the terms. Because of this finding, the district court did not consider whether the defendants had waived their right to arbitrate by bringing a motion to dismiss on the merits before moving to compel arbitration.]

DISCUSSION

We consider first whether there is a valid agreement to arbitrate between Meyer and Uber . . . .

I. The Arbitration Agreement

[. . .]

A. Applicable Law

1. Procedural Framework

Under the Federal Arbitration Act (the "FAA"), "[a] written provision in . . . a contract . . . to settle by arbitration a controversy thereafter arising out of such contract . . . shall be valid, irrevocable, and enforceable." 9 U.S.C. § 2. The FAA reflects "a liberal federal policy favoring arbitration agreements," *AT&T Mobility LLC v. Concepcion*, 563 U.S. 333, 346 (2011) (*quoting Moses H. Cone Mem'l Hosp. v. Mercury Constr. Corp.*, 460 U.S. 1, 24 (1983)), and places arbitration agreements on "the same footing as other contracts," . . . . It thereby follows that parties are not required to arbitrate unless they have agreed to do so. . . .

Thus, before an agreement to arbitrate can be enforced, the district court must first determine whether such agreement exists between the parties. . . . This question is determined by state contract law. . . .

[. . .]

2. *State Contract Law*

"State law principles of contract formation govern the arbitrability question." . . . . The district court applied California law in its opinion, but acknowledged that it "[did] not view the choice between California law and New York law as dispositive with respect to the issue of whether an arbitration agreement was formed." . . . . Defendants have not challenged the district court's choice of law but state that "if this Court concludes that New York law differs from California law with respect to any determinative issues, it should apply New York law." Appellants' Br. at 17 n.2. We agree with the district court's determination that California state law applies, and note that New York and California apply "substantially similar rules for determining whether the parties have mutually assented to a contract term." . . . .

To form a contract, there must be "[m]utual manifestation of assent, whether by written or spoken word or by conduct." [*Specht v. Netscape Commc'ns Corp.*, 306 F.3d 17, 20 (2d Cir. 2002).] California law is clear, however, that "an offeree, regardless of apparent manifestation of his consent, is not bound by inconspicuous contractual provisions of which he is unaware, contained in a document whose contractual nature is not obvious." *Id.* at 30 (*quoting Windsor Mills, Inc. v. Collins & Aikman Corp.*, 101 Cal. Rptr. 3d 347, 351 (Cal. Ct. App. 1972)). "Thus, California contract law measures assent by an objective standard that takes into account both what the offeree said, wrote, or did and the transactional context in which the offeree verbalized or acted." *Id.* at 30.

Where there is no evidence that the offeree had actual notice of the terms of the agreement, the offeree will still be bound by the agreement if a reasonably prudent user would be on inquiry notice of the terms. . . . *Nguyen v. Barnes & Noble Inc.*, 763 F.3d 1171, 1177 (9th Cir. 2014). Whether a reasonably prudent user would be on inquiry notice turns on the "[c]larity and conspicuousness of arbitration terms," *Specht*, 306 F.3d at 30; in the context of web-based contracts, as discussed further below, clarity and conspicuousness are a function of the design and content of the relevant interface. . . .

Thus, only if the undisputed facts establish that there is "[r]easonably conspicuous notice of the existence of contract terms and unambiguous manifestation of assent to those terms" will we find that a contract has been formed. *See Specht*, 306 F.3d at 35.

3. *Web-based Contracts*

"While new commerce on the Internet has exposed courts to many new situations, it has not fundamentally changed the principles of contract." *Register.com, Inc. v. Verio, Inc.*, 356 F.3d 393, 403 (2d Cir. 2004). "Courts around the country have recognized that [an] electronic 'click' can suffice to signify the acceptance of a contract," and that "[t]here is nothing automatically offensive about such agreements, as long as the layout and language of the site give the user reasonable notice that a click will manifest assent to an agreement." *Sgouros v. TransUnion Corp.*, 817 F.3d 1029, 1033-34 (7th Cir. 2016).

With these principles in mind, one way in which we have previously distinguished web-based contracts is the manner in which the user manifests assent—namely, "clickwrap" (or "click-through") agreements, which require users to click an "I agree" box after being presented with a list of terms and conditions of use, or "browsewrap" agreements, which generally post terms and conditions on a website via a hyperlink at the bottom of the screen. . . . Courts routinely uphold clickwrap agreements for the principal reason that the user has affirmatively assented to the terms of agreement by clicking "I agree." *See Fteja v. Facebook, Inc.*, 841 F. Supp. 2d 829, 837 (S.D.N.Y. 2012) (collecting cases). Browsewrap agreements, on the other hand, do not require the user to expressly assent. . . . . "Because no affirmative action is required by the website user to agree to the terms of a contract other than his or her use of the website, the determination of the validity of the browsewrap contract depends on whether the user has actual or constructive knowledge of a website's terms and conditions." . . . .

Of course, there are infinite ways to design a website or smartphone application, and not all interfaces fit neatly into the clickwrap or browsewrap categories. Some online agreements require the user to scroll through the terms before the user can indicate his or her assent by clicking "I agree." . . . . Other agreements notify the user of the existence of the website's terms of use and, instead of providing an "I agree" button, advise the user that he or she is agreeing to the terms of service when registering or signing up. . . .

In the interface at issue in this case, a putative user is not required to assent explicitly to the contract terms; instead, the user must click a button marked "Register," underneath which the screen states "By creating an Uber account, you agree to the TERMS OF SERVICE & PRIVACY POLICY," with hyperlinks to the Terms of Service and Privacy Policy. . . . Most recently in *Nicosia*, we held that reasonable minds could disagree regarding the sufficiency of notice provided to Amazon.com customers when placing an order through the website. [*Nicosia v. Amazon.com, Inc.*, 834 F.3d 220, 237 (2d Cir. 2016).]

Following our precedent, district courts considering similar agreements have found them valid where the existence of the terms was reasonably communicated to the user. *Compare Cullinane v. Uber Techs., Inc.*, No. 14-14750-DPW, 2016 WL 3751652, at *7 (D. Mass. July 11, 2016) (applying Massachusetts law and granting motion to compel arbitration);

. . . . *with Applebaum v. Lyft, Inc.*, No. 16-cv-07062 (JGK), 2017 WL 2774153, at *8-9 (S.D.N.Y. June 26, 2017) (applying New York law and denying motion to compel arbitration where notice of contract terms was insufficient to bind plaintiff). *See also* Woodrow Hartzog, *Website Design As Contract*, 60 Am. U. L. Rev. 1635, 1644 (2011) ("Courts oscillate on 'notice sentence browsewraps,' which provide users with a link to terms of use but do not require users to acknowledge that they have seen them.").

Classification of web-based contracts alone, however, does not resolve the notice inquiry. Insofar as it turns on the reasonableness of notice, the enforceability of a web- based agreement is clearly a fact-intensive inquiry. . . . Nonetheless, on a motion to compel arbitration, we may determine that an agreement to arbitrate exists where the notice of the arbitration provision was reasonably conspicuous and manifestation of assent unambiguous as a matter of law. . . .

B. Application

Meyer attests that he was not on actual notice of the hyperlink to the Terms of Service or the arbitration provision itself, and defendants do not point to evidence from which a jury could infer otherwise. Accordingly, we must consider whether Meyer was on inquiry notice of the arbitration provision by virtue of the hyperlink to the Terms of Service on the Payment Screen and, thus, manifested his assent to the agreement by clicking "Register."

[. . .]

1. Reasonably conspicuous notice

In considering the question of reasonable conspicuousness, precedent and basic principles of contract law instruct that we consider the perspective of a reasonably prudent smartphone user. . . . "[M]odern cell phones . . . are now such a pervasive and insistent part of daily life that the proverbial visitor from Mars might conclude they were an important feature of human anatomy." *Riley v. California*, 134 S. Ct. 2473, 2484 (2014). As of 2015, nearly two-thirds of American adults owned a smartphone, a figure that has almost doubled since 2011. . . .

Smartphone users engage in these activities through mobile applications, or "apps," like the Uber App. To begin using an app, the consumers need to locate and download the app, often from an application store. Many apps then require potential users to sign up for an account to access the app's services. Accordingly, when considering the perspective of a reasonable smartphone user, we need not presume that the user has never before encountered an app or entered into a contract using a smartphone. Moreover, a reasonably prudent smartphone user knows that text that is highlighted in blue and underlined is hyperlinked to another webpage where additional information will be found.

Turning to the interface at issue in this case, we conclude that the design of the screen and language used render the notice provided reasonable as a matter of California law. The Payment Screen is uncluttered, with only fields for the user to enter his or her credit card details, buttons to register for a user account or to connect the user's pre-existing PayPal account or Google Wallet to the Uber account, and the warning that "By creating an Uber account, you agree to the TERMS OF SERVICE & PRIVACY POLICY." The text, including the hyperlinks to the Terms and Conditions and Privacy Policy, appears directly below the buttons for registration. The entire screen is visible at once, and the user does not need to scroll beyond what is immediately visible to find notice of the Terms of Service. Although the sentence is in a small font, the dark print contrasts with the bright white background, and the hyperlinks are in blue and underlined. This presentation differs sharply from the screen we considered in *Nicosia*, which contained, among other things, summaries of the user's purchase and delivery information, "between fifteen and twenty-five links," "text . . . in at least four font sizes and six colors," and several buttons and advertisements. *Nicosia*, 834 F.3d at 236-37. Furthermore, the notice of the terms and conditions in *Nicosia* was "not directly adjacent" to the button intended to manifest assent to the terms, unlike the text and button at issue here. *Id.* at 236.

In addition to being spatially coupled with the mechanism for manifesting assent—i.e., the register button—the notice is temporally coupled. . . . Here, notice of the Terms of Service is provided simultaneously to enrollment, thereby connecting the contractual terms to the services to which they apply. We think that a reasonably prudent smartphone user would understand that the terms were connected to the creation of a user account.

That the Terms of Service were available only by hyperlink does not preclude a determination of reasonable notice. . . . Moreover, the language "[b]y creating an Uber account, you agree" is a clear prompt directing users to read the Terms and Conditions and signaling that their acceptance of the benefit of registration would be subject to contractual terms. As long as the hyperlinked text was itself reasonably conspicuous—and we conclude that it was—a reasonably prudent smartphone user would have constructive notice of the terms. While it may be the case that many users will not bother reading the additional terms, that is the choice the user makes; the user is still on inquiry notice. . . .

Accordingly, we conclude that the Uber App provided reasonably conspicuous notice of the Terms of Service as a matter of California law and turn to the question of whether Meyer unambiguously manifested his assent to those terms.

2. *Manifestation of assent*

Although Meyer's assent to arbitration was not express, we are convinced that it was unambiguous in light of the objectively reasonable notice of the terms, as discussed in detail above. . . . As we described above, there is ample evidence that a reasonable user would be on inquiry notice of the terms, and the spatial and temporal coupling of the terms with the registration button "indicate[d] to the consumer that he or she is . . . employing such services subject to additional terms and conditions that may one day affect him or her." . . . A reasonable user would know that by clicking the registration button, he was agreeing to the terms and conditions accessible via the hyperlink, whether he clicked on the hyperlink or not.

The fact that clicking the register button had two functions—creation of a user account and assent to the Terms of Service—does not render Meyer's assent ambiguous. The registration process allowed Meyer to review the Terms of Service prior to registration, unlike web platforms that provide notice of contract terms only after the user manifested his or her assent. Furthermore, the text on the Payment Screen not only included a hyperlink to the Terms of Service, but expressly warned the user that by creating an Uber account, the user was agreeing to be bound by the linked terms. Although the warning text used the term "creat[e]" instead of "register," as the button was marked, the physical proximity of the notice to the register button and the placement of the language in the registration flow make clear to the user that the linked terms pertain to the action the user is about to take.

The transactional context of the parties' dealings reinforces our conclusion. Meyer located and downloaded the Uber App, signed up for an account, and entered his credit card information with the intention of entering into a forward-looking relationship with Uber. The registration process clearly contemplated some sort of continuing relationship between the putative user and Uber, one that would require some terms and conditions, and the Payment Screen provided clear notice that there were terms that governed that relationship.

Accordingly, we conclude on the undisputed facts of this case that Meyer unambiguously manifested his assent to Uber's Terms of Service as a matter of California law.

[The court vacated the order of the district court denying the motion to compel and remanded the case to determine if the defendants had waived the right to arbitrate.]

CULLINANE V. UBER TECHS., INC.

893 F.3d 53 (1st Cir. 2018).

(footnotes omitted)

TORRUELLA, CIRCUIT JUDGE.

This case concerns the enforceability of an arbitration clause contained in an online contract. Plaintiffs-Appellants Rachel Cullinane, Jacqueline Núñez, Elizabeth Schaul, and Ross McDonagh, (collectively, "Plaintiffs"), filed this putative class action in Massachusetts Superior Court on behalf of themselves and other users of a ride-sharing service in the Boston area against Defendant-Appellee Uber Technologies, Inc. ("Uber"). In their complaint, Plaintiffs alleged that Uber violated a Massachusetts consumer-protection statute by knowingly imposing certain fictitious or inflated fees. Uber removed the case to the United States District Court for the District of Massachusetts, and filed a motion to compel arbitration and stay or dismiss the case. The district court granted Uber's motion to compel arbitration and dismissed the complaint. For the reasons explained below, we reverse and remand.

[. . .]

A. Factual Background

Uber provides a ride-sharing service that transports customers throughout some cities, including Boston, for a fee. Uber licenses the Uber mobile application (the "Uber App") to the public so that users may request transportation services from independent third party providers in the users' local area. To be able to request and pay for third party transportation services, Uber App users must first register with Uber by creating an account. At the time Plaintiffs created their accounts, prospective users could either register through the Uber App or register directly through Uber's website.

All four named Plaintiffs downloaded the Uber App on iPhones and used the Uber App to create Uber accounts between December 31, 2012 and January 10, 2014. [Each of the named plaintiffs alleged that they paid unnecessary toll fees on rides that they ordered using the Uber app.]

Now, the Plaintiffs seek to represent a class of Massachusetts-resident Uber passengers who have been charged the Massport Surcharge and East Boston toll, and have not received a refund for these charges.

B. Uber App Registration Process

All prospective Uber passengers must go through Uber's registration process. When Plaintiffs used the Uber App to register, the process included three different screens that asked for user information. The first screen, titled "Create an Account," asked users to enter an e-mail address, a mobile phone number, and a password for the account. Immediately above the phone's keyboard—which occupied half of the phone screen—written in dark gray against a black background, was the text: "We use your email and mobile number to send you ride confirmations and receipts."

The second screen, entitled "Create a Profile," prompted the user to enter their first and last name, and to upload a picture. This screen also included dark gray text on a black background which read: "Your name and photo helps [sic] your driver identify you at pickup."

The third screen varied slightly during the thirteen-month period during which the Plaintiffs registered. The first two plaintiffs to register, Nuñez and Schaul, saw a third screen titled "Link Card." The last two plaintiffs to register, Cullinane and McDonagh, saw a third screen titled "Link Payment." Irrespective of its title, the third and final screen prompted the user to enter the appropriate payment information for Uber's services. Because the design and content of both versions of the third screen are particularly relevant to this case, we discuss them in greater detail.

1. "Link Card"

When confronted with the third screen, Nuñez and Schaul were presented with the "Link Card" screen. . . .

As depicted in the screenshot above, the screen contained a thick gray bar at the top of the screen with the title "Link Card." To the left of the title was a "CANCEL" button and to the right was an inoperative and barely visible "DONE" button. Below the thick gray title bar was a blank text field where users could enter their credit card information. The blank text field was white, contrasting with the black background, horizontally traversing the screen, and included some light gray numbers to exemplify the type of information required. In addition, at the beginning of the blank text field, and to the left of the light gray numbers, there was an icon representing a credit card.

The "Link Card" screen automatically included a number pad, covering half of the screen, for users to type their credit card information into the blank text field.

The screen also included text, just below the blank text field, that instructed users to "scan your card" and "enter promo code." This text was written in light gray bolded font. The "scan your card" text had a bright blue camera icon to its left, and the "enter promo code" had a bright blue bullet-shaped icon enclosed in a circle. The record is unclear as to whether the "scan your card" and "enter promo code" texts were clickable buttons.

Finally, the "Link Card" screen also included dark gray text which read: "By creating an Uber account, you agree to the." Below this text was the phrase "Terms of Service & Privacy Policy" in bold white text enclosed in a gray rectangle. According to Uber, this rectangular box indicated that this phrase was a "clickable button."

2. "Link Payment"

Plaintiffs Cullinane and McDonagh confronted a third screen that looked like this: . . . .

The "Link Payment" screen was very similar to the "Link Card" screen, except that it provided for an additional payment option that altered the screen's initial presentation. Instead of a blank text field for credit card information and the aforementioned number pad, the "Link Payment" screen displayed the blank text field and a large blue button with the PayPal logo. The blue PayPal button was located immediately below a centralized dark gray text reading "OR," indicating the existence of two payment options. Below the PayPal button, at the bottom of the screen, the texts "[b]y creating an Uber account you agree to the" and "Terms of Service & Privacy Policy" were presented in the same manner as previously described. If the user selected the blank text field to input his or her credit card information, the user would then "engage[ ] the keyboard" and the "Link Payment" screen would resemble the "Link Card" screen.

Notwithstanding the differences in the third screen, the design and general mechanics of the Uber App interface remained fairly uniform. For example, all screens included a gray bar at the top. Within this bar the user was presented with the screen title written in capital letters in a dark colored font. Below the title, but within the gray bar, was an illustration of three circles connected by a green line. These circles indicated the user's progress through Uber's registration process.

In addition, on all screens, the gray bar incorporated two buttons: one to the left and one to the right of the screen's title. The left button was a "CANCEL" button, written in all capital letters. This button was enabled throughout the registration process, even before the user interacted with the screen. On the first two screens the right button was a "NEXT" button, also written in all capital letters. The "NEXT" button would remain barely visible and inoperative until after the user had entered the required information for each screen. In both versions of the third screen, the "NEXT" button was replaced by a "DONE" button. This "DONE" button also remained inoperative and barely visible until the user had entered the requested payment information.

C. Uber's Terms and Conditions

Uber's Terms and Conditions (the "Agreement") consisted of an approximately ten-page document that was available to Uber App users during the registration process via hyperlink. If the user "clicked" on the "Terms of Service & Privacy Policy" button in either version of the third screen, he or she would be taken to another screen that contained two additional clickable buttons entitled "Terms & Conditions" and "Privacy Policy." The Agreement was displayed on the user's screen once the "Terms & Conditions" button was clicked. However, the Uber App did not require prospective users to "click" any of these buttons or access the Agreement before they could complete the registration process.

The Agreement contained a "Dispute Resolution" section that provided that the user and Uber:

> [A]gree that any dispute, claim or controversy arising out of or relating to this Agreement or the breach, termination, enforcement, interpretation or validity thereof or the use of the Service or Application (collectively, **"Disputes"**) will be settled by binding arbitration. . . . **You acknowledge and agree that you and [Uber] are each waiving the right to a trial by jury or to participate as a plaintiff or class User in any purported class action or representative proceeding.**

(Emphasis in original). Furthermore, the Agreement stipulated that "[t]he arbitration [would] be administered by the American Arbitration Association ('AAA') in accordance with the Commercial Arbitration Rules and the Supplementary Procedures for Consumer Related Disputes (the 'AAA Rules')" and that the Federal Arbitration Act ("FAA") would govern the interpretation and enforcement of the Agreement's arbitration.

[. . .]

III. Discussion

Under the FAA, "[a] written provision in . . . a contract . . . to settle by arbitration a controversy thereafter arising out of such contract . . . shall be valid, irrevocable, and enforceable." 9 U.S.C. § 2 (2012). The Supreme Court has stated that the FAA reflects "a federal liberal policy favoring arbitration agreements." . . . Nevertheless, the "FAA does not require parties to arbitrate when they have not agreed to do so." *Volt Info. Scis., Inc. v. Bd. of Trs. of Leland Stanford Jr. Univ.*, 489 U.S. 468, 478, 109 S.Ct. 1248, 103 L.Ed.2d 488 (1989). Therefore, in deciding a motion to compel arbitration, a court must first determine "whether '. . . there exists a written agreement to arbitrate.' " . . . . The burden of making that showing lies on the party seeking to compel arbitration. . . .

It is well settled that "arbitration is a matter of contract." *Rent-A-Center, West, Inc. v. Jackson*, 561 U.S. 63, 67, 130 S.Ct. 2772, 177 L.Ed.2d 403 (2010). "When deciding whether the parties agreed to arbitrate a certain matter (including arbitrability), courts generally . . . should apply ordinary state-law principles that govern the formation of contracts." *First Options of Chi., Inc. v. Kaplan*, 514 U.S. 938, 944, 115 S.Ct. 1920, 131 L.Ed.2d 985 (1995). The district court applied Massachusetts law and the parties do not challenge that decision. *Cullinane v. Uber Techs., Inc.*, 2016

WL 3751652, at *5. In any event, we agree with the district court that Massachusetts contract law applies.

The Massachusetts Supreme Judicial Court ("SJC") has not addressed the issue of contract formation for online agreements. However, in *Ajemian v. Yahoo!, Inc.*, 83 Mass.App.Ct. 565, 987 N.E.2d 604, 611–15 (2013), the Massachusetts Appeals Court ("Appeals Court") addressed the enforceability of forum selection and limitation clauses within an online contract and that court's decision is "trustworthy data for ascertaining state law." . . . While the clauses at issue in *Ajemian* did not include an arbitration clause, "the essential question presented was the same: what level of notice and assent is required in order for a court to enforce an online adhesion contract?" *Cullinane*, 2016 WL 3751652, at *6. Consequently, we apply the principles stated in *Ajemian*.

In *Ajemian*, the Appeals Court determined that there was "no reason to apply different legal principles [of contract enforcement] simply because a forum selection clause . . . is contained in an online contract." 987 N.E.2d at 612. Therefore, "such clauses will be enforced provided they have been reasonably communicated and accepted." *Id.* at 611. The Appeals Court explained that "[r]easonably conspicuous notice of the existence of contract terms and unambiguous manifestation of assent to those terms by consumers are essential if electronic bargaining is to have integrity and credibility." *Id.* at 612. (emphasis added) (internal quotations marks omitted) (quoting *Specht v. Netscape Commc'ns Corp.*, 306 F.3d 17, 35 (2d Cir. 2002)). With this in mind, the Appeals Court set forth a two-step inquiry for the enforceability of forum selection clauses in online agreements. The first inquiry is whether the contract terms were "reasonably communicated to the plaintiffs." *Id.* at 612. The second is whether the record shows that those terms were "accepted and, if so, the manner of acceptance." *Id.* at 613. The court further clarified that the burden to show that the terms were reasonably communicated and accepted lies on the party seeking to enforce the forum selection clause. *See id.* at 611.

With the legal framework determined, we proceed to our analysis keeping in mind that our sole focus is on the enforceability of Uber's mandatory arbitration clause found in the Agreement.

A. Reasonable Notice

Uber makes no claim that any of the Plaintiffs actually saw the arbitration clause or even clicked on the "Terms of Service & Privacy Policy" button. Rather, it relies solely on a claim that its online presentation was sufficiently conspicuous as to bind the Plaintiffs whether or not they chose to click through the relevant terms. Therefore, we must determine whether the terms of the Agreement were "reasonably communicated" to the Plaintiffs. We note that "in the context of web-based contracts . . . clarity and conspicuousness are a function of the design and content of the relevant interface." *Meyer v. Uber Techs., Inc.*, 868 F.3d 66, 75 (2d Cir. 2017).

Under Massachusetts law, "conspicuous" means that a terms is "so written, displayed or presented that a reasonable person against which it is to operate ought to have noticed it." . . . . Whether or not a term is conspicuous is for the court to decide. . . . Several nonexhaustive examples of general characteristics that make a term conspicuous include using larger and contrasting font, the use of headings in capitals, or somehow setting off the term from the surrounding text by the use of symbols or other marks. . . .

In addition, when the terms of the agreement are only available by following a link, the court must examine "the language that was used to notify users that the terms of their arrangement with [the service provider] could be found by following the link, how prominently displayed the link was, and any other information that would bear on the reasonableness of communicating [the terms]." *Ajemian*, 987 N.E.2d at 612.

After reviewing the Uber App registration process, we find that the Plaintiffs were not reasonably notified of the terms of the Agreement. We note at the outset that Uber chose not to use a common method of conspicuously informing users of the existence and location of terms and conditions: requiring users to click a box stating that they agree to a set of terms, often provided by hyperlink, before continuing to the next screen. Instead, Uber chose to rely on simply displaying a notice of deemed acquiescence and a link to the terms. In order to determine whether that approach reasonably notified users of the Agreement, we begin our analysis with how this link was displayed.

Uber contends that the gray rectangular box with the language "Terms of Service & Privacy Policy" was reasonably conspicuous, both visually and contextually, because it was displayed in a larger font, in bold, contrasting in color, and highlighted by the box around it. Furthermore, Uber argues that the screen contained a total of twenty-six words, making it difficult for a user to miss it.

While the language and the number of words found on the "Link Card" and "Link Payment" screens could be seen to favor Uber's position, the reading of Uber's "Terms of Service & Privacy Policy" hyperlink must be contextualized. That is, it may not be read in a vacuum. Other similarly displayed terms presented simultaneously to the user in both versions of the third screen diminished the conspicuousness of the "Terms of Service & Privacy Policy" hyperlink. We explain.

First, Uber's "Terms of Service & Privacy Policy" hyperlink did not have the common appearance of a hyperlink. While not all hyperlinks need to have the same characteristics, they are "commonly blue and underlined."

. . . . Here, the "Terms of Service & Privacy Policy" hyperlink was presented in a gray rectangular box in white bold text. Though not dispositive, the characteristics of the hyperlink raise concerns as to whether a reasonable user would have been aware that the gray rectangular box was actually a hyperlink.

Next, the overall content of the "Link Card" and "Link Payment" screens show that the "Terms of Service & Privacy Policy" hyperlink was not a conspicuous term as defined by Massachusetts law. Again, this hyperlink was displayed in white bold font within a gray rectangular box. While these features may have been sufficient to accentuate a hyperlink found within a registration process interface with a plain design and limited content, that was not the case here.

Along with the "Terms of Service & Privacy Policy" hyperlink, the "Link Card" and "Link Payment" screens contained other terms displayed with similar features. For example, the terms "scan your card" and "enter promo code" were also written in bold and with a similarly sized font as the hyperlink. Both versions of the third screen also included the words "CANCEL" and "DONE,"—the latter being barely visible until the user had entered the required payment information—in all capital letters and dark colored font. Meanwhile, the top of the screens featured the terms "Link Card" or "Link Payment" in large capital letters and dark colored font. These had the largest-sized font in both versions of the third screen.

Uber's "Terms of Service & Privacy Policy" hyperlink was even less conspicuous on the "Link Payment" screen. The inclusion of the additional payment option and the placement of a large blue PayPal button in the middle of the screen were more attention-grabbing and displaced the hyperlink to the bottom of the screen.

It is thus the design and content of the "Link Card" and "Link Payment" screens of the Uber App interface that lead us to conclude that Uber's "Terms of Service & Privacy Policy" hyperlink was not conspicuous. Even though the hyperlink did possess some of the characteristics that make a term conspicuous, the presence of other terms on the same screen with a similar or larger size, typeface, and with more noticeable attributes diminished the hyperlink's capability to grab the user's attention. If everything on the screen is written with conspicuous features, then nothing is conspicuous. . . .

Furthermore, when we consider the characteristics of the text used to notify potential users that the creation of an Uber account would bind them to the linked terms, we note that this phrase was even less conspicuous than the "Terms of Service & Privacy Policy" hyperlink. This notice was displayed in a dark gray small-sized non- bolded font against a black background. The notice simply did not have any distinguishable feature that would set it apart from all the other terms surrounding it.

Because both the "Link Card" and "Link Payment" screens were filled with other very noticeable terms that diminished the conspicuousness of the "Terms of Service & Privacy Policy" hyperlink and the notice, we find that the terms of the Agreement were not reasonably communicated to the Plaintiffs. As such, Uber's motion to compel arbitration fails.

IV. Conclusion

Because the Plaintiffs were not reasonably notified of the terms of the Agreement, they did not provide their unambiguous assent to those terms. We therefore find that Uber has failed to carry its burden on its motion to compel arbitration. For these reasons we reverse the district court's grant of Uber's motion to compel arbitration, and remand the case for further proceedings consistent with this opinion.

Reversed and Remanded.

NOTES AND QUESTIONS

1. How do the two reported cases differ? How are they alike? Which do you think makes more sense? Why? Can you synthesize a consistent rule of law after reading them both?

2. What do you make of the Second Circuit's declaration in *Meyer* that "[w]hile it may be the case that many users will not bother reading the additional terms, that is the choice the user makes; the user is still on inquiry notice"? Does it matter that strong evidence exists that virtually all users make the "choice" not to read terms in boilerplate? One empirical study, for instance, found that only about one-tenth of one percent of customers visited terms and conditions pages. *See* Yannis Bakos, Florencia Marotta-Wurgler, and David R. Trossen, *Does Anyone Read the Fine Print? Consumer Attention to Standard-Form Contracts, 43* J. LEG. STUD. 1, 19 (2014).

3. Even if individuals read boilerplate, persuasive evidence exists that they may not understand it. For instance, one empirical study found that a majority of participants did not know if a given contract contained an arbitration provision even immediately after they read the contract. Jeff Sovern, Elayne Greenberg, Paul Kirgis & Yuxiang Liu, *'Whimsy Little Contracts' with Unexpected Consequences: An Empirical Analysis of Consumer Understanding of Arbitration Agreements*, 75 MD. L. REV. 1, 46 (2015).

4. If no one reads boilerplate—or understands it when they do—is there any material distinction between eight-pages of detailed boilerplate and zero pages? In other words, does the presence (or absence) of terms and conditions have any practical meaning or relevance for non-drafting parties? Does that matter? It is enough that these terms and conditions matter to the commercial party?

5. Look back at the arbitration clauses in *Meyer* and *Cullinane*. Are they clearly articulated? Do you think that an individual Uber user reading them

would or could understand what they mean? Do you think that the clauses are substantively fair?

* * *

These cases are recent examples of an ongoing trend of court decisions wrestling with various forms of hypothetical consent. Though technology has evolved, the core issue of standardized terms has been around for at least a couple of decades. For instance, in *Hill v. Gateway 2000, Inc.*, 105 F.3d 1147 (7th Cir.), *cert. denied*, 522 U.S. 808 (1997), the Hills purchased a Gateway 2000 computer over the telephone. The box that arrived contained the computer and a list of terms and conditions that would govern the transaction unless the customer returned the computer within thirty days. One of these terms was an arbitration clause. The Hills kept the computer more than thirty days before complaining about its components and performance. They filed suit in federal court arguing, *inter alia*, that the product's shortcomings made Gateway a racketeer under RICO. Gateway asked the district court to enforce the arbitration clause; the judge refused, ruling that "[t]he present record is insufficient to support a finding of a valid arbitration agreement between the parties or that the plaintiffs were given adequate notice of the arbitration clause."

On appeal, the Seventh Circuit disagreed, holding that the arbitration agreement "in the box" was binding on the Hills. Relying primarily on *ProCD, Inc. v. Zeidenberg*, 86 F.3d 1447 (7th Cir. 1996) (holding that terms inside a box of software bind consumers who use the software after an opportunity to read the terms and to reject them by returning the product), the court concluded that, by keeping the computer for more than thirty days, the Hills accepted Gateway's offer—including the arbitration clause—thereby creating an enforceable contract. In so ruling, the Seventh Circuit rejected the Hills' argument that the arbitration clause did not stand out, stating that, under *Doctor's Associates, Inc. v. Casarotto*, 517 U.S. 681 (1996), the Federal Arbitration Act does not require that an arbitration clause be prominent in order to be enforceable.

Problems with mutual assent may also turn on facts other than notice of boilerplate terms. Courts, in other words, may refuse to enforce arbitration agreements that have other mutual assent failings. Courts seem to be particularly attentive to such failings in adhesive contracts. For instance, the First Circuit recently refused to enforce an arbitration clause entered into by a song-writing contestant and Sony. *Cortes-Ramos v. Martin-Morales*, 894 F.3d 55 (1st Cir. 2018). The contestant submitted a song but did not win. Two years later, Ricky Martin, who had been involved with the contest, released the song "Vida." The contestant alleged that the "Vida" music video was similar to the video he submitted and violated federal copyright and trademark laws. In response, Ricky Martin moved to compel arbitration, relying on the arbitration agreement in the contest rules. The district court granted his motion, noting that Martin was a third-party beneficiary and referenced in many parts of the contest terms. On appeal, however, the First Circuit reversed, finding Ricky Martin was a non-signatory and thus not party to the agreement.

Similarly, the Fifth Circuit recently refused to compel an employee to arbitrate her claims against her employer because the employer did not sign the employment agreement containing the arbitral clause. *Huckaba v. Ref-Chem, L.P.*, 892 F.3d 686, 687 (5th Cir. 2018). Relying on Texas contract law, the court concluded that the parties intended not to be bound unless both parties signed the agreement. They demonstrated that intent by including a signature block for the employer that said, "by signing this agreement the parties are giving up any right they may have to sue each other" and requiring that any modifications be signed by all parties.

3. OBJECTIONS TO THE ARBITRAL PROCESS

Arbitration offers many comparative advantages to litigation in public courts. Courts can be slow, inefficient, and expensive, providing, in practice, limited justice for all but the wealthiest individuals. Arbitration allows parties to choose the procedural hurdles they would rather forgo in order to have a cost-efficient, prompt, and final mechanism to resolve their disputes. Most of the time, panels of unbiased arbitrators provide parties with a full and fair hearing. The threat of vacatur if a panel deprives parties of an equitable opportunity to present their evidence tends to keep the process honest.

The advantages of arbitration, however, can start to feel one-sided when the procedure gets chosen unilaterally by the commercial party. In addition to worrying that voluntary consent is no longer the touchstone of formation, as discussed in the previous Section, critics also have misgivings about the ways in which a commercial party might subtly (and not so subtly) tilt various aspects of the process in its favor. For instance, the commercial party could calibrate rights to discovery in ways that limit individuals' access to vital sources of proof. Or, the commercial party could impose barriers to bringing claims at all, by locating the arbitration in some far-flung place that is expensive or burdensome for the individual to reach. Additionally, the commercial party can insulate itself from aggregate liability, and perhaps from all liability, by imposing class action waivers and confidentiality provisions. Of course, other process inequities are imaginable.

Moreover some imbalances might be inherent to the system. Arbitration could be an insider's game. Commercial parties have repeat opportunities to get familiar with the procedures used and the arbitrators available, while individual parties will likely have only a single arbitration in their entire lives. Repeat players may be able to stockpile information, make short-term sacrifices for long-term gains, and cultivate relationships within arbitral institutions, if not with arbitrators directly.

Courts can rein in flagrant abuses of the arbitral process or correct for positional imbalances that permeate it by striking down specific terms in the arbitration agreement or denying enforcement entirely. To reach an assessment of enforceability, however, courts must distinguish between clauses that merely entail the sorts of tradeoffs involved when parties give up their access to courts in exchange for an alternative forum and those that are oppressive to the weaker party. Policing that boundary line can be challenging, as the U.S. Supreme Court has repeatedly emphasized that choosing an arbitral forum and its attendant streamlined procedures does not amount to a loss of rights. *See, e.g., Mitsubishi Motors Corp. v. Soler Chrysler-Plymouth, Inc.*, 473 U.S. 614, 628 (1985). Nevertheless, if a court concludes that the arbitration agreement unjustly harms the weaker party, it may intervene by using a variety of generally applicable contract law defenses.

Perhaps the defense most commonly brandished by courts looking to trim or invalidate arbitration agreements is unconscionability. Unconscionability applies in an amorphous range of situations, often where other process defects like fraud or duress cannot quite be established. Under the doctrine, courts will refuse to enforce a contract if, on balance, the combination of the bargaining process and the terms in the contract are so one-sided as to "shock the conscience." The unconscionability doctrine, in other words, is divided into procedural unconscionability and substantive unconscionability. *See, e.g., AT&T Mobility LLC v. Concepcion,* 563 U.S. 333, 340 (2011).

Procedural unconscionability focuses on contract formation and the ability of the weaker party to make a meaningful choice. Considering the procedural aspects of contract formation, a court might scrutinize the conspicuousness and intelligibility of terms offered, as well as the use of high-pressure sales tactics, the speed with which the transaction was rushed to conclusion, and the relative access of the parties to counsel.

Substantive unconscionability focuses on the actual terms of the deal. Courts analyze whether the terms impose unduly harsh or one-sided obligations on weaker party without offsetting commercial justification. While substantive unconscionability may take many forms, decisional law contains frequent examples of courts addressing lopsided obligations to arbitrate. Such arbitration agreements allow the commercial party recourse to courts for some or all claims that it might have against the individual while demanding that the individual arbitrate all claims she might have against the commercial party. In addition to watching out for asymmetrical arbitration agreements, courts are also sensitive to the ways that costs in arbitration may impede or prevent individuals from pursuing claims. Mutuality of the obligation to arbitrate and costs are not the only issues relevant to substantive unconscionability, but they are two of the more commonly discussed.

Importantly, the adhesive nature of a contract—the take-it-or-leave-it presentation of terms—does not, in isolation, render a contract unconscionable. Individuals are presumed to have a meaningful choice: they can walk away. In *Harper v. J.D. Byrider of Canton*, 772 N.E.2d 190 (Ohio Ct. App. 9th Dist. 2002), for example, the court explained that a used car buyer who believed that the car he purchased had a false odometer reading was bound to arbitrate his dispute with the car dealer: "Preprinted forms are a fact of commercial life and do not serve to demonstrate *prima facie* unconscionability with regard to arbitration clauses." *Id.* at 192. Normally, unconscionability comes into play only when significant disparities in bargaining power are coupled with terms unreasonably favorable to the stronger, drafting party.

The following cases illustrate these points. As you read them, be attentive to the specific alleged process defects and the legal justifications offered or used to invalidate the arbitration agreements. In combination, these cases make clear that positional advantage, combined with the abridgement of rights, can subdue the federal judicial policy on arbitration. Nevertheless, as you read these cases, ask yourself this: even if access to courts is available, are the individuals in these cases necessarily better off going to court?

ENGALLA V. PERMANENTE MEDICAL GROUP, INC.

15 Cal.4th 951, 938 P.2d 903, 64 Cal.Rptr.2d 843 (1997).

(footnotes omitted)

[**Summary of the Facts.** Mr. Engalla immigrated to the United States in 1980 and had been employed since that time by the Oliver Tire & Rubber Co. as a certified public accountant. At the time of his hiring, Engalla enrolled in the company's health plan. The health benefits were offered through Kaiser Permanente. The Service Agreement for the Plan provided for the resolution of disputes through Kaiser's self-administered arbitration procedures. According to the California Supreme Court, the arbitration procedure was "designed, written, and mandated by Kaiser." Moreover, "[t]he fact that Kaiser . . . administer[ed] its arbitration program from an adversarial perspective [was] not disclosed to Kaiser members or subscribers."

According to the Service Agreement, in the event of a dispute, Kaiser and the subscriber were to designate an arbitrator within thirty days of service of the claim and the two party-designated arbitrators would name a neutral arbitrator within another thirty days. Subscribers agreed to pay a $150 fee for the costs of the arbitration. Kaiser documents described the arbitration program as fair to both parties, allowing employees to resolve disputes quickly and economically. The materials further represented that a hearing would ensue within several months of filing a demand for arbitration. An independent statistical analysis, however, revealed that nearly all Kaiser arbitrations experienced substantial delays; on average, the appointment of a neutral arbitrator alone took some twenty-two months (rather than the two months provided for in the Service Agreement).

In March 1986, Engalla sought treatment from Kaiser for respiratory problems. Tests revealed a possible abnormality in the right lung, but further examination of the condition was not undertaken. Prior radiological studies on Mr. Engalla had been lost, and the radiologist's recommendation for further examinations was ignored. Despite repeated visits by Mr. Engalla for respiratory problems, Kaiser personnel did not perform further diagnostic tests. Mr. Engalla was treated by a variety of Kaiser medical personnel (doctors, nurses, and physicians assistants) during this time; his condition was repeatedly diagnosed as allergies or a cold. In 1991, a radiological test was administered and revealed that Mr. Engalla had inoperable lung cancer.

At the end of May 1991, the Engallas filed a demand for arbitration, alleging negligent diagnosis of Mr. Engalla's condition by Kaiser physicians. Thereafter, Kaiser employees who administered the arbitration procedure engaged in a course of systematic delay. The Engalla's attorney requested expedited processing in light of Mr. Engalla's terminal condition. Kaiser responded to the attorney's repeated entreaties with less than timely and cooperative replies. A variety of procedural matters—the appointment of arbitrators and the scheduling of depositions—were delayed. Kaiser's obfuscation was especially evident in the appointment of a neutral arbitrator. Until the parties agreed upon a neutral, discovery could not be conducted and a hearing date could not be set. Kaiser acknowledged the appointment of a neutral arbitrator in late October 1991 nearly five months after the demand for arbitration and some three months beyond the sixty-day period provided for in the Service Agreement. Mr. Engalla died the next day. The Engallas then filed a lawsuit against Kaiser, claiming *inter alia* fraud as a defense to the enforcement of the arbitration agreement. Kaiser responded with a petition to compel arbitration.]

MOSK, JUSTICE

[. . .]

After a hearing the trial court issued its order denying Kaiser's petition after making specific findings of fact on the issue of fraud both "in the inducement" and "in the application" of the arbitration agreement. The court further found that the arbitration agreement, as applied, was overbroad, unconscionable and a violation of public policy, inasmuch as Kaiser was arguing that the agreement could not be avoided on grounds of fraudulent inducement. The court further found that equitable considerations peculiar to this case required the invalidation of the arbitration provision.

The Court of Appeal reversed. It rejected the claim that Kaiser had defrauded the Engallas, finding *inter alia* that Kaiser's contractual representation of a 60-day time limit for the selection of arbitrators was not "a representation of fact or a promise by Kaiser because appointment of the neutral arbitrator requires the cooperation of and mutual agreement of the parties." . . . The court further concluded there was no evidence of actual reliance on these representations nor evidence that the Engallas would have been any better off had their claims been submitted for judicial resolution rather than arbitration. The court also found that the availability of section 1281.6, which permits one of the parties to petition the court to appoint an arbitrator when the parties fail to agree on one, undermined the Engallas' claim that Kaiser's alleged deliberate delay in selecting arbitrators was a ground for avoiding the arbitration agreement. The court further rejected the claim that Kaiser's special relationship as Engalla's insurer or as a fiduciary in the administration of his health plan created any special duty to disclose the workings of its arbitration program. Finally, the court held the Engallas' waiver and unconscionability claims to be without merit. We granted review.

[. . .]

III. Fraud in the Inducement of the Arbitration Agreement

The Engallas claim fraud in the inducement of the arbitration agreement and therefore that "[g]rounds exist for the revocation of the agreement" within the meaning of section 1281.2, subdivision (b). . . . We construe section 1281.2, subdivision (b), to mean that the petition to compel arbitration is not to be granted when there are grounds for rescinding the agreement. Fraud is one of the grounds on which a contract can be rescinded. (Civ. Code, § 1689, subd. (b)(*l*)) In order to defeat a petition to compel arbitration, the parties opposing a petition to compel must show that the asserted fraud claim goes specifically "to the 'making' of the agreement to arbitrate," rather than to the making of the contract in general. . . . In the present case, the Engallas do allege, and seek to show, fraud in the making of the arbitration agreement.

[. . .]

Here the Engallas claim (1) that Kaiser misrepresented its arbitration agreement in that it entered into the agreement knowing that, at the very least, there was a likelihood its agents would breach the part of the agreement providing for the timely appointment of arbitrators and the expeditious progress towards an arbitration hearing; (2) that Kaiser employed the above misrepresentation in order to induce reliance on the part of Engalla and his employer; (3) that Engalla relied on these misrepresentations to his detriment. The trial court found evidence supporting those claims. We examine each of these claims in turn.

First, evidence of misrepresentation is plain. "[F]alse representations made recklessly and without regard for their truth in order to induce action by another are the equivalent of misrepresentations knowingly and intentionally uttered." . . . As recounted above, section 8.B. of the arbitration agreement provides that party arbitrators "shall" be chosen within 30 days and neutral arbitrators within 60 days, and that the arbitration hearing "shall" be held "within a reasonable time thereafter." Although Kaiser correctly argues that these contractual representations did not bind it to appoint a neutral arbitrator within 60 days, since the appointment of that arbitrator is a bilateral decision that depends on agreements of the parties, Kaiser's contractual representations were at the very least commitments to exercise good faith and reasonable diligence to have the arbitrators appointed within the specified time. This good faith duty is underscored by Kaiser's contractual assumption of the duty to administer the health service plan as a fiduciary.

Here there are facts to support the Engallas' allegation that Kaiser entered into the arbitration agreement with knowledge that it would not comply with its own contractual timelines, or with at least a reckless indifference as to whether its agents would use reasonable diligence and good faith to comply with them. . . . [A] survey of Kaiser arbitrations between 1984 and 1986 submitted into evidence showed that a neutral arbitrator was appointed within 60 days in only 1 percent of the cases, with only 3 percent appointed within 180 days, and that on average the neutral arbitrator was appointed 674 days almost 2 years after the demand for arbitration. . . . [T]he depositions of two of Kaiser's in-house attorneys demonstrate that Kaiser was aware soon after it began its arbitration program that its contractual deadlines were not being met, and that severe delay was endemic to the program. Kaiser nonetheless persisted in its contractual promises of expeditiousness.

Kaiser now argues that most of these delays were caused by the claimants themselves and their attorneys, who procrastinated in the selection of a neutral arbitrator. But Kaiser's counterexplanation is without any statistical support, and is based solely on anecdotal evidence related by Kaiser officials. Moreover, the explanation appears implausible in view of the sheer pervasiveness of the delays. . . . It is, after all, the defense which often benefits from delay, thereby preserving the status quo to its advantage until the time when memories fade and claims are abandoned. Indeed, the present case illustrates why Kaiser's counsel may sometimes find it advantageous to delay the selection of a neutral arbitrator. There is also evidence that Kaiser kept extensive records on the arbitrators it had used, and may have delayed the selection process in order to ensure that it would obtain the arbitrators it thought would best serve its interests. Thus, it is a reasonable inference from the documentary record before us that Kaiser's contractual representations of expeditiousness were made with knowledge of their likely falsity, and in fact concealed an unofficial policy or practice of delay.

The systemwide nature of Kaiser's delay comes into clearer focus when it is contrasted with other arbitration systems. As the Engallas point out, many large institutional users of arbitration, including most health maintenance organizations (HMOs), avoid the potential problems of delay in the selection of arbitrators by contracting with neutral third party organizations, such as the American Arbitration Association (AAA). These organizations will then assume responsibility for administering the claim from the time the arbitration demand is filed, and will ensure the arbitrator or arbitrators are chosen in a timely manner. Though Kaiser is not obliged by law to adopt any particular form of arbitration, the record shows that it did not attempt to create within its own organization any office that would neutrally administer the arbitration program, but instead entrusted such administration to outside counsel retained to act as advocates on its behalf. In other words, there is evidence that Kaiser established a self-administered arbitration system in which delay for its own benefit and convenience was an inherent part, despite express and implied contractual representations to the contrary.

A fraudulent state of mind includes not only knowledge of falsity of the misrepresentation but also an " 'intent to . . . induce reliance' " on it. It can be reasonably inferred in the present case that these misrepresentations of expeditiousness, which are found not only in the contract but in newsletters periodically sent to subscribers touting the virtues of the Kaiser arbitration program, were made by Kaiser to encourage these subscribers to believe that its program would function efficiently. . . .

Kaiser also claims that the Engallas failed to demonstrate actual reliance on its misrepresentations.

[. . .]

In the present case, our assessment of the materiality of representations is somewhat complicated by the fact that the primary decision maker responsible for selecting the Kaiser health plan was not Engalla himself but his employer, Oliver Tire. The evidence shows that Engalla had little if any cognizance of the arbitration agreement, and that the form he signed to enroll in Kaiser merely stated that members' claims must be submitted to arbitration "[i]f the [health services plan] agreement so provides." On the other hand, Oliver Tire and its personnel employees were obviously aware of the arbitration provision and were responsible for scrutinizing the details of the health services plan before offering it to the company's employees. But this complication does not alter fundamentally our analysis of materiality. As we have recognized, an employer that negotiates group medical benefits for its employees acts as an agent for those employees during the period of negotiation.... An agency relationship is a fiduciary one, obliging the agent to act in the interest of the principal.... Accordingly, a material representation in this case is one that would have substantially influenced the health plan selection process of Oliver Tire, acting as an agent of its employees as a class.

Applying these principles to the present ease, we conclude that Kaiser's representations of expeditiousness in the arbitration agreement were not "so obviously unimportant" as to render them immaterial as a matter of law. We have recognized that expeditiousness is commonly regarded as one of the primary advantages of arbitration.... We have accordingly rejected, as a general proposition, the claim that arbitration agreements between an HMO and its participants are inherently one-sided in favor of the former. "The speed and economy of arbitration, in contrast to the expense and delay of a jury trial, could prove helpful to all parties...." ... The explicit and implicit representations contained in Kaiser's arbitration agreement serve to confirm to the reasonable potential subscriber that Kaiser has an efficient system of arbitration, in which what is lost in terms of jury trial rights would be gained in part by a swifter resolution of the dispute. If it is indeed the case that these representations were false, and concealed an arbitration process in which substantial delay was the rule and timeliness the rare exception, then we cannot say these misrepresentations were so trivial that they would not have influenced a reasonable employer's decision as to which among the many competing employee health plans it would choose for its employees.

Kaiser argues to the contrary that the existence of section 1281.6 negates any possible materiality that its misrepresentation of expeditiousness may have had. That section states in pertinent part that in the absence of an agreed method of appointing an arbitrator, "or if the agreed method fails or for any reason cannot be followed ... the court, on petition of a party to the arbitration agreement, shall appoint the arbitrator." ... But the mere fact that there is a statutory remedy to expedite the arbitrator selection process does not necessarily render the reality of Kaiser's systematic delay irrelevant to the selection of a health plan. A party's success in having a section 1281.6 petition granted is not necessarily assured, nor is it costless, nor is it in accord with normal expectations of arbitration participants, who view arbitration as an alternative to the courts. " 'Typically, those who enter into arbitration agreements expect that their dispute will be resolved without necessity for any contact with the courts.' " ... Given the reality that there exists a considerable number of roughly comparable group health plans ..., a reasonable employer choosing a health plan for its employees may very well decline to select a plan with a dysfunctional arbitration system requiring court supervision.

Nor is there any evidence to conclusively rebut the inference of Oliver Tire's reliance on Kaiser's representations of expedition. Kaiser claims to the contrary that the company paid scant attention to the arbitration clause, focusing in particular on the statement of Theodomeir Roy, a personnel officer with Oliver Tire who advised the company in its selection of employee health plans, that he "would not be concerned if [the plan] didn't [have an arbitration clause]. And in fact if it did, as it has here, [we] sort of look with favor on it, thinking that it was an expeditious way to resolve disputes." Yet although Roy may have been indifferent to whether arbitration or some other effective dispute resolution mechanism was available, the evidence suggests he would have looked unfavorably on a system such as Kaiser is alleged to have actually had, which delayed the resolution of claims, required constant action by the claimant, and failed to adhere to its own contractual terms. There is therefore sufficient evidence to support the claim that Oliver Tire actually relied on Kaiser's misrepresentations.

We turn then to the question of injury. A defrauded party has the right to rescind a contract, even without a showing of pecuniary damages, on establishing that fraudulent contractual promises inducing reliance have been breached. . . . The rule derives from the basic principle that a contracting party has a right to what it contracted for, and so has the right "to rescind where he obtain[ed] something substantially different from that which he [is] led to expect." . . . It follows that a defrauded party does not have to show pecuniary damages in order to defeat a petition to compel arbitration. Of course, the Engallas cannot defeat a petition to compel arbitration on the mere showing that Kaiser has engaged generally in fraudulent misrepresentation about the speed of the arbitration process. Rather, they must show that in their particular case, there was substantial delay in the selection of arbitrators contrary to their reasonable, fraudulently induced, contractual expectations. Here, there is ample evidence to support the Engallas' contention that Kaiser breached its arbitration agreement by repeatedly delaying the timely appointment of an available party arbitrator and a neutral arbitrator.

To be sure, the mere fact that the selection of arbitrators extended beyond their 30- and 60-day deadlines does not by itself establish that Kaiser breached its arbitration agreement. It is, after all, the malpractice claimant in arbitration, like the plaintiff in litigation, who bears the primary responsibility of exercising diligence in order to advance progress towards the resolution of its claim . . . , and Kaiser is under no obligation to press for appointment of arbitrators when a claimant is himself dilatory. Nor is the contract breached when delay in the selection of arbitrators is the result of reasonable disagreements over arbitrator selection.

Nonetheless, as explained above, Kaiser, by agreeing to 30- and 60-day periods for the appointment of arbitrators, committed itself to cooperate with reasonable diligence and good faith in the process of appointing the arbitrators within the specified times . . . Here, there is strong evidence that, despite a high degree of diligence on the part of Engalla's counsel in attempting to obtain the timely appointment of arbitrators, Kaiser lacked either reasonable diligence, good faith, or both, in cooperating on these timely appointments. Instead, the evidence shows that it engaged in a course of nonresponse and delay and added extracontractual conditions to the arbitration selection process, such as the requirement that the claimant name a party arbitrator first. Thus, strong evidence supports the conclusion that Kaiser did not fulfill its contractual obligations in this case to appoint arbitrators in a timely manner.

Nor does the presence of section 1281.6 excuse Kaiser's alleged misfeasance, as Kaiser contends. That section, as explained above, provides a statutory method for resolving breakdowns in the arbitrator selection process, and states in pertinent part that in the absence of an agreed method of appointing an arbitrator, "or if the agreed method fails or for any reason cannot be followed . . . the court, on petition of a party to the arbitration agreement, shall appoint the arbitrator." Kaiser contends that section 1281.6 is implicitly incorporated into the contract, which specifies that California law be followed. Yet the availability of section 1281.6 does not absolve Kaiser of its explicit and implicit contractual duties to timely select a neutral arbitrator and to not obstruct progress towards arbitration. All section 1281.6 provides is a remedy for the breach of those duties of which parties may avail themselves. As noted, this remedy compels claimants to go into superior court and seek specific performance of the arbitration agreement, forcing them to engage in at least some litigation in order to vindicate their rights and thereby violating the usual expectations of an arbitration agreement. . . . Nothing in the language of section 1281.6 compels a party to seek this remedy, nor does this language suggest that resort to section 1281.6 is a precondition to opposing successfully a petition to compel arbitration when the petitioning party has engaged in fraud. Rather, section 1281.6 appears to be simply a legislative means of implementing this state's policy in favor of arbitration by permitting parties to an arbitration contract to expedite the arbitrator selection process.

Of course, when a delay in the selection of arbitrators is the result of a reasonable and good faith disagreement between parties, or of some other reasonable cause, the remedy for such delay may indeed be a section 1281.6 petition rather than the abandonment of the arbitration agreement. But a party that imposes and administers its own arbitration program, that fraudulently misrepresents the speed of the arbitrator selection process so as to induce reliance, and that in fact engages in conduct forcing substantial delay, may not then compel arbitration by contending that the other party failed to resort to the court by filing a section 1281.6 petition.

In sum, we conclude there is evidence to support the Engallas' claims that Kaiser fraudulently induced Engalla to enter the arbitration agreement in that it misrepresented the speed of its arbitration program, a misrepresentation on which Engalla's employer relied by selecting Kaiser's health plan for its employees, and that the Engallas suffered delay in the resolution of its malpractice dispute as a result of that reliance, despite Engalla's own reasonable diligence. The trial court, on remand, must resolve conflicting factual evidence in order to properly adjudicate Kaiser's petition to compel arbitration.

IV. Waiver

The Engallas also claim the petition to compel arbitration should be denied on grounds of waiver. For reasons discussed below, we conclude that their waiver claims may have merit, but that the question of waiver must be determined by the trial court on remand.

Section 1281.2, subdivision (a), provides that a trial court shall refuse to compel arbitration if it determines that "[t]he right to compel arbitration has been waived by the petitioner." The Engallas argue that Kaiser's various dilatory actions constituted a waiver of its right to compel arbitration.

[. . .]

. . . [T]he question of waiver is one of fact, and an appellate court's function is to review a trial court's findings regarding waiver to determine whether these are supported by substantial evidence. The trial court in this case made no findings regarding the Engallas' waiver claim, focusing instead on their fraud claim, which has therefore been our primary focus as well. Given the summary-judgment-like posture of the present case, our sole task is to review the record to determine whether there are facts to support the Engallas' waiver claim. We conclude that the evidence of Kaiser's course of delay, reviewed extensively above, which was arguably unreasonable or undertaken in bad faith, may provide sufficient grounds for a trier of fact to conclude that Kaiser has in fact waived its arbitration agreement.

We emphasize, as we explained in our discussion of fraud, that the delay must be substantial, unreasonable, and in spite of the claimant's own reasonable diligence. When delay in choosing arbitrators is the result of reasonable and good faith disagreements between the parties, the remedy for such delay is a petition to the court to choose arbitrators under section 1281.6, rather than evasion of the contractual agreement to arbitrate. The burden is on the one opposing the arbitration agreement to prove to the trial court that the other party's dilatory conduct rises to such a level of misfeasance as to constitute a waiver . . . , and such waiver "is not to be lightly inferred". . . . In this case, there is ample evidence that the claimant was diligent in seeking Kaiser's cooperation, and instead suffered from Kaiser's delay, a delay which was unreasonable or in bad faith. We leave it to the trial court to determine on remand whether waiver of the right to compel arbitration has in fact occurred.

V. Unconscionability

. . . [A]lthough the present contract has some of the attributes of adhesion, it did not, on its face, lack " 'minimum levels of integrity.' " . . . The unfairness that is the substance of the Engallas' unconscionability argument comes essentially to this: The Engallas contend that Kaiser has established a system of arbitration inherently unfair to claimants, because the method of selecting neutral arbitrators is biased. They claim that Kaiser has an unfair advantage as a "repeat player" in arbitration, possessing information on arbitrators that the Engallas themselves lacked. They also argue that Kaiser, under its arbitration system, has sought to maximize this advantage by reserving for itself an unlimited right to veto arbitrators proposed by the other party. This method is in contrast to arbitration programs run by neutral, third party arbitration organizations such as the AAA, which give parties a very limited ability to veto arbitrators from its preselected panels.

Yet none of these features of Kaiser's arbitration program renders the arbitration agreement per se unconscionable. As noted above, section 1281.6 specifically contemplates a system whereby neutral arbitrators will be chosen directly by the parties. The alleged problem with Kaiser's arbitration in this case was not any defect or one-sidedness in its contractual provisions, but rather in the gap between its contractual representations and the actual workings of its arbitration program. It is the doctrines of fraud and waiver, rather than of unconscionability, that most appropriately address this discrepancy between the contractual representation and the reality. Thus, viewing the arbitration agreement on its face, we cannot say it is unconscionable.

VI. Conclusion and Disposition

For the foregoing reasons, the judgment of the Court of Appeal is reversed with directions to remand the case for proceedings consistent with this opinion.

GEORGE, C.J., and BAXTER, WERDEGAR and CHIN, JJ., concur.

KENNARD, JUSTICE, concurring.

I concur in the majority opinion. I write separately to note that this case illustrates yet again the essential role of the courts in ensuring that the arbitration system delivers not only speed and economy but also fundamental fairness.

Unfairness in arbitration sufficiently extreme to justify court intervention can take many forms. As I have previously stated, in my view courts have the power to overturn an arbitrator's decision if it contains manifest error that causes substantial injustice. . . . It is also my view that arbitrators are limited to the same remedies that a court could award under the circumstances of the case, and that a court may overturn an arbitrator's award of relief that exceeds that limit. . . .

This case illustrates the role that courts play in maintaining the procedural fairness, as well as the substantive fairness, of arbitration proceedings. Procedural manipulations can be used by a party not only to delay and obstruct the proceedings, thereby denying the other party the speed and efficiency that are the arbitration system's primary justification, but also to affect the possible outcome of the arbitration. As to speed and efficiency, the Kaiser arbitration provision provides for appointment of a neutral arbitrator within a 60-day period. . . . In reality, a neutral arbitrator was appointed within 60 days in less than 1 percent of Kaiser's arbitrations; the appointment occurred within 180 days (3 times the contractual time period) in less than 3 percent of Kaiser's arbitrations. Indeed, the average time for appointment of a neutral arbitrator was 674 days, more than 11 times the contractual time period. The average time for a Kaiser-administered arbitration hearing to begin (not conclude) was 863 days or almost 30 months. . . . Although the comparison is not exact, it is instructive to compare the "speed" of Kaiser's arbitration process to the speed of judicial proceedings in Alameda County Superior Court, where this action was filed. During the 1993–1994 fiscal year that court disposed of 96 percent of its civil cases in less than 24 months.

By delaying arbitration in this case until after Wilfredo Engalla died, Kaiser also affected the potential outcome of his malpractice claims. Engalla's death reduced Kaiser's potential liability for noneconomic damages to $250,000 from the $500,000 potential liability it would have faced had the claims been arbitrated during Engalla's life. . . .

As the majority opinion makes clear, courts must be alert to procedural manipulations of arbitration proceedings and should grant appropriate relief when such manipulations occur. As here, such conduct may give rise to claims of fraud in the inducement of the arbitration agreement or claims that the manipulating party has waived its right to enforce the arbitration agreement. Moreover, if such conduct affects the arbitration award, it may form the basis for vacating the award as one "procured by corruption, fraud or other undue means". . . .

Finally, it is worth noting that new possibilities for unfairness arise as arbitration ventures beyond the world of merchant-to-merchant disputes in which it was conceived into the world of consumer transactions (like the health care agreement in this case) and nonunion employment relationships. In such cases, the assumption that the parties have freely chosen arbitration as a dispute resolution mechanism in a process of arm's-length negotiation may be little more than an illusion. Unlike the traditional model of arbitration agreements negotiated between large commercial firms with equal bargaining power, consumer and employment arbitration agreements are typically "take it or leave it" propositions, contracts of adhesion in which the only choice for the consumer or the employee is to accept arbitration or forgo the transaction. And the fact that the business organization imposing the arbitration clause is a repeat player in the arbitration system, while the consumer or employee is not, raises the potential that arbitrators will consciously or unconsciously bias their decisions in favor of an organization or industry that hires them regularly as an arbitrator.

Here, neither plaintiffs' decedent nor his employer was afforded an opportunity to accept or reject arbitration as the means of resolving disputes. Rather, Kaiser's standard health care agreement, which included the arbitration requirement, was presented on a "take it or leave it" basis. . . . There was no true bargaining involved here. Moreover, although Kaiser appears to have led its members to believe that Kaiser administered its arbitration system fairly and as a "fiduciary", in reality the opposite may have been true. Kaiser "administered" its arbitration system through its defense attorneys who appear to have manipulated the process to Kaiser's advantage.

Private arbitration may resolve disputes faster and cheaper than judicial proceedings. Private arbitration, however, may also become an instrument of injustice imposed on a "take it or leave it" basis. The courts must distinguish the former from the latter, to ensure that private arbitration systems resolve disputes not only with speed and economy but also with fairness.

BROWN, JUSTICE, dissenting.

The intended target of the majority's wrath, the Permanente Medical Group, Inc., Kaiser Foundation Hospitals, and the Kaiser Foundation Health Plan (hereafter Kaiser) could not be more deserving. I write separately to represent the interests of the unintended victim of the majority's holding, private arbitration in California.

Introduction

Pursuant to the terms of a prior written agreement, the parties in this case submitted a medical malpractice dispute to private, or nonjudicial, arbitration. California law, like corresponding federal law under the United States Arbitration Act . . . , has long reflected a strong policy in favor of such arbitration.

As this court recently explained, "Title 9 of the Code of Civil Procedure, . . . as enacted and periodically amended by the Legislature, represents a comprehensive statutory scheme regulating private arbitration in this state. . . . Through this detailed statutory scheme, the Legislature has expressed a 'strong public policy in favor of arbitration as a speedy and relatively inexpensive means of dispute resolution.' . . . Consequently, courts will 'indulge every intendment to give effect to such proceedings.' " . . . Indeed, more than 70 years ago this court explained: "The policy of the law in recognizing arbitration agreements and in providing by statute for their enforcement is to encourage persons who wish to avoid delays incident to a civil action to obtain an adjustment of their differences by a tribunal of their own choosing. . . . 'Typically, those who enter into arbitration agreements expect that their dispute will be resolved without necessity for any contact with the courts.' " . . .

Although the majority purports to "affirm the basic policy in favor of enforcement of arbitration agreements" . . . , it nonetheless concludes that "the governing statutes place limits on the extent to which a party that has committed misfeasance in the performance of such an agreement may compel its enforcement." . . . I cannot agree with the majority's interpretation of the governing statutory framework. In my view, except for seeking statutorily prescribed court assistance in the arbitrator selection process . . . , once a private arbitration is pending, a party must seek relief for its adversary's "misfeasance in the performance" in the arbitral forum, not in the courts. Make no mistake about it. The majority's decision to validate a party's unilateral withdrawal from a pending arbitration based on the conduct of its arbitration adversary will wreak havoc on arbitrations throughout the state. Therefore, I respectfully dissent.

Factual and Procedural Background

Almost lost in the majority's exhaustive procedural summary is one key fact—namely, the arbitration process was already underway by the time the plaintiffs unilaterally withdrew. A brief review of the history of the arbitration is in order.

On May 31, 1991, pursuant to the terms of a "Group Medical and Hospital Services Agreement," Wilfredo Engalla, his wife, and their four children (hereafter the Engallas) demanded that Kaiser submit a medical malpractice dispute to binding private arbitration. On June 17, Kaiser submitted to the Engallas' arbitration demand. Two days later, the Engallas' counsel sent Kaiser the $150 check "required in order to initiate the arbitration proceeding."

The Engallas designated their party arbitrator on July 8, Kaiser designated its party arbitrator on July 17, and the parties confirmed their agreement on a neutral arbitrator on October 2. While the parties were in the process of designating arbitrators, they exchanged a number of discovery requests.

Thereafter, on October 28, the Engallas refused to continue with the pending arbitration. The reason the Engallas withdrew from the arbitration was that Kaiser declined to stipulate that Mrs. Engalla's separate loss of consortium claim survived her husband's death. It is this unilateral withdrawal from a pending arbitration that the majority's decision validates.

Discussion

In evaluating both the Engallas' fraudulent inducement claim and their waiver claim, the majority focuses on Kaiser's performance during the course of the aborted private arbitration. According to the majority, the sine qua non of successful fraudulent inducement and waiver claims is unreasonable or bad faith delay by Kaiser. . . . Thus, the majority permits the fraudulent inducement claim to proceed because "there is strong evidence that, despite a high degree of diligence on the part of [the Engallas'] counsel in attempting to obtain the timely appointment of arbitrators, Kaiser lacked either reasonable diligence, good faith, or both, in cooperating on these timely appointments." . . . Likewise, the majority permits the waiver claim to proceed because "there is ample evidence that the [Engallas were] diligent in seeking Kaiser's cooperation, and instead suffered from Kaiser's delay, a delay which was unreasonable or in bad faith." . . .

Although the majority's desire to penalize Kaiser's obduracy is understandable, the consequences of validating a party's unilateral withdrawal from a pending arbitration based on the conduct of its arbitration adversary will reverberate far beyond the bad facts of the instant case. In stark contrast to the legislative response, which enhances the procedures for keeping a case in private arbitration . . . , the majority expands the procedures for removing a case from arbitration. The majority maintains that section 1281.2 compels its decision. . . . I cannot agree. That statute delineates certain narrow circumstances in which a trial court may uphold a party's "refus[al] to arbitrate." (§ 1281.2.) Nothing in section 1281.2 permits a party that has previously submitted a dispute to arbitration, and thereby agreed to arbitrate, to withdraw from that arbitration at some later date based on the unreasonable or bad faith delay of its adversary.

To construe section 1281.2 in the sweeping fashion advanced by the majority will seriously compromise the integrity of the arbitral process and will impose an unpredictable and unnecessary burden on our trial courts. It is well established that "contractual arbitration has a life of its own outside the judicial system." . . . "It is the job of the arbitrator, not the court, to resolve all questions needed to determine the controversy. . . . The arbitrator, and not the court, decides questions of procedure and discovery.... It is also up to the arbitrator, and not the court, to grant relief for delay in bringing an arbitration to a resolution." ...

"This does not mean that a party to an arbitration proceeding has no remedy against dilatory tactics." ... Rather, a party who has suffered as a result of such tactics may seek appropriate relief in the arbitral forum....

Nor does the fact that the arbitrator selection process in a given private arbitration has not yet been completed preclude a party from obtaining appropriate relief. To the contrary, section 1281.6 provides a mechanism by which a party can seek limited assistance from the trial court in obtaining the appointment of an arbitrator or arbitrators.... "[O]nce there is an arbitrator appointed pursuant to section 1281.6, the party seeking to expedite the arbitration proceedings can apply to the arbitrator for [appropriate relief]." ...

I do not share the majority's view that requiring a party to a private arbitration to file a section 1281.6 petition would "violat[e] the usual expectations of an arbitration agreement." ... The majority's reliance on the statement in *Moncharsh* ... that " '[t]ypically, those who enter into arbitration agreements expect that their dispute will be resolved without necessity for any contact with the courts' " ... is misplaced. *Moncharsh* did not hold that a party to a private arbitration would never have to have any contact with the courts but rather that "judicial intervention in the arbitration process [should] be minimized...." ... Indeed, the very paragraph of *Moncharsh* quoted by the majority emphasizes that title 9 of part 3 of the Code of Civil Procedure which includes section 1281.6—"represents a comprehensive statutory scheme regulating private arbitration in this state ... " ...

Section 1281.6 is the statutory remedy that our Legislature has provided for resolving disputes in the arbitrator selection process, thereby preventing such disputes from becoming occasions for avoiding private arbitration agreements. The statute's evident purpose is to facilitate, not to hinder, private arbitration. Requiring a party to employ a legislatively prescribed remedy simply cannot be deemed contrary to the "normal expectations of arbitration participants." ... In fact, the arbitration provision at issue in the present case specifically alerts the signatories that "[w]ith respect to any matter not herein expressly provided for, the arbitration shall be governed by California Code of Civil Procedure provisions relating to arbitration."

The inclusiveness of the language of section 1281.6 belies the notion that it contains some sort of ill-defined exception for unreasonable or bad faith delay.... By its own terms, the statute comes into play whenever "the agreed method [of appointing an arbitrator] fails or for any reason cannot be followed." ... If there were any doubt that the statutory remedy was intended to apply broadly, the Legislature has now put it to rest. Largely in response to this very case, the Legislature recently enacted Health and Safety Code section 1373.20, subdivision (a)(2), providing that for nonindependent arbitration systems such as Kaiser's "[i]n cases or disputes in which the parties have agreed to use a tripartite arbitration panel consisting of two party arbitrators and one neutral arbitrator, and the party arbitrators are unable to agree on the designation of a neutral arbitrator within 30 days after service of a written demand requesting the designation, it shall be conclusively presumed that the agreed method of selection has failed and the method provided in Section 1281.6 of the Code of Civil Procedure may be utilized." The new legislation also provides for attorney fees and costs against a party that "has engaged in dilatory conduct intended to cause delay in proceeding under the arbitration agreement." . . .

In this case, having previously submitted their dispute to private arbitration and having already completed the arbitrator selection process, the Engallas should have sought relief for Kaiser's dilatory conduct in the pending arbitration. For example, the Engallas could have presented their fraud and waiver claims directly to the arbitrators and requested that they not enforce the arbitration provision. . . . Likewise, the Engallas could have requested that the arbitrators sanction Kaiser's dilatory conduct by deeming Mrs. Engalla's separate loss of consortium claim to have survived her husband's death. . . . In fact, at oral argument, the Engallas' counsel conceded that this case could likely have remained in private arbitration if Mrs. Engalla's economic loss had been ameliorated.

The one thing the Engallas should not be permitted to do, however, is to circumvent the arbitrators altogether. The consequences of validating a party's unilateral withdrawal from a pending arbitration will be dramatic. Jurisdictional disputes will inevitably arise. Suppose, for example, that following the Engallas' unilateral withdrawal, Kaiser had elected to continue to pursue the pending arbitration and that the arbitrators had ultimately entered a default judgment in favor of Kaiser. Would that default judgment have been valid? Would the same have been true if the trial court had simultaneously entered a default judgment in favor of the Engallas in the pending litigation?

In addition, as the Engallas' counsel acknowledged at oral argument, if this court validates the Engallas' unilateral withdrawal, other parties to pending arbitrations will doubtlessly engage in the same conduct. Counsel's answer to this dilemma was that this court should "trust the trial courts." The majority's answer is to "emphasize . . . that the delay must be substantial, unreasonable, and in spite of the claimant's own reasonable diligence" and not "the result of reasonable and good faith disagreements between the parties." . . .

Neither answer is satisfactory. Under the majority's holding, which has all the precision of a "SCUD" missile, the resolution of fraudulent inducement and waiver claims will necessarily entail fact-intensive, case-by-case determinations. . . . The disruptive, time-consuming nature of these determinations is well illustrated by the facts of the present case, in which "[t]he Engallas ultimately had five months to complete discovery [on the petition to compel arbitration], during which time thirteen motions were filed and more than a dozen depositions were taken." . . . Even assuring that the trial courts ultimately resolve all future claims correctly, the interim disruption to pending arbitrations will be simply intolerable.

Conclusion

"Great cases like hard cases make bad law. For great cases are called great, not by reason of their real importance in shaping the law of the future, but because of some accident of immediate overwhelming interest which appeals to the feelings and distorts the judgment. These immediate interests exercise a kind of hydraulic pressure which makes what previously was clear seem doubtful, and before which even well settled principles of law will bend." [Justice Holmes in *Northern Securities,* 193 U.S. 197, 400–01 (1904).]. . . . Although legislators, practitioners, and courts have all expressed concern that disparities in bargaining power may affect the procedural fairness of consumer arbitration agreements, this case amply demonstrates why any solutions should come from the Legislature, whose ability to craft precise exceptions is far superior to that of this court.

However well-intentioned the majority and however deserving its intended target, today's holding pokes a hole in the barrier separating private arbitrations and the courts. Unfortunately, like any such breach, this hole will eventually cause the dam to burst. Ironically, the tool the majority uses to puncture its hole is the observation that " 'those who enter into arbitration agreements expect that their dispute will be resolved without necessity for any contact with the courts.' " . . . Because I suspect that parties to private arbitrations will be having quite a bit more contact with the courts than they ever bargained for, I dissent.

HOOTERS OF AMERICA, INC. V. PHILLIPS

173 F.3d 933 (4th Cir. 1999).

(footnotes omitted)

WILKINSON, CHIEF JUDGE:

Annette R. Phillips alleges that she was sexually harassed while working at a Hooters restaurant. After quitting her job, Phillips threatened to sue Hooters in court. Alleging that Phillips agreed to arbitrate employment-related disputes, Hooters preemptively filed suit to compel arbitration under the Federal Arbitration Act, 9 U.S.C. § 4. Because Hooters set up a dispute resolution process utterly lacking in the rudiments of even-handedness, we hold that Hooters breached its agreement to arbitrate. Thus, we affirm the district court's refusal to compel arbitration.

I.

Appellee Annette R. Phillips worked as a bartender at a Hooters restaurant in Myrtle Beach, South Carolina. She was employed since 1989 by appellant Hooters of Myrtle Beach (HOMB), a franchisee of appellant Hooters of America (collectively Hooters).

Phillips alleges that in June 1996, Gerald Brooks, a Hooters official and the brother of HOMB's principal owner, sexually harassed her by grabbing and slapping her buttocks. After appealing to her manager for help and being told to "let it go," she quit her job. Phillips then contacted Hooters through an attorney claiming that the attack and the restaurant's failure to address it violated her Title VII rights. Hooters responded that she was required to submit her claims to arbitration according to a binding agreement to arbitrate between the parties.

This agreement arose in 1994 during the implementation of Hooters' alternative dispute resolution program. As part of that program, the company conditioned eligibility for raises, transfers, and promotions upon an employee signing an "Agreement to arbitrate employment-related disputes." The agreement provides that Hooters and the employee each agree to arbitrate all disputes arising out of employment, including "any claim of discrimination, sexual harassment, retaliation, or wrongful discharge, whether arising under federal or state law." The agreement further states that

> the employee and the company agree to resolve any claims pursuant to the company's rules and procedures for alternative resolution of employment-related disputes, as promulgated by the company from time to time ("the rules"). Company will make available or provide a copy of the rules upon written request of the employee.

The employees of HOMB were initially given a copy of this agreement at an all-staff meeting held on November 20, 1994. HOMB's general manager, Gene Fulcher, told the employees to review the agreement for five days and that they would then be asked to accept or reject the agreement. No employee, however, was given a copy of Hooters' arbitration rules and procedures. Phillips signed the agreement on November 25, 1994. When her personnel file was updated in April 1995, Phillips again signed the agreement.

After Phillips quit her job in June 1996, Hooters sent to her attorney a copy of the Hooters rules then in effect. Phillips refused to arbitrate the dispute.

Hooters filed suit in November 1996 to compel arbitration under 9 U.S.C. § 4. Phillips defended on the grounds that the agreement to arbitrate was unenforceable. Phillips also asserted individual and class counterclaims against Hooters for violations of Title VII and for a declaration that the arbitration agreements were unenforceable against the class. In response, Hooters requested that the district court stay the proceedings on the counterclaims until after arbitration, 9 U.S.C. § 3.

In March 1998, the district court denied Hooters' motions to compel arbitration and stay proceedings on the counterclaims. The court found that there was no meeting of the minds on all of the material terms of the agreement and even if there were, Hooters' promise to arbitrate was illusory. In addition, the court found that the arbitration agreement was unconscionable and void for reasons of public policy. Hooters filed this interlocutory appeal, 9 U.S.C. § 16.

II.

The benefits of arbitration are widely recognized. Parties agree to arbitrate to secure "streamlined proceedings and expeditious results [that] will best serve their needs." *Mitsubishi Motors Corp. v. Soler Chrysler-Plymouth, Inc.*, 473 U.S. 614, 633, 105 S.Ct. 3346, 87 L.Ed.2d 444 (1985). The arbitration of disputes enables parties to avoid the costs associated with pursuing a judicial resolution of their grievances. By one estimate, litigating a typical employment dispute costs at least $50,000 and takes two and one-half years to resolve.... Further, the adversarial nature of litigation diminishes the possibility that the parties will be able to salvage their relationship. For these reasons parties agree to arbitrate and trade "the procedures and opportunity for review of the courtroom for the simplicity, informality, and expedition of arbitration." *Gilmer v. Interstate/Johnson Lane Corp.*, 500 U.S. 20, 31, 111 S.Ct. 1647, 114 L.Ed.2d 26 (1991) (internal quotation marks omitted).

In support of arbitration, Congress passed the Federal Arbitration Act .... "Its purpose was to reverse the longstanding judicial hostility to arbitration agreements that had existed at English common law and had been adopted by American courts, and to place arbitration agreements upon the same footing as other contracts." *Gilmer*, 500 U.S. at 24, 111 S.Ct. 1647. The FAA manifests "a liberal federal policy favoring arbitration agreements." *Moses H. Cone Mem'l Hosp. v. Mercury Constr. Corp.*, 460 U.S. 1, 24, 103 S.Ct. 927, 74 L.Ed.2d 765 (1983). When a valid agreement to arbitrate exists between the parties and covers the matter in dispute, the FAA commands the federal courts to stay any ongoing judicial proceedings, 9 U.S.C. § 3, and to compel arbitration, id. § 4.

The threshold question is whether claims such as Phillips' are even arbitrable. The EEOC as amicus curiae contends that employees cannot agree to arbitrate Title VII claims in predispute agreements. We disagree. The Supreme Court has made it plain that judicial protection of arbitral agreements extends to agreements to arbitrate statutory discrimination claims. In *Gilmer v. Interstate/Johnson Lane Corp.*, the Court noted that " '[b]y agreeing to arbitrate a statutory claim, a party does not forgo the substantive rights afforded by the statute; it only submits to their resolution in an arbitral, rather than a judicial, forum.' " 500 U.S. at 26, 111 S.Ct. 1647 (alteration in original) (*quoting Mitsubishi Motors*, 473 U.S. at 628, 105 S.Ct. 3346). Thus, a party must be held to the terms of its bargain unless Congress intends to preclude waiver of a judicial forum for the statutory claims at issue. Such an intent, however, must "be discoverable in the text of the [substantive statute], its legislative history, or an 'inherent conflict' between arbitration and the [statute's] underlying purposes." *Id.*

[The court concludes that Congress did not intend to precluse waiver of Phillips' statutory claims.]

III.

Predispute agreements to arbitrate Title VII claims are thus valid and enforceable. The question remains whether a binding arbitration agreement between Phillips and Hooters exists and compels Phillips to submit her Title VII claims to arbitration. . . .

Hooters argues that Phillips gave her assent to a bilateral agreement to arbitrate. That contract provided for the resolution by arbitration of all employment-related disputes, including claims arising under Title VII. Hooters claims the agreement to arbitrate is valid because Phillips twice signed it voluntarily. Thus, it argues the courts are bound to enforce it and compel arbitration.

We disagree. The judicial inquiry, while highly circumscribed, is not focused solely on an examination for contractual formation defects such as lack of mutual assent and want of consideration. . . . Courts also can investigate the existence of "such grounds as exist at law or in equity for the revocation of any contract." 9 U.S.C. § 2. However, the grounds for revocation must relate specifically to the arbitration clause and not just to the contract as a whole. *Prima Paint Corp. v. Flood & Conklin Mfg. Co.*, 388 U.S. 395, 402–04, 87 S.Ct. 1801, 18 L.Ed.2d 1270 (1967) . . . . In this case, the challenge goes to the validity of the arbitration agreement itself. Hooters materially breached the arbitration agreement by promulgating rules so egregiously unfair as to constitute a complete default of its contractual obligation to draft arbitration rules and to do so in good faith.

Hooters and Phillips agreed to settle any disputes between them not in a judicial forum, but in another neutral forum-arbitration. Their agreement provided that Hooters was responsible for setting up such a forum by promulgating arbitration rules and procedures. To this end, Hooters instituted a set of rules in July 1996.

The Hooters rules when taken as a whole, however, are so one-sided that their only possible purpose is to undermine the neutrality of the proceeding. The rules require the employee to provide the company notice of her claim at the outset, including "the nature of the Claim" and "the specific act(s) or omissions(s) which are the basis of the Claim." Rule 6–2(1), (2). Hooters, on the other hand, is not required to file any responsive pleadings or to notice its defenses. Additionally, at the time of filing this notice, the employee must provide the company with a list of all fact witnesses with a brief summary of the facts known to each. Rule 6–2(5). The company, however, is not required to reciprocate.

The Hooters rules also provide a mechanism for selecting a panel of three arbitrators that is crafted to ensure a biased decisionmaker. Rule 8. The employee and Hooters each select an arbitrator, and the two arbitrators in turn select a third. Good enough, except that the employee's arbitrator and the third arbitrator must be selected from a list of arbitrators created exclusively by Hooters. This gives Hooters control over the entire panel and places no limits whatsoever on whom Hooters can put on the list. Under the rules, Hooters is free to devise lists of partial arbitrators who have existing relationships, financial or familial, with Hooters and its management. In fact, the rules do not even prohibit Hooters from placing its managers themselves on the list. Further, nothing in the rules restricts Hooters from punishing arbitrators who rule against the company by removing them from the list. Given the unrestricted control that one party (Hooters) has over the panel, the selection of an impartial decision maker would be a surprising result.

Nor is fairness to be found once the proceedings are begun. Although Hooters may expand the scope of arbitration to any matter, "whether related or not to the Employee's Claim," the employee cannot raise "any matter not included in the Notice of Claim." Rules 4–2, 8–9. Similarly, Hooters is permitted to move for summary dismissal of employee claims before a hearing is held whereas the employee is not permitted to seek summary judgment. Rule 14–4. Hooters, but not the employee, may record the arbitration hearing "by audio or videotaping or by verbatim transcription." Rule 18–1. The rules also grant Hooters the right to bring suit in court to vacate or modify an arbitral award when it can show, by a preponderance of the evidence, that the panel exceeded its authority. Rule 21–4. No such right is granted to the employee.

In addition, the rules provide that upon 30 days notice Hooters, but not the employee, may cancel the agreement to arbitrate. Rule 23–1. Moreover, Hooters reserves the right to modify the rules, "in whole or in part," whenever it wishes and "without notice" to the employee. Rule 24–1. Nothing in the rules even prohibits Hooters from changing the rules in the middle of an arbitration proceeding.

If by odd chance the unfairness of these rules were not apparent on their face, leading arbitration experts have decried their one-sidedness. George Friedman, senior vice president of the American Arbitration Association (AAA), testified that the system established by the Hooters rules so deviated from minimum due process standards that the Association would refuse to arbitrate under those rules. George Nicolau, former president of both the National Academy of Arbitrators and the International Society of Professionals in Dispute Resolution, attested that the Hooters rules "are inconsistent with the concept of fair and impartial arbitration." He also testified that he was "certain that reputable designating agencies, such as the AAA and Jams/Endispute, would refuse to administer a program so unfair and one-sided as this one." Additionally, Dennis Nolan, professor of labor law at the University of South Carolina, declared that the Hooters rules "do not satisfy the minimum requirements of a fair arbitration system." He found that the "most serious flaw" was that the "mechanism [for selecting arbitrators] violates the most fundamental aspect of justice, namely an impartial decision maker." Finally, Lewis Maltby, member of the Board of Directors of the AAA, testified that "This is without a doubt the most unfair arbitration program I have ever encountered."

In a similar vein, two major arbitration associations have filed amicus briefs with this court. The National Academy of Arbitrators stated that the Hooters rules "violate fundamental concepts of fairness . . . and the integrity of the arbitration process." Likewise, the Society of Professionals in Dispute Resolution noted that "[i]t would be hard to imagine a more unfair method of selecting a panel of arbitrators." It characterized the Hooters arbitration system as "deficient to the point of illegitimacy" and "so one sided, it is hard to believe that it was even intended to be fair."

We hold that the promulgation of so many biased rules-especially the scheme whereby one party to the proceeding so controls the arbitral panel-breaches the contract entered into by the parties. The parties agreed to submit their claims to arbitration-a system whereby disputes are fairly resolved by an impartial third party. Hooters by contract took on the obligation of establishing such a system. By creating a sham system unworthy even of the name of arbitration, Hooters completely failed in performing its contractual duty.

Moreover, Hooters had a duty to perform its obligations in good faith. See Restatement (Second) of Contracts § 205 (1981) ("Every contract imposes upon each party a duty of good faith and fair dealing in its performance and its enforcement.") . . . . Good faith "emphasizes faithfulness to an agreed common purpose and consistency with the justified expectations of the other party." Restatement (Second) of Contracts § 205 cmt. a. Bad faith includes the "evasion of the spirit of the bargain" and an "abuse of a power to specify terms." *Id.* § 205 cmt. d. By agreeing to settle disputes in arbitration, Phillips agreed to the prompt and economical resolution of her claims. She could legitimately expect that arbitration would not entail procedures so wholly one-sided as to present a stacked deck. Thus we conclude that the Hooters rules also violate the contractual obligation of good faith.

Given Hooters' breaches of the arbitration agreement and Phillips' desire not to be bound by it, we hold that rescission is the proper remedy. Generally, "rescission will not be granted for a minor or casual breach of a contract, but only for those breaches which defeat the object of the contracting parties." . . . . As we have explained, Hooters' breach is by no means insubstantial; its performance under the contract was so egregious that the result was hardly recognizable as arbitration at all. We therefore permit Phillips to cancel the agreement and thus Hooters' suit to compel arbitration must fail.

IV.

We respect fully the Supreme Court's pronouncement that "questions of arbitrability must be addressed with a healthy regard for the federal policy favoring arbitration." *Moses H. Cone*, 460 U.S. at 24, 103 S.Ct. 927. Our decision should not be misread: We are not holding that the agreement before us is unenforceable because the arbitral proceedings are too abbreviated. An arbitral forum need not replicate the judicial forum. "[W]e are well past the time when judicial suspicion of the desirability of arbitration and of the competence of arbitral tribunals inhibited the development of arbitration as an alternative means of dispute resolution." *Mitsubishi Motors*, 473 U.S. at 626–27, 105 S.Ct. 3346; *see also Gilmer*, 500 U.S. at 31–32, 111 S.Ct. 1647 (rejecting abbreviated discovery and lack of written opinions as reasons to inhibit arbitration of statutory claims).

Nor should our decision be misunderstood as permitting a full-scale assault on the fairness of proceedings before the matter is submitted to arbitration. Generally, objections to the nature of arbitral proceedings are for the arbitrator to decide in the first instance. Only after arbitration may a party then raise such challenges if they meet the narrow grounds set out in 9 U.S.C. § 10 for vacating an arbitral award. In the case before us, we only reach the content of the arbitration rules because their promulgation was the duty of one party under the contract. The material breach of this duty warranting rescission is an issue of substantive arbitrability and thus is reviewable before arbitration. . . . This case, however, is the exception that proves the rule: fairness objections should generally be made to the arbitrator, subject only to limited post-arbitration judicial review as set forth in section 10 of the FAA.

By promulgating this system of warped rules, Hooters so skewed the process in its favor that Phillips has been denied arbitration in any meaningful sense of the word. To uphold the promulgation of this aberrational scheme under the heading of arbitration would undermine, not advance, the federal policy favoring alternative dispute resolution. This we refuse to do.

The judgment of the district court is affirmed, and the case is remanded for further proceedings consistent with this opinion.

AFFIRMED AND REMANDED.

NOTES AND QUESTIONS

1. *Engalla* constitutes a significant case—perhaps an opinion of fundamental significance in elaborating a regulatory policy on consumer arbitration in the HMO and other service areas. Its reasoning and rationale also have implications for the regulation of employment arbitration. The importance of the opinion is heightened by the fact that California remains one of the most active and sophisticated ADR jurisdictions in the country. Moreover, California courts have a longstanding acquaintance with and an elaborate decisional law on arbitration and ADR.

The majority opinion holds that an arbitration agreement can be defeated, albeit in exceptional circumstances, by allegations of fraud. The concurring opinion adds that the expansion of arbitration into consumer affairs warrants greater judicial supervision of this use of arbitration.

2. *Phillips* has less systemic value as a precedent, but it demonstrates an extreme example of how a commercial party can attempt to pervert the arbitral process to its advantage. What, however, is the doctrinal basis for the court's refusal to enforce the arbitration agreement in *Phillips*? If you were thinking of the case as precedent, how would you describe its "rule"?

3. Imagine you are tasked with reworking the arbitration agreements for Kaiser and for Hooters. Both companies want to retain the arbitration agreements in some form. What features of the arbitral process, in each of these cases, are the most unfair or inequitable? Are there any features that are fair? How would you rewrite these agreements to make them enforceable?

4. The facts in *Engalla* are particularly damning as to Kaiser, but is the description of the company's litigious conduct surprising? Isn't this what insurance companies do whenever they are engaged in adjudication? Why should this conduct be viewed as so reprehensible in this case?

5. As to the *Engalla* court's assessment of the materiality of Kaiser's misrepresentation of its arbitral system, do you agree that Oliver Tire would have given substantial importance to the operation of Kaiser's arbitration system if it had been informed of the system's actual operation? Wouldn't the

level of premiums and the benefit coverage be much more significant considerations for a company subscriber? What does this analysis suggest about the majority opinion and its underlying objectives?

6. Are these cases fundamentally about fraud? The adhesive nature of the arbitration contract? Are the courts more concerned the "cloaking" of the true operation of the arbitration systems or with the fact that the commercial parties established, designed, and administered arbitral systems that generously favored their interests over those of the individuals? In other words, if the commercial parties had been more forthright about the details, would these clauses have been enforceable?

7. Are these cases both "great cases" in the sense that the dissent means in *Engalla*? Are they, in other words, extraordinary examples of such reprehensible conduct that they are of little assistance in deciding how to address more moderate cases?

AAMES FUNDING CORP. V. SHARPE

2004 WL 2418284 (E.D. Pa. 2004) (not rep. in F.Supp.2d).

PADOVA, J.

[. . .]

I. BACKGROUND

. . . On or about January 10, 2000, First Choice solicited Plaintiff to enter into a home improvement contract for her home in Philadelphia. Plaintiff and her daughter thereafter executed a "proposal" for home improvement work in the amount of $5,640. Upon executing the contract, First Choice informed Plaintiff that someone from his office would be contacting her to arrange financing for the home improvement work. Two days later, Borso visited Plaintiff at her home to request all documentary information on her outstanding debts. Although Plaintiff never wanted a loan for anything but home improvements, Borso insisted that she would have to pay off any other outstanding debts in order to obtain the home improvement loan. Borso did not provide Plaintiff with a broker contract, did not identify himself as a broker, and did not explain that, as a mortgage broker, he would be paid by Plaintiff for arranging a loan.

On or about March 3, 2000, a settlement agent for Petitioner closed a loan at Plaintiff's home for a principal amount of $25,000 and at an interest rate of 11%. The settlement statement for the loan reflects the pay-off of Respondent's consumer loan, utility, and tax debts, as well as a $2,500 broker fee for Brookside. The settlement statement did not account for the $5,500 balance of the principal of the loan. Weeks later, First Choice's agent visited Plaintiff's home to inquire about the loan proceeds for the home improvement work. Plaintiff and her daughter advised First Choice that they never received the funds. . . .

On or about March 17, 2000, Plaintiff received three checks, $2,855 in cash payable to Plaintiff, $891 payable to PECO Energy, and $117 payable to CitiBank. . . . Plaintiff returned the checks to the sender because they did not represent the cash amount she was supposed to receive from the home improvement loan. First Choice, Borso, and/or Brookside never responded to inquiries from Plaintiff nor visited her at her home ever again. The $1,700 remainder of the principal remains unaccounted for and Plaintiff never received any home improvements. . . .

[. . .]

On September 13, 2004, Petitioner commenced the instant action against Respondent by filing a Petition to Compel Arbitration under § 4 of the FAA. . . . Petitioner maintains that Respondent is required to arbitrate her dispute against Petitioner pursuant to an arbitration agreement entered into by the parties. Under the arbitration agreement, Petitioner and Respondent are required to arbitrate "any and all" claims, with the exception of:

> (i) foreclosure proceedings, whether by judicial action, power of sale, or any other proceeding in which a lien holder may acquire or convey title to or possession of any property which is security for this Transaction (including an assignment of rents or appointment of a receiver) or (ii) an application by or on behalf of the Borrower for relief under the federal bankruptcy laws or any other similar laws of general application for the relief of debtors, or (iii) any Claim where Lender seeks damages or other relief because of Borrower's default under the terms of a Transaction.

(Am.Pet., Ex. B.)

[. . .]

III. DISCUSSION

[. . .]

B. *Arbitrability*

Petitioner contends that Respondent is required to arbitrate the underlying dispute pursuant the agreement to arbitrate entered into by the parties in this action. . . . Before a reluctant party can be compelled to arbitrate, however, the court must "engage in a limited review to ensure that the dispute is arbitrable—*i.e.*, that a valid agreement to arbitrate exists between the parties and that the specific dispute falls within the substantive scope of that agreement." . . . Federal law presumptively favors the enforcement of arbitration agreements. . . .

Respondent contends that the arbitration agreement entered into by the parties in this case is void as unconscionable. Questions concerning the interpretation and construction of arbitration agreements are determined by reference to federal substantive law.... In interpreting such agreements, federal courts may apply state law pursuant to § 2 of the FAA.... Thus, generally applicable contract defenses may be applied to invalidate arbitration agreements without contravening the FAA.... A party challenging a contract provision as unconscionable generally bears the burden of proving that the provision is both procedurally and substantively unconscionable.... Procedural unconscionability pertains to the process by which an agreement is reached and the form of an agreement, including the use therein of fine print and convoluted or unclear language.... Substantive unconscionability refers to terms that unreasonably favor one party to which the disfavored party does not truly assent....

Respondent argues that the arbitration agreement is procedurally unconscionable as a contract of adhesion. An adhesion contract is defined as a "standard form contract prepared by one party, to be signed by the party in a weaker position, [usually] a consumer, who has little choice about the terms." ... Procedural unconscionability is generally established if the agreement at issue constitutes a contract of adhesion.... Petitioner does not dispute that the arbitration agreement at issue constitutes a contract of adhesion. Accordingly, Respondent has demonstrated that the agreement to arbitrate is procedurally unconscionable. Of course, "[a]n adhesion contract is not necessarily unenforceable," ... as Respondent must also demonstrate that the arbitration agreement is substantively unconscionable.

Respondent argues that the arbitration agreement is substantively unconscionable because it requires her to arbitrate the vast majority of her claims while allowing Petitioner to bring a foreclosure action in the courts. Respondent cites *Lytle v. CitiFinancial Services, Inc.*, 810 A.2d 643 (Pa. Super. Ct.2002), in support of her substantive unconscionability argument. *Lytle* involved a lender-borrower agreement which provided for arbitration of all claims by the parties, with the exception "[a]ny action to effect a foreclosure to transfer title to the property being foreclosed ... or [a]ny matter where all parties seek monetary damages in the aggregate of $15,000 or less in total damages (compensatory or punitive), costs and fees." ... The *Lytle* court noted that, in practice, the borrowers were required to arbitrate all disputes involving more than the modest sum of $15,000, while the lender remained free to enforce most of its substantive rights (*i.e.*, repayment of the debt and commencement of foreclosure proceedings) in court.... The court concluded that "under Pennsylvania law, the reservation by [a lender] of access to the courts for itself to the exclusion of the consumer creates a presumption of unconscionability, which in the absence of 'business realities' that *compel* inclusion of such a provision in an arbitration provision, renders the arbitration provision unconscionable and unenforceable under Pennsylvania law." . . . (emphasis in original).

The Court concludes that the Respondent's reliance on the Pennsylvania Superior Court's decision in *Lytle* is unpersuasive. The Court is bound by the decision of the United States Court of Appeals for the Third Circuit in *Harris,* wherein the court rejected the borrowers' contention that an arbitration clause in a loan agreement was substantively unconscionable because it provided the lender with the option of litigating certain disputes, while providing no such choice to the borrowers. . . . The court concluded that "the mere fact that [the lender] retains the option to litigate some issues in court, while the [borrowers] must arbitrate all claims does not make the arbitration agreement unenforceable. We have held repeatedly that inequality in bargaining power, alone, is not a valid basis upon which to invalidate an arbitration agreement." . . . ("It is of no legal consequence that the arbitration clause gives [the lender] the option to litigate arbitrable issues in court, while requiring the [borrowers] to invoke arbitration" because "mutuality is not a requirement of a valid arbitration clause"). . . . The Court concludes, therefore, that the arbitration agreement entered into by Petitioner and Respondent is valid and enforceable. The Court further finds that the underlying dispute between Petitioner and Respondent falls within the broad scope of the arbitration agreement. Accordingly, Petitioner's Amended Petition to Compel Arbitration is granted.

[. . .]

NOTES AND QUESTIONS

1. Is the contract at issue procedurally unconscionable? Do you agree with the court that the mere adhesive nature of the contract makes it procedurally one-sided? Particularly in a competitive market, like the mortgage market, doesn't an individual like Sharpe have other options? Couldn't he simply walk away from this lender and take his business somewhere else? Is the option to walk away a "meaningful choice"? Why or why not?

2. What, specifically, is the alleged substantive unconscionability in this case?

3. How is the decision in *Lytle* different from *Harris* (two cases discussed in *Aames Funding*)? Is the latter more compelling? Why or why not?

4. How does this arbitration agreement stack up against the agreements in *Engalla* and *Phillips*? Are its terms less fair? More fair?

5. Imagine for a moment that you are representing Aames Funding. You are trying to understand what the original drafter had in mind, but no one at the company knows or recalls why the arbitration agreement is drafted like it is. What explanations might there be for the imbalance in the agreement? Are

all of the possible explanations nefarious or designed to harm the borrower? Could you argue, in other words, that there's a legitimate business justification for the one-sidedness?

6. Not all courts are as generous to asymmetrical obligations to arbitrate as the Eastern District of Pennsylvania. For instance, the Montana Supreme Court concluded that an arbitration agreement between a debtor and a debt reduction company imposed an unfairly one-sided obligation to arbitrate on the debtor and refused to enforce it.

> The arbitration provision at issue in this case . . . obligates both parties to arbitrate any controversy or dispute arising out of the DAA, including matters with respect to breach or enforcement of the agreement. . . . However, a separate provision in the DAA provides that if [the debtor's] account has a negative balance at any time, "collection actions may be pursued against you. If any such collection action is undertaken, you agree to pay all court costs and collection fees, including reasonable attorney's fees, to the extent permitted by applicable law." Thus, . . . [the debtor] is obligated to arbitrate all controversies arising from the breach of the DAA, but if [the debtor] breaches the agreement, [the commercial party] has the right to sue her in a court of law and to recover damages plus court costs, collection fees, and attorney fees. . . . [The commercial party] is entitled to sue [the debtor] in a court of law for breach of the agreement, but she cannot sue it for breach of the agreement. In sum, the obligation to arbitrate is one-sided, not mutual.

Glob. Client Sols., LLC v. Ossello, 2016 MT 50, ¶ 37, 382 Mont. 345, 356–57, 367 P.3d 361, 370; *see also, e.g., Figueroa v. THI of N.M. at Casa Arena Blanca, LLC*, 306 P.3d 480 (N.M. Ct. App. 2012) (holding that notwithstanding the pronouncements in *Concepcion*, an arbitration agreement in which the drafter unreasonably reserved to itself the claims it would most likely bring for the courts while subjecting the weaker party to arbitration of all claims, was unenforceable) (*cert. denied by THI of New Mexico at Casa Arena Blanca, LLC v. Figueroa*, 569 U.S. 1004, 133 S. Ct. 2736, 186 L.Ed.2d 193 (2013)).

Still, a consensus exists that arbitration commitments do not need to be perfectly reciprocal. "Mutuality 'does not require an exactly even exchange of identical rights and obligations' between the parties," and that "arbitration agreements that more frequently bind the [individuals than commercial parties may be] valid despite the differences in the parties' rights." *Rose v. New Day Fin., LLC*, 816 F. Supp. 2d 245, 259 (D. Md. 2011).

ZEPHYR HAVEN HEALTH & REHAB CENTER, INC. V. HARDIN

122 So.3d 916 (Fla. Ct. App. 2013).

(footnotes omitted)

SILBERMAN, JUDGE.

Zephyr Haven Health & Rehab Center, Inc., and the other named appellants (all appellants are collectively referred to as "the Owners") challenge the trial court's order denying their motion to compel arbitration of Edna Hardin's claims against them. Because Hardin failed to establish that the arbitration agreement should not be enforced, we reverse.

I. Factual and Procedural Background

Hardin was admitted to the Owners' nursing facility on November 9, 2010. Two days later, she signed admissions documents, including an arbitration agreement. The arbitration agreement was conspicuously labeled and specified that its execution was not a precondition to receiving care at the nursing facility. It further specified that in any arbitration proceeding, the nursing facility would pay the first $500 of arbitration fees and costs and that all additional expenses would be split with the nursing facility responsible for 60% and Hardin responsible for 40%. The agreement provided that the parties would be responsible for their own attorney's fees.

One year later Hardin sued the Owners, alleging a variety of claims arising out of the care she received at the nursing facility. The Owners responded with a motion to dismiss the complaint and to compel arbitration. At a hearing on the motion, the Owners submitted the arbitration agreement into evidence and argued that the agreement required arbitration of Hardin's claims. Hardin responded that although there was no dispute that she signed the agreement, it would be impossible for her to perform under the agreement because she could not afford to pay 40 percent of the arbitration expenses. She provided to the trial court several invoices from unrelated arbitration proceedings. Although the invoices do not appear to have been admitted into evidence, Hardin argued that they were examples of the fees and costs that could be incurred in arbitration. Hardin also presented testimony from her stepson, who served as her caretaker, regarding her strained finances. No other evidence was presented.

Argument at the hearing largely addressed the doctrines of impossibility of performance and unconscionability. Although Hardin asserted that the issue was one of impossibility, the Owners maintained the matter should be analyzed instead under the doctrine of unconscionability. After the hearing, the trial court issued an order denying the motion to compel arbitration. The order found both that it was "financially impossible" for Hardin to participate in arbitration and that if

Hardin "were forced to pay 40 percent of arbitration costs, based on her income and her expenses, the amount would be unconscionable."

In this appeal, the Owners challenge the sufficiency of the evidence presented to the trial court and the court's findings that the arbitration agreement was unconscionable and impossible for Hardin to perform.

[. . .]

II. Unconscionability

To succeed in claiming that a contractual provision is unconscionable, a party must demonstrate both procedural and substantive unconscionability. . . . Procedural unconscionability addresses "the manner in which the contract was entered," including "consideration of facts such as the relative bargaining power of the parties and their ability to understand the contract terms." . . . Substantive unconscionability, on the other hand, requires assessment of the contract's terms to "determine whether they are so 'outrageously unfair' as to 'shock the judicial conscience.' " . . . Where the party alleging unconscionability establishes only one of the two prongs, the claim fails. . . .

In the context of unconscionability, the issue of the financial cost of arbitration is generally considered substantive, rather than procedural. . . . Hardin's alleged inability to pay that cost was the basis of her opposition to the motion to compel arbitration. Thus, while she addressed substantive unconscionability, she failed to present evidence of procedural unconscionability. Accordingly, to the extent the trial court determined that the agreement is unenforceable based on unconscionability, it erred.

III. Impossibility of Performance

Impossibility of performance "is a defense to nonperformance and refers to situations where the purpose for which the contract was made has become impossible to perform." . . . When determining impossibility, courts focus on " 'whether an unanticipated circumstance has made performance of the promise vitally different from what should reasonably have been within the contemplation of both parties when they entered into the contract.' " . . . Where the risk was foreseeable when the agreement was made and could have been expressly addressed in the agreement, "[t]he doctrine of impossibility of performance should be employed with great caution." . . .

Even where performance actually becomes impossible after execution of the agreement, the doctrine cannot be invoked as a defense if "knowledge of the facts making performance impossible" was available at the inception of the agreement to the party claiming impossibility. . . . In the specific context of arbitration, courts are "not empowered to rewrite a clear and unambiguous provision, nor should [they] attempt to make an otherwise valid contract more reasonable for one of the parties." . . . Further, "unexpected difficulty or expense will not excuse a party to a contract from performance" of an agreement to arbitrate. . . .

After reviewing the evidence submitted to the trial court and the applicable law, we cannot uphold the trial court's decision to deny the motion to compel arbitration on the basis of financial impossibility. First, Hardin failed to establish that performance was impossible. Hardin's stepson testified that her monthly income was approximately $3000 but that the monthly cost of her care exceeded that amount. However, he added that although paying the costs of arbitration would create a financial hardship, Hardin could receive care in a nursing home through "taxpayer dollars" rather than out-of-pocket spending. While it is understandable that Hardin may consider this option less desirable than private care, its existence undermines her effort to establish financial impossibility.

Second, the evidence indicated that Hardin's costs for care were significantly reduced at the time of the hearing as compared to what she had been paying when she was in the nursing facility. Thus, she did not establish an adverse change in circumstances from the time she entered into the agreement to the time the issue was presented to the trial court. Consequently, to the extent the trial court determined the agreement is unenforceable due to financial impossibility, we reverse.

[The court went on to evaluate the cost allocation formula in light of the U.S. Supreme Court's decision in *Green Tree Financial Corp.—Alabama v. Randolph*, 531 U.S. 79 (2000). Analogizing to *Green Tree*, the court noted that "there exists a threshold where the costs of arbitration in a fee-splitting agreement can become prohibitive and render the agreement unenforceable by denying the plaintiff access to the forum." A "case-by-case analysis is appropriate, focusing, 'among other things, upon the claimant's ability to pay the arbitration fees and costs, the expected cost differential between arbitration and litigation in court, and whether that cost differential is so substantial as to deter the bringing of claims.' "]

Here, Hardin has not met her burden under Green Tree. First, she has not presented evidence of the likely cost of arbitrating her claim. The invoices Hardin referred to were for unknown claims and do not establish what she could expect to incur if forced to arbitrate this matter. Second, even if Hardin's evidence had addressed the cost of arbitrating this specific claim, she did not attempt to compare that cost with what she would pay in litigation. She is correct that fees would be required to pay an arbitrator (or, under the agreement, more than one arbitrator if the parties could not agree on one arbitrator) while no fees would be paid to a judge. But she presented no evidence, and therefore failed to carry her burden, to show that her likely expenses in arbitration would exceed her likely expenses in litigation. . . .

Finally, we note that it is not clear from the record that Hardin would be required to pay anything at all if the matter proceeded to arbitration. During cross-examination of Hardin's stepson, the Owners sought to inquire into the financial arrangements between Hardin and her lawyer. Hardin objected based on the attorney-client privilege. The Owners argued that, customarily, a plaintiff in a case such as this one is represented by an attorney on a contingency fee basis, with the plaintiff's attorney advancing the expenses to prepare and try the case. The Owners asserted that the arbitration agreement must be upheld absent evidence as to the costs Hardin herself would likely incur and for which she claimed she could not make payment. The Owners submitted that to the extent Hardin contended that the arbitration expenses would be borne directly by her and that she was unable to pay them, then the Owners should be permitted to engage in discovery to determine the accuracy of those contentions.

Hardin's attorney did not respond directly to the contention that the law firm was representing Hardin under a contingency fee arrangement, maintaining that the fee agreement was protected by the attorney-client privilege. But the attorney stated that if the case proceeded to arbitration, the firm would not represent Hardin and Hardin would have to bear the costs of arbitration. The attorney then reiterated that the firm should not have to pay an arbitrator when it does not have to pay for a judge to be a decision-maker. The trial court sustained Hardin's objection based on attorney-client privilege.

To the extent Hardin has maintained that the costs of arbitrating her claim were prohibitively expensive, it was her burden to prove "the likelihood of incurring such costs." *Green Tree,* 531 U.S. at 92, 121 S.Ct. 513. The Owners argued, in essence, that if Hardin's attorneys were representing her on a contingency basis, advancing all costs and recouping them solely from any recovery, then this burden has not been met. Hardin did not refute that contention or present authority that such an analysis is irrelevant to the issue. Instead, she baldly asserted that the attorney-client privilege protected the payment arrangement. This attempt to use the payment arrangement as both a sword and a shield must fail. Even assuming that the fee agreement contains privileged material, that information could be redacted and the billing information could be produced to substantiate Hardin's claim. . . . Consequently, Hardin failed to carry her burden under *Green Tree.*

V. Conclusion

Because the trial court's findings are unsupported by the record, it erred in denying the motion to arbitrate. Accordingly, the trial court's order is reversed, and we remand with directions that an order be entered compelling arbitration.

Reversed and remanded.

NOTES AND QUESTIONS

1. The court relies on *Green Tree Financial Corp.—Alabama v. Randolph*, 531 U.S. 79 (2000), which is reproduced later in this Chapter. In *Green Tree*, the U.S. Supreme Court recognized that circumstances may arise such that "the existence of large arbitration costs could preclude a litigant . . . from effectively vindicating her federal statutory rights in the arbitral forum." *Id.* at 90. The fact that an agreement remains silent about arbitration costs and fees is not *per se* unenforceable. Instead, when a party seeks to invalidate an arbitration agreement on the ground that arbitration would be prohibitively expensive, that party bears the burden of showing the likelihood of incurring such costs.

Green Tree, however, is an employment case. Are there differences in the situations of consumers of goods or services and employees? Do these differences matter when thinking about the fairness of costs of arbitration? Another way of thinking about this is to ask whether the logic of *Green Tree* is limited to the employment context.

2. To the extent that comparatively high costs of arbitration might be unconscionable, commercial parties may be able to include a delegation clause and force the issue to be decided by arbitrators. For instance, in *Dean v. Draughons Junior Coll., Inc.*, student plaintiffs asked that a federal district court free them from having to arbitrate their claims because they were deeply indebted and could not afford the arbitrator's fees. No. 3:12–CV–0157, 2012 WL 3308370, at *7 (M.D. Tenn. Aug. 13, 2012). The arbitral clause stated that its "scope or enforceability . . . shall be determined by the arbitrator, and not by a court." *Id.* at *1 (emphasis omitted). Though under protest, the court felt compelled to send the matter to arbitration, saying:

> [T]his holding present[s] a serious fairness issue. . . . [T]he court is concerned that one or more of the named plaintiffs in this action will not be able to afford the out-of-pocket costs to arbitrate, even under conservative cost assumptions. Indeed, several of the plaintiffs have represented that they have no income and no unencumbered assets whatsoever. . . . While [compelling arbitration is] required by the FAA [and *Rent-A-Center, West, Inc. v. Jackson*], this result strikes the court as manifestly unjust and, perhaps, deserving of legislative attention.

Dean v. Draughons Junior Coll., Inc., 917 F. Supp. 2d 751, 765 (M.D. Tenn. 2013).

Is the court in *Dean* right? Would the pairing of a cost-allocation that might be unconscionable with a delegation clause be "manifestly unjust"?

3. If adhesive contracts are necessarily procedurally unconscionable—the position that the *Aames* court seems to have taken—why isn't the contract in *Zephyr* procedurally unconscionable? What, if anything, differs in the way that the contracts in *Aames* and *Zephyr* were formed?

4. Do you agree with the court in this case that Hardin could have or should have done more to establish the difficulty of paying for arbitration? What more, according to the court, was she supposed to have done?

5. How would you rate the fairness of the fee sharing arrangement set out in Zephyr's arbitration clause? Is it fair? Why or why not? Does your answer depend on who the individual receiving care is? How could the clause be fairer, if at all? In other words, if you were redrafting it, what might you change?

D.R. HORTON, INC. V. GREEN

120 Nev. 549, 96 P.3d 1159 (2004).

Opinion

PER CURIAM.

Appellant D.R. Horton, Inc., a real property developer, and respondents Michael Green, John Velickoff, and Tracy Velickoff (jointly the Homebuyers) entered into home purchase agreements containing a mandatory binding arbitration provision. In the ensuing dispute over the provision's validity, the district court found that the arbitration clause was adhesive and unconscionable. On appeal, Horton argues that the district court erred in concluding that the arbitration clause was unenforceable. We disagree. We conclude that the clause is void as unconscionable and affirm the district court's order denying Horton's motion to compel arbitration.

Facts and Procedural History

The arbitration clause dispute arose from a construction defect controversy between the Homebuyers and Horton. These parties entered into home purchase agreements containing a mandatory arbitration provision. In each case, a two-page form sales agreement constituted the agreement between the parties. The agreement was printed in a very small font. The front page contained the sales price, other financial information, and the signature lines. A clause at the bottom in capitalized bold letters stated that: "PARAGRAPHS 10 THROUGH 27 CONSTITUTE A PART OF THIS CONTRACT."

The back page included, among other things, a limited warranty clause and a mandatory binding arbitration provision. The font size on the back page was smaller than the font utilized on the front page. The arbitration provision read as follows:

> 11. This Contract Is Subject To The Nevada Arbitration Rules Governed Under Nevada Revised Statute Chapter 38 And The Federal Arbitration Act.
>
> Buyer and Seller agree that any disputes or claims between the parties, whether arising from a tort, this Contract, any breach

> of this Contract or in any way related to this transaction, including but not limited to claims or disputes arising under the terms of the express limited warranty referenced in Paragraph 10 of this Contract, shall be settled by binding arbitration under the direction and procedures established by the American Arbitration Association "Construction Industry Arbitration Rules" except as specifically modified herein or dictated by applicable statutes including the Nevada Revised Statute Chapter 38 and/or the Federal Arbitration Act. If Buyer does not seek arbitration prior to initiating any legal action, Buyer agrees that Seller shall be entitled to liquidated damages in the amount of ten thousand dollars . . . ($10,000.00). Any dispute arising from this Contract shall be submitted for determination to a board of three (3) arbitrators to be selected for each such controversy. The decision of the arbitrators shall be in writing and signed by such arbitrators, or a majority of them, and shall be final and binding upon the parties. Each party shall bear the fees and expenses of counsel, witnesses and employees of such party, and any other costs and expenses incurred for the benefit of such party. All other fees and expenses shall be divided equally between Buyer and Seller.

With the exception of the paragraph title, which was in bold capital letters like the other contract headings, nothing drew special attention to this provision.

Green testified that he only read the first page of the document. He indicated that he did not read the second page because "it was all fine print" and Horton's agent told him that it was a standard contract. The Velickoffs indicated that they read both sides of the contract, including the arbitration provision. They testified, however, that they did not understand that the provision constituted a waiver of their right to a jury trial or that it impacted their statutory rights under NRS Chapter 40 involving construction defect claims. Neither Green nor the Velickoffs understood that they would be required to fund one-half of the expenses of the arbitration and that these expenses could be more costly than standard litigation.

[. . .]

After hearing arguments and conducting an evidentiary hearing, the district court denied Horton's motion to compel arbitration, essentially granting judgment in favor of the Homebuyers on the declaratory relief action. The district court ruled that the arbitration clause was adhesive and fell short of Nevada's standards regarding jury trial waivers. The district court also determined that the clause was procedurally and substantively unconscionable because, if enforced, it operated to waive the right to a jury trial without even mentioning that right, and it failed "to inform homeowners of the costs associated with arbitration and the substantial difference between arbitration fees and filing fees for suits filed under Chapter 40." The district court struck the arbitration clause, reasoning that absent such disclosures, the Homebuyers could not give an informed consent. This appeal followed.

DISCUSSION

[. . .]

Strong public policy favors arbitration because arbitration generally avoids the higher costs and longer time periods associated with traditional litigation. Nevertheless, courts may invalidate unconscionable arbitration provisions. "Generally, both procedural and substantive unconscionability must be present in order for a court to exercise its discretion to refuse to enforce a . . . clause as unconscionable." However, less evidence of substantive unconscionability is required in cases involving great procedural unconscionability. A clause is procedurally unconscionable when a party lacks a meaningful opportunity to agree to the clause terms either because of unequal bargaining power, as in an adhesion contract, or because the clause and its effects are not readily ascertainable upon a review of the contract. Procedural unconscionability often involves the use of fine print or complicated, incomplete or misleading language that fails to inform a reasonable person of the contractual language's consequences. As the Ninth Circuit has recognized, "substantive unconscionability focuses on the one-sidedness of the contract terms." (All citations omitted.)

The district court determined that the arbitration clause was unenforceable because the Homebuyers had no realistic bargaining opportunity; that is, the agreement was an adhesion contract. This finding is not supported by substantial evidence. In fact, the record demonstrates that it was possible to negotiate for deletion of the arbitration provision. Nevertheless, the district court also concluded that the provision was procedurally deficient because it failed to indicate that by agreeing to binding arbitration, the Homebuyers were giving up significant rights under Nevada law. The district court also considered the fact that the clause was in fine print and indistinguishable from many other contractual provisions, and thus its significance was downplayed. Finally, the district court found that Horton's sales agent referred to the contract as a form agreement containing standard language, leading the Homebuyers to believe that the clause was simply a formality that did not significantly affect their rights. Based upon these findings, the district court concluded that the arbitration provision was procedurally unconscionable.

[. . .]

The contracts Horton presented to the Homebuyers were difficult to read and the arbitration clause was on the back page. The signature lines, in contrast, were on the front page. Other than the fact that the paragraph headings relating to the arbitration provision were in bold capital letters, just like every other heading in the contracts, nothing drew attention to the arbitration provision. To the contrary, although the termite and drainage provisions were capitalized throughout, the body of the arbitration clause was not capitalized. Instead, it was in an extremely small font. As in *Burch,* the arbitration provision was inconspicuous. Thus, even if an individual read the contract, there was nothing to draw the reader's attention to the importance of the arbitration provision. This failure to highlight the arbitration agreement, together with the representations made by Horton's agent that these were standard provisions, are key features in the district court's finding of procedural unconscionability.

Finally, even if any home purchasers noticed and read the arbitration provision, as did the Velickoffs, they would not be put on notice that they were agreeing to forgo important rights under state law. In addition to the right to a jury trial, . . . a construction defect claimant may recover attorney fees or other damages proximately caused by the construction defect controversy. In general, the right to request attorney fees would still exist in an arbitration proceeding because " '[b]y agreeing to arbitrate a statutory claim . . . , a party does not forgo the substantive rights afforded by the statute; it only submits to their resolution in an arbitral, rather than a judicial, forum.' " However, the arbitration provision provides that each party is to bear its own attorney fees and expenses. While Horton did not have a duty to explain in detail each and every right that the Homebuyers would be waiving by agreeing to arbitration, to be enforceable, an arbitration clause must at least be conspicuous and clearly put a purchaser on notice that he or she is waiving important rights under Nevada law.

Our 1989 decision in *Tandy Computer Leasing v. Terina's Pizza* is relevant to our analysis of the arbitration provision in this case. In *Tandy Computer Leasing,* a computer equipment lessor brought an action in Texas against a family of Nevada pizza parlor owners. The lessor initiated the action in Texas pursuant to a forum selection clause in the lease agreement and subsequently sought to enforce the judgment in Nevada. We invalidated the forum selection clause, in part because of the lessor's failure to make the clause conspicuous. We noted that binding a consumer under such circumstances was unrealistic because [the] clause was buried on the very bottom of the back page of the lease agreement, in very fine print, in a paragraph labelled MISCELLANEOUS. . . . Nothing on the front page notifies the reader of the specific forum selection clause on the back page. The clause is not even in bold print.

In the instant case, the district court did not err in finding procedural unconscionability. The arbitration provision was inconspicuous, downplayed by Horton's representative, and failed to adequately advise an average person that important rights were being waived by agreeing to arbitrate any disputes under the contract. We conclude that the district court did not err in finding the arbitration clause to be procedurally deficient.

We now turn to the issue of substantive unconscionability. Two provisions of the agreement implicate substantive unconscionability: the $10,000 penalty for refusing to arbitrate, and the requirement that each party pay equally for the costs of arbitration.

Ting v. AT & T, a recent Ninth Circuit case applying California law, provides guidance in determining substantive unconscionability. In *Ting,* the Ninth Circuit invalidated, among other things, a contract provision requiring customers to split arbitration fees with AT & T. The Ninth Circuit held that "[w]here an arbitration agreement is concerned, the agreement is unconscionable unless the arbitration remedy contains a 'modicum of bilaterality.' " The court went on to say that:

> "[a]lthough parties are free to contract for asymmetrical remedies and arbitration clauses of varying scope ... the doctrine of unconscionability limits the extent to which a stronger party may ... impose the arbitration forum on the weaker party without accepting that forum for itself." (*Ting quoting Armendariz v. Foundation Health Psychcare,* 24 Cal.4th 83, 99 Cal.Rptr.2d 745, 6 P.3d 669, 692 (2000)).

Ting is similar to the case at bar. Here, the arbitration provision is one-sided because it contained a liquidated damages provision penalizing the Homebuyers if they chose to forgo arbitration but imposed no such penalty upon Horton. Although the one-sidedness of the provision is not overwhelming, it does establish substantive unconscionability, especially when considered in light of the great procedural unconscionability present in this case.

[. . .]

CONCLUSION

We conclude that the arbitration provision was procedurally and substantively unconscionable because it was inconspicuous, one-sided and failed to advise the Homebuyers that significant rights under Nevada law would be waived by agreeing to arbitration. While the absence of language disclosing the potential arbitration costs and fees, standing alone, may not render an arbitration provision unenforceable, the district court properly considered that as a factor in invalidating the provision. As the arbitration provision is unenforceable, we affirm the district court's order denying Horton's motion to compel arbitration.

NOTES AND QUESTIONS

1. Is there an implied message in the court's reasoning and result? Does the arbitral clause—either in its making or content—exhibit gross unfairness? Do you suspect that there is a sort of "trigger mechanism" in the court's discussion?

2. What about the federal policy on arbitration? Should the opinion be deemed to violate FAA § 2 and be federally preempted? What arguments for and against that proposition can you make? What parts of the opinion might transgress the strictures of the federal policy? Which federal cases might be at play?

3. How are *Ting* and *Armendariz* relevant to the court's assessment of the facts and its ruling?

4. Could the arbitration agreement in this case be salvaged? How might you redraft it, if you represented the developer, in light of this decision?

* * *

Institutional Initiatives to Correct for Possible Unfairness in the Arbitral Process

Arbitration institutions have actively sought to offset worries about fairness in the arbitral process by passing various "due process" protocols. These protocols aim to correct for imbalances in mass-market arbitration agreements, though they do so in varying ways.

In 1998, for instance, the Council of Better Business Bureaus, Inc. (CBBB) made public its position on binding, pre-dispute arbitration clauses in consumer contracts. The policy, adopted by the CBBB membership, acknowledged that arbitration often is a highly effective means of resolving disputes between businesses and consumers, but it emphasized that ADR procedures, which restrict a consumer's access to courts, should be voluntary. Accordingly, the nation's Better Business Bureaus agreed to arbitrate consumer-business disputes only when the contract gave the consumer fair notice of the consequences of agreeing to arbitration and when the customer formally acknowledges its acceptance of the arbitration clause.

According to the CBBB, "pre-dispute, binding arbitration clauses" have been used historically in contracts involving two business entities or in collective bargaining, where both sides are represented by sophisticated negotiators. In more recent years, however, these clauses are appearing more frequently in consumer product and service contracts. The CBBB believes that it is essential that parties enter into these agreements voluntarily, with a clear understanding of what disputes will be subject to the arbitration agreement, what arbitration will cost, and what rights are compromised in return for the opportunity to arbitrate.

The obligation to arbitrate has frequently been buried in the contract or drafted poorly. As a result, "in these cases, it is difficult to say that the consumer's agreement to arbitrate is voluntary. Indeed, it is often a complete surprise to consumers when a dispute later arises and they discover the lengthy documents they signed included one of these clauses." When businesses use a binding pre-dispute arbitration clause and name the Better Business Bureau as Provider, they will be required to follow the BBB policy for fair disclosure to consumers and give the BBB notice when they draft such contract provisions.

JAMS/ENDISPUTE (now JAMS), a nationally recognized private provider of dispute resolution services, also announced in 1998 a policy designed to achieve greater fairness in the resolution of consumer disputes. The substance of the policy is contained in a document entitled "Minimum Standards of Procedural Fairness" which applies to binding consumer arbitrations conducted by JAMS.

Effectively, the policy attempts to address both formation concerns and concerns about the fairness of the arbitral process itself. With respect to formation, the policy requires that the consumer be given notice of the terms of the arbitration and that those terms be clear. With respect to the process, the policy requires a number of specific consumer protection measures be present in the arbitration agreement, including:

- Reciprocal obligations to arbitrate and carve outs allowing both sides recourse to small claims courts for appropriate cases;
- Full access to all the remedies that would otherwise be available in court;
- A reasonable opportunity for the consumer to participate in the process of selecting the arbitrator;
- A right to counsel and no provisions discouraging the participation of lawyers;
- The right of the consumer to have any in-person hearings conducted in her or his hometown area;
- A provision requiring the commercial party to bear all costs associated with the arbitration other than a $250 filing fee;
- A reasonable right to have access to discovery of non-privileged and relevant information; and
- A written and reasoned award stating the essential finding and conclusions of the arbitrator.

Like the BBB and JAMS, the National Consumer Disputes Advisory Committee of the American Arbitration Association, composed of seventeen of the nation's leading consumer affairs, business, government affairs, and alternative dispute resolution experts, developed a national *Due Process Protocol for Mediation and Arbitration of Consumer Disputes.* The development of the *Protocol* was in response to the pronounced trend toward incorporation of out-of-court conflict resolution processes in standardized agreements presented to consumers of goods and services. The *Consumer Due Process Protocol* includes a Statement of Fifteen Principles and is intended to protect the rights of consumers who are required to resolve disputes outside of court. The dispute can relate to the following types of transactions: banking, credit cards, financial services, home construction and improvements, insurance, communications, and the purchase and lease of motor vehicles and other personal property.

The American Arbitration Association announced in 1998 its endorsement of the *Consumer Due Process Protocol.* To ensure fairness and equity for consumer disputes resolved through mediation and arbitration, the American Arbitration Association has adopted the following policy:

> It is the policy of the American Arbitration Association to administer cases in accordance with the law. In following the law, the Association, as a matter of policy, will administer consumer dispute resolution programs that meet the standards outlined in the Consumer Due Process Protocol. If the Association determines that a consumer dispute resolution program on its face substantially and materially deviates from the minimum standards of the Consumer Due Process Protocol, the Association may decline to administer cases under that program.

The co-chair of the Advisory Committee stated: "The use of arbitration and mediation to resolve disputes between consumers and providers of goods and services is spreading rapidly as cost and delay in traditional court proceedings become more and more burdensome. . . . The role of the American Arbitration Association, an independent dispute resolution institution, in developing these standards is particularly appropriate because consumer arbitration is usually founded on contract terms specified by the seller of goods or services without any opportunity for negotiation or input from the consumer." Another co-chair stated that: "I would expect it to become a national standard for dispute resolution providers as mediation and arbitration grow as options for resolving disputes."

Finally, a consumer advocate stated: "I believe the Protocol takes an important step toward protecting the rights of consumers who are forced, typically without their knowledge or consent, to give up their right to bring a court action when they are harmed by a marketplace transaction. . . . While I firmly believe that it is improper to foreclose court access for consumers, especially through the use of small-print clauses in standardized form contracts, I am hopeful that the Protocol will place consumers on a more equal footing with providers than has been the case thus far."

Due Process Protocol for the Mediation and Arbitration of Consumer Disputes

—Statement of Principles—

Principle 1. Fundamentally-Fair Process

All parties are entitled to a fundamentally-fair ADR process. As embodiments of fundamental fairness, these Principles should be observed in structuring ADR Programs.

Principle 2. Access to Information Regarding ADR Program

Providers of goods or services should undertake reasonable measures to provide Consumers with full and accurate information regarding Consumer ADR Programs. At the time the Consumer contracts for goods or services, such measures should include: (1) clear and adequate notice regarding the ADR provisions, including a statement indicating whether participation in the ADR Program is mandatory or optional; and (2) reasonable means by which Consumers may obtain additional information regarding the ADR Program. After a dispute arises, Consumers should have access to all information necessary for effective participation in ADR.

Principle 3. Independent and Impartial Neutral; Independent Administration

1. **Independent and Impartial Neutral.** All parties are entitled to a Neutral who is independent and impartial.

2. **Independent Administration.** If participation in mediation or arbitration is mandatory, the procedure should be administered by an independent ADR Institution. Administrative services should include: the maintenance of a panel of prospective Neutrals, facilitation of Neutral selection, collection and distribution of [the] Neutral's fees and expenses, oversight and implementation of ADR rules and procedures, and monitoring of Neutral qualifications, performance, and adherence to pertinent rules, procedures[,] and ethical standards.

3. **Standards for Neutrals.** The Independent ADR Institution should make reasonable efforts to ensure that Neutrals understand and conform to pertinent ADR rules, procedures[,] and ethical standards.

4. **Selection of Neutrals.** The Consumer and Provider should have an equal voice in the selection of Neutrals in connection with a specific dispute.

5. **Disclosure and Disqualification.** Beginning at the time of appointment, Neutrals should be required to disclose to the Independent ADR Institution any circumstance likely to affect impartiality, including

any bias or financial or personal interest which might affect the result of the ADR proceeding, or any past or present relationship or experience with the parties or their representatives, including past ADR experiences. The Independent ADR Institution should communicate any such information to the parties and other Neutrals, if any. Upon objection of the party to continued service of the Neutral, the Independent ADR Institution should determine whether the Neutral should be disqualified and should inform the parties of its decision. The disclosure obligation of the Neutral and procedure for disqualification should continue throughout the period of appointment.

Principle 4. Quality and Competence of Neutrals

All parties are entitled to competent, qualified Neutrals. Independent ADR Institutions are responsible for establishing and maintaining standards for Neutrals in ADR Programs they administer.

Principle 5. Small Claims

Consumer ADR Agreements should make it clear that all parties retain the right to seek relief in a small claims court for disputes or claims within the scope of its jurisdiction.

Principle 6. Reasonable Cost

1. **Reasonable Cost.** Providers of goods and services should develop ADR programs which entail reasonable cost to Consumers based on the circumstances of the dispute, including, among other things, the size and nature of the claim, the nature of goods or services provided, and the ability of the Consumer to pay. In some cases, this may require the Provider to subsidize the process.

2. **Handling of Payment.** In the interest of ensuring fair and independent Neutrals, the making of fee arrangements and the payment of fees should be administered on a rational, equitable[,] and consistent basis by the Independent ADR Institution.

Principle 7. Reasonably Convenient Location

In the case of face-to-face proceedings, the proceedings should be conducted at a location which is reasonably convenient to both parties with due consideration of their ability to travel and other pertinent circumstances. If the parties are unable to agree on a location, the determination should be made by the Independent ADR Institution or by the Neutral.

Principle 8. Reasonable Time Limits

ADR proceedings should occur within a reasonable time, without undue delay. The rules governing ADR should establish specific reasonable time periods for each step in the ADR process and, where necessary, set forth default procedures in the event a party fails to participate in the process after reasonable notice.

Principle 9. Right to Representation

All parties participating in processes in ADR Programs have the right, at their own expense, to be represented by a spokesperson of their own choosing. The ADR rules and procedures should so specify.

Principle 10. Mediation

The use of mediation is strongly encouraged as an informal means of assisting parties in resolving their own disputes.

Principle 11. Agreements to Arbitrate

Consumers should be given:

a) clear and adequate notice of the arbitration provision and its consequences, including a statement of its mandatory or optional character;

b) reasonable access to information regarding the arbitration process, including basic distinctions between arbitration and court proceedings, related costs, and advice as to where they may obtain more complete information regarding arbitration procedures and arbitrator rosters;

c) notice of the option to make use of applicable small claims court procedures as an alternative to binding arbitration in appropriate cases; and,

d) a clear statement of the means by which the Consumer may exercise the option (if any) to submit disputes to arbitration or to [the] court process.

Principle 12. Arbitration Hearings

1. **Fundamentally-Fair Hearing.** All parties are entitled to a fundamentally-fair arbitration hearing. This requires adequate notice of hearings and an opportunity to be heard and to present relevant evidence to impartial decision-makers. In some cases, such as some small claims, the requirement of fundamental fairness may be met by hearings conducted by electronic or telephonic means or by a submission of documents. However, the Neutral should have discretionary authority to require a face-to-face hearing upon the request of a party.

2. **Confidentiality in Arbitration.** Consistent with general expectations of privacy in arbitration hearings, the arbitrator should make reasonable efforts to maintain the privacy of the hearing to the extent permitted by applicable law. The arbitrator should also carefully consider claims of privilege and confidentiality when addressing evidentiary issues.

Principle 13. Access to Information

No party should ever be denied the right to a fundamentally-fair process due to an inability to obtain information material to a dispute. Consumer ADR agreements which provide for binding arbitration should establish procedures for arbitrator-supervised exchange of information prior to arbitration, bearing in mind the expedited nature of arbitration.

Principle 14. Arbitral Remedies

The arbitrator should be empowered to grant whatever relief would be available in court under law or in equity.

Principle 15. Arbitration Awards

1. **Final and Binding Award; Limited Scope of Review.** The arbitrator's award should be final and binding, but subject to review in accordance with applicable statutes governing arbitration awards.

2. **Standards to Guide Arbitrator Decision-Making.** In making the award, the arbitrator should apply any identified, pertinent contract terms, statutes, and legal precedents.

3. **Explanation of Award.** At the timely request of either party, the arbitrator should provide a brief written explanation of the basis for the award. To facilitate such requests, the arbitrator should discuss the matter with the parties prior to the arbitration hearing.

NOTES AND QUESTIONS

1. How impartial and objective are the arbitral institutions' pronouncements on consumer arbitration? Are these institutions likely to lose business because of their high-mindedness? Is consumer arbitration a source of lucrative business? If these protocols are not about making money, what is their objective?

2. How effective do you think that these sorts of self-regulatory measures are at creating a "fundamentally fair" arbitration process? These sorts of protocols, of course, do not have the force of law. As such, they remain voluntary undertakings. Does that matter, especially if there is widespread agreement on at least core features of what a fundamentally fair arbitral process should look like?

3. When is notice of the agreement to arbitrate adequate? When are costs or other features of the arbitral process reasonable? Can a fundamentally fair arbitration procedure ever allay the injustice of an unfair contract formation process?

4. How would you explain "arbitration" to the average person? Can you develop a colloquial definition? At the same time, how would you describe public court adjudication? Both processes are obscure, but perhaps in different ways. Arbitration may seem foreign to average people because they have never

heard of it or have only heard of it in the context of consumer advocacy generally. At the same time, although average people have heard of public court litigation, they probably know next to nothing about how it functions. Given what you know about both processes—arbitration and public court litigation—which is easier to understand?

5. Debates about adhesive arbitration often take place against the implicit assumption that public court litigation is the gold-standard of adjudication. Do you think that is really true? As you think about your answer, consider what Chief Justice Warren E. Burger wrote in 1982

> [F]or at least the past 20 years there has been a slowly, all too slowly, developing awareness that the traditional litigation process has become too cumbersome, too expensive, and also burdened by many other disadvantages. In 1976 we took note of these problems in commemorating the 70th anniversary of Roscoe Pound's indictment of the American judicial and legal systems. . . . It is now clear that neither the federal nor the state court systems are capable of handling all the burdens placed upon them.

Warren E. Burger, *Isn't There a Better Way?*, 68 A.B.A. J. 274, 277 (Mar. 1982).

Legal traffic jams caused by bloated court dockets can limit access to justice for many people and businesses. Additionally, court congestion can make it difficult for judges to be as focused on civil cases as parties might want. Judges are busy generalists, with criminal cases, family law cases, juvenile cases, probate cases, and civil cases vying for their attention. Finally, although the ideal of a jury trial still holds some sway, the number of cases decided by juries at both the state and federal level has been declining sharply and consistently for more than fifty years. *See, e.g.*, Richard Lorren Jolly, *Expanding the Search for America's Missing Jury*, 116 MICH. L. REV. 925, 925 (2018) (reporting that, between 1962 and 2015, civil decided by a jury in the federal courts declined from 5.5% to 0.76% and that state courts have experienced a similar decline in jury trials).

Given that litigation in public courts may not be affordable or feasible for individuals, if due process protocols were taken seriously, might arbitration be a better form of justice for at least some individuals? Does it depend on what the stakes of the dispute are?

6. Assess the AAA Protocol rules on impartiality and disclosure. Must all arbitrators be free of any "leanings"? What about the institutional administrator? Are there minimal qualifications for arbitrators? How do they become part of an institutional list? When is disclosure sufficient?

7. How does the AAA Protocol protect statutory rights and procedural recourse in the form of class litigation and the awarding of exemplary damages?

8. Does the content of the AAA Protocol assist you in drafting a standard agreement for the arbitration of consumer disputes?

4. OBJECTIONS TO CLASS ACTION WAIVERS

Perhaps the most hotly contested issues related to the fairness of arbitration center on so-called class action waivers. Concerns about these waivers might be thought of as straddling the divide between concerns over the fairness of the arbitral process itself and concerns about the fairness of the outcomes in arbitration.

As U.S. Supreme Court jurisprudence was becoming more protective of consumer and employment arbitration contracts, forcing individuals to arbitrate claims rather than take them to court, the aggregation of claims in courts was on the rise. Various procedural tools allow for the aggregation or pooling of claims into a single package of "mass" litigation. One critical moment for mass litigation was the passage of Federal Rule of Civil Procedure 23, the class action rule, in 1966. Another was the adoption of the Multidistrict Litigation Act in 1968, which empowered a judicial panel to combine civil cases from across the federal system before a single judge. And finally, more liberal joinder rules have allowed for what some have labeled "mass actions," with hundreds or even thousands of claimants joined together.

For commercial parties, class actions and other forms of aggregation pose much greater financial risk than individual lawsuits, whether litigated or arbitrated. Class actions allow many similarly situated parties—usually plaintiffs—to aggregate their claims together. Pooled claims can create tremendous settlement pressure. Even if the merits of class action claims are dubious, rational commercial parties will settle many of them. For instance, imagine that a class of 500,000 consumers alleges that Big Company X engaged in a scheme of fraudulent behavior that deprived them each of $100. This class, then, has a total damage claim of $50 million. Even if these plaintiffs have only a 5% change of prevailing, Company X should settle for around $2.5 million plus whatever it would spend on attorneys' fees to defend itself through a trial.

As a result, class actions may incentivize entrepreneurial litigators to bring questionable claims against commercial parties because the threat of huge losses can extract quick settlements. Most class action attorneys are compensated by contingency fee arrangements, so they can stand to earn large payouts if they can leverage a concession by the commercial party.

Of course, this skeptical view of class actions has to be counterbalanced by the fact that without them, individuals may have no meaningful opportunity to protect themselves from predatory businesses. Without the threat of class action damages, commercial parties could be free to systematically defraud large numbers of individuals for small amounts. As Chief Justice Warren Burger explained in 1980

> The aggregation of individual claims in the context of a classwide suit is an evolutionary response to the existence of injuries unremedied by the regulatory action of government. Where it is not economically reasonable to obtain relief within the traditional framework of small individual suits for damages, aggrieved persons may be without any effective redress unless they may employ the class-action device.

Deposit Guaranty Nat. Bank v. Roper, 445 U.S. 326, 339 (1980). Chief Justice Burger also recognized that class actions often depended on contingent fee arrangements that were "a natural outgrowth of the increasing reliance on the 'private attorney general' for the vindication of legal rights; obviously this development has been facilitated by Rule 23." *Id.* at 338.

It is worth noting that the American approach to aggregative litigation is somewhat unique. The rest of the world generally takes a more reluctant approach to class actions, as illustrated by the following introduction by a Canadian professor at an international conference:

> U.S.-style class actions have become a flashpoint for debate over group litigation and the collective redress regimes emerging around the world. Everyone wants to develop better ways for consumers and others who suffer loss from mass harms to receive compensation for claims that are too small to litigate individually. Everyone wants to improve the means for encouraging responsible conduct on the party of those who might cause such harms. But everyone, at least outside the United States, seems also agree that they do not want to adopt U.S.-style class actions in their systems.

Janet Walker, *"General Report," in* CIVIL PROCEDURE IN CROSS-CULTURAL DIALOGUE: EURASIA CONTEXT 413 (Dmitry Maleshin ed. 2012).

Whatever one might think of the controversial debates regarding class actions and aggregation, commercial parties saw the U.S. Supreme Court's unwavering support of arbitration as an opportunity to avoid collective claims altogether. Commercial parties began including bars to class actions and aggregative processes in mandatory pre-dispute arbitration clauses. In other words, they began mandating that individuals arbitrate any and all disputes and do so on their own. These bars have come to be known as "class action waivers."

Initial judicial response to these waivers was mixed, with some courts allowing arbitrators to decide whether a clause contemplated class arbitration. Other courts voided the bars against class actions using the doctrine of unconscionability. For instance, in *Discover Bank v. Superior Court*, the California Supreme Court said:

> We do not hold that all class action waivers are necessarily unconscionable. But when the waiver is found in a consumer contract of adhesion in a setting in which disputes between the contracting parties predictably involve small amounts of damages, and when it is alleged that the party with the superior bargaining power has carried out a scheme to deliberately cheat large numbers of consumers out of individually small sums of money, then, at least to the extent the obligation at issue is governed by California law, the waiver becomes in practice the exemption of the party "from responsibility for [its] own fraud, or willful injury to the person or property of another." (Civ. Code, § 1668.) Under these circumstances, such waivers are unconscionable under California law and should not be enforced.

30 Cal.Rptr.3d 76, 87 (Cal. 2005).

The judicial uncertainty over class action waivers came to an end in 2011, with the U.S. Supreme Court's decision in *AT&T Mobility v. Concepcion*, it held that the *Discover Bank* rule was preempted by the FAA. Since then, the Court has systematically reinforced the right of parties to exclude class actions when they choose to arbitrate. The following cases are central to evolution of the Court's class action wavier jurisprudence.

AT&T MOBILITY LLC V. CONCEPCION

563 U.S. 333, 131 S.Ct. 1740, 179 L.Ed.2d 742 (2011).

JUSTICE SCALIA delivered the opinion of the Court.

Section 2 of the Federal Arbitration Act (FAA) makes agreements to arbitrate "valid, irrevocable, and enforceable, save upon such grounds as exist at law or in equity for the revocation of any contract." . . . We consider whether the FAA prohibits States from conditioning the enforceability of certain arbitration agreements on the availability of classwide arbitration procedures.

I

In February 2002, Vincent and Liza Concepcion entered into an agreement for the sale and servicing of cellular telephones with AT&T Mobility LCC (AT&T). [Footnote omitted.] The contract provided for arbitration of all disputes between the parties, but required that claims be brought in the parties' "individual capacity, and not as a plaintiff or class member in any purported class or representative proceeding."[2] . . . The agreement authorized AT&T to make unilateral amendments, which it did to the arbitration provision on several occasions. The version at issue in

[2] That provision further states that "the arbitrator may not consolidate more than one person's claims, and may not otherwise preside over any form of a representative or class proceeding." . . .

this case reflects revisions made in December 2006, which the parties agree are controlling.

The revised agreement provides that customers may initiate dispute proceedings by completing a one-page Notice of Dispute form available on AT&T's Web site. AT&T may then offer to settle the claim; if it does not, or if the dispute is not resolved within 30 days, the customer may invoke arbitration by filing a separate Demand for Arbitration, also available on AT&T's Web site. In the event the parties proceed to arbitration, the agreement specifies that AT&T must pay all costs for nonfrivolous claims; that arbitration must take place in the county in which the customer is billed; that, for claims of $10,000 or less, the customer may choose whether the arbitration proceeds in person, by telephone, or based only on submissions; that either party may bring a claim in small claims court in lieu of arbitration; and that the arbitrator may award any form of individual relief, including injunctions and presumably punitive damages. The agreement, moreover, denies AT&T any ability to seek reimbursement of its attorney's fees, and, in the event that a customer receives an arbitration award greater than AT&T's last written settlement offer, requires AT&T to pay a $7,500 minimum recovery and twice the amount of the claimant's attorney's fees.[3]

The Concepcions purchased AT&T service, which was advertised as including the provision of free phones; they were not charged for the phones, but they were charged $30.22 in sales tax based on the phones' retail value. In March 2006, the Concepcions filed a complaint against AT&T in the United States District Court for the Southern District of California. The complaint was later consolidated with a putative class action alleging, among other things, that AT&T had engaged in false advertising and fraud by charging sales tax on phones it advertised as free.

In March 2008, AT & T moved to compel arbitration under the terms of its contract with the Concepcions. The Concepcions opposed the motion, contending that the arbitration agreement was unconscionable and unlawfully exculpatory under California law because it disallowed classwide procedures. The District Court denied AT & T's motion. It described AT & T's arbitration agreement favorably, noting, for example, that the informal dispute-resolution process was "quick, easy to use" and likely to "promp[t] full or . . . even excess payment to the customer *without* the need to arbitrate or litigate"; that the $7,500 premium functioned as "a substantial inducement for the consumer to pursue the claim in arbitration" if a dispute was not resolved informally; and that consumers who were members of a class would likely be worse off. . . . Nevertheless, relying on the California Supreme Court's decision in *Discover Bank v. Superior Court,* 36 Cal.4th 148, 30 Cal.Rptr.3d 76, 113 P.3d 1100 (2005),

[3] The guaranteed minimum recovery was increased in 2009 to $10,000. . . .

the court found that the arbitration provision was unconscionable because AT & T had not shown that bilateral arbitration adequately substituted for the deterrent effects of class actions. . . .

The Ninth Circuit affirmed, also finding the provision unconscionable under California law as announced in *Discover Bank*. . . . It also held that the *Discover Bank* rule was not preempted by the FAA because that rule was simply "a refinement of the unconscionability analysis applicable to contracts generally in California." . . . In response to AT & T's argument that the Concepcions' interpretation of California law discriminated against arbitration, the Ninth Circuit rejected the contention that " 'class proceedings will reduce the efficiency and expeditiousness of arbitration' " and noted that " '*Discover Bank* placed arbitration agreements with class action waivers on the *exact same footing* as contracts that bar class action litigation outside the context of arbitration.' " . . .

We granted certiorari, 560 U.S. ___, 130 S.Ct. 3322, 176 L.Ed.2d 1218 (2010).

II

The FAA was enacted in 1925 in response to widespread judicial hostility to arbitration agreements. . . .

[. . .]

We have described this provision as reflecting both a "liberal federal policy favoring arbitration," . . . and the "fundamental principle that arbitration is a matter of contract,". . . . In line with these principles, courts must place arbitration agreements on an equal footing with other contracts, . . . and enforce them according to their terms. . . .

The final phrase of § 2, however, permits arbitration agreements to be declared unenforceable "upon such grounds as exist at law or in equity for the revocation of any contract." This saving clause permits agreements to arbitrate to be invalidated by "generally applicable contract defenses, such as fraud, duress, or unconscionability," but not by defenses that apply only to arbitration or that derive their meaning from the fact that an agreement to arbitrate is at issue. . . . The question in this case is whether § 2 preempts California's rule classifying most collective-arbitration waivers in consumer contracts as unconscionable. We refer to this rule as the *Discover Bank* rule.

Under California law, courts may refuse to enforce any contract found "to have been unconscionable at the time it was made," or may "limit the application of any unconscionable clause." Cal. Civ.Code Ann. § 1670.5(a) (West 1985). A finding of unconscionability requires "a 'procedural' and a 'substantive' element, the former focusing on 'oppression' or 'surprise' due to unequal bargaining power, the latter on 'overly harsh' or 'one-sided' results." . . .

In *Discover Bank,* the California Supreme Court applied this framework to class-action waivers in arbitration agreements and held as follows:

> "[W]hen the waiver is found in a consumer contract of adhesion in a setting in which disputes between the contracting parties predictably involve small amounts of damages, and when it is alleged that the party with the superior bargaining power has carried out a scheme to deliberately cheat large numbers of consumers out of individually small sums of money, then . . . the waiver becomes in practice the exemption of the party 'from responsibility for [its] own fraud, or willful injury to the person or property of another.' Under these circumstances, such waivers are unconscionable under California law and should not be enforced." . . .

California courts have frequently applied this rule to find arbitration agreements unconscionable. . . .

III

A

The Concepcions argue that the *Discover Bank* rule, given its origins in California's unconscionability doctrine and California's policy against exculpation, is a ground that "exist[s] at law or in equity for the revocation of any contract" under FAA § 2. Moreover, they argue that even if we construe the *Discover Bank* rule as a prohibition on collective-action waivers rather than simply an application of unconscionability, the rule would still be applicable to all dispute-resolution contracts, since California prohibits waivers of class litigation as well. . . .

When state law prohibits outright the arbitration of a particular type of claim, the analysis is straightforward: The conflicting rule is displaced by the FAA. *Preston v. Ferrer,* 552 U.S. 346, 353 (2008). But the inquiry becomes more complex when a doctrine normally thought to be generally applicable, such as duress or, as relevant here, unconscionability, is alleged to have been applied in a fashion that disfavors arbitration. In *Perry v. Thomas,* 482 U.S. 483 (1987), for example, we noted that the FAA's preemptive effect might extend even to grounds traditionally thought to exist " 'at law or in equity for the revocation of any contract.' " *Id.,* at 492, n. 9 (emphasis deleted). We said that a court may not "rely on the uniqueness of an agreement to arbitrate as a basis for a state-law holding that enforcement would be unconscionable, for this would enable the court to effect what . . . the state legislature cannot." *Id.,* at 493, n. 9.

An obvious illustration of this point would be a case finding unconscionable or unenforceable as against public policy consumer arbitration agreements that fail to provide for judicially monitored discovery. The rationalizations for such a holding are neither difficult to imagine nor different in kind from those articulated in *Discover Bank.* A court might reason that no consumer would knowingly waive his right to full discovery, as this would enable companies to hide their wrongdoing. Or the court might simply say that such agreements are exculpatory—restricting discovery would be of greater benefit to the company than the consumer, since the former is more likely to be sued than to sue. . . . And, the reasoning would continue, because such a rule applies the general principle of unconscionability or public-policy disapproval of exculpatory agreements, it is applicable to "any" contract and thus preserved by § 2 of the FAA. In practice, of course, the rule would have a disproportionate impact on arbitration agreements; but it would presumably apply to contracts purporting to restrict discovery in litigation as well.

Other examples are easy to imagine. The same argument might apply to a rule classifying as unconscionable arbitration agreements that fail to abide by the Federal Rules of Evidence, or that disallow an ultimate disposition by a jury (perhaps termed "a panel of twelve lay arbitrators" to help avoid preemption). Such examples are not fanciful, since the judicial hostility towards arbitration that prompted the FAA had manifested itself in "a great variety" of "devices and formulas" declaring arbitration against public policy. . . . And although these statistics are not definitive, it is worth noting that California's courts have been more likely to hold contracts to arbitrate unconscionable than other contracts. . . .

The Concepcions suggest that all this is just a parade of horribles, and no genuine worry. "Rules aimed at destroying arbitration" or "demanding procedures incompatible with arbitration," they concede, "would be preempted by the FAA because they cannot sensibly be reconciled with Section 2." . . . The "grounds" available under § 2's saving clause, they admit, "should not be construed to include a State's mere preference for procedures that are incompatible with arbitration and 'would wholly eviscerate arbitration agreements.' " . . . [Footnote omitted.]

We largely agree. Although § 2's saving clause preserves generally applicable contract defenses, nothing in it suggests an intent to preserve state-law rules that stand as an obstacle to the accomplishment of the FAA's objectives. . . . As we have said, a federal statute's saving clause " 'cannot in reason be construed as [allowing] a common law right, the continued existence of which would be absolutely inconsistent with the provisions of the act. In other words, the act cannot be held to destroy itself.' " . . .

We differ with the Concepcions only in the application of this analysis to the matter before us. We do not agree that rules requiring judicially monitored discovery or adherence to the Federal Rules of Evidence are "a far cry from this case." . . . The overarching purpose of the FAA, evident in the text of §§ 2, 3, and 4, is to ensure the enforcement of arbitration agreements according to their terms so as to facilitate streamlined proceedings. Requiring the availability of classwide arbitration interferes with fundamental attributes of arbitration and thus creates a scheme inconsistent with the FAA.

B

The "principal purpose" of the FAA is to "ensur[e] that private arbitration agreements are enforced according to their terms." . . . This purpose is readily apparent from the FAA's text. Section 2 makes arbitration agreements "valid, irrevocable, and enforceable" as written (subject, of course, to the saving clause); § 3 requires courts to stay litigation of arbitral claims pending arbitration of those claims "in accordance with the terms of the agreement"; and § 4 requires courts to compel arbitration "in accordance with the terms of the agreement" upon the motion of either party to the agreement (assuming that the "making of the arbitration agreement or the failure . . . to perform the same" is not at issue). In light of these provisions, we have held that parties may agree to limit the issues subject to arbitration . . . to arbitrate according to specific rules . . . , and to limit *with whom* a party will arbitrate its disputes. . . .

The point of affording parties discretion in designing arbitration processes is to allow for efficient, streamlined procedures tailored to the type of dispute. It can be specified, for example, that the decisionmaker be a specialist in the relevant field, or that proceedings be kept confidential to protect trade secrets. And the informality of arbitral proceedings is itself desirable, reducing the cost and increasing the speed of dispute resolution. . . .

The dissent quotes *Dean Witter Reynolds, Inc. v. Byrd,* 470 U.S. 213, 219 (1985), as " 'reject[ing] the suggestion that the overriding goal of the Arbitration Act was to promote the expeditious resolution of claims.' " . . . That is greatly misleading. After saying (accurately enough) that "the overriding goal of the Arbitration Act was [not] to promote the expeditious resolution of claims," but to "ensure judicial enforcement of privately made agreements to arbitrate," . . . *Dean Witter* went on to explain: "This is not to say that Congress was blind to the potential benefit of the legislation for expedited resolution of disputes. Far from it. . . ." It then quotes a House Report saying that "the costliness and delays of litigation . . . can be largely eliminated by agreements for arbitration." . . . The concluding paragraph of this part of its discussion begins as follows:

> We therefore are not persuaded by the argument that the conflict between two goals of the Arbitration Act—enforcement of private agreements and encouragement of efficient and speedy dispute resolution—must be resolved in favor of the latter in order to realize the intent of the drafters. . . .

In the present case, of course, those "two goals" do not conflict—and it is the dissent's view that would frustrate *both* of them.

Contrary to the dissent's view, our cases place it beyond dispute that the FAA was designed to promote arbitration. They have repeatedly described the Act as "embod[ying] [a] national policy favoring arbitration," . . . and "a liberal federal policy favoring arbitration agreements, notwithstanding any state substantive or procedural policies to the contrary," . . . Thus, in *Preston v. Ferrer,* holding preempted a state-law rule requiring exhaustion of administrative remedies before arbitration, we said: "A prime objective of an agreement to arbitrate is to achieve 'streamlined proceedings and expeditious results,' " which objective would be "frustrated" by requiring a dispute to be heard by an agency first. . . . That rule, we said, would "at the least, hinder speedy resolution of the controversy." . . . [Footnote omitted.]

California's *Discover Bank* rule similarly interferes with arbitration. Although the rule does not *require* classwide arbitration, it allows any party to a consumer contract to demand it *ex post.* The rule is limited to adhesion contracts, . . . but the times in which consumer contracts were anything other than adhesive are long past.[6] . . . The rule also requires that damages be predictably small, and that the consumer allege a scheme to cheat consumers. . . . The former requirement, however, is toothless and malleable . . . and the latter has no limiting effect, as all that is required is an allegation. Consumers remain free to bring and resolve their disputes on a bilateral basis under *Discover Bank,* and some may well do so; but there is little incentive for lawyers to arbitrate on behalf of individuals when they may do so for a class and reap far higher fees in the process. And faced with inevitable class arbitration, companies would have less incentive to continue resolving potentially duplicative claims on an individual basis.

Although we have had little occasion to examine classwide arbitration, our decision in *Stolt-Nielsen* is instructive. In that case we held that an arbitration panel exceeded its power under § 10(a)(4) of the FAA by imposing class procedures based on policy judgments rather than the arbitration agreement itself or some background principle of contract law that would affect its interpretation. . . . We then held that the agreement at issue, which was silent on the question of class procedures, could not be interpreted to allow them because the "changes brought about by the shift from bilateral arbitration to class-action arbitration" are "fundamental." . . . This is obvious as a structural matter: Classwide arbitration includes absent parties, necessitating additional and different procedures and

---

[6] Of course States remain free to take steps addressing the concerns that attend contracts of adhesion—for example, requiring class-action-waiver provisions in adhesive arbitration agreements to be highlighted. Such steps cannot, however, conflict with the FAA or frustrate its purpose to ensure that private arbitration agreements are enforced according to their terms.

involving higher stakes. Confidentiality becomes more difficult. And while it is theoretically possible to select an arbitrator with some expertise relevant to the class-certification question, arbitrators are not generally knowledgeable in the often-dominant procedural aspects of certification, such as the protection of absent parties. The conclusion follows that class arbitration, to the extent it is manufactured by *Discover Bank* rather than consensual, is inconsistent with the FAA.

First, the switch from bilateral to class arbitration sacrifices the principal advantage of arbitration—its informality—and makes the process slower, more costly, and more likely to generate procedural morass than final judgment. "In bilateral arbitration, parties forgo the procedural rigor and appellate review of the courts in order to realize the benefits of private dispute resolution: lower costs, greater efficiency and speed, and the ability to choose expert adjudicators to resolve specialized disputes." . . . But before an arbitrator may decide the merits of a claim in classwide procedures, he must first decide, for example, whether the class itself may be certified, whether the named parties are sufficiently representative and typical, and how discovery for the class should be conducted. A cursory comparison of bilateral and class arbitration illustrates the difference. According to the American Arbitration Association (AAA), the average consumer arbitration between January and August 2007 resulted in a disposition on the merits in six months, four months if the arbitration was conducted by documents only. . . . As of September 2009, the AAA had opened 283 class arbitrations. Of those, 121 remained active, and 162 had been settled, withdrawn, or dismissed. Not a single one, however, had resulted in a final award on the merits. . . . For those cases that were no longer active, the median time from filing to settlement, withdrawal, or dismissal—not judgment on the merits—was 583 days, and the mean was 630 days. . . . [Footnote omitted.]

Second, class arbitration *requires* procedural formality. The AAA's rules governing class arbitrations mimic the Federal Rules of Civil Procedure for class litigation. . . . And while parties can alter those procedures by contract, an alternative is not obvious. If procedures are too informal, absent class members would not be bound by the arbitration. For a class-action money judgment to bind absentees in litigation, class representatives must at all times adequately represent absent class members, and absent members must be afforded notice, an opportunity to be heard, and a right to opt out of the class. . . . At least this amount of process would presumably be required for absent parties to be bound by the results of arbitration.

We find it unlikely that in passing the FAA Congress meant to leave the disposition of these procedural requirements to an arbitrator. Indeed, class arbitration was not even envisioned by Congress when it passed the FAA in 1925; as the California Supreme Court admitted in *Discover Bank,* class arbitration is a "relatively recent development." . . . And it is at the very least odd to think that an arbitrator would be entrusted with ensuring that third parties' due process rights are satisfied.

Third, class arbitration greatly increases risks to defendants. Informal procedures do of course have a cost: The absence of multilayered review makes it more likely that errors will go uncorrected. Defendants are willing to accept the costs of these errors in arbitration, since their impact is limited to the size of individual disputes, and presumably outweighed by savings from avoiding the courts. But when damages allegedly owed to tens of thousands of potential claimants are aggregated and decided at once, the risk of an error will often become unacceptable. Faced with even a small chance of a devastating loss, defendants will be pressured into settling questionable claims. Other courts have noted the risk of "in terrorem" settlements that class actions entail . . . and class arbitration would be no different.

Arbitration is poorly suited to the higher stakes of class litigation. In litigation, a defendant may appeal a certification decision on an interlocutory basis and, if unsuccessful, may appeal from a final judgment as well. Questions of law are reviewed *de novo* and questions of fact for clear error. In contrast, 9 U.S.C. § 10 allows a court to vacate an arbitral award *only* where the award "was procured by corruption, fraud, or undue means"; "there was evident partiality or corruption in the arbitrators"; "the arbitrators were guilty of misconduct in refusing to postpone the hearing . . . or in refusing to hear evidence pertinent and material to the controversy[,] or of any other misbehavior by which the rights of any party have been prejudiced"; or if the "arbitrators exceeded their powers, or so imperfectly executed them that a mutual, final, and definite award . . . was not made." The AAA rules do authorize judicial review of certification decisions, but this review is unlikely to have much effect given these limitations; review under § 10 focuses on misconduct rather than mistake. And parties may not contractually expand the grounds or nature of judicial review. . . . We find it hard to believe that defendants would bet the company with no effective means of review, and even harder to believe that Congress would have intended to allow state courts to force such a decision. . . . [Footnote omitted.]

The Concepcions contend that because parties may and sometimes do agree to aggregation, class procedures are not necessarily incompatible with arbitration. But the same could be said about procedures that the Concepcions admit States may not superimpose on arbitration: Parties *could* agree to arbitrate pursuant to the Federal Rules of Civil Procedure, or pursuant to a discovery process rivaling that in litigation. Arbitration is a matter of contract, and the FAA requires courts to honor parties' expectations. . . . But what the parties in the aforementioned examples would have agreed to is not arbitration as envisioned by the FAA, lacks its benefits, and therefore may not be required by state law.

The dissent claims that class proceedings are necessary to prosecute small-dollar claims that might otherwise slip through the legal system. . . . But States cannot require a procedure that is inconsistent with the FAA, even if it is desirable for unrelated reasons. Moreover, the claim here was most unlikely to go unresolved. As noted earlier, the arbitration agreement provides that AT & T will pay claimants a minimum of $7,500 and twice their attorney's fees if they obtain an arbitration award greater than AT & T's last settlement offer. The District Court found this scheme sufficient to provide incentive for the individual prosecution of meritorious claims that are not immediately settled, and the Ninth Circuit admitted that aggrieved customers who filed claims would be "essentially guarantee[d]" to be made whole. . . . Indeed, the District Court concluded that the Concepcions were *better off* under their arbitration agreement with AT & T than they would have been as participants in a class action, which "could take months, if not years, and which may merely yield an opportunity to submit a claim for recovery of a small percentage of a few dollars." . . .

Because it "stands as an obstacle to the accomplishment and execution of the full purposes and objectives of Congress," . . . California's *Discover Bank* rule is preempted by the FAA. The judgment of the Ninth Circuit is reversed, and the case is remanded for further proceedings consistent with this opinion.

It is so ordered.

JUSTICE THOMAS, concurring.

Section 2 of the Federal Arbitration Act (FAA) provides that an arbitration provision "shall be valid, irrevocable, and enforceable, save upon such grounds as exist at law or in equity for the revocation of any contract." . . . The question here is whether California's *Discover Bank* rule . . . is a "groun[d] . . . for the revocation of any contract."

It would be absurd to suggest that § 2 requires only that a defense apply to "any contract." If § 2 means anything, it is that courts cannot refuse to enforce arbitration agreements because of a state public policy against arbitration, even if the policy nominally applies to "any contract." There must be some additional limit on the contract defenses permitted by § 2. . . .

I write separately to explain how I would find that limit in the FAA's text. As I would read it, the FAA requires that an agreement to arbitrate be enforced unless a party successfully challenges the formation of the arbitration agreement, such as by proving fraud or duress. . . . Under this reading, I would reverse the Court of Appeals because a district court cannot follow both the FAA and the *Discover Bank* rule, which does not relate to defects in the making of an agreement.

[. . .]

I

The FAA generally requires courts to enforce arbitration agreements as written. Section 2 provides that "[a] written provision in . . . a contract . . . to settle by arbitration a controversy thereafter arising out of such contract . . . shall be valid, irrevocable, and enforceable, save upon such grounds as exist at law or in equity for the revocation of any contract." Significantly, the statute does not parallel the words "valid, irrevocable, and enforceable" by referencing the grounds as exist for the "invalidation, revocation, or nonenforcement" of any contract. Nor does the statute use a different word or phrase entirely that might arguably encompass validity, revocability, and enforce-ability. The use of only "revocation" and the conspicuous omission of "invalidation" and "nonenforcement" suggest that the exception does not include all defenses applicable to any contract but rather some subset of those defenses. . . .

Concededly, the difference between revocability, on the one hand, and validity and enforceability, on the other, is not obvious. The statute does not define the terms, and their ordinary meanings arguably overlap. Indeed, this Court and others have referred to the concepts of revocability, validity, and enforceability interchangeably. But this ambiguity alone cannot justify ignoring Congress' clear decision in § 2 to repeat only one of the three concepts.

To clarify the meaning of § 2, it would be natural to look to other portions of the FAA. Statutory interpretation focuses on "the language itself, the specific context in which that language is used, and the broader context of the statute as a whole." . . . "A provision that may seem ambiguous in isolation is often clarified by the remainder of the statutory scheme . . . because only one of the permissible meanings produces a substantive effect that is compatible with the rest of the law." . . .

Examining the broader statutory scheme, § 4 can be read to clarify the scope of § 2's exception to the enforcement of arbitration agreements. When a party seeks to enforce an arbitration agreement in federal court, § 4 requires that "upon being satisfied that the making of the agreement for arbitration or the failure to comply therewith is not in issue," the court must order arbitration "in accordance with the terms of the agreement."

Reading §§ 2 and 4 harmoniously, the "grounds . . . for the revocation" preserved in § 2 would mean grounds related to the making of the agreement. This would require enforcement of an agreement to arbitrate unless a party successfully asserts a defense concerning the formation of the agreement to arbitrate, such as fraud, duress, or mutual mistake. . . .

Contract defenses unrelated to the making of the agreement—such as public policy—could not be the basis for declining to enforce an arbitration clause.*

II

Under this reading, the question here would be whether California's *Discover Bank* rule relates to the making of an agreement. I think it does not.

In *Discover Bank,* . . . the California Supreme Court held that "class action waivers are, under certain circumstances, unconscionable as unlawfully exculpatory." . . . The court concluded that where a class-action waiver is found in an arbitration agreement in certain consumer contracts of adhesion, such waivers "should not be enforced." . . . In practice, the court explained, such agreements "operate to insulate a party from liability that otherwise would be imposed under California law." . . . The court did not conclude that a customer would sign such an agreement only if under the influence of fraud, duress, or delusion.

The court's analysis and conclusion that the arbitration agreement was exculpatory reveals that the *Discover Bank* rule does not concern the making of the arbitration agreement. Exculpatory contracts are a paradigmatic example of contracts that will not be enforced because of public policy. . . . Indeed, the court explained that it would not enforce the agreements because they are " 'against the policy of the law.' " . . . Refusal to enforce a contract for public-policy reasons does not concern whether the contract was properly made.

Accordingly, the *Discover Bank* rule is not a "groun[d] . . . for the revocation of any contract" as I would read § 2 of the FAA in light of § 4. Under this reading, the FAA dictates that the arbitration agreement here be enforced and the *Discover Bank* rule is pre-empted.

JUSTICE BREYER, with whom JUSTICE GINSBURG, JUSTICE SOTOMAYOR, and JUSTICE KAGAN join, dissenting.

The Federal Arbitration Act says that an arbitration agreement "shall be valid, irrevocable, and enforceable, *save upon such grounds as exist at*

* The interpretation I suggest would be consistent with our precedent. Contract formation is based on the consent of the parties, and we have emphasized that "[a]rbitration under the Act is a matter of consent." . . .

The statement in *Perry v. Thomas,* . . . suggesting that § 2 preserves all state-law defenses that "arose to govern issues concerning the validity, revocability, and enforceability of contracts generally," . . . is dicta. . . . Similarly, to the extent that statements in *Rent-A-Center, West, Inc. v. Jackson* . . . can be read to suggest anything about the scope of state-law defenses under § 2, those statements are dicta, as well. This Court has never addressed the question whether the state-law "grounds" referred to in § 2 are narrower than those applicable to any contract.

Moreover, every specific contract defense that the Court has acknowledged is applicable under § 2 relates to contract formation. In *Doctor's Associates, Inc. v. Casarotto,* . . . this Court said that fraud, duress, and unconscionability "may be applied to invalidate arbitration agreements without contravening § 2." All three defenses historically concern the making of an agreement. . . .

law or in equity for the revocation of any contract." . . . (emphasis added). California law sets forth certain circumstances in which "class action waivers" in *any* contract are unenforceable. In my view, this rule of state law is consistent with the federal Act's language and primary objective. It does not "stan[d] as an obstacle" to the Act's "accomplishment and execution." . . . And the Court is wrong to hold that the federal Act pre-empts the rule of state law.

I

The California law in question consists of an authoritative state-court interpretation of two provisions of the California Civil Code. The first provision makes unlawful all contracts "which have for their object, directly or in-directly, to exempt anyone from responsibility for his own . . . violation of law." . . . The second provision authorizes courts to "limit the application of any unconscionable clause" in a contract so "as to avoid any unconscionable result." . . .

The specific rule of state law in question consists of the California Supreme Court's application of these principles to hold that "some" (but not "all") "class action waivers" in consumer contracts are exculpatory and unconscionable under California "law." *Discover Bank v. Superior Ct.*, 36 Cal.4th 148, 160, 162, 30 Cal.Rptr.3d 76, 113 P.3d 1100, 1108, 1110 (2005). In particular, in *Discover Bank* the California Supreme Court stated that, when a class-action waiver

> "is found in a consumer contract of adhesion in a setting in which disputes between the contracting parties predictably involve small amounts of damages, and when it is alleged that the party with the superior bargaining power has carried out a scheme to deliberately cheat large numbers of consumers out of individually small sums of money, then . . . the waiver becomes in practice the exemption of the party 'from responsibility for [its] own fraud, or willful injury to the person or property of another.' " . . .

In such a circumstance, the "waivers are unconscionable under California law and should not be enforced." . . .

The *Discover Bank* rule does not create a "blanket policy in California against class action waivers in the consumer context." . . . Instead, it represents the "application of a more general [unconscionability] principle." *Gentry v. Superior Ct.*, 42 Cal.4th 443, 457, 64 Cal.Rptr.3d 773, 165 P.3d 556, 564 (2007). Courts applying California law have enforced class-action waivers where they satisfy general unconscionability standards. See, *e.g., Walnut Producers of Cal. v. Diamond Foods, Inc.,* 187 Cal.App.4th 634, 647–650, 114 Cal.Rptr.3d 449, 459–462 (2010); *Arguelles-Romero v. Superior Ct.*, 184 Cal.App.4th 825, 843–845, 109 Cal.Rptr.3d 289, 305–307 (2010); . . . And even when they fail, the parties remain free to devise other dispute mechanisms, including informal mechanisms, that, in context, will not prove unconscionable. . . .

II

A

The *Discover Bank* rule is consistent with the federal Act's language. It "applies equally to class action litigation waivers in contracts without arbitration agreements as it does to class arbitration waivers in contracts with such agreements." . . . Linguistically speaking, it falls directly within the scope of the Act's exception permitting courts to refuse to enforce arbitration agreements on grounds that exist "for the revocation of *any* contract." 9 U.S.C. § 2 (emphasis added). The majority agrees. . . .

B

The *Discover Bank* rule is also consistent with the basic "purpose behind" the Act. . . . We have described that purpose as one of "ensur[ing] judicial enforcement" of arbitration agreements. . . . As is well known, prior to the federal Act, many courts expressed hostility to arbitration for example by refusing to order specific performance of agreements to arbitrate. . . . The Act sought to eliminate that hostility by placing agreements to arbitrate " '*upon the same footing as other contracts.*' " . . . (. . . emphasis added).

Congress was fully aware that arbitration could provide procedural and cost advantages. The House Report emphasized the "appropriate[ness]" of making arbitration agreements enforceable "at this time when there is so much agitation against the costliness and delays of litigation." . . . And this Court has acknowledged that parties may enter into arbitration agreements in order to expedite the resolution of disputes. . . .

But we have also cautioned against thinking that Congress' primary objective was to guarantee these particular procedural advantages. Rather, that primary objective was to secure the "enforcement" of agreements to arbitrate. . . . The relevant Senate Report points to the Act's basic purpose when it says that "[t]he purpose of the [Act] is *clearly set forth in section 2,*" S.Rep. No. 536, at 2 (emphasis added), namely, the section that says that an arbitration agreement "shall be valid, irrevocable, and enforceable, save upon such grounds as exist at law or in equity for the revocation of any contract," 9 U.S.C. § 2.

Thus, insofar as we seek to implement Congress' intent, we should think more than twice before invalidating a state law that does just what § 2 requires, namely, puts agreements to arbitrate and agreements to litigate "upon the same footing."

III

The majority's contrary view (that *Discover Bank* stands as an "obstacle" to the accomplishment of the federal law's objective, . . .) rests primarily upon its claims that the *Discover Bank* rule increases the complexity of arbitration procedures, thereby discouraging parties from entering into arbitration agreements, and to that extent discriminating in practice against arbitration. These claims are not well founded.

For one thing, a state rule of law that would sometimes set aside as unconscionable a contract term that forbids class arbitration is not (as the majority claims) like a rule that would require "ultimate disposition by a jury" or "judicially monitored discovery" or use of "the Federal Rules of Evidence." . . . Unlike the majority's examples, class arbitration is consistent with the use of arbitration. It is a form of arbitration that is well known in California and followed elsewhere. . . . Indeed, the AAA has told us that it has found class arbitration to be "a fair, balanced, and efficient means of resolving class disputes." . . . And unlike the majority's examples, the *Discover Bank* rule imposes equivalent limitations on litigation; hence it cannot fairly be characterized as a targeted attack on arbitration.

Where does the majority get its contrary idea—that individual, rather than class, arbitration is a "fundamental attribut[e]" of arbitration? . . . The majority does not explain. And it is unlikely to be able to trace its present view to the history of the arbitration statute itself.

When Congress enacted the Act, arbitration procedures had not yet been fully developed. Insofar as Congress considered detailed forms of arbitration at all, it may well have thought that arbitration would be used primarily where merchants sought to resolve disputes of fact, not law, under the customs of their industries, where the parties possessed roughly equivalent bargaining power. . . . This last mentioned feature of the history—roughly equivalent bargaining power—suggests, if anything, that California's statute is consistent with, and indeed may help to further, the objectives that Congress had in mind.

Regardless, if neither the history nor present practice suggests that class arbitration is fundamentally incompatible with arbitration itself, then on what basis can the majority hold California's law pre-empted?

For another thing, the majority's argument that the *Discover Bank* rule will discourage arbitration rests critically upon the wrong comparison. The majority compares the complexity of class arbitration with that of bilateral arbitration. . . . And it finds the former more complex. . . . But, if incentives are at issue, the *relevant* comparison is not "arbitration with arbitration" but a comparison between class arbitration and judicial class actions. After all, in respect to the relevant set of contracts, the *Discover Bank* rule similarly and equally sets aside clauses that forbid class procedures—whether arbitration procedures or ordinary judicial procedures are at issue.

Why would a typical defendant (say, a business) prefer a judicial class action to class arbitration? AAA statistics "suggest that class arbitration proceedings take more time than the average commercial arbitration, but may take *less time* than the average class action in court." . . . Data from California courts confirm that class arbitrations can take considerably less time than in-court proceedings in which class certification is sought. . . . And a single class proceeding is surely more efficient than thousands of separate proceedings for identical claims. Thus, if speedy resolution of disputes were all that mattered, then the *Discover Bank* rule would reinforce, not obstruct, that objective of the Act.

The majority's related claim that the *Discover Bank* rule will discourage the use of arbitration because "[a]rbitration is poorly suited to . . . higher stakes" lacks empirical support. . . . Indeed, the majority provides no convincing reason to believe that parties are unwilling to submit high-stake disputes to arbitration. And there are numerous counterexamples. . . .

Further, even though contract defenses, *e.g.,* duress and unconscionability, slow down the dispute resolution process, federal arbitration law normally leaves such matters to the States. . . . A provision in a contract of adhesion (for example, requiring a consumer to decide very quickly whether to pursue a claim) might increase the speed and efficiency of arbitrating a dispute, but the State can forbid it. . . . The *Discover Bank* rule amounts to a variation on this theme. California is free to define unconscionability as it sees fit, and its common law is of no federal concern so long as the State does not adopt a special rule that disfavors arbitration. . . .

Because California applies the same legal principles to address the unconscionability of class arbitration waivers as it does to address the unconscionability of any other contractual provision, the merits of class proceedings should not factor into our decision. If California had applied its law of duress to void an arbitration agreement, would it matter if the procedures in the coerced agreement were efficient?

Regardless, the majority highlights the disadvantages of class arbitrations, as it sees them. . . . But class proceedings have countervailing advantages. In general agreements that forbid the consolidation of claims can lead small-dollar claimants to abandon their claims rather than to litigate. I suspect that it is true even here, for as the Court of Appeals recognized, AT & T can avoid the $7,500 payout (the payout that supposedly makes the Concepcions' arbitration worthwhile) simply by paying the claim's face value, such that "the maximum gain to a customer for the hassle of arbitrating a $30.22 dispute is still just $30.22." . . .

What rational lawyer would have signed on to represent the Concepcions in litigation for the possibility of fees stemming from a $30.22 claim? . . . In California's perfectly rational view, nonclass arbitration over such sums will also sometimes have the effect of depriving claimants of their claims (say, for example, where claiming the $30.22 were to involve filling out many forms that require technical legal knowledge or waiting at great length while a call is placed on hold). *Discover Bank* sets forth circumstances in which the California courts believe that the terms of consumer contracts can be manipulated to insulate an agreement's author from liability for its own frauds by "deliberately cheat[ing] large numbers of consumers out of individually small sums of money." . . . Why is this kind of decision—weighing the pros and cons of all class proceedings alike—not California's to make?

Finally, the majority can find no meaningful support for its views in this Court's precedent. The federal Act has been in force for nearly a century. We have decided dozens of cases about its requirements. We have reached results that authorize complex arbitration procedures. . . . We have upheld nondiscriminatory state laws that slow down arbitration proceedings. . . . But we have not, to my knowledge, applied the Act to strike down a state statute that treats arbitrations on par with judicial and administrative proceedings. . . .

At the same time, we have repeatedly referred to the Act's basic objective as assuring that courts treat arbitration agreements "like all other contracts." . . . And we have recognized that "[t]o immunize an arbitration agreement from judicial challenge" on grounds applicable to all other contracts "would be to elevate it over other forms of contract." . . .

These cases do not concern the merits and demerits of class actions; they concern equal treatment of arbitration contracts and other contracts. Since it is the latter question that is at issue here, I am not surprised that the majority can find no meaningful precedent supporting its decision.

IV

By using the words "save upon such grounds as exist at law or in equity for the revocation of any contract," Congress retained for the States an important role incident to agreements to arbitrate. . . . Through those words Congress reiterated a basic federal idea that has long informed the nature of this Nation's laws. We have often expressed this idea in opinions that set forth presumptions. See, *e.g., Medtronic, Inc. v. Lohr,* 518 U.S. 470, 485, 116 S.Ct. 2240, 135 L.Ed.2d 700 (1996) ("[B]ecause the States are independent sovereigns in our federal system, we have long presumed that Congress does not cavalierly pre-empt state-law causes of action"). But federalism is as much a question of deeds as words. It often takes the form of a concrete decision by this Court that respects the legitimacy of a State's action in an individual case. Here, recognition of that federalist ideal, embodied in specific language in this particular statute, should lead us to uphold California's law, not to strike it down. We do not honor federalist principles in their breach.

With respect, I dissent.

NOTES AND QUESTIONS

1. How would you define the *Discover Bank* rule? It is hostile to arbitration and the arbitral process? When considering your answer, recall that neither AT&T nor the Concepcions were seeking to avoid arbitration. Unlike the situation in many of the other cases that you have read, everyone in this case understood that they were going to go to arbitration to resolve their dispute. So, what's the real problem?

2. What are the "fundamental attributes" of arbitration, and why does class litigation conflict with these attributes, in the majority's opinion? Do you agree?

3. Does it change your answer to know that consolidated and class arbitrations can and do occur? *See, e.g.,* RUAA § 10 (allowing for consolidation of arbitrations in certain circumstances); AAA Supplementary Rules for Class Arbitrations (2003). The majority recognizes this, but it still insists that bilateral arbitration is very different from multilateral arbitration. Do you agree? In framing your answer, be sure that you can follow the majority's logic.

4. *Concepcion* appears to reassert and expand the old-time religion on arbitration associated with the application of the federal preemption doctrine. The integrity of the federal right to arbitrate, which appears to be embedded in FAA § 2, must be protected from encroachment by provisions of state law. The parties' recourse to arbitration must be unimpeded by antagonistic state law rules and unobstructed by state law procedural barriers. California state courts, led by the California state Supreme Court, have displayed considerable resistance to embracing wholeheartedly arbitration and the "emphatic federal policy supporting arbitration." California has a standard, unremarkable state law of arbitration, but decisional results, especially in cases involving adhesive arbitration, often exhibit hostility to arbitration, arbitrability, and award enforceability. Despite the enormous ADR industry in the state, it is well settled that arbitral awards are most likely to be vacated in California than in any other U.S. jurisdiction. *Concepcion* slowed that practice.

5. *Concepcion*'s reach, however, was far greater than just California. At a practical level, the decision abrogated cases from various jurisdictions that had followed California's lead.[1] By making class action waivers in adhesive

---

[1] See, e.g, Homa v. Am. Express Co., 558 F.3d 225, 231 n.2, 233 (3d Cir. 2009), abrogation recognized by Litman v. Cellco P'ship, 655 F.3d 225, 231 (3d Cir. 2011); Lowden v. T- Mobile USA, Inc., 512 F.3d 1213, 1218–19 (9th Cir. 2008); Dale v. Comcast Corp., 498 F.3d 1216, 1224 (11th Cir. 2007) (applying Georgia law); Brewer v. Mo. Title Loans, Inc., 323 S.W.3d 18, 22–23 (Mo. 2010) (en banc), vacated and remanded, 131 S. Ct. 2875 (2011), aff'd in part, rev'd in part; 364 S.W.3d 486 (Mo. Mar. 6, 2012) (en banc); Fiser v. Dell Computer Corp., 188 P.3d 1215, 1222 (N.M. 2008); Tillman v. Commercial Credit Loans, Inc., 655 S.E.2d 362, 373 (N.C. 2008); Vasquez-Lopez v.

arbitration contracts enforceable, the court invited commercial parties to impose arbitration agreements in virtually all consumer and employment contracts. As a result, there has been an explosion of mass-market arbitration agreements.

6. Beyond its holding with respect to class action waivers, the case was also a dramatic shift in how the Court thinks about arbitration more generally. It is worth observing that the decision was highly partisan when it was issued. The majority includes the conservative justices and the more moderate Justice Kennedy; the dissent consists of the four liberal members of the Court. That ideological divide, however, would not remain in place, at least with respect to two core principles.

First, *Concepcion* has come to stand for the proposition that the FAA creates an "equal-treatment" principle:

> A court may invalidate an arbitration agreement based on 'generally applicable contract defenses' like fraud or unconscionability, but not on legal rules that 'apply only to arbitration or that derive their meaning from the fact that an agreement to arbitrate is at issue'

AT&T Mobility LLC v. Concepcion, 563 U.S. 333, 339 (2011). In 2017, a nearly unanimous Court—Justice Thomas being the sole dissenter—confirmed that this equal-treatment principle constitutes a firm part of arbitration. *See Kindred Nursing Centers Ltd. P'ship v. Clark*, 137 S. Ct. 1421, 1425, 197 L.Ed. 2d 806 (2017). Notably, despite dissenting in *Concepcion*, Justice Kagan authored the majority decision in *Kindred*.

Second, and more radically, *Concepcion* has come to stand for the proposition that the FAA "displaces any rule that covertly [regulates the recourse to arbitration] by disfavoring contracts that (oh so coincidentally) have the defining features of arbitration agreements." *Id.* at 1426 (citing *AT&T Mobility LLC v. Concepcion*, 563 U.S. 333, 342 (2011). In other words, "the saving clause [of FAA § 2] does not save defenses that target arbitration either by name or by more subtle methods, such as by 'interfer[ing] with fundamental attributes of arbitration.' " *Epic Sys. Corp. v. Lewis*, 138 S. Ct. 1612, 1622, 200 L.Ed. 2d 889 (2018) (referencing both *Concepcion* and *Kindred*).

These two principles—equal treatment and protection of the fundamental attributes of arbitration—have the effect of insulating the arbitration protocol. Even laws that appear facially neutral, like the *Discover Bank* rule, may be overridden by FAA § 2.

For instance, in *Kindred*, the Court preempted a common law rule that the Kentucky Supreme Court maintained was generally applicable. In that case, two nursing home residents had family members with general powers of

---

Beneficial Or., Inc., 152 P.3d 940, 948–54 (Or. App. 2007); Thibodeau v. Comcast Corp., 912 A.2d 874, 885–86 (Pa. Super. Ct. 2006), abrogation recognized by Brown v. Trueblue, Inc., No. 1:10–CV–0514, 2011 WL 5869773, at *3 (M.D. Pa. Nov. 22, 2011); Herron v. Century BMW, 693 S.E.2d 394, 399–400 (S.C. 2010), aff'd, 693 S.E.2d 394, 398–400 (S.C. 2010), vacated, Sonic Auto., Inc. v. Watts, 131 S. Ct. 2872 (2011).

attorney complete the paperwork necessary for them to move into the facility. That paperwork included an arbitration provision. When the two residents died, the families brought suit against the nursing home. The nursing home invoked the arbitration agreement, but the Kentucky courts all agreed that the arbitration agreement was not binding on the residents. These courts relied on a common law rule that required powers of attorney in Kentucky to specifically authorize agents to give up "fundamental constitutional rights." In the Kentucky Constitution, a right to a court trial with a jury is "sacred" and "inviolate." Because the family members had only general powers of attorney, they did not have the authorization to give up the residents' constitutional rights to a jury trial. The U.S. Supreme Court, however, did not believe that this common law rule was truly neutral. Instead, the Court found that it was a covert effort to regulate arbitration and therefore was preempted by FAA § 2.

7. The dissent in *Concepcion* believes that AT&T could eliminate any prospect of paying the $7,500 minimum premium by settling the $30 claims at the outset of the process. Does that really matter? If the $7,500 premium functions to guarantee that aggrieved customers will get serious settlement offers that address their alleged harms, why should anyone care? Moreover, is it not just as likely that such a $30 settlement offer will wind up being a larger sum of compensation, gotten more quickly, than the average customer would win if a class action lawsuit were settled?

In fact, one scholar has argued that the comparatively cheap and speedy access to individual justice provided by a system like AT&T's could be used to handle harms that are difficult to price. Erin O'Hara O'Connor, *Protecting Consumer Data Privacy with Arbitration*, 96 N.C. L. REV. 711, 731 (2018) (the "low-cost structure for resolving consumer disputes may be especially well-suited for handling subjective and heterogeneous harms, including privacy harms")

8. Does a class action waiver reduce the relief that is available in arbitration and thereby the remedy itself? Does it make consumer arbitration abusive? What are the counterarguments?

9. *Murlithi v. Shuttle Express, Inc.*, 712 F.3d 173 (4th Cir. 2013), involved claims by a driver of an airport shuttle for wages and overtime pay from Shuttle Express, Inc. The parties were linked by a franchise agreement. The latter contract contained an arbitral clause and a class action waiver within that clause. It also contained a fee-splitting provision that engendered claims of prohibitive costs. These claims were countered by allegations that the plaintiff failed to satisfy his burden of proof. The franchise agreement also contained a one-year statute of limitations. In assessing the validity of the class waiver, the Fourth Circuit analyzed *AT&T Mobility v. Concepcion* in the following manner:

> The Supreme Court's holding in *Concepcion* sweeps more broadly than [the plaintiff] suggests. In *Concepcion*, the Supreme Court cautioned that the generally applicable contract defense of unconscionability may not be applied in a manner that targets the

existence of an agreement to arbitrate as the basis for invalidating that agreement. . . . Applying that principle to the *Discover Bank* "rule" at issue, the Court explained that state law cannot "stand as an obstacle to the accomplishment of the FAA's objectives," by interfering with "the fundamental attributes of arbitration." . . .

We recently discussed the holding in *Concepcion* in our decision in *Noohi v. Toll Bros., Inc.*, . . . , 2013 WL 680690, at *6 (4th Cir. Feb. 26, 2013).[2] We explained that the holding "prohibited courts from altering otherwise valid arbitration agreements by applying the doctrine of unconscionability to eliminate a term barring classwide procedures." . . . Thus, contrary to [the plaintiff's] contention, the Supreme Court's holding was not merely an assertion of federal preemption, but also plainly prohibited application of the general contract defense of unconscionability to invalidate an otherwise valid arbitration agreement under these circumstances. The district court in the present case, deciding the same issue of unconscionability prior to *Concepcion*, reached the opposite conclusion.[3] Accordingly, we conclude that the district court erred in holding that the class action waiver was unconscionable.

Under this view of *AT&T Mobility v. Concepcion*, can unconscionability be the sole consideration used to invalidate an arbitration agreement? *Concepcion* appears to mean that there must be some other defect thwarting the enforceability of the arbitration contract. Doesn't this reasoning render unconscionability useless in the arbitration context? Does the reasoning mean that unconscionability has a special, more limited function in the circumstances of arbitration? How does the Maryland rule on consideration compare to the *Discover Bank* rule? Doesn't the Maryland rule discriminate blatantly against arbitration contracts? Does the Fourth Circuit distort *Concepcion* or refine and expose its underlying meaning? Does *Concepcion* really prohibit the use of unconscionability against arbitration contracts? Is footnote 2 clearer?

---

2 In *Noohi*, we addressed the issue whether a Maryland rule, requiring that an arbitration agreement be supported by mutual consideration irrespective whether the underlying contract was supported by mutual consideration, was preempted by the FAA. 2013 WL 680690, at *9, 11–12 (citing *Cheek v. United Healthcare of Mid-Atl., Inc.*, 835 A.2d 656 (Md. 2003)). We held that the Maryland rule did not increase procedural formality or risks to defendants, which were "primary concerns underlying *Concepcion*," nor did it involve, as in *Concepcion*, a state-law rule requiring class arbitration. *Id.* at *11. We concluded that the Maryland rule was not preempted by the FAA. *Id.* at *12.

3 In a case decided several years before *Concepcion*, we addressed a related question whether Congress, in enacting the FLSA, provided a right to class action relief that could not be waived. There, in *Adkins v. Labor Ready, Inc.*, 303 F.3d 496 (4th Cir. 2002), a plaintiff tried to avoid arbitration arguing that the arbitration clause, which included a class action waiver, "foreclose[d] redress" of his federal statutory rights under the FLSA. *Id.* at 502. We held that there was no indication "in the text, legislative history, or purpose of the FLSA that Congress intended to confer a nonwaivable right to a class action under that statute." *Id.* at 503. Thus, we concluded that the inability to pursue an FLSA claim as a member of a class proceeding is by itself insufficient to override "the strong congressional preference for an arbitral forum." *Id.*

AMERICAN EXPRESS CO. v. ITALIAN COLORS REST.

570 U.S. 228, 133 S.Ct. 2304, 186 L.Ed. 2d 417 (2013).

JUSTICE SCALIA delivered the opinion of the Court.

We consider whether a contractual waiver of class arbitration is enforceable under the Federal Arbitration Act when the plaintiff's cost of individually arbitrating a federal statutory claim exceeds the potential recovery.

I

Respondents are merchants who accept American Express cards. Their agreement with petitioners—American Express and a wholly owned subsidiary—contains a clause that requires all disputes between the parties to be resolved by arbitration. The agreement also provides that "[t]here shall be no right or authority for any Claims to be arbitrated on a class action basis." . . .

Respondents brought a class action against petitioners for violations of the federal antitrust laws. According to respondents, American Express used its monopoly power in the market for charge cards to force merchants to accept credit cards at rates approximately 30% higher than the fees for competing credit cards. [Footnote omitted.] This tying arrangement, respondents said, violated § 1 of the Sherman Act. They sought treble damages for the class under § 4 of the Clayton Act.

Petitioners moved to compel individual arbitration under the Federal Arbitration Act (FAA). . . . In resisting the motion, respondents submitted a declaration from an economist who estimated that the cost of an expert analysis necessary to prove the antitrust claims would be "at least several hundred thousand dollars, and might exceed $1 million," while the maximum recovery for an individual plaintiff would be $12,850, or $38,549 when trebled. . . . The District Court granted the motion and dismissed the lawsuits. The Court of Appeals reversed and remanded for further proceedings. It held that because respondents had established that "they would incur prohibitive costs if compelled to arbitrate under the class action waiver," the waiver was unenforceable and the arbitration could not proceed. . . .

We granted certiorari, vacated the judgment, and remanded for further consideration in light of *Stolt-Nielsen S.A. v. AnimalFeeds Int'l Corp.,* 559 U.S. 662, 130 S.Ct. 1758, 176 L.Ed.2d 605 (2010), which held that a party may not be compelled to submit to class arbitration absent an agreement to do so. . . . The Court of Appeals stood by its reversal, stating that its earlier ruling did not compel class arbitration. . . . It then *sua sponte* reconsidered its ruling in light of *AT&T Mobility LLC v. Concepcion,*

563 U.S. [321], 131 S.Ct. 1740, 179 L.Ed.2d 742 (2011), which held that the FAA pre-empted a state law barring enforcement of a class-arbitration waiver. Finding *AT&T Mobility* inapplicable because it addressed pre-emption, the Court of Appeals reversed for the third time.... It then denied rehearing en banc with five judges dissenting.... We granted certiorari, 568 U.S. ___, 133 S.Ct. 594, 184 L.Ed.2d 390 (2012), to consider the question "[w]hether the Federal Arbitration Act permits courts ... to invalidate arbitration agreements on the ground that they do not permit class arbitration of a federal-law claim." ...

II

Congress enacted the FAA in response to widespread judicial hostility to arbitration.... As relevant here, the Act provides:

> "A written provision in any maritime transaction or contract evidencing a transaction involving commerce to settle by arbitration a controversy thereafter arising out of such contract or transaction ... shall be valid, irrevocable, and enforceable, save upon such grounds as exist at law or in equity for the revocation of any contract." 9 U.S.C. § 2.

This text reflects the overarching principle that arbitration is a matter of contract.... And consistent with that text, courts must "rigorously enforce" arbitration agreements according to their terms ..., including terms that "specify *with whom* [the parties] [emphasis and brackets in the original] choose to arbitrate their disputes," ... and "the rules under which that arbitration will be conducted" ... That holds true for claims that allege a violation of a federal statute, unless the FAA's mandate has been " 'overridden by a contrary congressional command.' " ...

III

No contrary congressional command requires us to reject the waiver of class arbitration here. Respondents argue that requiring them to litigate their claims individually—as they contracted to do—would contravene the policies of the antitrust laws. But the antitrust laws do not guarantee an affordable procedural path to the vindication of every claim. Congress has taken some measures to facilitate the litigation of antitrust claims—for example, it enacted a multiplied-damages remedy.... In enacting such measures, Congress has told us that it is willing to go, in certain respects, beyond the normal limits of law in advancing its goals of deterring and remedying unlawful trade practice. But to say that Congress must have intended whatever departures from those normal limits advance antitrust goals is simply irrational. "[N]o legislation pursues its purposes at all costs." *Rodriguez v. United States,* 480 U.S. 522, 525–526, 107 S.Ct. 1391, 94 L.Ed.2d 533 (1987) (*per curiam*).

The antitrust laws do not "evinc[e] an intention to preclude a waiver" of class-action procedure. . . . The Sherman and Clayton Acts make no mention of class actions. In fact, they were enacted decades before the advent of Federal Rule of Civil Procedure 23, which was "designed to allow an exception to the usual rule that litigation is conducted by and on behalf of the individual named parties only." . . . The parties here agreed to arbitrate pursuant to that "usual rule," and it would be remarkable for a court to erase that expectation.

Nor does congressional approval of Rule 23 establish an entitlement to class proceedings for the vindication of statutory rights. To begin with, it is likely that such an entitlement, invalidating private arbitration agreements denying class adjudication, would be an "abridg[ment]" or "modif[ication]" of a "substantive right" forbidden to the Rules. . . . But there is no evidence of such an entitlement in any event. The Rule imposes stringent requirements for certification that in practice exclude most claims. And we have specifically rejected the assertion that one of those requirements (the class-notice requirement) must be dispensed with because the "prohibitively high cost" of compliance would "frustrate [plaintiff's] attempt to vindicate the policies underlying the antitrust" laws. *Eisen v. Carlisle & Jacquelin,* 417 U.S. 156, 166–168, 175–176, 94 S.Ct. 2140, 40 L.Ed.2d 732 (1974). One might respond, perhaps, that federal law secures a nonwaivable *opportunity* to vindicate federal policies by satisfying the procedural strictures of Rule 23 or invoking some other informal class mechanism in arbitration. But we have already rejected that proposition in *AT&T Mobility*. . . .

IV

Our finding of no "contrary congressional command" does not end the case. Respondents invoke a judge-made exception to the FAA which, they say, serves to harmonize competing federal policies by allowing courts to invalidate agreements that prevent the "effective vindication" of a federal statutory right. Enforcing the waiver of class arbitration bars effective vindication, respondents contend, because they have no economic incentive to pursue their antitrust claims individually in arbitration.

The "effective vindication" exception to which respondents allude originated as dictum in *Mitsubishi Motors,* where we expressed a willingness to invalidate, on "public policy" grounds, arbitration agreements that "operat[e] . . . as a prospective waiver of a party's *right to pursue* statutory remedies." 473 U.S., at 637, n. 19, 105 S.Ct. 3346 (emphasis added). Dismissing concerns that the arbitral forum was inadequate, we said that "so long as the prospective litigant effectively may vindicate its statutory cause of action in the arbitral forum, the statute will continue to serve both its remedial and deterrent function." . . . Subsequent cases have similarly asserted the existence of an "effective vindication" exception, see, *e.g., 14 Penn Plaza LLC v. Pyett,* 556 U.S. 247, 273–274, 129 S.Ct. 1456, 173 L.Ed.2d 398 (2009); *Gilmer v. Interstate/Johnson Lane Corp.,* 500 U.S. 20, 28, 111 S.Ct. 1647, 114 L.Ed.2d 26 (1991), but have similarly declined to apply it to invalidate the arbitration agreement at issue. [Footnote omitted.]

And we do so again here. As we have described, the exception finds its origin in the desire to prevent "prospective waiver of a party's *right to pursue* statutory remedies," *Mitsubishi Motors, supra,* at 637, n. 19, 105 S.Ct. 3346 (emphasis added). That would certainly cover a provision in an arbitration agreement forbidding the assertion of certain statutory rights. And it would perhaps cover filing and administrative fees attached to arbitration that are so high as to make access to the forum impracticable. . . . But the fact that it is not worth the expense involved in *proving* a statutory remedy does not constitute the elimination of the *right to pursue* that remedy. . . . [Footnote omitted.] The class-action waiver merely limits arbitration to the two contracting parties. It no more eliminates those parties' right to pursue their statutory remedy than did federal law before its adoption of the class action for legal relief in 1938. . . . Or, to put it differently, the individual suit that was considered adequate to assure "effective vindication" of a federal right before adoption of class-action procedures did not suddenly become "ineffective vindication" upon their adoption. [Footnote omitted.]

A pair of our cases brings home the point. In *Gilmer,* . . . we had no qualms in enforcing a class waiver in an arbitration agreement even though the federal statute at issue, the Age Discrimination in Employment Act, expressly permitted collective actions. We said that statutory permission did " 'not mean that individual attempts at conciliation were intended to be barred.' " . . . And in *Vimar Seguros y Reaseguros, S.A. v. M/V Sky Reefer,* 515 U.S. 528, 115 S.Ct. 2322, 132 L.Ed.2d 462 (1995), we held that requiring arbitration in a foreign country was compatible with the federal Carriage of Goods by Sea Act. That legislation prohibited any agreement " 'relieving' " or " 'lessening' " the liability of a carrier for damaged goods . . .—which is close to codification of an "effective vindication" exception. The Court rejected the argument that the "inconvenience and costs of proceeding" abroad "lessen[ed]" the defendants' liability, stating that "[i]t would be unwieldy and unsupported by the terms or policy of the statute to require courts to proceed case by case to tally the costs and burdens to particular plaintiffs in light of their means, the size of their claims, and the relative burden on the carrier." . . . Such a "tally[ing] [of] the costs and burdens" is precisely what the dissent would impose upon federal courts here.

Truth to tell, our decision in *AT&T Mobility* all but resolves this case. There we invalidated a law conditioning enforcement of arbitration on the availability of class procedure because that law "interfere [d] with fundamental attributes of arbitration." . . . "[T]he switch from bilateral to class arbitration," we said, "sacrifices the principal advantage of arbitration—its informality—and makes the process slower, more costly, and more likely to generate procedural morass than final judgment." . . . We specifically rejected the argument that class arbitration was necessary to prosecute claims "that might otherwise slip through the legal system." . . . [Footnote omitted.]

The regime established by the Court of Appeals' decision would require—before a plaintiff can be held to contractually agreed bilateral arbitration—that a federal court determine (and the parties litigate) the legal requirements for success on the merits claim-by-claim and theory-by-theory, the evidence necessary to meet those requirements, the cost of developing that evidence, and the damages that would be recovered in the event of success. Such a preliminary litigating hurdle would undoubtedly destroy the prospect of speedy resolution that arbitration in general and bilateral arbitration in particular was meant to secure. The FAA does not sanction such a judicially created superstructure.

The judgment of the Court of Appeals is reversed.

It is so ordered.

JUSTICE SOTOMAYOR took no part in the consideration or decision of this case.

JUSTICE THOMAS, concurring.

I join the Court's opinion in full. I write separately to note that the result here is also required by the plain meaning of the Federal Arbitration Act. In *AT&T Mobility LLC v. Concepcion,* 563 U.S. [321], 131 S.Ct. 1740, 179 L.Ed.2d 742 (2011), I explained that "the FAA requires that an agreement to arbitrate be enforced unless a party successfully challenges the formation of the arbitration agreement, such as by proving fraud or duress." . . . In this case, Italian Colors makes two arguments to support its conclusion that the arbitration agreement should not be enforced. First, it contends that enforcing the arbitration agreement "would contravene the policies of the antitrust laws." . . . Second, it contends that a court may "invalidate agreements that prevent the 'effective vindication' of a federal statutory right." . . . Neither argument "concern[s] whether the contract was properly made," . . . Because Italian Colors has not furnished "grounds . . . for the revocation of any contract," 9 U.S.C. § 2, the arbitration agreement must be enforced. Italian Colors voluntarily entered into a contract containing a bilateral arbitration provision. It cannot now escape its obligations merely because the claim it wishes to bring might be economically infeasible.

JUSTICE KAGAN, with whom JUSTICE GINSBURG and JUSTICE BREYER join, dissenting.

Here is the nutshell version of this case, unfortunately obscured in the Court's decision. The owner of a small restaurant (Italian Colors) thinks that American Express (Amex) has used its monopoly power to force merchants to accept a form contract violating the antitrust laws. The restaurateur wants to challenge the allegedly unlawful provision (imposing a tying arrangement), but the same contract's arbitration clause prevents him from doing so. That term imposes a variety of procedural bars that would make pursuit of the antitrust claim a fool's errand. So if the arbitration clause is enforceable, Amex has insulated itself from antitrust liability—even if it has in fact violated the law. The monopolist gets to use its monopoly power to insist on a contract effectively depriving its victims of all legal recourse.

And here is the nutshell version of today's opinion, admirably flaunted rather than camouflaged: Too darn bad.

That answer is a betrayal of our precedents, and of federal statutes like the antitrust laws. Our decisions have developed a mechanism—called the effective-vindication rule—to prevent arbitration clauses from choking off a plaintiff's ability to enforce congressionally created rights. That doctrine bars applying such a clause when (but only when) it operates to confer immunity from potentially meritorious federal claims. In so doing, the rule reconciles the Federal Arbitration Act (FAA) with all the rest of federal law—and indeed, promotes the most fundamental purposes of the FAA itself. As applied here, the rule would ensure that Amex's arbitration clause does not foreclose Italian Colors from vindicating its right to redress antitrust harm.

The majority barely tries to explain why it reaches a contrary result. It notes that we have not decided this exact case before—neglecting that the principle we have established fits this case hand in glove. And it concocts a special exemption for class-arbitration waivers—ignoring that this case concerns much more than that. Throughout, the majority disregards our decisions' central tenet: An arbitration clause may not thwart federal law, irrespective of exactly how it does so. Because the Court today prevents the effective vindication of federal statutory rights, I respectfully dissent.

I

Start with an uncontroversial proposition: We would refuse to enforce an exculpatory clause insulating a company from antitrust liability—say, "Merchants may bring no Sherman Act claims"—even if that clause were contained in an arbitration agreement. . . . Congress created the Sherman Act's private cause of action not solely to compensate individuals, but to promote "the public interest in vigilant enforcement of the antitrust laws." . . . Accordingly, courts will not enforce a prospective waiver of the right to gain redress for an antitrust injury, whether in an arbitration agreement or any other contract. . . . The same rule applies to other important federal statutory rights. . . . But its necessity is nowhere more evident than in the antitrust context. Without the rule, a company could use its monopoly power to protect its monopoly power, by coercing agreement to contractual terms eliminating its antitrust liability.

If the rule were limited to baldly exculpatory provisions, however, a monopolist could devise numerous ways around it. Consider several alternatives that a party drafting an arbitration agreement could adopt to avoid antitrust liability, each of which would have the identical effect. On the front end: The agreement might set outlandish filing fees or establish an absurd (*e.g.*, one-day) statute of limitations, thus preventing a claimant from gaining access to the arbitral forum. On the back end: The agreement might remove the arbitrator's authority to grant meaningful relief, so that a judgment gets the claimant nothing worthwhile. And in the middle: The agreement might block the claimant from presenting the kind of proof that is necessary to establish the defendant's liability—say, by prohibiting any economic testimony (good luck proving an antitrust claim without that!). Or else the agreement might appoint as an arbitrator an obviously biased person—say, the CEO of Amex. The possibilities are endless—all less direct than an express exculpatory clause, but no less fatal. So the rule against prospective waivers of federal rights can work only if it applies not just to a contract clause explicitly barring a claim, but to others that operate to do so.

And sure enough, our cases establish this proposition: An arbitration clause will not be enforced if it prevents the effective vindication of federal statutory rights, however it achieves that result. The rule originated in *Mitsubishi,* where we held that claims brought under the Sherman Act and other federal laws are generally subject to arbitration. . . . By agreeing to arbitrate such a claim, we explained, "a party does not forgo the substantive rights afforded by the statute; it only submits to their resolution in an arbitral, rather than a judicial, forum." . . . But crucial to our decision was a limiting principle, designed to safeguard federal rights: An arbitration clause will be enforced only "so long as the prospective litigant effectively may vindicate its statutory cause of action in the arbitral forum." . . . If an arbitration provision "operated . . . as a prospective waiver of a party's right to pursue statutory remedies," we emphasized, we would "condemn[ ]" it . . . Similarly, we stated that such a clause should be "set [ ] aside" if "proceedings in the contractual forum will be so gravely difficult" that the claimant "will for all practical purposes be deprived of his day in court." . . . And in the decades since *Mitsubishi,* we have repeated its admonition time and again, instructing courts not to enforce an arbitration agreement that effectively (even if not explicitly) forecloses a plaintiff from remedying the violation of a federal statutory right. See *Gilmer v. Interstate/Johnson Lane Corp.,* 500 U.S. 20, 28, 111

S.Ct. 1647, 114 L.Ed.2d 26 (1991); *Vimar Seguros y Reaseguros, S.A. v. M/V Sky Reefer,* 515 U.S. 528, 540, 115 S.Ct. 2322, 132 L.Ed.2d 462 (1995); *14 Penn Plaza,* 556 U.S., at 266, 273–274, 129 S.Ct. 1456.

Our decision in *Green Tree Financial Corp.—Ala. v. Randolph,* 531 U.S. 79, 121 S.Ct. 513, 148 L.Ed.2d 373 (2000), confirmed that this principle applies when an agreement thwarts federal law by making arbitration prohibitively expensive. The plaintiff there (seeking relief under the Truth in Lending Act) argued that an arbitration agreement was unenforceable because it "create[d] a risk" that she would have to "bear prohibitive arbitration costs" in the form of high filing and administrative fees. . . . We rejected that contention, but not because we doubted that such fees could prevent the effective vindication of statutory rights. To the contrary, we invoked our rule from *Mitsubishi,* making clear that it applied to the case before us. . . . Indeed, we added a burden of proof: "[W]here, as here," we held, a party asserting a federal right "seeks to invalidate an arbitration agreement on the ground that arbitration would be prohibitively expensive, that party bears the burden of showing the likelihood of incurring such costs." . . . Randolph, we found, had failed to meet that burden: The evidence she offered was "too speculative." . . . But even as we dismissed Randolph's suit, we reminded courts to protect against arbitration agreements that make federal claims too costly to bring.

Applied as our precedents direct, the effective-vindication rule furthers the purposes not just of laws like the Sherman Act, but of the FAA itself. That statute reflects a federal policy favoring actual arbitration—that is, arbitration as a streamlined "method of resolving disputes," not as a foolproof way of killing off valid claims. . . . Put otherwise: What the FAA prefers to litigation is arbitration, not *de facto* immunity. The effective-vindication rule furthers the statute's goals by ensuring that arbitration remains a real, not faux, method of dispute resolution. With the rule, companies have good reason to adopt arbitral procedures that facilitate efficient and accurate handling of complaints. Without it, companies have every incentive to draft their agreements to extract backdoor waivers of statutory rights, making arbitration unavailable or pointless. So down one road: More arbitration, better enforcement of federal statutes. And down the other: Less arbitration, poorer enforcement of federal statutes. Which would you prefer? Or still more aptly: Which do you think Congress would?

The answer becomes all the more obvious given the limits we have placed on the rule, which ensure that it does not diminish arbitration's benefits. The rule comes into play only when an agreement "operate[s] . . . as a prospective waiver"—that is, forecloses (not diminishes) a plaintiff's opportunity to gain relief for a statutory violation. . . . So, for example, *Randolph* assessed whether fees in arbitration would be "prohibitive" (not high, excessive, or extravagant). . . . Moreover, the plaintiff must make that showing through concrete proof: "[S]peculative" risks, "unfounded assumptions," and "unsupported statements" will not suffice. . . . With the inquiry that confined and the evidentiary requirements that high, courts have had no trouble assessing the matters the rule makes relevant. And for almost three decades, courts have followed our edict that arbitration clauses must usually prevail, declining to enforce them in only rare cases. . . . The effective-vindication rule has thus operated year in and year out without undermining, much less "destroy[ing]," the prospect of speedy dispute resolution that arbitration secures. . . .

And this is just the kind of case the rule was meant to address. Italian Colors, as I have noted, alleges that Amex used its market power to impose a tying arrangement in violation of the Sherman Act. The antitrust laws, all parties agree, provide the restaurant with a cause of action and give it the chance to recover treble damages. Here, that would mean Italian Colors could take home up to $38,549. But a problem looms. As this case comes to us, the evidence shows that Italian Colors cannot prevail in arbitration without an economic analysis defining the relevant markets, establishing Amex's monopoly power, showing anticompetitive effects, and measuring damages. And that expert report would cost between several hundred thousand and one million dollars. [Footnote omitted.] So the expense involved in proving the claim in arbitration is ten times what Italian Colors could hope to gain, even in a best-case scenario. That counts as a "prohibitive" cost, in *Randolph*'s terminology, if anything does. No rational actor would bring a claim worth tens of thousands of dollars if doing so meant incurring costs in the hundreds of thousands.

An arbitration agreement could manage such a mismatch in many ways, but Amex's disdains them all. As the Court makes clear, the contract expressly prohibits class arbitration. But that is only part of the problem. [Footnote omitted.] The agreement also disallows any kind of joinder or consolidation of claims or parties. And more: Its confidentiality provision prevents Italian Colors from informally arranging with other merchants to produce a common expert report. And still more: The agreement precludes any shifting of costs to Amex, even if Italian Colors prevails. And beyond all that: Amex refused to enter into any stipulations that would obviate or mitigate the need for the economic analysis. In short, the agreement as applied in this case cuts off not just class arbitration, but any avenue for sharing, shifting, or shrinking necessary costs. Amex has put Italian Colors to this choice: Spend way, way, way more money than your claim is worth, or relinquish your Sherman Act rights.

So contra the majority, the court below got this case right. Italian Colors proved what the plaintiff in *Randolph* could not—that a standard-form agreement, taken as a whole, renders arbitration of a claim "prohibitively expensive." . . . The restaurant thus established that the contract "operate[s] . . . as a prospective waiver," and prevents the "effective[ ] . . . vindicat[ion]" of Sherman Act rights. . . . I would follow our precedents and decline to compel arbitration.

II

The majority is quite sure that the effective-vindication rule does not apply here, but has precious little to say about why. It starts by disparaging the rule as having "originated as dictum." . . . But it does not rest on that swipe, and for good reason. As I have explained, . . . the rule began as a core part of *Mitsubishi*: We held there that federal statutory claims are subject to arbitration "*so long as*" the claimant "effectively may vindicate its [rights] in the arbitral forum." . . . ([E]mphasis added). The rule thus served as an essential condition of the decision's holding. [Footnote omitted.] And in *Randolph,* we provided a standard for applying the rule when a claimant alleges "prohibitive costs" . . . , and we then applied that standard to the parties before us. So whatever else the majority might think of the effective-vindication rule, it is not dictum.

The next paragraph of the Court's decision (the third of Part IV) is the key: It contains almost the whole of the majority's effort to explain why the effective-vindication rule does not stop Amex from compelling arbitration. The majority's first move is to describe *Mitsubishi* and *Randolph* as covering only discrete situations: The rule, the majority asserts, applies to arbitration agreements that eliminate the "right to pursue statutory remedies" by "forbidding the assertion" of the right (as addressed in *Mitsubishi*) or imposing filing and administrative fees "so high as to make access to the forum impracticable" (as addressed in *Randolph*). . . . Those cases are not this case, the majority says: Here, the agreement's provisions went to the possibility of "*proving* a statutory remedy." . . .

But the distinction the majority proffers, which excludes problems of proof, is one *Mitsubishi* and *Randolph* (and our decisions reaffirming them) foreclose. Those decisions establish what in some quarters is known as a principle: When an arbitration agreement prevents the effective vindication of federal rights, a party may go to court. That principle, by its nature, operates in diverse circumstances—not just the ones that happened to come before the Court. . . . It doubtless covers the baldly exculpatory clause and prohibitive fees that the majority acknowledges would preclude an arbitration agreement's enforcement. But so too it covers the world of other provisions a clever drafter might devise to scuttle even the most meritorious federal claims. Those provisions might deny entry to the forum in the first instance. Or they might deprive the claimant of any remedy. Or they might prevent the claimant from offering the necessary proof to prevail, as in my "no economic testimony" hypothetical—and in the actual circumstances of this case. . . . The variations matter not at all. Whatever the precise mechanism, each "operate[s] . . . as a prospective waiver of a party's [federal] right[s]"—and so confers immunity on a wrongdoer. . . . And that is what counts under our decisions. [Footnote omitted.]

Nor can the majority escape the principle we have established by observing, as it does at one point, that Amex's agreement merely made arbitration "not worth the expense." . . . That suggestion, after all, runs smack into *Randolph,* which likewise involved an allegation that arbitration, as specified in a contract, "would be prohibitively expensive." . . . Our decision there made clear that a provision raising a plaintiff's costs could foreclose consideration of federal claims, and so run afoul of the effective-vindication rule. The expense at issue in *Randolph* came from a filing fee combined with a per-diem payment for the arbitrator. But nothing about those particular costs is distinctive; and indeed, a rule confined to them would be weirdly idiosyncratic. Not surprisingly, then, *Randolph* gave no hint of distinguishing among the different ways an arbitration agreement can make a claim too costly to bring. Its rationale applies whenever an agreement makes the vindication of federal claims impossibly expensive—whether by imposing fees or proscribing cost-sharing or adopting some other device.

That leaves the three last sentences in the majority's core paragraph. Here, the majority conjures a special reason to exclude "class-action waiver[s]" from the effective-vindication rule's compass. . . . Rule 23, the majority notes, became law only in 1938—decades after the Sherman Act. The majority's conclusion: If federal law in the interim decades did not eliminate a plaintiff's rights under that Act, then neither does this agreement.

But that notion, first of all, rests on a false premise: that this case is only about a class-action waiver. . . . It is not, and indeed could not sensibly be. The effective-vindication rule asks whether an arbitration agreement *as a whole* precludes a claimant from enforcing federal statutory rights. No single provision is properly viewed in isolation, because an agreement can close off one avenue to pursue a claim while leaving others open. In this case, for example, the agreement could have prohibited class arbitration without offending the effective-vindication rule *if* it had provided an alternative mechanism to share, shift, or reduce the necessary costs. The agreement's problem is that it bars not just class actions, but also all mechanisms—many existing long before the Sherman Act, if that matters—for joinder or consolidation of claims, informal coordination among individual claimants, or amelioration of arbitral expenses. . . . And contrary to the majority's assertion, the Second Circuit well understood that point: It considered, for example, whether Italian Colors could shift expert expenses to Amex if its claim prevailed (no) or could join with merchants bringing similar claims to produce a common expert report (no again). . . . It is only in this Court that the case has become strangely narrow, as the majority stares at a single provision rather than considering, in the way the effective-vindication rule demands, how the entire contract operates. [Footnote omitted.]

In any event, the age of the relevant procedural mechanisms (whether class actions or any other) does not matter, because the effective-vindication rule asks about the world today, not the world as it might have looked when Congress passed a given statute. Whether a particular procedural device preceded or post-dated a particular statute, the question remains the same: Does the arbitration agreement foreclose a party—right now—from effectively vindicating the substantive rights the statute provides? This case exhibits a whole raft of changes since Congress passed the Sherman Act, affecting both parties to the dispute—not just new procedural rules (like Rule 23), but also new evidentiary requirements (like the demand here for an expert report) and new contract provisions affecting arbitration (like this agreement's confidentiality clause). But what has stayed the same is this: Congress's intent that antitrust plaintiffs should be able to enforce their rights free of any prior waiver. . . . The effective-vindication rule carries out that purpose by ensuring that any arbitration agreement operating as such a waiver is unenforceable. And that requires courts to determine in the here and now—rather than in ye olde glory days—whether an agreement's provisions foreclose even meritorious antitrust claims.

Still, the majority takes one last stab: "Truth to tell," it claims, *AT&T Mobility LLC v. Concepcion,* . . . "all but resolves this case." . . . In that decision, the majority recounts, this Court held that the FAA preempted a state "law conditioning enforcement of arbitration on the availability of class procedure." . . . According to the majority, that decision controls here because "[w]e specifically rejected the argument that class arbitration was necessary." . . .

Where to begin? Well, maybe where I just left off: Italian Colors is not claiming that a class action is necessary—only that it have *some* means of vindicating a meritorious claim. And as I have shown, non-class options abound. . . . The idea that *AT&T Mobility* controls here depends entirely on the majority's view that this case is "class action or bust." Were the majority to drop that pretense, it could make no claim for *AT&T Mobility*'s relevance.

And just as this case is not about class actions, *AT&T Mobility* was not—and could not have been—about the effective-vindication rule. Here is a tip-off: *AT&T Mobility* nowhere cited our effective-vindication precedents. That was so for two reasons. To begin with, the state law in question made class-action waivers unenforceable even when a party *could* feasibly vindicate her claim in an individual arbitration. The state rule was designed to preserve the broad-scale "deterrent effects of class actions," not merely to protect a particular plaintiff's right to assert her own claim. . . .

Indeed, the Court emphasized that the complaint in that case was "most unlikely to go unresolved" because AT & T's agreement contained a host of features ensuring that "aggrieved customers who filed claims would be essentially guaranteed to be made whole." . . . So the Court professed that *AT&T Mobility* did not implicate the only thing (a party's ability to vindicate a meritorious claim) this case involves.

And if that is not enough, *AT&T Mobility* involved a *state* law, and therefore could not possibly implicate the effective-vindication rule. When a state rule allegedly conflicts with the FAA, we apply standard preemption principles, asking whether the state law frustrates the FAA's purposes and objectives. If the state rule does so—as the Court found in *AT&T Mobility*—the Supremacy Clause requires its invalidation. We have no earthly interest (quite the contrary) in vindicating that law. Our effective-vindication rule comes into play only when the FAA is alleged to conflict with another *federal* law, like the Sherman Act here. In that all-federal context, one law does not automatically bow to the other, and the effective-vindication rule serves as a way to reconcile any tension between them. Again, then, *AT&T Mobility* had no occasion to address the issue in this case. The relevant decisions are instead *Mitsubishi* and *Randolph*.

* * *

The Court today mistakes what this case is about. To a hammer, everything looks like a nail. And to a Court bent on diminishing the usefulness of Rule 23, everything looks like a class action, ready to be dismantled. So the Court does not consider that Amex's agreement bars not just class actions, but "other forms of cost-sharing . . . that could provide effective vindication." . . . In short, the Court does not consider—and does not decide—Italian Colors's (and similarly situated litigants') actual argument about why the effective-vindication rule precludes this agreement's enforcement.

As a result, Amex's contract will succeed in depriving Italian Colors of any effective opportunity to challenge monopolistic conduct allegedly in violation of the Sherman Act. The FAA, the majority says, so requires. Do not be fooled. Only the Court so requires; the FAA was never meant to produce this outcome. The FAA conceived of arbitration as a "method of *resolving* disputes"—a way of using tailored and streamlined procedures to facilitate redress of injuries. *Rodriguez de Quijas,* 490 U.S., at 481, 109 S.Ct. 1917 (emphasis added). In the hands of today's majority, arbitration threatens to become more nearly the opposite—a mechanism easily made to block the vindication of meritorious federal claims and insulate wrongdoers from liability. The Court thus undermines the FAA no less than it does the Sherman Act and other federal statutes providing rights of action. I respectfully dissent.

NOTES AND QUESTIONS

1. *Italian Colors* may be understood as both a case about class action waivers and a case about the arbitrability of statutory rights. With respect to class action waivers, the case does little more than validate the holding of *Concepcion*. The real impact of the case was to do away with the effective vindication doctrine. This doctrine had been seen as a mechanism to override arbitration agreements that might amount to the functional equivalent of express waivers of statutory rights.

The U.S. Supreme Court, as you saw in Chapter 5, gradually unwound the holding and logic of *Wilko v. Swan*, making virtually all statutory rights arbitrable. In so doing, the Court repeatedly emphasized that the choice to arbitrate did not constitute a deprivation of substantive rights. Instead, arbitration was merely an alternative procedure for enforcing those rights. The effective vindication doctrine was seen by many as a safeguard, in light of this jurisprudential shift, against efforts by commercial parties to exempt themselves from responsibility for complying with the statutory directives.

2. To the extent that *Italian Colors* is seen as a case continuing the Court's erosion of subject matter limits to arbitrability, it is worth noting that other non-judicial efforts to reform adhesive arbitration have stalled over the past two decades. *See, e.g.*, Arbitration Fairness Act of 2013, S. 878, 113th Cong. (1st Sess. 2013) (providing that agreements to arbitrate certain types of claims are not enforceable); Arbitration Fairness Act of 2009, H.R. 1020, 111th Cong. (1st Sess. 2009) (providing the same).

Most recently, the Consumer Fraud Protection Bureau ("CFPB") established under the Dodd-Frank Wall Street Reform and Consumer Protection Act of 2010 ("Dodd-Frank"), Pub. L. No. 111–203, H.R. 4173, 111th Cong., conducted a study on the use of mandatory arbitration provisions in banking, credit card and other lending agreements. After years of study and public field hearings, on May 5, 2016 the CFPB released for public comment a proposed rule that would bar banks, lenders, and other providers of certain financial products from using mandatory arbitration provisions that include class-action waivers. The CFPB received over 110,000 comment letters on its proposal and, on July 19, 2017, published a final rule that banned the use of class-action waivers in consumer contracts with providers of banking, credit, and lending. Agreements, 82 Fed. Reg. 33210 (July 19, 2017).

The CFPB rule was, however, quite short-lived. On Nov. 1, 2017, the President signed a joint resolution passed by Congress disapproving the Arbitration Agreements Rule under the Congressional Review Act. 5 U.S.C. §§ 801–808 (1996).

Still, the passage of the rule, as well as the persistence of prior legislative efforts, evidences that there are constituencies who believe that some limits on what matters can be arbitrated need to exist.

3. Evaluate the majority's and dissent's assessment of the *Mitsubishi* precedent. In *Mitsubishi*, the Court said that

> By agreeing to arbitrate a statutory claim, a party does not forgo the substantive rights afforded by the statute; it only submits to their resolution in an arbitral, rather than a judicial, forum. It trades the procedures and opportunity for review of the courtroom for the simplicity, informality, and expedition of arbitration.

473 U.S. 614, 628 (1985). At the same time, the Court added that, "if the arbitration clause acted "as a prospective waiver of a party's right to pursue statutory remedies . . . we would have little hesitation in condemning the agreement as against public policy." *Id.* at 637 n.19. Is the 'effective vindication' doctrine the same as the 'prospective waiver' rule? How would you define each of these concepts? Does the majority in *Italian Colors* do justice to *Mitsubishi*?

4. What do you think of the affordability argument made by the merchants? What impact does affordability have on rights? What impact should it have? Must society provide an affordable means of vindicating rights to all plaintiffs?

5. The effective vindication doctrine, while it was recognized, was not necessarily a panacea. The doctrine might have created perverse incentives for lawyers getting paid through contingency fee arrangements to refuse to cover costs of arbitration, though they would cover the costs of litigation. *See* Christopher R. Drahozal, *Arbitration Costs and Contingent Fee Contracts,* 59 VAND. L. REV. 729, 734–35 (2006). In other words, some of the cost differentials between court litigation and arbitration could have been manufactured. If true, does this change your view of the value or importance of the doctrine?

EPIC SYSTEMS CORP. V. LEWIS

584 U.S. ___, 138 S.Ct. 1612, 200 L.Ed. 2d 889 (2018).

(footnotes omitted)

JUSTICE GORSUCH delivered the opinion of the Court.

Should employees and employers be allowed to agree that any disputes between them will be resolved through one-on-one arbitration? Or should employees always be permitted to bring their claims in class or collective actions, no matter what they agreed with their employers?

As a matter of policy these questions are surely debatable. But as a matter of law the answer is clear. In the Federal Arbitration Act, Congress has instructed federal courts to enforce arbitration agreements according to their terms—including terms providing for individualized proceedings. Nor can we agree with the employees' suggestion that the National Labor Relations Act (NLRA) offers a conflicting command. It is this Court's duty to interpret Congress's statutes as a harmonious whole rather than at war with one another. And abiding that duty here leads to an unmistakable conclusion. The NLRA secures to employees rights to organize unions and bargain collectively, but it says nothing about how judges and arbitrators must try legal disputes that leave the workplace and enter the courtroom or arbitral forum. This Court has never read a right to class actions into the NLRA—and for three quarters of a century neither did the National Labor Relations Board. Far from conflicting, the Arbitration Act and the NLRA have long enjoyed separate spheres of influence and neither permits this Court to declare the parties' agreements unlawful.

I

The three cases before us differ in detail but not in substance. Take *Ernst & Young LLP* v. *Morris*. There Ernst & Young and one of its junior accountants, Stephen Morris, entered into an agreement providing that they would arbitrate any disputes that might arise between them. The agreement stated that the employee could choose the arbitration provider and that the arbitrator could "grant any relief that could be granted by . . . a court" in the relevant jurisdiction. . . . The agreement also specified individualized arbitration, with claims "pertaining to different [e]mployees [to] be heard in separate proceedings." . . .

After his employment ended, and despite having agreed to arbitrate claims against the firm, Mr. Morris sued Ernst & Young in federal court. He alleged that the firm had misclassified its junior accountants as professional employees and violated the federal Fair Labor Standards Act (FLSA) and California law by paying them salaries without overtime pay. Although the arbitration agreement provided for individualized proceedings, Mr. Morris sought to litigate the federal claim on behalf of a nationwide class under the FLSA's collective action provision, 29 U. S. C. § 216(b). He sought to pursue the state law claim as a class action under Federal Rule of Civil Procedure 23.

Ernst & Young replied with a motion to compel arbitration. The district court granted the request, but the Ninth Circuit reversed this judgment. 834 F. 3d 975 (2016). The Ninth Circuit recognized that the Arbitration Act generally requires courts to enforce arbitration agreements as written. But the court reasoned that the statute's "saving clause," see 9 U. S. C. § 2, removes this obligation if an arbitration agreement violates some other federal law. And the court concluded that an agreement requiring individualized arbitration proceedings violates the NLRA by barring employees from engaging in the "concerted activit[y]," 29 U. S. C. § 157, of pursuing claims as a class or collective action.

Judge Ikuta dissented. In her view, the Arbitration Act protected the arbitration agreement from judicial interference and nothing in the Act's saving clause suggested otherwise. Neither, she concluded, did the NLRA demand a different result. Rather, that statute focuses on protecting unionization and collective bargaining in the workplace, not on guaranteeing class or collective action procedures in disputes before judges or arbitrators.

Although the Arbitration Act and the NLRA have long coexisted—they date from 1925 and 1935, respectively—the suggestion they might conflict is something quite new. Until a couple of years ago, courts more or less agreed that arbitration agreements like those before us must be enforced according to their terms. . . .

The National Labor Relations Board's general counsel expressed much the same view in 2010. Remarking that employees and employers "can benefit from the relative simplicity and informality of resolving claims before arbitrators," the general counsel opined that the validity of such agreements "does not involve consideration of the policies of the National Labor Relations Act." . . .

But recently things have shifted. In 2012, the Board—for the first time in the 77 years since the NLRA's adoption—asserted that the NLRA effectively nullifies the Arbitration Act in cases like ours. . . . Initially, this agency decision received a cool reception in court. . . . In the last two years, though, some circuits have either agreed with the Board's conclusion or thought themselves obliged to defer to it under *Chevron U. S. A. Inc.* v. *Natural Resources Defense Council, Inc.*, 467 U. S. 837 (1984). . . . More recently still, the disagreement has grown as the Executive has disavowed the Board's (most recent) position, and the Solicitor General and the Board have offered us battling briefs about the law's meaning. We granted certiorari to clear the confusion. 580 U. S. ___ (2017).

II

We begin with the Arbitration Act and the question of its saving clause.

Congress adopted the Arbitration Act in 1925 in response to a perception that courts were unduly hostile to arbitration. No doubt there was much to that perception. Before 1925, English and American common law courts routinely refused to enforce agreements to arbitrate disputes. *Scherk* v. *Alberto-Culver Co.*, 417 U. S. 506, 510, n. 4 (1974). But in Congress's judgment arbitration had more to offer than courts recognized—not least the promise of quicker, more informal, and often cheaper resolutions for everyone involved. *Id.*, at 511. So Congress directed courts to abandon their hostility and instead treat arbitration agreements as "valid, irrevocable, and enforceable." 9 U. S. C. § 2. The Act, this Court has said, establishes "a liberal federal policy favoring arbitration agreements." *Moses H. Cone Memorial Hospital* v. *Mercury Constr. Corp.*, 460 U. S. 1, 24 (1983) . . . .

Not only did Congress require courts to respect and enforce agreements to arbitrate; it also specifically directed them to respect and enforce the parties' chosen arbitration procedures. See § 3 (providing for a stay of litigation pending arbitration "in accordance with the terms of the agreement"); § 4 (providing for "an order directing that . . . arbitration proceed in the manner provided for in such agreement"). Indeed, we have often observed that the Arbitration Act requires courts "rigorously" to "enforce arbitration agreements according to their terms, including terms that specify *with whom* the parties choose to arbitrate their disputes and *the rules* under which that arbitration will be conducted." *American Express Co.* v. *Italian Colors Restaurant*, 570 U. S. 228, 233 (2013) (some emphasis added; citations, internal quotation marks, and brackets omitted).

On first blush, these emphatic directions would seem to resolve any argument under the Arbitration Act. The parties before us contracted for arbitration. They proceeded to specify the rules that would govern their arbitrations, indicating their intention to use individualized rather than class or collective action procedures. And this much the Arbitration Act seems to protect pretty absolutely. . . . You might wonder if the balance Congress struck in 1925 between arbitration and litigation should be revisited in light of more contemporary developments. You might even ask if the Act was good policy when enacted. But all the same you might find it difficult to see how to avoid the statute's application.

Still, the employees suggest the Arbitration Act's saving clause creates an exception for cases like theirs. By its terms, the saving clause allows courts to refuse to enforce arbitration agreements "upon such grounds as exist at law or in equity for the revocation of any contract." § 2. That provision applies here, the employees tell us, because the NLRA renders their particular class and collective action waivers illegal. In their view, illegality under the NLRA is a "ground" that "exists at law . . . for the revocation" of their arbitration agreements, at least to the extent those agreements prohibit class or collective action proceedings.

The problem with this line of argument is fundamental. Put to the side the question whether the saving clause was designed to save not only state law defenses but also defenses allegedly arising from federal statutes. . . . Put to the side the question of what it takes to qualify as a ground for "revocation" of a contract. . . . Put to the side for the moment, too, even the question whether the NLRA actually renders class and collective action waivers illegal. Assuming (but not granting) the employees could satisfactorily answer all those questions, the saving clause still can't save their cause.

It can't because the saving clause recognizes only defenses that apply to "any" contract. In this way the clause establishes a sort of "equal-treatment" rule for arbitration contracts. *Kindred Nursing Centers L. P.* v. *Clark*, 581 U. S. ___, ___ (2017) (slip op., at 4). The clause "permits agreements to arbitrate to be invalidated by 'generally applicable contract defenses, such as fraud, duress, or unconscionability.'" *Concepcion*, 563 U. S., at 339. At the same time, the clause offers no refuge for "defenses that apply only to arbitration or that derive their meaning from the fact that an agreement to arbitrate is at issue." *Ibid.* Under our precedent, this means the saving clause does not save defenses that target arbitration either by name or by more subtle methods, such as by "interfer[ing] with fundamental attributes of arbitration." *Id.*, at 344; see *Kindred Nursing, supra,* at ___ (slip op., at 5).

This is where the employees' argument stumbles. They don't suggest that their arbitration agreements were extracted, say, by an act of fraud or duress or in some other unconscionable way that would render *any* contract unenforceable. Instead, they object to their agreements precisely because they require individualized arbitration proceedings instead of class or collective ones. And by attacking (only) the individualized nature of the arbitration proceedings, the employees' argument seeks to interfere with one of arbitration's fundamental attributes.

We know this much because of *Concepcion*. There this Court faced a state law defense that prohibited as unconscionable class action waivers in consumer contracts. The Court readily acknowledged that the defense formally applied in both the litigation and the arbitration context. 563 U. S., at 338, 341. But, the Court held, the defense failed to qualify for protection under the saving clause because it interfered with a fundamental attribute of arbitration all the same. It did so by effectively permitting any party in arbitration to demand classwide proceedings despite the traditionally individualized and informal nature of arbitration. This "fundamental" change to the traditional arbitration process, the Court said, would "sacrific[e] the principal advantage of arbitration—its informality—and mak[e] the process slower, more costly, and more likely to generate procedural morass than final judgment." *Id.*, at 347, 348. Not least, *Concepcion* noted, arbitrators would have to decide whether the named class representatives are sufficiently representative and typical of the class; what kind of notice, opportunity to be heard, and right to opt out absent class members should enjoy; and how discovery should be altered in light of the classwide nature of the proceedings. *Ibid.* All of which would take much time and effort, and introduce new risks and costs for both sides. *Ibid.* In the Court's judgment, the virtues Congress originally saw in arbitration, its speed and simplicity and inexpensiveness, would be shorn away and arbitration would wind up looking like the litigation it was meant to displace.

Of course, *Concepcion* has its limits. The Court recognized that parties remain free to alter arbitration procedures to suit their tastes, and in recent years some parties have sometimes chosen to arbitrate on a classwide basis. *Id.*, at 351. But *Concepcion*'s essential insight remains: courts may not allow a contract defense to reshape traditional individualized arbitration by mandating classwide arbitration procedures without the parties' consent. *Id.*, at 344–351 . . . Just as judicial antagonism toward arbitration before the Arbitration Act's enactment "manifested itself in a great variety of devices and formulas declaring arbitration against public policy," *Concepcion* teaches that we must be alert to new devices and formulas that would achieve much the same result today. 563 U. S., at 342 (internal quotation marks omitted). And a rule seeking to declare individualized arbitration proceedings off limits is, the Court held, just such a device.

The employees' efforts to distinguish *Concepcion* fall short. They note that their putative NLRA defense would render an agreement "illegal" as a matter of federal statutory law rather than "unconscionable" as a matter of state common law. But we don't see how that distinction makes any difference in light of *Concepion*'s rationale and rule. Illegality, like unconscionability, may be a traditional, generally applicable contract defense in many cases, including arbitration cases. But an argument that a contract is unenforceable *just because it requires bilateral arbitration* is a different creature. A defense of that kind, *Concepcion* tells us, is one that impermissibly disfavors arbitration whether it sounds in illegality or unconscionability. The law of precedent teaches that like cases should generally be treated alike, and appropriate respect for that principle means the Arbitration Act's saving clause can no more save the defense at issue in these cases than it did the defense at issue in *Concepcion*. At the end of our encounter with the Arbitration Act, then, it appears just as it did at the beginning: a congressional command requiring us to enforce, not override, the terms of the arbitration agreements before us.

[. . .]

[The Court goes on to analyze whether a conflict between the NLRA and the FAA exists. If it did, the NLRA would trump as the more recent statute. The Court, however, concludes that Section 7 of the NLRA does not "speak" to group litigation procedures, such as class actions. In fact, the Court goes on to say, there is "no textually sound reason to suppose" that Section 7 "speaks to the procedures judges or arbitrators must apply in disputes that leave the workplace and enter the courtroom or arbitral forum." The Court concludes by noting that "[i]n many cases over many years, this Court has heard and rejected efforts to conjure conflicts between the Arbitration Act and other federal statutes. In fact, this Court has rejected every such effort to date (save one temporary exception since overruled)."]

IV

The dissent sees things a little bit differently. In its view, today's decision ushers us back to the *Lochner* era when this Court regularly overrode legislative policy judgments. The dissent even suggests we have resurrected the long-dead "yellow dog" contract. *Post,* at 3–17, 30 (opinion of Ginsburg, J.). But like most apocalyptic warnings, this one proves a false alarm. Cf. L. Tribe, American Constitutional Law 435 (1978) (" '*Lochnerizing*' has become so much an epithet that the very use of the label may obscure attempts at understanding").

Our decision does nothing to override Congress's policy judgments. As the dissent recognizes, the legislative policy embodied in the NLRA is aimed at "safeguard[ing], first and foremost, workers' rights to join unions and to engage in collective bargaining." *Post,* at 8. Those rights stand every bit as strong today as they did yesterday. And rather than revive "yellow dog" contracts against union organizing that the NLRA outlawed back in 1935, today's decision merely declines to read into the NLRA a novel right to class action procedures that the Board's own general counsel disclaimed as recently as 2010.

Instead of overriding Congress's policy judgments, today's decision seeks to honor them. This much the dissent surely knows. Shortly after invoking the specter of *Lochner*, it turns around and criticizes the Court for trying *too hard* to abide the Arbitration Act's " 'liberal federal policy favoring arbitration agreements,' " *Howsam* v. *Dean Witter Reynolds, Inc.*, 537 U. S. 79, 83 (2002), saying we " 'ski' " too far down the " 'slippery slope' " of this Court's arbitration precedent, *post,* at 23. But the dissent's real complaint lies with the mountain of precedent itself. The dissent spends page after page relitigating our Arbitration Act precedents, rehashing arguments this Court has heard and rejected many times in many cases that no party has asked us to revisit. . . .

When at last it reaches the question of applying our precedent, the dissent offers little, and understandably so. Our precedent clearly teaches that a contract defense "conditioning the enforceability of certain arbitration agreements on the availability of classwide arbitration procedures" is inconsistent with the Arbitration Act and its saving clause. *Concepcion, supra,* at 336 (opinion of the Court). And that, of course, is exactly what the employees' proffered defense seeks to do.

[. . .]

Ultimately, the dissent retreats to policy arguments. . . . This Court is not free to substitute its preferred economic policies for those chosen by the people's representatives. *That,* we had always understood, was *Lochner*'s sin.

[. . .]

The policy may be debatable but the law is clear: Congress has instructed that arbitration agreements like those before us must be enforced as written. While Congress is of course always free to amend this judgment, we see nothing suggesting it did so in the NLRA—much less that it manifested a clear intention to displace the Arbitration Act. Because we can easily read Congress's statutes to work in harmony, that is where our duty lies. The judgments in *Epic*, No. 16–285, and *Ernst & Young*, No. 16–300, are reversed, and the cases are remanded for further proceedings consistent with this opinion. The judgment in *Murphy Oil*, No. 16–307, is affirmed.

So ordered.

[. . .]

[Justices Ginsburg issued a scathing dissent in which Justices Breyer, Sotomayor, and Kagan joined. The focus most of the dissent, however, is on the proper interpretation of Section 7 of the NLRA. A portion of the dissent related to the FAA appears in the notes following *Circuit City Stores v. Adams* later in the Chapter.]

[. . .]

NOTES AND QUESTIONS

1. *Epic Systems* represents the most recent word by the U.S. Supreme Court on arbitration law and class action waivers. Despite the Court having addressed the class action issue from a variety of angles, the Court has taken another case for its 2019 term related to how specific the language of an arbitration agreement must be in order to authorize class arbitration. *See Lamps Plus, Inc. v. Varela,* 138 S. Ct. 1697, 200 L.Ed. 2d 948 (2018). Additionally, a Circuit split has been heating up about whether courts or arbitrators decide whether an arbitration agreement allows for class actions? The Third, Fourth, Sixth and Eight Circuits have all held that class arbitrability is an issue that is presumably for courts (not arbitrators) to decide, even if the parties incorporate rules that generally delegate issues of arbitrability to an arbitrator. *See Catamaran Corp. v. Towncrest Pharmacy,* 864 F.3d 966, 969 (8th Cir. 2017); *Del Webb Communities, Inc. v. Carlson*, 817 F.3d 867, 869 (4th Cir.), *cert. denied*, 137 S. Ct. 567, 196 L.Ed. 2d 444 (2016); *Opalinski v. Robert Half Int'l Inc.,* 761 F.3d 326 (3d Cir. 2014); *Reed Elsevier, Inc. ex rel. LexisNexis Div. v. Crockett*, 734 F.3d 594, 596 (6th Cir. 2013). The Second, Tenth, and Eleventh Circuits disagree. *See Dish Network L.L.C. v. Ray,* 900 F.3d 1240 (10th Cir. 2018); *Spirit Airlines, Inc. v. Maizes*, 899 F.3d 1230 (11th Cir. 2018); *Wells Fargo Advisors, LLC v. Sappington*, 884 F.3d 392, 393 (2d Cir. 2018).

The critical point is that the law surrounding class action waivers remains volatile and in flux.

2. In one sense, *Epic Systems* may feel a bit abstracted, having more to do perhaps with the NLRA than it does with arbitration. But the practical impact of the case should not be overlooked. A number of pending and potential class action suits have been dismissed or voluntarily abandoned in the wake of the decision. For instance, a pending 2014 class action by former employees against Chipotle alleging that the company systematically forced them to work "off the clock" will likely be divided into smaller sub-groups. Additionally, a

class of approximately 1,600 former employees of Kelly Services who had alleged violations of the Federal Fair Labors Standards Act have been compelled to go to individual arbitrations as a result of *Epic Systems. See Gaffers v. Kelly Services,* 900 F.3d 293 (6th Cir. 2018).

3. The majority takes an incredibly expansive view of the "savings clause" of FAA § 2. Take a moment to be sure that you see what is different and new about this view. Does this expansive reading line up with your understanding of the clause from prior cases? Do you agree with the majority? Why or why not?

4. Do you agree with the majority that the essential insight of *Concepcion* is that "courts may not allow a contract defense to reshape traditional individualized arbitration by mandating classwide arbitration procedures without the parties' consent"?

5. The majority denies that collective lawsuits by employees are equivalent to other forms of collective actions by employees. Do you agree that dispute resolution processes outside of employment are fundamentally different than bargaining and collection action rights before and during employment? Why or why not?

5. OBJECTIONS TO OUTCOMES

Arbitration substitutes for public courts. But sometimes the outcomes in arbitration might not be perceived as equal to what individuals would have received in court.

In particular, the arbitral process may result in individuals getting lower damages awards or having remedies otherwise stripped away. A commercial party might want to arbitrate precisely because it believes that arbitrators will be less emotional or extreme than courts or juries when awarding damages. As industry experts, arbitrators may be more dispassionate and potentially even biased in favor of the industry. Even in the absence of a remedy stripping provision in an arbitration agreement, arbitrators might be less inclined to award damages or punitive damages.

Additionally, awards can be private or even confidential. As a result, serial predators can be shielded from exposure. Victims can be given less access to patterns of misconduct relevant to their damages, and commercial parties can more easily downplay or conceal structural or systemic bias that gives safe harbor to predators.

These outcome-based concerns raise important empirical questions. Unfortunately, only limited empirical evidence exists. *See, e.g.,* Thomas J. Stipanowich, *The Third Arbitration Trilogy: Stolt-Nielsen, Rent-A-Center, Concepcion and the Future of American Arbitration,* 22 AM. REV. INT'L ARB. 323, 422 (2011) (noting that it is notoriously difficult to "obtain[ ] sufficient reliable data on largely private arbitration processes"); David S. Schwartz, *Mandatory Arbitration and Fairness,* 84 NOTRE DAME L. REV. 1247, 1283

(2009) ("Ten years of empirical research into the fairness of mandatory arbitration have produced only a handful of empirical studies, and these have told us very little.").

The dearth of information stems partly from the fact that many arbitrations are private, making it difficult to see what is going on inside of the process. On the other hand, even though court proceedings are public, not a lot of easily digestible data exists about civil verdicts generally or subcategories of cases involving disparate parties in particular. In short, comparisons between processes are impeded because of available information about the processes in isolation.

Compounding these basic empirical problems are a host of differences in how and when parties might pursue arbitration versus litigation. These differences could impact the relative strength of disputes that are fought to conclusion in an award or court verdict. Accordingly, comparing awards to verdicts could be like comparing apples to oranges.

On the one hand, you could imagine that if arbitration is cheaper and easier than court litigation—for instance, if the commercial party covers the costs of the arbitration and if the process takes place in the individual's hometown without need for a lot of burdensome discovery or motion practice—we might see more people asserting questionable claims in arbitration. After all, the barriers to asserting claims is low so individuals might feel willing to roll the dice. This might mean that we would expect to see fewer plaintiffs prevail in arbitration than in court litigation.

On the other hand, if arbitration, in fact, is opaque and deters individuals from bringing claims at all, as many critics contend, we might see only the strongest claims in arbitration. *See, e.g.,* Mark E. Budnitz, *The High Cost of Mandatory Consumer Arbitration,* 67 LAW & CONTEMP. PROBS. 133, 133, 161 (2004) (arguing that mandatory arbitration provisions dissuade individuals from bringing claims). If that hypothesis is true, we would expect to see more plaintiffs prevail in arbitration.

Along a slightly different dimension, because public court litigation is expensive and time-consuming, we might see more settlements, which means that cases would only be fully litigated in court when the plaintiffs had the strongest claims. In contrast, lower process costs in arbitration might mean that there would be less incentive for any side to settle, allowing more cases, strong and weak, to be fully arbitrated.

Finally, even defining "success" can be challenging. Measuring only monetary wins shortchanges the possibilities of equitable or injunctive relief or other practical changes in behavior that might result from legal action.

The bottom line is that, as important as data is making wise policy decisions, assessing the relative outcomes in courts and arbitration has proven quite challenging. A number of valiant efforts exist, but at present these studies provide only a glimpse into how outcomes might differ between courts and arbitration.

One very recent empirical effort has analyzed 40,775 arbitration cases filed between 2010 and 2016 with four major arbitration institutions. *See* Andrea Cann Chandrasekher & David Horton, *Arbitration Nation: Data from Four Providers*, 107 CAL. L. REV. ___ (forthcoming 2019). Based on their review, the authors conclude: (1) arbitration has become surprisingly affordable for individuals, with many individuals paying no arbitration fees or costs; (2) when plaintiffs are represented by lawyers, those lawyers have dramatically closed whatever gaps may exist between public court litigation and arbitration (though some differences in outcomes may persist); and (3) although arbitration does seem to favor repeat players, that effect applies to repeat plaintiff's lawyers as well as defendants. Ultimately, in many situations, no variable impacts win rates as dramatically as whether a plaintiff hires a lawyer.

This last finding may be particularly salient to ongoing discussions of the propriety of mass market arbitrations. It may be the case that access to justice concerns should focus more on the availability of competent counsel than on the forum where disputes are resolved. While no existing empirical comparison of success rates in pro se arbitration versus pro se litigation exist, parties without competent counsel are likely to experience worse outcomes than those with counsel in any forum. But arbitration is not necessarily dramatically worse at offering plaintiffs opportunities to be represented by counsel. *See, e.g.*, Judith Resnik, *"Vital" State Interests: From Representative Actions for Fair Labor Standards to Pooled Trusts, Class Actions, and MDLs in the Federal Courts,* 165 PENN. L. REV. 1765, 1774 (2017) (observing that, as of 2015, more than 25% of plaintiffs filing civil suits in public courts did so pro se and more than 50% of appellants were pro se, though these numbers include prisoner suits). Accordingly, it may be that the variable most likely to impact outcomes in both litigation and arbitration is access to counsel.

In addition to thinking about empirical data, an interesting line of cases from California explores the overlap between private remedies for plaintiffs and public remedies that benefit society at large.

Several California statutes, including the California Consumers Legal Remedies Act (CLRA), the California Unfair Competition Law (UCL), and the California False Advertising Law (FAL), permit any person who has suffered injury to also seek injunctive relief on behalf of the public. Two California cases interpreting the public injunctive relief aspect of those three laws developed what has become known in California as the *Broughton-Cruz* rule: claims for public injunctive relief may not be forced into arbitration. *See Broughton v. Cigna Healthplans of California*, 21

Cal.4th 1066, 90 Cal.Rptr.2d 334, 988 P.2d 67 (1999); *Cruz v. Pacificare Health Systems, Inc.*, 30 Cal. 4th 1157 (2003). The *Broughton-Cruz* rule distinguished between private injunctive relief—relief that primarily resolves a private dispute between the parties and rectifies individual wrongs and that benefits the public, if at all, only incidentally—and public injunctive relief—relief that by and large benefits the general public and that benefits the plaintiff, if at all, only incidentally and as a member of the general public.

The Ninth Circuit has held that the *Broughton-Cruz* rule is preempted by the FAA and the U.S. Supreme Court's decision in *Concepcion*. *Ferguson v. Corinthian Colls.*, 733 F.3d 928 (9th Cir. 2013). The California Court of Appeals agreed, saying

> the United States Supreme Court unmistakably declared the FAA preempts all state-law rules that prohibit arbitration of a particular type of claim because an outright ban, no matter how laudable the purpose, interferes with the FAA's objective of enforcing arbitration agreements according to their terms. The *Broughton-Cruz* rule falls prey to *AT&T Mobility*'s sweeping directive because it is a state-law rule that prohibits arbitration of UCL, FAL, and CLRA injunctive relief claims brought for the public's benefit.

McGill v. Citibank, N.A., 232 Cal. App. 4th 753, 181 Cal. Rptr. 3d 494, 497 (2014), *review granted and opinion superseded sub nom. McGill v. Citibank*, 345 P.3d 61 (Cal. 2015), *and rev'd*, 2 Cal. 5th 945, 393 P.3d 85 (2017).

The California Supreme Court, however, has taken a different approach. It has held that the *Broughton-Cruz* rule "is not a defense that applies only to arbitration or that derives its meaning from the fact that an agreement to arbitrate is at issue." *McGill v. Citibank, N.A.*, 2 Cal. 5th 945, 962, 393 P.3d 85, 94 (2017). Instead, "a provision in *any* contract—even a contract that has no arbitration provision—that purports to waive, in all fora, the statutory right to seek public injunctive relief under the UCL, the CLRA, or the false advertising law is invalid and unenforceable under California law." *Id.* In the California Supreme Court's view, FAA does not require enforcement of a provision in an arbitration agreement that, in violation of generally applicable California contract law, "limit[s] statutorily imposed remedies such as punitive damages and attorney fees." *Id.* (citing *Armendariz v. Foundation Health Psychcare Services, Inc.* (2000) 24 Cal.4th 83, 103, 99 Cal.Rptr.2d 745, 6 P.3d 669). So, the FAA also does not require the enforcement of a provision that would waive statutory rights to injunctive relief in any forum. *Id.*

This reconstruction of the *Broughton-Cruz* rule side-steps the problem, at least to some degree. In its original form, the *Broughton-Cruz* rule hinged on the fact that arbitrators simply do not have the power to issue public injunctive relief, as they can only bind the parties to the arbitration and lack the structural authority to manage an ongoing injunction for the benefit of non-parties. At least in some sense, then, the *Broughton-Cruz* rule does hinge on the unique characteristics of arbitration. Nevertheless, the court's point is also understandable. If arbitrators do, in fact, lack the power to issue public injunctions, and if certain statutes give individuals the right to pursue public injunctive relief, then mandating arbitration would amount to exempting commercial parties from at least a portion of those rights.

6. EMPLOYMENT ARBITRATION

Employment arbitration emerged in the 1990s, some thirty years after its labor counterpart. It does not involve unions and union representation; employees enter into arbitration agreements directly with the employer. The employee's acquiescence to the employer's arbitration provision is often a condition of employment or continued employment. The contracts for arbitration are generally adhesive. Accordingly, most of the same patterns of objections arise with respect to employment arbitration as with other forms of disparate party arbitration. Nevertheless, the employment context has generated some of its own important precedents, and it might implicate at least some unique issues.

The U.S. Supreme Court's decision in *Gilmer v. Interstate/Johnson Lane Corp.*, 500 U.S. 20 (1991), provided the impetus for the creation of "employment" arbitration. In *Gilmer*, however, the agreement to arbitrate employment disputes was not technically part of the employment contract. In order to secure work as a stock broker, Gilmer signed a U-4 Registration Form with the New York Stock Exchange that required him to submit disputes with his employer to arbitration under the rules of the Exchange. The obligation to arbitrate claims against the employer, therefore, was implied and indirect. Accordingly, the Court in *Gilmer* never directly addressed the question of whether employment contracts containing mandatory, employer-imposed arbitral clauses constituted valid contractual references to arbitration under the FAA. Employers both inside and outside the securities industry nonetheless began inserting such clauses into standard employment contracts, usually as part of a company ADR process to handle workplace disputes.

As in many other settings, arbitration in the employment context can be readily justified by practical considerations of resource allocation. The dysfunctionality of the judicial process as a dispute resolution mechanism—in terms of costs, time, and disruption to commercial and individual interests—constitute the most compelling argument for arbitration and ADR more generally. The EEOC has a staggering national backlog of cases, so it cannot be expected to protect the interests of more than a handful of employees each year. In these circumstances, employment arbitration or company-sponsored ADR frameworks may be the only realistic recourse available to employees.

The argument for employment arbitration has substantial appeal. The progression of the arbitration industry in employment, however, raises some reservations. A nagging suspicion and concern remain about the enthusiasm for arbitration and ADR. There may be larger societal interests at stake in the privatization of adjudication. Despite attempts to safeguard procedural due process in arbitration, many critics worry that consumers, employees, and society at large may be getting only second-class justice. How serious is U.S. society about integrating minorities, women, gay, and transgender individuals and into the workplace if claims of discrimination and harassment are submitted to private remedial mechanisms at the employer's choice? Are commands of political rights merely symbolic? Have we chosen to privilege functionality over all other values?

These sobering and important questions have meant that the employment context has thus far generated some the strongest challenges to the wisdom of the Court's endorsement of arbitration. A number of lower state and federal courts have demonstrated serious reluctance to enforce these unilateral dispute resolution compacts, and members of the U.S. Congress have proposed legislation to remedy the perceived inequities of these arbitration agreements.

In addition to policy issues, employment arbitration raises a number of analytical questions. First, does the exclusion of specific employment contracts in Section One of the FAA render the FAA and its accompanying decisional law inapplicable to employment arbitration?

Second, should arbitration be imposed unilaterally upon employees by their employers either as a pre-condition to employment or after-the-fact in a modified employee handbook? Employment arbitration, in other words, compels revisiting the issue of the validity of arbitration agreements.

Third, assuming that formation of an arbitration contract has occurred, do arbitral clauses in employment contracts constitute lawful waivers of judicial remedies in areas implicating fundamental rights? The U.S. Supreme Court has left little, if any, doubt that statutory and civil rights claims can be submitted to arbitration. But perhaps the one-sided and economically-coercive character of employment can or should give courts greater incentive to police the fairness of arbitral clauses in employment contracts, particularly when they impose significantly greater costs on employees than litigation would.

The following sections will consider these topics in more detail.

The Employment Contract Exclusion (FAA § 1)

The U.S. Supreme Court addressed the problem of the employment contract exclusion (FAA § 1) in its landmark ruling in *Circuit City Stores, Inc. v. Adams*, 532 U.S. 105 (2001). The Court held that the so-called employment contract exclusion applies only to the employment contracts of workers directly involved in the interstate transport of good and services. Employers, therefore, could require—under the supportive umbrella of the FAA—all other employees to submit employment-related disputes to arbitration. The Court rejected and reversed the Ninth Circuit holding that the language in FAA § 1 exempted all employment contracts from the FAA's scope of application.

CIRCUIT CITY STORES, INC. V. ADAMS

532 U.S. 105, 121 S.Ct. 1302, 149 L.Ed.2d 234 (2001).

(footnotes omitted)

JUSTICE KENNEDY delivered the opinion of the Court.

Section 1 of the Federal Arbitration Act (FAA) excludes from the Act's coverage "contracts of employment of seamen, railroad employees, or any other class of workers engaged in foreign or interstate commerce." . . . All but one of the Courts of Appeals which have addressed the issue interpret this provision as exempting contracts of employment of transportation workers, but not other employment contracts, from the FAA's coverage. A different interpretation has been adopted by the Court of Appeals for the Ninth Circuit, which construes the exemption so that all contracts of employment are beyond the FAA's reach, whether or not the worker is engaged in transportation. It applied that rule to the instant case. We now decide that the better interpretation is to construe the statute, as most of the Courts of Appeals have done, to confine the exemption to transportation workers. . . .

In October 1995, respondent Saint Clair Adams applied for a job at petitioner Circuit City Stores, Inc., a national retailer of consumer electronics. Adams signed an employment application which included the following provision:

> "I agree that I will settle any and all previously unasserted claims, disputes or controversies arising out of or relating to my application or candidacy for employment, employment and/or cessation of employment with Circuit City, *exclusively* by final and binding *arbitration* before a neutral Arbitrator. By way of example only, such claims include claims under federal, state, and local statutory or common law, such as the Age Discrimination in Employment Act, Title VII of the Civil Rights Act of 1964, as

> amended, including the amendments of the Civil Rights Act of 1991, the Americans with Disabilities Act, the law of contract and the law of tort."

App. 13 (emphasis in original).

Adams was hired as a sales counselor in Circuit City's store in Santa Rosa, California. . . .

Two years later, Adams filed an employment discrimination lawsuit against Circuit City in state court, asserting claims under California's Fair Employment and Housing Act . . . and other claims based on general tort theories under California law. Circuit City filed suit in the United States District Court for the Northern District of California, seeking to enjoin the state-court action and to compel arbitration of respondent's claims pursuant to the FAA. . . . The District Court entered the requested order. Respondent, the court concluded, was obligated by the arbitration agreement to submit his claims against the employer to binding arbitration. An appeal followed.

While respondent's appeal was pending in the Court of Appeals for the Ninth Circuit, the court ruled on the key issue in an unrelated case. The court held the FAA does not apply to contracts of employment. . . . In the instant case, following the rule announced in *Craft*, the Court of Appeals held the arbitration agreement between Adams and Circuit City was contained in a "contract of employment," and so was not subject to the FAA. . . . Circuit City petitioned this Court, noting that the Ninth Circuit's conclusion that all employment contracts are excluded from the FAA conflicts with every other Court of Appeals to have addressed the question. . . . We granted *certiorari* to resolve the issue. . . .

II

A

Congress enacted the FAA in 1925. As the Court has explained, the FAA was a response to hostility of American courts to the enforcement of arbitration agreements, a judicial disposition inherited from then-longstanding English practice. . . . To give effect to this purpose, the FAA compels judicial enforcement of a wide range of written arbitration agreements. . . .

We had occasion in *Allied-Bruce* . . . to consider the significance of Congress' use of the words "involving commerce" in § 2. The analysis began with a reaffirmation of earlier decisions concluding that the FAA was enacted pursuant to Congress' substantive power to regulate interstate commerce and admiralty . . . and that the Act was applicable in state courts and pre-emptive of state laws hostile to arbitration . . . Relying upon these background principles and upon the evident reach of the words "involving commerce," the Court interpreted § 2 as implementing Congress' intent "to exercise [its] commerce power to the full." . . .

The instant case, of course, involves not the basic coverage authorization under § 2 of the Act, but the exemption from coverage under § 1. The exemption clause provides the Act shall not apply "to contracts of employment of seamen, railroad employees, or any other class of workers engaged in foreign or interstate commerce." . . . Most Courts of Appeals conclude the exclusion provision is limited to transportation workers, defined, for instance, as those workers "actually engaged in the movement of goods in interstate commerce." . . . As we stated at the outset, the Court of Appeals for the Ninth Circuit takes a different view and interprets the § 1 exception to exclude all contracts of employment from the reach of the FAA. This comprehensive exemption had been advocated by *amici curiae* in *Gilmer,* where we addressed the question whether a registered securities representative's employment discrimination claim under the Age Discrimination in Employment Act of 1967 . . . could be submitted to arbitration pursuant to an agreement in his securities registration application. Concluding that the application was not a "contract of employment" at all, we found it unnecessary to reach the meaning of § 1. . . . There is no such dispute in this case; while Circuit City argued in its petition for *certiorari* that the employment application signed by Adams was not a "contract of employment," we declined to grant *certiorari* on this point. So the issue reserved in *Gilmer* is presented here.

B

Respondent, at the outset, contends that we need not address the meaning of the § 1 exclusion provision to decide the case in his favor. In his view, an employment contract is not a "contract evidencing a transaction involving interstate commerce" at all, since the word "transaction" in § 2 extends only to commercial contracts. . . . This line of reasoning proves too much, for it would make the § 1 exclusion provision superfluous. If all contracts of employment are beyond the scope of the Act under the § 2 coverage provision, the separate exemption for "contracts of employment of seamen, railroad employees, or any other class of workers engaged in . . . interstate commerce" would be pointless. . . . The proffered interpretation of "evidencing a transaction involving commerce," furthermore, would be inconsistent with *Gilmer* . . . where we held that § 2 required the arbitration of an age discrimination claim based on an agreement in a securities registration application, a dispute that did not arise from a "commercial deal or merchant's sale." Nor could respondent's construction of § 2 be reconciled with the expansive reading of those words adopted in *Allied-Bruce* . . . If, then, there is an argument to be made that arbitration agreements in employment contracts are not covered by the Act, it must be premised on the language of the § 1 exclusion provision itself.

Respondent, endorsing the reasoning of the Court of Appeals for the Ninth Circuit that the provision excludes all employment contracts, relies on the asserted breadth of the words "contracts of employment of . . . any other class of workers engaged in ... commerce." Referring to our construction of § 2's coverage provision in *Allied-Bruce*—concluding that the words "involving commerce" evidence the congressional intent to regulate to the full extent of its commerce power—respondent contends § 1's interpretation should have a like reach, thus exempting all employment contracts. The two provisions, it is argued, are coterminous; under this view the "involving commerce" provision brings within the FAA's scope all contracts within the Congress' commerce power, and the "engaged in . . . commerce" language in § 1 in turn exempts from the FAA all employment contracts falling within that authority.

This reading of § 1, however, runs into an immediate and, in our view, insurmountable textual obstacle. Unlike the "involving commerce" language in § 2, the words "any other class of workers engaged in . . . commerce" constitute a residual phrase, following, in the same sentence, explicit reference to "seamen" and "railroad employees." Construing the residual phrase to exclude all employment contracts fails to give independent effect to the statute's enumeration of the specific categories of workers which precedes it; there would be no need for Congress to use the phrases "seamen" and "railroad employees" if those same classes of workers were subsumed within the meaning of the "engaged in . . . commerce" residual clause. The wording of § 1 calls for the application of the maxim *ejusdem generis*, the statutory canon that "where general words follow specific words in a statutory enumeration, the general words are construed to embrace only objects similar in nature to those objects enumerated by the preceding specific words." . . . Under this rule of construction the residual clause should be read to give effect to the terms "seamen" and "railroad employees," and should itself be controlled and defined by reference to the enumerated categories of workers which are recited just before it; the interpretation of the clause pressed by respondent fails to produce these results.

. . . The application of the rule *ejusdem generis* in this case, however, is in full accord with other sound considerations bearing upon the proper interpretation of the clause. For even if the term "engaged in commerce" stood alone in § 1, we would not construe the provision to exclude all contracts of employment from the FAA. . . .

[. . .]

The Court's reluctance to accept contentions that Congress used the words "in commerce" or "engaged in commerce" to regulate to the full extent of its commerce power rests on sound foundation, as it affords objective and consistent significance to the meaning of the words Congress uses when it defines the reach of a statute. To say that the statutory words "engaged in commerce" are subject to variable interpretations depending upon the date of adoption, even a date before the phrase became a term of art, ignores the reason why the formulation became a term of art in the first place: The plain meaning of the words "engaged in commerce" is narrower than the more open-ended formulations "affecting commerce" and "involving commerce." . . . It would be unwieldy for Congress, for the Court, and for litigants to be required to deconstruct statutory Commerce Clause phrases depending upon the year of a particular statutory enactment.

In rejecting the contention that the meaning of the phrase "engaged in commerce" in § 1 of the FAA should be given a broader construction than justified by its evident language simply because it was enacted in 1925 rather than 1938, we do not mean to suggest that statutory jurisdictional formulations "necessarily have a uniform meaning whenever used by Congress." . . . As the Court has noted: "The judicial task in marking out the extent to which Congress has exercised its constitutional power over commerce is not that of devising an abstract formula." . . . We must, of course, construe the "engaged in commerce" language in the FAA with reference to the statutory context in which it is found and in a manner consistent with the FAA's purpose. These considerations, however, further compel that the § 1 exclusion provision be afforded a narrow construction. As discussed above, the location of the phrase "any other class of workers engaged in . . . commerce" in a residual provision, after specific categories of workers have been enumerated, undermines any attempt to give the provision a sweeping, open-ended construction. And the fact that the provision is contained in a statute that "seeks broadly to overcome judicial hostility to arbitration agreements," . . . which the Court concluded in *Allied-Bruce* counseled in favor of an expansive reading of § 2, gives no reason to abandon the precise reading of a provision that exempts contracts from the FAA's coverage.

In sum, the text of the FAA forecloses the construction of § 1 followed by the Court of Appeals in the case under review, a construction which would exclude all employment contracts from the FAA. While the historical arguments respecting Congress' understanding of its power in 1925 are not insubstantial, this fact alone does not give us basis to adopt, "by judicial decision rather than amendatory legislation," . . . an expansive construction of the FAA's exclusion provision that goes beyond the meaning of the words Congress used. While it is of course possible to speculate that Congress might have chosen a different jurisdictional formulation had it known that the Court would soon embrace a less restrictive reading of the Commerce Clause, the text of § 1 precludes interpreting the exclusion provision to defeat the language of § 2 as to all employment contracts. Section 1 exempts from the FAA only contracts of employment of transportation workers.

C

As the conclusion we reach today is directed by the text of § 1, we need not assess the legislative history of the exclusion provision. . . . We do note, however, that the legislative record on the § 1 exemption is quite sparse. . . .

[. . .]

We see no paradox in the congressional decision to exempt the workers over whom the commerce power was most apparent. To the contrary, it is a permissible inference that the employment contracts of the classes of workers in § 1 were excluded from the FAA precisely because of Congress' undoubted authority to govern the employment relationships at issue by the enactment of statutes specific to them. By the time the FAA was passed, Congress had already enacted federal legislation providing for the arbitration of disputes between seamen and their employers . . . When the FAA was adopted, moreover, grievance procedures existed for railroad employees under federal law . . . and the passage of a more comprehensive statute providing for the mediation and arbitration of railroad labor disputes was imminent. . . . It is reasonable to assume that Congress excluded "seamen" and "railroad employees" from the FAA for the simple reason that it did not wish to unsettle established or developing statutory dispute resolution schemes covering specific workers.

As for the residual exclusion of "any other class of workers engaged in foreign or interstate commerce," Congress' demonstrated concern with transportation workers and their necessary role in the free flow of goods explains the linkage to the two specific, enumerated types of workers identified in the preceding portion of the sentence. It would be rational for Congress to ensure that workers in general would be covered by the provisions of the FAA, while reserving for itself more specific legislation for those engaged in transportation. . . . Indeed, such legislation was soon to follow, with the amendment of the Railway Labor Act in 1936 to include air carriers and their employees. . . .

III

Various *amici,* including the attorneys general of 22 States, object that the reading of the § 1 exclusion provision adopted today intrudes upon the policies of the separate States. They point out that, by requiring arbitration agreements in most employment contracts to be covered by the FAA, the statute in effect pre-empts those state employment laws which restrict or limit the ability of employees and employers to enter into arbitration agreements. It is argued that States should be permitted, pursuant to their traditional role in regulating employment relationships, to prohibit employees like respondent from contracting away their right to pursue state-law discrimination claims in court.

It is not our holding today which is the proper target of this criticism. The line of argument is relevant instead to the Court's decision in *Southland Corp. v. Keating* . . . holding that Congress intended the FAA to apply in state courts, and to pre-empt state antiarbitration laws to the contrary. . . .

[. . .]

Furthermore, for parties to employment contracts[,] . . . there are real benefits to the enforcement of arbitration provisions. We have been clear in rejecting the supposition that the advantages of the arbitration process somehow disappear when transferred to the employment context. . . . Arbitration agreements allow parties to avoid the costs of litigation, a benefit that may be of particular importance in employment litigation, which often involves smaller sums of money than disputes concerning commercial contracts. These litigation costs to parties (and the accompanying burden to the Courts) would be compounded by the difficult choice-of-law questions that are often presented in disputes arising from the employment relationship . . . and the necessity of bifurcation of proceedings in those cases where state law precludes arbitration of certain types of employment claims but not others. The considerable complexity and uncertainty that the construction of § 1 urged by respondent would introduce into the enforceability of arbitration agreements in employment contracts would call into doubt the efficacy of alternative dispute resolution procedures adopted by many of the Nation's employers, in the process undermining the FAA's proarbitration purposes and "breeding litigation from a statute that seeks to avoid it." . . . The Court has been quite specific in holding that arbitration agreements can be enforced under the FAA without contravening the policies of congressional enactments giving employees specific protection against discrimination prohibited by federal law; as we noted in *Gilmer*, "by agreeing to arbitrate a statutory claim, a party does not forgo the substantive rights afforded by the statute; it only submits to their resolution in an arbitral, rather than a judicial, forum." . . .

For the foregoing reasons, the judgment of the Court of Appeals for the Ninth Circuit is reversed, and the case is remanded for further proceedings consistent with this opinion.

It is so ordered.

JUSTICE STEVENS, with whom JUSTICE GINSBURG and JUSTICE BREYER join, and with whom JUSTICE SOUTER joins as to Parts II and III, dissenting.

JUSTICE SOUTER has cogently explained why the Court's parsimonious construction of § 1 of the Federal Arbitration Act (FAA or Act) is not consistent with its expansive reading of § 2. I join his opinion, but believe that the Court's heavy reliance on the views expressed by the Courts of

Appeals during the past decade makes it appropriate to comment on three earlier chapters in the history of this venerable statute.

I

Section 2 of the FAA makes enforceable written agreements to arbitrate "in any maritime transaction or a contract evidencing a transaction involving commerce." . . . If we were writing on a clean slate, there would be good reason to conclude that neither the phrase "maritime transaction" nor the phrase "contract evidencing a transaction involving commerce" was intended to encompass employment contracts.

The history of the Act, which is extensive and well-documented, makes clear that the FAA was a response to the refusal of courts to enforce commercial arbitration agreements, which were commonly used in the maritime context. . . .

[. . .]

Nevertheless, the original bill was opposed by representatives of organized labor, most notably the president of the International Seamen's Union of America, because of their concern that the legislation might authorize federal judicial enforcement of arbitration clauses in employment contracts and collective-bargaining agreements. In response to those objections, the chairman of the ABA committee that drafted the legislation emphasized at a Senate Judiciary Subcommittee hearing that "it is not intended that this shall be an act referring to labor disputes at all," but he also observed that "if your honorable committee should feel that there is any danger of that, they should add to the bill the following language, 'but nothing herein contained shall apply to seamen or any class of workers in interstate and foreign commerce.' " . . . Similarly, another supporter of the bill, then Secretary of Commerce Herbert Hoover, suggested that "if objection appears to the inclusion of workers' contracts in the law's scheme, it might be well amended by stating 'but nothing herein contained shall apply to contracts of employment of seamen, railroad employees, or any other class of workers engaged in interstate or foreign commerce.' " . . . The legislation was reintroduced in the next session of Congress with Secretary Hoover's exclusionary language added to § 1, and the amendment eliminated organized labor's opposition to the proposed law.

That amendment is what the Court construes today. History amply supports the proposition that it was an uncontroversial provision that merely confirmed the fact that no one interested in the enactment of the FAA ever intended or expected that § 2 would apply to employment contracts. It is particularly ironic, therefore, that the amendment has provided the Court with its sole justification for refusing to give the text of § 2 a natural reading. Playing ostrich to the substantial history behind the amendment. . . . ("We need not assess the legislative history of the exclusion provision"), the Court reasons in a vacuum that "if all contracts of employment are beyond the scope of the Act under the § 2 coverage provision, the separate exemption" in § 1 "would be pointless" . . . But contrary to the Court's suggestion, it is not "pointless" to adopt a clarifying amendment in order to eliminate opposition to a bill. Moreover, the majority's reasoning is squarely contradicted by the Court's approach in *Bernhardt v. Polygraphic Co. of America* . . . where the Court concluded that an employment contract did not "evidence 'a transaction involving commerce' within the meaning of § 2 of the Act," and therefore did not "reach the further question whether in any event petitioner would be included in 'any other class of workers' within the exceptions of § 1 of the Act."

The irony of the Court's reading of § 2 to include contracts of employment is compounded by its cramped interpretation of the exclusion inserted into § 1. As proposed and enacted, the exclusion fully responded to the concerns of the Seamen's Union and other labor organizations that § 2 might encompass employment contracts by expressly exempting not only the labor agreements of "seamen" and "railroad employees," but also of *"any other class of workers* engaged in foreign or interstate commerce." . . . (emphasis added). Today, however, the Court fulfills the original—and originally unfounded—fears of organized labor by essentially rewriting the text of § 1 to exclude the employment contracts *solely* of "seamen, railroad employees, or any other class of *transportation* workers engaged in foreign or interstate commerce." . . . In contrast, whether one views the legislation before or after the amendment to § 1, it is clear that it was not intended to apply to employment contracts at all.

[. . .]

III

Times have changed. Judges in the 19th century disfavored private arbitration. The 1925 Act was intended to overcome that attitude, but a number of this Court's cases decided in the last several decades have pushed the pendulum far beyond a neutral attitude and endorsed a policy that strongly favors private arbitration. The strength of that policy preference has been echoed in the recent Court of Appeals opinions on which the Court relies. In a sense, therefore, the Court is standing on its own shoulders when it points to those cases as the basis for its narrow construction of the exclusion in § 1. There is little doubt that the Court's interpretation of the Act has given it a scope far beyond the expectations of the Congress that enacted it. . . .

It is not necessarily wrong for the Court to put its own imprint on a statute. But when its refusal to look beyond the raw statutory text enables it to disregard countervailing considerations that were expressed by Members of the enacting Congress and that remain valid today, the Court misuses its authority. As the history of the legislation indicates, the potential disparity in bargaining power between individual employees and large employers was the source of organized labor's opposition to the Act, which it feared would require courts to enforce unfair employment contracts. That same concern . . . underlay Congress' exemption of contracts of employment from mandatory arbitration. When the Court simply ignores the interest of the unrepresented employee, it skews its interpretation with its own policy preferences.

[. . .]

I respectfully dissent.

JUSTICE SOUTER, with whom JUSTICE STEVENS, JUSTICE GINSBURG, and JUSTICE BREYER join, dissenting.

Section 2 of the Federal Arbitration Act (FAA or Act) provides for the enforceability of a written arbitration clause in "any maritime transaction or a contract evidencing a transaction involving commerce," . . . while § 1 exempts from the Act's coverage "contracts of employment of seamen, railroad employees, or any other class of workers engaged in foreign or interstate commerce." Whatever the understanding of Congress's implied admiralty power may have been when the Act was passed in 1925, the commerce power was then thought to be far narrower than we have subsequently come to see it. As a consequence, there are two quite different ways of reading the scope of the Act's provisions. One way would be to say, for example, that the coverage provision extends only to those contracts "involving commerce" that were understood to be covered in 1925; the other would be to read it as exercising Congress's commerce jurisdiction in its modern conception in the same way it was thought to implement the more limited view of the Commerce Clause in 1925. The first possibility would result in a statutory ambit frozen in time, behooving Congress to amend the statute whenever it desired to expand arbitration clause enforcement beyond its scope in 1925; the second would produce an elastic reach, based on an understanding that Congress used language intended to go as far as Congress could go, whatever that might be over time.

In *Allied-Bruce Terminix Cos. v. Dobson* . . . we decided that the elastic understanding of § 2 was the more sensible way to give effect to what Congress intended when it legislated to cover contracts "involving commerce," a phrase that we found an apt way of providing that coverage would extend to the outer constitutional limits under the Commerce Clause. The question here is whether a similarly general phrase in the § 1 exemption, referring to contracts of "any . . . class of workers engaged in foreign or interstate commerce," should receive a correspondingly evolutionary reading, so as to expand the exemption for employment contracts to keep pace with the enhanced reach of the general enforceability provision. . . .

The number of courts arrayed against reading the § 1 exemption in a way that would allow it to grow parallel to the expanding § 2 coverage reflects the fact that this minority view faces two hurdles, each textually based and apparent from the face of the Act. First, the language of coverage (a contract evidencing a transaction "involving commerce") is different from the language of the exemption (a contract of a worker "engaged in . . . commerce"). Second, the "engaged in . . . commerce" catchall phrase in the exemption is placed in the text following more specific exemptions for employment contracts of "seamen" and "railroad employees." The placement possibly indicates that workers who are excused from arbitrating by virtue of the catchall exclusion must resemble seamen and railroad workers, perhaps by being employees who actually handle and move goods as they are shipped interstate or internationally.

Neither hurdle turns out to be a bar, however. The first objection is at best inconclusive and weaker than the grounds to reject it; the second is even more certainly inapposite, for reasons the Court itself has stated but misunderstood.

[. . .]

The Court tries to deflect the anomaly of excluding only carrier contracts by suggesting that Congress used the reference to seamen and rail workers to indicate the class of employees whose employment relations it had already legislated about and would be most likely to legislate about in the future. . . . This explanation, however, does nothing to eliminate the anomaly. On the contrary, the explanation tells us why Congress might have referred specifically to the sea and rail workers; but, if so, it also indicates that Congress almost certainly intended the catchall phrase to be just as broad as its terms, without any interpretive squeeze in the name of *ejusdem generis*.

The very fact, as the Court points out, that Congress already had spoken on the subjects of sailors and rail workers and had tailored the legislation to the particular circumstances of the sea and rail carriers may well have been reason for mentioning them specifically. But making the specific references was in that case an act of special care to make sure that the FAA not be construed to modify the existing legislation so exactly aimed; that was no reason at all to limit the general FAA exclusion from applying to employment contracts that had not been targeted with special legislation. Congress did not need to worry especially about the FAA's effect on legislation that did not exist and was not contemplated. As to workers uncovered by any specific legislation, Congress could write on a clean slate, and what it wrote was a general exclusion for employment contracts within Congress's power to regulate. The Court has understood this point before, holding that the existence of a special reason for emphasizing specific examples of a statutory class can negate any inference that an otherwise unqualified general phrase was meant to apply only to matters *ejusdem generis*. On the Court's own reading of the history, then, the explanation for the catchall is not *ejusdem generis*; instead, the explanation for the specifics is *ex abundanti cautela*, abundance of caution. . . .

Nothing stands in the way of construing the coverage and exclusion clauses together, consistently and coherently. I respectfully dissent.

NOTES AND QUESTIONS

1. In *Epic Systems*, Justice Ginsburg writing for the dissent, challenges the wisdom and rationale of *Adams*.

> The legislative hearings and debate leading up to the FAA's passage evidence Congress' aim to enable merchants of roughly equal bargaining power to enter into binding agreements to arbitrate *commercial* disputes. See, *e.g.*, 65 Cong. Rec. 11080 (1924) (remarks of Rep. Mills) ("This bill provides that where there are commercial contracts and there is disagreement under the contract, the court can [en]force an arbitration agreement in the same way as other portions of the contract."); Joint Hearings on S. 1005 and H. R. 646 before the Subcommittees of the Committees on the Judiciary, 68th Cong., 1st Sess. (1924) (Joint Hearings) (consistently focusing on the need for binding arbitration of commercial disputes).
>
> The FAA's legislative history also shows that Congress did not intend the statute to apply to arbitration provisions in employment contracts. In brief, when the legislation was introduced, organized labor voiced concern. . . . Herbert Hoover, then Secretary of Commerce, suggested that if there were "objection[s]" to including "workers' contracts in the law's scheme," Congress could amend the legislation to say: "but nothing herein contained shall apply to contracts of employment of seamen, railroad employees, or any other class of workers engaged in interstate or foreign commerce." *Id.*, at 14. Congress adopted Secretary Hoover's suggestion virtually verbatim in § 1 of the Act . . .
>
> Congress, it bears repetition, envisioned application of the Arbitration Act to voluntary, negotiated agreements. . . . Congress never endorsed a policy favoring arbitration where one party sets the terms of an agreement while the other is left to "take it or leave it." . . .

Epic Sys. Corp. v. Lewis, 138 S. Ct. 1612, 1643, 200 L.Ed. 2d 889 (2018).

Do you agree with Justice Ginsburg or the majority in *Adams*? What is the best reading of FAA § 1? What is the significance of legislative history? Why does the majority in *Adams* seem to ignore it?

2. Though the holding in *Adams* appears to be settled law, the First Circuit recently held that the term "contracts of employment" for purposes of

Section 1 includes transportation-worker agreements that establish or purport to establish independent-contractor relationships. *Oliveira v. New Prime, Inc.*, 857 F.3d 7, 16 (1st Cir. 2017). The U.S. Supreme Court will be reviewing this decision in its 2019 term. *See* 138 S. Ct. 1164, 200 L.Ed. 2d 313 (2018) (granting review).

Perhaps the more interesting question rasied by *Olivera* is whether a district court or the arbitrator decides the applicability of the FAA § 1 exemption. The First Circuit concluded that "whether the § 1 exemption applies presents a question of 'whether the FAA confers authority on the district court to compel arbitration" and not a question of arbitrability.' " *Oliveira*, 857 F.3d at 14 (citations omitted). The Eighth Circuit has taken the opposite view and find that the applicability of the § 1 exemption is a question of arbitrability that can be delegated to arbitrators. *Green v. SuperShuttle International, Inc.*, 653 F.3d 766 (8th Cir. 2011).

3. In subsequent litigation to *Adams*, the Ninth Circuit—perhaps to express its resistance to the U.S. Supreme Court's decision in *Adams*—held that the contract of a delivery driver who worked for a courier service was not covered by the FAA because it fell within the interstate transportation concept of the employment contract exclusion. A district court, therefore, could not compel arbitration. *See Harden v. Roadway Package Systems, Inc.*, 249 F.3d 1137 (9th Cir. 2001); *see also Palcko v. Airborne Express Inc.*, 372 F.3d 588 (3d Cir. 2004) (although an employment arbitration agreement could not be enforced under FAA § 1, the FAA did not preempt state law and the arbitration agreement could be enforced under state law).

4. As to *Adams* itself, on remand, the Ninth Circuit found the reference to arbitration flawed on another (more doctrinally acceptable) basis: It concluded that Circuit City's arbitration agreement was an unconscionable contract of adhesion and, therefore, unenforceable. As a result, the court reversed the order compelling Adams to arbitrate. The court found that, although federal policy favored arbitration, state contract defenses could still invalidate arbitration agreements. The Dispute Resolution Agreement (DRA) was procedurally unconscionable. Circuit City had greater bargaining power, drafted the contract, and made it a condition of employment. The court also found that the DRA forced employees to arbitrate claims against Circuit City but did not require Circuit City to arbitrate its claims against employees. The court, therefore, determined that the DRA lacked the necessary mutuality of obligation.

The lack of mutuality was compounded by other restrictions: the limitation placed on available damages, the requirement that employees share the arbitration fees, and the strict one-year statute of limitations. Under current federal arbitration law, arbitrating parties must be given basically the same relief that would have been available in court. Moreover, an employee need not pay unreasonable costs and arbitrators' fees in order to engage in arbitration. *See Circuit City Stores, Inc. v. Adams*, 279 F.3d 889 (9th Cir. 2002).

Accord Circuit City Stores, Inc. v. Ahmed, 283 F.3d 1198 (9th Cir. 2002) (the court held that, if an employee is given a meaningful opportunity to opt out of an employer's binding arbitration program and fails to do so, the arbitration agreement is not procedurally unconscionable under California state contract law and the employee can be compelled to arbitrate). The Ninth Circuit focused upon whether the arbitration agreement was procedurally unconscionable. Determining that the agreement was not procedurally unconscionable, the court pointed out that "Ahmed was not presented with a contract of adhesion because he was given the opportunity to opt-out of the Circuit City arbitration program by mailing in a simple one-page form." Ahmed would have been allowed to keep his job if he had chosen not to participate in the arbitration program. The court further stated that the arbitration agreement "lacked any other indicia of procedural unconscionability" because the terms of the agreement were clearly spelled out in the written agreement. The court also noted that the employees had thirty days in which to opt-out and were encouraged to contact counsel or Circuit City representatives before deciding whether to participate in the program. Finally, the court, in refuting Ahmed's claim that he lacked the sophistication to be given a meaningful opportunity to opt-out of the arbitration program, emphasized the general rule that "one who signs a contract cannot [thereafter] complain of unfamiliarity with the language of the instrument."

5. In *Circuit City Stores, Inc. v. Mantor*, 335 F.3d 1101 (9th Cir. 2003), the Ninth Circuit held that an arbitration agreement between Circuit City Stores and an employee was procedurally unconscionable; that provisions of the agreement concerning statute of limitations, class actions, cost-splitting, and the employer's unilateral power to modify or terminate the agreement rendered the arbitration agreement substantively unconscionable; that the filing fee provision of the agreement was also substantively unconscionable despite a waiver provision; and that the agreement was unenforceable in its entirety because the unconscionable provisions were not severable from the remainder of the agreement.

The main issue before the Ninth Circuit was whether the arbitration agreement was unconscionable under California contract law. The court noted that the FAA provides that arbitration agreements "shall be valid, irrevocable and enforceable" except when grounds "exist at law or equity for the revocation of any contract." The court also referred to *Ingle v. Circuit City Stores, Inc.*, 328 F.3d 1165, 1174 n.10 (9th Cir. 2003), in which it stated that federal law "does not supplant state law governing the unconscionability of adhesive contracts." Under California state contract law, unconscionability consists of a lack of meaningful choice in entering a contract or in negotiating its terms. As a result, the terms were unreasonably favorable to one party and oppressive to the other.

The Ninth Circuit held the arbitration agreement procedurally unconscionable because Mantor had no meaningful choice in accepting the arbitration agreement. The court found the terms of the arbitration agreement oppressive. Oppression, the court said, springs "from inequality of bargaining power [that] results in no real negotiation and an absence of meaningful choice." Circuit City had argued that the agreement was not oppressive because Mantor was given an opportunity to "opt-out" of the arbitration program. The court held that, although Mantor was given an "opt-out" form, Circuit City management impliedly and expressly pressured Mantor not to exercise his right. According to the court, when one of the parties possesses far greater bargaining power than the other or when the stronger party pressures, harasses, or compels the other party into entering into a contract, " 'oppression and therefore, procedural unconscionability, are present.' " In the court's view, "A meaningful opportunity to negotiate or reject the terms of a contract must mean something more than an empty choice. At a minimum, a party must have an actual, meaningful, and reasonable choice to exercise that discretion." Mantor had no meaningful choice because he could either participate in the arbitration program or lose his job.

The Ninth Circuit also held that the agreement was substantively unconscionable. Substantive unconscionability, the court said, concerns "the terms of the agreement and whether or not those terms are so one-sided as to shock the conscience." The court found the terms concerning the statute of limitations, class actions, cost-splitting, and the employer's unilateral power to modify or terminate the agreement substantively unconscionable. The Ninth Circuit also held that the Filing Fee/Waiver provision of Circuit City's arbitration agreement was substantively unconscionable. It held the fee waiver rule was "manifestly one-sided" and, therefore, unconscionable because it "(1) provides that an employee must pay an interested party 'for the privilege of bringing a complaint' and (2) assigns Circuit City, an interested party, the responsibility for deciding whether to waive the filing fee." Finally, the court refused to sever the unconscionable provisions. They were too numerous and severance would obligate the court to assume the role of "contract author rather than interpreter."

6. In *Al-Safin v. Circuit City Stores, Inc.*, 394 F.3d 1254 (9th Cir. 2005), the Ninth Circuit reaffirmed its long-standing negative evaluation of Circuit City's Dispute Resolution Rules and Procedures (DRRP) by holding a Circuit City arbitration agreement unconscionable and unenforceable under Washington state contract law. In so doing, it identified the provisions that could render an arbitration agreement unconscionable: Limitations on remedies and class actions, high costs for employees, binding employees exclusively to arbitration while allowing Circuit City to pursue disputes in court and giving Circuit City the right to modify terms at will.

Under Washington state law, a contract clause need only be substantively unconscionable to be unenforceable. Substantive unconscionability refers to the terms themselves; by contrast, procedural unconscionability refers to how the agreement is negotiated and presented. The court of appeals concluded that Circuit City's DRRP "requires employees to forgo essential substantive and procedural rights and that clauses regarding coverage of claims, remedies, arbitration fees, cost-splitting, the statute of limitations, class actions, and modifications, render the agreement excessively one-sided and unconscionable."

In reaching this conclusion, the court relied upon its prior dispositions in *Ingle*, *Mantor*, and *Adams*. The cases involved the same Circuit City DRRP. Moreover, Washington and California law regarding substantive unconscionability were basically the same; each of them used a definition of substantively unconscionability that emphasized that the terms of the contract were so "one-sided" as to "shock the conscience." Additionally, Circuit City's DRRP did not meet *Gilmer*'s minimum requirements that arbitration agreements embody "basic procedural and remedial protections so that claimants can effectively pursue their statutory rights." Circuit City's agreement, the Ninth Circuit said, failed in this regard because it restricted remedies that would be available in a judicial forum.

Handbook Agreements

The decisional law on the validity and enforceability of employment arbitrations has grown dramatically over the past couple of decades. It is becoming clear that the agreement to arbitrate workplace disputes is a self-contained, autonomous contract that governs regardless of whether there is an underlying employment contract documenting the basic relationship between the employer and the employee. An employer and an at-will employee can agree in a written instrument to arbitrate disputes, including statutory discrimination claims, without undermining the at-will status of the employee. The arbitral clause, therefore, stands on its own as a contract and does not affect, and is not affected by, the circumstances of employment. At times, the arbitral clause remains enforceable even though the employment agreement or relationship has expired. The employment arbitration agreement can govern all aspects of the association between the employer and the employee.

The employment arbitration contract can take a variety of forms. In most circumstances, however, these contracts are far removed from the model of mutual, bilateral agreements. Like other mass-market contracts, they are typically adhesive in nature and unilaterally imposed by the employer. Accordingly, many of the same issues regarding mutual assent exist.

One particular and somewhat unique feature of employment arbitration agreements, however, arises when they are imposed through employee handbooks. Though most courts find that arbitration agreements in handbooks may be enforced, there are some wrinkles.

* * *

In *Towles v. United HealthCare Corp.*, 338 S.C. 29, 524 S.E.2d 839 (Ct. App. 1998), United sought to compel the arbitration of a former employee's claim pursuant to the Employee Handbook Acknowledgment Form that had been issued to the employee. The relevant portion of the Acknowledgment Form stated that "[a]rbitration is the final, exclusive and required forum for the resolution of all employment related disputes which are based on legal claim." The court of appeals held that the arbitration provision was a binding arbitration agreement that mandated the use of arbitration as the final and exclusive forum for resolving the employment dispute between Towles, the former employee, and United.

Towles raised a notice-based argument to challenge the enforceability of the Acknowledgment Form as an arbitration agreement. He argued that an employee handbook constituted a contract only if actual notice of the handbook's provisions was provided to the employee. The court rejected the contention, stating that precedent did "not focus on the need for actual notice when an employee handbook creates an employment contract, but rather holds that an employee must receive actual notice when an employer modifies an existing handbook." Further, the court stated that "the law does not impose a duty to explain a document's contents to an individual when the individual can learn the contents from simply reading the document."

The court then examined the Employee Handbook Acknowledgment Form. The court concluded that the Acknowledgment Form created a valid, binding contract requiring arbitration; it constituted a "specific communication of an offer" to Towles which "conditioned his acceptance of the Employment Arbitration Policy as part of his employment contract." Further, the court stated that Towle's continued employment with United amounted to a valid acceptance of the contractual offer.

* * *

In *Dumais v. American Golf Corp.*, 150 F. Supp. 2d 1182 (D.N.M. 2001), the court was asked to determine if an arbitration provision contained in an employment handbook was enforceable. It concluded that the arbitration agreement was illusory because it was executed over two months after the employee began her employment. *Id.* at 1193. The agreement also modified the employment terms—it divested the employee's right to have disputes heard in an Article III court—without consideration. *Id.* Finally, the language of the agreement was inconsistent and unclear, making it unclear whether the commitment to arbitrate was reciprocal. This too potentially rendered the clause illusory and unenforceable. The Tenth Circuit affirmed, noting that "[w]e join other circuits in holding that an arbitration agreement allowing one party the unfettered right to alter the arbitration agreement's existence or its scope is illusory." *See Dumais v. American Golf Corp.*, 299 F.3d 1216, 1220 (10th Cir. 2002).

* * *

In contrast, the Tenth Circuit later held that so long as some limitations were in place, the employer's ability to modify its handbook provisions would not necessarily render an arbitration agreement in the handbook illusory. *Hardin v. First Cash Fin. Servs., Inc.*, 465 F.3d 470 (10th Cir. 2006). In *Hardin*, the arbitration agreement required the employer to provide ten-days' notice to its current employees before amending or terminating the arbitration agreement, and provided that the employer could not amend the agreement if it had actual notice of a potential dispute or claim, nor could it terminate the agreement as to any claims which arose before the termination date. Applying Oklahoma contract law, the court concluded that "[t]he . . . limitations [were] sufficient to avoid rendering the parties' Agreement to arbitrate illusory." *Id.* at 478.

* * *

The New Jersey state Supreme Court, however, refused to enforce an arbitration clause contained in an employee handbook. The employee failed to sign the "Employee Handbook Receipt and Agreement," which would have indicated his express intent to be bound by the terms of the handbook, including the arbitration provision. The court rejected the notion that an employee could impliedly consent to such an agreement and held that, for a waiver of rights provision to be valid, an express and unambiguous manifestation of intent on the part of an employee was needed.

In *Leodori v. CIGNA Corp.*, 175 N.J. 293, 814 A.2d 1098 (2003), Leodori brought suit against his employer alleging violations of the New Jersey Conscientious Employee Protection Act. Prior to his dismissal, Leodori had been employed as in-house counsel. In 1994, almost a year before Leodori began his employment, the company instituted an arbitration program for resolving employment disputes. A handbook was distributed to employees at several times. In 1998, the company distributed an updated handbook, containing specific language regarding arbitration. Two acknowledgment forms also accompanied this handbook—a receipt form and a second form entitled "Employee Handbook Receipt and Agreement." The former simply acknowledged that employees had received their copy of the July 1998 employee handbook. Leodori signed this form in September 1998. The latter form contained language reiterating that the employee had received the handbook, but also stated that employees agreed to two further provisions: (1) that their employment could be terminated at any time, and (2) that the employees would use CIGNA's internal and external dispute resolution procedures to resolve claims against the company rather than a court or government agency. Leodori did not sign this second form.

Leodori alleged that he was dismissed from his job because he engaged in whistleblowing. He filed a complaint in the New Jersey courts. The action was dismissed and then reinstituted. CIGNA appealed and the New Jersey state Supreme Court granted certifications.

In an unanimous decision, the high court affirmed the appellate ruling that Leodori be allowed to proceed in court. In reaching its decision, the court emphasized that state law could not impose more burdensome requirements for the formation of arbitration agreements than for the formation of other contracts. Also, a waiver of rights provision must clearly and unambiguously demonstrate that an employee has agreed to arbitrate any disputed claim.

To determine whether Leodori agreed to arbitrate his CEPA claims, the court asked two questions: (1) did the waiver of rights provision in the handbook clearly reflect an intention to arbitrate a CEPA claim; and, if so, (2) did the evidence indicate that Leodori clearly agreed to such a provision? The court found the language of the waiver of rights clause sufficient to include all applicable federal and state law claims, but not to compel arbitration.

The court thereby rejected CIGNA's contention that Leodori's receipt of the handbook and continued employment constituted an implied agreement to abide by the arbitration policy. The court held that an employee's implied consent to a waiver of rights provision was not sufficient and that a valid waiver only results from an "explicit, affirmative agreement that unmistakably reflects the employee's assent" to the waiver provision. The court concluded that, without Leodori's signature on the "Employee Receipt and Agreement," it could not enforce the arbitration provision unless it found some other affirmative assent on Leodori's part to be bound by the arbitration provision. While the court agreed with the company's assertion that Leodori was aware of the arbitration policy (as it was publicized in numerous documents distributed by the defendant), it stated that it could not find evidence that he intended to be bound by it. Absent such a finding, the court felt constrained to conclude that the record did not demonstrate that Leodori had surrendered his statutory rights knowingly and voluntarily.

CIGNA asserted that the court's holdings contradicted the FAA. The company also expressed concern that the court's decision would drastically alter an employer's ability to use arbitration agreements as a means of workplace dispute resolution. The court rejected both arguments stating that it was merely requiring employee acknowledgment in the form of a signature and that the employer obtain a clear indication of the intent to be bound by the employee. The resources necessary to fulfill these requirements were neither impractical nor excessive.

* * *

Similarly, a Pennsylvania superior court ruled that employees who sign an acknowledgment form are not bound by an arbitration agreement contained in an employee handbook when the totality of the circumstances makes clear that the agreement is unenforceable. In *Quiles v. Financial Group, Inc.*, 879 A.2d 281 (Pa. Super. Ct. 2005), Quiles sued Dollar for wrongful termination. Dollar sought arbitration pursuant to the company's Dispute Resolution Program described in the employee handbook. In addition, Dollar argued that Quiles signed the acknowledgment form, which stated "she had received . . . and carefully read this handbook . . . before signing below."

The court held that, because of the totality of the circumstances, Quiles had not "knowingly and voluntarily" accepted the terms of the agreement; thus, the contract was unenforceable. The court considered the following factors: Although the arbitration process was described in the employee handbook, Quiles never received or saw a copy of the handbook; Quiles and other employees were not provided with a copy of the handbook when they requested one; Quiles was from Puerto Rico and had difficulty with English; the acknowledgment form merely mentioned that the company had provisions relating to arbitration, but failed to provide a substantive explanation of the arbitration provision; and, lastly, Quiles was pressured into signing the form by her manager.

The Allocation of Costs in Employment Arbitration Agreements

Cost-splitting provisions can also make employment arbitration agreements suspect. The payment of costs by the employee creates a barrier to the accessibility of the arbitral remedy. Some courts have found that even the partial allocation of costs to the employee can render the agreement substantively unconscionable. Once the defective provision is identified and combined with a lack of mutuality and the employer's unilateral ability to modify the terms of the agreement, severance is excluded as a means of salvaging the arbitral clause.

In the California decisional law, the allocation of costs has special significance: "[A]n employee seeking to vindicate unwaivable [public law] rights may not be compelled to pay forum costs that are unique to arbitration." *Armendariz v. Foundation Health Psychcare Services, Inc.*, 24 Cal.4th 83, 99 Cal.Rptr.2d 745, 6 P.3d 669, 703 (2000). The contemplated rights are created by California legislation (*e.g.*, the Fair Employment and Housing Act [FEHA]). The California state Supreme Court in *Armendariz* ruled that arbitration agreements that affect such rights "must be subject to particular scrutiny"; the decision in *Little v. Auto Stiegler, Inc.*, 29 Cal.4th 1064, 130 Cal.Rptr.2d 892, 63 P.3d 979 (2003), extended the *Armendariz* ruling to non-statutory rights. Moreover, even if an arbitration agreement satisfies the requirements in *Armendariz*, it could still be unconscionable. In *Abramson v. Juniper Networks, Inc.*, 115 Cal.App.4th 638, 9 Cal.Rptr.3d 422 (2004), a California court of appeal held an employment arbitration agreement involving unwaivable, nonstatutory public law rights unenforceable because the cost-sharing provision required the employee to pay half of the costs of arbitration. "When an employer imposes arbitration as a condition of employment, the arbitration agreement or arbitration process cannot generally require the employee to bear any *type* of expense that the employee would not be required to bear if he or she were free to bring the action in court."

In *Cole v. Burns Int'l Security Services*, 105 F.3d 1465 (D.C. Cir. 1997), the court held that the payment of arbitral costs by the employer was instrumental to the enforceability of a contract for the arbitration of workplace disputes. In fact, to render an otherwise unenforceable agreement valid, the employer was obligated to pay all of the costs for arbitration. The D.C. Circuit seemed to reason that contract unfairness was permissible as long as the culprit paid for it. The fact of the case indicate clearly the equity dilemma that was at the core of the litigation:

[. . .]

Clinton Cole used to work as a security guard at Union Station in Washington, D.C. for a company called LaSalle and Partners ("LaSalle"). In 1991, Burns Security took over LaSalle's contract to provide security at Union Station and required all LaSalle employees to sign a "Pre-Dispute Resolution Agreement" in order to obtain employment with Burns. The Pre-Dispute Resolution Agreement ("agreement" or "contract"), in relevant part, provides:

> In consideration of the Company employing you, you and the Company each agrees that, in the event either party (or its representatives, successors or assigns) brings an action in a court of competent jurisdiction relating to your recruitment, employment with, or termination of employment from the Company, the plaintiff in such action agrees to waive his, her or its right to a trial by jury, and further agrees that no demand, request or motion will be made for trial by jury.
>
> In consideration of the Company employing you, you further agree that, in the event that you seek relief in a court of competent jurisdiction for a dispute covered by this Agreement, the Company may, at any time within 60 days of the service of your complaint upon the Company, at its option, require all or part of the dispute to be arbitrated by one arbitrator in accordance with the rules of the American Arbitration Association. You agree that the option to arbitrate any dispute is governed by the Federal Arbitration Act, and fully enforceable. You understand and agree that, if the

> Company exercises its option, any dispute arbitrated will be heard solely by the arbitrator, and not by a court.
>
> This pre-dispute resolution agreement will cover all matters directly or indirectly related to your recruitment, employment or termination of employment by the Company; including, but not limited to, claims involving laws against discrimination whether brought under federal and/or state law, and/or claims involving co-employees but excluding Worker's Compensation Claims.
>
> The right to a trial, and to a trial by jury, is of value.
>
> YOU MAY WISH TO CONSULT AN ATTORNEY PRIOR TO SIGNING THIS AGREEMENT. IF SO, TAKE A COPY OF THIS FORM WITH YOU. HOWEVER, YOU WILL NOT BE OFFERED EMPLOYMENT UNTIL THIS FORM IS SIGNED AND RETURNED BY YOU.

. . . On August 5, 1991, Cole signed the agreement and began working for Burns.

In October 1993, Burns Security fired Cole. After filing charges with the Equal Employment Opportunity Commission, Cole filed the instant complaint in the United States District Court for the District of Columbia, alleging racial discrimination, harassment based on race, retaliation for his writing a letter of complaint regarding sexual harassment of a subordinate employee by another supervisor at Burns, and intentional infliction of emotional distress. Burns moved to compel arbitration of the dispute and to dismiss Cole's complaint pursuant to the terms of the contract.

The District Court found that the arbitration agreement clearly covered Cole's claims. The court also rejected Cole's suggestions (1) that the Pre-Dispute Resolution Agreement was excluded from coverage under the Federal Arbitration Act under 9 U.S.C. § 1, and (2) that the agreement was an unenforceable and unconscionable contract of adhesion. As a result, the trial court granted Burns Security's motion to compel arbitration and dismissed Cole's complaint. . . .

* * *

After extensive discussion and reasoning, the court reaches its cryptic holding:

> In sum, we hold that Cole could not be required to agree to arbitrate his public law claims as a condition of employment if the arbitration agreement required him to pay all or part of the arbitrator's fees and expenses. In light of this holding, we find that the arbitration agreement in this case is valid and enforceable. We do so because we interpret the agreement as requiring Burns Security to pay all of the arbitrator's fees necessary for a full and fair resolution of Cole's statutory claims.

It seems that the court lacked confidence in its own determination. In her concurring-dissenting opinion, Judge LeCraft Henderson stated: "[I]f the majority believes that the arbitration agreement was reached under duress or that it is unconscionable, it should say so straight out and declare it unenforceable."

NOTES AND QUESTIONS

1. You should evaluate the pre-dispute resolution agreement imposed by Burns Int'l Security Services. The company's objective is to avoid jury trials and to maintain its own option to avoid judicial litigation altogether. It includes an admonishment that prospective employees should agree to these conditions only upon the basis of informed consent.

Is there any balance to the agreement or mutuality to the contemplated exchange? Why would the company seek to eliminate a prospective employee's litigation leverage except to compromise the employee's rights?

2. Throughout its discussion, the court appears preoccupied with the parties' payment of arbitrator fees. In doing so, is the court advancing a legal value? Is it expressing in an indirect fashion its misgivings about the validity of the agreement? The court reasons that obliging employees to pay all or part of the arbitrators' fee would amount to a "*de facto* forfeiture of employee's statutory rights." Why should the payment of arbitrator fees be more significant in this regard than the agreement itself? While litigants do not pay judges' salaries directly, is that factor the most critical difference between arbitral and judicial adjudication?

3. The court expresses some level of confidence in the integrity of the arbitration process and arbitrators. The court implies that the availability of judicial review of awards legitimizes the arbitration agreement in *Cole*. How persuasive is that argument? It also admonishes arbitrators to adapt to their functions in resolving workplace disputes, presumably because of the importance of the statutory rights that are at stake. It further states that it is "misguided to mourn" the U.S. Supreme Court's doctrine on the arbitrability of statutory rights. How do you interpret these remarks?

In a more cogent assessment of the cost factor in *Shankle v. B-G Maintenance Management of Colorado, Inc.*, 163 F.3d 1230 (10th Cir. 1999), the U.S. Court of Appeals for the Tenth Circuit ruled that an arbitration agreement was unenforceable when it functioned as a condition of employment or of continued employment and required the employee to pay a prohibitively expensive part of the fees for arbitration. In the court's view, the agreement, as written, deprived the employee of any remedy by prohibiting recourse to the courts and by making arbitration unaffordable.

Matthew Shankle was a shift manager for B-G Maintenance Management of Colorado, Inc. B-G required Shankle to sign an arbitration agreement as a condition of continued employment. Under the agreement, the parties substituted arbitration for judicial recourse. In addition, the agreement provided that Shankle would pay half of the arbitrator's fee.

When B-G terminated Shankle, he filed a demand for arbitration. After receiving the arbitrator's fee arrangements, Shankle canceled the arbitration and filed suit under Title VII of the Civil Rights Act of 1964. B-G moved to compel arbitration, but the district court and the Tenth Circuit ruled that the arbitration agreement was invalid because it "actually prevent[ed] an individual from effectively vindicating his or her statutory rights." The court emphasized that, if an agreement prohibits the use of the judicial forum for a statutory claim, it must provide "an effective and reasonable alternative forum." Because so few employees could afford to pay their share of the fees, the use of arbitration was a limited, even useless remedy. The court dismissed B-G's claim that fee-splitting promoted neutrality. Even if fee-splitting did promote neutrality, that benefit was "substantially outweighed" by the restrictions placed on the employee's right of recourse.

In late 2000, the U.S. Supreme Court rendered its decision in *Green Tree Financial Corp.—Alabama v. Randolph*, 531 U.S. 79 (2000). In its opinion, the Court—speaking through Chief Justice Rehnquist—addressed the impact of arbitral costs upon the validity of arbitration agreements. In contrast to the ruling in *Cole* and *Armendariz*, the Court held—in a divided segment of its opinion—that the fact that a consumer bears some of the costs of the arbitral process "alone is plainly insufficient to render [the arbitration agreement] unenforceable. . . . To invalidate the agreement would undermine the 'liberal federal policy favoring arbitration agreements' . . . [and] would conflict with [this Court's holdings, for example,] . . . that the party resisting arbitration bears the burden of proving that Congress intended to preclude arbitration of the statutory claims at issue. . . . Thus, a party seeking to invalidate an arbitration agreement on the ground that arbitration would be prohibitively expensive bears the burden of showing the likelihood of incurring such costs. Randolph did not meet that burden."

The members of the Court were quite divided on this issue. The ruling appears to have been decided by a slim 5 to 4 majority. The emerging view that argued that the allocation of the costs was a critical factor in determining the legitimacy of the reference to arbitration, as previously articulated in *Cole, Shankle*, and *Armendariz*, was clearly chilled by the holding in *Green Tree*. If the costs of arbitration were burdensome, the party being burdened did not get a pass, but rather needed to establish the existence and the extent of the financial burden. What was important to the majority of the Court in *Green Tree* was preserving the right to engage in arbitration, not to create and enlarge due process exceptions to it.

The concurring and dissenting opinions concluded that the lower court opinion should have been vacated and remanded for "closer consideration of the arbitration forum's [financial] accessibility." According to Justice Ginsburg, "As I see it, the case in its current posture is not ripe for [the majority's] disposition." Justice Ginsburg emphasized the disparity of position between the parties, the form contract presented on a take-it-or-leave-it basis, and Green Tree's position as a repeat player in arbitration. She concluded that "the Court . . . reached out prematurely to resolve the matter in the lender's favor."

GREEN TREE FINANCIAL CORP.—ALA. V. RANDOLPH

531 U.S. 79, 121 S.Ct. 513, 148 L.Ed.2d 373 (2000).

(footnotes omitted)

CHIEF JUSTICE REHNQUIST delivered the opinion of the Court.

In this case we first address whether an order compelling arbitration and dismissing a party's underlying claims is a "final decision with respect to an arbitration" within the meaning of § 16 of the Federal Arbitration Act, 9 U.S.C. § 16, and thus is immediately appealable pursuant to that Act. Because we decide that question in the affirmative, we also address the question whether an arbitration agreement that does not mention arbitration costs and fees is unenforceable because it fails to affirmatively protect a party from potentially steep arbitration costs. We conclude that an arbitration agreement's silence with respect to such matters does not render the agreement unenforceable.

I

Respondent Larketta Randolph purchased a mobile home from Better Cents Home Builders, Inc., in Opelika, Alabama. She financed this purchase through petitioners Green Tree Financial Corporation and its wholly owned subsidiary, Green Tree Financial Corp.—Alabama. Petitioners' Manufactured Home Retail Installment Contract and Security Agreement required that Randolph buy Vendor's Single Interest insurance, which protects the vendor or lienholder against the costs of repossession in the event of default. The agreement also provided that all disputes arising from, or relating to, the contract, whether arising under case law or statutory law, would be resolved by binding arbitration.

Randolph later sued petitioners, alleging that they violated the Truth in Lending Act (TILA) . . . by failing to disclose as a finance charge the Vendor's Single Interest insurance requirement. She later amended her complaint to add a claim that petitioners violated the Equal Credit Opportunity Act . . . by requiring her to arbitrate her statutory causes of action. She brought this action on behalf of a similarly situated class. In lieu of an answer, petitioners filed a motion to compel arbitration, to stay the action, or, in the alternative, to dismiss. The District Court granted petitioners' motion to compel arbitration, denied the motion to stay, and dismissed Randolph's claims with prejudice. The District Court also denied her request to certify a class. . . . She requested reconsideration, asserting that she lacked the resources to arbitrate and as a result, would have to forgo her claims against petitioners.... The District Court denied reconsideration.... Randolph appealed.

The Court of Appeals for the Eleventh Circuit first held that it had jurisdiction to review the District Court's order because that order was a final decision.... The Court of Appeals looked to § 16 of the Federal Arbitration Act (FAA) ... which governs appeal from a District Court's arbitration order, and specifically § 16(a)(3), which allows appeal from "a final decision with respect to an arbitration that is subject to this title." The Court determined that a final, appealable order within the meaning of the FAA is one that disposes of all the issues framed by the litigation, leaving nothing to be done but execute the order. The Court of Appeals found the District Court's order within that definition.

The court then determined that the arbitration agreement failed to provide the minimum guarantees that respondent could vindicate her statutory rights under the TILA. Critical to this determination was the court's observation that the arbitration agreement was silent with respect to payment of filing fees, arbitrators' costs, and other arbitration expenses. On that basis, the court held that the agreement to arbitrate posed a risk that respondent's ability to vindicate her statutory rights would be undone by "steep" arbitration costs, and therefore was unenforceable. We granted *certiorari* ... and we now affirm the Court of Appeals with respect to the first conclusion, and reverse it with respect to the second.

II

[. . .]

III

We now turn to the question whether Randolph's agreement to arbitrate is unenforceable because it says nothing about the costs of arbitration, and thus fails to provide her protection from potentially substantial costs of pursuing her federal statutory claims in the arbitral forum. Section 2 of the FAA provides that "[a] written provision in any maritime transaction or a contract evidencing a transaction involving commerce to settle by arbitration a controversy thereafter arising out of such contract ... shall be valid, irrevocable, and enforceable, save upon such grounds as exist at law or in equity for the revocation of any contract." ... In considering whether respondent's agreement to arbitrate is unenforceable, we are mindful of the FAA's purpose "to reverse the longstanding judicial hostility to arbitration agreements ... and to place arbitration agreements upon the same footing as other contracts." ...

In light of that purpose, we have recognized that federal statutory claims can be appropriately resolved through arbitration, and we have enforced agreements to arbitrate that involve such claims.... We have likewise rejected generalized attacks on arbitration that rest on "suspicion of arbitration as a method of weakening the protections afforded in the substantive law to would-be complainants." . . . These cases demonstrate that even claims arising under a statute designed to further important social policies may be arbitrated because " 'so long as the prospective litigant effectively may vindicate [his or her] statutory cause of action in the arbitral forum,' " the statute serves its functions. . . .

In determining whether statutory claims may be arbitrated, we first ask whether the parties agreed to submit their claims to arbitration, and then ask whether Congress has evinced an intention to preclude a waiver of judicial remedies for the statutory rights at issue. . . . In this case, it is undisputed that the parties agreed to arbitrate all claims relating to their contract, including claims involving statutory rights. Nor does Randolph contend that the TILA evinces an intention to preclude a waiver of judicial remedies. She contends instead that the arbitration agreement's silence with respect to costs and fees creates a "risk" that she will be required to bear prohibitive arbitration costs if she pursues her claims in an arbitral forum, and thereby forces her to forgo any claims she may have against petitioners. Therefore, she argues, she is unable to vindicate her statutory rights in arbitration. . . .

It may well be that the existence of large arbitration costs could preclude a litigant such as Randolph from effectively vindicating her federal statutory rights in the arbitral forum. But the record does not show that Randolph will bear such costs if she goes to arbitration. Indeed, it contains hardly any information on the matter. As the Court of Appeals recognized, "we lack . . . information about how claimants fare under Green Tree's arbitration clause." . . . The record reveals only the arbitration agreement's silence on the subject, and that fact alone is plainly insufficient to render it unenforceable. The "risk" that Randolph will be saddled with prohibitive costs is too speculative to justify the invalidation of an arbitration agreement.

To invalidate the agreement on that basis would undermine the "liberal federal policy favoring arbitration agreements." . . . It would also conflict with our prior holdings that the party resisting arbitration bears the burden of proving that the claims at issue are unsuitable for arbitration. . . . We have held that the party seeking to avoid arbitration bears the burden of establishing that Congress intended to preclude arbitration of the statutory claims at issue. . . . Similarly, we believe that where, as here, a party seeks to invalidate an arbitration agreement on the ground that arbitration would be prohibitively expensive, that party bears the burden of showing the likelihood of incurring such costs. Randolph did not meet that burden. How detailed the showing of prohibitive expense must be before the party seeking arbitration must come forward with contrary evidence is a matter we need not discuss; for in this case neither during discovery nor when the case was presented on the merits was there any timely showing at all on the point. The Court of Appeals therefore erred in deciding that the arbitration agreement's silence with respect to costs and fees rendered it unenforceable.

The judgment of the Court of Appeals is affirmed in part and reversed in part.

It is so ordered.

JUSTICE GINSBURG, with whom JUSTICE STEVENS and JUSTICE SOUTER join, and with whom JUSTICE BREYER joins as to Parts I and III, concurring in part and dissenting in part.

I

I join Part II of the Court's opinion, which holds that the District Court's order, dismissing all the claims before it, was a "final," and therefore immediately appealable, decision. . . . On the matter the Court airs in Part III . . .—allocation of the costs of arbitration—I would not rule definitively. Instead, I would vacate the Eleventh Circuit's decision, which dispositively declared the arbitration clause unenforceable, and remand the case for closer consideration of the arbitral forum's accessibility.

II

The Court today deals with a "who pays" question, specifically, who pays for the arbitral forum. The Court holds that Larketta Randolph bears the burden of demonstrating that the arbitral forum is financially inaccessible to her. Essentially, the Court requires a party, situated as Randolph is, either to submit to arbitration without knowing who will pay for the forum or to demonstrate up front that the costs, if imposed on her, will be prohibitive. . . . As I see it, the case in its current posture is not ripe for such a disposition.

The Court recognizes that "the existence of large arbitration costs could preclude a litigant such as Randolph from effectively vindicating her federal statutory rights in the arbitral forum." . . . But, the Court next determines, "the party resisting arbitration bears the burden of proving that the claims at issue are unsuitable for arbitration" and "Randolph did not meet that burden." . . . In so ruling, the Court blends two discrete inquiries: First, is the arbitral forum *adequate* to adjudicate the claims at issue; second, is that forum *accessible* to the party resisting arbitration.

Our past decisions deal with the first question, the *adequacy* of the arbitral forum to adjudicate various statutory claims. . . . These decisions hold that the party resisting arbitration bears the burden of establishing the inadequacy of the arbitral forum for adjudication of claims of a particular genre. . . . It does not follow like the night the day, however, that the party resisting arbitration should also bear the burden of showing that the arbitral forum would be financially inaccessible to her.

The arbitration agreement at issue is contained in a form contract drawn by a commercial party and presented to an individual consumer on a take-it-or-leave-it basis. The case on which the Court dominantly relies, *Gilmer*, also involved a nonnegotiated arbitration clause. But the "who pays" question presented in this case did not arise in *Gilmer*. Under the rules that governed in *Gilmer*—those of the New York Stock Exchange—it was the standard practice for securities industry parties, arbitrating employment disputes, to pay all of the arbitrators' fees. . . . Regarding that practice, the Court of Appeals for the District of Columbia Circuit recently commented:

"In *Gilmer*, the Supreme Court endorsed a system of arbitration in which employees are not required to pay for the arbitrator assigned to hear their statutory claims. There is no reason to think that the Court would have approved arbitration in the absence of this arrangement. Indeed, we are unaware of any situation in American jurisprudence in which a beneficiary of a federal statute has been required to pay for the services of the judge assigned to hear her or his case." . . .

III

The form contract in this case provides no indication of the rules under which arbitration will proceed or the costs a consumer is likely to incur in arbitration. Green Tree, drafter of the contract, could have filled the void by specifying, for instance, that arbitration would be governed by the rules of the American Arbitration Association (AAA). Under the AAA's Consumer Arbitration Rules, consumers in small-claims arbitration incur no filing fee and pay only $125 of the total fees charged by the arbitrator. All other fees and costs are to be paid by the business party. . . . Other national arbitration organizations have developed similar models for fair cost and fee allocation. It may be that in this case, as in *Gilmer*, there is a standard practice on arbitrators' fees and expenses, one that fills the blank space in the arbitration agreement. Counsel for Green Tree offered a hint in that direction. . . . But there is no reliable indication in this record that Randolph's claim will be arbitrated under any consumer-protective fee arrangement.

As a repeat player in the arbitration required by its form contract, Green Tree has superior information about the cost to consumers of pursuing arbitration. . . . In these circumstances, it is hardly clear that Randolph should bear the burden of demonstrating up front the arbitral forum's inaccessibility, or that she should be required to submit to arbitration without knowing how much it will cost her.

As I see it, the Court has reached out prematurely to resolve the matter in the lender's favor. If Green Tree's practice under the form contract with retail installment sales purchasers resembles that of the employer in *Gilmer*, Randolph would be insulated from prohibitive costs.

And if the arbitral forum were in this case financially accessible to Randolph, there would be no occasion to reach the decision today rendered by the Court. Before writing a term into the form contract, as the District of Columbia Circuit did . . . or leaving cost allocation initially to each arbitrator, as the Court does, I would remand for clarification of Green Tree's practice.

The Court's opinion, if I comprehend it correctly, does not prevent Randolph from returning to court, post arbitration, if she then has a complaint about cost allocation. If that is so, the issue reduces to when, not whether, she can be spared from payment of excessive costs. Neither certainty nor judicial economy is served by leaving that issue unsettled until the end of the line.

For the reasons stated, I dissent from the Court's reversal of the Eleventh Circuit's decision on the cost question. I would instead vacate and remand for further consideration of the accessibility of the arbitral forum to Randolph.

NOTES AND QUESTIONS

1. The dissent, to some extent, makes the D.C. Circuit's ruling in *Cole* the centerpiece of its reasoning. Does the majority opinion contradict or embrace *Cole*? What could possibly be wrong with requiring proof of financial hardship? Is Justice Ginsburg right to think that Green Tree is a better source of the requisite information?

2. How can you square this case with *Italian Colors*? Although the Court in *Adams* finds that the arbitration agreement at issue is enforceable, it also says that "[i]t may well be that the existence of large arbitration costs could preclude a litigant such as Randolph from effectively vindicating her federal statutory rights in the arbitral forum." In light of the decision in *Italian Colors*, do you think that this possibility still exists? Is *Italian Colors* distinguishable because it does not involve an employment contract and individual civil rights? Should that distinction matter? Are some statutory rights more important than others? Even if the answer is yes, does that necessarily mean that the most important statutory rights will appear in the employment context?

3. The U.S. Fourth Circuit Court of Appeals has held that a fee-splitting provision which divided the cost of arbitration between all parties did not *per se* render an arbitration agreement unenforceable. *See Bradford v. Rockwell Semiconductor Sys., Inc.*, 238 F.3d 549 (4th Cir. 2001) (determining whether such a provision had an impact upon the validity of the arbitration agreement required a case-by-case analysis that focused upon the claimants' ability to pay arbitration fees and costs).

At the end of its analysis, the Fourth Circuit acknowledged that the federal circuits were divided on whether fee-splitting provisions were *per se* invalid. Both the Eleventh Circuit and the D.C. Circuit concluded that "fee-splitting provisions render arbitration agreements unenforceable because the cost of fee splitting deters or prevents employees from vindicating their statutory rights in arbitral forums." The First, Fifth, and Seventh Circuits, however, have refused to endorse that position. These courts prefer to assess the validity of fee-splitting provisions on a case-by-case basis. *See Perez v. Globe Airport Sec. Services, Inc.*, 253 F.3d 1280 (11th Cir. 2001), *reh'g and reh'g en banc denied* (Aug. 16, 2001). *But see LaPrade v. Kidder, Peabody & Co., Inc.*, 246 F.3d 702 (D.C. Cir. 2001) (court found that plaintiff misinterpreted *Cole* to provide "a virtually cost-free alternative to traditional court proceedings"; under *Cole*, an employee may be assessed reasonable forum fees because, even if the employee filed in federal court, he or she would still have to pay some costs; further, plaintiff failed to meet the burden of proof).

In comparing the two approaches, the Fourth Circuit turned to the various circuit interpretations of *Gilmer*. Bradford's argument relied heavily upon the statement in *Cole* that, "under *Gilmer*, arbitration is supposed to be a reasonable substitute for a judicial forum. Therefore, it would undermine Congress' intent to prevent employees who are seeking to vindicate statutory rights from gaining access to a judicial forum and then require them to pay for the services of an arbitrator when they would never be required to pay for a judge in court." The Fourth Circuit adopted the Fifth Circuit's interpretation of *Gilmer*, that "the crucial inquiry under *Gilmer* is whether the particular claimant has an adequate and accessible substitute forum in which to resolve his statutory rights and that *Gilmer* does not call for the conclusion that fee-splitting in all cases deprives the claimant of such a forum." *See Williams v. Cigna Fin. Advisors, Inc.*, 197 F.3d 752 (5th Cir. 1999), *cert. denied*, 529 U.S. 1099 (2000); *Bradford*, 238 F.3d at 556.

Having endorsed the case-by-case analysis, the court found that the employee had "failed to demonstrate any inability to pay the arbitration fees and costs, much less prohibitive financial hardship, to support his assertion that the fee-splitting provision deterred him from arbitrating his statutory claims." The court, therefore, refused to invalidate the arbitration provision because of the fee-splitting requirement. The court invoked language in the *Green Tree* decision to justify its ruling, namely that "some showing of individualized prohibitive expense would be necessary to invalidate an arbitration agreement on the ground that fee-splitting would be prohibitively expensive."

4. In contrast, the Sixth Circuit, in *Morrison v. Circuit City Stores, Inc.*, 317 F.3d 646 (6th Cir. 2003), held that the cost splitting provisions in two separate employment arbitration agreements were unenforceable. In so doing, the court articulated a new standard by which to address the cost issue when a case involved federal antidiscrimination statutes such as Title VII. It rejected the case-by-case approach under which the costs of arbitration and judicial litigation are compared or the impact of costs upon rights protection is assessed by the court after the plaintiff has engaged in arbitration. The Sixth Circuit held that "potential litigants must be given an opportunity, prior to arbitration on the merits, to demonstrate that the potential costs of arbitration are great enough to deter them and similarly situated individuals from seeking to

vindicate their federal statutory rights in the arbitral forum." In the court's view, the focus should be upon a group of similarly situated individuals, rather than solely upon the plaintiff, in order to further the goal of the federal statutes to deter discrimination.

The Sixth Circuit's "similarly situated individuals" approach involves several steps of analysis. The court establishes the group of similarly situated plaintiffs by identifying similar "job description[s] and socioeconomic background[s]." In addition, it looks to the average costs of arbitration when determining whether a group of similarly situated people would be deterred from bringing their claims to arbitration. The court also compares the total arbitration costs to the costs of bringing the same claims to court. For example, while arbitrators' fees represent the additional expense of arbitration, court proceedings generally involve more depositions, interrogatories, and motions for discovery. The critical question is whether the total costs of arbitration might deter a group of similarly situated individuals from going to arbitration.

The court was not willing to discount the cost of arbitration when the arbitration agreement authorized the arbitrator to award attorney's fees to the prevailing party. Moreover, in considering whether a group of similarly situated individuals would be prevented from vindicating their statutory rights in an arbitral forum, the court indicated that higher-level employees, such as managers, would be more likely to have a cost-splitting provision enforced against them as compared to lower level employees.

Applying the "similarly situated individuals" approach to one of the cost-splitting provisions in the instant case, the court held that the provision was unenforceable. Although the cost-splitting provision gave Morrison the choice of paying either $500 or 3% of her yearly salary, whichever amount was greater, the court found that these costs were substantial enough to prohibit Morrison and similarly situated people from bringing their statutory claims to arbitration. The evidence indicated that Morrison earned approximately $54,060 annually; thus, she would have had to pay $1,622 within ninety days of the rendering of the arbitral award. The court felt that this amount was high enough to hinder Morrison and others from bringing a claim to arbitration. The court also noted that the average costs for the arbitration of employment discrimination claims were much higher than court costs.

CHAPTER 7

THE ENFORCEMENT OF DOMESTIC ARBITRAL AWARDS

■ ■ ■

1. INTRODUCTION

Parties frequently comply with arbitral awards. Arbitration constitutes a voluntary choice to opt out of publics courts, and parties are often content to abide by the adjudication that they preferred. If they comply with the award, no further judicial action is needed.

Of course, things are not always so simple. One party—usually the loser—may not be satisfied with the award or the process used to reach it. That party could seek to vacate the award in a court or merely ignore it. In either case, the prevailing party will likely seek to have the award confirmed. When a court enters a judgment confirming an award, "[t]he judgment so entered shall have the same force and effect, in all respects, as . . . a judgment in an action." FAA § 9; *see also* RUAA § 25(a). Confirmation allows the prevailing party to harness the coercive police power of the state for enforcement. This means that the winner may obtain judicial liens on property and garnish income, among other things.

Vacatur and confirmation, then, are two sides of the same coin. When one party seeks to confirm an award, the other usually seeks to vacate it, or vice versa. Both motions to vacate or confirm involve a court reviewing the arbitral award and determining whether it should be enforced.

The enforcement of arbitral awards constitutes a critical part of the arbitration process. The reasons are self-evident: Without the ability to achieve enforcement, arbitration would lose its practical appeal. The process would be reduced to a preliminary, non-binding exercise, the cost of which in terms of time and money would preclude recourse. More delays and protracted proceedings at the enforcement stage would also eviscerate arbitration. By choosing arbitration, parties bargain for economical, expert, efficient, and enforceable private adjudication.

To maintain the benefits of arbitration, courts tend to be deferential to arbitrators and the arbitral process, acknowledging a clear presumption in favor of enforcement. The presumption can be defeated in only those exceptional circumstances in which the arbitrators fail to provide the parties with basic adjudicatory fairness. Accordingly, the post-award review that courts undertake focuses on the arbitral process and not its results.

The first step in the arbitral process involves parties opting out of public courts and committing to resolve their disputes in arbitration. Accordingly, during the review and enforcement stage, courts may review *de novo* whether a party consented to arbitration. *See First Options, Inc. v. Kaplan*, 514 U.S. 938, 943–44 (1995); RUAA § 23(a)(5). To preserve this sort of review, however, a party must promptly object to the arbitrability of the dispute during the arbitration. Failure to object results in a court concluding that the complaining party has waived the objection.

The remaining standards for judicial supervision of arbitral awards are primarily statutory. FAA § 10, mirrored in RUAA § 23, articulates these standards. As construed by courts, the statutory grounds for review and enforcement are neither rigorous nor demanding. Arbitrators must not be corrupt, exceed their powers, or ignore the parties' essential adjudicatory rights or the content of the arbitration agreement. The statutory grounds provide minimal guarantees of procedural due process.

In *Hall Street Associates, L.L.C. v. Mattel, Inc.*, the U.S. Supreme Court made it clear that the standards provided by FAA § 10 are mandatory and exclusive in federal courts—the statutory grounds are the floor and the ceiling of judicial supervision of awards. Federal courts called upon to review an arbitral award must follow the § 10 standards and only those standards.

FAA § 10, however, may not apply directly in state courts. That matters because many arbitral awards cannot be reviewed or enforced in federal court. Recall that the mere fact that FAA § 2 applies does not confer federal question subject matter jurisdiction. *See Moses H. Cone Mem'l Hosp. v. Mercury Constr. Corp.,* 460 U.S. 1, 26, n.32 (1983). Instead, an independent jurisdictional ground must exist for parties to get through the federal courts' door. Parties unable to get into federal court, or who prefer review and enforcement in state courts, must comply with state arbitration law.

A recurring theme throughout this book has been that the FAA preempts inconsistent state regulation of arbitration. With respect to judicial review and enforcement of arbitral awards, however, things could be more complicated. In dicta, the Court in *Hall Street* indicated that the FAA does not preempt state laws with differing standards for post-award review:

> [t]he FAA is not the only way into court for parties wanting review of arbitration awards: they may contemplate enforcement under state statutory or common law, for example, where judicial review of different scope is arguable.

Hall St. Assocs., L.L.C. v. Mattel, Inc., 552 U.S. 576, 590 (2008). In practice, most states' review and enforcement statutes, including those based on the RUAA, are indistinguishable from FAA § 10. Moreover, state courts tend to interpret their statutes in harmony with U.S. Supreme Court's reading of FAA § 10. But, relying on *Hall Street*, several states have recently engaged in more rigorous review than would be required or permitted by FAA § 10.

An additional wrinkle with review and enforcement arises because of "manifest disregard of the law." Courts differ in their specific interpretations of the doctrine, but most agree that, for an award to be vacated, a party must demonstrate that the arbitrator was aware of some applicable legal standard but consciously chose to ignore or disregard it. In federal courts, this common law ground for review and enforcement would seem to be foreclosed by the holding in *Hall Street*. The Court, however, discussed the manifest disregard standard at length in the case and then pointedly refused to decide if it survived the holding. *See also, e.g., Stolt-Nielsen S.A. v. AnimalFeeds Int'l Corp.*, 559 U.S. 662, 672, 130 S. Ct. 1758, 1768, 176 L.Ed. 2d 605 (2010) ("We do not decide whether " 'manifest disregard' " survives our decision in [*Hall Street*] as an independent ground for review or as a judicial gloss on the enumerated grounds for vacatur set forth at 9 U.S.C. § 10."). As a result, courts and commentators are divided about whether the doctrine continues to exist.

The following materials explore the core doctrine and concepts at the heart of judicial review and enforcement of arbitral awards. They also address, briefly, the ability of courts to modify arbitral awards.

2. THE GENERAL POLICY

The boundaries of judicial supervision of arbitral awards are highly circumscribed. Courts construe the grounds for review narrowly, reinforcing the finality of awards. In effect, this makes courts far more deferential to arbitral awards than appellate courts are to the holdings of lower courts. Appellate courts typically review factual findings to determine if they were clearly erroneous and procedural rulings to determine if the court abused its discretion. They then review legal findings *de novo*. When it comes to arbitral awards, the deference given is significantly greater and extends to legal as well as factual and procedural determinations.

As one court has explained:

> [T]he question for decision by a federal court asked to set aside an arbitration award . . . .is not whether the arbitrator or arbitrators erred in interpreting the contract; it is not whether they clearly erred in interpreting the contract; it is not whether they grossly

erred in interpreting the contract; it is whether they interpreted the contract.

Hill v. Norfolk & W. Ry. Co., 814 F.2d 1192, 1194 (7th Cir. 1987). Thus, even if a judge would have reached a different conclusion on the merits, she is not supposed to substitute her judgment for that of the arbitrator.

The following excerpts evidence this general policy. But you should also be alert to it in the subsequent sections. Notwithstanding the discussion of judicial review issues in this Chapter, constantly bear in mind that such review is *extremely* limited and that courts vacate arbitration awards infrequently. This approach is reflected not only in legal doctrine, but also in the basic attitude of judges toward challenges of arbitration award.

FINE V. BEAR, STEARNS & CO., INC.

765 F.Supp. 824, 827 (S.D.N.Y. 1991).

[. . .]

It is well-settled that a court's power to vacate an arbitration award must be extremely limited because an overly expansive judicial review of arbitration awards would undermine the litigation efficiencies which arbitration seeks to achieve. . . .

[. . .]

REMMEY V. PAINEWEBBER, INC.

32 F.3d 143, 146 (4th Cir. 1994), *cert. denied*, 513 U.S. 1112, 115 S.Ct. 903, 130 L.Ed.2d 786 (1995).

[. . .]

We must underscore at the outset the limited scope of review that courts are permitted to exercise over arbitral decisions. Limited judicial review is necessary to encourage the use of arbitration as an alternative to formal litigation. This policy is widely recognized, and the Supreme Court has often found occasion to approve it. . . .

A policy favoring arbitration would mean little, of course, if arbitration were merely the prologue to prolonged litigation. If such were the case, one would hardly achieve the "twin goals of arbitration, namely, settling disputes efficiently and avoiding long and expensive litigation." . . . Opening up arbitral awards to myriad legal challenges would eventually reduce arbitral proceedings to the status of preliminary hearings. Parties would cease to utilize a process that no longer had finality. To avoid this result, courts have resisted temptations to redo arbitral decisions. As the Seventh Circuit put it, "[a]rbitrators do not act as junior varsity trial courts where subsequent appellate review is readily available to the losing party." . . .

Thus, in reviewing arbitral awards, a district or appellate court is limited to determining " 'whether the arbitrators did the job they were told to do—not whether they did it well, or correctly, or reasonably, but simply whether they did it.' " . . . Courts are not free to overturn an arbitral result because they would have reached a different conclusion if presented with the same facts. . . .

[. . .]

* * *

In *Borop v. Toluca Pacific Securities Corp.*, 1997 WL 790588 (N.D. Ill. 1997), the court held that NASD arbitral awards are enforceable even though a party has not been represented effectively by counsel. Review for vacatur can only take place on the basis of the limited grounds in FAA §§ 10 and 11.

In an NASD arbitral proceeding, Borop alleged that his brokers, Toluca and Gucciardo, misrepresented the speculative character of securities and thereby induced him to enter into a high-risk transaction. The arbitral tribunal rendered an award in his favor. In a challenge to the award, Gucciardo contended that he had been denied effective counsel during the proceeding. His lawyer failed to appear at the hearing and to file an answer on his behalf.

Ruling upon a motion to confirm the award, the court recognized that confirmation was to be granted "unless the award is vacated, modified, or corrected as prescribed in Sections 10 and 11 of the FAA." FAA § 10 provides for the vacatur of awards on limited grounds (corruption, fraud, or undue means; evident partiality; procedural misconduct; or excess of arbitral authority). In the absence of a violation of Section 10, courts engage in a deferential standard of review. The court, therefore, granted the motion to confirm despite the alleged deficiencies of representation:

> Notwithstanding Gucciardo's unfortunate situation, the denial of effective counsel simply does not fall within the enumerated grounds in Section 10. . . . Furthermore, this Court is mindful that the Seventh Circuit has consistently refused to entertain claims of ineffective counsel as a basis of relief from an unfavorable result. . . . ("Litigants whose lawyers fall asleep at crucial moments may seek relief from the somnolent agents; inexcusable inattention to the case[ ] does not justify putting the adversary to the continued expense and uncertainty of litigation."). . . .

* * *

NOTES AND QUESTIONS

1. The case excerpts and summary describe the general judicial policy of restrained review for arbitral awards and articulate the underlying policy rationale. As *Fine* demonstrates, the application of the policy usually results in the enforcement of awards.

2. Would a less deferential approach better serve the interests of the parties, arbitration, and justice? The *Remmey* court describes the judicial function as determining "whether the arbitrators did the job they were told to do." Is that enough supervision? What if the arbitrators truly misunderstand a central point of the applicable law? Or what if the arbitrators make critical factual errors when rendering their decision and issuing an award?

3. As you know, arbitrators are not required to give detailed reasons for their awards, especially in domestic arbitrations. (Parties may impose such an obligation on arbitrators in their agreement, but no legal requirement exists.) In addition, arbitrators are not generally required or permitted to testify regarding their award or the process by which it was reached. *See, e.g.,* RUAA § 14(d). Not surprisingly, the absence of evidence of the arbitrator's reasoning can make judicial review of an award very difficult.

Considering this difficulty, some courts have concluded that a presumption should exist that "the arbitrators took a permissible route to the award where one exists." *Am. Tel. & Tel. Co. v. United Computer Sys., Inc.*, 7 F. App'x 784, 789 (9th Cir. 2001) (*quoting A.G. Edwards & Sons, Inc. v. McCollough*, 967 F.2d 1401, 1403 (9th Cir. 1992)).

4. In *Green v. Ameritech Corp.*, 200 F.3d 967 (6th Cir. 2000), the court went even further and upheld an arbitral award despite claims that it did not satisfy the requirements established by the arbitration agreement. According to the plaintiffs, the arbitral award failed to set forth a full explanation as to each theory of the complaint as required by the arbitration agreement.

The parties proceeded to arbitration on a number of discrimination claims. All of the plaintiffs except Green settled within a few days. After the arbitral hearing, Green and Ameritech filed post-arbitration briefs. The arbitrator indicated that he hoped to meet with counsel for each party separately to attempt to have the parties settle. The parties did not settle. The arbitrator never rendered an award and did not contact the parties for almost a year. At that point, Green filed a motion to remove the arbitrator and appoint another or to reinstate the case to federal court, arguing that the arbitrator's failure to render an award breached the submission agreement.

Before the district court ruled on the motion, the arbitrator rendered an award in favor of the employer. The opinion described the plaintiff's claims, provided an account of the allegations of discrimination, and reached conclusions as to each claim. The arbitrator concluded that the plaintiff had not satisfied his burden of proof. Green filed an action to vacate the arbitral award because it deviated from the parties' agreement, was untimely, and in excess of the arbitrator's authority. In particular, it failed to comply with the requirement for an explanation of the decision.

The district court vacated the award for excess of authority because it did not provide a reasoned explanation as required by the parties' agreement. The appellate court disagreed. The Sixth Circuit determined that the award "explain[ed] the arbitrator's decision with respect to each theory advanced by each Plaintiff." Because the language was so general, the court was "left with little guidance as to how to determine whether the arbitrator explained his decision so as to meet the requirements of the agreement."

By ruling that the plaintiff failed to meet his burden of proof, the arbitrator had "explained" the result reached in the award. According to the court, "[i]f parties to an arbitration agreement wish a more detailed arbitral opinion, they should clearly state in the agreement the degree of specificity required." Terms like "conclusions of law" and "finding of facts" would convey the demand for a formal judicial discussion of the facts and law. Such terminology would require the arbitrator to set forth the record and explain systematically the application of the law to the facts.

Even though the court upheld the award, it should be noted that the arbitrator's attempt to force the parties to settle or delay rendering an award could have been readily construed as misconduct. The AAA Rules, for example, are absolutely clear that an arbitrator is not to function as a mediator or participate in the parties' efforts to settle. Withholding the award until the parties resolved their own dispute appears to exceed even the arbitrator's wide discretion to fashion an appropriate remedy for the dispute. These deficiencies seem to constitute a more apposite basis for challenging the award than the would-be failure to provide a sufficient explanation of the result in the award.

3. CORRUPTION, FRAUD OR UNDUE MEANS

Awards are seldom vacated on the basis of "corruption, fraud, or undue means." FAA § 10(a)(1); RUAA § 23(a)(2)(B). The movant must show the misconduct was: (1) not discoverable by the exercise of due diligence prior to the award; (2) materially related to the issue in the arbitration; and (3) established by clear and convincing evidence. *Envtl. Barrier Co., LLC v. Slurry Sys., Inc.*, 540 F.3d 598, 608 (7th Cir. 2008) (*quoting Gingiss Int'l v. Bormet*, 58 F.3d 328 (7th Cir. 1995)).

In *Environmental Barrier*, the defendant argued that the plaintiff had concealed an affidavit that contradicted the testimony of the plaintiff's sole witness at the arbitration hearing. According to the defendant, this "newly discovered evidence" tended to show that the award in the plaintiff's favor had been "procured by fraud, corruption or other means." In the defendant's view, it needed only to show that the withheld evidence was material to some issue in the arbitration, not necessarily to the outcome. The Seventh Circuit disagreed. It held that "we must find a nexus between the purported fraud and the arbitrator's final decision." *Id.*

Similarly, in an Eleventh Circuit case, an arbitral award was vacated on the basis that an expert witness whose testimony influenced the arbitral award had committed perjury. The circumstances were unusual in that there was very clear evidence of perjury with respect to a central issue in the case, and the aggrieved party was not in a position to discover the evidence until after the arbitration proceedings ended. *Bonar v. Dean Witter Reynolds, Inc.*, 835 F.2d 1378 (11th Cir. 1988). Interestingly, the court in *Bonar* did not require "the movant to establish that the result of the proceedings would have been different had the fraud not occurred." *Id.* at 1383. Nevertheless, the court made several findings about the influence of the expert witness: "The arbitrators' written award, although brief, reflects the influence of [the expert's] testimony. . . . The arbitrators' award of punitive damages against [against one party but not another] unquestionably reflects the influence of this testimony." *Id.* at 1385.

In most cases where claims of perjury or improper evidence are raised after arbitrators have ruled, courts find that they do not need to "reopen" proceedings and hear such "new" evidence. *See, e.g., Terk Techs. Corp. v. Dockery*, 86 F. Supp. 2d 706 (E.D. Mich. 2000), *aff'd*, 3 F. App'x 459, 2001 WL 128317 (6th Cir. Feb. 7, 2001) (arbitration award was not procured by fraud, even if party agreed to arbitration only after witness gave perjured testimony, where witness's testimony was not considered by arbitrators). Instead, courts emphasize finality, giving parties and lawyers incentives to present all evidentiary problems, including claims of perjured testimony, to the arbitrators themselves.

4. IMPARTIALITY AND DISCLOSURES

Arbitrators must be neutral and independent adjudicators. It is rare, however, to find cases in which a court concludes that the behavior of arbitrators demonstrated actual partiality or bias. Instead, arbitration law focuses on the evident partiality of arbitrators. *See* FAA § 10(a)(2); RUAA § 23(a)(2)(A)–(B). The term "evident" centers the inquiry on whether the parties reasonably perceived the arbitrators to be impartial.

This focus on evident partiality derives from an inherent tension in arbitration. Of course, parties have a right to be judged impartially. But this right strains against another fundamental attribute of arbitration—the parties' right to choose their arbitrator. There's a tradeoff, in short, between impartiality and expertise. As Judge Richard Posner has noted, an "expert adjudicator is more likely than a judge or juror not only to be precommitted to a particular substantive position but to know or have heard of the parties (or if the parties are organizations, their key people)." *Merit Insurance Co. v. Leatherby Insurance Co.*, 714 F.2d 673 (7th Cir. 1983). The commentary to the RUAA echoes this, adding

> [t]he problem of arbitrator partiality is a difficult one because consensual arbitration involves a tension between abstract concepts of impartial justice and the notion that parties are entitled to a decision maker of their own choosing, including an expert with the biases and prejudices inherent in particular worldly experience.

RUAA § 12, cmt. 1.

Arbitration law balances these sometimes-competing attributes of arbitration by requiring that arbitrators disclose to parties all information that might reasonably be seen as affecting their impartiality. The parties can then make an informed choice about whether they have qualms with a given personal, social, financial or professional conflict of interest.

An arbitrator's failure to disclose actual or perceived conflicts of interest may justify judicial intervention. In *Commonwealth Coatings Corp. v. Continental Casualty Co.*, 393 U.S. 145 (1968), the U.S. Supreme Court determined that an arbitrator's failure to disclose a business relationship with one of the parties was sufficient to support vacation of a subsequent award on the ground of "evident partiality." The case involved a tribunal made up of two arbitrators chosen by each of the parties and a third "neutral" arbitrator. That third arbitrator had a previous business relationship with one of the parties. The third arbitrator voted with the panel for an award in favor of the party with whom he had done business.

The losing party challenged the award, claiming that the failure of the third arbitrator to disclose his significant business relationship with the winning party amounted to "evident partiality" under FAA § 10. A majority of the Court concluded that vacatur was warranted even though there was no proof of actual bias or partiality on the part of the arbitrator. Moreover, there was no evidence that the undisclosed connection had any direct impact on the deliberations leading to the award. Still, according to the Court, the mere fact that the relationship had not been disclosed on a timely basis justified a finding of "evident partiality."

COMMONWEALTH COATINGS CORP. V. CONTINENTAL CASUALTY CO.

393 U.S. 145, 89 S.Ct. 337, 21 L.Ed.2d 301 (1968).

MR. JUSTICE BLACK delivered the opinion of the Court.

At issue in this case is the question whether elementary requirements of impartiality taken for granted in every judicial proceeding are suspended when the parties agree to resolve a dispute through arbitration.

The petitioner, Commonwealth Coatings Corporation, a subcontractor, sued the sureties on the prime contractor's bond to recover money alleged to be due for a painting job. The contract for painting contained an agreement to arbitrate such controversies. Pursuant to this agreement petitioner appointed one arbitrator, the prime contractor appointed a second, and these two together selected the third arbitrator. This third arbitrator, the supposedly neutral member of the panel, conducted a large business in Puerto Rico, in which he served as an engineering consultant for various people in connection with building construction projects. One of his regular customers in this business was the prime contractor that petitioner sued in this case. This relationship with the prime contractor was in a sense sporadic in that the arbitrator's services were used only from time to time at irregular intervals, and there had been no dealings between them for about a year immediately preceding the arbitration. Nevertheless, the prime contractor's patronage was repeated and significant, involving fees of about $12,000 over a period of four of five years, and the relationship even went so far as to include the rendering of services on the very projects involved in this lawsuit. An arbitration was held, but the facts concerning the close business connections between the third arbitrator and the prime contractor were unknown to petitioner and were never revealed to it by this arbitrator, by the prime contractor, or by anyone else until after an award had been made. . . .

[FAA § 10] does authorize vacation of an award where it was 'procured by corruption, fraud, or undue means' or '(w)here there was evident partiality . . . in the arbitrators.' These provisions show a desire of Congress to provide not merely for any arbitration but for an impartial one. It is true that petitioner does not charge before us that the third arbitrator was actually guilty of fraud or bias in deciding this case, and we have no reason, apart from the undisclosed business relationship, to suspect him of any improper motives. But neither this arbitrator nor the prime contractor gave to petitioner even an intimation of the close financial relations that had existed between them for a period of years. We have no doubt that if a litigant could show that a foreman of a jury or a judge in a court of justice had, unknown to the litigant, any such relationship, the judgment would be subject to challenge. This is shown beyond doubt by *Tumey v. State of Ohio*, 273 U.S. 510, 47 S.Ct. 437, 71 L.Ed. 749 (1927), where this Court held that a conviction could not stand because a small part of the judge's income consisted of court fees collected from convicted defendants. Although in *Tumey* it appeared the amount of the judge's compensation actually depended on whether he decided for one side or the other, that is too small a distinction to allow this manifest violation of the strict morality and fairness Congress would have expected on the part of the arbitrator and the other party in this case. Nor should it be at all relevant, as the Court of Appeals apparently thought it was here, that '(t)he payments received were a very small part of (the arbitrator's) income. . . .' For in *Tumey* the Court held that a decision should be set aside where there is 'the slightest pecuniary interest' on the part of the judge, and specifically rejected the State's contention that the compensation involved there was 'so small that it is not to be regarded as likely to influence improperly a judicial officer in the discharge of his duty. . . .' Since in the case of courts this is a constitutional principle, we can see no basis for refusing to find the same concept in the broad statutory language that governs arbitration proceedings and provides that an award can be set aside on the basis of 'evident partiality' or the use of 'undue means.' . . . It is true that arbitrators cannot sever all their ties with the business world, since they are not expected to get all their income from their work deciding cases, but we should, if anything, be even more scrupulous to safeguard the impartiality of arbitrators than judges, since the former have completely free rein to decide the law as well as the facts and are not subject to appellate review. We can perceive no way in which the effectiveness of the arbitration process will be hampered by the simple requirement that arbitrators disclose to the parties any dealings that might create an impression of possible bias.

While not controlling in this case, Section 18 of the Rules of the American Arbitration Association, in effect at the time of this arbitration, is highly significant. It provided as follows:

> *Section 18.* Disclosure by Arbitrator of Disqualification—At the time of receiving his notice of appointment, the prospective Arbitrator is requested to disclose any circumstances likely to create a presumption of bias or which he believes might disqualify him as an impartial Arbitrator. Upon receipt of such information, the Tribunal Clerk shall immediately disclose it to the parties, who if willing to proceed under the circumstances disclosed, shall, in writing, so advise the Tribunal Clerk. If either party declines to waive the presumptive disqualification, the vacancy thus created shall be filled in accordance with the applicable provisions of this Rule.

And based on the same principle as this Arbitration Association rule is that part of the 33d Canon of Judicial Ethics which provides:

> 33. Social Relations.
>
> . . . (A judge) should, however, in pending or prospective litigation before him be particularly careful to avoid such action as may reasonably tend to awaken the suspicion that his social or business relations or friendships, constitute an element in influencing his judicial conduct.

This rule of arbitration and this canon of judicial ethics rest on the premise that any tribunal permitted by law to try cases and controversies not only must be unbiased but also must avoid even the appearance of bias. We cannot believe that it was the purpose of Congress to authorize litigants to submit their cases and controversies to arbitration boards that might reasonably be thought biased against one litigant and favorable to another.

Reversed.

MR. JUSTICE WHITE, with whom MR. JUSTICE MARSHALL joins, concurring.

While I am glad to join my Brother BLACK'S opinion in this case, I desire to make these additional remarks. The Court does not decide today that arbitrators are to be held to the standards of judicial decorum of Article III judges, or indeed of any judges. It is often because they are men of affairs, not apart from but of the marketplace, that they are effective in their adjudicatory function. . . . This does not mean the judiciary must overlook outright chicanery in giving effect to their awards; that would be an abdication of our responsibility. But it does mean that arbitrators are not automatically disqualified by a business relationship with the parties before them if both parties are informed of the relationship in advance, or if they are unaware of the facts but the relationship is trivial. I see no reason automatically to disqualify the best informed and most capable potential arbitrators.

The arbitration process functions best when an amicable and trusting atmosphere is preserved and there is voluntary compliance with the decree, without need for judicial enforcement. This end is best served by establishing an atmosphere of frankness at the outset, through disclosure by the arbitrator of any financial transactions which he has had or is negotiating with either of the parties. In many cases the arbitrator might believe the business relationship to be so insubstantial that to make a point of revealing it would suggest he is indeed easily swayed, and perhaps a partisan of that party. But if the law requires the disclosure, no such imputation can arise. And it is far better that the relationship be disclosed at the outset, when the parties are free to reject the arbitrator or accept him with knowledge of the relationship and continuing faith in his objectivity, than to have the relationship come to light after the arbitration, when a suspicious or disgruntled party can seize on it as a pretext for invalidating the award. The judiciary should minimize its role in arbitration as judge of the arbitrator's impartiality. That role is best consigned to the parties, who are the architects of their own arbitration process, and are far better informed of the prevailing ethical standards and reputations within their business.

Of course, an arbitrator's business relationships may be diverse indeed, involving more or less remote commercial connections with great numbers of people. He cannot be expected to provide the parties with his complete and unexpurgated business biography. But it is enough for present purposes to hold, as the Court does, that where the arbitrator has a substantial interest in a firm which has done more than trivial business with a party, that fact must be disclosed. If arbitrators err on the side of disclosure, as they should, it will not be difficult for courts to identify those undisclosed relationships which are too insubstantial to warrant vacating an award.

MR. JUSTICE FORTAS, with whom MR. JUSTICE HARLAN and MR. JUSTICE STEWART join, dissenting.

I dissent and would affirm the [lower court] judgment.

[. . .]

The arbitration was held pursuant to provisions in the contracts between the parties. It is not subject to the rules of the American Arbitration Association. It is governed by the United States Arbitration Act. . . .

[. . .]

The third arbitrator was not asked about business connections with either party. Petitioner's complaint is that he failed to volunteer information about professional services rendered by him to the other party to the contract, the most recent of which were performed over a year before the arbitration. Both courts below held, and petitioner concedes, that the third arbitrator was innocent of any actual partiality, or bias, or improper motive. There is no suggestion of concealment as distinguished from the innocent failure to volunteer information.

The third arbitrator is a leading and respected consulting engineer who has performed services for 'most of the contractors in Puerto Rico.' He was well known to petitioner's counsel and they were personal friends. Petitioner's counsel candidly admitted that if he had been told about the arbitrator's prior relationship 'I don't think I would have objected because I know Mr. Capacete (the arbitrator).'

Clearly, the District Judge's conclusion, affirmed by the Court of Appeals for the First Circuit, was correct, that "the arbitrators conducted fair, impartial hearings; that they reached a proper determination of the issues before them, and that plaintiff's objections represent a 'situation where the losing party to an arbitration is now clutching at straws in an attempt to avoid the results of the arbitration to which it became a party.' "

The Court nevertheless orders that the arbitration award be set aside. It uses this singularly inappropriate case to announce a *per se* rule that in my judgment has no basis in the applicable statute or jurisprudential principles: that, regardless of the agreement between the parties, if an arbitrator has any prior business relationship with one of the parties of which he fails to inform the other party, however innocently, the arbitration award is always subject to being set aside. This is so even where the award is unanimous; where there is no suggestion that the nondisclosure indicates partiality or bias; and where it is conceded that there was in fact no irregularity, unfairness, bias, or partiality. Until the decision today, it has not been the law that an arbitrator's failure to disclose a prior business relationship with one of the parties will compel the setting aside of an arbitration award regardless of the circumstances.

I agree that failure of an arbitrator to volunteer information about business dealings with one party will, *prima facie*, support a claim of partiality or bias. But where there is no suggestion that the nondisclosure was calculated, and where the complaining party disclaims any imputation of partiality, bias, or misconduct, the presumption clearly is overcome.

[. . .]

Arbitration is essentially consensual and practical. The United States Arbitration Act is obviously designed to protect the integrity of the process with a minimum of insistence upon set formulae and rules. The Court applies to this process rules applicable to judges and not to a system characterized by dealing on faith and reputation for reliability. Such formalism is not contemplated by the Act nor is it warranted in a case where no claim is made of partiality, of unfairness, or of misconduct in any degree.

NOTES AND QUESTIONS

1. You should recognize that arbitrator impartiality is inextricably linked to arbitrator disclosures. Arbitrators have a duty to investigate and disclose facts that a reasonable person would consider likely to affect the arbitrator's impartiality in the arbitral proceeding. No one debates this fundamental proposition. But what are the precise contours of the duty to investigate? How thorough do arbitrators need to be? Additionally, what particular dealings or relationships trigger a duty to disclose?

2. Do you agree with the plurality of the Court that the business relationship between the third arbitrator and the prime contractor was so significant that should have been disclosed? Do you think that the relationship actually had any impact on the decision of the third arbitrator? If not, what would the point of disclosure be?

3. Justice Black's opinion in *Commonwealth Coatings* provides a strong incentive for arbitrators to disclose. If a party later discovers a non-disclosed conflict, a court may presume that the conflict demonstrates evident partiality, even if the conflict is relatively minor. It then becomes the burden of the party seeking to enforce the award to rebut the presumption by showing that the award was not tainted by the non-disclosure or there in fact was no prejudice. *See, e.g.,* RUAA § 12(e) (a neutral arbitrator's failure to disclose "a known, direct, and material interest in the outcome or a known, existing, and substantial relationship with a party," gives rise to a presumption of "evident partiality.") Justice Black's approach, in other words, is information forcing—it requires the party with the best access to the relevant information to share it.

4. *Commonwealth Coatings* is a plurality opinion. The plurality and concurring opinions are challenging to synthesize, which leaves the case open to interpretation. Additionally, note the date of the opinion—1968. Issued one year after *Prima Paint*, the case was decided on the cusp of the modern era of arbitral law. Accordingly, *Commonwealth Coatings* bears some of the hallmarks of a more antiquated approach to arbitration, reminiscent in some respects of *Bernhardt* (decided in 1956, which has been relegated to insignificance) and *Wilko* (decided in 1953, which was overruled). Whatever the reasons, the Court has never confirmed the position it took in *Commonwealth Coatings* so many years ago.

Because of its uncertain foundations, courts have not read the case uniformly. Some courts have chosen not to follow Justice Black's opinion, finding that it was without support from a majority of the Justices. These courts have instead often followed the concurring opinion of Justice White to the effect that failure to disclose a trivial or insubstantial relationship would not be grounds for setting aside an award. *Legacy Trading Co. v. Hoffman*, 363 F. App'x 633, 635 (10th Cir. 2010) (*quoting Ormsbee Dev. Co. v. Grace*, 668 F.2d 1140, 1147 (10th Cir. 1982)) (an appearance of bias is not enough to set aside an award—the challenging party must also present "evidence of bias [that is] . . . direct, definite and capable of demonstration"). Several states, however, have gone in the opposite direction and imposed even more rigorous standards. California, for instance, has created by statute a virtual strict liability vacatur standard for the non-disclosure of specified information. See CAL. CODE CIV. P. § 1281.9 (a)–(b).

5. Should the same standard of impartiality apply to all arbitrators? Are party-designated arbitrators and the neutral indistinguishable for this purpose? Is tribunal-wide impartiality necessary, desirable, indispensable?

CERTAIN UNDERWRITING MEMBERS OF LLOYDS OF LONDON V. FLORIDA, DEPARTMENT OF FINANCIAL SERVICES

892 F.3d 501 (2nd Cir. 2018).

(footnotes omitted)

DENNIS JACOBS, CIRCUIT JUDGE:

Insurance Company of the Americas ("ICA") appeals the order vacating the arbitral award (the "Award") issued in a reinsurance dispute between ICA and Certain Underwriting Members of Lloyds of London including those members subscribing to Treaty No. 02072/04 (the "Underwriters"). The issue on appeal is whether the Award is void for evident partiality under the Federal Arbitration Act ("FAA"), 9 U.S.C. § 10(a)(2), by reason of the failure by ICA's party-appointed arbitrator to disclose close relationships with former and current directors and employees of ICA. The district court concluded under our reasonable person standard that the ICA-appointed arbitrator was impermissibly partial to

ICA. We hold that a party seeking to vacate an award under Section 10(a)(2) must sustain a higher burden to prove evident partiality on the part of an arbitrator who is appointed by a party and who is expected to espouse the view or perspective of the appointing party. *See Scandinavian Reinsurance Co. Ltd. v. Saint Paul Fire and Marine Ins. Co.*, 668 F.3d 60, 76 n.21 (2d Cir. 2012).

The district court weighed the conduct of ICA's party-appointed arbitrator under the standard governing neutral arbitrators. We therefore vacate and remand for the district court to reconsider under the proper standard. An undisclosed relationship between a party and its party-appointed arbitrator constitutes evident partiality, such that vacatur of the award is appropriate if: (1) the relationship violates the contractual requirement of disinterestedness (*see Sphere Drake Ins. v. All American Life Ins.*, 307 F.3d 617, 620 (7th Cir. 2002)); or (2) it prejudicially affects the award (*see Delta Mine Holding Co. v. AFC Coal Properties, Inc.*, 280 F.3d 815, 821–22 (8th Cir. 2001)).

BACKGROUND

ICA insures workers compensation claims in the construction industry. The Underwriters in turn provide ICA with second and third layer reinsurance under a series of treaties, each of which contains an arbitration clause requiring that disputes be adjudicated by an arbitration panel consisting of three members: one party-appointed arbitrator for each party, and the neutral umpire. The only contractual qualification is that the arbitrators "be active or retired disinterested executive officers of insurance or reinsurance companies or Lloyd's London Underwriters." . . . Each party bears the expense of its own arbitrator and is permitted to engage in *ex parte* discussion with its party-appointed arbitrators during discovery.

ICA requested coverage from the Underwriters under the treaties for claims arising out of multiple construction site injuries exceeding in total $12.5 million. The Underwriters declined the claim . . . . In December 2014, ICA demanded arbitration pursuant to the treaty. ICA appointed Alex Campos as its arbitrator, and the two party-appointed arbitrators selected Ben Hernandez as neutral umpire.

At the May 11, 2015 organizational meeting, each arbitrator was called upon to disclose pre-existing or concurrent relationships with a party. ICA was represented at the disclosure meeting by Gary Hirst, Chairman and Chief Investment Officer, and arbitration counsel. Campos disclaimed any appreciable link to ICA:

> I don't know anyone here except for Mr. [Gary Hirst, Chairman of ICA]. I had some potential business dealings with him about ten years ago that never really materialized. He had an associate that I was trying to do a deal with but it never went anywhere and

other than that contact I don't have any other related contacts with Mr. Hirst.

.... Between the organizational meeting and the conclusion of the arbitration, Campos let pass several opportunities to come forward with additional disclosures.

As the district court found, Campos's pre-existing and concurrent relationships with ICA's representatives were considerably more extensive than Campos disclosed. The court emphasized undisclosed dealings between ICA and a human resources firm named Vensure Employee Services ("Vensure") of which Campos was President and CEO. Specifically, the court found that: ICA and Vensure operate out of the same suite in a business park in Mesa, Arizona; John Iorillo, a former director of ICA, was CFO of a firm that provided consulting services to Vensure; and Ricardo Rios, a Director of ICA, was hired as the CFO of Vensure in the summer of 2015. Rios testified as a witness at the arbitration, and Iorillo's name was mentioned repeatedly.

The panel favored ICA's interpretation of the treaty language, and the Award granted ICA net damages of over $1.5 million. The Underwriters moved to vacate the Award on several grounds, including "evident partiality" on the part of Alex Campos .... ICA cross-moved to confirm.

The district court granted the motion to vacate the award and denied the cross-motion to confirm.... Campos's "undisclosed relationships" with ICA representatives were found to be "significant enough to demonstrate evident partiality." ... The district court "note[d] that the relationships here are far more significant, more numerous, and involve more financial entanglements than are present in" other cases from this Circuit.... (citing the "number and variety" of relationships with former ICA employees, which were "longstanding" and "ongoing at the time of the arbitration"). Additionally, the court was "troubl[ed]" by the apparent willfulness of the non-disclosures, in particular Campos's silence during the testimony of Ricardo Rios.... The court did not take issue with the substance of the Award, did not connect Campos's conduct to the panel's decision, and made no finding that Campos had a personal or financial interest in the outcome of the arbitration.

DISCUSSION

I

"When reviewing a district court's decision to vacate an arbitration award, we review findings of fact for clear error and questions of law *de novo*." ... Our review of an arbitration award is "severely limited" in view of the strong deference courts afford to the arbitral process.... A "stringent standard for vacating awards is a necessary corollary to the federal policy favoring arbitration." ...

"Under the FAA, the validity of an award is subject to attack only on those grounds listed in [Section] 10, and the policy of the FAA requires that the award be enforced unless one of those grounds is affirmatively shown to exist." . . . We may vacate under Section 10 "where there was evident partiality . . . in the arbitrator." *Morelite Const. Corp. v. New York City Dist. Council Carpenters Ben. Funds*, 748 F.2d 79, 82 (2d Cir. 1984) ("*Morelite*") (internal quotation marks omitted); *see* 9 U.S.C. § 10(a)(2). "[E]vident partiality within the meaning of 9 U.S.C. § 10 will be found where a reasonable person would have to conclude that an arbitrator was partial to one party to the arbitration." *Id.* at 84. The party challenging the award must prove the existence of evident partiality by clear and convincing evidence. . . .

The Supreme Court established in *Commonwealth Coatings* that "an arbitrator's failure to disclose a material relationship with one of the parties can constitute 'evident partiality' requiring vacatur of the award." . . . But "Commonwealth Coatings does not establish a *per se* rule requiring vacatur of an award whenever an undisclosed relationship is discovered." . . . It is "the materiality of the undisclosed conflict [that] drives a finding of evident partiality, not the failure to disclose or investigate *per se*." . . .

A neutral arbitrator's relationship with a party is material if it goes "so far as to include the rendering of services on the very projects involved in th[e] lawsuit," . . . or contemporaneous investments that create a vested financial stake in that party. . . . A reasonable person could also conclude that the arbitrator is unduly partial to the side of a close family relation. . . .

But even with respect to neutral arbitrators, "we have not been quick to set aside the results of an arbitration because of an arbitrator's alleged failure to disclose information." . . . "[W]e have declined to vacate awards because of undisclosed relationships where the complaining party should have known of the relationship, or could have learned of the relationship 'just as easily before or during the arbitration rather than after it lost its case.' " . . . "We have concluded in various factual settings that the evident-partiality standard was not satisfied because the undisclosed relationship at issue was 'too insubstantial to warrant vacating the award.' " . . .

For example, past contacts do not amount to material bias. When an arbitrator's "relationship with [a party] materially end[s] before [the party] appointed him as an arbitrator," one "cannot say that a reasonable person would have to conclude that an arbitrator was partial to one party to the arbitration." . . . Thus an arbitrator is not disqualified from selection as the neutral umpire by having received compensation from one of the parties for past service as a party-appointed arbitrator. . . .

In broader strokes, the FAA does not proscribe all personal or business relationships between arbitrators and the parties. . . . "[T]he balance of case law in the Second Circuit supports the proposition that when a purported financial interest or financial relationship between an arbitrator and a party to arbitration is indirect, general[,] or tangential, courts should not vacate arbitration awards." . . .

We therefore "requir[e] a showing of something more than the mere 'appearance of bias' to vacate an arbitration award," . . . and will not vacate arbitration awards for evident partiality when the party opposing the award "identifies no direct connection between [the arbitrator] and the outcome of the arbitration." . . .

Judicial tolerance of relationships between arbitrators and party representatives reflects competing goals in partiality decisions. Complete candor and transparency help root out bias and fraud. But reinsurers and ceding insurers affirmatively seek arbitral panels with expertise. "[T]he best informed and most capable potential arbitrators" are repeat players with deep industry connections, *Commonwealth Coatings*, 393 U.S. at 150 (White, J., concurring), who will "understand the trade's norms of doing business and the consequences of proposed lines of decision," *Sphere Drake Ins. v. All American Life Ins.*, 307 F.3d 617, 620 (7th Cir. 2002) . . . . "Familiarity with a discipline often comes at the expense of complete impartiality," and "specific areas tend to breed tightly knit professional communities." . . . "[T]o disqualify any arbitrator who had professional dealings with one of the parties (to say nothing of a social acquaintanceship) would make it impossible, in some circumstances, to find a qualified arbitrator at all." . . .

II

The principles and circumstances that counsel tolerance of certain undisclosed relationships between arbitrator and litigant are even more indulgent of party-appointed arbitrators, who are expected to serve as de facto advocates. "[I]n the main party-appointed arbitrators are supposed to be advocates." *Sphere Drake*, 307 F.3d at 620. . . . The ethos of neutrality that informs the selection of a neutral arbitrator to a tripartite panel does not animate the selection and qualification of arbitrators appointed by the parties. . . .

Of equal importance, arbitration is a creature of contract, and courts must hold parties to their bargain. ICA and the Underwriters have chosen a tripartite panel with party-appointed arbitrators who are "relieved of all judicial formalities and may abstain from following the strict rules of law." . . . "[P]arties are free to choose for themselves to what lengths they will go in quest of impartiality," including the various degrees of partiality that inhere in the party-appointment feature. *Sphere Drake*, 307 F.3d at 622 (noting that the impartiality protections of Section 10(a)(2) may be altered or waived by mutual consent); *see also Volt Information Sciences, Inc. v. Board of Trustees of Leland Stanford Junior Univ.*, 489 U.S. 468, 478–79

(1989) (emphasizing how "parties are generally free to structure their arbitration agreements as they see fit," including "specify[ing] by contract the rules under which the arbitration will be conducted"). . . .

Many of our sister circuits have therefore held that the disclosure requirements for neutral arbitrators "do[ ] not extend to party-appointed arbitrators." . . . Some courts have gone so far as to suggest that when parties contract to allow selection of their own arbitrators, the FAA's evident partiality rules do not apply. *Sphere Drake*, 307 F.3d at 622 ("To the extent that an agreement entitles parties to select interested (even beholden) arbitrators, [Section] 10(a)(2) has no role to play.").

The Second Circuit has not had occasion to decide the standard for a Section 10(a)(2) evident partiality challenge to a party-appointed arbitrator. In [a previous case], we acknowledged that the issue remained unresolved; but we reserved decision on "whether the FAA imposes a heightened burden of proving evident partiality in cases in which the allegedly biased arbitrator was party-appointed" because the arbitrator in that case had made sufficient disclosures even under the more relaxed standard for neutrals. . . . Here the question is squarely and unavoidably presented because the district court's sound findings on Campos's improprieties are substantial under the traditional *Morelite* test. Moreover, the district court expressly declined ICA's invitation to apply a heightened burden for the Underwriters' evident partiality challenge in view of Campos's role as a party-appointed arbitrator, and ruled that "Campos's conduct must be considered under the same evident partiality standard as is required in all arbitrations." . . .

We respectfully part ways with the district court, and instead join the circuits that distinguish between party-appointed and neutral arbitrators in considering evident partiality. This distinction is salient in the reinsurance industry, where an arbitrator's professional acuity is valued over stringent impartiality. It also meshes with our case law and takes into account the FAA, which restricts "evident partiality" as opposed to "partiality" or "appearance of bias." 9 U.S.C. § 10(a)(2); *Morelite*, 748 F.2d at 83–84 (requiring "something more than the mere 'appearance of bias' to vacate an arbitration award"); *Sphere Drake*, 307 F.3d at 621 ("only evident partiality, not appearances or risks, spoils an award"). Expecting of party-appointed arbitrators the same level of institutional impartiality applicable to neutrals would impair the process of self-governing dispute resolution.

That said, a party-appointed arbitrator is still subject to some baseline limits to partiality. We decline to catalogue all "material relationship[s]" that may bear upon the service of a party-appointed arbitrator. . . . But it can be said that an undisclosed relationship is material if it violates the arbitration agreement. *See Sphere Drake*, 307 F.3d at 622. In this case, the qualification in the contract is "disinterested," which would be breached if the party-appointed arbitrator had a personal or financial stake in the outcome of the arbitration. . . . An undisclosed fact is also material, and therefore warrants vacatur, if the party opposing the award can show that the party-appointed arbitrator's partiality had a prejudicial effect on the award. . . . In the absence of a clear showing that an undisclosed relationship (or the non-disclosure itself) influenced the arbitral proceedings or infected an otherwise-valid award, that award should not be set aside even if a reasonable person (or court) could speculate or infer bias. . . .

We vacate and remand for the district court to determine whether the Underwriters have shown by clear and convincing evidence that the failure to disclose by party-appointed arbitrator Campos either violates the qualification of disinterestedness or had a prejudicial impact on the award. At the district court's discretion, this undertaking may necessitate additional proceedings. . . .

CONCLUSION

For the foregoing reasons, we hereby **VACATE** the judgment of the district court and **REMAND** for further proceedings consistent with this opinion.

POSITIVE SOFTWARE SOLUTIONS, INC. V. NEW CENTURY MORTGAGE CORP.

436 F.3d 495 (5th Cir. 2006).

REAVLEY, CIRCUIT JUDGE:

The question here is whether an arbitrator's failure to disclose that seven years before the arbitration, he and his former law firm were co-counsel in a lengthy litigation matter with one of the law firms and counsel in this matter, justifies vacating the award. We hold that the arbitrator was required to disclose the relationship because it might have created an impression of possible bias, and we affirm the district court's judgment vacating the arbitration award; but we vacate the portion of the district court's judgment that regulates a subsequent arbitration.

I.

A.

New Century Mortgage Corporation ("New Century") is in the mortgage business. It generates business through telephone contacts with prospective borrowers. Positive Software Solutions, Inc. ("Positive Software") develops, markets, and manufactures computer-software products for the mortgage industry. It developed "LoanForce," a software product that is a relational database for use in the mortgage lending business. Positive Software licensed LoanForce to New Century pursuant to a Software Subscription Agreement ("SSA"). Positive Software learned that New Century was allegedly copying LoanForce and was incorporating it into different software products. Thereafter, Positive Software filed this lawsuit alleging, *inter alia,* claims of copyright infringement, theft of trade secrets, breach of contract, seeking specific performance, money damages, and preliminary and permanent injunctive relief. The district court granted Positive Software's motion for a preliminary injunction enjoining New Century from using LoanForce. In addition, the district court compelled arbitration pursuant to the SSA.

B.

Arbitration of this matter took place under the auspices of the American Arbitration Association ("AAA"). Pursuant to AAA procedures, the AAA provided the parties with a list of candidate arbitrators, along with their *curricula vitae,* and requested that the parties rank the candidates. Both parties provided their lists of acceptable arbitrators to the AAA, ranking them in the order of preference as instructed. . . .

The AAA contacted [party chosen arbitrator] Shurn by letter to determine his availability. That letter listed the names of the parties and counsel, including designating Susman Godfrey L.L.P. ("Susman Godfrey") as the firm representing New Century, and one if its partners, Ophelia F. Camiña, as New Century's arbitration counsel. At the bottom of the letter, there was an "important reminder" advising arbitrators of their "obligation to disclose any circumstance likely to affect impartiality or create an appearance of partiality." The same "important reminder" appeared in two subsequent letters addressed to Shurn.

Shurn signed and returned the standard "Notice of Appointment" form to the AAA, which advised arbitrators to "please disclose any past or present relationship with the parties, their counsel, or potential witnesses, direct or indirect, whether financial, professional, social or any other kind. . . ." That letter included twelve questions to assist arbitrators in determining whether any "past or present relationship" required disclosure, including the following question, "Have you had any professional or social relationship with counsel for any party in this proceeding or with the firms for which they work?" Shurn indicated that he had nothing to disclose.

After a seven-day hearing, in a written ruling, Shurn found that New Century did not infringe Positive Software's copyrights, did not misappropriate Positive Software's trade secrets, did not breach the SSA, and did not defraud or conspire against Positive Software. Shurn ordered that Positive Software take nothing.

C.

Following the arbitration award, Positive Software conducted a detailed investigation into Shurn's background. It discovered that Shurn and his former law firm, Arnold White & Durkee ("Arnold White"), had been involved in a professional relationship with Susman Godfrey and Camiña, New Century's arbitration counsel, for a period of time.

Soon thereafter, Positive Software filed a motion to vacate the arbitration award. The district court granted Positive Software's motion on the ground that Shurn failed to disclose that he had "served as co-counsel with New Century's counsel over a period of years in significant litigation," and that this prior relationship "might create a reasonable impression of possible bias." Further, Shurn's "failure to disclose that relationship deprived Positive Software of the opportunity to make an informed choice of arbitrators and requires vacatur of the award."

[. . .]

The district court further found that had Positive Software been aware of Shurn's prior relationship with Susman Godfrey and Camiña, it would not have ranked Shurn highly, and he would not have been chosen as the arbitrator. The district court outlined the numerous reminders and opportunities that Shurn had to disclose his past professional relationship with Susman Godfrey and Camiña, and that he failed to do so.

The district court held that any reasonable lawyer selecting a sole arbitrator for arbitration would have wanted to know that the arbitrator chosen had a prior association with opposing counsel, given the contentious nature of the dispute between the parties and the duration and importance of the prior litigation with which both arbitrator and opposing counsel were associated. . . .

II.

We review a district court's decision to vacate an arbitration award under the same standard as any other district court decision. We accept findings of fact that are not clearly erroneous and decide questions of law *de novo*. We also review the application of law to fact *de novo*.

III.

A.

Congress promulgated the United States Arbitration Act . . . in 1925 to delineate the thorny relationship between the role of private arbitration and the federal courts. Section 10 of the Act provides the grounds upon which a court may vacate an arbitrator's award, and for our purposes, states that such a basis exists "[w]here there was evident partiality . . . in the arbitrator[ ]. . . ."

Deciding what constitutes "evident partiality" in an arbitrator and the use of "undue means" has proved troublesome. The case law in this area is confusing and complicated. While this court has not previously determined the scope of this standard,[20] numerous courts in other jurisdictions, including the Supreme Court, have done so. We analyze those cases.

The case of *Commonwealth Coatings Corp. v. Continental Cas. Co.* involved an arbitration panel composed of two arbitrators chosen by each of the parties and a third "neutral" arbitrator who had previously worked for one of the parties to the arbitration. The neutral arbitrator voted with the panel for an award in favor of the party with whom he had done business. Thereafter, the party that lost the arbitration challenged the award, claiming that the failure of the arbitrator to disclose his significant business relationship resulted in "evident partiality" under 9 U.S.C. § 10, warranting vacatur of the award.

Justice Black, in delivering the Court's opinion, concluded that the arbitrator's failure to disclose warranted vacating the award for evident partiality even though there was no evidence of actual bias. The Court noted that arbitrators are not expected to sever ties with the business world, but nevertheless, it must be scrupulous in safeguarding the impartiality of arbitrators, as they have "completely free rein to decide the law as well as the facts and are not subject to appellate review." As a result, the Court imposed "the simple requirement that arbitrators disclose to the parties any dealings that might create an impression of possible bias."

In a concurring opinion, Justice White, joined by Justice Marshall, specifically stated that he joined the Court's "majority opinion," and he emphasized that the parties must be cognizant of all non-trivial relationships in order to exercise full and fair judgment. Justice White agreed on a rule of full disclosure. . . .

Although Justice White indicated that he was "glad to join" Justice Black's opinion and that he desired to make "additional remarks," and Justice Black's opinion was designated the "opinion of the court," some lower federal courts have seen a conflict between the two writings. Accordingly, by treating Justice Black's opinion as a plurality opinion, some courts have felt free to reject Justice Black's statement that "evident partiality" is met by an "appearance of bias," and to apply a much narrower standard.

An early example of this occurred in *Morelite Constr. Corp.* . . . There, the court referred to Justice Black's opinion as a mere plurality of four justices and read much of that opinion as *dicta*. The court reasoned that

[20] The closest this court came to addressing the "evident partiality" standard was in *Bernstein Seawell & Kove v. Bosarge,* 813 F.2d 726 (5th Cir.1987). There, this court stated in dicta that the "appearance of bias" is insufficient to warrant vacatur. *Id.* at 732. The standard for vacating an arbitration award for evident partiality has not been definitively addressed in this circuit.

something more than an "appearance of bias" was necessary to disqualify an arbitrator, but this was not a case of failure to disclose. Other federal circuits have adopted a similar "evident partiality" standard.[33]

Other federal circuits, centering on the need for full disclosure to parties who are choosing their own arbitrators, have adopted a much broader standard. One such case is *Schmitz,* wherein the Ninth Circuit held that an arbitrator had a duty to disclose that his law firm had represented the parent company of a party to the arbitration. After determining that Justice Black's opinion in *Commonwealth Coatings* was controlling precedent, the court stated that the "best expression" of the Supreme Court's holding is that evident partiality exists when "undisclosed facts show a reasonable impression of partiality." The court discussed the important distinction between cases in which actual bias is alleged and those involving allegations of failure to disclose, observing that although the "reasonable impression of partiality" standard may not be appropriate in actual bias cases (though it has, confusingly, been used by some courts in those cases), it is the correct standard for nondisclosure cases:

> The policies of 9 U.S.C. § 10 . . . support the notion that the standard for nondisclosure cases should differ from that used in actual bias cases. In a nondisclosure case, the integrity of the process by which arbitrators are chosen is at issue. Showing a "reasonable impression of partiality" is sufficient in a nondisclosure case because the policy of section 10(a)(2) instructs that the parties should choose their arbitrators intelligently. The parties can choose their arbitrators intelligently only when facts showing potential partiality are disclosed. Whether the arbitrators' decision itself is faulty is not necessarily relevant. But in an actual bias determination, the integrity of the arbitrators' decision is directly at issue. That a reasonable impression of partiality is present does not mean the arbitration was the product of impropriety.

[. . .]

[33] *See Peoples Sec. Life Ins. Co. v. Monumental Life Ins. Co.*, 991 F.2d 141, 146 (4th Cir.1993) (adopting the *Morelite* standard and holding that the arbitrator was unaware of the questioned relationship); *Apperson,* 879 F.2d at 1358 (adopting the *Morelite* standard and holding that the objection to the arbitrator had been waived); *Nationwide Mut. Ins. Co. v. Home Ins. Co.,* 429 F.3d 640 (6th Cir.2005) (declining to deviate from *Apperson*); *Health Servs. Mgmt. Corp. v. Hughes,* 975 F.2d 1253, 1264 (7th Cir.1992) (holding that the objection to the arbitrator was waived); *Ormsbee Dev. Co. v. Grace,* 668 F.2d 1140, 1147 (10th Cir.1982) ("only clear evidence of impropriety [ ] justifies the denial of summary confirmation of an arbitration award. . . . For an award to be set aside, the evidence of bias or interest of an arbitrator must be direct, definite and capable of demonstration rather than remote, uncertain or speculative.") (internal citations omitted); *ANR Coal Co., Inc. v. Cogentrix of N. Carolina, Inc.,* 173 F.3d 493, 500 (4th Cir.1999) (holding that mere nondisclosure does not itself justify vacatur).

B.

Having analyzed the case law, we address what standard to apply in this case. This is a nondisclosure case in which the parties chose the arbitrator. Striking the balance of the competing goals of expertise and impartiality in the selection process, maintaining faithfulness to the Court's opinion in *Commonwealth Coatings,* and agreeing with the policy arguments set out in *Schmitz,* we hold that an arbitrator selected by the parties displays evident partiality by the very failure to disclose facts that might create a reasonable impression of the arbitrator's partiality. The evident partiality is demonstrated from the nondisclosure, regardless of whether actual bias is established.

Such a demanding disclosure rule ensures that the parties will be privy to a potential arbitrator's biases at the outset, when they are "free to reject the arbitrator or accept him with knowledge of the relationship and continuing faith in his objectivity," and allow the parties, who are "far better informed of the prevailing ethical standards and reputations within their business," to be the "architects of their own arbitration process." A simple disclosure requirement minimizes the role of the courts in weighing arbitrators' potential conflicts, and at the same time, minimizes the discretion of the arbitrators in determining what to reveal. In addition, as the district court stated, "the full disclosure rule of *Commonwealth Coatings* reinforces the parties' expectations that arbitrators will abide by the Rule of the American Arbitration Association (and related rules), which the Supreme Court deemed 'highly significant.' "

The standard we adopt comports with Canon II of the AAA's Code of Ethics for Arbitrators in Commercial Disputes ("Code of Ethics"), which provides, in relevant part:

> A. Persons who are requested to serve as arbitrators should, before accepting, disclose:
>
> * * *
>
> (2) Any existing or past financial, business, professional, family or social relationships which are likely to affect impartiality or which might reasonably create any appearance of partiality or bias. . . .
>
> * * *
>
> B. The obligation to disclose interests or relationships described in the preceding paragraph A is a continuing duty which requires a person who accepts appointment as an arbitrator to disclose, at any stage of the arbitration, any such interests or relationships which may arise, or which are recalled or discovered.

We note that we are not adopting an inflexible *per se* rule in nondisclosure cases. While an arbitrator to be selected by the parties need not disclose relationships that are trivial, an arbitrator should always err in favor of disclosure.

C.

We now apply the standard we adopt to the facts of this case. Based on the facts of this case, New Century contends that no matter what standard this court adopts, including the standard above, Positive Software cannot meet that standard. We disagree.

[. . .]

After reviewing the facts, we hold, like the district court did, that Shurn's past professional relationship with Susman Godfrey and Camiña might have conveyed an impression of possible partiality to a reasonable person. It is important to remember that the issue is only whether Shurn's prior professional relationship might reasonably give someone who is considering his services as an arbitrator the impression that he might favor one litigant over the other. It is not hard to think that Positive Software might not want to employ his services in an arbitration hearing with New Century once it discovered his prior relationship with the law firm and counsel representing New Century. On the other hand, Positive Software might decide that Shurn's qualifications as an arbitrator outweigh whatever concerns it might have. The point is simply that the information should have been disclosed to Positive Software so that it could make that decision. The integrity of the arbitral process demands no less.

New Century argues that a finding of evident partiality under the facts of this case would make the job of finding a qualified arbitrator burdensome and would disqualify most attorneys from large firms from acting as arbitrators. We disagree. Qualified arbitrators would not be disqualified from acting as arbitrators, rather, they would merely have to disclose their past relationships, and then it would be for the parties to decide whether, based on the disclosure, the arbitrator merits objection.

We conclude that the district court properly vacated the arbitration award by reason of Shurn's failure to reveal to the parties his prior professional relationship with Susman Godfrey and Camiña. We hasten to add that we do not imply that Shurn was guilty of any wrongdoing or that he was in fact biased or influenced by reason of the relationship. Nevertheless, as Justice Black emphasized in *Commonwealth Coatings,* such relationships must be disclosed to the parties if the integrity and effectiveness of the arbitration process is to be preserved.

IV.

New Century maintains that Positive Software waived its nondisclosure objection by failing to raise the issue until after the arbitration award. The district court found that Positive Software was unaware of the undisclosed relationship until after the arbitration, and accordingly, held that Positive Software did not waive its objection to the nondisclosure.

This court has not considered the issue of waiver of a nondisclosure objection. Our sister circuits require *actual knowledge* of an arbitrator's potential partiality on the part of the complaining party prior to the arbitration proceeding as foundational to waiver.[50] We agree with our sister circuits and hold that one must have actual knowledge of the presence of a conflict of interest before one can waive the conflict. To hold otherwise, would turn the arbitration process on its head by shifting the onus from requiring an arbitrator to assume the duty of disclosure to requiring a party to assume a duty to investigate.

Turning to the facts of this case, there is no evidence that Positive Software had actual knowledge of Shurn's past professional relationship with Susman Godfrey and Camiña. . . . Based on these facts, we will not disturb the district court's finding that Positive Software did not learn of the professional relationship until after the arbitration, and therefore, did not waive its objection to the nondisclosure.

V.

In vacating the arbitration award, the district court ordered that in the second arbitration, the parties must refrain from certain practices, including referring to any ruling of the first arbitrator and advising the new arbitrator of the first arbitrator's award. New Century argues that the district court did not have the authority to dictate procedures for a second arbitration. We agree and hold that the district court erred in specifying procedures for the second arbitration. Here, the district court lacked authority to go beyond vacating the award and dictating how the parties and the arbitrator should proceed in the second arbitration.

VI.

The district court's judgment vacating the arbitration award is modified to vacate the portion of the district court's judgment that regulates a subsequent arbitration and, as modified, is affirmed.

---

[50] *See, e.g., Apperson,* 879 F.2d at 1359 (affirming the district court's conclusion that, "as a general rule, a grievant must object to an arbitrator's partiality at the arbitration hearing before such an objection will be considered by the federal courts" but highlighting that "[t]he successful party . . . may not rely on the failure to object for bias . . . unless '[a]ll the facts now argued as to [the] alleged bias were known . . . at the time the joint committee heard their grievances' "); *Middlesex,* 675 F.2d at 1204 ("Waiver applies only where a party has acted with full knowledge of the facts.").

NOTES AND QUESTIONS

1. How does *Positive Software* compare to *Certain Underwriting Members of Lloyds of London*? Is the Second or Fifth Circuit more faithful to *Commonwealth Coatings*?

2. Why do you think that Shurn, in *Positive Software*, failed to reveal his prior professional relationship with Susman Godfrey and Camiña? Do you believe that he withheld information in order to gain the appointment? Do you agree with the court that, although there was no evidence of actual bias or partiality, "[t]he integrity of the arbitral process demands no less" than that he be obligated to reveal his prior relationships?

3. How do you assess the AAA's twelve-question form? What is the purpose of the document? Is it likely to be effective? How would you advise prospective arbitrators and clients?

4. The court references the AAA. Rule 17 of the AAA Commercial Arbitration Rules and Mediation Procedures imposes a generalized and continuing obligation of disclosure, but it does not provide any details about the content of the disclosure. The Canon II of the AAA The Code of Ethics for Arbitrators in Commercial Disputes (2004), cited by the court, does provide a more robust set standards for disclosure.

Perhaps the most specific guidance available regarding disclosures is provided by the International Bar Association's (IBA) Guidelines on Conflicts of Interest in International Arbitration (2014). These Guidelines provide a detailed list of potential conflicts and then hierarchically color codes them in terms of their significance: Non-Waivable Red, Waivable Red, Orange, and Green.

5. In your evaluation of the case law, you should remember that the consequence of a finding of evident partiality results in the vacatur of the award. There is no possibility of retrieval or other means of lessening the consequences of the finding. The award is absolutely null and without effect. Also, there is no arbitrator malpractice. In fact, arbitrators are immune from civil liability for acts arising out of or related to their duties. *See, e.g., Pfannenstiel v. Merrill Lynch, Pierce, Fenner & Smith,* 477 F.3d 1155 (10th Cir. 2007) (noting that every other circuit that has considered the issue of arbitral immunity recognizes the doctrine and that supreme court precedent also supports the doctrine of arbitral immunity). Therefore, the only available relief is to begin another arbitration and select more professional arbitrators.

6. Did the challenging party wait too long to state its opposition to the arbitrator? When should such challenges be made? The court discusses this issue, without providing a lot of guidance, at the end of the opinion. It concludes that there was no wavier of the right to object to the arbitrator's partiality under the circumstances.

That said, a party to an arbitration with knowledge of facts possibly indicating bias or prejudice on the part of an arbitrator should object at the earliest moment, giving the arbitrator an opportunity to decide whether to continue in the appointment. *See, e.g., Delta Mine Holding Co. v. AFC Coal Properties, Inc.,* 280 F.3d 815, 821 (8th Cir. 2001) ("Even when a neutral arbitrator is challenged for evident partiality, the issue is deemed waived unless the objecting party raised it to the arbitration panel."). Requiring a timely objection preserves the functionality of the arbitral process. A party cannot hold onto a potential conflict that she knows about, waiting to see if the arbitration turns out in her favor, before objecting. She must, instead, act swiftly or be deemed to have abandoned her right to object.

7. Imagine that you need to explain the law of impartiality to a novice associate or client. Is the applicable standard statutory or decisional? What role do disclosures play? Do they, once made, absolve the arbitrator of any failing in regard to impartiality? How does the reasonable person gauge factor into the process? Do presumptions exist? Is timing important? Write out your understanding of this area of law in detail.

5. ARBITRAL MISCONDUCT

Parties may give up their "day in court" when they agree to arbitrate, but they still have a reasonable right to be heard. FAA § 10(a)(3) permits courts to vacate an arbitration award where "the arbitrators were guilty of misconduct in refusing to postpone the hearing, upon sufficient cause shown, or in refusing to hear evidence pertinent and material to the controversy; or of any other misbehavior by which the rights of any party have been prejudiced." *See also* RUAA § 23(a)(3), (a)(6). This provision may be summarized as requiring arbitrators to provide the parties with a "fundamentally fair hearing."

In practice, misconduct issues come up infrequently for at least two reasons. First, arbitrators enjoy broad discretion regarding the management of hearings and the receipt of evidence under the law of arbitration, and such discretion is reinforced by standard arbitration rules. *See, e.g., DFM Investments, LLC v. Brandspring Sols., LLC,* No. 17–2447, 2018 WL 3569353, at *2 (8th Cir. July 25, 2018) (refusing to vacate for misconduct merely because the arbitrator concluded that certain additional evidence was not material); *Hyatt Franchising, L.L.C. v. Shen Zhen New World I, LLC,* 876 F.3d 900, 902 (7th Cir. 2017) ("§ 10(a)(3) does not provide for substantive review of an arbitrator's decisions. It provides for judicial intervention when an arbitrator commits "misbehavior", but an error differs in kind from misbehavior.").

For instance, in *Campbell v. American Family Life Assurance Co. of Columbus, Inc.*, 613 F. Supp. 2d 1114 (D. Minn. 2009), the arbitrators granted the defendant's motion for summary judgment instead of conducting an evidentiary hearing. In the underlying dispute, two state sales coordinators had brought claims in arbitration against their employer for wrongful termination. After discovery, the employer brought and won a motion for summary judgment. The plaintiffs sought to vacate the award for a failure to hear pertinent and material evidence.

The court concluded that summary judgment is permissible in arbitration. The court also found that the plaintiffs had waived any objections to the use of summary judgment by failing to go on the record with objections. Finally, even if such objections were not subject to waiver, "the [p]laintiffs were afforded an opportunity to present arguments and evidence to the arbitrators, and they [did] not demonstrate[ ] any prejudice resulting from the arbitrators' use of summary judgment." *Id.* at 1120.

Similarly, in *Akpele v. Pac. Life Ins. Co.*, 646 F. App'x 908 (11th Cir. 2016), a widow arbitrated negligence and intentional torts claims against defendants after she discovered that she was not named as a beneficiary in three of her husband's retirement accounts. At the hearing, the plaintiff offered into evidence a defined benefit plan and its trust document, sponsored by her late husband's medical practice. Ostensibly, she wanted to show that spousal consent was required to change a beneficiary. The panel, however, excluded the two documents because the plaintiff did not produce the documents in a timely manner in violation of FINRA discovery rules.

After the plaintiff lost in arbitration, she moved to vacate the award under this section, claiming the panel's preclusion of the two documents was arbitrator misconduct under section 10(a)(3). The Eleventh Circuit held that the exclusion of the documents was reasonable because of the discovery violation. Further, the court agreed with the district court that the panel's decision was not made in bad faith, and did not deprive the plaintiff of a fair hearing. *Id.* at 913.

The second reason misconduct issues rarely arise is because arbitrators tend to err on the side of allowing all evidence to be heard. Arbitrators have strong professional incentives to make sure that their awards are enforceable, and one of the easiest ways to do this is by allowing all evidence to be considered. A court might be tempted to vacate an award because an arbitrator excluded evidence, but no court will vacate an award because an arbitrator allowed irrelevant evidence to be used in a hearing.

6. EXCESS OF AUTHORITY

Arbitrators' power derives from the arbitration agreement. Arbitrators can do only what the parties have authorized. FAA § 10(a)(4) permits courts to vacate an arbitration award where "the arbitrators exceeded their powers." *See also* RUAA § 23(a)(5). The inquiry "focuses on whether the arbitrators had the power, based on the parties' submissions or the arbitration agreement, to reach a certain issue, not whether the arbitrators correctly decided the issue." *Westerbeke Corp. v. Daihatsu Motor Co.*, 304 F.3d 200, 220 (2d Cir. 2002).

In theory, this ground for review appears to offer the greatest opportunity for aggrieved parties to overturn awards. *See, e.g.,* Thomas J. Brewer, Lawrence R. Mills, *When Arbitrators "Exceed Their Powers" A New Study of Vacated Arbitration Awards,* DISP. RESOL. J., FEBRUARY-APRIL 2009, AT 46 (noting that their earlier 2004 study found that excess of authority was the most frequently raised and successful challenge to arbitral awards). In practice, as with the other grounds for review, courts are careful not to let parties who are merely disappointed with the outcome escape the consequences of their choice to arbitrate. *See id.* (finding that over than 90% of awards are confirmed).

STOLT-NIELSEN S.A. V. ANIMALFEEDS INTERNATIONAL CORP.

559 U.S. 662, 130 S.Ct. 1758, 176 L.Ed.2d 605 (2010).

JUSTICE ALITO delivered the opinion of the Court.

We granted certiorari in this case to decide whether imposing class arbitration on parties whose arbitration clauses are "silent" on that issue is consistent with the Federal Arbitration Act. . . .

I

A

Petitioners are shipping companies that serve a large share of the world market for parcel tankers-seagoing vessels with compartments that are separately chartered to customers wishing to ship liquids in small quantities. One of those customers is AnimalFeeds International Corp. (hereinafter AnimalFeeds), which supplies raw ingredients, such as fish oil, to animal-feed producers around the world. AnimalFeeds ships its goods pursuant to a standard contract known in the maritime trade as a charter party. [Footnote omitted.] Numerous charter parties are in regular use, and the charter party that AnimalFeeds uses is known as the "Vegoilvoy" charter party. Petitioners assert, without contradiction, that charterers like AnimalFeeds, or their agents-not the shipowners-typically select the particular charter party that governs their shipments. . . .

Adopted in 1950, the Vegoilvoy charter party contains the following arbitration clause:

"Arbitration. Any dispute arising from the making, performance or termination of this Charter Party shall be settled in New York, Owner and Charterer each appointing an arbitrator, who shall be a merchant, broker or individual experienced in the shipping business; the two thus chosen, if they cannot agree, shall nominate a third arbitrator who shall be an Admiralty lawyer. Such arbitration shall be conducted in conformity with the provisions and procedure of the United States Arbitration Act [*i.e.,* the

FAA], and a judgment of the Court shall be entered upon any award made by said arbitrator." . . .

In 2003, a Department of Justice criminal investigation revealed that petitioners were engaging in an illegal price-fixing conspiracy. When AnimalFeeds learned of this, it brought a putative class action against petitioners in the District Court for the Eastern District of Pennsylvania, asserting antitrust claims for supracompetitive [sic] [supercompetitive] prices that petitioners allegedly charged their customers over a period of several years.

Other charterers brought similar suits. In one of these, the District Court for the District of Connecticut held that the charterers' claims were not subject to arbitration under the applicable arbitration clause, but the Second Circuit reversed. See *JLM Industries, Inc. v. Stolt-Nielsen S.A.,* 387 F.3d 163, 183 (2004). While that appeal was pending, the Judicial Panel on Multidistrict Litigation ordered the consolidation of then-pending actions against petitioners, including AnimalFeeds' action, in the District of Connecticut. . . . The parties agree that as a consequence of these judgments and orders, AnimalFeeds and petitioners must arbitrate their antitrust dispute.

B

In 2005, AnimalFeeds served petitioners with a demand for class arbitration, designating New York City as the place of arbitration and seeking to represent a class of "[a]ll direct purchasers of parcel tanker transportation services globally for bulk liquid chemicals, edible oils, acids, and other specialty liquids from [petitioners] at any time during the period from August 1, 1998, to November 30, 2002." . . . The parties entered into a supplemental agreement providing for the question of class arbitration to be submitted to a panel of three arbitrators who were to "follow and be bound by Rules 3 through 7 of the American Arbitration Association's Supplementary Rules for Class Arbitrations (as effective Oct. 8, 2003)." . . . These rules (hereinafter Class Rules) were developed by the American Arbitration Association (AAA) after our decision in *Green Tree Financial Corp. v. Bazzle,* 539 U.S. 444, 123 S.Ct. 2402, 156 L.Ed.2d 414 (2003), and Class Rule 3, in accordance with the plurality opinion in that case, requires an arbitrator, as a threshold matter, to determine "whether the applicable arbitration clause permits the arbitration to proceed on behalf of or against a class." . . .

The parties selected a panel of arbitrators and stipulated that the arbitration clause was "silent" with respect to class arbitration. Counsel for AnimalFeeds explained to the arbitration panel that the term "silent" did not simply mean that the clause made no express reference to class arbitration. Rather, he said, "[a]ll the parties agree that when a contract is silent on an issue there's been no agreement that has been reached on that issue." . . .

After hearing argument and evidence, including testimony from petitioners' experts regarding arbitration customs and usage in the maritime trade, the arbitrators concluded that the arbitration clause allowed for class arbitration. They found persuasive the fact that other arbitrators ruling after *Bazzle* had construed "a wide variety of clauses in a wide variety of settings as allowing for class arbitration," but the panel acknowledged that none of these decisions was "exactly comparable" to the present dispute. . . . Petitioners' expert evidence did not show an "inten[t] to preclude class arbitration," the arbitrators reasoned, and petitioners' argument would leave "no basis for a class action absent express agreement among all parties and the putative class members." . . .

The arbitrators stayed the proceeding to allow the parties to seek judicial review, and petitioners filed an application to vacate the arbitrators' award in the District Court for the Southern District of New York. . . . The District Court vacated the award, concluding that the arbitrators' decision was made in "manifest disregard" of the law insofar as the arbitrators failed to conduct a choice-of-law analysis. . . . Had such an analysis been conducted, the District Court held, the arbitrators would have applied the rule of federal maritime law requiring that contracts be interpreted in light of custom and usage. . . .

AnimalFeeds appealed to the Court of Appeals, which reversed. . . . As an initial matter, the Court of Appeals held that the "manifest disregard" standard survived our decision in *Hall Street Associates, L.L.C. v. Mattel, Inc.*, 552 U.S. 576, 128 S.Ct. 1396, 170 L.Ed.2d 254 (2008), as a "judicial gloss" on the enumerated grounds for vacatur of arbitration awards under 9 U.S.C. § 10. . . . Nonetheless, the Court of Appeals concluded that, because petitioners had cited no authority applying a federal maritime rule of custom and usage *against* class arbitration, the arbitrators' decision was not in manifest disregard of federal maritime law. . . . Nor had the arbitrators manifestly disregarded New York law, the Court of Appeals continued, since nothing in New York case law established a rule against class arbitration. . . .

We granted certiorari. 557 U.S. ___ (2009). [Footnote omitted.]

II

A

Petitioners contend that the decision of the arbitration panel must be vacated, but in order to obtain that relief, they must clear a high hurdle. It is not enough for petitioners to show that the panel committed an error-or even a serious error. . . . "It is only when [an] arbitrator strays from interpretation and application of the agreement and effectively 'dispense[s] his own brand of industrial justice' that his decision may be unenforceable." . . . In that situation, an arbitration decision may be vacated under § 10(a)(4) of the FAA on the ground that the arbitrator "exceeded [his] powers," for the task of an arbitrator is to interpret and enforce a contract, not to make public policy. In this case, we must conclude that what the arbitration panel did was simply to impose its own view of sound policy regarding class arbitration.[3]

B

1

In its memorandum of law filed in the arbitration proceedings, AnimalFeeds made three arguments in support of construing the arbitration clause to permit class arbitration:

"The parties' arbitration clause should be construed to allow class arbitration because (a) the clause is silent on the issue of class treatment and, without express prohibition, class arbitration is permitted under *Bazzle*; *(b) the clause should be construed to permit class arbitration as a matter of public policy*; and (c) the clause would be unconscionable and unenforceable if it forbade class arbitration." . . .

The arbitrators expressly rejected AnimalFeeds' first argument . . . and said nothing about the third. Instead, the panel appears to have rested its decision on AnimalFeeds' public policy argument. Because the parties agreed their agreement was "silent" in the sense that they had not reached any agreement on the issue of class arbitration, the arbitrators' proper task was to identify the rule of law that governs in that situation. Had they engaged in that undertaking, they presumably would have looked either to the FAA itself or to one of the two bodies of law that the parties claimed were governing, *i.e.,* either federal maritime law or New York law. But the panel did not consider whether the FAA provides the rule of decision in such a situation; nor did the panel attempt to determine what rule would govern under either maritime or New York law in the case of a "silent" contract. Instead, the panel based its decision on post-*Bazzle* arbitral decisions that "construed a wide variety of clauses in a wide variety of settings as allowing for class arbitration." . . . The panel did not mention whether any of these decisions were based on a rule derived from the FAA or on maritime or New York law.[4]

---

[3] We do not decide whether " 'manifest disregard' " survives our decision in *Hall Street Associates, L.L.C. v. Mattel, Inc.,* 552 U.S. 576, 585, 128 S.Ct. 1396, 170 L.Ed.2d 254 (2008), as an independent ground for review or as a judicial gloss on the enumerated grounds for vacatur set forth at 9 U.S.C. § 10. AnimalFeeds characterizes that standard as requiring a showing that the arbitrators "knew of the relevant [legal] principle, appreciated that this principle controlled the outcome of the disputed issue, and nonetheless willfully flouted the governing law by refusing to apply it." . . . Assuming, *arguendo,* that such a standard applies, we find it satisfied for the reasons that follow.

[4] The panel's reliance on these arbitral awards confirms that the panel's decision was not based on a determination regarding the parties' intent. All of the arbitral awards were made under

Rather than inquiring whether the FAA, maritime law, or New York law contains a "default rule" under which an arbitration clause is construed as allowing class arbitration in the absence of express consent, the panel proceeded as if it had the authority of a common-law court to develop what it viewed as the best rule to be applied in such a situation. Perceiving a post-*Bazzle* consensus among arbitrators that class arbitration is beneficial in "a wide variety of settings," the panel considered only whether there was any good reason not to follow that consensus in this case. . . . The panel was not persuaded by "court cases denying consolidation of arbitrations,"[5] by undisputed evidence that the Vegoilvoy charter party had "never been the basis of a class action," or by expert opinion that "sophisticated, multinational commercial parties of the type that are sought to be included in the class would never intend that the arbitration clauses would permit a class arbitration."[6] . . . Accordingly, finding no convincing ground for

the AAA's Class Rules, which were adopted in 2003, and thus none was available when the parties here entered into the Vegoilvoy charter party during the class period ranging from 1998 to 2002. . . . Indeed, at the hearing before the panel, counsel for AnimalFeeds conceded that "[w]hen you talk about expectations, virtually every one of the arbitration clauses that were the subject of the 25 AAA decisions were drafted before *[Bazzle]*. So therefore, if you are going to talk about the parties' intentions, pre-*[Bazzle]* class arbitrations were not common, post *[Bazzle]* they are common." . . . Moreover, in its award, the panel appeared to acknowledge that none of the cited arbitration awards involved a contract between sophisticated business entities. . . .

[5] See *Government of United Kingdom v. Boeing Co.,* 998 F.2d 68, 71, 74 (C.A.2 1993); see also *Glencore, Ltd. v. Schnitzer Steel Prods. Co.,* 189 F.3d 264, 268 (C.A.2 1999); *Champ v. Siegel Trading Co.,* 55 F.3d 269, 275 (C.A.7 1995). Unlike the subsequent arbitration awards that the arbitrators cited, these decisions were available to the parties when they entered into their contracts.

[6] Petitioners produced expert evidence from experienced maritime arbitrators demonstrating that it is customary in the shipping business for parties to resolve their disputes through bilateral arbitration. See, *e.g.,* . . . (expert declaration of John Kimball) ("In the 30 years I have been practicing as a maritime lawyer, I have never encountered an arbitration clause in a charter party that could be construed as allowing class action arbitration"); *id.,* . . . (expert declaration of Bruce Harris) ("I have been working as a maritime arbitrator for thirty years and this matter is the first I have ever encountered where the issue of a class action arbitration has even been raised"). These experts amplified their written statements in their live testimony, as well. See, *e.g.,* . . . (Mr. Kimball) (opining that the prospect of a class action in a maritime arbitration would be "quite foreign" to overseas shipping executives and charterers); *id.,* . . . (Mr. Harris) (opining that in the view of the London Corps of International Arbitration, class arbitration is "inconceivable").

Under both New York law and general maritime law, evidence of "custom and usage" is relevant to determining the parties' intent when an express agreement is ambiguous. See *Excess Ins. Co. v. Factory Mut. Ins. Co.,* 3 N.Y.3d 577, 590–591, 789 N.Y.S.2d 461, 822 N.E.2d 768, 777 (2004) ("Our precedent establishes that where there is ambiguity in a reinsurance certificate, the surrounding circumstances, including industry custom and practice, should be taken into consideration"); *Lopez v. Consolidated Edison Co. of N. Y.,* 40 N.Y.2d 605, 609, 389 N.Y.S.2d 295, 357 N.E.2d 951, 954–955 (1976) (where contract terms were ambiguous, parol evidence of custom and practice was properly admitted to show parties' intent); *407 East 61st Garage, Inc. v. Savoy Fifth Avenue Corp.,* 23 N.Y.2d 275, 281, 296 N.Y.S.2d 338, 244 N.E.2d 37, 41 (1968) (contract was "not so free from ambiguity to preclude extrinsic evidence" of industry "custom and usage" that would "establish the correct interpretation or understanding of the agreement as to its term"). See also *Great Circle Lines, Ltd. v. Matheson & Co.,* 681 F.2d 121, 125 (C.A.2 1982) ("Certain long-standing customs of the shipping industry are crucial factors to be considered when deciding whether there has been a meeting of the minds on a maritime contract"); *Samsun Corp. v. Khozestan Mashine Kar Co.,* 926 F.Supp. 436, 439 (S.D.N.Y.1996) ("[W]here as here the contract is one of charter party, established practices and customs of the shipping industry inform the court's analysis of what the parties agreed to"); Hough, Admiralty Jurisdiction—Of Late Years, 37 departing from the post-*Bazzle* arbitral consensus, the panel held that class arbitration was permitted in this case. . . . The conclusion is inescapable that the panel simply imposed its own conception of sound policy.[7]

2

It is true that the panel opinion makes a few references to intent, but none of these shows that the panel did anything other than impose its own policy preference. The opinion states that, under *Bazzle,* "arbitrators must look to the language of the parties' agreement to ascertain the parties' intention whether they intended to permit or to preclude class action," and the panel added that "[t]his is also consistent with New York law." . . . But the panel had no occasion to "ascertain the parties' intention" in the present case because the parties were in complete agreement regarding their intent. In the very next sentence after the one quoted above, the panel acknowledged that the parties in this case agreed that the Vegoilvoy charter party was "silent on whether [it] permit[ted] or preclude[d] class arbitration," but that the charter party was "not ambiguous so as to call for parol evidence." . . . This stipulation left no room for an inquiry regarding the parties' intent, and any inquiry into that settled question would have been outside the panel's assigned task.

The panel also commented on the breadth of the language in the Vegoilvoy charter party, . . . but since the only task that was left for the panel, in light of the parties' stipulation, was to identify the governing rule applicable in a case in which neither the language of the contract nor any other evidence established that the parties had reached any agreement on the question of class arbitration, the particular wording of the charter party was quite beside the point.

In sum, instead of identifying and applying a rule of decision derived from the FAA or either maritime or New York law, the arbitration panel imposed its own policy choice and thus exceeded its powers. As a result, under § 10(b) of the FAA, we must either "direct a rehearing by the arbitrators" or decide the question that was originally referred to the panel.

Harv. L.Rev. 529, 536 (1924) (noting that "maritime law is a body of sea customs" and the "custom of the sea . . . includes a customary interpretation of contract language").

7 The dissent calls this conclusion "hardly fair," noting that the word " 'policy' is not so much as mentioned in the arbitrators' award." . . . But just as merely saying something is so does not make it so, . . . the arbitrators need not have said they were relying on policy to make it so. At the hearing before the arbitration panel, one of the arbitrators recognized that the body of post-*Bazzle* arbitration awards on which AnimalFeeds relied involved "essentially consumer non-value cases." . . . In response, counsel for AnimalFeeds defended the applicability of those awards by asserting that the "vast majority" of the claimants against petitioners "have negative value claims . . . meaning it costs more to litigate than you would get if you won." . . . The panel credited this body of awards in concluding that petitioners had not demonstrated the parties' intent to preclude class arbitration, and further observed that if petitioners' anticonsolidation precedents controlled, then "there would appear to be no basis for a class action absent express agreement among all parties and the putative class members." . . .

Because we conclude that there can be only one possible outcome on the facts before us, we see no need to direct a rehearing by the arbitrators.

[. . .]

IV

While the interpretation of an arbitration agreement is generally a matter of state law, . . . the FAA imposes certain rules of fundamental importance, including the basic precept that arbitration "is a matter of consent, not coercion." . . .

A

In 1925, Congress enacted the United States Arbitration Act, as the FAA was formerly known, for the express purpose of making "valid and enforceable written provisions or agreements for arbitration of disputes arising out of contracts, maritime transactions, or commerce among the States or Territories or with foreign nations." . . . Reenacted and codified in 1947 [footnote omitted], . . . the FAA provides, in pertinent part, that a "written provision in any maritime transaction" calling for the arbitration of a controversy arising out of such transaction "shall be valid, irrevocable, and enforceable, save upon such grounds as exist at law or in equity for the revocation of any contract," . . . Under the FAA, a party to an arbitration agreement may petition a United States district court for an order directing that "arbitration proceed in the manner provided for in such agreement." . . . Consistent with these provisions, we have said on numerous occasions that the central or "primary" purpose of the FAA is to ensure that "private agreements to arbitrate are enforced according to their terms." . . .

Whether enforcing an agreement to arbitrate or construing an arbitration clause, courts and arbitrators must "give effect to the contractual rights and expectations of the parties." . . . In this endeavor, "as with any other contract, the parties' intentions control." . . . This is because an arbitrator derives his or her powers from the parties' agreement to forgo the legal process and submit their disputes to private dispute resolution. . . .

Underscoring the consensual nature of private dispute resolution, we have held that parties are " 'generally free to structure their arbitration agreements as they see fit.' " . . . For example, we have held that parties may agree to limit the issues they choose to arbitrate, . . . and may agree on rules under which any arbitration will proceed. . . . They may choose who will resolve specific disputes. . . .

We think it is also clear from our precedents and the contractual nature of arbitration that parties may specify *with whom* they choose to arbitrate their disputes. . . . It falls to courts and arbitrators to give effect to these contractual limitations, and when doing so, courts and arbitrators must not lose sight of the purpose of the exercise: to give effect to the intent of the parties. . . .

B

From these principles, it follows that a party may not be compelled under the FAA to submit to class arbitration unless there is a contractual basis for concluding that the party *agreed* to do so. In this case, however, the arbitration panel imposed class arbitration even though the parties concurred that they had reached "no agreement" on that issue. . . . The critical point, in the view of the arbitration panel, was that petitioners did not "establish that the parties to the charter agreements intended to *preclude* class arbitration." . . . Even though the parties are sophisticated business entities, even though there is no tradition of class arbitration under maritime law, and even though AnimalFeeds does not dispute that it is customary for the shipper to choose the charter party that is used for a particular shipment, the panel regarded the agreement's silence on the question of class arbitration as dispositive. The panel's conclusion is fundamentally at war with the foundational FAA principle that arbitration is a matter of consent.

In certain contexts, it is appropriate to presume that parties that enter into an arbitration agreement implicitly authorize the arbitrator to adopt such procedures as are necessary to give effect to the parties' agreement. Thus, we have said that " ' "procedural" questions which grow out of the dispute and bear on its final disposition' are presumptively not for the judge, but for an arbitrator, to decide." . . . This recognition is grounded in the background principle that "[w]hen the parties to a bargain sufficiently defined to be a contract have not agreed with respect to a term which is essential to a determination of their rights and duties, a term which is reasonable in the circumstances is supplied by the court." Restatement (Second) of Contracts § 204 (1979).

An implicit agreement to authorize class-action arbitration, however, is not a term that the arbitrator may infer solely from the fact of the parties' agreement to arbitrate. This is so because class-action arbitration changes the nature of arbitration to such a degree that it cannot be presumed the parties consented to it by simply agreeing to submit their disputes to an arbitrator. In bilateral arbitration, parties forgo the procedural rigor and appellate review of the courts in order to realize the benefits of private dispute resolution: lower costs, greater efficiency and speed, and the ability to choose expert adjudicators to resolve specialized disputes. . . . But the relative benefits of class-action arbitration are much less assured, giving reason to doubt the parties' mutual consent to resolve disputes through class-wide arbitration. . . .

Consider just some of the fundamental changes brought about by the shift from bilateral arbitration to class-action arbitration. An arbitrator chosen according to an agreed-upon procedure . . . no longer resolves a single dispute between the parties to a single agreement, but instead resolves many disputes between hundreds or perhaps even thousands of parties. . . . Under the Class Rules, "the presumption of privacy and confidentiality" that applies in many bilateral arbitrations "shall not apply in class arbitrations." . . . The arbitrator's award no longer purports to bind just the parties to a single arbitration agreement, but adjudicates the rights of absent parties as well. . . . And the commercial stakes of class-action arbitration are comparable to those of class-action litigation . . . even though the scope of judicial review is much more limited. . . . We think that the differences between bilateral and class-action arbitration are too great for arbitrators to presume, consistent with their limited powers under the FAA, that the parties' mere silence on the issue of class-action arbitration constitutes consent to resolve their disputes in class proceedings.[10]

The dissent minimizes these crucial differences by characterizing the question before the arbitrators as being merely what "procedural mode" was available to present AnimalFeeds' claims. . . . If the question were that simple, there would be no need to consider the parties' intent with respect to class arbitration. . . . But the FAA requires more. Contrary to the dissent, but consistent with our precedents emphasizing the consensual basis of arbitration, we see the question as being whether the parties *agreed to authorize* class arbitration. Here, where the parties stipulated that there was "no agreement" on this question, it follows that the parties cannot be compelled to submit their dispute to class arbitration.

V

For these reasons, the judgment of the Court of Appeals is reversed, and the case is remanded for further proceedings consistent with this opinion.

It is so ordered.

JUSTICE SOTOMAYOR took no part in the consideration or decision of this case.

JUSTICE GINSBURG, with whom JUSTICE STEVENS and JUSTICE BREYER join, dissenting.

[. . .]

NOTES AND QUESTIONS

1. What is the majority's primary objection to the arbitrators' award? The arbitrators were not disabled by the parties' arbitration agreement from imposing class arbitration. To the contrary, the agreement was silent about

[10] We have no occasion to decide what contractual basis may support a finding that the parties agreed to authorize class-action arbitration. Here, as noted, the parties stipulated that there was "no agreement" on the issue of class-action arbitration. . . .

the matter. Given this silence, why couldn't the arbitrators fill in a gap in the agreement and decide that class arbitration was appropriate? Does the Court's holding mean that arbitrators have less power than common law courts to interpret and apply contracts?

2. What does the Court mean to say when it invokes the ground of excess of authority under FAA § 10(a)(4)? Did the arbitrators commit an error of law?

3. *Stolt-Nielsen* pre-dates *Concepcion* by a year. You should recognize, in its discussion, many of the predicate concepts that would inform the *Concepcion* holding, including that "class-action arbitration changes the nature of arbitration to such a degree that it cannot be presumed the parties consented to it by simply agreeing to submit their disputes to an arbitrator."

4. In *Bazzle*, discussed in *Stolt-Nielsen* at some length, the Supreme Court granted certiorari to resolve the following question: "Whether the Federal Arbitration Act, 9 U.S.C. § 1 *et seq.*, prohibits class-action procedures from being superimposed onto an arbitration agreement that does not provide for class-action arbitration." Technically, the question presented was one of preemption, because the class arbitration rule was based on state law. The Court, however, did not resolve the preemption question. In fact, only the dissenting Justices even reached it. Instead, the Court issued four separate opinions none of which commanded a majority.

The plurality in *Bazzle*, comprised of Justices Breyer, Scalia, Souter, and Ginsburg, concluded that the FAA required the arbitrator to determine "whether the arbitration contracts forbid class arbitration," vacating the South Carolina Supreme Court's judgment and remanding for further proceedings. Justice Stevens had a slightly different view, concluding that "nothing in the Federal Arbitration Act" conflicted with South Carolina court's finding that the parties' agreement was silent on class arbitration and therefore, as a matter of state law, class arbitration was permissible. He nevertheless concurred so that there would be a controlling judgment of the court.

Chief Justice Rehnquist dissented, joined by Justices O'Connor and Kennedy. The dissenting justices construed the parties' agreement as precluding class arbitration: petitioner's "contractual right to choose an arbitrator for each dispute with the other 3,734 individual class members . . . was denied when the same arbitrator was foisted upon petitioner to resolve those claims as well." Because "the Supreme Court of South Carolina imposed a regime that was contrary to the express agreement of the parties as to how the arbitrator would be chosen," its decision was contrary to the FAA. (Justice Thomas also dissented on the ground that the FAA does not apply in state court and so "the FAA cannot be a ground for pre-empting a state court's interpretation of a private arbitration agreement.")

Given this background, what, if anything does *Bazzle* stand for? Is anything left of the decision after *Stolt-Nielsen*?

5. *Stolt-Nielsen* is, itself, a complicated and somewhat confusing case. Read narrowly, the only issue was whether the arbitrators exceeded their authority by looking to public policy when the parties had stipulated that there was no agreement to class arbitration. If the answer was "yes," as the Court found, then the doctrinally appropriate response was to vacate the award and send the matter back to the arbitrators. Instead, the Court went further and decided, for itself, whether the parties had agreed to class arbitration.

In so doing, the Court failed to provide much guidance about the caliber and quantity of evidence necessary to establish an agreement to arbitrate on a classwide basis. Additionally, confusion persists about who decides whether an agreement authorizes class arbitration.

Both of these issues should have some resolution soon. As discussed in Note 1 after *Epic Systems*, a Circuit split has been heating up about whether courts or arbitrators decide whether an arbitration agreement allows for class actions? The Third, Fourth, Sixth and Eight Circuits have all held that class arbitrability is an issue that is presumably for courts (not arbitrators) to decide, even if the parties incorporate rules that generally delegate issues of arbitrability to an arbitrator. The Second, Tenth, and Eleventh Circuits disagree. This split seems ripe for consideration by the Supreme Court. Moreover, the Supreme Court will address, in its 2019 term, how specific the language of an arbitration agreement must be in order to authorize class arbitration. *See Lamps Plus, Inc. v. Varela,* 138 S. Ct. 1697, 200 L.Ed. 2d 948 (2018).

OXFORD HEALTH PLANS LLC V. SUTTER

569 U.S. 564, 133 S. Ct. 2064, 186 L.Ed. 2d 113 (2013).

JUSTICE KAGAN delivered the opinion of the Court.

Class arbitration is a matter of consent: An arbitrator may employ class procedures only if the parties have authorized them. See *Stolt-Nielsen S.A. v. AnimalFeeds Int'l Corp.,* 559 U.S. 662, 684, 130 S.Ct. 1758, 176 L.Ed.2d 605 (2010). In this case, an arbitrator found that the parties' contract provided for class arbitration. The question presented is whether in doing so he "exceeded [his] powers" under § 10(a)(4) of the Federal Arbitration Act (FAA or Act). . . . We conclude that the arbitrator's decision survives the limited judicial review § 10(a)(4) allows.

I

Respondent John Sutter, a pediatrician, entered into a contract with petitioner Oxford Health Plans, a health insurance company. Sutter agreed to provide medical care to members of Oxford's network, and Oxford agreed to pay for those services at prescribed rates. Several years later, Sutter filed suit against Oxford in New Jersey Superior Court on behalf of himself and a proposed class of other New Jersey physicians under contract with Oxford. The complaint alleged that Oxford had failed to make full and prompt payment to the doctors, in violation of their agreements and various state laws.

Oxford moved to compel arbitration of Sutter's claims, relying on the following clause in their contract:

> "No civil action concerning any dispute arising under this Agreement shall be instituted before any court, and all such disputes shall be submitted to final and binding arbitration in New Jersey, pursuant to the rules of the American Arbitration Association with one arbitrator." . . .

The state court granted Oxford's motion, thus referring the suit to arbitration.

The parties agreed that the arbitrator should decide whether their contract authorized class arbitration, and he determined that it did. Noting that the question turned on "construction of the parties' agreement," the arbitrator focused on the text of the arbitration clause quoted above. . . . He reasoned that the clause sent to arbitration "the same universal class of disputes" that it barred the parties from bringing "as civil actions" in court: The "intent of the clause" was "to vest in the arbitration process everything that is prohibited from the court process." . . . And a class action, the arbitrator continued, "is plainly one of the possible forms of civil action that could be brought in a court" absent the agreement. . . . Accordingly, he concluded that "on its face, the arbitration clause . . . expresses the parties' intent that class arbitration can be maintained." . . .

Oxford filed a motion in federal court to vacate the arbitrator's decision on the ground that he had "exceeded [his] powers" under § 10(a)(4) of the FAA. The District Court denied the motion, and the Court of Appeals for the Third Circuit affirmed. . . .

While the arbitration proceeded, this Court held in *Stolt-Nielsen* that "a party may not be compelled under the FAA to submit to class arbitration unless there is a contractual basis for concluding that the party *agreed* to do so." . . . The parties in *Stolt-Nielsen* had stipulated that they had never reached an agreement on class arbitration. Relying on § 10(a)(4), we vacated the arbitrators' decision approving class proceedings because, in the absence of such an agreement, the arbitrators had "simply . . . imposed [their] own view of sound policy." . . .

Oxford immediately asked the arbitrator to reconsider his decision on class arbitration in light of *Stolt-Nielsen*. The arbitrator issued a new opinion holding that *Stolt-Nielsen* had no effect on the case because this agreement authorized class arbitration. Unlike in *Stolt-Nielsen,* the arbitrator explained, the parties here disputed the meaning of their contract; he had therefore been required "to construe the arbitration clause in the ordinary way to glean the parties' intent." . . . And in performing that task, the arbitrator continued, he had "found that the arbitration clause unambiguously evinced an intention to allow class arbitration." . . . The arbitrator concluded by reconfirming his reasons for so construing the clause.

Oxford then returned to federal court, renewing its effort to vacate the arbitrator's decision under § 10(a)(4). Once again, the District Court denied the motion, and the Third Circuit affirmed. The Court of Appeals first underscored the limited scope of judicial review that § 10(a)(4) allows: So long as an arbitrator "makes a good faith attempt" to interpret a contract, "even serious errors of law or fact will not subject his award to vacatur." . . . Oxford could not prevail under that standard, the court held, because the arbitrator had "endeavored to give effect to the parties' intent" and "articulate[d] a contractual basis for his decision." . . . Oxford's objections to the ruling were "simply dressed-up arguments that the arbitrator interpreted its agreement erroneously." . . .

We granted certiorari, 568 U.S. ___, 133 S.Ct. 786, 184 L.Ed.2d 526 (2012), to address a circuit split on whether § 10(a)(4) allows a court to vacate an arbitral award in similar circumstances.[1] Holding that it does not, we affirm the Court of Appeals.

II

Under the FAA, courts may vacate an arbitrator's decision "only in very unusual circumstances." . . . (citation to *Kaplan*). That limited judicial review, we have explained, "maintain[s] arbitration's essential virtue of resolving disputes straightaway." . . . (citation to *Hall Street Assoc.*). If parties could take "full-bore legal and evidentiary appeals," arbitration would become "merely a prelude to a more cumbersome and time-consuming judicial review process." . . . (*id.*).

Here, Oxford invokes § 10(a)(4) of the Act, which authorizes a federal court to set aside an arbitral award "where the arbitrator[ ] exceeded [his] powers." A party seeking relief under that provision bears a heavy burden. "It is not enough . . . to show that the [arbitrator] committed an error—or even a serious error." . . . (citation to *Stolt-Nielson*). Because the parties "bargained for the arbitrator's construction of their agreement," an arbitral decision "even arguably construing or applying the contract" must stand, regardless of a court's view of its (de)merits . . . (citation to *Eastern Association Coal et al.*). Only if "the arbitrator act[s] outside the scope of his contractually delegated authority"—issuing an award that "simply reflect[s] [his] own notions of [economic] justice" rather than "draw[ing] its essence from the contract"—may a court overturn his determination . . . (*id.*). So the sole question for us is whether the arbitrator (even arguably)

[1] Compare 675 F.3d 215 (C.A.3 2012) (case below) (vacatur not proper), and Jock v. Sterling Jewelers Inc., 646 F.3d 113 (C.A.2 2011) (same), with Reed v. Florida Metropolitan Univ., Inc., 681 F.3d 630 (C.A.5 2012) (vacatur proper).

interpreted the parties' contract, not whether he got its meaning right or wrong.[2]

And we have already all but answered that question just by summarizing the arbitrator's decisions . . . ; they are, through and through, interpretations of the parties' agreement. The arbitrator's first ruling recited the "question of construction" the parties had submitted to him: "whether [their] Agreement allows for class action arbitration." . . . To resolve that matter, the arbitrator focused on the arbitration clause's text, analyzing (whether correctly or not makes no difference) the scope of both what it barred from court and what it sent to arbitration. The arbitrator concluded, based on that textual exegesis, that the clause "on its face . . . expresses the parties' intent that class action arbitration can be maintained." . . . When Oxford requested reconsideration in light of *Stolt-Nielsen,* the arbitrator explained that his prior decision was "concerned solely with the parties' intent as evidenced by the words of the arbitration clause itself." . . . He then ran through his textual analysis again, and reiterated his conclusion: "[T]he text of the clause itself authorizes" class arbitration. . . . Twice, then, the arbitrator did what the parties had asked: He considered their contract and decided whether it reflected an agreement to permit class proceedings. That suffices to show that the arbitrator did not "exceed[ ] [his] powers." § 10(a)(4).

Oxford's contrary view relies principally on *Stolt-Nielsen.* As noted earlier, we found there that an arbitration panel exceeded its powers under § 10(a)(4) when it ordered a party to submit to class arbitration. . . . Oxford takes that decision to mean that "even the 'high hurdle' of Section 10(a)(4) review is overcome when an arbitrator imposes class arbitration without a sufficient contractual basis." . . . Under *Stolt-Nielsen*, Oxford asserts, a court may thus vacate "as *ultra vires*" an arbitral decision like this one for misconstruing a contract to approve class proceedings. . . .

But Oxford misreads *Stolt-Nielsen*: We overturned the arbitral decision there because it lacked *any* contractual basis for ordering class procedures, not because it lacked, in Oxford's terminology, a "sufficient" one. The parties in *Stolt-Nielsen* had entered into an unusual stipulation

---

[2] We would face a different issue if Oxford had argued below that the availability of class arbitration is a so-called "question of arbitrability." Those questions—which "include certain gateway matters, such as whether parties have a valid arbitration agreement at all or whether a concededly binding arbitration clause applies to a certain type of controversy"—are presumptively for courts to decide. Green Tree Financial Corp. v. Bazzle, 539 U.S. 444, 452, 123 S.Ct. 2402, 156 L.Ed.2d 414 (2003) (plurality opinion). A court may therefore review an arbitrator's determination of such a matter de novo absent "clear[ ] and unmistakabl[e]" evidence that the parties wanted an arbitrator to resolve the dispute. AT & T Technologies, Inc. v. Communications Workers, 475 U.S. 643, 649, 106 S.Ct. 1415, 89 L.Ed.2d 648 (1986). Stolt-Nielsen made clear that this Court has not yet decided whether the availability of class arbitration is a question of arbitrability. See 559 U.S., at 680, 130 S.Ct. 1758. But this case gives us no opportunity to do so because Oxford agreed that the arbitrator should determine whether its contract with Sutter authorized class procedures. See Brief for Petitioner 38, n. 9 (conceding this point). Indeed, Oxford submitted that issue to the arbitrator not once, but twice—and the second time after Stolt-Nielsen flagged that it might be a question of arbitrability.

that they had never reached an agreement on class arbitration. . . . In that circumstance, we noted, the panel's decision was not—indeed, could not have been—"based on a determination regarding the parties' intent." . . . Nor, we continued, did the panel attempt to ascertain whether federal or state law established a "default rule" to take effect absent an agreement. . . . Instead, "the panel simply imposed its own conception of sound policy" when it ordered class proceedings. . . . But "the task of an arbitrator," we stated, "is to interpret and enforce a contract, not to make public policy." . . . In "impos[ing] its own policy choice," the panel "thus exceeded its powers." . . .

The contrast with this case is stark. In *Stolt-Nielsen,* the arbitrators did not construe the parties' contract, and did not identify any agreement authorizing class proceedings. So in setting aside the arbitrators' decision, we found not that they had misinterpreted the contract, but that they had abandoned their interpretive role. Here, the arbitrator did construe the contract (focusing, per usual, on its language), and did find an agreement to permit class arbitration. So to overturn his decision, we would have to rely on a finding that he misapprehended the parties' intent. But § 10(a)(4) bars that course: It permits courts to vacate an arbitral decision only when the arbitrator strayed from his delegated task of interpreting a contract, not when he performed that task poorly. *Stolt-Nielsen* and this case thus fall on opposite sides of the line that § 10(a)(4) draws to delimit judicial review of arbitral decisions.

[. . .]

. . . All we say is that convincing a court of an arbitrator's error—even his grave error—is not enough. So long as the arbitrator was "arguably construing" the contract—which this one was—a court may not correct his mistakes under § 10(a)(4). . . . The potential for those mistakes is the price of agreeing to arbitration. As we have held before, we hold again: "It is the arbitrator's construction [of the contract] which was bargained for; and so far as the arbitrator's decision concerns construction of the contract, the courts have no business overruling him because their interpretation of the contract is different from his." . . . The arbitrator's construction holds, however good, bad, or ugly.

In sum, Oxford chose arbitration, and it must now live with that choice. Oxford agreed with Sutter that an arbitrator should determine what their contract meant, including whether its terms approved class arbitration. The arbitrator did what the parties requested: He provided an interpretation of the contract resolving that disputed issue. His interpretation went against Oxford, maybe mistakenly so. But still, Oxford does not get to rerun the matter in a court. Under § 10(a)(4), the question for a judge is not whether the arbitrator construed the parties' contract correctly, but whether he construed it at all. Because he did, and therefore did not "exceed his powers," we cannot give Oxford the relief it wants. We accordingly affirm the judgment of the Court of Appeals.

It is so ordered.

JUSTICE ALITO, with whom JUSTICE THOMAS joins, concurring.

As the Court explains, "[c]lass arbitration is a matter of consent," . . . and petitioner consented to the arbitrator's authority by conceding that he should decide in the first instance whether the contract authorizes class arbitration. The Court accordingly refuses to set aside the arbitrator's ruling because he was " 'arguably construing . . . the contract' " when he allowed respondent to proceed on a classwide basis. . . . Today's result follows directly from petitioner's concession and the narrow judicial review that federal law allows in arbitration cases. . . .

But unlike petitioner, absent members of the plaintiff class never conceded that the contract authorizes the arbitrator to decide whether to conduct class arbitration. It doesn't. If we were reviewing the arbitrator's interpretation of the contract *de novo,* we would have little trouble concluding that he improperly inferred "[a]n implicit agreement to authorize class-action arbitration . . . from the fact of the parties' agreement to arbitrate." . . . (citation to *Stolt-Nielsen*).

With no reason to think that the absent class members ever agreed to class arbitration, it is far from clear that they will be bound by the arbitrator's ultimate resolution of this dispute. Arbitration "is a matter of consent, not coercion," . . . (citation to *Volt*), and the absent members of the plaintiff class have not submitted themselves to this arbitrator's authority in any way. It is true that they signed contracts with arbitration clauses materially identical to those signed by the plaintiff who brought this suit. But an arbitrator's erroneous interpretation of contracts that do not authorize class arbitration cannot bind someone who has not authorized the arbitrator to make that determination. As the Court explains, "[a]n arbitrator may employ class procedures only if the parties have authorized them." . . .

The distribution of opt-out notices does not cure this fundamental flaw in the class arbitration proceeding in this case. "[A]rbitration is simply a matter of contract between the parties," . . . (citation to *Kaplan*), and an offeree's silence does not normally modify the terms of a contract, 1 Restatement (Second) of Contracts § 69(1) (1979). Accordingly, at least where absent class members have not been required to opt *in,* it is difficult to see how an arbitrator's decision to conduct class proceedings could bind absent class members who have not authorized the arbitrator to decide on a classwide basis which arbitration procedures are to be used.

Class arbitrations that are vulnerable to collateral attack allow absent class members to unfairly claim the "benefit from a favorable judgment without subjecting themselves to the binding effect of an unfavorable one,". . . . In the absence of concessions like Oxford's, this possibility should give courts pause before concluding that the availability of class arbitration is a question the arbitrator should decide. But because that argument was not available to petitioner in light of its concession below, I join the opinion of the Court.

NOTES AND QUESTIONS

1. Do you agree with Justice Kagan's characterization of *Stolt-Nielsen* and how she distinguishes it from *Sutter*? Are the cases so different from a factual and analytical perspective? Why does 'excess of authority' apply to one and not the other?

2. Did the arbitrator in *Sutter* provide a legal basis for his interpretation of the arbitral clause? Looking at the arbitral clause, which is recited in the opinion, do you agree with the arbitrator that class arbitration was authorized?

3. In *Southern Communications Services Inc. v. Thomas*, 720 F.3d 1352 (11th Cir. 2013), the Eleventh Circuit interpreted and applied *Oxford Health Plans LLC v. Sutter*, 133 S.Ct. 2064 (2013), and upheld an arbitrator's interpretation of a cellular phone contract as authorizing class action proceedings and his certification of a class. The dispute involved the assessment of early termination fees by the company against a customer. The court concluded that the contract was silent on the issue of class litigation. Referring to the standard established in *Sutter*, the appellate court further held that the arbitrator did not "stray from his delegated task"; the arbitrator took the language of the contract into account in determining the parties' intent on the matter of class action. Moreover, the parties agreed to arbitrate and were seeking an arbitrator's resolution of contract interpretation difficulties. It was clear to the court that the arbitrator had reached its decision on the basis of the provisions in the contract and his decision was final and binding, no matter its would-be quality.

Plaintiff bought three lines of service over a period of several years (for himself, his wife, and his son). He refused to pay the early termination fees for the third cancellation and eventually filed putative class action arbitration under AAA Rules. He argued, *inter alia*, that the fees were an illegal penalty under Georgia law and the Federal Communications Act. The consumer then sought a Clause Construction Award under Article 3 of the AAA Supplementary Rules for Class Arbitration. The appointed arbitrator rendered an award permitting the arbitration to proceed as a class proceeding under Georgia law, which he held even favored class proceedings in these circumstances. Upon the plaintiff's motion, the arbitrator certified the class, concluding that his determination complied with the rigorous requirement of *Stolt-Nielsen* that an arbitrator's decision to allow class proceedings have a basis in law.

Citing extensively the U.S. Supreme Court's decision in *Sutter*, the Eleventh Circuit reasoned that

> . . . [T]he Partial Final Clause Construction Award reveals that the arbitrator in this case arguably 'interpreted the parties' contract.' . . . The arbitrator began his award by recounting the text of the contract's arbitration clause. He acknowledged that the contract is 'silent with respect to class actions' and went on to examine the text of AAA Supplementary Rule 3, which was incorporated by reference into the contract by the parties' choice, stated in the arbitration clause, to 'conduct the arbitration . . . pursuant to applicable Wireless Industry Arbitration Rules of the American Arbitration Association.' . . . After parsing the language of that rule, the arbitrator went on to consider the meaning of the words 'any disputes' in the clause itself. . . . He then, in a section headed 'Application of Georgia Contract Construction Law,' interpreted the meaning of silence as to class arbitration within the clause and determined that 'it is fair to conclude that the intent [of the clause] was not to bar class arbitration.' . . . Engaging as he did with the contract's language and the parties' intent, the arbitrator did not 'stray [ ] from his delegated task of interpreting a contract,' . . . 'arguably construing' the contract.' . . . It is not for us to opine on whether or not that task was done badly, for '[i]t is the arbitrator's construction [of the contract] which was bargained for. . . .' The arbitrator's construction holds, however good, bad, or ugly.' . . .

4. Similarly, in *Dish Network L.L.C. v. Ray*, 900 F.3d 1240 (10th Cir. 2018), an employee brought putative collective and class action with the American Arbitration Association against former employer, alleging violation of the Fair Labor Standards Act (FLSA) and state laws. The arbitrator concluded that the arbitration agreement permitted class arbitration. Upholding the arbitrator's decision, the Tenth Circuit cited to *Sutter* and said that determining whether the arbitrator even arguably interpreted the contract "can almost always be answered by simply ' "summarizing the arbitrator's decisions.' " *Id.* at *7. Because the arbitrator had "spent ten pages laboring over this issue and analyzing it in depth," the court concluded that, although it did not "necessarily agree," the arbitrator "interpreted the parties' contract." *Id.* at *7, *10.

THI OF NEW MEXICO AT VIDA ENCANTADA, LLC V. LOVATO

864 F.3d 1080 (10th Cir. 2017).

(footnotes omitted)

PHILLIPS, CIRCUIT JUDGE.

Under the Federal Arbitration Act (FAA), we may vacate an arbitrator's decision "only in very unusual circumstances." *Oxford Health*

Plans LLC v. Sutter, ___ U.S. ___, 133 S.Ct. 2064, 2068, 186 L.Ed.2d 113 (2013) (*quoting First Options of Chicago, Inc. v. Kaplan*, 514 U.S. 938, 942, 115 S.Ct. 1920, 131 L.Ed.2d 985 (1995)). "That limited judicial review . . . 'maintain[s] arbitration's essential virtue of resolving disputes straightaway.' " *Id.* . . . Section 10(a) of the FAA delineates the four "very unusual circumstances" for vacating arbitration awards. *Oxford Health Plans LLC*, 133 S.Ct. at 2068; *see* 9 U.S.C. § 10(a). Here, we consider whether an arbitrator exceeded his authority under § 10(a)(4) and whether he manifestly disregarded the law in awarding certain costs and fees to the prevailing party. Under our restrictive standard of review, we conclude that the arbitrator did not exceed his authority or manifestly disregard the law. So we affirm.

I

1. Standard of Review

. . . . Our task is to assess whether the district court correctly followed the restrictive standard that governs judicial review of an arbitrator's award:

> "[W]e must give extreme deference to the determination of the [arbitrator] for the standard of review of arbitral awards is among the narrowest known to law.". . . . "By agreeing to arbitrate, a party trades the procedures and opportunity for review of the courtroom for the simplicity, informality, and expedition of arbitration." *Gilmer v. Interstate/Johnson Lane Corp.*, 500 U.S. 20, 31, 111 S.Ct. 1647, 114 L.Ed.2d 26 (1991).

. . . . So our review is extremely limited. . . . In addition, we have emphasized that a court should exercise "great caution" when a party asks for an arbitration award to be set aside. . . .

The Supreme Court has emphasized that "only . . . extraordinary circumstances" warrant vacatur of an arbitral award. . . . The Court has also said that if "the arbitrator is even arguably construing or applying the contract and acting within the scope of his authority, that a court is convinced he committed serious error does not suffice to overturn his decision." . . . *Oxford Health Plans LLC*, 133 S.Ct. at 2068 (describing "the sole question" for courts as "whether the arbitrator (even arguably) interpreted the parties' contract, not whether he got its meaning right or wrong"). Even so, "[t]he arbitrator may not ignore the plain language of the contract." . . .

In practice, courts "are 'not authorized to reconsider the merits of an award even though the parties may allege that the award rests on errors of fact or on misinterpretation of the contract.' " . . . "The arbitrator's construction holds, however good, bad, or ugly." *Oxford Health Plans LLC*, 133 S.Ct. at 2071.

Any "less deference would risk 'improperly substitut[ing] a judicial determination for the arbitrator's decision that the parties bargained for.' " . . . It would also create a system in which "arbitration would become 'merely a prelude to a more cumbersome and time-consuming judicial review process.' " *Oxford Health Plans LLC*, 133 S.Ct. at 2068 . . . .

2. Grounds for Reversal

Alongside this highly deferential standard of review, the law sets a high hurdle for reversal of an arbitral award. Enforcing the "strong federal policy favoring arbitration," this court has required parties seeking to set aside an arbitration award to establish a statutory basis or a judicially created exception for doing so. . . . Aside from these "limited circumstances," § 9 of the FAA requires courts to confirm arbitration awards. . . .

Section 10(a) of the FAA, 9 U.S.C. § 10(a), delineates four statutory grounds for vacating arbitral awards—grounds that require very unusual circumstances. *Oxford Health Plans LLC*, 133 S.Ct. at 2068. The first three grounds encompass various types of "corruption, fraud, or undue means" and arbitrator misconduct. 9 U.S.C. § 10(a)(1)–(3). The fourth ground, which is the only ground that THI of New Mexico at Vida Encantada (THI) invokes, applies "where the arbitrators exceeded their powers, or so imperfectly executed them that a mutual, final, and definite award upon the subject matter submitted was not made." *Id.* § 10(a)(4).

A party seeking relief under § 10(a)(4) "bears a heavy burden." *Oxford Health Plans LLC*, 133 S.Ct. at 2068. "[C]onvincing a court of an arbitrator's error—even his grave error—is not enough." *Id.* at 2070. "Because the parties 'bargained for the arbitrator's construction of their agreement,' an arbitral decision 'even arguably construing or applying the contract' must stand, regardless of a court's view of its (de)merits." *Id.* . . . Thus, in considering whether the arbitrator exceeded his powers, we consider one question: whether the arbitrator arguably interpreted the parties' contract, regardless of whether that interpretation was correct. *Id.*

To supplement these statutory grounds, we have recognized a judicially created exception to the rule that even an erroneous interpretation or application of law by an arbitrator is not reversible. . . . For instance, this court has held that "manifest disregard of the law"—which requires "willful inattentiveness to the governing law"—is subject to reversal. . . . "It is not enough . . . to show that the [arbitrator] committed an error—or even a serious error." *Stolt-Nielsen S.A. v. Animalfeeds Int'l Corp.*, 559 U.S. 662, 671, 130 S.Ct. 1758, 176 L.Ed.2d 605 (2010). "To warrant setting aside an arbitration award based on manifest disregard of the law, 'the record must show that the arbitrators knew the law and explicitly disregarded it.' " . . .[1]

II

With this framework in mind, we turn to the facts of this case. In May 2007, ninety-two-year-old Guadalupe Duran was admitted to THI of New Mexico at Vida Encantada, LLC, a nursing home in Las Vegas, New Mexico, to obtain nursing-home care. During her stay at THI, Ms. Duran fell several times. During one fall, she broke her femur and hip. She suffered a stroke soon after undergoing surgery for her injuries. Less than five months after admission, Ms. Duran died while in THI's care.

Before admitting Ms. Duran to THI, her daughter and personal representative, Mary Ann Atencio, executed on her behalf an Admission Agreement and an Arbitration Agreement. In the Arbitration Agreement, the parties agreed to submit to "arbitration, as provided by the National Arbitration Forum Code of Procedure or other such association," and to allow an arbitrator to resolve "any Dispute(s)" between them, including "any controversy or dispute . . . arising out of or relating to" the Admission Agreement or "the provision of care or services to" Ms. Duran, and "all issues pertaining to the scope of" the Arbitration Agreement. . . . The Arbitration Agreement also said that it "shall be governed by and interpreted under the [FAA]." . . .

Acting on behalf of Ms. Duran's estate, Mary Louise Lovato, Ms. Duran's granddaughter and the personal representative of the estate, sued THI (and others who are not parties to this appeal) in New Mexico state court for wrongful death and other tort claims. In response, THI filed a motion in federal court to compel arbitration, which the district court granted over Ms. Lovato's opposition. . . .

The parties participated in a four-day arbitration, at which Ms. Lovato prevailed on the wrongful-death claim. The arbitrator awarded her $475,000 in compensatory damages and authorized a post-arbitration motion for further relief and costs. After extensive briefing by the parties concerning Ms. Lovato's Post-Arbitration Motion for Fees and Costs, the arbitrator awarded Ms. Lovato an additional $245,462.75: $62,100.89 in costs and expenses, which included $39,051.25 in arbitrator's fees (half of the total fees of $78,102.49); $170,087.98 in pre-judgment interest; and

---

[1] This exception's viability has been uncertain, however, since the Supreme Court's decision in *Hall Street*. There, the Court questioned whether "manifest disregard" names a new ground for review or refers to the § 10 grounds collectively. 552 U.S. at 585, 128 S.Ct. 1396. It then emphasized that "expanding the detailed categories would rub too much against the grain of the § 9 language, where provision for judicial confirmation carries no hint of flexibility." *Id.* at 587, 128 S.Ct. 1396; *see also Abbott v. Law Office of Patrick J. Mulligan*, 440 Fed.Appx. 612 (10th Cir. 2011) (unpublished) (explaining the uncertainty as to whether manifest disregard is still a viable ground to overturn an arbitration award after *Hall Street*).

$13,273.88 in post-judgment interest, with additional post-judgment interest continuing to accrue from the date of the award.

THI filed a motion in district court to vacate or modify the arbitrator's award, and Ms. Lovato filed a motion to confirm it. The district court upheld the award. THI appealed, challenging only the confirmation of the costs and interest award.

III

The district court applied the "maximum deference" standard of review within the framework of § 10(a)(4) of the FAA and appropriately deferred to the arbitrator in confirming the award of costs and interest. . . . The district court correctly stated that "irrespective of whether the Court concurs with the Arbitrator's interpretation of the underlying arbitration agreement, it is obvious that the Arbitrator here construed the relevant contract." . . . The arbitrator did so when he reasoned that the Arbitration Agreement "states that it is governed by and interpreted under the [FAA]" but "does not exclude jurisdiction for the arbitration under the [NMUAA,] a statute which applies to all arbitration agreements contracted within New Mexico." Thus, unless this conclusion ignored the plain language of the parties' agreement, the arbitrator's award must stand.

1. The Terms of the Arbitration Agreement

Relying extensively on cases from other circuits, THI argues that the costs and interest award—which the arbitrator issued under the NMUAA—is "in direct contradiction to the Arbitration Agreement's plain language" such that he exceeded his powers under § 10(a)(4). . . . THI argues that the Arbitration Agreement designates the FAA, not the NMUAA, as the governing law, and the FAA does not authorize the recovery of costs and interest by the prevailing party.

In assessing the Arbitration Agreement, "[w]e consider the plain language of the relevant provisions, giving meaning and significance to each word or phrase within the context of the entire contract, as objective evidence of the parties' mutual expression of assent." . . . THI focuses only on one sentence: "This Agreement shall be governed by and interpreted under the Federal Arbitration Act, 9 U.S.C. Sections 1–16." . . .

As a threshold matter, THI has not established that the FAA affirmatively prohibits an award of costs and interest—only that it does not expressly authorize one. Although the FAA displaces conflicting state law, . . . state law is preempted only "to the extent that it actually conflicts with federal law" and "would undermine the goals and policies of the FAA," *Volt Info. Sciens., Inc. v. Bd. of Trs. of Leland Stanford Junior Univ.*, 489 U.S. 468, 477–78, 109 S.Ct. 1248, 103 L.Ed.2d 488 (1989). We have previously recognized that the FAA and the NMUAA may apply to the same arbitration agreement so long as the NMUAA doesn't conflict with the FAA. . . . The Arbitration Agreement poses no such conflict.

Two contractual terms support the arbitrator's award of costs and interest. First, as THI itself emphasized in moving to compel arbitration, the Arbitration Agreement delegates broad authority to the arbitrator: "The parties agree that all issues pertaining to the scope of this Agreement . . . shall be determined by the arbitrator," . . . language that appears to include the determination of available legal and equitable remedies. "[C]ourts favor the arbitrator's exercise of . . . broad discretion in fashioning remedies." . . . "Parties who agree to submit matters to arbitration are presumed to agree that everything, both as to law and fact, necessary to render an ultimate decision is included in the authority of the arbitrators." . . .

Second, the Arbitration Agreement directs that the National Arbitration Forum Code of Procedure (NAF Code) applies. . . . Rule 20 of the NAF Code allows an arbitrator to "grant any legal, equitable or other remedy or relief provided by law in deciding a Claim." NAF Code, Rule 20.D (2008). Also, under Rule 37, an arbitrator's final award "may include fees and costs . . . as permitted by law" if the party seeking them makes a timely request, though the opposing party has an opportunity to object. *Id.*, Rule 37.C; *see also id.*, Rule 37.D ("An Award may include arbitration fees awarded by an Arbitrator. . . ."). By referencing the applicable law, the NAF Code authorized the application of New Mexico law governing costs and interest.

We acknowledge the parties did not arbitrate under the NAF Code, and the district court found they were not "[bound] . . . to follow the rules and procedures of the NAF." . . . But the Arbitration Agreement's reference still shows that an award of costs and interest was within the realm of their agreement. . . .

Section 10(a)(4) "permits courts to vacate an arbitral decision only when the arbitrator strayed from his delegated task of interpreting a contract." *Oxford Health Plans LLC*, 133 S.Ct. at 2070. Where, as here, the arbitrator's decision has "any" contractual basis, it should not be overturned under the deferential standard of review afforded to arbitration awards. *See id.* at 2069–70. Because the costs and interest award finds support in the terms of the Arbitration Agreement, the district court did not err in confirming it.

2. *Manifest Disregard of the Law*

Finally, THI asks us to apply the judicially created manifest disregard of the law exception to vacate the arbitrator's costs and interest award. Again, we apply the required deferential standard of review. We assume (without deciding) the viability of that exception. For the reasons discussed above explaining why the arbitrator did not exceed his authority, we affirm the district court's conclusion that the arbitrator did not act in manifest disregard of the law. THI has presented no evidence showing the arbitrator's "willful inattentiveness to the governing law." . . . Nor has THI shown that the arbitrator "knew the law and explicitly disregarded it." . . .

IV

Under the restrictive standard of review applicable to this appeal, THI falls short of the exceptional showing required to upset the finality of arbitration. We affirm the district court's order confirming the arbitrator's award of costs and interest.

NOTES AND QUESTIONS

1. How does this case square with your understanding of *Sutter* and *Stolt-Nielsen*? Why does the court, in this case, allow the arbitrator to fill in a gap left by the parties' agreement when the court did not permit such gap-filling in *Stolt-Nielsen*? Notice that, although the court identifies several arguable contractual grounds that could indicate authorization for the fees and costs that the arbitrator awarded, the court never says that the arbitrator actually considered these grounds. Does that matter? Is it sufficient that the award might have been based on these grounds?

2. As *Lovato* illustrates, excess of authority issues can and do arise outside of the class arbitration context. In fact, many excess of authority cases turn on the arbitrator's power to award particular forms of relief or damages.

For instance, in *Saturn Telecommunications Servs., Inc. v. Covad Commc'ns Co.*, 560 F. Supp. 2d 1278, 1282 (S.D. Fla. 2008), the court was faced with a motion to vacate an arbitration award because the arbitrator had exceeded his powers in awarding Saturn damages for lost revenue and profits. The defendant argued that a clause in the container contract limited liability under any theory of recovery, including breach of contract or tort. This limited liability clause expressly provided that neither party would be liable for "ANY LOST REVENUE, LOST PROFITS, INCIDENTAL, PUNITIVE, INDIRECT OR CONSEQUENTIAL DAMAGES WITH RESPECT TO ANY SUBJECT MATTER OF THIS AGREEMENT. . . ." *Id.* at 1283.

The court rejected the defendant's position. It held that "when parties vest the arbitrator with the power to resolve all disputes arising from their agreement, the arbitrator may interpret the agreement and apply relevant state law to determine whether certain provisions of the contract are enforceable." *Id.* at 1286. Because the arbitrator had an arguable basis for not applying the limitations provision, the court confirmed the award.

3. A later section in this Chapter addresses manifest disregard, but as *Lovato* suggests, there is some overlap between that concept and excess of authority. As you review the excess of authority cases, try to decipher what boundary, if any, exists between these doctrines.

HYATT FRANCHISING, L.L.C. V. SHEN ZHEN NEW WORLD I, LLC

876 F.3d 900 (7th Cir. 2017).

EASTERBROOK, CIRCUIT JUDGE.

In September 2012 Hyatt and Shen Zhen New World I entered into an agreement providing that Shen Zhen would renovate a hotel in Los Angeles and operate it using Hyatt's business methods and trademarks. Two years later Hyatt declared that Shen Zhen had not kept its promises. An arbitrator concluded that Shen Zhen owes Hyatt about $7.7 million in damages plus about $1.3 million in attorneys' fees and costs. Hyatt filed this suit under the diversity jurisdiction and asked a district court to enforce the award. The court did just that. . . . Shen Zhen appeals.

Shen Zhen's principal arguments concern the arbitrator's rulings with respect to Lynn Cadwalader, who represented it during the negotiations that led to the contract with Hyatt. Shen Zhen asked the arbitrator to issue a subpoena that would have required Cadwalader to give a deposition; the arbitrator said no. The arbitrator stated that Cadwalader lacked any information bearing on the parties' contractual dispute, which arose two years after she had stopped working for Shen Zhen. The arbitrator also declined to disqualify Hyatt's law firm, DLA Piper, which Cadwalader joined in July 2015, about three years after the contract was signed. Cadwalader had not represented Shen Zhen since October 2012. The arbitrator concluded that DLA Piper's ethics screen ensured that no confidential information would reach the lawyers representing Hyatt in 2015 and 2016.

Shen Zhen maintains that it is entitled to relief under 9 U.S.C. § 10(a)(3), which provides that a judge may set aside an arbitrator's award "where the arbitrators were guilty of misconduct in refusing to postpone the hearing, upon sufficient cause shown, or in refusing to hear evidence pertinent and material to the controversy; or of any other misbehavior by which the rights of any party have been prejudiced". Like the district court, we do not see how either branch of Shen Zhen's argument comes within this language.

The statutory phrase "refusing to hear evidence" concerns the conduct of the hearing, not the conduct of discovery. Indeed, nothing in the Federal Arbitration Act requires an arbitrator to allow any discovery. Avoiding the expense of discovery under the Federal Rules of Civil Procedure and their state-law equivalents is among the principal reasons why people agree to arbitrate. That Hyatt's attorneys' fees in the arbitration exceeded $1 million shows that plenty of discovery occurred; an argument that the arbitrator had to allow more rings hollow.

Whether Cadwalader furnished good advice when negotiating the contract might be relevant in a malpractice action against her but does not bear on Hyatt's contention that Shen Zhen broke its promises. The contract has an integration clause that forecloses resort to the negotiating history as an interpretive tool. Shen Zhen tells us that Cadwalader might have helped bolster its contention that the contract is unconscionable, but in a commercial transaction between sophisticated parties the defense of unconscionability, if available at all, is an objective one that depends on the agreement's terms, not on what either side's lawyer may say about the negotiations. . . .

As for the motion to disqualify DLA Piper: a decision by an arbitrator on that subject may or may not be mistaken, either as a matter of fact (is DLA Piper's ethics screen as good as the arbitrator thought?) or as a matter of law (state rules could require disqualification no matter how good the ethics screen), but § 10(a)(3) does not provide for substantive review of an arbitrator's decisions. It provides for judicial intervention when an arbitrator commits "misbehavior", but an error differs in kind from misbehavior. Perhaps Shen Zhen believes that Cadwalader or other lawyers at DLA Piper have engaged in misbehavior, and if so it can complain to the state bar, but the arbitrator is free of any plausible charge of misbehavior—and only misbehavior by the arbitrator comes within the residual clause of § 10(a)(3).

For a fallback argument, Shen Zhen contends that the award disregards federal and state franchise law and therefore should be set aside under 9 U.S.C. § 10(a)(4), which covers situations in which "the arbitrators exceeded their powers, or so imperfectly executed them that a mutual, final, and definite award upon the subject matter submitted was not made." Yet § 10(a)(4) does not make legal errors a ground on which a judge may refuse to enforce an award. . . . Just as an arbitrator is entitled to interpret the parties' contract without judicial review, so an arbitrator is entitled to interpret the law applied to that contract. An agreement to arbitrate is an agreement to move resolution of the parties' disputes out of the judicial system. An arbitrator is not like a magistrate judge, whose recommendations are subject to plenary judicial review.

[Two previous cases] hold that an arbitrator acts as the parties' joint agent and may do anything the parties themselves may do. . . . If they may reach a compromise over some legal issue without being accused of "violating the law," then the arbitrator may do so on their behalf. That was the situation in [*Watts & Son, Inc. v. Tiffany & Co.*, 248 F.3d 577 (7th Cir. 2001)], another franchise case in which the arbitral loser accused the arbitrator of misapplying state franchise law.

One party in *Watts* contended that state law entitled it to an award of attorneys' fees, although the arbitrator had ordered each side to bear its own fees. We replied that, because the parties could have settled their dispute and agreed to cover their own fees and costs, an arbitrator likewise had that power. Arbitrators "exceed[ ] their powers" under § 10(a)(4) if they order the parties to violate the rights of persons who have not agreed to arbitrate—if, for example, an arbitrator purports to allow businesses to fix prices, to the detriment of consumers. But when an arbitrator does only what the parties themselves could have done by mutual consent, § 10(a)(4) does not intervene.

None of Shen Zhen's arguments concerns the rights of third parties. Consider, for example, its contention that Hyatt violated one of the FTC's franchise-disclosure rules, 16 C.F.R. § 436.9(g), by not furnishing changes in the draft agreement at least seven days in advance of signing. Shen Zhen concedes that it possessed the final version more than seven days in advance but maintains that Hyatt did not do enough to flag changes for attention. Suppose that Shen Zhen and Hyatt disagreed about that subject and, after negotiations, concluded that Hyatt was entitled to enforce the agreement. (A concession on damages could have produced such an agreement, even if Shen Zhen was unconvinced on the legal point.) No one else could have complained. *Watts* . . . hold[s] that the arbitrator may do what the parties could have done. That's exactly what this arbitrator did when concluding that Hyatt had satisfied § 436.9(g). Other provisions of federal and California law that Shen Zhen invokes need not be discussed separately.

Shen Zhen cannot make headway by relabeling its "violation of law" arguments as "violation of public policy." Law reflects public policy, to be sure, but the sort of "public policy" that judges may use to annul an award is policy designed to protect the public against the parties to the arbitration. To repeat an example from *Watts*. . . : in a contest between a truck driver and an employer, an arbitrator could not conclude that a driver whose license has been revoked can continue to drive a truck.

The parties cannot use arbitration to get around rules designed for the protection of people who have not agreed to arbitrate. That's the point of decisions such as *W.R. Grace & Co. v. Rubber Workers Union*, 461 U.S. 757, 766, 103 S.Ct. 2177, 76 L.Ed.2d 298 (1983). But when the parties are free under the law to agree on some outcome, the arbitrator's decision as their agent does not violate public policy. That's the holding of *Eastern Associated Coal Corp. v. United Mine Workers*, 531 U.S. 57, 121 S.Ct. 462, 148 L.Ed.2d 354 (2000), which concluded that an arbitrator was entitled to reinstate a driver who had twice tested positive for marijuana. It was lawful for such a person to continue driving, so it was permissible, the Court held, for an arbitrator to reinstate that worker to a driver's job even though the use of marijuana was unlawful and contrary to public policy.

More than 25 years ago, this court held that commercial parties that have agreed to final resolution by an arbitrator, yet go right on litigating, must pay their adversaries' attorneys' fees. . . . The American Rule requires each side to bear its legal fees in an initial round, but an entity that insists on multiplying the litigation must make the other side whole for rounds after the first. . . . Section 14.4 of the contract between Hyatt and Shen Zhen includes a fee-shifting clause, so it is unnecessary to make a separate fee-shifting order. . . , but if the parties cannot agree on how much Shen Zhen owes for pointlessly extending this dispute through the district court and the court of appeals, Hyatt should apply for an appropriate order.

AFFIRMED

NOTES AND QUESTIONS

1. What does the decision in *Hyatt Franchising* add to your understanding of excess of authority? How do you understand the court's admonition that "[t]he parties cannot use arbitration to get around rules designed for the protection of people who have not agreed to arbitrate"? Does the court's example make sense: "in a contest between a truck driver and an employer, an arbitrator could not conclude that a driver whose license has been revoked can continue to drive a truck"?

2. What is the alleged "excess of authority?" What did the arbitrator do wrong, in Shen Zhen's view? Why does the court disagree?

3. The first portion of the decision addresses arbitrator misconduct, the subject of the previous section of this Chapter. Do you agree with the court that the arbitrator error "differs in kind from misbehavior"? Does that distinction make sense to you?

4. With respect to arbitrator misconduct, the decision also points out that FAA § 10(a)(3) focuses on the arbitrator's conduct, not misbehavior by opposing parties or third parties. That distinction derives from the text of the FAA. Not all courts agree, however. *See, e.g., Hayne, Miller & Farni, Inc. v. Flume,* 888 F. Supp. 949, 952 (E.D. Wis. 1995) ("Misconduct by a party can be a basis for setting aside an arbitration award."). When, if ever, might party misconduct could be so problematic as to implicate the enforceability of an arbitral award?

HASBRO, INC. V. CATALYST USA, INC.

367 F.3d 689 (7th Cir. 2004).

DIANE P. WOOD, CIRCUIT JUDGE.

Although companies often choose arbitration with the hope of avoiding the (presumed) greater time and expense of litigating in court, that was not the fate of the parties in this case. Hasbro, Inc. and Catalyst USA, Inc. waited more than two years for a final award from an arbitration panel that was adjudicating a dispute between them about a software license. After the award was finally issued, the losing party, Catalyst, asked the district court to vacate the arbitral award. The court agreed that this was appropriate on the ground that the arbitrators had exceeded their authority by waiting too long to issue their decision. While we appreciate the frustration caused by the delay, a closer look at the proceedings shows that no one objected at the crucial time to the panel's conduct of the proceedings. Whatever errors with respect to deadlines may have been committed were either waived or harmless. We therefore reverse and remand for entry of an order enforcing the award.

I

In 1993, Hasbro and Catalyst entered into a software licensing contract, in which they agreed to arbitrate any disputes that arose that could not be resolved amicably. Any such dispute was to be submitted to arbitration pursuant to the Federal Arbitration Act (FAA) and the rules of the American Arbitration Association (AAA).

Six years later, dissatisfied with the performance of Catalyst's software, Hasbro filed a demand for arbitration on October 8, 1999. A hearing was conducted in Milwaukee between October 2000 and March 2001 before a panel of arbitrators from the Commercial Arbitration Tribunal of the AAA. . . .

The parties did not hear again from the AAA or the panel until October 2, 2001, when the AAA sent a bill to the parties seeking compensation for the arbitrators' "post-hearing time" from July to September 2001. In response, Catalyst requested an explanation of the bill. On October 10, 2001, the AAA sent the parties an itemization of charges—a communication that raised red flags for Catalyst. Catalyst found questionable the hours and increased rate charged by the panel chair, Alan Wernick. The itemization of the charges also brought to light other key information. Among the many entries were ones that stated "review and revise damage calculations to provide interest" and "extended conferences with panel regarding damage calculations and award." Because only Hasbro had requested damages, Hasbro alleges that these references to damage calculations should have signaled to Catalyst that Hasbro was the prevailing party.

On October 26, 2001, Catalyst wrote to the AAA challenging the propriety of Wernick's charges. In that letter, it also asserted for the first time that under Rule 37 of the AAA rules, the hearing had been closed on July 10, 2001, "as of the final date set by the arbitrator for the receipt of briefs," and that under Rule 43, the arbitrator had until August 11, 2001, "30 days from the date of closing the hearing," to make the award. The panel's failure to issue the award by August 11, 2001, Catalyst charged, raised "serious questions about the validity of the entire process."

On November 8, 2001, Catalyst received additional information concerning the Wernick bills. Again it wrote to the AAA requesting further information that would help it to analyze the propriety of the charges. It also, at that point, inquired specifically about the status of the overdue award. Not receiving word from the AAA, on November 13, 2001, Catalyst formally objected to the untimeliness of the award. Perhaps prompted by this inquiry, or perhaps for their own reasons, the arbitrators declared the hearing closed on December 5, 2001, and issued their award on January 2, 2002. The panel awarded Hasbro $799,839.93, plus interest; denied Catalyst's counterclaims; and divided arbitration fees, expenses, and compensation equally between the two parties, requiring Hasbro to pay the remaining $2,083.63 and Catalyst the remaining $22,083.63 outstanding. It declined to award attorneys' fees to either side.

Catalyst moved in district court to vacate the arbitration award on the ground that the arbitrators exceeded their power by issuing an untimely award. The district court agreed, and this appeal followed.

II

Generally, a court will set aside an arbitration award only in "very unusual circumstances," . . . Judicial review of arbitration awards is "tightly limited" . . . and confirmation is "usually routine or summary." . . . "With few exceptions, as long as the arbitrator does not exceed [her] delegated authority, her award will be enforced." . . . This is so even if the arbitrator's award contains a serious error of law or fact. . . . We review the district court's decision to vacate the arbitration award *de novo*, . . . accepting findings of fact that are not clearly erroneous. . . .

The FAA makes arbitration agreements enforceable "to the same extent as other contracts, so courts must 'enforce privately negotiated agreements to arbitrate, like other contracts, in accordance with their terms.' " . . . Under Wisconsin law, which applies to this diversity action, . . . untimely performance of a contractual obligation does not result in the harsh penalty of forfeiture or rescission, unless the parties agree that "time is [ ] of the essence." . . . Thus, even assuming that the panel's performance was untimely, whether the arbitration agreement was thereby rendered unenforceable depends on whether the parties agreed that time would be of the essence.

Whether this was indeed the parties' agreement is generally a question of fact that, if there was some sign of a material dispute, we would need to remand to the district court as fact-finder. . . .

Under Wisconsin law, time is generally not of the essence, "unless it is expressly made so by the terms of the contract, or by the conduct of the parties." . . . In this case, nowhere either in the arbitration agreement or in the AAA rules does it expressly say that time was of the essence. Wisconsin law further indicates that the fact that the AAA rules specify a 30-day deadline is not enough to support the inference that time is of the essence. . . .

Nor does the conduct of the parties in this case support a finding that time was of the essence. . . . Although Catalyst asserts that the hearing should have been declared closed on July 10, 2001, and an award should have been issued by August 11, 2001, Catalyst itself waited until October 26, 2001, before raising the issue of untimely performance, and until November 13, 2001, before formally objecting to the arbitrators' delay.

Indeed, all indications suggest that Catalyst, the party now complaining of untimely performance, benefited from the delay, given the fact that it was able to hold off payment to Hasbro for several months at no cost (apart from the questionable arbitrators' fees, which we discuss in a moment). A conclusion that time was not of the essence under these circumstances comports with Wisconsin's additional consideration of equity in construing the parties' agreement, by allowing Hasbro to avoid the harsh penalty of forfeiture when the delay caused no prejudice to Catalyst.

[. . .]

For these reasons, we find that time was not of the essence under this arbitration agreement. Therefore, the arbitrators did not exceed their authority by issuing an untimely award to the extent that the harsh penalty of forfeiture or rescission was warranted. . . .

This is not to say, obviously, that arbitrators may indefinitely delay issuance of an award, in open violation of the AAA rules, without the parties' consent. Under Wisconsin law, "time may be made of the essence after breach of the contract by reasonable notice to the person in default to perform." . . . But the prejudiced party must make its objection known, which Catalyst failed to do here. This entire problem stemmed from the panel's original failure to declare the hearing closed in accordance with Rule 37. Such a declaration would have triggered the 30-day deadline under Rule 43. From the time Catalyst gave notice of its position that the panel had breached Rule 37, however, there was no further delay or failure to perform to which Catalyst can point. . . . Upon receiving notice from Catalyst, the panel promptly invited Hasbro to respond. Soon after, it declared the hearing closed and issued an award within 30 days thereafter.

Notwithstanding our enforcement of the arbitral award, we do not condone the panel's substandard performance. The AAA (and judicial tribunals) have good reasons for rules that clarify when a proceeding is concluded. These rules allow all parties to know whether there is still time remaining to raise points with the original tribunal, whether the time has come to appeal, and how much time exists for all such steps. Just as Federal Rule of Civil Procedure 58, which requires a specific document memorializing a final judgment, avoids countless problems with the appellate process that arise when a separate final judgment is missing, the AAA's rules also structure the process so that parties will know at all times where they stand.

III

We therefore *vacate* the judgment of the district court and *remand* for enforcement of the arbitral award.

NOTES AND QUESTIONS

1. Why do you think that the court minimizes the arbitrators' blunder in these circumstances? Is that the right decision? Does this decision mean that parties are effectively at the mercy of the arbitrators? Remember, arbitrators and institutions enjoy civil immunity on par with judges.

2. Are there circumstances when arbitrator delay could result in vacatur? When? Think about it this way, if you were drafting an arbitral clause, in light of this decision, and you were concerned about getting a timely award, what could you do?

3. The court references the AAA Rules, but the numbering has since changed. The decision cites Rule 37, which requires the panel to close the hearings. That is now R-39. The decision also cites Rule 43, which required a decision within 30 days of the closing of the hearing. That is now R-45.

7. STATE DEPARTURES FAA § 10

Most state laws of arbitration provide for functionally equivalent standards of judicial review to the FAA. For instance, RUAA § 23 maps onto FAA § 10 with no substantive differences. As the Introduction discussed, however, FAA § 10 may not apply in state court and dicta from the U.S. Supreme Court appears to authorize states to impose more rigorous or searching standards of review on arbitral awards. *See Hall St. Assocs., L.L.C. v. Mattel, Inc.,* 552 U.S. 576, 590 (2008).

The Supreme Court's expansive reading of FAA § 2 means that states have no power to regulate the recourse to arbitration on the front end of the process. But several states have relied on *Hall Street*'s dicta to place greater judicial supervision on arbitral awards.

It would be premature to say that a trend exists towards greater state judicial intervention in the backend of the process, but the threat of more searching standards of review is real.

CABLE CONNECTION, INC. V. DIRECTV, INC.

44 Cal. 4th 1334, 1343, 190 P.3d 586, 591 (2008).

(footnotes omitted)

CORRIGAN, J.

This case presents two questions regarding arbitration agreements. (1) May the parties structure their agreement to allow for judicial review of legal error in the arbitration award? (2) Is classwide arbitration available under an agreement that is silent on the matter?

On the first question, the United States Supreme Court has held that the Federal Arbitration Act (FAA; 9 U.S.C. § 1 et seq.) does not permit the parties to expand the scope of review by agreement. (Hall Street Associates, L.L.C. v. Mattel, Inc. (2008) 552 U.S. 576, ___–___ [170 L.Ed.2d 254, 128 S.Ct. 1396, 1404–1405] (Hall Street).) However, the high court went on to say that federal law does not preclude "more searching review based on authority outside the [federal] statute," including "state statutory or common law." (*Id.* at p. ___ [170 L.Ed.2d 254, 128 S.Ct. at p. 1406].) In Moncharsh v. Heily & Blasé (1992) 3 Cal.4th 1 [10 Cal.Rptr.2d 183, 832 P.2d 899] (Moncharsh), this court reviewed the history of the California Arbitration Act (CAA; Code Civ. Proc., § 1280 et seq.) . . . We concluded that the California Legislature "adopt[ed] the position taken in case law . . . that is, 'that in the absence of some limiting clause in the arbitration agreement, the merits of the award, either on questions of fact or of law, may not be reviewed except as provided in the statute.' " (*Moncharsh,* at p. 25, ...)

We adhere to our holding in *Moncharsh,* recognizing that contractual limitations may alter the usual scope of review. The California rule is that the parties may obtain judicial review of the merits by express agreement. There is a statutory as well as a contractual basis for this rule; one of the grounds for review of an arbitration award is that "[t]he arbitrators exceeded their powers." (§§ 1286.2, subd. (a)(4), 1286.6, subd. (b).) Here, the parties agreed that "[t]he arbitrators shall not have the power to commit errors of law or legal reasoning, and the award may be vacated or corrected on appeal to a court of competent jurisdiction for any such error." This contract provision is enforceable under state law, and we reverse the contrary ruling of the Court of Appeal. . . .

I. BACKGROUND

Defendant DIRECTV, Inc., broadcasts television programming nationwide, via satellite. It contracts with retail dealers to provide customers with equipment needed to receive its satellite signal. In 1996, DIRECTV employed a "residential dealer agreement" for this purpose. A new "sales agency agreement" was used in 1998. Both agreements included arbitration clauses . . . .

In 2001, dealers from four states filed suit in Oklahoma, asserting on behalf of a nationwide class that DIRECTV had wrongfully withheld commissions and assessed improper charges. DIRECTV moved to compel arbitration. As the Oklahoma court was considering whether the arbitration could be conducted on a classwide basis, the United States Supreme Court decided Green Tree Financial Corp. v. Bazzle (2003) 539 U.S. 444 [156 L.Ed.2d 414, 123 S.Ct. 2402] (Bazzle). A plurality in *Bazzle* held that the arbitrator must decide whether class arbitration is authorized by the parties' contract. (*Id.* at pp. 451–452 . . . .) Accordingly, the Oklahoma court directed the parties to submit the matter to arbitration in Los Angeles as provided in the sales agency agreement. . . .

After the dealers presented a statement of claim and demand for class arbitration in March 2004, a panel of three AAA arbitrators was selected. Following the procedure adopted by the AAA in response to *Bazzle,* the panel first addressed whether the parties' agreement permitted the arbitration to proceed on a classwide basis.

After briefing and argument, a majority of the panel decided that even though "the contract is silent and manifests no intent on this issue," arbitration on a classwide basis was authorized under [California law]. . . . The award emphasized that class arbitration was not necessarily required in this case; it was merely permitted by the contract. Whether the arbitration would actually be maintained on a classwide basis would be the subject of a future hearing.

The dissenting arbitrator found that the sales agency agreement provided "ample indication" the parties had contemplated arbitration only on an individual basis. . . . The dissent considered the availability of classwide arbitration to be a procedural issue subject to the FAA and AAA rules, under the terms of the arbitration clause.

DIRECTV petitioned to vacate the award, contending (1) the majority had exceeded its authority by substituting its discretion for the parties' intent regarding class arbitration; (2) the majority had improperly ignored extrinsic evidence of contractual intent; and (3) even if the majority had not exceeded the authority generally granted to arbitrators, the award reflected errors of law that the arbitration clause placed beyond their powers and made subject to judicial review. The dealers responded that the majority had properly applied California law and had not refused to receive extrinsic evidence. The trial court vacated the award, essentially accepting all of DIRECTV's arguments.

The Court of Appeal reversed, holding that the trial court exceeded its jurisdiction by reviewing the merits of the arbitrators' decision. Although in the trial court the dealers did not question whether a contract may provide for an expanded scope of judicial review, the Court of Appeal deemed it an important matter of public policy, suitable for consideration for the first time on appeal. The court agreed with two previous Court of Appeal decisions holding such provisions unenforceable. . . . It concluded that the provision for judicial review in this case was severable from the remainder of the arbitration agreement, and directed the trial court to confirm the award.

We granted DIRECTV's petition for review.

II. DISCUSSION

A. *Contract Provisions for Judicial Review of Arbitration Awards*

1. *The CAA, the FAA, and Prior Case Law*

(1) "In most important respects, the California statutory scheme on enforcement of private arbitration agreements is similar to the [FAA]; the similarity is not surprising, as the two share origins in the earlier statutes of New York and New Jersey" . . . . The CAA, like the FAA, provides that arbitration agreements are "valid, enforceable and irrevocable, save upon such grounds as exist for the revocation of any contract." (§ 1281; see 9 U.S.C. § 2.) This provision was intended "to overcome an anachronistic judicial hostility to agreements to arbitrate, which American courts had borrowed from English common law." . . .

Consistent with that purpose, the CAA and the FAA provide only limited grounds for judicial review of an arbitration award. Under both statutes, courts are authorized to vacate an award if it was (1) procured by corruption, fraud, or undue means; (2) issued by corrupt arbitrators; (3) affected by prejudicial misconduct on the part of the arbitrators; or (4) in excess of the arbitrators' powers. . . .

As noted at the outset, and discussed further below, in *Moncharsh* we declared that " 'in the absence of some limiting clause in the arbitration agreement, the merits of the award, either on questions of fact or of law, may not be reviewed except as provided in the statute.' " . . . (Moncharsh, supra, 3 Cal.4th at p. 25.) . . . . In each of these cases, however, the courts noted that an expanded scope of review *would* be available under a clause specifically tailored for that purpose. . . .

Nevertheless, when the issue has been squarely presented, no Court of Appeal has enforced a contract clause calling for judicial review of an arbitration award on its merits. . . . *In* Old Republic Ins. Co. v. St. Paul Fire & Marine Ins. Co. (1996) 45 Cal.App.4th 631 [53 Cal.Rptr.2d 50] (Old Republic), a stipulation for binding arbitration provided that a special master would enter findings of fact and conclusions of law, which would be reviewed by the trial court under the CAA, entered as a judgment, and " 'treated as a judgment of the Superior Court for all purposes, including, without limitation, the right of any party adversely affected by said judgment to seek review of the findings of fact, conclusions of law, or judgment as if this matter had been tried to the Court without a jury and judgment entered thereon.' " (45 Cal.App.4th at pp. 634–635.) The Court of Appeal refused to review the merits, because the stipulation was "inconsistent with some of the primary purposes of arbitration, quicker results and early finality." (*Id.* at p. 638.) Moreover, "the flexibility in the consideration of both evidence and law afforded to arbitrators" made plenary review on appeal problematic. (*Ibid.*) The court also held that the limitations on the scope of the trial court's review precluded more extensive appellate review, and that the parties could not create appellate jurisdiction by consent. (*Id.* at pp. 638–639.)

[. . .]

Before the *Hall Street* decision was handed down, the federal circuits were split on whether the FAA grounds for judicial review are exclusive. The First, Third, Fourth, Fifth, and Sixth Circuits held or indicated that contract provisions for expanded review of arbitration awards were enforceable. . . . The Seventh, Eighth, Ninth, and Tenth Circuits took the opposite view. . . . As we discuss next, a majority of the Supreme Court in *Hall Street* decided the FAA was intended to provide exclusive criteria for review of arbitration awards.

2. Hall Street *and the Question of Preemption*

The *Hall Street* case arose from an arbitration agreement negotiated during litigation, to resolve an indemnification claim. The agreement was approved and entered as an order by the trial court. It provided: " 'The Court shall vacate, modify or correct any award: (i) where the arbitrator's findings of facts are not supported by substantial evidence, or (ii) where the arbitrator's conclusions of law are erroneous.' " . . .

A majority of the court [held] that the grounds for vacatur and modification provided by sections 10 and 11 of the FAA are exclusive. (Hall Street, supra, 552 U.S. at p. ___ [128 S.Ct. at p. 1401].) First, the majority rejected the argument that the nonstatutory "manifest disregard of the law" standard of review recognized by some federal courts supports the enforceability of contract provisions for additional grounds to vacate or modify an arbitration award. (*Id.* at p. ___ [128 S.Ct. at p. 1403].) It reasoned that the "manifest disregard" exception presumes a rule against general review for legal error, and should not be seen as a "camel's nose" under the arbitration tent. (*Id.* at pp. ___–___ [128 S.Ct. at pp. 1403–1404] . . . .

Next, the *Hall Street* majority disposed of the contention that allowing parties to contract for an expanded scope of review is consistent with the FAA's primary goal of ensuring the enforcement of arbitration agreements. "[T]o rest this case on the general policy of treating arbitration agreements as enforceable as such would be to beg the question, which is whether the FAA has textual features at odds with enforcing a contract to expand judicial review following the arbitration." (Hall Street, supra, 552 U.S. at p. ___ [128 S.Ct. at p. 1404].) The majority decided that, indeed, those textual features exist. It characterized the statutory grounds for review as remedies for "egregious departures from the parties' agreed-upon arbitration," such as corruption and fraud. (*Ibid.*) It viewed the directive in section 9 of the FAA, that the court " 'must grant' " confirmation " 'unless the award is vacated, modified, or corrected as prescribed in sections 10 and 11,' " as a mandatory provision leaving no room for the parties to agree otherwise. (*Hall Street,* at p. ___ [128 S.Ct. at p. 1405].) . . . .

Despite this strict reading of the FAA, the *Hall Street* majority left the door ajar for alternate routes to an expanded scope of review. "In holding that §§ 10 and 11 provide exclusive regimes for the review provided by the statute, we do not purport to say that they exclude more searching review based on authority outside the statute as well. The FAA is not the only way into court for parties wanting review of arbitration awards: they may contemplate enforcement under state statutory or common law, for example, where judicial review of different scope is arguable. But here we speak only to the scope of the expeditious judicial review under §§ 9, 10, and 11, deciding nothing about other possible avenues for judicial enforcement of arbitration awards." (Hall Street, supra, 552 U.S. at p. ___ [128 S.Ct. at p. 1406].)

[. . .]

The dealers in this case urge us to follow the rationale of the *Hall Street* majority. They contend that any other construction of the CAA would result in its preemption by the FAA. Alternatively, they argue that *Hall Street* provides a persuasive analysis of the FAA that should be applied to the similar CAA provisions governing judicial review. We consider first the question of preemption, because if the dealers are correct on that point, it would be fruitless to consider alternate interpretations of state law. . . .

(3) Section 2 of the FAA, declaring the enforceability of arbitration agreements, "create[s] a body of federal substantive law of arbitrability, applicable to any arbitration agreement within the coverage of the Act." . . . The FAA governs agreements in contracts involving interstate commerce, like those in this case. . . . The United States Supreme Court has frequently held that state laws invalidating arbitration agreements on grounds applicable only to arbitration provisions contravene the policy of enforceability established by section 2 of the FAA, and are therefore preempted. . . .

However, "the United States Supreme Court does not read the FAA's procedural provisions to apply to state court proceedings." . . . Sections 3 and 4 of the FAA, governing stays of litigation and petitions to enforce arbitration agreements, do not apply in state court. . . . As we have noted, the provisions for judicial review of arbitration awards in sections 10 and

11 of the FAA are directed to "the United States court in and for the district wherein the award was made." . . . We have held that similar language in sections 3 and 4 of the FAA reflects Congress's intent to limit the application of those provisions to federal courts. . . .

Thus, . . . the FAA's procedural provisions are not controlling, and the determinative question is whether CAA procedures conflict with the FAA policy favoring the enforcement of arbitration agreements. . . .

(4) Before *Hall Street,* we would have had no difficulty concluding that enforcing agreements for judicial review on the merits is consistent with the fundamental purpose of the FAA. . . .

The *Hall Street* majority, however, brushed aside policy considerations favoring the enforcement of contractual arbitration arrangements, concentrating instead on whether "the FAA has textual features at odds with enforcing a contract to expand judicial review following the arbitration." (Hall Street, supra, 552 U.S. at p. ___ [128 S.Ct. at p. 1404].) Underlying the FAA provisions governing judicial review, it discerned "a national policy favoring arbitration with just the limited review needed to maintain arbitration's essential virtue of resolving disputes straightaway." (552 U.S. at p. ___ [128 S.Ct. at p. 1405].)

Nevertheless, we do not believe the *Hall Street* majority intended to declare a policy with preemptive effect in all cases involving interstate commerce.[14] *Hall Street* was a federal case governed by federal law; the court considered no question of competing state law. It reviewed the application of FAA provisions for judicial review that speak only to the federal courts. The court unanimously left open other avenues for judicial review, including those provided by state statutory or common law. . . . While the court, of course, *decided* nothing about the viability of these alternatives, their mention in the majority opinion indicates that *Hall Street*'s holding on the effect of the FAA is a limited one. . . .

(5) We conclude that the *Hall Street* holding is restricted to proceedings to review arbitration awards under the FAA, and does not require state law to conform with its limitations. Furthermore, a reading of the CAA that permits the enforcement of agreements for merits review is fully consistent with the FAA "policy guaranteeing the enforcement of private contractual arrangements." . . .

---

[14] Such an effect would be sweeping indeed in the commercial setting. Not only would state courts be barred from giving a more expansive interpretation to state law as it applies to agreements for merits review of arbitration awards, but state legislatures would be unable to specifically permit contract provisions for expanded review. (See, e.g., N.J. Stat. Ann. § 2A:23B-4(c) ["nothing in this act shall preclude the parties from expanding the scope of judicial review of an award by expressly providing for such expansion . . ."].) Arguably, statutory provisions for review of the merits in particular contexts, such as public contract arbitrations (see § 1296), would be precluded. The viability of public policy exceptions to the general rule of limited review would also be called into question. . . .

[. . .]

[The court went on to conclude that parties could, under California law, contract for expanded judicial review of arbitral awards.]

The benefits of enforcing agreements like the one before us are considerable, for both the parties and the courts. The development of alternative dispute resolution is advanced by enabling private parties to choose procedures with which they are comfortable. Commentators have observed that provisions for expanded judicial review are a product of market forces operating in an increasingly "judicialized" arbitration setting, with many of the attributes of court proceedings. The desire for the protection afforded by review for legal error has evidently developed from the experience of sophisticated parties in high stakes cases, where the arbitrators' awards deviated from the parties' expectations in startling ways. . . .

The judicial system reaps little benefit from forcing parties to choose between the risk of an erroneous arbitration award and the burden of litigating their dispute entirely in court. Enforcing contract provisions for review of awards on the merits relieves pressure on congested trial court dockets. . . . Courts are spared not only the burden of conducting a trial, but also the complications of discovery disputes and other pretrial proceedings. Incorporating traditional judicial review by express agreement preserves the utility of arbitration as a way to obtain expert factual determinations without delay, while allowing the parties to protect themselves from perhaps the weakest aspect of the arbitral process, its handling of disputed rules of law. . . .

There are also significant benefits to the development of the common law when arbitration awards are made subject to merits review by the parties' agreement. . . .

(11) These advantages, obtained with the consent of the parties, are substantial. . . . The Court of Appeal erred by refusing to enforce the parties' clearly expressed agreement in this case.

[. . .]

NOTES AND QUESTIONS

1. Recall that *Hall Street* involved an arbitration clause providing, in pertinent part that:

> The United States District Court for the District of Oregon may enter judgment upon any award, either by confirming the award or by vacating, modifying or correcting the award. The Court shall vacate, modify or correct any award: (i) where the arbitrator's findings of facts are not supported by substantial evidence, or (ii) where the arbitrator's conclusions of law are erroneous.

Hall St. Assocs., LLC v. Mattel, Inc., 552 U.S. 576, 579 (2008). This sort of expanded judicial review is not permitted by the FAA. Why might parties ever want this sort of expanded review? Does the California court's explanation make sense?

2. Prior to *Hall Street,* United States courts had generally held that parties could not preclude courts from vacating an award when one of the statutory grounds for vacating the award is met. In other words, parties could not opt out of the review provided by FAA § 10. *Hall Street* confirms that this approach is mandated by the FAA. Thus, parties cannot avoid judicial review of an award by providing (as many arbitration rules commonly do) that "[a]ll awards shall be final and binding on the parties" or that the "parties also waive irrevocably their right to any form of appeal, review or recourse to any state court or other judicial authority, insofar as such waiver may be validly made." *See* LCIA Arbitration Rules, art. 26.8. Rather, U.S. Courts read language like 'final' and 'binding' in arbitration agreements merely as a reflection of contractual intent that the issues joined and resolved in the arbitration may not be tried *de novo* in any court. The statutory grounds for review and enforcement are mandatory and exclusive.

Given the holding in *Cable Connection*, do you think that this would be true under California law? Could the parties, in other words, opt into less judicial review of arbitral awards? Does the *Cable Connection* approach work both ways?

3. At least three other states have followed California's lead and allow parties to do, under their laws, what they cannot under the FAA. *See Raymond James Fin. Servs., Inc. v. Honea,* 55 So. 3d 1161, 1169 (Ala. 2010) (a court may conduct a de novo review of an award if the agreement provides for judicial review on that basis); *Nafta Traders Inc. v. Quinn,* 339 S.W.3d 84, 101 (Tex. 2011) (the FAA does not preempt enforcement of an agreement for expanded judicial review of an arbitration award enforceable under state law); N.J. Stat. Ann. § 2A:23B-4 (authorizing parties to contract for expanded judicial review of awards).[1]

The Texas Supreme Court's decision in *Nafta Traders* parallels, in may respects, the court's reasoning in *Cable Connection*, but the Texas court added that expanded review could be justified by a proper understanding of the role played by excess of authority. According to the Texas Court, the U.S. Supreme Court in *Hall Street* mistakenly overlooked this ground for review, which can encompass situations where the "parties have agreed that an arbitrator should not have authority to reach a decision based on reversible error—in other

---

[1] Connecticut may also allow for expanded review. In a decision released only two months after *Hall Street*, the Connecticut Supreme Court said in a footnote that "[p]arties to agreements remain, however, free to contract for expanded judicial review of an arbitrator's findings." *HH East Parcel, LLC v. Handy & Harman, Inc.*, 947 A.2d 916, 926 n.16 (Conn. 2008). This dicta seemed to reaffirm a position taken earlier by the Connecticut court in 2006 in *Stutz v. Shepard*, 901 A.2d 33 (Conn. 2006). In *Stutz*, the court unceremoniously and without any detailed analysis upheld a contractual provision that invested a court with the power to review an arbitral award under a "clearly erroneous" standard.

words, that an arbitrator should have no more power than a judge." *Nafta Traders Inc.,* 339 S.W.3d at 92. In the Texas court's opinion, this express statutory ground for review coupled with the underlying purposes of the federal and Texas acts—to ensure that private agreements are enforced according to their terms—rendered *Hall Street*'s analysis and conclusion flawed.

4. Not all courts agree that state law applies to review and enforcement of arbitral awards. Instead, some state courts apply FAA § 10 grounds to proceedings in state court. *See, e.g., U.S. Elecs., Inc. v. Sirius Satellite Radio, Inc.,* 17 N.Y.3d 912, 913, 958 N.E.2d 891, 892 (2011) ("As this matter affects interstate commerce, the vacatur of the arbitration award is governed by the Federal Arbitration Act."); *Vold v. Broin & Assocs., Inc.*, 2005 S.D. 80, ¶ 17, 699 N.W.2d 482, 487 (same).

FINN V. BALLENTINE PARTNERS, LLC

143 A.3d 859, 871–72 (N.H. 2016).

(footnotes omitted)

LYNN, J.

The plaintiff, Alice Finn, appeals an order of the Superior Court. . . denying her motion to affirm and granting the motion of the defendants, Ballentine Partners, LLC (BPLLC), Ballentine & Company, Inc., Roy C. Ballentine, Kyle Schaffer, Claudia Shilo, Andrew McMorrow, and Gregory Peterson, to vacate a final arbitration award in part pursuant to RSA 542:8 (2007). Because we conclude that the trial court did not err in ruling that RSA 542:8 is not preempted by the Federal Arbitration Act (FAA), *see* 9 U.S.C. §§ 2, 9–11 . . . , and in ruling, pursuant to RSA 542:8, that the arbitration panel committed a plain mistake of law by concluding that res judicata did not bar Finn's claim, we affirm.

I

The record supports the following facts. Ballentine and Finn founded Ballentine Finn & Company, Inc. (BFI), a New Hampshire subchapter S corporation, in 1997. Each owned one half of the company's stock, and Finn served as the Chief Executive Officer. Later, four other individuals became shareholders of BFI. In 2008, Ballentine and the other shareholders forced Finn out of the corporation and terminated her employment. BFI asserted that the termination was for cause, and exercised its right to purchase Finn's shares at the price assigned to "for cause" terminations pursuant to the Shareholder Agreement (Agreement). At the time of her termination, Finn held 37.5% of the shares of BFI. BFI gave Finn a promissory note in the amount of $4,635,684, which represented 1.4 times earnings for her shares for the 12 months before her termination. This amount was below the fair market value of Finn's shares.

Pursuant to the Agreement, Finn challenged her termination before an arbitration panel in 2009. . . . This first arbitration panel found that Finn's termination was unlawful and awarded her $5,721,756 for the stock that BFI forced her to sell and $720,000 in lost wages. The panel recognized that BFI likely did not have sufficient liquidity to pay the award immediately, so it authorized BFI to make periodic payments through December 31, 2012.

After the first panel award, BFI formed BPLLC, contributed all of its assets and some of its liabilities to BPLLC, and became its sole member. BFI then changed its name to Ballentine & Company (Ballentine & Co.). After the reorganization, Ballentine & Co. sold 4,000 preferred units, a 40% membership interest in BPLLC, to Perspecta Investments, LLC (Perspecta). Perspecta paid $7,000,000 to Ballentine & Co. and made a $280,000 capital contribution to BPLLC. The defendants asserted that the membership interest had to be sold in order to raise funds to pay the arbitration award to Finn.

In 2013, Finn filed a complaint and a motion to compel arbitration in superior court, alleging that she was entitled to relief under the "Claw Back" provision of the Agreement. That provision provides, in essence, that if a founding shareholder of BFI sells shares back to the corporation and those shares are resold at a higher price within eight years, the founder is entitled to recover a portion of the additional price paid for the shares. The defendants moved to dismiss Finn's complaint, arguing that it was barred by res judicata. The trial court did not rule on the motion to dismiss; instead, it stayed the court proceedings and granted Finn's motion to compel arbitration, concluding that the issue of res judicata must be decided by arbitration in the first instance.

A second arbitration panel held a five-day hearing to decide Finn's new claims, which included breach of contract and unjust enrichment. It ruled that "[t]he findings of the first panel essentially resolve[d] Finn's contract claim for 'Claw Back' benefits because the predicate facts needed to support a contractual 'Claw Back' claim were found against Finn by that panel.". . . . The second panel concluded, however, that Finn was entitled to an award based upon her unjust enrichment claim. Although it agreed with the defendants' argument that a party cannot be awarded relief under a theory of unjust enrichment when "there is an available contract remedy identified," the panel stated that this "legal principle cannot equitably pertain where the breaching party has, because of its wrongdoing, effectively eliminated the opposing party's contractual remedy, as happened here.". . . . Therefore, the panel concluded that the defendants had been unjustly enriched by the sale of shares to Perspecta. Using the "Claw Back" provision in the Agreement as a guide only, the second panel awarded Finn $600,000 in equitable relief.

Returning to court, Finn moved to affirm, and the defendants moved to vacate in part, the second arbitration award. Applying the plain mistake standard of review found in RSA 542:8, the trial court ruled that the second panel's award of additional damages to Finn on her unjust enrichment claim was barred, under settled principles of res judicata, by the award of damages she received from the first panel.

Finn moved for reconsideration, arguing that the FAA applied to this case because the Agreement affected interstate commerce. Therefore, she argued, the trial court should have applied the more deferential FAA standard in reviewing the arbitration award because the FAA preempts state law. The trial court denied the motion, and this appeal followed.

II

On appeal, Finn asserts that the trial court erred in applying RSA 542:8 to review the second arbitration panel's award because state law is preempted by the FAA. Alternatively, she argues that, even if RSA 542:8 applies, the trial court erred because it did not afford sufficient deference to the panel's findings of fact and rulings of law. Finally, she argues that the trial court misapplied the doctrine of res judicata to her unjust enrichment claim. We examine her arguments in turn. . . .

A

Finn argues that the trial court erred in reviewing the second panel's award under RSA 542:8 instead of §§ 9 and 10 of the FAA. Relying primarily upon the decision of the United States Supreme Court in *Hall Street Associates, L.L.C. v. Mattel, Inc.*, 552 U.S. 576, 128 S.Ct. 1396, 170 L.Ed.2d 254 (2008), she asserts that RSA 542:8 is impliedly preempted by the FAA because the Agreement is a contract affecting interstate commerce, . . . to which the FAA applies, and that failing to employ the more deferential federal standard of judicial review of arbitration awards "foils the objective Congress seeks to advance with the FAA." "Because the trial court's determination of federal preemption is a matter of law, our review is *de novo*." . . .

The federal preemption doctrine effectuates the Supremacy Clause of the United States Constitution. . . . It ensures that federal law "shall be the supreme law of the land; and the judges in every state shall be bound thereby, anything in the Constitution or laws of any state to the contrary notwithstanding," U.S. CONST. art. VI, by invalidating state laws that conflict with federal legislation. . . . Congress may expressly preempt a state law, or it may implicitly preempt a state law through "field" preemption or "conflict" preemption. . . .

The Supreme Court has held that "[t]he FAA contains no express preemptive provision, nor does it reflect a congressional intent to occupy the entire field of arbitration." *Volt Info. Sciences v. Leland Stanford Jr.*

U., 489 U.S. 468, 477, 109 S.Ct. 1248, 103 L.Ed.2d 488 (1989). Therefore, Finn presses conflict preemption, which "arises when compliance with both federal and state regulations is a physical impossibility, or when state law stands as an obstacle to the accomplishment and execution of the full purposes and objectives of Congress." . . .

The trial court reviewed the second panel's award pursuant to RSA 542:8, which creates a procedure for parties to seek confirmation, modification, or vacatur of an arbitral award:

> At any time within one year after the award is made any party to the arbitration may apply to the superior court for an order confirming the award, correcting or modifying the award for plain mistake, or vacating the award for fraud, corruption, or misconduct by the parties or by the arbitrators, or on the ground that the arbitrators have exceeded their powers. Where an award is vacated and the time within which the agreement required the award to be made has not expired, the court may in its discretion, direct a rehearing by the arbitrators or by new arbitrators appointed by the court.

We have construed this statute to grant a court the authority to vacate an award for plain mistake if it "determine[s] that an arbitrator misapplied the law to the facts." . . . Similarly, the FAA creates "mechanisms for enforcing arbitration awards: a judicial decree confirming an award, an order vacating it, or an order modifying or correcting it." . . .

Section 2 of the FAA provides:

> A written provision in . . . a contract evidencing a transaction involving commerce to settle by arbitration a controversy thereafter arising out of such contract or transaction, or the refusal to perform the whole or any part thereof, or an agreement in writing to submit to arbitration an existing controversy arising out of such a contract, transaction, or refusal, shall be valid, irrevocable, and enforceable, save upon such grounds as exist at law or in equity for the revocation of any contract.

9 U.S.C. § 2. Thus, the FAA applies to state courts insofar as § 2 prohibits state courts from refusing to enforce agreements to arbitrate. *Southland Corp. v. Keating*, 465 U.S. 1, 14–16, 104 S.Ct. 852, 79 L.Ed.2d 1 (1984).

Finn's argument relies upon §§ 9, 10 and 11 of the FAA. In *Hall Street,* the Supreme Court held that the listed grounds for vacation, correction or modification of an arbitral award by a federal court, as set forth in §§ 10 and 11 of the FAA, may not be supplemented by the terms of the arbitration agreement entered into by the parties. *Hall Street*, 552 U.S. at 590, 128 S.Ct. 1396. These provisions provide much more limited grounds for review of an arbitration award than does "plain mistake" review under RSA 542:8.

We do not agree with Finn's first argument that the FAA is the exclusive method by which to review the second panel's award because we conclude that §§ 9–11 of the FAA apply only to arbitration review proceedings commenced in federal courts. As we have already noted, the FAA creates some substantive rules that apply to arbitration agreements in both federal and state courts when the contract to arbitrate affects commerce. . . . Section 2 of the act applies in state courts to prevent anti-arbitration laws from invalidating otherwise lawful arbitration agreements. . . . However, it does not follow that the FAA applies to state courts in its entirety. In fact, the Supreme Court has suggested that some of the statute's provisions apply only in federal courts. . . . In considering whether other sections of the FAA apply in state courts, the Court noted that it has "never held that §§ 3 and 4, which by their terms appear to apply only to proceedings in federal court, . . . are nonetheless applicable in state court." . . . This comment clearly contemplates that the Court considers the application to the states of each section individually, rather than the application of the Act as a whole. Therefore, we consider whether §§ 9–11 of the FAA also use language that limits their application to federal courts.

[FAA §§ 3 and 4 make] reference to either "the courts of the United States" or "any United States district court." . . . Likewise, §§ 10 and 11, the sections that establish the limited grounds upon which arbitration awards may be upset, reference only the federal courts. 9 U.S.C. §§ 10, 11. Although § 9 of the FAA could be read to encompass state courts as well as federal courts, and to contemplate that state courts reviewing covered arbitration awards (*i.e.,* those involving contracts affecting interstate commerce) must utilize exclusively the standards set forth in §§ 10 and 11, the Court has not interpreted the FAA in this fashion. In *Hall Street,* the Court . . . acknowledged the potential for review of arbitration awards under state law. . . . If the FAA were, in all circumstances, the exclusive grounds for review of arbitration awards subject to the FAA, these possible alternative paradigms of judicial review that the Court described would have been completely foreclosed. Indeed, the Texas Supreme Court has specifically recognized the limited applicability of the FAA to state courts: "The mere fact that a contract affects interstate commerce, thus triggering the FAA, does not preclude enforcement under [state law] as well." *Nafta Traders, Inc. v. Quinn*, 339 S.W.3d 84, 98 (Tex.2011).

Here, the FAA applied to the extent that it required the parties to arbitrate their dispute, as the trial court noted when it referred Finn's claim to the second arbitration panel. That does not mean that all aspects of the FAA are applicable to this proceeding. Based upon our review of the pertinent case law, we conclude that neither *Hall Street,* nor any other precedents by which we are bound, requires that we accept plaintiff's position that §§ 10 and 11 provide the exclusive grounds for state court review of arbitration awards subject to the FAA.

We next consider Finn's argument that so-called "obstacle preemption" supports her assertion that RSA 542:8 is invalidated by the FAA. The "obstacle" branch of conflict preemption requires more than a showing that some tension between the state and federal laws exists. . . . A party must show that "the repugnance or conflict is so direct and positive that the two acts cannot be reconciled or consistently stand together." . . . "What is a sufficient obstacle is a matter of judgment, to be informed by examining the federal statute as a whole and identifying its purpose and intended effects." . . .

The Supreme Court has provided guidance regarding the purpose of the FAA. It has described the primary purpose of the FAA as "foreclos[ing] state legislative attempts to undercut the enforceability of arbitration agreements." *Southland Corp.*, 465 U.S. at 16, 104 S.Ct. 852. This purpose is rooted in § 2 of the FAA. *Id.* at 10, 104 S.Ct. 852. By establishing that agreements to arbitrate "shall be valid, irrevocable, and enforceable," 9 U.S.C. § 2, Congress "withdrew the power of the states to require a judicial forum for the resolution of claims which the contracting parties agreed to resolve by arbitration." *Southland Corp.*, 465 U.S. at 10, 104 S.Ct. 852. For example, the Court held preempted a state law that required notice of an arbitration clause upon the first page of the contract, *Doctor's Associates, Inc. v. Casarotto*, 517 U.S. 681, 683, 116 S.Ct. 1652, 134 L.Ed.2d 902 (1996), and a law that required administrative procedures before a case could proceed to arbitration, *Preston v. Ferrer*, 552 U.S. 346, 349–50, 128 S.Ct. 978, 169 L.Ed.2d 917 (2008). Thus, at the heart of the Court's FAA preemption doctrine is its effort to enforce Congressional intent by thwarting the recurring refusal of state courts to enforce an otherwise valid contract because it embodied the parties' agreement to arbitrate. . . . In short, preemption under the FAA is at its apex when parties cannot get to arbitration because state law attempts to force them to resolve their dispute in court. . . .

In *AT&T Mobility LLC v. Concepcion*, 563 U.S. 333, 338, 131 S.Ct. 1740, 179 L.Ed.2d 742 (2011), the Court considered California's application of the doctrine of unconscionability to an arbitration agreement. . . . The California law held unconscionable arbitration agreement provisions that waived class proceedings—both in litigation and arbitration—if the state court found that bilateral proceedings would not adequately substitute for the deterrent effect of a class action. . . . The Court had to decide whether the FAA preempted the California law, which was generally applicable but was "alleged to have been applied in a fashion that disfavors arbitration." . . . In reaching its conclusion, the Court emphasized that "[t]he overarching purpose of the FAA . . . is to ensure the enforcement of arbitration agreements according to their terms so as to facilitate streamlined proceedings." . . . Reiterating that "our cases place it beyond dispute that the FAA was designed to promote arbitration," the Court examined whether the California rule "interferes with arbitration." . . . It concluded that, by requiring that class actions be available in a particular subset of arbitration agreements, California courts had "sacrifice[d] the principal advantage of arbitration—its informality." . . . Class arbitrations take more time to reach a final award on the merits than bilateral arbitration and require procedural formality to make the award binding upon absent parties. . . . These complications, the Court determined, departed significantly from arbitration as envisioned by the FAA and, therefore, were a thinly veiled refusal to enforce arbitration agreements. . . . The California rule was therefore preempted because it required drastic procedural changes before the court would enforce the agreement to arbitrate. . . .

In contrast, state rules that slow or change procedures without the potential consequence of invalidating an arbitration agreement are not preempted. . . .

The fact that a state law affecting arbitration is less deferential to an arbitrator's decision than the FAA does not create an obstacle so insurmountable as to preempt state law. *Volt* demonstrates that not all obstacles to arbitration are repugnant to the FAA. The procedural rule in *Volt* delayed arbitration, and simplified it, by staying the proceedings until non-arbitral issues had been resolved. . . . On the other hand, the state rule at issue in *AT&T Mobility* contemplated an extreme alteration of arbitration procedure, risks, and efficiency, and failure to comply with its requirement would make the agreement to arbitrate unenforceable. . . . It thus had such a profound effect upon arbitration as to effectively deter parties from choosing arbitration.

RSA 542:8 is more like the rule at issue in *Volt* than that at issue in *AT & T Mobility*. "[T]he FAA does not preempt all state-law impediments to arbitration; it preempts state-law impediments to arbitration agreements." Nafta Traders, 339 S.W.3d at 100. Thus, "[f]or the FAA to preempt [state law], state law must refuse to enforce an arbitration agreement that the FAA would enforce." *Id.* at 98 (quotation omitted). RSA 542:8's more rigorous standard of judicial review of arbitral decisions is not an impediment to enforcement of the parties' *agreement to arbitrate* as per the terms of the Agreement. In fact, it does not even slow the enforcement of an agreement to arbitrate, but instead applies *after* an agreement to arbitrate has already been enforced, arbitration conducted, and a final award issued. It allows the trial court to ensure that no plain mistakes made by the arbitrators will go uncorrected.

In this case, the trial court did not refuse to enforce the parties' agreement to arbitrate. Instead it applied RSA 542:8 to review the second panel's award, which was produced because the trial court had complied with the FAA and enforced their agreement to arbitrate. RSA 542:8 does not interfere with the FAA's principal purpose of protecting arbitration agreements from perceived judicial hostility. Because our state standard of review does not impede the enforcement of an arbitration agreement nor mandate drastic changes to the procedures by which arbitration is to be conducted, it is not preempted by the FAA.

Finn nonetheless insists that the Court's discussion in *Hall Street* about the dangers of "full-bore legal and evidentiary appeals that can render informal arbitration merely a prelude to a more cumbersome and time-consuming judicial review process," thus "bring[ing] arbitration theory to grief in postarbitration process," . . . demands that we hold RSA 542:8 preempted by the FAA. She argues that, although the Court acknowledged that parties may seek review of arbitral decisions through other avenues of enforcement, these "are only permissible where they are *more restrictive* than federal standards of review." . . . We do not believe that *Hall Street* stands for this proposition. . . .

[T]he parties could not contract to expand the scope of review applied to the award under the FAA because "it makes more sense to see the three provisions . . . as substantiating a national policy favoring arbitration with just the limited review needed to maintain arbitration's essential virtue of resolving disputes straightaway." . . . But the Court limited the reach of this national policy:

> In holding that §§ 10 and 11 provide exclusive regimes for the review provided by the statute, we do not purport to say that they exclude more searching review based on authority outside the statute as well. The FAA is not the only way into court for parties wanting review of arbitration awards: they may contemplate enforcement under state statutory or common law, for example, where judicial review of different scope is arguable. But here we speak only to the scope of the expeditious judicial review under §§ 9, 10, and 11, deciding nothing about other possible avenues for judicial enforcement of arbitration awards.

. . . . Accordingly, *Hall Street* does not support Finn's contention that the Court has held preempted state standards of review that are more rigorous than the FAA. Instead, the caveat of *Hall Street* supports our conclusion that RSA 542:8 is not preempted. *Hall Street* was a question of statutory interpretation, not preemption. . . . It considered only federal law as it applied to a federal court. . . .

The California Supreme Court reached a similar conclusion [in *Cable Connection, Inc. v. DIRECTV, Inc.*, 44 Cal.4th 1334, 82 Cal.Rptr.3d 229, 190 P.3d 586, 599 (2008)]. We agree with the California court. To conclude from *Hall Street* that the Court intended to establish a new policy with preemptive effect is unreasonable given both the context and express limitation of the case's holding, as well as the federalism concerns that would be implicated by such a broad reading of the case.

. . . . We therefore conclude that the FAA does not preempt RSA 542:8, and that the trial court did not err by applying it to the second arbitral award.

B

Finn next argues that the trial court erred because it did not give deference to the second panel's findings of fact and rulings of law. She contends that the trial court erred by failing to accept the second panel's finding that Finn could not have brought her unjust enrichment claim in the first arbitration. She also contends that the trial court was entitled to vacate the second panel's award for mistake of law only if it found that the panel did not know what the law was. We are not persuaded by these arguments.

We have construed RSA 542:8 to grant the trial court the power to vacate an arbitration award for a "plain mistake" of law or fact. . . . "It must be shown that the arbitrators manifestly fell into such error concerning the facts or law, and that the error prevented their free and fair exercise of judgment on the subject." . . . We therefore consider arbitral awards with deference to the arbitrators. . . . In past cases we have defined a "plain mistake" as "an error that is apparent on the face of the record and which would have been corrected had it been called to the arbitrators' attention." . . . Although we have recited this language, we have reversed arbitration awards when the errors, although not subtle, were not so obvious as to satisfy the literal meaning of this language. Indeed, we have found plain mistake in circumstances where the correct legal analysis was presented to the arbitrator(s) but was rejected. . . .

The trial court did not misapply the standard of review for an arbitration panel's findings of fact because it did not upset the second panel's findings as to any factual issues. The panel asked the parties to brief whether Finn "[c]ould and therefore should . . . have . . . advanced a claim for unjust enrichment in [the first] action and if she did not, is she foreclosed from advancing such a claim . . . in the current action." This question is, in essence, merely a rephrasing of the doctrine of res judicata, which is an issue of law. . . . Therefore, we consider the question by applying the standard for plain mistakes of law.

A trial court may vacate an award for plain mistake of law under two circumstances. First, the court may find a plain mistake of law when the law has changed after the issuance of an award, but before the award is reduced to final judgment, if the court concludes that the panel would not have reached the same conclusion had it known of the change in the law. . . . Second, the court may find a plain mistake of law when the panel clearly misapplied the law to the facts. . . . RSA 542:8 does not require, as

Finn contends, a scouring of the record for proof as to the panel's understanding of general legal principles that may be pertinent to the issues before it. Nor must it assume proper application of the law from the panel members' resumes. Rather, although judicial review is deferential, it is the court's task to determine whether the arbitrators were plainly mistaken in their application of law to the specific facts and circumstances of the dispute they were called upon to decide.

. . . .[W]e reject Finn's contention that the trial court misapplied the plain mistake standard by conducting an overly searching review of the panel's decision.

[. . .]

NOTES AND QUESTIONS

1. *Finn* carries the logic and reasoning of *Cable Connections* further and finds that state law, irrespective of the parties' agreement, may impose stricter standards of review than would be required under FAA § 10.

Rhode Island's Supreme Court has taken a similar view. In *Nappa Constr. Mgmt., LLC v. Flynn*, 152 A.3d 1128, 1132 (R.I. 2017), the expansively defined excess of authority to include situations where an award "fails to 'draw its essence from the agreement, if it was not based upon a passably plausible interpretation thereof, if it manifestly disregarded a contractual provision, *or if it reached an irrational result.*' " *Id.* at 1132 (citations omitted) (emphasis added). The court went on to say that "[a]n arbitrator may misconstrue a contract; however, he may not manifestly disregard a contractual term or ignore 'clear-cut contractual language.' " *Id.* at 1133.

2. Notice how the court in *Finn* justifies its departure from the FAA. Do you agree that "RSA 542:8's more rigorous standard of judicial review of arbitral decisions is not an impediment" to the goals of the FAA? Is the holding in *Finn* more like the situation in *Volt* or more like the situation in *Concepcion*?

3. Does *Finn* authorize a court in New Hampshire to review the merits of the arbitrator's decision? If so, does the case seem to square with your understanding of the U.S. Supreme Court's view of arbitration?

4. The drafters of the Restatement (Third) U.S. Law of Int'l Comm. Arb. § 1–5 TD No 9 (2016) believe that federal law will preempt state law grounds for post-award relief to the extent that: (1) they substantially impair the parties' agreement to arbitration; or (2) they interfere with a fundamental attribute of arbitration.

8. MANIFEST DISREGARD OF THE LAW

Manifest disregard, to the extent that it survives the holding in *Hall Street*, applies when there is a well-defined contract term or law, the term or law was not a matter of dispute, and the arbitrator declined to apply the term or law. The phrase "manifest disregard" originated in *Wilko v. Swan*. *Wilko* was decided prior to the U.S. Supreme Court's contemporary jurisprudence and the strong federal policy favoring enforcement of arbitration agreements. Indeed, *Wilko* was eventually overruled. The real legacy of *Wilko*, however, is manifest disregard of the law. In the case, the Court stated that "the interpretations of the law by the arbitrators in contrast to *manifest disregard* are not subject, in the federal courts, to judicial review for error in interpretation" *Wilko v. Swan*, 346 U.S. 427, 436–37 (1953). Lower courts have relied on this language to fashion the modern manifest disregard of the law doctrine.

Currently, a Circuit split exists about whether manifest disregard exists, at least in federal courts. The Second, Fourth, Seventh, Ninth, and Tenth Circuits all maintain that some variant of the manifest disregard ground for review of arbitral awards survived *Hall Street*.[2] The Fifth, Eighth, and Eleventh Circuits hold that manifest disregard is no longer an applicable ground for vacating an arbitration award.[3] The First and DC Circuits have only addressed the issue in dicta.[4]

RODRIGUEZ V. PRUDENTIAL-BACHE SECURITIES, INC.

882 F.Supp. 1202, 1209 (D.P.R. 1995).

(footnotes omitted)

[. . .]

Prudential's next contention is that the award represents a manifest disregard of the law. In essence, Prudential argues that claimants were terminated for "just cause," in accordance with Commonwealth Law 80, . . . which provides the exclusive remedy for wrongfully discharged employees, and therefore are not entitled to any compensation. The "manifest disregard" language derives from *dicta* employed by the U.S. Supreme Court in *Wilko v. Swan*. . . . *See Advest, Inc.* at 9 n.5. "The lane of review that has opened out of this language is a judicially created one, not to be found in 9 U.S.C. § 10." *Id.*

---

[2] *See, e.g., A & G Coal Corp. v. Integrity Coal Sales, Inc.*, 565 Fed. Appx. 41 (2d Cir. 2014), *cert. denied*, 135 S. Ct. 368, 190 L.Ed. 2d 252 (2014); *Dewan v. Walia*, 544 Fed. Appx. 240, 36 I.E.R. Cas. (BNA) 1672 (4th Cir. 2013), *cert. denied*, 134 S. Ct. 1788, 188 L.Ed. 2d 757, 37 I.E.R. Cas. (BNA) 1716 (2014); *Renard v. Ameriprise Financial Services, Inc.*, 778 F.3d 563 (7th Cir. 2015); *Wetzel's Pretzels, LLC v. Johnson*, 567 Fed. Appx. 493 (9th Cir. 2014); *Adviser Dealer Services, Inc. v. Icon Advisers, Inc.*, 557 Fed. Appx. 714 (10th Cir. 2014).

[3] See *McVay v. Halliburton Energy Servs., Inc.*, 608 F. App'x 222, 225 (5th Cir. 2015); *Med. Shoppe Int'l, Inc. v. Turner Invs., Inc.*, 614 F.3d 485, 489 (8th Cir. 2010); *Frazier v. CitiFinancial Corp.*, 604 F.3d 1313, 1322–24 (11th Cir. 2010).

[4] *See Raymond James Fin. Servs., Inc. v. Fenyk*, 780 F.3d 59, 65 (1st Cir. 2015) (acknowledging that the circuit has "not squarely determined whether our manifest disregard case law can be reconciled with *Hall Street*") (internal quotation and citation omitted); *Affinity Fin. Corp. v. AARP Fin., Inc.*, 468 F. App'x 4, 5 (D.C. Cir. 2012) (assuming without deciding that manifest disregard of the law standard survived *Hall Street*).

In *Advest, Inc.*, the First Circuit identified two classes of cases where an arbitral award is subject to review under this standard. The first category, usually involving labor arbitration, is where an award is contrary to the plain language of the collective bargaining agreement. *Advest, Inc.* at 9. The second category involves instances where it is clear from the record that the arbitrator recognized the applicable law—and then ignored it. *Id.* As in *Advest*, Prudential is making a claim of the second type, asserting that the arbitrators' award is so irreconcilable with the provisions of Law 80 that the panel must have disregarded the law, and "embarked on a flight of fancy." *Id.* at 10. As expressly stated by the court in *Advest* however, the hurdle is a high one. In order to vacate an arbitration award, there must be some showing in the record, other than the result obtained, that the arbitrators knew the law and expressly disregarded it. *Id.* . . . The court construed the term "disregard" to imply that the arbitrators appreciated the existence of a governing legal rule but willfully decided not to apply it. [*Id.*] As arbitrators need not explain the reasons justifying their award, and did not do so in this case, "it is no wonder that [Prudential] is hard pressed to satisfy the exacting criteria for invocation of the doctrine." *Id.*

Prudential's argument that it had just cause to terminate its relationship with claimants was considered and, judging from the award, rejected by the arbitrators. Furthermore, it is not disputed that Law 80 was not the only cause of action asserted by claimants in their quest for relief. Nor is it contested that claimants presented evidence regarding damages under Law 80 which directly contradicted that which was presented by Prudential. We therefore decline Prudential's invitation to revisit the merits of their factual contentions regarding just cause and the damages resulting from the termination of claimants.

[. . .]

NOTES AND QUESTIONS

1. The excerpt from *Rodriguez* provides a straightforward representation of the function of the "manifest disregard" basis for review. The reference to *Advest* explains the role of "manifest disregard" in the setting of labor arbitration and illustrates that it is available against any type of arbitral award "when it is clear from the record that the arbitrator recognized the applicable law—and then ignored it." Given this description of the means of recourse, the standard set of concerns surface. Should "manifest disregard" be available outside the context of labor arbitration, especially when the standard practice in nonlabor domestic arbitration is to render awards without opinions? Does the ground's origination in the *dicta* of *Wilko v. Swan* justify making it applicable in all arbitral contexts? Even assuming a wide application, should "manifest disregard" be employed only when the award involves the application of statutory law?

2. In any event, the elements of the ground make it difficult to invoke: (1) there must be a record, and (2) that record must indicate clearly that the arbitrator (a) recognized the law and (b) disregarded it in reaching a determination. None of these elements is readily established. The award may not be accompanied by an opinion and usually there is no transcript of the proceedings. Few arbitrators are likely to provide a written statement of the applicable law and then reach a determination that completely ignores it as a guiding principle. Commercial arbitrators may describe the law or apply it in a judicially erroneous manner, but they are not likely simply to dismiss it once it has been presented and argued, unless they are authorized by the parties to rule as amiable compositors. Amiable compositors are given the right by the contract of arbitration to decide the matter according to their own sense of justice, provided they find the legal answer and then conclude it is unjust or untoward. Essentially, amiable compositors rule in equity after they discover the law and reject it. Outside the context of labor or maritime arbitration, "manifest disregard" appears to be misplaced and to have an obtuse function.

3. The *Advest* court notes that, if arbitrators do not render reasons with the award, the party challenging the award on the basis of "manifest disregard" is extremely unlikely to prevail. On this basis, the court in *Rodriguez* concludes that the attempt to vacate the award for "manifest disregard" constitutes an unwarranted invitation to the court to "revisit the merits" of the litigation. Do you agree with these assessments?

BARAVATI V. JOSEPHTHAL, LYON & ROSS, INC.

28 F.3d 704, 706 (7th Cir. 1994).

[. . .]

Judicial review of arbitration awards is tightly limited; perhaps it ought not be called "review" at all. By including an arbitration clause in their contract the parties agree to submit disputes arising out of the contract to a nonjudicial forum, and we do not allow the disappointed party to bring his dispute into court by the back door, arguing that he is entitled to appellate review of the arbitrators' decision. . . . There are, nevertheless, limited grounds on which an arbitral award can be set aside, such as that the arbitrators "exceeded their powers." . . .

A number of courts, including our own, have said that they can set aside arbitral awards if the arbitrators exhibited a "manifest disregard of the law." . . . Two courts, however, have declined to adopt this formula, . . . though without rejecting it. Two have criticized it. . . . This formula is dictum, as no one has found a case where, had it not been intoned, the result would have been different. It originated in *Wilko v. Swan*, . . . a case the Supreme Court first criticized for mistrust of arbitration and confined to its narrowest possible holding . . . and then overruled. . . . Created *ex nihilo* to be a nonstatutory ground for setting aside arbitral awards, the *Wilko* formula reflects precisely that mistrust of arbitration for which the

Court in its two *Shearson/American* opinions criticized *Wilko*. We can understand neither the need for the formula nor the role that it plays in judicial review of arbitration (we suspect none—that it is just words). If it is meant to smuggle review for clear error in by the back door, it is inconsistent with the entire modern law of arbitration. If it is intended to be synonymous with the statutory formula that it most nearly resembles—whether the arbitrators "exceeded their powers"—it is superfluous and confusing. There is enough confusion in the law. The grounds for setting aside arbitration awards are exhaustively stated in the statute. Now that *Wilko* is history, there is no reason to continue to echo its gratuitous attempt at nonstatutory supplementation. So it will be enough in this case to consider whether the arbitrators exceeded their powers.

[. . .]

NOTES AND QUESTIONS

1. *Baravati* is one of the more interesting judicial variations on the theme of the judicial supervision of awards and on the concept of "manifest disregard." What do you think of the court's assertion that the judicial supervision of arbitral awards does not or should not constitute "judicial review"? What term or description do you think might be more appropriate or accurate?

2. The court justifies the limited availability of judicial scrutiny in terms of the need for arbitral autonomy. What are the other elements of its justification?

3. The court then engages in a critical review of the origins and function of the "manifest disregard" basis for review. Did "manifest disregard" die with the reversal of *Wilko* in *Rodriguez*?

4. As noted in at the outset of this section, the Seventh Circuit is currently among those recognizing the continued viability of some variation of the manifest disregard standard. As *Baravati* may suggest, however, the Seventh Circuit is not an unabashed fan of the doctrine.

In *George Watts & Son, Inc. v. Tiffany & Co.*, 248 F.3d 577 (7th Cir. 2001), the Seventh Circuit addressed *Baravati*. In *George*, the Seventh Circuit acknowledged that *Baravati* "concluded that the statutory list of reasons for setting aside an award is exclusive, that *Wilko* has after all been overruled, and that as a result 'manifest disregard' of the law is not an independent reason to set aside an award." *Id.* at 580. The court went on to observe that the year after *Baravati* was decided, the Supreme Court issued its ruling in *First Options of Chicago, Inc. v. Kaplan*, which "repeated the *Wilko* dictum, and in 1999 another panel of this court stated in dictum (without citing *Baravati*) that the statutory list is not exclusive and that 'manifest disregard of the law' is one non-statutory ground for setting aside an award." *Id.*

After noting the confusing state of the law and the Supreme Court's "opaque" handing of the issue, the court went on to say that "[t]here is, however, a way to understand 'manifest disregard of the law' that preserves the established relation between court and arbitrator and resolves the tension in the competing lines of cases. It is this: an arbitrator may not direct the parties to violate the law." *Id.*

In 2015, the Seventh Circuit repeated this language, citing *George* and clarifying that " 'manifest disregard of the law' exists only if the arbitrator directs the parties to violate the law." *Renard v. Ameriprise Fin. Servs., Inc.*, 778 F.3d 563, 567 (7th Cir. 2015).

PATTEN V. SIGNATOR INS. AGENCY, INC.

441 F.3d 230 (4th Cir.), *cert. denied* 549 U.S. 975, 127 S.Ct. 434, 166 L.Ed.2d 308 (2006).

KING, CIRCUIT JUDGE:

Appellant Ralph F. Patten, Jr., appeals from the district court's denial of his motion to vacate an arbitration award rendered in favor of John Hancock Mutual Life Insurance Company, Signator Insurance Agency, Incorporated, and Signator Investors, Incorporated (collectively the "respondents"). . . . By this appeal, Patten seeks only to vacate that aspect of the arbitration award dismissing as time-barred his claims against Signator Investors. Patten asserts that the arbitrator acted without authority when he unilaterally imposed an implied one-year limitations period onto the governing arbitration agreement between Patten and Signator Investors. As explained below, the arbitration agreement does not explicitly prescribe any limitations period with respect to an arbitration demand, and it supersedes all other agreements between the parties. In the circumstances presented, the arbitrator's ruling constituted a manifest disregard of the law and was not drawn from the essence of the governing arbitration agreement. As a result, we vacate the district court's refusal to vacate the arbitration award as to Signator Investors, and we remand for further proceedings.

I.

A.

Patten first began working as a sales agent for Hancock in the Washington, D.C. area in 1972. In 1989, he became a General Agent for Hancock in Bethesda, Maryland. In 1992, he entered into an agreement with Hancock and its affiliates, designated as a "Mutual Agreement to Arbitrate Claims" (the "Mutual Agreement"). The Mutual Agreement required, *inter alia*, that any claims arising between Patten and Hancock (or any of Hancock's affiliates or subsidiaries) were to be resolved by mandatory arbitration. The Mutual Agreement specifically provided, in a section captioned "Required Notice of all Claims and Statute of Limitations," that an "aggrieved party must give written notice of any claim to the other party within one (1) year of . . . the event giving rise to the claim," or the claim would be deemed waived. . . . It is undisputed that Signator Investors was an "affiliate" of Hancock and thus a party to the Mutual Agreement.

In 1998, Patten entered into a new and superseding agreement with Signator Investors, to become its branch manager in Bethesda (the "Management Agreement"). The Management Agreement provided, *inter alia*, that "Signator [Investors] and Branch Manager [Patten] mutually consent to the resolution by arbitration of all claims or controversies." The Management Agreement was silent, however, on any requirements of timing or manner with respect to an arbitration demand. The Management Agreement also provided that it "supersedes all previous agreements, oral or written, between the parties hereto regarding the subject matter hereof." Finally, the Management Agreement mandated that it was to "be governed by and construed in accordance with the laws of the Commonwealth of Massachusetts."

On October 18, 1999, Hancock reprimanded Patten for alleged deficiencies in his performance as a General Agent—specifically, for advancing premiums on behalf of his clients, in violation of company policy. On December 13, 2000, the respondents each terminated Patten, effective January 2, 2001. On August 2, 2001, Patten sent a letter to the respondents advising them that he had been wrongfully terminated and discriminated against because of his age, and that he was preparing to file a lawsuit on the basis of these claims. The respondents, by letter of August 30, 2001, advised Patten that his allegations were "unequivocally denie[d]," and the parties then apparently entered into unsuccessful settlement negotiations.

On March 4, 2002, Patten forwarded the respondents a demand for arbitration, asserting claims of discrimination, wrongful termination, and breach of contract. On March 13, 2002, the respondents informed Patten by letter that they would not arbitrate because his demand for arbitration was made fourteen months after his termination, and thus was not "timely or proper" under the Mutual Agreement's one-year limitations period. On March 14, 2002, Patten replied that the Management Agreement (rather than the Mutual Agreement) governed his claims against Signator Investors, and that he would seek judicial enforcement of his rights if the respondents refused to arbitrate.

B.

On May 20, 2002, Patten filed a complaint for enforcement of arbitration in the District of Maryland, seeking to compel arbitration. The parties thereafter filed cross-motions for summary judgment and, on November 5, 2002, the court ruled in favor of Patten and directed the respondents to submit to arbitration. . . . Because the court concluded that arbitration should be compelled "under the Mutual Agreement, the Court [found] it unnecessary to address Plaintiff's argument regarding the Management Agreement." . . . In its opinion, the court observed that all other questions concerning the arbitration—including the satisfaction of time and notice requirements—were "within the arbitrator's purview." *Id.* at 2.

The parties entered into arbitration in 2003 under the auspices of the American Arbitration Association (the "AAA"). On January 24, 2003, Patten filed a demand for arbitration with the AAA, making allegations of (1) wrongful termination, (2) breach of contract, (3) breach of the implied covenant of good faith and fair dealing, and (4) unlawful discrimination in violation of federal law as well as the law of Massachusetts and Maryland. After selecting an arbitrator under the procedures of the AAA, the parties engaged in discovery and exchanged witness lists. On December 8, 2003, the respondents filed a motion for summary judgment in the arbitration proceedings, asserting, *inter alia*, that Patten had failed to comply with the one-year notice provision of the Mutual Agreement. On December 18, 2003, Patten filed an opposition to the respondents' summary judgment request, asserting that the arbitration proceedings arose under both the Management Agreement and the Mutual Agreement. Patten contended that he had complied with the applicable notice requirements of each agreement—maintaining that his August 2, 2001 letter substantially complied with the one-year notice requirement in the Mutual Agreement, and that the Management Agreement contained no limitations period governing when an arbitration demand was to be made.

By his arbitration award of January 10, 2004, the arbitrator dismissed the arbitration proceedings as time-barred and entered summary judgment for the respondents, without conducting a hearing on the merits. As a preliminary matter, he determined that the arbitration proceedings were governed by both the Mutual Agreement and the Management Agreement. While the arbitrator accurately observed that the Management Agreement contained no notice requirement, he determined that it "necessarily contain[ed] an implied term limit." The arbitrator then "look[ed] to the Mutual Agreement for guidance," and "adopt[ed]" its one-year limitations period. Because Patten sent his demand for arbitration fourteen months after his termination in January 2001, the arbitrator dismissed Patten's claims "on the sole ground that Claimant's March 4, 2002 Demand for Arbitration is time-barred."

C.

On April 9, 2004, Patten filed a motion in the district court proceedings seeking to vacate the arbitration award's determination that the claims in arbitration under the Management Agreement were time-barred. By this motion, Patten contended that the arbitrator had acted in manifest disregard of the law, and had failed to draw his award from the essence of the agreement, by concluding that the Management Agreement contained an implied one-year limitations period on the filing of an arbitration demand. Patten asserted that the Management Agreement explicitly provided that it "supersede[d]" all previous agreements, and its lack of any limitations period had to be construed against Signator Investors, which had drafted it. On January 4, 2005, the district court denied the motion to vacate, concluding that the arbitrator had not ignored any governing legal principles, and that, in any event, an arbitrator's misinterpretation of an arbitration agreement is not a basis for vacating an arbitration award. . . . Patten has filed a timely notice of appeal, and we possess jurisdiction pursuant to 28 U.S.C. § 1291.

II.

The process and extent of federal judicial review of an arbitration award are substantially circumscribed. As a general proposition, a federal court may vacate an arbitration award only upon a showing of one of the grounds specified in the Federal Arbitration Act . . . or upon a showing of certain limited common law grounds. The permissible common law grounds for vacating such an award, which constitute the essential premises of this appeal, include those circumstances where an award fails to draw its essence from the contract, or the award evidences a manifest disregard of the law. . . . In reviewing a denial of a motion to vacate an arbitration award, we review the district court's determinations of law *de novo*. . . .

III.

A.

This dispute was submitted to arbitration pursuant to two separate agreements: first, the Mutual Agreement of 1992, which Patten entered into with Hancock and its affiliates (which included Signator Investors); and second, the Management Agreement, which Patten and Signator Investors entered into in 1998. On appeal, however, Patten seeks only to vacate the arbitrator's dismissal of his claims under the Management Agreement against Signator Investors. Importantly, he does not, in this appeal, take issue with those aspects of the arbitration award dismissing his claims against Hancock and Signator Insurance as time-barred under the Mutual Agreement. Thus, the governing arbitration agreement in this appeal is contained in Paragraph 11 of the Management Agreement between Patten and Signator Investors. That arbitration agreement provides, in pertinent part:

> Signator [Investors] and Branch Manager [Patten] mutually consent to the resolution by arbitration of all claims or controversies ("claims") . . . that Signator [Investors] may have against Branch Manager or that Branch Manager may have against Signator [Investors]. . . . The claims covered by this

consent to arbitration include all claims arising out of or in connection with the business of Signator [Investors]. . . .

B.

Patten contends that the arbitration award should be vacated as to Signator Investors because the arbitrator's most crucial ruling—that the governing arbitration provision in the Management Agreement contained an implied time limitation on an arbitration demand—constituted a manifest disregard of the law, and failed to draw its essence from the agreement. In seeking to vacate an arbitration award, of course, an appellant "shoulders a heavy burden." . . . Put simply, an arbitrator's legal determination "may only be overturned where it is in manifest disregard of the law," and an arbitrator's interpretation of a contract must be upheld so long as it "draws its essence from the agreement." . . . Under our precedent, a manifest disregard of the law is established only where the "arbitrator[ ] understand[s] and correctly state[s] the law, but proceed[s] to disregard the same." . . . Moreover, an arbitration award does not fail to draw its essence from the agreement merely because a court concludes that an arbitrator has "misread the contract." . . . An arbitration award fails to draw its essence from the agreement only when the result is not "rationally inferable from the contract." . . .

In supporting the district court's ruling on the motion to vacate, Signator Investors relies solely on the circumscribed scope of review which we are obliged to apply in assessing an arbitration award. And although the authority of an arbitrator is broad, and subject to great deference under the applicable standard of review, "it is not unlimited." . . . For example, an arbitrator has acted in manifest disregard of the law if he "disregard[s] or modif[ies] unambiguous contract provisions." . . . Moreover, an award fails to draw its essence from the agreement if an arbitrator has "based his award on his own personal notions of right and wrong." . . . In such circumstances, a federal court has "no choice but to refuse enforcement of the award." *Int'l Union, United Mine Workers of Am. v. Marrowbone Dev. Co.*, 232 F.3d 383, 389 (4th Cir.2000) (internal quotation marks omitted) (affirming district court's vacatur of award where arbitrator refused to conduct hearing as required by agreement).

In this case, as explained below, the arbitrator disregarded the plain and unambiguous language of the governing arbitration agreement when he concluded that it included an implied one-year limitations period. In so doing, the arbitrator acted in manifest disregard of the law and failed to draw his award from the essence of the agreement.

C.

In assessing the timeliness of Patten's arbitration demand, the arbitrator correctly recognized that the Management Agreement contained no explicit time limitation. The arbitrator nonetheless determined, however, that the Management Agreement "necessarily contain[ed] an implied term limit." In certain instances, when the contracting parties have failed to specify a term that is essential to the determination of their rights and duties under an arbitration agreement, the arbitrator may supply a term that is "reasonable in the circumstances." . . . In the circumstances of this case, however, the one-year limitations period imposed by the arbitrator was not reasonable, in that it contradicted the plain and unambiguous terms of the Management Agreement.

The Management Agreement unambiguously provided that, as to its parties (Patten and Signator Investors), it "supersede[d]" the Mutual Agreement. . . . Despite this clear repudiation of the Mutual Agreement by both Patten and Signator Investors, the arbitrator proceeded to "look to the Mutual Agreement for guidance" and "adopt[ed]" its one-year limitations period. In so doing, he failed to heed the plain and unambiguous terms of the Management Agreement—not only had Patten and Signator Investors contractually agreed that the Mutual Agreement was superseded, they had also chosen to omit certain of its terms from the Management Agreement, including the one-year limitations period.

Moreover, the arbitrator ignored the fact that the Management Agreement provided that it was to "be governed by and construed in accordance with the laws of the Commonwealth of Massachusetts." If the arbitrator felt the need to import a limitations period into the Management Agreement, the most obvious source was that which governed their agreement: Massachusetts law. And under Massachusetts law, claims of wrongful termination and discrimination are subject to a three-year statute of limitations . . . and contract claims must be filed within a six-year period. . . . Utilizing either of these limitations periods, Patten's March 2, 2002 demand for arbitration—submitted to Signator Investors within fourteen months of his termination—would have been timely.

Put succinctly, the arbitrator appears to have revised the governing arbitration agreement on the basis of his own "personal notions of right and wrong," and imposed a limitations period on the parties that they had specifically rejected. *See Upshur Coals,* 933 F.2d at 229; *see also U.S. Postal Serv.,* 204 F.3d at 527 ("When the arbitrator ignores the unambiguous language chosen by the parties, the arbitrator simply fails to do his job."). Consequently, this dispute does not fall into the category of awards based on "misapplication of principles of contractual interpretation [or] erroneous interpretation," which are not to be disturbed by judicial review. . . . Rather, the arbitrator in this instance simply "amend[ed] or alter[ed] the agreement," and thus he "act[ed] without authority." . . . The arbitrator's ruling thus resulted in an award that . . . simply was "not rationally inferable from the contract." . . .

Although our standard of review of an arbitration award is properly a limited and deferential one, it does not require that we affirm an award that contravenes the plain and unambiguous terms of the governing arbitration agreement. . . . In these circumstances, the arbitration award as to Patten and Signator Investors failed to draw its essence from the governing arbitration agreement and was made in manifest disregard of the law.

IV.

Pursuant to the foregoing, we vacate the district court's denial of Patten's motion to vacate the arbitration award as to Signator Investors. We remand for such other and further proceedings as may be appropriate.

VACATED AND REMANDED.

NOTES AND QUESTIONS

1. What does the choice-of-law provision in the contract say about the parties' *contractual* relationship? How does it factor into the court's reasoning in regard to manifest disregard? Is the court's assessment proper and persuasive?

2. Can there be any dispute about whether Patten followed the precise language of the agreement in filing his compliant and demand for arbitration? Does the arbitrator misunderstand the facts? Does he engage in a creative interpretation of the applicable agreement? Is this fundamentally deviant? Has he "manifestly disregarded the law"? Is there any law at play? Was it stated and then ignored in the ruling?

3. Given the succession of positions and agreements between the same parties, why is it wrong for the arbitrator to see the parties' relationship as a unitary transaction with an abstract overarching contract? How can it be wrong for the arbitrator to imply a term in the parties' contract relationship? How can gap-filling or boot-strapping constitute manifest disregard of the law?

4. The court also concludes in a parallel determination that the arbitrator's ruling that Patten's claims were prescribed could not be drawn from the essence of the contract. Can you explain the significance of this ruling? Is it a misplaced and ill-conceived conclusion? Is an employment contract equivalent to a collective bargaining agreement?

COMEDY CLUB, INC. V. IMPROV WEST ASSOCS.

553 F.3d 1277 (9th Cir. 2009).

GOULD, CIRCUIT JUDGE:

On June 13, 1999, Comedy Club, Inc. and Al Copeland Investments, Inc. (collectively "CCI") executed a Trademark License Agreement ("Trademark Agreement") with Improv West Associates ("Improv West") that granted CCI an exclusive nationwide license to use Improv West's trademarks. A few years later, CCI breached the agreement and sought to protect its interests in the trademarks in federal district court by filing a declaratory judgment action. After a complex procedural history, the parties were left with an arbitration award and two district court orders, one order compelling the parties to arbitrate, and another order confirming the arbitration award. CCI appealed both district court orders. . . .

In a prior opinion, . . . we determined that we lacked jurisdiction to review the district court's order compelling arbitration. We affirmed in part and vacated in part the district court's order confirming the arbitration award. The Supreme Court vacated that opinion and remanded this case to us for reconsideration in light of *Hall Street Associates L.L.C. v. Mattel, Inc.* . . . . We determine that *Hall Street Associates* does not undermine our prior precedent, *Kyocera Corp. v. Prudential-Bache T. Servs.* . . . . As a result, in this circuit, an arbitrator's manifest disregard of the law remains a valid ground for vacatur of an arbitration award under § 10(a)(4) of the Federal Arbitration Act. Therefore, we adhere to the outcome in our prior decision.

I

Improv West is the founder of the Improv Comedy Club and the creator and owner of the "Improv" and "Improvisation" trademarks ("Improv marks"). CCI owns and operates restaurants and comedy clubs nationwide. On June 13, 1999, CCI and Improv West entered a Trademark Agreement [footnote omitted] that provided, *inter alia*: (1) that Improv West granted CCI an exclusive nationwide license to use the Improv marks in connection with the opening of new comedy clubs; (2) that, according to a development schedule, CCI was to open four Improv clubs a year in 2001 through 2003 [footnote omitted]; and (3) that CCI was prohibited from opening any non-Improv comedy clubs during the term of the Trademark Agreement. [Footnote omitted.] The Trademark Agreement also had an arbitration clause:

> All disputes relating to or arising under this Agreement or the Asset Purchase Agreement shall be resolved by arbitration in Los Angeles, California in accordance with the commercial arbitration rules of the American Arbitration Association. In any such arbitration, the parties shall be entitled to discovery in the same manner as if the dispute was being litigated in Los Angeles Superior Court. Notwithstanding this agreement to arbitrate, the parties, in addition to arbitration, shall be entitled to pursue equitable remedies and agree that the state and federal courts shall have exclusive jurisdiction for such purpose and for the purpose of compelling arbitration and/or enforcing any arbitration award. The parties agree to submit to the jurisdiction of such courts and agree that service of process in any such action may be

made by certified mail. The prevailing party in any arbitration or action to enforce this Agreement or the Asset Purchase Agreement shall be entitled to its costs, including reasonable attorneys' fees.

CCI concedes that it failed to open eight Improv clubs by 2002, [footnote omitted] and that it was in default of amended § 12.a. of the Trademark Agreement. Consistent with Improv West's sole remedy, as stated in § 13.b., [footnote omitted] Improv West sent CCI a letter asserting that CCI was in default of the Trademark Agreement, withdrawing CCI's license to use the Improv marks and rights to open more Improv clubs, and informing CCI that Improv West intended to begin opening its own Improv clubs.

In response to Improv West's letter, CCI filed a complaint in federal district court seeking declaratory relief. CCI's complaint sought a declaration that the covenant that CCI could not open any non-Improv comedy clubs was void under California Business and Professions Code ("CBPC") § 16600, and that CCI's failure to meet the development schedule did not revoke CCI's license to the Improv marks or right to open Improv clubs. Improv West then filed a demand for arbitration seeking damages. [Footnote omitted.]

On August 2, 2004, the district court ordered the parties to arbitrate their dispute. CCI did not appeal that order until May 16, 2005. On February 28, 2005, the arbitrator entered a Partial Final Arbitration Award that stated: (1) that CCI defaulted on the Trademark Agreement by failing to adhere to the development schedule listed in amended § 12.a.; (2) that CCI forfeited its rights to open Improv clubs and its use of the Improv marks license in connection with any clubs not open or under construction as of October 15, 2002; (3) that Improv West could open or license to third parties new Improv clubs; (4) that § 9.j. of the Trademark Agreement was "a valid and enforceable in-term covenant not to compete" and remained valid "for the remaining term of the Agreement"[footnote omitted]; (5) that CCI and its "Affiliates" [footnote omitted] were enjoined from opening or operating any other comedy clubs other than those open or under construction as of October 15, 2002 for the duration of the Trademark Agreement; (6) that neither CCI nor its Affiliates could change the name on any of its current clubs; and (7) that Improv West was entitled to attorneys fees and costs. On April 14, 2005, the district court confirmed the Partial Award. CCI timely appealed, tendering to us the issues addressed in this opinion. [Footnote omitted.]

In an opinion filed on September 7, 2007 and amended on January 23, 2008, we held that we did not have jurisdiction to review the district court's order compelling the parties to arbitrate; that the arbitrator did not exceed his authority by arbitrating the equitable claims; that the arbitrator did exceed his authority by issuing permanent injunctions that enjoined relatives who were not parties to the agreement; that the arbitrator's award was not completely irrational; and that the arbitrator's enforcement of the covenant not to compete was a manifest disregard of the law. The Supreme Court granted a petition for a writ of *certiorari*, vacated our prior opinion, and remanded this case to us to reconsider our decision in light of *Hall Street Associates v. Mattel.*

Both parties agree that this remand only affects the portion of the prior opinion in which we found the arbitrator acted with a "manifest disregard of the law." Therefore, we continue to hold that we do not have jurisdiction over the district court's order compelling arbitration. We also determine that the arbitrator did not exceed his authority when he arbitrated the equitable claims, but that he exceeded his authority regarding the permanent injunction that enjoined non-parties to the agreement. We also decide that the arbitrator's award was not completely irrational. Finally, addressing the issue raised by the Supreme Court's remand, we conclude that *Hall Street Associates* did not undermine the manifest disregard of law ground for vacatur, as understood in this circuit to be a violation of § 10(a)(4) of the Federal Arbitration Act, and that the arbitrator manifestly disregarded the law.

[. . .]

Finally, we address CCI's claim that the partial arbitration award should be vacated because it is in violation of CBPC § 16600. CCI argues that the arbitrator's validation of § 9.j. is in manifest disregard of the law. Improv West counters that after the recent Supreme Court case, *Hall Street Associates,* 128 S. Ct. 1396 (2008), manifest disregard of the law is not a valid ground for vacatur. In *Hall Street Associates,* the Supreme Court held that the FAA provided exclusive grounds to modify or vacate an arbitration award. *Id.* at 1404. Improv West argues that manifest disregard of the law is not among the statutory grounds for vacatur, and therefore we must amend our prior opinion that vacated this part of the arbitrator's award for that reason.

We have already determined that the manifest disregard ground for vacatur is shorthand for a statutory ground under the FAA, specifically 9 U.S.C. § 10(a)(4), which states that the court may vacate "where the arbitrators exceeded their powers." *Kyocera Corp. v. Prudential-Bache T. Servs.,* 341 F.3d 987, 997 (9th Cir. 2003) (en banc) (holding that "arbitrators 'exceed their powers' . . . when the award is 'completely irrational,' or exhibits a 'manifest disregard of law' ") (citations omitted). The Supreme Court did not reach the question of whether the manifest disregard of the law doctrine fits within §§ 10 or 11 of the FAA. *Hall Street Associates,* 128 S. Ct. at 1404. Instead, it listed several possible readings of the doctrine, including our own. *Id.* ("Or, as some courts have thought, 'manifest disregard' may have been shorthand for § 10(a)(3) or § 10(a)(4), the subsections authorizing vacatur when the arbitrators were 'guilty of misconduct' or 'exceeded their powers.' ") (*citing Kyocera,* 341 F.3d at 997). We cannot say that *Hall Street Associates* is "clearly irreconcilable" with *Kyocera* and thus we are bound by our prior precedent. . . . Therefore, we conclude that, after *Hall Street Associates*, manifest disregard of the law remains a valid ground for vacatur because it is a part of § 10(a)(4). We note that we join the Second Circuit in this interpretation of *Hall Street Associates. Stolt-Nielsen Transportation,* 548 F.3d 85, 96 (2d Cir. 2008). *But see Ramos-Santiago v. UPS,* 524 F.3d 120, 124 n.3 (1st Cir. 2008).

We have stated that for an arbitrator's award to be in manifest disregard of the law, "[i]t must be clear from the record that the arbitrator[ ] recognized the applicable law and then ignored it." *Mich. Mut. Ins. Co. v. Unigard Sec. Ins. Co.,* 44 F.3d 826, 832 (9th Cir. 1995).

[. . .]

CITIGROUP GLOBAL MKTS. INC. V. BACON

562 F.3d 349 (5th Cir. 2009).

E. GRADY JOLLY, CIRCUIT JUDGE:

An arbitration panel ordered Citigroup Global Markets to pay Debra Bacon $256,000. Citigroup moved the district court to vacate the award, and the district court obliged on the basis that the arbitrators had manifestly disregarded the law. On appeal, we consider whether manifest disregard of the law remains a valid ground for vacatur of an arbitration award in the light of the Supreme Court's recent decision in *Hall Street Associates, L.L.C. v. Mattel, Inc.,* 128 S. Ct. 1396, 1403, 170 L. Ed. 2d 254 (2008). [Footnote omitted.] We conclude that *Hall Street* restricts the grounds for vacatur to those set forth in § 10 of the Federal Arbitration Act (FAA or Act), 9 U.S.C. § 1 et seq., and consequently, manifest disregard of the law is no longer an independent ground for vacating arbitration awards under the FAA. *Hall Street* effectively overrules our previous authority to the contrary, so we must VACATE the district court's judgment and REMAND for reconsideration in accord with the exclusivity of the statutory grounds.

I.

Debra Bacon's quarrel with Citigroup began in 2002 when she discovered that her husband had withdrawn funds from her Citigroup Individual Retirement Accounts without her permission. By forging her signature, he made five withdrawals totaling $238,000. As soon as Bacon discovered the unauthorized withdrawals, she notified Citigroup.

In 2004, Bacon submitted a claim in arbitration against Citigroup seeking reimbursement for the unauthorized withdrawals. The arbitration panel granted Bacon $218,000 in damages and $38,000 in attorneys' fees.

Citing § 10 of the FAA, Citigroup made an application to the district court requesting vacatur of the award.

The district granted the motion to vacate, holding that the award was made in manifest disregard of the law. The court based its holding on three grounds: 1) Bacon was not harmed by the withdrawals because her husband used the money for her benefit and subsequently promised to pay her back; 2) Bacon's claims were barred by Texas law, which permits such claims only if the customer reports the unauthorized transaction within thirty days of the withdrawal; and 3) Texas law requires apportionment among the liable parties, which, in this case, includes Bacon's husband.

Bacon appeals. We review *de novo* the vacatur of an arbitration award. . . .

II

A.

Although *Hall Street* clearly has the effect of further restricting the role of federal courts in the arbitration process, there is nothing revolutionary about its holding.

Even before the enactment of the United States Arbitration Act in 1925, [footnote omitted] courts of equity would set aside an arbitration award only in narrowly defined circumstances. . . . If the arbitration award was "within the submission, and contain[ed] the honest decision of the arbitrators, after a full and fair hearing of the parties, a court of equity [would] not set it aside for error, either in law or fact." . . . This deference was appropriate because a submission agreement—a document executed by both parties and presented to the arbitrators in order to outline the dispute and the desired arbitration procedures—was a valid and enforceable contract. . . . Thus, a provision in the submission agreement requiring the parties to abide by the arbitrator's decision made the arbitration award binding. Even when a submission agreement did not contain an express agreement to adhere to the decision of the arbitrators, courts implied such an agreement and enforced the awards as binding. . . . Although arbitration was binding and final, awards could be set aside in the following circumstances: (1) where the arbitrators engaged in fraud, corruption, or improper conduct; (2) where the arbitrators failed to decide all of the issues submitted; (3) where the arbitrators exceeded their powers by deciding issues not submitted; and (4) where the award was not certain, final, and mutual. . . . These limited grounds are akin to the provisions of § 10 of the FAA.

Importantly, awards were affirmed even if based upon error in law or fact. . . . "A contrary course would be a substitution of the judgment of the chancellor in place of the judges chosen by the parties, and would make an award the commencement, not the end, of litigation." . . . [The case law] also cautioned against assuming improper conduct from mere error: "We are all too prone, perhaps, to impute either weakness of intellect or corrupt motives to those who differ with us in opinion." . . . The Supreme Court has continued to emphasize the importance of respecting the arbitration process. In *Hall Street,* the Court explained: permitting vacatur and modification of arbitration awards on more expansive grounds "opens the door to the full-bore legal and evidentiary appeals that can rende[r] informal arbitration merely a prelude to a more cumbersome and time-consuming judicial review process, and bring arbitration theory to grief in post-arbitration process." . . .

In short, strictly confining the perimeter of federal court review of arbitration awards is a widely accepted practice that runs throughout arbitration jurisprudence—from its early common law and equity days to the present.

B.

1.

Congress embraced this notion that arbitration awards should generally be upheld barring some sort of procedural injustice, and §§ 10 and 11 of the FAA enumerate the circumstances under which an award may be vacated, modified, or corrected when the action is one brought under the Act. . . .

[. . .]

Based both on the text and on the legislative history, *Hall Street* concluded that §§ 10 and 11 provide the exclusive regimes for review under the FAA. The Court reiterated this holding several times: "We hold that the statutory grounds are exclusive"; "We agree with the Ninth Circuit that they are [exclusive] . . ."; "We now hold that §§ 10 and 11 respectively provide the FAA's exclusive grounds for expedited vacatur and modification"; "In holding that §§ 10 and 11 provide exclusive regimes for the review provided by the statute. . . ." *Hall Street,* 128 S.Ct. at 1400, 1401, 1403, 1406. This rule, *Hall Street* determined, is consistent with the "national policy favoring arbitration with just the limited review needed to maintain arbitration's essential virtue of resolving disputes straightaway." . . .

2.

[. . .]

. . . In short, *Hall Street* rejected manifest disregard as an independent ground for vacatur, and stood by its clearly and repeatedly stated holding, as noted in the earlier paragraph, that §§ 10 and 11 provide the exclusive bases for vacatur and modification of an arbitration award under the FAA.

C.

It is certainly true that over the years this circuit, like most other circuits, [footnote omitted] ultimately came to recognize manifest disregard of the law as a nonstatutory basis for vacatur. . . . Even so, manifest disregard of the law was defined as a standard difficult to satisfy. Manifest disregard of the law

> means more than error or misunderstanding with respect to the law. The error must have been obvious and capable of being readily and instantly perceived by the average person qualified to serve as an arbitrator. Moreover the term "disregard" implies that the arbitrator appreciates the existence of a clearly governing principle but decides to ignore or pay no attention to it.

. . . In addition, we have stated that an award may be vacated for manifest disregard of the law only when "the award resulted in, a 'significant injustice.' " . . .

Our circuit did not accept manifest disregard of the law as a nonstatutory ground for vacatur with immediate confidence and certainty. . . . Indeed, manifest disregard of the law does not have a compelling origin as a ground for vacatur. Its modest debut occurs in a vague phrase found in *Wilko v. Swan*: "the interpretations of law by the arbitrators in contrast to manifest disregard are not subject, in the federal courts, to judicial review for error in interpretation." . . . That is all *Wilko* said about it.

Thus, it is not surprising that the lower courts initially grappled with the uncertain implications of this clause. . . . Uncertain about the propriety of vacating an award for manifest disregard of the law, some courts avoided the issue by assuming, without deciding, that it was a valid ground for vacatur, but declining to vacate the award nonetheless. . . . Some circuits continued to maintain the exclusivity of the statutory grounds, in the face of *Wilko,* for decades. . . . However, despite its uncertain genesis, most circuits eventually accepted manifest disregard of the law as a valid extra statutory ground for vacatur. . . .

We were among the very last to adopt manifest disregard. . . . But in *Williams v. CIGNA,* nearly fifty years after *Wilko,* we finally embraced manifest disregard as a nonstatutory ground for vacating arbitration awards. . . . We concluded that the departure from precedent was necessary and justified in the light of the Supreme Court's opinion in *First Options of Chicago, Inc. v. Kaplan,* which cited 9 U.S.C. § 10 and *Wilko* for the proposition that courts will set arbitration awards aside "only in very unusual circumstances." . . .

III.

A.

The question before us now is whether, under the FAA, manifest disregard of the law remains valid, as an independent ground for vacatur, after *Hall Street*. The answer seems clear. *Hall Street* unequivocally held that the statutory grounds are the exclusive means for vacatur under the FAA. Our case law defines manifest disregard of the law as a *nonstatutory* ground for vacatur. . . . Thus, to the extent that manifest disregard of the law constitutes a nonstatutory ground for vacatur, it is no longer a basis for vacating awards under the FAA.

Four other circuits have considered this issue. The First Circuit, in dictum and with little discussion, concluded that *Hall Street* abolished manifest disregard of the law as a ground for vacatur. [Footnote omitted.] *See Ramos-Santiago v. United Parcel Serv.*, 524 F.3d 120, 124 n.3 (1st Cir. 2008) ("We acknowledge the Supreme Court's recent holding in *Hall Street Assocs., L.L.C. v. Mattel* that manifest disregard of the law is not a valid ground for vacating or modifying an arbitral award in cases brought under the [FAA]."). . . . The Sixth Circuit, in an unpublished opinion, reached the opposite conclusion by narrowly construing the holding of *Hall Street* to apply only to contractual expansions of the grounds for review. *Coffee Beanery, Ltd. v. WW, L.L.C.*, . . . 2008 WL 4899478, at *4 (6th Cir. 2008). The Second Circuit has also held that manifest disregard survives *Hall Street. Stolt-Nielsen SA v. AnimalFeeds Int'l Corp.*, 548 F.3d 85, 93–95 (2d Cir. 2008). The court, however, recognized that *Hall Street's* holding was in direct conflict with the application of manifest disregard as a nonstatutory ground for review, but resolved the conflict by recasting manifest disregard as a shorthand for § 10(a)(4). . . . Finally, the Ninth Circuit has concluded that *Hall Street* did not abolish manifest disregard because its case law defined manifest disregard as shorthand for § 10(a)(4). *See Comedy Club Inc. v. Improv West Assocs.*, 553 F.3d 1277, 1290, . . . (9th Cir. 2009) (*"Comedy Club II"*). We now turn to discuss the opinions of the Sixth, Second, and Ninth Circuits.

1.

Coffee Beanery only briefly considered the effect of *Hall Street* on manifest disregard of the law. . . . In what we view as an understatement, the Sixth Circuit acknowledged that *Hall Street* "significantly reduced the ability of federal courts to vacate arbitration awards for reasons other than those specified in 9 U.S.C. § 10. . . ." Citing *Hall Street's* discussion of *Wilko*, which *Coffee Beanery* thought demonstrated a "hesitation to reject the 'manifest disregard' doctrine," and noting the acceptance of the standard by each and every court of appeals, the court concluded that it would be imprudent to cease vacating arbitration awards made in manifest disregard of the law. . . .

This decision suffers from two significant flaws. First, the opinion utterly fails to address *Hall Street*'s express holding that the grounds for vacatur found in § 10 are exclusive. Instead, the court narrowly construed *Hall Street* as applying only to contractual expansions of the grounds for vacatur. . . . In the light of *Hall Street*'s repeated statements that "*We hold* that the statutory grounds are exclusive," we think it incorrect so narrowly to construe *Hall Street*'s holding. 128 S. Ct. at 1400 (emphasis added).

Second, we believe that *Coffee Beanery* misread *Hall Street*'s discussion of *Wilko*. We do not see hesitation by *Hall Street* to reject manifest disregard of the law as an independent ground for vacating an award under the FAA; instead, *Hall Street's* discussion of *Wilko* demonstrates the Supreme Court's unwillingness to give any significant meaning to *Wilko's* vague language. *Hall Street* observed that *Wilko* dealt with an entirely separate issue and, noting the vagueness of *Wilko's* statement, concluded that: "When speaking as a Court, we have taken the *Wilko* language as we found it, without embellishment, and now that its meaning is implicated, we see no reason to accord it the significance that [the petitioner] urges." . . .

2.

Unlike *Coffee Beanery,* the Second Circuit in *Stolt-Nielsen* did not shy from *Hall Street*'s holding. The court acknowledged that *Hall Street* "held that the FAA sets forth the 'exclusive' grounds for vacating an arbitration award." . . . The court also recognized that this holding was in conflict with its own prior statements regarding manifest disregard, which the court discounted as *dicta*. . . . Instead of directly concluding that *Hall Street* eliminated manifest disregard as a ground for vacatur under the FAA, the court reasoned that manifest disregard of the law should be "reconceptualized as a judicial gloss on the specific grounds for vacatur enumerated in section 10 of the FAA. . . ."

Describing its "reconceptualization," the court stated:

> We must therefore continue to bear the responsibility to vacate arbitration awards in the rare instances in which "the arbitrator knew of the relevant [legal] principle, appreciated that this principle controlled the outcome of the disputed issue, and nonetheless willfully flouted the governing law by refusing to apply it." . . . At that point the arbitrators have "failed to interpret the contract at all," . . . for parties do not agree in advance to submit to arbitration that is carried out in manifest disregard of the law. Put another way, the arbitrators have thereby "exceeded their powers, or so imperfectly executed them that a mutual, final, and definite award upon the subject matter submitted was not made." . . .

Stolt-Nielsen, 548 F.3d at 95. Thus, the court seems to conclude that manifest disregard—as the court describes it—does not add to the statutory grounds. The court simply folds manifest disregard into § 10(a)(4).[5] In the full context of the Second Circuit's reasoning, this analysis is not inconsistent with *Hall Street's* speculation that manifest disregard may, among other things, "have been shorthand for § 10(a)(3) or § 10(a)(4). . . ." . . . . .

We should be careful to observe, however, that this description of manifest disregard is very narrow. Because the arbitrator is fully aware of the controlling principle of law and yet does not apply it, he flouts the law in such a manner as to exceed the powers bestowed upon him. This scenario does not include an erroneous application of that principle. [Footnote omitted.]

3.

. . . In a decision issued prior to *Hall Street,* the Ninth Circuit found that the arbitration award at issue constituted a manifest disregard of the law. . . . The Supreme Court then vacated the decision in *Comedy Club I* and remanded for reconsideration in the light of its recently issued decision in *Hall Street*. . . .

On remand, the Ninth Circuit, unlike the Second Circuit, had no need to reconceptualize manifest disregard because its own case law had already defined it as a shorthand for § 10(a)(4). *Comedy Club,* 553 F.3d at 1290. The court therefore held that manifest disregard of the law, as a shorthand for § 10(a)(4), survived *Hall Street*. . . .

B.

In the light of the Supreme Court's clear language that, under the FAA, the statutory provisions are the exclusive grounds for vacatur, manifest disregard of the law as an independent, nonstatutory ground for setting aside an award must be abandoned and rejected. Indeed, the term itself, as a term of legal art, is no longer useful in actions to vacate arbitration awards. *Hall Street* made it plain that the statutory language means what it says: "courts *must* [confirm the award] unless the award is vacated, modified, or corrected as prescribed in sections 10 and 11 of this title," . . . and there's nothing malleable about "must" . . . Thus from this point forward, arbitration awards under the FAA may be vacated only for reasons provided in § 10.

To the extent that our . . . precedent holds that nonstatutory grounds may support the vacatur of an arbitration award, it is hereby overruled.

---

[5] The court relies heavily upon the Seventh Circuit's decision in *Wise v. Wachovia Securities, LLC,* which noted that the Seventh Circuit has defined manifest disregard "so narrowly that it fits comfortably under the first clause of the fourth statutory ground." 450 F.3d 265, 268 (7th Cir. 2006).

IV.

The district court, which issued its opinion before *Hall Street,* held that the arbitrators in this case manifestly disregarded the law. The judgment of the district court is therefore VACATED. The court, however, did not consider whether the grounds asserted for vacating the award might support vacatur under any of the statutory grounds. Accordingly, we REMAND for further consideration not inconsistent with this opinion. The judgment of the district court is VACATED and the case REMANDED. . . .

9. MECHANICS OF MOTIONS UNDER THE FAA

While the FAA creates federal substantive law, it does not confer independent subject matter jurisdiction on federal courts. Accordingly, federal courts must have an independent jurisdictional basis before hearing cases involving arbitration. To have any possibility of getting into federal court for review and enforcement of an arbitral award, the underlying claim in the arbitration must qualify for federal court jurisdiction. *See Vaden v. Discover Bank,* 556 U.S. 49 (2009).

In *Vaden,* the Court held that an action to compel arbitration under FAA § 4 may be brought in federal court if the underlying claim states a federal cause of action. A current Circuit split exists regarding whether this "look through" doctrine can be used to establish federal jurisdiction at the review and enforcement stage.[5]

In *Cortez Byrd Chips, Inc. v. Bill Harbert Constr. Co.,* the U.S. Supreme Court held that the FAA's venue provisions, §§ 9–11, were permissive in character. The ruling allowed motions to confirm, vacate, or modify an arbitration award to be brought either in the district where the award had been rendered or in any proper district under the general venue statute. The general venue statute provides for venue in either "a judicial district in which any defendant resides, if all defendants are residents of the State in which the district is located" or "a judicial district in which a substantial part of the events or omissions giving rise to the claim occurred, or a substantial part of property that is the subject of the action is situated."[6] The Court explained that "the three venue sections of the FAA [were] best analyzed together, owing to their contemporaneous enactment and the similarity to their pertinent language."

---

[5] The Court in *Vaden Compare Ortiz-Espinosa v. BBVA Sec. of Puerto Rico, Inc.,* 852 F.3d 36, 46–47 (1st Cir. 2017) (looking through to the underlying claim in the arbitration to find jurisdiction for review and enforcement); *Doscher v. Sea Port Grp. Sec., LLC,* 832 F.3d 372, 388–89 (2d Cir. 2016) (same) *with Goldman v. Citigroup Global Mkts., Inc.,* 834 F.3d 242, 251 (3d Cir. 2016) (declining to use the "look through" doctrine to establish federal jurisdiction at the review and enforcement stage); *Magruder v. Fid. Brokerage Servs. LLC,* 818 F.3d 285, 288 (7th Cir. 2016) (same).

[6] 28 U.S.C. § 1391(b)(1)–(2). If neither option provides an appropriate venue, venue is proper any judicial district in which any defendant is subject to the court's personal jurisdiction with respect to such action. *Id.* (b)(3).

After *Cortez*, the Second Circuit created a split regarding the permissiveness of the one-year limitations period for confirming awards listed in FAA § 9. According to the Second Circuit, the provision constitutes a mandatory limitations period. The Fourth and Eight Circuits, prior to *Cortez* held that the provision should be seen as permissive.

CORTEZ BYRD CHIPS, INC. V. BILL HARBERT CONSTR. CO.

529 U.S. 193, 120 S.Ct. 1331, 146 L.Ed.2d 171 (2000).

(footnotes omitted)

JUSTICE SOUTER delivered the opinion of the Court.

This case raises the issue whether the venue provisions of the Federal Arbitration Act (FAA or Act) . . . are restrictive, allowing a motion to confirm, vacate, or modify an arbitration award to be brought only in the district in which the award was made, or are permissive, permitting such a motion either where the award was made or in any district proper under the general venue statute. We hold the FAA provisions permissive.

I

Petitioner Cortez Byrd Chips, Inc., and respondent Bill Harbert Construction Company agreed that Harbert would build a wood chip mill for Cortez Byrd in Brookhaven, Mississippi. One of the terms was that "[a]ll claims or disputes between the Contractor and the Owner arising out [of] or relating to the Contract, or the breach thereof, shall be decided by arbitration in accordance with the Construction Industry Arbitration Rules of the American Arbitration Association currently in effect unless the parties mutually agree otherwise." . . . The agreement went on to provide that "[t]he award rendered by the arbitrator or arbitrators shall be final, and judgment may be entered upon it in accordance with applicable law in any court having jurisdiction thereof," . . . that the agreement to arbitrate "shall be specifically enforceable under applicable law in any court having jurisdiction thereof," . . . and that the law of the place where the project was located, Mississippi, governed. . . .

After a dispute arose, Harbert invoked the agreement by a filing with the Atlanta office of the American Arbitration Association, which conducted arbitration in November 1997 in Birmingham, Alabama. The next month, the arbitration panel issued an award in favor of Harbert. . . .

In January 1998, Cortez Byrd filed a complaint in the United States District Court for the Southern District of Mississippi seeking to vacate or modify the arbitration award, which Harbert then sought to confirm by filing this action seven days later in the Northern District of Alabama. When Cortez Byrd moved to dismiss, transfer, or stay the Alabama action, the Alabama District Court denied the motion, concluding that venue was proper only in the Northern District of Alabama. . . .

The Court of Appeals for the Eleventh Circuit affirmed. It held itself bound by pre-1981 Fifth Circuit precedent . . . to the effect that under the Act's venue provisions . . . venue for motions to confirm, vacate, or modify awards was exclusively in the district in which the arbitration award was made. . . . The arbitration here having been held in Birmingham, the rule as so construed limited venue to the Northern District of Alabama.

We granted *certiorari* . . . to resolve a split among the Courts of Appeals over the permissive or mandatory character of the FAA's venue provisions. . . . We reverse.

II

Section 9 of the FAA governs venue for the confirmation of arbitration awards:

> "If the parties in their agreement have agreed that a judgment of the court shall be entered upon the award made pursuant to the arbitration, and shall specify the court, then at any time within one year after the award is made any party to the arbitration may apply to the court so specified for an order confirming the award, and thereupon the court must grant such an order unless the award is vacated, modified, or corrected as prescribed in sections 10 and 11 of this title. If no court is specified in the agreement of the parties, then such application may be made to the United States court in and for the district within which such award was made." 9 U.S.C. § 9.

Section 10(a), governing motions to vacate arbitration awards, provides that

> "the United States court in and for the district wherein the [arbitration] award was made may make an order vacating the award upon the application of any party to the arbitration [in any of five enumerated situations]."

And under § 11, on modification or correction,

> "the United States court in and for the district wherein the award was made may make an order modifying or correcting the award upon the application of any party to the arbitration."

The precise issue raised in the District Court was whether venue for Cortez Byrd's motion under §§ 10 and 11 was properly laid in the southern district of Mississippi, within which the contract was performed. It was clearly proper under the general venue statute, which provides, among other things, for venue in a diversity action in "a judicial district in which a substantial part of the events or omissions giving rise to the claim occurred, or a substantial part of property that is the subject of the action is situated." 28 U.S.C. § 1391(a)(2). If §§ 10 and 11 are permissive and thus supplement, but do not supplant, the general provision, Cortez Byrd's motion to vacate or modify was properly filed in Mississippi, and under principles of deference to the court of first filing, the Alabama court should have considered staying its hand. . . . But if §§ 10 and 11 are restrictive, there was no Mississippi venue for Cortez Byrd's action, and the Northern District of Alabama correctly proceeded with the litigation to confirm. Although § 9 is not directly implicated in this action, since venue for Harbert's motion to confirm was proper in the northern district of Alabama under either a restrictive or a permissive reading of § 9, the three venue sections of the FAA are best analyzed together, owing to their contemporaneous enactment and the similarity of their pertinent language.

Enlightenment will not come merely from parsing the language, which is less clear than either party contends. Although "may" could be read as permissive in each section, as Cortez Byrd argues, the mere use of "may" is not necessarily conclusive of congressional intent to provide for a permissive or discretionary authority. . . . Cortez Byrd points to clearly mandatory language in other parts of the Act as some indication that "may" was used in a permissive sense. . . . Each party has a point, but neither point is conclusive. The answer is not to be had from comparing phrases.

Statutory history provides a better lesson, though, which is confirmed by following out the practical consequences of Harbert's position. When the FAA was enacted in 1925, it appeared against the backdrop of a considerably more restrictive general venue statute than the one current today. At the time, the practical effect of 28 U.S.C. § 112(a) was that a civil suit could usually be brought only in the district in which the defendant resided. . . . The statute's restrictive application was all the more pronounced due to the courts' general inhospitality to forum selection clauses. . . . Hence, even if an arbitration agreement expressly permitted action to be brought in the district in which arbitration had been conducted, the agreement would probably prove to be vain. The enactment of the special venue provisions in the FAA thus had an obviously liberalizing effect, undiminished by any suggestion, textual or otherwise, that Congress meant simultaneously to foreclose a suit where the defendant resided. Such a consequence would have been as inexplicable in 1925 as it would be passing strange 75 years later. The most convenient forum for a defendant is normally the forum of residence, and it would take a very powerful reason ever to suggest that Congress would have meant to eliminate that venue for postarbitration disputes.

The virtue of the liberalizing nonrestrictive view of the provisions for venue in the district of arbitration is confirmed by another obviously liberalizing venue provision of the Act, which in § 9 authorizes a binding agreement selecting a forum for confirming an arbitration award. Since any forum selection agreement must coexist with §§ 10 and 11, one needs to ask how they would work together if §§ 10 and 11 meant that an order vacating or modifying an arbitration award could be obtained only in the district where the award was made. The consequence would be that a proceeding to confirm the award begun in a forum previously selected by agreement of the parties (but outside the district of the arbitration) would need to be held in abeyance if the responding party objected. The objecting party would then have to return to the district of the arbitration to begin a separate proceeding to modify or vacate the arbitration award, and if the award withstood attack, the parties would move back to the previously selected forum for the confirming order originally sought. Harbert, naturally, is far from endorsing anything of the sort and contends that a court with venue to confirm under a § 9 forum selection clause would also have venue under a later filed motion under § 10. But the contention boils down to denying the logic of Harbert's own position. The regime we have described would follow from adopting that position, and the Congress simply cannot be tagged with such a taste for the bizarre.

Nothing, indeed, would be more clearly at odds with both the FAA's "statutory policy of rapid and unobstructed enforcement of arbitration agreements," . . . or with the desired flexibility of parties in choosing a site for arbitration. Although the location of the arbitration may well be the residence of one of the parties, or have some other connection to a contract at issue, in many cases the site will have no relation whatsoever to the parties or the dispute. The parties may be willing to arbitrate in an inconvenient forum, say, for the convenience of the arbitrators, or to get a panel with special knowledge or experience, or as part of some compromise, but they might well be less willing to pick such a location if any future court proceedings had to be held there. Flexibility to make such practical choices, then, could well be inhibited by a venue rule mandating the same inconvenient venue if someone later sought to vacate or modify the award.

A restrictive interpretation would also place § 3 and §§ 9–11 of the FAA in needless tension, which could be resolved only by disrupting existing precedent of this Court. Section 3 provides that any court in which an action "referable to arbitration under an agreement in writing" is pending "shall on application of one of the parties stay the trial of the action until such arbitration has been had in accordance with the terms of the agreement." 9 U.S.C. § 3. If an arbitration were then held outside the district of that litigation, under a restrictive reading of §§ 9–11 a subsequent proceeding to confirm, modify, or set aside the arbitration award could not be brought in the district of the original litigation (unless that also happened to be the chosen venue in a forum selection agreement). We have, however, previously held that the court with the power to stay the action under § 3 has the further power to confirm any ensuing arbitration award. *Marine Transit Corp. v. Dreyfus,* 284 U.S. 263, 275–276, 52 S.Ct. 166, 76 L.Ed. 282 (1932) ("We do not conceive it to be open to question that, where the court has authority under the statute . . . to make an order for arbitration, the court also has authority to confirm the award or to set it aside for irregularity, fraud, *ultra vires* or other defect"). Harbert in effect concedes this point, acknowledging that "the court entering a stay order under § 3 retains jurisdiction over the proceeding and does not 'lose venue.' " . . . But that concession saving our precedent still fails to explain why Congress would have wanted to allow venue liberally where motions to confirm, vacate, or modify were brought as subsequent stages of actions antedating the arbitration, but would have wanted a different rule when arbitration was not preceded by a suit between the parties.

Finally, Harbert's interpretation would create anomalous results in the aftermath of arbitrations held abroad. Sections 204, 207, and 302 of the FAA together provide for liberal choice of venue for actions to confirm awards subject to the 1958 Convention on the Recognition and Enforcement of Foreign Arbitral Awards and the 1975 Inter-American Convention on International Commercial Arbitration. . . . But reading §§ 9–11 to restrict venue to the site of the arbitration would preclude any action under the FAA in courts of the United States to confirm, modify, or vacate awards rendered in foreign arbitrations not covered by either convention. . . . Although such actions would not necessarily be barred for lack of jurisdiction, they would be defeated by restrictions on venue, and anomalies like that are to be avoided when they can be. . . .

Attention to practical consequences thus points away from the restrictive reading of §§ 9–11 and confirms the view that the liberalizing effect of the provisions in the day of their enactment was meant to endure through treating them as permitting, not limiting, venue choice today. . . .

The judgment of the Court of Appeals is reversed, and the case is remanded for further proceedings consistent with this opinion.

It is so ordered.

NOTES AND QUESTIONS

1. Justice Souter delivered the opinion for a unanimous Court. How does the reasoning and determination fit into the federal policy on arbitration? What are the practical advantages of the ruling?

2. What could be said in favor of a restrictive view of the venue provisions? What did Harbert argue?

3. How do the statutory provisions on international commercial arbitration influence the result in the case? How significant a factor are they?

PHOTOPAINT TECHN., LLC V. SMARTLENS CORP.

335 F.3d 152 (2d Cir. 2003).

JACOBS, CIRCUIT JUDGE.

Photopaint Technologies, LLC, ("Photopaint") appeals from a final judgment entered in the United States District Court for the Southern

District of New York . . . denying Photopaint's motion to confirm an arbitration award under the Federal Arbitration Act . . . and granting the cross-motion for summary judgment of Smartlens Corporation and Steven Hylen (collectively, "Smartlens") on the grounds that section 9 of the FAA imposes a one-year statute of limitations on an application for an order of confirmation and that Photopaint (which moved for confirmation more than one year after the award was made) was not entitled to relief from this limitation period. . . .

We reverse, holding that the FAA does impose a one-year statute of limitations, but that Photopaint is entitled to relief from the statutory period. For the reasons that follow, the judgment of the district court is vacated and the case remanded for further proceedings not inconsistent with this opinion.

BACKGROUND

In December 1997, Photopaint and Smartlens entered into a license agreement containing a clause under which they agreed that their disputes would be submitted to arbitration. When a dispute arose in October 1999, they duly submitted it to an arbitrator selected by the American Arbitration Association ("AAA"). In an August 1999 "Partial/Interim Award," the arbitrator ruled largely in Photopaint's favor and ordered it to submit an accounting of costs associated with the license agreement. After reviewing these accounting submissions, the arbitrator signed a "Final Award" on May 26, 2000. The Final Award provided that the License Agreement was voidable; that either party could elect to rescind it within thirty days from receipt of the award; and that Smartlens would make a payment to Photopaint if either party elected to rescind. The amount of this payment was to depend on which party rescinded: if Smartlens rescinded first, it would pay approximately $384,000 plus Photopaint's share of the AAA costs; if Photopaint rescinded first, Smartlens would pay approximately $320,000.

Although the arbitrator signed the Final Award on May 26, 2000 and promptly sent it to the AAA for distribution, the AAA failed (for some reason) to deliver the award to the parties until October 3, 2000—more than four months later. The parties ultimately found out that the award had issued when Smartlens asked to have the arbitration hearing reopened for additional submissions; in denying that request on October 23, 2000, the arbitrator treated it as one for modification of the Final Award, noting that this award had been rendered on May 26, 2000.

Since the Final Award provided that either party could rescind within thirty days of *receiving* the award, and since the parties first received it on October 3, 2000, the option to rescind was initially scheduled to expire on

November 2, 2000. As this date neared, the parties entered into a series of letter agreements to allow for continued settlement discussions.

During the negotiations, Smartlens and Photopaint exchanged several drafts of a settlement agreement, in which they agreed that Smartlens would pay Photopaint a lump-sum of $360,000, but differed as to other provisions. In April, negotiations appeared close to resolution, and on April 16, 2001, Photopaint circulated a revised draft reflecting the $360,000 lump-sum payment and acceding to the remaining changes sought by Smartlens. Shortly afterward, however, Smartlens advised that, due to sharp financial reverses, it could offer no more than a lump-sum payment of $100,000, together with a promissory note. On May 1, Smartlens sought a further time extension "under exactly the same terms" as the parties' prior agreements, to "discuss [the] alternative proposal further and attempt to achieve a final resolution." Photopaint agreed. On the basis of this and subsequent letter agreements, the parties continued discussions into May, June, and July 2001—beyond the May 26 one-year anniversary of the rendering of the Final Award.

Negotiations broke down in July 2001, and on July 27, Photopaint rescinded the license agreement and demanded from Smartlens the $320,000 payment provided for under the terms of the Final Award. Smartlens refused to pay, and Photopaint filed this petition to confirm the Final Award pursuant to the FAA.

In the district court, Smartlens argued against confirmation on the ground that the application was time-barred, under section 9 of the FAA, because it was filed more than one year after the date the Final Award was made. The district court agreed, granted Smartlens summary judgment on this ground, and dismissed the petition. . . . Photopaint appealed.

DISCUSSION

We review *de novo* a ruling granting summary judgment . . . construing the evidence in the light most favorable to the non-moving party (here, Photopaint) and drawing all reasonable inferences in that party's favor. . . .

I

Section 9 of the FAA provides, in pertinent part:

> If the parties in their agreement have agreed that a judgment of the court shall be entered upon the award made pursuant to the arbitration, and shall specify the court, then *at any time within one year after the award is made* any party to the arbitration *may* apply to the court so specified for an order confirming the award, and thereupon the court *must* grant such an order [confirming the award] unless the award is vacated, modified, or corrected as prescribed in sections 10 and 11 of this title.

9 U.S.C. § 9 (emphasis added). The threshold question on appeal is whether this wording creates a one-year statute of limitations—a question of first impression in this Court.

As Photopaint emphasizes, the permissive verb "may," rather than the mandatory verb "must," is used in the clause affording one year to the party wishing to confirm an award, while "must" is used elsewhere in the same section and in other sections of the FAA. In section 12, for example, Congress used "must" in relation to the three-month period for filing a motion to vacate an arbitration award.[3]

We have recognized in another context that "when the same [statute] uses both 'may' and 'shall', the normal inference is that each is used in its usual sense—the one act being permissive, the other mandatory." . . . Both the Fourth and the Eighth Circuits have relied on this "normal inference" in holding that "may" in section 9 is permissive only, and that petitions to confirm arbitral awards under the FAA may be filed beyond the "one year" period. *See Sverdrup Corp. v. WHC Constructors, Inc.*, 989 F.2d 148, 151–56 (4th Cir.1993). . . . *But see In re Consol. Rail Corp.*, 867 F.Supp. 25, 30–32 (D.D.C.1994) (relying on considerations of finality to hold that section 9 imposes a mandatory one-year statute of limitations). In the Fourth Circuit's *Sverdrup* decision, which was relied on heavily by the Eighth Circuit in *Val-U Construction,* the court cited the ordinary permissive meaning of "may," as well as considerations of judicial economy, in holding that section 9's limitations period is not mandatory. *Sverdrup,* 989 F.2d at 151–52, 156; *accord Val-U Constr.,* 146 F.3d at 581.

We respectfully disagree, particularly in light of the Supreme Court's intervening decision in *Cortez Byrd Chips, Inc. v. Bill Harbert Construction Co.,* 529 U.S. 193, 120 S.Ct. 1331, 146 L.Ed.2d 171 (2000). *Cortez Byrd* considered whether the word "may" is used permissively in the context of the FAA's venue provisions, under which (whenever the parties do not specify otherwise) proceedings "may" be conducted in the district where the award was made. . . . Although the Court held that the venue provisions are permissive, it expressly declined to rely on the permissiveness of "may" as a matter of plain meaning. . . . Instead, *Cortez Byrd* relied on considerations particular to venue: the overall structure of the FAA (a narrow reading of the venue provisions would have created "needless tension" with other parts of the FAA, . . . and the statutory history of the general federal venue provision . . . (which was considerably more restrictive when the FAA was enacted, suggesting that Congress used "may" in § 9 to broaden venue under the FAA. . . .)). And the Court rejected

---

[3] "Notice of a motion to vacate, modify, or correct an award *must* be served upon the adverse party or his attorney within three months after the award is filed or delivered." 9 U.S.C. § 12 (emphasis added).

the idea that use of "may" in some provisions of the FAA (including § 9)—and not in others—carries definitive significance. . . .

We therefore consider the text of section 9 without affording decisive effect to the ordinary permissive meaning of "may." Although the word "may" in a statute "usually implies some degree of discretion[, t]his common-sense principle of statutory construction . . . can be defeated by indications of legislative intent to the contrary or by obvious inferences from the structure and purpose of the statute." . . . One indication of legislative intent to the contrary here is that, unless the adverbial phrase beginning "at any time within one year" creates a time limitation within which one "may" apply for confirmation, the phrase lacks incremental meaning. . . . We read statutes to avoid rendering any words wholly superfluous. . . . Photopaint suggests that section 9 can be read to say that enforcement is mandatory if the application is made within one year, and that it is discretionary thereafter. We are unpersuaded. Photopaint gives no support for this reading, no explanation as to how such discretion would be guided, and no theory as to why Congress would want to do that.

In *Seetransport Wiking Trader Schiffarhtsgesellschaft MBH & Co. v. Navimpex Centrala Navala,* 989 F.2d 572 (2d Cir.1993), we construed section 207 of the International Convention on the Recognition and Enforcement of Foreign Arbitral Awards (the "Convention") . . . which is analogous to section 9 of the FAA, and held that a clause using the word "may" created a statute of limitation notwithstanding that "shall" was used elsewhere in the same provision. *See Seetransport,* 989 F.2d at 580–81 (reversing judgment enforcing foreign arbitral award on ground that cause of action seeking enforcement of arbitral award under the convention was time-barred). *Seetransport* construed the Convention, not the FAA, but is otherwise difficult to distinguish.

Dicta in our previous cases is to the same effect. In *The Hartbridge,* 57 F.2d 672 (2d Cir.1932), we suggested that, even though section 9's language was permissive, "the privilege conferred by section 9" was a privilege "to move 'at any time' *within the year.*" *Id.* at 673 (emphasis added). Similarly, in *Kerr-McGee Refining Corp. v. M/T Triumph,* 924 F.2d 467 (2d Cir.1991), we cited section 9 for the proposition that, "[u]nder the Arbitration Act, *a party has one year* to avail itself of summary proceedings for confirmation of an award." *Id.* at 471 (emphasis added).

In light of these authorities, we read the word "may" in section 9 as permissive, but only within the scope of the preceding adverbial phrase: "[a]t any time within one year after the award is made." We therefore hold that section 9 of the FAA imposes a one-year statute of limitations on the filing of a motion to confirm an arbitration award under the FAA. Our construction of the text is not inevitable, but it is intuitive: for example, tax returns may be filed anytime up to April 15, but one senses at once that the phrase is permissive only up to a point. Moreover, this result advances important values of finality:

> One of the FAA's purposes is to provide parties with an effective alternative dispute resolution system which gives litigants a sure and expedited resolution of disputes while reducing the burden on the courts. Arbitration should therefore provide not only a fast resolution but one which establishes conclusively the rights between the parties. A one year limitations period is instrumental in achieving this goal.

In re Consol. Rail, 867 F.Supp. at 31; *see also Young v. United States,* 535 U.S. 43, 47, 122 S.Ct. 1036, 152 L.Ed.2d 79 (2002) (describing the "basic policies [furthered by] all limitations provisions" as "repose, elimination of stale claims, and certainty about a plaintiff's opportunity for recovery and a defendant's potential liabilities" (modification in original)).

In arriving at an opposite conclusion, the Fourth Circuit's opinion in *Sverdrup* made contextual and policy arguments that merit consideration. The *Sverdrup* court noted that Congress used "may" in the section 9 context of the one-year period for filing a motion to confirm an award, and "must" in the section 12 context of the three-month period for filing a motion to vacate, modify, or correct an award. *Sverdrup,* 989 F.2d at 151. Concluding that these sections are otherwise parallel, the court concluded that Congress "understood the plain meaning of 'may' [in section 9] to be permissive," *id.* at 151, and that section 9 "must [therefore] be interpreted as its plain language indicates, as a permissive provision which does not bar the confirmation of an award beyond a one-year period." *Id.* at 156.

Sections 9 and 11, however, are not otherwise parallel. Sections 10 and 11 of the FAA govern the filing of motions to vacate or modify; both describe the circumstances under which a court "may" make an order vacating, modifying or correcting an award "upon the application of any party to the arbitration. . . ." . . . Because section 12 comes into play only in the event that a party makes such an application, "must" in section 12 unambiguously bears on *when* a party can file a motion to vacate, modify, or correct, and not *whether* the party has discretion to bring such a motion. (Such discretion is provided by the "may" in sections 10 and 11.) In section 9, by contrast, "may" *can* be read to reflect a party's discretion as to *whether* to "apply to the court . . . for an order confirming the award." *See Kentucky River Mills v. Jackson,* 206 F.2d 111, 120 (6th Cir.1953) ("The language of [section 9] as to application to the court for an order is not mandatory, but permissive. A party may, therefore, apply to the court for an order confirming the award, but is not limited to such remedy.").

Sverdrup also relied on considerations of judicial economy: "[b]ecause remedies do exist outside the FAA's framework to enforce [an arbitral] award, reading § 9 as a strict statute of limitations would be an exercise in futility" because it would "merely encourage, at the expense of judicial economy, the use of another analogous method of enforcing awards." *Sverdrup,* 989 F.2d at 155. We agree with the Fourth Circuit that an action at law offers an alternative remedy to enforce an arbitral award, but we draw a different conclusion from the existence of that alternative. An action at law is not identical to the summary confirmation proceeding established by the FAA, which was intended to streamline the process and eliminate certain defenses. *See generally* Robert J. Gruendel, *Domestic Law and International Conventions, the Imperfect Overlay: The FAA as a Case Study,* Admiralty Law Institute Symposium: A Sea Chest for Sea Lawyers, 75 Tulane L.Rev. 1489, 1504–07 (2001) (noting that burdens and defenses available in an action at law to confirm an arbitration award differ from those in a statutory summary proceeding under the FAA). It was therefore not "futile" for Congress to have specified a statute of limitations for the filing of summary proceedings: consistent with the wording of the statute, a party to an arbitration is entitled to the benefits of the streamlined summary proceeding only if, as it may do, it files at any time within one year after the award is made.

II

It is undisputed in this case that Photopaint filed its motion to confirm the Final Award more than one year from the date on which the award was made, and that Photopaint's motion to confirm the award is therefore barred absent some relief from the limitations period. Photopaint asserts several grounds for such relief, largely framed in terms of equity. We need not consider, the availability of equitable relief, however, because the undisputed record establishes, as a matter of law, that Smartlens and Photopaint agreed to toll any applicable limitations periods imposed under the FAA.

It is undisputed that the parties entered into a series of agreements extending the time in which to conduct settlement negotiations; the parties, however, contest the scope of these agreements. The meaning of contract provisions is a question of law over which we exercise *de novo* review. . . . Under New York law, which applies here, judgment as a matter of law is appropriate if the contract language is unambiguous. . . . "Contract language is unambiguous when it has 'a definite and precise meaning, unattended by danger of misconception in the purport of the [contract] itself, and concerning which there is no reasonable basis for a difference of opinion.'" . . . Unambiguous contract language is not rendered ambiguous by competing interpretations of it urged in litigation. . . .

The letter agreements at issue were entered into after the parties received the Final Award, which provided that for a thirty day period, ending on November 2, 2000, either party could rescind the license agreement. In an October 31, 2000 letter memorializing previous oral discussions, however, the parties extended the rescission deadline as well as other (unspecified) dependent deadlines:

> [W]e both understand that the 30 day time period specified in section 2(A) of the Final Award would have required action by the parties on or before 2 November 2000. Our agreement to extend the time would therefore extend this date to on or before 16 November 2000. *All other dependent times, if any, would be extended a like amount. The agreed extension shall apply to all acts or failures to act permitted or required to or by either party.* (Emphasis added.)

Smartlens argues that this wording is insufficient to extend the statute of limitation under the FAA. But the scope of the extension is broad and undifferentiated—"all acts and failures to act permitted or required to or by either party"—and at oral argument, counsel for Smartlens was unable to come up with an alternative formulation that would have been any broader. Moreover, the letter agreement was drafted by counsel for Smartlens, and we generally interpret contractual ambiguities against the drafter. . . .

We need not rely on the breadth of this initial letter agreement, however, because the parties' intent was clarified in subsequent letter agreements—each of which recited that the extension of time is on the same terms as before. Specifically, the parties' November 13, 2000 letter extending their initial tolling agreement explicitly references the FAA: Smartlens, the drafter, warned that in the absence of a further extension of time, it would be forced "to complete the Motion [pursuant to section 12 of the FAA] to Vacate the Award and the Interpleader, both items [it] would like to avoid." Smartlens "therefore propose[d]" a further extension, "under exactly the same terms as were set out in [the] previous letter," emphasizing that the agreement would extend "the time within which action must be taken by either of us *to rescind the license, or otherwise.*" (Emphasis added.) And Smartlens required that Photopaint sign an acknowledgment that "[t]he above terms accurately state[d]" the parties' agreement. More letter agreements followed, each expressly predicated on the ones before, and each extending the time within which the parties had "to rescind the license agreement, or otherwise." The initial series of letter agreements was followed by an "indefinite extension" for several months, and then by further periodic extensions.

This series of agreements and extensions, which continued until several months before Photopaint filed the instant petition for confirmation under the FAA, extended the one-year limitations period for filing the petition to confirm in this case.

It is undisputed that the period covered by the tolling agreements—the approximately nine months from October 31, 2000 through July 27,

2001—is long enough to make Photopaint's motion to confirm timely. Smartlens therefore cannot prevail on its statute of limitations defense.

CONCLUSION

For the reasons stated above, we agree with the district court's ruling that the FAA imposes a one-year statute of limitations, but reverse the judgment dismissing Photopaint's petition as untimely, and remand for further proceedings not inconsistent with this opinion.

NOTES AND QUESTIONS

1. How does the reasoning in *Cortez Byrd Chips, Inc.* influence the court in *Photopaint Techn.*? Is the language of the FAA subject to strict construction? When? What do you make of the court's distinction between an "inevitable" and "intuitive" interpretation of a statutory text?

2. Is the proceeding described in *Photopaint Techn.* an arbitration, an adjudication, arb-med, or a mini-trail—or even structured negotiation? Why? Why does the court not address that problem?

3. The Circuit split identified in *Photopain Techn.* remains unresolved, though it has not deepened since 2003. Why do you think that the issue seems to arise relatively infrequently in practice?

4. Note *Photopain* focuses on the limitations period for confirming an award. In contrast, no real debate exists about the fact that the three-month limitation period for motions to vacate or modify an arbitration award is mandatory. *See* FAA § 12 ("Notice of a motion to vacate, modify, or correct an award *must* be served upon the adverse party or his attorney within three months after the award is filed or delivered.") (emphasis added); *Pfannenstiel v. Merrill Lynch, Pierce, Fenner & Smith*, 477 F.3d 1155, 1158 (10th Cir. 2007) (failure to file within three months waived judicial review, and loss of evidence did not toll deadline); *Corey v. New York Stock Exchange*, 691 F.2d 1205, 1212 (6th Cir. 1982) ("failure to comply with the statutory precondition of timely service of notice forfeits the right to judicial review of the award.").

10. MODIFICATION OR CLARIFICATION OF AN AWARD

Courts have extremely limited power to fix non-substantive mistakes in arbitral awards. FAA § 11 and RUAA § 24 make possible the enforcement of awards containing minor mistakes. At the request of one of the parties, courts have the power to modify or correct awards for inadvertent technical errors that might otherwise preclude enforcement. The errors in question must be "evident" and unrelated to the merits of the award.

Additionally, and more importantly, although the Federal Arbitration Act does not expressly provide for remand of arbitration awards to the arbitrators for clarification, some authority exists for the proposition that courts have such power. *See, e.g.,* RUAA § 24. Where the arbitrators' true intentions cannot be discerned, a remand to the arbitrators preserves the integrity of arbitration, bolstering the efficacy and efficiency of the process.

M & C CORP. V. ERWIN BEHR GMBH & CO., KG

326 F.3d 772 (6th Cir. 2003).

OPINION

PER CURIAM.

This case is before us on appeal for the third time since an international arbitrator rendered an award in favor of the plaintiff, M & C Corporation. That award was confirmed by the district court, and judgment was entered. The instant appeal arises from a dispute regarding enforcement of a specific portion of the award. The defendant, Erwin Behr GmbH & Co., KG, interprets the award one way, and the plaintiff interprets it another. The district court initially had found the award to be unambiguous but, after attempting to determine the precise amount owed under the award, held that the award was "unclear as to its application" and entered an order of remand to the original arbitrator to clear up the problem. Behr appeals from this order, arguing that remand is inappropriate and that it has satisfied the award. In response, M & C contends that the district court's order of remand is not a "final order" and that this court therefore has no jurisdiction over Behr's appeal. In addition, M & C argues that remand is appropriate.

For the reasons set out below, we conclude that we have jurisdiction over Behr's appeal but that we are unable to review the order of remand on its merits because the district court failed to identify in what respect(s) the arbitration award was ambiguous and in need of clarification. Without this guidance, we cannot determine whether remand is proper and, moreover, the arbitrator would be left to speculate about how to interpret the award. Hence, we find it necessary to remand this case to the district court for further clarification.

[. . .]

2. *Did The District Court Err By Entering Its Order Of Remand?*

The bulk of Behr's brief is spent making a complex, fact-intensive argument that it has paid M & C all commissions due under the Eighth Award. According to Behr, the district court's principal error was in failing to grant Behr's motion for partial satisfaction of the judgment. This argument is premature and, in our judgment, misses the point. The district court did not expressly *deny* Behr's motion for partial satisfaction of the judgment. Instead, it is apparent that the court was in the process of determining whether Behr had satisfied the judgment when it encountered an ambiguity in the award, necessitating a remand to the arbitrator. That brings us to the most pressing question raised by this appeal: whether that remand was proper. Behr argues that remand is inappropriate, while M & C disagrees.

"A remand is proper, both at common law and under the federal law of arbitration contracts, to clarify an ambiguous award or to require the arbitrator to address an issue submitted to him but not resolved by the award." *Green v. Ameritech Corp.,* 200 F.3d 967, 977 (6th Cir.2000). The authority to order a remand derives from a recognized exception to the *functus officio* doctrine, which holds that an arbitrator's duties are generally discharged upon the rendering of a final award, when the arbitral authority is terminated.... However, " '[w]here the award, although seemingly complete, leaves doubt whether the submission has been fully executed, an ambiguity arises which the arbitrator is entitled to clarify.' " *Id.* at 977 (quoting *La Vale Plaza, Inc. v. R.S. Noonan, Inc.,* 378 F.2d 569, 573 (3d Cir.1967)). *See also Hyle v. Doctor's Assoc.,* 198 F.3d 368, 370 (2d Cir.1999) ("[A] district court can remand an award to the arbitrator for clarification where an award is ambiguous.").

The propriety of remanding an ambiguous award to the arbitrator is reinforced by the strong federal policy favoring arbitration. *See Behr II,* 143 F.3d at 1041 (Daughtrey, J., dissenting) ("I am led to th[e] conclusion [that remand of ambiguous award was proper] by the Supreme Court's pronouncement that 'any doubts concerning the scope of arbitrable issues should be resolved in favor of arbitration' ") (quoting *Moses H. Cone Memorial Hosp. v. Mercury Constr. Co.,* 460 U.S. 1, 24–25, 103 S.Ct. 927, 74 L.Ed.2d 765 (1983)); *Mutual Fire, Marine & Inland Ins. Co. v. Norad Reinsurance Co.,* 868 F.2d 52, 58 (3d Cir.1989) ("A district court itself should not clarify an ambiguous arbitration award but should remand it to the arbitration panel for clarification."). Of course it is true that "[w]hen possible, . . . a court should avoid remanding a decision to the arbitrator because of the interest in prompt and final arbitration." *Publicis Communication v. True North Communications Inc.,* 206 F.3d 725, 730 (7th Cir.2000). At the same time, however, a court simply should not "engag[e] in impermissible interpretation" of an ambiguous award. *Tri-State Bus. Mach., Inc. v. Lanier Worldwide, Inc.,* 221 F.3d 1015, 1020 (7th Cir.2000) (reversing and remanding order executing post-arbitration judgment where district court erred in not remanding the ambiguous award to arbitration panel for clarification). *See also Americas Insurance Co. v. Seagull Compania Naviera, S.A.,* 774 F.2d 64, 67 (2d Cir.1985) ("An ambiguous award should be remanded to the arbitrators so that the court will know exactly what it is being asked to enforce."); *Ganey v. Raffone,* No. 90–00871, 1996 WL 382278, at *3 (6th Cir. July 5, 1996) ("There are limited circumstances under which a district court can remand a case to the arbitrators for clarification. While a remand is to be used sparingly, it may be employed to avoid judicial guessing of the meaning of arbitral awards.") (citations and quotations omitted). In short, for a court to engage in guesswork as to the meaning and application of an ambiguous arbitration award is inconsistent not only with federal policy, but also with the parties' own agreement to submit their dispute to arbitration.

In *Behr II,* the majority decided that remand was inappropriate because it determined that the award was *not* ambiguous. There, the portion of the arbitrator's award subject to dispute was easily identified: The district court determined that "Behr had raised a good faith issue of what constitutes an 'order' under the commission contract, and that the prior arbitration award had not addressed that issue." *Behr II,* 143 F.3d at 1036. Here, on the other hand, the district court's order lacks any indication of precisely how the Eighth Award is "unclear as to its application", or which issue submitted to the arbitrator was "not fully adjudicate[d]." Nor with any confidence can we divine the answers from the circumstances; prior to its remand order, the district court had expressly held that the arbitrator's opinion and award were *not* ambiguous with respect to Behr's obligation to pay commissions on the 1996 EK parts and 1997 K parts. If the district court has changed its mind about *this* issue, it needs to say so and explain it. If there is *another* ambiguity in the award that makes enforcement impossible, the district court needs to identify it. Until it does so, we cannot undertake a meaningful review of whether the award is ambiguous or whether the circumstances are appropriate for a remand to the arbitrator. Moreover, the district court's vague order creates a substantial risk that the arbitrator will have insufficient guidance as to how to clarify its award, creating the potential for yet another journey to the district court, to this court on appeal, and back yet again to the arbitrator. Accordingly, we find it necessary to remand this case to the district court for clarification of the precise issue or issues that remain for the arbitrator on remand.

Because the case will be remanded to the district court, two other issues raised by Behr merit discussion in the interest of judicial economy.

3. Should Remand Be To The Same Arbitrator?

Behr argues that, assuming remand was appropriate, it was error for the district court to remand the award to the original arbitrator rather than directing the parties to start the whole process over again before a brand new arbitrator. In making this argument, Behr fails to account for our observation in *Green* that "[c]ourts usually remand to the *original* arbitrator for clarification of an ambiguous award when the award fails to address a contingency that later arises or when the award is susceptible to more than one interpretation." *Green,* 200 F.3d at 977 (emphasis added). The district court characterized its remand order as "simply . . . requir[ing the arbitrator] to complete his duties by applying his reasoning to the facts and . . . not reopen[ing] the merits of the case." Assuming that the district court's revised order on remand is consistent with this characterization, remand to the original arbitrator is the right result.

4. *Can This International Arbitration Be Remanded?*

Hoping to avoid remand, Behr makes a two-pronged argument that remand is improper even if the award is ambiguous. First, Behr contends that the International Chamber of Commerce (ICC) Rules that govern this dispute pursuant to the parties' arbitration agreement do not expressly permit remand. Behr points out that the 1988 version of the ICC Rules "made no provision for reconsideration, reinterpretation, or remand." According to Behr, remand is therefore disallowed.

However, as M & C points out, Article 35 of the same rules demonstrates that a guiding principle behind the rules is to ensure that the award is ultimately susceptible of enforcement, providing, as it does, that "[i]n all matters not expressly provided for in these rules, the court and the Arbitral Tribunal shall act in the spirit of these Rules and shall make every effort to make sure that the Award is enforceable at law." We read this provision to permit remand in this case, given that clarification by the original arbitrator is critical in order to make the Eighth Award enforceable at law.

Moreover, as M & C indicates, the parties' terms of reference for the arbitration provide that "[w]here the Rules are silent then such rules shall apply as may be made from time to time by the Arbitrator consistent with any mandatory requirement of the law of the place of arbitration. . . ." The "place of arbitration" in this case was London, England, and English law appears to require remand under the circumstances presented by this case. In this regard, M & C points to the English Arbitration Act of 1996, in which Parliament provided that where there is "uncertainty or ambiguity as to the effect of the award," it may be "remit[ted] to the tribunal, in whole or in part." English Arbitration Act of 1996, 1996 Chapter 23, § 68(2)(f) and (3)(a). In the absence of a clear indication that remand is disallowed by the applicable rules, we find no merit to this argument by Behr.

Behr's final argument is based on the Convention on the Recognition and Enforcement of Foreign Arbitral Awards ("New York Convention"). *See* 9 U.S.C. § 201. Behr observes that "[t]he Convention makes no provision for a remand after an arbitration award is rendered." Making this same observation, the district court below concluded in a separate order entered almost six years ago that it had no authority to order a remand, saying that "[b]ecause the arbitration award is governed by the [New York Convention], and because that convention makes no provision for a remand after an arbitration award is rendered, there is no basis in law for this court to remand." In addition, Behr cites our holding in *Behr I* that the New York Convention applied to prevent a party from moving in the United States courts to *vacate* an arbitration award made in a foreign nation. 87 F.3d at 847.

Contrary to what Behr argues, however, neither the New York Convention itself nor our holding in *Behr I* compels a holding that the district court lacks authority to remand an ambiguous award. First, we note that the New York Convention is utterly silent on the issue, as it is on many other issues dealing with the nuts and bolts of international arbitration procedure. At bottom, a remand of an ambiguous award under the circumstances presented here is not inconsistent with any provision of the New York Convention, and we have been unable to locate any authority suggesting that it is. Moreover, our holding in *Behr I* is inapposite. There, we were faced with a motion to *vacate* a foreign arbitration award and held that the district court lacked jurisdiction to enter such an order because, "[p]ursuant to the Convention, an application for setting aside or suspending an arbitral award may be made only to a 'competent authority of the country in which, or under the law of which, that award was made.' " *Behr I,* 87 F.3d at 847 (quoting New York Convention, Art. VI). Here, by contrast, the parties do not seek to *vacate* the confirmed arbitration award, nor did the district court enter such an order. Rather, the district court ordered a remand so that an award that it determined to be ambiguous could be rendered enforceable.

CONCLUSION

The district court's order remanding this case to the original arbitrator for clarification of an apparent ambiguity fails to identify the issue or issues that supposedly need the arbitrator's attention. We cannot conduct a meaningful review of the propriety of the district court's order of remand without a statement by the district court of what it perceives to be the ambiguity in the award. In addition, the arbitrator's job on remand will be needlessly complicated in the absence of clear direction from the district court. Accordingly, we REMAND this case to the district court with instructions to enter an order specifying in what respects the Eighth Award is unclear as to its application.

NOTES AND QUESTIONS

1. Generally, once an award has been issued, the arbitrators have completed their work. The arbitration is "*functus officio*." The doctrine of *functus officio* ("a task performed") provides that an arbitrator may not revisit the merits of an award once it has issued. Or, as an English court put it, "[w]hen an arbitrator makes a valid award, his authority as an arbitrator comes to an end and, with it, his powers and duties in the reference: he is then said to be *functus officio*." *Five Oceans Salvage Ltd v Wenzhou Timber Company* [2011] EWHC 3282 (Comm). Who or what created the "recognized exception to the *functus officio* doctrine?

2. Although arbitrators are not permitted to revisit the merits of the dispute, many arbitration associations have adopted rules that permit arbitrators to modify their awards after they have been issued. *See, e.g.*, AAA Commercial Arbitration Rules and Mediation Procedures R-50 (authorizing the arbitrator, upon the request of any party within 20 days of the award, to modify the award, though the arbitrator may not "redetermine the merits of any claim already decided").

This can become tricky if the arbitrators separate the proceeding into multiple stages—a liability stage and then a damages stage, for instance. The award at the end of each stage may simply be preliminary, in which case, the arbitrators remain free to revisit or revise their rulings. In some cases, however, arbitrators will issue a final award at the end of a stage. Even though other stages remain open, a final award puts an end to whatever issues it resolves. These sorts of awards are subject to the same review and enforcement rules as any other final award.

3. Clarification of an award does not constitute an explanation of an award. Arbitrators are not required to explain their awards. Courts cannot remand an award merely to obtain an explanation as to why the arbitrators ruled the way they did.

4. Who determines ambiguity? Can the court and the arbitrators disagree on the issue? What result would such disagreement entail?

5. If the remand is submitted to a new arbitrator, does it then constitute appeal?

HARDY V. WALSH MANNING SECURITIES, LLC

341 F.3d 126 (2d Cir. 2003).

(footnotes omitted)

POOLER, CIRCUIT JUDGE.

Respondent-Appellant Frank James Skelly, III appeals from the September 4, 2002 judgment of the U.S. District Court for the Southern District of New York (Lynch, J.), granting Petitioner-Appellee Warren A. Hardy's motion to confirm an arbitration award, and denying Skelly's and Respondent-Appellant Walsh Manning Securities, L.L.C.'s cross-motion to vacate the award. Skelly also appeals from the September 6, 2002 order denying his motion for reconsideration. Walsh Manning filed a Notice of Appeal, but has not pursued its appeal. We therefore affirm the district court's confirmation of the arbitration as it applies to Walsh Manning.

FACTS

Hardy, a British national, opened an investment account in 1997 at the Westbury, Long Island branch office of Walsh Manning, a New York City brokerage firm. Skelly is Walsh Manning's "Chief Executive Officer," although it is uncontested that he is actually an employee of Walsh

Manning, not an officer. Hardy's account was handled by Barry Cassese, who recommended stocks and made trades on Hardy's behalf.

In November 1998, Hardy filed a Statement of Claim with the National Association of Securities Dealers (NASD) claiming that Cassese, Skelly, and Walsh Manning, among others, engaged in various improprieties with regard to his account. In brief, Hardy charged that the respondents had misrepresented the fiscal health of certain companies whose stock Hardy was urged to buy, and did not disclose that these securities were "house stocks," which Walsh Manning had an interest in selling.

Before Hardy's claim proceeded to arbitration, Cassese agreed to settle with Hardy for $250,000.00. The settlement agreement also provided that Cassese would testify at any subsequent arbitration hearing with respect to Hardy's claims against the other respondents.

The NASD arbitration panel ("the Panel") consisted of three members, only one of whom is an attorney. The Panel's award was based upon an extensive documentary record and twenty-five days of testimony. Cassese testified extensively, charging that the malfeasance with respect to Hardy's account was undertaken at the behest, or with the connivance, of Walsh Manning and Skelly.

The Panel issued its award on February 2, 2002 ("the Award"). In the section of the Award relevant to this appeal, the Panel stated as follows:

> After considering the pleadings, the testimony and evidence presented at the hearing, and the post-hearing submissions, the Panel has decided in full and final resolution of the issues submitted for determination as follows:
>
> 1. Respondents Walsh Manning and Skelly be and hereby are jointly and severally liable for and shall pay to Claimant compensatory damages in the amount of $2,217,241.00 **based upon the principles of respondeat superior.** It is noted that this amount reflects deductions for the amounts previously paid by settling respondents.
>
> 2. Respondents Walsh Manning and Skelly be and hereby are jointly and severally liable for and shall pay to Claimant interest in the amount of $548,767.00.
>
> 3. Respondents Walsh Manning and Skelly be and hereby are jointly and severally liable for and shall pay to Claimant the sum of $250.00 to reimburse Claimant for the non-refundable filing fee previously paid to NASD Dispute Resolution, Inc. (emphasis added)

The Award is problematic. In addition to asserting various grounds of primary liability as to Skelly, Hardy asserted in his Statement of Claim that Skelly was liable to him "in [Skelly's] capacity as the Chief Executive Officer and Manager of Walsh Manning, under Section 20 of the Securities & Exchange Act [*sic*] of 1934 and under the common law theory of respondeat superior." But in their post-hearing brief, the respondents argued that Skelly could not be liable to Hardy under respondeat superior because of the undisputed fact that Skelly is an employee, not an officer, of Walsh Manning. In his own post-hearing brief, Hardy asserts respondeat superior as a ground for liability *only* with respect to Walsh Manning, but he does not explicitly repudiate the assertion of respondeat superior as to Skelly. Confusingly, Hardy also asserts in his post-hearing brief that Skelly and others "are secondarily liable for Cassese's misconduct. Such secondary liability is based on Section 20 of the Securities Exchange Act of 1934 and agency law." In any event, the only basis of liability as to Walsh Manning and Skelly stated in the Award is secondary liability pursuant to respondeat superior.

Hardy moved in the district court to confirm the Award, and Walsh Manning and Skelly cross-moved to vacate the Award. Judge Lynch found all of Walsh Manning's and Skelly's claims to be wholly without merit except for the application of respondeat superior liability to Skelly. Judge Lynch held that although "Skelly was the CEO of Walsh Manning, he was technically only an employee, and vicarious personal liability cannot be imposed on individual supervisors based solely on the conduct of their underlings, when both are fellow employees of a common employer." . . . Judge Lynch nevertheless concluded that the language employed by the Panel in the Award as to Skelly's liability can be read to mean that the Panel did not find Skelly liable pursuant to respondeat superior alone:

> It is possible to find that the phrase "based upon . . . respondeat superior" refers not to the finding of *liability* of each respondent, but to the conclusion that both respondents are "jointly and severally liable." This is essentially the reading adopted by petitioner, who would read the sentence as saying, "[Skelly is liable in damages, based on his own conduct, and] both respondents are jointly and severally liable, based on respondeat superior." While the words chosen may not be the most direct or grammatical way of expressing this thought, it is worth noting that the sentence ("Respondents . . . be and hereby are . . . liable") isn't grammatical in the first place.

. . . Finding therefore that Hardy's reading of the Award was "a plausible one . . . supported by a permissible view of the evidence," Judge Lynch ordered that the Award should be enforced as written. . . .

Skelly immediately moved for reconsideration, asserting that the Award should be remanded to the Panel for an explanation of the grounds of his liability. In his unreported denial of the motion, Judge Lynch held it would not be proper to remand the Award to the Panel for clarification as to its intent regarding Skelly's liability. Such action might be warranted, Judge Lynch held, if there were ambiguities in the nature and extent of the relief awarded. Here, however, "[t]he arbitrators were crystal clear in directing the respondents to pay a sum certain."

DISCUSSION

I. Was the District Court Correct in Holding That the Panel's Award Should Be Confirmed as Written?

As a general matter, "[a]rbitration awards are subject to very limited review in order to avoid undermining the twin goals of arbitration, namely, settling disputes efficiently and avoiding long and expensive litigation." . . . It is nevertheless the case that an arbitration award should not be confirmed where it can be shown that the arbitration panel acted in "manifest disregard of the law" to such an extent that "(1) the arbitrators knew of a governing legal principle yet refused to apply it or ignored it altogether and (2) the law ignored by the arbitrators . . . [was] well defined, explicit, and clearly applicable." . . .

We are fully aware that this is not an easy standard to meet for a party challenging confirmation of an arbitration award. . . . In *Duferco International Steel Trading v. T. Klaveness Shipping A/S,* 333 F.3d 383, 389 (2d Cir.2003), it was calculated that "since 1960 we have vacated some part or all of an arbitral award for manifest disregard in . . . four out of at least 48 cases where we applied the standard." (collecting cases) Yet, even though this standard "gives extreme deference to arbitrators," . . . we believe that it is satisfied here, at least to the extent of warranting a remand of the Award to the Panel for clarification of what it intended regarding Skelly's liability.

It is certainly possible to find that the Panel disregarded the principles of respondeat superior, the same principles that it purported to apply. Although the Panel did not explicitly say so, it is agreed by all parties that these are meant to be the principles of New York law. The principle that respondeat superior is a form of secondary liability that cannot be imposed upon the fellow employee of a wrongdoer is certainly well-defined and explicit in New York. . . . Indeed, it has been noted that the very possibility of liability *between* employees for acts committed in connection with their employment was an anomalous development in New York's tort law meant as a means of limiting the reach of respondeat superior liability. That is, "[t]he onerous 'fellow-servant' rule, [was] developed at common law to preclude respondeat superior claims against an employer by an employee injured in the workplace due to the negligence of a co-worker." . . .

As already noted, the Panel was made aware of the argument that Skelly could not be found liable for the acts of Cassese because both men were employees of Walsh Manning. Walsh Manning explicitly made this argument in their post-hearing brief, and Hardy impliedly agreed by raising respondeat superior as to Walsh Manning, but remaining silent as to Skelly's liability pursuant to the doctrine. . . .

Judge Lynch asserts that the Award can be read as holding that Skelly is liable "based on his own conduct." This reading reduces the Panel's explicit reference to respondeat superior to "a stray and unnecessary remark," as Judge Lynch terms it. But this reading is simply untenable. The Award is *silent* as to the issue of Skelly's primary wrongdoing, and it states no other ground of liability but respondeat superior. The untenability is implicitly confirmed by Hardy himself. He asserts that "[t]he Panel elected not to discuss the rationale for its finding of primary wrongdoing." . . . But he later acknowledges that "[t]he Award is completely silent regarding the primary wrongdoer." Hardy Brief at 14. Hardy gets it right the second time. The Panel made no finding of primary wrongdoing.

Judge Lynch himself acknowledges that "[t]he arbitrators nowhere made a finding that Skelly had committed no misconduct." . . . He nevertheless asserts that it is proper to infer that the arbitrators concluded that Skelly *had* committed misconduct because this is "a permissible view of the evidence." . . . But this "permissible" view is by no means necessarily equivalent to the view of the evidence actually taken by the Panel and . . . the latter view is dispositive. That is, a reviewing court is bound to accept the facts considered by an arbitrator "*as those facts have been determined by the arbitrator*." . . .

Indeed, Judge Lynch found that Walsh Manning's assertion that *it* could not properly be found liable under respondeat superior is without merit because the assertion "ask[ed] the Court to reassess the evidence." . . . But what is Judge Lynch's holding that Skelly was found to be primarily liable? It is an assessment of the evidence. We note also that Hardy's brief is largely devoted to assessing the evidence so as to assure this Court that there is indeed substantial evidence in the record to find that Skelly is primarily liable. Such evidence may exist. But since the award makes no mention of it, we will not assess this evidence.

Judge Lynch is correct that "[t]he arbitrators were crystal clear in directing the respondents to pay petitioner a sum certain." But, once again, it is also crystal clear that the award states no other basis for liability than respondeat superior. The district court correctly found that a court must "confirm [an arbitrator's] award if [it is] able to discern any colorable justification for the arbitrator's judgment, even if that reasoning would be based on an error of fact or law." . . . There may indeed be more than enough evidence in the record to find that Skelly should have been found primarily liable. But that is not what "the arbitrator's judgment" is in the instant case. The arbitrator's judgment is that Skelly was liable "upon the principles of respondeat superior," and no one points us to any evidence in the record that provides a colorable justification for this conclusion.

[. . .]

Finally, we disagree with Judge Lynch's contention that there is anything relevant in the fact that the Award "isn't grammatical." . . . The Award may fail in terms of usage, but it succeeds in stating a ground of liability in a manner that is manifestly intelligible.

It is true that the Award does not contain anything that can be termed "legal reasoning." But it *does* contain an explicit legal conclusion. To this extent, the award is not ambiguous and is not susceptible to more than one plausible reading. Nor does it rest on "a colorable interpretation of the law." . . . The award indeed contains a fundamental mistake of law.

II. Since This Court Holds That the Award Cannot Be Enforced as Written, What Should Be Done?

Voiding an award because an arbitration panel acted in manifest disregard of the law "requires more than a mistake of law or a clear error in fact finding." . . . We are reluctant to announce that the Award is void outright as written.

Although certainly not the normal course of things, we do have the authority to remand to the Panel for purposes broader than a clarification of the terms of a specific remedy. That is, we have the authority to seek a clarification of whether an arbitration panel's intent in making an award "evidence[s] a manifest disregard of the law." . . . The Panel should be afforded such an opportunity. . . .

. . . In this case, the Panel chose to make an explicit legal conclusion in the award, a conclusion that may very well be wrong. It should be given the opportunity to explain themselves. We are emphatically opening no floodgates here. We simply wish for more clarity because we think that substantial financial liability should not be imposed upon an individual without a clear basis in law.

The inquiries to the Panel on remand are not extensive and its response need not be, and should not be, detailed. We merely ask the Panel to do the following: (1) Confirm that Skelly is liable only under the principles of respondeat superior because there are indeed facts which have not been brought to our attention which support this holding; (2) In the alternative, assert that some other ground of secondary liability applies to Skelly; or (3) Failing both of these, acknowledge that it erred in finding Skelly secondarily liable and that the record does or does not support a finding that Skelly is primarily liable to Hardy.

CONCLUSION

The judgment of the district court is AFFIRMED in so far as the award applies to Walsh Manning. In so far as the award applies to Skelly, the district court's judgment is VACATED and REMANDED for proceedings consistent with this opinion.

STRAUB, CIRCUIT JUDGE, dissenting.

By remanding to the arbitration panel for clarification as to the underlying legal basis for liability, the majority, in my most respectful view, disregards the well-settled precedent establishing our severely limited review of arbitration awards. It is precisely because arbitration is designed to provide parties with an expedited process for conclusively resolving their disputes, that judicial review of arbitration awards is so narrow. . . . Accordingly, I dissent.

While the majority fully recognizes that substantial deference must be given to the arbitrator's finding of liability under the governing manifest disregard standard, it fails to acknowledge that equal deference must be accorded in interpreting the arbitration award itself. As this Court has recently reaffirmed, "where an arbitral award contains more than one plausible reading, manifest disregard cannot be found if at least one of the readings yields a legally correct justification for the outcome." . . . Thus, mere ambiguity in the award itself is not a basis for denying confirmation, so long as the award can be interpreted as having a colorable factual or legal basis. . . . Moreover, in interpreting an arbitration award, deference mandates that "we look only to *plausible* readings of the award, and not to *probable* readings of it." . . . Our goal, then, is not to discern the actual subjective intent of the arbitration panel, but only to determine if the award can be sustained under any plausible reading. . . .

Although the majority suggests that this is somehow an extraordinary case, we are presented at most with an arbitration award that is ambiguous and susceptible of more than one plausible reading. Because the award need not be read as stating that respondeat superior is the sole basis for Skelly's primary liability, affirmance is required under the established standard of this Circuit. Even if the majority is correct that there is no ambiguity, and the award must be read as erroneously holding Skelly liable under the principles of respondeat superior, then the appropriate remedy is to vacate the judgment of the District Court and remand for vacatur of the arbitration award. To suggest that we may remand for clarification despite finding that the arbitrator has manifestly disregarded the law has little support in prior precedent. Indeed, such a rule fatally frustrates the very goals which arbitration seeks to advance: the efficient resolution of disputes and the avoidance of prolonged expensive litigation.

I.

In this case, the disputed portion of the arbitrators' decision simply states: "Walsh Manning and Skelly be and hereby are jointly and severally liable . . . based upon the principles of respondeat superior." The majority's interpretation, while conceivable, ignores the fact that the critical phrase "based upon the principles of respondeat superior" may simply explain the basis for Walsh Manning's joint and several liability, without referring to the basis for Skelly's primary liability. Indeed, the phrase may indicate Walsh Manning's liability for *Skelly's* actions, not just Cassese's wrongful conduct, based upon the theory of respondeat superior. In other words, the award may specify the form of liability, joint and several, while remaining completely silent as to the underlying claims on which Skelly was actually found liable.

Not only is this a *plausible* interpretation of the decision, but also a completely *probable* one, for Hardy presented substantial evidence during the arbitration hearing that Skelly, who was Cassese's direct supervisor, failed to properly supervise Cassese, that Skelly was personally aware of Cassese's unauthorized trading, and that Skelly violated federal securities laws by engaging in direct market manipulation. In addition, as the majority points out, Hardy did not argue that Skelly faced direct liability on the basis of respondeat superior in his post-hearing brief, an argument, which nonetheless, Skelly directly refuted in his opposing brief. Finally, although Walsh Manning and Skelly did request that the Panel specify the damages awarded as to each particular claim for indemnification purposes, arbitrators have no obligation to provide such explanations for their decisions. . . .

[. . .]

III.

In sum, in "wish[ing] for more clarity," the majority's decision overlooks our limited role in reviewing arbitration decisions and encourages the very type of protracted litigation that arbitration seeks to avoid.

For all of the foregoing reasons, I respectfully dissent and would affirm the decision of the District Court.

NOTES AND QUESTIONS

1. There are three competing interpretations of the NASD award in *Hardy*: The district court's, the majority, and the dissent. Which do you find most persuasive? Why?

2. How does the majority align the remand with manifest disregard of the law? Is this a legitimate use of the manifest disregard ground? Is the court using remand as a veiled threat to have the arbitrators rule the way it believes the law should be applied?

3. In your view, did the arbitrators get the law wrong? What might constitute a legally correct determination? Is plausibility a more realistic

standard than correctness? Can you distinguish objective error from opinion? Illustrate your answer.

4. Does the court's reasoning comply with the dictates of the federal policy on arbitration? Is the district court's ruling more acceptable from this perspective?

11. PENALTIES FOR FRIVOLOUS VACATUR ACTIONS

Courts in the United States are committed to the "bedrock" principle that litigants are responsible for their own attorneys' fees, whether they win or lose. The U.S. Supreme Court recently reaffirmed this principle, saying that it will not depart from it absent express statutory authority or a valid contractual provision. *Baker Botts L.L.P. v. ASARCO LLC,* 135 S. Ct. 2158, 2164, 192 L.Ed. 2d 208 (2015).

Despite this abiding dedication to the "American Rule," courts have been penalizing attorneys and their clients who engage in meritless attempts to undermine the arbitration process through collateral litigation. Such penalties discourage vexatious litigation tactics designed to thwart the parties' agreed dispute resolution method.

B.L. HARBERT INTERNATIONAL, LLC V. HERCULES STEEL CO.

441 F.3d 905 (11th Cir. 2006).

CARNES, CIRCUIT JUDGE:

The Federal Arbitration Act (FAA) liberally endorses and encourages arbitration as an alternative to litigation. . . .

The laudatory goals of the FAA will be achieved only to the extent that courts ensure arbitration is an alternative to litigation, not an additional layer in a protracted contest. If we permit parties who lose in arbitration to freely relitigate their cases in court, arbitration will do nothing to reduce congestion in the judicial system; dispute resolution will be slower instead of faster; and reaching a final decision will cost more instead of less. This case is a good example of the poor loser problem and it provides us with an opportunity to discuss a potential solution.

I.

B.L. Harbert International, LLC, is a Delaware corporation based in Birmingham, Alabama, which makes money in large construction projects including some done for the government. Hercules Steel Company is a North Carolina corporation based in Fayetteville, North Carolina, that manufactures steel used in construction.

On August 25, 2000, the United States Army Corp of Engineers, Savannah District, awarded Harbert a contract to construct an office complex for the Special Operations Forces at Fort Bragg, North Carolina. Harbert, in turn, awarded Hercules a $1,197,000 steel fabrication and erection subcontract on September 21, 2000.

The subcontract between the parties includes a provision that disputes between them will be submitted to binding arbitration under the auspices of the American Arbitration Association, using the Construction Industry Arbitration Rules. Later, the parties executed a separate Agreement to Arbitrate, which recognizes that the Federal Arbitration Act, 9 U.S.C. § 1, would control arbitration proceedings.

The subcontract further provides that Harbert will issue a "Progress Schedule" for the project and will provide a copy to each subcontractor. It states that the subcontractor must perform all work "in accordance with Progress Schedule as prepared by [Harbert] and as it may be revised from time to time with the Subcontractor's input." . . .

Harbert's failure to define those terms might have gone unnoticed if it had created only one schedule for the project, but Harbert developed two, which it referred to as the 2000 and 3000 schedules. . . . [N]either schedule is mentioned in the subcontract.

The dispute-generating problem is that the 2000 schedule contained earlier completion dates than the 3000 one. According to the 2000 schedule, Hercules was to begin work on March 5, 2001, and finish it by June 6, 2001. That did not happen. Hercules began work in April of 2001, and did not finish it until January of 2002. That completion of the work was, however, within the more lenient deadlines of the 3000 schedule.

[. . .]

After considering the parties' opposing arguments and a voluminous record, the arbitrator issued his "Award of Arbitrator" on September 8, 2004. That award denied Hercules' delay damages claim, denied all of Harbert's counterclaims, denied both parties' claims for attorney's fees, and awarded Hercules $369,775, representing the subcontract balance and the interest on that sum. Because the award, not counting interest, was nearly $100,000 less than the amount the parties had agreed was the subcontract balance, Hercules believed that the arbitrator had made a scrivener's or mathematical error. It submitted a request for clarification which pointed out the problem.

[. . .]

On October 18, 2004, the arbitrator issued his "Disposition for Application of Modification/Clarification of the Award," a decision document which corrected the scrivener's error by increasing the award from $369,775 to $469,775. The document also revealed the arbitrator's findings on the six issues, stating in answer to the first one that Hercules was contractually bound to the more generous "project schedule submitted to the Corps of Engineers which was used to build the project [the 3000 schedule] . . . not the sixteen week schedule unilaterally set by Harbert [the 2000 schedule]." The arbitrator stated in answer to another of the six issues that Harbert was not entitled to any damages because "[t]he delay and acceleration damages are necessarily dependent on the claimed project schedule which has been found not applicable."

On November 18, 2004, Harbert filed in the district court a motion to vacate the arbitration award, contending that the arbitrator's rationale reflected a manifest disregard of the applicable law. Hercules opposed Harbert's motion with one of its own, asking the court to confirm the award pursuant to 9 U.S.C. § 9.

On February 7, 2005, the district court entered an order denying Harbert's motion to vacate the award and granting Hercules' motion to confirm it. . . .

[. . .]

II.

Judicial review of commercial arbitration awards is narrowly limited under the Federal Arbitration Act. . . . The FAA presumes the confirmation of arbitration awards . . . and federal courts should defer to an arbitrator's decision whenever possible. . . . The FAA sets out four narrow bases for vacating an award, none of which are even remotely applicable in this case. . . .

Harbert's challenge to the arbitrator's award rests solely on its contention that the arbitrator acted in manifest disregard of the law. This ground for vacating an arbitration award requires clear evidence that the arbitrator was "conscious of the law and deliberately ignore[d] it." . . . A showing that the arbitrator merely misinterpreted, misstated, or misapplied the law is insufficient. . . . We review *de novo* the district court's legal conclusions on this issue. . . .

This Court first adopted manifest disregard for the law as a basis for challenging an arbitration award in the *Montes* case. 128 F.3d at 1461. It remains the only case in which we have ever found the exceptional circumstances that satisfy the exacting requirements of this exception. . . .

The *Montes* litigation arose out of a dispute between an employer and employee about overtime pay. . . . The controlling law, the Fair Labor Standards Act, was against the employer's position, and during the arbitration proceedings its attorney repeatedly urged the arbitrators to disregard the requirements of the Act and rule for the employer on the basis of equitable considerations. . . . He told the arbitrators that: "you as an arbitrator are not guided strictly to follow case law precedent . . . you can also do what's fair and just and equitable and that is what [my client] is asking you to do in this case." . . . Instead of contending that the law could be applied favorably to his client's position, the attorney argued to the arbitrators that "in this case this law is not right," and "[t]he law says one thing. What equity demands and requires and is saying is another." . . . He explicitly asked the arbitrators not to follow the law. . . .

The arbitrators in *Montes* found in favor of the employer, and in their award they repeated the plea of the employer's attorney that they disregard the law. . . . There was nothing in the transcript of the proceedings or the award itself to indicate that the arbitrators had not heeded that plea, and the evidence and law did not support the award. . . .

In holding that the arbitrators had acted in manifest disregard of the law in *Montes,* we disavowed any notion that an arbitrator's decision "can be reviewed on the basis that its conclusion or reasoning is legally erroneous." *Id.* at 1461; *accord id.* at 1460 ("This does not mean that arbitrators can be reversed for errors or misinterpretations of law."). And we emphasized the rare nature of the circumstances in that case. *Id.* at 1461–62. Four facts came together in *Montes* and will seldom recur:

> Those facts are that: 1) the party who obtained the favorable award had conceded to the arbitration panel that its position was not supported by the law, which required a different result, and had urged the panel not to follow the law; 2) that blatant appeal to disregard the law was explicitly noted in the arbitration panel's award; 3) neither in the award itself nor anywhere else in the record is there any indication that the panel disapproved or rejected the suggestion that it rule contrary to law; and 4) the evidence to support the award is at best marginal.

. . . While *Montes* shows the exception, the rule is shown in every other case where we have decided if the arbitration loser had established manifest disregard of the law. In all of those other cases the loser in arbitration was the loser in our decision. . . .

The facts of this case do not come within shouting distance of the *Montes* exception. This is a typical contractual dispute in which the parties disagree about the meaning of terms of their agreement. There are arguments to be made on both sides of the contractual interpretation issue, and they were made to the arbitrator before being made to the district court and then to us. Even if we were convinced that we would have decided this contractual dispute differently, that would not be nearly enough to set aside the award. *See Peebles,* 431 F.3d at 1326 ("[A] litigant arguing that an arbitrator acted in manifest disregard of the law must show something more than a misinterpretation, misstatement, or misapplication of the law."); *Brown,* 211 F.3d at 1223 ("Arbitration awards will not be reversed due to an erroneous interpretation of law by the arbitrator."); *Montes,* 128

F.3d at 1461 ("An arbitration board that incorrectly interprets the law has not manifestly disregarded it. It has simply made a legal mistake.").

Harbert's argument that the arbitration award clearly contradicts an express term of the contract is simply another way of saying that the arbitrator clearly erred, and even a showing of a clear error on the part of the arbitrator is not enough. The arbitration loser must establish more than that in order to have the award set aside, the more being that the arbitrator actually recognized a clear rule of law and deliberately chose to ignore it. *Peebles,* 431 F.3d at 1326 ("A manifest disregard for the law involves a conscious and deliberate decision to ignore the applicable law."); *id.* at 1327. . . . On the record before us, we cannot find proof that the arbitrators recognized a clear rule of law and chose to ignore it. . . .

[. . .]

There is no evidence that the attorney for Hercules urged the arbitrator to disregard the law, and Harbert does not even suggest that happened. There is no evidence that the arbitrator decided the dispute on the basis of anything other than his best judgment—whether right or wrong—of how the law applies to the facts of the case. There is, in short, no evidence that the arbitrator manifestly disregarded the law. The only manifest disregard of the law evident in this case is Harbert's refusal to accept the law of this circuit which narrowly circumscribes judicial review of arbitration awards. By attacking the arbitration award in this case Harbert has shown at best an indifference to the law of our circuit governing the subject. Harbert's refusal to accept that there is no basis in the law for attacking the award has come at a cost to the party with whom Harbert entered into the arbitration agreement and to the judicial system.

In litigating this case without good basis through the district court and now through this Court, Harbert has deprived Hercules and the judicial system itself of the principal benefits of arbitration. Instead of costing less, the resolution of this dispute has cost more than it would have had there been no arbitration agreement. Instead of being decided sooner, it has taken longer than it would have to decide the matter without arbitration. Instead of being resolved outside the courts, this dispute has required the time and effort of the district court and this Court.

When a party who loses an arbitration award assumes a never-say-die attitude and drags the dispute through the court system without an objectively reasonable belief it will prevail, the promise of arbitration is broken. Arbitration's allure is dependent upon the arbitrator being the last decision maker in all but the most unusual cases. The more cases there are, like this one, in which the arbitrator is only the first stop along the way, the less arbitration there will be. If arbitration is to be a meaningful alternative to litigation, the parties must be able to trust that the arbitrator's decision will be honored sooner instead of later.

Courts cannot prevent parties from trying to convert arbitration losses into court victories, but it may be that we can and should insist that if a party on the short end of an arbitration award attacks that award in court without any real legal basis for doing so, that party should pay sanctions. A realistic threat of sanctions may discourage baseless litigation over arbitration awards and help fulfill the purposes of the pro-arbitration policy contained in the FAA. It is an idea worth considering.

We have considered ordering Harbert and its counsel to show cause why sanctions should not be imposed in this case, but have decided against doing so. That decision is the product of the combined force of three reasons, which we list in reverse order of weight. First, there is speculative dicta in the *University Commons* opinion that provided Harbert with a little cover for its actions, although this factor alone does not carry much weight. The rule that prior panel precedent trumps later decisions, to say nothing of later dicta, is so well known and well established that lawyers and their clients should be held responsible for knowing that rule and acting accordingly. Second, Hercules did not move for sanctions against Harbert in either the district court or in this Court. While we can raise and consider the issue of sanctions on our own, after giving the parties notice and an opportunity to be heard, the lack of interest in sanctions shown by the party to whom any monetary sanctions would be paid is a factor to consider.

Third, and most importantly, when Harbert took its arbitration loss into the district court and then pursued this appeal, it did not have the benefit of the notice and warning this opinion provides. The notice it provides, hopefully to even the least astute reader, is that this Court is exasperated by those who attempt to salvage arbitration losses through litigation that has no sound basis in the law applicable to arbitration awards. The warning this opinion provides is that in order to further the purposes of the FAA and to protect arbitration as a remedy we are ready, willing, and able to consider imposing sanctions in appropriate cases. While Harbert and its counsel did not have the benefit of this notice and warning, those who pursue similar litigation positions in the future will.

Affirmed.

NOTES AND QUESTIONS

1. Are sanctions for perfunctory, speculative, or frivolous vacatur litigation a good idea? How might the prospect of legal malpractice affect the imposition of sanctions? How onerous do such sanctions need to be?

2. Might imposition of sanctions have an over-deterence effect? Do you think that Harbert's objections were truly frivolous?

3. The Eleventh Circuit no longer recognizes "judicially-created bases for vacatur." *Frazier v. CitiFinancial Corp.*, 604 F.3d 1313, 1324 (11th Cir. 2010). In *Frazier*, the specific basis at issue was manifest disregard. Because

manifest disregard is no longer recognized in the Elventh Circuit, *B.L. Harbert* has been technically abrogated, but its reasoning with respect to sanctions for frivolous challenges to arbitration awards has remained influential.

HUNT V. MOORE BROTHERS, INC.

861 F.3d 655 (7th Cir. 2017).

WOOD, CHIEF JUDGE.

James Hunt worked as a truck driver in Nebraska. On July 1, 2010, he signed an Independent Contractor Operating Agreement with Moore Brothers, a small company located in Norfolk, Nebraska. Three years later, Hunt and Moore renewed the Agreement. Before the second term expired, however, relations between the parties soured. Hunt hired Attorney Jana Yocum Rine to sue Moore on his behalf. She did so in federal court, raising a wide variety of claims, but paying little heed to the fact that the Agreements contained arbitration clauses. Rine resisted arbitration, primarily on the theory that the clause was unenforceable as a matter of Nebraska law. Tired of what it regarded as a flood of frivolous arguments and motions, the district court granted Moore's motion for sanctions under 28 U.S.C. § 1927 and ordered Rine to pay Moore about $7,500. The court later dismissed the entire action without prejudice.

I

Rine has appealed from that order.

[. . .]

The relevant part of the arbitration clauses in the Agreements reads as follows:

> This Agreement and any properly adopted Addendum shall constitute the entire Agreement and understanding between us and it shall be interpreted under the laws of the State of Nebraska. . . . To the extent any disputes arise under this Agreement or its interpretation, we both agree to submit such disputes to final and binding arbitration before any arbitrator mutually agreed upon by both parties.

When Rine decided to take formal action on Hunt's part, she ignored that language and filed a multi-count complaint in federal court. The complaint was notable only for its breadth: it accused Moore of holding Hunt in peonage in violation of 18 U.S.C. § 1581 (a criminal statute), and of violating the Racketeer Influenced and Corrupt Organizations Act (RICO), 18 U.S.C. § 1962; the federal antitrust laws, 15 U.S.C. §§ 1, 4, 14; the Illinois Employee Classification Act, 820 ILCS 185/1 et seq.; and for good measure, the Illinois tort of false representation.

Relying on the Federal Arbitration Act (FAA), 9 U.S.C. § 1 et seq., Moore responded with a motion to compel arbitration and to stay the litigation; it also sought the appointment of an arbitrator pursuant to section 5 of the FAA, 9 U.S.C. § 5. Rine objected on several grounds. First, she asserted that Hunt had no obligation to comply with the arbitration clause because Moore had materially breached the Agreements. Second, she asserted that the Agreements fell outside the scope of the FAA because Hunt was a transportation worker. See 9 U.S.C. § 1; *Circuit City Stores, Inc. v. Adams*, 532 U.S. 105, 119, 121 S.Ct. 1302, 149 L.Ed.2d 234 (2001) ("Section 1 exempts from the FAA only contracts of employment of transportation workers."). Third, Rine resisted Moore's request for a court-appointed arbitrator, noting that the clause provided for a person "mutually agreed on by the parties."

The district court made short shrift of Rine's arguments. It rejected the assertion that an alleged breach of the underlying contract relieves a party from an arbitration agreement; by that reasoning no one would ever arbitrate a contract dispute, because the arbitration agreement would go up in smoke as soon as the dispute arose. Rine's effort to bring Hunt under the transportation-worker exception also failed, the court said, because the complaint conceded that he was an "independent truck owner operator," not an employee. Rine prevailed only on her procedural argument against a court-appointed arbitrator: the judge found this step premature, and directed the parties to try to do this themselves. They took some steps in that direction, but they never agreed on anyone.

This was the backdrop to Rine's ill-fated return to the district court. Less than two months after the judge told the parties to agree on an arbitrator, Rine filed a motion reporting that their efforts had failed. This revealed, she said, that the arbitration clause was nothing more than an "agreement to agree," unenforceable under Nebraska law. The district court rejected this reasoning. It noted that Rine should have raised this argument earlier and that in any event it was wholly without merit. The FAA preempts conflicting state law, and a delay in the selection of an arbitrator does not affect the enforceability of an arbitration clause.... This was the point at which the court imposed the sanctions that are the subject of Rine's appeal.

III

Rine offers several reasons for setting aside the district court's order of sanctions, even as she acknowledges that the court has wide discretion over such matters.... She complains that the court based its order exclusively on a finding of objective unreasonableness, without finding subjective bad faith on her part. Her premise—that both are needed—is mistaken: while subjective bad faith is sufficient to support section 1927 sanctions, "such a finding is not necessary; 'objective bad faith' will also support a sanctions award." . . .

Rine insists that the arbitration clause was not enforceable as a matter of Nebraska law, and so she was justified in resisting its application. She also attacks the district court's conclusion that the FAA preempts whatever Nebraska law has to say on the subject, and asserts that her motion to lift the stay and vacate the order compelling arbitration was justified. This is so, she says, because she pointed to some precedent for the position that if an arbitration agreement is found to be unenforceable after a stay pursuant to FAA section 3 is entered, the party opposing arbitration is entitled to file a motion to lift the stay. See 9 U.S.C. § 3.

We are unpersuaded by Rine's arguments. The fundamental flaw underlying her entire course of conduct is her disregard of the long line of Supreme Court decisions upholding the enforceability of arbitration clauses exactly like the one in the Hunt-Moore Agreements. As we noted earlier, Rine's theory in the district court was that the arbitration clause was only an agreement to agree in the future and thus was unenforceable under Nebraska law. For support, she pointed to [two cases]. Yet neither of those cases has anything to do with arbitration, and so neither is of any use to Rine, which perhaps is why she has not cited them on appeal.

As the Supreme Court repeatedly has said—most recently in *Kindred Nursing Centers Ltd. Partnership v. Clark*, ___ U.S. ___, 137 S.Ct. 1421, 197 L.Ed.2d 806 (2017)—"[t]he Federal Arbitration Act . . . requires courts to place arbitration agreements on equal footing with all other contracts." *Id.* at 1424 (internal quotation marks omitted). In *Kindred Nursing*, the Kentucky Supreme Court held that its state constitution forbade a person with a general power of attorney from entering into an arbitration agreement for his principal. The Supreme Court found this state law to be incompatible with the FAA because it singled out arbitration agreements for disfavored treatment, in violation of the equal-treatment principle that applies to arbitration agreements. . . . And there is more: the Court has also held that arbitration clauses should be generously construed. . . . Rine's position is inconsistent with this guidance.

The fact that an agreement to arbitrate leaves for later negotiations the selection of the particular arbitrator does not render that agreement so vague as to be unenforceable. If that were the case, then section 5 of the FAA, which provides for the court to appoint an arbitrator in some circumstances, would be pointless. Provisions in which the parties must agree on one or more arbitrators are common. If they cannot do so, as apparently happened in this case, the court is empowered to step in and "designate and appoint an arbitrator or arbitrators or umpire, as the case may require, who shall act under the said agreement with the same force and effect as if he or they had been specifically named therein. . . ." 9 U.S.C. § 5 . . . .

That is enough to show that Rine's effort to avoid arbitration was doomed. But if we had any doubts about the district court's imposition of sanctions, the remainder of Rine's conduct in the litigation would resolve them. Section 1927 permits sanctions against a lawyer who "so multiplies the proceedings in any case unreasonably and vexatiously" that the lawyer should be responsible for the excess costs, expenses, and attorney'/s fees borne by the other side. 28 U.S.C. § 1927. This is the authority on which the district court relied. As we said earlier, the court has broad discretion in implementing this statute. We will reverse only if no reasonable person could have come to the same conclusion, in these circumstances.

This was a simple commercial dispute between Hunt and Moore, but one would never know that from reading Rine's complaint. She blew it up beyond all rational proportion. One count asserted that there was an unspecified civil right of action to enforce the criminal laws against peonage. 18 U.S.C. § 1581. There is no support whatsoever for that theory. As far as we can tell, only one court has considered it, and that judge rejected the argument that section 1581 creates a civil right of action. . . . Her RICO and antitrust arguments were also beyond the pale. There is no RICO enterprise in sight, no pattern of racketeering activity, and no conspiracy between Moore and any other entity, as far as this record shows. And it is clear under the antitrust laws that a simple decision by one firm to stop dealing with another firm at a different point along the distribution chain does not violate Sherman Act § 1, 15 U.S.C. § 1. . . . It is also frivolous to imply that Moore had the kind of market power necessary to support a claim under Sherman Act § 2, 15 U.S.C. § 2. As for the Illinois Employee Classification Act, 820 ILCS 185/1 et seq., while it does at least address the "practice of misclassifying employees as independent contractors," *id.* § 3, nothing hints at why Illinois law governs this relationship between a Nebraska truck driver and a small Nebraska company. The same is true of the claim that relies on Illinois common law.

So Rine was off to a bad start, even before she filed the motion that prompted the district court's sanctions: her complaint was a disaster, and her efforts to avoid arbitration were meritless. Moreover, the key motion was one under Federal Rule of Civil Procedure 60(b), but Rine failed to show the exceptional circumstances required by that rule. . . . As the district court pointed out, Rine was "not offering newly discovered evidence, or arguing fraud or misconduct. . . . Nor [was] counsel arguing that the Court's prior findings . . . [were] incorrect." She was instead introducing a meritless theory that the arbitration clause was unenforceable as a matter of Nebraska law.

This court had already squarely rejected Rine's theory [in a previous case]. The district court, though not compelled to do so, was entitled to regard Rine's approach as so objectively unreasonable that it called for some kind of sanction under section 1927.

To determine the amount of sanctions it was prepared to impose, the court ordered Moore to submit an affidavit describing all fees that it had incurred in responding to Rine's motion. Moore did so, and based on the materials it submitted, the court settled on $7,427 (representing 27.6 hours of work) as the money Rine had to pay. This is a reasonable measure of the cost Rine imposed on her opponent. She argues that the sanction was too high, but she offers no support for that position other than a convoluted argument to the effect that Moore should be compensated only for the pages of its brief that (she thinks) the district court adopted. As the district court put it, "it is unfathomable why she would invent an algorithm rather than relying on the information supplied in the Defendants' affidavit."

IV

We have no need to consider whether the sanctions imposed by the district court were also justified under the court's inherent power. . . . Nor are we saying that the district court would have erred if it had denied Moore's sanctions motion. We hold only that it lay within the district court's broad discretion, in light of all the circumstances of this case, to impose a calibrated sanction on Rine for her conduct of the litigation, culminating in the objectively baseless motion she filed in opposition to arbitration. We therefore AFFIRM the district court's order imposing sanctions.

NOTES AND QUESTIONS

1. Federal courts derive power to issue sanctions from three primary sources: (1) 28 U.S.C. § 1927; (2) Federal Rule of Civil Procedure 11; and (3) the court's inherent authority to manage its docket, the parties and cases. In state court, the RUAA § 25 provides that in judicial proceedings to confirm or vacate an arbitration award, the court may add to its judgment "reasonable attorneys' fees and other reasonable expenses of litigation incurred."

Each of these sources has unique features, but all turn on some combination of bad faith motive and objective unreasonableness. While the later concept, in theory, hinges on more objective criteria, district courts have broad discretion to determine when sanctions are appropriate.

2. There are other examples cases imposing penalties on lawyers and parties for imprudent challenges to arbitration agreements or awards. For instance, stating that a baseless vacatur action against an arbitral award broke the "promise of arbitration," the Tenth Circuit in *DMA Int'l Inc. v. Qwest Communications Int'l Inc.*, 585 F. 3d 1341 (10th Cir. 2009), ordered DMA Int'l's lawyers to pay their opponent's attorney's fees. The case involved a dispute

over the amount owed by Qwest for DMA's services. The arbitrator adopted Qwest's interpretation of the payment clause and ruled in its favor. DMA's lawyer launched the proverbial laundry list of objections to the award, claiming the ruling was made in manifest disregard of the law, violated public policy, and reflected arbitrator bias and excess of authority. The Tenth Circuit concluded that the *pro forma* invectives were "completely meritless," 585 F. 3d at 1346, and that the lawyers who authored the objections had no reasonable basis for believing that their strategy would succeed. Their empty litigiousness violated the expedition and economy of arbitration and the 'emphatic federal policy favoring arbitration.' *Id.*

Similarly, in *Digitelcom, Ltd. v. Tele 2 Sverige AB*, 12 Civ. 3082, 2012WL3065345 (S.D.N.Y. July 25, 2012), the parties disagreed about the effective performance of their obligation to expand mobile services in the Russian Federation. The matter was submitted to arbitration and the arbitral tribunal ruled in favor of Tele2, awarding them nearly $2 million in attorney's fees and costs. DigiTelCom sought to vacate the award, alleging imperfect execution of the arbitral mandate, manifest disregard of law, and bias. Tele2 filed a motion to confirm the award and to impose sanctions on the opposing attorneys because of the improper challenge to the award. The federal district court confirmed the award and granted the motion for sanctions. It deemed the motion for vacatur to be based on "pure speculation" and to lack any reasonable justification. The attack on the award merely indicated that the moving party disagreed with the arbitrator's conclusions and added unwarranted expense to the arbitral process to express that position. According to the court:

> Sanctions must not be imposed lightly. At the same time, where parties agree to arbitration as an efficient and lower-cost alternative to litigation, both the parties and the system itself have a strong interest in the finality of those arbitration awards. Thus, although courts should be careful not to chill parties' good-faith challenges to arbitration awards where there are serious questions of the tribunal's impartiality or authority, litigants must be discouraged from defeating the purpose of arbitration by bringing such petitions based on nothing more than dissatisfaction with the tribunal's conclusions. For this reason, "sanctions are peculiarly (sic) (particularly) appropriate in the context of a challenge to an arbitration award which appears to be a largely dilatory effort."

Conclusions

Enforcement is the stage at which the force of law meets arbitration head-on. The topic, therefore, warrants thorough treatment. Legal issues here may render an entire arbitration useless. Without voluntary compliance, the law is necessary to give operative effect to the arbitral process.

While the objective of FAA § 10 is limpid, its construction by courts attests to a surfeit of disfiguring judicial interest. With an abundance of judicial pronouncements, FAA § 10 has mutated into a complex regime. Despite the activity, the presumption in favor of enforcement remains generally steadfast.

Manifest disregard complicates the matter of enforcement, if only by generating ambiguity and indecision in applicable concepts. Still, the basic result has never really in doubt no matter how it was reached—courts rarely overturn arbitral awards.

The more recent assaults on arbitral autonomy come at the state level. Some state courts have determined that they are free to depart from FAA § 10, imposing different and potentially more stringent requirements on arbitral awards. This approach, while seemingly at odds with at least the spirit of most U.S. Supreme Court decisions from the past five decades and counting, finds support in dicta from *Hall Street.* Unless and until the Supreme Court addresses the preemptive force of federal law on the review and enforcement process, these state incursions are likely to become bolder and more frequent. States are disabled from regulating arbitration on the front end, for instance by removing some subjects from the domain of arbitration. But states may be able to regulate arbitration on the backend, for instance by authorizing courts to conduct a de novo review of an arbitrator's application of law.

INDEX

References are to Pages